DICTIONARY OF AMERICAN HISTORY

DICTIONARY
OF
AMERICAN HISTORY

DICTIONARY OF AMERICAN HISTORY

REVISED EDITION

VOLUME I

Aachen–Chattanooga Campaign

Charles Scribner's Sons · New York

Published simultaneously in Canada
by Collier Macmillan Canada, Inc.

13 15 17 19 AG/H 20 18 16 14

Printed in the United States of America
Library of Congress Catalog Card Number 76-6735
ISBN 0-684-13856-5 (set)

ISBN 0-684-15071-9 (vol. 1)
ISBN 0-684-15072-7 (vol. 2)
ISBN 0-684-15073-5 (vol. 3)
ISBN 0-684-15074-3 (vol. 4)
ISBN 0-684-15075-1 (vol. 5)
ISBN 0-684-15076-X (vol. 6)
ISBN 0-684-15077-8 (vol. 7)
ISBN 0-684-15078-6 (Index)

EDITORIAL STAFF

LOUISE BILEBOF KETZ, *Managing Editor*

JOSEPH G. E. HOPKINS, *Editorial Adviser*

COPY EDITORS

PATRICIA R. BOYD

NORMA FRANKEL

ROBERT HAYCRAFT

LELAND S. LOWTHER

PROOFREADERS

MARGARET DONOVAN

ROGER GREENE

PAULINE PIEKARZ

ANDREW J. SMITH

DORIS A. SULLIVAN

MARSHALL DE BRUHL, *Director, Reference Editorial*

FOREWORD

In the last few decades our history has been almost completely rewritten. New facts have been discovered; new interests have developed. A generation ago historians had done the merest spade work in many departments of our national life. They were still chiefly concerned with political and military events. Today our whole culture is their province, and the public which reads history has widened with the widening of the historian's vision. . . . History is no longer the concern of a few. If the interests of scholars have broadened, so has the use of the results of their researches, until historical facts are sought for in business offices as well as in halls of learning.

Until now the facts of the new history have not been readily available. They are scattered through thousands of volumes of general histories or special studies. There has been an increasingly insistent demand for some one source to which an inquirer might go to find, and quickly, what he wishes to know as to specific facts, events, trends or policies in our American past, without searching for hours, perhaps unsuccessfully, through stacks of books, even should he have access to them. It is this which the Dictionary of American History *is intended to fill.*

From James Truslow Adams' Foreword
to the first edition (Jan. 2, 1940)

On Dec. 29, 1936, Charles Scribner's Sons announced that James Truslow Adams, noted historian and Pulitzer Prize winner, had been appointed editor in chief of a board of scholars that, with the cooperation of the leading state historical societies and other learned organizations, would produce a dictionary of American history. As indicated in Adams' Foreword, the project was undertaken in response to the demands of historians and librarians for a reference work of American history in which exact information about the thousands of separate facts of American history that are so difficult to locate elsewhere could be found easily and quickly. The plan, therefore, for the first edition of the *Dictionary of American History* was to bring within an accessible reference work a vast amount of historical data.

The announcement of the preparation of the *Dictionary* came shortly after the publication by Scribners of the *Dictionary of American Biography*. The intent of Adams, his highly capable managing editor, R. V. Coleman, associate editors Thomas Robson Hay and Ralph Foster Weld, and the seventeen-member advisory council was to do for factual history what the *Dictionary of American Biography* did for biography. As Adams said, ". . . the very richness of our historical background, as revealed by the *Dictionary of American Biography,* has made a dictionary of American history necessary."

The editors of the first edition of the *Dictionary of American History* realized that only by the cooperation of historical scholars in every part of the country could the work hope to attain such inclusiveness as to make it a really national history, and several hundred historians were enlisted in the major task of composing a list of entries. A tentative list of 6,000 entries was then reviewed by the advisory council and the historians and a final list of 6,425 entries was completed. The subjects selected included not only those commonly looked on as important in American history, but also those subjects previously overlooked but that are as much a part of American history as those more traditionally accepted. Hence, an article was included on barbed wire, the invention and use of which revolutionized the development of the Plains country and made possible the transition from cattle range to settled farm.

The 6,425 entries were then assigned to more than 1,000 contributors for the preparation of articles. The editors sought in every instance to assign a subject to the scholar most familiar with it. Commissioned to prepare articles from 50 to 5,000 words in length, the authors were asked to keep the articles within their brief assigned lengths without a loss in informational value.

In January 1940, Volume I of the first edition of the *Dictionary of American History* was published. The remaining volumes appeared at brief intervals thereafter; Volume V, the final volume, appeared in May 1940. After four years of editorial work, Adams and his staff had succeeded in bringing together facts scattered in thousands of volumes in a readily accessible, readable, and reliable five-volume reference work. The reaction of librarians and historians was exceptionally favorable. A letter addressed to Coleman from Milton James Ferguson, chief librarian of the Brooklyn Public Library and former president of the American Library Association, is indicative of the reaction generated by the publication of Volume I: "I cannot picture any public or school library so small that the *Dictionary of American History* will not be indispensable." Several one-volume compilations of American historical facts have appeared since 1940, but none matches the scope of the *Dictionary of American History,* nor its inherent interest, despite the necessary brevity of many of its articles.

In 1961 a supplement volume to the *Dictionary* was published as an extension of the first edition to cover the facts, events, and trends of the American national experience during the years 1940–60, to replace certain of the articles from the first edition that, although excellent at the time written, had become obsolete, and to include subjects not included in the original *Dictionary*.

Since its first publication, the *Dictionary* has continued to be regarded by the historical profession as the best work of its kind available. In order to maintain that estimation, it was decided in 1970 to publish a complete revision, in the light of historiographical changes over the past thirty years, rather than publish a second supplementary volume. This decision was based not only on the reexamination of historical data and the occurrence of events since 1940 that would be required in a revised edition, but also on a number of factors that revealed inadequacies in the first edition. First, it was determined as imperative that the brief coverage of science and technology be greatly expanded. Second, the lack of coverage of the history of the arts would also need to be corrected. Third, a review of the entries revealed that too many of them required revision or replacement for a one-volume second supplement. Fourth, the coverage of the native American Indian was obviously inadequate and often biased. Finally, the coverage of Afro-Americans, despite a corrective article prepared for the supplement volume, did not adequately discuss or point up their role and influence in the course of nearly 400 years of American history. It was therefore decided that while the first edition of the *Dictionary* in many respects was still an excellent reference work, a revised edition that would completely supersede it was imperative.

Work on the revised edition began with the selection of an Editorial Board comprising authorities in military history, science and technology, political science, economics, the arts, and general history. This board reviewed every entry in the first edition and the supplement and determined which of the articles could be retained after rechecking, editing, and updating; which articles needed to be revised completely, either because the entries in the first edition or supplement were unsatisfactory or because recent research indicated that a different approach was needed; and which entries were no longer important and could thus be deleted from the *Dictionary*. The Editorial Board then proceeded, with the help of colleagues in the various disciplines, to draw up the list of 500 entirely new entries, bringing the total number of entries for the revised edition to 7,200. The new or revised entries were then assigned to approximately 800 authors.

Important advances in the field of American prehistory and the inadequacy in the first edition of the articles on the American Indian necessitated a complete revision of all articles pertaining to native Americans. This task was undertaken by Robert F. Spencer of the University of Minnesota and Kenneth M. Stewart of the University of Arizona. Professors Spencer and Stewart guided the editorial staff in completely revising one-half of the first-edition articles; and in collaboration with scholars they undertook the preparation of new articles on the remaining 50 percent. In addition, twenty-five new entries on the history of the American Indian were prepared for inclusion in this revised edition.

Henry N. Drewry of Princeton University reviewed the coverage of the history of the Afro-Americans and prepared a new essay on this subject. He also commissioned some forty new articles and supervised the complete revision of approximately sixty additional entries from the original *Dictionary* and supplement.

The Index of the revised edition of the *Dictionary* is not simply a listing of proper names, but a thorough analytical listing of every item of information in the *Dictionary* under all its possible headings.

Throughout the work on the revised edition, it has been the goal of the staff and Editorial Board to maintain the high standards set by the first edition. Although the work is now greatly expanded, it retains the format of a dictionary—providing quick identification of a subject and related information. We have endeavored to comply with the demands of students, scholars, and librarians for an accessible, accurate, informative, and interesting reference work of American history.

Louise Bilebof Ketz
July 4, 1976

DICTIONARY OF AMERICAN HISTORY

Aachen–Chattanooga Campaign

AACHEN (Aix-la-Chapelle), first major German city to fall to American troops in World War II; birthplace and reputed burial place of the Emperor Charlemagne; also renowned for its medicinal waters. In pursuit of German forces defeated in France, troops of the American First Army crossed the German frontier near Aachen on Sept. 11, 1944. Unknown to the Americans, the German commander responsible for Aachen had abandoned the city. The commander of the U.S. VII Corps, Maj. Gen. J. Lawton Collins, chose to bypass the city in order to overcome formidable frontier fortifications of the Westwall, or Siegfried Line. Although Collins' troops penetrated the defenses, reinforcements reaching the German Seventh Army forced a halt. By that time, German troops had reoccupied Aachen. With the help of the U.S. XIX Corps north of Aachen, the VII Corps closed a circle about the city on Oct. 16. Meanwhile, after the commander of the German garrison, Col. Gerhard Wilck, had refused a surrender ultimatum, the First Infantry Division under Maj. Gen. C. Ralph Huebner on Oct. 13 launched a systematic assault on the city. Intense fighting and heavy bombardment by American planes and artillery followed. Infantrymen had to blast their way from one building to the next and sometimes to enter sewers to eliminate diehard resistance. Particularly intense fighting occurred at St. Elizabeth's Church; a *Kurhaus*—the Palast-Hotel Quellenhof; and two hill parks, the Salvatorberg and the Lousberg. In later stages of the fighting, contingents of tanks from the Third Armored Division participated. When American troops had pressed to almost every corner of the city, Col. Wilck on Oct. 21 at last surrendered. Amid the mass of rubble that the city had become, the Aachen Cathedral, which houses Charlemagne's coronation chair, escaped with remarkably little damage.

[Charles B. MacDonald, *The Siegfried Line Campaign.*]

CHARLES B. MACDONALD

ABC CONFERENCE, held at Niagara Falls, May 18–July 2, 1914. The ABC powers (Argentina, Brazil, and Chile) tendered mediation to prevent a conflict between the United States and the Victoriano Huerta regime in Mexico (*see* Vera Cruz). The conference failed because revolution leader Venustiano Carranza, victorious in recent battles, rejected its proposal for a provisional government chosen by agreement between the contending factions. Huerta, however, resigned on July 15 and Carranza assumed the presidency on Aug. 22.

DANA G. MUNRO

ABILENE, an early cow town in Kansas, established by Joseph G. McCoy in 1867 as a depot to which Texas cattle might be driven for shipment by rail to Kansas City (*see* Abilene Trail; Chisholm Trail). Attempts of trail drivers to reach market in 1866 had failed largely because of the hostility of the settlers of Missouri and eastern Kansas, who feared the introduction of Texas fever. Located on the Kansas Pacific Railway west of all settlement, Abilene was for four or five years a popular shipping point until the westward advance of settlers forced the drovers to new cow towns farther west.

[Joseph G. McCoy, *Historic Sketches of the Cattle Trade and Southwest.*]

EDWARD EVERETT DALE

ABILENE TRAIL, a cattle trail leading from Texas to Abilene, Kans. Its exact route is disputed owing to its many offshoots, but it crossed the Red River a little east of Henrietta, Tex., and continued north across the Indian Territory to Caldwell, Kans., and on past Wichita and Newton to Abilene. The first herds were probably driven over it in 1866, though it was not named until Abilene was established in 1867.

EDWARD EVERETT DALE

AB-INITIO MOVEMENT, a controversy that originated during Reconstruction in Texas in 1866. In the constitutional convention of that year the question arose, Was secession null and void from the beginning (*ab initio*) or did it become null and void as a result of the Civil War? The staunch unionists took the position that it was null and void from the beginning and therefore all laws based upon secession were null and void and all public and private relations based upon such laws were null and void. This contention was rejected by the governor, military officers, both constitutional conventions, and the Republican state convention, but it seriously divided the party of Reconstruction. Two brothers assumed leadership of the respective groups, Morgan Hamilton of the Ab-Initios and former Gov. A. J. Hamilton of the anti-Ab-Initios. This heated controversy continued over a period of three years. A. J. Hamilton and the conservatives finally emerged victorious but not until compromise had been made.

[C. W. Ramsdell, *Reconstruction in Texas.*]

J. G. SMITH

ABLEMAN* V. *BOOTH, 21 Howard 506 (1859), provided Chief Justice Roger B. Taney with an opportunity for a masterly analysis of federal and state powers. Sherman Booth, sentenced to jail by a federal court for assisting in the rescue of a fugitive slave at Milwaukee, was released on a writ of habeas corpus issued by a judge of the Wisconsin Supreme Court on the ground that the Fugitive Slave Act was unconstitutional. The case was carried to the U.S. Supreme Court, which rendered a unanimous opinion pronouncing the Fugitive Slave Act valid and forbidding a state to interfere with federal prisoners by habeas corpus writs.

[Homer Cummings and Carl McFarland, *Federal Justice;* C. B. Swisher, *Roger B. Taney.*]

JOHN G. VAN DEUSEN

ABNAKI (from *Wabnaki,* "those of the sunrise"), a tribe of Algonkin-speaking Indians generally resident in western and central Maine. Although a population of 3,000 is estimated for them in 1600, some confusion arises because of the identification of the Abnaki with various adjacent Algonkins, such as the Malecite, Pennacook, Penobscot, Passamaquoddy, and Micmac. Possessing marked similarity in both language and culture, these groups tend to blend into one another, and all may be assigned to the Eastern Woodlands (Northeast) culture area. They were not drawn into the modified agricultural mode of life characteristic of some of the Algonkins to the south and of the intruded Iroquois but rather reflected a basic adaptation to the subarctic boreal forest. Hunting was the primary basis of subsistence of the Abnaki and their neighbors. Skill in hunting, together with its associated technology, permitted exploitation of available land and fauna, such as moose, beaver, deer, mink, and otter, and the development of extensive freshwater fishing. Wild foods were gathered, especially roots and berries; and wildfowl, taken in many ways, were important. Although village sites are listed for them in 17th-century sources, it was not the village but rather the hunting territory that identified both the Abnaki and their neighbors: the localized patrilineal family was identified with a specific hunting area that it owned and jealously guarded against trespass, and social units were thus made up of kindred people identified with a particular region. Birch bark canoes; wigwams and bark-covered houses; birch bark containers; snowshoes of rawhide; and a wide variety of traps and snares, again employing the subarctic rawhide, characterized the culture.

Although Abnaki political organization was family-centered, the strong political influences exerted by the intruded Iroquois made themselves felt early in the historic period. Political relations with other tribes began to be marked by the exchange of wampum, the tubular beads signifying ambassadorial status, as well as by the appearance of the calumet ("peace pipe"), suggesting increased emphasis in historic times on political and chiefly authority. Contacted in the 17th century and missionized by the French in the 18th century, the Abnaki identified with French interests. They were unsuccessful in hindering British expansion in 1724–25, and severe defeats (*see* Norridgewock Fight) reduced their numbers and forced their movement to the St. Francis River, in Quebec, along with many other Algonkin groups.

The Abnaki are best known through a dictionary compiled prior to their dispersion, by the missionary Sebastian Rasles.

[John R. Swanton, *The Indian Tribes of North America.*]

ROBERT F. SPENCER

ABOLITION. *See* **Antislavery.**

ABOMINATIONS, TARIFF OF. *See* **Tariff.**

A. B. PLOT. The political enmity between Sen. Ninian Edwards of Illinois and William H. Crawford, secretary of the treasury, produced this "plot." Crawford had employed the unstable western banks to collect public land revenues in fluctuating banknote currencies. This policy, though justifiable, resulted in losses to the government, while he doubtless used his banking connections to advance his political influence. In 1823 the *Washington Republican,* a John C. Calhoun publication, published a series of articles signed A. B., which attacked Crawford for malfeasance in his relations with certain banks, and accused him of suppressing letters on the subject, for which the House had called. These articles were written by Edwards. Some thought he desired to damage Crawford in the 1824 presidential campaign; John Quincy Adams believed the real object was to remove W. W. Seaton and Joseph Gales, Crawford supporters, from the post of public printers. Early in 1824, while on his way west as the newly appointed minister to Mexico, Edwards sent formal charges against Crawford to the House. He was at once recalled to testify before an investigating committee of seven, resigning his ministership. The committee report not only exonerated Crawford but left Edwards' reputation severely blemished.

[Ninian W. Edwards, *History of Illinois From 1778 to 1833,* and *Life and Times of Ninian W. Edwards;* J. E. D. Shipp, *Giant Days, or the Life and Times of William H. Crawford.*]

ALLAN NEVINS

ABRAHAM, PLAINS OF, on the west side of the city of Quebec, were named after Abraham Martin, a Quebec pilot, who once owned part of the land. They were the scene, in 1759, of the battle (*see* Quebec, Capture of) that brought an end to the dream of French empire in North America, and, incidentally, resulted in the death of two great generals, James Wolfe and Louis Joseph de Montcalm. The site is now a national park.

LAWRENCE J. BURPEE

ABRAHAM LINCOLN, FORT, built by Gen. George A. Custer in 1873, on the Missouri River, just below Heart River in North Dakota. Fort McKean, on a hill above this fort, was an infantry post, and though built first, was usually considered part of Fort Abraham Lincoln. In 1895 the fort was abandoned.

[Francis P. Prucha, S.J., *A Guide to Military Posts of the United States, 1798–1895.*]

CARL L. CANNON

ABSENTEE OWNERSHIP is a situation in which the actual ownership of an asset is divorced from day-to-day management and control. Historically, the asset consisted of land, especially agricultural land worked by tenants, although in modern times it may also include urban rental dwellings and mineral lands. All corporate stockholders who are not officeholders in a firm can be considered "absentee owners," but the term is not customarily used in this sense. Absentee property owners may occasionally participate in management activities, but typically they employ real estate or rental agencies to supervise their property, pay taxes, handle legal obligations, and collect rents.

Absentee ownership has been an integral part of the American land-holding pattern since the earliest colonial times, although unencumbered home ownership—the idea that everyone should have an opportunity to enjoy life "under his vine and under his fig tree"—remains the popular ideal. Initially, the colonial proprietors and colonization companies that acquired land charters from the English crown attempted to lease their lands to colonists under feudal tenure patterns or, as in New England, to distribute freeholds only through town governments on the basis of individual family need. But the desire to attract settlers brought down the barriers against a free and open land system, and, as historians have convincingly shown, men of means—and many without means—speculated in land from the earliest days and acquired large acreages. In the southern colonies the "headright" system, whereby any individual who brought in an immigrant received a negotiable title to fifty acres of unseated land, provided the basis for the large plantations that gradually developed. During the 18th century, as the colonies became more fully settled and developed, land values rose sharply and large landowners were able to attract propertyless farmers as tenants on their land. The tenants were customarily new immigrants or younger sons of farmers who lacked the capital resources to purchase farms. They rented until such time as they could climb the "agricultural ladder" to ownership.

By the early 19th century, "landlordism" and tenancy were common features of American land tenure, especially on the frontier. In New York and Pennsylvania from about 1810 to 1820, tenants outnumbered freeholders in more than a dozen western counties, where the land was largely owned by a foreign corporation—the Holland Land Company. Along the Hudson River, the Rensselaers, Livingstons, and Schuylers controlled entire counties and populated them with Yankee tenants. In the antebellum South, absentee plantation owners were relatively few; where they existed they were found most frequently among the large estates in coastal South Carolina and Georgia, and in the new sugar and cotton plantations of the Southwest. As the pace of government land sales quickened on the mid-continent frontier, absentee ownership likewise increased. Most notable were such "Prairie Kings," described by Paul Wallace Gates, as Henry O. Ellsworth, former U.S. commissioner of patents, and William Scully, an alien landowner residing in Ireland, who engrossed upwards of 100,000 and 200,000 acres respectively of prairie land, most of which was leased to tenants. By 1860, eastern capitalists and local townsmen owned more than half of the land in Iowa, which comprised the richest soil in the nation; and further west the government subsequently granted to railroad companies some 130 million acres. Land was the avenue to wealth in the 19th century, both for residents and nonresidents alike.

Absentee landowners frequently felt the sting of agrarian attacks, especially during the periodic "hard times." The campaign against nonresident land "monopolists" came to a head in the 1880's, when most midwestern states and finally Congress adopted laws banning alien ownership of land in the several states and territories. In 1890 Congress also enacted legislation to force railroads to forfeit unearned land grants, but the railroad companies effectively blocked the law in the courts. The bill of indictment against absentee landowners usually charged them with creating "speculator's deserts" of vacant land held for a price rise, with refusing to carry their fair share of the local property tax burden, and with fostering the un-American institution of tenancy on the frontier. The latter question awaits careful study, but recent research reveals that nonresident landowners eagerly pressed sales at reasonable prices and that they paid more than their share of property taxes because local assessors traditionally overvalued nonresident lands.

Absentee landownership is an inevitable and necessary aspect of any free market economic system where land is a valuable asset. In 1970 almost half of all residential units were leased and 40 percent of U.S. farms were wholly or partially rented. According to land economist Raleigh Barlowe, absentee landlords are needed in the American tenure system "to facilitate the operation of our agricultural and residential ownership ladders, to permit an orderly retreat from owner-operatorship on the part of our elderly owners, and to fill the continuing demand for commercial and residential rental properties in urban areas."

[Raleigh Barlowe, *Land Resource Economics;* Marion Clawson, *The Land System of the United States;* Leslie E. Decker, "The Great Speculation," in David M. Ellis, ed., *The Frontier in American Develcpment;* Paul Wallace Gates, *Frontier Landlords and Pioneer Tenants;* Robert P. Swierenga, *Pioneers and Profits: Land Speculation on the Iowa Frontier,* esp. chap. 1 for bibliographic essay.]

ROBERT P. SWIERENGA

ACADEMIC FREEDOM is a term descriptive of a group of rights claimed by teachers: to study, to communicate ideas, and to publish the results of reflection and research without external restraints—in short, to assert the truth as they perceive it. Academic freedom developed in the universities of Western Europe in the 17th and 18th centuries, as a result of the gradual growth of an atmosphere of tolerance nurtured by various factors: the spread of scientific inquiry; the reaction to the fiercely destructive religious conflicts that had for so long plagued Europe; the growth of commerce, which drew attention to the value of competitive enterprise; and the evolution of the liberal state, with its general bias toward liberty, including intellectual freedom. Academic freedom is now recognized in most countries except those with totalitarian governments. In most places the concept of academic freedom emphasizes the autonomy of the institution and its independence from external restraints; in the United States, in accordance with the individualistic bent of its constitutional law, the claim to academic freedom is usually asserted in terms of the individual teacher's freedom from interference with the free play of the intellect.

The principal justification of academic freedom is that through the unhampered interplay of ideas, the world's stock of usable knowledge is enlarged. Thus, while academic freedom benefits the teacher, in a larger and much more significant sense it serves vital public interests. The concept of academic freedom is now well established in the jurisprudence of the U.S. Supreme Court. The first case in which a majority of the Court's justices ruled that academic freedom is protected by the due process clauses of the Constitution was *Sweezy* v. *New Hampshire,* 354 U.S. 234 (1957). A decade later, to cite one of a number of cases, the Court held invalid a statute requiring the dismissal of "subversive" professors on the ground that the Constitution "does not tolerate laws that cast a pall of orthodoxy over the classroom" (*Keyishian* v. *Board of Regents of University of State of New York,* 385 U.S. 589, 603 [1967]).

Academic freedom is invariably tied to the concept of tenure (status granted after a trial period, protecting a teacher from summary dismissal), since without security of employment a teacher cannot safely exercise his intellectual freedom. Tenure does not mean, however, that the teacher granted it can never be dismissed but rather that he can be dismissed only for adequate cause, established according to the exacting requirements of due process, and including at some stage a judgment by one's professional peers.

There are many associations throughout the world that are concerned with the defense of academic freedom and tenure, for example, the American Association of University Professors. Such defense is needed because academic freedom is often under great pressure from a wide variety of sources: political parties, politicians, economic interests, religious and racial groups, alumni, donors, and members of governing boards. For publicly supported institutions, pressures are often generated in the legislative bodies that control the purse strings. Furthermore, with the rise of the social sciences, teachers have become involved with issues on which people are deeply divided—issues such as foreign policy, war and peace, race relations, the elements of human inequality, and fundamental economic policy—and such involvement can result in threats against academic freedom. Thus, academic freedom does not exist in a vacuum, and its viability varies from time to time and from place to place. In the United States and Western Europe it seems to be well understood and generally respected.

[Richard Hofstadter and Walter P. Metzger, *The Development of Academic Freedom in the United States;* Louis Joughin, ed., *Academic Freedom and Tenure.*]

DAVID FELLMAN

ACADEMIES. There have been three types of secondary schools in the United States: the Latin grammar school of the colonial period; the academy, which began about the middle of the 18th century and continued for nearly a century; and the public high school. The Latin grammar school was displaced by the academy, and the academy was largely displaced by the public high school.

An early school of this kind grew out of the work of Benjamin Franklin, one of the founders, in 1751, of Franklin's Academy in Philadelphia, which offered a more diversified course of studies than that of the Latin schools. Most of the early academies, however, seem to have been the fruits of denominational interests, and most of them were private institutions, although some states undertook to provide for county systems of academies. Academies were also under the control of self-perpetuating boards of trustees, were often chartered by the legislatures of the various states, and had the right to own and control property, to receive gifts and endowments, and to engage and dismiss their teachers. These institutions went by a variety of names, such as academy, institution, seminary, collegiate institute, and sometimes college. There were academies for boys, for girls, and in some cases, coeducational academies. Tuition fees were usually charged, but occasionally the legislature would charter an academy or grant it other privileges with the provision that poor children should be taught gratuitously. The academy movement spread widely. It was reported that by 1830 there were 1,000 such incorporated institutions in the United States and within two decades about 6,000, instructing more than 260,000 pupils.

The academies stimulated interest in the training of teachers and may be considered the forerunners of the normal schools. Many became the nuclei from which collegiate institutions developed. They served also to encourage the education of girls and women. Variants of the academy appeared in the vocational schools and in military schools.

[Edgar W. Knight, *Education in the United States.*]

EDGAR W. KNIGHT

ACADIA, a former French colony in Canada (now Nova Scotia). The name Acadia, whether of European origin or a derivative of the American Indian word *aquoddiake,* was first applied in letters-patent to the grant obtained by Pierre de Guast, Sieur de Monts, from the king of France, Nov. 18, 1603. The boundaries of Acadia, never clearly defined, roughly embraced the North American coast from Cape Breton to the shores below the Hudson River (forty to forty-six degrees north latitude) and overlapped considerably the land claimed by England by virtue of John Cabot's discovery (*see* Cabot Voyages) and Sir Humphrey Gilbert's possessory claim in the 16th century. Such was the basis for the conflicting claims of England and France to North America, which resulted in a hundred and fifty years of predatory warfare, during which time Acadia, unproductive and desolate, was traded back and forth between the two powers as English and French diplomats sought to adjust the balance of losses and acquisitions elsewhere.

Acadians. Although by the Treaty of Utrecht, 1713, "all Nova Scotia with its ancient boundaries" was ceded to England, French empire builders saw the advantage of tacitly narrowing the indefinite limits of Nova Scotia to what is now the peninsula bearing that name, and England, faced with the necessity of holding the land from the Kennebec River to the Saint Croix, came to view the French inhabitants of the peninsula, the Acadians, with alarm. The Acadians, both the victims and oftentimes the participators in maundering warfare, charged by the English with disloyalty undoubtedly fostered by Jesuit priests, were believed to menace the English colonial possessions from within. By an act of extreme severity, immortalized by Henry Wadsworth Longfellow in the poem *Evangeline,* over 4,000 of these Acadians were uprooted from their homes and dispersed to other English colonies, principally Maryland and Virginia. Some made their way to the West Indies and Louisiana. Many found their way back and today their descendants may be found in Nova Scotia and Maine.

ELIZABETH RING

Acadians in Louisiana. It is not known that any of the Acadians came directly from Nova Scotia to Louisiana. They came in irregular groups and at irregular intervals, having first attempted to settle at other places without success. Some came by ship to New Orleans from the New England and Atlantic seaboard colonies, but the majority came overland, from Maryland, Pennsylvania, and Virginia, by trail across the mountains and by flatboat down the Tennessee, Ohio, and Mississippi rivers. This accounts for the fact that some came after the first deportation while others did not arrive until 1776. From New Orleans the Acadians were first sent some fifty miles up the Mississippi to what is now Saint James parish, and they gave the name of Acadian Coast to that section of the river. Others pushed up the river as far as Pointe Coupée, in the parish of that name. Later arrivals were sent westward into southern Louisiana, from 70 to 100 miles from New Orleans, along Bayou Lafourche and Bayou Teche, into the region protected by the frontier *postes* of Attakapas and Opelousas.

At Attakapas they largely founded the town of Saint Martinville, which quickly became and has remained the center of Acadian life in Louisiana. Land was given them in this frontier region; they built their homes and furnished them mainly with handmade furniture that may still be seen throughout south Louisiana. As industrious and prolific people, they rapidly increased in numbers and spread westward into the parish which bears their name, Acadia, and the surrounding territory. They and their descendants, who are called Cajuns, have been largely farmers, but some became merchants and stock raisers, while others entered the professions. In the region of the Teche and Lafourche they developed a characteristic culture that exists today despite modern changes. Until 1900 French was the language of the Acadians, but with public education and the compulsory speaking and study of English in the schools, English has become the first language.

Saint Martinville is one of the most charming towns in Louisiana, and a mecca for tourists. Here on the banks of the Teche stands the "Evangeline Oak," and nearby in the churchyard of Saint Martin is the grave of Evangeline, marked by a life-size bronze statue, for here lived Emmeline Labiche, the original of Longfellow's heroine. Not far distant is the Evangeline State Park, a beautiful tract along the Teche, where there is preserved a typical Acadian farm dwelling, furnished as it originally stood.

No record was kept of the numbers of Acadians who arrived in Louisiana. Dudley Le Blanc, in his *True Story of the Acadians,* states that 2,500 came by way of France, and that the total number was 5,000. This appears to be an exaggeration, for in 1787, thirty-two years after the beginning of the deportations, colonial Governor E. R. Miró of Louisiana had a census of the Acadians taken, and reported the number in the province as 1,587. It would appear that the number did not exceed 2,000 altogether, or at most 2,500.

[J. B. Brebner, *New England's Outpost;* F. Parkman, *A Half-Century of Conflict,* and *Montcalm and Wolfe;* Oscar William Winzerling, *Acadian Odyssey.*]

J. FAIR HARDIN

ACADIAN COAST, the section of Louisiana along the Mississippi River settled by the exiled Acadians after about 1760. While applying particularly to the present parish of Saint James, the term is sometimes used to designate the scattered Acadian settlements on the Mississippi as far as the mouth of Red River.

[Oscar William Winzerling, *Acadian Odyssey.*]

WALTER PRICHARD

ACCIDENTS. Deaths from accidents in the United States in 1973 totaled 116,000, and injuries resulting from accidents incapacitated 11.4 million persons beyond the day of the injury. Economic losses from accidents totaled $40 billion. One-half the fatalities resulted from traffic accidents, about one-fourth from home accidents, one-fifth from public non-motor-vehicle accidents, and one-eighth from occupational accidents. Only three diseases—heart disease, cancer, and stroke—kill more Americans than accidents do. In terms of productive years of life wiped out, accidents are the nation's worst killer. Although all ages suffer heavily from accidents, it is the elderly who have the highest accidental death rate. Young people from fifteen to twenty-four years of age have next to the worst record, and infants under one year have the third worst record. Statistically, those from five to fourteen years of age are safest from accidents.

Organized accident-prevention activities began early in the 20th century. In 1912 a small group of interested people—mainly from the steel, railroad, and mining industries—met in the first National Safety Congress, in Milwaukee. This group called for creation of a national safety organization. The organization, called the National Industrial Safety Council, was established in 1913 at the second National Safety Congress. At the third congress, in 1914, the name was changed to the National Safety Council, and the organization's mission was expanded to include efforts to combat all kinds of accidents.

The achievements of the organized safety movement have been impressive. The 1908–12 death rate per 100,000 in population from all accidents was 83.1. By 1973 it had been reduced to 55.3—despite the fact that in the meantime the motor-vehicle death rate had risen from 2.1 to 26.4. National work fatality figures go back only to 1926, but since that time there has been a substantial decline in the number of occupational accident fatalities, despite a great increase in the working force. On a population basis, the work death rate has been more than cut in half. From the early 1960's to the early 1970's, however, progress in reducing accident rates slowed markedly; motor vehicle and public non-motor-vehicle accidents actually increased slightly.

The federal government began to take a greatly increased interest in safety. The Highway Safety Act of 1966 represented the first major entry of the federal government into safety. Subsequently the Occupational Safety and Health Act of 1970 placed almost all employers under the obligation to obey safety and health standards—and was backed by penalties. The Consumer Safety Product Act of 1972 established a federal commission with authority to set standards and bar hazardous products from the marketplace. Certain individual industries are regulated under other federal safety laws. Moreover, there has been a constant extension of the coverage and benefits provided by the workmen's compensation laws established in the second decade of the 20th century in most states.

Despite the recently more active government role in accident prevention, the voluntary safety movement is stronger than ever. The National Safety Council has more than 15,000 members, most of them industrial corporations. In addition to extensive and sophisticated programs in the area of industrial safety, the council maintains a variety of safety programs, each with a special focus—farm, home, public, traffic, youth, women, and school and college.

[National Safety Council, *Accident Facts.*]

NATIONAL SAFETY COUNCIL

ACKIA, BATTLE OF. On May 26, 1736, the Chickasaw, with aid from British traders, decisively defeated the French under Jean Baptiste Le Moyne, Sieur de Bienville, at Ackia, near present Tupelo, Miss. This defeat reduced French prestige in that quarter, where French and English traders were engaged in a contest for control of Indian trade. (*See also* Chickasaw-French War.)

WALTER PRICHARD

ACOMA. Bounded by Zuni and Hopi on the west and by the Tanoan Pueblo to the north and east, the seven Keresan-speaking towns occupied the center of the present-day Pueblo area. (The Keresan language appears to be an independent linguistic family, having no known relationships elsewhere.) On the Rio Grande and its Jemez tributary are the towns of Cochiti, Santo Domingo, San Felipe, Santa Ana, and Zia, while to the west are the pueblos of Laguna and Acoma. Acoma falls into the general Pueblo cultural domain. It is a single town, located on a rock mesa 357 feet in height, about sixty miles west of the Rio Grande.

Like other pueblos Acoma stresses its independence, its endogamy, and the ritual character of intensive agriculture. Acoma, like its neighbors, retained its primary conservatism. Its intensive maize cultivation, ritual calendar, and priestly cults reflect a basic emphasis on the retention of a pre-Columbian cultural system, as happens elsewhere in the Pueblo region.

Acoma was contacted early by Spanish explorers, Francisco Vásquez de Coronado in 1540, Antonio de Espéjo in 1583, and Juan de Oñate in 1598, and subjected to Franciscan missionization. In December 1598, thirty of Oñate's men visited Acoma and were attacked by the Indians, resulting in the death of fifteen Spaniards. The following month a force of seventy scaled the high wall to the mesa and, during a three-day battle, killed nearly 1,500 Acoma. The Acoma also participated in the Pueblo Revolt of 1680, but were not dealt with as severely as other pueblos because of the inaccessibility of their town.

[L. A. White, "The Acoma Indians," *Annual Reports, Bureau of American Ethnology,* vol. 47.]

ROBERT F. SPENCER

ACRE RIGHT. *See* **Cabin Rights.**

ACT FOR THE IMPARTIAL ADMINISTRATION OF JUSTICE (one of the Coercion Acts). Passed by Parliament in May 1774, this act provided that whenever the governor of Massachusetts doubted whether a person accused of misconduct in suppressing a riot or executing the law could secure a fair trial in Massachusetts, he might, with consent of the council, transfer the trial to another colony or to Great Britain. This act—known in America as the "Murder Act"—aroused the colonists' apprehensions that the British government intended to establish a military despotism by giving British soldiers the privilege of shooting down Whigs with impunity.

[C. H. Van Tyne, *The Causes of the War of Independence.*]

JOHN C. MILLER

ACTING. *See* **Theater.**

ACTION, a federal agency created by executive order on July 1, 1971, to help solve social and economic problems at home and abroad through the cooperative efforts of a number of different volunteer programs. The overall commitment of ACTION is helping people to help themselves.

Originally ACTION included six volunteer programs formerly administered by several federal agencies: Peace Corps, Volunteers in Service to America (VISTA), Foster Grandparent Program, Retired Senior Volunteer Program (RSVP), Service Corps of Retired Executives (SCORE), and Active Corps of Executives (ACE). By mid-1974 ACTION had developed three additional programs—the Senior Companion Program, University Year for ACTION (UYA), and ACTION Cooperative Volunteers (ACV)—and was testing several others. During the same period it had increased its volunteer strength from 22,830 to 127,000. Agency headquarters are in Washington, D.C. Ten regional offices located throughout the nation oversee the efforts of all domestic programs operating within the respective regions. In the ACTION international program, Peace Corps volunteers serve in sixty-nine developing nations around the world.

Peace Corps volunteers serve for two-year terms in host countries, working in a wide variety of projects relating to agriculture; education; health; and economic, community, and natural-resources development and conservation. More than 8,000 Peace Corps volunteers provide these nations with trained manpower and help to promote peace and friendship through mutual understanding. Since its beginning in 1961, more than 50,000 Americans have served in the Peace Corps, which serves only at the request of the host country governments.

VISTA volunteers serve in the United States to mobilize community resources to solve problems that poverty communities have themselves identified. In mid-1974 more than 4,400 VISTA volunteers were working in locally administered projects in an attempt to upgrade health care, education, housing, and social and legal services. VISTA volunteers also give aid in the areas of community planning and economic development. One-year VISTA assignments are made at the request of, and under the sponsorship of, public or private nonprofit organizations.

Both the Foster Grandparent Program and RSVP tap the skills and experience of retired persons sixty years of age and older while providing them with opportunities for personal reward. In the Foster Grandparent Program, 12,000 such men and women who need supplementary income provide companionship and guidance on a one-to-one basis to physically, mentally, or emotionally handicapped children. The volunteers visit their "grandchildren" in an institutional setting four hours a day, five days a week, and receive a stipend of $1.60 an hour. Older Americans also find an outlet for their talents in RSVP, the fastest growing of all ACTION programs. As RSVP volunteers, retired persons give part-time service to schools, courts, libraries, hospitals, nursing homes, museums, day-care centers, and social welfare agencies. They are reimbursed only for transportation and on-site meals. Based on the Foster Grandparent model the Senior Companion Program enables low-income older people to serve needy adults in nursing homes and other group settings or in the homes of the needy adults for a stipend of $1.60 an hour.

SCORE and ACE bring the expertise of business people, retired or active, to struggling small businesses and minority-owned enterprises at no charge. These programs operate under a cooperative management agreement between the federal government's Small Business Administration and ACTION. Between 1964 and 1974 SCORE volunteers handled nearly 200,000 cases, providing individual counseling on management and financial and operational problems to small businessmen and nonprofit organizations. In 1974 there were more than 4,600 SCORE and 2,700 ACE volunteers.

In 1972 ACTION developed, tested, and established UYA. It utilizes the energies of students and the resources of their universities in a joint effort to help solve some of the problems which cause poverty. The volunteers spend one year off campus, living and working in low-income communities, guided by supervisors from sponsoring community organizations, and receive academic supervision and course credit from their colleges or universities. In mid-1974 1,900 students from forty-three schools were participating in the program.

Another program, ACV, allows community groups to sponsor volunteers for one year by sharing the overall costs with ACTION. Still modest in scale in mid-1974, the program included approximately 220 volunteers serving in thirty-three states.

JOAN KELLEY

***ACTIVE* CASE,** *Olmstead et al.* v. *Rittenhouse's Executives,* raised the question of prerogative as between federal and state courts. Gideon Olmstead of Connecticut and others seized the British sloop *Active* (1777), which was later captured by the Pennsylvania armed brig *Convention,* commanded by Capt. Houston. Award of prize money to Houston and his crew by state courts of Pennsylvania was set aside by the Supreme Court (1809) after a bitter dispute regarding jurisdiction.

WHEELER PRESTON

ACTS OF TRADE. *See* **Navigation Acts.**

ADAIR* V. *UNITED STATES, 208 U.S. 161 (1908). In violation of a federal law of 1898, William Adair, acting for the Louisville & Nashville Railroad, dismissed O. B. Coppage because he was a member of a labor union. The Supreme Court declared this law unconstitutional because it violated the due process clause of the Fifth Amendment.

[Charles Warren, *The Supreme Court in the United States.*]

E. MERTON COULTER

ADAMS, FORT, built 1798–99 by Maj. Thomas Freeman eight miles above the thirty-first parallel on the east bank of the Mississippi River (Loftus Heights), was an earthwork, magazine, and barracks for boundary defense against the Spanish, just removed from Natchez and confined to Louisiana and Florida (*see* Pinckney's Treaty). It was the United States port of entry on the Mississippi.

Here Gen. James Wilkinson negotiated a treaty with the Choctaw (Dec. 12, 1801) for resurveying the British line from the Yazoo River southward marking limits of the Natchez district, and for a road (Natchez Trace) north through Choctaw country to the Chickasaw, thence to Nashville. Negotiations for a road to Mobile were opened but abandoned for fear of Spanish hostility. Wilkinson completed the resurvey in 1803. Congress appropriated $6,000 for the Natchez Trace (1806). After American acquisition of Louisiana and Florida, Fort Adams was abandoned.

[C. E. Carter, *Territorial Papers of the United States,* vol. V; Dunbar Rowland, *Mississippi,* vol. I.]

MACK SWEARINGEN

ADAMS EXPRESS COMPANY. In 1839 Alvin Adams, a produce merchant ruined by the panic of 1837, began carrying letters, small packages, and valuables for patrons between Boston and Worcester. He began with a partner named Burke, who soon withdrew, and as Adams and Company, Adams rapidly extended his territory to New York, Philadelphia, and other eastern cities. By 1847 he had penetrated deeply into the South, and by 1850 he was shipping by rail and stagecoach to Saint Louis. In 1854 his company was reorganized as the Adams Express Company, having merged with several rival firms. Meanwhile, a subsidiary concern, Adams and Company of California, had been organized in 1850 and spread its service along the Pacific coast; but not being under Adams' personal management, it was badly handled and failed in 1854, causing a panic in California. The South was almost entirely covered by the Adams express service in 1861, when the Civil War necessitated the splitting off of another company, which, for politic reasons, was given the name of Southern. There was a mysterious kinship between the two ever afterward; they had joint offices at common points. Southern stock was never quoted in the market, and it was even charged by some Adams stockholders that the Southern was secretly owned by Adams. The parent company held a strong position from New England and the mid-Atlantic coast to the far western plains. Its stock holdings were enormous. In 1910 it was the second largest stockholder in the Pennsylvania Railroad and the third largest in the New Haven, besides owning large blocks of American Express and Norfolk & Western. Its antebellum employment of Allan Pinkerton to solve its robbery problems was a large factor in building up that noted detective agency. Along with the other expresses, in 1918 it merged its shipping interests into the American Railway Express Company, but continued its corporate existence as a wealthy investment trust.

[Alvin F. Harlow, *Old Waybills;* Henry Pickering Walker, *The Wagonmasters: High Plains Freighting From the Earliest Days of the Santa Fe Trail to 1880.*]

ALVIN F. HARLOW

ADAMSON ACT, enacted under administration pressure backed by a strike threat, was passed Sept. 2, 1916. It established, in place of a ten-hour day, an eight-hour day for trainmen. The alternative of 100 miles of run remained unchanged. The railroads claimed the law raised wages rather than regulated hours, as normal operation required over eight hours' work. The law was upheld, in *Wilson* v. *New,* 243 U.S. 332 (1917), as hour legislation in the interests of interstate commerce.

[J. R. Commons and J. B. Andrews, *Principles of Labor Legislation.*]

JAMES D. MAGEE

ADAMS-ONÍS TREATY. Signed at Washington, Feb. 22, 1819, by John Quincy Adams, secretary of state, and Luis de Onís, Spanish minister, the treaty closed the first era of United States expansion by providing for the cession of East Florida, the abandonment of the controversy over West Florida, which had previously been seized by the United States, and a boundary delineation along the Sabine River from the Gulf of Mexico north to the 32nd parallel; thence north to the Red River, along it to the 100th meridian; north to the Arkansas River and along it to its source; thence directly north or south as the case might be to the 42nd parallel; and west on that line to the Pacific Ocean. The United States assumed claims of its own citizens against Spain, prorating them down to a maximum of $5 million. Nonconflicting articles of Pinckney's Treaty of 1795 were to remain in force. Spanish goods received certain tariff privileges in Florida ports.

Spain, weakened by European wars and colonial revolutions, was obliged to sacrifice her interests, especially after Andrew Jackson's seizure of Spanish property in the Floridas in 1818 (*see* Arbuthnot and Ambrister, Case of). Other nations declined to assist Spain in the negotiations. Ferdinand VII's ministers at first refused to ratify the treaty, using as a pretext the nullification of certain land grants made by Ferdinand in the Floridas. Evasion failed, and after a revolt made Ferdinand a constitutional monarch in 1820, his council was obliged to approve the treaty. Ratifications were exchanged at Washington on Feb. 22, 1821.

[Samuel Flagg Bemis, *John Quincy Adams and the Foundations of American Foreign Policy;* R. W. Van Alstyne, *The Rising American Empire.*]

PHILIP COOLIDGE BROOKS

"ADDRESS OF THE SOUTHERN DELEGATES." Southern delegates in Congress, aroused by hostile resolutions on slavery, called a caucus for Dec. 23, 1848. John C. Calhoun submitted an address "moderate in manner" but calculated to unite the South which, with three amendments that did not "affect the truth of its narrative, or materially change its character," was finally adopted on Jan. 22, 1849, after a substitute proposal by John M. Berrien had been rejected. Calhoun's address relates entirely to the sectional contest over slavery and recounts the aggressions of the North on the South. These aggressions were of two kinds: nullification of constitutional guarantees for the return of fugitive slaves, and the exclusion of slavery and southerners from the common territories (*see* Wilmot Proviso). Calhoun maintained that these aggressions threatened ultimate abolition and the complete overturn of southern society unless the South united and brought them to an end. Fewer than half the southern delegates signed the address, and it accomplished little. (*See also* Tarpley Letter.)

[T. H. Benton, *Thirty Years' View;* John C. Calhoun, *Works,* vol. VI; W. M. Meigs, *Life of John Caldwell Calhoun.*]

FLETCHER M. GREEN

ADDYSTON PIPE COMPANY CASE, 175 U.S. 211 (1899). The Supreme Court, by a unanimous decision based on the Sherman Antitrust Act, permanently enjoined six producers of cast-iron pipe from continuing an agreement eliminating competition among themselves. Justice Rufus Peckham, speaking for the Court, denied that the *United States* v. *E. C. Knight Company* decision obtained, saying that here was a definite conspiracy to interfere with the flow of interstate commerce and a positive scheme to limit competition and fix prices. This decision indicated that the Sherman Antitrust Act possessed teeth, and tended to restrain similar activities.

[Eliot Jones, *The Trust Problem in the United States;* W. Z. Ripley, *Trusts, Pools and Corporations.*]

ALLEN E. RAGAN

ADENA. The Adena culture was the first of a series of spectacular Early and Middle Woodland cultures in prehistoric eastern North America. Dating from about 1000 B.C. to A.D. 200, Adena sites are mainly concentrated in the central Ohio valley within 150 miles of Chillicothe, Ohio. The classic heartland includes sections of southern Ohio, eastern Indiana, northern Kentucky, northwestern West Virginia, and southwestern Pennsylvania. Even though the geographic extent of this prehistoric culture was severely restricted, the Adena experienced a cultural florescence that influenced the development of other Eastern Woodland cultures. The persistence of Adena art motifs, artifact forms, and ceremonial and burial rituals, particularly in the South and East, indicates the extent of this influence. For example, the raptorial bird, the hand-eye design, the death motif, and the circular eye remained dominant themes in Eastern Woodland art into the historic period.

Archaeologists have concentrated their excavations on the impressive burial and ceremonial centers of the Adena, which is why this aspect of their lifeway is known in greatest detail. The centers often contain both conical earthen burial mounds and large circular, square, and pentagonal earthworks. Open areas enclosed by the earthworks may have been the focus of ritual activities within the centers. Wooden palisades and round houses 20 to 80 feet in diameter are associated with some mounds and earthworks. The mounds vary widely in size and pattern of use. Some small mounds were built quickly to cover the body of a single individual. Other, larger, mounds were built up through successive interments over an extended period of time. Dozens of these burials were recovered in West Virginia from the 20-meter-high Grave Creek Mound. The famous Robbins Mounds site near Big Bone Lick, Ky., also has a large mound and more than fifty-two tombs. Graves ranged in Adena mounds from simple pits to clay-lined crematory basins and large log-lined cribs containing several extended skeletons. Important individuals were apparently buried in the larger tombs. Unlike later Hopewell mounds, Adena mounds did not usually contain grave goods.

The Adena people lived in clusters of small hamlets near these burial and ceremonial centers. Among the more unusual Adena artifacts are bowls made from human crania, rectangular stone tablets engraved with zoomorphic figures, stone chest ornaments in a variety of geometric shapes, shell beads, tubular pipes, and stone atlatl weights. Woodland cord-marked pottery and some southern check-stamped wares were used as containers. Evidence of the subsistence base that supported the construction of the impressive mounds and earthworks is still inconclusive. Varieties of pumpkin, gourd, sunflower, and goosefoot that may have been domesticated were found in association with Adena artifacts in Newt Kash Shelter, Ky. Small amounts of corn, a potentially more significant domesticate, were recovered in Kentucky from the Daines Mound 2, which has been dated by radiocarbon to 250 B.C. The basic subsistence pattern seems to have continued the broadly exploitive collecting emphasis characteristic of the Archaic. Although Mexican influence has been suggested as the source of the stimulus that led to the emergence of classic Adena, it seems more likely that the roots of the florescence will eventually be found in increased sedentism, population growth, and other indigenous Eastern Woodland processes. The Middle Woodland Hopewell cultures were in part a later elaboration of classic Adena.

[Don W. Dragoo, "Mounds for the Dead," *Annals of the Carnegie Museum,* vol. 37; William S. Webb and Raymond S. Baby, *The Adena People.*]

GUY GIBBON

***ADKINS* V. *CHILDREN'S HOSPITAL*,** 261 U.S. 525 (1923), a Supreme Court decision holding invalid an act of Congress creating a minimum wage board to ascertain and fix adequate wages for women employees in the District of Columbia. The question before the Court was whether the act of Congress constituted a deprivation of "life, liberty or property without due process of law" under the Fifth Amendment. The Court held by a vote of five to three that the act was an unjustified interference by Congress with the freedom of employer and employee to contract as they pleased. Justices William H. Taft, Edward Sanford, and Oliver Wendell Holmes, dissenting, took the view that the Fifth Amendment did not stand in the way of reasonable legislation calculated to correct admitted evils. The case was expressly overruled by *West Coast Hotel Company* v. *Parrish,* 57 Supreme Court 578 (1937).

[Roscoe Pound and others, *The Supreme Court and Minimum Wage Legislation.*]

GEORGE W. GOBLE

ADMINISTRATIVE DISCRETION, DELEGATION OF. The design of the U.S. Constitution incorporating the separation of legislative, executive, and judicial powers was a deliberate attempt to limit the use and abuse of executive discretion in government by a formal differentiation and separation of governmental functions. Regardless of the formal separation of powers, however, the First Congress made delegations of discretionary powers to the Treasury and War departments respecting taxes and pensions. Since that time delegations of discretionary powers to the president or subordinate executive officers, such as the postmaster general or the commissioner of Indian affairs, have occurred so frequently as to be commonplace. Discretionary powers pervade the executive branch.

The increasing complexity of society, especially in economic matters, has resulted in increased demands for governmental regulation and for services. A great acceleration in delegation of powers to specialized administrative agencies has been the response of all levels of government. The device of the specialized agency probably results from the necessity for detailed technical knowledge and for continuing supervision, both to a degree beyond the capacity of Congress and the courts. Since the creation of the Interstate Commerce Commission in 1887, at least eight major regulatory agencies have been created, with a host of service agencies.

The hallmark of delegation of administrative powers, particularly in the regulatory agencies, has been the merging of governmental functions ostensibly separated constitutionally. Thus discretion is conferred not only in executive powers (investigation, supervision, prosecution), but also in the legislative (rulemaking) and judicial spheres. Criticism of this merger of functions led Congress in the Administrative Procedure Act of 1946 to require separate performance of adjudicatory functions by special personnel.

The historic quest for controls on discretion has continued. Substantial constitutional limitations exist, especially the requirement of due process of law. For delegations to be effective, Congress must by statute provide standards for the exercise of the delegated power. Substantive legislation establishing agencies frequently contains specific limitations on the scope of their authority, and specific procedural requirements for its exercise. The Administrative Procedure Act establishes broad procedural requirements generally applicable to most administrative agencies. Agency acts, as well as adjudication, are subject to judicial review within limits.

[C. H. Kinnane, *Anglo-American Law.*]

ROBERT E. GOOSTREE

ADMINISTRATIVE JUSTICE, or, more commonly, administrative adjudication, is the exercise by an administrative agency of judicial powers delegated to the agency by a legislative body. Agencies that have these judicial powers are often termed "administrative tribunals" to distinguish them from those which do not have judicial powers, and from the regular courts.

The distinction which modern usage makes between administrative tribunals and the courts of law was not made historically. For example, the English Court of Exchequer evolved from the administrative Exchequer, a tax-assessing and collecting agency. American usage derives from the separation of powers in the U.S. Constitution, and from the limitation therein of the "judicial power of the United States" to certain types of "cases . . . and controversies." It was this interpretation of Article III that led certain judges in Hayburn's case (1792) to refuse to pass on veterans' claims, as authorized by Congress. The veterans' claims were felt by the judges to be administrative, rather than judicial. On the other hand, the U.S. Court of Claims originated as an administrative tribunal, but is now defined as a constitutional court. The Tax Court, however, is not a court in the usual sense, but an administrative appellate tribunal, dealing with appeals from administrative determinations of officers of the Internal Revenue Service.

Administrative tribunals are not ordinarily engaged in determining the rights and duties of individuals as against other individuals. Rather, they typically deal with individuals in relation to government, in terms of benefits sought or disabilities incurred from government action. It is this function that chiefly distinguishes the administrative tribunal from the civil courts. In contrast to the criminal courts, administrative tribunals are typically empowered to assess various penalties, such as forfeiture of licenses, for violation of statutory or administrative regulation. Some administrative agencies, however, are not vested with adjudicative powers and must proceed through the regular courts for civil or criminal punishment of violations.

A second fundamental difference between the administrative tribunals and the courts is the nature of subject matter jurisdiction. The subject matter of administrative regulation and adjudication by an agency is normally a single economic activity, a set of closely related economic activities, or specific benefits conferred by government. The concern of the National Labor Relations Board with labor relations is an example of the first; the jurisdiction of the Federal Communications Commission over radio, television, and telephone, of the second; and adjudication of the validity of claims to benefits by such agencies as the Veterans Administration, of the third. In contrast, the subject matter jurisdiction of courts embraces a broad spectrum of civil and criminal law.

Adjudication by administrative tribunals has, especially in the 1930's, been violently criticized on the ground that the merger of the judicial with the legislative and executive functions in an administrative agency was contrary to the constitutional separation of powers. The Administrative Procedure Act of 1946, applicable to most U.S. administrative tribunals, imposes uniform procedural requirements on the agencies, and requires the judicial function to be separated from the legislative and executive aspects. Some agencies, not covered by this act, have substitute provisions in their organic statutes; some have had additional procedural requirements imposed.

The act specifies requirements as to notice and hearing for covered agencies. It provides that decision must be made upon a record established in the hearing, and that an initial decision be made by the officer who hears the evidence. This hearing examiner moves written findings of fact and conclusions of law and the initial decision is based thereon. The initial decision is frequently subject to appeal to intraagency boards or to the commission or board which is the highest administrative authority of the agency. The act further provides for a broad right of review of agency adjudication by the courts. In general, judicial review is limited to questions of law, and administrative findings of fact are conclusive on the courts unless unsupported by substantial evidence. Questions of law include allegations of denial of constitutional or statutory rights, failure to observe procedures required, and scope of authority of the agency. An administrative adjudication may be set aside if a court finds it to be arbitrary, capricious, or an abuse of discretion.

Administrative regulation and adjudication is not limited to the national governmental level. It has become widespread in the states and municipalities, embracing such subjects as public utilities, natural resources, banking, securities, workmen's compensation, unemployment insurance, employment discrimination, rents, automobile operation and inspection, corporations, elections, welfare, commercial insurance, land use, and environmental and consumer protection. Some states have administrative procedure acts comparable to the federal act of 1946; but in the states, judicial review is characteristically broader than under the federal act.

[Louis L. Jaffe, *Judicial Control of Administrative Action.*]

ROBERT E. GOOSTREE

ADMINISTRATIVE OFFICE OF U.S. COURTS. *See* **Federal Agencies.**

ADMIRALS AND COMMODORES. Prior to the Civil War, the small number of U.S. warships did not justify having admirals, the naval equivalent of generals. The highest rank was that of captain, equal to an army colonel. As a practical matter when two or more vessels operated together, the senior captain temporarily assumed the flag-pendant and title of commodore, an honorary title equal to brigadier general. At the onset of the Barbary War, Thomas Truxtun, hero-leader in the Quasi-War with France, sought to make the rank of commodore permanent, but was forced into retirement for presumed pretensions.

Lingering republican abhorrence for aristocratic titles led to the invention of the ambiguous title "flag officer" for the first year of the Civil War. It was unsatisfactory for senior naval officers cooperating with army leaders holding clear-cut and traditional general ranks. On July 16, 1862, Congress established the ranks of rear admiral (two-star flag and insignia) and commodore (one star). In 1864 David Farragut was made the first vice admiral (three stars) and, a year later, the first "full" admiral (four stars). His protégé, David Dixon Porter, became vice admiral, heading ten rear admirals. Following the deaths of Farragut and Porter, the two senior grades remained unfilled for some years. (The Confederacy also had flag officers but commissioned only Admiral Franklin Buchanan and Rear Admiral Raphael Semmes.) In 1899 George Dewey was given the four-star rank Admiral of the Navy. The eighteen rear admirals he headed displaced the need for commodores, and the grade was abolished in 1912.

The navy entered World War I with thirty rear admirals. Three billets had the temporary rank of admiral—Chief of Naval Operations, or CNO (William S. Benson), Commander-in-Chief, Atlantic Fleet (Henry T. Mayo), and Commander of Naval Forces Operating in European Waters (William S. Sims). Congress did not make the rank permanent for Benson, Mayo, and Sims, who after the war completed service as rear admirals, the highest rank at which they could retire, although the temporary admiral rank continued with the billets of CNO or fleet command, and vice admiral for seconds-in-command. World War II opened the purse for permanent higher ranks and even created the super, five-star rank of fleet admiral for the remaining lifetimes of Ernest J. King, Chester W. Nimitz, William D. Leahy, and William F. Halsey, who had led to victory 252 line and staff (supply, etc.) admirals and 111 commodores (whose one-star grade was reinstituted for command of wartime convoys).

The Korean War had some 200 line and 60 staff admirals, and in 1972, the navy had 9 four-star, 40 three-star, and 313 two-star admirals. There was some newspaper criticism that 362 flag officers commanding 602,000 men was excessive in comparison to the same number of flag officers in World War II leading five times as many men, 3,381,000, and in 1973 a 10-percent reduction took place.

R. W. Daly

ADMIRALTY LAW AND COURTS. Admiralty law consists of the norms governing traffic by water. In America its sources were British admiralty law, the less restricted colonial vice-admiralty jurisdiction of the crown, and the broad and ancient European maritime legal traditions.

Ancient maritime law derived from cosmopolitan commercial customs and from compilations. Phoenician and Rhodian sea rules—historically vague but traditionally acknowledged—and Roman marine practice were threaded into medieval compilations (for example, Amalfi, Consolato del Mar, Oleron), which were of great significance. These compilations represented customary rules, sometimes set forth initially by tribunals of merchant-consuls in the commercial centers, and were independent of the local sovereigns. With the rise of modern states, the customary sea rules ran afoul of change. States incorporated the maritime laws into sovereign codes, the most celebrated of which was the 1681 French Marine Ordinance. In England this development came earlier, but was more piecemeal. Somewhat before the reign of Richard II (1377–1400), an admiralty court had come to function under the principal royal maritime authority, although tribunals based on the merchant-consul model continued to function for a time. Eventually, common law courts, viewing admiralty with jaundiced eye, achieved limitations on admiralty jurisdiction.

Most American colonial courts were common law, but colonial admiralty tribunals enjoyed a jurisdiction less restricted than in England. That and the fact that juries were not utilized under admiralty tribunals—certainly advantageous to the crown—contributed to the grievances of the colonists. Immediately following American independence, most admiralty concerns were placed under state authority; but the Articles of Confederation did provide for courts governing piracy, sea felonies, and prize. National jurisdiction was, however, implemented only in prize cases.

Under the Constitution, federal authority "extends to all cases of admiralty and maritime jurisdiction" (including inland waterways) and the district courts have original jurisdiction by law. Admiralty law embraces the various legal concerns, public and private, of marine industry and activity but omits certain related areas, for example, shipbuilding contracts. Admiralty jurisdiction includes insurance, bills of lading, charters, general average, seamen's rights, collision, salvage, maritime liens, ships' mortgages, liability limitations, piracy, and the laws of sea warfare. It remains to be noted that some aspects of maritime law have a near universal quality due not only to ancient practice, but also to recent shipping conventions under which generalized procedures are very widely employed, for example, the York-Antwerp rules of general average.

[C. John Colombos, *The International Law of the Sea*, 6th ed.; Grant Gilmore and Charles L. Black, Jr., *The Law of Admiralty;* Arnold W. Knauth and Christopher R. Knauth, *Benedict on Admiralty*, 6–7th eds., 7 vols. supplemented, 1940–69; William McFee, *The Law of the Sea;* John Henry Wigmore, *A Panorama of the World's Legal Systems*, vol. III.]

H. B. JACOBINI

ADMISSION OF STATES. *See* **State-making Process.**

ADOBE, a type of construction used principally in the Rocky Mountain plateau and the southwestern United States. The method came from North Africa via Spain and was introduced by the Spanish conquerors into the Southwest in the 16th century. Most of the Spanish mission buildings were made of this material. Wet clay and chopped hay or other fibrous material were mixed and the mass tramped with bare feet. This was molded into bricks and sun dried. The walls were laid up with mud mortar. In the Rocky Mountain plateau adobe houses were made by molding clay directly into the wall instead of making it into bricks. Adobe was widely used to build forts and trading posts as far east and north as Nebraska. Adobe was corrupted to "dobie" by the Americans.

EVERETT DICK

ADOBE WALLS, BATTLE OF (June 27, 1874). In retaliation against hunters who were killing buffalo—the Indians' source of food, clothing, and shelter—Comanche, Cheyenne, and Kiowa Indians attacked Adobe Walls, a trading post on the north side of the Canadian River in the Texas Panhandle. The Indians abandoned the attack after suffering heavy losses.

J. EVETTS HALEY

ADULT EDUCATION. *See* **Education.**

ADVENTIST CHURCHES. The adventist movement was a response to the prophecies of William Miller in the 1830's and early 1840's. Miller was a farmer and devoted Bible student from Low Hampton, N.Y., who maintained that the Second Coming of Christ would occur in 1843. After the failure of this prediction (and two dates he set in 1844), his disciples, also known as Millerites, divided over such issues as the name of the denomination, the dating of the end, and whether Saturday or Sunday should be observed as the day of rest. The two largest Adventist groups are the Advent Christian Church and the Seventh Day Adventists.

The Advent Christian Church, organized in 1860 by Jonathan Cummings, holds doctrines similar to those of other Protestant denominations with the exception of the church's understanding of the Second Coming and of the nature of man. Its members believe that the soul sleeps until the end of the age, when it is reunited with the body for the Last Judgment. The church had 30,000 members in 1973. The Seventh Day Adventists were organized as a denomination in 1863. They adopted the seventh-day pattern of worship after a study of the Decalogue (Ten Commandments) and in deference to Mrs. Rachael D. Preston, a former Seventh Day Baptist. The Seventh Day Adventists believe that the scriptures are an infallible guide to faith and they abstain from tobacco, liquor, and sometimes tea and coffee. Each member is expected to contribute a full tithe to the work of the church. The group had 448,000 members in 1973. Other adventist denominations are the Church of God (Abrahamic Faith) with 6,700 members and the Primitive Advent Christian Church with 600 members in 1973.

[*Seventh-Day Adventist Encyclopedia;* Sylvester Bliss, *Memoirs of William Miller;* Arthur W. Spalding, *Origin and History of Seventh-Day Adventists;* E. G. White, *The Story of Patriarchs and Prophets*.]

GLENN T. MILLER

ADVENTURE, a sloop built in the winter of 1791–92 at Clayoquot on Nootka Sound in southwest British Columbia by Asa Gray and John Kendrick of Boston, who were on an exploring and trading expedition in the Northwest. It was the first American sailing vessel built on the Pacific coast.

[K. Coman, *Economic Beginnings of the Far West*.]

CARL L. CANNON

ADVENTURERS. The term "adventurer" runs far back into English history when there appeared a body of traders known as merchant adventurers. The very name, adventurer, denoted a new age and spirit in mercantile life. With money to invest, these enterprising merchants sought opportunities beyond England's shores. They adventured or risked their capital in foreign trade. Groups of merchant adventurers existed in Bristol, London, York, Chester, and other leading ports.

Colonization in the New World demanded labor and capital. Settlers had to be transported across a hostile sea, properly equipped to build life anew in a virgin land, and supplied with food until self-sustaining. Many were able to help themselves, venturing both life and money. Many others were dependent upon financial assistance. The demands upon capital were heavy.

The adventurers supplied the capital and enterprise which built up England's profitable commercial dominion in the Old World in the 16th century. The New World offered increased opportunities. The merchants of Bristol aided Sir Humphrey Gilbert's futile colonial venture in Newfoundland in 1583, and a few London merchants assisted Sir Walter Raleigh in his ill-fated attempt to settle Roanoke Island in 1585. A larger capital was necessary and the familiar device of the joint-stock company was employed (*see* Trading Companies). Adventurers of Plymouth subscribed to the stock of the Plymouth Company, whose colonial effort in Maine in 1607 promptly failed. London adventurers took stock in the company, which by persistent effort succeeded in making Virginia a permanent colony (*see* Virginia Company of London). A group of London merchants risked their capital in aiding the Pilgrims to settle the colony of Plymouth in 1620. The colony of Massachusetts originated in an association of merchants living in and about Dorchester, England. Not all those who risked their capital were merchants. The charter of 1609 to the Virginia Company of London incorporated fifty-six companies of the city of London and 659 persons gathered from various walks of life.

[C. M. Andrews, *Colonial Period of American History;* C. P. Nettels, *Roots of American Civilization.*]

WINFRED T. ROOT

ADVERTISING. Colonial Period to the 1880's. Before the advent of newspapers, signboards on inns, taverns, and coffeehouses constituted the only advertising medium. In the larger towns portrait artists frequently painted these to earn a livelihood. The first newspaper to appear continuously, the *Boston News-Letter,* was established in 1704; and its third issue contained the first advertisements, an offer for the sale of real estate and two notices of lost articles. The number of such notices increased in subsequent issues. Reward offers for runaway apprentices were common, as were announcements of sale of cordage, wine, and cloth. A substantial percentage of early advertisements were notices of slaves for sale.

From its founding in 1728 Benjamin Franklin's *Pennsylvania Gazette* published more advertisements than any other contemporary colonial newspaper. Franklin introduced the use of 14-point headings; the separation of advertisements with space; and, after 1750, the illustration of shipping notices, slave auctions, and horologers' shops by the insertion next to the notices of small woodcuts of ships, blacks, and clock faces, respectively. John Dunlap followed Franklin's example in his *Pennsylvania Packet and General Advertiser,* which in 1784 became the first daily in the United States. Newspaper advertisements are an important source for the social and economic history of the colonial and early national period, since they describe the imported and domestically manufactured commodities for sale, give sailing vessel, stagecoach, and after 1800 steamboat schedules, and indicate the wide variety of services available. Amusement notices and "wanted" advertisements were featured first in separate sections in the 1830's by the tabloid *New York Sun,* which also started the practice of printing marriage and death announcements for revenue.

The onset of the Revolution provoked a severe paper shortage, which continued until about 1830, when the Fourdrinier papermaking machine came into general use. The necessity of conserving space precluded display advertising and led to the use of advertisements of the legal-notice variety. These single-column agate advertisements remained the standard until the 1860's, when large display advertisements by bond houses to stimulate the sale of western railroad securities and by dry goods stores began to appear continuously. Column rules, previously strictly adhered to by publishers, were thus broken.

The Civil War period also saw a large increase in circulation, the genesis of Sunday newspapers, the introduction of paper from wood pulp, and important improvements in the printing process, all of which contributed to a significant rise in advertising volume. Magazine advertising also began at this time, and advertising occupied much space in religious and farm periodicals until 1890. P. T. Barnum's promotional successes were largely responsible for a sizable increase in outdoor advertising in the form of posters and handbills. The mail-order catalog was introduced in 1870 by E. C. Allen of Augusta, Maine, a manufacturer of a washing powder recipe.

In the 1830's James Gordon Bennett of the *New York Herald* essentially initiated the modern line rate—establishing a minimum advertising unit and setting rates on a daily, weekly, monthly, or annual basis—although bargaining for space continued for another half-century. The early advertising agents, who appeared before 1850, negotiated with newspapers for space, paying either in cash or in printing materials, and then sold the space to advertisers at a profit. By estimating the circulation of newspapers and thus their value, the agents acted in effect as rate makers.

Advent of Modern Advertising. The industrialization of the United States was well under way in the 1880's. Such new products as cameras, bicycles, and safety razors began to compete for the consumer's dollar with the staples—sugar, flour, clothing, and patent medicines. Between 1880 and 1910 the population almost doubled, increasing from 50 to 92 million. The growth of cities and, later, the development of suburbs, aided by the introduction of street railways and automobiles, created large urban markets. The introduction of rural free delivery in 1896 and of parcel post in 1913 aided widespread contact with the farming population. The completion of a nationwide rail network, affording rapid transport of goods, provided the basis for a mass national market.

The department store, largely a metamorphosis from the retail dry goods establishment, came into existence in the late 1870's. By 1880 R. H. Macy and Company and Lord and Taylor—both in New York City—had book, china, silverware, shoe, and furniture departments. In Philadelphia John Wanamaker had opened the "New Kind of Store." Department stores were particularly influential in establishing the fixed retail price, introduced by A. T. Stewart of New York City, whose "Marble Palace" was purchased by Wanamaker in 1896. Wanamaker built his business on newspaper advertising; he instituted the money-back guarantee; and his innovative advertising ideas influenced the advertising practices of retail merchants countrywide. Retail advertising, particularly that of department stores, made possible the emergence of the two-cent newspaper of forty-eight or more pages. By 1905 daily newspaper circulation had risen to 21 million from 8 million in 1890.

In their quest for a mass national market, manufacturers sought to break with the tradition of depending upon jobbers to sell their products to retailers, who in turn offered the merchandise to the public. Instead, it became their strategy to create widespread consumer demand through national advertising, obliging retailers to order goods from wholesalers. George Eastman was among the first to adopt this idea, spending $25,000 to advertise the Kodak in 1888. In the 1890's Procter and Gamble (Ivory soap), Sapolio (cleaning powder), and the Royal Baking Powder Company led in such promotion, the latter expending $500,000 for advertising in 1893 alone. These efforts not only increased the number and circulation of weekly and monthly periodicals, but also augmented the volume and expense of advertising. By 1900 the *Ladies' Home Journal,* established by Cyrus H. K. Curtis in 1883, had 850,000 subscribers, followed by *Munsey's* with a circulation of 700,000. The Crowell Publishing Company founded *Farm and Fireside, Women's Home Companion,* and *Collier's,* while William Randolph Hearst offered competition with *Cosmopolitan, Good Housekeeping, Harper's Bazar,* and *Town & Country.* Between 1890 and 1905 the monthly circulation of periodicals increased from 18 million to 64 million.

Other advertising media were being exploited at the same time. Montgomery Ward's first mail-order catalog, an eight-page pamphlet, was issued in 1874, and by 1890 company sales were almost $9 million. Ward was joined in 1893 by Sears, Roebuck, whose sales volume surpassed Ward's within a decade. Carleton and Kissam of New York City was the agency leader in systematic streetcar advertising, and by 1905 it controlled this medium in fifty-four cities served by 9,000 cars. To achieve its success the agency had to persuade manufacturers of streetcars to design and build vehicles affording liberal and prominent space for advertising cards. Outdoor advertising also prospered, the increased number of billboards paralleling the growth of automobile use.

Accompanying the vast increase in the circulation of newspapers and periodicals and the substantially increased advertising expenditures were significant changes in the advertising trade. Reliable systems for checking circulation were established; a complete modification of the role of the advertising agency occurred; more attention was paid to the design and message of advertisements; and critical appraisal of the advertised products and advertising practices began.

From the time that advertising became a substantial factor in the financial success of newspapers, publishers kept their actual circulation figures secret. To maintain high advertising rates it was common practice to claim grossly exaggerated numbers of subscribers. George P. Rowell, a New York City agent, made the initial attempt to ascertain the advertising value of newspapers in 1869 by publishing his *American Newspaper Directory,* which listed 5,411 publications in the United States and 367 in Canada. Following each name was a symbol that indicated Rowell's estimate of the newspaper's actual circulation. Rowell published subsequent issues of this directory, and others followed his lead in the periodicals field. The pressure from advertisers, working through agencies, to gain access to information concerning quantity and quality of the circulation of publications led to the formation of the Audit Bureau of Circulations in 1914. Member publishers submit biennial statements of circulation calculated according to a common standard of measurement, and bureau auditors make an annual examination of circulation records.

The practice of purchasing space from publishers at the lowest possible cost and selling it at the highest price to potential advertisers placed agents in the position of middlemen, who profited to the extent of their bargaining ability. To gain a more professional status a few agencies, notably N. W. Ayer and Son of Philadelphia, about 1880 began to offer advertisers an "open contract." Under this arrangement the advertiser contracted to allow the agent to handle his entire advertising budget for an unspecified period of time. On his part the agent agreed to purchase the most valuable space in the advertiser's behalf, invoicing him for his cost plus a certain percentage as a commission. In 1893 the American Newspaper Publishers Association agreed to pay a commission to recognized independent agencies and not to allow discounts on space to direct advertisers. Curtis Publishing Company inaugurated the same practice in 1901, and other periodical publishers soon followed suit. The cost-plus-commission basis for the agency was accepted industrywide in 1919, and the commission was standardized at 15 percent.

In order to justify the commission and to retain the loyalty of the client, the agent, in the early period of the open contract, began to perform services that had previously been the responsibility of the advertiser. One of the first was the coining of slogans and brand names. Ivory soap's slogan "99 44/100ths percent pure" appeared in 1885; Prudential's "Rock of Gibraltar" originated in 1896; and N. W. Ayer and Son suggested the brand name "Uneeda" to the National Biscuit Company in 1900. Brand names did not become common until 1905, when federal legislation provided for the registration of trademarks for a period of twenty years with provision for renewal. To a large extent, product packaging developed so that the trademark could be applied to a commodity for easy recognition.

By 1900 the preparation of plans for an advertising campaign, the preparation of copy, and the supervision of artwork became regular services offered by the agent. Shortly thereafter agencies began to make comprehensive surveys of the entire industry of the prospective advertiser in order to assess the strength and tactics of his competitors; to discuss his marketing problems and strategy; and to become familiar with his products in an attempt to find features or suggest improvements that might be used as selling points.

Until the agencies took over the responsibility of the entire preparation of advertisements, the designs of most were uninspired; the messages bland, loquacious, and at times obscure; and the illustrations scarcely better than in the days of Franklin. In the 1880's John E. Powers, Wanamaker's advertising counsel, stressed the merit of a simple and clear presentation of the product's advantages or virtues. Beginning in 1888, John Irving Romer, editor of *Printer's Ink*—founded in that year by Rowell—undertook to train readers on the design of advertisements, besides disseminating information on every phase of the profession. It was then recognized that women not only controlled the buying of household necessities, but were also highly influential in the purchase of luxuries and men's clothing. The appeal of advertisements featuring illustrations of babies or of handsome young women also began to be appreciated. However, the transformation of the structure and nature of advertisements did not occur until about 1900, when psychologists entered the field and convinced the industry that there was great value in their analyses of appeals, of the placement of advertisements, and of the most satisfactory balance between the message space and the illustration space.

It was soon ascertained that right-hand pages have an advantage of from 5 to 10 percent in attracting attention over left-hand pages, that outside columns are preferable to inside columns, and that the upper half of the page has greater advertising value than the lower half. Advertisements in which space is about equally divided between message and illustration appeared to gain the most attention. Movement as opposed to rest in illustrations, and various typefaces and colors, were also examined to determine their effectiveness as stimuli in provoking reader notice. Most studies involved analyses of the various kinds of appeals that would impress consumers and motivate them to purchase. Although psychologists disagreed on relative importance in terms of selling power of the appeals, they generally concurred that advertisements stressing health, appetite, sex, and ambition were likely to produce the most satisfactory results.

One consequence of these studies was the establishment of courses in the techniques and practices of advertising in the curricula of colleges and business schools. Textbooks on these subjects began to proliferate in the 1920's. The studies also confirmed what had been known in the trade since the days of Barnum—that the average consumer bought products on an emotional rather than a rational basis, that purchases were often made compulsively, and that the consumer was easily persuaded. The striking success of advertisements of medical nostrums had actually demonstrated the validity of these facts for years.

Disgusted by the deceptive and false claims for patent medicines, Curtis finally refused to accept such advertisements in the *Ladies' Home Journal* in 1892. Beginning in 1904 his editor, Edward Bok, began to print chemical analyses of widely advertised nostrums, demonstrating that many contained habit-forming drugs, and *Collier's* soon joined the campaign. The passage of the federal Food and Drug Act of 1906 was aided by these efforts, which also led to the "truth in advertising" movement and the *Printer's Ink* model statute in 1910. Several states acted to make false advertising a misdemeanor; Better Business Bureaus were established in many cities; and the Post Office Department, the Department of Agriculture, and the Federal Trade Commission also sought to prevent fraudulent and deceptive advertising. The most serious misrepresentations were suppressed by these means, but the knowledge of the power of appeals to basic motivations encouraged subtler forms of deception. In the depression of the 1930's efforts to stimulate sales caused further excesses, leading to the passage in 1938 of the Wheeler-Lea amendments to the Federal Trade Commission Act, which gave the commission power over false advertising, and called for special attention to be given to food, drug, and cosmetic advertisements.

Total advertising expenditures rose from an estimated $39 million in 1880 to about $1 billion in 1929 and $5.7 billion in 1950. Just after 1900, agencies launched successful campaigns to stimulate the advertising of staples, which resulted in marked increases in the advertising of soft drinks, baby foods, and tobacco products. The automobile industry soon assumed the leading position among advertisers, and by 1929, automobiles, gasoline, and tires accounted for almost half the advertising volume. Commencing in the 1920's, consumer durable goods—refrigerators, stoves, and washing machines—further aided growth. Institutional advertising, designed to build favorable attitudes toward the advertiser's organization, originated after 1900 with Western Union and American Telephone and Telegraph Company. Beginning in the 1920's such advertisements usually stressed the extensive research conducted by the company—connoting dependability of products and services—and contained ideas leading to the expectation of honesty and fair dealing.

Full-page advertisements became common after 1906, and in 1910 the halftone, permitting two- and three-color processes, began to be used extensively. This was a new device for attracting attention by creating more realism and by imparting an aura of richness and splendor in illustrations of luxuries. With better reproduction such artists as Rockwell Kent and N. C. Wyeth were commissioned to paint portraits or scenes.

Radio became an additional advertising medium in 1922, and the sale of radio advertising rose steadily in the following twenty-five years. Agencies easily accommodated themselves to radio, not only creating the advertising messages, but also, before the establishment of networks, producing the programs. Rather than employing radio to compete with other media, agencies used it as an integral part of an advertising campaign.

Age of Television. Television, in its infancy prior to World War II, expanded rapidly in the early 1950's and received additional impetus when color sets became available. By 1968, 94 percent of the homes in the country had at least one television set, and more than 20 percent had color television. From 1946 television became the fastest growing medium, absorbing over $4 billion of the $21 billion expended on advertising in 1973. Almost every other medium prospered also. With the introduction of computerized mailing lists and autotypewriters, direct mail advertising increased substantially after 1955, rising to almost $4 billion spent in 1973. The circulation of newspapers and periodicals, as well as their advertising revenues, mounted, even though the number of publications declined. Only network radio advertising showed a substantial decrease; however, advertising through the large number of independent radio stations established after 1950 more than compensated for this reduction.

Consumer surveys became common in the 1930's, not only to determine product preferences, but also to measure the extent to which advertising was effective. After 1950, increased rates in newspapers and periodicals and the substantial cost of television advertising, particularly during the prime time of the early evening hours, led to the establishment of additional consumer research organizations. These used various techniques to determine effectiveness, although most depended on statistical sampling. One employed trained door-to-door questioners. Another relied on diaries in which the householder entered the dates, times, and programs viewed when the television set was in operation. A third installed a device on television sets that automatically recorded the viewer's station selections and times on tapes, which were periodically replaced, and from which the most popular programs could be computed. A fourth research firm continually audited the inventories and wholesale orders of supermarkets and drugstores in order to compute actual sales of advertised products during and after campaigns. Yet another rewarded families for keeping detailed records of every item purchased during a specified period. Several specialized in soliciting consumer responses to new advertisements in order to perfect their appeals.

As the volume of advertising rose, attacks against it increased. Reacting to complaints that outdoor advertising despoiled the landscape, Congress passed the Highway Beautification Act (1965), which regulated placement of billboards near interstate highways. The long-criticized practice of appealing to the authority of scientists and physicians practically ceased after the Television Code in 1967 forbade actors from assuming these roles in food and drug commercials. The ruling of the Federal Trade Commission in 1965 requiring cigarette companies to include the notice that smoking might be dangerous to health was followed in 1971 by the agreement of these companies, in reaction to widespread criticism, to cease television advertising altogether. Political advertising came particularly under fire—both the carefully prepared and produced question-and-answer session, and the twenty-second spot announcements, first used in the 1952 Dwight D. Eisenhower presidential campaign, that presented simplistic views of complicated political questions.

Beyond the specific issues of fraud, deceit, peril to health, and vulgarity, a larger question has arisen since the advent of modern advertising, that of its social value. In the 1920's Thorstein Veblen termed advertising "the production of systematized illusions," and Stuart Chase, estimating that 90 percent of advertising expenditures was a waste, concluded that advertising should be limited to the dissemination of information about new products and services. In the 1950's David Potter argued that although advertising was comparable in the magnitude of its social influence to the school and the church, it had no social usefulness whatever; he argued further that it promoted conformity and "exalted the materialistic values of consumption." Others have asserted that advertising, in accentuating health or personality defects, creates insecurity and severe neurosis in human beings. Supporters of advertising give little credence to such indictments. Although admitting defects in its practice, which they point out are common to all human institutions, they agree fully with the statement of business educator Ralph Hower that "advertising is one of the influences leading to the opening of new vistas, the pursuit of new interests, and the material enrichment of life."

[Neil Borden, *The Economic Effects of Advertising;* George B. Hotchkiss, *An Outline of Advertising: Its Philosophy, Science, Art and Strategy;* Ralph M. Hower, *The History of an Advertising Agency;* Martin Mayer, *Madison Avenue, U.S.A.;* Frank Presbrey, *The History and Development of Advertising.*]

John G. Burke

A.E.F. *See* **American Expeditionary Forces.**

AEOLUS. One of the early experiments in railroad cars, the yachtlike *Aeolus* was designed to sail before the wind. It was tried on the Baltimore and Ohio Railroad in 1830. On one occasion the *Aeolus* failed to stop when it reached the end of the finished track and ran into an embankment.

[Edward Hungerford, *The Story of the Baltimore and Ohio Railroad.*]

Frank Freidel

AERONAUTICS. *See* **Aviation.**

AERONAUTICS AND SPACE ADMINISTRATION, NATIONAL. *See* **National Aeronautics and Space Administration.**

AERONAUTICS BOARD, CIVIL. *See* **Federal Agencies.**

AFL. *See* **American Federation of Labor–Congress of Industrial Organizations.**

AFRICAN-AMERICAN RELATIONS originated through slavery and the slave trade. Although Africans were among the early 15th-century explorers and settlers of what are today parts of the American Southeast and Southwest, sustained interaction between Africa and America dates from 1619, when nineteen Africans were brought to Virginia as indentured servants. African indenture developed formally into African slavery by 1662. Americans themselves had participated increasingly in the lucrative African slave trade from the early 17th century. Although Congress outlawed the importation of slaves in 1808, Americans continued to do so clandestinely right up to the Civil War. It is estimated that some 427,000 Africans were landed in the United States during the entire period of slavery.

In the antebellum period, there was some diversification of African-American relations resulting from legitimate trade, the founding of Liberia, and the beginning of American missionary activities. From the early 19th century, Americans participated in the legitimate trade to West and East Africa: rum, tobacco, and cotton goods were exchanged for gold dust, ivory, peanuts, and spices. But this trade declined during the Civil War. The idea of settling free black Americans in West Africa was advocated by certain Afro-American spokesmen, who argued that even free blacks in the "free" North were intensely discriminated against. The colonization idea won support among whites—for altruistic as well as less charitable reasons—and led to the formation of the American Colonization Society in 1817 and the founding of Liberia in 1822. Up to the outbreak of the Civil War some 12,000 Afro-Americans emigrated to Liberia through the society. In 1847 Liberia declared itself independent as a black republic, but it was not until 1862, when southern slaveholding interests were removed during the Civil War, that the United States recognized Liberia's independence. As yet, American emigrants and missionaries went largely to Liberia, but a few were to be found in other parts of West Africa, notably Sierra Leone and Nigeria.

Between the end of the Civil War and World War I, the United States, in contrast to Europe, showed little general or governmental interest in Africa. Trade was desultory, but spurted somewhat during World War I. Among Americans, blacks were most interested in Africa. Because Afro-Americans, for the most part, were disfranchised, jim crowed, and discriminated against, some Afro-American leaders, notably Bishop Henry McNeal Turner, again advocated Afro-American emigration to Africa, even after its partition by the major European powers in the late 19th century. They argued that at least Liberia was independent and that it was easier to end white minority rule in Africa than to revolutionize the attitude of white Americans toward blacks. Hundreds of thousands of Afro-Americans expressed the desire to emigrate to Africa, but only a small percentage could afford to do so. Some 3,000 emigrated to Liberia in the post-Civil War 19th century and a few to other parts of the continent. Afro-Americans showed their interest in Africa in other ways too: they helped to protest against the atrocities in King Leopold's Congo between 1885 and 1908 and they applauded when the ancient kingdom of Ethiopia thwarted Italy's colonial ambition by defeating that nation's invading forces at the Battle of Adowa (1896). But the major impact of Afro-Americans on Africa came through their use as missionaries, particularly in West Africa and southern Africa. Here they were agents either of white denominations or of two black churches: the African Methodist Episcopal Church and the African Methodist Episcopal Zion Church. These missionaries arranged for dozens of African students to study at Afro-American colleges in the United States.

African-American relations remained essentially the same between the two world wars as in the post-Civil War decades. Commercially, the most important development was the grant by the Liberian government of a million acres to the U.S. Firestone Company in 1926 for plantations to grow rubber. Since then, Firestone has played a dominant role in the Liberian economy. Politically, Marcus Garvey's mass American-based Universal Negro Improvement Association (UNIA), founded in 1914, with its bold cry of "Africa for the Africans," served to stimulate African nationalism—particularly in the urban areas of West and South Africa. Branches of the UNIA were formed, and Garvey's militant weekly newspaper, *The Negro World* (1918–23), was read—clandestinely after it had been banned in several European colonies in Africa. Additionally, a few African leaders did participate in the four Pan-African conferences organized between 1919 and 1927 by Dr. W. E. B. Du Bois, the Afro-American intellectual and activist. Italy's conquest of Ethiopia in 1935–36 called forth widespread expressions of Pan-African solidarity and served to stimulate greater American interest in Africa. In the United States several organizations—racial and interracial—were formed to give aid to Ethiopia and Ethiopian refugees. In 1937 the Council on African Affairs was founded under the leadership of Paul Robeson and

Max Yergan, with the goal of influencing United States policy in favor of African colonials. The council remained active until 1955.

American interest in Africa grew enormously during and after World War II, mainly because of the strategic importance of Africa during the war, the desire for African friendship during the postwar period of cold war politics with the Soviet Union, and the economic interest in Africa as a major source of strategic raw materials. This new interest expressed itself in vastly increased investments; in the establishment of a military base in Ethiopia; in the founding of such educational and cultural organizations as the African-American Institute, the African Studies Association, the American Society for African Culture, and Cross Roads Africa; in the increased activities of American labor organizations in Africa; and in the operation of Peace Corps Africa.

By 1970 U.S. investments in sub-Saharan Africa had grown to a substantial $2.25 billion, about 40 percent of which was invested in the white-dominated territories of southern Africa, particularly South Africa and Angola. As a result the United States was charged with supporting the minority white ruling elements against the legitimate aspirations of Africans for freedom. Also, through NATO as well as bilateral agreements, the U.S. government supplied arms to Portugal; and critics have charged that these arms were used against African freedom fighters in Angola, Mozambique, and Portuguese Guinea in the 1960's and early 1970's.

The feeling of Afro-Americans for Africa continued to be of a special kind. After World War II there was a marked increase in the interaction between African and Afro-American leaders, notably at the 1945 Manchester Pan-African Conference, which plotted a strategy for the independence movement in black Africa. Independent black Africa, and particularly independent and progressive leaders like the late Kwame Nkrumah of Ghana and Julius Nyerere of Tanzania, helped Afro-Americans to lose much of their historic ambivalence toward their ancestral continent and thus stimulated their pride in blackness. Since black African countries started to achieve independence, beginning with Ghana in 1957, hundreds of Afro-Americans, including major leaders, have visited the continent each year. In such centers as New York and Washington, D.C., constant informal contacts and expressions of mutual support take place between Afro-American and African leaders. Thus, in the Nigerian-Biafran Civil War (1967–70), Afro-American leaders sought to play a reconciling role. In the 1970's they were concerned with seeing an end to white minority rule in southern Africa and criticized U.S. policy in this area as being prowhite.

The 1970's also saw a relative diminution of U.S. governmental and public interest in Africa. The end of the cold war, the rapprochement with China and Russia, preoccupation with the Vietnam conflict concluded in 1973 and with domestic problems are all factors in this slackening of attention to Africa. But growing U.S. investments, the steady interest of Afro-Americans in that continent, and the potentially explosive struggle in southern Africa ensure a continuing major American interest in, and interaction with, Africa.

[American Society of African Culture, *Africa Seen By American Negro Scholars;* Vernon McKay, *Africa in the United States;* Eric Rosenthal, *Stars and Stripes in Africa;* Robert G. Weisbord, *Ebony Kinship: Africa, Africans and the Afro-American.*]

HOLLIS R. LYNCH

AFRICAN COMPANY, ROYAL, an English trading company, one of a series granted a monopoly of the African slave trade. In 1672 it took over the charter and African trading posts of the Company of Royal Adventurers to Africa established by the Duke of York and associates in 1662. In 1697 its monopoly was destroyed when independent merchants were permitted to engage in the trade upon payment for fourteen years of export duties which were turned over to the company to maintain its posts. From this time the trade was largely absorbed by the independents. During the 18th century most of the slaves were carried to the West Indies and North America in ships owned by Bristol, Liverpool, and colonial merchants. The company endeavored to prevent independent traders from bargaining directly with the dealers in Africa. Most of the slaves it secured were sold to the independents, to the English South Sea Company after it was granted the Asiento (1713), or even to foreign traders. The destruction of the monopoly, the competition of independent traders, the expense of maintaining its posts, and the imposition of poll duties on slave importations by Virginia, South Carolina, Jamaica, and Barbados, all proved so disastrous to the company that, in spite of annual grants by Parliament of £10,000 beginning in 1729, its affairs were ended in 1750. By that year, of the 155 British ships in the trade, 20 were North American, nearly half from Rhode Island.

[L. H. Gipson, *The British Before the American Revolution.*]

CHARLES F. MULLETT

AFRICAN METHODIST EPISCOPAL CHURCH, the oldest and largest denomination of Afro-American Methodists, organized in 1816 in Philadelphia with Richard Allen as its first bishop. The origins of the group lie in Allen's unsuccessful efforts to set up a separate place of worship for blacks soon after his arrival in Philadelphia in 1786. In this initial step he was opposed by blacks and whites. When friction developed around efforts to segregate blacks attending St. George's Methodist Episcopal Church, Allen, Absolom James, William White, and other blacks withdrew. Under Allen's leadership they organized the Free African Society, which developed into the Bethel African Methodist Episcopal church in 1794. Branches of the church were established in Baltimore, Md.; Wilmington, Del.; and several Pennsylvania and New Jersey cities; by 1816 a formal denominational organization was possible. Opposition to Afro-American organizations after Denmark Vesey's insurrection in 1822 checked the church's growth in the South. After several decades of slow growth the African Methodist Episcopal church grew rapidly during the latter half of the 19th century. In 1974 there were 1.1 million members and 6,000 churches. In doctrine that church is similar to the Methodist Episcopal, from which it separated.

[Harry A. Ploski and Ernest Kaiser, *Negro Almanac;* J. Beverly F. Shaw, *The Negro in the History of Methodism;* Charles H. Wesley, *Richard Allen, Apostle of Freedom.*]

HENRY N. DREWRY

AFRO-AMERICAN CHURCH, the most important black institution in pre–Civil War days. It dates back to the federal period, when in Savannah, Philadelphia, Richmond, Baltimore, and New York, separatist black churches were constituted among free black Baptists, Presbyterians, Methodists, and Episcopalians. A sign of the spirit of the times was that they universally adopted the descriptive adjective "African," for example the First African Baptist Church of Savannah (1785), the First African Meeting House in Philadelphia (1788), and the First African Presbyterian Church of Philadelphia (1804); so also the first denomination, the African Methodist Episcopal church, established in Philadelphia in 1816 by Richard Allen.

Organization of separate churches received impetus from contradictions in the attitudes of whites: they did not want Afro-Americans to worship with them, but they did not want them to worship alone. Whites felt an obligation to Christianize Africans but were unwilling to apply the concept of Christian brotherhood in dealing with the converts.

Among slaves, plantation churches developed, sometimes served by white ministers. Religious services offered rare opportunities for blacks to get together and undoubtedly provided important emotional release. At first whites expressed discomfort with the idea of holding as slaves those who had been Christianized, but later they claimed to find full support in the Bible for chattel slavery. Slaveowners increasingly fostered religious services as Christianity came to be used as an instrument for teaching obedience. When abolitionists began their activity, planters became more cautious about scheduling religious services. Restrictions followed the insurrection led by the Virginia black preacher Nat Turner in 1831. In most slave states, black preachers were outlawed and slaves were required to attend church with their owners, or, if black religious services were held, a white person had to be present.

After the emancipation of slaves, the church emerged as the only institution—except for the Afro-American family—which was not under the direct influence or control of whites. Religious organizations provided opportunities for leadership by Afro-Americans—which, except during the brief Reconstruction period, they were almost completely deprived of. Furthermore, religion served as a refuge and center of hope for those who were discriminated against in their day-to-day activities. Added to the general movement toward segregated activities, these factors gave rise to separate Afro-American denominations among the former slaves. Whereas the Methodist Episcopal Church South had had 207,000 Afro-American members in 1860, the number had dropped to 78,000 by 1866, as the membership of the African Methodist church had swelled; the remaining group withdrew in 1870 to form the Colored Methodist Episcopal church. By 1880 black and white Baptists had split. Where denominational separation did not take place, as with the Presbyterians and Catholics, Afro-American communicants usually worshipped in separate churches.

Churches were in the forefront of the Afro-American self-help programs of the post-Reconstruction period. They were instrumental in the establishment of a number of schools and colleges and were among the few places that offered opportunities to the graduates of such institutions to make use of their education. Black Methodists alone established eleven colleges between 1870 and 1902.

As Afro-Americans migrated to the North in great

numbers during and after World War I, their religious institutions changed. Among the significant characteristics of the religious life of the developing ghettos of large cities were the creation of numerous "storefront" churches and the appearance of a number of non-Christian sects. Among this latter group were the Black Muslims, the peace movement of Father Divine, and the United House of Prayer of Daddy Grace.

In the post–World War II period much of the leadership in civil-rights activity came from the clergy. Noteworthy among these clergymen were Martin Luther King, Jr., Adam Clayton Powell, Jr., Ralph D. Abernathy, Nathan Wright, Jesse L. Jackson, and Leon Sullivan. Black churches in the South frequently served as the rallying points for planning and action and often bore the brunt of hostile reactions. Bombings and burnings of church buildings were common. The height of these attacks took place in 1965 during a voter registration drive in Mississippi, where thirty-five black churches were burned in that year alone.

Although still an important institution, Afro-American churches had lost some of their influence by the 1970's, as part of a general move away from religion, but also because of the limited success of the church-oriented civil-rights activity of the 1950's and 1960's. The disillusionment that earlier caused blacks to turn to religion may be the cause of their turning away.

In the 1970's Baptists formed the largest of the Afro-American church groups, with a membership of 7,253,000. Three Methodist groups formed the bulk of the 2,067,000 Afro-American members of that denomination. Afro-American membership in other Christian churches was distributed as follows: Catholic, 774,000; Presbyterian, 107,000; other groups, 1,050,000. The rest of the religious membership among Afro-Americans consisted of 190,000 non-Christians, of whom 9,000 were Jewish.

[E. Franklin Frazier, *The Negro Church in America;* Ruby Johnston, *The Development of Negro Religion;* Benjamin Mays and Joseph W. Nicholson, *The Negro Church.*]

HENRY N. DREWRY

AFRO-AMERICAN CULTURE. Of the dozens of subcultures that contribute to American civilization, the Afro-American is one of the largest and most distinctive. In the 1970's black Americans made up about 11 percent of the U.S. population. Since World War II the black emigration from the agrarian South, which began with the Civil War, has redefined the black population as essentially northern and urban rather than southern and rural. The scope and richness of Afro-American culture thus reflects the fusion of these two dissimilar experiences.

The black presence in America predates that of most ethnic groups, although black culture probably did not begin to take on distinctive configurations until the restrictions of slavery enforced the separation of blacks from the general community.

People of African descent first arrived in the New World in significant numbers with the Spanish *conquistadores* in the 16th century. They were sailors, soldiers, servants, and explorers. Some were slaves. They hunted gold in Peru; participated in the conquest of Mexico; and helped build Saint Augustine, Fla., the oldest city in America. One of them, Estevanico, led an expedition into what is now Arizona and New Mexico and planted the first wheat crops ever harvested in the American Southwest. Other blacks were members of French expeditions that opened up the Mississippi valley; for example, Jean Baptiste Point du Sable established the trading post on Lake Michigan that in time became the city of Chicago. But the African peoples had relatively little contact with the French, and Spanish interests were quickly displaced by those of the English. As the English and their Anglo-American successors came to be the chief colonizers of what is now the United States, the introduction of millions of Africans to fill the labor needs of the colonies linked the black experience in America to that of Anglo-Americans.

Whether or not the developing subculture among the African diaspora was significantly influenced by antecedent African cultures, despite continual reinforcement of the African population in America over a period of two centuries, is an issue still debated. The two best-known schools of thought on this problem have been led by anthropologist Melville J. Herskovits and sociologist E. Franklin Frazier. The former holds that survivals of African tribal cultures play an important role in the shaping of the contemporary Afro-American culture. The latter contends that the peculiar conditions of slavery in America and the resulting cultural shock were so intense as to eliminate effectively the African past as a meaningful source of cultural influence for the African diaspora in America. According to Frazier, Afro-American culture is that aggregation of concepts, skills, arts, and habits that Afro-Americans have acquired in the course of their experience in America, and intracultural borrowing and contributions mark the Afro-Americans' association with other subcultures with whom they have had sustained contact. But since the black experience in America is in many important ways a unique experience, the Afro-American subculture has certain unique features—most pronounced perhaps in religion, music, art, speech, and certain life styles.

Since World War II the cultural image of the black American has been under continuous restructuralization. The traditional self-concept of most blacks from the Civil War until the mid-20th century was one closely identified with the American mainstream and its values. A sharp reversal toward ethnocentricity emerged with the civil rights struggles of the 1950's and 1960's, and this revived sense of "Africanness" expressed itself in such slogans as "Black is Beautiful" and in demands for "black power" in political and economic affairs. A serious school of black theologians emerged. "Black religion" as a corrective approach to traditional American interpretations of Christianity became popular, especially among the younger and better educated black Americans. Black ethnocentricity became a pronounced theme in the works of such leading black artists as Charles White and Vertis Hayes; the writers Ralph Ellison, Langston Hughes, John A. Williams, John O. Killens, Gwendolyn Brooks, Imamu A. Baraka, Margaret G. Burroughs, and Nikki Di Giovanni. The music of black Americans has always been distinctive and remains so in spite of heavy borrowings by other groups. In dance, Katherine Dunham and Alvin Ailey have been greatly influential and Arthur Mitchell's Dance Theatre of Harlem provided classical training and careers for blacks. Black arts centers grew up around the country, a notable example being the center founded by Alma Lewis in Boston. The Negro Ensemble Company in New York fostered black playwrights and delineated the black experience for playgoers.

The commercialization of distinctive Afro-American life styles (including dress) through film and television in the 1960's and 1970's extended the range of the impact of black culture, though many of the facets of Afro-American culture that were given attention were faddish. Even so, the overall recognition of black distinctiveness and its appreciation increased dramatically during that period and reinforced the sensitivity of black Americans to the legitimacy and merit of values and inventions deriving from their distinctive experience. The direction of Afro-American culture seems, however, toward a unicultural norm with the rest of America.

[Leonard Bloom and Norval Glen, *Transformation of the Negro American;* W. E. B. Du Bois, *The Dusk of Dawn;* E. Franklin Frazier, *The Negro in the United States;* Melville J. Herskovits, *The Myth of the Negro's Past;* C. Eric Lincoln, *The Negro Pilgrimage in America;* Benjamin Muse, *The American Negro Revolution.*]

C. Eric Lincoln

AFRO-AMERICAN MIGRATION. In 1860, 95 percent of American blacks were rural dwellers and 92 percent lived in the South. In 1960, 14 percent were rural and approximately 60 percent lived in the South. Ten years later 28 percent were either suburban or rural dwellers and 52 percent still lived in the South. This movement from farms to cities of the South and from southern farms and cities to northern urban areas has been one of the major American population shifts. Although the shift of blacks to the urban North is part of the general urbanization of the American population, blacks became urbanized at a faster rate than others. Beginning after the Civil War, movement was at first within the South. By 1900 blacks outnumbered whites in Charleston, Vicksburg, Baton Rouge, Savannah, Montgomery, Jacksonville, Shreveport, and other cities. When white segregationists regained control of southern state governments following Reconstruction, the movement to northern cities began. Small at first, it continued throughout the 1880's and 1890's and significantly increased when wartime industrial needs boosted the demand for labor during World War I. The war almost completely cut off the flow of European immigrants who had supplied industrial labor, and the restrictive immigration policies of the 1920's prevented the return to the high prewar influx. The net black out-migration from the South was 454,000 between 1910 and 1920. The number rose to 969,000 in the following decade, declined to 348,000 in the 1930's, then spurted to 1,597,000 in the 1940's. It remained a high 1,457,000 during the 1950's, then declined slightly to 1,380,000 in the 1960's.

When migrating North, blacks tended to concentrate in large cities. New York's black population rose from 60,000 in 1910 to 1,660,000 in 1970. In Chicago the increase during this period was from 30,000 to 1,103,000; in Baltimore from 79,000 to 420,000; and in Washington, D.C., from 86,000 to 538,000. Even greater increases occurred in Detroit and Los Angeles, where the black population increased from 4,000 and 2,000, respectively, in 1910 to 660,000 and 523,000 in 1970. The 1970 census reported 72 percent of all blacks lived in cities, compared with 70 percent for the total population.

The causes of the migration were mainly but not entirely economic. The wage rate fell rapidly in the 1910's as a result of declining farm prices. In 1915 and 1916 a succession of floods and crop failures and increased destruction by the boll weevil drove many out of agriculture. Add to these the precarious economic condition of black tenant farmers and sharecroppers even in "good times" and the pressures to leave the South were clear. When war-stimulated industries offered opportunities for gainful employment at wages higher than those paid in the South, large numbers of blacks responded.

Also, less overt discrimination in day-to-day activities, better public school facilities, suffrage, possibilities for justice in the courts, and access to public places were available to a greater degree in the North. A contemporary effort to assess the cause and nature of the black migration, sponsored by the U.S. Department of Labor in 1917, pointed to the treatment blacks received at the hands of southern whites as an important factor.

While migration to the North allowed blacks to improve their condition, it was not without its problems. Northern life failed to fulfill the democratic expectations held by Afro-Americans. Crime, the shortage of housing, limitations on occupational advancement, and the breakdown of family and community under pressures of urban living became major concerns. In addition the increased numbers of blacks stimulated latent racism among white northerners. The creation of black ghettos, high unemployment among blacks, and a series of urban riots reflect the nature and intensity of white reactions.

HENRY N. DREWRY

AFRO-AMERICANS. The 1970 census identified 22,672,570 Afro-Americans, or black Americans, in the United States, constituting slightly more than 11 percent of the total population. This group is significantly different from the white majority in ways other than the obvious one of physical features. The life span of the average Afro-American is seven years less than that of the average white American; the infant mortality rate is twice as high; and the Afro-American is twice as likely to die of tuberculosis, influenza, and pneumonia. Also, the black American is twice as likely to be unemployed, has an average family income that is a third less than that of the average white, and is often paid less for performing the same job. He has two to three years less formal education and will have lifetime earnings in excess of 35 percent less than his white counterpart with the same formal education. In addition, the average black is more likely to be an urban dweller than is the average white.

A variety of theories exist about the reasons for these differences between the white majority and the largest U.S. racial minority. At one extreme all fault is placed on Afro-Americans themselves. At the other extreme the causes are seen in the actions of whites and in the influence of the environment in which blacks must live and work. The attitudes of nonblacks and the policies of government and private organizations throughout the history of the country reflect the degree to which blacks are viewed as personally responsible for their unfavorable condition.

As is the case in all such broad coverages, any brief overview of the 350-year history of blacks in North America requires an effort to periodize events. Students of American history have become familiar with certain general periods in their study of the North American English colonies and the United States and the consistency with which these divisions appear in the works of historians has helped to shape the way students consider America's past. For the person who does not make a serious study of history the generalized understanding of the label attached to a period comes to represent the chief characteristics of the period and, collectively, the surface and widely accepted view of the overall history of the country. These divisions, for which we use such titles as "European Migration to the New World," "Colonial Experience," "American Revolution and the Origins of a New Nation," "Jeffersonian and Jacksonian Democracy," "Rise of the Common Man," and "Progressive Period," fail to be useful for a study of black history. Although Afro-American history is part of the warp and woof of American history, different period designations are needed to reflect the Afro-American experience. Periods entitled "Slavery," "Civil War and Reconstruction," "Search for Direction in a Hostile Society," "World War I and the Black Migration to the Cities," and "Prelude and Protest in the Mid-20th Century" correctly designate the black experience in North America and suggest differences from the white experience in the same place during the same 350 years.

Africans were first brought to the territory that became the United States in 1619, when the captain of a Dutch man-of-war sold nineteen blacks as indentured servants to Englishmen at Jamestown, Va. Others followed in Dutch and later English bottoms, as England moved to dominate the African slave depots and the slave trade. Between 5 million and 10 million Africans were transported to the Americas and the West Indies between 1619 and 1865. The vast majority of these people came from that stretch of the West African coast extending from present-day Senegal to Angola; a small percentage came from Madagascar and East Africa. Coming as they did from such an extensive area, they were not of one physical or cultural type. Significant differences existed among them, but they shared a general set of characteristics. They were tall and had dark skin, tight woolly hair, full lips, broad noses, and limited facial and body hair. Their social, political, and economic organization tended to be on a tribal basis and was often complex and subtle in the established relationships.

It is the descendants of these Africans brought to North America by force who now form the 11 percent of the U.S. population that has been variously called colored, Negro, Afro-American, and black. If in determining "Americanness" such measures as length of residence, separation from contacts with the native land and culture, and loyalty to the country are used, then it can be argued that the Afro-Americans are the most American of any U.S. racial or ethnic group. But this unencumbered attachment to the United States was offset by the ethnocentrism of the white majority, so that the experience of descendants of Africans in the United States has been very different from that of descendants of Europeans. The forceful removal from Africa to North America, two and a half centuries of slavery, and a century of institutionalized segregation and discrimination produced a unique human experience that scholars have only recently begun to probe in depth.

The first Africans introduced at Jamestown probably worked off their indentures as did other servants. For half a century they competed with, and were outnumbered by, indentured servants from Europe, as landowners in the colonies sought an ever increasing supply of labor. But maintaining white servants was difficult. The laws, customs, and sentiment in the countries from which they came made it difficult to work white servants beyond the time of their indenture. More important, if news of maltreatment spread among European servants, the number of such servants declined. For Africans the situation was different. Their presence as servants was not voluntary: they had been captured and sold. Moreover, the areas from which they came were not comparable to European nations in terms of military power and, even if they had desired to do so, they could not influence the English North American colonies to provide protection for Africans equal to that provided various Europeans. As a result the relative number of black servants continuously increased, and their status changed. By 1670 servants of African descent were generally viewed as slaves. By the middle of the 18th century the evolution of the institution of slavery had reduced Africans to the status of personal property. As a 1740 Virginia law states, slaves were "chattles personal in the hands of their owners to all intents, construction and purpose whatsoever."

The American Revolution and a declining profit from slaves led to the end of slavery in the area north of Maryland. Movements to curb slavery took place in the South but came to a halt with the invention of the cotton gin by Eli Whitney in 1793. His invention led to an increase in the amount of land planted in cotton and in the demand for slaves as cotton became "king" in the Deep South. Thus, despite the ideals of the Declaration of Independence, slavery continued, and the slaveholding interests increased in influence well into the 19th century.

The Constitution recognized the existence of slavery, and federal legislation protected property in slaves, as did the constitutions of the new states of Mississippi and Alabama in 1817 and 1819; free blacks were discriminated against in both North and South. The position of the Afro-American in the United States at mid-century was articulated in 1857 in the Supreme Court decision of *Dred Scott* v. *Sandford*. The Court held that people of African descent "were not intended to be included under the word 'citizen' in the Constitution and can, therefore, claim none of the rights and privileges which that instrument provides for and secures to citizens of the United States whether emancipated or not."

The process of making slaves out of Africans and maintaining control over them occupied the attention of slaveowners and nonslaveowners alike. Initial steps had to be taken to break down the tribal attachments of new imports, to destroy the sense of individuality of each slave, and to establish an attitude of submission to the will of the slaveowner. Violence and brutality often played a part in the achievement of these objectives by slaveowners and were often carried out by persons who owned no slaves. It is one of the peculiarities of American history that the nonslaveowners—in 1860, three-quarters of the southern white families owned no slaves—gave such support to the system. All southern states enacted slave codes and enforced them with varying degrees of severity, and each community maintained a patrol to enforce these codes. Since the monied slaveholders could hire people to work for them, the patrols were composed mainly of nonslaveowners. It was not rare for slaveowners to challenge members of patrols in court for abusing slaves without cause.

Psychologists have provided evidence that members of minority groups react in odd ways to their subordinate position in society. The reactions of blacks to slavery have been examined, but perhaps the actions and reactions of poor whites toward slaves need more study.

Blacks sought a variety of means to counter physical and psychological bondage. Efforts to escape or commit suicide were common during the voyage from Africa. There were revolts in transit, as with the slave ship *Creole* en route from Virginia to New Orleans. A mutiny on Nov. 7, 1841, by the slaves gave them control of the ship, and they sailed it to Nassau, a British port in the West Indies. Conspiracies and revolts continued as long as the institution of slavery existed, among them those of Denmark Vesey in 1822 and Nat Turner in 1831. Escapes to the North and to Canada were common. No firm statistics exist on the number of escapees, but a variety of evidence shows it to be high. Notable among escaped slaves is Frederick Douglass, who fled from slavery in Maryland in 1838 and became an outstanding abolitionist activist and publisher in the North. Black opposition to slavery also took such forms as vandalism, sabotage, and work slowdowns.

Opposition to slavery among free persons also existed from the earliest days of the institution. In the 19th century abolition became an influential force, largely through the activities of Douglass, Benjamin Lundy, David Walker, William Lloyd Garrison, and Theodore D. Weld. In its early stages the abolition movement concentrated on colonization of freed slaves in Africa; it had some support in all sections of the country, though with few exceptions, blacks did not support the colonization concept. After 1820 one group of abolitionists began to talk of equal rights for blacks within the American society, and the activities of this group played an important part in bringing the issue of slavery to center stage in the years before the Civil War.

The effect the Civil War would have on slavery was not clear at the start of the conflict. Southern states went to war determined to maintain slavery, and President Abraham Lincoln announced that he had no intention to interfere with slavery in the states. In 1861 and early 1862 the federal government ignored the efforts of abolitionists to make the end of slavery a war aim. Not until military conditions made it seem beneficial did the Lincoln administration issue the Emancipation Proclamation, in January 1863, and allow the enlistment of blacks in the military. Some 140,000 blacks served in the Union army and navy during the remaining years of the conflict.

The Emancipation Proclamation and the Thirteenth, Fourteenth, and Fifteenth amendments to the Constitution provided the legal basis for full citizenship for blacks, and for a brief period they enjoyed these benefits under federal protection. Several factors combined to prevent their new status from becoming effectively established. First, blacks lacked political experience, education, and independent economic activity. Second, despite notable accomplishments in each of these areas the opposition of southern whites to citizenship rights for blacks was almost unanimous, and no broad base of support existed in the North. When the war ended, support for the rights of blacks gave way in favor of national unity, and the federal retreat from the civil rights field placed protection of the rights of blacks in the hands of the southern states—in some cases in the hands of the same men who had fought to maintain the institution of slavery. Also, the allegiance of blacks to the Republican party in power was on shaky ground from the start. For the most part the Republican party was supported by northern conservatives whose economic concerns centered on industrial development, whereas the more than 4 million freed slaves were largely dwellers in the rural South who depended on agriculture for their livelihood. The frailty of the mutual support that supposedly existed between Republicans and blacks became clear with the compromise of 1876. This bargain between Republican and Southern Democratic conservatives put Rutherford B. Hayes in the presidency in return for the withdrawal of federal troops from the South, northern capital investment in the South, and a federal hands-off policy with regard to the rights of blacks.

Considering the limited experience of the blacks and the hostility of much of the population of the South, blacks made impressive steps in the areas of education and politics. Reconstruction governments developed new state constitutions and established the first public school systems in most of the southern states. Blacks and their white supporters established a number of institutions of higher education, among them Fisk University, Talladega College, Morehouse College, Atlanta University, Johnson C. Smith University, and Shaw University. A number of blacks held political office and voting was widespread. Economic success was far more limited. Blacks sought to secure land for farming, but with no capital accumulation and no federal or state programs to compensate for the years of labor taken from them by force, they were unsuccessful. They had to turn to former slaveowners for employment, land rentals, or sharecropping arrangements; consequently, there was little chance to become self-sufficient. Economic dependency in turn weakened chances for effective use of politics and education to protect their interests and promote their welfare.

The gains blacks were able to maintain after the end of the Reconstruction period came under a new series of attacks in the 1890's, after southern Populists threatened and sometimes overthrew the political control of the old southern elite. Legislative and judicial action reduced the political influence and civil rights of blacks in every state in the Old South. A new constitution adopted in 1901 in Alabama, incorporating a poll tax and literacy test requirement, reduced the number of blacks registered to vote from 181,471 to 3,000. A constitutional amendment in Louisiana reduced 120,334 registered blacks in 1866 to 1,342 in 1901. Other techniques used to effect reduction in black political power included "lily white" primaries, complicated and confusing ballots and balloting procedures, and "grandfather clauses," which relieved whites of tax and literacy restrictions placed on blacks. At the same time school funds for black education came under serious attack in all legislatures. Laws requiring segregation by race became commonplace. Court tests of Jim Crow laws produced no relief. In the case of *Plessy* v. *Ferguson* (1896) the Supreme Court put its stamp of approval on the use of the police power of the states to enforce racial separation in public accommodations. In the years following, the increase in the number of legislative actions aimed at separating blacks from whites affected almost every aspect of public and private life.

World War I represents a watershed in the experience of black Americans. Most significant was the impetus given to the urbanization of blacks by the labor needs of northern industries. This movement of blacks to the cities began in the years immediately after emancipation. The freedom of movement afforded by the end of slavery resulted in a large migration to some southern cities; by 1900 blacks outnumbered whites in Charleston, S.C., Savannah, Ga., Montgomery, Ala., Jacksonville, Fla., Vicksburg, Miss., and Baton Rouge, La.; Louisville, Ky., and Atlanta, Ga., had large and rapidly growing black populations. When Southern Democrats regained political control of state governments in the 1870's, a similar move to northern cities began. Northern cities by no means provided equality of opportunity for black citizens but they differed in their treatment of blacks in important ways. When war in Europe stopped the flow of immigrants for industrial labor, job opportunities for blacks increased. As a result the trickle of blacks to the cities of the Northeast and West became a flood. By 1920 half a million southern blacks had relocated. The movement continued in the 1920's, slowed somewhat during the depression, but revived during and after World War II. At the outbreak of the Civil War 92 percent of the black population lived in the South, and 95 percent on farms. At the turn of the century the South still claimed almost 90 percent of all blacks. By 1970 blacks in the South had declined to 52 percent with less than 12 percent living on farms. Blacks had come to be more urbanized than the general population.

The presence of blacks in large numbers in major population centers had both benefits and drawbacks. More political influence based on increased numbers led to the election of some black officials in municipal, state, and federal governments, beginning with the elections of Oscar DePriest as Chicago alderman in 1915 and Edward Austin Johnson as New York state legislator in 1917. But increased numbers meant greater pressure on the limited housing available to blacks and greater antiblack feeling as Afro-Americans tried to move out of traditionally black areas. The usual social ills of ghetto life expanded with population density. Blacks were employed mainly in unskilled positions, were the last hired and first fired, and were, for the most part, refused membership in the established labor unions. There were also more violent reactions to the increased number of blacks, namely, race riots. A series of riots spread across the country in the first two decades of the 20th century: Springfield, Ohio (1904), Atlanta (1906), Springfield, Ill. (1908), and East Saint Louis, Mo. (1917).

When World War I began in 1914 there were 20,000 blacks among the 750,000 men in the regular army and National Guard. Before November 1918 there were 2,290,000 registered blacks and 367,000 of them were called into service. They served in segregated units in the army and were excluded from the navy except for menial jobs. None were admitted to the Marine Corps. Discriminatory practices in housing, assignment, promotions, and provisions for recreation accompanied the segregation into separate units. Nevertheless, blacks served with distinction; the all-black 369th, 371st, and 372nd regiments received the Croix de Guerre for valor.

Any hopes that the demonstration of loyalty and support for the war effort at home and abroad would convince Americans that blacks were entitled to equal rights disappeared in the years immediately after the war. The Ku Klux Klan was revived as early as 1915, and the number of lynchings, which had dropped considerably after reaching a peak of 235 in 1892, turned upward again. Among the 70 blacks lynched in 1919 were ten veterans, some still in uniform. Another series of race riots spread across the country: Longview, Tex., in 1919, and Chicago, Ill., Knoxville, Tenn., and Elaine, Ark., in 1920.

Despite the absence of appreciable progress in the area of civil rights, there were significant cultural developments among blacks. A growing sense of racial pride, of which the Universal Negro Improvement Association (1920) was the prime example, and the desire to dissent in the American system of racial justice resulted in important works of literature and art. The Harlem Renaissance, as the post–World War I movement came to be called, centered in New York City, in the nation's largest ghetto. Among its leaders were novelists James Weldon Johnson and Claude McKay, poets Langston Hughes and Countee Cullen, and scholars W. E. B. Du Bois, Alain Locke, and Charles S. Johnson.

The Great Depression temporarily set back race pride and dissent. For many blacks the hard times were only more of the same, with the usual discriminatory racial practices influencing the distribution of jobs and welfare in most places. As part of the larger humanitarian concern for the welfare of all the underprivileged in society, the welfare of blacks did receive some attention. Symbolically Eleanor Roosevelt, wife of the New Deal president, demonstrated genuine concern and friendship for blacks, as did some executive appointees, although no New Deal legislation was specifically concerned with the civil rights of Afro-Americans. Some measures actually increased the economic hardship of rural blacks (tenant farmers and sharecroppers) who were forced off the land as a result of legislation aimed at assistance to agriculture (subsidies withdrawing land from cultivation). As a result the migration of blacks to cities continued throughout the 1930's, though at a slower pace than it had in the 1920's.

When World War II began, there were 10,000 blacks in the regular army and National Guard. An amendment to the Selective Service Act of 1940 forbade discrimination in the drafting or training of men. The War Department interpreted this to mean that blacks should be received into the army in proportion to their percentage of the population but should be organized in separate units. No serious effort was made to prevent discrimination in training or treatment, though the number of black officers reached 7,768, as against only 1,400 in World War I. In all, 750,000 blacks served in the army, 165,000 in the navy, and between 20,000 and 25,000 in the Coast Guard and Marine Corps. Approximately 500,000 saw service in Europe, Africa, Asia, or the South Pacific.

For blacks, World War II offered the questionable privilege of fighting abroad in defense of a system whose benefits they were denied at home. In spite of, or because of, the clarity with which this conflict set forth the issue, blacks expressed hopes that participation in the war against the racist policies of Nazism would aid America to see the brutality of its own racial patterns and to move to change them. The clarity of the issue produced ever greater disillusionment among blacks as the majority's desire to return to prewar conditions became evident in the late 1940's and early 1950's. The few positive signs, such as those shown in the executive branch of government during the administration of President Harry S. Truman, were too little and too late to make it possible for blacks to return to their prewar optimism. The result was a stepping-up of the activity of the National Association for the Advancement of Colored People (NAACP), the National Urban League, and other organizations long in existence, and the creation of new organizations and approaches to deal with civil rights issues. Judicial process continued to be considered a means toward racial justice, but direct protest characterized the actions of blacks on these matters in the 1950's, 1960's, and 1970's.

Protest by blacks between World War II and 1960 reflected the aim and desire to convince the American majority of the immorality of its racial position and to win its support. The chief characteristics were a moderate, nonviolent approach, opposition to physical confrontation, a willingness of protesters to suffer physically to make their point, and an implied and expressed desire to find for blacks a place in the mainstream of American life, in which political and economic structures remained essentially unchanged. A series of court cases instituted by the NAACP led eventually to the 1954 and 1955 Supreme Court decisions in *Brown* v. *Board of Education of Topeka, Kansas,* stating that separate but equal education was unconstitutional and ordering the desegregation of educational facilities "with all deliberate speed." Former servicemen created an organization, Negroes and Allied Veterans, that supported Henry Wallace in the presidential election of 1948. The 386-day Montgomery bus boycott that began in December 1955 spawned the Southern Christian Leadership Conference (SCLC) and produced the foremost civil rights leader and exponent of nonviolent protest of the nation, the Rev. Dr. Martin Luther King, Jr. The SCLC joined the Congress of Racial Equality (CORE), in existence since 1942, and the Student Nonviolent Coordinating Committee (SNCC), organized in 1960 to exert pressure by nonviolent protest, urging the United States to move to a new level of morality on the issue of race.

These groups and others like them had limited success in changing laws, customs, and policies regarding race, but they had considerable success in sensitizing a wide range of Americans to the need for opposition to institutionalized racial prejudice. The result was a shift in the nature of black protest and the rise of protests among other nonwhite ethnic groups, women, and students.

Black protest after 1960 differed from earlier protest in several important ways. It fostered confrontation, expressed objection to much in the existing political and economic structure, placed less emphasis on integration than had previously been the case, and placed more emphasis on self-help and work through all-black organizations. This new wave of "creative disorder" was introduced by the sit-in of four black college students at the North Carolina Agricultural and Technical College in Greensboro, N.C., February 1960. Sit-ins became stand-ins at segregated theater box offices, kneel-ins at segregated churches, and wade-ins at segregated beaches. A series of "freedom rides" was organized by CORE to protest segregation in interstate travel, and voter registration drives and demonstrations were organized against discriminatory practices in voting. Major demonstrations took place in Birmingham and Selma, Ala., Albany, Ga., and numerous other places.

In spite of some white support of black protest, many among the white majority reacted with hostility and violence to both phases of the movement. In 1955, Emmet Till, a fourteen-year-old black boy, was kidnapped and lynched in Mississippi and the National Guard had to be used to quell mobs attempting to prevent the implementation of court orders to desegregate educational facilities in Tennessee and Kentucky (1956), Arkansas (1957), Mississippi (1962), and Alabama (1963). Dozens of churches and homes were bombed and burned, and peaceful demonstrators were beaten and gassed. Both black and white civil rights workers were killed in Mississippi (1964) and Alabama (1965).

One expression of the frustration of blacks, their hostility to white reaction to their movement, and the slow pace of change was a series of riots beginning in 1963. In Birmingham, Ala., a riot followed the May 11, 1963, bombing of a black church. In Manhattan on July 18, 1964, a fifteen-year-old black youth was shot to death by a policeman who alleged that the boy was threatening him with a knife—whereupon rioting followed, spread to Brooklyn, and continued until July 26. Actions by police—alleged to have used more than the necessary force in arresting three blacks—set off rioting in the Watts section of Los Angeles on Aug. 11, 1965, and the conflict continued for five days. In July 1967 riots were sparked by police arrest of blacks in Detroit, Mich., and Newark, N.J. Forty-three people were killed and more than 1,500 injured in four days (July 23–27) in Detroit, and twenty-six were killed and more than 1,000 injured during five days (July 14–19) in Newark. Other disorders took place in Cambridge, Md.; Chicago, Ill.; Philadelphia, Pa.; Rochester, N.Y.; Atlanta, Ga.; Plainfield, N.J.; Nashville, Tenn.; and Boston, Mass.

Race riots before 1963 had been characterized by attacks of whites on blacks. Unlike these earlier riots the conflicts after 1963 represented the lashing out of blacks at examples and symbols of discrimination and segregation. Attacks on the persons of whites were rare. The majority of those killed were black, the deaths resulting from the actions of police and troops in putting down the riots, frequently using excessive force. In its report to the president submitted in February 1968 the National Advisory Commission on Civil Disorders, appointed by President Lyndon B. Johnson in July 1967, found no organized conspiracy behind the riots and listed among the major grievances of blacks in the cities in which disorders took place (1) police activities, (2) unemployment, (3) inadequate housing, (4) inadequate education, (5) absence of quality recreational programs and facilities, and (6) unresponsiveness of the political structure to grievances of blacks.

Another round of riots occurred in 1968 after the assassination of Martin Luther King on Apr. 4 in Memphis, Tenn., where he had gone to lead a march of garbage workers seeking recognition for their union and higher pay. As King was spiritual leader of the civil rights movement, his death stunned many Americans. (His assassin was later arrested in England, extradited to the United States, pleaded guilty, and was sentenced without trial to ninety-nine years in jail.) Racial violence erupted in about 110 cities in the days following King's death: 39 people were killed; nearly 2,500, injured; and almost 15,000, arrested. Thirty-five of those killed and the vast majority of those wounded and arrested were black. The most serious conflicts took place in Washington, D.C.; Chicago; Detroit; Newark; Baltimore; Pittsburgh, Pa.; Kansas City, Mo.; New York; Saint Louis; and Philadelphia. Sixty-five thousand National Guardsmen and federal troops were used to restore order.

Despite efforts during the post–World War II period, by 1974 only moderate progress had been made toward racial justice. The major accomplishments at the national level were the Civil Rights Act of 1964 and the Voting Rights Act of 1965. Also, a series of Supreme Court decisions had been made supporting the rights of blacks to equality of treatment and protecting the right to protest in an effort to secure that equality. On the local level white-collar job opportunities, the availability of housing to middle-class blacks, and the availability of higher education to blacks improved somewhat. Little was changed for the majority of blacks, who were poor and who now lived in urban areas. Custom, economic conditions, and violations of the law—plus the effect of centuries of unequal opportunity—were responsible for differences between blacks and whites. In the 1970's some school districts were more segregated than they had been at the time of *Brown* v. *Board of Education,* and although the average income of blacks had increased, the difference in the average for the two races was greater than it had been in the 1960's.

Characteristic of the 1970's was a growing race consciousness and pride among black people; continued opposition to legal or *de facto* segregation, coupled with less attention to integration as a solution to problems; and growing political activity and awareness, especially in those areas in which blacks formed a large part of the population. One positive result was the election of black mayors in several large U.S. cities: Los Angeles, Newark, Atlanta, and Cleveland among them.

[*Report of the National Advisory Commission on Civil Disorders;* John Blassingame, *The Slave Community;* John Hope Franklin, *From Slavery to Freedom;* E. Franklin Frazier, *The Negro in the United States;* Loren Miller, *The Petitioner: The Story of the Supreme Court of the United States and the Negro;* Gunnar Myrdal, *An American Dilemma;* C. Vann Woodward, *The Strange Story of Jim Crow;* Carter G. Woodson, *The Negro in Our History.*]

HENRY N. DREWRY

AGAMENTICUS. Successively known as Bristol (1632), Agamenticus (1641), Gorgeana (1642), and York (1652), this early Maine settlement, equidistant from Mount Agamenticus and the Piscataqua River, has the distinction of being the first municipal corporation in America (1642), created so by Sir Ferdinando Gorges, whose special favor the settlement enjoyed. Settled about 1624, it was one of the few substantial settlements in the province of Maine during the trying period of colonial wars.

[C. E. Banks, *History of York, Maine.*]

ELIZABETH RING

AGENCIES, FEDERAL. *See* **Federal Agencies.**

AGENT, COLONIAL. *See* **Colonial Agent.**

AGRARIAN MOVEMENT. Even before formation of the federal system, American agrarianism developed into one of the major forces shaping the policies of the new nation. The early agrarian movement was a mixture of philosophic idealism rooted in the 18th-century Enlightenment and in the hard, practical demands of colonial farmers, who were essentially a debtor class. As the nation evolved, agrarianism became a tradition of independence and self-reliance, of progress and scientific improvement, tinged with a sentimental romanticism that reached its height among American writers and artists of the 19th century.

Ten years before the Declaration of Independence, Thomas Jefferson expressed the classic ideal of agrarianism in his *Notes on Virginia:* "Those who labor in the earth are the chosen people of God, if He ever had a chosen people, whose breasts He has made His peculiar deposit for substantial and genuine virtue. It is the focus in which He keeps alive that sacred fire, which otherwise might escape from the face of the earth." Jefferson viewed the growth of industrialism and the concentration of population in cities as a menace to the fledgling republic, and he wanted to keep the Industrial Revolution confined to Europe. "It is better to carry provisions and materials to workmen there than bring them to the provisions and materials, and with them their manners and principles. . . . The mobs of great cities add just so much to the support of pure government, as sores do to the strength of the human body."

Although the population of the new nation at the end of the Revolution was mostly agricultural, the powerful merchant and trader class along the eastern seaboard attempted to dominate the debt-ridden farmers of the backcountry. This rivalry between agricultural and commercial interests was an important factor in the development of the two-party political system. The Federalists, led by Alexander Hamilton, advocated a strong central government favorable to commerce and opposed the rights of state governments, which agrarians sometimes controlled. The Jeffersonian Republicans, following the philosophy of their leader, represented the agrarians. After Jefferson was elected president in 1800, restrictive excise duties were repealed, and the purchase of the Louisiana Territory widened the land area for agrarian expansion and assured use of the Mississippi River as a market route to New Orleans for Jefferson's idealized "yeoman farmers."

From these beginnings the agrarian movement continued to be closely involved with political movements. In the 1830's, when urban business interests gained power among National Republicans, the agrarians shifted to the Jacksonian Democrats. After slavery and the coming of the Civil War caused a split between plantation owners of the South and free-soil farmers of the North and West, the Republican party of President Abraham Lincoln won strong agrarian support with passage of the Homestead Act, creation of the U.S. Department of Agriculture, and passage of the Morrill Act establishing land grant colleges. During the agricultural depression of the 1890's many farmers turned to a third-party movement—the Populist—but they soon followed William J. Bryan to the Democratic party. In the 1920's other third-party movements had agrarian backing, but the New Deal measures of the Democrats in the 1930's won back a majority of the nation's farmers to that party.

Agrarianism was also a major force in the national expansionist movement that began with Jefferson's Louisiana Purchase (1803) and reached its zenith with the doctrine of Manifest Destiny (1845) and the conquest of Mexican and Indian lands. The expanding frontier, where there was always land for landless Americans, was regarded as a natural right, and the image of the farmer-settler became the national ideal. In 1858, Ralph Waldo Emerson was extolling the strength and dignity of the countryman, advising those poisoned by urban life and urban vices to go back to the land. By this time, however, the countrymen themselves were expressing skepticism about the traditional myths of rural life and its virtues as portrayed by poets, artists, and politicians, who never mentioned the endless toil, discomforts, and deprivations of farm life as compared with the social amenities, cultural opportunities, and higher standard of living of urban areas.

In the period after the Civil War, the contrasts between rural and urban life were so extreme that the agrarian movement became a movement of farmer organizations—such as the Grange and various alliances, unions, and bureaus—designed to improve the position of farmers in American society. These organizations forced passage of many laws favorable to agriculture, with the Department of Agriculture responsible for execution.

As an intellectual movement agrarianism again flowered briefly in the 1930's after a group of southern writers known as the Fugitives issued a statement of principles advocating rejection of industrialism and a national reacceptance of agrarianism. Instead of emancipating laborers, industry "evicts them," the Fugitives charged, and they expressed the belief "that the culture of the soil is the best and most sensitive of vocations and that therefore it should have the economic preference and enlist the maximum number of workers." With the deepening of the economic depression of the 1930's, which brought about a back-to-the-land movement among thousands of unemployed industrial workers, the theories of the Fugitives were widely debated. After World War II, however, the South—which the agrarians had viewed as the base for their movement—turned rapidly away from its agricultural tradition toward industrialization.

Technological changes, which had begun during the 19th century, accelerated after the war and revolutionized agriculture nationally. By 1960, two-thirds of all Americans lived in urban areas as compared with the extreme minority of Jefferson's time. Distinctions between urban and rural life vanished as the result of automobiles and paved highways, farm price supports, mechanized farming, standardized education, and a wide diffusion of information and entertainment through print and the electronic media. Cultural deprivations and social aridities were virtually eliminated from rural life, and farmers became businessmen with attitudes and values similar to those of their counterparts in cities. In the 20th century farm organizations adopted the methods of big business—some of them using the same pressure politics of industrial corporations—as well as extolling free enterprise and opposing excessive government regulation.

[Solon J. Buck, *The Agrarian Crusade;* U.S. Department of Agriculture, *Farmers in a Changing World.*]

DEE BROWN

AGRICULTURAL ADJUSTMENT ADMINISTRATION. *See* **Agriculture; New Deal.**

AGRICULTURAL MACHINERY. The Industrial Revolution affected all aspects of human life but none more dramatically than the raising of food and fiber. Although Thomas Jefferson wrote a treatise on the design of the moldboard plow in 1788 and the first cast-iron plow was patented in 1797, opening the way for mass production of that tool, the first major impact of the Industrial Revolution on American agriculture came from a different direction. Eli Whitney's cotton gin, patented in 1794, was the last link in the industrialization of the cotton textile industry. Cotton farming boomed, and the dying institution of slavery acquired a brief new lease on life. Arising from the conflict over this very institution, the Civil War, by creating a shortage of labor, brought on a mechanical revolution in farming, followed by the introduction of power machinery near the turn of the century.

Preparing the Soil, Planting, and Cultivating. The invention of the steel plow by John Deere in 1837 solved the problem of how to plow the rich earth of the primeval American prairie, in which the cast-iron plows and the iron-patched wooden plows brought from the East had heavy going. Shaped over a log at Deere's shop in Grand Detour, Ill., the steel plow, intrinsically lighter than its predecessors, had the special advantage of scouring and significantly increasing the speed of plowing. The powerful but plodding ox team was therefore replaced by the faster horse and mule.

The challenge of the prairie soil sparked a proliferation of tools for soil preparation, later to be given added impetus by the Civil War, with its demand for more food produced by less labor. In 1864 a two-wheeled sulky plow was invented. For the first time, the plowman rode instead of walked. Iron and steel replaced wood, with consequent improvements in efficiency and durability. A disk plow, today one of the most widely used types of plow, was patented as early as 1847 but did not become popular for many years. The harrow, long nothing more than a bush weighted by a log, or at most a wooden frame armed with pegs or spikes, became a family of specialized tools during the middle of the 19th century. At the same time the lister, or double moldboard plow, was developed. This plow made it possible to plant row crops in furrows and came to be sometimes used for planting as well as ground-breaking.

Though most of the elements of the modern drill were present in a machine developed in Italy about 1600 and in a more advanced machine developed by the British agronomist Jethro Tull in 1733, lack of an effective metering device hindered the machine's acceptance. Several such devices were patented in the United States in the early 1840's, and in 1851 a force-feed device utilizing a rotating fluted cylinder was developed. This device was the most important invention of the drill industry in America.

By the time of the Civil War, improvements in other agricultural implements had made hand seeding the limiting factor in the number of acres a farmer might cultivate. It was said that mechanization of seeding during the war freed one man in three for other duties. Improvements and variations of mechanical metering continued to be made, but it was more than a century before any fundamentally new approach appeared. In 1971 the International Harvester Company introduced a machine invented by two Minnesota farmers, Claude and Leo Loesch, that utilizes a flow of air to select and transport the seed.

As the plow is the basic tool of soil preparation, the hoe is that of cultivation. A horse hoe, designed to be drawn between rows by a single horse, was developed about 1820. A second hoe blade was added about 1850, and a two-horse straddle-row cultivator, which doubled productivity, was patented in 1856.

Harvesting. The sickle, later improved as the scythe and the cradle, remained the tool of the grain harvest throughout the preindustrial period. All crops except small grains were harvested completely by hand. Cyrus McCormick developed his famous reaper in 1831. Patented in 1834, the machine did not achieve great commercial success until McCormick moved from his Virginia homeland to Chicago, where he began the manufacture of an improved reaper. Three thousand reapers were sold in 1850, and 40,000 were sold in the labor-short war year of 1863. Although far from a perfected harvesting machine, the reaper was a great step forward. It cut harvest time in half—saving much labor and, equally significantly, lessening the risk of weather damage to the ripe and vulnerable grain.

By the early 1800's small stationary mechanical threshing machines were in use in America. In 1837 a machine was developed that combined the old "groundhog" thresher with a fanning mill, thus performing both threshing and winnowing operations. Two Michigan men, H. Moore and J. Hascall, developed the first combine in 1836. Horse-drawn and ground-driven, the machine was improved to the point at which it could cut and thresh twenty-five acres a day. After ten years of work the developers abandoned the project, and the combine did not achieve wide acceptance for nearly a century.

There were two problems with Moore and Hascall's combine. First, Michigan's cool and damp climate produced a high-moisture grain, and there was much spoilage in combine-processed grain. Other less efficient systems permitted a drying time between cutting and threshing. Second was the problem of power. The horse-drawn and ground-driven machine did not have the power to make efficient use of the combine principle. The first objection did not hold in the drier western areas, and the original combine was shipped around Cape Horn to San Francisco in time to cut 600 acres of California wheat in 1854. The combine achieved local success there and was put into commercial production in 1880. Drawn by teams of more than thirty mules, such machines were harvesting two-thirds of the California wheat crop by 1900. Wide acceptance of the combine principle had to wait for the mechanically powered, self-propelled machine developed by Thomas Carroll, an engineer for the Massey-Harris Company, in 1938. This machine reached mass production in time to play a significant role in World War II food production. The self-propelled combine has become the prime tool in the grain harvest, and with variations and special attachments it is used to harvest such other crops as corn, soybeans, rice, and peanuts.

In 1971 the acreage devoted to hay in the United States was second only to that in corn. The basic hay harvesting tool is a mower with a serrated, reciprocating knife much like a barber's clippers. A mowing machine was first patented in the United States in 1822, following by two years a horse-drawn revolving rake. Early mowing machine development quickly blended with that of the reaper, which had similar requirements. In the 1850's their development moved apart again with the invention of a flexible mower bar that could be used over rougher ground. By 1865 nearly all haymowing in the United States was done mechanically.

A baling press was developed in 1853, but growth in the field of hay-handling machinery was less rapid than in hay harvesting. The advent of powered machinery, particularly the development of the automatic pick-up baler by the New Holland Company in 1940, made possible a much more efficient use of hay. Hay use varies widely around the country, and an equally wide variety of powered and self-propelled machines has been developed to swath, windrow, condition, chop, and otherwise prepare the forage for storage or immediate use.

Cotton resisted mechanical harvesting longer than any other major crop. A stripper was patented in 1871, but stripping is suitable only to the arid high plains. Picking is the method of choice for most cotton regions. A third method, brush harvesting, has found some adherents. The modern cotton picker is based upon the use of a rotating spindle, patented by Angus Campbell in 1895. Two brothers, John and Mack Rust, are credited with the first successful machine in 1927. Commercial success, however, did not come until the International Harvester Company introduced a machine of somewhat different design in 1942. Both types of machines are used.

Mechanical harvesters for many root and specialty crops were developed after the internal combustion engine became available. Harvesters for root crops such as potatoes require large amounts of power and were developed only when more powerful and versatile tractors became available in the 1930's. A notable modern effort was the collaboration of an equipment maker, Blackwelder Manufacturing Company, with two University of California scientists, Coby Lorenson, Jr., and Gordie C. Hanna, to develop simultaneously a mechanized tomato harvester and a tomato amenable to such harvest. Within five years of its introduction, more than 80 percent of California's tomatoes were being mechanically harvested. Efforts to develop mechanical harvesters for tree and vine crops have been less successful for the most part.

Mechanical Power. The introduction and improvement of mechanical power gave impetus to the development of farm machinery. Steam plowing had been attempted in England as early as 1836; a successful effort was reported in Illinois in 1860. The first major application to farm machinery was in the operation of threshers. Portable but not self-propelled engines for this purpose were built as early as 1849 in Philadelphia. Joseph McCune is credited with converting such a machine to self-propulsion in 1855. It was not until the 1880's that steam traction engines attained widespread success and use.

In 1892 the J. I. Case Company introduced the first true gasoline traction engine. The first commercially successful machine (1906) was the Hart-Parr Company's "Old No. 1." This machine, for which the name "tractor" was coined, developed 22/45 horsepower. Many improvements were made during the next several years, but the tractor remained chiefly a pulling vehicle until the development of the power take-off in 1918. This device made it possible to power by the tractor's engine many implements that had formerly been ground-propelled. A tricycle-type all-purpose tractor introduced by the International Harvester Company in 1924 widened the application of the principle to cultivation. In 1936 Harry Ferguson's 3-point hitch made it possible to tractor-mount many implements that formerly had been trailed. After World War II many advances in the use of hydrostatics and hydraulics broadened the tractor's versatility as a power source for many agricultural activities. In addition, development occurred in the self-propulsion of many specialized machines, such as combines, cotton pickers, and various forage processors.

Many of the bulk-handling procedures already used in mining and manufacturing have been applied to animal agriculture. It has become possible not merely to mechanize but also to automate agriculture. Increasing labor costs, governmental and consumer resistance to price increases, and a growing unwillingness to perform arduous labor have tended to accelerate the trend. In 1790 it took nearly ten workers on the farm to support one worker in a trade. In 1972 only 4.6 percent of the population was employed on the farm.

[Stewart H. Holbrook, *Machines of Plenty;* E. P. Neufeld, *A Global Corporation;* C. B. Richey, Paul Jacobson, and Carl W. Hall, *Agricultural Engineers' Handbook;* Harrison Pearson Smith, *Farm Machinery and Equipment.*]

RICHARD E. UPTON

AGRICULTURE. *This article consists of an essay on the history of* American Agriculture *and the following related topics:* Influence of Transportation; Farm Tenancy; Agricultural Societies and Farm Organizations; Agricultural Policies and Legislation; Federal Farm Credit Agencies; Department of Agriculture; Farm Periodicals; Scientific Aid to Agriculture; Agricultural Experiment Stations; *and* Agricultural Education.

When the first European settlers arrived in America, they attempted to use Old World agricultural methods but were unable to provide themselves with adequate food supplies until they combined their skills with the American Indians' ways of growing and processing crops. At first the colonists subsisted mainly on wild plants, game, and fish, and many would have starved but for supplies obtained from the Indians. The basic food crop of the Indians was maize (Indian corn) but their fields also contained peanuts, pumpkins, squash, potatoes, tobacco, tomatoes, and wild cotton—all indigenous to the North American continent.

Faced with a shortage of metal tools, the pioneer farmers adopted the Indians' digging stick, flint or bone hoe, winnowing basket, and cornhusking peg, and they imitated the design of the Indian corncrib set on posts to dry the grain. They also followed the native custom of planting beans and corn in hills with pumpkins and squash between the hills. From the Indians they learned the art of maple sugaring; the use of native dye plants, such as indigo; and the making of pemmican for storage as a winter food resource.

The first farms were set in clearings along the coastal plain, land probably previously used by Indians for maize plantings and abandoned. The soil was seldom good, and soon the colonists were moving into the interior, resorting to primitive slash-and-burn methods to clear forests for farming.

From the beginning labor scarcities influenced American agricultural practices—and except for periods of economic depression the shortage has existed to the present, becoming so acute at times that it has acted as an incentive for the development of labor-saving tools, equipment, and machinery. Because of the abundance and easy accessibility of cheap land, almost all farmers worked their own fields, and there was almost no hiring-out. In the northern colonies the labor shortage was compensated for in some measure by community cooperation. During the 17th and 18th centuries apprenticeship systems brought thousands of indentured servants and redemptioners into the middle colonies as farm laborers, but since most of these immigrants soon gained their independence and acquired farms of their own, the labor shortage persisted. In 1619 the first African slaves were landed by a Dutch privateer at Jamestown, and they were sold to Virginia planters as agricultural laborers. By the time of the American Revolution, almost half a million slaves had been brought to the colonies; because they were found to be best suited to the plantation system of the South, three-fourths of them were located in that area. Eventually slave labor drove out most of the free labor in the South, although only one-fourth of the population there owned slaves. Thus, in the first decades of colonization, agriculture established labor patterns that were to affect the stream of American history.

Dependent upon the Old World for manufactured articles, the first colonial farmers worked with simple hoes, pitchforks, axes, harrows, shovels, and scythes. Plows were always scarce, the first one on record in America having arrived in Plymouth Colony twelve years after its establishment. Owners of plows could earn a good living by plowing for their neighbors—setting a precedent for the modern practice of custom-hiring power machinery. In the South tobacco farming required only the capital investment of huge plantations consisting of the land, slaves, work animals, plows, carts, and a few tools that could be contrived by plantation blacksmiths.

Agriculture during the colonial period was characterized by the misuse of soil, forests, and water. To the immigrants, the New World appeared an inexhaustible continent. Land was so plentiful and so cheap that it was acquired with the expectation of wearing it out by continuous cropping. The pioneer farmer was a migrant, always moving westward, claiming new ground when his old fields lost their fertility. Before the end of the 18th century, however, the best of the farmlands east of the Alleghenies were under cultivation, and agricultural experimenters—a notable one being Thomas Jefferson—were beginning to advocate rotation and fertilization practices.

As the colonists moved inland, clearing forests as they went, maize was almost invariably the first crop; wheat and rye followed when the ground had been worked sufficiently. The South, which was to become the primary agricultural region of the new nation, was exporting great quantities of tobacco, sugar, rice, and indigo before the revolutionary war. Cotton, grown for home use from the time of the Jamestown settlements, did not become a commercial crop until after the war.

Because the American Indian had no domesticated animal except the dog, farm livestock had to be imported. Since wild game provided a meat supply for the colonists, the first importations consisted mainly of oxen and a few draft horses. But by the 18th century the typical northern farm was equipped with a few cattle, swine, and sheep to provide milk, meat, and wool for the farm family.

In the South the livestock industry was slow to develop; it was actually discouraged in several colonies because of the desire of land grant owners to concentrate production of staple crops on their plantations. When cattle proved to be profitable in Virginia and the Carolinas, the open-range system was generally used. Thus, it was in the South that the pattern of later far-western ranching was established—with brands and marks to denote ownership, annual roundups, and overland drives to markets.

As the young nation moved into the 19th century, agriculture expanded rapidly westward, in ever sharper competition for labor with the Industrial Revolution. In northern areas the manpower shortage had become so acute by 1840 that inventors of improved farm implements and machinery found ready markets for their contrivances. The period from 1840 to the Civil War saw a ferment of inventions for the farm, hundreds of new patents being registered for implements designed to save labor (*see* Agricultural Machinery).

One side result of the emergence of improved agricultural machinery was the gradual disappearance of the ox, that now almost forgotten beast of burden that hauled families by the thousands to frontier claims, plowed the first fields, carried wood and water, and was eventually sacrificed for food and leather. In 1840 oxen outnumbered horses by three to two on American farms; by 1860 their numbers were about equal. Soon after the Civil War the ox had nearly vanished, and for the next sixty years the horse was to reign supreme as the power source on farms.

During the first half of the 19th century livestock production gradually developed into importance in areas just west of the Alleghenies. Between 1840 and 1860, a large-scale beef cattle industry flourished in Ohio and in the Kentucky Bluegrass regions, the finished animals being trailed overland to markets in the East. Sheep and swine production also shifted westward, whereas dairying remained concentrated in the East, closer to markets. By mid-century the South was taking the lead in animal husbandry, the great breeding centers being in the pasture regions of Kentucky and Tennessee. The best types of animals were imported from abroad—Henry Clay was one of the active leaders in improving livestock breeds—and from Kentucky and Tennessee livestock farming spread to other sections of the South. During the 1850's Texans were beginning to drive cattle into the Midwest for fattening, foreshadowing the great western beef cattle industry that was to develop after the Civil War.

The years immediately preceding the Civil War became the era of Currier and Ives prints, of John Greenleaf Whittier's "Barefoot Boy," of Stephen Foster's ballads—romanticizing and idealizing rural life. It was also the era of agricultural societies and fairs and of many new farm periodicals—all spreading the gospel of better tillage, improved livestock breeding, crop rotations, and conservation practices. The burgeoning cities and manufacturing centers provided ready markets for farm products. Though not all American farmers were prosperous, by comparison with the times before the advent of new labor-saving inventions, life was easygoing, the future seemed bright, and rural life was the national ideal.

As the era came to a close with the outbreak of the Civil War, the center of agriculture was shifting to the West, to the vast new prairie lands. John Deere's invention of a steel plow that would scour in the clinging black humus of prairie soils opened the richest grain-growing region in the world, millions of acres that earlier settlers had avoided or passed over as unsuited to agriculture. There the farms were more isolated, social events less frequent. Populations were of mixed nationalities. There was more machinery, but overproduction and uncertain markets created tensions and insecurities.

In the South, also, the plantation system was exploding westward on the basis of cotton production—made possible by Eli Whitney's cotton gin—moving out of the Carolinas and Georgia across the black prairies of Alabama to the rich deltas of the Mississippi and Red rivers. With the westward movement marched the burning question of slavery. Would the farms of the western territories, future American states, be worked by free men or slaves?

The old rivalry between western and eastern agriculture was diminished by the greater rivalry between the North and South. Indeed, from colonial days onward the North and South had been moving in different directions, and the South's commercial cotton cultivation of the 19th century accelerated the differences. In addition to its cotton the South produced more than half the nation's corn, almost all of the tobacco, and all of the rice and sugar. As the Civil War approached, the self-sufficient northern farmers were also struggling toward commercial agriculture; but they were hindered by habits and traditions and most of all by lack of working capital.

The war's outbreak had little effect on the agricultural labor supply in the South, few slaves being diverted to direct military efforts; the major change was a switch from large cotton crops to corn and other food crops. In the North, however, many rural young men went into the army, creating a great labor shortage on farms at a time when produce was bringing high prices because of increased demands. To solve the dilemma, output of farm machines was increased sharply; old men, boys, and women could operate horsepowered cultivators, mowers, and reapers. The pressure of wartime thus served as a further impetus to lighten human labor, and the latter years of the struggle and the decades following it saw a new wave of inventions.

In the 1880's, when huge bonanza grain farms were opened on the Great Plains, steam-powered machines were developed to reduce the back-breaking work of harvesting. Shortly after the turn of the century the gasoline engine reached the farm as a replacement for the vanishing "handy man." Though hailed as a deliverer of the farmer from drudgery, it served only a generation—to be replaced after World War I by the electric motor.

During this period of rapid mechanization the farm frontier moved across the western plains ten times as fast as it had moved across the wooded regions of the East. The Homestead Act of 1862, which had provided free land for settlers who would live on it for five years (military service being deductible), was an accelerating force to settlement. A flood of emigrants from Europe, mainly Germans and Scandinavians, joined this westward-moving army. Specialization of crops became relatively more important, increasing the need for additional capital to finance risks and necessary machinery.

Wheat was the principal crop in the West, and once again the old story of land abuse was repeated. In the wake of crop failures resulting from drought or pests, overextended debts were claimed and mortages foreclosed. Prices of commodities began falling, and the postwar boom failed. Farm life on the new frontier turned almost as hard and barren as that on the old frontier of a century earlier.

The late 19th century also saw a major shift of livestock production from East to West, the corn-hog pattern of farming developing in the Middle West; the cattle kingdom, in the Southwest and on the Great Plains. The rise of the western cattle industry was the most picturesque of all American agricultural endeavors—the long drives from Texas to Kansas railheads and Montana ranges, the romantic cowboys, and the wars between cattlemen and sheepmen, and between cattlemen and homesteaders. Shorthorns and Herefords gradually replaced the scrawny Texas longhorns; the open range was closed; and in the mountain states sheep outnumbered cattle. By the late 1880's, western stockmen were in as dire straits as were the homesteaders. Blizzards, droughts, and overproduction brought threats of economic disaster to cattle barons and homesteaders alike.

From the end of the Civil War to the late 1880's prices of commodities gradually fell, farmers receiving less and less for what they had to sell and paying more and more for what they had to buy. In 1867 agricultural leaders organized the Patrons of Husbandry, or National Grange, to fight for lower railroad rates, more favorable banking practices, and the elimination of middlemen. During the 1880's an outbreak of farm unrest resulted in the organization of the militant Farmers' Alliance, differing in policy from region to region but united in a determination to better the farmer's lot through political action. The power of these movements was concentrated in the central plains, where grain and livestock prices were most depressed. Under the leadership of such colorful political figures as "Sockless Jerry" Simpson and Mary E. Lease in Kansas, they won a series of surprise political victories in 1890. By 1892 the various groups comprehended by the Farmers' Alliance had united into the People's party, or Populist movement, and two years later—after the panic of 1893—it doubled its vote, and a national third party loomed on the political horizon. But in 1896 the weakened Democratic party moved to add Populists to its ranks by nominating William Jennings Bryan as candidate for president and almost won the election. After the turn of the century, however, demand for commodities caught up with supply. Many farm workers had gone to the cities to become factory workers; immigration had increased, the newcomers remaining in cities because there was no more frontier land. As a result, prices of farm products were rising, and pressures for a radical agrarian party was ended. During the early years of the 20th century much of the old Populist program was put into law, just as much of the program of the unsuccessful Farmer-Labor party of the 1920's became law during the New Deal of the 1930's.

Vast as were the changes in American agriculture from colonial days to 1900, the first half of the 20th century brought an even more startling transformation—an agricultural revolution comparable in scope to the Industrial Revolution of the 19th century. As early as 1850 the nation's industrial structure had begun to challenge the supremacy of agriculture. By the time of the Civil War 60 percent of the population was engaged in agriculture; in 1900 it was only 37 percent. By 1930 the figure was 24.9 percent and in 1972 it was 4.6 percent. Not only did this percentage drop sharply; the total farm population declined by more than 10 million during the first half of the 20th century. Although considerably more land was converted to farming acreage, the total number of farms declined from 6.4 million in 1910 to 2.8 million in 1973. During this period the average size of farms increased from 138 to 385 acres.

Production per acre and per man-hour increased significantly for many of the staple crops: in 1940 one farm worker could supply only eleven persons with the agricultural products they required; in 1970 one worker could supply forty-seven persons, more than a fourfold increase. Except in the harvesting of some perishable fruit and vegetable crops, mechanization and automation replaced hand labor. Tractors increased from fewer than 1,000 in 1910 to 5.5 million in 1970. During the same period the number of horses and mules on farms decreased from 25 million to about 2.4 million, the draft horse becoming almost as rare as its predecessor the ox. Rural electrification brought power to more than 98 percent of the nation's farms. Daily mail service, telephones, radio and television, paved highways, and consolidated schools greatly lessened the differences between urban and rural life.

At the same time federal controls growing out of the depression of the 1930's eliminated many of the economic risks of farming. Price and income support programs, along with soil conservation programs, acted as stabilizing forces. In the half century preceding 1970, the value of farm assets rose from $40 billion to more than $300 billion. More and more capital was required to operate farms, to acquire and maintain powerful tractors and implements, and to house and service livestock. Corporation farming was on the increase, and various farmer organizations expressed fears for the future of the traditional family farm. In the 1970's agriculture entered the space age, with orbiting satellites carrying remote sensing equipment that monitored crops through the growing seasons, estimating yields, detecting insect and disease outbreaks, observing soil nutrient and moisture conditions, and warning of pollution patterns.

Influence of Transportation. For more than a century and a half after the first colonists settled in America, the limited transportation confined commercial agriculture to the narrow strip of eastern seacoast. Navigable rivers were the natural travel routes westward, and as immigration and the demand for farmland increased, settlers moved inland by water. The pattern of agricultural production for markets was therefore restricted to lands bordering these river routes. For many years Indian trails that led from one stream to another were used by travelers, but these land routes were unsuited for transporting agricultural commodities. Even after the narrow trails were widened into roads, the costs of moving grain were prohibitive for farmers who lived several miles from a river landing. In the colonial South the greatest obstacle to expanding tobacco production was poor transport, a problem that was only partially alleviated by rolling the product overland in hogsheads attached to mules by an ingenious pole arrangement.

Not until the beginning of the 19th century were any considerable amounts of public monies spent for building and improving roads, the greatest single contribution to agriculture being the Cumberland, or National, Road, which was completed westward to Columbus, Ohio, by 1833. As late as 1840, however, most of the so-called highways were still cluttered by stumps and brush and were without weatherproof surfacing, with the result that loaded wagons could not pass over them during many months of the year. It was only natural that, discouraged by such overland means of transporting their products, frontier farmers should turn to canals as the answer to the problem of reaching markets.

As early as 1784 George Washington had urged construction of a canal to connect the tidewaters of the Potomac with the Ohio River, as an aid to development of the Northwest Territory, but not until 1850 was the Chesapeake and Ohio Canal completed to Cumberland, Md. Meanwhile, in New York State, the Erie Canal had opened a new era for western agriculture. During its first ten years of operation from 1825 to 1835, the Erie reduced its rates from $22 per ton to $4 per ton, so cheapening transportation costs that an immense wilderness was opened for agricultural exploitation. For almost half a century a flood of agricultural commodities moved through the canal from Lake Erie to the Hudson River, contributing to the establishment of New York City as the great port and commercial center of the nation.

Although the success of the Erie encouraged canal construction in almost all the northern states and some of the southern ones, neither these man-made water routes nor rivers and turnpikes combined were ever adequate to meet the demands of expanding agricultural production. Not until railroads were extended to the interior during the period between 1840 and 1860 was commercial agriculture able to begin its great development west of the Alleghenies. By the time of the Civil War more than two-thirds of middlewestern farm products marketed in the East were transported there by rail. After the war railroads and agriculture moved westward simultaneously. Such refinements in railroad transport services as faster trains and the development of refrigerated cars made it possible to ship meats and other perishables thousands of miles. Specialty crops could be grown in the most suitable climate and soil zones and shipped to centers of population, giving rise to the vast fruit and vegetable farms in Florida, in the Rio Grande valley, and along the Pacific coast.

The 20th century saw another complete revolution in agricultural transport—the introduction of the motor truck. By 1967, 51 percent of foods and kindred products were transported by trucks, 47 percent by rail, and 2 percent by water. Trucks hauled most of the perishable crops whereas railroads continued to transport grains and other semiperishables. By the 1970's barges and other methods of water transportation were offering considerable competition to railroads as grain carriers and airplanes were competing with trucks as carriers of perishables, such as fresh fruits, vegetables, and horticultural products.

Farm Tenancy. Since the first settlement of the United States, farm tenancy has existed, although for many years the number of tenants remained relatively small because of an abundance of land. No statistical information on land tenure was available until 1880, when the census of agriculture reported that 25 percent of farms were operated by tenants. By 1900 the percentage of tenant farmers had grown to 35 percent and in the 1930's it had grown to 42 percent. In the cotton-growing states of the South tenancy was as high as 62 percent.

A fairly close relationship has always existed between the prevalence of farm tenancy and the various stages of agricultural development in different parts of the country. When a given area was newly settled, with free land available, little tenancy existed; but as sections became settled and agriculture well established, the practice of renting farms tended to accelerate. In the southern states tenancy evolved from the plantation system, which used slave labor and tended to crowd the nonslaveholding population onto poor land. At the end of the Civil War thousands of freed but impoverished and poorly educated blacks could find no means of support except by remaining on the land. A tenancy arrangement was then devised whereby these tenants were given a share of the crop, usually one-half, in return for their labor. They became known as sharecroppers. Gradually the economic aspects of the sharecropper system were extended to poor white farmers. By 1930 there were more white than black sharecropper families in the principal cotton states of the South.

The advent of the depression intensified the poverty of tenant farmers, who then composed one-fourth of the population living outside urban areas. Year by year their standard of living decreased and their indebtedness to landowners increased. Housing, nutrition, and health conditions became intolerable, and more than a million rural families were on the welfare rolls. In 1934 the Southern Tenant Farmers Union was organized with the objective of alleviating conditions among sharecroppers. Although its membership remained small, the union helped bring the attention of the nation to the plight of sharecroppers and other tenants. Recognizing the economic maladjustments affecting farm tenants, President Franklin D. Roosevelt in 1936 set up a Farm Tenancy committee and from its recommendations arose the 1937 Bankhead-Jones Farm Tenant Act. This act provided for loans to tenants for the purchase of farms, livestock, equipment, and supplies.

After 1940 major changes took place in the tenure status of American farmers, many of the changes resulting from the revolution in farming methods that virtually eliminated marginal farms and drastically reduced requirements for labor. By 1969 the number of farms worked by tenants had dropped to 12.9 percent. In the South the number had fallen to 11.7 percent. The sharecroppers had either migrated to urban centers or had become owners or part-owner–operators. Tenancy was relatively low for livestock farms and was highest for cash-grain, tobacco, and cotton farms. The primary shift in tenure relationships after 1940 was toward part-ownership. The number of farms in this tenure group remained small; but in terms of acreage operated and percentage of farm production, part-owners by 1969 had become the largest tenure group, leasing farmland mainly on a cash basis. Between 1940 and 1969 the percentage of farms owned by part-owners increased from 10.1 percent to 24.6 percent.

Agricultural Societies and Farm Organizations. Although agriculture is generally considered to be an individualistic way of life, American farmers have been quick to organize for mutual advantage when circumstances have warranted. During colonial days they joined forces to fight Indians, to improve schools, and to secure roads and canals. Shays's Rebellion of 1786–87 was largely an organized farmers' revolt against disproportionate taxation in Massachusetts. The Whiskey Rebellion of 1794 was a Pennsylvania farmers' revolt against taxes on distilled spirits; Fries's Rebellion of 1799, also in Pennsylvania, was an uprising against a federal land tax.

As the nation moved into the 19th century, such violent rural protest movements declined and a more calm type of organization arose—the agricultural society. The Philadelphia Society for Promoting Agriculture and the South Carolina Society for Promoting and Improving Agriculture were formed in 1785. During the following half century almost every state, region, and county organized a society or farmers' club to promote agriculture or its branches of horticulture, dairying, animal breeding, and so forth. For the most part agricultural society members were gentlemen farmers—distinguished intellectuals and political figures. Originally very few rank-and-file farmers were active; in fact, agricultural societies at first were ridiculed by frontier farmers, who had little use for scientific theories of improving production in a time of cheap land and scarce markets.

Nevertheless the societies flourished, gradually winning the support of practicing farmers. They sponsored annual fairs and exhibits and supported agricultural journals that spread information about new experiments and discoveries. In the 1840's efforts were made to establish a national society, and in 1852 representatives from local organizations met in Washington, D.C., to form the U.S. Agricultural Society, which was largely responsible for passage of the law creating the U.S. Department of Agriculture a decade later.

In 1867 Oliver Hudson Kelley and six associates founded a national secret organization of farmers, the National Grange of the Patrons of Husbandry, or simply the Grange. Originally intended as a fraternal and educational organization, the Grange within ten years attracted a membership of nearly a million and gave its name to the Granger movement of the 1870's. During that period of agrarian discontent the Grange fought against low commodity prices, high freight charges, and political corruption. The organization was considered too conservative in its political action by many farmers, and the membership greatly decreased during the rise of the more radical Farmers' Alliance of the late 1880's. But after the Farmers' Alliance became part of the Populist movement, the Grange came back into influence. In 1974 it was the second largest farmers' organization in America, with about 600,000 members.

The National Farmers Union, founded by Newt Gresham at Point, Texas, in 1902, was considered the natural successor to the 19th-century Farmers' Alliance. Flourishing in the South during its first decade, the Farmers Union gradually moved into the wheat-growing states of the West, where it was especially strong during the 1950's. Its national membership in 1974 included about 250,000 farm families. Over the years the organization's policies have been directed toward preservation of the family farm, an increase in bargaining power with the federal government for farm operations, close relationships between farmer and labor groups, and special aids for low-income farmers.

In the years immediately preceding World War I several county farm committees or bureaus were organized in various states to support the county agent and extension services of the Department of Agriculture. The first organization to work with a county agent was formed in Broome County, N.Y., in 1911, as a bureau of the Binghamton Chamber of Commerce. With the passage of the Smith-Lever Act in 1914, increased federal funds became available to finance the work, and the rapid increase of local units led to the formation of state federations, first in New York in 1917. When agricultural prices began falling after the war, several state representatives decided to create a farmers' organization that would be national in scope, and the American Farm Bureau Federation was formally organized in Chicago, Mar. 1, 1920.

In 1921 the Farm Bureau organized the first farm bloc in Congress, and two years later was urging action to solve the mounting problem of farm surpluses. During the 1920's the bureau supported the McNary-Haugen bills to control overproduction and with the coming of the Great Depression proposed a price-parity, production-control bill similar in its essential features to the Agricultural Adjustment Act of 1933.

During World War II the Farm Bureau was active in protecting farmers' interests under price controls and in directing programs necessary in the war effort. After 1947 the bureau's attitude toward government controls shifted, and it began to advocate a reduction in the use of public funds to increase farm productive capacity and a return to policies that would allow prices to respond to supply and demand. In the 1970's the Farm Bureau was the largest American farmers' organization, having a membership of more than 2 million families.

The National Farmers Organization began in Iowa in September 1955 to protest low farm prices, and within a few months it became an organization of 71,000 members. The goal of the NFO was a collective bargaining system whereby farmers would set prices for their produce, and to accomplish this end, it initiated a system of withholding products from market until prices were met. During the 1960's NFO membership figures were not released, and estimates vary from 115,000 to 270,000. The United Farm Workers Union developed out of the California farm labor movements of the 1960's, and in 1974 claimed a membership of 60,000.

Agricultural Policies and Legislation. When the first census was taken in 1790, about 95 percent of the population was rural, and for a century afterward most aspects of national policy were influenced by agricultural interests. As the percentage of farmers in the population declined, agricultural legislation that established policies became a series of compromises resulting from the constant shifting of attitudes and purposes of conflicting groups.

Early land policies were hardly more than modifications of customary patterns of ownership and tenure established by the feudal systems of Western Europe, tending to perpetuate strongly entrenched privileged classes. Gradually, however, American land policy came to favor the settlers of the land, founders of family farms. After the cession of the western lands to the Union, the federal government transferred these holdings as soon as possible to farmer-settlers, enacting liberal credit provisions and yielding to pressures from squatter-settlers through preemption acts.

During the twenty years before the Civil War, Congress considered successive bills designed to grant free lands to settlers. Land grant policy was closely linked with the slavery question, and no effective act was passed until after the war had begun. The Homestead Act of 1862 provided a free title grant for 160 acres of land to a settler who maintained residence for five years. After 1900 this act was modified by a series of laws that granted larger tracts in arid regions of the western states. With the virtual disappearance of the nation's once vast public domain, 20th-century land policies have involved efforts to conserve and reconstruct soils and to exercise more public control over forest lands, waters, and mineral resources.

American farmers have always been concerned with federal tariff policies, quantitative trade restrictions, transportation subsidies, and credit and monetary systems—any national policy that might affect either the prices of agricultural commodities or the costs of manufactured articles used in agricultural production. Not until after the Civil War, however, did farmers form organizations to represent them in the creation of new national policies. The Granger movement developed out of farmer opposition to the railroad monopoly and high interest rates. The Greenback movement, the Farmers' Alliance, and the People's party attempted to formulate new, or to change old, national policies affecting agriculture. After 1900 the National Farmers Union, the National Nonpartisan League, and the American Farm Bureau Federation arose as spokesmen for the farmers in policy matters. In 1955 the National Farmers Organization was formed to protest current policies, and during the 1960's the United Farm Workers Union began formulating policies for farm laborers.

During World War I the government encouraged expansion of farm output, but when foreign and military demands declined, a collapse of export markets followed and American agriculture fell into a severe economic depression that continued long after urban and industrial segments of the population were enjoying restored prosperity. To adjust the sharp differences, several proposals for farm relief legislation—notably the McNary-Haugen bills—were actively discussed and promoted during the 1920's. "Orderly marketing" of farm products was encouraged by passage of the Co-operative Marketing Act of 1922; other laws provided special credit facilities for farmers. The Agricultural Marketing Act of 1929 created a Federal Farm Board, designed to stabilize prices of commodities. Although the Farm Board failed in its objectives, its experiences led to more successful legislation during the depression of the 1930's, when farm prices fell to their lowest levels.

In an attempt to raise prices by restricting supplies, the Agricultural Adjustment Act of 1933 established quotas limiting production of basic agricultural commodities. Declared unconstitutional by the U.S. Supreme Court in 1936, the original act was superseded by the act of 1938. From the 1940's into the 1960's this act was amended several times, the basic aims being formation of a price-support program to bring farm income into balance with the national income. The original "parity" formula underlying the program was based on market statistics for the years 1910–14, a period during which farm and nonfarm prices were considered to be in reasonable balance. In 1950 the formula was changed to permit use of average prices paid and received during the ten-year period immediately preceding any current year.

The 1956 act established the Soil Bank program, which was designed to reduce surpluses by removing land from production. In 1959 Congress terminated the acreage reserve section of the Soil Bank, leaving the conservation reserve program in effect until 1965, when the entire act was repealed by passage of the Food and Agriculture Act of 1965. This latter legislation established a long-term land-retirement policy, the Cropland Adjustment program; the 1965 act also established a new four-year price-adjustment program. The Agriculture Act of 1970 included a payment limitation of $55,000 for price supports to any one person or company. Other agricultural legislation of the 1960's and early 1970's indicated a shift away from price supports and an enlarged role for American agriculture in producing food under government subsidies for export to underdeveloped countries.

The Commodity Credit Corporation, formed in 1933 to replace the Federal Farm Board, was the principal agency through which price-support activities of the government were carried out. When it was not possible to support prices through loans or purchase agreements, the CCC bought farm commodities outright. Commodities thus acquired were usually disposed of in ways that would not disrupt price levels: for instance, storable commodities were held for future resale into commercial channels whenever demand increased; perishable commodities were disposed of outside normal commercial channels—by donation to relief agencies, by transfer to the national school-lunch program, or through special export sales or exchanges. To increase exports of surplus products, Congress in 1954 passed the Agricultural Trade Development Act (Public Law 480), authorizing the secretary of agriculture to accept up to $700 million in foreign currencies as repayment for commodities shipped abroad to friendly nations.

During the years following World War II the national agricultural policy turned toward improvement of standards of living, not only for the rural population but also for American society as a whole. Some significant legislation passed during the period included the National School Lunch Act of 1946, extension of Social Security coverage to farm operators in 1954, the Great Plains Conservation program of 1956, the Humane Slaughter Act of 1958, provision for food distribution to the needy in 1961, and the Food Stamp Act of 1964. In 1966 the Child Nutrition Act was passed; the federal minimum wage was extended to farm workers; and the President's Committee on Rural Poverty was established. In 1967 and 1968 legislation was passed providing food packages for expectant mothers and special food services for children. In the 1970's the Department of Agriculture through its extension service began to expand nutrition and 4-H programs into urban areas of the nation. In 1972, after more than 400 million bushels of wheat were sold to the Soviet Union by six grain corporations, the Department of Agriculture became embroiled in controversy over the pricing arrangements and management of the sale. To keep export prices low, subsidies were paid by the department, and a $750 million credit was established to facilitate the Soviet Union's financing of the purchase. The Soviet wheat deal, plus large shipments of other grain products to China and other countries in 1972–73, depleted surplus stocks of American grains for the first time in a generation. The resulting low supplies led to sharply higher domestic prices for meat, bread, milk, and other farm products. A new farm program, enacted in 1973, ended the system of acreage restrictions and government purchases to support prices. Under the new program, the Department of Agriculture established "target prices" for certain commodities; and if a farmer's average sale prices fell below the targets, the government paid the difference to the farmer. The objective of the legislation was increased production to meet worldwide demands for American food crops.

Federal Farm Credit Agencies. Throughout American history one of the major problems of American agriculture has been that of financing the farmer. As a political issue during the nation's first century, agricultural credit was overshadowed only by slavery and the tariff. After the Civil War high interest rates and the unavailability of long-term mortgage loans brought farmer support to a succession of cheap money schemes, notably those of the National Greenback party and the Free Silver movement. When these movements faded with the political defeat of William Jennings Bryan, agricultural leaders turned to the federal government for a solution of their continuing credit difficulties.

In 1913 the Federal Reserve Act increased facilities of rural banks to make seasonal credit available to farmers, and in that same year, as a preliminary to establishing adequate farm mortgage credit facilities, Congress appointed a special commission to study European experiences in the field. Three years later the Federal Farm Loan Act established a national system of twelve federal land banks. The operational method of the land banks was to pool the mortgages of individual farmers and issue bonds with the mortgages as security; to keep mortgage interest low, the bonds were exempted from taxation.

As a result of the price depression that affected farmers immediately after World War I, a demand arose for short-term credit. This led to passage in 1923 of an amendment to the Federal Farm Loan Act, establishing twelve federal intermediate credit banks. Largely because of a continued decline in prices of farm commodities, these credit agencies failed to solve the problem, and in an effort to provide farmers with both a greater share of the market price of their products and adequate credit facilities for production, Congress in June 1929 established the Federal Farm Board. One of the board's major functions was to advance loans to agricultural cooperatives from a revolving fund of $500 million.

With the Great Depression, however, both the bank credit and Farm Board programs ran into serious difficulties. Sharp declines in farm income and real estate values brought on such an accelerated rate of foreclosures in farm property that emergency measures became necessary. In 1932 the Reconstruction Finance Corporation was authorized to establish twelve agricultural credit corporations to make loans directly to farmers and stockmen in their respective areas. At the same time the federal land bank system relaxed loan requirements.

In June 1933 the Farm Credit Administration was created to consolidate all farm credit functions of the federal government. The agency operated independently until 1939, when it became a part of the Department of Agriculture. The Farm Credit Act of 1953 made the FCA again an independent agency, with a thirteen-member policy board. Additional legislation enacted in 1955, 1966, and 1968 transferred complete ownership of the FCA to farmers and their cooperatives. Farmers elected local boards of directors of the federal land bank associations, production credit associations, and cooperatives which owned and used the banks for cooperatives. The local boards from the twelve farm credit districts made nominations for the president to consider in appointing members of the national board. The thirteenth member was appointed by the governor of the FCA with the advice and consent of the federal board.

Although the FCA was intended to combine all credit operations, only four months after its establishment the Commodity Credit Corporation was created as an independent agency to make loans on commodities in connection with crop control and marketing problems. The CCC operated in close affiliation with the Reconstruction Finance Corporation until a general reorganization of governmental functions in 1939 transferred it to the Department of Agriculture. The CCC was managed by a board of six directors appointed by the president; members included the secretary of agriculture and five other administrative officials of the department. An additional five-member advisory board, consisting of persons with broad business and agricultural experience, no more than three of whom could belong to the same political party, was also appointed by the president. Capitalized at $100 million, the CCC was authorized to borrow up to $14.5 billion to carry out its programs, which supported prices of agricultural commodities by payments to farmers, procured agricultural commodities for sale to other agencies and foreign governments, and attempted to increase consumption of agricultural commodities through development of new markets at home and abroad.

In 1935 the Resettlement Administration was created to provide funds for relief and rehabilitation of low-income farm families; the Rural Electrification Administration was also established in 1935 to make loans for financing construction and operation of plants and lines to provide electric power for rural areas. A 1949 amendment authorized the REA to make loans for providing and improving rural telephone service. In 1937 the Resettlement Administration was succeeded by the Farm Security Administration, which became the Farmers Home Administration in 1946, with authority to provide credit to farmers who could not obtain financing elsewhere at reasonable rates and terms. Legislation in 1961 and 1964 broadened the credit authority of the FHA. In addition to loans for farm operation and ownership, improvement of farm housing, and soil and water conservation, the FHA provided funds for income-producing recreational enterprises and for rural community water and waste disposal systems for rural towns of not more than 5,500 in population.

Department of Agriculture. In his last message to Congress in 1796, George Washington recommended the establishment of a national board of agriculture. "In proportion as nations advance in population," observed Washington, "the cultivation of the soil becomes more and more an object of public patronage." Although a bill was brought up for consideration in that session, it never reached a vote, and forty years passed before agriculture was represented by a federal agency. From 1835 to 1862, national agricultural interests were promoted through the Patent Office. Henry Leavitt Ellsworth, commissioner from 1835 to 1845, helped to lay the foundations for a department of agriculture by collecting and distributing seeds and by gathering and publishing statistical and other information on agricultural subjects. An agricultural division was established within his agency.

Largely through the efforts of state and national agricultural societies a bill establishing the Department of Agriculture was passed by Congress and signed into law by President Abraham Lincoln on May 15, 1862. Isaac Newton, who had served as superintendent of the Patent Office agricultural division, became the first commissioner of the new department.

The department was organized into divisions of chemistry, entomology, statistics, botany, forestry, pomology, and vegetable physiology and pathology. In 1884 the Bureau of Animal Industry was created, and in 1890 the Weather Bureau was transferred from the War Department. After the Hatch Act of 1887 established agricultural experiment stations, an Office of Experiment Stations was formed in the department. The head of the Department of Agriculture achieved cabinet status in 1889 after a long campaign by the Grange.

The department entered many new fields of activity in the 20th century. Its rural development and conservation activities include operation of the Forest Service, Soil Conservation Service, Rural Electrification Administration, and Farmers Home Administration. Marketing and consumer services include the food stamp and other nutritional programs, the standardization of farm products, and the regulation of packers and stockyards. The department conducts scientific research in all areas of agriculture and transmits its findings through the various extension services in the states. It gathers and publishes agricultural statistics, administers price-support programs, and promotes exports through its Foreign Agricultural Service. The library of the department, organized in 1862, has become the national agricultural library with a collection of 1.3 million volumes.

Farm Periodicals. The *Agricultural Museum,* published at Georgetown, D.C. (1810–12), was the first farm periodical in the United States. Its two-year span was about the average survival time for such publications in the 19th century. Since there was little specialized agriculture, early agricultural periodicals were general in coverage, with departments or columns on horticulture, crops, poultry, and dairying. The same pattern was followed generally in agricultural publishing until the appearance of specialized periodicals, which were founded to serve the widely diversified agricultural operations of the 20th century.

A few 19th-century farm periodicals were national in scope and thrived for many years, among them *American Farmer, American Agriculturist, Country Gentleman, Colman's Rural World,* and *Farm Journal*. Most periodicals, however, were regional in their appeal—for example, *New England Farmer, Southern Cultivator, Prairie Farmer, Rural New Yorker*—and the last of the national monthlies, *Farm Journal,* was divided into various regional editions in 1952.

In the commissioner of agriculture's report for 1867, an attempt was made to list all periodicals "devoted to the advancement of agriculture, horticulture, and kindred interests within the United States." There were only fifty-six. A century later the National Agricultural Library was receiving annually several thousand such periodicals. This increase in numbers reflects the specialization resulting from scientific and mechanized agriculture. In addition to popular periodicals large numbers of trade magazines and research journals began publication in the 20th century, all dealing with such specific divisions of agriculture as livestock by breeds, crops by varieties, fruits, vegetables, dairying, poultry, soils, and farm machinery.

Scientific Aid to Agriculture. During the colonial period the importance of science in agriculture was recognized by the more successful farmers, and extensive agricultural experiments were conducted by Thomas Jefferson and George Washington on their Virginia estates. When the Department of Agriculture was established in 1862, the first commissioner was directed "to acquire and preserve . . . all information concerning agriculture which he [could] obtain by means of books and correspondence, and by practical and scientific experiments."

Because of the widespread influence of the German chemist Justus von Liebig's monumental work on agricultural chemistry, published in 1840, the first experiments backed by federal funds were chemical analyses of soils and plants. Grasshopper plagues, blights, and other epidemics affecting crops and livestock led to entomological research and studies of animal and plant diseases later in the 19th century. A tremendous impetus to agricultural research came in 1887 with the passage of the Hatch Act, which provided for the establishment of experiment stations in connection with land grant colleges. Funds were appropriated to each state "to promote scientific investigations" in various branches of agricultural endeavor and to publish results of the experiments.

Some of the dramatic results of federally financed research were Marion Dorset's discovery that hog cholera was viral in origin; Theobald Smith's research showing that ticks transmitted cattle fever, which led to the control of malaria, yellow fever, and other insect-borne diseases; the bacteriological studies of Henry Ayers, L. A. Rogers, and C. E. Gray, which improved the purity and palatability of dairy products; S. M. Babcock's butterfat tests, which insured the quality of dairy products; T. J. Burrill, Merton B. Waite, and Erwin F. Smith, who demonstrated that bacteria could cause diseases in plants and that some of these diseases were spread by insects; William A. Orton's and E. C. Stakman's breeding of plants resistant to disease and C. M. Woodworth's work on plants resistant to disease-spreading insects; C. V. Riley's demonstration that harmless insects could be used to destroy harmful insects; W. O. Atwater's invention of the first calorimeter to study metabolism in relation to food consumed and energy expended; Curtis F. Marbut's development of soil classification; and the early work on hybrid corn by William James Beal, George Harrison Shull, and Edward Murray East.

The application of Mendel's laws of genetics transformed American agriculture. Through crossbreeding and artificial insemination new varieties and breeds were created, thus increasing production and disease resistance and improving the quality of the product. In 1926 the first hybrid seed corn company was organized, and by the 1960's more than 96 percent of corn acreage was planted with hybrids and production was almost tripled.

The increased complexity of scientific agriculture led the Department of Agriculture to establish several regional laboratories and field stations during the 1930's, each to deal with some specific area of research. The Agricultural Research Center at Beltsville, Md., became the national experimental station for basic research, the new discoveries generally being applied elsewhere.

Between the 1940's and the 1970's the use of chemical fertilizers quadrupled and the use of pesticides, defoliants, and chemical additives became widespread. This extensive application of chemicals brought about a great increase in agricultural production but their effects upon the environment created such concern that controls were put upon unrestricted use of certain chemicals.

Other scientific aids that have been adopted by agriculture include ultrasonics for research on plants, livestock, and insects; use of hormones both to increase the number of multiple births and the size of livestock; brain stimulation devices to increase milk production; electronic data-processing; infrared photography for identification of crops, forests, and soils; and earth satellites to monitor disease, insect infestations, and drought.

Agricultural Experiment Stations. The Hatch Act of 1887 gave federal support to agricultural experiment stations throughout the country. The act allotted $15,000 per year to each land grant college for the purpose of conducting experiments in agriculture and publishing results of the research. Previous to passage of the act, Wesleyan University in Middletown, Conn., had established the first state agricultural station in 1875, and during the early 1880's several states organized similar stations. The Office of Experiment Stations, which was established within the Department of Agriculture in 1888, acted as a center for exchange of information among the various stations. In a reorganization of the department in 1961, functions of the Office of Experiment Stations were assigned to the Cooperative State Experiment Station Service. Although the original $15,000 allotment per station had increased to average annual allotments of more than one million dollars to each station by the 1970's, the major source of support remained appropriations of state legislatures, state funds averaging about three times federal appropriations.

Agricultural Education. State agricultural societies and farm papers both promoted agricultural education and were influential in establishing a nationwide system of education to improve farming practices. As early as 1754, King's College in New York (now Columbia University) was offering a course in husbandry, and during the first half of the 19th century Rensselaer Polytechnic Institute and Amherst College provided instruction in scientific courses relating to agriculture.

A major force in agricultural education was the passage of the Agricultural Land Grant College Act, known as the Morrill Act, of 1862. It gave public lands to each state, to be used either as a source of funds or as a college site, to aid the states in establishing colleges for the teaching of "such branches of learning as are related to agriculture and the mechanic arts." Although hampered at first by a lack of qualified instructors, adequate texts, and a body of research to draw upon, by 1900 most of the colleges were firmly established and supported by federal subsidies.

Between 1880 and 1900 farmers' institutes in many states attempted to bring new discoveries directly to farmers by cooperating with agricultural colleges; and out of this specialized model for adult education came the agricultural extension movement, which received federal support in 1914 with passage of the Smith-Lever Act. In 1928 additional federal funds to be used mainly in employment of county agents were provided under the Capper-Ketcham Act.

The teaching of agriculture at the secondary school level was given federal support under the Smith-Hughes Act of 1917, which provided for systematic instruction for all persons over fourteen years of age who had entered upon or who were preparing for work on the farm or in the farm home. The vocational education acts of 1946 and 1963 considerably broadened the original Smith-Hughes Act, the 1963 act providing funds for vocational education in any occupation involving knowledge and skills in agricultural subjects, whether or not the occupation involved work on a farm. This last change resulted from the decline in the farm population and the corresponding increase in agriculture-related industries requiring large numbers of trained workers.

[Gladys L. Baker et al., *Century of Service, the First 100 Years of the United States Department of Agriculture;* Murray R. Benedict, *Farm Policies of the United States, 1790–1950;* Percy W. Bidwell and John I. Falconer, *History of Agriculture in the Northern United States, 1620–1860;* George Brandsberg, *The Two Sides in NFO's Battle;* D. A. Brown, "Agricultural Periodicals," *Library Trends,* vol. 10 (1962); Solon Buck, *The Agrarian Crusade;* Gilbert C. Fite, *The Farmers' Frontier, 1865–1900;* Paul W. Gates, *The Farmer's Age: Agriculture 1815–1860;* E. A. Goldenweiser and Leon E. Truesdell, *Farm Tenancy in the United States;* Lewis C. Gray, *History of Agriculture in the Southern United States to 1860;* O. M. Kile, *The Farm Bureau Movement;* David Lindstrom, *American Farmers' and Rural Organizations;* Aaron G. Nelson and William G. Murray, *Agricultural Finance;* Wayne D. Rasmussen, *Liberal Education and Agriculture;* Wayne D. Rasmussen, ed., *Readings in the History of American Agriculture;* Robert D. Reinsel and Bruce Johnson, *Farm Tenure and Cash Rents in the United States* (Agricultural Economic Report 190); S. C. Stuntz, *List of Agricultural Periodicals of the United States and Canada . . . July 1810 to July 1910;* A. C. True, *A History of Agricultural Education in the United States;* A. C. True and V. A. Clark, *The Agricultural Experiment Stations in the United States;* Luther Tweeten, *Foundations of Farm Policy;* U.S. Department of Agriculture, *Farmers in a Changing World, the Yearbook of Agriculture, 1940,* and *Science in Farming, the Yearbook of Agriculture, 1947;* U.S. Farm Credit Administration, *Annual Reports.*]

DEE BROWN

AGRICULTURE, AMERICAN INDIAN. Native America, long before European discovery, had developed its own distinctive agricultural complex, one wholly independent of European and Asian agriculture in both form and product. A basic triad of food plants was developed. The primary staple was Indian corn, or maize (*Zea mays*), generally augmented by various beans, the common kidney bean (*Phaseolus vulgaris*) appearing most frequently, and by many different species of cucurbits, such as pumpkins and squashes. Although there were many other plants domesticated for food in both North America and South America, their appearance was local, whereas the basic triad was universal. Associated with the maize complex was tobacco, the primary narcotic, which tended to spread considerably beyond the boundaries of agricultural specialization.

The origins of maize are open to question, but on the basis of intensity of development and botanical evaluation and evidences of antiquity, the heartland of cultivation lay in Middle America, southern Mexico, Guatemala, and possibly northern South America. Radiocarbon dating has established the presence of beans, gourds, and squashes in prehistoric Mexican caves as early as 5500 B.C.; a cave in Puebla, Mexico, offers specimens of maize as early as 5000 B.C. The Bat Cave discoveries in New Mexico show an unhusked pod and popcorn as early as 4000 B.C. South American specimens date from somewhat later but still point to considerable antiquity. It can be suggested that seed gathering in desert or temperate and tropical highland conditions led to domestication by the Paleo-Indians.

In later times, Middle America, with centers in Yucatán and Guatemala, in the Valley of Mexico, and in Colombia and Peru, developed elaborate urbanized and religiopolitical structures. The Maya, Aztec, and Inca and their precursors depended on the essentially predictable food supply provided by well-regulated agricultural patterns. Given a Middle-American center for the origins of New World farming, it follows that the greatest intensity of development lay there; other areas, both north and south, were marginally agricultural, with farming becoming less and less significant at increasing distances from the focal center and at length giving way to hunting and gathering modes of life. Middle America also showed the greatest diversity of food plants: pineapples, tomatoes, bananas, guavas, peanuts, chile peppers, and cacao were included in the inventory of pre-Columbian products. Potatoes of many varieties originated in the South American highlands. These, along with the botanically different sweet potato, cotton (independently evolved in the Old World), manioc, and corn itself attest a world debt to the American Indian, considering the economic importance of these items in post-Columbian times.

Despite the early appearance of maize in the American Southwest, North America generally lagged behind Middle America in the development of agriculture. The maize complex moved slowly northward from Mexico to the Gulf states and so up the Mississippi, the Ohio, and the Missouri river systems. Still intensive in the Southwest and the lower Mississippi region, farming patterns were considerably less well focused by the time they had reached the Algonkin-speaking peoples of New England and the St. Lawrence River valley. There, as among the tribes of the eastern Plains, agriculture and hunting stood side by side. Maize, beans, squash, and tobacco constituted the entire farming array in those areas, but tobbacco farming spread quickly, many nonfarming groups planting and cultivating it as their sole agricultural endeavor. Native Indian modes of planting in corn hills—small mounds with bean and squash vines trained against the growing corn—were adopted from local tribes by the settlers of Massachusetts; they also adopted the corn crib from the Indian.

The technology of native American farming is also unique to the New World. Lacking domesticated animals, the wheel, and the plow, native American farming depended entirely on human labor. Fields were cleared by hand or by slashing the brush cover to kill it and then burning it off, a method still practiced in the tropics. Depending on water resources, irrigation might be practiced, although this was limited to the areas of intensive cultivation in the American Southwest. The principal tool was the digging stick, or dibble, a pointed stick allowing a five- to six-inch perforation of the soil; the general practice was to drop in a few seed kernels of corn, to thin the growing corn, and to follow it with bean and squash planting. Generally associated with native American farming was pottery, always made in the New World by women by a paddle-and-anvil method—that is, smoothing roped or coiled clay to shape the vessel. In some instances pottery spread to hunting peoples. In many shapes, designs, and colors, pottery was important in its use as containers and as cooking and storage vessels among settled farming peoples.

Patterns of land tenure among the various tribes of American Indians admit no general rule. In Mexico and Peru some attempt was apparently made to regulate and allocate land. Elsewhere the tendency was toward usufruct holdings, or land might be associated with an extended social unit, clan, or household. The concept of land ownership in the European sense was alien.

[Robert F. Spencer, Jesse D. Jennings, and others, *The Native Americans.*]

ROBERT F. SPENCER

AGUAYO EXPEDITION (1720–22). Marquis San Miguel de Aguayo, governor of Coahuila and Texas, left Monclova in 1720 with an expedition of 500 soldiers to reestablish the Spanish missions and presidios in East Texas which had been abandoned in 1719 because of trouble with the French at Natchitoches. Joined by eighty refugees at San Antonio, Aguayo continued northeast, reestablished six missions, and fortified Adaes (now Robeline, La.) near the French. On his return in 1722, he erected a mission near the site of Fort Saint Louis, in Texas. Thus Aguayo in effect put an end to French claims in Texas.

[Eleanor Buckley, "The Aguayo Expedition in Texas and Louisiana," *Texas Historical Quarterly,* vol. 15.]

L. W. NEWTON

AGUE, or shakes and ague, a fever of malarial origin prevalent on the frontier from the Appalachian to the Rocky Mountains. It was thought to be caused by the dew or by gases from newly plowed virgin soil. The patient was afflicted with chills lasting an hour or two, succeeded by a fever, severe headache, and delirium lasting six to eight hours. Then came a devitalizing sweat and temporary recovery only to be followed by the same process in from one to three days. Hardly a person in low territory escaped it. Quinine was the best of innumerable remedies.

[Everett Dick, *The Sod-House Frontier*.]

EVERETT DICK

AIR CAVALRY. On June 16, 1965, the U.S. Army received Department of Defense authorization to organize the 1st Cavalry Division (Airmobile). The authorized strength of this division was 15,787 men equipped with 434 aircraft, mainly helicopters, and 1,600 land vehicles; as compared with 15,900 men, 101 aircraft, and 3,200 land vehicles in the standard infantry division. The obvious purpose was to recapture with air transport the relatively high mobility formerly enjoyed by horse cavalry. Although the intensifying war in Vietnam provided the immediate impetus, the army had been contemplating such a division for several years. Army planners believed the Korean War could have been fought more effectively if American technology had been better exploited to provide superior mobility; moreover, lack of mobility had been fatal to the French at Dien Bien Phu in 1954. In Vietnam, terrain, vegetation, and climate badly impeded American ground mobility, yet the army needed to move swiftly to be able to offset the enemy's initiative and familiarity with the country.

The airmobile concept proved to be one of the more successful American innovations of the Vietnam War. In late 1965 the 1st Cavalry Division (Airmobile) entered the Ia Drang Valley campaign aimed at destroying the enemy's buildup in the Central Highlands, which threatened to cut South Vietnam in two; in the battle of Plei Me of that campaign, units of the division were uplifted to new positions at least forty times, as they mauled three enemy regiments and pushed them into Cambodia. Increasingly thereafter, although the 1st Cavalry and later the 101st Airborne Division (Airmobile) retained special air mobility, the army sought enough helicopters to give all infantry units air mobility whenever operations made it desirable.

The air mobility concept involved airborne maneuvers during an engagement, as well as long-distance moves, airborne logistical and medical support, flexible and informed command through aerial command posts, and superior firepower through both helicopter-lifted artillery and aerial gunships. In a theater such as Vietnam, where American control of the air afforded protection from enemy fighter aircraft, helicopter and propeller-driven gunships could offer ground troops sustained gunnery support of a kind impossible for jet-powered airplanes. Transports given side-firing weapons could circle a ground target while maintaining extended fire at a constant altitude and range. By the spring of 1966 the C-47, the military version of the old Douglas DC-3 transport, was armed with three 7.62mm miniguns, electrically powered versions of the Gatling gun, each capable of firing 6,000 rounds per minute. The appearance of its tracers (one round in five) gave this gunship the name "Puff the Magic Dragon." Versions of the C-119 and C-130, and other types of gunships, were progressively more heavily armed. The AC-130, for example, had eight miniguns and four 20mm Vulcan cannons.

The usual gunship, however, was a helicopter, if only because it could start from the same field used by air cavalry. As the American ground buildup in Vietnam began, the standard helicopter gunship was a heavily armed version of the UH-1B Huey, carrying fourteen rockets and door-mounted M-60 7.62mm machine guns. Later the AH-1G Cobra helicopter gunship appeared, carrying seventy-six air-to-ground rockets, a 7.62mm minigun, and a 40mm grenade launcher capable of firing 400 rounds a minute. With this weaponry and still more powerful weapons planned for it, the Cobra gunship in the early 1970's figured heavily in Army tests of the 1st Cavalry Division, further reorganized as a TRICAP (triple capability) unit, adding tank battalions and intended with its combination of tanks and attack helicopters to challenge Soviet armored superiority in Europe. Whatever the future of the TRICAP division, there was considerable merit in the Army's contention that the helicopter had already opened a new era in the history of land warfare.

RUSSELL F. WEIGLEY

AIR COMMERCE ACT OF 1926. *See* **Civil Aeronautics Act.**

AIR CONDITIONING. *See* **Heating and Air Conditioning.**

AIRCRAFT, BOMBER. America's first bomber, the Martin MB-1, was developed late for World War I. In the 1920's the United States had only a few British DH-4's and Martin NBS-1's, which the celebrated Col. William (Billy) Mitchell used to prove his theories. These were replaced by the twin-engine, 107-mph Keystone biplane, which was standard until 1932, and a few superior but expensive Curtiss B-2 Condors. The Boeing Y1B-9 twin-engine all-metal 188-mph monoplane replaced the Keystone but was eclipsed by the Martin B-10, which, at 210 mph, was faster than any existing American pursuit plane. Its replacements were the Douglas twin-engine 218-mph B-18 and the Boeing four-engine B-17.

World War II was fought with bombers planned during the later 1930's and early 1940's. These were designed either for strategic bombardment, or for tactical and supplemental strategic tasks. The main strategic bombers were the Boeing B-17 Flying Fortress and Consolidated twin-tailed B-24 Liberator. These were both used in Europe, but the B-24's greater range made it more acceptable in the Pacific area. The B-17F and B-17G, armed with twelve .50-caliber guns, carried 4,000 pounds of bombs over 2,000 miles at 300 mph; the B-24H and B-24J, similarly armed, carried a 2,500-pound payload about 1,925 miles at 300 mph. The Boeing B-29 Superfortress was the war's largest bomber: armed with twelve .50-caliber guns, both the B-29A and B-29B carried 20,000 pounds of bombs and had a range of 5,000 miles. Its development was justified in that it helped reduce Japan in nine months; although introduced before this, the bomber's full effectiveness was not realized until it could be used in mass from Pacific island bases.

Tactical and supplemental strategic tasks were carried out by medium and attack bombers. The medium bombers were the North American B-25 Mitchell, which made the first raid on Tokyo, and the Martin B-26 Marauder. Both were heavily armed, twin-engine, midwing planes capable of 285 mph and a range of 1,100 miles. The B-25 carried 3,100 and the B-26 4,100 pounds of bombs. Attack bombers operated at low altitudes and were noted for speed and maneuverability. The Douglas A-20 Havoc was a 325-mph twin-engine monoplane armed with up to nine .50-caliber guns and bearing up to 4,000 pounds of bombs. The Douglas A-26 Invader, appearing in 1944, though classed as an attack bomber, was the war's most advanced medium—a 360-mph twin-engine midwing carrying eighteen .50-caliber guns, 6,000 pounds of bombs, and fourteen rockets, and having a range of over 1,000 miles.

The first intercontinental bomber, the Consolidated-Vultee B-36, appeared in 1946. It had six piston engines, later augmented by four jets, attained a maximum speed of 383 mph, cruised at 225 mph, and carried 10,000 pounds of bombs 7,500 miles. Fully jet-powered bombers came late because of the jet engine's high fuel consumption. The first jet bomber, in 1948, was the North American B-45 Tornado: the B-45C's four jets pushed it to a maximum speed of 579 mph with a cruising speed of 457 mph and carried 10,000 pounds of bombs 1,910 miles. The second fully jet-powered bomber was the Boeing B-47 Stratojet, which, with six jets, cruised at 500 mph (maximum speed, over 630 mph) with 10,000 pounds of bombs, had a range of 3,870 miles, and was armed with twin radar-aimed .50-caliber tailguns. The B-47 replaced the B-29 and B-50 (an improved B-29) as a medium bomber until retired in the 1960's. The Korean War had demonstrated the need for an attack jet to replace the B-26: the Martin B-57, a copy of the RAF Canberra, and the Douglas B-66 Destroyer, a version of the U.S. Navy Skywarrior, were chosen.

In 1954 the Boeing B-52 Stratofortress began replacing the B-36 as the mainstay of the Strategic Air Command. Powered by eight jets, the B-52G has a maximum speed of 650 mph carrying 65,000 pounds of bombs. General Dynamics' B-58 Hustler also served the Strategic Air Command until it was retired in 1970. Powered by four jets, its maximum speed was 1,324 mph with a 1,200-mile combat radius. It carried "mission pods" under the fuselage, or four nuclear weapons underwing, as it had no internal bomb bay.

The U.S. Air Force mid-1970 bomber force comprised the B-52G, B-52H, B-56G, and a few General Dynamics FB-111A's. Derived from the F-111 fighter-bomber, the FB-111A carries 37,000 pounds externally and internally at subsonic speeds; once the ordnance is dropped, the maximum speed is Mach 2.2. It is to be operational until the B-1 joins the force.

[Wesley F. Craven and James L. Cate, eds., *The Army Air Forces in World War II*, vol. VI, *Men and Planes;* Ray Wagner, *American Combat Planes*.]

WARNER STARK

AIRCRAFT, DEVELOPMENT OF. On Dec. 17, 1903, after four and a half years of study and experiment, Orville and Wilbur Wright flew a biplane that achieved sustained, powered, and controlled flight. The Wright invention underwent rapid improvement. The aileron, a movable surface at the rear of the wing (sometimes between wings), supplanted the Wrights's method of controlling flight by a combination of wing warping and rudder movement. The yoke-and-wheel control column and the control stick replaced the body harness devised by the Wrights to coordinate the position of wings and rudder. Wheels proved superior to the launching rail and landing skid.

Before the outbreak of World War I, tests showed the military potential of airplanes. Glenn Curtiss experimented with aerial bombing as early as 1910; Eugene Ely performed shipboard takeoffs and landings (1910–11); James McCurdy demonstrated the feasibility of two-way radio contact between air and ground (1911); and Riley Scott invented a bombsight (1914). Monoplanes appeared in Europe, as did the elongated fuselage and the enclosed cabin. The first tailless, swept-wing biplane was designed in 1908 by J. W. Dunne, an Englishman, and built in 1913 by the Burgess Company of Massachusetts.

Glenn Curtiss pioneered in seaplane construction in 1911. One of his most successful craft, *America* (1914), was designed with the aid of J. C. Porte, a British naval officer, and manufactured in Britain for wartime use. With guidance from Rear Admiral David Taylor of the U.S. Navy, Curtiss built the postwar, four-engine navy Curtiss seaplane. In May 1919, one of these, the NC-4, completed a flight from St. John's, Newfoundland, to Plymouth, England, by way of the Azores and Portugal.

America's principal technological accomplishment of World War I was the liquid-cooled, mass-produced Liberty engine, developed in 1917 under the direction of Jesse F. Vincent. A series of successful engines followed, including the liquid-cooled Curtiss, and the Pratt and Whitney and Wright air-cooled radials. Technological development of aircraft continued unabated after the war. The National Advisory Committee for Aeronautics (NACA), founded in 1915, opened a modern laboratory in 1920 and over the years made numerous discoveries, among them, a cowling to streamline radial engines and a variety of airfoils. The armed forces and industry called upon men like John Macready, Apollo and Zeus Soucek, and Wiley Post for experiments involving supercharged engines, oxygen equipment, and high-altitude clothing.

Wright engines powered two remarkable American planes, the Ryan Aeronautical *Spirit of St. Louis,* designed by Donald Hall for Charles Lindbergh's May 1927 nonstop flight from New York to Paris, and the Wright-Bellanca, designed by Giuseppe Bellanca. In June of that year, Clarence Chamberlain, accompanied by Charles Levine, flew a Wright-Bellanca nonstop from the United States to Germany. These two planes overshadowed such single-engine, Liberty-powered craft as the 1924 Douglas World Cruisers, in which army aviators circled the earth, and Grover Loening's amphibian, used on an aerial goodwill tour of Latin America in 1926–27.

The Lockheed Vega, a single-engine monoplane designed by Allan Loughhead and John Northrop, was first flown in 1927 and later used by Wiley Post on two around-the-world flights. Of wooden monocoque construction, the Vega marked the successful revival of a building technique introduced in France before World War I. Post's second around-the-world flight was a 1933 solo effort made possible by an automatic pilot built by Sperry Gyroscope Company. Lawrence Sperry, a pioneer instrument maker, had tested a crude prototype as early as 1912.

The most significant American contribution to the development of the dirigible was the introduction of helium, a nonflammable lifting gas found only in the United States. A metalclad airship flew successfully, but loss of the navy's *Shenandoah, Akron,* and *Macon*—followed by the destruction in 1937 of Germany's hydrogen-filled *Hindenburg*—brought to an end the era of the great dirigibles.

First in a series of distinguished American commercial aircraft was the Ford trimotor transport of 1926. This all-metal plane, inspired by William Stout, was more famous for its rugged dependability than for aerodynamic innovation. More important in terms of technology was the highly streamlined, twin-engine Boeing 247 of 1933, credited to a team led by William E. Boeing and Robert Minshall. Donald Douglas, using a Northrop-designed wing, produced the bigger and faster DC-2, which with its successor, the DC-3, came to dominate the airways of the world. Lockheed introduced its own series of transports, one of which, Model 14 of 1937, boasted flaps designed by Harlan Fowler to increase wing area by deploying on rails from the trailing edge. In addition to these land planes, a number of successful seaplane transports were built by Igor Sikorsky, Glenn L. Martin, and Boeing.

The advance in transports accompanied similar achievements in bombers, as the twin-engine biplane gave way to the fast, all-metal, low-wing monoplane.

The army also began acquiring the four-engine bombers that, after extensive modification, performed so effectively in World War II. Boeing's B-17 prototype flew in 1935 and the Consolidated B-24 in 1940. The latter featured a high aspect ratio wing, developed by David R. Davis, that reduced drag, thus increasing range.

In 1939, Hungarian-born Theodore von Kármán launched research into rocket-propelled airplanes, but progress in this area lagged; during World War II American aviation concentrated on piston-powered craft. Two transports, the Lockheed C-69 Constellation and the Douglas C-54 Skymaster, and two propeller-driven combat planes were noteworthy accomplishments. One of the latter was the North American P-51, built to fight at medium altitude, then fitted with a supercharged British-designed Merlin engine to become a successful escort for the high-altitude American bombers that were battering Germany by day. The other was the Boeing B-29, the largest bomber to see combat in the war—a plane that combined such innovations as remote-controlled gun turrets, four twin-row radial engines developing 2,200 horsepower each, and a pressurized cabin. Pressurization had worked well on the experimental Lockheed XC-35 and on the Boeing 307 transport, but never before on a heavy bomber.

The first practical helicopter appeared during World War II, but too late to see much service. Sikorsky introduced a craft that did not require twin main rotors turning in opposite directions. By installing a light, vertically mounted propeller at the rear of the fuselage to compensate for the torque of the blades rotating overhead, Sikorsky saved enough weight to enable the helicopter to carry a worthwhile payload.

German data on jet propulsion became available to American engineers as a result of the war. These data showed that a swept wing would delay the buildup of shock waves at extreme speeds. Building on the German foundation, Americans made further discoveries, such as Richard Whitcomb's area rule, which demonstrated that a wasp-waisted fuselage was the most efficient shape for supersonic flight.

In the postwar advance of aviation technology several experimental craft were trailblazers, such as the rocket-powered Bell X-1—suggested by John Stack of NACA and Robert Woods of Bell Aircraft—in which Charles Yeager exceeded the speed of sound in level flight. The Bell X-5 turbojet had a wing whose degree of sweep could be adjusted for various flight conditions. Most famous of the series was the North American X-15 rocket plane, in which Joseph Walker and Peter Knight exceeded 4,000 mph and both Walker and Robert White climbed above 300,000 feet.

C. L. Johnson of Lockheed Aircraft supervised the design of two famous reconnaissance planes: the U-2 and the SR-71. The U-2 resembled a jet-propelled sailplane and was able to take photographs from altitudes that interceptors could not reach. In contrast to the long, narrow U-2 wing was the small, modified delta wing of Johnson's SR-71. Powered by two engines in large nacelles on either side of the fuselage, this plane could attain a speed of 2,000 mph and an altitude of 80,000 feet.

American-designed transports continued to dominate the world's commercial airlines. First came the long-range, piston-powered types, culminating in the Lockheed Super Constellation and the Douglas DC-7C, a descendant of the wartime Skymaster. Britain in 1951 introduced the first practical jet transport, the Comet, but a series of tragic accidents caused its grounding and tarnished the reputation of a modified version. The expectation of military orders persuaded Boeing to build a prototype jet transport that was completed in 1954. When the U.S. Air Force purchased a tanker model, the KC-135, Boeing arranged to lease government-owned tools to build a commercial type, the successful 707. Along with the larger Douglas DC-8, the 707 fulfilled the promise shown by the Comet.

Progress in general aviation, including business and personal planes, culminated in the production of William P. Lear's Learjet (1964), a jet-powered executive transport designed exclusively for the civilian market. Lockheed had already produced a business jet, but its 1959 JetStar was inspired by military needs. Other milestones in general aviation included the twin-engine Beechcraft Model 18 (1937), the Stinson Reliant (1936), and Cessna Airmaster (1934) single-engine monoplanes, and the Beechcraft Model 17 Staggerwing single-engine biplane (1932). The most popular of American light planes was the two-place, single-engine Cub, designed in 1932 by C. Gilbert Taylor. Piper Aircraft later took over Taylor's design, which remained in production for two decades.

In the early 1970's, the American aircraft industry concentrated on big transports such as the Boeing 747, McDonnell Douglas DC-10, and Lockheed L-1011 TriStar. They owed their success to powerful new turbofan engines that displace huge volumes of air, and to the ingenious use of wing slots, flaps, and other devices for increasing lift, especially at low speed.

After winning a federally supervised design competition with Lockheed Aircraft, Boeing began preliminary work on a supersonic transport (SST). Despite the investment of an estimated $900 million, the government in March 1971 ended its subsidy, in effect halting the development of an American SST to compete with those being built by an Anglo-French consortium and by the Soviet Union. Many of the same ecological and economic problems that led to termination of the Boeing project may prevent widespread acceptance of the foreign SST's.

[Charles H. Gibbs-Smith, *The Aeroplane: An Historical Summary;* Alvin Josephy, ed., *The American Heritage Book of Flight;* H. F. King and John W. R. Taylor, *Milestones of the Air: Jane's 100 Significant Aircraft;* Robert Schlaifer and S. D. Heron, *Development of Aircraft Engines and Aviation Fuels.*]

BERNARD C. NALTY

AIRCRAFT, FIGHTER. The first American-built fighter, the Thomas-Morse MB-1 Scout, appeared in 1919. The U.S. Army relied on the Curtiss Hawk series until 1930, when the Martin B-10 bomber outran existing fighters. To gain higher speeds, the army switched to monoplanes: the Boeing P-26—an all-metal low-wing, carrying two .30-caliber guns and traveling at 233 mph—was the first. World tension and technical advances led to an "international" fighter type—an all-metal, low-wing monoplane with enclosed cockpit, retractable landing gear, and increasingly heavier armament. In 1935 the Republic P-35, a 259-mph, four-gun fighter, and the Curtiss P-36 (Hawk 75), both of the international type, replaced the P-26.

The Army Air Corps's interest in bombers and policies that held aircraft to close-support and coast defense roles retarded development of U.S. fighters, so that the standard fighters—the Curtiss P-40 Warhawk (introduced May 1940) and the Bell P-39 Airacobra (introduced February 1941)—were obsolescent in 1941 when the United States entered World War II. The first advanced U.S. fighter (ordered in August 1939) was the Lockheed P-38 Lightning, a twin-engine, 414-mph, twin-tailed plane, armed with one 20mm and four .50-caliber guns. The Republic P-47 Thunderbolt (introduced in April 1943) was the Army Air Force's only radial-engined fighter. Traveling at 460 mph, armed with six or eight .50-caliber guns plus rockets and bombs, it was widely used in the ground-support role. Perhaps the war's best fighter, the North American P-51 Mustang, was in British service before the AAF's need for bomber escorts brought widespread American use. The P-51 fighter, delivered in March 1943, was the AAF's fastest operational plane at 487 mph maximum. Armed with six .50-caliber guns and having a 1,500-mile range with drop tanks, it excelled in a variety of roles; many P-51's were still in use during the Korean War. The Northrop P-61 Black Widow, first American plane specifically designed as a night fighter, was a three-place, twin-engine plane that looked like a giant P-38; it was delivered in October 1943. Traveling at 360 mph, it carried four .50-caliber and four 20mm guns. Ground-support duties required supplementing the medium and attack bombers with single-engine types. The army modified 500 P-51's into A-36 fighter-bombers, which performed so well that unmodified P-51's and P-47's were also pressed into that role.

Unlike Britain and Germany, the United States used no jet aircraft operationally during World War II, although the development of jets had begun. The first U.S. jet, the Bell XP-59 Airacomet (October 1943), copied a British engine and was capable of only 418 mph. It was soon relegated to a transition training role. The Lockheed P-80 (553 mph) was the AAF's fastest World War II fighter; in production as the Shooting Star, it arrived too late for combat. The last AAF propeller fighter was the P-82 Twin Mustang, two P-51H's joined together, which saw service in Korea. The first postwar fighter was the Republic F-84 Thunderjet, which began in 1947 as a 587-mph fighter and evolved into the 693-mph F-84F Thunderstreak. The Strategic Air Command (SAC) used the latter for its escort groups until 1957, when escorts were deemed unnecessary. It then became Tactical Air Command's (TAC) main fighter-bomber until the F-100C. The North American F-86 Sabre was the first American-built jet with swept wings and tail surfaces, which overcame the effects of compressibility. Armed with six .50-caliber guns and traveling at 675 mph maximum, the Sabre participated in the first jet-versus-jet battles over Korea. The first jet night fighter and the first fighter with an afterburner was the Lockheed F-94. The Northrop F-89 Scorpion was the first successful all-weather jet.

The Soviet 1949 nuclear tests spurred interceptor development; since even one bomber could inflict a major blow, the first hit had to bring the enemy down. This was ensured by guiding the interceptor from the ground to the target and then firing the weapons. The first automatic interceptor was the YF-86; its twenty-four 2.75-inch rockets were fired by ground command. Next was the Lockheed F-94C Starfire with 48 rockets, followed by the Scorpion, armed with 104 rockets.

The U.S. Air Force ordered its first supersonic aircraft in the early 1950's. The Century series consisted of the North American F-100 Super Sabre, McDonnell Douglas F-101A Voodoo, Convair F-102 Delta Dagger (first with area-rule or "Coke bottle" configuration), and the Lockheed F-104 Starfighter. The TAC's first specially designed aircraft—the Republic F-105 Thunderchief—was delivered in 1956; it was the first fighter with a bomb bay. Traveling at Mach 2, it carried a 12,000-pound payload. Other attack aircraft include the Vought A-7D Corsair II, which replaced the A-1E Skyraider, a World War II vintage propeller plane recycled for Vietnam; the Northrop F-5 series; and the Cessna A-37, an interim support plane. Three cargo planes, the AC-47 Spooky, the AC-119 Shadow, and the AC-130 Super Spooky—all with side-mounted, rapid-fire, multibarreled weapons—are also in the attack category. The Convair 1,526-mph F-106 Delta Dart, an almost fully automatic fighter, appeared in 1956.

A new generation of aircraft began to appear in the 1960's. The first was the McDonnell Douglas F-4 Phantom II series, a twin-engine jet carrying a 20mm rapid-fire cannon and performing both as interceptor and attack plane. The Lockheed YF-12A, an advanced interceptor that was to have traveled over 2,000 mph, never went past the prototype stage. Two additional fighters of this generation are General Dynamics F-111, an all-weather fighter-bomber, and the McDonnell Douglas F-15 Eagle, built to replace the Phantom II.

[Wesley F. Craven and James L. Cate, eds., *The Army Air Forces in World War II*, vol. VI, *Men and Planes;* Ray Wagner, *American Combat Planes*.]

WARNER STARK

AIRCRAFT CARRIERS AND NAVAL AIRCRAFT. Carriers. The first airplane ever launched from a ship flew from a jury-rigged platform on the bow of the American light cruiser *Birmingham,* Nov. 10, 1910. The civilian pilot, Eugene B. Ely, subsequently made the first shipboard landing, Jan. 18, 1911, on a platform over the stern guns of the cruiser *Pennsylvania*. During World War I, however, it was the British Royal Navy that took the imaginative steps essential to the development of a true aircraft carrier, succeeding in taking to sea fighter aircraft that scored kills on German zeppelins over the sea approaches to Britain.

The first U.S. carrier was *Langley,* converted in 1922 from the collier *Jupiter*. *Langley* could operate thirty-four aircraft and steam at 15 knots. It was sunk by Japanese planes, Feb. 27, 1942, while ferrying U.S. Army Air Force planes to Java.

The foundation of American carrier air power was laid at the Washington Naval Conference of 1922, which limited construction of capital warships. Two U.S. battle cruisers were completed as aircraft carriers. *Lexington* and *Saratoga* were big and fast, at 33,000 tons and 33 knots, and carried a normal complement of nearly a hundred planes. They not only provided a training base for the first generations of carrier pilots but also enabled U.S. naval strategists to develop the doctrine and tactics that could project air power across oceans. The competition of carrier aviation with land-based aviation brought the United States into World War II with a broadly based aviation industry.

Lexington and *Saratoga* were classic attack carriers (CV's) extending the striking power of the fleet while protecting it from enemy action. During the early months of World War II they both took the war to the southwest Pacific. *Lexington* was sunk May 8, 1942, in the Battle of the Coral Sea, and *Saratoga* served through the war, only to become a target vessel for the Bikini atomic bomb evaluations of 1946. Additional CV's were added to the fleet beginning with *Ranger* in 1934, *Yorktown* in 1937, *Enterprise* in 1938, *Wasp* in 1940, and *Hornet* in 1941.

Essex defined a class of twenty-four 27,000-ton vessels completed from 1942 to 1946, almost all of which saw service in the Pacific. None was ever sunk. The last on active duty, *Ticonderoga,* was retired in 1973.

Wartime conversions from light cruiser hulls added nine light carriers (CVL's) to the fleet in one year (1943). These 15,000-ton ships operated at 31 knots or more with the fast carrier task force but had a complement of only some forty-five airplanes—half that of *Essex*. Concurrently a class of escort carriers (CVE's) sprang from conversions of merchant hulls. Some 112 of these were built, 28 being transferred to the British. The CVE's made less than 20 knots and carried fewer than thirty planes. In their primary role as submarine hunter-killers, American CVE's accounted directly for the destruction of thirty-three U-boats and participated in the destruction of twelve more. More important, their presence kept the German undersea force in a state of defense, which rendered it increasingly ineffective. The *Guadalcanal* actually captured a U-boat, now on display in Chicago's Grant Park. The support role of CVE's in amphibious landings took some in harm's way, and five in all were sunk—variously by submarine, kamikaze, or cruiser gunfire.

Aircraft. The development of naval carrier aircraft before World War II produced three basic types of planes: the fighter (VF), the scout bomber (VSB), and the torpedo plane (VT). Fighters tended to become fighter-bombers (VBF's) near the end of the war as the skies were cleared of enemy fighter opposition.

By 1929 a typical carrier complement included either F2B-1 or F3B-1 fighters by Boeing (450 h.p.; 158 mph max. speed), T4M-1 torpedo planes by Martin (525 h.p.; 116 mph), and O2U-1 scout bombers by Chance Vought (410 h.p.; 150 mph). All were fabric-covered biplanes.

The early 1930's produced the first of the Grumman fighter series—FF-1, F2F, and F3F (650 h.p.; 230 mph)—which broke the 200-mph barrier. Still, all were biplanes. The Douglas TBD torpedo plane began the trend to low-wing monoplanes, reaching the fleet in 1935. It could not reach 200 mph in level flight despite an 850-horsepower engine. Scout dive-bombers of the 1930's included the SBU biplane and the SB2U low-wing by Chance Vought, last of the fabric-covered combat planes. The biplane Curtiss SBC also saw service for a limited time. The dive-bombers were in the 200-mph class.

World War II spurred engine development. Horsepower doubled, reaching 2,000 for fighters, and maximum speed finally reached 300 mph and better. Biplanes passed into history.

Fighters evolved from the prewar F2A Brewster Buffalo, which was a hopeless mismatch for contemporary Japanese fighters, and the F4F Grumman Wildcat, which attained a 7:1 kill ratio over seemingly better Japanese planes, to the F6F Grumman Hellcat, which destroyed 75 percent of all enemy planes shot down by navy pilots in World War II (with a kill ratio of 19:1), and the F4U Chance Vought Corsair, flown chiefly by U.S. Marine pilots from advanced island bases (with a kill ratio of 11:1).

Scout bombers progressed from the fabric-covered SB2U Vought Vindicator, last in action at Midway; through the SBD Douglas Dauntless, which turned the tide at Midway and in many of the battles for the southwest Pacific; to the SB2C Curtiss Helldiver, a problem from its introduction on the first *Essex* carriers in 1943 until the end of the war. All were designed particularly for 60-degree dive-bombing, a navy specialty for accuracy.

Torpedo planes entered the war with the inadequate TBD Douglas Devastator, which carried Torpedo Squadron 8 to extinction at Midway. Its replacement, the TBF Grumman Avenger, performed notably, seeing postwar service as an interim antisubmarine warfare (ASW) platform.

Patrol planes (VP's), operating from land or water, supplemented carrier aircraft chiefly for search, ASW patrols, and antishipping attacks. Among these, the PBY Consolidated Catalinas—the famed Black Cats of the southwest Pacific—performed well all over the world, including the USSR, throughout the war. The PBM Martin Mariner provided better performance after 1943, and the PB4Y Consolidated Privateer, a navy version of the Liberator, which operated in both Atlantic and Pacific theaters, gave improved radar periscope detection.

Scout observation aircraft (VSO–VOS) contributed a minor but unique role in naval operations, from the first days of aviation to the advent of helicopters—their replacement after World War II. Catapulted from battleships, cruisers, and (rarely) destroyers and retrieved on a sea-sled towed by the mother ship, they could provide spotting capability for naval shore gunfire. They also rescued downed pilots from the sea, even under the guns of enemy-held atolls. Two types of these planes served all during the war—the venerable biplane SOC Curtiss Seagull and the newer OS2U Vought Kingfisher.

Carrier Battles of World War II. The three major carrier battles of World War II were the Coral Sea, Midway, and the Philippine Sea. In addition, the three-month campaign for Okinawa was a continuing deadly struggle between the fleet and kamikazes, resulting in major damage to nine CV's, one CVL, and three CVE's, but the destruction of more than 2,000 enemy aircraft by carrier-based planes. Carrier raids against Japanese positions commenced early in 1942, the most notable being the "Shangri-La" raid on Tokyo itself, on April 18, 1942; these raids increasingly inhibited Japanese initiatives. Equally important, air strikes from carriers spearheaded the North African landings in 1942 as well as every Pacific assault.

The Battle of the Coral Sea, May 4–8, 1942, kept Japan from its goal of landing forces at Port Moresby, New Guinea, and marked the end of southward expansion. But U.S. forces came off second best, losing the CV *Lexington* in exchange for the CVL *Shoho*. The Battle of Midway, June 3–7, 1942, reversed the offensive-defensive roles of the two combatants and frustrated Japanese strategic plans from then on.

Yorktown was sunk, but Japan lost all four of its CV's in the operation, together with their planes, pilots, and mechanics. Plane losses favored the Americans, 322 to 150. The Battle of the Philippine Sea, June 19–21, 1944, was the largest carrier battle in history. The Japanese defeat in this battle marked the end of Japanese carrier intervention: three Japanese carriers were lost, two to U.S. submarines, whereas no U.S. ships were lost; Japanese aircraft losses totaled 500 as against some 100 for the United States; most significant, only sixteen American pilots and thirty-three aircrewmen were lost, whereas Japan lost almost all its remaining carrier pilots.

After World War II. U.S. carrier air power has had no real foreign counterpart since World War II; nonetheless, carrier forces have remained an active, major arm of U.S. foreign policy. The western Pacific has not been without a carrier task force since V-J Day. The Truman Doctrine, enunciated in 1947, was supported immediately by the assignment of carriers to the Mediterranean, and they have been an integral part of the Sixth Fleet ever since.

Three new, larger classes of carrier have evolved since the war: *Midway,* 45,000 tons (1945); *Forrestal,* 60,000 tons (1955); and the nuclear-powered *Enterprise,* 75,000 tons (1961). With them have come jet aircraft (1948), nuclear bomb delivery capability (1951), and true all-weather operational capability (in the late 1960's). Further technological progress came in the 1950's with the adoption from the British Royal Navy of the angled deck (which permits simultaneous launch and recovery and power-on landings) and the steam catapult, which provides the greater launch capability needed for the jets. At the same time optical landing systems were introduced and have evolved from the mirror through the Fresnel lens, encompassing a closed-circuit television monitor and advancing toward an automatic landing system, not yet perfected. The Tactical Air Navigational System (TACAN) rose from needs of carriers. The Navy Tactical Data System arrived on the Vietnam scene, utilizing many ancillary electronic, computerized command, and control features.

Antisubmarine warfare carriers (CVS's) entered the postwar fleet as replacement for the CVE's. The ASW carrier mission began to take on renewed importance with the growth of the Soviet submarine fleet. Some CVE's and CVL's were used in ASW operations, but after the early 1950's they were replaced by converted *Essex* class ships. The CVS became the nucleus of a carrier-destroyer force utilized to sanitize the operating area for a carrier strike force, to search out and destroy enemy submarines (hunter-killer), or to close off a potential route for enemy submarines to reach an objective area. Aircraft complements aboard CVS's have stabilized with S2F Grumman Tracker twin-engine aircraft, helicopters, and an early-warning detachment of specially configured electronic S2F's. The Tracker was introduced in 1954. More advanced versions, the S2F-3 and S2F-3s (now designated S-2D and S-2E), began to reach the fleet in 1962.

Helicopters became operational aboard carriers with the first helicopter ASW (HS) squadron in 1952, although the XOP-1 autogiro was tested on *Langley* in 1931. The first ASW squadron was equipped with the Piasecki HUP-1, to be replaced in time with the Sikorsky HSS-1 piston engine Seabat and then the HSS-2 turbine-powered Sea King. Also, most major vessels carry utility helicopters for such chores as stores movement and replenishment, personnel transfers, and lifeguard missions.

A period of international significance in carrier history was the development in the 1950's of nuclear bomb delivery capability for carriers. With attack planes on board available for nuclear missions, the carriers could cover the European peninsula, including the Ukraine and Caucasus, most of China, and eastern Siberia. Naval aircraft shared the national nuclear deterrent responsibility with the Strategic Air Command through the 1950's and into the 1960's, when the Polaris fleet and ICBM's took over the major burden. The most significant technological development for carriers after World War II was that of nuclear power, but Secretary of Defense Robert S. McNamara's decisions of 1962 delayed its exploitation. However, with the commissioning of *Nimitz* (1972) and *Eisenhower* (1974), proponents of an increased nuclear-powered carrier force had won part of their struggle.

Naval aircraft since World War II have been predominantly jet-powered but the propeller dive-bomber AD Douglas Skyraider persisted as the world's best attack airplane from the late 1940's into the 1970's, excelling both in Korea and in Vietnam. With a single piston engine, the AD carries a bigger bomb load than the famous B-17 Flying Fortress.

From the variety of naval jet aircraft tested in high-accident-rate programs during the 1950's, three attack planes and two outstanding fighters emerged. The A4 McDonnell Douglas Skyhawk, designed originally as a super-simple atomic delivery vehicle, was modified substantially for effective conventional weapons delivery. The twin-engine A-6 Grumman Intruder, a superbly electronically equipped all-weather plane with several unique electronic countermeasure versions, was introduced in 1963. The A-7 Vought Corsair II, a single-engine jet designed to carry either nuclear or conventional weapons, first saw combat in 1967 in the Tonkin Gulf. It is basically a day-attack plane. In the fighter field, the F8U-1 Vought Crusader, a day fighter gun platform with missile capability, became operational in 1957. The F4 McDonnell Douglas Phantom II, an all-weather missile fighter, was first produced in 1961 and also adopted by the U.S. Air Force as its primary fighter.

Historically carrier participation in both the Korean and Vietnam wars was similar. Both were peninsular wars, from the start characterized by a lack of land bases. As a result, in both, U.S. carriers were responsible for a major part of the air fighting over enemy territory—exploiting their quick and self-contained reaction capability, mobility, and wide choice of launch areas—the flanking position behind the enemy's ground battlelines being peculiarly advantageous. Because they could get in and out of target areas more easily, carrier planes rather than land-based planes took out the Yalu River bridges and Hwachon Reservoir Dam in 1951 and the Haiphong and Hanoi power plants in 1965. In both conflicts, carriers have operated free from enemy damage.

Carrier force levels fluctuate with need. V-J Day found ninety-nine carriers of all types in commission. When war broke out in Korea, fifteen carriers, but only seven CV's, were left. By 1953 thirty-nine carriers were in commission, of which seventeen were of *Essex* or *Midway* class. On-station commitments in Southeast Asia went from three CVA's to five CVA's in the first months of the air war in Vietnam, but Department of Defense analysts were successful in keeping the attack carrier level at fifteen; meanwhile ASW carrier strength declined from nine in 1965 to three in 1972.

[*Dictionary of American Fighting Ships*, vol. II; Norman Polmar, *Aircraft Carriers;* Clark G. Reynolds, *The Fast Carriers*.]

WILLIAM C. CHAPMAN

AIRCRAFT ARMAMENT, the weapons carried on a plane for attacking or defense against enemy aircraft and ground targets. Early warplanes were equipped either with a small-caliber weapon capable of a high number of strikes per second or with a larger, slower-firing weapon capable of high penetration and destruction; later aircraft were often equipped with both.

The early low-powered American fighter aircraft of World War I carried a single drum-fed Lewis gun, which was difficult for the pilot to reload. With the development of more powerful engines and synchronized guns, planes were armed with twin belt-fed machine guns, such as the British Vickers. Between the world wars, American fighters carried either two Browning air-cooled .30-caliber machine guns, or one .30- and one .50-caliber machine gun. Although aerial cannon were employed in World War I, the first practical models appeared only in World War II. The P-39 Airacobra, for example, carried a 37mm coaxial cannon, but the most widely used was the Swiss 20mm Oerlikon, as carried by the P-38 Lightning. The largest was the 75mm M-4 cannon mounted on some B-25 bombers for attacking ground targets.

Flexible guns mounted to defend heavier aircraft remained small and light until the development of a mount that allowed the gunner to overcome slip-stream interference. During and immediately following World War I, one or two Lewis guns mounted on a Scarff ring were standard. Enclosed turrets first appeared in 1930 on the B-10 bomber, followed by American adoption of the British power turret, usually mounting twin .50-caliber guns. Remote-controlled turrets came in 1942 and were standard after World War II, as in the retractable twin turrets with 20mm cannon on the B-36.

After World War II, bombers such as the B-52 were equipped with radar-aimed 20mm cannon, while fighters carried radar-guided and computer-fired air-to-air rockets—the earliest being the Folding Fin Aircraft Rocket (Mighty Mouse) carried by a modified F-86. Such has been the impact of rockets that they have generally replaced guns as the primary fighter weapon, although most fighters continue to carry at least one gun. The F-14, however, carries only the Phoenix missile. Further developments in air-to-air ordnance include the infrared-homing Sidewinder, the beam-riding Sparrow I, and the radar-homing Sparrow III. Also developed were the Falcon GAR-3 or GAR-4 heat-seeking missiles and the MB-1 Genie, with a nuclear warhead capable of destroying any aircraft within 1,000 feet of detonation. Gunnery developments include the 20mm T-171 Vulcan multi-barreled cannon firing 6,000 rounds per minute and a similar 37mm cannon.

[Ray Wagner, *American Combat Planes*.]

WARNER STARK

AIR DEFENSE. Although American cities were not in danger of attack by air during World War I, the ordeal of Great Britain in the face of such attack was not overlooked by American military planners. Remote as the possibility of air attack against the United States was during the interwar period, war studies contemplated the use of fighter aircraft, antiaircraft artillery (AAA), and ground observers against that possibility. In the 1920's and 1930's studies were made of electronic aircraft warning, culminating in the 1930's in the development of radar. In 1935 the War Department ordered the establishment of regional air defense systems, to which radar was added at the end of the decade. The operation of the regional systems was considerably improved by the adoption of British organization and procedures observed by U.S. officers during the Battle of Britain in 1940. During World War II certain radar improvements, independently developed by the British, were added to the American systems to the great advantage of the latter. By Dec. 7, 1941, air defense systems—including radar, fighters, AAA, ground observers, and control centers—had been established along both continental coasts, in Panama, and in Hawaii. After the Japanese attack on Pearl Harbor, these defenses were greatly expanded, resulting in a total of more than 100 radar stations, about a million volunteer civilian ground observers and control center operators, and substantial numbers of fighters and AAA batteries. By 1943 it was evident that both Germany and Japan were virtually incapable of inflicting serious damage on American cities and the air defenses were demobilized by war's end.

The Air Defense Command (renamed the Aerospace Defense Command in 1968) was established in 1946, but it was not until 1948 that serious efforts were made to reconstruct air defenses in the continental United States. Thereafter progress was rapid, stimulated by the international tensions of the cold war. By 1950 work on construction of a modern, improved radar network had begun, and by 1960 several hundred modern radar stations blanketed the country (*see* Radar). Until the electronic network came into full operation, about 500,000 civilian volunteers constituted a Ground Observer Corps (GOC), providing backup warning capability—especially around the nation's perimeters. Jet fighters were similarly deployed. To extend radar surveillance northward, a Canada–United States agreement in 1950 permitted U.S.-manned radar stations to be erected on Canadian soil, including a line of Distant Early Warning (DEW) radars along the Arctic Circle. To extend radar surveillance seaward, navy radar picket ships patrolled the coasts, and radar-bearing platforms (Texas Towers) were embedded in shoals off the East Coast. By the end of the 1950's, antiaircraft guns had been replaced by surface-to-air missiles (Nike and Bomarc) to defend cities and military installations. These extensive resources were severely limited, however, by their dependence on human reactions, which were not accurate or quick enough for the era of atomic warfare. In the early 1950's intensive research and development in the application of electronic computers to air defense were undertaken with great success, culminating in the early 1960's in the deployment of about twenty Semi-Automatic Ground Environment (SAGE) combat operation centers throughout the country, integrating all air defense operations both regionally and nationally.

The coming of the space age caused much emphasis to be placed on intercontinental ballistic missiles (ICBM's) by the world powers. To counter the new threat, a Ballistic Missile Early Warning System (BMEWS) was erected, with special radar stations in Alaska, Greenland, and the United Kingdom. By the early 1960's the ICBM had replaced the manned bomber as the chief instrument of intercontinental air warfare. In consequence, air defense priorities were readjusted to favor the new threat. Since the art of anti-ICBM defense was still in its infancy, reliance had to be placed on the deterrent of overwhelming ICBM retaliation in the event of an attack. The readjustment of priorities in air defense also saw the progressive dismantling of defenses against the manned bomber, although this was accompanied by qualitative improvement of the remaining resources. Attention was also given to the possibility of attack by earth-orbiting satellites, and an elaborate network of space sensors, the Space Detection and Tracking System (SPADATS), was deployed worldwide.

In 1969 Congress approved a decision to construct a Ballistic Missile Defense System (BMDS), which was given the code name Safeguard. Elements of the system included radars, short-range and long-range missiles, and supporting automatic data processing equipment. Plans called for large-scale deployment throughout the United States; but the Strategic Arms Limitation Treaty (SALT I) between the United States and the Soviet Union, ratified by the Senate in July 1972, limited each country to only two antiballistic missile (ABM) defenses, one to protect each nation's capital and the other to defend one ICBM complex. The United States constructed its Safeguard missile site in North Dakota, completed in 1974, but Congress did not authorize construction of the Washington, D.C., site. The control facility for the Safeguard system was the Missile Defense Center near Colorado Springs. The entire system began operations in 1975.

Because all three services were operating air defense equipment, the Continental Air Defense Command (CONAD) was established in 1954 to coordinate their efforts. In 1958 the United States and Canada pooled their air defense resources for the common defense of their territories and established the North American Air Defense Command (NORAD), into which CONAD was integrated. NORAD Headquarters was established in a cavern under Cheyenne Mountain near Colorado Springs, Colo. By 1974 the U.S. Army and Navy had ceased their participation in CONAD, which was inactivated, leaving the USAF's Aerospace Defense Command the only U.S. component of NORAD.

[Wesley F. Craven and James L. Cate, eds., *The Army Air Forces in World War II,* vol. I, *Plans and Early Operations,* vol. VI, *Men and Planes;* Alfred Goldberg, ed., *A History of the United States Air Force, 1907–1957.*]

DENYS VOLAN

AIR FORCE, UNITED STATES. Although the U.S. Air Force did not achieve independent status until 1947, the history of American military aviation reaches back to the Civil War, when civilian aeronauts and enlisted ground crews operated observation balloons for Union forces. The War Department became interested in heavier-than-air flight, funding the efforts of Samuel P. Langley in 1898, but was slow to exploit the work of the Wright brothers after their first powered flights in 1903. On Aug. 1, 1907, the U.S. Army created an aeronautical division within the Signal Corps, to take charge "of all matters pertaining to military ballooning, air machines, and all kindred subjects," and in 1909 it purchased its first airplane from the Wrights. Subsequent funding for aviation was tight, and weaknesses in this new military field were revealed in the 1916 Mexican border campaign. When the United States entered World War I, the American aviation arm possessed only thirty-five pilots and fifty-five mechanics.

The wartime Congress voted large sums for aviation, envisioning a decisive American air contribution. Results were disappointing, mainly because of American inexperience in aircraft design and production. Fewer than 200 planes of 740 in use by American squadrons at the close of hostilities were American built. The brief combat record was nevertheless creditable, over seventy American pilots qualifying as "aces" by destroying five or more enemy craft. In August 1918 certain French and all American frontline air units were placed under a single commander, Brig. Gen. William (Billy) Mitchell. Supported by other Allied units, Mitchell directed the war's heaviest concentration of air power in attacks against the German lines and rear areas about Saint-Mihiel. A similar, though smaller, air concentration was effected under Mitchell for the final Meuse-Argonne campaign.

The air arm was separated from the Signal Corps in May 1918 and by legislation in 1920 became the Air Service, one of seven combatant arms of the army. The reform fell short of that recommended by air officers, and the energetic Mitchell promoted projects to increase awareness of the potential of aviation. A mass transcontinental flight in 1919, tests against battleships in 1921 and 1923, and a global circumnavigation advanced aviation, but failed to win further reform. Embittered, Mitchell invited the 1925 court-martial that ended his military career. Modest gains were detectable in the Air Corps Act of 1926, which changed the Air Service to the Air Corps, increased air representation on the General Staff, and authorized expansion. Funding remained tight, and when in 1934 the Air Corps undertook to fly the nation's airmail, a series of crashes ensued, revealing the arm's poor condition. Partial reorganization followed, establishing a single headquarters for control of most Air Corps combat units. In the 1930's aircraft and doctrine for "strategic" (or independent) air warfare emerged. The new heavy bomber, the XB-17, flew nonstop from Seattle to Dayton in August 1935. In contemplating employment of the new weapon, Air Corps officers avoided the idea of attacking civilian populations, but spoke of long-range coastal defense and, more circumspectly, of daylight, precision attacks against vulnerable joints of an enemy's economic system.

The collapse of France in 1940 shocked the United States into a massive air rearmament effort. The Army Air Forces (AAF) was created in June 1941, becoming coequal the following year with the army ground forces and the services of supply. The air arm thus attained a position of autonomy not far short of full independence.

World War II. The Japanese attackers on Dec. 7, 1941, badly surprised the AAF defenders of Hawaii. Later in the day, Japanese planes destroyed two B-17 squadrons on the ground in Luzon, soon thereafter establishing full command of the air over the Philippines. More psychological than strategic was the AAF reply—an attack on Tokyo on Apr. 18, 1942, by sixteen twin-engine bombers led by Lt. Col. James Doolittle and launched from the carrier *Hornet*. After building up forces in Australia, the AAF progressively regained command of the air over the southwest Pacific, attacking Japanese airfields, interdicting sea communications, and spearheading Gen. Douglas MacArthur's amphibious and airborne advance toward the Philippines. Seven days after the Oct. 20, 1944, landings at Leyte, P-38 fighters flew into a beachhead strip at Tacloban; after several weeks, Allied carrier- and land-based air units gained full dominance over Japanese air strength in the Philippines. Meanwhile, AAF transport aircraft based in India were sustaining Allied forces in difficult campaigns in Burma and were performing massive lifts of matériel into China, encouraging the Chinese to continue a war effort.

In the Mediterranean theater, AAF bombers contributed to late-1942 victories at both ends of North Africa. After assembling superior air forces and placing them under centralized control, the Allies asserted air supremacy over Tunisia, contributing massive tactical air support during the final ground offensive in April 1943. During the campaigns in Sicily and Italy, the AAF steadily pounded enemy communications (the extent of success is still controversial). Attacks against the Ploesti oil fields in Romania began with a historic raid on Aug. 1, 1943, carried out by more than 170 B-24's and costing 54 bombers. The Mediterranean air campaigns weakened Axis air power, but delayed both the campaign against the Luftwaffe over Germany, seen as an essential preliminary to the cross-channel assault, and the full buildup of the AAF in Britain.

The daylight air battle of Germany opened in 1943, although AAF heavy bombers regularly attacked France in 1942 and the RAF Bomber Command had long operated over Germany by night. The Americans were nearly defeated in their daylight air offensive, since escort fighters could accompany the bombers only as far as the German border. Over sixty four-engine heavies were lost on Aug. 17, 1943, in attacking ball-bearing factories at Schweinfurt and the fighter assembly plant at Regensburg, both deep inside Germany. A second Schweinfurt raid on Oct. 14 cost another sixty bombers. The tide turned in early 1944, when the Americans began using long-range P-47's (Thunderbolts) and P-51's (Mustangs), modified with external fuel tanks that eventually extended escort fighter radius beyond Berlin. These high-performance craft attacked the Luftwaffe in the air and on the ground, defeating an enemy already weakened by shortages of fuel and experienced pilots. In June 1944 the Normandy invasion proceeded without enemy air interference; the assault began with a two-division night parachute drop from AAF transports. Massive Allied tactical air forces supported the ensuing ground campaign. The heavy bombers, finally at full strength in mid-1944, returned to attacks against Germany, smashing the German economy by systematic efforts against transportation and synthetic oil targets. By April 1945 German oil production was 5 percent that of a year earlier. German jet interceptors, which in 1943 might have changed the course of the air war, appeared too late to impede the huge Allied fleets.

Strategic bombing of Japan by B-29 Superfortresses from bases in the Marianas began in November 1944, after logistics difficulties plagued an earlier effort from China. In early 1945, the AAF broke from its pattern in Europe, and the B-29's began night incendiary area attacks on Japanese cities. Ships flew at medium altitudes to increase bomb loads, engine life, and accuracy, without benefit of formation or close escort. Devastation was utter, over 600 B-29's bombing on certain nights. The atomic bombs, delivered accurately by a special B-29 unit, ended the resolution of Japan's leaders, confronted already with sea blockade, Russian war entry, and the prospect of continued bombing.

The wartime AAF was a citizen's air force, although its higher leadership was mainly from the few prewar professionals. Peak strength in 1944 was 2,400,000 persons. The immediate postwar demobilization was precipitate (as in 1919), strength declining to 485,000 by April 1946.

Postwar Years. The National Security Act of July 26, 1947, established a single Department of Defense, with three departments—the army, the navy (which retained naval and marine aviation), and the air force. Stuart Symington was sworn in as first secretary of the air force on Sept. 18, 1947; Gen. Carl Spaatz became the USAF's first chief of staff. Strategic and budget controversies quickly loomed, naval leaders challenging the usefulness of the new B-36 heavy bomber and the efficacy of strategic bombing itself.

The emergent cold war confirmed that the atomic bomb and the means to deliver it were militarily insufficient. After witnessing the subversion of non-Communist governments in Eastern Europe, American leaders became resolute in the face of Soviet closure of surface routes to occupied Berlin in June 1948. The Berlin airlift kept the city supplied with coal, foodstuffs, and other necessities through the winter of 1948–49, presenting the USAF with its first major test. Pilots overcame difficult weather and crowded airspace, while innovation and tight organization made possible an enormous aircraft maintenance effort. During the 11-month period of the blockade, beginning on June 25, 1948, nearly 2 million tons were airlifted into Berlin, most of it in USAF C-54's. The single-day peak occurred on Apr. 16, 1949, when 1,398 transports delivered nearly 13,000 tons.

Soviet detonation of an atomic device in 1949 emphasized that the USAF's first responsibility was the nation's nuclear deterrent. For nine years under the single-minded leadership of Gen. Curtis E. LeMay (1948–57), the Strategic Air Command (SAC) gained a reputation for the highest standards in professional airmanship and readiness. Jet-propelled B-47's entered SAC in early 1953, their limited range extended by a complex of overseas bases and a force of aerial tankers. For most SAC personnel, the frequent overseas deployments and the demanding alert requirements left little time for normal family life.

Korean War. The United States again reacted firmly when the North Koreans attacked South Korea on June 25, 1950. Two days later, USAF units in the Far East began munitions lifts into Korea, and commenced strikes against airfields, bridges, and targets of opportunity. A U.S. Army battalion was airlifted to Korea on the sixth day of the war. The Americans quickly won air superiority over the poorly equipped North Korean air force and persisted in attacks against the enemy's extended lines of communication, thus aiding the Allied defense of the southern tip of the peninsula and the return north. The USAF transports lifted forces into Seoul soon after the Inchon landings and made deliveries to units advancing up the mud-clogged North Korean roadways. During the late-year retreat from the Yalu River, air force and Marine Corps transports made resupply paradrops and landed at hastily prepared strips to evacuate over 4,000 wounded.

The entry of the Communist Chinese brought the latest Soviet-built MIG-15 fighters, far superior to the opposing USAF F-80 jets. The U.S. Fourth Fighter-Interceptor Wing was sent quickly to the Far East. Equipped with F-86A craft, the wing's pilots claimed their first MIG on Dec. 17, 1950. The MIG's and F-86's met regularly near the Yalu thereafter, the Americans claiming 792 MIG kills, with the loss of 78 F-86's in air-to-air combat. The jet battles served to preserve Allied command of the air over most of Korea. Through the protracted stalemate, USAF and navy jet and propeller fighters (including P-51's) attacked interdiction and close-support targets by day, while propeller bombers ranged by night. The Communists were resourceful—exploiting camouflage and darkness, and patiently making road repairs—but were unable to sustain another strong ground offensive. Allied difficulties in giving close support to ground troops grew out of poor radio equipment and divergent army and air force concepts, but were eased by use of airborne forward air controllers in light, Mosquito aircraft. For the air force, the Korean conflict was another citizen's war, involving many World War II veterans recalled from civilian reservist status.

From 1954 to 1965. The experience of the limited conflict in Korea stimulated reemphasis on tactical air forces during the next decade. The development of nuclear weapons small enough to be carried on fighter aircraft promised a means for deterring or overcoming future stalemates like the one in Korea. During the late 1950's, the Tactical Air Command remained ready to deploy nuclear-capable composite air task forces from the United States to overseas trouble spots. After 1960, interest in attaining greater flexibility produced expansion of air transport forces for hauling airborne troop units. By mid-1965, the Military Air Transport Service possessed 550 four-engine transports, including all-jet C-141 cargo carriers. Tactical fighter forces included twenty-three wings (over 1,000 aircraft) in the United States, with another eight wings overseas.

Task forces of fighter, reconnaissance, and airlift craft moved overseas in response to crises in Taiwan in 1958, in the Middle East in 1958, and in Laos in 1962. The USAF transports hauled extensively during emergencies in the Congo in 1960 and 1964, and moved 16,000 troops and equipment into the Dominican Republic in 1965. In 1962, photography by USAF pilots in U-2 reconnaissance craft permitted detection of missile construction in Cuba. During the ensuing crisis, tactical air forces moved to bases in Florida for possible operations against Cuba, and U.S. Army troop units moved to the southeast United States, in part by USAF airlift.

Most fundamentally, however, U.S. diplomacy continued to rest on the retaliatory capabilities of SAC. During the Cuban crisis, the command remained in highest alert status for four weeks, keeping some fifty thermonuclear-carrying B-52 bombers aloft around the clock. The B-52 had entered the inventory in 1956, replacing the B-36, as SAC moved toward an all-jet force. The SAC strength in bomber and tanker aircraft grew through 1957, and the command worked steadily to reduce SAC's vulnerability by dispersion, alert systems, and better communications. Transition into a mixed bomber-missile force began in 1957, upon activation of a unit equipped with Snark intercontinental cruise missiles. Overseas deployment of Thor and Jupiter intermediate-range ballistic missiles commenced in 1958; the first intercontinental ballistic missile unit, equipped with Atlas, approached operational status late in 1959. By mid-1965 the manned bomber force had declined to 900 aircraft, with over 800 intercontinental missiles (mostly solid-fuel Minutemen) on alert.

The Air Defense Command in the early 1950's consisted of fighter-interceptor squadrons and a net of radar and control units across the United States and Alaska. These were tied into radar lines crossing Canada, and in 1957 USAF completed construction of a 3,000-mile Distant Early Warning (DEW) line, entirely within the Arctic Circle. Airborne and sea-emplaced radar sites completed the net. The combined North American Air Defense Command (NORAD), with a USAF commander and a Canadian deputy, was created on Sept. 12, 1957. A large computerized control system became operative in 1958. Construction of huge antennae for the Ballistic Missile Early Warning System (BMEWS) was begun in 1959 in Greenland and Alaska; a third installation was built later in Britain. These were supplemented by "over-the-horizon" radar equipment, revealed in 1964. Fighter-interceptors carried air-to-air nuclear-tipped missiles, but the manned interceptors gradually relinquished their roles to ground-to-air missiles, including the Bomarc and Nike series.

Events in Southeast Asia claimed increasing attention. Reacting to what seemed an avowed Kremlin policy encouraging wars of national liberation, the air force in 1961 organized a sublimited warfare unit, equipped with low-performance aircraft and trained to operate in primitive environments. A detachment of twelve propeller-driven strike aircraft and four transports moved into Vietnam late in the year, soon joined by a line squadron of C-123 transports, several dozen U.S. Army helicopters, and a few aerial spray ships. The strike aircraft, painted with Vietnamese insignia, performed combat missions with combined American-Vietnamese crews. The American air package expanded modestly, but the basic objective remained that of vitalizing Vietnamese efforts, while various test projects sought ways of applying air power to problems of insurgency and nation building. Political instability in Saigon compromised the counterinsurgency program and compounded American frustration. Jet strike aircraft of USAF entered Vietnam following the Tonkin Gulf affair of August 1964 and they began attacks on Communist lines of communication in Laos that December. Communist actions in South Vietnam triggered further retaliation in early 1965, USAF planes for the first time joining navy jets against the North on Feb. 8. The first American ground units entered Vietnam in March, one marine battalion deploying by sea, a second by USAF C-130 lift from Okinawa.

From 1965 to 1973. The American air campaign against North Vietnam was designed to discourage and impede assistance to the Communist effort in the South. Air strikes were closely controlled from the White House, which gradually escalated pressure in hopes of gaining limited political objectives. Early missions were limited to military and transportation targets in the southern part of North Vietnam, with occasional forays against rail bridges farther north. In early 1966, petroleum targets near Hanoi were attacked, followed by systematic attacks on the rail lines from China. After several bombing pauses failed to start negotiations, targeting expanded in 1967 to include the North's only steel mill, electric power generating facilities, and transportation targets around Haiphong and Hanoi. North Vietnamese air defenses, initially weak, were strengthened by aid from the Soviet Union and China. MIG-17's and surface-to-air missiles appeared in 1965—the missiles were the more deadly, forcing the Americans to low levels where vulnerability to antiaircraft fire was high. By 1967 improved American electronic devices had reduced the effectiveness of the missiles, while recent attacks on airfields eased the MIG threat. Navy and air force fighter-bombers attacked the North almost daily, averaging more than 10,000 sorties per month during the summers of 1966 and 1967. Assisting the strike force were a variety of specialized aircraft, designed to provide air refueling, rescue, reconnaissance, electronic countermeasures, or radar-warning support, along with other fighters equipped to attack missile installations or engage enemy interceptors.

In South Vietnam, jet and propeller fighters provided heavy firepower for close support of ground troops, usually guided to targets by airborne controllers. B-52 heavy bombers pounded carefully selected areas with 30-ton loads of conventional bombs. Air force transports, including large numbers of four-engine C-130 turboprops, moved and resupplied brigade forces engaged in search-and-destroy operations, staging into forward airheads in remote regions. Some transports were modified as gunships, for night defense of friendly installations. Despite the enemy's use of Cambodian sanctuaries and its proven skill in camouflage and dispersion, the Allied air and ground steamroller in South Vietnam rendered hopeless the enemy's protracted strategy and prompted him to launch his 1968 Tet offensive. Allied air firepower and airlifts were instrumental in the recovery from the Tet attacks, as well as in the simultaneous defense of isolated Khe Sanh.

President Lyndon Johnson's 1968 decisions, to curtail and then suspend the bombing of the North, led to redirection of the Allied air effort toward the Laos panhandle. Acoustic and seismic sensors were placed along Communist infiltration routes, to detect movements and relay signals to a computerized ground center. American strike and gunship aircraft, many equipped with infrared and light-amplification devices for night target detection, became effective in destroying trucks despite improving antiaircraft and missile opposition. Elsewhere in Laos, USAF strike aircraft provided support for Laotian government forces. Interdiction operations by USAF helped the armed forces of Cambodia to retain control of key areas after 1970, and the Khmer regime was further bolstered by periodic C-130 airlifts of food and petroleum.

The USAF and Vietnamese air power was apparently a decisive factor in halting the North Vietnamese 1972 Easter offensive against the South. The USAF, which had severely reduced its strength in the Far East, brought back over 250 aircraft and 7,000 personnel from the United States during the crisis. Most dramatic were the air resupply and strikes about An Loc, sustaining an isolated and desperate garrison in the face of Communist surface-to-air missiles. The Communist invasion resulted in a modification of U.S. restraint, and determined air and mining campaigns helped produce terms of peace. Final Communist resistance to a settlement was eroded apparently by a twelve-day B-52 bombing campaign about Hanoi, in which fifteen of the giant planes were lost.

Most career personnel served one or more twelve-month tours in Southeast Asia; the air force avoided a major expansion. The conflict had painful aspects, including numerous covert programs leading to cases of deceptive strike reporting, and resulted in wide criticism of indiscriminate effects of air operations. The ending was not entirely bitter; the obvious courage and integrity of the returning prisoners of war (a majority of them USAF members) reminded the divided nation of its traditions.

The 660,000-man air force in early 1974 looked ahead to continued change. SAC maintained fewer than 450 manned bombers, along with over 1,000 intercontinental missiles in hardened silos, under limitations set in the 1972 strategic arms treaty with the Soviets. The worldwide tactical air forces anticipated a major role in post-Vietnam national strategy. Hostilities in the Middle East late the previous year called forth a major logistics effort, to marshal quantities of matériel and airlift them to Israel. Especially valuable in this effort were the load capacity and range of the huge C-5A's, their history stained by cost overruns and metal fatigue problems.

The history of the U.S. Air Force has mirrored the temper and aspirations of American society. The nation has found the promise of air power appealing, in hopes of avoiding heavy manpower losses in ground fighting. The military air arm, like the surface forces, was poorly prepared for combat in 1917, 1941, and 1950, but in each case underwent fast and substantial wartime expansion. Since the formal creation of USAF, roughly coinciding with American assumption of global responsibilities, air power and the air force have been keystones of the nation's military posture and diplomacy.

Research and Space Activities. From its birth, the air force's technical orientation was apparent in the emphasis given to research and development. Most effort has focused toward future air weaponry, such work drawing from and often contributing to general scientific knowledge. Meteorological research, aerial geodetic surveys, and various aeromedical research efforts have had wide application. Air force transports have provided essential airlift for scientific projects in the Arctic and Antarctic, including paradrops at the South Pole station.

Air force space activities have included numerous unmanned research, weather, detection, and communications satellite projects, as well as systematic surveillance and tracking of space objects. Upon cancellation of air force manned projects—a piloted space glider in 1963 and the Manned Orbital Laboratory in 1969—the USAF supported the manned ventures of the National Aeronautics and Space Administration. The air force contributed numerous technical personnel and astronauts for projects Mercury, Gemini, Apollo, and Skylab. Capt. Virgil I. Grissom in July 1961 became the second American in space, and Col. Edwin E. Aldrin with Neil A. Armstrong on July 20, 1969, became the first men on the moon. Air force ballistic missiles were transformed into reliable space-launch systems—Atlas and Titan boosters launched certain Mercury and all Gemini flights, respectively—and the early Thors propelled over 400 space launches, beginning in 1958. The United States adhered to a treaty signed by eighty-four nations in 1967, which provided against military exploitation of space.

Air Force Organizations. The basic USAF tactical unit has been the squadron, consisting of aircrews and enough ground crewmen for routine flight-line maintenance of the twelve to twenty-four assigned aircraft. The First Aero Squadron was organized in 1913, representing the only tactical air unit in the army prior to 1917. During World War II, tactical squadrons were combined into groups; later, they were placed under a wing headquarters, which also included heavy maintenance, supply, and sometimes base housekeeping units. A wing could occupy a single base, or its units could be dispersed at several locations.

Several wings could be organized into an air division, or be placed directly under the next echelon, the numbered air force. Several numbered air forces became famous in World War II, including the Eighth Air Force in Britain, the Fifteenth in the Mediterranean, and the Fifth in the South Pacific. The B-29 units in the Marianas were organized as XXI Bomber Command. The Fifth Air Force fought in Korea; the Seventh in Vietnam.

Reorganizations after World War II brought into being the major air commands, including SAC, the Air Defense Command, and the Tactical Air Command. The Air Materiel Command and the Air Research and Development Command were reorganized in 1961 as the Air Force Logistics Command (responsible for maintenance, supply, and procurement) and the Air Force Systems Command (applied research and development). Overseas, air force component commands served in unified theater commands, parallel with army and navy component commands. Headquarters, USAF, headed by the chief of staff and under the office of the secretary of the air force, is located in Washington, D.C.

Air University. Formal professional education for air officers evolved from the Air Service Field Officers' School, created in 1920 at Langley Field, Va., to prepare officers for direction of air units in operations with other branches. Early classes were small, but included officers from first lieutenant through lieutenant colonel. The school was renamed Air Service Tactical School in 1922, and Air Corps Tactical School in 1926, moving to Maxwell Field, Ala., in 1931. Students from other arms and services were enrolled, and the school became an important breeding ground for ideas on the proper employment of the air weapon.

The Air University was established in September 1946 at Maxwell, with three main component schools. An Air Tactical School (later renamed Squadron Officer School) was designed for regular officers in their first five years, essentially to prepare them for squadron command or equivalent staff responsibility. The Air Command and Staff School (later College) was designed for selected officers prior to their twelfth year. At the apex was the ten-month Air War College, with annual classes selected from the best-qualified officers prior to their twentieth year of service; its first class, numbering fifty-five, graduated in June 1947. Despite temporary reductions during the Korean and Southeast Asian conflicts, all three schools have functioned continuously. Individuals could complete each of the three schools either in residence at Maxwell or by correspondence. Air force officers attended parallel institutions of the other services, as well as the National War College and the Industrial College of the Armed Forces, both located in Washington, D.C.

Air Reserve Forces. The Air National Guard and the Air Force Reserve constitute the air reserve forces of the United States. The first National Guard aviation unit was organized in New York in 1915. Although no such units were mustered into federal service in World War I, postwar National Guard regulations established air observation, balloon, and photo units. All twenty-nine observation squadrons were ordered to federal duty in September 1940. The Air National Guard separated from the National Guard upon USAF independence in 1947. Three-fourths of Air National Guard strength was brought to active duty in 1950–51; guard fighter squadrons mobilized and were deployed overseas during the 1961 Berlin crisis and after the *Pueblo* affair in early 1968. Guard squadrons began participating in the continental air defense system in 1954. Although the primary mission of the guard was to provide combat-ready units for the air force, the organization also afforded the individual states an organized military body, a role specified in the U.S. Constitution. The Air National Guard in 1974 included over 90,000 personnel and was principally equipped with Vietnam-vintage aircraft, including the F-100, F-102, F-105, and C-130.

The Air Force Reserve includes individuals assigned as augmentees for active duty units and members of reserve squadrons equipped with transport and other aircraft. Individuals (like certain guardsmen) receive pay for training and short active-duty periods. Organized reservists in 1949 numbered 42,000; another 60,000 were unpaid Volunteer Air Reservists. During the Korean War, all twenty-five reserve troop carrier and light bomber wings were recalled, although most personnel were redistributed among other units. Four squadrons were recalled in 1961, and eight during the Cuban missile crisis. Huge C-124's with Air Force Reserve crews proved vital during the 1965 Dominican intervention and routinely flew trans-Pacific hauls during the war in Southeast Asia. An "associate unit" system was begun in 1968, whereby reserve unit members helped fly and maintain aircraft belonging to an active unit. Under this plan the active unit's workload capacity could be raised instantly by calling the associate unit to active status. In early 1974, the Air Force Reserve numbered thirty-eight squadrons, mostly equipped with C-130's, as well as eighteen associate squadrons affiliated with active units of Military Airlift Command.

[Wesley F. Craven and James L. Cate, eds., *The Army Air Forces in World War II;* Robert Frank Futrell, *The United States Air Force in Korea;* Alfred Goldberg, ed., *A History of the United States Air Force, 1907–1957;* John H. Scrivner, Jr., *A Quarter Century of Air Power;* U. S. G. Sharp and William Westmoreland, *Report on the War in Vietnam;* U.S. Department of Defense, *Annual Reports* (1948–68).]

RAY L. BOWERS

AIR FORCE ACADEMY, UNITED STATES. President Dwight D. Eisenhower signed legislation creating the U.S. Air Force Academy on Apr. 1, 1954, fulfilling recommendations that had been made by air-minded leaders since World War I. The academy was conceived as a four-year undergraduate institution, leading to the B.S. degree and a regular air force commission. The first class entered in summer, 1955, using facilities at Denver, Colo., prior to occupation of the permanent site at Colorado Springs three years later. The group, numbering 207, graduated on June 3, 1959. The full authorized enrollment of 2,500 was reached in 1962, and in 1964 legislation set the authorizations for the Military and Air Force academies at 4,417, the same as the Naval Academy's. Each congressman was authorized five appointments to each academy at any one time, and could nominate several individuals to compete for each vacancy. The 1964 legislation also increased the period of obligatory service after graduation from three to five years, beginning with the class of 1968.

From its start, the Air Force Academy departed from service academy tradition by providing advanced and accelerated studies beyond the prescribed curriculum. In 1964, the academy instituted a system of specialized majors programs, whereby every cadet elected a substantial part of his course work in one of several dozen areas. The academy has retained an all-military faculty, subsidizing graduate work for line officers at civilian institutions prior to faculty tours of about four years. A severe cheating incident in 1965 received national attention and resulted in over 100 cadets leaving the academy. Reassessment of the academy's academic, athletic, and military systems left the traditional honor code unchanged, although certain rigidities in cadet life were reduced.

Over two-thirds of all graduates (including 85 percent of those physically qualified) have entered pilot training. An optional 36-hour flying program in light aircraft was instituted for upperclassmen in 1968, and cadets could participate in glider and parachute activities. The academy has vigorously recruited minority youths, and in 1973 reached accommodation to the end of compulsory chapel attendance. Graduates received numerous decorations in Southeast Asia, where ninety lost their lives. Academy graduates through 1973 number 6,942, including sixteen Rhodes scholars.

RAY L. BOWERS

AIRMAIL. The first test of airmail service was made in May 1918, when the U.S. Army and the Post Office Department together set up an experimental line between New York and Washington, D.C., using army pilots. After three months, the Post Office assumed entire control of the line, and employed civilian aviators. This route was too short to give the plane much advantage over the railway and did not continue long. Other disconnected lines were tried, between New York and Cleveland, Cleveland and Chicago, Chicago and Omaha, but all had the same fault—they were too short to attract mail at high rates. In 1920 the Post Office installed a service between New York and San Francisco, whereon the planes flew only by daylight, the mail being transferred at dusk to railway trains and rushed on, to take to the air again early next morning. This was replaced on July 1, 1924, by a continuous, day-and-night service across the continent. In 1926–27 the department turned over the handling of airmail to private corporations as contractors. Branch lines and north-and-south lines were rapidly added. In 1930 when two new routes—New

York to Los Angeles via St. Louis and Los Angeles to Atlanta—were designated, there were only two bids for the former contract and one for the latter. Charging that there had been collusion among airline owners in the bidding, Postmaster General James A. Farley on Feb. 9, 1934, canceled all airmail contracts, and for four months army planes carried the mail, while an official investigation was conducted. There were several fatal accidents to army fliers. New contracts were signed in June, and the service, which by this time covered the United States pretty thoroughly and connected with lines to Canada, the West Indies, Mexico, and Central and South America, was returned to private planes.

In 1935 regular mail service was established across the Pacific between San Francisco and Manila, and in 1939 transatlantic service between New York and London.

[Paul T. David, *The Economics of Air Mail Transportation;* Alvin F. Harlow, *Old Post Bags.*]

ALVIN F. HARLOW

AIR NAVIGATION AGREEMENTS. *See* **Aviation.**

AIRPLANE. *See* **Aviation.**

AIRPLANE DISASTERS. *See* **Aviation.**

AIRPLANE RACES. *See* **Aviation.**

AIRPORTS. *See* **Air Transportation.**

AIR POWER, STRATEGIC. The concept of strategic air power involves the employment of aerial weapons to bypass the surface battlefield and strike at the key industries that permit a country to carry on its war effort. Typical target systems for strategic bombardment are the transportation network, including railroads, bridges, marshaling yards, and harbors; the petroleum industry, including refineries and tank farms; the electrical generating system; and the aerospace industry. Intensive strategic bombardment campaigns, such as those conducted against Germany and Japan in World War II, embrace many target systems and can be compared to a traditional siege, in which all elements of a nation's economy and military strength—including its means of sustenance and its civilian labor force—come under attack.

Because the industrial strength of a nation lies principally in its cities, cities themselves are targets in an all-out strategic bombardment campaign. Heavy air attacks such as those in World War II against London, Hamburg, and Tokyo caused much criticism because of the vast firestorms generated and the great loss of life among civilians. Opponents of the strategic air power concept claimed that the will to resist was strengthened in those subjected to bombardment and that the raids were inconclusive militarily. Proponents argued that by shortening the war or obviating a land invasion, lives were saved on both sides. Moreover, it was claimed, in a total war the whole population is involved in supporting the war effort.

Strategic bombardment was first attempted by Germany in World War I with zeppelin and Gotha raids on London, although the aerial vehicles were too limited to do much more than terrify the population. However, the British people visualized the future development of air power and in 1917 established an air force independent of the army and navy, with a section under Gen. Hugh Trenchard charged with bombing industrial and rail targets far behind the enemy lines.

Seeking answers to the riddle of the stabilized western front in France that had taken such a heavy toll of lives, the then Maj. William (Billy) Mitchell, an aviator with the advance echelon of the U.S. Army, visited Trenchard and became an exponent of the new doctrine. But American air power was slow in coming and did not achieve a bombing capability of significance before the war was over.

Even though Mitchell continued to write and lecture after World War I about the need for strategic air power, the concept all but vanished. American military aviation was confined to an observation role for surface forces. In the 1930's a small group of Billy Mitchell disciples were researching the concept of strategic air power at the Air Corps Tactical School, Maxwell Field, Ala. These airmen discovered a prophetic book, *Command of the Air,* written in 1921 by an Italian artillery officer, Giulio Douhet. The school made a translation and this theoretical work was argued and refined by the officers who were to become the American air leaders of World War II.

The early years of World War II provided some rude shocks to traditionalists who had disparaged the role of air power in war. The Battle of Britain demonstrated the possibility of losing a war through air action alone. In the Pacific, the Japanese air attack on

Pearl Harbor of Dec. 7, 1941, sank or immobilized most of America's Pacific fleet. A few hours later in the western Pacific, Japanese bombers sank the new British battleship *Prince of Wales* and the battle cruiser *Repulse*. The age of the battleship ended, giving place to air power.

The German air attack on England in 1940 was a strategic offensive to defeat the Royal Air Force and pave the way for a cross-channel invasion. Fortunately for the British, Germany had no strategic bombers, its aircraft all having been designed to support armies. This, combined with the heroic defense put up by the RAF Fighter Command, assured a defeat for the Luftwaffe.

Later, the British were unable to bring any force to bear against the Axis powers on the Continent except through strategic bombardment. At first this effort was considered a diversion to draw defensive fighters from Russia and the Middle East, but as the RAF Bomber Command grew in size, its raids began to cripple the German economy. To minimize its losses the RAF turned exclusively to night operations, with a consequent degradation of bombing accuracy. Thus "area" bombing against cities to destroy civilian morale became the modus operandi of the RAF.

By the time the United States entered the war in 1941, the concept of strategic air power had found its way into war plans. A requirement for 63,467 aircraft was set and the B-17 Flying Fortress strategic bomber was put into mass production. It was believed that this heavily armed aircraft could survive in daylight raids and bomb accurately.

In January 1943, President Franklin D. Roosevelt met with Prime Minister Winston Churchill at Casablanca and agreed to the Combined Bomber Offensive against Germany. The U.S. Eighth Air Force would strike Germany in daylight and the RAF Bomber Command would strike at night, allowing Germany no respite. Although the tempo of the strategic air offensive increased during the year and a half before the Normandy invasion, Germany grimly held out—but by the end of the war the economy was in complete collapse. To determine whether this economic collapse had been caused by air power or by armies, President Roosevelt appointed the Strategic Bombing Survey Board. After extensive studies the board reported: "Allied air power was decisive in the war in Western Europe. By the beginning of 1945, before the invasion of the homeland itself, Germany was reaching a state of helplessness. . . . Germany was mortally wounded." The Strategic Bombing Survey reported failures in achieving objectives against a number of target systems; however, the bombing of the petroleum industry and the transportation system was eminently successful in bringing Germany's economy to a standstill. With the lessons learned in Europe and the advent of a still larger strategic bomber, the B-29, the results of strategic air power were more conclusive in the war in the Pacific. Even before the first atomic bombs were dropped the Japanese were seeking channels for surrender. Although an invasion of Japan had been planned, none was necessary.

With the advent of nuclear weapons and the development of rocket missiles, there seemed little doubt that total wars of the future would be won by air power alone. While rocketry was being developed, the United States organized the Strategic Air Command (SAC) with aircraft of intercontinental capabilities. Gen. Curtis E. LeMay is credited with creating the global nuclear force of SAC. By 1973 SAC was composed primarily of B-52 jet bombers and Minuteman intercontinental ballistic missiles (ICBM's). Although Russia forged ahead of the United States in numbers of ICBM's and warhead yield, the United States still held a slight lead in missile-launching submarines. (*See also* Air Defense.)

[Bonner Fellers, *Wings for Peace;* R. H. Fredette, *The Sky on Fire;* Sir Arthur Harris, *Bomber Offensive;* Curtis E. LeMay, *America Is in Danger;* Dale O. Smith, *U.S. Military Doctrine*.]

DALE O. SMITH

AIR TRANSPORTATION developed slowly after the first controlled flight in 1903. Commercial passenger service was launched Jan. 1, 1914, between Saint Petersburg and Tampa, on a seasonal basis, but World War I halted development of commercial air transportation. During 1919–23, Aeromarine Airways made the only impressive record among commercial air companies, carrying mail and passengers between Miami and the Bahama Islands and between Key West and Havana during the winter, and passengers between New York and Cleveland during the summer. No aircraft at that time was reliable for year-round commercial service; airports were almost nonexistent; airways consisted of visual flying; and investors were unwilling to underwrite the necessarily expensive development.

Beginning May 15, 1918, the federal government provided airmail service, and for the first three months army pilots were used. In August the U.S. Post Office took over the service until Aug. 31, 1927. A coast-to-coast route was opened on Sept. 8, 1920, and the first night mail began July 1, 1924. Both beacon lights and radio beacons were used in navigation. The Kelly Air Mail Act of 1925 quickly stimulated the rise of commercial airlines; twenty small, privately owned companies contracted to carry the mail, the payment including an unspecified amount of subsidy. Only two carriers showed much interest in transporting passengers.

Nevertheless, the public became enthusiastic about the potential of aviation following Charles A. Lindbergh's 1927 solo flight from New York to Paris. Within two years Pan American World Airways and the "big four" domestic air transportation companies were formed: United Airlines, Eastern Airlines, Transcontinental Air Transport (later Trans World Airlines), and American Airlines. In an effort to develop a few strong rival companies instead of the forty-four small contractors carrying the mail, Postmaster General Walter Folger Brown, in effect, tried to operate as a one-man public utility commission. Many of his ideas were incorporated in the Air Mail Act of 1930, which enabled Brown to exchange certain contracts for ten-year certificates and to eliminate practically all competitive bidding. In 1934 these contracts were cancelled; after an interim during which the Air Corps flew the mail, new contracts were issued and the Interstate Commerce Commission was authorized to determine the mail pay, including a subsidy.

The expansion of air passenger traffic, the reliability of the DC-3 and other aircraft, and discontent with the Post Office contracts led to the Civil Aeronautics Act of 1938. The sixteen domestic airlines, with their 38,500 miles of routes, and Pan American were placed under the economic regulation of the Civil Aeronautics Authority, soon renamed the Civil Aeronautics Board (CAB).

With the country's entry into World War II, all air carriers placed much of their equipment and personnel on military assignments. Fortunately, because the Instrument Landing System had finally been perfected by the government in 1940, it was possible to complete a greater percentage of civilian and military flights. Although the war retarded technological advancement in commercial aircraft, the volume of passenger and mail traffic increased rapidly. Thereupon, the CAB reduced the mail pay rate, which, at least for the big four, became a nonsubsidized payment.

During the war there was much enthusiasm about the coming air age. Feeder lines were authorized by the CAB, first as an experiment to supplement the trunk lines, then by 1947 as the components of a national network constituting a second level of scheduled services. These feeder lines were aided by such subsidy payments as were needed. The first twenty feeder lines have been combined or replaced over the years, until by 1974 there were nine identified as local service airlines; all had increased financial strength and two were no longer subsidized. In the early 1940's all trunk lines except United worked for the elimination of the "chosen instrument" policy, whereby Pan American and its half-owned subsidiary, Panagra, were the only significant American-flag carriers outside the United States. When the war ended, both Pan American and Trans World Airlines (TWA) were authorized to expand as round-the-world carriers; Northwest Orient Airlines obtained a route across the northern Pacific; American Airlines into the southern Pacific; and Braniff Airways into South America. Beginning in 1946 several domestic carriers were permitted to operate scheduled flights into the Caribbean. The Chicago and Southern Air Lines, which has since merged with Delta Airlines, obtained the longest routes. In 1974, Pan American, Eastern, American, and Delta were the American-flag carriers in that area.

During 1945–46, about 3,000 small nonscheduled carriers were formed, usually using inexpensive war surplus aircraft. The CAB authorized 142 to be large irregular carriers. Since 1959 this group has been relabeled supplemental air carriers, and the number has dwindled to eight. Besides offering irregular domestic service they may engage in irregular service to specified foreign areas. Some of the early nonscheduled companies became all-cargo carriers. That number decreased to three, which in 1974 were sound and doing well. Air taxis have developed since 1962 as the third level of scheduled air carriers. Within seven years there were some 3,500 such operators; by mid-1973 the number had declined to less than 2,000, which included 124 commuter air carriers transporting passengers on an individually ticketed basis.

All of the American air transportation companies grossed an aggregate revenue exceeding $13.5 billion for the twelve months ending March 1974, of which more than $10 billion was received for traffic within the fifty states and border traffic adjacent to the states. Their routes have been modified, with many new nonstop schedules and more one-carrier service, thus increasing competition. Additional competition has resulted from the rapid introduction of three generations of jet aircraft; the turboprops of the mid-1950's; the turbojets, such as the Boeing 707 and the Douglas DC-8 of the late 1950's; and, beginning in 1970, the widebodied aircraft (Boeing 747, DC-10, Lockheed 1011). In 1973, commercial supersonic jet flights were banned over the United States and its territorial waters because of noise and sonic boom. A current problem is that the seat capacity of planes has exceeded the demand, with the result that in 1971–72 temporary agreements were permitted among American, TWA, United, Eastern, and Pan American to limit the number of flights. These were replaced by a similar agreement in 1973 designed to lessen both financial difficulties and fuel consumption. Meanwhile, passenger rates decreased relative to most other consumer prices. It was estimated in 1973 that 23 percent of adults were using scheduled airlines each year with an average of 5.5 flights each.

Air cargo has become an increasing proportion of the airline business. During the twelve months ending June 1974, air cargo constituted 20 percent of the payload by weight on the domestic trunk lines, 9 percent on the local service carriers, and 32 percent on the international trunk lines. The rapid expansion of both passenger and freight traffic led airline management to begin its big swing to widebodied aircraft, which disrupted the patterns of flight frequencies and the balances between the larger capacity of the new planes and the limitations of the market. The consequent decrease of net revenues was sufficient in 1972 to cause managements to ground various aircraft, including some widebodies, and offer them for sale. The fuel crisis during the winter of 1973–74 brought deficits and accelerated the trend of grounding planes. Another cost-cutting effort in 1974 was the exchange of routes between carriers, with CAB permission, and proposals for more route revisions to reduce expensive competition. Especially significant by late 1974 was the willingness of airline managements for the first time to tell their stockholders that they had overexpanded and must now retrench.

On Dec. 31, 1958, all aspects of federal regulation of aviation were gathered under the Federal Aviation Agency (Federal Aviation Administration since 1966), except that the CAB has retained authority over its basic transport regulations and over determination of probable causes of aircraft accidents. Air safety always has commanded major attention and the carriers and aircraft manufacturers have logged a remarkable safety record. This is due in part to the increase in sophistication of the airspace system since the development of radar in the early 1940's. The number of flights under instrument flight rules and the use of advanced types of communications, navigation, and radar facilities have increased greatly.

Revenue Passenger-Miles

(in billions)

Year	In 48 States: Railroad Commutation	In 48 States: Railroad Intercity	In 48 States: Commercial Air Transport	All Other Commercial Air Transport by U.S.-Owned Carriers
1925	6.6	29.4	[a]	none
1930	6.7	20.2	0.07	0.01
1935	4.1	14.4	0.3	0.05
1940	4.0	19.8	1.2	0.1
1945	5.4	86.3	3.4	0.5
1950	5.0	26.8	8.4	2.2
1955	4.8	23.7	21.0	5.2
1960	4.2	17.1	31.2	10.4
1965	4.1	13.3	53.2	22.0
1970	4.6	6.2	108.6	49.0
1974 [b]	4.5	5.6	125.0	55.2

[a] Los Angeles-San Diego air passenger service beginning March 1925.

[b] Year-ending date is June 30.

Source: Association of American Railroads, Civil Aeronautics Board, *Aviation Daily*.

Many of the new airports constructed near the major cities under the Federal Airport Act of 1946 are becoming inadequate. Consequently, a few mammoth regional airports are now planned or under construction. The first one, between Dallas and Fort Worth, is already completed. Construction on the new Miami airport was stopped in the summer of 1974 because of disagreements on ecological effects on the Everglades National Park. Federal funds available under the airport development aid program for fiscal year 1975 were $310 million, an amount considered inadequate by many local airport authorities. State expenditures for airports were nearly one-half that amount. By July 1974 there were 12,676 airports in the United States, of which 452 were used for scheduled airline service, and 386 of the latter had FAA control towers.

[R. E. G. Davies, *Airlines of the United States Since 1914;* William A. Jordan, *Airline Regulation in America: Effects and Imperfections;* Charles J. Kelly, Jr., *The Sky's the Limit: The History of the Airlines.*]

CHARLES JOHNSTON KENNEDY

AISNE DEFENSIVE (May 27–June 5, 1918), a sequel to the operations on the Somme in March, the Germans making a new attack southward between Soissons and Reims with the intention of drawing French reserves south so that they could renew their attacks in the north. The attack was successful even beyond their hopes, and reached the Marne near Château-Thierry, only forty miles from Paris. The Germans then attempted to establish a bridgehead on the Marne, and also to push westward toward Paris; both efforts were unsuccessful. Two American divisions took part in the defense: the Third, opposing the crossing of the Marne; and the Second, being very heavily engaged at Belleau Wood and at Vaux, west of Château-Thierry.

[Oliver L. Spaulding, *The United States Army in War and Peace.*]

OLIVER LYMAN SPAULDING

AISNE-MARNE OPERATION (July 18–Aug. 6, 1918), the Franco-American counteroffensive following the German offensive of July 15 in the Marne salient (*see* Aisne Defensive). The French Tenth Army (under Gen. Mangin) opened the attack, striking eastward into the salient just south of Soissons. The main attack was made by the XX Corps, with three divisions in front line, two American and one Moroccan. The Germans were taken by surprise, and their outpost line made little resistance, but the line soon stiffened and the fighting was severe. It was not until July 21 that control of the Soissons–Château-Thierry highway was gained. The total penetration was eight miles.

From July 21 on, the armies farther east joined in the advance—the Sixth (Degoutte) and the Fifth (Berthelot), along both faces of the salient. With the Sixth Army there were two American corps headquarters—the I (Liggett) and the III (Dickman)—and eight American divisions. The Germans conducted their retreat skillfully, making an especially strong stand on the Ourcq on July 28. But early in August they were back behind the Vesle.

The operations since July 15 had changed the whole aspect of the war. A German offensive had been stopped suddenly in mid-career, and the advance changed to a retreat. The Marne salient had ceased to exist, and the Germans were never again able to undertake a serious offensive.

[John J. Pershing, *Final Report as Commander-in-Chief, A.E.F.;* Oliver L. Spaulding, *The United States Army in War and Peace.*]

OLIVER LYMAN SPAULDING

AIX-LA-CHAPELLE, TREATY OF (Oct. 18, 1748), ended the War of the Austrian Succession (*see* King George's War). The term chiefly concerning American history was the restoration of Louisburg to France, which irritated the New Englanders who had been active in the capture. The peace was merely an intermission in the protracted struggle for control of the Saint Lawrence and Mississippi basins. Its final phase, the French and Indian War, began in 1754.

[Adolphus Ward and G. P. William, eds., *Cambridge History of British Foreign Policy,* vol. IX.]

EDMUND K. ALDEN

AKRON. *See* **Dirigibles.**

AKRON LAW (Feb. 8, 1847). As a result of a movement for a better public school system in Akron, Ohio, the Ohio General Assembly passed a special law for the city, which provided for an elected board of education of six members, the organization of the city as a single school district, free admission of all children to the public schools, the adoption of a system for the classification of pupils and their promotion by examinations, and local taxation for financing the schools. The law was broadened in 1848 to apply to any incorporated town, if the voters by a two-thirds vote chose to adopt the plan. In 1849 a general law, modeled on the Akron Law, reduced this requirement to a majority vote, required that schools be kept in operation not less than thirty-six nor more than forty-four weeks per year, and limited the amount of taxes to be raised for school purposes in any one year. In 1850 townships and special districts were permitted to make use of this system. Thus the Akron Law, with some modifications, came to be applied generally throughout the state.

[Edward A. Miller, "The History of Educational Legislation in Ohio Before 1850," *Ohio Archaeological and Historical Quarterly,* vol. 27 (1918).]

EUGENE H. ROSEBOOM

ALABAMA. The first white men to reach the region that became Alabama were the Spanish explorers Alonzo Alvares de Piñeda (1519) and Pánfilo de Narváez (1528). In the 1540's Hernando de Soto crossed through the region and won a Pyrrhic victory over the Indians at Mabila. The first permanent settlement was established by the French under Jean Baptiste Le Moyne, Sieur de Bienville, in 1702 at Mobile Bay, which was then considered a part of Louisiana. In 1763 France ceded the territory to Great Britain, and in 1783 the southern portion was ceded to Spain and the remainder to the United States. Mobile, the seat of Spanish power, was taken by the United States in 1813. In 1817 the Alabama Territory was organized out of the Mississippi Territory, of which it had been a part since 1798, and was admitted to the Union on Dec. 14, 1819, as the ninth state in order after the original thirteen.

Alabama was settled principally by farmers, planters, and professional men, who came mostly from Georgia and the Carolinas. The warm climate, rich land, and abundant rainfall made it especially well suited for general farming and particularly for the cultivation of cotton. As a result, the economic and social life of Alabama prior to 1860 was centered on agriculture, and, as in other states of the South, cotton farming and the plantation system prevailed.

The predominance of agriculture expressed itself in the politics of the period before 1860. Although the Democratic and Whig parties were both ably led and campaigns were vigorously fought, the Democrats were dominant, with a basically Jeffersonian and proslavery philosophy. Andrew Jackson was the political idol of the masses, but many Alabamians supported Henry Clay and John C. Calhoun. In the decades prior to 1860 states' rights sentiment grew rapidly, and defense of southern rights became a dominant issue under the fiery leadership of William L. Yancey. By 1860 the supporters of sectional reconciliation, who had been led by Henry W. Hilliard, were unable to stem the tide, and Alabama and its neighboring states were ready to secede from the Union. On Jan. 11, 1861, Alabama threw in its lot with the Confederate states.

The Confederate government was organized at Montgomery (Feb. 4, 1861), which became its first capital and has since been called the "Cradle of the Confederacy." In the war that followed, soldiers and civilians of the state distinguished themselves in battle and high posts of the Confederacy, both military and civil. Estimates of property losses during the Civil War run as high as $500 million; losses among the white male population, which was heavily enrolled in the Confederate army, were one in ten. After the Civil War the state attempted to reenter the Union under President Andrew Johnson's plan of reconstruction, but the provisional government which had been functioning under its new constitution drafted in September 1865 was repudiated by the newly elected Radical Republicans in the U.S. Congress. The congressional plan of reconstruction brought the state under federal military control on Mar. 2, 1867. A new constitution was drafted in November 1867, and the state was readmitted to the Union in June 1868. The decade following the Civil War saw Alabama torn by party dissension and its government characterized by extravagance and dishonesty in official circles. The 1870's heralded the end of the Reconstruction era, and the return of economic and political stability marked the beginning of the state's postwar growth and prosperity.

From 1876 through 1944 Alabama was controlled politically by the Democratic party, and the state has been a stronghold of the party in both state and national politics. In 1948 the state joined other southern states in leaving the Democratic national convention, an abandonment of party owing to the stand on civil rights taken by the national Democratic party and by Harry S. Truman, the presidential nominee, who staunchly supported the national party position. Later at a convention in Birmingham the southern states organized the States' Rights Democratic party, rejecting Truman and giving their votes to their own nominees, J. Strom Thurmond and Fielding Lewis Wright. The state political leaders prevented the electors of the national Democratic party from appearing on the Alabama ballot. In 1952 the state returned to the Democratic party to remain until 1968. In that year the state supported the American Independent party, organized and led by George C. Wallace, who had been in secure political control of the state since his election to the governorship in 1962. The state was again projected into the national political arena in 1972, when Wallace attempted to capture the presidential nomination of the national Democratic party. The traditionally Democratic structure of the state is now broken; several congressmen hold seats as Republicans.

Disturbances in Alabama's traditional allegiance to the Democratic party in the 20th century reflect, in large measure, controversy over civil rights issues, starting in the 1940's and reaching a climax in the 1950's and 1960's. In 1956 the state was a focus of national attention as Afro-American residents of Birmingham, under the leadership of Martin Luther King, carried through a successful boycott of local buses, prompted by discriminatory practices. In 1961 a confrontation of busloads of representatives of the Congress of Racial Equality and local mobs necessitated the imposition of martial law. In 1963, after years of conspicuous resistance to the racial integration of schools, Alabama was forced by federal court order to grant admission to Afro-Americans at the University of Alabama and various public schools in Birmingham, Mobile, and Tuskegee. In 1965 Alabama again became a center of national attention, by the Selma-to-Montgomery march of some 25,000 civil rights proponents from all over the nation, again under the leadership of Martin Luther King.

International, as well as national, attention has been focused on Alabama as a space-age center: Explorer 1—the first U.S. satellite to be set in orbit, Jan. 31, 1958—was developed at Huntsville; and the George C. Marshall Space Flight Center was established at Huntsville in 1960.

Cotton has remained the chief money crop of Alabama, which ranked sixth among the states in cotton production in 1970, but since World War II less and less land and manpower have been devoted to cotton farming. More farmland has been turned over to the raising of livestock, especially chickens—in which enterprise Alabama was the fifth-ranking state in 1971. Two-thirds of the state's land area has come to be devoted to timber, leading to the development of related industries, such as paper, pulp, and paperboard. Iron and steel manufacture, begun in the late 19th century, have expanded rapidly, especially in Birmingham, but more than 50 percent of the state's mineral production is constituted of bituminous coal. Thus, Mobile, a major cotton port before the Civil War, has regained a prominent rank among American ports—but principally in the handling of coal.

The Afro-American population of Alabama has continued to decline since 1900, from 50 percent in 1900 to 30 percent in 1970. Alabama has, however, followed the national trend toward urbanization: in 1900, the state had an urban population of only 12 percent; in 1950, 40 percent; and in 1970, 58 percent. The overall population has increased since 1920 from less than 2.5 million to nearly 3.5 million.

[Thomas P. Abernathy, *The Formative Period in Alabama;* Walter L. Fleming, *Civil War and Reconstruction in Alabama;* Malcolm C. McMillan, *Constitutional Development in Alabama, 1798–1901;* Albert B. Moore, *History of Alabama;* Thomas M. Owen, *History of Alabama and Dictionary of Alabama Biography;* Albert J. Pickett, *History of Alabama.*]

GORDON T. CHAPPELL

ALABAMA. In June 1861, Capt. J. D. Bulloch reached England as Confederate agent to contract with private builders for warships. He first obtained the *Florida,* and on May 15, 1862, a second and more powerful ship, the *Alabama,* was launched at Liverpool. The U.S. minister, C. F. Adams, who had previously demanded the detention of the *Florida,* now presented, on June 23, what he thought full evidence of the illegal character of the *Alabama;* but the British authorities were exceedingly slow, and the sudden insanity of a law officer of the crown caused a five-day delay. Finally orders were telegraphed to hold the vessel, but it had already sailed under pretense of a trial trip. Earl Russell and other cabinet members felt a sincere desire to keep it from leaving, and deeply regretted the evasion. Guns, munitions, and coal were put aboard ship at the Azores, and it became the terror of American vessels. Under Capt. Raphael Semmes, before its destruction in June 1864 in the English channel (*see Kearsarge-Alabama* Fight), it sank, burned, or captured more than sixty ships.

[Ephraim D. Adams, *Great Britain and the American Civil War;* Allan Nevins, *Hamilton Fish.*]

ALLAN NEVINS

ALABAMA CLAIMS. American grievances against Great Britain during and just after the Civil War all clustered about this generic phrase; but they filled a broad category. The queen's proclamation of neutrality, giving the South belligerent rights, was regarded by Secretary of State William H. Seward and most northerners as hasty and unfriendly. The Confederate cruisers, built or armed by Britons, not only destroyed northern shipping, but did indirect damage by driving insurance rates high and forcing many northern ships under foreign flags. The Confederates raised large sums of money in Great Britain and outfitted blockade runners there.

Early in the war Seward instructed Minister C. F. Adams to lay before the British government, with a demand for redress, the losses caused by the *Alabama.* As a result the British authorities showed greater care. In April 1863 they halted the *Alexandra* when Adams proved it was intended for the Confederacy; in September, British Secretary Lord John Russell issued orders to detain the two armored rams which John Laird and Sons was building. Only one other ship, the *Shenandoah,* clearly violated the British neutrality laws and only after refitting at Melbourne. Ultimately, the United States entered claims against Great Britain for damage wrought by eleven vessels, totaling $19,021,000. Of these the damage done by the *Alabama* was estimated at $6,547,609; that by the *Shenandoah* at $6,488,320; and that by the *Florida* at $3,698,609.

The claims were repeated from time to time but met no response until 1868. The Johnson-Clarendon Convention, signed that year under Seward's close supervision, made no mention of the *Alabama* damages but provided for a settlement of all Anglo-American claims since 1853. Partly because of the unpopularity of the Andrew Johnson administration, the convention was overwhelmingly defeated by the Senate (Apr. 13, 1869). Sen. Charles Sumner seized the opportunity to make a speech reviewing the whole case against Great Britain. He declared that the *Alabama* and other cruisers had not only done heavy damage, direct and indirect, but with the queen's proclamation and other moral and material support given by England to the South had doubled the duration of the war. His object in thus implying that the total U.S. bill reached $2,125,000,000 was to lay a basis for demands which could be met only by the cession of Canada. Fortunately Hamilton Fish, becoming secretary of state in March 1869, took a saner position. Playing for time, he soon adopted the view that the whole set of Alabama Claims could be met by the payment of a moderate lump sum, an apology, and a definition of maritime international law meeting U.S. wishes. When he mildly urged Canadian independence, the British government refused to admit that the two questions could be connected. The impasse between the two nations was brief. Great Britain advanced to a more conciliatory position when Lord Granville succeeded the Earl of Clarendon as foreign minister, and when the Franco-Prussian War and Russia's denunciation of its Black Sea pledges threatened European complications. Washington became more amenable when Canada showed distinct hostility to the United States, when the Santo Domingo controversy destroyed Sumner's influence over President Ulysses S. Grant and when financial interests pressed for a settlement. With Sir John Rose, a Canadian prominent in London, acting as intermediary, Fish and Granville decided that a joint commission should settle the whole nexus of disputes—Canadian fisheries, northwestern boundary, and Alabama Claims. The commission, meeting under Fish and Earl DeGrey, drew up the Treaty of Washington (signed May 8, 1871), which expressed British regret for the escape of the *Alabama* and other cruisers, laid down three rules of maritime neutrality, and provided for submission of the Alabama Claims to a board of five arbitrators, American, British, Italian, Swiss, and Brazilian. This tribunal decided, Sept. 14, 1872, that Great Britain had failed in its duties as a neutral and awarded the United States $15,500,000 in gold to meet its direct damages, all indirect claims having been excluded. American opinion accepted the award as adequate.

[S. F. Bemis, ed., *American Secretaries of State;* Caleb Cushing, *The Treaty of Washington;* Bancroft Davis, *Mr. Fish and the Alabama Claims;* John Bassett Moore, *International Arbitrations;* Allan Nevins, *Hamilton Fish.*]

ALLAN NEVINS

ALABAMA PLATFORM, adopted by the Democratic state convention in 1848 and approved by other southern groups, was W. L. Yancey's answer to the Wilmot Proviso and squatter sovereignty principles. It demanded congressional protection of slavery in the Mexican cession. Rejected by the Democrats in 1848, the principle was adopted by a majority of the Democratic Convention at Charleston in 1860. With the disruption of that convention, it became a basic issue of the southern secessionists.

[C. P. Denman, *The Secession Movement in Alabama.*]

WENDELL H. STEPHENSON

ALAMANCE, BATTLE OF (May 16, 1771). To punish and suppress the Regulators of North Carolina, Gov. William Tryon ordered Gen. Hugh Waddell to Hillsboro with a force of about 1,000 militia.

Two thousand Regulators had assembled on the Alamance River, about one-half without arms and with no officer higher than captain. The provincial army had artillery and was adequately equipped. The battle lasted two hours and ended in disaster to the Regulators. The provincials lost nine killed and sixty-one wounded, while the Regulators had about twenty killed and a greater number wounded. As a result of their defeat, many of the Regulators migrated to the trans-Allegheny region, to Tennessee in particular.

[E. W. Caruthers, *Life of Rev. David Caldwell.*]

SAMUEL C. WILLIAMS

ALAMO, SIEGE OF THE (Feb. 23–Mar. 6, 1836). When the revolting province of Texas swept its soil clear of weak Mexican garrisons in 1835 the commander-in-chief, Sam Houston, ordered a concentration on the theory that the Mexicans would return (*see* Texas Revolution). He recommended the destruction and abandonment of the fortifications at San Antonio. For this cautious counsel Houston was deposed from command. A twenty-seven-year-old lawyer, Lt. Col. William Barret Travis, found himself in joint command, with James Bowie, of about 145 men at San Antonio when on Feb. 23 Antonio López de Santa Anna appeared with between 3,000 and 4,000 men.

Travis and Bowie could have retreated safely. Instead they moved into the stout-walled Alamo mission, answered a demand for surrender with a cannon shot, and sent couriers for reinforcements. A message signed by Travis read: "I have sustained a continual Bombardment and a cannonade for 24 hours and have not lost a man. . . . Our flag still proudly waves from the wall. I shall never surrender or retreat. . . . VICTORY OR DEATH." On the eighth day of battle thirty-two recruits crept through the Mexican lines, the last reinforcements the garrison was to receive. This brought their number to about 187. Though suffering from want of sleep, and with ammunition running low, the Texans had lost the services of only one man, Bowie, ill and disabled by a fall.

At four in the morning of Mar. 6, the thirteenth day of battle, Santa Anna stormed the Alamo on all sides. The first and second assaults were broken up. At dawn the Mexicans attacked again. The Texans' guns were hot from heavy firing in the two assaults, their ammunition nearly out, and, though casualties had not been numerous, men were dropping from exhaustion. The walls were breached. The defenders fought throughout the mission compound, clubbing rifles and drawing knives. The last point taken was the church. There fell David Crockett and twelve volunteers who had followed him from Tennessee. By eight o'clock the last of the 187 defenders was dead, though the Mexicans spared about thirty noncombatants. Mexican losses were about 1,500 killed.

The fall of the Alamo sowed panic through Texas, precipitating a flight of the civilian population and of the government toward U.S. soil. Inwardly raging against Travis' disastrous stand, Houston gathered an army. Six weeks later, marching to meet Santa Anna, Houston paraded his men and in an impassioned address abjured them to "Remember the Alamo!" With that cry they vanquished the Mexicans at San Jacinto, establishing the independence of the Texas Republic.

[Marquis James, *The Raven.*]

MARQUIS JAMES

ALASKA, the northwestern extension of the North American continent, 586,000 square miles in extent, acquired by purchase from Russia in 1867, became the forty-ninth state of the Union in 1958. It was the last important area on earth to be "discovered." As late as the beginning of the 18th century the circumpolar regions and the North Pacific had not been charted. On all maps of that day the west coast of North America vanished just north of Cape Mendocino in the northern part of California. It was not known whether the continental masses of Asia and North America converged or were separated by a narrow body of salt water, with perhaps an island lying between them. It was this unanswered question that motivated Peter the Great and, after his death in 1725, his widow, Empress Catherine I, to send exploratory expeditions under naval captain Vitus Bering, leading to discoveries that completed the outlines of the habitable world and to the exploration of Alaska itself in 1741.

In long past millennia of prehistory it was across the Bering Sea and over the stepping-stones of the Aleutian Islands that the course by which Asians migrated to the Americas probably lay. These Asians became the indigenous "Indians" that Columbus found. In the 18th century they were followed by Russians lured by the potentially abundant harvest of furs. And so Russian America came to be.

That the newly discovered terrain was part of North America was established by Georg Wilhelm Steller, the Bering expedition's German-born scientist, who, while briefly ashore on Kayak Island, recognized the similarity between a crested blue jay and a colored picture of one in the recently published *Natural History of the Carolinas and Florida,* which had reached Saint Petersburg's scientific circles before the expedition's departure.

The Russian rule lasted 126 years. Its legacy now consists only in a substantial number of place names, a few sparsely attended Russian Orthodox churches, and a steadily attenuating stream of Slavic blood, found chiefly among the Aleut—the Eskimoid people inhabiting the Alaska Peninsula and its fractured continuation, the Aleutian Islands.

The real significance of the Russian occupation was that it made possible the negotiated acquisition of Alaska by the United States a century and a quarter later; but for Russia's hegemony, Alaska would have become a province of Canada. The secret instruction the British Admiralty had given Capt. James Cook regarding his 1774 expedition in quest of the Northwest Passage was to take possession of countries sparsely inhabited for the British crown, even if previously visited and discovered by another European power. But the Russians had already established the Russian-American Company in Alaska and under the management of Aleksandr Baranov had extended the czar's dominions far eastward. On an island that would bear his name in the Alexander Archipelago—as the islands of southeastern Alaska, the Panhandle, were named—Baranov had founded a settlement, including a military and trading post named New Archangel, later named Sitka, which became the capital of Russian America. In 1804, after Sitka's inhabitants had been massacred by Tlingit Indians (1802), the Indians were no less bloodily put down with the assistance of a Russian naval vessel.

While a rival British concessionaire, the Hudson's Bay Company, was advancing westward with the similar objective of exploiting the region's resources, clashes between the two companies were averted by a convention signed by Britain and Russia in 1828, which provided that neither should trespass on each other's domain and fixed Russia's boundary at 54°40′ north latitude and at the 141st meridian.

In 1861 William Henry Seward became secretary of state. A firm believer in extending U.S. sovereignty over the entire continent, as early as Sept. 18, 1860, he had revealed his thinking about Alaska:

> Looking far off into the northwest I see the Russian as he busily occupies himself by establishing seaports and towns and fortifications on the verge of this continent . . . and I can say, 'go on and build up your outposts all along the coast and even up to the Arctic Ocean—they will yet become the outposts of my own country—monuments to the civilization of the United States. . . .'

The Russian-American Company had not fared well; its deficits could be more than wiped out by a sale of Russian America, and Russia's expansion more profitably diverted into the Amur River region on the Manchurian border. The Russian crown, in contrast to the British crown, had favored the cause of the Union in the American Civil War; there was thus an element of reciprocity in the proposed transfer of sovereignty. On Mar. 29, 1867, after some weeks of negotiation, Seward and Baron Eduard Stoeckl, Russia's minister to the United States, completed the draft of a treaty of cession of Russian North America, and it was signed at 4 A.M. the next day. The price was $7.2 million.

The problem was to secure Senate ratification. Charles Sumner of Massachusetts, chairman of the Foreign Relations Committee, in a three-hour speech spelled out all the advantages of the acquisition and gave the area its name, Alaska, based on an Aleut word meaning "the great land." Yet the vote for ratification was only one more than the required two-thirds. The first session of the Fortieth Congress then adjourned, and the ceremonies of transfer took place on Oct. 18, 1867. This circumstance was a fortunate one because it made it difficult for the House in the second session to deny the appropriation for payment to Russia. The debate, beginning on June 20, 1868, made clear that there was substantial opposition. Unfavorable epithets that had been given currency in a press hostile to the transaction were reechoed. Alaska was called many harsh names: Icebergia, Polaria, Walrussia, Seward's Polar Bear Garden; but the most enduring one was Seward's Folly.

Decades had passed before it was realized that the United States had consummated one of the greatest real estate bargains in history. At the price of less than two cents an acre it had acquired an area one-fifth as large as the continental United States, with a 26,000-mile coastline, longer than the combined Atlantic, Gulf, and Pacific coastlines. A map of Alaska superimposed on that of the mainland shows Alaska touching the Atlantic and Pacific coasts, as well as the Canadian and Mexican borders. The area has many unique features. It contains four time zones and there would be a fifth except that the international dateline was obligingly bent westward so that no part of Alaska would be in tomorrow. At Alaska's boundaries are the northernmost and westernmost reaches of the nation—and since it extended into the eastern hemisphere, also the easternmost. Its vertical dimension is no less striking. It contains the continent's loftiest peak, 20,300-foot Mount McKinley. Alaska also possesses the widest range of temperatures under the American flag, in a community just north of the Arctic Circle, 100° in summer, −76° in winter.

"The great land" disclosed untold natural resources. The nation's greatest fishery, it offered a wealth of marine, fluvial, and lacustrine life: the Pacific salmon, halibut, king crab, sea otter, fur seal, rainbow trout, and grayling. It also offered abundant and diversified terrestrial wildlife: moose, caribou, sheep, goat, deer, wolverine, and brown, grizzly, and black bears. Alaska possesses subsoil deposits of gold, copper, and other minerals; oil and natural gas; forests of spruce, hemlock, birch, and cottonwood; the greatest water-power potential in the United States; and with its superlative scenery unlimited opportunities for recreation.

Giving currency to the presumption of Alaska's worthlessness, the Congress proceeded to forget Alaska and to usher in a period of neglect. In the seventeen years following the purchase some twenty-five bills were introduced in Congress providing civil government for Alaska, but none of them was deemed worthy of debate and they remained buried in committees. Indeed in those seventeen years Congress enacted only two bills dealing with Alaska. One extended to it the commerce and navigation laws and provided a collector of customs who at that period was its principal government official. The other act turned over administration of the abundant fur seal fisheries of the Pribilof Islands to the secretary of the treasury, who leased them to a private enterprise in San Francisco. During those seventeen years no Alaskan settler could secure title to property; no prospector could stake a mining claim; no marriage could be celebrated; no injured party could secure redress for a grievance unless he took the law into his own hands; no crime could be punished. This situation did not exist in the other western territories of the United States.

Such authority as there was in Alaska was exercised without legal proviso by the general commanding the U.S. forces stationed at Sitka. When in 1877 he and his troops were removed to quell an uprising of Nez Perce in the Northwest, not even that authority remained.

Various violent incidents in Sitka and Wrangell between Indians and whites deepened apprehension in Sitka concerning another Indian uprising. The ancestor and namesake of one of the more militant of the local chiefs, Katlean, had played a leading role in the 1802 Sitka massacre. The Sitkan settlers' request for the stationing of a U.S. naval vessel in Alaskan waters to prevent a recurrence was supported by the collector of customs, Mottram D. Ball. When repeated pleas went unheeded, appeal was made to the Canadian authorities at Victoria, where British Capt. H. Holmes A'Court consulted the U.S. consul, who wired Secretary of State William Evarts and secured his approval, provided the situation was urgent. The consul left the decision to A'Court, who promptly took his warship, H.M.S. *Osprey,* to Sitka and announced he would stay until a U.S. warship arrived. Thirty-four days later the U.S. corvette *Alaska* arrived, permitting the *Osprey* to depart. The commander of the *Alaska* had no instructions for a permanent stay, and so the Sitkans' pleas were renewed. On June 14, 1878, the U.S.S. *Jamestown* under Comdr. L. A. Beardslee arrived, with no terminal date set for its sojourn in Alaskan waters. It had been one year since the departure of the army. The incident was illustrative of the indifference of the federal authorities to the Alaskans' needs. But for the kindly intervention of A'Court, another massacre might well have occurred. For the next two years Beardslee was *de facto,* and without any legal authority whatever, the highest government authority in Alaska, as for three years thereafter would be his successors aboard.

Establishment of Government. Following repeated proddings by three presidents, Congress in 1884 gave Alaska its first vestige of government and law. The Organic Act of 1884 provided a governor, a federal district judge, and five lesser magistrates called commissioners. The act extended to this newly established civil and judicial district the nation's mining laws and appropriated $25,000 for education under the supervision of the secretary of the interior. It extended the laws of the state of Oregon to Alaska. But it specifically forbade the application of U.S. land laws, the establishment of a legislature and of an office of delegate to Congress, and the creation of counties.

Drawn up with little knowledge of or concern for Alaska, the act of 1884 proved worthless. Land acquisition, and hence settlement, were impossible under it. The Oregon code contained frequent references to county officials and county functions: for example, school districts were established by county commissioners. But since there could be no county commissioners in Alaska, there could be no school districts. The Oregon code provided that in order to serve on a jury one had to be a taxpayer, and since the act provided no taxes for Alaska, it could have no juries. Thus the administration of justice under the American system was precluded.

For the next twenty years the annual reports of six successive governors and their messages and communications to the presidents, to the secretaries of the interior, and to members of Congress—as well as the communications of Alaskan private citizens—voiced condemnation of the omissions and restrictions in the Organic Act. No attention was paid to these complaints until the discovery of gold in the Klondike in the 1890's and other gold strikes in Alaska brought a rush of prospectors to the Far North. These prospectors were voters in their own states and their complaints consequently registered with their senators and representatives. Bills to provide a delegate in Congress for Alaska were introduced in several congresses, making a better showing each time, and finally one was enacted in the Fifty-ninth Congress on May 7, 1905. In addition to providing an official spokesman for Alaska in the national capital, the law established voting—for the office of delegate to Congress only—limited to males who had resided in Alaska for one year. Meanwhile gold, copper, and coal mining brought capital to Alaska and gave Alaska nationwide attention. The fisheries—salmon and fur seal—had earlier been preempted by powerful stateside interests. They would play an important part in shaping the forthcoming legislation in Congress, which at last permitted Alaska to have a legislature.

The Organic Act of 1912, while a substantial improvement over its unworkable predecessor of 1884, was still notable for what it forbade Alaskans to do. The lobbies of the powerful absentee interests had made it the least generous act granted any territory, facilitating their control of Alaska's actions. The act denied Alaska the control and management of its fisheries and wildlife; forbade the enacting of any basic land laws; kept the judiciary in federal control, while still denying the lesser court judges—the commissioners—a salary and compelling them to subsist on the meager fees they would collect from the public; and again forbade the creation of counties without the prior consent of Congress. The composition of the legislature followed no approved pattern. In an earlier day, when mining had been virtually the only economic activity, Alaska had been divided into four judicial districts to permit the judge or commissioner to "get around" once a year to settle mining claims, using dog teams in winter and river transportation in summer. These judicial districts were now made the electoral districts, each with two senators and four representatives, disregarding the disparity in their populations and creating a duplication of upper- and lower-house constituencies. Such a small number of senators, it was thought, would facilitate control by a few, control sufficient to block legislation.

Despite the self-serving precautions of outside interests, local self-government began promisingly, and the early legislature performed admirably. The first legislature in 1913 enfranchised women, thus anticipating federal action under the Nineteenth Amendment by seven years. The second legislature in 1915 enacted what appears to have been the first old-age pension system in the United States. Under it, indigents who did not desire to go to the Pioneers' Home (established by the first legislature) could, if qualified, receive a monthly pension of $12.50. The pension was made available to women. The two legislatures established a modest revenue system by a series of license and poll taxes. Having created a structure of territorial government and having found vast fields requiring legislation in which they were forbidden to act, the legislatures pleaded with Congress to make the necessary laws. Their pleas were directed at the larger objectives of developing Alaska and promoting settlement. Repeatedly, by sequential legislatures, Congress was asked: to revise the land laws to promote homesteading, as had been done for the West decades earlier; to transfer to Alaska the management of the fisheries, which were inadequately protected against depletion under federal management; to make appropriations for highway construction, a logical request in a territory that was totally in public domain; and to pay the federal lower court judges a salary. There was much else that was reasonable and scarcely controversial in the requests of the Alaskan legislators. Yet not one of these requests was honored by the Congress during the next forty years, although they were pressed in session after session by Alaska's voteless delegates to do so.

It was this rejection that led Alaska's delegate, James Wickersham, in 1908, a towering figure in Alaskan history (federal judge, delegate, explorer, author, bibliographer), to conclude as early as 1916 that only statehood would satisfy Alaska's needs; and he introduced the first legislation to achieve it. Despite congressional rejections there was some progress in Alaska. Wickersham secured the establishment of a land grant college, which became the University of Alaska. Moreover, he secured congressional passage of legislation to provide a railroad from Seward on the Pacific coast to Fairbanks, a new community born of the gold discoveries in the Tanana

Valley. Also, a low-grade wagon road named the Richardson Highway, 371 miles long, was completed in 1913 from Valdez to Fairbanks.

With the exception of these two enterprises—the railroad and the wagon road—it was in the area of transportation that Alaska suffered most grievous discrimination. When, coincident with the increasing use of the automobile, Congress in 1916 enacted the first Federal Aid Highway Act, designed to give the nation a system of roads on a uniformly high standard, Alaska was uniquely excluded for the next forty years. In maritime transportation, until the start of air service between Alaska and the lower states in 1940, the only link connecting them with Alaska, there was such flagrant discrimination in the connecting transcontinental railroad freight rates that budding Alaskan enterprises depending on shipments to and from Alaska had to suspend. On appeal, the U.S. Supreme Court held that nothing in the Constitution forbade discrimination against a territory.

Alaska's strategic position in World War II gave it unprecedented attention at that time and brought about its first defenses, with resulting economic benefits. An increase in population also resulted when many of the GI's stationed there decided to stay.

Statehood. During the 1940's the struggle between the absentee interests and those who wanted to develop Alaska as a place of permanent abode reached a new intensity. The legislature's structure made it easy for the former to block legislation sought by the latter, including—and especially—revenue measures. But the 1948 election broke the blockade; the resulting 1949 session enacted a comprehensive tax program and prepared the way for assuming the responsibilities of statehood. In 1946 a referendum on this issue showed Alaskans favoring it by a three-to-two majority. Statehood legislation sponsored by Alaska's delegates, Anthony J. Dimond and his successor, E. L. (Bob) Bartlett, was introduced, with similar action for Hawaii. President Harry S. Truman vigorously supported both. President Dwight D. Eisenhower favored Hawaiian but not Alaskan statehood on the assumption—then generally held in Washington but later disproved in the case of Hawaii—that Alaska would elect Democrats to Congress and Hawaii, Republicans. Bills to achieve statehood for both were unable to secure approval of both houses for a decade, but public sentiment for both was increasing.

The final push that resulted in success for both originated with an idea and action by an Alaska legislature. During World War II an enlightened New Orleans businessman, George Lehleitner, a student of American history who had volunteered for service in the navy, was stationed at Pearl Harbor. Sympathetic with Hawaii's statehood aspirations he called a little-known episode from America's past to the attention of the Hawaiian leaders who favored statehood. Lehleitner's idea was based on the historical fact that a number of territories had successfully dispensed with the customary procedure for achieving statehood. The first had been Tennessee. Anxious to achieve statehood and envious of Kentucky's admission to the Union in 1792, Tennessee had called a constitutional convention and elected two "senators" who were sent to the national capital in 1796 to present the cause of statehood—and returned with it. The same procedure was followed by Michigan in 1835; Iowa in 1846; California in 1850; Minnesota in 1858; Oregon in 1859; and Kansas in 1861. But few Americans knew about this intriguing bit of history. The Hawaiian leaders rejected the idea; they felt they would achieve statehood without it. Lehleitner turned his attention to Alaska and brought his proposal to former Gov. Ernest Gruening, who had been active in Alaska's statehood cause.

The 1955 Alaska legislature had passed an act calling for a constitutional convention, which was to draft a constitution for the hoped-for state. The convention was then in session and, after hearing Lehleitner's proposal, adopted it, setting an election date for the voters to nominate what became known as the Tennessee Plan delegation. Both parties nominated their candidates, and the people elected as senators William Egan, president of the convention and a state legislator since 1941, and Gruening; and as representative, Ralph J. Rivers, also a state legislator. All three were Democrats. When they arrived in Washington in 1957, they were not seated, as had been some of the earlier Tennessee Plan legislators from other territories, and were informed that if statehood was to be secured they would have to run again. For the next two sessions of the Eighty-fifth Congress, the three lobbied the unconvinced or opposed members of Senate and House, mainly refuting the opposing arguments of noncontiguity and small population. The House passed the statehood bill by a vote of 217 to 172; the Senate passed it on June 30, 1958, by 64 to 20. The following January President Eisenhower signed the bill, with the recently elected Alaska congressional delegation looking on. They were senators-elect Bartlett and Gruening, and Representative Rivers. William Egan had been elected governor and with him a Democratic state legislature, with eighteen

Democrats to two Republicans in the senate and thirty-four Democrats to six Republicans in the house.

The Democratic landslide victory was only a temporary harbinger of the future of party politics in Alaska, however. Whereas the Democrats retained control in 1962, though by smaller majorities, they were toppled in 1966 when Gov. Egan, running for a third term, was defeated by Republican Walter Hickel and Republican majorities were elected to both houses. Thereafter the pendulum swung back and forth between the two parties.

A constitution was written by the constitutional convention of 1956 and Alaska has enjoyed the progress that self-government was expected to carry with it. One important benefit of statehood was the recapturing of control over Alaska's most valuable resource, the fisheries, which had been seriously depleted under federal administration. Other relations with the federal government, dealing with the public domain and subsoil resources and the power of the Department of Interior to make reservations and withdrawals, continue to be an unsolved problem.

Status of Native Population. Economically the native population of Alaska (including Eskimos, Aleuts, and several tribes of Indians—Athapascan, Tlingit, Haida, and Tsimshian) was long disadvantaged. It experienced social and political discrimination, and indeed federally established segregation in the schools was a factor in this discrimination. In 1944, however, as a result of executive initiative in the state capital, two Indians from southeastern Alaska were elected to the house. In the 1945 legislature, likewise in response to executive prodding, exclusion of natives from restaurants and barber shops, segregation in theaters, and similar discriminatory practices were made illegal. The first state legislature dramatized the change in 1958 by electing an Eskimo, William Beltz, as president in the predominantly white senate and, following his death, an Indian, Frank Peratrovich, as president—one of the two Indians first elected to the house in 1944.

Economically the position of the native Alaskans showed little improvement. Most of them lived in dire poverty under extremely substandard conditions. This problem, affecting one-fifth of Alaska's population, was a long-standing one. The Organic Act of 1884 had provided that the aboriginal inhabitants should "not be disturbed in the possession of any lands actually in their use and occupation or claimed by them": in other words, their right of occupancy was affirmed. The act continued: "The terms under which such persons may acquire title to such lands is reserved to future action by Congress."

For nearly ninety years no action was taken to validate this congressional mandate. Action would have been easy when so few had migrated from the states to the new territory—the first reasonably reliable Alaska census in 1890 listed a population of 23,531 native, 4,298 white, and 1,823 mixed. No federal (or other) reservations or withdrawals had taken place. The federal agency that had the responsibility for the aborigines, the Department of the Interior, and specifically its Bureau of Indian Affairs, showed no interest. Its critics charged that it had no desire to emancipate its wards, preferring to perpetuate their wardship in order to maintain its own security as their warden. But by the 1960's the disparity between the living conditions of the native population of Alaska and the immigrant whites had become increasingly apparent and challenging. Two decades earlier Alaska's governor had brought Indians and Eskimos into the territorial legislature; they and their white colleagues had raised the issue of federal failure to carry out the 1884 congressional design. By the 1960's legislation to validate their rights was introduced in Congress; hearings on bills to achieve them were held in both houses, becoming steadily more generous; and finally, far-reaching legislation was enacted on Dec. 18, 1971, and signed by the president. The act provided a financial settlement of $962.5 million and 40 million acres of land and provided that all Alaskans of one-quarter "native" blood, including those born in but no longer residing in Alaska, should participate in the settlement. Their number is estimated at 75,000. It was provided that each participant should receive 100 shares of stock in the profit-making corporation (one of twelve) that represents his village. For those living outside Alaska a thirteenth corporation was visualized, to distribute cash rather than land. Even with the complications anticipated, there was no question that the act would give an impetus to Alaska's economy. The social and economic effects on the native population were harder to gauge.

Conservation. Concomitantly, other conflicts in Alaska were in the making: developers versus conservationists. This conflict arose briefly in the late 1950's with the discovery of vast oil and gas deposits in the Kenai Peninsula midway along Alaska's gulf coast. During the 1950's Alaska's economy had been in trouble. Its mainstays had been mining and fisheries. Gold mining had been suspended by presidential order as a World War II measure (although gold-producing allies of the United States, Canada and

Australia, took no such step), and Alaska's gold mining had not recovered. Alaska's fisheries, principally salmon, had been depleted, and statehood had not yet come to enable their restoration. Alaska sorely needed a new economic prop. So a group of Anchorage citizens sought to develop the Kenai subsoil deposits. The obstacle was that some years earlier Secretary of the Interior Harold Ickes had, without consultation with Alaskans, withdrawn 200,000 acres there as a moose range. Secretary of the Interior Fred Seaton was confronted with the opposition of all but one conservation organization (the Izaak Walton League), the conservationists claiming that drilling for oil would destroy the moose's habitat and the moose. Proponents denied this danger existed. They argued that man also requires a habitat and that without a viable economy there would be none. Seaton decided to open half the moose range for drilling. Alaska's economy was restored, and the moose not only multiplied but also spread over Alaska.

The conservationist issue recurred in the 1960's concerning the vast oil discoveries at Prudhoe Bay on the Arctic Coast. To get the oil to market, a pipeline to Alaska's gulf coast was planned. Transporting the oil by a specially designed tanker, the *Manhattan*, had been tried and found impractical. The conservation societies began fighting the pipeline. They argued that the pipeline would pass through earthquake-prone terrain, that it would impede migration of animals, and that oil spills from tankers operating from Valdez, the terminal port of the pipeline, would be perilous to the fisheries. The conservation societies' efforts to block the pipeline were defeated in successive court actions; Congress approved legislation authorizing its construction, and the legislation became law on Nov. 16, 1973.

A similar fight occurred in the mid-1970's to prevent establishment of a pulp mill in the northern end of the Tongass National Forest—which covers Alaska's Panhandle. The proponents of the operation, most Alaskans, argued that the timber was overripe and dying on the stump and that harvesting is the essence of good conservation practice; in addition, they pointed out that two mills, at Ketchikan and Sitka, had been operating for years. The Alaska district court allowed the project, but opponents vowed to continue their fight in the courts. At the same time a similar conflict began to emerge in connection with a project to extract iron ore from a large deposit near Haines.

A further and even more intense conflict arose in 1973 with the withdrawal by Secretary of the Interior Rogers Morton of 83 million acres of public domain in Alaska, for national parks, national forests, wildlife refuges, and wild rivers, to be managed by federal agencies. Morton's action followed the last-minute insertion in conference between the Senate and House on the Native Claims Settlement legislation of authorization for his action. This acreage was subsequently increased to 106 million acres by legislation sponsored by Sen. Henry M. Jackson of Washington at the request of the Sierra Club. The issue will ultimately be decided by Congress, which has until 1978 to make its finding. The issue meanwhile has aroused widespread and intense opposition in Alaska. The legislation was denounced by Gov. William Egan and Walter Hickel, former governor of Alaska and secretary of the interior. It has led to a proposal in Alaska for secession from the Union, if Congress approves, and will be a hotly contested issue intensified by the energy crisis, since it forecloses exploration for and development of energy and mineral resources in most of the withdrawn acreage.

[Hubert Howe Bancroft, *History of Alaska;* Ernest Gruening, *The State of Alaska;* Jeannette P. Nichols, *Alaska: A History of Its Administration During Its First Half Century Under the Rule of the United States;* Morgan E. Sherwood, *Alaska and Its History*.]

ERNEST GRUENING

ALASKAN INDIANS. Alaska is the gateway from Asia by which man undoubtedly entered the North American continent as much as 25,000 years ago. In Alaska, early man appears to have depended basically for his subsistence on mammal hunting, particularly of the caribou. Thus, in the Alaskan interior, there is a suggestion of a continuity of tradition, a retention of the same primary subarctic ecological adaptation. But such a dependence is characteristic only of the Alaskan subarctic interior, a region of boreal forest rather than tundra conditions. In the valleys of the Yukon and Kuskokwim, shut off from the sea by the Eskimo, are to be found such Athapascan (Na-Déné)–speaking groups as the Koyukon, Tanaina, Tanana, Han, Ingalik, Kutchin, Nabesna, and Ahtena, dialect and regional groups rather than tribes as such. They are divided into socioeconomic hunting groups or bands, and the bases of their societal organization lie in caribou hunting. The same socioeconomic pattern and the Athapascan languages spread out into the northwestern Canadian forest and tundra.

There are other cultural patterns in the Alaskan domain. Perhaps the most significant is that of the Eskimo, who, judging from archaeological evidence, did not reach the Alaskan coasts until about A.D. 1000 and whose contacts with other native American peoples already resident remained minimal. The various groups of Eskimo, also organized as hunting societies, moved to such northern islands as St. Lawrence, the Diomedes in the Bering Strait, Nunivak, and King and were distributed from the south Alaskan coasts to the east of Cook Inlet and around the peninsula to the north. Different in language from the interior peoples, the Eskimo relate linguistically to the Aleut, the native inhabitants of the Aleutian archipelago. These groups, decimated early by Russian contacts, offer an old insular substratum of culture, one adapted especially to seal hunting.

Still another native American cultural focus appears in southeastern Alaska, where both topography and climate change markedly. There the rich cultures of the Indians of the Northwest Coast, with their basic salmon dependence, their extensive use of wood, and their complexities of social organization, suggest yet another cultural focus. Some of these tribes—Tlingit, for example—represent an Athapascan intrusion, while the Eyak, to the north of the coastal cultural region, are clearly an interior group that spread into the salmon-fishing domain. But the Eskimo-Aleut and Northwest Coast cultural developments in Alaska are recent and tangential to the major interior focus of the native Athapascan (Na-Déné) peoples. (*See also* Alaska.)

[C. Osgood, *Contributions to the Ethnography of the Kutchin;* Robert F. Spencer, Jesse D. Jennings, and others, *The Native Americans.*]

ROBERT F. SPENCER

ALASKA-PACIFIC-YUKON EXPOSITION, Seattle, 1909, a notable achievement of the Pacific Northwest. The federal government spent $600,000 for exhibits on the Philippines, Hawaii, and Alaska to reveal to the American people, by the first comprehensive demonstration, the peoples, arts, and industries of these possessions. Japan presented the largest foreign exhibit it had ever attempted; China and Oceania were well represented. An estimated $20 million secured by taxation, appropriations, gifts, and revenues was spent on the entire enterprise. It was a minor, but highly successful, American exposition.

FRANK MONAGHAN

ALBANY. In September 1609, Henry Hudson moored his ship, the *Half Moon,* near the site of the present city of Albany, New York. No serious attempt at settlement was made until the spring of 1624, when the Dutch West India Company sent over a group of eighteen families, mostly Walloons, who built Fort Orange on the site of the present capitol. During the years 1630–36 the colony was augmented by the arrival of groups of colonists sent over by Kiliaen Van Rensselaer, who had been granted a large tract of land near Fort Orange. In 1652 the village of about a hundred houses, which had grown up in the protection of the fort, was declared independent of the patroon's colony, and became known as Beverwyck. Shortly afterward, the fur trade, which had been under the control of the Dutch West India Company, having been thrown open to the citizens, rapidly increased.

On Sept. 24, 1664, Fort Orange surrendered to the English and Beverwyck became Albany, after the Scottish title of the Duke of York. On July 22, 1686, Gov. Thomas Dongan granted the city a charter. For many years Albany was the key in the regulation of Indian affairs; since the early days of the colony relations with the Iroquois had been friendly. During the period of the colonial wars many conferences, including the famous Albany Congress of 1754, were held there. The fur trade continued to be important.

On the eve of the Revolution, Albany was a prosperous city of 3,000 inhabitants, laid out in a wide strip along the Hudson River. The Albanians entered into the struggle with ardor. The position of the city made it strategically important, and throughout the war the inhabitants were in fear of attack. The year 1777 was an anxious one as Gen. John Burgoyne advanced toward the city by way of Lake Champlain and Col. Barry St. Leger by way of the Mohawk Valley (*see* British Campaign of 1777). At the request of Gen. Philip Schuyler, lead window weights were melted down and made into bullets in preparation for attack. The surrender of Burgoyne at Saratoga and the retreat of St. Leger from Fort Stanwix relieved the anxiety of the people, but conditions in the city were wretched. It was crowded with refugees and sick or wounded soldiers. In addition a conspiracy among the Afro-Americans, British prisoners, and Tories was feared. News of the provisional peace was received with great rejoicing, and the citizens set to work with zest to build up their neglected trade. By a law enacted on Mar. 10, 1797, Albany became the capital of the state of New York.

Because of its strategic location on the Hudson River, 145 miles north of New York City, Albany has been a crossroads since colonial times. The two-day passage of Robert Fulton's *Clermont* from New York to Albany in August 1807 laid the basis for the first commercial steamboat line in the United States and the expansion of Albany as a transportation center. In 1825 the completion of the Erie Canal made Albany the junction of the water route from the East to the Great Lakes, and also a point of departure for the Northwest. The completion of the Albany-Schenectady Railroad in 1831 began Albany's role as a rail center. In the 20th century Albany became a highway and air crossroads. The first municipal airport in the United States was opened in Albany in 1919.

In 1970 about one-fourth of Albany's work force worked in manufacturing—principally felt and woolen goods, meat products, paper, iron and brass castings, and pharmaceuticals. The government of the state of New York, centered in Albany, employed about 35,000. The city's population in 1970 was 114,873.

[Codman Hislop, *Albany, Dutch, English and American.*]

A. C. FLICK

ALBANY CONGRESS (1754), called by order of the British government for the purpose of conciliating the Iroquois and securing their support in the war against France, was more notable for the plans that it made than for its actual accomplishments. In June commissioners from New York, Massachusetts, Rhode Island, Connecticut, Pennsylvania, New Hampshire, and Maryland met with the chiefs of the Six Nations. Encroachment on their lands, the trading of Albany with Canada, and the removal of Johnson (later Sir William Johnson) from the management of their affairs had aroused a dangerous spirit of disaffection among the Indians. Gifts and promises were bestowed and the alliance renewed, but the Iroquois went away only half satisfied.

For the better defense of the colonies and control of Indian affairs it had long been felt that a closer union was needed than occasional meetings of governors or commissioners. Discussion of such a union now became one of the principal subjects of the congress. Massachusetts indeed had granted its delegates authority to "enter into articles of union . . . for the general defense of his majesty's subjects." The plan adopted was one proposed by Benjamin Franklin and frequently referred to at the time as the Albany Plan. It provided for a voluntary union of the colonies with "one general government," each colony to retain its own separate existence and government. The new government was to be administered by a president general appointed by the crown and a grand council of delegates from the several colonial assemblies, members of the council to hold office for three years. This federal government was given exclusive control of Indian affairs, including the power to make peace and declare war, regulate Indian trade, purchase Indian lands for the crown, raise and pay soldiers, build forts, equip vessels, levy taxes, and appropriate funds. The home government rejected this plan because it was felt that it encroached on the royal prerogative. The colonies disapproved of it because it did not allow them sufficient independence. Nevertheless this Albany Plan was to have far-reaching results. It paved the way for the Stamp Act Congress of 1765 and the Continental Congress of 1774, and when the need of a closer union was felt, it served as a guide in the deliberations of the representatives of the colonies.

[E. B. O'Callaghan, ed., *Documentary History of the State of New York.*]

A. C. FLICK

ALBANY CONVENTION (1689–90), a convention of the civil and military officers of Albany, which, convening on Aug. 1, 1689, set itself up as an emergency government until the intentions of William and Mary were made known. Fearful of attack by the French, the convention sought a promise of aid from Jacob Leisler, who had seized control of southern New York, but was rebuffed by Leisler, whose subsequent demand that he be recognized as commander in chief was rejected. Badly frightened by a French attack on Schenectady, the convention sought aid from New England and in the spring yielded to renewed demands from Leisler.

[V. H. Paltsits, "Transition From Dutch to English Rule," in A. C. Flick, *History of the State of New York,* vol. II.]

A. C. FLICK

ALBANY REGENCY, the first American political machine. It was organized in 1820 under Martin Van Buren and acquired its name because his first aides, residing in Albany and nearby, managed the machine during his absence in the U.S. Senate. The regency developed party discipline and originated the control of party conventions through officeholders and others subservient to it. The spoils system was the core of its philosophy. The regency waned following Van Buren's unsuccessful bid for the presidency in 1848.

[Denis Tilden Lynch, *An Epoch and a Man, the Times of*

Martin Van Buren, and *The Growth of Political Parties, 1777–1850.*]

DENIS TILDEN LYNCH

ALBATROSS, the Yankee-owned ship which brought news of the outbreak of the War of 1812 to W. P. Hunt, partner of the Pacific Fur Company, at its Astoria post. Hunt chartered the ship and removed the furs from Astoria to avoid possible British capture, thus abandoning the first American fur post on the Columbia River.

[H. M. Chittenden, *History of the American Fur Trade.*]

CARL L. CANNON

ALBEMARLE, Confederate ram, built on the Roanoke River in 1853. Under command of James W. Cooke in April 1864, it sank the gunboat *Southfield,* put the *Miami* to flight, and captured Plymouth, N.C. On May 5 it fought, indecisively, Capt. Melancton Smith's seven blockaders at the mouth of the Roanoke. But on the night of Oct. 27 Lt. William B. Cushing, with fifteen men in a small launch, bearing a torpedo ingeniously attached to a spar, sank it.

[J. Thomas Scharf, *History of the Confederate States Navy.*]

CHARLES LEE LEWIS

ALBEMARLE AND CHESAPEAKE CANAL, built by a corporation in 1856–60 to afford inland navigation between Chesapeake Bay and Albemarle Sound. It is really two canals, thirty miles apart; one is eight and one-half miles long, connecting the Elizabeth River with North Landing River in Virginia, and the other five and one-half miles long, connecting Currituck Sound with the North River in North Carolina.

ALVIN F. HARLOW

ALBEMARLE SETTLEMENTS. The first permanent settlement in North Carolina was made in the Albemarle Sound region about the middle of the 17th century by Virginians in search of good lands and engaged in trade with Indians. Nathaniel Batts, who was trading there by 1653, had a house at the western end of Albemarle Sound in 1655. Other settlers soon followed, and in 1662 Capt. Samuel Stephens of Virginia was made commander of the Southern Plantation with authority to appoint a sheriff. When it was learned in 1665 that the Albemarle settlements were not included in the Carolina proprietary grant of 1663, a new charter was granted that included them. Government was instituted in 1664 with the appointment of William Drummond as governor of the county of Albemarle, and an assembly met the following year. Land grants were issued by Sir William Berkeley, governor of Virginia, who was also one of the eight proprietors of Carolina, and settlers in large numbers began to move into the region after the Concessions and Agreement issued by the proprietors in 1665 promised a stable government. Within a few years Quaker missionaries appeared, and their converts soon prevailed in many areas. By 1689 the settled portion of Carolina had expanded beyond the original Albemarle section, and the county of Albemarle was abolished as a unit of government.

[William S. Powell, *Ye Countie of Albemarle.*]

WILLIAM S. POWELL

ALBUQUERQUE, the largest city in New Mexico, with a population of 243,751 (1970), originated April 1706 as the Spanish villa San Felipe de Albuquerque, named for King Philip V and the viceroy, Duke of Albuquerque. It was on the Chihuahua Trail and dominated the Rio Abajo (downriver) part of the province. Exposed to Apache and Navajo inroads, the settlers were "reduced" (1779) to the plaza arrangement which survives in Old Town.

New Albuquerque started a century later (1880) a mile to the east, as a railroad center. That year, the Santa Fe system (*see* Railroads, Sketches), built along the Rio Grande, and the Atlantic and Pacific headed westward over the old U.S. survey (1853) along the 35th parallel. Connection southeast into Texas came only in 1907. The automobile and airplane also have made Albuquerque an important crossroads of transcontinental routes.

[L. B. Bloom, "Albuquerque and Galisteo," *New Mexico Historical Review,* vol. 10 (1935); C. F. Coan, *History of New Mexico.*]

LANSING B. BLOOM

ALCALDES, mayors of Mexican towns. Under the American provisional government in California these officers were recognized by military governors and continued in office until 1850.

[T. H. Hittell, *History of California.*]

WILLIAM S. LEWIS

ALDER GULCH. Gold was discovered at Alder Gulch, Mont., and the first stampede reached there

June 6, 1863. The people lived in brush wickiups, dugouts, and among the rocks, but later in the year a town sprang up nearby which was named Virginia City. The diggings were the richest gold placer deposits ever discovered and in three years $30 million was taken from them.

[G. Stuart, *Forty Years on the Frontier.*]

CARL L. CANNON

ALDRICH COMMISSION. *See* **National Monetary Commission.**

ALDRICH-VREELAND ACT, an emergency currency law enacted May 30, 1908, as a result of the so-called bankers' panic of 1907. Its aim was to give elasticity to the currency through the next six years by permitting national banks to issue circulating notes on securities additional to federal bonds. It permitted issuance, under strict supervision, of additional currency, on bonds of states, cities, towns, and counties, and on commercial paper. A tax graduated up to 10 percent discouraged abundant issues. The act also created the National Monetary Commission to investigate systems of money and banking abroad and to advise Congress of desirable changes in the American banking system.

JEANNETTE P. NICHOLS

ALEUT. Together with the Eskimo, the Aleut, native inhabitants of southwestern Alaska, the Shumagin Islands, and the long Aleutian archipelago, form the single language family of Eskaleut. This relationship, reflecting no mutual intelligibility, suggests that the two peoples may have common backgrounds and origins. The population estimate for 1740 of 16,000 Aleut points to a dispersal of maritime hunters over a wide and insular geographic area. Living in sod houses, often semisubterranean, the Aleut made capital of seal, sea otter, walrus, and occasional whales; they also depended in some measure on wildfowl and fishing. Skilled sailors, the Aleut made their way over great fog- and storm-bound distances in open skin-covered boats. The many local groups of Aleut developed, as did the Eskimo, small semipermanent villages. Kinship relationships rather than political organization were the rule.

The Aleut were known to the Russians through the voyages of Alexei Chirikov and Vitus Bering in 1741. Russian exploitation, especially in the quest for seal fur, worked early to the detriment of the Aleut. Societal disorganization and population decline have marked the two centuries of their contact with Asians and Europeans.

[John R. Swanton, *The Indian Tribes of North America.*]

ROBERT F. SPENCER

ALEUTIAN ISLANDS extend westward in a long, sweeping curve about 1,200 miles from the tip of the Alaska Peninsula. They are largely of volcanic composition and unsuitable for agriculture. Although the islands appear to provide a natural bridge between North America and Asia, the function of the archipelago as a bridge is more apparent than real since population migration from Siberia to Alaska appears to have taken place to the north and the constant fog and severe storms obviate any real strategic significance.

Before the Russian-sponsored exploration of the area by Alexei Chirikov and Vitus Bering in 1741, the islands were peopled exclusively by Aleut, who numbered about 16,000 or more. The Russian-American Fur Company exploited the region—indiscriminately hunting, buying, and stealing the locally plentiful seals and sea otters and their pelts and massacring and enslaving the Aleut. By 1900 the Aleut population had been reduced to nearly 3,000, through murder, illness, and the gradual destruction of the food supply. Added to the Russian incursions were British and American slaughtering of seals, stemming from the late 18th-century explorations of James Cook, George Vancouver, Alexander Mackenzie, Robert Gray, and John Kendrick. After the U.S. purchase of Alaska (and the Aleutians) from Russia in 1867, controversies over hunting rights in the Bering Sea proliferated; a political settlement by a court of arbitration in Paris in 1893 left the sea open. Not until 1911 was a viable American-Canadian-Japanese agreement reached to protect the seals—and in 1941 Japan withdrew.

In June 1942 a Japanese task force moved into the Aleutians to destroy military bases at Dutch Harbor, the principal city, and to occupy the undefended islands of Attu and Kiska. This maneuver was an unsuccessful gambit to draw the U.S. Pacific Fleet north away from Midway Island, the principal objective of a Japanese second-phase offensive. Although airfields and fortifications were constructed, without the capture of Midway these outposts were of little use in the Japanese defense perimeter. In March 1943 the Japanese attempted to bring in reinforcements but were turned back off the Komandorskiye Islands.

Thereafter, Attu and Kiska had to be supplied solely by submarines. Two months later the U.S. Seventh Infantry Division invaded Attu in heavy fog and, after eighteen days of bitter combat, captured the island. The ratio of American to Japanese casualties was second only to that at Iwo Jima. Under cover of fog and darkness late in July, the Japanese evacuated their 5,183-man garrison at Kiska by surface ships. Unaware of this development, U.S. forces bombarded the island at length on Aug. 15, and a combined American-Canadian force landed unopposed.

After World War II a U.S. Coast Guard fleet was stationed at Unalaska Island to patrol the sealing grounds and, after 1956, to supervise the effectuation of a convention signed by the United States, Canada, Japan, and the Soviet Union for the protection of the seals. The Aleut in the islands had been reduced to about 500 by 1970. (*See also* Alaska.)

[Brian Garfield, *The Thousand-Mile War: World War II in Alaska and the Aleutians.*]

GEORGE L. MACGARRIGLE

ALEXANDRIA, city in Virginia on the Potomac River, below Washington, D.C., was an important trading center until early in the 19th century, particularly as a tobacco warehousing and deep-sea shipping port. First settled in 1695, it was established as a town in 1749 on an original grant of 6,000 acres awarded in 1669; the site had been owned for nearly a century by the Alexander family. It was situated on the main stage route, the King's Highway, running southward into Virginia. Gen. Edward Braddock departed from there on his fatal expedition in 1755. The Fairfax Resolves were signed in Alexandria, July 18, 1774. Alexandria was incorporated in 1779. From 1791 to 1847 the city was under federal jurisdiction as part of the District of Columbia. Thomas Jefferson's Embargo Act of 1807 destroyed its tobacco trade. During the Civil War it was occupied by Union troops. Alexandria was the home of many prominent Virginia families. Alexandria's population greatly increased in the 20th century (in 1970, 110,938) and it has become a largely residential city noted for its colonial architecture.

[Mary G. Powell, *The History of Old Alexandria, Virginia.*]

ETHEL ARMES

ALEXANDRIA CONFERENCE (March 28, 1785), between Maryland and Virginia, dealt with navigation and commerce in Chesapeake Bay and the Potomac and Pocomoke rivers. Scheduled to be held at Alexandria on March 21, it actually met at George Washington's invitation at Mount Vernon. Daniel of St. Thomas Jenifer, Thomas Stone, and Samuel Chase represented Maryland, George Mason and Alexander Henderson, Virginia. In ratifying the agreement, Maryland urged the inclusion of Pennsylvania and Delaware, while Virginia urged a meeting of all the states to adopt uniform commercial regulations. This produced the Annapolis Convention, the origin of the Convention of 1787.

[J. Thomas Scharf, *History of Maryland.*]

WALTER B. NORRIS

ALGECIRAS CONFERENCE. In 1904 France made agreements with England and Spain which allowed it to increase its influence in Morocco. Germany, angered because it was not consulted, demanded a conference of the signatories of the Morocco agreement negotiated at Madrid in 1880. Among the signatories was the United States, to whom the German government now appealed for an extension of the open door policy to Morocco. President Theodore Roosevelt, in an attempt to obtain a peaceful solution, helped Germany by persuading England and France to attend a conference at Algeciras, Spain, in 1906. In the conference, however, the Germans appeared so uncompromising that Roosevelt supported France, which in the end won out by obtaining a privileged position in Morocco. The U.S. Senate ratified the resulting treaty but declared that this action was taken solely to protect American interests and should not be interpreted as an abandonment of a nonintervention policy toward Europe.

[E. N. Anderson, *First Moroccan Crisis;* A. L. P. Dennis, *Adventures in American Diplomacy.*]

LYNN M. CASE

ALGIERS, WAR WITH. *See* **Barbary Wars.**

ALGONQUIN. The Algonquin tribe, located with the Ottawa on the northern tributaries of the Ottawa River in southwestern Quebec, is to be contrasted with the extensive North American speech family, Algonkin (or Algonquian, or Algonquin), to which it has lent its name. The tribe itself was always small, a relatively isolated Eastern Woodlands (Northeastern) people. Like others in the woodlands pattern, the Algonquin were a nonagricultural hunting people, exploiting such faunal resources as moose, deer, beaver, otter, bear, fish, and wildfowl. Extensive use of birch bark for housing, canoes, and containers characterized their culture.

Most closely related in language to the Ojibwa (or Chippewa) of Ontario, Wisconsin, and Minnesota, the Algonquin, along with the neighboring Ottawa, appear to be a remnant of various Ojibwa bands that gradually shifted westward as a result of the pressures of European settlement. The tribe, perhaps 6,000 in 1600, was divided into various paternal groups associated with hunting territories. Originally lacking any political solidarity, the tribe was drawn gradually into the French orbit and patterned a series of political alliances with other tribes on the model of the Iroquois federation. But the group was never a potent military or political force, suffering decimation and dispersion at the hands of the hostile Iroquois. Members of the group surviving in the 20th century are identified only with difficulty.

The language phylum to which the Algonquin lent their name is, however, one of the most widely spread and important of the American continent. Careful philological analyses and comparisons demonstrate the language affiliation to an Algonkin family of such widely spread peoples as the Arapaho, Cheyenne, and Blackfoot in the Plains and the Yurok and Wiyot in California. There is also the suggestion that certain Gulf languages—for example, those formerly classified as Muskogean (or Muskhogean)—may have remote connections with the major Algonkin grouping. When to this is added the suggestion that some languages of Central America, such as Coahuiltecan, may derive from a proto-Algonkin, it seems clear that considerable antiquity is implied. The source of the name of both the tribe and the language family is uncertain.

[John R. Swanton, *The Indian Tribes of North America.*]

ROBERT F. SPENCER

ALIEN AND SEDITION LAWS. In June and July, 1798, the Federalists, fearful of French invasion and certain they were only spelling out the details of the proper restraints on free speech and press implied by common law and American statute, introduced four bills designed to impede political opposition. Although they were debated as war measures, three of them were applicable in peacetime as well.

Skepticism of aliens and of their ability to be loyal to the nation permeated these laws. In place of the five-year residency requirement, the Naturalization Act of June 18, 1798, substituted fourteen years, five of which were to be spent in the state or territory in which the individual was being naturalized. The alien was required to declare an intention of becoming a citizen five years before the ultimate application. As a measure of control all aliens were to be registered with the clerk of their district court. This law was repealed in 1802. The Alien Friends Act (June 25, 1798) gave the president the power to deport aliens "dangerous to the peace and safety of the United States." Its terms were sweeping because it was passed in the context of an undeclared war with France. But it was limited to two years, and it was never enforced. On July 6, 1798, the Alien Enemies Act was passed—the only one of the group that gathered strong Republican support as a clearly defensive measure in time of declared war. It gave the president the power to restrain, arrest, and deport male citizens or subjects of a hostile nation.

The Act for the Punishment of Certain Crimes, signed into law on July 14, 1798, was the nation's first sedition act. It made it a high misdemeanor "unlawfully to combine and conspire" in order to oppose legal measures of the government, to interfere with an officer in the discharge of his duty, to engage in or abet "insurrection, riot, or unlawful assembly or combination, whether such conspiracy . . . shall have the proposed effect or not." The penalty was a fine of not more than $5,000 and imprisonment of up to five years. Moreover, the writing or printing of "any false, scandalous and malicious writing" with intent to bring the government, Congress, or the president "into contempt or disrepute, or to excite against them . . . the hatred of the good people of the United States," was punishable by a fine of up to $2,000 and imprisonment for up to two years. The Sedition Act carefully specified, however, that truth might be admitted as a defense, that malicious intent had to be proved, and that the jury had the right to judge whether the matter was libelous. Although President John Adams had not urged that the bills be enacted, he signed them into law without serious protest, and they were supported by most Federalists.

Enforcement against critics of the administration was pressed by Secretary of State Timothy Pickering. Ten Republicans were convicted; they included Congressman Matthew Lyon, political writer James T. Callender, the lawyer Thomas Cooper, and newspaper editors William Duane and John Daly Burk. Because Federalist judges frequently conducted the trials in a partisan manner, and because the trials demonstrated that the Sedition Act had failed to distinguish between malicious libel and the expression of political opinion, the laws were the catalyst in prompting a broader definition of freedom of the press.

The protest against these laws received its most significant formulation in the Kentucky and Virginia resolutions, drafted by Vice-President Thomas Jefferson and James Madison, which claimed for the states the right to nullify obnoxious federal legislation. The resolutions, however, did not seriously question the concept of seditious libel; they merely demanded that such prosecutions be undertaken in state courts, as indeed they were during Jefferson's own presidency.

[Leonard W. Levy, *Legacy of Suppression;* James Morton Smith, *Freedom's Fetters: The Alien and Sedition Laws and American Civil Liberties.*]

LINDA K. KERBER

ALIEN CONTRACT LABOR LAW. *See* **Contract Labor, Foreign.**

ALIEN LANDHOLDING. The common-law disability of aliens to inherit lands in the United States has always been removable by statute and by treaty. Alienage occasioned by the Revolution was excepted by the Definitive Treaty of Peace, which also required Congress to "recommend to the State Legislatures" restitution of confiscated estates. The Jay Treaty went a step further by guaranteeing existing titles wherever held and treating British subjects with respect thereto as equal to citizens. But the guarantee did not hold for lands acquired thereafter or for other than British aliens. The Convention of 1800 removed the disability of alienage for French citizens in all the states. A treaty with Switzerland (1850) similarly affected Swiss citizens. But in the absence of such a treaty state laws applied, as in Kansas, where the disability was expressed in the state constitution. In California, on the other hand, the state constitution authorized aliens to acquire, transmit, and inherit property equally with citizens; and this provision, like similar ones in other states, was upheld by the Supreme Court.

A vast increase in European immigration, an extensive flow of British capital into the purchase of land and cattle companies in western states, and, along with this capital, establishment of Old World systems of land tenure produced a contrary sentiment. The Nimmo Report of 1885 on range and ranch cattle traffic in the West included a table showing the purchase by foreign companies of some 20 million acres of land, mostly in the West. Though the table of ownership was somewhat exaggerated, it did reveal how the benevolent land system had enabled English and Scottish capitalists to take over large segments of the ranch and cattle business (*see* Foreign Investment in the United States). Even more startling to many who were concerned about the way large owners of foreign capital were benefiting from American policies was the action of William Scully, a notorious Irish landlord, in buying 220,000 acres of prime agricultural land in Illinois, Kansas, Nebraska, and Missouri—much of which was purchased from the government at a cost of $1.25 or less an acre. This huge acreage was rented to 1,200 tenants under a modification of the Irish land system, the tenants being required to make all improvements and to pay the taxes and a cash rent. These requirements kept the tenants in poverty, their improvements substandard, and the social amenities of the Scully districts limited. Leaders of the growing antimonopoly movement excoriated Scully and joined with others troubled about the large foreign ownerships in the Great Plains to demand legislation to outlaw further acquisition of land by aliens. Illinois led in 1887 in denying aliens the right to acquire land. Nine other states rapidly followed suit either by constitutional amendment or by legislation, and Congress banned further acquisition of land by aliens in the territories. Since the measures could not apply retroactively, they succeeded only in halting further expansion of alien ownership.

[Everett Dick, *The Lure of the Land: A Social History of the Public Lands From the Articles of Confederation to the New Deal;* Paul W. Gates, *Landlords and Tenants on the Prairie Frontier.*]

PAUL W. GATES

ALIENS. *See* **Naturalization.**

ALIENS, RIGHTS OF. For the first hundred years the U.S. government imposed no restrictions on the entry of aliens. Commencing in 1819, some federal statutes sought to improve conditions on ships bringing immigrants to the United States. A law passed by Congress in 1864 sought to encourage immigration to the United States. Various states enacted laws to control immigration, but these state laws were declared unconstitutional, being an infringement of exclusive federal power. The first federal controls appeared in an 1875 statute that barred convicts and prostitutes; the first general immigration statute was passed in 1882 and introduced a number of additional restrictions. Thereafter, the classes of aliens barred from entry were steadily enlarged, and these qualitative controls remain an important feature of U.S. immigration laws. In 1882 Congress also passed the Chinese Exclusion Act, which, in various forms, remained effective until it was repealed in 1943.

A substantial increase in the volume of immigration early in the 20th century led to increasing sentiment for restriction of the number of immigrants who could be admitted. The first numerical limitation was adopted in 1921, as a temporary measure. This was succeeded by the National Origins Quota Act of 1924, which imposed quotas on immigration from each country outside the Western Hemisphere. This law was criticized as discriminatory but remained in effect until 1965, when it was superseded by a single allocation of 170,000 immigrants for all countries outside the Western Hemisphere, to be available on a first-come, first-served basis, without regard to the immigrant's race or nationality. The 1965 act also imposed a separate limitation of 120,000 for immigrants born in the Western Hemisphere; this limitation became effective in 1968.

Pursuant to the constitutional provision authorizing it to establish a uniform rule of naturalization, Congress has enacted laws, commencing with the first Congress, providing procedures for the naturalization of aliens (*see* Naturalization). These procedures are relatively simple and enable aliens who are lawfully in the United States to become American citizens after a prescribed period of residence, usually five years, and the establishment of good moral character and attachment to the principles of the Constitution.

Aliens residing in the United States enjoy many constitutional protections. Their status in regard to judicial proceedings, civil and criminal, is virtually the same as that of U.S. citizens. The protections of the Fifth and Fourteenth amendments relate to "persons," a term that unquestionably includes aliens. Therefore, the Supreme Court has declared unconstitutional various state laws that sought to limit the employment opportunities available to aliens. Early Supreme Court decisions, however, permitted the states to exclude aliens from public employment and to deny them licenses for certain occupations. However, the soundness of these early decisions was questioned in *Graham* v. *Richardson,* 403 U.S. 365 (1971), and such state restrictions were declared unconstitutional in 1973 in *Sugarman* v. *Dougall,* involving public employment, and *In re Griffiths,* involving an applicant for admission to the bar. *Graham* v. *Richardson* also declared unconstitutional various state statutes that denied welfare benefits to resident aliens. Moreover, a federal statute prohibits discrimination on the ground of race, color, or national origin under any program receiving federal financial assistance.

[Charles Gordon and Harry H. Rosenfield, *Immigration Law and Procedure*.]

CHARLES GORDON

ALLATOONA PASS, BATTLE AT (Oct. 5, 1864). After the fall of Atlanta, Confederate commander J. B. Hood moved his army north to destroy Gen. William T. Sherman's communications. Sherman followed. Hood detached S. G. French's division to destroy a railroad bridge. On his march French stopped to destroy stores at Allatoona and attacked federal troops stationed there under the command of J. M. Corse, but without success. The popular song "Hold the Fort" was based on messages exchanged between Corse and Sherman.

[R. U. Johnson and C. C. Buel, *Battles and Leaders of the Civil War,* vol. IV.]

THOMAS ROBSON HAY

ALLEGHENY MOUNTAINS, ROUTES ACROSS. The steep eastern escarpment of the Allegheny Mountains (3,000–5,000 feet high and extending from the Mohawk Valley to the Tennessee River) was a serious impediment to the westward movement. Routes across the Alleghenies depended upon gaps and approaches along the tributaries of rivers. Probably buffalo first trod these routes. Later the Indians followed them as trails. In turn they were used by explorers and fur traders.

The West Branch of the Susquehanna, extending close to the Allegheny River, furnished a route used by the Indians, though only fur traders made much use of it during the early period. The branches of the Juniata River led to two historic routes across the Alleghenies: one, the Frankstown Path, much used by Pennsylvania fur traders; and the other, the Traders Path, followed by the Pennsylvania Road and Gen. John Forbes's expedition (Forbes's Road). The route used by Christopher Gist, George Washington, and Edward Braddock ran from the Potomac River at Wills Creek over the Alleghenies. From the headwaters of the Potomac also ran a route over the mountains, which was used in later times as the Northwestern Pike. The headwaters of the James River determined a route overland to branches of the Great Kanawha, one branch of which, the New River, also provided a route from the headwaters of the Roanoke River. Farthest south, Cumberland Gap offered easy passage from eastern Tennessee to central Kentucky, making possible the greatly used Wilderness Road. In the light of the extensive use made of Forbes's Road, Braddock's Road, and the Wilderness Road in the westward movement, probably no routes in the United States are more properly known as historic highways. The transportation of the 20th century follows closely the old routes across the Alleghenies.

[Archer Butler Hulbert, *Historic Highways of America;* Alfred P. James, "Approaches to the Early History of Western Pennsylvania," *Western Pennsylvania Historical Magazine,* vol. 19 (1936).]

ALFRED P. JAMES

ALLEGHENY PORTAGE RAILWAY, a thirty-six-mile span between Hollidaysburg and Johnstown that linked the eastern and western canals of the Pennsylvania System. Constructed in 1831–35, when the ascent of 1,400 feet within 10.1 miles—from Hollidaysburg to Blair's Gap, at the summit of the Allegheny Mountains—seemed a prohibitive gradient for a continuous roadbed, the railway consisted of eleven level stretches and ten inclined planes, five on each side of the crest. The planes were operated by stationary engines. Locomotives quickly replaced horses as motive power. In 1856 the planes were superseded by a continuous railway. The portage railway was sold to the Pennsylvania Railroad in 1857 and abandoned shortly thereafter.

[W. B. Wilson, *History of the Pennsylvania Railroad Company.*]

E. DOUGLAS BRANCH

ALLEGHENY RIVER. Rising in Potter County, Pa., the Allegheny flows in an arc through New York and back into Pennsylvania, where it unites with the Monongahela to form the Ohio River. About 325 miles long, it is navigable for about 200 miles. It was considered by the French and early English explorers as a part of the Ohio River. The Delaware and Shawnee settled along its course soon after 1720; white settlement followed after 1790. It was an important highway for settlers and freight in the keelboat and flatboat era. Its name is probably a corruption of *Alligewi-hanna,* "stream of the Alligewi," from a tribe that Indian tradition says once inhabited the region.

LELAND D. BALDWIN

ALLIANCE, a Continental frigate carrying thirty-six guns, built in Salisbury, Mass., 1778. It carried the Marquis de Lafayette and Thomas Paine to France. Its first commander, Pierre Landais, showed doubtful loyalty in the *Bonhomme Richard–Serapis* engagement and was relieved of his command. Disobeying orders, he sailed the *Alliance* from France to America; the crew mutinied twice during the voyage and was brought into Boston by its lieutenant. Capt. John Barry cruised in the *Alliance* from 1780 through the last sea fight of the Revolution with the *Sybil,* Mar. 10, 1783.

[G. W. Allen, *Naval History of the American Revolution.*]

WALTER B. NORRIS

ALLIANCE FOR PROGRESS, a policy statement calling for a concentrated joint effort to accelerate the economic and social development of Latin America within a democratic political framework. The ten-year plan was proposed in a speech by President John F. Kennedy to the Latin-American diplomatic corps at a White House reception on Mar. 13, 1961. President Kennedy stressed that "only the most determined efforts of the American nations themselves" would insure the success of the ambitious proposal, which included comprehensive economic and social planning, land and tax reform, strengthened education and health services, commodity stabilization arrangements, expanded training of technical and scientific personnel, economic integration, and improved hemispheric defense arrangements coupled with arms limitation. President Kennedy's proposal stressed that the material objectives of the alliance should be paralleled by efforts to preserve and expand political freedom and effect social change.

The alliance speech was a powerful political statement marking a definite shift in U.S. policy that began in the late 1950's, at least partially in response to the growing revolutionary activity epitomized by Fidel Castro's overthrow of Fulgencio Batista in Cuba. The speech, the Kennedy personality, and the positive response of popular Latin-American leaders combined to produce a remarkable mass psychological impact throughout the hemisphere. Its immediate effect was to improve dramatically the political relations between the United States and Latin America, especially with the "democratic Left." The speech electrified the masses and gave encouragement to progressive political and intellectual forces within Latin America, but it also engendered bitterness and obdurate opposition among those who, for selfish or ideological reasons, resisted strongly, if not always publicly, the fundamental changes called for.

Between 1961 and 1969 public economic assistance to the Latin-American countries in the form of grants and loans from all external sources was about $18 billion, of which about $10 billion came directly from official U.S. sources. However, on a net basis, that is, after taking account of loan repayments and interest, official U.S. direct aid is estimated to have been about $4.8 billion in the same period. This relatively small net transfer of official capital is explained by the fact that public indebtedness in Latin America in 1960 was more than $10 billion, the servicing of which diverted resources away from new investment.

Although profound changes in the economic, social, and political structures in Latin America began to take place in 1961 under the impetus of the alliance, a variety of forces within Latin America and a major shift in U.S. energies and resources associated with the Vietnam War drained the alliance effort of its vitality. These factors, combined with the intrinsic difficulty of bringing about radical social change within a free and democratic framework, resulted in a failure to meet early expectations concerning performance; the Alliance for Progress is more appropriately viewed as a major shift in U.S. hemispheric policy and should be evaluated in a longer sweep of history.

[William D. Rogers, *The Twilight Struggle: The Alliance for Progress and the Politics of Development in Latin America;* Arthur M. Schlesinger, Jr., *A Thousand Days: John F. Kennedy and the White House.*]

RALPH A. DUNGAN

ALLISON COMMISSION, a joint, bipartisan congressional committee chaired by Sen. William B. Allison that investigated four federal scientific agencies from 1884 to 1886. In addition to examining a jurisdictional dispute between the Navy Hydrographic Office and the Coast and Geodetic Survey over the charting of offshore waters, the commission inquired into the charge that the Geological Survey, the Coast Survey, and the Weather Service, which was then part of the Army Signal Corps, were doing research for abstract, not strictly practical, purposes. Scientists testified that their work was wholly practical. Some who argued that the legitimacy of research could not be judged by laymen called for a reorganization of federal science to keep its administration out of the hands of mere political functionaries. Congressman Hilary A. Herbert, a Southern Democrat on the commission, insisted on the principle of maintaining direct democratic control over the scientific agencies. A devotee of limited government, he proposed sharp reductions in the activities of the two surveys, the award of the Coast Survey's offshore work to the Hydrographic Office, and the transfer of the Weather Service from the Army Signal Corps to a civilian department. But the majority of the commission favored retaining the status quo in federal science, and the Congress upheld the majority report.

[A. Hunter Dupree, *Science in the Federal Government;* Thomas G. Manning, *Government in Science.*]

DANIEL J. KEVLES

"ALL QUIET ALONG THE POTOMAC," the opening words of a poem published as "The Picket Guard" by Mrs. Ethel Lynn Beers in *Harper's Weekly,* Nov. 30, 1861. It refers to official telegrams reporting "all is quiet tonight" to the secretary of war by Maj. Gen. George B. McClellan.

FRED A. EMERY

ALMANACS. In colonial days the almanac was a publication of great importance second only to the Bible and widely used by farmers. Beginning as a publication of astronomical information and prophecy, it later grew into one of culture, occupying the position in the 18th century later taken by the magazine.

The first almanac printed in America was the *Almanacke for New England for the Year 1639,* printed by Stephen Daye at Cambridge; in 1676 an almanac was published in Boston; and in 1686 in Philadelphia, Samuel Atkins, "Student in the mathamaticks and astrology," compiled the *America's Messenger.* Almanacs were published in New York in 1697, in Rhode Island in 1728, and in Virginia in 1731. In content these almanacs were similar to earlier ones in Europe containing prophecies concerning human beings and the weather, based on astrology. The early almanacs were preserved from year to year and the blank spaces used for diaries, recording accounts, and attempts at poetry.

The most famous of the early almanacs are *The Astronomical Diary and Almanack* published by Nathaniel Ames in Boston (1726–75); and *Poor Richard's Almanac* by Benjamin Franklin in Philadelphia (1732–57). The latter was unequaled in reputation for proverbs, wit, and wisdom, not all original. Ames, in his *Astronomical Diary and Almanack,* furnished perhaps a greater versatility than appeared in any other almanac of the century. Its tide charts, solar table calculations and eclipses, and changes of the moon were definite assets. The most enduring American almanac is *The Farmer's Almanac,* begun in 1793 by Robert Bailey Thomas. For over 180 years it has retained much of its old form and content, combining weather prophecies with anecdotes, old jokes, and verse. Supposedly, Abraham Lincoln, as an Illinois lawyer, used *The Farmer's Almanac* to prove the lack of moonlight on the night of a murder, thus discrediting a witness and winning his case. Foreign language almanacs were widely used. A prominent example was the *Hoch Deutsch Americanische* in 1739 and various almanacs published by the Pennsylvania Germans.

In the 19th century, almanacs were frequently issued for political and other propaganda and advertising purposes as indicated by the *Sun Anti-Masonic Almanac* (1831); *Harrison Almanacs* (1840–41); *Henry Clay Almanac* (1844); *General Taylor's Rough and Ready Almanac* (1848); *Cass and Butler Almanac* (1849); *Common School Almanac* (1842); and *Temperance Almanac* (1834). *The Confederate Almanac and Register* (1862) and *Uncle Sam's Union Almanac* (1863) gave military statistics somewhat as did *Hutchin's Almanac* of New York in the later 18th century. The first comic almanac appeared in Boston in 1831 and was quickly imitated, one example being *Davy Crockett's Almanack of Wild Sports of the West.* H. W. Shaw, under the pseudonym of Josh Billings, published a very successful satirical version of *The Farmer's Almanac* in 1870, calling it *The Farmer's Allminax.*

All the major religious denominations published almanacs giving denominational statistics and other information. Medical almanacs of all types have been widely distributed. Astronomical almanacs for use in sea and air navigation are prepared by official organizations of the United States (beginning in 1849 by an act of Congress) and other major countries because of the expense of accurate astronomical research. Encyclopedic information appeared in the *Tribune Almanac and Political Register* (1846); and *The World Almanac* (1868) continues to cover a wide range of statistical and historical information.

[C. S. Brigham, *An Account of American Almanacs and Their Value for Historical Study;* Milton Drake, *Almanacs of the United States;* Bessie W. Johns, *Poor Richard Comes to Life;* George Lyman Kittredge, *The Old Farmer and His Almanack.*]

H. H. SHENK

ALPHADELPHIA ASSOCIATION, a Fourierist community established in Comstock township, Kalamazoo County, Mich., in 1844. A German, Dr. H. R. Schetterly, was the leading spirit. Three thousand acres of land were purchased, a large "mansion" built, and at one time probably 300 members were admitted. The common property was valued at $43,897.21 in 1846. It was disbanded in 1848.

WILLIS DUNBAR

ALTA CALIFORNIA. Under Spain (1533–1822), California embraced the whole Pacific coast of North America from Cape San Lucas to the Oregon country. Until the middle of the 18th century it was frequently represented on maps as an island some 3,000 miles long. Early in the 18th century the Jesuit Father Eusebio Kino proved by actual exploration that the southern portion of the area was a peninsula and the rest of it mainland. Thereafter the peninsula came to be called Baja (Lower) and the rest Alta (Upper) California.

[H. E. Bolton, *Outpost of Empire;* C. E. Chapman, *California, The Spanish Period.*]

HERBERT E. BOLTON

ALTA VELA CLAIM, a flimsy claim against the Dominican government by American adventurers ejected on the eve of the unsuccessful Spanish reoccupation (1861–65) of the guano island by that name located fifteen miles south of the Dominican Republic. It has both a sinister and an auspicious significance in U.S. political history because former Secretary of State Jeremiah S. Black resigned as defending counsel in the impeachment trial of President Andrew Johnson in 1868 when the latter would not order Secretary of State William H. Seward to approve the claim.

[Samuel Flagg Bemis, *Diplomatic History of the United States.*]

SAMUEL FLAGG BEMIS

ALTON PETROGLYPHS. Near the present town of Alton, Ill., the Jesuit Jacques Marquette in 1673 saw painted upon the face of a rocky bluff the figure of a "monster" which terrified him and interested later travelers until its destruction about 1856. Called "Piasa" by the Indians, the figure was that of an imaginary bird legendary with many tribes.

[F. W. Hodge, *Handbook of American Indians.*]

CLARK WISSLER

ALUMINUM, the most useful of the nonferrous metals, was first isolated in metallic form in 1825 by

Hans Christian Oersted in Denmark. The metal remained a laboratory curiosity until 1854, when Henri Sainte-Claire Deville discovered a process using metallic sodium as a reductant that led to the first commercial production of aluminum. The price of the metal fell from $545 per pound in 1852 to $8 per pound in 1885, and uses for the lightweight metal began to increase greatly. Emperor Napoleon III considered outfitting his army with lightweight aluminum armor and equipment. However, the price of the metal was still too high for widespread use. In 1886, an American, Charles Martin Hall, and a Frenchman, Paul Heroult, independently discovered that aluminum could be produced by electrolyzing a solution of aluminum oxide in molten cryolite (sodium aluminum fluoride). The electrolytic process won immediate acceptance by the commercial industry and remains the sole commercial method used throughout the world for making aluminum.

Hall's invention led to the formation of the Pittsburgh Reduction Company in 1888. This company, now known as the Aluminum Company of America (ALCOA), produced 50 pounds of aluminum per day at first. It became the world's largest producer of aluminum by the turn of the century and continues to be so today. Growth of the aluminum industry in Europe was more diverse. Within ten years there were firms operating in Switzerland, Germany, Austria, France, and Scotland—all having obtained rights to Heroult's patents to make the metal. By 1900 total world production was about 7,500 short tons; American production was 2,500 tons.

With the advent of the airplane in World War I, quantities of the lightweight metal were needed. In 1918 the primary capacity in the United States had grown to 62,500 short tons; world production amounted to 143,900 tons. Steady growth of the aluminum industry continued, and in 1939 the United States produced 160,000 tons of the metal and world production amounted to 774,000 tons. The airplane became a prime factor in waging World War II, and aluminum production throughout the world tripled; in the United States it grew sixfold. Another major period of growth in the industry took place during the Korean War; by 1954 world production of primary aluminum was 3,069,000 tons, with the United States producing almost half that amount, 1,460,000 tons. In 1972 total world production of aluminum came to 12,103,000 tons, but the American share, produced by twelve companies, had dropped to 34 percent, or 4,122,000 tons.

Aluminum is the most abundant metallic element in the earth's crust. It is made from the mineral bauxite—hydrated aluminum oxide—which is found in plentiful supply throughout the tropic areas of the world. Five countries—Jamaica, Surinam, Guyana, Guinea, and Australia—mined about 61 percent of the world's supplies in 1972, with the remainder coming from twenty-two other countries. The United States produces less than 13 percent of its bauxite needs and relies upon imports.

The great growth in the use of aluminum metal indicates its versatility. It has a unique combination of useful properties: lightness, good thermal and electrical conductivity, high reflectivity, malleability, resistance to corrosion, and excellent tensile strength in alloyed form. It is extensively employed in building and construction, where almost 400 pounds of the metal are used per house for such items as windows, doors, and siding. Another major market is transportation: almost 80 pounds were used in the average automobile in 1970. Aluminum is used extensively in truck and railroad car bodies, in which each pound of weight saved permits an extra pound of revenue-producing payload. For similar reasons, the airplane and aerospace industries are also large consumers of aluminum. There are many electrical applications because it is one-third as heavy and roughly two-thirds as conductive as copper. Applications for the metal are also growing rapidly for containers and packaging, where it is used in cans, foil, and frozen-food containers. Indeed, the metal's versatility leads to a never-ending list of other possible applications.

[Kent R. Van Horn, *Aluminum*, vol. 2, Design and Application.]

KENNETH B. HIGBIE

AMANA COMMUNITY. Born of religious enthusiasm, this unique community was founded in Germany in 1714 as the Community of True Inspiration in protest against the arbitrary rule of church and state. For mutual protection the Inspirationists congregated on several large estates, but high rents and unfriendly governments forced them to seek a new home in America.

Under the leadership of Christian Metz the Inspirationists crossed the Atlantic in the early 1840's and settled near Buffalo in Erie County, N.Y. Here they laid out six villages, called the settlement Ebenezer, built mills and factories, tilled the soil, and formally adopted communism as a way of life.

The rapid expansion of nearby Buffalo threatened that isolation which the Inspirationists had sought in the New World and in 1855 they moved to the frontier state of Iowa. They located in Iowa County, incorporated as the Amana Society, and once more built houses, churches, schools, stores, and mills, and continued their community life of "brothers all." Consisting of approximately 1,500 people, living in seven villages and owning 26,000 acres of land in one of the garden spots of Iowa, the Amana community conducted for nearly a century the most successful experiment in communism recorded in the annals of American history.

Once the frontier disappeared, isolation became impossible, memories of the founding forefathers faded, the old idealism grew dim, and spiritual enthusiasm waned. In 1932 by unanimous vote the community reorganized on the basis of cooperative capitalism as a joint stock company where stockholders are both owners and employees.

[Bertha M. H. Shambaugh, *Amana, The Community of True Inspiration,* and *Amana That Was and Amana That Is.*]

BERTHA M. H. SHAMBAUGH

AMBASSADORS. Through the great-power Congress of Vienna (1815) and the Congress of Aix-la-Chapelle (1818) four standardized diplomatic grades were established: ambassadors were given the highest rank, followed, first, by ministers plenipotentiary and envoys extraordinary; second, by ministers resident; and third, by chargés d'affaires. Under the revised rules of the Vienna Convention on Diplomatic Relations of 1961, reducing the ranks to three by eliminating ministers resident, ambassadors remain senior. Ambassadors are accredited directly to the sovereign or the head of state, and they represent the highest authority of their own governments. Thus, American ambassadors represent the president of the United States even though they normally communicate with the president through the secretary of state. The ambassador longest accredited in a foreign capital is known as the dean, or doyen, of the international diplomatic corps, and as such represents it for certain purposes. The doyen may act to convey the corps's collective congratulations on occasions such as national holidays, thus simplifying the scale of protocol requirements. The doyen is likely to be the spokesman for any widespread diplomatic corps complaint. U.S. ambassadors rarely attain this distinction because of frequent rotation.

Until well into the 19th century only great powers exchanged ambassadors; other nations exchanged envoys of the rank of minister (plenipotentiary). Because the United States did not aspire to great-power rank, because it played only a small role in international affairs, and because ambassadors were associated with monarchy in the public mind, the United States did not exchange ambassadors until almost the close of the 19th century, sending ministers instead. The first U.S. ambassador, Thomas F. Bayard of Delaware, was commissioned to Great Britain on Mar. 30, 1893. In exchange, Sir Julian Pauncefote, minister plenipotentiary since 1889, presented his credentials as ambassador to President Grover Cleveland on Apr. 11, 1893.

The choice of Great Britain for the first U.S. ambassador reflected that nation's importance to America as well as Great Britain's determination to cultivate closer relations with the United States, in view of its increasingly difficult international position. By 1939 the United States was exchanging ambassadors with twenty nations. After World War II the number increased steadily, both because many new nations were coming into existence and because, as a matter of national pride, smaller nations were more and more demanding the equality of status signified by an exchange of ambassadors; the rank of minister came to be rarely used. In 1974 the United States exchanged ambassadors with 124 nations, sending ministers to none. Also, eight ambassadors were accredited to international organizations, such as the United Nations and North Atlantic Treaty Organization.

FREDERICK H. HARTMANN

AMBRISTER. *See* **Arbuthnot and Ambrister, Case of.**

AMELIA ISLAND AFFAIR. The Embargo Act (1807) and the abolition of the American slave trade (1808) made Amelia Island, off the coast of Spanish Florida, a resort for smugglers with sometimes as many as 300 square-rigged vessels in its harbor.

In June 1817 Gregor McGregor arrived in Amelia, styling himself the "brigadier general" of the United Provinces of the New Granada and Venezuela and general-in-chief of the armies of the two Floridas. He left for Nassau in September, but his followers were soon joined by Luis Aury, formerly associated with McGregor in South American adventures but later leader of a piratical band on Galveston Island, Tex. Aury assumed control of Amelia, got a legislature elected, set a committee to drawing up a constitution, and invited all Florida to unite in throwing off the Spanish yoke. The United States, becoming tired of having its laws violated, sent a naval force that captured Amelia Island on Dec. 23, 1817, and put an end to the miniature republic. The island was returned to the Spaniards prior to 1821.

[Carolina Mays Brevard, *History of Florida;* James Parton, *Andrew Jackson.*]

W. T. CASH

AMEN CORNER, a celebrated niche in the corridor of the old Fifth Avenue Hotel (1859–1908), New York City, where politicians and reporters gathered to discuss coming political events. It was here that Sen. Thomas C. Platt's "Sunday school class" was held in the late 1890's; when the senator announced his decisions his associates would say "Amen."

[Louis J. Lang, ed., *The Autobiography of Thomas Collier Platt.*]

HAROLD F. GOSNELL

AMENDMENT. Those amendments to the U.S. Constitution that are discussed in individual articles are listed under the number of the amendment, such as **Fourteenth Amendment** and **Twenty-second Amendment.**

AMENDMENTS TO THE CONSTITUTION. Twenty-six amendments have been adopted since 1789. The first ten were drafted to meet the protests in numerous state ratifying conventions against the absence of a bill of rights in the Constitution. To fill this void, the First Congress, chiefly on the initiative of James Madison, submitted twelve amendments to the states; ten of these were ratified (1791) and constitute the Bill of Rights, which limits the powers of the federal government but not the powers of the states (*see Barron* v. *Baltimore*). These amendments—which guarantee the people's civil liberties—provide that Congress shall make no law infringing freedom of speech, the press, religion, assembly, or petition; reaffirm the right of trial by jury; protect against unreasonable searches or seizures; and assure that no individual shall be compelled to testify against himself in a criminal case or "be deprived of life, liberty, or property, without due process of law."

The Eleventh Amendment (1798) was designed to override the Supreme Court decision in the case of *Chisholm* v. *Georgia* (1793). It provides that the federal judiciary cannot accept jurisdiction of a suit against a state by a citizen of another state or by a citizen of a foreign state.

The Twelfth Amendment (1804) altered Article II, Section 1, of the Constitution, which had permitted presidential electors to vote for two persons without designating which was to be president and which vice-president, and instructed them to cast separate ballots for each of these executive officers. The election of 1796 and particularly the canvass of 1800, when Thomas Jefferson and Aaron Burr received an equal number of electoral votes, had demonstrated the inadequacy of the original presidential election machinery and stimulated interest in a reform to prevent such difficulties.

Three amendments were ratified during the Reconstruction period following the Civil War. The Thirteenth Amendment (1865) abolished slavery and involuntary servitude. The Fourteenth Amendment (1868) for the first time defined citizenship, which included Afro-Americans. It stipulates that no state can deny individuals equal protection of the laws or deprive them of life, liberty, or property without due process of law, and provides for reduced representation in Congress for states that deny the right to vote in federal elections to adult male citizens. It also barred certain Confederate officers from holding state or federal offices unless pardoned by Congress and repudiated the Confederate debt. Disagreement over the meaning of this amendment continues to the present day, and it has been the subject of more Supreme Court cases than any other provision of the Constitution. The Fifteenth Amendment (1870), which secured the right to vote against denial or abridgment on the basis of race, color, or previous condition of servitude, was adopted when it was clear that the Fourteenth Amendment would not guarantee freedmen the right to the franchise.

Several amendments reflect the widespread desire for economic, political, and social reform during the early 20th century. The Sixteenth Amendment (1913), which overruled the Supreme Court decision in *Pollock* v. *Farmers' Loan and Trust Company* (1895), gives Congress the power to tax incomes from any source and without apportionment among the states according to population. The Seventeenth Amendment (1913) provides for direct, popular election of senators, revising Article I, Section 3, of the Constitution. It was thought that this method of election would make senators more responsive to the will of the people. Success for two other reform measures came at the conclusion of World War I. The Eighteenth Amendment (1919) prohibited the sale of intoxicating liquors and was the first amendment to specify a period of years (seven) within which it had to be ratified. Suffrage for women was guaranteed by the Nineteenth Amendment (1920), fulfilling a central demand of the women's rights movement.

The Twentieth, or "Lame Duck," Amendment (1933) set the dates for the beginning of presidential terms (Jan. 20) and congressional sessions (Jan. 3) and settled certain points with respect to presidential succession. The Twenty-first Amendment (1933) repealed the Eighteenth but gives the states power to regulate the use of intoxicating liquors; it is the only amendment to be ratified by special state conventions instead of state legislatures.

A two-term limit for presidents was established by the Twenty-second Amendment (1951), which was originally proposed by Republicans after the Democrat Franklin D. Roosevelt had been elected to a fourth term in office (1944) but was later endorsed by many who were wary of strong executive leadership.

The Twenty-third Amendment (1961) enables residents of the District of Columbia to vote for president and vice-president and gives the capital city three electoral votes, the number selected by each of the least populous states. State use of poll taxes in federal elections as a voting requirement, a device often employed to disfranchise Afro-Americans in the South, was banned by the Twenty-fourth Amendment (1964). Subsequently, the Supreme Court outlawed all poll taxes. Both amendments reflected the concern of the 1960's that all citizens should be guaranteed basic civil rights. One result of the assassination of President John F. Kennedy (1963) was the adoption of the Twenty-fifth Amendment (1967), which provides that whenever there is a vacancy in the office of the vice-president, the chief executive is authorized to nominate a successor who must be confirmed by a majority of both houses of Congress. It also empowers the vice-president to serve as acting president if the president is incapacitated. The Twenty-sixth Amendment (1971) lowered the voting age to eighteen, bypassing the traditional state control of that requirement.

A twenty-seventh amendment, known as the Equal Rights Amendment, was proposed by Congress on Mar. 22, 1972. It states that "Equality of rights under the law shall not be denied or abridged by the United States or by any State on account of sex." As of April 1975, thirty-four states had ratified the amendment; thirty-eight ratifications are needed by March 1979 for the amendment to succeed.

Three amendments proposed by Congress failed of ratification. The first, proposed to the states in May 1810, stated that any citizen accepting a title of nobility or honor from the head of a foreign nation would "cease to be a citizen of the United States." The Corwin amendment, proposed in March 1861, was an attempt to "freeze" the Constitution with regard to slavery by barring amendments that would give Congress "the power to abolish or interfere, within any State, with the domestic institutions thereof, including that of persons held to labor or service by the laws of said State." A child labor amendment, proposed in 1924, would have given Congress the power to regulate labor by persons under eighteen years of age, but the Fair Labor Standards Act was passed in 1938 before the necessary thirty-six ratifications had been achieved.

[Alfred H. Kelly and Winfred A. Harbison, *The American Constitution.*]

JOHN J. TURNER, JR.

"AMERICA." *See* **"My Country, 'tis of Thee."**

***AMERICA*, ** an American yacht which in 1851 won the trophy cup presented by the Royal Yacht Squadron; from 1857 the trophy was called the America's Cup. The *America* served later as a Confederate dispatch boat, was captured, and served as practice ship at the Naval Academy. It defended the cup in 1870, was sold to Gen. B. F. Butler in 1873, and in 1917 to Charles H. W. Foster of the Eastern Yacht Club. It was permanently docked at the Naval Academy in 1921, and was broken up in 1946.

[J. S. Hughes, *Famous Yachts;* W. M. Thompson, *The Yacht America.*]

LOUIS H. BOLANDER

AMERICA, DISCOVERY AND EARLY EXPLORATION OF. Norse Exploration. About the year A.D. 1000, roving Norsemen, starting from the Scandinavian colonies in Greenland, may have reached the coast of North America somewhere between Labrador and the Chesapeake. If they did, they left no undisputed archaeologic evidence of their visit. The legends of the voyages of Leif Ericson and Thorfinn Karlsefni depend upon three manuscripts of sagas written more than three hundred years after the possible discovery of that part of America which Leif called Vinland the Good. Admitting Leif to have been the discoverer of America, Edward Channing aptly said, "The history of America would have been precisely what it has been if Leif Ericsson had never been born and if no Northman had even steered his knorr west of Iceland."

Spanish Exploration. It is, however, undisputed historic fact that on Aug. 3, 1492, the Genoese Christopher Columbus, sailed from Palos, Spain, under the authority of the Spanish king and queen. On Oct. 12, 1492, Columbus saw some island in the Bahamas which the Indians called Guanahani, and which Columbus rechristened San Salvador. Its exact identity never has been conclusively established, but many scholars have accepted Watling Island as his first landfall. Following this, Columbus made three other voyages to the New World (1493, 1498, and 1502), during which he touched the coasts of South and Central America. But it must be remembered there is a documented story that one of the factors which induced Columbus to make his voyage was his actual meeting with, or knowledge of, a Spanish pilot who brought back news of having been wrecked on an island far west of the Madeiras as early as 1484.

In 1499, Alonso de Ojeda and Juan de la Cosa visited South America, and with them went Amerigo Vespucci who wrote such popular accounts of his own deeds that the German geographer Martin Waldseemüller coined the word "America" in a book published in 1507. The inevitability of the so-called discovery of America by Europeans is illustrated by the fact that the Portuguese Pedro Cabral, in 1500, tried to reach India by way of the African coast, and was accidentally blown to the west where unintentionally he reached the coast of Brazil.

The island of Española (now Hispaniola) became the Spanish outpost from which further discoveries of the mainland were made. From there Vasco Núñez de Balboa went to Central America, crossed the Isthmus of Panama, and discovered the Pacific Ocean, Sept. 25, 1513. The eastern coast of the mainland of North America had been seen and was cartographically traced by 1502. On Easter Sunday, 1513, Juan Ponce de León, from Española, found his way to the site of the present city of St. Augustine, Fla. Francisco Gordillo coasted as far north as Cape Fear (1521) and Lucas Vásquez de Ayllón followed and got as far as the James River in Virginia (1526). Meantime Hernando Cortés had landed in Mexico and conquered it in one of a series of the most amazing expeditions in all history (1519). Pánfilo de Narváez explored western Florida and possibly Georgia (1528) while his treasurer Álvar Núñez Cabeza de Vaca walked overland from Pensacola Bay, Fla., to the Gulf of California. In 1539 Hernando de Soto took an expedition from Tampa Bay, Fla., marched north to the Savannah River, turned west and proceeded overland until he reached the Mississippi River in 1541.

By this time Antonio de Mendoza had become viceroy of New Spain (Mexico, as opposed to Peru) and from his bailiwick, Franciscan friars were pushing up into what is now the Southwest of the United States. Fray Marcos de Niza (1539) brought back such reports of wealth in that region that Francisco Vásquez de Coronado started out in April 1540 on an expedition which took him as far north as central Kansas (1541).

French Exploration. Giovanni da Verrazano, acting under the favor of Francis I, came to North America in 1524 and possibly saw the Lower Bay of New York. Jacques Cartier coasted Labrador in 1534 and in the next year entered and explored the St. Lawrence River to the Lachine Rapids above Quebec. The discovery of much of the present area of the United States from the north was the work of Samuel de Champlain, who found Maine in 1603–04, and Cape Cod in 1605, and got as far as central New York State in 1615.

English Exploration. Most effective of the discovering nations was England. In May 1497 John Cabot sailed from Bristol, England, under a patent from Henry VII, and some time in June probably discovered the continent of North America, first sighting land near Newfoundland. The Hawkinses—William, John, and James—explored the West Indies in the late 16th century. Sir Francis Drake doubled Cape Horn and reached the coast of California near, if not at, San Francisco Bay in June 1579. In 1602 Bartholomew Gosnold reached the coast of Maine near Cape Porpoise, skirted Cape Cod (which he named), and found Narragansett Bay. George Weymouth in 1605 sighted Nantucket and then headed north to find the coast of Maine in the neighborhood of Monhegan and Georges islands.

Other Exploration. Mention should be made of an alleged discovery of America by Swedes and Norwegians from Greenland in the 13th century, through Hudson Bay and the Red River of the North into the present state of Minnesota. This theory rests on an inscribed stone and certain artifacts which need further study (*see* Kensington Stone). There are also stories of pre-Columbian discoveries of America by the Chinese, Welsh, Irish, Phoenicians, and others. These are all legendary.

[Edward Channing, *History of the United States*, vol. I; Justin Winsor, *Narrative and Critical History of America*.]

RANDOLPH G. ADAMS

AMERICA, NAMING OF. The earliest explorers and historians designated America as the Indies, the West Indies, or the New World, and these terms remained the favorites in Spain and Portugal for over two centuries. Beyond the Pyrenees the chief source of information on the discoveries was Amerigo Vespucci's account of his voyages, translated into Latin. A coterie of scholars at Saint-Dié, in Lorraine, chiefly Martin Waldseemüller and Mathias Ringmann, printed this in 1507 in *Cosmographiae Introductio,* a small work designed to accompany and explain a wall map and globe executed by Waldseemüller. In their work two names were suggested for the new "fourth part" of the world, one *Amerige* (pronounced A-mer-i-gay, with the *-ge* from the Greek, meaning "earth"), and the other *America* (in the feminine form, parallel to *Europa* and *Asia*). The latter form was placed on Waldseemüller's maps of 1507, and their wide circulation brought about the gradual adoption of the name. Waldseemüller was aware of only South America as a continent, but Gerhardus Mercator in 1538 extended the designation to both continents.

Although Vespucci was not responsible for the giving of the name, the injustice to Columbus has aroused a series of protests since 1535. Various impossible origins of the name America have been suggested, such as that it comes from a native Indian word or from a sheriff of Bristol named Richard Ameryk. The etymology of *Amerigo* can be traced to the old Germanic, meaning "ruler of the home." The name America is today highly ambiguous, since it often, as determined by the context, refers to the United States alone.

[Edward Gaylord Bourne, "The Naming of America," *American Historical Review*, vol. 10 (1904).]

ALLEN WALKER READ

AMERICA FIRST COMMITTEE. Founded in 1940 to fight against U.S. participation in World War II, it was endorsed at the outset by Henry Ford and the historian Charles A. Beard. Isolationists in all parts of the United States were involved, but the committee was especially active in Chicago. By October 1941 the organization began to disintegrate.

WAYNE ANDREWS

AMERICAN ACADEMY OF ARTS AND SCIENCES, the second oldest learned society in the United States (*see* American Philosophical Society). Plans for "a society for the cultivation and promotion of arts and sciences" were initiated by John Adams in 1779, and a charter was granted to the academy by the Massachusetts House of Representatives in 1780. The first president of the academy was Gov. James Bowdoin of Massachusetts. Its avowed purpose was "to promote and encourage medical discoveries, mathematical disquisitions, philosophical inquiries and experiments; astronomical, meteorological, and geographical observations, and improvements in agriculture, arts, manufactures, and commerce; and, in fine, to cultivate every art and science which may tend to advance the interest, honor, dignity, and happiness of a free, independent, and virtuous people."

The American Academy of Arts and Sciences has no fixed home although it has owned its own building in the past. It has occupied a number of sites in the Boston area. From 1817 to 1829 the academy joined the Boston Athenaeum in moving to various buildings in Boston; after that time it rented various quarters, until 1904, when it bought its own building at 28 Newbury Street in Boston. The academy stayed at this location until 1955, when city business and parking presented insuperable problems and the building was sold. In 1974 academy headquarters occupied the Brandegee Estate at 165 Allandale Street in the Jamaica Plain section of Boston. The academy also has a Western Center branch, located at the Center for Advanced Study in Behavioral Sciences at Stanford, Calif.; and monthly meetings are held during the academic year at both locations.

Publications of the academy began with a quarto series of *Memoirs,* four volumes of which appeared between 1785 and 1821. In 1833 a new series was begun, and nineteen volumes in this series were issued in the next 113 years. In 1848 a series of octavo *Proceedings* were added, which appeared at more frequent intervals over the next century. In 1955 the academy began publication of the quarterly *Daedalus,* intended not only to capitalize on the wide interests and expertise of the academy fellows but also to serve as a medium for publication for the large number of special studies and commissions sponsored by the academy. Many of the issues of *Daedalus* have been republished in book form.

The academy gives three prizes on a continuing basis: the Rumford Premium, set up by Benjamin Thompson, Count Rumford, in 1797 to honor "the author of the most important discovery or useful improvement . . . in heat and light"; the Emerson-Thoreau medal in the humanities; and the Social Science Prize.

As of August 1973 there were 2,389 fellows and

418 foreign honorary members elected for their contributions to science, humanities, and the arts.

SANBORN C. BROWN

AMERICAN ASSOCIATION FOR THE ADVANCEMENT OF SCIENCE. The AAAS was voted into existence in 1847 and held its first meeting in Philadelphia in 1848. It was shaped by earlier efforts toward a national science organization. Inspired by the example of the British Association for the Advancement of Science, several geologists founded the Association of American Geologists in 1840, with the specific intention of gradually broadening the scope of their organization. They paralleled the British association by holding peripatetic annual meetings, giving reports on advances in specific fields, and opening sessions to the general public. After seven years the geologists decided that gradualism was not the best technique and determined to move directly to an organization "for the advancement of science."

From 1848 to 1860 the AAAS was the preeminent scientific organization in the United States. Nearly all practicing scientists were members and most attended the annual meetings; the leadership included older naturalists like Benjamin Silliman and Edward Hitchcock, as well as such younger natural and physical scientists as William Barton Rogers, Alexander Dallas Bache, and Joseph Henry. The younger men in particular were insistent that the new association establish high professional standards in its published *Proceedings* and monitor the oral presentations. The organization had two sometimes divergent goals—to promote (popularize) and to advance (sponsor research in) science. Disagreement concerning the distribution of decision-making power and the implementation of new standards sparked internal dissension. These arguments also bred hostility toward a prominent group of scientists whose friendship manifested itself privately in a clique, the so-called Lazzaroni, and publicly in the control of the Standing Committee, the principal executive body of the association. As a result of tensions between amateurs and professionals, between some natural and physical scientists, and between regions—tensions not all directly related to the AAAS itself—attendance and membership began to drop at the end of the decade. The outbreak of the Civil War caused the cancellation of the scheduled Nashville meeting for 1861. When the organization regrouped in 1866, it faced competition from the new National Academy of Sciences and from a movement toward scientific societies organized in specialized fields.

For the rest of the 19th century the AAAS sought to reformulate its role in the scientific community. The annual presidential addresses (the office cycled between natural and physical sciences) became an index to American science. In 1873 the association adopted a revised constitution that, among other changes, distinguished between fellows and members, and established new possibilities for more diversified sections. Incorporation in 1874 by the Commonwealth of Massachusetts meant that the association could accumulate a fund for research. Membership gradually increased through the next two decades as more Americans took graduate degrees in science. In 1900 the AAAS took James McKeen Cattell's *Science* as its official journal, supplementing the annual volumes of *Proceedings*.

In 1907 the Smithsonian Institution gave the AAAS free office space; not until 1945 was land purchased in Washington, D.C., where the permanent headquarters are now located. In 1915 the association organized *The Scientific Monthly,* an illustrated nontechnical magazine that, like *Science,* was owned and edited by Cattell. (In 1957 the two periodicals were merged.) Cattell wanted the AAAS to be an increasingly responsible "House of Commons" for American science, while the National Academy of Sciences would become a less powerful but prestigious "House of Lords." In 1920 he helped rewrite the constitution of the AAAS, giving more influence to independent, specialized societies in the hope of better coordination of scientific efforts.

The AAAS served as an integrating organization for science during a century that witnessed increasing specialization. From World War II on, it concentrated its efforts both to provide a common ground on which scientists from different disciplines could share related knowledge on specific topics and to make science more available to the public. In spite of new tactics and a shift in emphasis from advancement to promotion of science, the association maintained its tradition as the most broad-based spokesman for science in America.

[Ralph S. Bates, *Scientific Societies in the United States;* Sally Kohlstedt, "The Formation of a National Scientific Community: The American Association for the Advancement of Science, 1848–1860," unpublished dissertation, University of Illinois (1972).]

SALLY GREGORY KOHLSTEDT

AMERICAN AUTOMOBILE ASSOCIATION. The AAA, a federation of state and local automobile clubs, has been the principal spokesman for American motorists since its formation in 1902. Until that time, the automobile club movement in the United States was dominated by the Automobile Club of America (ACA)—an elite group of New York City automobilists who organized in 1899 with the intention of exerting national influence. Early clubs in other cities also followed the ACA pattern of restricted memberships, elaborate clubhouse and garage facilities, and emphasis on social functions—along with making significant efforts to secure improved roads and rational regulation of the motor vehicle. The AAA was the outcome of nine local clubs recognizing the need for a national federation to coordinate their efforts on the many matters of concern to motorists that transcend municipal and state boundaries. By its 1909 annual meeting the AAA represented 30 state associations with 225 affiliated clubs and had 25,759 members.

With the widespread use of the automobile after 1910, the clubs constituting the AAA increasingly became mass membership organizations, offering special services to members but concerned with a wide range of matters affecting all motorists. Emergency road service for its members was inaugurated by the Automobile Club of Missouri in 1915 and soon came to be offered by all AAA clubs. The AAA issued its first domestic tour book in 1917 and in 1926 published its first series of tour books, issued the first modern-style AAA road maps, and began rating tourist accommodations. From the 1916 Federal Aid Highway Act, through the Interstate Highway Act of 1956, to the present, the AAA has lobbied for toll-free improved highways, for highway beautification programs, and against the diversion of motor vehicle use taxes into nonhighway expenditures. Over the years the AAA has been the nation's leading advocate of highway safety. In 1955 the AAA discontinued its long-standing sanction and supervision of all automobile racing as being inconsistent with the organization's many highway safety activities. In 1972 the AAA had 875 clubs and branches throughout the United States and Canada, and membership passed the 15 million mark.

JAMES J. FLINK

AMERICAN BAR ASSOCIATION. With approximately 160,000 members in 1973, the ABA is the largest and most influential association of lawyers in the United States. It directly or indirectly publishes some 150 periodicals and receives revenues of over $10 million annually.

Founded in 1878, under the leadership of Simeon Baldwin of the Connecticut Bar Association, the ABA originated as an instrument of social intercourse for lawyers and as a means of improving American jurisprudence. In 1936 the present constitution of the ABA was adopted by a national convention of delegates in Boston. The constitution provides for a house of delegates, elected at the state and local levels, which is the association's principal governing body; between sessions the house acts through a board of governors. The ABA's principal publication, the monthly *American Bar Association Journal,* publishes news of general interest to the legal profession. More than twenty sections of the ABA carry on the work of the association in specific fields of law (for example, antitrust law, criminal law, family law, and tax law), and many sections issue their own publications in their respective fields. Through its Committee on the Federal Judiciary, the association judges the qualifications of prospective nominees to the federal bench. In some administrations the association has had close to a veto power on such nominations. But even where it has not had such veto power, it has had enough influence to prevent some appointments. Knowledgeable observers believe the association's interest has on the whole been beneficial to the selection process.

The stated objectives of the ABA are "to advance the science of jurisprudence; to promote the administration of justice and the uniformity of legislation and of judicial decisions throughout the nation; to uphold the honor of the profession of law; to apply its knowledge and experience in the field of law to the promotion of public good; . . . and to correlate and promote such activities of the bar organizations in the nation and in the respective states as are within these objects, in the interest of the legal profession and the public." Clearly the ABA has taken a broad view of its objective "to apply its knowledge . . . to the promotion of public good." Along with its yeoman service in providing insights on public policy issues where knowledge and experience in the law are helpful, it has taken stands on many issues where such a claim is less than persuasive.

[Harold W. Chase, *Federal Judges: The Appointing Process;* Leon Jaworski, "The American Bar Association: A Quasi-Public Institution," *American Bar Association Journal,* vol. 58 (1972); John R. Schmidhauser, *The Supreme Court.*]

HAROLD W. CHASE
ERIC L. CHASE

AMERICAN BATTLE MONUMENTS COMMISSION. *See* **Federal Agencies.**

AMERICAN BIBLE SOCIETY was organized in 1816 by Elias Boudinot, who also served as its first president, to promote the distribution of the Holy Scriptures without doctrinal note or comment and without profit. In its first year forty-three state, county, regional, and local Bible societies already in existence became associated with it as auxiliaries, to share the tasks of supplying the needs of the westward-expanding nation for the Scriptures in English and other European languages and of preparing translations for Indians, such as the Delaware, Cherokee, Seneca, and Mohawk. The program's emphasis gradually shifted from national to worldwide distribution, until today the American Bible Society cooperates with the United Bible Societies in a global coordination of Scripture translation, production, and distribution on every continent.

Through the labors of individual scholars and the coordination of their efforts in a variety of programs and resources provided by the Bible societies and other Christian organizations—translators' institutes and workshops, critical editions of texts, reference tools, and regional technical consultants—the entire Bible has been translated and published in 255 languages, the complete New Testament in 359 more, and at least one book in another 912 languages and dialects, to make a total of 1,526 languages, representing over 97 percent of the world's population. To meet the challenge of presenting the biblical message with fresh impact to new generations unfamiliar with traditional expressions, translators are preparing new popular-language translations in the style of *Good News for Modern Man: The New Testament in Today's English Version.* These new translations will be published in more than 230 languages.

New production techniques have enabled the American Bible Society to reproduce the Scriptures on tapes, records, and cassettes, as well as in braille, and to provide them in contemporary formats: four-page illustrated selections, paperback portions, large-print New Testaments, and whole Bibles.

Distribution rates have soared. In 1973, Bible distribution in the United States totaled more than 117 million copies (more than doubling the 1968 record), and overseas, working in more than 150 nations and territories, the United Bible Societies reported more than 249 million Bibles distributed in over 500 languages. The total number of Bibles distributed by the American Bible Society since its founding passed 1.6 billion in 1973.

The society's headquarters is in New York City, with regional offices in New York, Chicago, Atlanta, and Los Angeles. It is interconfessional; governed by its own duly elected officers, managers, and committees; and is supported by churches and individual donors.

[Annual Reports of the American Bible Society.]

AMERICAN BOTTOM, a narrow Mississippi River flood plain, extending roughly 100 miles between Chester and Alton, Ill., which took its name jointly perhaps from the first American settlers in the Old Northwest and from serving as part of the territorial boundary before the Louisiana Purchase. Site of preeminent burial and ceremonial mounds, the bluff-hemmed strip became a lifeline of settlers in the wilderness with settlements at Cahokia, Kaskaskia, Fort de Chartres, Bellefontaine, and Prairie du Rocher, among others. Frontier travelers found the pond-dotted flat "miasmatic" but extremely fertile.

[L. C. Beck, *Gazetteer of Illinois and Missouri;* H. I. Priestly, *The Coming of the White Man.*]

IRVING DILLIARD

AMERICAN CIVIL LIBERTIES UNION, founded in 1920 to defend constitutional freedoms, especially freedom of expression, due process, the right to privacy, and equal protection under the law. Supplemented by congressional lobbying, the ACLU's main activity consists of court litigation of test cases selected on the basis of constitutional principles involved. Counsel is provided without charge from a staff of about 5,000 volunteer lawyers, with expenses paid by contributions from the organization's 275,000 (1975) members. Policy is established by an elected board of directors.

During its early years the ACLU defended the right to teach evolution in public schools and the right of labor unions to organize; was defense counsel in the controversial Sacco-Vanzetti case; and won major Supreme Court cases in the 1930's protecting the right of public protest. More recently the ACLU has focused its efforts on such issues as amnesty for Vietnam War resisters, abortion and birth control, equal rights for women and children, sexual privacy, humane treatment of mental patients, and prison reform. (*See also* Civil Rights and Liberties.)

[Charles L. Markmann, *The Noblest Cry: A History of the American Civil Liberties Union.*]

JOEL HONIG

AMERICAN COLONIZATION SOCIETY. Formed in 1817 to alleviate the plight of free Afro-Americans by removing them from the United States to Africa, the American Colonization Society also worked to aid the manumission of slaves and to suppress the African slave trade. Throughout its existence the society believed that the race question superseded the questions of slavery and discrimination, and was unable to visualize a biracial society. This led the society into conflicts with the abolitionists, the Radical Republicans, and most Afro-American leaders.

Various colonization schemes appeared in the late 18th century. These plans, increasingly centered in the upper South, emphasized what many felt to be the incompatibility of blacks and whites and proposed colonization as a solution to the problem created by the presence of free blacks as well as the evils of slavery. Following the War of 1812 the idea received impetus from the actions of Paul Cuffe, a black shipowner, who in 1815 transported thirty-eight American blacks to Africa at his own expense.

Colonization was taken up in 1816 by a New Jersey Presbyterian minister, Robert Finley, who convened a series of meetings that led to the formation of the society the following year. As one of the benevolent societies that appeared after the War of 1812, it gained the support of Congregational and Presbyterian clergy, along with that of most of the prominent politicians of the day. Among its early members were Supreme Court Justice Bushrod Washington, Henry Clay, and John Randolph. Official recognition was given to the society by several state legislatures, among them Virginia, Maryland, and Kentucky.

In 1822 the American Colonization Society established the colony of Liberia on the west coast of Africa. In the following decade the number of auxiliary societies increased yearly; receipts grew; and although a total of only 2,638 blacks migrated to Liberia, the number jumped every year. Yet during the decade efforts to secure federal support were rebuffed and the triumph of Jacksonian Democracy blocked the support necessary for a successful program. At the same time, opposition to the society from both abolitionists and proslavery forces combined with mounting debts and internal strife to undermine the organization.

The independence of Liberia after 1846 lifted a great financial burden, and in the 1850's, under the leadership of William McLain, the fortunes of the society revived. Prominent politicians once again endorsed colonization, and for the first time there was some support for the idea from blacks. Although the Civil War might have boosted the fortunes of the society further, it in fact had the opposite effect. Republicans reviled the society and most blacks—including Martin R. Delany, who had at times supported colonization—rejected it. Under the leadership of its secretary, William Coppinger, the society stressed its educational and missionary activities, sending fewer than 2,000 blacks to Liberia in the decade after 1870.

In the 1890's, when rising racial tensions gave voice to back-to-Africa sentiments among southern blacks, the society, which was constantly plagued by a lack of funds and in 1892 was deprived of the services of both the resourceful Coppinger and its longtime president J. H. B. Latrobe, found itself unequal to the task. After a brief period during which the society focused on an unsuccessful attempt to remodel the educational system of Liberia, the organization languished; by 1910, it had all but ceased to exist.

[Willis Dolmond Boyd, "Negro Colonization in the Reconstruction Era, 1865–1870," *Georgia Historical Quarterly,* vol. 40 (1956); George M. Frederickson, *The Black Image in the White Mind;* Edwin S. Redkey, *Black Exodus;* P. J. Staudenraus, *The African Colonization Movement: 1816–1865.*]

William G. Shade

AMERICAN EXPEDITIONARY FORCES. This term was used to designate the American troops serving in Europe during World War I. The declaration of war found the United States without plans for organizing a force that would be capable of offensive action in modern warfare. On May 26, 1917, Maj. Gen. John J. Pershing, who had been selected by President Woodrow Wilson to command American land forces abroad, was directed to proceed with his staff to France. Shortly after his arrival, convinced that military assistance on a vast scale would be necessary to Allied success, Pershing cabled the War Department that its minimum undertaking should contemplate one million men in France by the following May, and that plans should be based on an ultimate force of three million. When the armistice came, approximately two million men had been transported to Europe, where they were trained, subsisted, and were equipped through their own supply system, and took a decisive part in bringing the war to a successful conclusion.

In the spring and early summer of 1918 a series of powerful German offensives threatened defeat of the Allies. In the crisis Pershing placed the entire resources of the American Expeditionary Forces at the disposal of the Allied High Command, postponing until July 24, 1918, the formation of the American First Army.

The assistance the United States gave the Allies in

combat began in May with the capture of Cantigny by an American division in the first independent American offensive operation of the war. This was followed early in June by the entrance into battle of two divisions that stopped the German advance on Paris near Château-Thierry. In July two American divisions, with one Moroccan division, formed the spearhead of the counterattack against the Château-Thierry salient, which marked the turning point of the war. Approximately 300,000 American troops were engaged in this second Battle of the Marne. In the middle of September the American First Army of 550,000 men reduced the Saint-Mihiel salient. The Meuse-Argonne offensive began in the latter part of September. After forty-seven days of intense fighting, this great battle ended brilliantly for the First and Second armies on Nov. 11. More than 1,200,000 American soldiers had participated.

With the cessation of hostilities, attention was immediately turned to repatriating the troops. By the end of August 1919 the last American division had embarked, leaving only a small force in occupied Germany, and on Sept. 1, 1919, Pershing and his staff sailed for the United States.

JOHN J. PERSHING

AMERICAN EXPEDITIONARY FORCES IN ITALY. As tangible proof of American cooperation in World War I, the Italian minister of war urged that American units be sent to Italy. The 332nd Infantry Regiment, the 331st Field Hospital, and the 102nd Base Hospital were so dispatched. With headquarters at Treviso, the 332nd Infantry made numerous marches to the front line, there to be observed by Austrians and Italians. The regiment participated in the attack to force a crossing of the Piave River (Oct. 26, 1918) and in the Battle of the Tagliamento River (Nov. 4). In March 1919 American troops sailed from Italy.

ROBERT S. THOMAS

AMERICAN EXPRESS COMPANY. In 1850 two express companies then operating in the Northeast—Wells, Butterfield and Company and Livingston, Fargo and Company—were united to form a joint stock association with a capital of $150,000 known as the American Express Company. Henry Wells and William G. Fargo were the real governing geniuses of the company, and Wells became its first president. It operated on important lines in New England, followed the Great Lakes into the Midwest and Northwest, and even thrust fingers into Canada. It played no small part in the commercial development of the state of Michigan. Its incorporators organized Wells, Fargo and Company in 1852 as a sister organization for the western half of the country. The United States Express Company was organized in 1854 as a subsidiary, but in the course of two decades the two companies drifted apart and became sharp competitors. In 1915 the American Express operated on 61,500 miles of steam and electric railroads, water, and stage lines, this being the second largest territory among the express companies. In 1918 all the companies merged their shipping interests in the American Railway Express Company, which was taken over in 1929 by the railroad-owned Railway Express Agency. The American Express Company, which had begun selling money orders in 1882 and traveler's checks in 1891, continued as a banking and tourist bureau. In 1958 the company introduced the American Express card, which became the leading travel and entertainment credit card in the world.

[Alvin F. Harlow, *Old Waybills.*]

ALVIN F. HARLOW

AMERICAN FEDERATION OF LABOR–CONGRESS OF INDUSTRIAL ORGANIZATIONS. The AFL and CIO were united in 1955 after almost twenty years of often intense and bitter rivalry. Forces leading to the merger were many and varied, including a hostile political environment (evident to labor leaders by the passage of the Taft-Hartley Act in 1947 and the election of a Republican president in 1952) and the conviction that the combined resources of the two organizations were required if the benefits of unionism were to be extended to burgeoning groups of white-collar workers, public employees, professionals, and others.

The merger did not change in any fundamental way the decentralized and essentially economic nature of the labor movement. The AFL-CIO does not itself engage in collective bargaining or issue strike calls (there are minor exceptions), this power residing, as it always has, with the autonomous national and international unions affiliated with the parent body. Power of the AFL-CIO over its affiliates did expand in important ways, however; this centralizing trend is best illustrated in the explicit constitutional authority given the AFL-CIO to expel unions for corruption or domination by Communist, Fascist, or other totalitarian forces. The AFL-CIO also adopted a vigorous antidiscrimination vow, created a single political arm (the Committee on Political Education), and moved with renewed spirit and a sizable bankroll into electioneering politics—officially on a nonpartisan basis but in reality in close alliance with the Democratic party.

In the late 1950's, the AFL-CIO's attention was focused on internal problems of corruption and racketeering. Televised hearings of Senator John L. McClellan's Select Committee on Improper Activities in the Labor or Management Field revealed dramatically the firm hold corrupt, and sometimes gangster-ridden, elements had taken of some AFL-CIO affiliates. Although President George Meany moved forthrightly against the racketeers and expelled several unions, including the huge International Brotherhood of Teamsters, the AFL-CIO could not prevent the passage of the Landrum-Griffin Act (1959). The act regulated internal union affairs and guaranteed democratic rights to union members.

In the 1960's, the AFL-CIO identified with the New Frontier and Great Society domestic programs of presidents John F. Kennedy and Lyndon Johnson. Its leadership and lobbying support contributed to legislative successes in such areas as civil rights, voting rights, housing, education, health and medical care, urban redevelopment, and poverty programs. Similar success did not follow its determined efforts to amend the Taft-Hartley Act (that is, repeal of section 14b).

The AFL-CIO found itself in opposition to much of the domestic legislation and policies of President Richard Nixon, particularly his anti-inflationary wage- and price-control program. Nevertheless, labor remained neutral in the 1972 presidential race, the first time in years that the Democratic candidate did not win the endorsement and heavy financial support of the AFL-CIO. After the 1972 election and the Watergate scandals, the AFL-CIO moved vigorously on two political fronts, reasserting its influence in the Democratic party and calling for the impeachment of President Nixon.

Approximately 13 million men and women were members of AFL-CIO unions in 1974. Some national and international unions have always remained independent of the AFL-CIO or have been expelled or suspended from it. Two of the biggest independent unions in the early 1970's were the International Brotherhood of Teamsters and the United Automobile Workers. The AFL-CIO has made some progress in organizing white-collar, public, and professional workers, but these groups are still among the largest potential sources for new union recruits.

American Federation of Labor. Launched in 1886, the AFL was in philosophy, structure, goals, and tactics the expression of a long process of evolution, its roots going as far back as the 1790's, when the first local unions emerged in the United States. Other streams of influence were European in origin, debts to the "new unionism" of the British labor movement and to "economic" Marxism being especially significant. Moreover, the philosophy, structure, and fundamental goals of the fledgling AFL have been remarkably successful and durable and continue to describe, in essence but with some important exceptions, the nature of the American labor movement today.

In technical language, the AFL was a trade union center, meaning that it was a "roof organization" under whose banner a large number and variety of other union organizations rallied in order to achieve greater economic and political strength and to pursue certain minimal, common objectives. The most powerful of these affiliates were the national and international unions (so called because they enrolled Canadian, as well as U.S., workers), such as the United Brotherhood of Carpenters and Joiners and the United Mine Workers. Initially their jurisdictions tended to cover a single trade or craft of skilled workers but—under pressures of technological change, changes in the skill mix of the labor force, and the emergence of the mass-production industries in the 20th century—they came to exercise jurisdiction over several trades or crafts, entire industries, and even related industries. Eventually well over a hundred national and international unions became affiliated with the AFL. They in turn were composed of local unions centered in towns, cities, or counties. Local unions from different national unions frequently formed city centrals to pursue common local political, educational, and community goals. Likewise, within each state, city centrals and local unions were the chief pillars upon which state federations of labor were erected, largely for political interaction with state governments.

Sovereign units within this structure were the national and international unions. They were the principal founders of the AFL, and they carried primary responsibility for the achievement of labor's overwhelmingly economic goals of higher wages, shorter hours, and improved conditions of work. Their strategy was to organize enough of the trade or industry to gain control over the supply of labor, use that power position to force employers (via the strike or threat of it) to bargain collectively over the terms of their workers' employment, and sign a trade agreement embodying such terms. Unionism of this type has variously been called "business" unionism, "job control" unionism, or "pure and simple" unionism.

Within such a decentralized, essentially economic structure as described above, the AFL itself carried out limited functions of a service, political, and representative nature. For example, the AFL lobbied for or against legislation in the Congress, carried major responsibility for labor's international activities, helped organize the unorganized, and performed the role of labor's spokesman to the public. These functions were handled through an annual convention, an elected executive council, a president, a secretary-treasurer, and a growing number of service departments. Samuel Gompers, generally accepted as the father of the modern American labor movement, was the first president of the AFL (1886–94, 1895–1924). He was followed by William Green (1925–52) and George Meany (1953–55). The AFL merged with the Congress of Industrial Organizations in 1955 to form the current trade union center, the AFL-CIO.

Congress of Industrial Organizations. The CIO emerged as a strong rival and competitor of the AFL in the 1930's, although there had long before been dissatisfaction with AFL leadership and policies. From its earliest days, the AFL was challenged by Marxist organizations like the Socialist Labor party of Daniel DeLeon and the Socialist party of Eugene V. Debs. These leftist political groups believed that the primary battle facing American workers was on the political rather than the economic front and that major structural changes in the capitalist system were required in order to end exploitation and wage slavery. In addition, the Industrial Workers of the World, a militant but tiny anarchosyndicalist movement, sought to free workers through a cataclysmic general strike and the subsequent erection of a decentralized society run by the unions. Many of the AFL's own national unions were won over to the Socialist cause, yet none of these radical challenges ever succeeded in substituting its program for the procapitalist, job-control unionism of the AFL majority.

The CIO did not pretend to challenge the AFL on radical ideological or philosophical grounds, and it was therefore qualitatively a quite different movement from some of the AFL's earlier antagonists. The major quarrel CIO leaders had with the AFL concerned structure, organizing, and power. They wanted to organize the largely unorganized workers in the mass-production industries (auto, rubber, steel, glass, aluminum, chemical), which had grown explosively since the turn of the century. Moreover, they wanted to organize all of them, regardless of skills, into industrial unions rather than into the traditional craft unions of skilled workers. That the CIO was a successful movement is traceable both to the procapitalist philosophy it shared with the AFL and to the accuracy of its views on structure and organizing. Indeed, as the CIO began to leap forward in membership in the late 1930's, the AFL saw itself forced to abandon antiquated policies and compete vigorously with the CIO for members in the mass-production industries.

Lesser, but still very important, divergences of program between the rival AFL and CIO movements concerned the role of government and legislation, partisan politics, racial discrimination, corruption, and international affairs. The role of the federal government had changed from the laissez-faire concept to that of the general welfare state; unskilled workers in national market industries needed government protection more than skilled workers in local markets; finally, the victorious New Deal coalition of the Democratic party, resting in large part upon worker, black, and urban support, contained a clear message to politically minded union leaders, who wished to turn out huge metropolitan pluralities for friendly Democratic candidates—thus assuring favorable social and economic legislation and a friendly White House.

An effort to reform the AFL from within began in 1933 after recovery legislation had rekindled the union spirit. Failing to achieve the success they desired during 1933–35, the labor progressives set up the Committee for Industrial Organization in November 1935. Unions supporting the committee were suspended from the AFL the following year, and after spectacular organizing successes in the steel, automobile, rubber, and other industries, the committee became the Congress of Industrial Organizations in November 1938. Its first president and undoubtedly most dramatic and forceful leader was John L. Lewis (1938–40). He was succeeded by Philip Murray, who died in office in 1952, and by Walter P. Reuther (1952–55). The CIO merged with the AFL in 1955 to form the AFL-CIO.

[Irving Bernstein, *The Turbulent Years;* Walter Galenson, *The CIO Challenge to the AFL;* Arthur J. Goldberg, *AFL-CIO: Labor United;* Samuel Gompers, *Seventy Years of Life and Labor;* Joseph C. Goulden, *Meany: The Unchallenged Strong Man of American Labor;* Edward Levinson, *Labor on the March;* Lewis L. Lorwin, *The American Federation of Labor;* James O. Morris, *Conflict Within the AFL;* Philip Taft, *The AF of L in the Time of Gompers,* and *The AF of L From the Death of Gompers to the Merger.*]

JAMES O. MORRIS

AMERICAN FORCES IN GERMANY. *See* **Army of Occupation; Germany, American Occupation of.**

AMERICAN FUR COMPANY, incorporated for a period of twenty-five years, under the laws of the state of New York by an act passed on Apr. 6, 1808. Its capital stock was not to exceed $1,000,000 for two years; thereafter it might not exceed $2,000,000. John Jacob Astor was the sole stockholder. From a poor, immigrant German lad in 1784, Astor had risen by 1808 to a position where he felt he could challenge unaided and successfully the two great fur-trading companies of Canada that were securing a large part of their furs within the limits of the United States—the North West Company, with a capital of $1,200,000, and the Michilimackinac Company, capitalized at about $800,000. All that he needed was incorporation as a company. This might have seemed presumptuous on Astor's part, but events were to prove that his belief in himself was justified.

To get control of the fur trade of the Great Lakes, the American Fur Company first came to an agreement with the North West Company and the Michilimackinac Company, whereby the Southwest Fur Company, representing the three companies, was constituted Jan. 28, 1811, to last for five years. It was to confine its operations to the region south of the Canadian frontier. The War of 1812 stopped the normal course of the fur trade, and by 1817 Astor was able to buy out his partners in the Southwest Company at a very low price. Thereupon the Northern Department of the American Fur Company was established, with headquarters at Mackinac.

The next aim of the company was to secure the St. Louis and Missouri River trade. In 1817 it made a tentative arrangement with powerful St. Louis firms, but it was not until 1822 that the company established its own branch in St. Louis. This became known as the Western Department of the American Fur Company.

Still another obstacle to be overcome in securing monopoly of the fur trade of the United States was the abolition of the federal government's Indian factory system, which had been in existence since 1795 and which was a step in the direction of a safe, enlightened, and humane Indian policy. Because the Indians could compete successfully with Astor for the trade, he determined to get rid of the system. With the aid of such interested men as Lewis Cass and Thomas Hart Benton, he campaigned successfully. In 1822 the system was abolished.

Private traders and other companies were treated in the same high-handed manner. Competition was stifled by fair means or foul. An act excluding foreigners from the trade was passed by Congress in 1816, probably at the instigation of the American Fur Company. In 1824 Congress passed another act, designating certain places at which trade might be carried on, which greatly hampered the company's competitors while favoring the company men.

In 1827 the greatest rival of the company—the Columbia Fur Company, which operated between the upper Mississippi and the upper Missouri rivers—united with it and was known thenceforth as the Upper Missouri Outfit of the American Fur Company.

By 1828 the company had a virtual monopoly of the fur trade of the United States. In 1834, however, it became politic for the company to withdraw from the Rocky Mountain area. In that year, too, Astor withdrew from the company, whose charter had lapsed in April 1833, though no notice had been taken of that fact. During the last decade of its existence, the company made profits and declared dividends of over $1,000,000. After 1817 the company had consisted (until 1823) of Astor, Ramsay Crooks, and Robert Stuart. After 1823 and until 1827 the only new partners were the St. Louis firms. In 1827 the Columbia Fur Company's men were added. In 1834 Astor sold out his interests: those in the Western Department to Pratte, Chouteau and Company; and those in the Northern Department to a group headed by Ramsay Crooks. This second group, of some ten stockholders, now became the American Fur Company. It lasted until 1842. During these eight years Ramsay Crooks was president of the company. Its operations were confined roughly to the area between Detroit, the Ohio River, and the Red River of the North. It built vessels on the upper Great Lakes, established extensive fisheries on Lake Superior, marketed the furs of the St. Louis firm of Pratte, Chouteau and Company (after 1838 Pierre Chouteau, Jr., and Company), tried desperately to oust such important rivals as W. G. and G. W. Ewing of Fort Wayne, and maintained something of a banking business throughout the area of its operations. After its failure in 1842 it seems to have been reconstituted once more in 1846 as a commission house. Its papers end for all practical purposes in 1847. (*See also* Astoria; Pacific Fur Company.)

[Grace Lee Nute, Papers of the American Fur Company, *American Historical Review* (1927); P. C. Phillips, *The Fur Trade;* Kenneth W. Porter, *John Jacob Astor, Business Man.*]

GRACE LEE NUTE

AMERICAN HISTORICAL ASSOCIATION. The AHA was founded Sept. 9, 1884, in Saratoga Springs, N.Y., at an annual meeting of the American Social Science Association. Of the forty original members, only thirteen were trained in history, yet they were confident that the future of historical studies belonged to the "teachers of history." During the first decade of its existence, the AHA did little more than meet annually to hear scholarly papers and publish a series of volumes called *The Papers of the American Historical Association.* Although there was and is an elected council and a president (the first of whom was the president of Cornell, Andrew Dickson White), it was Herbert Baxter Adams of Johns Hopkins University, secretary from 1884–1900, who was the leading figure during the early years of the association's history. In 1889 Adams obtained a charter of incorporation from Congress, thus securing the AHA a permanent home in Washington, D.C., as well as its claim to being a national organization. In 1895 the association began to take on more professional tasks, such as establishing a Historical Manuscripts Commission to edit, index, and collect information about unprinted documents relating to American history. In 1899 it formed a Public Archives Commission, which, spurred on by J. Franklin Jameson and Waldo Gifford Leland, stimulated twenty-four states to establish archives and led the movement to establish the National Archives and Records Service. In 1895 the *American Historical Review* began publication, with J. Franklin Jameson as editor; the *Review* was closely affiliated with the AHA until 1915, when it became the association's official organ. Through the report of its Committee of Seven on the Teaching of History in the Secondary Schools (1899) the AHA established the long-enduring four-year curriculum. Since then the association has taken a continuing interest in the teaching of history in schools and colleges, publishing a variety of reports and guides, issued through its Service Center for Teachers of History. It also publishes an annual report and an annual bibliography of writings on American history, as well as a variety of other bibliographies. The AHA is generally recognized as the official representative of historians in the United States, and anyone interested in history may join the organization.

[John Higham, Leonard Krieger, and Felix Gilbert, *History: The Development of Historical Studies;* Boyd C. Shafer, Michel Francois, Wolfgang J. Mommsen, and A. Taylor Milne, *Historical Study in the West.*]

DAVID D. VAN TASSEL

AMERICAN INDEPENDENT PARTY, a third political party, organized in 1968 by George C. Wallace, governor of Alabama (1963–66; 1971–), in support of his presidential candidacy. Wallace and his running mate, Gen. Curtis E. LeMay, opposed forced integration of the races and the enhancement of federal power. The party was popular in the South and among some working-class groups in the North. It won 13.53 percent of the popular vote and forty-six electoral votes, all save one from the five states of the Deep South.

JACOB E. COOKE

AMERICAN INDIAN DEFENSE ASSOCIATION, organized in 1923 with John Collier as executive secretary, was the forerunner of the Association on American Indian Affairs. With many writers and social scientists among its members, it emphasized the rights of Indians to religious freedom and opposed bills proposing to take Indian lands. It promoted the Act of June 2, 1924 (also known as the Curtis Act), which granted United States citizenship to all Indians not yet enfranchised. Collier became U.S. commissioner of Indian affairs in 1933 and administered the Indian New Deal policies of the Indian Reorganization Act of 1934, also known as the Wheeler-Howard Act, until 1946.

[John Collier, *Indians of the Americas;* Stephen J. Kunitz, "The Social Philosophy of John Collier," *Ethnohistory,* vol. 18.]

KENNETH M. STEWART

AMERICAN INDIAN MOVEMENT, a militant movement, called AIM, which uses tactics of direct confrontation, including picketing and disruption, in seeking full rights and redress for Indians. AIM was organized in Minneapolis in 1968 to protest alleged police brutality to Indians, and it attempts to point out instances of discrimination and racism. It seeks the return of federal lands to Indians and opposes what it considers to be the exploitation of Indians in performing tribal dances at the annual Inter-Tribal Indian Ceremonial in Gallup, N.Mex. AIM has played a leading role in a number of Indian protests, including the forceful occupation by hundreds of Indians of the Washington, D.C., headquarters of the Bureau of Indian Affairs in November 1972. (The movement that brought them to Washington was called the Trail of Broken Treaties.) Three months later members of

AIM seized the village of Wounded Knee, S.Dak., scene of a massacre of Sioux Indians by U.S. troops in 1890, and occupied it by force of arms for seventy-one days. After an eight-month trial in 1974, a federal judge dismissed charges against Russell Means and Dennis Banks, AIM leaders and key organizers of the siege at Wounded Knee.

[Alvin Josephy, *Red Power*.]

KENNETH M. STEWART

AMERICANISM. By an apostolic letter, entitled *Testem benevolentiae* (from the first two words of the text), addressed by Leo XIII to the American hierarchy on Jan. 22, 1899, the pontiff, while expressing praise for the progress Catholicism had made in the United States, took occasion to point out some dogmatic and moral tendencies which he singled out for correction. The three main points of discussion were the adaptation of Christian teaching to our advancing civilization, freedom of spirit in matters of faith and of Christian life, and the division of virtues into active and passive. Principal among these was the alleged effort on the part of some American ecclesiastics to have the church adapt its teaching to contemporary religious thought. Hence the name as used in the brief. The term "Americanism" is vague, although it was defined at the time as "a spirit that is democratic, tolerant, anti-medieval, up-to-date, individualistic, believing chiefly in good works, and lastly, very ultramontane" (Adrian Fortescue, *Folia Fugitiva*, 1907). The Latin and English text of the brief will be found in the *American Catholic Quarterly Review*, vol. 24 (1899).

[Winthrop S. Hudson, *Religion in America;* Peter Guilday, "The Church in the United States: 1870–1920," *Catholic Historical Review* (1921).]

PETER GUILDAY

AMERICAN JOINT COMMISSION TO FRANCE. *See* **France, American Joint Commission to.**

AMERICAN LABOR PARTY. The ALP was formed in July 1936 as the New York State unit of the Nonpartisan League. Circumstances specific to New York dictated the creation of a separate party rather than a Committee for Industrial Organization campaign body allied to the Democratic party: a Tammany machine unsympathetic to President Franklin D. Roosevelt and the New Deal; a large ethnic bloc that was traditionally socialistic; and a state law permitting dual nominations. The successful campaigns of Fiorello H. La Guardia for New York City mayor in 1937 and Herbert H. Lehman for governor in 1938 demonstrated that the ALP held the balance of power between the two major parties. Nevertheless, this potent position, displayed in the elections of the next five years, eroded because of factional disputes and a loss of union support and voter allegiance—all the result primarily of Communist influence in the ALP. In 1944 the right wing split off to form the Liberal party, and subsequently the ALP lost its swing position in New York politics. Although it recorded its highest vote in the national election in 1948, as the New York unit of the Progressive party, the ALP thereafter declined rapidly and disbanded in 1954. The New York pattern of third-party pressure politics that it had pioneered continued, however, through the activities of the Liberal party and, from the opposite end of the political spectrum, of the Conservative party, founded in 1962.

[Warren Moscow, *Politics in the Empire State*.]

DAVID BRODY

AMERICAN LAND COMPANY, one of a score or more of large land companies speculating in public lands in the 1830's. It became the object of a severe political attack because its best-known promoters were leading New York Democratic politicians who, it was charged, used their influence to secure public deposits for banks they controlled. With the credit made available to them, promoters of these favored institutions invested extensively in federal lands. It was even charged that they were given special advantages when there were crowds lined up at the land offices. Best known of these promoters were Attorney General Benjamin F. Butler and Postmaster General Amos Kendall in Andrew Jackson's cabinet; and E. Corning, John Van Buren, John A. Dix, Silas Wright, and Edwin Crosswell, all members of the Albany Regency. The American Land Company, capitalized at one million dollars, purchased some 322,000 acres of public land in Mississippi, Arkansas, Michigan, Wisconsin, and Illinois and town lots in Chicago, Toledo, and some less promising sites during the frenzy of speculation that affected almost everybody in 1835 and 1836. The company fell into financial difficulty following the issue of the Specie Circular in 1836 and the panic of 1837, when little of its land was in demand and its costs were multiplying.

However, the partial record of its dividends suggests that stockholders who held on to their investment may not have done badly. Almost from its inception the American Land Company was criticized as a "gigantic monopoly" that was corrupting public officials, cheating Indians, preventing competitive bidding at public land sales, preventing the distribution of the public funds in order to retain them in the "pet banks," and charging outrageous prices up to $10 an acre for lands that it had bought less than a year before for $1.25 an acre.

[Irene D. Neu, *Erastus Corning: Merchant and Financier, 1794–1872*.]

PAUL W. GATES

AMERICAN LEGION. The American Legion is the largest U.S. veterans' organization, with membership open to any person, male or female, who has served honorably on active duty in the U.S. armed forces during the hostilities of World War I, World War II, the Korean conflict, or the war in Vietnam.

The Legion was founded in February 1919 by a group of Allied Expeditionary Forces staff officers at Paris. Led by Col. Theodore Roosevelt, Jr., the founders sought both to bolster soldier morale during the postarmistice period and to provide an alternative to veterans' groups being set up in the United States. They enunciated the organization's purposes at the Paris Caucus and saw them reaffirmed at the Continental Caucus, held three months later at St. Louis, Mo. The Legionnaires dedicated themselves to perpetuating the principles for which they had fought, to inculcating civic responsibility to the nation, to preserving the history of their participation in the war, and to binding together as comrades all those who had fought. Among other aims, they pledged themselves to defending law and order, to developing "a one hundred percent Americanism," and to working to help others.

The Legion soon assumed the role of spokesman for all former doughboys, although its 1920 membership of 840,000 represented only about 18.5 percent of eligible veterans. Over the next half-century the Legion's membership fluctuated from a low of 610,000 in 1925 to a high of 3,325,000 in 1946, followed by a general decline, leveling off by 1972 to 2,700,000.

Pursuit of its goals of Americanism, military preparedness, and extending veterans' benefits has led the Legion into many controversies. It has striven to rid school textbooks and public libraries' shelves of alien, Communist, syndicalist, or anarchist influences. During the "red scare" of 1919–20, four Legionnaires were killed in a shootout with Industrial Workers of the World organizers at Centralia, Wash. Its advocacy of preparedness during the late 1930's, when isolationism was dominant nationally, made the organization unpopular with many, as did its support of universal military training in the 1950's. Similarly its condemnation of U.S. participation in United Nations Economic and Social Council activities and its call for a total blockade of Communist Cuba during the 1960's sparked debates.

The Legion's strenuous efforts to obtain benefits for veterans earned for it the reputation by the late 1930's of being one of the nation's most effective interest groups. Its demand for a bonus for World War I veterans, finally met in 1936 over the objections of four successive presidents, and its promotion of the GI Bill of Rights for World War II veterans, achieved in 1944, testified to its highly publicized dedication to all veterans—not just its members. Other, less controversial activities of the Legion include support of programs for children's welfare and for physical and vocational rehabilitation; sponsorship of Cub Scouts, Boy Scouts, and Explorer Scout troops; and promotion of school oratorical and essay-writing contests on patriotic subjects.

The Legion has some 16,100 local posts throughout the world. These posts are bound together into departments at the state level, which send representatives to the annual national convention. The convention in turn sets policy for the organization and elects the national commander and national executive committee. The latter directs the organization from national headquarters at Indianapolis, Ind., between conventions. The Legion's charter forbids formal political activity by the organization or its elective officers. Nonetheless the Legion does maintain a liaison office in Washington, D.C., and publishes the monthly *American Legion Magazine* from its New York branch.

[Raymond Moley, Jr., *The American Legion Story*.]

DAVIS R. B. ROSS

AMERICAN LIBERTY LEAGUE, organized in August 1934, with the express purpose of fighting radicalism and defending property rights and the U.S. Constitution. Among its organizers were many lifelong, though conservative, Democrats, but it was clearly inimical to the New Deal and, because of this and its many wealthy members, was denounced by the Franklin D. Roosevelt administration as reactionary. It was dissolved in 1940.

["Fifty-Eight Lawyers," *United States Law Review*, vols. 69–70.]

ALVIN F. HARLOW

AMERICAN LITERATURE. *See* **Literature.**

AMERICAN MATHEMATICAL SOCIETY. In 1887 Thomas Scott Fiske, a graduate student at Columbia College, who was visiting the University of Cambridge, attended meetings of the London Mathematical Society, founded in 1865. Upon returning to Columbia, he and a handful of faculty and students met on Thanksgiving Day, Nov. 24, 1888, to organize the New York Mathematical Society, with Dean J. H. Van Amringe as president and Fiske as secretary-treasurer. In 1892 the society published the first volume of its *Bulletin*, with Fiske as editor. The name of the organization was changed to the American Mathematical Society in 1894, and on May 3, 1923, the society was incorporated under the laws of the District of Columbia. At the World's Columbian Exposition in Chicago in 1893, lecture series were initiated; these resulted in the publication by the society of its *Colloquium Publications*. In 1900 the society established the *Transactions*, for longer research papers; in 1950 publication of the *Proceedings*, for papers of moderate length, and the *Memoirs*, for monographs or a group of cognate papers, was begun. The society in 1940 undertook the publication of *Mathematical Reviews*, a monthly abstracting journal now sponsored also by a dozen other organizations. In 1954 housekeeping details were transferred from the *Bulletin* to still another publication, the *Notices*. The society has also initiated series of translations, including *Soviet Mathematics—Doklady* (from 1960) and *Chinese Mathematics—Acta* (from 1962), and in 1962 it took over the publication of *Mathematics of Computing*.

Sectional meetings of the society were initiated with the formation in 1897 of the Chicago section; the activity of members of this group resulted in 1915 in the founding of the Mathematical Association of America. The society represents the research interests of mathematicians, while the association—especially through the publication of *The American Mathematical Monthly*—meets the interests of teachers and students on the college level.

[R. C. Archibald, *A Semicentennial History of the American Mathematical Society*, and "History of the American Mathematical Society," *Bulletin of the American Mathematical Society*, vol. 45 (1939); K. O. May, ed., *A Fifty-Year History of the Mathematical Association of America*.]

CARL B. BOYER

AMERICAN-MEXICAN MIXED CLAIMS COMMISSIONS. For over a century after the United States recognized Mexico's independence in 1822, claims by citizens of each nation for losses attributed to the actions of the other complicated relations between the two governments. In 1839 a joint commission was established to settle these claims, and by 1842 it had awarded $2,026,139 to Americans. Mexico's failure to honor the adjudication contributed to President James K. Polk's decision to ask Congress for a declaration of war in 1846. By the terms of the Treaty of Guadalupe Hidalgo (1848) the U.S. government assumed liability for American claims to the amount of $3,250,000. Claims accruing during the next twenty years were examined by a second mixed commission (1869–76), which granted $4,125,633 to Americans and $150,498 to Mexicans. The chaotic decade following the outbreak of the 1910 revolution generated thousands of claims from aggrieved Americans and a smaller number from Mexicans. The Bucareli accords of 1923 instituted a Special Commission on Revolutionary Claims and a Mexican–United States General Claims Commission. Working in the glare of emotional publicity, neither body accomplished its task. The general commission resolved only 148 of 3,617 cases; the special commission disposed of only 18 of 3,176 claims and made no monetary awards. Both commissions suspended work in 1931. In 1934 the United States accepted a settlement of most revolutionary claims for a lump payment equivalent to 2.64 percent of their face value. By another agreement in 1941 Mexico paid remaining American claims to the amount of $40 million and agreed to the appointment of a joint commission to determine the value of U.S. oil holdings expropriated in 1938. The commissioners completed their work to the satisfaction of both governments in 1942. Occasional claims filed after that year were arbitrated by normal diplomatic procedures.

[H. F. Cline, *The United States and Mexico;* F. S. Dunn, *The Diplomatic Protection of Americans in Mexico*.]

DAVID C. BAILEY

AMERICAN PARTY, or the **Know-Nothing party,** enjoyed a meteoric career during the 1850's. It was founded in New York in 1849 as a secret patriotic society known as the Order of the Star Spangled Banner, but experienced little success until after 1852. Expansion from that time on was so rapid that by 1854 a national organization could be perfected.

This phenomenal growth was due partly to the charm of secrecy with which the party clothed itself. Members were initiated and sworn not to reveal its mysteries; their universal answer to questions was "I know nothing about it," thus giving their organization its popular name—the Know-Nothing party. All who joined were pledged to vote only for native Americans, to work for a twenty-one-year probationary period preceding naturalization, and to combat the Catholic church.

More important in accounting for the party's success was the period in which it thrived. Older party lines had been disrupted by the Kansas-Nebraska Act, and many voters, unwilling to cast their lot either with proslavery Democrats or antislavery Republicans, found refuge with the Know-Nothings. At this time, too, anti-Catholic sentiment, long fostered by churches, societies, and the press, was reaching its height. The American party attracted thousands of persons who sincerely believed that Catholicism and immigration menaced their land.

These factors account for the startling strength shown by the party. In the elections of 1854 and 1855 it was successful in a number of New England and border states, and its supporters fully expected to carry the country in 1856.

By this time, however, the slavery issue had caused a split in Know-Nothing ranks. A proslavery resolution, pushed through the 1855 convention by southern delegates, caused a lasting breach, and the American party entered the election of 1856 so hopelessly divided that its presidential candidate, Millard Fillmore, carried only the state of Maryland. This crushing defeat and the growing sectional antagonism over slavery brought about the party's rapid end.

[C. Beals, *Brass-Knuckle Crusade: The Great Know-Nothing Conspiracy;* Ray Allen Billington, *The Protestant Crusade, 1800–1860;* L. F. Schmeckebier, *History of the Know-Nothing Party in Maryland.*]

Ray Allen Billington

AMERICAN PHILOSOPHICAL SOCIETY is the oldest learned society in America. The proposal for a general scientific society in Philadelphia was first made by the botanist John Bartram in 1739; but Benjamin Franklin issued a public call to found a society of "Virtuosi or ingenious Men," offering himself as secretary. Several meetings were held in 1743; members were elected from neighboring colonies; learned papers were read and plans made to publish them. But, Franklin complained, the members were "very idle"; consequently the society languished and by 1746 it was dead. In 1766, stimulated by the feelings of American nationalism engendered by the Stamp Act, some younger Philadelphians—many of Quaker background and, in politics, belonging to the Assembly party—formed the American Society for Promoting Useful Knowledge, which meant better agricultural methods, domestic manufactures, and internal improvements. Survivors of the 1743 group and some others, Anglican and Proprietary in sentiment, then revived the "dormant" American Philosophical Society. Wisely the rival societies merged in 1769 as the American Philosophical Society, Held at Philadelphia, for Promoting Useful Knowledge. In a contested election Franklin, then in London, was chosen president.

The society's first important scientific undertaking was to observe the transit of Venus (June 3, 1769). Its reports were first published in the *Philosophical Transactions* of the Royal Society, then, in full, in its own *Transactions* (1771), which, distributed among European academies and philosophers, quickly established the society's reputation. Reorganized in 1784–85 after wartime interruption, the society expanded its membership, erected a hall (still in use), and resumed publication of the *Transactions*. In the ensuing half-century it was the most important single scientific forum in the United States. Its tone was Jeffersonian, republican, deistic, and pro-French. By the loan of its facilities, it encouraged such other learned bodies in Philadelphia as the College of Physicians, the Historical Society of Pennsylvania, the Academy of Natural Sciences, and the Agricultural Society. Thomas Jefferson, president of the United States and the society simultaneously, used the society as a national library, museum, and academy of sciences, asking it to draft instructions for Meriwether Lewis and William Clark and, after the explorers' return, depositing their specimens and report in its museum and library. Materials on American Indian languages collected by Jefferson and another society president, Peter S. Du Ponceau, also went into the library. Joel R. Poinsett donated an impressive collection of ancient Mexican artifacts. During the 19th century, the *Transactions* carried many descriptive articles on American natural history: by Isaac Lea on malacology, Edward D. Cope on paleontology, F. V. Hayden on geology, Joseph Leidy on anatomy, Leo Lesquereux on botany. Joseph Henry's experiments on electromagnetism were often reported in the society's *Proceedings*.

The society lost preeminence during the second third of the century, when the specialized learned societies arose; the federal government created its own learned institutions like the Smithsonian; and the *American Journal of Science* was founded, which ensured prompt publication. At mid-century the society seemed without imagination or energy—Henry Thoreau called it "a company of old women"—but it continued to meet, publish, and elect persons to membership, overlooking hardly any outstanding scientist.

The bicentennial of Franklin's birth in 1906 brought a renewal of activity, especially in historical publication. In 1927–29 plans were drafted to reorganize the society as a clearinghouse for scientific knowledge—with popular lectures, a newsletter, and a publications office designed to disseminate "authoritative news of forward steps in all branches of learning." Those plans collapsed with the economic depression that began in 1929. After 1940 private bequests and gifts produced striking changes. While retaining its old organization and traditional practices, the society extended its activities in several directions. It expanded its scholarly publications program, inaugurated a program of research grants to individuals (406 grants amounting to $344,202 were made in 1973), and developed its library into one of the principal collections on the history of science in America.

[American Philosophical Society, *Year Books;* Brooke Hindle, *The Pursuit of Science in Revolutionary America, 1735–1789*.]

WHITFIELD J. BELL, JR.

AMERICAN PROTECTIVE ASSOCIATION, a secret anti-Catholic society, founded at Clinton, Iowa, in 1887 by Henry F. Bowers. It grew slowly in the Midwest until the panic of 1893 brought home to native Americans the economic rivalry of second-generation immigrants, and this, combined with rural antagonism toward urban Catholics, the effective propaganda of nativistic newspapers and speakers, revived Catholic demands for a share in public school funds, and political instability following the Democratic victory in 1892, attracted a million members by 1896. This voting strength was utilized to gain control of local Republican organizations and carry elections throughout the Midwest, but in 1896 the association split over the question of supporting William McKinley. Its members deserted rapidly amidst the greater excitement of the free silver campaign. It lingered on despite steadily declining support until 1911.

[H. J. Desmond, *The A.P.A. Movement. A Sketch*.]

RAY ALLEN BILLINGTON

AMERICAN RAILWAY ASSOCIATION, originated in meetings of general managers and ranking railway operating officials known as Time Table Conventions, the first of which was held on Oct. 1, 1872, at Louisville, Ky. One of the major achievements of these meetings was the railroads' decision to establish the four zones of standard time in the United States. In 1875 the group changed its name to General Time Convention and in October 1891 to American Railway Association. In January 1919 ten separate groups of operating officers were amalgamated with the association and carried on their activities as divisions, sections, or committees of the larger group. In 1934 it was included in the Association of American Railroads.

HARVEY WALKER

AMERICAN RAILWAY UNION, started by Eugene V. Debs in June 1893 in an attempt to unite all railroad workers. In June 1894 it ordered its members not to handle Pullman cars in sympathy with the Pullman shop strikers. Violence resulting, President Grover Cleveland sent troops to stop interference with the mails. The union officers were jailed for violating an injunction secured by the railroads under the Sherman Antitrust Act. The strike was lost, and the union collapsed.

[McAlister Coleman, *Eugene V. Debs*.]

JAMES D. MAGEE

AMERICAN REPUBLICAN PARTY, a minor nativistic political organization, launched in New York in June 1843, largely as a protest against immigrant voters and officeholders. In 1844 it carried municipal elections in New York City and Philadelphia and expanded so rapidly that by July 1845 a national convention was called. This convention changed the name to the Native American party and drafted a legislative program calling for a twenty-one-year period preceding naturalization and other sweeping reforms in the naturalization machinery. Failure to force congressional action on these proposals, combined with the growing national interest in the Mexican problem, led to the party's rapid decline.

[Ray Allen Billington, *The Protestant Crusade;* L. D. Scisco, *Political Nativism in New York State*.]

RAY ALLEN BILLINGTON

AMERICAN REPUBLICS, BUREAU OF. *See* **Pan-American Union.**

AMERICAN REVOLUTION. *See* **Revolution, American.**

AMERICAN SAMOA. *See* **Samoa, American.**

AMERICAN STUDIES, an approach to the study of American civilization (sometimes described as a method, a discipline, or even a philosophy) that achieved grudging institutional acceptance in American universities in the 1930's and growing popularity in the period immediately following World War II. As described by Robert H. Walker in his *American Studies in the United States: A Survey of College Programs* (1958), the American studies movement was bred in the minds of certain professors (more often in history than in literature departments despite a contrary impression held by many) who were impatient with the rigid institutional boundaries maintained by traditional departments. These scholars sought to approach American culture in the most comprehensive fashion possible, primarily through its history and literature, but also through its fine arts, religion, and philosophy. The American studies approach was also characterized by a concern with myth and symbol, as in Henry Nash Smith's pioneering work *Virgin Land: The American West as Symbol and Myth* (1950), the product of his studies toward the first Ph.D. in American civilization to be granted at Harvard University.

American studies programs at both undergraduate and graduate levels were at first under the control of interdepartmental committees consisting of representatives from such departments as English, history, fine arts, philosophy, and government. More recently a number of institutions have created separately funded and independently organized American studies departments. The American studies movement acquired a journal in 1949, when the first issue of *American Quarterly* appeared under the auspices of the Program in American Studies at the University of Minnesota. The *American Quarterly* soon moved to the University of Pennsylvania, where in 1952 it became the official journal of the newly organized American Studies Association, the national organization of those professionally concerned with research and teaching in the field of American studies.

Despite the rapid growth of the American studies movement (242 colleges and universities in 1974; 30 with Ph.D. programs), its supporters have usually been ill at ease with themselves and with the movement. As noted by Robert Merideth, in his introduction to a collection of essays entitled *American Studies: Essays on Theory and Method* (1968), the tone of those involved has been "frustrated, combative, urgent, at times hopeful, the tone of men with a cause engaged in struggle." All practitioners of American studies have been forced to face the question propounded by Henry Nash Smith in an article published in the *American Quarterly* in 1957 entitled "Can 'American Studies' Develop a Method?" While accepting the validity of a comprehensive, culture-oriented approach to the study of American life, Smith concluded that no existing method, including that of cultural anthropology, provided a ready-made method of American studies. Rather, Nash concluded, "The best thing we can do, in my opinion, is to conceive of American Studies as a collaboration among men working from within existing academic disciplines but attempting to widen the boundaries imposed by conventional methods of inquiry."

As American studies programs expanded in number and influence, criticism increased. In the 1950's the charge was made that American studies reflected a jingoistic exaltation of American virtues and a concealment of American vices. While some support for American studies programs has come from patriotically inclined men of substance, few practitioners of American studies would accept, or even recognize, the charge that American studies is merely a reflection of crude ethnocentric pride. Another criticism has been that the followers of American studies are distinguished less by their knowledge of America than by their ignorance of Europe. Partly in response to this charge, most doctoral programs in American studies require that competence in at least one non-American field be demonstrated. A practical criticism has been that recipients of Ph.D.'s in American studies, although they must normally find a niche in university departments of history or literature, are neither fitted for, nor welcomed by, such departments. The evidence of placement of American studies Ph.D.'s tends to belie the assertion.

Perhaps the most serious criticism of the American studies approach has been that writers in the field play fast and loose with symbols and myths, with notions of national character, and with a few literary works thought by literary critics, but not the public to which they were directed, to be particularly representative of American thought. Roy Harvey Pearce, himself the author of a significant study in the field, *Savagism and Civilization: The Indian and the American Mind* (1967; a revision of his 1953 work, *The Savages of America*), has warned of the tendency of writers in the movement "to use words as magic: Name it, the formula goes, and you have it." Literary critic Alfred Kazin, in an outspoken review of Alan Trachtenberg's *Brooklyn Bridge: Fact and Symbol,* in the *New York Review of Books* (July 15, 1965), was even more vitriolic in indicting American studies for producing "junkheaps of unnecessary and even cynical publication." Kazin charged that writers in the American studies tradition did not deal with basic social, economic, or literary history, that they were content to juggle symbols extracted from the work of others. Kazin's skepticism was echoed by Bruce Kuklick, in an article entitled "Myth and Symbol in American Studies," which appeared in the October 1972 issue of the *American Quarterly*. Kuklick denied that American studies was a true historical enterprise and concluded that American studies scholars, including himself, had "no business masquerading as historians at all."

American studies scholars in the 1970's tended to accept the limitations of the American studies method but to remain loyal to it. Leo Marx, in an appropriately titled article, "American Studies—A Defense of an Unscientific Method," in *New Literary History* (vol. I, 1969), defended the humanistic rather than scientific analysis of images—intellectual constructions that fuse concept and emotion and connote more than they denote—as a valid intellectual contribution of the American studies approach.

American studies in the 1960's and 1970's did not retreat in the face of its critics, but rather extended its grasp. Anthropology, sociology, historical archaeology, industrial archaeology, folk culture, material culture, museum studies, and popular culture, as well as urban, minority, and women's studies, were all included within the purview of American studies, both as subjects of study and as sources of theories and methods of approach to American culture. Henry Wasser's aphorism, that American studies "often has the appearance of six disciplines in search of a methodology," may have to be modified by enlarging the number of disciplines engaged in the search. The variety of techniques and theories characterizing the American studies approach is both a strength and a weakness. An unsophisticated approach to the disparate and homely aspects of American culture can degenerate into antiquarianism and casual inquiry. On the other hand, a disciplined and comprehensive approach to the multifarious facts of American civilization, utilizing the methods and insights of various disciplines and exploiting the constantly enlarging sources for such a study, can provide the opportunity for syntheses not liable to emerge from any of the separate disciplines concerned with American life.

[Hennig Cohen, ed., *The American Culture,* and *The American Experience;* Marshall W. Fishwick, ed., *American Studies in Transition;* Stuart Levine, "Art, Values, Institutions and Culture: An Essay in American Studies Methodology and Relevance," *American Quarterly,* vol. 24 (1972); Jay Mechling, Robert Merideth, and David Wilson, "American Culture Studies: The Discipline and the Curriculum," *American Quarterly,* vol. 25 (1973); Robert Merideth, ed., *American Studies: Essays on Theory and Method;* Cecil F. Tate, *The Search for a Method in American Studies;* Robert H. Walker, *American Studies in the United States: A Survey of College Programs.*]

WILCOMB E. WASHBURN

AMERICAN SYSTEM, a term applied by Henry Clay, in his tariff speech of March 30–31, 1824, by which he sought to justify the greater measure of protection that he was trying to secure in the tariff bill under discussion. His object was to create a home market and "to lay the foundations of a genuine American policy"; he wished to check the decline of American industry and offered a remedy, which, he said, "consists in modifying our foreign policy, and in adopting a genuine American system." By this he proposed to eliminate the dependence upon the foreign market with the result that American industries would flourish and a home market for the surplus of agricultural products would develop. Such a program was presumed to offer attractions not only to the eastern manufacturer but also to the western farmer. Implicit in the arrangement was the availability of more revenue for internal improvements, upon which Clay had already taken a leading position.

Since Clay became known as the father of the American system, the practice soon developed of applying this label to collateral measures for which he stood. With his tariff and internal improvement policies was combined his proposal to have the national government distribute among the states the proceeds of the sale of public lands. Clay's contemporary biographer, Calvin Colton, declared (I, 428): "There are collateral measures, and measures of affinity, having more or less of an intimate connection. There are numerous measures of result emanating from this system. But internal improvement, and protection of American interests, labor, industry and arts, are commonly understood to be the *leading* measures, which constitute the *American system.*"

[T. H. Clay, *Henry Clay;* Calvin Colton, *The Life and Times of Henry Clay.*]

ARTHUR C. COLE

AMERICAN TOBACCO CASE, 221 U.S. 106 (1911). In this decision the Supreme Court, following the same line of reasoning as in the Standard Oil decision of the same year, found that the American Tobacco Company had attempted to restrain commerce and monopolize the tobacco business in violation of the Sherman Antitrust Act. "Restraint of trade," the Court declared, did not embrace "all those normal and usual contracts essential to individual freedom, and the right to make which was necessary in order that the course of trade might be free," but on the other hand, in view of "the general language of the statute, and the public policy which it manifested, there was no possibility of frustrating that policy by resorting to any disguise or subterfuge of form, since resort to reason rendered it impossible to escape by any indirection the prohibitions of the statute."

[E. D. Durand, *The Trust Problem;* J. A. McLaughlin, *Cases on the Federal Anti-Trust Laws of the United States.*]

W. A. ROBINSON

***AMERICA'S* CUP RACES.** *See* **Yacht Racing.**

AMIENS, TREATY OF, signed Mar. 27, 1802 (after agreement in October 1801 on preliminary articles), between France and Great Britain, ended the war declared by France on Feb. 1, 1793, and terminated the first phase of the war of the French Revolution. Its significance for American history is that it afforded a short breathing spell in the controversy with the belligerents over neutral rights, and offered an interval of peace during which Napoleon turned to the newly acquired province of Louisiana as a field for the building of a great colonial empire. On the eve of war again with Great Britain in 1803, he sold Louisiana to the United States to cash in on the territory before it should be captured by superior British sea power.

[Henry Adams, *History of the United States During the First Administration of Thomas Jefferson,* vols. I, II.]

SAMUEL FLAGG BEMIS

AMISH MENNONITES. *See* **Mennonites.**

***AMISTAD* CASE.** In 1839 fifty-four slaves on the Spanish schooner *Amistad* mutinied near Cuba, murdered part of the crew, and attempted to cause the remainder to sail to Africa. They landed on Long Island Sound in the jurisdiction of American courts. Piracy charges were quashed, it being held that it was not piracy for persons to rise up against those who illegally held them captive. Salvage claims, initially awarded by legal proceedings in Connecticut, were overturned by the Supreme Court in 1841 and the Africans were freed. Former President John Quincy Adams represented the Africans before the Supreme Court. Private charity provided their transportation back to Africa, and the organized support on their behalf played a part in the later establishment of the American Missionary Association. This case offers an interesting comparison with the *Creole* affair.

[J. W. Barber, *A History of the Amistad Captives.*]

HENRY N. DREWRY

AMITE, BATTLE OF (August 1808), a skirmish fought on the Amite River in Mississippi Territory between nineteen frontier settlers and thirty Choctaw Indians. Regular troops and militia were called out, but the Indians disappeared.

WALTER PRICHARD

AMNESTY, the decision of a government not to punish certain offenses, typically of a political nature. Amnesty is usually general, applies to certain groups or communities of people, and relates to a particular historical event. It overlooks both the offense and the offender. Amnesty is based upon the theory that forgiveness can be more in the interest of general welfare than prosecution. The U.S. Constitution gives the president the authority to grant pardon and, by interpretation, amnesty.

Amnesty was used by President George Washington to quell the Whiskey Rebellion of 1794. He offered amnesty to citizens of several Pennsylvania counties who refused to pay taxes levied upon the manufacture of alcohol. In 1807, President Thomas Jefferson pardoned army deserters outside the country if they turned themselves in within four months and resumed their duties. President James Madison issued three amnesty proclamations for deserters after the War of 1812. President Andrew Jackson issued an amnesty proclamation in 1830, but recipients were precluded from serving in the military.

Following the Civil War, no action was taken

against southern deserters. Moreover, President Abraham Lincoln granted amnesty to all Union deserters; they were to return to their units within sixty days and serve out their enlistment or lose their citizenship. Although some Radical Republicans branded them traitors, the Confederates were entitled to the protection accorded participants in a recognized war. The establishment of the Confederacy was the deliberate act of an entire people through their organized state governments.

The executive branch of the government attempted, even during the Civil War, to provide genuine relief to those allied to the southern cause. Lincoln believed that through the use of his amnesty power he could facilitate reunion and ease sectional hatreds. He attempted—unsuccessfully—to establish a parole system for political prisoners and offered a pardon to southerners who would take an oath of allegiance to the federal government.

Following Lincoln's assassination, his successor, Andrew Johnson, a Tennessee Democrat, indicated he would be more reluctant to grant amnesty, especially to Confederate military and civilian leaders. However, during his three years in office he proclaimed three executive amnesties, each more liberal than the former. His final proclamation, on Christmas of 1868, was a universal amnesty that even included Jefferson Davis in its provisions.

Congress was at the opposite pole from the executive branch on the issue of clemency, both before and after the war. In addition to providing criminal and civil penalties for Confederates during the Civil War, Congress continued to press the southerners after the war by passing the Fourteenth Amendment (1868), the third section of which effectively precluded southerners who had previously served in federal or state offices from ever serving in a government position again. Another law passed by Congress denied all active supporters of the Confederacy the right to vote, even those who had been pardoned by the president. Although the Supreme Court declared this law invalid, a later act effectively denied the right to vote to those southerners who had been pardoned by the president.

One important reason why Congress was reluctant to grant amnesty was that the Radical Republicans believed that a lenient policy toward the South would ultimately undermine their numerical supremacy in Congress. Consequently, not until May 22, 1872, did Congress pass a limited amnesty law. Congress also enacted laws precluding Confederates from serving on juries and from receiving military commissions. Indeed, it was not until 1898 that the last political disability of southerners was removed by Congress, when it repealed the third section of the Fourteenth Amendment. The amnesty issue was a major reason for the impeachment and near removal of President Johnson. It created bitterness toward the Republicans that is still evident in the South and encouraged the founding of the Ku Klux Klan.

After World War I, there was no general amnesty for deserters, although President Woodrow Wilson did grant full amnesty to nearly 5,000 persons serving federal sentences for conscription violations. In 1924, President Calvin Coolidge restored citizenship to those who had deserted after the actual fighting in Europe stopped and before a final peace treaty was signed. Following World War II, President Harry S. Truman established an amnesty board, which recommended individual consideration of each amnesty request. Only 1,523 out of 15,000 persons were pardoned—most of them on religious grounds. No amnesty was granted to draft evaders or deserters following the Korean War.

The Vietnam War was one of America's longest and most divisive wars. It was a cold war battleground in which the United States, as the military leader of the non-Communist world, was unable to wear down a Communist guerrilla army sheltered in dense Asian jungles. Eventually, the universities and the mass media within the United States began to ignite internal dissent, which adversely affected public opinion regarding the merits of pursuing the struggle. Over 500,000 men deserted the armed services during this increasingly unpopular war. An additional 8,000 men were convicted of draft violations. On Sept. 16, 1974, President Gerald R. Ford proclaimed a conditional form of clemency, providing for a method by which draft dodgers and military deserters would be forgiven following a prescribed time of public service. A presidential clemency board, with specific guidelines, was designated to carry out the task. On Mar. 31, 1975, the last day on which applications for clemency could be accepted, the clemency board had received approximately 25,000 applications (20 percent of the 125,000 persons eligible).

[Jonathan T. Dorris, *Pardon and Amnesty Under Lincoln and Johnson*.]

EDWARD M. BYRNE

AMUNDSEN POLAR EXPEDITIONS. Roald Amundsen gained his first experience as an explorer in the Belgian Antarctic Expedition, 1897–99. He led the first expedition to sail through the Northwest Passage from the Atlantic to the Pacific and fixed the position of the north magnetic pole, feats he accomplished in the sloop *Gjoa,* 1903–06. He discovered the South Pole in December 1911, beating Capt. Robert F. Scott to the goal by a month. He sailed through the Northeast Passage from Norway to Alaska in the *Maud,* 1918–20, on an unsuccessful attempt to drift across the pole from the New Siberian Islands. In an effort to attain the North Pole with Lincoln Ellsworth by air from Spitsbergen in 1925, he reached latitude eighty-eight degrees. With Ellsworth and Col. Umberto Nobile he navigated the airship *Norge* from Spitsbergen to Alaska in 1926. He was lost in 1928 while flying across the Arctic wastes in search of Nobile and the *Italia's* crew, over the North Pole. (Nobile and the crew were eventually rescued.)

[R. Amundsen, *The North West Passage; The South Pole; Nordost Passagen;* and *My Life as an Explorer;* R. Amundsen and L. Ellsworth, *Our Polar Flight;* and *First Crossing of the Polar Sea.*]

N. M. Crouse

***AMY WARWICK* ADMIRALTY CASE,** 2 Black 635 (1863), one of the prize cases in which the Supreme Court upheld the power of the president to recognize the existence of a civil war and thereupon to establish a blockade, without awaiting congressional action.

[Charles Warren, *The Supreme Court in United States History.*]

Charles Fairman

ANACONDA COPPER, one of the largest copper mining companies of the world, and the principal producer of the Butte district of Montana. It was organized in 1881 as the Anaconda Silver Mining Company, Marcus Daly having persuaded James B. Haggin, Lloyd Tevis, and George Hearst to purchase for $30,000 the small Anaconda silver mine, then only sixty feet deep. The ore contained just enough copper to facilitate the recovery of the silver for which it was being worked, but at greater depth it became evident that its principal content was copper. A copper smelter was erected in 1884 and 3,000 tons of ore were being treated daily by 1889. Continuing to expand through the purchase of other mines it was reorganized as the Anaconda Mining Company in 1891, with a capital of $25,000,000. The Hearst interests were sold to the Exploration Company, London, and the company was reorganized in 1895 as the Anaconda Copper Mining Company.

T. T. Read

ANAHUAC, ATTACK ON (June 1832). Anahuac was a Mexican military post on the northeast shore of Galveston Bay. To effect the release of William B. Travis and other Americans held there, a group of American settlers in Texas attacked the post. The resulting negotiations led the Texans to declare for the Santa Anna party in Mexico. The incident was an important preliminary to the Texas Revolution.

[E. C. Barker, *Mexico and Texas, 1821–1835.*]

E. C. Barker

ANANIAS CLUB, an expression employed by the press in 1906–07, following President Theodore Roosevelt's accusations of inveracity against reporters. Taken from the biblical story of Ananias, who was struck dead for lying, persons were eligible for membership in the "club" once they had been called a liar by Roosevelt. Membership grew to include opponents of Roosevelt's policies, including railroad magnate E. H. Harriman, Judge Alton Brooks, and, most notably, Sen. Benjamin Tillman.

ANARCHISTS. Anarchism is a political philosophy that rejects rule and particularly the rule of the state. To the anarchist, the modern state stands for everything he repudiates—centralization, harsh coercion, economic exploitation, and war. In the United States, anarchist views began to be expressed very early. The statement "That government is best which governs least," associated with Thomas Jefferson, while not anarchist, moves strongly in an anarchist direction. Josiah Warren (1798–1874), with his philosophy of the "sovereignty of the individual," was a good representative of early 19th-century anarchism.

Classical American anarchism—which evolved from the post–Civil War period to about World War I—developed two schools of thought about its goals and two about means. In terms of goals, some anarchists, like Benjamin E. Tucker (1854–1939), were "individualists." Their great fear was that the individual would be lost in the organized group. But other anarchists were "communists," tending to follow the teachings of men like Peter Kropotkin (1842–1921). Emma Goldman (1869–1940) and Alexander Berkman (1870–1936) were two of the best-known communist anarchists. Goldman was a pioneer in the birth-control movement and did much to advance the cause of freedom of expression. Many of her ideas were developed in her journal *Mother Earth* (1906–17). Berkman was an able advocate of communist anarchism in such books as *Now and After:*

The ABC of Communist Anarchism (1929). In terms of means and strategies, there were "anarchists of the deed," who thought physical violence was permissible, and anarchists who stressed the importance of nonviolent methods. Leon Czolgosz, the assassin of President William McKinley, was an anarchist of the deed; and Berkman, in his 1892 attempt on the life of steel magnate Henry Clay Frick, seemed to espouse the same position. But many anarchists insisted on principles of nonviolence: thus, Tucker, in his magazine *Liberty* (1881–1908) and in books like *Instead of a Book* (1893), argued that the state must be abolished by education and nonviolent resistance; and in the latter part of his life Berkman emphasized nonviolent approaches. American anarchist followers of the Russian novelist Leo Tolstoy were, of course, radical pacifists. The Industrial Workers of the World (IWW), founded in 1905 and particularly active to the end of World War I, was often said to be anarchosyndicalist in its outlook: it distrusted the state and hoped to reorganize society along syndicalist (industrial union) lines.

Anarchism left its imprint on American legislation and administrative practice. Thus, immigration legislation excluded anarchists, and so in 1919 Goldman and Berkman were deported to the Soviet Union. Legislators have often mistakenly assumed that all anarchists advocate overthrow of the government by force or violence.

Anarchist influence declined between World War I and World War II. After World War II, it was reflected in Dwight MacDonald's well-edited but short-lived journal *Politics*. Many in the so-called New Left movement of the 1960's, during their attacks on the largely Marxist Old Left, developed an outlook that, in its stress on decentralization and its distrust of organization, reminded some of certain classical anarchist positions.

[Paul Eltzbacher, *Anarchism;* Emma Goldman, *Living My Life;* Benjamin Tucker, *Individual Liberty;* Robert Paul Wolff, *In Defense of Anarchism;* George Woodcock, *Anarchism.*]

MULFORD Q. SIBLEY

ANASAZI. The prehistoric Anasazi culture developed on the high mesas and in the deep canyons surrounding the Four Corners, the juncture of Arizona, New Mexico, Utah, and Colorado. The spectacular ruins of cliff dwellings and large apartment houses built hundreds of years ago by the Anasazi have attracted thousands of visitors yearly, making the Anasazi the best-known prehistoric culture in the Southwest. However, their isolated northern position impeded prehistoric Middle American stimulus and resulted in a lag in development compared with other contemporary Southwestern cultures. Rooted in a Desert culture base, the Anasazi cultural continuum evolved through earlier Basketmaker and later Pueblo phases. A distinctive way of life began to emerge by Basketmaker II (A.D. 1–500) with the addition of cultigens (corn and squash) and pithouses to the Desert culture base. During the Pueblo I and II periods (A.D. 750–1100), domesticated plant foods became the staple of the economy and large settlements of contiguous rooms began to replace the earlier pithouses, paralleling a trend in the Mogollon region. Pithouses continued to survive as ceremonial structures or "kivas." During the Classic period of Anasazi culture (A.D. 1100–1300) most of the population lived in towns. Pueblo Bonito in Chaco Canyon, N.Mex., was the largest of these towns. This D-shaped, semicircular apartment contained about 800 rooms and increased from one story around several interior plazas to four stories along the curved rear wall. As many as 1,200 people may have lived in Pueblo Bonita at one time. Cliff Palace in Mesa Verde contained more than 200 rooms and 23 kivas. By this time, advanced agricultural techniques, including the use of dams and irrigation canals up to 6.5 kilometers long, were known. The Classic period was also an age of craft specialization. High-quality ceramics, textiles, ornaments of turquoise, and many other exquisite artifacts demonstrate the skill and artistry of the Classic Anasazi. After A.D. 1300 complex climatic and social factors resulted in the abandonment of these flourishing towns and a southward displacement of their inhabitants.

[Jesse D. Jennings, *Prehistory of North America;* John C. McGregor, *Southwestern Archaeology.*]

GUY GIBBON

***ANDERSON* V. *DUNN*,** 6 Wheaton 204 (1821). The right of the House of Representatives to charge, hear, and punish contempt, and detain, arrest, and imprison those so charged, was unanimously upheld on the analogy of the right of the judiciary to punish contempt—for the self-preservation of the institutions of the state.

PHILLIPS BRADLEY

ANDERSONVILLE PRISON, established February 1864 in Georgia, was the largest and best known of Confederate military prisons. Hastily established because the number of prisoners constituted a military danger and a serious drain on the food supplies of Richmond, no adequate preparations were made for housing the captives. The poverty of the Confederacy, a defective transportation system, and the concentration of all resources on the army prevented the prison officials from supplying barracks, cooked food, clothing, or medical care to their charges. The prison consisted solely of a log stockade of sixteen and one-half acres (later enlarged to twenty-six acres) through which ran a stream of water. Rations to the prisoners generally consisted of cornmeal and beans, and seldom included meat. Bad sanitary conditions, lack of cooking facilities, poor food, crowding, and exposure soon produced respiratory diseases, diarrhea, and scurvy. The inadequate medical staff, without drugs, could not cope with the situation. During the summer the number of prisoners increased to 31,678. There are 12,912 graves in the national cemetery at Andersonville. Estimates place the total number of deaths at even higher figures. In September, the approach of Gen. W. T. Sherman's army caused the removal of all well prisoners to Charleston, S.C. Only enlisted men were confined at Andersonville; commissioned officers were held at Macon, Ga.

To the prisoners and to their friends in the North it appeared that the Confederates were deliberately murdering the captives. As a result of this belief, Capt. Henry Wirz, commander of the interior of the prison, was tried in August 1865 on charges of murder and conspiring with Jefferson Davis to murder. Although found guilty by a military commission and hanged, Nov. 10, 1865, subsequent investigation has revealed much in Wirz's favor. For many years Andersonville prison was a vital element in the "bloody shirt" issue in politics.

[W. B. Hesseltine, *Civil War Prisons: A Study in War Psychology*.]

W. B. HESSELTINE

ANDRÉ, CAPTURE OF. Maj. John André, adjutant-general of the British Army in North America during the Revolution, was entrusted by Sir Henry Clinton with the correspondence between the British headquarters and the American traitor Brig. Gen. Benedict Arnold, in the years 1779–80. On Sept. 21, 1780, he met Arnold at Joshua Hett Smith's house, just south of West Point on the Hudson River, to complete the arrangements for the betrayal of West Point to the British. He had arrived on the British vessel *Vulture*, which anchored opposite Haverstraw. While Arnold and André were in conference, American artillery fire compelled the *Vulture* to fall downstream. Having lost his means of transport, André was persuaded to change his costume for a disguise and carry the treasonable papers back overland by horseback. He crossed the Hudson, started down the east bank, and was captured (Sept. 23) by three American irregulars, John Paulding, Isaac van Wart, and David Williams, who searched him, discovered the papers, and turned him over to the American army. André explained himself to Gen. George Washington, and Sir Henry Clinton demanded his release on the ground that he had gone to consult with Arnold under a flag of truce, which was true. But, in fact, his conduct had made him a spy, as he said in his own words: "The events of coming within an Enemy's posts and of changing my dress which led me to my present Situation were contrary to my own Inclination as they were to [Clinton's] orders. . . ." André was tried before a court-martial (Sept. 29), of which Maj. Gen. Nathanael Greene was the president, convicted of being a spy, and ordered to be hanged. Washington refused to intercede in his behalf, and he was executed on Oct. 2, 1780, at Tappan, N.Y.

[James Thomas Flexner, *The Traitor and the Spy;* Carl Van Doren, *Secret History of the American Revolution*.]

RANDOLPH G. ADAMS

ANDREWS' RAID. On April 12, 1862, twenty-two Union spies attempted to destroy the strategic railroad between Atlanta, Ga., and Chattanooga, Tenn. After a race in the engine *General* they were captured by men from the pursuing engine *Texas*. Eight were subsequently hanged.

[John R. Hornady, *Atlanta, Yesterday, Today, and Tomorrow*.]

HAYWOOD J. PEARCE, JR.

ANDROS REGIME. *See* **New England, Dominion of.**

ANESTHESIA, DISCOVERY OF. Throughout history surgeons have attempted to deaden the pain of operations through the use of drugs—chiefly mandrake, opium, and alcohol—with indifferent results; chilling, nerve compression, and hypnotism were also tried. Late in the 18th century, physicians began experimenting with various newly discovered gases as possible therapeutic agents. They discovered the exhilarating properties of nitrous oxide, which Sir Humphry Davy suggested might be useful in surgical operations to prevent pain. His suggestion was ignored, but nitrous oxide parties and "ether frolics" became popular in the United States.

In 1824 Henry Hill Hickman in England operated on experimental animals after anesthetizing them with carbon dioxide, but he could not arouse any interest in this procedure among surgeons in London or Paris. William E. Clarke of Rochester, N.Y., is said to have administered ether successfully for a tooth extraction in January 1842, but he did not continue to use ether. In March 1842, Crawford W. Long, a Georgia surgeon familiar with ether from student frolics, removed a small tumor from the neck of James Venable while the latter was under the influence of ether inhalation. Venable later testified that he felt no pain, and Long performed several other operations with ether anesthesia in the next four years. He did not publish his results until 1849 or demonstrate them publicly, so that his work had no influence on the introduction or adoption of anesthesia into surgery.

In December 1844, after witnessing a nitrous oxide entertainment in which a young man injured himself but felt no pain, the Hartford, Conn., dentist Horace Wells had the gas administered to himself and had a tooth extracted while under its influence; he felt no pain. Wells clearly grasped the idea of inhalation anesthesia and experimented on several patients. He then attempted to demonstrate the technique publicly in Boston, but the demonstration failed. Following this, his former student and partner, William T. G. Morton, a Boston dentist, began experimenting with sulfuric ether. Morton received some useful, but not crucial, advice from a Boston chemist, Charles T. Jackson. After succeeding with a dental patient, Morton received permission to demonstrate his procedure at the Massachusetts General Hospital; and on Oct. 16, 1846, Dr. John C. Warren operated on a patient after Morton had anesthetized him. The demonstration was an unqualified success. Promptly reported in the newspapers and reported in the *Boston Medical and Surgical Journal* on Nov. 18, anesthesia was quickly tried and accepted by leading surgeons in Europe and America. An unfortunate controversy arose when Jackson tried to claim that Morton was merely his agent (as earlier he had claimed that he gave Morse the idea for the telegraph) and when Wells put forward his own claims to priority. Later, others were to argue the priority of Crawford Long. Despite Wells's real contribution, however, as Sir William Osler wrote, "Before October 16, 1846, surgical anaesthesia did not exist; within a few months it became a world-wide procedure; and the full credit for its introduction must be given to William Thomas Green Morton."

[Barbara M. Duncum, *The Development of Inhalation Anaesthesia With Special Reference to the Years 1846–1900;* Thomas E. Keys, *The History of Surgical Anesthesia.*]

JOHN B. BLAKE

ANGLICAN CHURCH. *See* **Church of England in the Colonies.**

ANGLO-AMERICAN RELATIONS. For more than a century and a half prior to the American Revolution, America had been an intimate, if dependent, part of Great Britain. Although the Revolution snapped the political ties that had bound the two peoples together and began a century of rivalry, the Revolution could not alter the fact that Americans and Britons shared a common language and history, read the same books, operated similar political systems, and harked back to common ancestors. Nor could it destroy the trade ties that were so profitable to both nations. These factors, surviving the century of rivalry, provided the foundation for the special relationship between Great Britain and the United States in the 20th century, the closest and most significant association between two nations in modern times.

Although the United States sought to lessen its economic dependence on Great Britain immediately after the Revolution, Americans quickly found this impossible. British merchants were the only source of credit that capital-poor Americans could find, and long-standing commercial relationships between American and British merchants were difficult to replace. In the first few years after the Revolution, Britain actually supplied 90 percent of America's imports. By 1795, the figure had declined to the more normal range of 30–40 percent, where it remained until 1850. During this same period, the United States sent between 30 percent and 50 percent of its exports to Great Britain. The United States accounted for 15–20 percent of Britain's trade—more than any other single foreign nation and almost as much as all England's imperial possessions combined. Most important of the products sent to England were cotton and, after the Corn Laws and other navigation acts were repealed in the late 1840's, foodstuffs. After 1850, American exports to Britain maintained their high level, but American manufactures began to replace British imported goods on the U.S. market, and British exports to America steadily dwindled.

These strong Anglo-American economic ties existed throughout most of the first century of America's existence without much encouragement from either government. During the peace negotiations following the Revolution, the British government had considered offering an excellent commercial treaty to the United States. But the outcry of Parliament and newspapers against excessive liberalism toward the former colonies quickly brought the British to the position that the United States was more a rival than a potential ally. This mood was made apparent to America when England refused to send a diplomatic representative to the United States in response to America's dispatch of John Adams as minister to St. James's. Adams tried to settle outstanding diplomatic problems and to conclude a trade treaty with Britain. But the British refused to negotiate. They closed Canada and the West Indies to American ships and to most American products; they also refused to turn over the military posts that the Peace of 1783 had placed on the American side of the Canadian-American border. These posts controlled the Great Lakes, attracted Indian trade and support, and gave England a jumping-off point in the contest with the United States for control of western North America. The stage was set for a century of rivalry. Great Britain—with its wealth, its navy, and its colonies adjacent to the United States—was the only nation capable of mounting an American invasion, permanently thwarting America's march to the Pacific, or destroying America's foreign commerce. England saw the United States as a threat to Canada and the West Indies and as a valuable source of supplies for Britain's European enemies. Since the trade and territorial issues involved areas very close to the United States but geographically remote from England, the United States took the rivalry more seriously than did Britain. England was in the center of America's consciousness in the 18th and 19th centuries; America was on the fringes of Britain's.

Under the Articles of Confederation, the United States found itself impotent in the face of British power and intransigence. The thirteen states were persuaded to accept a new Constitution and turn over to the federal government the power to control foreign trade, and Congress began to debate the restriction of British commerce as a means of forcing Great Britain toward a more friendly policy. In response, Britain finally dispatched a diplomatic representative to the United States in 1791, but it still refused to give up the Canadian border posts or open its empire to American ships.

When war broke out between revolutionary France and Great Britain in 1793, new issues were added to the old, and the United States and Great Britain teetered on the brink of war. American ships and goods intended for France were captured by the British in defiance of what the United States considered its rights as a neutral. In 1794, George Washington sent John Jay to England on an emergency mission to salvage the peace. Jay got the British to give up the border posts and to submit other outstanding border issues to arbitration; he did not get agreement to America's conception of its proper neutral rights, nor did he succeed in opening much of the British empire to American trade. Although Jay's Treaty saved the peace, it reaped a torrent of criticism from his fellow Americans.

France objected to the treaty even more than Jay's American constituents. It retaliated by capturing American ships, and America was driven into waiting British arms. British warships even convoyed American merchant vessels to protect them during this brief, but undeclared, Franco-American naval war of 1797–1800. But the rapprochement with Britain did not last long. In 1800 the United States and France made peace, and in 1803 Britain and Napoleonic France renewed their war. By 1805 the British once again began wholesale captures of American merchant ships. President Thomas Jefferson embargoed all American exports in a vain attempt to coerce British respect for America's neutral rights. But when commercial measures failed, the United States declared war on England in 1812. Since the British were supreme on the sea, the United States aimed its major blow at Canada. Not only did this invasion fail miserably, but the British invaded the United States and burned the Capitol, the White House, and other federal buildings in Washington. The Americans, who had begun the war with dreams of capturing both Canada and Florida, were lucky to make peace without loss of any of their own territory.

The Treaty of Ghent, ending the war in 1815, did nothing more than restore the *status quo antebellum,* but it marked the beginning of a new era. America acknowledged that Canada was not likely to leap at the chance of annexing itself to the American Union, and England acknowledged that the United States was not going to disintegrate into a myriad of squabbling little independent states. By restoring prewar boundaries, no problem of territorial irredenta was created. A new time of peace in Europe, combined with British naval supremacy on the Atlantic, prevented foreign wars from intruding into the profitable commercial relationship between England and America and freed the United States to turn its attention westward. Trade and territorial rivalries still existed. And literary figures in both countries expanded on the already unflattering images the peoples of each country held of each other. Englishmen caricatured the Americans as a whittling, spitting, gambling, slave-beating, dram-drinking people. Americans responded that this British spleen was the natural response of a nation to which a government of liberty and equality stood as an eternal reproach. But these ill feelings and conflicts were slowly overcome as the two governments, recognizing many common interests, came to one agreement after another. In 1817, they restricted naval armaments on the Great Lakes, beginning the march toward a completely unfortified Canadian-American border. The following year, they settled the location of the Canadian border at forty-nine degrees north latitude between the Lake of the Woods and the Rocky Mountains and agreed to joint occupation of the Oregon Territory beyond the mountains. Also in 1818, the British showed admirable restraint in their response to Andrew Jackson's arbitrary hanging of two British citizens during his punitive foray into Spanish Florida (*see* Arbuthnot and Ambrister, Case of).

By 1823, the British government was so convinced of the importance of America to England that Foreign Secretary George Canning offered to ally with the United States against a possible European invasion of Latin America. President James Monroe and Secretary of State John Quincy Adams decided to decline the invitation in favor of a unilateral declaration, the Monroe Doctrine, which was aimed at England as well as the rest of Europe. This stopped the movement toward any formal intimate Anglo-American connection, but the amicable settlement of particular points of conflict continued. In 1830, the British opened the West Indies to American ships, ending decades of contention over that question. The Webster-Ashburton Treaty of 1842 settled the simmering dispute over the Canadian border in Maine and around the Great Lakes. And in 1846 the Oregon Treaty ended years of controversy over the proper division of that territory. The British had demanded that the Columbia River form the border while the United States had insisted that the border simply continue west along the 49th parallel directly to the Pacific. With England making the major concessions, the border was run along the 49th parallel but bent southward at the Juan de Fuca Strait to give the British all of Vancouver Island.

At the same time, the British were forced to abandon any hopes of forming independent buffer states in Texas and California. The Texas Republic accepted annexation to the United States rather than ratify a treaty calling for British mediation with Mexico to guarantee the independence of Texas. The resulting Mexican War saw the United States invade California, ending whatever hopes Great Britain had entertained there. British activities in Texas left a bad taste in the mouth of the Americans, but Anglo-American rivalry for western North America was at an end.

Not so the rivalry in Latin America. Both nations had an interest in controlling any projected canal across the isthmus of Central America, and the two came close to blows over British occupation of critical sites in the area. The Clayton-Bulwer Treaty of 1850 reached a compromise on the issue by providing joint Anglo-American control of any isthmian canal and nondiscrimination in traffic fees charged the two nations.

The American Civil War imposed new strains on Anglo-American relations. First the Americans forcibly removed two Confederate diplomats from the British ship *Trent*. War was avoided only when President Abraham Lincoln ordered the two diplomats released. Then the British failed to stop the *Alabama*, a ship built and outfitted by the Confederates in England, from leaving port to begin its maraudings against the Union. Union protests were finally settled when the Geneva Arbitration of 1871 awarded more than $15 million in damages to the American claimants (*see* Alabama Claims). But the Civil War also produced some promising signs. The British did not try to break the Union blockade of the South, despite Britain's need for southern cotton, but chose to store up precedents should the United States protest a British blockade in the future. In addition, the secession of the South allowed the British and the Union to agree to searches of one another's ships in African waters to destroy the slave trade. Southern objections, along with America's historical antagonism to British naval searches and seizures, had blocked such an agreement for decades.

Anglo-American relations were relatively quiet for thirty years after the Civil War. Disputes over the cod fisheries off Newfoundland and the seal fisheries in the Bering Strait were settled by arbitration; economic relations were good; and the only potential area of rivalry, Latin America, was quiescent. Yet on the surface the old attitudes of defensive superiority on the part of England and aggressive inferiority on the part of America remained. It took a serious crisis to jar attitudes into line with the fact that serious points of conflict had disappeared and new areas of common interest had developed. That crisis came in 1895, when President Grover Cleveland and Secretary of State Richard Olney intervened in a boundary dispute between Great Britain's colony of Guiana and the independent republic of Venezuela. Cleveland and Olney demanded that the controversy be submitted to American arbitration, proclaiming that if Britain refused, America would draw the boundary unilaterally and fight if the British crossed it. Britain was already apprehensive about the rise of German power in Europe. It had always sought a balance of power in Europe to prevent any single country from being in a position to invade the British Isles. Not only did the British wish to avoid war with America at such a juncture, but they looked forward to a time when America might be in a position to help them maintain the balance of power in Europe. So Britain swallowed its pride and submitted the question to arbitration. From thence forward, Britain avoided any challenge to America in the Western Hemisphere. When America went to war with Spain in 1898, the British government gave the coup de grâce to any possibility that the continental powers might aid the Spanish. The British also agreed to the abrogation of the Clayton-Bulwer Treaty and permitted the United States to have sole control of the projected Panama Canal (the Hay-Pauncefote Treaty of 1901).

American attitudes toward the British changed more slowly. But even during the Venezuelan crisis, the original enthusiasm for the challenge to Great Britain soon diminished. During the Spanish-American War, Great Britain became almost popular. Americans also found points of agreement with the British in Asia. In 1899 Anglophile Secretary of State John Hay proclaimed the Open Door policy in China, at least partially in response to the requests of some of his English friends. Great Britain, however, knowing that the United States would not back up its policy in China with force, concluded an alliance with Japan that obligated Japan and England to fight together if either were challenged by more than one enemy in China. This Anglo-Japanese Alliance of 1902 was an embarrassment to the growing amity between England and the United States, as Japan and the latter were becoming increasingly estranged. But the British let it be known in several ways that the alliance would never commit the British to fight the Americans. America's benevolent neutrality toward England during the Boer War, when Germany sent a challenging telegram of sympathy to the Boers, further solidified the Anglo-American friendship. Even President Theodore Roosevelt's uncompromising stand and sharp tactics in the arbitration of the Canada-Alaska border dispute in 1902 did not interrupt it.

By the time World War I broke out, American public opinion was thoroughly ready to favor the British, especially after Germany's invasion of Belgium. Although Americans resented the British blockade of Germany and the interruption of America's trade with the Continent, they resented Germany's submarine warfare even more, so there was no disposition to do more than protest British naval policy. Meanwhile, supplies, arms, and loans to the British flowed in ever-increasing amounts. Some sophisticated American analysts saw that German domination of the Continent might lead to a long-range threat to American dominance in the Western Hemisphere; they reasoned that Britain's attempt to maintain a balance of power there was almost as valuable to the United States as to Britain itself. When the Germans resumed their submarine warfare in 1917, sinking American ships, killing American civilians aboard belligerent ships, and threatening the flow of supplies to Great Britain, the United States entered the war.

Still the Americans held themselves somewhat aloof from their European allies. The United States referred to itself as an "associated" rather than an "allied" power. The American army kept itself together as an operational unit in Europe instead of dispersing its men into the French and British armies as the Allies had wanted. President Woodrow Wilson was only very reluctantly drawn into the Allied intervention in Russia after the October Revolution. During the peace conference after the war, Wilson tried to resist Allied demands for new colonies and large-scale reparations; but ultimately he had to compromise with these Allied demands. The Americans, deeply disillusioned, rejected the Treaty of Versailles and association with Great Britain in the League of Nations.

World War I also marked a turning point in the Anglo-American economic relationship. The exigencies of war had forced the British to spend most of the assets that they had held in America and to borrow a great deal of money from the United States as well. By the end of the war, in a startling reversal, England was the debtor and America the creditor. In addition,

American need for British imports was declining. Between 1920 and 1950, British imports fell from 19 percent to 3.5 percent of the American market. England now found it difficult to afford American goods, and America's exports fell from 21 percent of the British market in the early 1920's to 5.5 percent in 1950. Nonetheless, America refused to scale down British debts, and therefore Great Britain refused to scale down the reparations owed it by Germany. These developments helped to bring on the worldwide depression of the 1930's.

Despite the dwindling economic relationship and America's refusal to join the League of Nations, Anglo-American political relations remained good. At the Washington Naval Conference of 1922, England and the United States agreed to accept naval parity with one another, and the Anglo-Japanese Treaty was formally abrogated, eliminating that potential embarrassment to Anglo-American friendship. A far-reaching Anglo-American trade treaty was signed in 1938, offsetting somewhat the disappointment of America's refusal to coordinate its economic attack on the depression with England and the rest of the world at the London Monetary Conference of 1933. Thus, when World War II broke out in 1939, there was no doubt as to where American sympathies lay.

At first, President Franklin Roosevelt was wary of concrete measures to aid Great Britain, because he feared American public opinion. But both he and public opinion advanced along the road toward more and more aid to the Allies. In late 1939, by executive agreement, Roosevelt traded fifty destroyers for permission to build U.S. bases on various British possessions in the Western Hemisphere. In 1941, America began lend-lease aid to the British, making America Britain's arsenal. Meanwhile, in early 1941, British and American military representatives began joint planning for war if America should come in. They made the momentous decision to give the European theater priority over the Far East, a decision vital to England's survival.

Once in the war, the United States fought in close collaboration with England. Command of the European theater was united under Gen. Dwight D. Eisenhower, and American arms flowed in a torrent to England. Of course there were problems. Military rivalries between British and American generals in North Africa, Europe, and Burma caused some hard feelings. Winston Churchill had to be thwarted in his desire to invade southern Europe rather than Normandy. The United States used the economic leverage of lend-lease to force open some of Great Britain's colonial markets and to coerce Britain's agreement to postwar economic arrangements. Roosevelt and Churchill clashed repeatedly over the disposition of the British and other European empires in Asia and the Middle East; they differed also over support for the return of the monarchies in Italy and Greece. Yet, despite these conflicts, the wartime Anglo-American alliance operated with remarkable smoothness and good feeling.

The end of the war placed great strains on the Anglo-American relationship. Americans did not understand that the war had exhausted the British economically. Expecting a much faster recovery than the British could possibly achieve, the United States continued to drive hard bargains in its economic dealings with Great Britain. The British desperately needed American goods but had trouble exporting enough to pay for them. Formerly, they had been able to make up this deficit in their trade with the empire, but now that they were abandoning their colonies, this was no longer possible. The British became increasingly reliant on American economic aid and loans, causing them to seek new markets anywhere, even in areas that were politically very unpopular with the United States.

Another postwar strain on Anglo-American relations was the issue of sharing atomic information. In 1940, the British and Americans had begun pooling their knowledge of nuclear physics, and Churchill had agreed that production of actual weapons should be concentrated in the United States. These agreements were formalized in the Quebec Conference of 1943, and cooperation of the British remained good throughout the war, despite problems created by the secrecy and anti-British actions of the military production unit headed by American Gen. Leslie Groves. But after the war, the Americans insisted on keeping to themselves the "secret" of the atomic bomb. Some argued that sharing with the British would endanger attempts to establish international controls on the bomb; Congress responded with the McMahon Act, prohibiting dissemination of most atomic information. The defection of Klaus Fuchs and the growth of anti-Communist hysteria in America doomed Britain's chances of reversing this decision. Only when the British produced first an atomic bomb and later a hydrogen bomb on their own was the sharing of atomic information gradually resumed between the two countries, with full nuclear partnership established by revisions to the Atomic Energy Act in 1958.

Another bitter postwar quarrel between Great Britain and the United States arose over Palestine. As Britain worked desperately for an agreement between Jews and Arabs to allow a graceful British exit, President Harry Truman intervened to push the Jewish case while refusing any responsibility for making a settlement work. With both Arabs and Jews now refusing to compromise, the British abandoned the question to the United Nations and pulled out in 1947, taking with them many bitter feelings about the role of the United States in the whole affair.

Despite these quarrels, the mutual fear of the Soviet Union and the rising cold war helped to maintain the special Anglo-American relationship. In 1947 the British notified the Americans that they could no longer assume responsibility for the defense of Greece; the United States responded with the Truman Doctrine, extending American military and economic aid to Greece and Turkey. This was soon followed by the Marshall Plan, giving economic aid to England and the rest of Europe. Meanwhile, in 1948, Great Britain agreed to permit American atomic air bases on British soil. Finally, England and America joined other Western European nations to form the North Atlantic Treaty Organization (NATO). After this, Anglo-American cooperation in Europe was very close.

Cooperation was not so close in Asia and the Middle East. The United States wanted a strong line against communism in Asia and, without changing policy toward Israel, a more moderate stance toward the Arab states in the Middle East. Great Britain, having a large stake in the Suez Canal and in the oil-producing sheikdoms of the Middle East; having given independence to India, Pakistan, and Burma; and having set Malaya on the road to independence, wanted the priorities reversed. Britain recognized Mao Tse-tung's regime in China on Jan. 6, 1950, and refused to honor the American economic boycott. This gave rise to much bitterness in America, particularly after the Chinese intervened on the side of North Korea during the Korean War. General Douglas MacArthur, who resented British pressure against extension of the Korean conflict to Chinese territory, even read to the Senate Foreign Relations Committee a list of strategic items the British were supposedly supplying the Chinese without revealing that the notation "nil" or "virtually nil" appeared opposite many of them. Shortly after the war in Korea, when the French empire in Indochina was crumbling and particularly after the siege of Dien Bien Phu, Secretary of State John Foster Dulles publicly chastised the British for refusing a joint intervention there; he then in turn refused a full commitment to the Geneva Settlement, which was supposed to end the war.

Meanwhile, in the Middle East, the British sought desperately to stave off Mohammed Mossadegh's coup in Iran, which could endanger their oil interests there. The Americans, with that same oil in mind, at first sympathized with Mossadegh, but Dulles reversed that policy and aided in Mossadegh's overthrow in 1953. The Suez crisis was far more serious. Egypt reacted to the withdrawal of United States financial aid to finance the Aswan High Dam by seizing the Suez Canal in 1956. Great Britain then joined France and Israel in an attempt to regain the canal. The United States publicly rebuked the British and their allies and, with Soviet threats in the background, forced an abandonment of the invasion. This was the nadir of Anglo-American relations in the 20th century.

Anglo-American relations were soon mended, however, and remained close. The United States encouraged England toward association with the European Common Market. The British allowed the stationing of American Intermediate Range Ballistic Missiles and Polaris submarines in Great Britain, while the United States supplied atomic plants and delivery systems for British nuclear weapons. A brief crisis in 1963 caused by America's cancellation of Skybolt, the proposed delivery system for British warheads, was resolved by an American offer of Polaris submarines and by the new Labour government's inclination to abandon entirely an independent British nuclear deterrent. In the Middle East, the British and Americans cooperated in the intervention in Lebanon and Jordan to prevent the spread of the Iraqi revolution of 1958, and together they suffered the steady erosion of Anglo-American influence in that area. In Asia, the British were reluctant supporters of American policy in Vietnam, although even that reluctant support was endangered by American resumption of bombing in North Vietnam in 1967 during delicate discussions between the British and the Soviets aimed at paving the way for negotiations between the warring parties. In Europe, Anglo-American cooperation remained close, in spite of some dispute over the proper rate of disarmament there. With British entry into the Common Market, Great Britain would doubtless take a more and more independent line toward the United States, and the "special relationship" would lose some of its importance for both countries. But strong cultural, economic, political, and historical ties would doubtless continue between the two nations.

[H. C. Allen, *Great Britain and the United States,* and *The Anglo-American Relationship Since 1783;* Basil Collier, *The Lion and the Eagle: British and Anglo-American Strategy, 1900–1950;* Richard Gardner, *Sterling-Dollar Diplomacy;* H. G. Nicholas, *Britain and the USA;* Andrew J. Pierre, *Nuclear Politics: The British Experience With an Independent Strategic Force, 1939–1970;* Bruce M. Russett, *Community and Contention: Britain and America in the Twentieth Century;* Harold Wilson, *The Labour Government, 1964–1970.*]

JERALD A. COMBS

ANGLO-CHINESE WAR (1839–42). American interests in this war center about the initiative of Commodore Lawrence Kearny that led to opening several Chinese ports to American commerce. Arriving off Canton with the *Constellation* and *Boston* in March 1842, Kearny found the war, precipitated by the opium dispute, nearly ended. He cultivated friendly relations with both sides, and when the victorious British demanded special trade privileges, he pleaded with the Chinese that equal privileges be granted Americans. This principle was accepted by the Chinese and formed the basis of the first U.S. treaty with China, negotiated by Caleb Cushing at Canton in 1844.

[C. O. Paullin, *Diplomatic Negotiations of American Naval Officers.*]

DUDLEY W. KNOX

ANIÁN, STRAIT OF. A mythical strait, supposed to connect the Atlantic and Pacific, sought by the Spaniards in the 16th and 17th centuries. In 1601 they tried to find a harbor on it beyond Quivira for direct intercourse with Spain. Until 1742 the Gulf of California was believed by many to join the west end of the strait.

[C. E. Chapman, *A History of California: Spanish Period.*]

LANSING B. BLOOM

ANIMAL PROTECTIVE SOCIETIES are incorporated under such headings as humane societies, anticruelty societies, animal rescue leagues, and societies for the prevention of cruelty to animals. They operate animal shelters either independently or in conjunction with local city governments. Many have animal hospitals and clinics. These protective societies work to secure and enforce laws that prevent cruelty to animals. Their workers may also become involved in investigating cases of cruelty to animals. They inspect facilities and monitor treatment where animals are housed and used. Much of their effort is devoted to promoting humane education to the general public.

The American Society for the Prevention of Cruelty to Animals, the first of its kind in the United States, was organized by Henry Bergh in New York City in 1866. Concerned over the mistreatment of animals and the squalor in which they were often kept, he also secured the first effective animal protective legislation that same year. Within ten years there were twenty-seven local humane organizations in operation from New Hampshire to California. In 1877 the American Humane Association was organized in Cleveland as a federation of animal protective societies. The following year the organization's declaration of organization was revised to include children. The humane movement has continued to grow, and the American Humane Association, headquartered in Denver, Colo., provides printed materials and services to more than 1,100 local humane groups. Incorporated in 1903, its charter purpose is the prevention of cruelty to children and animals and the distribution of humane education materials. In contrast to those groups opposed to the utilization of animals for man's benefit for specified purposes—antivivisectionists, antizoo groups, vegetarians—because some individuals may inflict suffering, the policy of the American Humane Association is to develop standards and controls applicable to individuals to prevent cruelty, rather than to seek to abolish any specific use of animals by mankind.

In recent years, animal protective agencies have worked closely with the packing and transportation industries to secure legislation for more humane treatment of animals in shipping and slaughtering. The protection of exotic pets and wildlife, particularly endangered species, has emerged as a major area of emphasis. Also, the current overpopulation of unwanted dogs and cats has led the humane movement to support research to find a suitable, inexpensive birth inhibitor, and education programs heavily stress the need for spaying or neutering pets.

Humane organizations are supported primarily by membership fees, contributions, and bequests. They are governed, at either local or national levels, by boards of directors.

[Eileen Schoen, *Early Years: A History of the American Humane Association.*]

DONALD M. HEGG

ANNAPOLIS. *See* **Naval Academy, United States.**

ANNAPOLIS CONVENTION, the precursor of the Constitutional Convention of 1787. On Sept. 11, 1786, twelve commissioners from New York, New Jersey, Pennsylvania, Delaware, and Virginia met in the State House at Annapolis, Md., to discuss reform of the vexatious restrictions placed upon interstate commerce by the various states. Among those present were Alexander Hamilton, John Dickinson, and James Madison. The convention took no action except to recommend that a larger convention be held in Philadelphia the following May.

[A. C. McLaughlin, *The Confederation and the Constitution.*]

WALTER B. NORRIS

ANNAPOLIS ROYAL. *See* **Port Royal.**

ANNEXATION OF TERRITORY. No specific provision was made in the Constitution for the annexation of territory. It is doubtful that the founding fathers in 1783 contemplated expansion across the empty continent beyond the ample boundaries set down in the Definitive Treaty of Peace. All the region beyond the Mississippi River, north of the Great Lakes and south of thirty-one degrees north latitude, was then in the hands of strong European monarchies. But Europe's distresses were America's advantage. The wars which followed the outbreak of the French Revolution and convulsed the Old World from 1793 to 1815 exhausted the energies of Great Britain and Spain, and also of France, which had intervened in Louisiana in 1800–1803 and enabled the United States first to clear its own territory of foreign troops and then to expand. By the twin treaties of George Washington's administration, Jay's Treaty with England (1794) and Pinckney's Treaty with Spain (1795), the West was cleared. Practice discovered four different means of annexation, all of which proved to be constitutional: (1) treaties of purchase; (2) treaties for frontier settlement; (3) joint resolution of annexation, accepted by the republic of Texas reciprocally in 1845; and (4) presidential proclamation.

A lucky break in the European constellation of 1800–1803 enabled President Thomas Jefferson unexpectedly by treaty to purchase the vast territory of Louisiana and thus to annex it to the United States. After 1815 England was so exhausted that, as Viscount Castlereagh said, it needed a long period of repose; reposing it made a boundary treaty in 1818 (*see* Convention of 1818) which accepted the line of forty-nine degrees north latitude to the Rocky Mountains and acknowledged the equal claim of the United States to the Pacific Northwest. Spain, harassed by South American revolutions, in 1819 gave up Florida to the United States in a treaty which also established a most favorable transcontinental frontier line from Texas to California (*see* Adams-Onís Treaty).

These new boundaries were soon expanded in both directions: to the southwest, by the annexation of Texas, and by the purchase of Mexican territory in the Treaty of Guadalupe Hidalgo, 1848, following a war the fundamental cause of which was the Texas question; to the northwest, by the Oregon Treaty in which England recognized full American sovereignty south of forty-nine degrees north latitude to the Pacific Ocean. Great Britain was opposed to both of these expansions, but preferred to accept them because at that time it was not in a position to fight, either for Texas or Oregon. In 1853 the United States bought from Mexico a comparatively small strip of territory, the Gadsden Purchase.

Two other treaties of purchase vastly expanded American territory: Alaska, from Russia in 1867 (Russia preferred to sell an unprofitable colony rather than see it some day conquered by the British navy); and the Philippines (later given independence) from Spain in 1899, as a result of the war of 1898. In the same treaty of peace, Puerto Rico and Guam were ceded as outright conquests. The Hawaiian Islands were meanwhile annexed by joint resolution of Congress, which was reciprocally voted by the Hawaiian legislature, as in the case of Texas. The Danish West Indies were acquired by a treaty of purchase in 1917. A number of small islands in the Atlantic and Pacific were annexed by presidential proclamation.

[Ray Allen Billington, *Westward Expansion;* Walter LaFeber, *The New Empire;* Ernest May, *American Imperialism;* Frederick Merk, *Manifest Destiny and Mission in American History.*]

SAMUEL FLAGG BEMIS

ANTARCTIC EXPLORATION. *See* **Amundsen Polar Expeditions; Byrd's Polar Flights; Polar Expeditions; Wilkes Exploring Expedition.**

ANTELOPE, a Spanish vessel taken March 1820 by an American privateer, seized by a United States revenue cutter with a cargo of slaves captured from Spanish and Portuguese ships. Vessel and Africans were claimed by Spanish and Portuguese vice-consuls on behalf of their citizens. Chief Justice John Marshall, declaring for the U.S. Supreme Court (10 Wheaton 66) that the African slave trade was not contrary to the law of nations, that the American cruiser had no right of search and seizure in a time of peace, and that it was not the duty of the United States to execute the penal laws of another country, directed that the slaves be restored to the foreigner in possession at the time of the capture.

LIONEL H. LAING

ANTHRACITE STRIKE. In May 1902, after vain efforts to secure an agreement, 150,000 anthracite miners, members of the United Mine Workers, under the leadership of John Mitchell, went on strike for higher wages, shorter hours, and recognition of the union. Most of the mines were owned by corporations that also controlled the coal-carrying railroads. Though the strike forced a complete shutdown, practically paralyzing the industry, the owners refused any dealings with the striking miners. There was little violence, and because they had real grievances, the miners won a large measure of public sympathy and support. As winter approached acute coal shortage developed. A widespread public demand arose for prompt settlement. Prices rose steadily. The coal operators still refused to meet the miners' representatives, their spokesman, George F. Baer, declaring in June: "We will give no consideration to any plan of arbitration or mediation or to any interference on the part of any outside party." On July 17 Baer wrote: "The rights and interests of the laboring men will be protected and cared for, not by the labor agitators, but by the Christian men to whom God in his infinite wisdom has given the control of the property interests of the country." Two months later, Baer again stated the operators would not yield. Soon afterward President Theodore Roosevelt intervened and called for a conference of the warring elements. The operators resented this action and accused the president of failure to send troops to protect the mines from violence. The president was not guilty of this charge because the governor of Pennsylvania had refused to call for federal troops; instead he called out the Pennsylvania Guard. The situation was becoming dangerous. After a secret but unsuccessful attempt had been made to intercede through a commission of which former President Grover Cleveland was to be chairman, the president was ready to send regular troops, even to take over and operate the mines. This determination was allowed to be known, and as a result the owners and operators yielded and in a stormy conference agreed to a committee of arbitration to be appointed by the president. The miners returned to work and, in March 1903, the commission awarded them a 10 percent increase in wages and other concessions, but refused to recognize the union. This strike is notable in that it emphasized that in struggles between capital and labor, the interests of a third party, the public, are paramount.

[John R. Commons, *History of Labour in the United States*.]

THOMAS ROBSON HAY

ANTHRACITE-TIDEWATER CANALS. Anthracite was discovered in northeastern Pennsylvania in the late 18th century, but for years it could be gotten to market only by floating it in arks or flatboats down the turbulent streams flowing out of the coal region—a difficult and expensive method. Josiah White in 1818 improved the upper Lehigh River with dams, but, this not proving adequate, he built the Lehigh Canal, completing it to the Delaware River at Easton in 1829. From there the Delaware Division of the Pennsylvania Canals continued the haul to tidewater at Bristol. Later, some of the coal crossed New Jersey to New York harbor through the Morris Canal, built 1824–32. The Schuylkill Canal, completed in 1825, was not conceived as a coal carrier, but it became one of the greatest in the country. The Delaware and Hudson Canal, built 1825–29, hauled coal out of the Lackawanna region, which was also served by the North Branch of the Pennsylvania State Canals, following down the Susquehanna, transferring some of its coal at Middletown to the Union Canal, whence it passed via the Schuylkill to Philadelphia and New York; or it carried on to Columbia, where the Susquehanna and Tidewater, built 1835–38, took over and hauled the coal down to Baltimore, sometimes through the Chesapeake and Delaware Canal, Delaware River, and Delaware and Raritan Canal to New York. These canals in their heyday, during the 1860's and 1870's, may each have carried from one to three million tons yearly; but the greater speed of the railroads destroyed them, one by one. The Lehigh-Delaware was the longest-lived of all. In 1931, after it had transported nearly fifty million tons of anthracite, not to mention other freight, all in horse-drawn boats, its traffic was abandoned.

[Alvin F. Harlow, *Old Towpaths*.]

ALVIN F. HARLOW

ANTHROPOLOGY AND ETHNOLOGY. The distinctive character of American anthropological inquiry was determined largely by the prior and continuing presence of the Indians on the North American continent—a physical and moral fact that defined theoretical controversies and gave focus to empirical research until well into the 20th century. Although ethnographic material appeared in various writings of the colonial period, systematic inquiry emerged contemporaneously with the Republic in the work of men associated with the American Philosophical Society, among them Benjamin Smith Barton, Samuel Stanhope Smith, and Thomas Jefferson. The focal issues of their inquiry were inherited from biblical assumption, the Age of Discovery, and the philosophical speculation of the Enlightenment. Had the Indians always been in America, a distinct species of mankind? Or had they migrated to the American continent? Were they perhaps one of the ten lost tribes of Israel? Had they degenerated, either physically or culturally, in the American wilderness? Or did they mirror the ancestral state of Europe, the bottom of a uniform ladder of social progress? A variety of data—physical, archaeological, cultural, and linguistic—could be brought to bear on such questions, although within the dominant monogenetic tradition, similarities of language were the primary means used to establish ethnic relationships. In 1797 the Standing Committee on Antiquities was formed in the American Philosophical Society, and in 1805 a precedent-setting questionnaire on Indians was sent with Lewis and Clark. In the decades that followed, the society played a major role in what came to be called ethnology—a study exemplified by the linguistic scholar Albert Gallatin, whose *Synopsis* of 1836 provided the ground plan for subsequent ethnological classification and who in 1842 founded the American Ethnological Society in New York City.

During this same period—in a context of religious revival, westward expansion, and Indian removal—the more optimistic aspects of the Enlightenment conception of the Indian were called into question. Henry Schoolcraft's researches, culminating in the government-sponsored *Indian Tribes of the United States* (1851–57), were couched in degenerationist terms; Samuel G. Morton's *Crania Americana* (1839) suggested that the Indians were one of a number of distinct species of mankind; and the impressive Indian mounds of the Mississippi Valley were used to buttress both degenerationist and (by the pioneer archaeologist E. G. Squier) polygenetic arguments. As the slavery debate reached a climax, Morton's followers J. C. Nott and George Gliddon propagated an extreme racialist view of the *Types of Mankind* (1854) and became known as "the American school of anthropology," a term that at this point connoted primarily the physical study of man.

Although large amounts of anthropometric data were collected on Union soldiers, physical anthropology lagged somewhat after the Civil War. In the context of the Darwinian revolution, social-evolutionary viewpoints of the 18th century were reasserted in a synthesis of psychic unity and racial assumption that correlated skin color, cultural stage, and mental development. The evolutionary viewpoint continued to dominate American anthropological thought until after the Indians of the West had been reduced to reservation half-life. The leading proponent was Lewis Henry Morgan, a lawyer who began by studying the Iroquois near his home in Rochester, N.Y., and whose later extensive collection of data on *Systems of Consanguinity* (1871) provided the basis for much modern social anthropology. When the Bureau of (American) Ethnology was founded under John Wesley Powell in 1879, Morgan's *Ancient Society* (1877) became the intellectual manual for the remarkable corps of government researchers whose collective efforts were marked by such works as Powell's *Indian Linguistic Families of America* (1891) and the *Handbook of American Indians* (1907), as well as the ethnographic riches of the bureau's *Reports* and *Bulletins*. Although work was also carried on in Cambridge, Mass., under the archaeologist F. W. Putnam at the Peabody Museum (founded 1866) and in Philadelphia by the independent scholar Daniel G. Brinton, the government anthropologists dominated the field until about 1900.

By that time, a new style and a new viewpoint had emerged under the aegis of the German-born scientist Franz Boas at the American Museum of Natural History and at Columbia University in New York. Boas' systematic critique of prevailing points of view in cultural, linguistic, and physical anthropology culminated in 1911 with the publication of three landmark works: *Changes in Bodily Form of the Descendants of Immigrants* attacked the assumptions of traditional physical anthropology; the "Introduction" to the *Handbook of American Indian Languages* provided the charter for modern descriptive linguistics; and *The Mind of Primitive Man* established the basis for modern anthropological thought on race and cultural determinism. Boas' embracive conception of anthropology was unified by its relativistic historical viewpoint, its skepticism of traditional categories, its reluctance to theorize, and its strong empirical emphasis. He opposed the founding of the American Anthropological Association in 1902 for fear of amateur domination and made his active institutional role and his graduate teaching potent factors in the professionalization of the discipline; indeed, much of its history in the first half of the 20th century is contained in the activities of his students.

During the first decades of the century, when much of their work was still carried on—with the support of museums—among the remnants of American tribes on western reservations, Boas' students were sometimes spoken of as the "American historical school." The characteristic focus of their researches was the geographical distribution and historical diffusion of culture elements, exemplified in the work of Robert Lowie and Leslie Spier and in the "culture area" concept of Clark Wissler and A. L. Kroeber and culminating in Kroeber's *Cultural and Natural Areas of Native North America* (1939). In the late 1920's, however, when the primary institutional locus was beginning to shift to the university department and the influence of Bronislaw Malinowski began to be felt on fieldwork method, other lines of inquiry began to develop out of the Boasian tradition. On the one hand, there was the study of the integration of whole cultures, most notably in Ruth Benedict's popularly influential *Patterns of Culture* (1934), and the related development of the culture and personality school, to which Edward Sapir and Margaret Mead made important contributions. On the other hand, as aboriginal ethnic identities receded more and more into the past, there was increasing emphasis on "acculturation" studies, exemplified by Melville Herskovits.

The work of all American anthropologists, including men like Robert Redfield and Ralph Linton, who stood somewhat apart from Boas, continued to be unified by the culture concept. But in the immediate pre– and post–World War II period, important new influences of a more sociological and scientistic character began to be asserted. This was especially true at Chicago, where the British social anthropologist A. R. Radcliffe-Brown taught from 1931 to 1937; at Yale, where George Murdock worked on the statistical study of *Social Structure* (1949); at Harvard, where the influence of Talcott Parsons was felt; at Michigan, where Leslie White contributed to a minor revival of cultural evolutionary theory; and even at post-Boas Columbia, where cultural ecological viewpoints were introduced by Julian Steward. By 1952, when the state of the discipline was inventoried in the symposium *Anthropology Today,* American anthropology—although still distinctively embracive in its totality—had clearly begun to fragment into a variety of conceptual orientations and subdisciplinary specializations.

This tendency was accelerated by various events of the succeeding decades. Major new intellectual influences continued to be felt, most notably the structuralism associated with Claude Levi-Strauss. The broadening of the areal range of research, which had really begun in the 1920's with the work of Mead and Herskovits in Oceania and Africa, was given great impetus by World War II. In the postwar decades of American global commitment, major inputs of government and private philanthropic research money enabled American anthropologists to carry on fieldwork on every continent. Simultaneously, the academic boom contributed to the explosive numerical growth of the profession and each of its various subdisciplines, the major ones of which have in effect become distinct fields of inquiry. Paradoxically, a rising reaction of subject-peoples, including American Indians, against a study closely tied to the historical phase of European overseas expansion has helped to create a strong sense of crisis in the discipline, the resolution of which cannot be clearly foreseen.

[J. O. Brew, ed., *One Hundred Years of Anthropology;* Marvin Harris, *The Rise of Anthropological Theory;* R. H. Lowie, *The History of Ethnological Theory;* B. J. Siegel, ed., *Biennial Review of Anthropology* (1959–71), and *Annual Review of Anthropology;* William Stanton, *The Leopard's Spots;* George W. Stocking, Jr., *Race, Culture, and Evolution.*]

GEORGE W. STOCKING, JR.

ANTIBANK MOVEMENT OF THE WEST. Opposition to banks of issue existed from the beginning of such institutions in America in the late 18th century. It was a marked characteristic of the Jeffersonian movement. After the panic of 1837, however, the sentiment reached the stage of a movement to abolish banks. It was rooted in Jacksonian fear, debtor distress, and a bullionist or "hard money" theory (*see* Jacksonian Democracy). The movement was centered in the new Jacksonian states of the Mississippi Valley and reached its climax in the constitutional conventions of the 1840's and 1850's. Between 1845 and 1863 banks were abolished in Illinois, Wisconsin, Iowa, Missouri, Arkansas, Louisiana, Texas, and on the Pacific coast.

The movement is properly interpreted as an early example of agrarian protest similar to the Populist movement of a later date.

[L. C. Helderman, *National and State Banks: A Study of Their Origins.*]

L. C. HELDERMAN

ANTIETAM, BATTLE OF (Sept. 17, 1862). Early in September 1862, Gen. Robert E. Lee's Army of Northern Virginia crossed the Potomac into Maryland (*see* Maryland, Invasion of). He concentrated at Frederick, then sent T. J. (Stonewall) Jackson's corps south to take Harpers Ferry, and Gen. James Longstreet's corps westward across the South Mountain. On the 14th Union Gen. G. B. McClellan's Army of the Potomac forced the mountain passes.

Lee began to concentrate toward the Potomac and took position at Sharpsburg, on the Antietam Creek. While Longstreet was assembling here, Lee heard that Jackson had captured Harpers Ferry and took the bold decision to stand and fight behind the creek, with the Potomac at his back. Longstreet took the right of the line; Jackson's troops, as they arrived, the left.

McClellan planned to strike Lee's left with three corps (Joseph Hooker's, Joseph Mansfield's, and Edwin Sumner's); to follow this blow with an attack by A. E. Burnside's corps on the Confederate right; and to hold Fitz-John Porter's and W. B. Franklin's corps, with Alfred Pleasonton's cavalry, in reserve in the center.

But Hooker, Mansfield, and Sumner attacked successively, not simultaneously, and each in turn was beaten. Burnside's attack on the other flank came still later. Longstreet's line had been weakened to reinforce Jackson, for Lee had no real reserve; hence Burnside made some progress at first, but when fully engaged he was struck in flank by A. P. Hill's division, the last of Jackson's troops returning from Harpers Ferry. Burnside was driven back to the bridge by which he had crossed the creek, and darkness ended the fighting.

On the 18th Lee stood fast and McClellan did not renew his attack. On the 19th Lee effected his withdrawal across the Potomac. The numbers engaged are uncertain; perhaps a fair estimate is 50,000 Union, 40,000 Confederate. But this was Lee's entire strength, and McClellan had 20,000 in reserve, never used. The losses may be estimated as over 12,000 for each side. In 1890 Antietam was made a national battlefield site.

[Official Records, War of the Rebellion; R. U. Johnson and C. C. Buel, eds., *Battles and Leaders of the Civil War;* J. C. Palfrey, *The Antietam and Fredericksburg.*]

OLIVER LYMAN SPAULDING

ANTIFEDERALISTS. The name Antifederalists was fixed upon the opponents of the adoption of the Constitution of the United States (1787–88) by the supporters of the Constitution, who appropriated the more attractive designation Federalists. Although Antifederalism thus came to be defined in relation to the Constitution, it originated as a political force during and after the American Revolution and represented those who favored the retention of power by state governments, in opposition to those who wanted a strong central government. The Federalists sought to assume the role of proponents of a federal form of government, but the Antifederalists were not opposed to such a system. Indeed, they insisted that in opposing the Constitution they were seeking to preserve the federal system created by the Articles of Confederation (1781–88), whereas the advocates of the new Constitution were attempting to replace federalism with nationalism and centralization. Some historians argue that a more appropriate name for the Federalists would be the nationalists, and for the Antifederalists, the federalists.

Philosophically, the Antifederalists suspected strong central governments and believed that the greatest gain of the Revolution was throwing off the central power of Great Britain and establishing the power of the states. They had no desire to see the power that had been centered in London transferred to Philadelphia or New York. Believing that freedom could be maintained only by governments close to the people, they supported the doctrine of lodging power in the legislative branch of government on the basis of its being more responsive to public opinion than the executive and the judicial branches. Antifederalist beliefs in the desirability of a weak central government and in the extension of democratic control were fundamental in their opposition to the Constitution. Nearly all Antifederalists were convinced that the Constitution established a national, not a federal, government and would produce a consolidation of previously independent states. They believed that concentrated power led to aristocracy and that power diffused led to democracy.

The Antifederalists published no group of papers comparable to *The Federalist*—authored by James Madison, Alexander Hamilton, and John Jay—but their political philosophy can be reconstructed from scattered articles in newspapers and pamphlets and from the debates in state ratifying conventions. These sources show a prevailing belief that republican government could exist only in a small geographical area and could not be extended successfully over a large territory with a numerous and heterogeneous population. Antifederalists believed that Americans were too diverse to be governed by a single national government and that the sheer size of the country was too great for one republican government. They favored a more rigid system of separation of powers and more extensive checks and balances than provided by the Constitution.

Antifederalists, including such leaders as George Mason, Patrick Henry, and George Clinton, decisively outnumbered Federalists in Rhode Island, New York, North Carolina, and South Carolina and were slightly more than a majority in Massachusetts and Virginia. In spite of the Antifederalist majority in at least six of the thirteen states—and the approval of nine states was required for ratification of the Constitution—the Antifederalists lost to the superior organization of the Federalists, who were aided also by the greater prestige of Federalist leaders, including George Washington and James Madison; by a pro-Constitution newspaper press; by the momentum of early ratification in certain states; by the promise of amendments to the new Constitution; and by the argument posed in some states in terms of union or no union.

The most extensive studies of the sources of strength of the two factions indicate that Antifederalism drew its greatest support from noncommercial interests isolated from the major paths of commerce and little dependent on the mercantile community or foreign markets, whereas the Federalists found their strongest support among the commercial elements, embracing merchants, townspeople, farmers dependent on major cities, and those who exported their surplus production.

With the ratification of the Constitution the Antifederalists did not persist as a group and did not form the basis for political party alignments in the new nation. Although Federalists in the 1790's frequently referred to their Republican opponents as Antifederalists, this usage reflected partisan tactics rather than evidence of historical continuity. Antifederalist ideas, however, did persist and can be seen in the growing concern over the centralized power of the national government that developed during the early decades under the Constitution and continued to some extent throughout American history.

[Noble E. Cunningham, Jr., *The Jeffersonian Republicans: The Formation of Party Organization 1789–1801;* Cecelia M. Kenyon, ed., *The Antifederalists;* Jackson Turner Main, *The Antifederalists: Critics of the Constitution, 1781–1788;* Robert A. Rutland, *The Ordeal of the Constitution: The Antifederalists and the Ratification Struggle of 1787–1788.*]

NOBLE E. CUNNINGHAM, JR.

ANTI-HORSE THIEF ASSOCIATION, organized at Fort Scott, Kans., in 1859 to provide protection against marauders thriving on border warfare. It resembled vigilance societies in organization and methods. After the Civil War gangs of outlaws made their hideaways in the inadequately policed Indian Territory and preyed on the livestock, chiefly horses, of the neighboring states. During the period 1869 to 1875 officers were unable to cope with the bandits and few sheriffs ventured south of the Marion County line, 150 miles north of the Indian Territory. The organization spread to other sections of the state as necessity arose, and probably to other states, but eventually turned into a social organization.

[E. Dick, *Sod House Frontier;* J. A. McClellan, "Joseph McClellan," *Kansas Historical Collection,* vol. 17.]

CARL L. CANNON

ANTI-IMPERIALISTS, a term given to Americans who opposed U.S. colonial expansion after the Spanish-American War. Although a number of anti-imperialists had first opposed the acquisition of island territories during the administration of Ulysses Grant and others survived to proclaim the faith in the 1920's, anti-imperialism as a movement of political significance is limited to the years 1898–1900.

Many anti-imperialists rejected organizational activity, but a majority claimed membership in one of the branches of the Anti-Imperialist League that was founded in Boston in November 1898. By 1900 the league claimed to have 30,000 members and over half a million contributors. An organization whose primary goal was the education of public opinion, the league published hundreds of pamphlets denouncing the acquisition of an island empire and the abandonment of America's unique "mission" to hold before the nations of the world the model of the free and self-governing society. George S. Boutwell, Erving Winslow, Edwin Burritt Smith, David Starr Jordan, and Carl Schurz were prominent leaders of the league, and its chief financial contributor was Andrew Carnegie. The most important anti-imperialists working outside the league were William Jennings Bryan and George Frisbie Hoar.

Although diverse in motives and party affiliation, the anti-imperialists shared common fears and beliefs. They were convinced that imperialism threatened the ideals and institutions of their own country, and they believed that it was unjust to dictate the political goals and institutions of foreign peoples. Although many anti-imperialists shared the racial bias of their imperialist opponents and some urged the expansion of foreign markets as a solution to domestic surplus, for most, racial "difference" did not require racial subordination nor did trade expansion demand gunboat diplomacy. The anti-imperialists insisted that it was as wrong for a republic to have colonies as it was for a representative government to have subject peoples. Tyranny abroad, they believed, could only undermine democracy at home. They also offered arguments against the constitutionality, economic wisdom, and strategic safety of a policy of insular imperialism. Colonial expansion not only denied the practice of the past, it would waste American resources, undermine the Monroe Doctrine, and embroil the United States in the rivalries of the European powers. Although hampered by having to preach a doctrine of abnegation to a nation of optimists and weakened by a failure to agree on a single policy alternative for the disposition of the Philippine Islands, the anti-imperialists were participants in one of the most intelligently reasoned debates in American history.

Even though they were important as a moral and educational force, the anti-imperalists must be classified among the political failures of American history. The heavy cost of the Philippine-American War and the labors of the anti-imperialists may have helped to check the territorial ambitions of the more zealous imperialists, but none of the immediate goals of the anti-imperialists was secured. The new island territories were officially annexed; President William McKinley easily won reelection in 1900, despite the opposition of the Anti-Imperialist League; and the Philippine Insurrection was mercilessly crushed.

[Robert L. Beisner, *Twelve Against Empire: The Anti-Imperialists, 1898–1900;* E. Berkeley Tompkins, *Anti-Imperialism in the United States: The Great Debate, 1890–1920.*]

RICHARD E. WELCH, JR.

ANTI-MASONIC MOVEMENTS. Suspicion of secret societies was marked at an early date but the fact that George Washington and other patriots were Masons seemed proof that the order was not dangerous. In 1826, however, when William Morgan, a Freemason and author of a book revealing secrets of the order, disappeared, there was a widespread reaction in western New York, which assumed national importance with the organization of the Anti-Masonic party. Many Masons renounced their vows, membership in New York dwindling from 20,000 to 3,000 between 1826 and 1836. The number of lodges was reduced from 507 before 1826, to 48 in 1832. In Vermont the Grand Lodge voted down a proposal for dissolution, but agreed to receive charters from chapters desiring to surrender them and provided that funds of such lodges should go to the state public school fund. Many congregations were divided, especially Presbyterian, Baptist, Methodist, and Congregational. Masons were excluded from membership, and pastors were barred from their pulpits. In Pennsylvania, Anti-Masonry found favor among Quakers, Mennonites, Dunkers, Moravians, and some Lutheran and German Reformed groups. A Vermont law of 1833 forbade extrajudicial oaths; and elsewhere Masons were deprived of local office and dropped from jury rolls.

Anti-Masonic newspapers were an index of the rapid growth of the Anti-Masonic party. Charging intimidation of printers and suppression of facts of the Morgan trials, party leaders urged the establishment of "free presses." Thurlow Weed, who in 1828 had started the Rochester *Anti-Masonic Enquirer,* was given financial backing in 1830 for his *Albany Evening Journal,* the principal party organ. In 1832 there were forty-six Anti-Masonic papers in New York and fifty-five in Pennsylvania. In September 1831 a national Anti-Masonic convention was held at Baltimore, the first national nominating convention of any party, naming William Wirt of Maryland for president. This, the first third party, only drew support away from Henry Clay, and helped the sweep for Andrew Jackson in 1832. It received seven electoral votes from Vermont. The party also gained adherents in Pennsylvania, Ohio, New Jersey, Massachusetts, Connecticut, and Rhode Island; but only Pennsylvania, through the leadership of Thaddeus Stevens, and Vermont elected Anti-Masonic governors. In the late 1830's the excitement subsided, or was replaced by the antislavery agitation. By 1838 the party had merged with the Whigs.

After the Civil War there was another movement directed against secret societies. The National Christian Association was founded at Aurora, Ill., in 1868 to oppose secret orders, "Jesuitism, Mormonism, atheism, spiritualism and free love." It maintained a national organization and published a weekly, *The*

Christian Cynosure (1867–71). This crusade was unsuccessful, and the 1880's and 1890's witnessed a great increase of fraternal orders.

[Charles McCarthy, *The Anti-Masonic Party,* and *The Anti-Masonic Scrapbook, 1883;* J. C. Palmer, *The Morgan Affair and Anti-Masonry.*]

MILTON W. HAMILTON

ANTIMONOPOLY PARTIES (1873–76), sometimes called Independent or Reform parties, were political parties organized by farmers, especially Grange members, in Indiana, Illinois, Michigan, Wisconsin, Minnesota, Iowa, Missouri, Kansas, Nebraska, California, and Oregon. Their platforms demanded government reform, economy, and reduced taxation; all but two also demanded state regulation of corporations, particularly railroads. In some states the new parties fused with the Democrats; thus they had some success in Iowa and elected the whole state ticket in Wisconsin. In other states, as in Oregon, and to some extent in Illinois, they remained independent and won local victories. In Illinois, Kansas, and California they secured the election of "Reformers" as U.S. senators. In Wisconsin, Iowa, and Minnesota, in 1874, the Antimonopolists obtained enactment of Granger railroad laws. Though these were soon repealed or moderated, their passage evoked court decisions establishing the right of states to regulate railway corporations. The Antimonopoly parties did not survive the presidential campaign of 1876.

[S. J. Buck, *The Granger Movement,* and "Independent Parties in the West," *Essays in American History Dedicated to Frederick Jackson Turner.*]

SOLON J. BUCK

ANTINOMIAN CONTROVERSY, a theological dispute begun in Boston by Anne Hutchinson in the fall of 1636. She had been a parishioner and devout admirer of John Cotton in Boston, England, and with her husband followed him to the new Boston, where they were admitted to membership in the First Church. She was exceptionally intelligent, kind, learned, and eloquent and began innocently to repeat on weekdays to small gatherings the substance of Cotton's sermons, but soon commenced delivering opinions of her own. At the height of her influence, about eighty persons were attending lectures in her house.

She caused turmoil by putting a different conclusion from that maintained by the clergy upon the doctrine of the covenant of grace. The standard view held that the elect entered a covenant with God on the condition of their believing in Christ, in return for which God contracted to give them salvation, but that thereafter the justified saints devoted themselves to good works, not in order to merit redemption, but as evidence of their having been called. Mrs. Hutchinson declared that stating the matter thus put too much emphasis upon works and denied the fundamental Protestant tenet of salvation by faith alone. Consequently she preached that the believer received into his soul the very substance of the Holy Ghost and that no value whatsoever adhered to conduct as a sign of justification.

This conclusion made for a disregard of morality such as Protestant theologians had everywhere endeavored to resist, and it could clearly lead to disastrous social consequences; the New England clergy, recognizing in her teachings a form of "Antinomianism," that is, a discarding of the moral law, could not possibly have tolerated her. She made matters worse by accusing all the clergy except Cotton of preaching a covenant of works, so that Gov. John Winthrop stated it began to be as common in Massachusetts to distinguish the party of works and the party of grace "as in other countries between Protestants and papists." Thus she threatened to split the colony into factions, particularly when she was supported by her brother-in-law, the Rev. John Wheelwright, and the new young governor, Henry Vane. The other clergy and magistrates believed that the existence of the whole colony was at stake; led by Winthrop, and employing consummately clever tactics, they regained control of the government in May 1637, then proceeded to disarm Anne's partisans and suppress the movement. Anne was examined by a synod of the ministers, which found her guilty of eighty erroneous opinions; John Cotton publicly repudiated her. Wheelwright was banished to New Hampshire; Anne was arraigned before the general court, where she boasted of having received explicit revelations from the Holy Ghost, a possibility which no orthodox Protestant community could for a moment admit. She was excommunicated from the First Church in March 1638, John Cotton pronouncing sentence upon her, and banished from the colony by the court, whereupon she fled to Rhode Island.

[C. F. Adams, *Antinomianism in the Colony of Massachusetts Bay,* and *Three Episodes of Massachusetts History;* Emery Battis, *Saints and Sectaries: Anne Hutchinson and the Antinomian Controversy in the Massachusetts Bay Colony;* Perry Miller, *Orthodoxy in Massachusetts;* E. S. Morgan, "The Case Against Anne Hutchinson," *New England Quarterly,* vol. 10 (1937).]

PERRY MILLER

ANTIRENT WAR (1839–46), a culmination of the resentment of farmers in upstate New York against the leasehold system, whereby the great landlords and land companies collected yearly tribute in produce, labor, or money and exacted a share ("quarter sales") of one-quarter or one-third the amount realized from the sale of a leasehold. In 1839, when the heirs of Stephen Van Rensselaer tried to collect some $400,000 in back rent, the farmers rebelled. Gov. William H. Seward called out the militia and issued a proclamation of warning. This sobered the rioters and ended the so-called Helderberg War. Similar disturbances, however, soon broke out in the counties south of Albany.

In Columbia and Delaware counties groups of men disguised as Indians tarred and feathered sheriffs and deputies who attempted to serve writs of ejectment. The murder of a deputy sheriff, August 1845, led Gov. Silas Wright to proclaim Delaware County in a state of insurrection. Antirent secret societies spread rapidly and became a political influence, electing John Young to the governorship. The amended constitution of 1846 prohibited new feudal tenures, and a court decision declared quarter sales illegal. There followed a general conversion of old leases into fee simple ownership.

[E. P. Cheney, "The Antirent Movement," in A. C. Flick, *History of the State of New York,* vol. VI.]

A. C. Flick

ANTI-SALOON LEAGUE, founded at Oberlin, Ohio, May 24, 1893. Creating this statewide organization was the idea of the Rev. H. H. Russell. This "Ohio plan" was copied by many states, and in 1895 a national organization, the Anti-Saloon League of America, was established at the Calvary Baptist Church, Washington, D.C. Soliciting and securing aid from the Protestant Evangelical churches, the league grew rapidly and came to regard itself as the "Church in Action Against the Saloon."

Prior to the Eighteenth Amendment the league centered its attention upon destroying the liquor traffic by legislation. To this end it sought and obtained local option, county option, state prohibition, regulation of interstate liquor shipments, and finally national prohibition. Following national prohibition the league sought by propaganda and pressure to achieve enforcement and the maintenance of this policy. For the first time in its history it was completely on the defensive. Accused of responsibility for the development of bootleg gangs, disrespect for law, and all of the undesirable social practices of the postwar period, the league slowly lost support. The depression of 1929 brought a diminution in the league's revenues. Faced by a public willing to try anything which might reestablish prosperity, and weakened internally, it lost ground rapidly. When in 1933 the Eighteenth Amendment was repealed, the league campaigned again for local option, but was no longer significant in national politics. In 1948 the league changed its name to the Temperance League of America; in 1950 it merged with the National Temperance Movement, forming the National Temperance League.

[E. H. Cherrington, *History of the Anti-Saloon League;* Peter Odegard, *Pressure Politics;* Justin Stewart, *Wayne Wheeler, Dry Boss.*]

Dayton E. Heckman

ANTISLAVERY in the United States took several forms during its evolution from the quiet protest of the Germantown Quakers in 1688 through the tragic and violent Civil War, which spawned the Thirteenth Amendment in December 1865. Response to slavery varied from mild doubts concerning the wisdom of the institution to militant hostility toward what was viewed as a sinful and unjust practice. It was intimately connected to conceptions of the meaning of the American experience and intertwined with white racial attitudes, since slavery in the United States was almost exclusively black slavery. As a consequence, different elements within the society perceived the problem of slavery in radically different ways and proposed sometimes contradictory solutions.

In the United States, there existed not one antislavery impulse but rather several distinct movements whose makeup, organization, and objectives differed radically. Throughout the history of antislavery in the United States there were a small number of men and women who may with justice be called abolitionists. Their primary goals were the abolition of slavery throughout the country and the ultimate incorporation of the freed blacks into American society. In the 18th century, abolitionists generally supported plans for gradual emancipation, but a new generation of abolitionists who appeared in the 1830's demanded an immediate end to slavery and advocated the integration of American society. A much larger group among the opponents of slavery were those who feared that blacks neither could nor should be incorporated into American society as equals; it proposed instead the colonization of free blacks outside the United States. These colonizationists were centered in the states of the upper South and the Ohio Valley; increasingly they shifted away from their early opposition to slavery, to focus upon the removal of free blacks. What came to be the largest element in the antislavery crusade were the northern sectionalists, who opposed slavery as the basis of the social and political power of an aristocratic class that unfairly dominated the political process to the disadvantage of northern whites. The racial attitudes of this group covered a broad spectrum, and their main efforts centered upon restricting the expansion of slave territory.

Gradualism. Although the first antislavery tract in the colonies was written by a New England Puritan, Samuel Sewell, the early history of antislavery in America consisted primarily of the agitation of certain English and American Quakers. But even among the Friends, antislavery sentiments grew slowly. Many wealthy Quakers were slaveholders; and in the first half of the 18th century, they caused both Ralph Sandiford and Benjamin Lay to be repudiated by their coreligionists for their antislavery activities. Only at midcentury, when the Society of Friends faced a severe internal crisis brought on by the effects of the Great Awakening and the French and Indian War, did opposition to slavery increase measurably among Quakers. In 1758 the two foremost antislavery Quakers, John Woolman and Anthony Benezet, induced the Philadelphia Yearly Meeting of New Jersey and Pennsylvania Friends to report "an unanimous concern [over] the buying, selling and keeping of slaves." Their activities eventually led to similar actions by the New England and New York Quakers, but it was not until the 1780's that the major meetings could announce that none of their members held slaves.

By that time the opposition to slavery had spread beyond the Society of Friends to other men whose response to slavery was rooted in the secular thought of the Enlightenment. Because of its underlying republican ideology, emphasizing liberty and the rights of man, the American Revolution encouraged antislavery sentiments. James Otis, John Dickinson, and Thomas Paine equated the situation of the American colonists with the plight of their African bondsmen. Thomas Jefferson, although he excluded his attack on the African slave trade from the final draft of the Declaration of Independence, argued that abolition of slavery was a "great object" of the colonists. During these years all the states abolished the African slave trade and most moved toward the ultimate eradication of slavery.

This movement proceeded most rapidly in the states north of the Mason-Dixon line, where slavery was of minor economic importance. Vermont explicitly outlawed slavery in 1777; and the Massachusetts courts similarly interpreted that state's new constitution of 1780. In the same year, Pennsylvania freed, under certain restrictions, all future children of slaves; Rhode Island and Connecticut passed similar laws four years later. After a good deal of controversy, New York (1799) and New Jersey (1804) also accepted proposals for gradual emancipation. With the enactment of the Northwest Ordinance in 1787, slavery was confined to the area that increasingly became known as the South.

Gradual emancipation in the northern states was not achieved without opposition; and the newly formed antislavery societies, which by the 1790's could be found scattered from Massachusetts to North Carolina, played a crucial role in these early achievements. Pennsylvania Quakers established the first such society in 1775. In 1794 a national organization, the American Convention for Promoting the Abolition of Slavery and Improving the Condition of the African Race, held its first meeting. Aside from supporting gradual emancipation, these early antislavery societies attacked the Fugitive Slave Law and the African slave trade, distributed antislavery literature, and encouraged education of blacks. Although their membership included such prominent political figures as Benjamin Franklin, John Jay, Alexander Hamilton, and Benjamin Rush, these early organizations were generally dominated by Quakers. Because of this narrow sectarian base and the ideological limitations of early antislavery sentiment, the movement rapidly waned following its victories in the northern states.

Colonization. During the three decades following 1800, opposition to slavery entered a new phase. Efforts at gradual emancipation gave way to proposals for the colonization of free blacks, and the center of antislavery activity shifted to the upper South. By 1827 Benjamin Lundy could report that more than three-quarters of the members of active antislavery societies lived in the southern states. Although the most vocal opponents of slavery during these years—men such as David Rice, David Barrow, George Bourne, and John Rankin—were active in these states, true abolitionism never gained a foothold anywhere in the South. In the two decades following the Revolution all the southern states except Georgia and South Carolina moved toward emancipation by easing the process of private manumission, and between 1800 and 1815 societies devoted to gradual emancipation sprouted in all the states of the upper South. After

1800 the tide turned and flowed in the opposite direction. By 1830 nearly all the vocal abolitionists were forced to leave the South. Levi Coffin, James G. Birney, the Grimké sisters, Rankin, and even Lundy had to carry their antislavery activities north. As the crucial debate in the Virginia legislature in 1832 revealed, the only antislavery advocates remaining in the South by then were the rapidly dwindling supporters of the American Colonization Society (ACS).

The ACS had originated in response to fears that free blacks could not be successfully incorporated into American society. Its activities typified the conservative reform emanating from a period of fairly modest social and economic change, but its early membership included, along with some of the South's leading politicians, such abolitionists as Lundy, the Tappan brothers, Gerrit Smith, and the young William Lloyd Garrison. Abolitionists formed only a minor element in the ACS, however; although in the early years colonization was usually related to schemes for manumission and gradual emancipation, most advocates of these proposals cared little about the plight of the slave and hoped to rid the country of the troublesome presence of a race generally deemed inferior and degraded. The doctrine of gradualism based on a faith in the perfectibility of all men gave way to the racist perspectives that typified the 19th century. As the ACS became increasingly dominated by those whose main purpose was the deportation of free blacks and shed its antislavery character, the abolitionists turned against the organization.

Immediatism. The appearance of Garrison's *Thoughts on African Colonization* in 1832, and the debates held at Lane Seminary two years later under the direction of Theodore Dwight Weld, signaled a major shift in American antislavery and the emergence of the movement for immediate abolition. One can trace the roots of the doctrine of immediatism to the basic elements of 18th-century antislavery thought and relate its appearance in the United States in the 1830's to such causes as English influence, increasing black militancy, and the failure of gradual emancipation in the South. But the new intensity and enthusiasm that characterized the drive for immediate, uncompensated abolition came about primarily from evangelical perfectionism. Although abolitionists were often ambivalent about their precise programs, their new approach connoted a direct response to the recognition of the sinfulness of slavery and epitomized the abolitionist movement of this period. In rejecting the detached 18th-century perspective that had governed the psychology of gradual emancipation, the advocates of immediate abolition "made a personal commitment to make no compromise with sin."

In the decade of the 1830's, antislavery sentiments spread throughout the northern states and a new network of abolition societies appeared. The New England Anti-Slavery Society was formed in 1831; two years later at a meeting in Philadelphia, delegates from Massachusetts, New York, and Pennsylvania established a national organization, the American Anti-Slavery Society (AAS). In rapid order, auxiliaries appeared in all the eastern states and an energetic effort was made to revive western abolitionism. Following the Lane debates, Weld served as an agent for the AAS, lecturing and organizing local groups throughout Ohio and the western portions of New York and Pennsylvania. His success prompted the AAS to extend the agency system, sending out a new host of agents, the "Seventy," to further expand the number of local societies and advance the idea of immediate abolition of slavery. Many of this group were former Lane students: "Their method was the evangelism of the Great Revival; their doctrine was a doctrine of sin; and their program was to convert congregations of the North to the duty of testimony against the slaveholders of the South."

As a result of such activities the number of state and local societies multiplied rapidly. By 1835 there were 225 auxiliaries of the AAS, a number that grew to 1,346 in the next three years; and by 1840 there were 1,650 such organizations, with a total of between 130,000 and 170,000 members. Little is known about the makeup of these societies except that they proliferated in rural Yankee areas "burned over" by the Great Revival and that a majority of their members were women. Abolitionist leaders were highly educated and moderately prosperous men of some importance in their communities. Their most significant characteristics were an intense religious commitment and Yankee origins. Nearly two-thirds were pastors, deacons, and elders of evangelical churches, and an even larger proportion of white abolitionist leaders traced their family origins to New England.

A distinctive group within the movement was made up of the free blacks who were prominent in the activities of the underground railroad and who provided a crucial element of abolitionist leadership. During the 1830's men such as James Forten, Theodore S. Wright, and Samuel Ringgold Ward cooperated with white abolitionists and held positions of power within the abolition societies. However, blacks were generally denied positions of power in these organizations and resented the racism and paternalism of the whites. During the 1830's and 1840's a series of all-black National Negro Conventions acted to focus the efforts of black abolitionists.

The major activity of the abolitionists in the 1830's consisted in the dissemination of antislavery arguments in the hope that moral suasion would effect the end of slavery in the United States. Birney estimated that in 1839 there were "upwards of a hundred" abolitionist newspapers, but most were short-lived and only a handful maintained continued existence during this period. The most famous of these were Garrison's *Liberator,* published in Boston from 1831 to 1865, and the *Emancipator,* which functioned as the major organ of the AAS. Aside from its newspaper, the AAS issued a quarterly, two monthlies, and a children's magazine. It also supported a yearly antislavery almanac and a series of pamphlets that included the classics of antislavery literature, such as Angelina Grimké's *Appeal to the Christian Women of the South* and James Throme and J. Horace Kimball's *Emancipation in the West Indies*. While it was not until the 1840's and 1850's that slave narratives, like that of Frederick Douglass, and sentimental antislavery novels, such as Harriet Beecher Stowe's *Uncle Tom's Cabin,* appeared, the appeal to sentiment was central to the most powerful of the abolitionist attacks on slavery published in the 1830's, Weld's *Slavery As It Is*. In this volume Weld chose to limit those characterizations of slavery that were "merely *horrid*" in order to "give place to those which are absolutely diabolical." Yet he drew most of these tales of cruelty directly from southern sources and insisted that they each could be thoroughly authenticated.

In 1835 the AAS launched its postal campaign under the direction of Lewis Tappan. The society hoped to inundate the South with publications and convince southerners to rid themselves of the wretched evils of slavery. In that year the AAS produced over a million copies of their publications and thousands of copies were mailed to whites in the South. Although the intention of the literature was to sway the minds and sentiments of the slaveholders, it was immediately viewed as incendiary. In July 1835, a mob attacked the Charleston, S.C., post office and burned a number of abolitionist newspapers. In the following year a law excluding antislavery literature from the mails, which Andrew Jackson strongly favored, failed in Congress by a narrow margin; but with the cooperation of the Jackson administration, local postmasters effectively eliminated the circulation of abolitionist material in the South.

When the postal campaign failed, the AAS shuffled its organizational structure and turned to a campaign to present Congress with petitions on a variety of subjects related to slavery. The petition was a traditional antislavery instrument, but in 1835 John C. Calhoun and his South Carolina colleague in the House, James Hammond, moved against hearing any antislavery pleas. In an effort to disassociate themselves from this attack on the civil rights of northern whites, northern Democrats accepted the more moderate gag rule that automatically tabled all antislavery petitions. Undaunted the AAS, using the numerous societies established by the Seventy, flooded Congress with petitions. Between January 1837 and March 1838, the AAS presented petitions signed by more than 400,000 people. The largest number of these opposed the annexation of Texas and called for the abolition of slavery in the District of Columbia. Yet by 1840, the gag rule had effectively stifled the petition campaign.

Political Antislavery. Although it had grown rapidly during the 1830's, at the end of the decade the abolition movement remained unpopular and generally weak. The abolitionists had encountered mob violence in the North; no major politician dared associate himself with their cause; and the leading religious denominations rejected their teachings. Factional bickering and financial reverses further undermined the movement. The theoretical Seventy agents had never reached full strength, and after 1838 their numbers dwindled drastically. Because the panic of 1837 and the subsequent depression dried up their sources of funds, the local societies were forced to curtail numerous activities. Then in 1840, after several years of bickering over the relation of abolitionism to the churches and to other reform movements, particularly women's rights, the AAS split into warring factions. In that year the radical followers of Garrison took over the AAS; the moderate element—led by Tappan, Birney, and Henry B. Stanton—formed a new organization, the American and Foreign Anti-Slavery Society (AFAS). By this time the Great Revival, which had fired the growth of abolitionism in the previous decade, had run its course, and neither of these organizations retained the vitality that had characterized the AAS in the first five years of its existence.

In 1839 the majority of American abolitionists, faced with the distinct possibility of failure and agreeing with Alvan Stewart that the tactics of the 1830's had "never . . . gained truth an advocate, or humanity a friend,'' decided to follow the urgings of those who advocated the establishment of a political party devoted to their cause. After an unsuccessful attempt to get New York gubernatorial candidates to respond publicly to their inquiries, Stewart, Gerrit Smith, and Myron Holley moved to form the Liberty, or Human Rights, party, which nominated Birney for president in 1840. At its inception the Liberty party was devoted to bringing the slavery question into politics and hoped to keep the doctrine of immediatism alive by offering individuals an opportunity to go on record against slavery. Through 1844 the new party retained its abolitionist character, attacking the immorality of slavery and demanding equal justice for free blacks. During these years its support grew among the moderate abolitionists associated with the AFAS; and in 1844 Birney, who was again the party's candidate, received 63,000 votes. While the Liberty party had clearly induced most abolitionists to join its ranks, it is doubtful that abolition sentiment grew in the North during these years. At the height of its popularity, the party's votes came mainly from men who had earlier converted to abolitionism but had voted Whig in 1840. It was strongest in the small, moderately prosperous Yankee farming communities that had earlier been touched by evangelical revivalism and had been centers of organized abolition activities. After 1844 the Liberty party split over the question of broadening the party's appeal, and the majority of its members drifted into the Free Soil party, which appeared in 1848.

The failure of both moral suasion and political activity led many blacks and a few whites to greater militancy. In 1843 Henry Highland Garnet's advocacy of self-defense and slave revolt was nearly adopted by the Buffalo National Convention; and within a decade, especially after the passage of the Fugitive Slave Law in 1850, numerous local conventions of blacks echoed his sentiments. In Christiana, Pa., Boston, and Syracuse, attempts by both blacks and whites to aid fugitive slaves became the focus of sporadic violence. However, it was not until 1859 that anyone connected with the abolition movement attempted to encourage rebellion among the slaves. After several years of planning, John Brown, with financial aid from white abolitionists and accompanied by sixteen whites and five blacks, launched his unsuccessful raid on Harpers Ferry.

Although individual abolitionists continued to agitate throughout the 1850's, organized abolitionism passed from the scene. As it emerged in the 1840's and 1850's political antislavery compromised abolitionist goals in order to present a program moderate and broad-gauged enough to attract voters in the North whose opposition to slavery arose from their desire to keep blacks out of the territories and slaveholders out of positions of power in the federal government. The final phase of antislavery activity in the United States was based primarily on hostility toward the slaveholder and the values of the society in which he lived. Antisouthernism provided a vehicle through which the Republican party could unite all forms of northern antislavery feeling by 1860.

The growth of popular antagonism toward the South in the northern states can be dated from the controversy over the gag rule. While the abolitionists had constantly attacked the slave power (the excessive political power wielded by slaveholders), Whig politicians in the early 1840's made the most use of the issue to define a moderate pro-northern position between the abolitionists and the Democrats. In numerous constituencies in the North this strategy forced Democratic candidates to oppose the gag rule and even, in a few cases, the annexation of Texas, to avoid depiction as ''doughfaces,'' subservient to the interests of the southern slaveholders. The events associated with the Mexican War and actions of James Polk's administration caused a split in the Democratic party and the enunciation of the Wilmot Proviso, which would have excluded slavery from the territory gained by the war. The followers of Martin Van Buren in New York, increasingly enraged by the power of slaveholders within their party, joined with the so-called Conscience Whigs of Massachusetts and the majority of the Liberty party to form the Free Soil party. In 1848 Van Buren ran as the party's candidate for president and garnered nearly 300,000 votes. While its members included many true abolitionists, its platform represented both a broadening of the appeal of antislavery and a turning away from the earlier goals of the abolitionists. The party focused almost entirely on limiting the expansion of slavery to keep the territories free for the migration of whites. Its platform avoided traditional abolitionist demands, and its followers spanned the wide spectrum of contemporary racist opinion. Following the election, the party's largest faction, the New York Barnburners, returned to the Democratic fold; the Free Democratic party, as it was called in 1852, could manage only 150,000 votes for its presidential candidate, John P. Hale.

During the years between 1850 and 1854 not only abolitionism but also antisouthernism seemed to fade. Northerners generally accepted the terms of the Compromise of 1850; and a leading southern paper noted "a calm comparatively in the political world." Yet at that very moment a surge of nativism and anti-Catholicism throughout the North shattered traditional party alignments. Then in 1854 and 1855 the fights over the Kansas-Nebraska Act and the chaos in Kansas Territory revived antisouthernism and channeled it through the new Republican party, which ran John C. Frémont for president in 1856. Although it deserves credit for ending slavery in the United States, the Republican party was by no means an abolitionist party nor one devoted solely to antislavery. Its platform touched on a wide variety of economic and social questions and appealed to a diverse group of northerners.

The new party was made up primarily of ex-Whigs, with smaller but crucial groups of free-soil and nativist ex-Democrats, and the remnants of the Free Democratic party; consequently, it included both vicious racists and firm believers in racial justice. Although most Republicans had moderately liberal racial views for the day, many were attracted by colonization schemes and nearly all expressed reservations about the total integration of the society. The main focus of their antislavery sentiments was the southern slaveholder, and the only antislavery plank in their platform demanded the exclusion of slavery from the territories. In this limited form a majority of northerners could embrace antislavery, and in 1860 Abraham Lincoln received 54 percent of the section's vote. Yet the party shied away from any direct attack on slavery; when secession threatened, many Republicans were willing to guarantee the existence of slavery in the southern states through a constitutional amendment.

The needs of war, as much as the constant agitation of the small abolitionist element within the Republican party, propelled the country toward emancipation. Lincoln, who had long doubted the feasibility of social integration, prosecuted the war primarily to maintain the Union. Caught between the radical and conservative wings of his own party, the president moved cautiously toward the enunciation of the Emancipation Proclamation on Jan. 1, 1863, freeing the slaves in areas still in rebellion. Subsequently, with a good deal more forthrightness, he lent his support to the Thirteenth Amendment, which declared that "neither slavery nor involuntary servitude . . . shall exist within the United States, or any place subject to their jurisdiction."

[Gilbert Hobbs Barnes, *The Anti-Slavery Impulse;* David B. Davis, *The Problem of Slavery in Western Culture;* Martin Duberman, ed., *The Antislavery Vanguard;* Dwight Lowell Dumond, *Antislavery;* Louis Filler, *The Crusade Against Slavery, 1830–1860;* Betty Fladeland, *James G. Birney;* James McPherson, *The Struggle for Equality;* Benjamin Quarles, *Black Abolitionists;* Gerald Sorin, *New York Abolitionists;* John L. Thomas, *The Liberator;* Bertram Wyatt-Brown, *Lewis Tappan and the Evangelical War Against Slavery;* Arthur Zilversmit, *The First Emancipation.*]

WILLIAM G. SHADE

ANTITRUST LAWS. The broad purpose of the federal antitrust laws is the maintenance of competitive conditions in the American private enterprise economy. The basic antitrust statutes are the Sherman Antitrust Act, the Clayton Act, and the Federal Trade Commission Act. This legislation, with its related body of case law, rests on the credo that competition is the most desirable regulator of economic activity and that restrictive trade practices and monopoly power are detrimental to the public interest and incompatible with the promotion of business opportunity in an open market. The origins of antitrust legislation lie in the post–Civil War era of industrial expansion and consolidation, with its accompanying wider use of the corporate form of organization, including the "trust." The rise of industrial trusts and monopolies brought a train of business abuses and political corruption that aroused the hostility of farmers, small proprietors, and consumers, all of whom feared economic and social domination by the large corporation. Some of the states enacted antitrust laws, which, however, proved inadequate for checking huge combinations doing business across state lines. Agricultural depression and rural opposition to monopoly sharpened a concern over the growing concentration of industrial and financial power.

The Sherman Antitrust Act, passed in 1890, was largely a response to public opinion—not least to the lively agitation of the trust issue by the Populist movement in the West and South. The act declared illegal every combination in restraint of interstate or foreign commerce and prohibited monopolization of any part of such trade. The U.S. attorney general was authorized to institute civil or criminal proceedings in the federal circuit courts, and injured private parties were allowed to bring civil suits for recovery of triple damages. Criminal violations were made punishable as a misdemeanor carrying a fine of up to $5,000 (increased in 1955 to $50,000) and/or imprisonment of up to one year. For the first decade or more of the Sherman Act, its enforcement against business combinations was generally feeble, save in cases of collusive price fixing, chiefly because of a negative attitude in the executive branch. The act was revitalized during the administrations of Theodore Roosevelt and William Howard Taft. A landmark in its judicial interpretation was the "rule of reason" applied in the Standard Oil and American Tobacco cases in 1911, when the Supreme Court drew a distinction between reasonable and unreasonable restraints of trade that influenced subsequent decisions.

The legislative, administrative, and judicial history of the Sherman Act indicates an intent to preserve competition while reaping the material benefits of the large corporate enterprise. This ambivalence has left its stamp on the evolution of American antitrust policy in the 20th-century era of big business. The Sherman Act has been amended in important respects, notably by the Webb-Pomerene Export Trade Act of 1918, which with certain qualifications allows American exporters to enter into agreements in foreign commerce that would otherwise violate the statute, and by the Miller-Tydings Act of 1937 and the McGuire-Keogh Act of 1952, both of which give federal sanction to resale price maintenance, or so-called fair-trade laws, where these are authorized by the states. Official enforcement of the Sherman Act is the jurisdiction of the Antitrust Division, a unit of the Department of Justice dating from 1903.

Trust regulation was still a national issue in the election of 1912; it was evident that the Sherman Act had failed to halt the trend toward concentrated economic power. Dissatisfied with the vague and ambiguous language of the Sherman Act and with the uncertainty of judicial application of the rule of reason, Progressive reformers pressed for legislation prohibiting specific trade practices. The result was the Clayton Act of 1914, whose main provisions forbade price discrimination, exclusive dealing and tying contracts, stock acquisitions of other companies, and interlocking directorates in industry and banking, where the "effect may be to substantially lessen competition or to create a monopoly." The Clayton Act was amended by the Robinson-Patman Act of 1936, which outlawed unreasonably low prices tending to destroy competition, and the Celler-Kefauver Act of 1950, which strengthened the provision against anticompetitive mergers. The Federal Trade Commission Act of 1914 established a five-member independent regulatory agency, the Federal Trade Commission (FTC), which was empowered to investigate unfair methods of competition and to issue cease and desist orders, subject to judicial review, aimed at preventing unfair business practices. The scope of the FTC was broadened by the Wheeler-Lea Act of 1938, which banned "unfair or deceptive acts or practices in commerce."

In October 1974 a more vigorous enforcement policy was announced in the economic message sent to Congress by President Gerald R. Ford, who in the following December signed into law the Antitrust Procedures and Penalties Act. This legislation, the most significant reform of the federal antitrust laws in a quarter-century, changed some criminal violations, notably price-fixing, from misdemeanors to felonies; raised maximum allowable fines from $50,000 to $1,000,000 for corporations and from $50,000 to $500,000 for individuals; and increased the maximum prison sentence from one to three years. It also contained important provisions concerning the public disclosure and judicial affirmation of antitrust case settlements negotiated by the Department of Justice.

Opinion on the effectiveness of the antitrust laws is divided. Some contend that the very existence of an antitrust policy has discouraged excessive concentration of business power. Others, pointing to a post-World War II trend toward oligopoly and conglomeration, have proposed the establishment of explicit and statutory standards for the determination of monopoly power and for the structural deconcentration of giant enterprise through divestiture or dissolution. Such recommendations have not been enacted into law, and the federal government continues to adhere to its traditional approach. Some critics, maintaining that public acceptance of big business has muted the antitrust reform fervor of an earlier day, hold that antitrust policy is merely a ceremonial device that serves the purpose of appeasing the social consensus on free competition.

[*Report of the Attorney General's National Committee to Study the Antitrust Laws;* J. M. Blair, *Economic Concentration;* W. Letwin, *Law and Economic Policy in America;* A. D. Neale, *The Antitrust Laws of the United States of America;* H. B. Thorelli, *The Federal Antitrust Policy.*]

WILLIAM GREENLEAF

ANTWERP, Belgium, one of the world's great ports, which in later stages of World War II accounted for one-third of American and Allied supplies discharged in Europe. Located fifty-five miles inland on the Schelde estuary, Antwerp was captured by British troops on Sept. 4, 1944, with its wharves and docks generally intact. Yet by holding the banks of the Schelde, the Germans denied the Allies use of the port for almost three months. The Germans subsequently bombarded the city with 2,500 V-1 and V-2 rockets, killing 734 soldiers and some 2,900 civilians among a population of 270,000 but interfering only minimally with port operations. Capture of the port was a major, but unrealized, German objective during the Battle of the Bulge.

[Roland G. Ruppenthal, *Logistical Support of the Armies*, vol. II, United States Army in World War II.]

CHARLES B. MACDONALD

ANZA EXPEDITION (Oct. 23, 1775–Jan. 4, 1776), sent out by Antonio Bucareli, viceroy of New Spain, to provide Alta California with the white population essential to its occupation in face of English and Russian threats. Led by Juan Bautista de Anza, who in 1774 had proved that a route existed from Sonora to California, 244 persons crossed the Colorado desert and reached San Gabriel. Local jealousies prevented Anza from founding the city he had laid out, but his capable lieutenant, José Joaquin Moraga, Sept. 17, 1776, dedicated a presidio on the site of modern San Francisco, and there, Oct. 9, 1776, the mission San Francisco de Asís was started.

[H. E. Bolton, *Anza's California Expeditions*.]

OSGOOD HARDY

ANZIO, a town on the west coast of Italy, thirty-three miles south of Rome, which became a battleground in the spring of 1944 during the Italian campaign of World War II. The Germans under Field Marshal Albert Kesselring were stubbornly defending southern Italy between Naples and Rome in the fall of 1943, and the Anglo-American ground forces under Gen. Sir Harold Alexander sought to outflank the German defenses by an amphibious end run to be made by part of Gen. Mark Clark's Fifth U.S. Army. By sending a seaborne invasion force northward from Naples around the German defensive line to land at Anzio, the Allies hoped to loosen the German grip on the mountainous terrain around Cassino, precipitate a battle for Rome, and compel the Germans to retreat to positions north of Rome.

The operation was risky because the Anzio forces would be distant from the main front and isolated in German-held territory. By January 1944 enough landing ships and craft had been gathered to transport a corps-sized force to Anzio. Bitter fighting had moved the main front to the German Gustav Line anchored on Cassino, and this was deemed close enough to promise a relatively rapid linkup with the landing force. Under pressure from Prime Minister Winston Churchill, who wished to capture Rome before the cross-Channel invasion into Normandy took place, the Sixth Corps under Gen. John Lucas landed British and American troops at Anzio and neighboring Nettuno against virtually no opposition on Jan. 22.

The Germans rallied quickly; penned the invaders into a small beachhead; brought reinforcements from northern Italy, France, Yugoslavia, and Germany; and almost drove the Anglo-American force into the sea, without ever losing their hold on the Gustav Line. The Allies built up their beachhead forces, instituted a seaborne shuttle service to keep the troops supplied, and held their precarious positions for four months.

Alexander's spring offensive of May 11 broke the German Gustav Line, and Clark's units linked up with the beachhead fourteen days later. The Sixth Corps, now under Gen. Lucian Truscott, Jr., joined the main forces, and Allied troops entered Rome on June 4, two days before the cross-Channel attack.

[Martin Blumenson, *Anzio: The Gamble That Failed*.]

MARTIN BLUMENSON

APACHE. With their linguistic relatives the Navaho, the Athapascan-speaking Apache pushed into New Mexico in prehistoric times, later fanning out into Arizona and western Texas and ranging over sections of northern Mexico. Unlike the Navaho, who were more strongly affected by Pueblo culture, the various groups of Apache became noted for the depredations they carried on against both their Indian neighbors and Spanish, Mexican, and U.S. settlers in the Southwest. Their very name apparently derives from the Zuni word for "enemy." Their war orientation reached a climax in the 19th century under the famous Chiricahua chiefs Cochise and Geronimo, and this somewhat sensational side of Apache life has made the group one of the best known of American Indians (*see* Apache Wars).

In the various sections of the Southwest in which the Apache settled, several distinct, closely related linguistic groupings appear. Moreover, some Apache adapted to a modified agriculture and others to hunting-gathering modes of subsistence. In the north of New Mexico the Jicarilla Apache took on Plains traits—the tipi and bison hunting. In central Arizona and New Mexico the San Carlos, White Mountain, Tonto, Mescalero, Chiricahua, and other groups, all divided in several bands. The Lipan Apache are a Mexican remnant. It has been suggested that the difficulties of living in a harsh desert environment led to the Apache "raiding economy."

Major Apache ceremonies involved the girls' rite

and masked spirit impersonation, a probable borrowing from the Pueblo. Never effectively politically organized, the Apache had war chiefs only late in their history, and even they had only an ephemeral following.

[Robert F. Spencer, Jesse D. Jennings, and others, *The Native Americans;* M. E. Opler, *An Apache Life-Way.*]

ROBERT F. SPENCER

APACHE, FORT, INCIDENT AT (Sept. 13, 1886), one of the last episodes in the Apache Wars. Some 480 Chiricahua and Mimbreño Apache who were living near Fort Apache in Arizona were believed to be actively aiding hostiles under Geronimo, who had broken away from the San Carlos Reservation. After Geronimo surrendered on Sept. 4, 1886, the other Chiricahua were summoned to Fort Apache for counting by Col. J. F. Wade and were surrounded by troops. With Geronimo's band they were shipped to Fort Marion, Fla., for internment.

[Odie B. Faulk, *The Geronimo Campaign;* Dan L. Thrapp, *The Conquest of Apachería.*]

KENNETH M. STEWART

APACHE PASS EXPEDITION (Feb. 4–23, 1861), led by Lt. George N. Bascom of the Seventh Infantry against Cochise, a chief of the Chiricahua Apache, who was falsely accused of having kidnapped a boy from a ranch. Cochise had been friendly to the Anglo-Americans and had not opposed the establishment of an overland stage route through Apache territory in eastern Arizona. Cochise went voluntarily under a flag of truce with several of his friends and relatives to the U.S. Army encampment to deny the charge, but Bascom ordered Cochise and those with him seized and bound. Cochise managed to escape and then led attacks on the nearby stage station and a wagon train. Bascom ordered the hanging of the six Apache who had been held as hostages. This blunder turned Cochise into an implacable foe of the whites. Joining forces with Mangas Coloradas, chief of the Mimbreño Apache, he fought the whites until 1872, when after a meeting with military authorities he agreed to the establishment of a reservation for the Chiricahua in southeastern Arizona.

[Odie B. Faulk, *The Geronimo Campaign;* Dan L. Thrapp, *The Conquest of Apachería.*]

KENNETH M. STEWART

APACHE WARS. The Apache of Arizona and New Mexico remained somewhat aloof from the Spaniards until after the Pueblo Revolt of 1680, when they intensified their raiding activities upon sedentary Indians and upon the Spanish towns along the Rio Grande, as well as raiding deep into Mexico, into Sonora and Chihuahua. By the 1690's the Apache were in control of a strip of territory 250 miles wide in which there were no Spanish settlements.

The Mexicans were no more successful in contending with the Apache menace than the Spaniards had been, despite an attempt to exterminate the predatory bands in the 1830's. By 1837 Mexican states were offering bounties for Apache scalps, but the Apache retaliated by stepping up their raids.

After the Mexican War (1846–48) the Anglo-Americans inherited the Apache problem. At first the Apache were more favorably disposed toward the Anglos, but Apache enmity was incurred when American authorities forbade raids into Mexico, the raids having become a vital part of Apache economy.

Among the famous Apache chiefs were Cochise of the central Chiricahua, who kept the peace until the Apache Pass expedition of 1861, and Mangas Coloradas, chief of the Mimbreño. Cochise and Mangas Coloradas joined forces to harass the whites.

War broke out also between the whites and the Tonto Apache when gold was discovered near Prescott, Ariz., in 1863. A ring of American forts was established, but it proved to be relatively ineffective either in protecting the settlers or in preventing Apache raids into Mexico. To many of the settlers and military men of the time, the only solution to the Apache problem was extermination.

Atrocities were committed by both sides, including the Camp Grant massacre in 1871. With the announcement of President Ulysses S. Grant's peace policy toward the Indians, Gen. George Crook was ordered into the Southwest with 3,000 soldiers to round up the Apache. This was a difficult directive to execute, but by 1875 some 5,000 Apache had been concentrated on the San Carlos Reservation in Arizona. Most of the Apache were willing to settle down by that time, but restless warriors repeatedly escaped from the reservation and resumed raiding under such leaders as Victorio of the Mimbreño and Geronimo of the southern Chiricahua. Victorio was killed in a fight with Mexican troops in 1880, but Geronimo eluded pursuit repeatedly, escaping to strongholds in the Sierra Madre in Mexico when hard-pressed. The Apache wars were finally ended with Geronimo's surrender in 1886.

[Odie B. Faulk, *The Geronimo Campaign;* Ralph H. Ogle, *Federal Control of Western Apaches, 1848–1886;* Dan L. Thrapp, *The Conquest of Apachería.*]

KENNETH M. STEWART

APALACHE MASSACRE (1704), an episode in Queen Anne's War. Having failed to take St. Augustine, Fla. (1702), former Gov. James Moore of Carolina with 50 Englishmen and 1,000 Creek Indians invaded the Apalache district in western Florida, defeating Captain Mexia's force of 30 Spaniards and 400 Apalache, destroying all but one of the fourteen Franciscan mission settlements and carrying off considerable loot including about 1,400 Christian Indians.

[J. T. Lanning, *The Spanish Missions of Georgia.*]

FRANCIS BORGIA STECK

APARTMENT HOUSES. Horizontal dwelling was a new concept in the United States—except for the lowly tenement—when Arthur Gilman, in 1858, designed the Hotel Pelham in Boston for Dr. John D. Dix. This was the prototype of apartment houses, borrowed from the French, complete with mansard roof. New York followed suit in 1869, when Richard Morris Hunt, recently returned from Paris, designed the five-story Stuyvesant Apartments on East 18th Street for Rutherford Stuyvesant. This was the first apartment house of note in New York City and was followed by ever-increasing numbers each year. The apartment hotel was the true forerunner of the apartment house; however, it rarely had cooking facilities in the apartments; residents ate in the main dining room or were served in their apartment. By the early 1880's apartments had been built in Washington, D.C., Chicago, and other major cities.

Acceptance of the apartment house in the United States was delayed by the odium connected with the squalid tenement house, which had been introduced in New York City as early as 1833. The post-Civil War housing shortage, followed by the massive influx of immigrants in the 1880's and 1890's, was aggravated by rapidly diminishing available land. Attempts to reduce the width of lots occasionally yielded ridiculously narrow houses, their floors connected by ladderlike stairs. Real estate developers followed the tentacles of newly extended rapid-transit lines away from congested districts, and blocks of five- and six-story apartment houses began springing up along their routes, in formerly "suburban" areas. Following the example of Paris and Berlin, many were built around a central court, garden, or playground, affording variety to an otherwise restrictive architectural form.

By the end of the 19th century, with the cost of building, furnishing, and staffing the average private home becoming prohibitive, middle-class families came to see apartment living as a desirable solution. It had at first been thought immoral for several families to live under one roof in these "French flats," and it took the well-to-do to render them fully respectable. Here Stuyvesant had pioneered with his apartments, which were followed by Haight House in 1871 (probably the first elevator apartment in the city), the Grosvenor, and Hunt's Stevens House—all on Fifth Avenue. Stevens House rose to a height of eight stories, made possible by the elevator, and was completely French in its concept, with stores on the first floor and a towering mansard roof. Built around a central courtyard, the Dakota, at 72nd Street and Central Park West—designed by Henry Janeway Hardenbergh and begun in 1880—was the prototype of the superblock apartment house.

The cooperative apartment was introduced as a "home club" in 1879 with Rembrandt House at 152 West 57th Street, designed by Hubert, Pirsson and Company. A New York State law (Jan. 23, 1881) made it possible for tenants to purchase their apartments, and the Knickerbocker, the Gramercy, and finally the great Central Park Apartments, designed for José de Navarro by Hubert, Pirsson and Company, followed in rapid succession. Known as the "Spanish flats," the Central Park Apartments consisted of eight units, surrounding a central courtyard and separated by open breezeways. Their spectacular failure in 1886 so discredited home clubs that the cooperative movement remained in disfavor until the late 1890's. In the early years of the 20th century, "studio cooperatives" began to appear, and during the building boom of the 1920's luxury cooperatives began supplanting private mansions in more desirable residential areas. Often overlooking a park or lake and soaring to twenty stories or more, many of these brick behemoths boasted block-long duplex or triplex apartments, with separate entrances for servants. The lesson of their troubles in the depression of the 1930's was not lost on the wise builders of cooperatives after World War II.

In 1800 about 4 percent of the population was urban; in 1880, 25 percent; in 1970, almost 69 percent. The growth of the apartment house was rapid. New housing units for five or more families numbered 780,900 in 1971 and rose to 906,200 in 1972, as contrasted with 1,151,000 and 1,309,200 single-family dwellings for the same years. Building was most prevalent in the South and lowest in the Northeast.

[Junius H. Browne, "Problem of Living in New York," *Harpers New Monthly Magazine*, vol. 65 (1882); Ernest Flagg, "A Fish Story—An Autobiographical Sketch of the Education of an Architect," *Journal of the American Institute of Architects*, vol. 3 (1945); James H. Richardson,

"New Homes of New York," *Scribner's Monthly*, vol. 3 (1874); R. W. Sexton, *American Apartment Houses, Hotels and Apartment Hotels of Today*.]

ALAN BURNHAM

APIA, DISASTER OF. On Mar. 16, 1889, one British, three American, and three German warships were crowded into Apia Harbor in Samoa, ready for hostilities because of the German attempt to set up a protectorate under a puppet native king. A clash was averted by a hurricane that swept in, destroying the German *Eber, Adler,* and the *Olga,* with the loss of 134 men, and the U.S. *Trenton* and the *Vandalia,* with a loss of 52 lives. The U.S. *Nipsic* was run ashore. The British *Calliope* escaped by steaming out to sea. The Berlin Conference followed, establishing for Samoa a tripartite government.

[G. H. Ryden, *The Foreign Policy of the United States in Relation to Samoa*.]

J. W. ELLISON

APOSTOLIC DELEGATION, established in Washington, D.C., by Pope Leo XIII, Jan. 14, 1893. Archbishop Francesco Satolli, representative of the Holy See at the World's Columbian Exposition, was appointed as the first apostolic delegate.

[Winthrop S. Hudson, *Religion in America*.]

T. E. HEWITT

APPALACHIA, a largely mountainous region in the eastern United States, extending generally from southwestern Pennsylvania southward through West Virginia and eastern Kentucky, and including western portions of Virginia, North Carolina, and South Carolina, eastern portions of Tennessee, and northern portions of Georgia and Alabama. It was settled in the 1790's and early 1800's—largely from the areas of eastern Pennsylvania, tidewater Virginia, and North Carolina—by people of English, Scotch-Irish, and German descent, joined by a scattering of other ethnic groups fleeing Western Europe during and after the Bonapartist disturbances. The settlers built their log cabins and clapboard houses on land lying generally between the Blue Ridge Mountains and the southern extension of the Allegheny Mountains. To the east of the Blue Ridge were landed estates and to the west were dense forests and hostile Indians. Many of the original settlers and their descendants remained in the area, engaging in logging, coal mining, small local industries, handicraft operations, and agricultural pursuits.

After many years of comparative isolation and neglect, Appalachia (since the 1930's) has come to the attention of the public and has gained government support for its efforts to improve its economy and living conditions. An aggressive and well-publicized attempt to control and curtail the strip mining of coal, principally in West Virginia and eastern Kentucky, and a return to the conventional method of shaft and drift mining, which leaves relatively few marks on the land surface and increases employment opportunities, have also fostered a new awareness of the region. Strip mining leaves physical surface scars marked by deep, bare gullies and ravines, treeless surface stretches, polluted waters, and destroyed home sites. In many cases in which there has been no restoration of the stripped surface, the environment is marred by destructive landslides, acid-polluted waters, and unsightly surface remains.

During the 1960's Appalachia became a *cause célèbre* for many former members of the Peace Corps, VISTA, and similar organizations, who went there to help improve living conditions, giving great impetus to the fight against strip mining and the allied environmental destruction and helping in other efforts to upgrade the region, particularly in efforts to improve the extent and quality of education.

[H. M. Candell, *My Land Is Dying;* T. D. Clark, *Settlers on the Cumberland;* E. C. Semple, *American History and Its Geographical Conditions*.]

THOMAS ROBSON HAY

APPALACHIAN MOUNTAINS BOUNDARY. *See* **Indian Barrier State; Proclamation of 1763; Quebec Act.**

***APPAM* CASE,** 243 U.S. 124 (1917). On Jan. 15, 1916, a German cruiser captured the *Appam,* a British merchantman, on the high seas and took it into Hampton Roads, Va. There its British crew was released by order of the American government, and on Feb. 16 the shipowner filed a libel suit in the proper U.S. district court, which ultimately decreed restitution of ship and cargo. On appeal by the German government to the Supreme Court the decree was affirmed on the ground that the capture, being a prize, of which the lower court had jurisdiction, the ship's detention in port was a breach of American neutrality, unauthorized by any treaty.

C. SUMNER LOBINGIER

APPEAL OF THE INDEPENDENT DEMOCRATS, a manifesto issued in January 1854, inspired by the Kansas-Nebraska Act, then pending. The signers, led by Sen. Salmon P. Chase, were free-soilers. Chase had tried to convert northern Democrats into a Wilmot Proviso party. Now, by a master stroke, precisely timed, he helped to create the Republican party. The "appeal" was sincere and effective, though it contained exaggerated statements and unsound prophecies relative to the possible influence of the measure, introduced by Sen. Stephen A. Douglas, on the spread of slavery.

WILLIAM O. LYNCH

APPEALS FROM COLONIAL COURTS. In the latter part of the 17th century the new colonial charters, proprietary and royal, reserved for the king-in-council the right to hear cases on appeal from provincial courts where the sum litigated exceeded £300 sterling. In the New England colonies particularly, the appellate authority was at best grudgingly conceded, as the Connecticut and Rhode Island charters made no provision for judicial review. At times, as in *Frost* v. *Leighton* (1739), an order of the privy council was deliberately ignored by the Massachusetts authorities. Pending appeals, executions of the colonial courts were suspended. Such appeals were both costly and protracted.

Through this appellate procedure the privy council sought to bring the legal systems of the colonies into conformity with that of England, particularly in such matters as the rules of evidence and the jury system. Major issues of colonial policy were reviewed in litigation brought on appeal, notably Indian relations, the colonial currency laws, and intestate succession. Currency practices in the colonies were more generally dealt with by the privy council under its authority to disallow colonial legislation or by Parliament (*see* Royal Disallowance). In the suit of the Virginia clergy instituted to recover back salaries resulting from the disallowance of the "two penny act," the council, in view of the constitutional storms raised by the Stamp Act, was prompted by political considerations to dismiss the appeal on a technicality. In the notable case of *Winthrop* v. *Lechmere* (1728) the council held the Connecticut custom of divisible descent of intestate estates invalid as contrary to the common law, but reversed itself in *Clark* v. *Tousey* and in the Massachusetts case of *Phillips* v. *Savage* (1737), a great victory for egalitarian property concepts in New England.

[R. B. Morris, *Studies in the History of American Law;* G. A. Washburne, *Imperial Control of the Administration of Justice in the Thirteen American Colonies.*]

RICHARD B. MORRIS

APPLESEED, JOHNNY. As the American frontier moved into Ohio, Indiana, and Illinois, the settlers were deprived of fruit until orchards could be grown. Since the people lacked money, they could not have bought young trees had nurseries been available; and horticulture languished. John Chapman therefore consecrated himself from 1801 to 1847 to the mission of bringing seed from Pennsylvania and planting flowers and fruits, especially apple seed, in the forests to be ready for the free use of the settlers when they arrived. Meager documentary evidence and rich tradition have preserved Chapman's fame under the sobriquet of Johnny Appleseed.

[W. A. Duff, *Johnny Appleseed, An Ohio Hero;* Henry Chapin, *The Adventures of Johnny Appleseed.*]

BLISS ISELY

APPLIANCES, ELECTRICAL HOME. *See* **Electrification, Household.**

APPOINTMENT, COUNCIL OF. *See* **Council of Appointment, New York.**

APPOINTMENTS TO GOVERNMENT OFFICE AND APPOINTING POWER. Whether appointment to government positions should be used mainly to reward party service and assist in executing party policies or to obtain the "best qualified man" has been an issue for continuing debate in American history. In his early appointments President George Washington emphasized "fitness of character," selecting men of high reputation. As the party system developed, however, Washington and his successors sought men of their own political persuasion. Thomas Jefferson devised the doctrine of "due participation" of each party in appointments (1801), thereby justifying the removal of Federalists and appointment of Republicans in their place. Even so, the use of federal appointments for party patronage was muted in those early years. Within the states, however, vigorous political battles occurred over patronage, marked by the wholesale replacement of administrative officials by the victorious faction at each turn of the political wheel.

President Andrew Jackson argued in his first message to Congress (1829) that "rotation" in office every few years was needed to keep officials sensitive to popular needs and that the duties of all government positions were "so plain and simple that men of intelligence [might] readily qualify . . . ." Responding to widespread criticism of his predecessors' tendency to make appointments from the social elite, Jackson replaced hundreds of officials with men of his own party of working-class origins.

During the next fifty years federal and state appointments were largely based upon party service and personal connections. By the 1870's this "spoils system" was widely condemned as having caused a sharp decline in competence and honesty in government service. After President James A. Garfield was killed by a disappointed office-seeker (1881), Congress yielded to public pressure and approved the Pendleton Civil Service Act (1883). The act created the Civil Service Commission to establish rules for "open, competitive examinations" to test job applicants. Initially only 10 percent of all federal positions were to be filled through examination, but as a result of sustained reformist pressure, 45 percent of federal jobs were covered by 1900 and 80 percent by 1932. During the period between 1933 and 1936, this percentage dropped, ranging between 60 and 65 percent, as 300,000 exempt positions were created in New Deal agencies. President Dwight D. Eisenhower, finding little room for policy and party appointments in 1953, created a new category, Schedule C, which included several hundred new positions exempt from civil service examination.

Since 1950, 85–90 percent of all federal employees have been covered by civil service rules; other merit systems include several thousand additional employees. Only a few thousand exempt positions remain—a small number at the top of each federal agency to permit discretionary appointment of men to carry out administration policies and a few other positions available to meet demands to reward party loyalty and interest-group support. Below the national level, evolution toward a merit system has been slower, and patronage appointments remain widespread in some states and cities and in many county governments. (*See also* Patronage, Political.)

[W. S. Sayre, ed., *The Federal Government Service;* P. P. Van Riper, *History of the United States Civil Service;* L. D. White, *The Federalists; The Jacksonians; The Jeffersonians;* and *The Republican Era.*]

JAMESON W. DOIG

APPOMATTOX, former courthouse (county seat) of the county of the same name in Virginia, 20 miles east southeast of Lynchburg, and scene of the surrender of the Confederate Army of Northern Virginia to the Union Army of the Potomac, April 9, 1865. Gen. Robert E. Lee, commanding the Confederate forces which evacuated Petersburg and Richmond on the night of April 2–3, had planned to withdraw into North Carolina, via Danville, and to join Gen. Joseph E. Johnston; but on the third day of retreat, Lee found the federal troops across his front at Jetersville, on the Richmond and Danville Railroad. As he was dependent on the railways for supplies, he determined to move westward across country to the Southside Railroad at Farmville, where he hoped to procure rations for a march to Lynchburg. Thence he would turn south again toward Danville. En route to Farmville, Lee was attacked heavily on April 6, at Sayler's Creek, where he lost about 6,000 men. The next day at Farmville he was again assailed before he could victual all his troops. By that time, long marches without food had so depleted the Confederate ranks that Gen. Ulysses S. Grant addressed Lee a proposal for the surrender of the army. Lee did not consider the situation altogether hopeless and pushed on toward Lynchburg by the Richmond Stage Road. When the army bivouacked around Appomattox Courthouse on the evening of April 8, the reflection of federal campfires against the clouds showed that the surviving Confederates, now reduced to two small corps, were surrounded on three sides. Lee closed his column and prepared to cut his way out, but, when he found the next morning that the corps of John B. Gordon faced impossible odds on the Stage Road, he sent a flag of truce to Grant. A suggestion that the army break into small bands and attempt to slip through the enveloping lines was rejected by Lee on the ground that it would carry a hopeless struggle into country that had escaped the ravages of war. After some delay in communicating with Grant, who had made his dispositions with the greatest skill, Lee rode, on April 9 at about 1 P.M., into the village and, at the house of Maj. Wilmer McLean, formally arranged the surrender of all forces then under arms in Virginia. Grant's generous terms, which allowed officers to retain their side arms and provided for the parole of all surrendered troops, were executed with the least humiliation to the defeated army. A full day's rations were issued the prisoners of war. When the troops marched into an open field to lay down their weapons and their flags (April 12), the federal guard presented arms. The number of Confederate infantrymen surrendered at Appomattox with arms in their hands was 7,892; the total number of troops paroled was about 28,000. In an interview with Lee on April 10, Grant sought to prevail on the Confederate commander to advise that all the remaining Confederate troops cease resistance, but Lee insisted that this was a question to be decided by the civil authorities.

Appomattox became a national historic site in 1954.

[D. S. Freeman, *R. E. Lee,* vol. 4; U. S. Grant, *Personal Memoirs,* vol. 2; R. U. Johnson and C. C. Buel, eds., *Battles and Leaders of the Civil War,* vol. 4.]

DOUGLAS SOUTHALL FREEMAN

APPORTIONMENT is the decennial computation and assignment of seats in the House of Representatives to the individual states, or the allocation of legislative seats within a state. The constitutional law governing congressional apportionment differs somewhat from that governing the apportionment of state legislatures.

Congressional Apportionment. Article I, Section 2, Clause 3, of the U.S. Constitution as amended by the Fourteenth Amendment provides for the apportionment of seats in the U.S. House of Representatives every ten years on the basis of population, except for the rule that each state shall have at least one representative. However, this constitutional provision is silent on how the congressmen are to be elected. To remedy the common practice of at-large or "winner take all" elections, the Apportionment Act of 1842 required single-member congressional districts composed of "contiguous" or adjoining territory. In 1872 Congress legislated that all districts should contain "as nearly as practicable an equal number of inhabitants," and in 1901 it passed a law requiring that districts should be of "compact territory."

Technically speaking, Congress apportions its House membership, and the states district themselves for the election of representatives. After the 1920 census, which showed for the first time that urban Americans outnumbered rural Americans, Congress was deadlocked on how to reapportion its House seats. To avoid future impasses, Congress in 1929 provided for a so-called permanent system of reapportionment that would discourage further growth in the size of the House and would obviate the necessity for further congressional action on the subject. As amended in 1941, the 1929 act required that (1) the size of the House be fixed at 435; (2) the Bureau of Census prepare for the president a table showing the number of inhabitants of each state and the number of representatives to which each state is entitled; and (3) the president transmit the information to Congress, with the proposed distribution becoming effective in fifteen days unless Congress enacts a different distribution. If a state fails to redraw district lines after gaining or losing seats, the expediency of using at-large elections for the added members in the case of a gain in seats or at-large elections for all members in the case of a loss in seats is authorized.

Unfortunately, the 1929 reapportionment act did not specify that districts were to be contiguous, compact, and of equal size; and the Supreme Court in *Wood* v. *Broom* (1932) ruled that those provisions were no longer in force. Thus, voters complaining of the inequity of districts of grossly unequal population and of gerrymandering could find no law in effect to prevent such practices. The remaining remedy of judicial relief was blocked by the 1946 Supreme Court decision in *Colegrove* v. *Green,* which prevented judicial consideration of issues pertaining to apportionment. Not until *Baker* v. *Carr* in 1962 did the Court reverse itself and rule that federal courts could review apportionment cases. In 1964, in a six-to-three decision, the Supreme Court decided the case of *Wesberry* v. *Sanders,* ruling that congressional districts must be substantially equal in population. Departing from the precedent established in *Baker* and also in *Reynolds* v. *Sims* earlier in the same year, the Court did not use the Fourteenth Amendment as its justification, but based its decision on the history and wording of Article I, Section 2, of the Constitution. The Court stated that this language means that "as nearly as is practicable, one man's vote in a congressional election is to be worth as much as another's."

Apportionment of State Legislatures. Until the Supreme Court ruling in *Baker* v. *Carr,* constitutional standards by which apportionment should be measured were not established. In a group of six state legislative reapportionment cases—collectively known by the name of the first case, *Reynolds* v. *Sims* (1964)—the Supreme Court made these major points: the Fourteenth Amendment's equal protection clause "requires that the seats in both houses of a bicameral state legislature must be apportioned on a population basis"; "mathematical exactness of precision" in carving out legislative districts may be impossible, but apportionments must be "based substantially on population"; "the so-called federal analogy is inapplicable as a sustaining precedent for state legislative apportionments"; and deviation from the one man, one vote rule for both houses is unconstitutional even if endorsed in a statewide initiative process or referendum because "a citizen's constitutional rights can hardly be infringed upon because a majority of the people choose to do so."

The equal population (one man, one vote) principle enunciated in *Reynolds* brought relief from decades of malapportionment. In spite of the 1920 census, which made clear that the population of urban America was exceeding that of rural America, and in spite of state constitutional requirements in some states for periodic reapportionment, many state legislatures had refused to reapportion either congressional districts or state legislatures to reflect the change in population, thus allowing the rural areas to continue to hold the reins of political power. Rural areas were also legally favored in those states in which the state constitutions provided apportionment based partly or wholly on counties or towns rather than on population. The majority opinion in *Reynolds* did not attempt to spell out precise state constitutional tests because "what is marginally permissible in one state may be unsatisfactory in another." It endorsed a case-by-case development of standards and seemed to be requiring a good-faith effort to achieve "precise mathematical equality." Left unresolved were requirements for compactness and contiguousness of districts, and the constitutionality of multimember districts.

[R. B. McKay, *Reapportionment*.]

CALVIN B. T. LEE

APPRENTICESHIP, a system of occupational training for a specific period and under written contract whereby a young person learns a skill on the job, in a classroom, or in a combination of both. Apprentice training, based on ancient and medieval practice, was systematized in England under Elizabeth I by the Statute of Artificers (1563) and the Poor Law (1601), and transferred to the American colonies. In 1642, the Virginia legislature ordered that children of poor parents be apprenticed to learn "carding, knitting and spinning," while Massachusetts passed a similar law that became the prototype of legislation in the North. The binding out of such children and the voluntary contracts or indentures often included instruction in reading, writing, and religion, and later in language and arithmetic. Among the prominent Americans who underwent apprentice training were Benjamin Franklin and Andrew Johnson. The system even prevailed in the professions of law and journalism.

With the Industrial Revolution and the expansion of educational opportunity, the need for apprenticeship began to decline. It was not always certain that the provisions of indenture were carried out. Late in the 19th century, many masters were unwilling to teach their apprentices and the latter were often reluctant to spend long years to master a trade. Industrialists and educators felt increasingly that vocational and industrial training could do a better job of preparing skilled workers.

During the 20th century, apprenticeship was revived and refined, especially after the National Apprenticeship Act (1937), which established a Bureau of Apprenticeship and Training in the U.S. Department of Labor. The experiences of World War II also contributed to the retention of apprentice training. By the mid-1970's the system of formal training was widely recognized in many industries. Hundreds of skills were being taught to over 300,000 apprentices in such industries as printing, metalworking, and building and construction, and in such trades as baking, mechanics, and jewelry. Apprenticeship information centers in thirty large cities, union locals, and trade groups were providing information to prospective apprentices.

[H. F. Clark and H. S. Sloan, *Classrooms in the Factories;* P. H. Douglas, *American Apprenticeship and Industrial Education;* M. W. Jernegan, *Laboring and Dependent Classes in Colonial America, 1617–1783;* U. S. Bureau of Apprenticeship and Training, *The National Apprenticeship Program.*]

WILLIAM W. BRICKMAN

APPROPRIATIONS BY CONGRESS. Congressional appropriations provide much of the money laid out by the federal government. Procedures for appropriating money have been changed several times by Congress, but according to present practice, programs and expenditure ceilings are authorized through legislation processed initially by congressional committees, such as those responsible for agriculture and the armed services. However, appropriations committees in each house of Congress are responsible for the actual appropriation of money for these programs; they may appropriate all the money authorized or only part of it.

The appropriations process begins each year with the president's budget requests. Within Congress itself the appropriations process is fragmented, and individual appropriations bills are not considered as part of a coherent and cohesive package. Several attempts—especially in the late 1940's and in the 1950's—to formulate a single legislative budget or to consider all appropriations bills together were abortive or short-lived. Currently about twelve separate appropriations bills are considered each year: customarily first by the subcommittees of the House Appropriations Committee, then by the full committee, and then by the full House. Similar units act in the Senate, and conference committees attempt to resolve House-Senate differences. Their recommendations return to each house for approval. The president then accepts or rejects each bill. In appropriations decision making, the power of the appropriations committees and subcommittees is substantial.

Congress exercises its appropriations power under few limits in law but under severe restrictions in practice. Initially Congress acts in the context of the executive budget: it is free to accept, amend, or reject the president's proposals. Normally, Congress accepts them or amends them only incrementally. Full consideration of each item is never feasible, and each year's appropriation provides a reliable guide for the next year's. Other limitations on congressional control over appropriations are the presidential veto (rarely used, partially because there is no item veto); the practice of impounding funds (presidents have from time to time refused to spend money appropriated for specific programs); and the series of devices collectively labeled "backdoor spending" (for example, Congress grants long-term contractual authority to executive departments, placing a ceiling only on total expenditures over the life of the program and thus obligating itself to appropriate money annually without further inspection).

[Congressional Quarterly, *Guide to the Congress of the United States;* R. F. Fenno, Jr., *The Power of the Purse;* A. Wildavsky, *The Politics of the Budgetary Process.*]

MORRIS S. OGUL

AQUIDNECK ISLAND, an Indian name for Rhode Island, the largest of the islands in Narragansett Bay. The island's purchase from the Narragansett sachems was witnessed by Roger Williams on March 24, 1638. Portsmouth was founded at the northern end, and in 1639 Newport was established on the southern end.

[S. G. Arnold, *History of Rhode Island.*]

ARTHUR R. BLESSING

ARAB-AMERICAN RELATIONS. Before World War I the United States had no important political connection with the Arab world, which extended from the Persian Gulf to Morocco and was under foreign (Ottoman, British, French, and Italian) domination. However, during the 19th century, American missionaries established enduring religious and educational ties with the Arabs, which generated friendship for the United States and helped spark Arab nationalism. Following the Ottoman Empire's dismemberment after World War I, Egypt, Yemen, and Saudi Arabia achieved independence, and other Arab areas became French and British mandates. Nevertheless, the United States, persisting in its isolationist policy, remained generally uninterested—politically and economically—in the Arab world, even though American oil companies were acquiring a stake in Arab oil fields.

Political interest in the Arabs was awakened by World War II and the resulting change in America's global role. Recognizing the importance of the Arab world's strategic location and vast oil reserves, the United States strengthened its political ties with Arab countries; obtained air bases in Saudi Arabia, Morocco, and Libya; and backed American oil companies' efforts to expand their oil holdings in Arab areas. Yet for several years after the war, the United States avoided deep involvement in Arab affairs—despite the decline in Anglo-French power, Russian threats to Iran and Turkey, the outbreak of the cold war, and mounting domestic political and emotional concern with the Palestine question. While extending major commitments to Turkey and Iran, the United States preferred working through Britain and France to protect its interests in the Arab world. Meanwhile, deepening American association with the European colonial powers and President Harry Truman's strong support for Israel produced the first serious strains between the United States and the Arabs. Nevertheless, because Arab governments were generally anti-Communist and maintained close economic and cultural links with the West and because the United States began to sympathize with Arab nationalism and reform movements in some areas, such as in Gamal Abdel Nasser's Egypt, overall Arab-American relations remained reasonably good.

These relations deteriorated during 1955 and 1956 after Secretary of State John Foster Dulles, deciding to play a more active role in the Middle East, encouraged the pro-Western Iraqi monarchy to help form the Baghdad Pact, despite Arab nationalist opposition; condemned Nasser's espousal of nonalignment; refused to sell Egypt arms; and abruptly withdrew an American offer to assist in financing the High Dam at Aswan, which led to the nationalization of the Suez Canal Company by Egypt. The Soviet Union, switching support from Israel to the Arabs and taking advantage of Dulles' actions, made its first major penetration into the Arab world by providing weapons to Egypt and financing the Aswan High Dam.

American opposition to the British-French-Israeli invasion of Egypt in late 1956 brought about some improvement in Arab-American relations. But during 1957 and 1958 tensions developed between the United States and Egypt, Syria, and Iraq. The primary causes of tension were Nasser's move toward socialism, which initiated an ideological conflict within the Arab world; the increased influence of anti-Western elements in Syria; the overthrow of the Iraqi monarchy; American efforts to strengthen the conservative, pro-Western regimes by providing them with economic and arms aid and promising them military support against any "Communist" threat under the Eisenhower Doctrine; and the landing of U.S. Marines in Lebanon to back the anti-Nasser government during the 1958 civil war.

After Dulles resigned in 1959, American officials, believing that Arab nationalism and nonalignment could be exploited against the Soviet Union, sought a modus vivendi with the progressive Arabs. In 1961 President John F. Kennedy initiated an even more liberal policy toward the Arabs: he recognized the new republican regime in Yemen, provided wheat to Egypt on favorable terms, and took a more neutral position both in the conflict between Israel and the Arabs and in the contention between conservative and Socialist Arab leaders.

After Lyndon B. Johnson became president in late 1963, the progressive Arabs were antagonized because he revived partisan backing for the conservative Arabs and withheld badly needed economic aid to Egypt. American relations with all Arabs—including those friendly to the West—worsened when Johnson gave especially strong support to Israel just before, during, and after the June 1967 war, which led to an Arab defeat and Israeli occupation of Egyptian, Syrian, and Jordanian territories.

Initially the administration of Richard M. Nixon assumed a more balanced position on the Arab-Israeli question, which the Arabs considered the key to improved relations with the United States. Because of their military weakness and the Soviet unwillingness to supply offensive weapons on a large scale, the more moderate leaders, including President Nasser and his successor Anwar Sadat, sought both closer ties with, and the aid of, the United States—despite protests from the Palestinian commandos and other militant Arabs—for they realized that only the United States was able to help them regain their lost territories. But the U.S. failure to promote the return of Arab lands, the resumption of large-scale American arms and economic aid to Israel in 1971, and continued U.S. support of Israel at the United Nations caused Arab-American relations to deteriorate once again. These developments also encouraged Egypt and Syria to resort to war with Israel in October 1973 in a desperate attempt to compel the superpowers to make more determined efforts to break the Arab-Israeli impasse and to implement those UN resolutions that called for both an Israeli withdrawal and respect for the rights of the Palestinians.

The Arabs were so aroused when the Nixon administration airlifted arms to Israel during the October war and decided to grant it up to $2.2 billion in military aid that they initiated an oil embargo against the United States, whose need for Middle Eastern oil had been rapidly growing. However, by early 1974 Secretary of State Henry Kissinger was able to obtain the lifting of the oil embargo and to enhance significantly America's position in much of the Arab world by personally assuming a major role in dealing with Arab-Israeli differences and by convincing President Sadat and some other Arab leaders that he was sincerely trying to be evenhanded. In the first half of 1974, Kissinger succeeded in arranging two disengagement agreements which enabled Egypt and Syria to regain for the first time some of their occupied lands and raised Arab hopes and expectations. However, on Mar. 25, 1975, one of the staunchest and most influential friends of the United States in the Middle East, King Faisal of Saudi Arabia, was assassinated. Arab distrust became intensified and Arab-American relations entered a period of uncertainty and strain as a result of the failure of Kissinger's step-by-step diplomacy to bring about further Israeli withdrawals from Arab territories and to provide in any way for the nationalist aspirations of the Palestinians. To most Arabs, good relations on a lasting basis depended primarily on how resolutely the American government would strive to maintain a more evenhanded posture and to induce Israel to accept a peace settlement based on past UN resolutions.

[John S. Badeau, *The American Approach to the Arab World;* John C. Campbell, *Defense of the Middle East;* Charles Cremeans, *The Arabs and the World;* Robert Daniel, *American Philanthropy in the Near East, 1820–1960;* John De Novo, *American Interests and Policies in the Middle East, 1900–1939;* Parker T. Hart, ed., "America and the Middle East," *The Annals* (May 1972); George Lenczowski, ed., *United States Interest in the Middle East;* William Polk, *The United States and the Arab World;* William Quandt, *United States Policy in the Middle East: Constraints and Choices.*]

FRED J. KHOURI

ARABIAN GOLD, gold coins—mostly *pagodas,* from the India pagodas on their reverse side, or gold *mohurs* of India or Persia—captured by colonial pirates from Arabian or Indian ships in the Arabian Sea after 1685. New York merchants got much more by trading with the Madagascar pirates; and these "Arabian" gold coins were common in New York, Philadelphia, and Rhode Island in 1690. Pirate Avery in 1698 brought his huge "Arabian" loot to the West Indies, whence the colonies got their supply of specie.

[Charles J. Bullock, *The Monetary History of the United States;* George Francis Dow and John Henry Edmonds, *The Pirates of the New England Coast.*]

GEORGE WYCHERLEY

***ARABIC* CASE.** On Aug. 19, 1915, a German submarine torpedoed without warning the British White Star passenger liner *Arabic,* with the loss of two U.S. citizens. This attack occurred soon after the exchange of notes that followed the similar torpedoing of the *Lusitania,* in which the United States had insisted that the lives of noncombatants could not lawfully be put in jeopardy by the capture or destruction of unresisting merchantmen. The German act indicated that it was still uncertain whether Germany had accepted the American position. After seeking to justify the attack on the ground that the *Arabic* was attempting to ram the submarine, the German government disavowed the act and offered indemnity. Claims of U.S. citizens arising out of this and similar cases were eventually adjudicated by a mixed claims commission, United States and Germany, following the war between the two nations.

[Alexander DeConde, *A History of American Foreign Policy.*]

SAMUEL FLAGG BEMIS

ARANDA MEMORIAL, statements of regret that Spain and France entered the Revolution in behalf of the American colonies, said to have been presented by Pedro Pablo Abarca y Bolea, Count of Aranda, to Charles III of Spain in 1783 or 1784. The memorial contains a striking prediction that the new "federated republic" would become an "irresistible colossus" endangering Spain's possessions. Hence the author suggested that new kingdoms, bound to Spain by marriage and commercial ties, be created from the Spanish colonies. Aranda's authorship of the memorial has been questioned by some historians.

[Arthur P. Whitaker, "The Pseudo-Aranda Memoir of 1783," *The Hispanic American Historical Review* (1937); Almon R. Wright, "The Aranda Memorial, Genuine or Forged," *ibid.* (1938).]

ALMON R. WRIGHT

ARANJUEZ, CONVENTION OF (April 12, 1779), provided for the entrance of Spain, as an ally of France, into the revolutionary war, in case Great Britain should reject (which it did) Spain's impossibly intrusive offer of mediation. Spain and France made a pact to fight the war jointly, and not to negotiate peace separately, and in any peace Gibraltar was to go to Spain. Other desirable acquisitions were stipulated for both allies out of anticipated conquests from Great Britain.

[Samuel Flagg Bemis, *Diplomacy of the American Revolution.*]

SAMUEL FLAGG BEMIS

ARAPAHO. One of the more important of the bison-hunting Plains tribes, the Arapaho spoke an Algonkin language. They were closely connected with another Algonkin people, the Atsina, and appear to have been resident in the Red River Valley in early historic times. With the Atsina and followed by the Cheyenne, the Arapaho pushed into the Dakotas and northeastern Wyoming. There they adapted exclusively to bison hunting and assimilated the Plains war pattern, carrying on intermittent warfare with the Ute, Shoshone, and Pawnee, having also fought various of the Dakota and Comanche. A general peace was maintained with the Cheyenne. The tribe was generally dispersed following treaty and reservation allocation.

Like other Indians of the Plains, the Arapaho made capital of the horse, the tipi, and the general material inventory of the nomadic Plains. Theirs was a tightly knit societal organization, paralleling that of the Cheyenne. Five main subdivisions of the tribe were recognized, virtually autonomous tribelets, which met for the bison hunt and organized raiding parties. The Arapaho lost contact with their close relatives, the Atsina, when the latter, separated by the incursions of the Crow, became associated with the Assiniboine. The tribe offers a classic example of the interaction and movement of peoples in the Plains area.

[Alfred L. Kroeber, *The Arapaho.*]

ROBERT F. SPENCER

***ARBELLA*,** the flagship of the "Winthrop Fleet" on which, between April 8 and June 12, 1630, Gov.

John Winthrop, other members of the Massachusetts Bay Company, and Puritan emigrants transported themselves and the charter of the company from England to Salem, thereby giving legal birth to the commonwealth of Massachusetts. (*See also* Great Migration.)

[C. M. Andrews, *The Colonial Period of American History;* James K. Hosmer, ed., *Winthrop's Journal, History of New England: 1630–1649.*]

RAYMOND P. STEARNS

ARBITRATION. In early literature the term "arbitration" was often used as a synonym for "conciliation" or "mediation" and to designate other forms of dispute-settling. In modern times, it has come to mean a judicial, if somewhat informal, process: the disputants agree to forgo other methods of resolving an issue—for example, by strikes in labor conflicts or by courtroom litigation in business controversies—in favor of the decision of an impartial person or board, whose judgment they have agreed in advance to accept as final and binding.

With very few exceptions (custody of children, for example, in which matter the state is presumed to have a predominant interest) any dispute may be arbitrated if the parties are willing. In general, however, arbitration practice in the United States falls into one of two categories: labor and commercial.

Labor arbitration is concerned principally with employee grievances—disputes over whether an employee was discharged for just cause, over whether a senior employee had sufficient ability to claim the job of a junior during a period of slack work, over whether certain employees were given their contractual share of overtime work, and the like. Such cases are said to involve arbitration of "rights," because they involve the interpretation and application of collective bargaining agreements. In labor arbitration there is also a small, but growing, practice of "interest" arbitration—impartial determination of new contract terms after union and management negotiators have reached an impasse. Such interest arbitration occurs most frequently in controversies involving public employment or privately owned transportation and power companies, when interruption of service is thought to be intolerable.

Commercial arbitration takes many forms: it ranges from the small claims procedures in an increasing number of cities, in which cases involving small amounts of money are systematically sent for a decision to an attorney who presides over an informal hearing, to international trade arbitration cases, which may involve many millions of dollars. The latter are usually conducted by three-man panels, and proceedings approach the formality that is characteristic of courts of law. The largest single group of commercial arbitration cases in the United States grows out of automobile accidents. In most states the law requires automobile insurance companies to offer policyholders coverage against personal injury inflicted by uninsured motorists, and in some states insured motorists have no option but to buy this coverage. These "uninsured-motorist endorsements" usually provide for arbitration of a dispute between the motorist and his own insurance company over the amount of damages inflicted by the uninsured driver or the degree of fault on the part of the insured person. It is possible, though, that with the rapid development of no-fault automobile insurance, arbitration of disputes over reimbursement for personal injury caused by uninsured motorists will cease to be an important feature of arbitration practice in the United States.

Whether in labor or in commercial matters, the agreement of the parties is the source of the arbitrator's authority; his award, therefore, must be rendered within the boundaries set by the parties. Law and the rules of the American Arbitration Association require that the arbitrator dispose of every claim and counterclaim to the best of his understanding. When he does so, the successful party may seek to have the award enforced by court order. But if the arbitrator has rendered an imperfect award—either by failure to decide all issues or by exceeding his authority—the courts may direct a new arbitration, send the case back to the same or another arbitrator, or under some circumstances modify the decision. Thus, although the arbitrator's award is final and not subject to review on the merits, the parties and their attorneys can appeal to the courts on the ground that the arbitrator has committed a procedural error that seriously prejudices their rights.

Although labor arbitration and commercial arbitration (including the accident-claims variant of commercial arbitration) have many features in common, there are differences between them in tradition and in the very reasons for the existence of each.

Labor-grievance arbitration is a creature of the collective-bargaining era. Its history in the United States dates back at least 100 years, for even in the middle of the 19th century there were some unions and some impartial determination of disputes. But the modern era of collective bargaining began in 1933 with the passage by Congress of section 7a of the National Industrial Recovery Act and, two years later, of the National Labor Relations Act. By means of these and subsequent laws collective bargaining became not merely a permissible activity but rather a practice that was advocated as national policy.

It was from 1942 to 1945, during American participation in World War II, that grievance arbitration received its strongest impetus. As during World War I, there was a no-strike pledge by labor. Disputes were brought to the National War Labor Board and to its regional boards throughout the country, all established on a tripartite basis (that is, each included representatives of labor, management, and the public). When efforts at mediation failed, the boards issued decisions that, under wartime government policy, labor and management regarded as binding. The National War Labor Board rendered more than 25,000 decisions in dispute cases, and decisions by third parties were, in a sense, the order of the day. Moreover, in hundreds of the cases that came before it, the board directed or strongly recommended the inclusion of a grievance procedure, culminating in arbitration, in the parties' agreements. Before the war was over, thousands of companies and unions had acquired their first experience of arbitration; they had discovered that it was possible to accommodate themselves to decisions by outsiders and that such decisions, even when adverse, were usually less harmful than work stoppages. Another direct consequence of the National War Labor Board's activities was the recruiting and training of arbitrators. By the war's end there were several hundred men, both in and outside government, with practical experience in resolving labor-management controversies. They had not only a personal interest in encouraging continued demand for their skills but also a professional desire to advance principles in which they believed.

Substantially more than 90 percent of all collective bargaining contracts in the United States arrived at since the 1960's (the number is estimated at upward of 100,000) contain arbitration clauses. No exact figure is available showing the number of times these clauses are invoked, but the figure is probably more than 50,000 a year; the American Arbitration Association alone administers about 10,000 cases a year, including arbitration cases in public employment.

Commercial arbitration is a much older practice than labor arbitration, evidence of its use being found in antiquity. A more direct origin of modern business arbitration is found in the informal courts through which merchants in preindustrial England resolved disputes over quality of merchandise, and the tradition was naturally carried over into colonial America. One of the earliest of such tribunals in the New World was that of the New York Chamber of Commerce, one of the organizations that had much to do with the founding of the American Arbitration Association in 1926.

The early attitude of the courts and the legal profession to commercial arbitration was one of hostility, and according to prevailing law an agreement to arbitrate was revocable at will. This circumstance naturally had a deterring effect. The common law doctrine of revocability was first challenged in New York in 1920, when a group of businessmen, led by the New York Chamber of Commerce, persuaded the state legislature to enact what became the first modern arbitration law in the United States. A future-dispute arbitration clause was given equal status with other contractual provisions as far as enforcement through the courts was concerned. Other states soon followed the new pattern, as did the federal government with the enactment of an arbitration law governing maritime transactions and business disputes arising out of interstate commerce. In 1955 the National Conference of the Commissioners on Uniform State Laws and the House of Delegates of the American Bar Association approved a uniform arbitration act that has since been adopted by several states. The thirty-three modern arbitration laws now in effect in the United States differ in some respects, but they are alike in that they permit enforcement of agreements to arbitrate future disputes, as well as enforcement of the awards themselves. The laws also establish expeditious procedures for such enforcement so that the presumed intention of the parties to bring their controversies to quick determination may be given effect. By the same token modern arbitration laws establish minimum standards of fair procedure and permit judges to vacate awards when a determination is made that rights of parties have been violated in any substantial way.

The modern attitude of the judiciary to arbitration has had the anticipated effect. Most arbitration in the United States is now statutory arbitration, occurring in states having laws that facilitate the enforcement of the results. Many trade associations and commodity exchanges have established their own procedures for resolving disputes among members or between members and nonmember firms. Arbitrations outside these organized bodies are mostly conducted under the rules of the American Arbitration Association. The association also conducts a publication and educational program, to advance knowledge of the uses of arbitration to dispose of disputes of all kinds.

Overwhelmingly the practice of voluntary arbitration in the United States now results from arbitration clauses in contracts that provide for this method of resolving disputes. A typical arbitration clause reads: "Any controversy or claim arising out of or relating to this contract, or the breach thereof, shall be settled by arbitration in accordance with the Rules of the American Arbitration Association, and judgment upon the award rendered by the Arbitrator(s) may be entered in any court having jurisdiction thereof." To a lesser extent, arbitration is also conducted under the agreements of disputing parties who either have no contractual relationship with one another or have failed to incorporate a future-disputes clause in their contract.

[Merton C. Bernstein, *Private Dispute Settlement;* Martin Domke, *The Law and Practice of Commercial Arbitration;* Steven Lazarus et al., *Resolving Business Disputes: The Potential of Commercial Arbitration;* Paul Prasow and Edward Peters, *Arbitration and Collective Bargaining: Conflict Resolution in Labor Relations;* Morris Stone, *Managerial Freedom and Job Security.*]

MORRIS STONE

ARBOR DAY. On the motion of the agriculturist J. Sterling Morton, the Nebraska State Board of Agriculture designated the tenth day of April, 1872, as a day to plant trees, naming it Arbor Day. In 1875 the state legislature changed the day to April 22, the birthday of Morton, and made it a legal holiday. It is now observed in every state except Alaska, usually on the last Friday in April. Arbor Day is also a legal holiday in Utah and Florida, the latter observing it in January.

[Addison E. Sheldon, *Nebraska Old and New.*]

EVERETT DICK

ARBUTHNOT AND AMBRISTER, CASE OF, an incident of Gen. Andrew Jackson's raid into East Florida in 1818. Believing himself tacitly authorized to seize the Floridas in view of Spain's delay in diplomacy, Jackson attacked the Seminole in Spanish territory. At St. Mark's, Fla., he captured Alexander Arbuthnot, a Scottish trader who had warned the Indians to escape. At the village of Chief Bowlegs on the Suwanee River Jackson captured Robert Ambrister, an English trader who had plotted an Indian uprising. After courts-martial, Ambrister was shot and Arbuthnot hanged, both at St. Mark's on April 29, 1818. The British government took no action, but Spain protested the invasion. Secretary of State John Quincy Adams vigorously defended Jackson in his published dispatches to the U.S. minister at Madrid, and thus helped to force Spanish signature of the Adams-Onís Treaty of Feb. 22, 1819, which included the cession of East Florida.

[John S. Bassett, *Life of Andrew Jackson.*]

PHILIP COOLIDGE BROOKS

ARCHAEOLOGY AND PREHISTORY, NORTH AMERICAN. Man is not indigenous to the New World. His biologic and cultural evolution began in the Old World and spanned millions of years before he first entered the Western Hemisphere during a phase of geographic expansion that also included the first settlement of Australia. Some of the most perplexing problems that archaeologists have worked to resolve concern the origins and nature of the earliest inhabitants of the New World. Other problems that still puzzle archaeologists concern the major adaptations that the descendants of these first Americans subsequently made to their changing natural and social environments.

Although archaeologists do not yet agree among themselves on the answers to individual questions, they do in general agree that certain major trends not unlike those that occurred in the Old World are apparent throughout the prehistoric period. These trends are those of population growth, regional differentiation, gradual elaboration of culture, increasing societal complexity, and greater energy control and consumption. Different classification frameworks based on these trends have been used as aids in answering various questions, but nearly all archaeologists recognize the presence of three major stages or fundamental lifeways among North America's prehistoric cultures. These stages, which are not time-dependent or limited to any one ecosystem, are called the Lithic, the Archaic, and the Formative.

The Lithic was characterized by small bands of hunters and gatherers with game-focused subsistence patterns. The hunters in part exploited now-extinct fauna in Pleistocene environments 10,000 years ago and earlier. In general, Lithic peoples roamed large hunting territories and left widely scattered camps containing only small numbers of artifacts. The comparatively simple tool kits of these early Americans were composed primarily of chipped stone artifacts, a cultural practice that led to the use of the stage designation Lithic. For convenience this stage can be divided into three hypothetical time periods: early (more than 28,000 years ago), middle (from 28,000 to 11,800 years ago), and late (from 11,800 to about 10,000 years ago).

The existence of widespread early Lithic cultures characterized by the absence of projectile points and by rough, percussion-flaked stone choppers, scrapers, and knives has been both vigorously proposed and denied. These latter tools have been equated on typological grounds with the Eurasian Lower and Middle Paleolithic, but the absence of secure radiocarbon dates has continued to cast doubt on their existence at an equally early phase in the New World Ice Age. In the mid-1970's not a single site was generally agreed upon by prehistorians as dating from this time period, although several are intriguing possibilities. For example, the Lewisville site in northeast Texas has two of the oldest radiocarbon dates purportedly associated with artifacts in North America. These dates of more than 37,000 and 38,000 years ago were obtained from possible fire hearths containing a crude pebble-chopper, a hammerstone, and a flake scraper. Remains of now-extinct animals, including glyptodon, horse, camel, and mammoth, were in the surrounding soil matrix. However, it has been argued that rodents dragged the artifacts down into lower stratigraphic layers containing naturally burned vegetation in more recent times. Unfortunately, the site is now under water. Among other widely discussed sites that may indicate the presence of an early Lithic substratum from which subsequent cultures in the Americas developed are Friesenhahn Cave, Tex.; Calico Hills, Santa Rosa Island, and San Miguel Island, Calif.; American Falls, Idaho; and Taber, Alberta, Canada. Many other assemblages of crude, heavy pebble tools from California, northeastern Arizona, and eastern North America are now considered quarry materials and implements associated with more recent cultures.

In contrast to the diminishing evidence for the presence of early Lithic man, the middle Lithic witnessed an upsurge in both number of sites and dating control during the 1960's and 1970's. Although most new sites are in Middle and South America, similar sites have been found in North America. For example, at Old Crow Flats, an intermontane basin in the northern Yukon, a toothed skin flesher made on a caribou tibia, mammoth and horse bone artifacts, a few possible stone artifacts, and hundreds of allegedly artificially broken bones were found among several tons of vertebrate fossils. Apatite dates on two mammoth bone artifacts and the tibia suggest a date of 25,000 to 30,000 years ago. Among other North American sites indicating the presence of middle Lithic cultures are Wilson Butte Cave (14,500 years ago), Idaho; the Dutchess Quarry Cave (14,500 years ago), N.Y.; and Fort Rock Cave (13,000 years ago), Oreg. Leaf-shaped stone projectile points may have been used by some of these Lithic peoples. A series of human skulls also has been dated to this period, including the Laguna Beach (17,000 years ago) and Los Angeles man (about 23,000 years ago) skulls in California.

The late Lithic was a time of big-game hunting throughout the High Plains and in the Southwest. The Clovis culture, characterized by the use of fluted lanceolate projectile points and the exploitation of mammoth, was the earliest and most widespread of the late Lithic cultures, dating about 11,250 years ago. In the Plains this vigorous culture was succeeded by the bison-hunting Itama culture, which persisted in some areas for about 3,000 years. Regional variants of Clovis fluted points are also widespread in forested eastern North America and on the West Coast. They are apparently associated with these areas' earliest cultures about the time of the mid-continent Clovis culture. By the late Lithic there is abundant evidence of man's presence in many areas of the New World.

From this often inconclusive and fragmentary evidence nearly all archaeologists agree that man's major early movement into the Americas was across a dry land bridge that periodically stretched between Siberia and Alaska, and that the primary penetration southward was probably through an intermittently open corridor between the western Cordilloid and the eastern Laurentian ice masses. Because the land bridge and corridor were both open for varying lengths of time in each of the three periods of the Lithic, each has been declared the initial period of man's occupation of the New World. Some archaeologists view the Southeast Asian chopper-chopping tool tradition as a likely source for the proposed, but still elusive, early Lithic chopper-scraper cultures. Others point to the middle Lithic and favor the advanced hunting Mousteroid cultures that were spreading eastward across the northern Eurasian plains in the late Pleistocene as a source for the first Americans. Still other archaeologists have argued that Old World Upper Paleolithic peoples were the New World's first residents during the late Lithic. Although there is no conclusive proof for these or other hypotheses, accumulating evidence indicates that man was in the Americas as a generalized Mongoloid physical type by at least 20,000 or 25,000 years ago.

In contrast to the game-focused economy of the Lithic, the Archaic emphasized the exploitation of a broad spectrum of seasonally available resources. A variety of specialized tool kits evolved in North America's major biomes to procure these resources efficiently; as a result distinguishable regional traditions eventually emerged throughout the continent. Although the biomes offered widely varying potential for cultural and social development, a number of stage trends can be identified. These include population growth, more efficient and varied resource procurement and preparation procedures, reduction in size of hunting and food-gathering territories, increased burial ceremonialism, and elaboration of trade and communication networks. Besides displaying a greater degree of material wealth, Archaic settlements were usually larger and more stable than their Lithic counterparts. Exceptions to these trends occurred mainly in regions with severe natural limitations.

There were several widespread Archaic traditions in North America, all of which continued in some areas up to the historic period. In the East the progressive adaptations to forest, riverine, and coastal conditions begun at the end of the Pleistocene culminated in the appearance of an array of developed broad-spectrum hunter-gatherer lifeways some 5,000 years ago. This Eastern Archaic was characterized by extensive assemblages of polished and chipped stone artifacts and a semisedentary, or even sedentary, existence in some localities. Although most sites remained relatively small and scattered, huge and complex settlements such as Poverty Point, La., were also constructed. West of the Rockies the Western Archaic, or Desert, culture was essentially an adaptation to arid land with sparse vegetation, although semisedentary societies based on fishing and acorn-gathering emerged along the Pacific coast. In the Desert West lifeways were geared to seed-collecting and seed-grinding subsistence patterns; typical artifacts were baskets and milling stones. Still other traditions developed on the Plains and in the northern Boreal forest.

Chronologically, most Archaic traditions had their beginnings at the end of the Pleistocene with the shift to modern environments. An example is the Eastern Archaic, where a transition from the late Lithic between 10,000 and 7,000 years ago is documented in southern sites, such as the Stanfield-Worley Bluff Shelter in Alabama and the Hardaway site in North Carolina. In other areas, the two lifeways apparently overlapped considerably. The Lithic persisted for an additional 4,000 to 5,000 years on the Plains and an early Archaic lifeway may have coexisted with both middle and late Lithic cultures in the West. These diverse temporal roots for the Archaic raise questions concerning the origins of the lifeway. In the mid-1970's these roots were considered to be the early chopper-scraper substratum, big-game hunters, or new arrivals from an Asian circumpolar complex. Probably all three explanations are correct, depending on the particular geographic areas involved.

The Formative lifeway was molded by the potentials and demands of intensive plant cultivation. Unlike the Lithic and the Archaic, the Formative was not a continentwide stage, for the adoption of this lifeway was limited by climatic and, in some areas, cultural factors. Even though this stage was geographically limited, its attainment was one of man's great achievements, for cultigen yields can be readily increased to a degree unattainable with natural plant and animal populations. In turn these yields offered the potential in suitable localities for the appearance of settled village-farming complexes, for great population increases, and, eventually, for the emergence of civilizations and the Classic stage.

In North America this lifeway was confined to regions of the Eastern Woodlands with summer growing seasons of more than 120 frostfree days, to the eastern Plains periphery, and to the Southwest. The date for the initial appearance of the Formative in these regions remains uncertain for several reasons. First, the transition from the Archaic to the Formative was not rapid, but spanned thousands of years. Traits that later became diagnostic of the Formative—in particular, pottery, cultigens, earthworks, and large stable settlements—made their first appearance during this transition. Second, there was considerable overlap in the cultural and demographic potential of advanced Archaic peoples possessing these traits and those with an early Formative agricultural lifeway. These overlaps are documented in material wealth, organizational complexity, occupational division of labor, and the ability to maintain complex exchange networks and densely inhabited settlements. And finally, the presence of pottery, earthworks, sedentism, and some cultigens, either individually or in combination, was taken at one time as an indication of the existence of the village-farming complex. This assumption, along with the absence of essential evidence, has tended to impede the separation of advanced Archaic and early Formative economic systems. Although the relationship between these two lifeways remains complicated and unclear, a reconstruction of past events is emerging that forecasts a resolution of these problems.

The incipient domestication of native North American plants began as early as 3,000 years ago in the Mississippi Valley and other midcontinent riverine areas. This innovation was either an indigenous development or the result of stimulus from Middle America, where Desert Archaic people had begun cultivating corn 6,000 years earlier. The eastern North American cultigens, which include sunflower, goosefoot, sumpweed, and pumpkin (*Cucurbita pepo*), were soon supplemented by Middle American domesticates that had already reached the Southwest between 3000 and 2000 B.C. Primitive corncobs appear in the Southwest at Bat Cave, N.Mex., in a Desert culture context by this early period. Squash and gourd may have been present as early, for both were apparently introduced into the East from the Southwest by about 1000 B.C. Squash has been tentatively identified from a Poverty Point site dating about then, and both are associated at Salts Cave, Ky., by 700 B.C. Although corn may have spread eastward with these domesticates, the earliest evidence of its actual presence is from a site in Kentucky dating to the third century B.C.

The earliest pottery vessels north of Mexico are fiber-tempered, soft-paste wares found in southeastern sites, where they have been dated as early as 2500 B.C. at Stallings Island, Ga. These vessels have counterparts in Middle America that date at least 500 years earlier. A second eastern ceramic tradition became well established in more northerly states between 1000 and 500 B.C. The origins of this Woodland tradition remain undemonstrated, although suggestions run the gamut from indigenous developments to derivation from the southeastern tradition, an Asiatic circumpolar complex, or a European source via a northern transatlantic route. The source of the earliest pottery vessels in the Southwest that appear by 300 B.C. is generally believed to be Middle America, although the impetus seems to have been stimulus diffusion rather than the direct introduction of southern vessel types.

A cultural florescence was experienced by the Adena and Hopewell cultures in the Eastern Woodlands between about 600 B.C. and A.D. 250. This florescence was apparently based on an advanced Archaic subsistence system in which increasingly efficient hunting and gathering techniques, including the harvesting of wild food resources, was practiced. The Adena and Hopewell Woodland people made pottery, planted some domesticates, constructed impressive mounds and earthworks, maintained complex exchange networks for the procurement of exotic raw resources, and probably had ranked societies and craft specialists. Cultigens were apparently not yet a staple or major determinant in their economic systems. Evidence for increased sedentism, population growth, and cultural creativity is found in other areas of native America in which the cultivation of food plants was not practiced at all. For example, settled villages and dense populations developed on the Northwest Coast and in the interior and coastal valleys of California following the development of subsistence systems focused on the harvesting of acorns and the exploitation of marine animals.

The threshold of a lifeway sustained primarily by cultivated plant foods apparently was not crossed in the East and Southwest until the second half of the first millennium A.D. When it did occur, this development was relatively rapid and probably in part the result of the sizable managerial problems generated by the substantial growth in size of advanced Archaic population aggregates. Complex interactions of other relevant factors were also important, including the availability of improved varieties of corn, new farming techniques, and continued stimulus from Middle America, where the Formative village-farming complex was already in existence by 2000 B.C. The complex and unclear relationships between village farming in Middle America and in North America are further obscured shortly after A.D. 500 by influences from the Middle American town-and-temple complex, which dates back to about 800 B.C. in Mexico. In general, Formative settlements can be distinguished from earlier Archaic settlements by their greater size, complexity, and permanence, by expanded food storage capacities, and by new, more complex patterns of social organization capable of handling large population aggregates. Other Formative tendencies include the construction of substantial houses, craft specialization and increased division of labor, major technological improvements in the crafts, elaboration of agricultural techniques, simplification of tool kits associated with hunting, and population growth.

Formative developments can be traced in the three major cultural traditions of the Southwest—the Anasazi, the Mogollon, and the Hohokam. Towns reached their apogee of construction in the Anasazi Pueblo III and IV periods and in the Classic Hohokam phases. Although strong and direct influence from Mexico is clearly evident in the presence of exotic artifacts, stepped pyramids, and ball courts, the Middle American institutions of the priest-ruler and the centralized political bureaucracy were apparently never adopted. The town-and-temple, mound-and-plaza complex developed in the bottom lands of the major rivers of the lower Mississippi Drainage system sometime between A.D. 500 and 800; the complex climaxed with the appearance of Mississippian cultures shortly afterward. The spectacular site of Cahokia in East Saint Louis, Ill., was the largest of the Mississippian settlements, covering six square miles. Cahokia was the main center of a chiefdom or even an urban-state society. Both Woodland- and Mississippian-influenced village-farming communities had become widespread throughout the East to the Plains periphery by A.D. 1000–1200. Thus, the thresholds of the village-farming and the town-and-temple complexes seem to have been crossed almost synchronously in both the East and the Southwest by A.D. 800 or shortly thereafter. By about A.D. 1300, the cultural climaxes in the East and Southwest had waned under the impact of changing climatic and social conditions, although a village-farming lifeway continued to dominate both areas to the historic period.

The trends in North America's prehistoric cultural development were not markedly different in broad outline from those in Europe. Although man entered the New World at a much more recent date, the game-focused hunters and gatherers of the two areas went through a comparable transition from the use of crude, percussion-flaked stone tools to the manufacture of specialized hunting tools used in the exploitation of big game and—where possible—herd animals. In both areas a broad-spectrum hunting and gathering lifeway developed at the end of the Pleistocene in response to the decimation of megafauna and the appearance of new environments. The subsequent importance of southern nuclear areas as sources of pottery, cultigens, religious symbolism, and many other cultural elements also has fundamental parallels. There were significant differences. The large-scale movements of people that characterized later European prehistory seem absent. Metallurgy, writing, and wheeled transport were also missing. More important, perhaps, the lack of a significant domesticated animal in North America lessened the immediate impact of cultigens by sustaining the importance of social institutions revolving around the hunt. Major secondary trends that distinguish prehistoric North America from ancient Europe include the large-scale reinterpretation of borrowed innovations, the absence of an early and dramatic change in social organization following the introduction of domesticates, the continued importance of hunting among Formative lifeways, and gradual indigenous development.

[Jesse D. Jennings, *Prehistory of North America;* Gordon R. Willey, *An Introduction to American Archaeology,* vol. I.]

GUY GIBBON

ARCHANGEL, U.S. TROOPS AT. On Mar. 16, 1918, revolution-shattered Russia was compelled by Germany to ratify the Treaty of Brest-Litovsk. The Allies were concerned because the treaty gave the German army entry into Finland, thus positioning it for marches upon the Russian ports of Murmansk and Archangel, where military supplies had been stockpiled from Allied ships. There was also fear that U-boat bases might be established on the North Cape. The unstable new government of Bolsheviks in Moscow was appalled by the rapacity of the German treaty and welcomed Allied troop landings at Murmansk in March 1918 as support against further demands by Berlin. The Allies proposed to form a shield in desolate northern Russia behind which the Russians could build a new, Red army. On this premise British officers led a push nearly 400 miles southward and firmly secured the railroad approach to Murmansk.

By Aug. 3, 1918, the Allied posture had become anti-Bolshevik, and Archangel was seized by 1,500 British and French troops. Three officers and forty-one seamen from the U.S. cruiser *Olympia* participated as Bolshevik authority over this most ancient of Russian ports was dissolved. The United States went from a token to a major role on Sept. 5, when Americans began debarking—4,477 strong—mainly in three battalions of the 339th Infantry Regiment of Lt. Col. George E. Stewart, which were reinforced a few weeks later by two additional companies. Although constituting 40 percent of the Allied troops under the command of British Maj. Gen. Frederick C. Poole, Americans had little say in planning operations.

The original American mission as envisioned by President Woodrow Wilson was "to guard military stores which [might] subsequently be needed by Russian forces and to render such aid as [might] be acceptable to the Russians in the organization of their own self-defense." By September 1918, however, civil war was raging in Russia, and Britain and France favored the Whites. Wilson's urge toward strict neutrality was compromised by the presence in turbulent Russia of a Czechoslovak legion that favored the Allies and was reportedly eager to get to the fighting in France (*see* Siberian Expedition). Poole was ordered to make a shorter exit for the legion than by way of Vladivostok, and thus, U.S. soldiers left Archangel in an Allied effort to reach a Trans-Siberian Railroad link at Vyatka, 600 miles to the southeast.

In the summer the Bolshevik army had been too feeble to prevent the Allied seizure of Archangel, but by autumn Mikhail S. Kedrov had two understrength rifle divisions around which was swiftly formed the Sixth Army. Poole's advance in columns via the Archangel railroad and the Dvina River penetrated a province larger than Texas, and a continuous front was impossible for the 10,000 or so Allied troops, since the Reds had ample spaces for flanking maneuvers. The advance was stalled about halfway to the objective of Vyatka in mid-October, when British Brig. William E. Ironside assumed command and realistically went to the defensive before the winter frost and snow. The U.S. 339th by then was responsible for a front of nearly 450 miles. The principal combats, trifles compared to the colossal battles in the main theaters of World War I, were at Tulgas and Kodish. (Trotsky was falsely rumored to have been present.)

The general armistice on the western front on Nov. 11, 1918, removed the anti-German rationale for the campaign. Continuation would be clearly an intervention in the Russian domestic struggle. Wilson was absorbed in his plans for Versailles; the American public had little enthusiasm for a new commitment to restore order in Russia; and so, the 339th held place through a more or less peaceful winter and spring, and, with the French, began sailing for home on June 2, 1919. (The British withdrew on Sept. 28th.) This ambiguous venture cost the United States 144 men killed in action and about 100 more dead from illness or accident. Soviet history still refers to the venture as a defeat of American "imperialism."

[E. M. Halliday, *The Ignorant Armies;* William Edmund Ironside, *Archangel, 1918–1919;* L. I. Strakhovsky, *Intervention at Archangel.*]

R. W. DALY

ARCHITECTURE in America changed from varied provincial patterns amid the New World wilderness in the 16th, 17th and 18th centuries, to its first unified expression—the Federal style—about 1800. Beginning in the late 19th century, American architects achieved a leading creative role in international architecture.

American Indian Contacts. Although it is known that European settlers in the New World used Indian buildings and building techniques, there are only a few remnants of 16th-century Spanish-Indian pueblos in the Southwest. At both Saint Augustine, Fla. (1565), and Saint Mary's City, Md. (1634), for instance, the first settlers bought an Indian village and moved in, but nothing remains aboveground or is documented of these early buildings on either site. (*See also* Architecture, American Indian.)

Spanish Colonial Styles. Although the North European explorers and fishermen who probably preceded the dated explorations of the New World may have constructed buildings, the first major European buildings of which there is evidence were those of the Spanish in the Southwest, in Florida, and on the Texas Gulf coast. From the 1540's in the Southwest the Spaniards, employing Indian labor, built religious, civil, and military buildings in which Indian adobe (mud layer, mud brick, and mudstone) techniques were combined with baroque decorative forms that the Spanish brought from Spain and Mexico. The lack of trained master builders among the 16th-century Spanish settlers sent north from Mexico is suggested by the absence of the arch, the vault, and the dome in their buildings. The uneven rectangular character of these earliest European buildings in what is now the United States is seen in the pueblo at San Geronimo de Taos, N.Mex., of which portions may date from the mid-16th century: the governor's palace (1610–14) at Santa Fe, N.Mex.; and the church and *convento* of San Estevan (ca. 1629–42) at Acoma, N.Mex., built on a mesa 357 feet above the desert, for which all the materials were carried up to the site, including the soil for the burial ground and for the padre's garden in the patio.

Forts and mission churches were built mainly of wood at Saint Augustine and elsewhere in Florida and along the Gulf coast from the 1560's onward, but the greatest work of Spanish Florida was the stone fort at Saint Augustine, the Castillo de San Marcos, begun in 1672 and completed in 1756. As in the Spanish fortifications at San Juan, Puerto Rico, the basic form is derived from the international Renaissance fortification style, with the slight touches of ornament drawn both from Spanish baroque and 18th-century international classicism.

The last major phase of Spanish colonial architecture in the area of the United States was that of the mission settlements in Texas (18th century) and Arizona and California (late 18th and early 19th centuries). Within a few miles of one another, in or near San Antonio, Tex., five major mission churches were built between 1718 and 1757, incorporating the arch, the vault, and the dome, as well as rich Spanish baroque stone carving. Finest of these is San José y San Miguel de Aguayo (built 1720–31), with churrigueresque details carved by the Mexican sculptor Pedro Huizar.

The one surviving Arizona mission is the remarkable San Xavier del Bac, near Tucson (built 1784–97), its six-domed interior and heavy provincial baroque details a distant reflection of the brilliant Italian Counter-Reformation style.

Many missions and a number of ranch houses remain in the coastal California area, which was settled beginning in 1769. The ranch houses (although most extant ones were built in the postcolonial era, after the Mexican Revolution of 1821) constitute the only substantial group of domestic architectural remains derived from Spanish styles; these low-profile adobe, stone, and tile buildings, with their balconies, porches, and patios, are well known as a symbol of a Mediterranean life pattern adapted to the American situation.

In addition to governors' houses of simple construction in Santa Fe and San Antonio, examples of Spanish colonial styles are the extraordinary pair of administrative buildings on either side of the cathedral in New Orleans, La., the Cabildo and the Presbytere, built in 1795 during the period of Spanish rule of the Louisiana Territory and utilizing an interesting provincial version of Palladian classical themes in designs probably stemming from Mexico.

French Colonial Styles. Of the network of forts, trading posts, and towns established by the French across the Great Lakes and down the Mississippi River in the late 17th and early 18th centuries, New Orleans became the greatest center and retains the strongest French traditions, although the great fires of the late 18th century destroyed most of the specifically French-style buildings. Other French colonial buildings in what is now the United States have also almost totally disappeared.

In the Quebec-centered years around 1700, Duluth, Minn.; Detroit, Mich.; Saint Louis, Mo.; Kaskaskia, Ill.; and Arkansas Post, Ark., may each have had a Quebec-style church; but none such remains. Many churches and dwelling houses in the Great Lakes and Mississippi areas were probably built in the French colonial version of log construction, with squared logs set upright (*poteaux-en-terre*) and chinked with stone, as in the one important surviving example, the Holy Family Church in Cahokia, Ill. (1799). Cahokia also has the most important surviving example of a French colonial small house, of the same upright-post construction, the Cahokia Courthouse, originally a private dwelling, built about 1737.

Other French colonial buildings reflect late medieval French (principally Norman) traditions in form and construction: massive framing; well-developed support systems for high, sloping roofs, flared at the eaves and often heavy with tile coverings; and stucco or boarding over stone-chinked or brick-filled frames. The *galerie* is a prominent feature of these houses, on from one to four sides, usually covered by a second pitch from the eave flare; it may be the principal source of the porch, an important feature of American architecture from the late 18th century onward. In the wet and often flooded Mississippi lands, houses were frequently raised on a fully exposed basement, and thus the two-story galleried form of raised cottage or plantation house was developed. Important reflections of these traditions and Franco-American developments are to be found in the Pascal house ("Madame John's Legacy") built about 1727 and rebuilt in the 1780's, in New Orleans; Parlange (1750) in Pointe Coupee Parish, La.; the Keller Mansion (ca. 1801) in Saint Charles Parish, La.; and Connelly's Tavern, probably built between 1796 and 1799, in Natchez, Miss.

In the 18th century, New Orleans grew to be the great city of the Mississippi River valley. Designs for official and religious buildings there came directly from the civil and religious headquarters in Paris, but of all the 18th-century French official buildings only the second Ursuline Convent survives (in altered form). Built of stucco-covered brick between 1748 and 1752, its mid-18th-century French style is seen in the reduction of ornament to the heavy, mannered rustication of the quoins and central pavilion. Documentation of the official Parisian character of many other New Orleans religious and civil buildings is to be found in the original architects' drawings in the Archives Nationales and other Paris repositories.

Late Medieval and Early Renaissance Traditions. The first settlers' primary shelters were whatever protections against the weather they could most quickly devise: dugouts roofed with sod; cabins of poles woven with willow withes and daubed with clay; Indian-style wigwams (round-roofed structures of bent poles, covered with bark, mats, or skins); and, probably, houses of squared timbers or hewn planks. Straight trees were plentiful for logs, but the round-log and squared-log houses are difficult to document for the earliest years of settlement and may have been widespread only generations later, dispersed by the Scotch-Irish who learned the use of these North European techniques from Swedish and German settlers. By the mid-18th century squared-log construction may have accounted for as many as half the buildings on the East Coast.

As soon as they could—probably within the first decade of settlement—the settlers built houses as much like their former homes as possible: in New England, English-style half-timbered frames covered with clapboards or shingles (a fine late example is the Parson Capen House, built in 1683, in Topsfield, Mass.); in New Netherlands, Dutch, Flemish, and Huguenot houses of brick, stone, and wood; in New Sweden, log, frame, and stone buildings; and in Maryland, Virginia, and Carolina, brick and frame English houses (for instance, the Adam Thoroughgood House, built between 1636 and 1640, in Princess Anne County, Va.). These houses—and meeting houses, parish churches, trading posts, barns, mills, and other buildings—contained a few Renaissance technical advances (developed flues and chimneys, plastered walls, and glass windows, for instance), but they followed late-medieval national traditions in the basic shape and technique of framing and covering. As late as the mid-18th century, for example, German settlers built the religious community at Ephrata, Pa., in a medieval German style.

The influence of Renaissance classicism did show itself in ornament, in gradual style changes, and in technique; specifically imitative buildings began to appear by the end of the 17th century. Renaissance classical details in otherwise late-medieval buildings appeared in fragments of Stuart plasterwork (complete with Italianate *putti*) excavated at Jamestown, Va., and in the triangular pediment of Saint Luke's Church (before 1657), Isle of Wight County, Va. Full-scale Jacobean baroque forms appeared in such buildings as the Arthur Allen House, known as Bacon's Castle (about 1655), Surry County, Va., and the Peter Sergeant House (1676–79, since demolished), Boston, Mass.

Jones-Wren English Classical Style. Even as the first English colonists were leaving England for America, a pure Italian Renaissance style was appearing in England, with the building in London of the Banqueting Hall at Whitehall, designed by Inigo Jones. This style—as developed by the leading 17th-century English classicists, Jones, John Webb, Roger Pratt, Hugh May, and Sir Christopher Wren—was influential in a number of buildings in the growing ports and governmental centers of the seaboard colonies. The facade of the long-demolished Foster-Hutchinson House, built about 1688 in Boston, was decorated with a giant order of Ionic pilasters and, probably, an eaveline balustrade to hide the roof and make the house look as much as possible like a rectangular Italian palace. Other examples are the Second Town-House (1712–13), Boston; McPhedris-Warner House (1718–23), Portsmouth, N.H.; Royall House (1733–50), Medford, Mass.; and Independence Hall, originally the State House of Pennsylvania (1731–36 and later), Philadelphia. At Williamsburg, Va., the town plan and capitol, the college, and the governor's palace form the greatest single American monument to Italian Renaissance style; indeed there is a tradition that the design of the College of William and Mary (1693) came from the office of Wren himself.

As fine examples of the style as any provincial houses in England are Stratford, known as the Lee Mansion (ca. 1725–30), in Westmoreland County, Va.; Brafferton Hall (1723), in Williamsburg, inspired by the governor's palace; and William Byrd's Westover (ca. 1730–34), in Charles City County, Va., in which the horizontal composure of the classical form is accented by the strong verticals of the corner chimneys and the subtle vertical diminutions in windowpanes and roof slates. The serene elegance of the period is also seen in such buildings as Saint James Church (1711), Goose Creek, S.C.; Christ Church (1732), Lancaster County, Va.; and the courthouse (1735), at Hanover Court House, Va.

Later Anglo-Palladianism. The classical villas and other works designed by the 16th-century Italian architect Andrea Palladio had a widespread influence in their own time and in the 17th century, but it was the 18th-century revival of Palladio's designs by the group around Richard Boyle, Lord Burlington, that left the greatest mark on England and the colonies. The two-story portico of Drayton Hall (1738–42), near Charleston, S.C., is the earliest American example of the pedimented projecting pavilion that became a hallmark of gentlemanly architecture in the 1750's and 1760's. As a temple-form portico with a giant order, the pedimented projecting pavilion appeared in Gov. Horatio Sharpe's Whitehall (1764), near Annapolis, Md., and in the Jumel Mansion (1765), in New York City. In an attenuated form the same feature appears in The Lindens, built in 1754, in Danvers, Mass., moved to Washington, D.C., in 1937. A plainer version of this pedimented projection is the major architectural feature of many college and official buildings of the same period—for example, Hollis Hall (1762–63), at Harvard University, Cambridge, Mass.

The most noted other Palladianism, the five-part plan (two blocks on each side of a central block, connected with narrow "hyphens"), appeared during the same period, for instance, in London architect John Hawks's plans for Gov. William Tryon's palace (1757), at New Bern, N.C., and in such southern plantation houses as Mount Airy (1758–62), Richmond County, Va.

Knowledgeable Americans were changing, under the English Palladian influence, from the use of classical details to the use of entire classical forms, particularly the temple form as adapted by Palladio and then by the English Palladians. The master builder and his client had previously relied on a design book or builders' guide as a source for touches of classical ornament. In this period the change toward forms with sophisticated proportions (often requiring the hiding of actual form or construction) and integrated decorations, led to the appearance of the architect along more or less modern lines—a designer with the ability to set out drawings or other directions by which the builder could achieve the desired unified (and "correct") classical effect in a whole building. Peter Harrison, a ship captain of Newport, R.I., who was also a collector of architectural books and an amateur designer, was the first American architect in this sense. In designing the Redwood Library at Newport (1748–50), he made highly imaginative use of a Palladian variation on the temple form and devised a wooden board covering cut to look like the shaped stone of English Palladian buildings, using paint with sand in it to achieve a stony texture. Harrison's designs give him a place in architectural history as the leading American architect of this phase of American Anglo-Palladianism. In addition to the Redwood Library, his works include King's Chapel (1749–54), Boston; Christ Church (1759–61), Cambridge, Mass.; Touro Synagogue (1759–63), Newport; and the bold Brick Market (1761–62), Newport, modeled on Jones and Webb's Somerset House in London.

Many of the Anglo-Palladian ideas came to the English colonies in design books by various architects. James Gibbs's *Book of Architecture* (1728) was one of the most influential of these for all sorts of buildings, but particularly churches. Gibbs palladianized the church form by applying a portico to Wren's "box with a spire," and Gibbsian Palladian churches are among the greatest 18th-century works all along the eastern seaboard: to name a few, Christ Church (1727–54), Philadelphia; Saint Michael's Church (1752–61), Charleston, S.C.; the First Baptist Meeting House (1774–75), Providence, R.I.; and Saint Paul's Chapel (1764–66, 1794–96), New York City.

Another method for the transfer of architectural ideas was the immigration of a master builder. Ezra Waite, for example, builder of the Miles Brewton House, advertised in the Charleston *Gazette* in 1769 as "Civil Architect, House-builder in general, and Carver, from London. . . ." William Buckland, trained in London as a builder and carver, came as an indentured servant to carve the woodwork for George Mason's house, Gunston Hall (1755–58), at Lorton, in Fairfax County, Va., where he used classical, Chinese, and Gothic themes. His other work in Virginia and then in Maryland (he established himself at Annapolis about 1770) was capped by the Hammond-Harwood House (1773–74), a provincial masterpiece of plan and ornament.

Neoclassicism and the Federal Style. The international neoclassicism moving swiftly to bold new forms in Europe in the second half of the 18th century was a precisely right source of design for the new United States. Drawing anew on the severest architecture of republican Rome, democratic Greece, and other historic styles (Egyptian, Oriental, Gothic), romantic classicism provided the framework for the first great American national style.

The plan and buildings for the new capital city of Washington provided—for the first time—a single American focus for architectural ideas and for architects themselves. A leading role was played by Thomas Jefferson, who had already shown himself a master of the use of the neoclassical style in his design (with C. L. Clérisseau) of the Virginia state capitol (1785), at Richmond, as a temple-form building based on the Roman Maison Carrée at Nîmes, France.

Washington was a magnet for designers and builders—an immense new city to be hewn out of the woods, orchards, and fields of its naturally romantic site on the Maryland side of the Potomac River just below the river's falls. There came, among others, the American Andrew Ellicott to survey the district; Pierre Charles L'Enfant, French engineer, to lay out the city; James Hoban, Irish architect, to design and build the White House; Stephen (Étienne) Hallet, French architect, and William Thornton, West Indian amateur, to design the Capitol; Louis de Toussard, French engineer, to plan the marine barracks; George Hadfield, Scottish architect, to build the official U.S. departmental buildings and the city hall; and, greatest of these figures, Benjamin Henry Latrobe, an imaginative young English architect who had also studied in Germany. Latrobe had been working in Virginia and then in Philadelphia in the late 1790's, in the latter city introducing the severest neoclassical and Gothic styles. Brought to Washington by Jefferson to consult on navy drydocks, Latrobe was appointed by Jefferson as both architect of the Capitol and surveyor of the public buildings. The finest interiors of the Capitol are his, most notably the old House of Representatives (Statuary Hall). His imaginative designs included three new "classical orders" based on the corn plant, the tobacco plant, and the cotton plant, of which the first two were utilized in the Capitol as completed. Latrobe's many other works include the Baltimore Cathedral (1804–ca. 1818); the neo-Gothic Christ Church (1806), in Washington, D.C.; and the boldly scaled entrance hall to Decatur House (1817), also in Washington.

But Latrobe was only first among many architects who built important works in the international neoclassical styles of the period. Another great figure was Charles Bulfinch, whose first great work was the Massachusetts State House (1795), in Boston, in Adamesque style and who later succeeded Latrobe as architect of the Capitol (1817). Jefferson's own architecture continued to develop through this period, in his rebuilding of Monticello as a Franco-Palladian villa (1793–1809) and his brilliant designs for the University of Virginia (1817–26) as "an academical village."

Growing Eclecticism. A unified classical style was rapidly superseded by the use of multiple styles in the first half of the 19th century. The period 1825–50 was dominated by the mighty Greek revival: Robert Mills's Washington Monument (1836–78) and U.S. Treasury Building (1836–79) in Washington, D.C.; Thomas U. Walter's Girard College (1833–47) and Andalusia (1834–47) in Philadelphia; and many handsome southern plantation houses, whose tall white-columned porticos created a powerful national image. The Greek revival was the first continentwide style, elements of it appearing, for instance, in buildings in Monterey, Calif., in the 1830's, 1840's, and 1850's.

Along with the Greek revival there was an ever-stronger Gothic revival, with such milestones as Alexander J. Davis' Lyndhurst (1838–41, 1864–66) at Tarrytown, N.Y., and the beginning of the use of "correct" Gothic styles for churches, which continued for more than a century. Important early examples are Richard Upjohn's Trinity Church (1846) and James Renwick's Saint Patrick's Cathedral (1858–79), both in New York City. The great engineer-architect Ithiel Town's young partner Alexander J. Davis became, he said, an "architectural compositor," and he listed twenty-three styles in which he could work. Town and Davis helped popularize the Egyptian and Italian-villa styles, and Davis' designs were principal parts of Andrew J. Downing's popularization of the Gothic cottage as an inexpensive house style—one that was successfully built from coast to coast. The Romanesque revival was introduced by Renwick in the Smithsonian Institution building (1846–55) at Washington, D.C., and another English-trained architect, John Notman, introduced a new phase of the Renaissance revival, notably in the Atheneum (1845–57), in Philadelphia. This changing and mixing of styles was much accelerated by the greater ease of national and international travel and by the development of illustrated histories of architecture and illustrated popular magazines. Stylistic change was also accelerated by technical change. Most important was the invention of the "balloon" frame at Chicago in the 1830's, in which lightweight prefabricated members were nailed together, rather than heavy frame timbers dressed, jointed, and fitted by hand. This method made building quicker and cheaper, and it allowed wood to be used to create almost any shape easily. The rapidly expanding middle class, which wanted extended cultural and social meaning in its architecture, pushed forward these changes from a handicraft America of unified styles to an industrial America of varied styles.

Beaux Arts and the Rise of Modern Architecture. Some Americans participating in the rapid changes of their industrial society sought a sense of social stability among the welter of designs. Thus, it is not surprising that they took up the Platonic idea that good design would make good people. In England, Augustus W. N. Pugin, John Ruskin, and William Morris preached these themes, and a measure of American acceptance of these ideas is the power of Gothic, vernacular, and handicraft themes from the 1840's forward. The English writer Sir Charles Locke Eastlake, whose *Hints on Household Taste* (1868) had its greatest effect in the United States, stressed the moral necessity that furniture should show the grain of the wood and the cut of the joint. The power of these ideas is evidenced in their long life into the mid-20th century.

Academic architectural training and illustrated professional periodicals were new factors in the stylistic developments of the 1850's and after. The École des Beaux Arts in Paris was the leading architectural training ground from the 1850's to the 1920's. Richard Morris Hunt was the first American architect trained there. From the 1850's through the 1890's he created a series of trend-setting designs in academic French and English Gothic and Renaissance styles, of which the finest examples were The Breakers (1892), in Newport, R.I.; Biltmore (1895), near Asheville, N.C.; and the Tribune Building (1873–75), in New York City.

Henry Hobson Richardson, who returned from the École des Beaux Arts just after the Civil War, was, by the 1870's, the major source of new American styles, using Romanesque and other motives in a highly personal manner. Richardsonian Romanesque was the first American-created style that had a strong influence elsewhere in North America and in Europe. Trinity Church in Boston (1873–77) was the first great success in the style, and there were hundreds—perhaps thousands—of imitations throughout the country and abroad. Richardson's libraries and railroad stations, in Massachusetts, and governmental designs, such as the Allegheny County buildings (1884–86), in Pittsburgh, were sources of many other designs of the late 19th century. In the 1870's he followed the English Queen Anne style in the revival of vernacular details, notably in the Watts Sherman House (1874), at Newport; exterior use was made of stone, brick, shingles, slates, and half-timbering, and the interior was dominated by a central living hall with a big fireplace, a multipaned window wall, and a great stair rising to one side. Richardson died in early middle age in 1886, but even in the last year of his life he continued to innovate, in the John Ames Office Building in Boston and the design for a Marshall Field wholesale store in Chicago, first steps on the way to a new American business-building style.

Among the first Americans trained at the École des Beaux Arts was Louis H. Sullivan—who also studied at the Massachusetts Institute of Technology, where the first American architectural school was established. Sullivan went to booming Chicago and there developed Richardsonian themes into his own business-building style, as in the powerful Auditorium Building (1887–89), now Roosevelt University (with its theater a great restored auditorium), and the Schlesinger and Meyer department store (1899–1906), now Carson, Pirie, Scott. There the young Frank Lloyd Wright worked as a draftsman for Sullivan, before establishing his own office in 1893.

Variety and a Changing Future. In the late 19th and 20th centuries, following the vernacular forms and details brought together in the Queen Anne and colonial styles, American architects developed many important changes in the plan, form, and decoration of the detached house—the suburban house. Two of the variations that evolved in the late 19th century were the Stick style and the Shingle style. Charles McKim and Stanford White, both of whom had worked for Richardson, were the principal design members of the highly successful firm of McKim, Mead and White, which introduced specific American colonial revival details into such houses in the 1880's, beginning the colonial revival style, which remained a major influence through the mid-20th century. In such works as the New York Herald Building (1878, since demolished) and the Boston Public Library (1887), McKim and White turned to the Italian Renaissance for inspiration. They took their version of Renaissance classicism to the planning sessions of the World's Columbian Exposition to be held in Chicago in 1893, and the design committee chose it for the fair. The "White City" classical setting for the fair—where millions of Americans were rowed around an Illinois lagoon in Venetian gondolas, with a unified Renaissance style in view wherever they looked—convinced a generation that that was the way to build cities. For sixty years thereafter the classical civic center was a theme of American architecture, often pedestrian but occasionally reaching the great quality of the San Francisco city hall (1915) done by the firm of Bakewell and Brown or of the Departmental Auditorium group in Washington, D.C. (1935), done by Arthur Brown, Jr.

In the middle and late 19th century, technical developments of iron and steel construction had permitted the designing of cast-iron buildings, notably by James Bogardus, and the suspension structure of John Roeblings' Brooklyn Bridge (1860–83). In Chicago and New York in the late 19th century and in the 20th century, a new business-building architecture was created, using these and other developments: steel frame; pipes in the floor slabs; elevators; and prefabricated window walls. From the Chicago system of the late 19th century, a straight-line development carried to the great skyscrapers of the 20th century. The most important of these are in New York: the Woolworth Building (Cass Gilbert, 1913); the first McGraw-Hill Building (Raymond Hood, 1929–30); the Chrysler Building (William Van Alen, 1930); the Empire State Building (Shreve, Lamb, and Harmon, 1931); and Rockefeller Center (various architects, 1931–39). A catalog of the skyscraper style is the series of designs submitted by both American and foreign architects in the competition for the Chicago Tribune Tower (1922), the winning design built in Gothic style by John Mead Howells and Raymond Hood.

Chicago was the center for the most significant developments in the detached house around 1900, the year in which Frank Lloyd Wright designed "A House in a Prairie Town" for the *Ladies' Home Journal,* a codification of the prairie style that was one of his many major contributions to American architecture. For six decades of the 20th century Wright created buildings whose influences permeated American and international architecture: the Larkin Building (1904, since demolished), Buffalo, N.Y.; Unity Temple (1906), Oak Park, Ill.; the Robie House (1909), Chicago; Midway Gardens (1913, since demolished), Chicago; the Imperial Hotel (1915–22, since demolished), Tokyo, Japan; the Mayan-influenced and patterned-block buildings of the 1910's and 1920's; the Johnson Building (1936–58), Racine, Wis.; the Guggenheim Museum (1943, 1956–59), New York City; Beth Sholom Synagogue (1959), Elkins Park, Pa.; and the prairie and Usonian house types—Taliesin (1925), Spring Green, Wis.; Taliesin West (1925–38), Scottsdale, Ariz.; Fallingwater, the Edgar S. Kaufmann House (1936–39), Bear Run, Pa. Wright's innovations encompassed the architectural process—the shaping of space and plan, the design of ornament, the buildings techniques themselves. The Kaufmann House, its planes of concrete cantilevered from its core of concrete and stone, is a sculptural form, one of the great art works of the 20th century.

In the early 20th century, important experiments in the detached house were made on the West Coast, fusing Queen Anne, Wrightian, Oriental, and Mission ideas, in the work of the firm of Greene and Greene, Bernard Ralph Maybeck, and Irving Gill. Also on the West Coast, in California, the early 20th-century expositions, emphasizing the Spanish history of the area, were the sources of a Spanish colonial revival that continued through the mid-20th century.

International Style. The ideas of Wright and of the European avant-garde architects of the 1910's and 1920's culminated in the style named the International style by Henry-Russell Hitchcock and Philip Johnson, in their important 1931 exhibition for the Museum of Modern Art in New York City. This crisp, plain style was slowly accepted, and what appeared shocking to many in the 1920's was widely admired by the 1950's. Important examples of the development of the International style in America include the Lovell House (1929) by Richard J. Neutra, Los Angeles; the Museum of Modern Art (1939) by Philip L. Goodwin and Edward Durell Stone, with annex and sculpture court (1964) by Philip Johnson, New York; the campus and buildings for the Illinois Institute of Technology (1939–56), by Ludwig Mies van der Rohe, Chicago; and various churches and campuses by Eliel and Eero Saarinen in the 1940's and 1950's. The style reached a peak in the period after World War II, in such works as the Kaufmann (Desert) House (1946) by Neutra, Palm Springs, Calif.; the United Nations buildings (1947–53), by a committee of international architects headed by Wallace K. Harrison, New York City; the Equitable Building (1948), by Pietro Belluschi, Portland, Oreg.; Charles Eames's Case Study House (1949), Pacific Palisades, Calif.; Philip Johnson's house (1949), New Canaan, Conn.; Lever House (1952), by Skidmore, Owings, and Merrill, New York City; and the Seagram Building (1955–58) by Mies van der Rohe and Johnson, also in New York City. Johnson's house exhibits the startling and beautiful innate classicism of the International style: a steel-framed glass box, architecturally decorated with only elegant proportions, a beautiful setting, and a small group of carefully chosen art objects. The continuing freshness of the International style can be seen in such buildings as Lake Point Tower (1968), by George Schipporeit and John Heinrich, Chicago, in which the undulating glass exterior draws on futurist and Corbusian ideas of four or five decades earlier.

In the 1960's and 1970's virtually every city had at least one tall building built in the International style, and the "tallest" buildings of the former skyscraper phase were all surpassed, although with no major additions to skyscraper styles. The growing densities, and generally pedestrian architecture, of many cities gave new impetus to the preservation and restoration movements, which had been changing from their century-old foci on the saving of individual structures of the highest quality or historic importance, to the saving of whole streets and districts for reuse and renewed contact with the past—in some cases, the very recent past.

Major architectural changes of the 1950's, 1960's, and 1970's occurred through experiments in the sculptural forming of space, in structural techniques, and in the pursuit of ornamentation through textured materials. Examples are Buckminster Fuller's tetrahedron domes and allied structures and Louis Kahn's exploitation of structure in the Yale Art Gallery (1951–53), New Haven, Conn., and the Richards Medical Research Building (1961–64), Philadelphia, Pa. A complete freedom with steel-supported concrete was demonstrated by many architects, notably Wright and Eero Saarinen in the Trans World Airlines Terminal (1962) at J. F. Kennedy Airport, New York City, and the brilliant Dulles Airport (1958–62) for

Washington, D.C., at Chantilly, Va. The boldest architecture of the period was that of the "new brutalism"—experiments in tough and overpowering forms and textured finishes, epitomized by Paul Rudolph's Temple Street Parking Garage (1962), New Haven, Conn., and his Art and Architecture Building (1963) for Yale University. Other examples of variations on these themes include the Everson Gallery of Art (1968) by I. M. Pei, in Syracuse, N.Y.; the East Building for the National Gallery of Art (1973–75), by Pei, in Washington, D.C.; and, within the historic core of Boston, the bold form of the new city hall (1969), by Kallman, McKinnell and Knowles; and Campbell, Aldrich and Nulty.

[*Journal of the Society of Architectural Historians;* Henry-Russell Hitchcock, *Architecture, Nineteenth and Twentieth Centuries;* Edgar Kaufmann, Jr., ed., *The Rise of an American Architecture;* Albert Manucy, *The Houses of St. Augustine;* Hugh Morrison, *Early American Architecture;* William H. Pierson, Jr., and William H. Jordy, *American Buildings and Their Architects;* Marcus Whiffen, *American Architecture Since 1780.*]

JOHN PEARCE

ARCHITECTURE, AMERICAN INDIAN. The great public and ceremonial structures of native America consist mainly of Maya and Aztec temples, pyramids, palaces, and ball courts in Mexico and Inca citadels in Peru. A North American exception is to be seen in the mounds and earthworks of the Mississippi Valley. There, especially in the southern reaches, there is prehistoric evidence of ceremonial buildings, never so elaborate as in Mexico, of wood rather than stone, placed on mounds. They seem to evidence a direct borrowing of a Mexican form.

The Indians of North America north of Mexico tended generally to concentrate on dwellings. These, together with a few random ceremonial structures, varied so greatly according to the raw materials available for building and the kind of economic and ecological specializations in various regions that a general statement on house types is impossible. Hunting peoples tended to favor the transportable skin tent, banked or even covered with snow in the far north; this gave rise to the hide-covered conical tipi of the bison-hunting Plains Indians. (Such skin tents may have been the kind of dwelling imported to the Americas by the original migrants from Asia.) With seasonal movement for the gathering of wild seeds, such as occurred in the Great Basin, a domed brush shelter, the wickiup, was developed. Permanently settled gatherers—in California and the Plateau, for example—depended basically on brush, straw, matting, or other available materials for their houses. But in those areas there was great variation in house form. Thatched, round houses in central California, domed or conical, contrast with multiple-family elongated tents of matting, each family possessing a single segment, or with semisubterranean earth lodges in the Plateau and sporadically in California.

Several distinctive house types emerged in various areas. While only the central Eskimo made extensive use of the domed ice lodge, the so-called igloo, this constituted a distinctive invention, being the one native American instance of the use of the architectural principle of the keystone arch. The Maya, lacking this principle, employed the corbelled arch, which accounts in some measure for the essentially cumbersome styles of Mexican architecture. The western Eskimo made sod houses, usually circular, over an excavation, having either an entrance passage or a roof entrance and an interior bench construction with a central firepit—a house type that seems to have parallels in Asia. The beautifully elaborate plank houses of the Northwest Coast, however much overt form and materials differ, appear to be variants of this pattern, especially since they have an interior bench structure and a central firepit and smokehole. Of split cedar planks, gabled, usually with the totem pole, houses of the Northwest Coast area depart from the Asian form in their rectangular ground plan. But the same semisubterranean style appears among the Pueblo, not in the dwellings, but in the ceremonial underground chamber, the kiva, center of all ritual. The erstwhile firepit in the center becomes the sacred place from which the ancestors are thought to emerge. (Pueblo dwellings, whether of one or several stories, were originally made of adobe and stone; adobe bricks are post-Spanish.) Familiar in all American Indian literature is the birch bark lozenge-shaped tent, the wigwam, a house generally appearing among the Algonkin-speaking peoples of the Northeast. The Iroquois offer a variation on the wigwam pattern—more elaborate, with elm bark covering. This was the famous longhouse, intimately linked with forms of societal organization, as is usually the case. Wicker structures covered with earth, wattle-and-daub houses, appear in the round, rectangular, or L-shaped cabins of the Gulf peoples.

Among the Pueblo, the kiva was a permanent structure. The same was true of the temple of such groups as the Creek or Natchez in the Southeast, the repository of the tribal palladia, built on an earth mound. Elsewhere, temporary dance houses or ceremonial structures might be erected, for example the Sun

Dance lodge of the Plains Indians. The western Eskimo of Alaska had structures for men's activity, a feature repeated in parts of California. A chief's house might be used for meetings in California and the Plateau, but in general the American Indian carried on political and ceremonial activities in the open and gave his principal architectural attention to the dwelling place of the social unit, however conceived.

[Harold E. Driver, *Indians of North America.*]

ROBERT F. SPENCER

ARCHIVES. The body of records and papers officially produced or received by a government, and filed and preserved by it for future reference, constitutes its archives. In the United States government archives, also called public records, are accumulated by the federal government, state governments, and local governments (such as county, municipal, and town). The term "archives" may be applied also to records similarly accumulated and preserved by semipublic and private organizations—those of greatest importance historically being records of business organizations, educational institutions, religious bodies, political parties, and fraternal organizations.

The National Archives. The National Archives of the United States consists of the records of all agencies of the federal government—legislative, executive, and judicial. In contrast to other nations the United States until relatively recently left noncurrent records in the custody of agencies that had created or inherited them, with the result that some were inadvertently destroyed and many were stored in unsuitable places where they were subject to deterioration and practically inaccessible to scholars or officials. In 1926 Congress made provision for the construction of the National Archives building in Washington, D.C., which, though not fully completed until 1937, was occupied in 1935. The National Archives was created by law in 1934 as an independent agency of the executive branch, to have the custody and administration of the records transferred to this building.

Under the direction of Robert D. W. Connor, the first Archivist of the United States, 1934–41, a comprehensive survey was made of federal records both at the capital and in field offices throughout the states. The information assembled about the location, quantity, nature, custody, physical condition, and research value of these records was important in gauging the size and nature of the task ahead and in establishing priorities for accessioning. Space needs for burgeoning New Deal agencies and even greater needs for World War II agencies caused the older records to be transferred to the archives building at a much faster rate than anticipated. All but a few of the 19th-century records and, in bulk, even greater quantities of 20th-century records were in the building by the end of the war. The *Guide to the Records in the National Archives,* published in 1948, described the more than 800,000 cubic feet of records accessioned by June 30, 1947. For the first time scholars had a single agency in Washington to which they might go to consult the older records of the federal government, or to learn whether or not such records existed and where they might be if not in the National Archives. Such a center of information was serving the federal government in many other ways also—by cleaning up disorderly attics and basements, eliminating fire hazards, providing Congress with a systematic review of records proposed for disposal, and in general bringing order and economy into record practices and administration.

Greatly increased responsibilities were given the National Archives under Connor and his successors, Solon J. Buck, 1941–48, and Wayne C. Grover, 1948–65. The Federal Register Act of 1935 provided that all regulations intended to have the force of law must be filed at the National Archives and published in the daily *Federal Register* before being put into effect. Those of continuing effect are also printed in a cumulative *Code of Federal Regulations*. Responsibility for receiving the original laws and publishing the *Statutes at Large* was transferred from the Department of State to the National Archives in 1950. Another area of responsibility has been that of presidential libraries, beginning with the Franklin D. Roosevelt Library in Hyde Park, N.Y. The Roosevelt Library was built with private funds but, together with its contents, including papers of Roosevelt and of many of his associates, was donated to the federal government and accepted by joint resolution of Congress in 1939. A resolution of 1955 provided generally for the acceptance, maintenance, and administration of such presidential libraries. In accordance with its provisions, the privately constructed Harry S. Truman Library at Independence, Mo., was opened in 1957; the Dwight D. Eisenhower Library at Abilene, Kans., in 1962; the Herbert Hoover Library at West Branch, Iowa, later the same year; and the Lyndon Baines Johnson Library at Austin, Texas, in 1971. Plans have been approved for the construction of the John Fitzgerald Kennedy Library adjacent to Harvard University in Cambridge, Mass. Pending completion of the building, date indefinite, the

Kennedy Library is located in a temporary facility at nearby Waltham. All six libraries are administered by the Archivist of the United States, and their holdings serve to supplement the strictly archival material in his custody.

The National Archives lost its independent status in 1949, when it was made a bureau of the newly created General Services Administration, an agency established upon the recommendation of the first Hoover Commission on the Reorganization of the Executive Branch. It was renamed the National Archives and Records Service.

Still greater expansion of the Archivist's duties and responsibilities came with the Federal Records Act of 1950, the first comprehensive records act ever passed by the federal government. The Archivist was directed to assist agencies in the control and maintenance of their current records. An Office of Records Management was created to work in this area. Authority was also granted for the establishment of intermediate records centers to house records not needed immediately at hand, in expensive space and equipment, by operating agencies but still having to be kept for an extended period or possibly permanent preservation. One such intermediate center, serving headquarters offices in the Washington area, is located in Suitland, Md., just outside the District of Columbia. There is also a National Personnel Records Center in St. Louis, where the records of former civilian and military personnel are concentrated and serviced. In addition, there are thirteen regional records centers that take care of records of field offices of federal agencies and records of a few agencies whose headquarters are outside the Washington area. In earlier years it was thought field office records of permanent value should be sent to Washington to be available with the headquarters records, but this idea has now been abandoned, and archives divisions have been established in each regional center to take over records determined worthy of permanent preservation.

Outside the National Archives building, national and regional intermediate centers now hold nearly 12,000,000 cubic feet of records in custody, of which more than 500,000 cubic feet are already in the archives divisions. Future appraisals will result in more being transferred to these divisions, but probably more than 90 percent can be destroyed in time. Including records kept in the National Archives building in Washington, the Archivist of the United States in 1973 had in his custody about 13,000,000 cubic feet of records, or well over 40 percent of the approximately 30,000,000 cubic feet of federal records reported to be in existence. It should be added that permanent records in the custody of the Archivist included about 1,600,000 maps; 4,600,000 still pictures; 69,000 sound recordings; and 52,000 motion pictures.

The records in the National Archives and in the intermediate centers have been divided into over 400 "record groups," reflecting the federal agencies, existing or once existing, that created them. Inventories have been published covering at least 140 of these groups, along with "special lists," information circulars, and other finding aids. There are special guides to records of both Union and Confederate governments during the Civil War, to records relating to both world wars, and to cartographic records. A new comprehensive guide in several volumes is in press, and a quarterly magazine entitled *Prologue* is published, which features articles based on the records, reports on current accessions, and other news.

Selected series of records having high research value are made available to libraries and scholars through a program of microfilm publication, whereby the National Archives prepares a master negative and sells positive prints for a modest sum. More than 150,000 rolls, totaling more than 150,000,000 pages, are thus available. Consultation of the records by scholars, administrators, attorneys, and ordinary citizens has increased steadily over the years.

State and Local Archives. Many of the states preceded the federal government in making some provision for the centralized custody and administration of noncurrent records, but the provisions were extremely diverse and frequently inadequate. Usually the archival functions have been assigned to a state historical society or commission, a state department of archives and history, a state library, or the secretary of state and are merely part of a larger program that absorbs most of the meager appropriations. In recent years there has been some tendency, following the federal example, to place the archives function in a department of administration or general services. Delaware, Georgia, Hawaii, Illinois, Maryland, North Carolina, and South Carolina have modern, especially constructed, buildings to house the state archives. In other states—for example, Virginia, Tennessee, and Nebraska—the archives are incorporated into a modern state library or historical society building that has specially planned stacks and service areas. Often, however, the quarters for archives are woefully inadequate and most of the noncurrent records perforce remain in the custody of the offices that have accumulated them.

Most state archival agencies have some authority over the records of counties, municipalities, and other state-created local governing bodies. In the East there has been some tendency to centralize the older local records—say, of the colonial period—at the state archives, or at least to assure security by assembling photographic copies of them there. Some states have full-time inspectors or examiners of local records. Municipal archival programs exist in some of the larger cities, notably New York and Philadelphia, but, given the present emphasis on urban history and government, the movement has not progressed as rapidly as might be expected.

Archives of Private Organizations. Greatly increased interest in business, social, and cultural history in recent years has led to more widespread concern for the archives of all influential organizations of the past. No longer are archivists engaged solely in the preservation of the documents of political history. After World War II, for instance, a number of leading business corporations (Firestone Tire and Rubber Company, Ford Motor Company, Du Pont) established well-considered archives and equipment for their older records. *A Directory of Business Archives in the United States and Canada,* published in 1969 by the Society of American Archivists, contained entries for 135 companies, nearly one-half of them manufacturing firms. Few had full-time archivists in charge, however. Often the company archives were the part-time responsibility of the staff of a company library, museum, or records management office. Many older companies have also transferred their early records to manuscript repositories.

College and university archives, another group of private archives, have expanded significantly. A directory of these, published by the Society of American Archivists in 1966, showed that 558 educational institutions in the United States had archival programs. Older ones include Harvard, Yale, Columbia, Princeton, Cornell, the University of Pennsylvania, Georgetown University, Catholic University, Duke, Vanderbilt, and many state universities. Some have well-developed programs administered by full-time professional archivists, but in most cases responsibility for the archives is an added function of the institutional library—usually of its division of manuscripts or "special collections." In addition to institutional records university archives usually include personal papers of faculty members.

A third group of private archives of considerable importance is the archives of religious organizations; the Society of American Archivists issued a directory of these in 1963. They ranged from the archives of denominational headquarters organizations to those of individual churches. Of special interest are the records of home and foreign missionary societies.

The profession of archivist, although an ancient and honorable one in Europe, could hardly be said to exist in the United States in the first third of this century. With the establishment of the National Archives, expansion of state archival activities, and growing interest in the subject in educational, business, and other organizations, a need for meetings and publication channels developed that led to the formation in 1936 of the Society of American Archivists, which in 1974 had some 2,400 members. Its quarterly journal, *The American Archivist,* published without break since 1938, is the chief source for the history of archival development in America for these years.

[H. G. Jones, *The Records of a Nation;* Ernst Posner, *American State Archives.*]

OLIVER WENDELL HOLMES

ARCHIVE WAR (1842), a contest between Austin and Houston, Tex., over the state archives. Austin had been designated as the capital in 1839, but President Sam Houston, after a Mexican raid on San Antonio in 1842, fearing the archives might be lost, undertook to remove them to Houston. The citizens of Austin overtook the wagons and forced them to be returned to Austin.

[H. H. Bancroft, *History of the North Mexican States and Texas,* vol. II.]

J. G. SMITH

ARCTIC EXPLORATION. *See* **Amundsen Polar Expeditions; Byrd's Polar Flights; Polar Expeditions.**

d'ARGES COLONY. In 1787 Pierre Wouves d'Arges acted as agent of Diego de Gardoqui, Spanish minister to the United States, in forwarding a plan to protect Florida and Louisiana from American encroachment by inducing Kentucky families to settle within those Spanish domains (*see* Spanish Conspiracy; Western Separatism). Liberal grants of land, freedom of religion, and free importation of slaves, stock, farming implements, and provisions for two years were promised to prospective settlers. Although the governor of Louisiana, Esteban Rodríguez Miró, opposed the plan, which conflicted with his intrigues with James Wilkinson, a considerable number of Americans took advantage of the offer and became Spanish subjects (*see* Forman's Colony).

[C. Gayarré, *History of Louisiana,* vol. III.]

WALTER PRICHARD

ARGONAUTS OF CALIFORNIA. *See* **Forty-niners.**

***ARGUS-PELICAN* ENGAGEMENT** (Aug. 14, 1813). Off Saint David's Head, Wales, the British brig *Pelican* captured the American brig *Argus,* which had sunk more than 20 ships in the English Channel in one month. The American loss was six killed and seventeen wounded; the British had two killed and five wounded.

[Theodore Roosevelt, *The Naval War of 1812.*]

CHARLES LEE LEWIS

ARID REGIONS. Definition has been the central problem in the history of the arid regions of the United States. The need to ascertain the limits of arability and the difficulty of establishing such boundaries where precipitation fluctuates unpredictably over a wide zone of marginal productivity constitute a basic developmental theme for more than half the nation. Archaeological evidences of prehistoric Indian communities indicate that droughts occasioned recurrent disaster to agricultural societies long ago, as now, in border areas. In 1803 President Thomas Jefferson, seeking congressional support for exploration of the upper Missouri River, summarized existing knowledge of newly purchased Louisiana in describing it as a region of "immense and trackless deserts" but also, at its eastern perimeter, as "one immense *prairie*"—a land "too rich for the growth of forest trees." The subsequent expedition of Meriwether Lewis and William Clark (1804–06) marked the official beginning of American efforts to elaborate the description.

Until the 1860's a conception prevailed that the vast province west from the meridian of Council Bluffs, on the Missouri River, to the Rocky Mountains, between thirty-five and forty-nine degrees north latitude, was a "Great American Desert." The explorations of Lewis and Clark, Zebulon Pike, and Stephen Harriman Long, followed by the experiences of traders to Santa Fe, Rocky Mountain fur trappers, immigrants to Oregon and California, soldiers along the Gila Trail, surveyors for transcontinental railroads, and prospectors throughout the West confirmed the appellation.

While commentators agreed that agriculture could have no significant role in the region, they did occasionally recognize that the Great Plains, the mountain parks, and the interior valleys of California and the Northwest afforded excellent pasturage. As livestock industry developed in these areas during the period from 1866 to 1886, redefinition of the limits of aridity evolved. Maj. John Wesley Powell's surveys and, notably, his *Report on the Lands of the Arid Region* (1878) expressed the new point of view; agriculture, Powell asserted, could be profitably conducted in many parts of the West, but only as an irrigated enterprise and generally as a supplement to stock growing. The collapse of open-range ranching in the mid-1880's emphasized the need for expanded hay and forage production and gave impetus to development of irrigation programs. But Powell's efforts to classify the public lands and the passage of the Carey Desert Land Grant Act of 1894 raised controversy. States east of the 104th meridian were excluded, at the request of their representatives, from the application of the Carey legislation. Farmers during the 1880's had expanded cultivation without irrigation nearly to that meridian in the Dakotas and even beyond it in the central plains. Many were convinced that "rainfall follows the plow." They saw no need to assume the costs and the managerial innovations of supplemental watering. A new conception of the boundaries of aridity was emerging.

Drought in the mid-1870's had driven a vanguard of settlers eastward from the James River Valley, a prairie zone normally receiving more than twenty inches of annual rainfall. Drought in the period 1889–94 forced thousands back from the plains farther west, where average precipitation ranges between fifteen and twenty inches annually. As normal conditions returned, however, farmers in the first two decades of the 20th century expanded cultivation across the plains to the foothills of the Rockies—in Montana, Colorado, and New Mexico—and in many areas beyond—Utah, Idaho, the interior valleys of California, and eastern Oregon and Washington. Irrigation supplied water to only a small portion of these lands. Dry farming—a specialized program that, ideally, combines use of crop varieties adapted to drought resistance, cultivation techniques designed to conserve moisture, and management systems that emphasize large-scale operations—provided a new approach to the problem of aridity. The deserts, promoters claimed, could be made to "blossom like the rose."

When severe droughts again returned from 1919 to 1922, and from 1929 to 1936, assessment of the effectiveness of dry farming raised new concern for defining the limits of aridity—an outlook most strongly expressed in the reports of the National Resources Board of the mid-1930's but one that still permeates the writings of agricultural scientists. Long-term precipitation records, with adjustment for seasonality and rate of variability in rainfall, humidity, temperature, and soil conditions, now afford some guidance to the mapping of cultivable areas.

By established criteria a zone of outright desert (less than five inches average annual precipitation) ranges from southeastern California, northward through the western half of Nevada, nearly to the Oregon border. Because cropping without irrigation is impracticable when rainfall averages less than ten inches annually, climatic pockets found in all states west of the 104th meridian—most prevalently in Arizona, central New Mexico, eastern Nevada, Utah, and the lee side of the Cascades in Oregon and Washington—may also be defined as arid. Semiaridity—an average precipitation of from ten to fifteen inches annually—characterizes the western Dakotas, much of Montana, and large sections of eastern New Mexico, Colorado, Wyoming, Idaho, Oregon, and Washington. There dry farming may be successful but only when management programs include allowances for recurrent drought. Throughout much of the semiarid region livestock production predominates, with cropping to afford feed and forage supplementary to native short-grass pasturage. In many areas, however, the possibility of raising wheat of superior milling quality, which commands premium prices, encourages alternative land utilization. The costs of marginal productivity must be carefully weighed.

Eastward, roughly from the Missouri River to the ninety-eighth meridian and curving to the west through the central and southern plains, is a subhumid zone, in which rainfall averages from fifteen to twenty inches annually, an amount sufficient, if well distributed, to permit cultivation without recourse to specialized programs but so closely correlated to the margin of general farming requirements that a deficiency occasions failure. Almost every spring, alarms are raised that some areas of the vast wheat fields extending from the central Dakotas, through western Kansas and Nebraska and eastern Colorado and New Mexico, into the panhandles of Oklahoma and Texas have suffered serious losses. There the problem of defining limits of arability is yet unresolved; the boundaries of aridity remain uncertain.

[Gilbert C. Fite, *The Farmers' Frontier, 1865–1900;* William H. Goetzmann, *Exploration and Empire: The Explorer and the Scientist in the Winning of the American West;* Mary W. M. Hargreaves, *Dry Farming in the Northern Great Plains, 1900–1925;* Howard W. Ottoson and others, *Land and People in the Northern Plains Transition Area;* U.S. Department of Agriculture, *Climate and Man: Yearbook of Agriculture.*]

MARY W. M. HARGREAVES

ARIKARA. A tribe in the northern Plains, the Arikara are significant because they were river-bottom farmers in an area otherwise devoted to bison hunting and also because they represent the northernmost movement of Caddoan speech. French sources in the 18th century locate them in Nebraska, along with the Pawnee and the Skidi, but Meriwether Lewis and William Clark met them in the western Dakotas in 1804. In the course of their migration northward from the Caddoan focus of the lower Mississippi, the Arikara adopted characteristic Plains traits, although retaining their agricultural inclination. In the 19th century they became associated in North Dakota with the Siouan-speaking Mandan and Hidatsa, Missouri River tribes that probably adopted farming practices from the Arikara. The three tribes are usually linked, not only because of their agriculture but also because the three were assigned the North Dakota Fort Berthold Reservation in the 1880's.

[J. C. Ewers, "Of the Arickaras," *Bulletin of the Missouri Historical Society,* vol. 6 (1950); John R. Swanton, *The Indian Tribes of North America.*]

ROBERT F. SPENCER

ARIZONA, the forty-eighth state, contains three geographic regions—northern plateau; central mountain belt; and dry, southern desert. In each of these regions ancient cultures flourished from ca. 500 B.C. to ca. A.D. 1350 and then mysteriously decayed. The principal groups of inhabitants that emerged later were the Piman peoples (the Pima and the Papago), who lived in the central and southern river valleys, and the Athapascan (the Apache and the Navajo), who roamed the eastern mountain-plateau country. Spaniards from central Mexico entered Arizona at an early date, Fray Marcos de Niza venturing into the eastern mountains in 1539; he was followed a year later by Francisco Vásquez de Coronado, whose captains discovered the Grand Canyon and ascended the Colorado River to Yuma. Exploring west from the Rio

Grande, Antonio de Espejo in 1583 discovered copper and silver deposits in central Arizona; twenty years later Juan de Oñate crossed over Espejo's route and descended the Colorado to its mouth. In the 1630's Franciscans tried to spread Roman Catholicism among the Hopi. In the 1690's the Jesuit missionary Eusebio Kino introduced the faith to the Pima; in the late 1760's, Francisco Garcés, a Franciscan, carried Christianity west to Yuma.

Rich silver discoveries in 1736 at Arizonac ("Small Spring"), a Pima village near present Nogales, drew the first settlers into the region and gave it a name. Spain established its first presidio-town in Arizona at Tubac in 1752 but moved the garrison north to Tucson in December of 1775, to cope with the increasing Apache threat. Beginning in the 1790's Arizona enjoyed nearly twenty years of relative peace. Spanish soldiers collected Apache on reservations (one was at Tucson); mines were discovered; ranches were started; and churches were erected at San Xavier del Bac and San Jose del Tumacácori. In 1821, however, Arizona became a part of Mexico and entered a period of extended neglect.

American fur parties began trapping along the Gila and its tributaries in the late 1820's. During the Mexican War, Gen. Stephen W. Kearny marched from New Mexico along the Gila to California and dispatched the Mormon Battalion through Tucson (occupied on Dec. 16, 1846) to San Diego. By the Treaty of Guadalupe Hidalgo of 1848, Arizona north of the Gila passed to the United States; on Sept. 9, 1850, it became a part of New Mexico Territory; and by the Gadsden Purchase of Dec. 30, 1853, southern Arizona was added to New Mexico. American troops reached Tucson in November of 1856. Army expeditions (1851–58) explored and constructed forts in the region, and federal subsidies promoted stage and steamboat traffic. In the late 1850's mining companies were developing mines near Tubac (silver) and at Ajo (copper); gold placers were discovered near Yuma. By 1856, mining interests in the Tubac-Tucson area were pushing for a separate territory. In the spring of 1862, Confederate troops briefly occupied Tucson but later withdrew with the advance of Union forces from California. Influenced by mining interests, Congress on Feb. 24, 1863, established Arizona Territory (which initially included the southern tip of Nevada). Gold discoveries in the central mountains in the mid-1860's and silver bonanzas a decade later, particularly at Tombstone, spurred population growth. The army forced hostile Indians onto reservations; a cattle industry arose; and transcontinental railroads were built. Large-scale copper mining and commercial irrigation followed. Arizona entered the Union on Feb. 14, 1912.

During the early 20th century the history of Arizona mirrored the impact of two world wars. In 1917–18 copper, cotton, and beef found ready markets, while mining labor unrest resulted in deportations from Jerome and Bisbee. Although the 1920's brought depression, a thriving tourist industry took root. In the following decade federal monies buoyed the local economy. World War II ushered in a new age. The military services established training camps and subsidiary industries, which stimulated a surge in manufacturing. A viable two-party system arose in the late 1950's, the Republicans steadily gaining influence. During the 1960's Arizona enjoyed an unprecedented prosperity from mining (producing nearly 50 percent of the nation's copper), agriculture, manufacturing, and tourism. In 1970 the population was 1,772,482; 50 percent of the inhabitants were concentrated around Phoenix, the state capital.

[University of Arizona Faculty, *Arizona: Its People and Resources;* Rufus K. Wyllys, *Arizona, the History of a Frontier State*.]

HARWOOD P. HINTON

***ARK* AND *DOVE*,** the two vessels that brought the first colonists, about 200 in number, to Maryland. These pioneers left England at the suggestion of and under instruction from Cecil Calvert, to whom, on June 20, 1632, Charles I had granted a charter which conferred proprietary powers and authorized the colonization of the territory in the vicinity of the Chesapeake Bay. Sailing from Cowes, on the Isle of Wight, Nov. 22, 1633, the *Ark* and the *Dove* laid their course to the Chesapeake by way of the Canary Islands and the West Indies. Entering the Potomac during the first week in March 1634, they explored the northern bank of this river until, on March 25, it was finally decided to make the first permanent settlement on a river which empties into the Potomac not very far from its mouth. This settlement was and still is known as St. Marys.

[C. C. Hall, *Narratives of Early Maryland, 1633–1684*.]

RAPHAEL SEMMES

ARKANSAS. First explored by Hernando de Soto in 1541, visited by Jacques Marquette and Louis Jolliet in 1673, and claimed for France by Robert Cavelier, Sieur de La Salle, and Henry de Tonti in 1682, the first permanent settlement, Arkansas Post, was founded in

1686 by Tonti. The name Arkansas was derived from that of the tribe of Indians living along the Arkansas River near its junction with the Mississippi. As a part of Louisiana, Arkansas was a French possession until 1762 and a Spanish possession from 1762 to 1800, when France again acquired it. The region became American territory with the Louisiana Purchase in 1803. A part of Missouri Territory, Arkansas became a separate territory in 1819, after Missouri applied for statehood. The first capital was Arkansas Post, but in 1821 Little Rock became the permanent capital. In 1836, although the move was not authorized by Congress, citizens of Arkansas prepared a constitution and successfully petitioned for statehood.

Two state banks, chartered in 1836, failed in the aftermath of the panic of 1837, leaving the state with a debt of more than $3 million. Meanwhile the southeastern part of Arkansas was settled mostly by slaveholders from the older South, while the northwestern, mountainous part was populated mostly by nonslaveholding farmers. Accordingly the secession crisis of 1860–61 found the state divided. A Unionist-controlled convention in March 1861 defeated a movement for secession but resolved against coercion of the Confederate states and agreed to submit "secession" or "cooperation" to a vote in August. When Abraham Lincoln asked Arkansas for troops after Fort Sumter fell in April, the convention reassembled, voted secession, and put Arkansas into the Confederacy.

By September 1863, the northern half of the state was in Union hands, and early in 1864 a loyal state government was organized at Little Rock under Lincoln's plan of Reconstruction. Congress refused to recognize this government, primarily because it failed to enfranchise black freedmen, and in 1868 set up a new state government that extended full citizenship to blacks. The Republican party controlled the state until 1874, when a division in its ranks permitted the Democratic party, which had ruled Arkansas prior to the Civil War, to return to power and write a new constitution. The Democrats, although hotly opposed by agrarian-labor parties in the 1880's and 1890's, controlled the state until 1966, when a Republican was elected governor for the first time since the Reconstruction era.

The railroad age of the late 19th century opened the rich coal, bauxite, and timber resources of Arkansas to northern industrial exploitation but brought little industry to the state. An extensive, disorganized road-building program between 1900 and 1930 left the state with a heavy bonded indebtedness. Refunded in the 1930's and 1940's, this debt has now been retired.

The 20th century has seen much change in Arkansas. An agriculture based on cotton farming, sharecropping, and mule-drawn implements has given way to a highly diversified, mechanized agriculture in which both the sharecropper and the mule have almost disappeared. The state government is mainly concerned with financing public schools, higher education, public welfare programs, and highways. Much emphasis is also placed on attracting new industry to the state and encouraging tourism. The loss of population that accompanied the agricultural revolution during the 1930's and World War II has been followed by a subsequent steady increase, approaching 20 million in the early 1970's.

[*Arkansas: A Guide to the State;* Walter L. Brown, *Our Arkansas;* John L. Ferguson and J. H. Atkinson, *Historic Arkansas;* David Y. Thomas, ed., *Arkansas and Its People.*]

WALTER L. BROWN

***ARKANSAS*, DESTRUCTION OF THE** (Aug. 5, 1862). After the Confederate ironclad *Arkansas* passed through the federal fleet before Vicksburg to cooperate in Gen. John C. Breckinridge's attempt to recapture Baton Rouge, its machinery became disabled when it was within five miles of its destination. The ship was run ashore and blown up to escape federal capture.

[A. Fortier, *History of Louisiana.*]

WALTER PRICHARD

ARKANSAS POST. When Robert Cavelier, Sieur de La Salle, laid claim to the entire Mississippi Valley for France in 1682, he granted to Henry de Tonti a large concession at the Quapaw villages on the Arkansas River, and in 1686 Tonti established the Arkansas Post as the earliest French settlement in the lower Mississippi Valley. In 1689 Tonti established a Catholic mission at the post, and by 1700 Jean Couture, who was left in command of the post, had developed an extensive trade with the English of Carolina. The subsequent history of the post is obscure until the Western Company took possession of Louisiana in 1718 and John Law sent 700 German colonists to develop his large concession on the Arkansas River. But Law's venture collapsed a few years later, and his colonists abandoned the settlement and located at the "German Coast" (*see* Côte des Allemands) near New Orleans. When French Louisiana was divided into nine districts in 1721, Arkansas Post became the administrative center for the Arkansas District, and in 1722 Benard de la Harpe strengthened the stockade and placed a regular garrison there. Until the end of the French regime in 1762 Arkansas Post remained important as the administrative and commercial center of the extensive Arkansas District and as the site of a Jesuit mission. Following the Civil War, the village declined. In 1960, the Arkansas Post National Memorial was created.

[M. W. Benjamin, "French History of Arkansas," *Publications of the Arkansas Historical Association* (1908); Dallas T. Herndon, ed., *Centennial History of Arkansas;* David Y. Thomas, ed., *Arkansas and Its People: A History, 1541–1930.*]

WALTER PRICHARD

ARKANSAS POST, BATTLE OF. Arkansas Post (Fort Hindman) was fortified by the Confederates for the protection of Little Rock. After the repulse of Union Gen. W. T. Sherman's attack upon Vicksburg (Dec. 29, 1862) it was considered essential to capture the post. Union Gen. John A. McClernand, with 30,000 men backed by Adm. David D. Porter's fleet of ironclads, forced Gen. Thomas J. Churchill to surrender Jan. 11, 1863.

[David Y. Thomas, *Arkansas in War and Reconstruction.*]

DAVID Y. THOMAS

ARKANSAS RIVER. Known to the early French as Rivière des Ark or d'Ozark, the 1,450-mile river derived its name from the Arkansas Indians who lived on its banks. The river was first discovered and explored by Hernando de Soto in 1541 on his journey into the Southwest. The French explorers, Louis Jolliet and Jacques Marquette, reached its mouth in 1673, in their search for a river "coming in from California on the southern sea." The Arkansas Post, established in 1686 by Henry de Tonti, was the first permanent settlement in the Arkansas River region, and the early history of the river centers around the post.

The Arkansas River, to the French, was the highway leading into the Spanish Southwest—Taos and Santa Fe. French traders preferred waterways as highways. The headwaters of the Arkansas were in Spanish territory. The Spanish explorer Uribarri in 1696 called the upper Arkansas Rio Napestle, probably of native Indian origin. This name was applied to the river by the Spanish until the 19th century. The treaty with Spain in 1819 (*see* Adams-Onís Treaty) made the Arkansas River west of the 100th meridian a part of the western boundary of the United States. The name Arkansas, which had applied only to lower reaches of the stream, was carried westward by American traders and trappers and succeeded in replacing the name Rio Napestle, or Napeste.

The Arkansas River was navigable with keelboats as far west as Grand River. In early days "Arkansas" and "Ozark" were used interchangeably and were applied to the Arkansas River, the mountains north of it, and the post near its mouth.

[Anna Lewis, *Along the Arkansas;* A. B. Thomas, *Spanish Exploration of Oklahoma, 1599–1792.*]

ANNA LEWIS

ARKANSAS RIVER, GREAT BEND OF THE, an important landmark on the Santa Fe trail, marking the first point at which the river was encountered, 278 miles from the start of the trail at Independence, Kans., and roughly halfway to Bent's Fort in Colorado, which was 530 miles from Independence. At Walnut Creek, which joined the Arkansas at the apex of the bend, travelers commonly encountered the first fringe of the buffalo herds; and Pawnee Rock, fifteen miles beyond, was regarded as the beginning of the hostile Indian country. One hundred miles from Walnut Creek was the Cimarron Crossing where a shortcut to Santa Fe could be obtained.

[Henry Inman, *The Old Santa Fe Trail.*]

PAUL I. WELLMAN

ARKANSAS RIVER ROUTE, the mountain or Pikes Peak division of the Santa Fe Trail, which avoided the dangerous Jornada desert of the Cimarron cutoff. Instead of turning south at Cimarron Crossing near the present site of Dodge City, this route followed up the Arkansas River to old Bent's Fort near present-day La Junta and there turned southwesterly to the mountains and crossed the difficult Raton Pass. Choice was now open to continue southward rejoining the other trail and going through Las Vegas to Santa Fe, or to proceed westward, past the Maxwell Ranch, along the base of the mountains and over the range to Taos. The trail then followed the Rio Grande down to Santa Fe. The Arkansas River route, though longer, was extensively used because of the importance of Bent's Fort, the trading center of the trappers and Indians; the presence of water; and the demand for freight at the settlements along the way. Also it was the route to the Colorado goldfields in 1858 (*see* Pikes Peak Gold Rush) and later and to Denver-Auraria.

[Henry Inman, *The Old Santa Fe Trail.*]

MALCOLM G. WYER

"ARKANSAS TRAVELER," Arkansas's best-known piece of folklore as well as the favorite of all old-time breakdown fiddle tunes in America. The rollicky dialogue and more rollicky tune go back to the days of Davy Crockett. It was first published in 1847, but neither the author of the dialogue nor the composer of the tune has been determined. Newspapers, books, and articles of commerce have taken the title. As the tradition goes, a stranger traveling in Arkansas comes to a roofless tavern before which the proprietor sits fiddling. "Where does this road go?" asks the stranger. "It's never gone anywhar since I been here," the squatter answers, going on fiddling. Finally, after more such colloquy, the stranger asks, "Why don't you play the rest of that tune?" Immediately the squatter makes the stranger dismount and play. This "turn of the tune" brings forth civil, though still comical, answers, whiskey, food, shelter, and horse provender, a hospitality having all the gusto of a country hoedown.

[Fred W. Allsopp, *Folklore of Romantic Arkansas*, vol. II.]

J. FRANK DOBIE

ARKS (also known as flatboats, broadhorns, Kentucky or Orleans boats). These craft until 1860 carried a large part of the downstream traffic on the rivers of the West. They were cheaply constructed of green wood, shaped like boxes with raked bows, roofed over in whole or in part, and were sold for lumber or firewood at their destinations. They were steered by a long oar, and two or more sweeps, or broadhorns, were used to move them into or out of the current. Three to five men constituted the crew. They averaged about fifteen by fifty feet and held forty to fifty tons of flour.

[Leland D. Baldwin, *The Keelboat Age on Western Waters*.]

LELAND D. BALDWIN

ARKWRIGHT MACHINERY, a spinning machine developed, rather than invented, by Richard Arkwright in England about 1770. It was a marked improvement over earlier forms of spinning machines. The English government prohibited the exportation of machines or drawings, but a young immigrant, Samuel Slater, carried the idea to Providence, R.I., and under his direction William Almy and Moses Brown constructed a set of Arkwright machines carrying seventy-two spindles. These were installed in 1790 in a small building at Pawtucket, introducing the modern factory to this country. The building is now the Slater Museum which displays the still operable original equipment.

[Dexter S. Kimball, *Principles of Industrial Organization*.]

DEXTER S. KIMBALL

ARLINGTON NATIONAL CEMETERY, on the Virginia bank of the Potomac River, directly opposite Washington, D.C. Originally part of the estate of George Washington, it passed to his adopted son, G. W. Parke Custis. In 1831 Robert E. Lee married Mary Ann Custis, and she inherited a life interest in the estate from her father, which after her death was to go to her eldest son, G. W. Custis Lee.

Upon the outbreak of the Civil War, the estate was seized by the United States, which acquired an alleged tax title, built a fort and hospital on the site, and used the grounds as a cemetery. In 1882, after suit which reached the Supreme Court, G. W. Custis Lee was declared the legal owner of the property. The government acquired the land by paying Custis Lee $150,000 indemnity.

The estate has become the site of one of the most important shrines maintained by the United States. In the cemetery are buried the dead of every war since the Revolution, and distinguished statesmen, including President John F. Kennedy. Arlington House has been restored and a Memorial Amphitheater erected. The Tomb of the Unknowns (known until 1958 as the Tomb of the Unknown Soldier) commemorates the dead of the two world wars and the Korean War.

[John V. Hinkle, *Arlington: Monument to Heroes*.]

L. C. HELDERMAN

ARMAMENTS. *See* **Defense, National.**

ARMED MERCHANTMAN. *See* **Merchantmen, Armed.**

ARMED NEUTRALITY OF 1780, a declaration by Catherine II, Empress of Russia, who desired to free neutral trade from the interference of belligerents. Her declaration sought to overturn the Rule of the War of 1756 and secure for neutrals the freedom of navigation even to the ports of belligerents; it restricted the category of contraband to munitions and the essential instruments of war; it asserted as an established rule of international law the principle that free ships make free goods and set forth a new theory of blockade. The declaration was followed by the arming of the neutrals of northern Europe to protect their commerce in accordance with the principles to which they had subscribed.

The United States, on Oct. 5, 1780, accepted unreservedly the rules of the armed neutrality declaration as a basis for its instructions to the commanders of its armed vessels. This action by Congress was intended to pave the way for the United States to become a party to the League of Neutrals. Francis Dana was appointed minister to Russia to secure the twin objectives of recognition of the independence of the United States and its admission "as a party to the convention for maintaining the freedom of the seas." His mission was in vain. The United States could not, while a belligerent, become a party to the armed neutrality, and Catherine II refused to receive Dana as long as the independence of the colonies was not recognized by Great Britain. The Definitive Treaty of Peace in 1783 altered the situation, and the primary object of the mission to Russia was removed. James Madison pointed out that, although Congress approved the principles of the armed neutrality, it would be "unwise to become a party to a confederacy which might thereafter complicate the interests of the United States with the politics of Europe." Congress finally resolved (June 12, 1783) upon a clear distinction between the principles of the armed neutrality and a confederation for their enforcement. That the United States should have escaped from participation in a confederacy of this sort was fortunate. All the members of the armed neutrality abandoned, upon the very next opportunity of their becoming belligerents, the creed which they had sought to enforce by arms when they were neutrals. Whatever advantage might have been gained for American commerce by membership in the league would not have compensated for the political embarrassments of such an alliance.

[W. S. Carpenter, "The United States and the League of Neutrals of 1780," *American Journal of International Law,* vol. 15.]

WILLIAM S. CARPENTER

ARMIES, DISBANDING OF THE. *See* **Demobilization.**

"ARM IN ARM" CONVENTION. *See* **National Union "Arm in Arm" Convention.**

ARMINIANISM, the Reformed theology which arose in opposition to the prevailing Calvinism, and received its name from Jacobus Arminius (1560–1609), a mild and liberal-spirited Dutch theologian. It places chief emphasis upon man's freedom and holds that God's sovereignty is so exercised as to be cooperable with the freedom of man. Introduced into America in the early 18th century, its influence spread rapidly in spite of able opposition. Those who accepted it became the advocates of a larger tolerance. On the frontier it made even more rapid headway than elsewhere, since it emphasized the natural human duties, rather than speculative theology, and the equality of all men in the sight of God, rather than limited grace and the possibility of salvation only for the few, which was the Calvinistic position.

[G. L. Curtiss, *Arminianism in History.*]

WILLIAM W. SWEET

ARMISTICE OF NOV. 11, 1918. On Oct. 4, 1918, the German government appealed to President Woodrow Wilson for an armistice with a view to peace on the basis of the Fourteen Points. As a prerequisite, Wilson insisted on the practical democratization of the German government and hinted openly at the abdication of Kaiser William II. Gen. John Pershing, the American commander in France, wished to continue the war until Germany was thoroughly beaten, but the Allied commanders, including Marshal Ferdinand Foch, agreed to an armistice and Wilson accepted this view. On Nov. 5, the United States notified Germany that the Fourteen Points were accepted as the basis of peace, subject to two reservations: (1) the freedom of the seas was not to be discussed at that time; (2) Germany must make reparation for the damage done to the property of Allied nationals during the war. The terms of armistice were communicated to Germany on Nov. 8 and signed on Nov. 11 at 5 A.M., to take effect at 11 A.M. Germany had to evacuate all territory west of the Rhine, which was to be occupied by Allied troops; a neutral zone was established ten kilometers east of the Rhine. Germany surrendered large quantities of artillery, machine guns, airplanes, motor trucks, and railway rolling stock, as well as most of its navy: it was made impossible for Germany to resume fighting. It had also to renounce the treaties of Brest-Litovsk and Bucharest and to withdraw its troops from Russia, Rumania, and Turkey. The blockade was to continue until peace was made, and a blanket financial reservation was added that "any future claims and demands of the Allies and the United States of America remain unaffected." The armistice was for one month and was renewed from time to time until peace was signed in 1919.

[Charles Seymour, *American Diplomacy During the World War*.]

BERNADOTTE E. SCHMITT

ARMORED VEHICLES. The efforts of soldiers throughout history to protect themselves while delivering decisive blows to the enemy have been manifest since World War I in the development of armored fighting vehicles and the concomitant development of tactics and the organization of armored units. Although Americans have learned much from Europeans in this military endeavor, many of the early developments took place in the U.S. Army.

In 1915 and 1916 the British developed armored tracked vehicles to assist their infantry in breaking the stalemate on the western front. Initially called caterpillar machine-gun destroyers, after the American-built caterpillar tractor, these vehicles soon came to be known as tanks. Originally, advancing with the infantry, they were used to make paths through the barbed wire that protected the enemy trenches and, with their guns, to engage and destroy the enemy machine guns. When the United States entered the war in April 1917, tanks had achieved only limited success. Nevertheless, the American Expeditionary Forces (AEF) in France turned to the British and French for equipment and for ideas on tank corps organization and tank tactics.

Only three American tank battalions saw combat in World War I. One battalion, equipped with British-made heavy tanks, supported American troops in an attack on the Hindenburg Line in late September 1918. During that fall two other battalions, equipped with French-made light tanks and commanded by Col. George S. Patton, participated in the two major offensives of the AEF, Saint-Mihiel and the Meuse-Argonne. American tanks played a role in the success of these operations despite poor cooperation with the infantry, numerous mechanical breakdowns, heavy casualties, and an inability to operate in difficult terrain. Tanks were assured a role in the postwar U.S. Army by these small successes, the more spectacular successes of British tanks at Cambrai in 1917 and at Amiens in 1918, and the planning for the expected 1919 offensive, which envisioned the operation of tanks beyond the range of infantry and striking the enemy's rear areas—not merely assaulting its trenches.

The National Defense Act of 1920 disbanded the wartime American tank corps and relegated tactical and organizational control of tanks to the infantry. Although official doctrine stressed the use of tanks only in close support of infantry, the development of faster vehicles, able to operate beyond the range of infantry, suggested a more independent role for tank units. In 1927 Secretary of War Dwight Davis witnessed the maneuvers of a British experimental mechanized force. When he returned to the United States, he ordered the army to organize a similar unit to test tanks, armored cars, self-propelled artillery, and auxiliary vehicles operating as an independent, self-sufficient force and including troops from all branches of the service. Davis wanted the force to develop adequate equipment and proper doctrine before the army organized additional tank units. Based on the performance of the U.S. experimental force, in 1930 the army created a permanent mechanized force for missions requiring great tactical and strategic mobility.

But within a year Gen. Douglas MacArthur, then army chief of staff, disbanded the mechanized force, revised the army's mechanization policy, and ordered all branches to use armored, mechanized vehicles as far as practical. The infantry kept its tanks for close support. The cavalry began employing armored vehicles to carry out its traditional missions of reconnaissance, pursuit, and exploitation. In early 1933 the army organized a mechanized cavalry regiment, expanded to brigade size in 1936, at Fort Knox, Ky. The regiment tested prototypes of new, faster tanks; developed tactics to exploit the mobility, firepower, and shock effect of armored vehicles; and organized flexible units composed of troops of all arms of the service capable of self-sustained action over a period of time.

During the 1930's Col. Adna R. Chaffee, foremost among mechanized cavalry leaders, developed a tactical doctrine assigning independent roles to mechanized units and thus expanded the dimensions of armored warfare. Although the cavalry emphasis on mobility and mounted combat remained, the tactical doctrine of mechanized cavalry gradually changed. To increase self-sufficiency, the army added motorized infantry, engineers, artillery, and other support units to the mechanized cavalry, and it became, in effect, a new force that combined elements of all the traditional arms of the service. Although it existed de facto, the institutionalization, and expansion, of this new force was opposed by the infantry and the cavalry, and it took graphic examples of the power of mechanized forces to overcome their opposition to expanding the existing tank and mechanized units.

In 1939 and 1940 the impetus for change and expansion in American armored organizations came from several sources. German panzer forces in the invasions of Poland and France demonstrated the offensive power of combined arms built around armored fighting vehicles. U.S. Army maneuvers in Louisiana confirmed the German experience. The beginning of World War II in Europe also improved the American political climate for expanding the army in general and new, modern units in particular. Gen. George C. Marshall, army chief of staff, ordered a separate armored force organized on July 10, 1940, and all mechanized cavalry and infantry tank units were combined into this force to form two armored divisions.

The U.S. Army's two original armored divisions had a preponderance of tanks in relation to infantry or artillery. Experience in maneuvers during 1941 and 1942 necessitated organizational changes. Additional infantry, transported in armored half-tracks, and self-propelled artillery improved the fighting power of the armored division. The most significant feature of the new divisional organization was the introduction of two tactical headquarters, Combat Commands A and B; each could assume command of any combination of the units organic to the division, giving the division commander great flexibility in deploying his forces. For instance, Combat Command A could use all the divisional infantry as a holding force against an enemy's front while Combat Command B employed all the tank battalions to strike the enemy flank. In another situation the combat commands, using equal forces, could support one another in a leapfrog action. A third, or reserve, combat command headquarters was added to all armored divisions in 1943, further improving their flexibility.

Also during 1943 overall control for armored development passed from the armored force to the commanding general of the army ground forces, Lt. Gen. Lesley J. McNair. Unlike the armored force leaders who envisioned divisions, corps, and field armies organized as armored units capable of striking deep into the enemy's rear, McNair wanted a more limited role for armor. He believed armor was chiefly a weapon of exploitation to be used as cavalry: only after the infantry broke the enemy's front would armor be unleashed to extend the break and mop up already disrupted defenses; tanks, artillery, and tactical air power would support the infantry in achieving the breakthrough; artillery, air power, and infantry would assist the tanks in the exploitation phase. But in McNair's view there would be few independent missions for armor. He emphasized that point by increasing the number of tank battalions and tank destroyer battalions providing immediate support for infantry divisions. By 1945 there were 128 such battalions, while there were only 50 tank battalions among the independent armored divisions. McNair also reduced the number of armored divisions from the approximately 50 proposed by the armored force early in the war to 16 actually organized. These 16 divisions, moreover, were not to be used in separate corps but were combined with infantry divisions under the tactical control of corps, army, and army group commanders in the field.

American armor saw action in every theater during World War II, usually performing the exploitation role that McNair had envisioned. Armored divisions were most successful in this respect following the Normandy invasion. After infantry, artillery, and air power broke the German defenses at Saint-Lô in July 1944, armored divisions exploited the break and led American armies across France. American armored divisions in North Africa and Italy demonstrated an ability to fight in terrain previously thought unsuitable for tanks. Although no armored divisions served in the Pacific, tank battalions and armored landing vehicles provided essential close support for the infantry during the island-hopping campaigns in that theater. When required, as in the Battle of the Bulge, armor fought effectively in a defensive role and was capable of heavy, sustained combat, as it demonstrated during the final campaign in Germany. Armor made a significant contribution to the Allied victory in World War II and was largely responsible for preventing a return to the tactical stalemate that had characterized the western front in World War I.

After 1945 American armored tactics and organization remained much the same as during the war. Although the divisions included more men and equipment, they retained a flexible command structure similar to that of the wartime combat commands. On the tactical level, tank battalions provided close support for American infantry divisions in Korea. In Vietnam an armored cavalry regiment, as well as tank battalions, performed the same support function. Armored divisions were not used in the Korean and Vietnam conflicts, but they remained the bulwark of the American ground deterrent in Europe. Even in the 1970's the U.S. Army considered the plains of western and central Europe a likely theater for a war of large-scale tank battles similar to those fought there thirty years before.

Technological advances—such as rocket-propelled grenades, antitank missiles, and rocket-firing helicopters—may necessitate changes in tank tactics and design. Thicker armor to protect crews and more widely dispersed tactical formations could be necessary in the face of the new antitank weaponry, but armor is likely to remain a mobile, decisive element in ground combat.

[Mildred Gillie, *Forging the Thunderbolt;* Kenneth Macksey, *Tank Warfare;* Richard Ogorkiewicz, *Armor*.]

TIMOTHY K. NENNINGER

ARMOR PLATE. Credit for the first proposal for an iron-plated ship belongs to Col. John Stevens of Hoboken, N.J., who, early in the War of 1812, designed a floating battery protected with iron plates. In 1820 Stevens fired thirty-two-pound shot at seventy yards without damage against targets protected with iron one-half inch thick, and in July 1841 his sons, Edwin A. and Robert L. Stevens, fired sixty-four-pound solid shot at thirty yards without damage against targets protected with wrought-iron boiler plates riveted together to four and one-half inches thickness. Steel supplanted wrought iron for armor plate in 1876, the first all-steel plates being made at Creusot, France. The Creusot process was brought to the United States in 1887 by the Bethlehem Steel Company. In 1890 tests at Annapolis proved definitely the superiority of steel over compound (wrought iron faced with steel) plates. In 1891 the Harvey process increased the resistance of steel by nearly 50 percent, but was supplanted by the Krupp process in 1900.

[J. P. Baxter, *Introduction of the Iron-Clad Warship;* William Hovgaard, *Modern History of Warships*.]

LOUIS H. BOLANDER

ARMS RACE WITH THE SOVIET UNION. The United States began a rapid postwar demobilization when Japan surrendered at the end of World War II. The 1945 war machine, with 12,123,444 men under arms, dropped in a year to 3,030,088—a number halved in 1947 to a norm of 1,583,000. Although there were U.S. government leaders who saw that Soviet-style totalitarianism was flourishing wherever Joseph Stalin's troops had advanced into Europe, the new threat was only slowly recognized by an American public sated with war, serene in sole possession of atomic bombs, and beguiled by the propaganda image of a kindly "Uncle Joe" Stalin. To many, President Harry Truman seemed alarmist in obtaining, in March 1947, legislation for aid to Greece and Turkey, which effectively stopped Communist takeovers. However, apologists for Stalin were largely silenced by his June 1948 attempt to squeeze the United States, Britain, and France out of Berlin, foiled by the ingenuity of the Berlin airlift. An anti-Communist reaction began, intensified by the 1949 Communist victory in China and the explosion of the Soviet Union's first atomic bomb. Thenceforward a congressional majority was assured for passage of any major legislation intended to arrest the spread of Communism.

In January 1950 Truman funded research to develop hydrogen bombs, meeting success in November 1952, a bare nine months before the Russians—and against the backdrop of the Korean conflict. By his April 1951 dismissal of Gen. Douglas MacArthur, Truman plainly signaled the continuance of U.S. moderation; but Stalin was implacable. Truman therefore accepted a policy of "containment" and in February 1952 welcomed the foundation of the North Atlantic Treaty Organization, establishing a European army of fifty divisions. Uneasiness in the American electorate contributed to the 1952 election of Gen. Dwight D. Eisenhower to the presidency. Two months after his inauguration, however, hopes soared upon the sudden death of Stalin—and fell when Stalin's successors relentlessly continued the drive for military primacy.

During the period immediately after the Korean conflict U.S. defense rested on improving the air power of the strategic bomber force and aircraft-carrier navy developed during World War II, neither seriously rivaled by the Soviet Union, whose strength was in a huge, tank-centered army. Owing to the persistence of Rear Adm. Hyman C. Rickover, the U.S. Navy made a quantum jump in submarines by the harnessing of atomic energy, shown in the January 1954 unveiling of the *Nautilus*. But the Soviet Union took another road in the race for primacy. Having in 1945 overrun the Nazi rocket development center at Peenemünde, Soviets made good use of German engineering to astonish the world in August 1957 by demonstrating a 4,000-mile intercontinental ballistic missile (ICBM) as the follow-up to World War II V-2 rockets, realizing Hitler's dream of being able to bombard the U.S. mainland. This achievement was technologically dwarfed in October of the same year, when the Soviets sent into orbit the first artificial satellite, Sputnik.

A contest then began to perfect rockets for lofting nuclear warheads from one continent to another—across mountain, ocean, any barrier to any distance—at supersonic speeds, compressing into mere minutes the flight times between Moscow and Washington. In sheer size and payload of missiles, the Soviets maintained their early lead, while U.S. engineers used superior miniaturization to obtain greater sophistication and accuracy. For the United States the first advantage stemmed from the July 1960 launch of a missile from the submerged *George Washington,* the original Polaris nuclear-powered submarine.

In October 1962 the world teetered toward holocaust after U.S. aerial surveillance of Cuba uncovered the presence of Russian medium-range weapons that could reach northward as far as Detroit. President John F. Kennedy's firm stand and his naval quarantine of Cuba compelled the withdrawal of the missiles. Such triumph as there may have been for the United States in this encounter vanished in the subsequent steady buildup of a new Soviet navy, displaying the Kremlin's resolve never again to be faced down by a quarantine. The naval competition imposed yet another huge burden upon taxpayers, as the Soviets developed their own Polaris submarines and the requisite covering ships.

During these developments and despite the pre-World War II failures of all solemn treaties to limit arms, American presidents repeatedly tried to control the burgeoning atomic arms race. In November 1948 Truman tried for controls through the fledgling United Nations, only to be foiled by the Soviet Union. Soviet persistence in seeking atomic weapons was matched by U.S. efforts to control them. Eisenhower was apparently successful in October 1958, when the Soviet Union was finally persuaded to sit with the United States and Britain at Geneva to work out a treaty to outlaw nuclear testing. To display good will, Eisenhower suspended U.S. testing and Soviet Premier Nikita Khrushchev ostentatiously agreed to a moratorium. The talks, however, were futile because of Soviet intransigence over inspection methods to ensure future compliance. Khrushchev was buying time to gain secret momentum for a series of tests, in September 1961, of more than forty bombs, climaxed by the detonation in the polar sky of an unprecedented 50-megaton hydrogen bomb. Khrushchev gloated that a 100-megaton bomb was in the Soviet arsenal. Notwithstanding such bad faith, Kennedy persisted in trying to reach an agreement upon effective controls. His credibility attested by the Cuban missile crisis, Kennedy, in July 1963, brought about with the Soviet Union and Britain an agreement banning every type of test except underground tests.

This vital, if partial, success owed much to enormous advances in reconnaissance by orbiting satellites, which could substitute for on-site inspectors. For the Soviet Union, perhaps the dominant motive was to take a giant step toward nonproliferation of nuclear weapons, inasmuch as a hundred nations accepted the invitation to subscribe to the treaty. Communist China did not, however. In October 1964 China also had "the bomb," and the strange Sino-Soviet dispute suddenly had genocidal teeth. Ironically it was the Soviet Union that had set for China the precedent of refusal to guarantee mankind a future by making nuclear war impossible. China would agree to no limitation. In the Strategic Arms Limitation Talks (SALT) with the Soviet Union, the United States tacitly acknowledged the Soviet Union's worry over China—a worry that was rooted in the historic enslavement of Russia for 257 years by Batu Khan and the Mongols. The U.S.–Soviet SALT-1 treaty of May 26, 1972, found the United States agreeing to a five-year freeze on production of weapons, which superficially gave the Soviet Union some superiority—enough, it was hoped, to deter China while keeping a stand-off mutual deterrence with the United States. Then, in November 1974, President Gerald R. Ford and Leonid Brezhnev in furtherance of "détente" signed an agreement at Vladivostok. Ostensibly defining "nuclear parity," the agreement raised weapons levels. Some critics thought that the terms heavily favored the USSR, and alarm about the Soviet threat persisted.

[Ernest M. Eller, *The Soviet Sea Challenge;* Raymond L. Garthoff, *Soviet Strategy in the Nuclear Age;* Malcolm Mackintosh, *Juggernaut;* Abdul A. Said, ed., *America's World Role in the 1970's.*]

R. W. Daly

ARMSTRONG, FORT, one of a chain of frontier defenses erected after the War of 1812. It was located at the foot of Rock Island, in the Mississippi River, five miles from the principal Sauk and Fox village on Rock River, Ill. Of stone and timber construction, 300 feet square, the building commenced in May 1816 and was completed the following year. The fort was garrisoned until 1836, usually by two companies of U.S. regulars.

[D. W. Flagler, *History of the Rock Island Arsenal.*]

Paul M. Angle

ARMY, CONFEDERATE, officially, the Army of the Confederate States of America, was the small regular force established by an act of the Confederate Provisional Congress on Mar. 6, 1861, to consist of one corps of engineers, one of artillery, six regiments of infantry, one of cavalry, and four staff departments (adjutant and inspector general's, quartermaster general's, subsistence, and medical). This force, incompletely organized when war began, was soon overshadowed by the volunteer forces known officially as the provisional army. Other acts of Feb. 28 and Mar. 6 authorized the president to assume control over military operations, to accept state forces and 100,000 volunteers for twelve months. By the end of April President Jefferson Davis had called for 82,000 men. On May 8 the Confederate congress authorized enlistments for the war and on Aug. 8, four more states having joined the Confederacy, 400,000 volunteers for one or three years' service. After the passage of the first conscription act in April 1862, men were taken into the provisional army directly without the necessary aid of the state authorities.

The highest office in the regular army was that of brigadier general until congress, May 16, 1861, established the rank of general in order to give higher Confederate commanders control over major generals of state troops in the field. On Aug. 31 Davis nominated and the congress confirmed Samuel Cooper, Albert Sidney Johnston, Robert E. Lee, Joseph E. Johnston, and G. T. Beauregard as generals of the regular army. On April 12, 1862, Braxton Bragg became a general in that army, and in May 1864 E. Kirby Smith became a general in the provisional army. Major generals in the provisional army, under the act of Feb. 28, 1861, were first appointed in May of that year. In September 1862 the rank of lieutenant general in the provisional army was created.

Serious difficulties were encountered in arming, clothing, and feeding the troops. Most of the arms available in May 1861 were obsolete or inferior, and even these could not supply all the men. There was little powder. Only one foundry could cast cannon, and only one small powder mill was in operation. The chief reliance for improved arms was in purchases abroad, but getting them through the Union blockade was a slow, risky, and expensive process. The Confederate government made contracts with private firms for arms and set up its own arsenals and powder mills. Shoes, clothing, and blankets were hard to procure, for wool and leather were scarce and importations did not fill requirements. Food supplies, much more plentiful in the South, were often reduced by weak transportation facilities. By 1863 horses and mules had become scarce, thus reducing the mobility of the cavalry, artillery, and baggage trains. Although the Confederate soldier was often poorly armed, clothed, and fed, discipline in the larger armies was good and morale high until near the end.

The Confederacy was divided into military departments, fluctuating in number and extent, under commanders responsible only to the war department and the president. Prompt coordination between these departments was often lacking. Other than President Davis himself, there was no commander in chief until Lee was appointed on Feb. 6, 1865, although Lee had been Davis' military adviser for a short time early in 1862 and Braxton Bragg from February to October in 1864.

Because of incomplete surviving records the number of enlistments in the Confederate armies has long been in dispute. Southern writers have estimated them at from 600,000 to 800,000 men, some northern students at from 1,100,000 to 1,500,000. This last figure is obviously too high for a white population of about 5,000,000. The U.S. census for 1860 indicates approximately 1,100,000 men of military age in the seceded states, but these figures are deceptive. Many sections where hostility to the Confederacy developed furnished few soldiers; other large areas were soon overrun by the Union armies. Apparently more men from the seceded states went into the Union Army than came to the Confederate colors from the nonseceding slave states. Exemptions, details for industrial work, and other evasions of service cut down enlistments. Probably between 800,000 and 900,000 actually enrolled, but so many were never in service at any given date. Consolidated returns in the war department showed

	Total present and absent	*Total present*	*Total effective present for duty*
Dec. 31, 1862	449,439	304,015	253,208
Dec. 31, 1863	464,646	277,970	233,586
Dec. 31, 1864	400,787	196,016	154,910

Liberal allowances for scattered commands not reported and for irregular organizations would not bring the total enrolled to more than 600,000 at any of these dates. The state militia, serving short terms, uncertain in number and of dubious value, probably fell short of 100,000 at any given date. Losses from battle, disease, capture, and desertion so reduced the numbers with the colors that only 174,223 surrendered in April and May of 1865.

[*War of the Rebellion: Official Records of the Union and Confederate Armies;* T. L. Livermore, *Numbers and Losses in the Civil War in America, 1861–65;* R. H. McKim, *The Numerical Strength of the Confederate Army.*]

CHARLES W. RAMSDELL

ARMY, UNION. When Fort Sumter was fired on, the United States had an army barely exceeding 16,000 enlisted men and officers, and the effectiveness of this organization was soon lessened by the resignations of Robert E. Lee and other southern officers. Northern states were feverishly passing laws for the raising, equipping, and training of volunteers for three years of the war. By April 1861, the governors had offered some 300,000 such troops to the federal government. Although determined to restore the Union by force, President Abraham Lincoln would not assemble Congress before July 4. Without new legislation there was no authority for an increase in the army, so all the recruiting fervor of the early spring was wasted.

The 75,000-man militia, called for on April 15, could be used for only three months, the term of enlistment, and hence was rushed into battle at Bull Run in a futile effort to show the strength of the Union. The defeat at Bull Run finally aroused federal activity as it had not been stirred by the earlier agitation in the states. On July 22, 1861, and following, Congress authorized the creation of a volunteer army of 500,000 men and legalized the president's call of May 3 for 42,000 three-year volunteers and 22,700 regulars. The regular army at an authorized strength of 42,000, which was halfway approximated, was used throughout the war for border defense against the Indians. The volunteer army, with which the war was fought, was officered mainly by political generals chosen by the governors, and in the early months, at least, by regimental officers elected by the enlisted men. The result was a needlessly slow development of discipline and efficiency. Also, the competition of state governments with the War Department in bidding for uniforms, munitions, food, and supplies led to a scandalous series of contract grafts, high prices, and shoddy products.

The volunteering spirit so cooled off after Bull Run that the remainder of 1861 had passed before an acceptable army could be whipped into rudimentary shape. By the middle of 1862 the first army had been so badly depleted by disease and battle that on July 2 an additional 300,000 volunteers were called for, the governors again being left to care for recruiting and management of the new contingents until they were mustered into service. The troops were urgently needed, and on Aug. 4, when volunteering proved sluggish, a draft of a 300,000-man nine months' militia was ordered under terms of an act of July 17, 1862. As a direct means of getting soldiers this draft proved a failure, only about 65,000 men being provided. But federal, state, and local bounties lured enough volunteers during the next few months to tide over the emergency.

Early in 1863 it was seen that continued heavy casualties, desertions, the expiration of short-term enlistments, and scanty volunteering were likely to cause a collapse of the army before the close of the year. Consequently, the Enrollment Act of Mar. 3, 1863, was passed to provide men by draft. The act was intended mainly to stimulate volunteering by threat of conscription, thus encouraging the states and localities to avoid this stigma by the offering of adequate bounties. Men of means were given an easy escape from the draft by the payment of a $300 commutation fee or the hiring of substitutes. By a later amendment the commutation fee was limited to conscientious objectors, but substitution was permitted until the end of the war. The direct product of two years of repeated drafting was about 50,000 conscripts and 120,000 substitutes. But in the same period over a million volunteers were procured by bounties. Thus for the last half of the war the army was relieved from the constant danger of extinction which had threatened the first half.

The total effective strength of the army on Jan. 1, 1863, before federal conscription was begun, was just under 700,000. On May 1, 1865, at its highest point, the number was nearly 800,000. Including all men not fit for active service, each of these figures would be increased by about 200,000. The commissioning of 2,537 generals alone (including brevet brigadiers) for an army of this size may be taken as an indication of the part spoilsman politics played in army organization. Nevertheless, after the first year the weeding out of incapable officers in high positions went on apace, proved capacity began to replace political favoritism and regimental elections for minor officers, and a tolerable degree of discipline was evolved. Contract grafts continued to lessen the efficiency of the army, but in a diminishing degree. An obtuse policy of the War Department prevented the supplying of the soldiers with modern weapons, which were available to the Union but not to the Confederacy, thus further restricting military efficiency.

[F. A. Shannon, *The Organization and Administration of the Union Army, 1861–1865.*]

FRED A. SHANNON

ARMY, UNITED STATES. *This article discusses the U.S. Army under the following headings:* Revolutionary War (1775–82); War of 1812; Establishment of a Peacetime Army (1815–45); Mexican War (1846–48); Civil War (1861–65); Post–Civil War Period (1866–98); Spanish-American War (1898) and Subsequent Reforms; World War I (1917–18) and

Postwar Years; World War II (1940–45); Since 1945; Peacetime Work; Army Aviation; Army General Staff; Insignia of Rank; Army Logistics; Army Posts; Army School System; Army War College; Army Hospitals.

The United States Army has traditionally consisted of a small professional force, the Regular Army, augmented in wartime by citizen soldiers—militia, National Guard, Organized Reserve, volunteers, or draftees. The army of today is the lineal descendant of the Continental army of the American Revolution, the first American national military organization. Its antecedents go back to the colonial period, when each of the colonies had militia laws requiring military service from every able-bodied male and recruited volunteer forces mainly from this militia base for protracted campaigns, such as those of the French and Indian War.

Revolutionary War (1775–82). The accepted birthdate of the U.S. Army is June 14, 1775, the day the Second Continental Congress appointed a committee to draw up rules and regulations to govern the New England army that had gathered near Boston and also voted to enlist ten rifle companies from colonies to the south as a reinforcement directly in the Continental service. The next day Congress selected George Washington to be commander in chief. This first national army, formed by Washington in 1775, became "Continental in every respect" on Jan. 1, 1776, with about 8,000 men enlisted to the end of the year, in contrast to the 20,000 men in twenty-six battalions Congress had authorized. In October 1776 Congress voted a new and larger establishment—to contain eighty-eight battalions of infantry, about 60,000 men, enlisted to serve for three years or "during the present war." Each of the states was assigned a quota in proportion to its population, and each of the battalions (or regiments, for the terms were practically synonymous) was given a numbered designation in that state's line. In December 1776 Congress voted twenty-two additional battalions to be recruited directly by Washington's officers into the Continental service.

These 110 battalions, or roughly 75,000 men, remained the authorized strength of the Continental army until 1781, when Congress, recognizing its inability to raise or support this number of battalions, reduced it to 59. It seems doubtful that there were ever more than 30,000 men in the Continental service at any one time, despite bounties for enlistment and the limited application of a draft. In order to maintain sufficient numbers in the field, Congress and Washington had constantly to call on the states for short-term militia; and the Continental army, in practice, was always a mixed force of militia and Continentals.

Despite the fact that it suffered from inadequate numbers and constant shortages of supplies, the Continental army matured as a military organization during the course of the war. It was composed mainly of infantry and artillery, with a small contingent of cavalry, a small corps of engineers, and an even smaller contingent of artificers to service and repair ordnance. It adopted an English system of staff and line organization and a system of drill introduced by the Prussian Gen. Friedrich Von Steuben, at Valley Forge. Steuben's "Blue Book" of drill regulations left its permanent mark on the 19th-century army.

At the end of the Revolution the Continental army was almost entirely disbanded, reaching its nadir of eighty men guarding stores at West Point and Fort Pitt in 1784. The need for protection of the frontiers led to some modest augmentation, but the new government under the Constitution inherited an army of only 718 officers and men from the Confederation. The Constitution gave Congress power to raise an army and to levy taxes to support it and designated the president as commander in chief. The War Department, charged with administering the army, was one of the first four cabinet departments established by Washington. Washington believed that a small regular army was necessary, backed by a "well regulated" citizens' militia for war or emergency. His doctrine became the nation's basic military policy in its formative years, although the well-regulated militia never became a reality. The small regular establishment, ranging between 2,000 and 4,000 men in the 1790's, proved its worth when Gen. Anthony Wayne achieved a decisive victory over the Northwest Indians at Fallen Timbers in 1794 after earlier efforts with ill-trained troops had failed. Thus began a task of policing the frontier that was to absorb most of the Regular Army's energies for a century afterwards.

War of 1812. During the troubled years leading to the War of 1812, the Regular Army was expanded to about 6,000–7,000 officers and men, and during the war the authorization was increased to 62,274. But, as in the Revolution, recruitment fell short, and the regulars numbered only slightly more than 38,000 in 1814. Perhaps an equal number was recruited in volunteer units raised by the states for the federal service, and larger numbers yet served as short-term militia for periods from a few weeks to a few months. Many of the same problems plagued the army of the

War of 1812 as had afflicted the Continental army thirty years before. Leadership was at first incompetent, both in the field and at the seat of government; and the performance of regulars, volunteers, and militia alike was poor. The emergence of leaders who insisted on high standards of training and discipline—including Winfield Scott, Jacob Brown, and Andrew Jackson—produced much improvement by 1815. And lessons learned in the war—among them, that masses of untrained militia were a weak reed on which to rely—played a major role in developing greater military competence in the postwar army.

Establishment of a Peacetime Army (1815–45). In the wake of the War of 1812 the Regular Army developed the professionalism and efficient administration it had largely lacked during the war. John C. Calhoun, as secretary of war between 1817 and 1825, established an administrative structure that was to endure in its essentials until after the Spanish-American War. It consisted of a group of War Department bureaus responsible for supply and administration throughout the army, territorial departments and divisions under their respective commanders, and a commanding general of the army responsible for directing operations. Calhoun also had the army regulations refined and standardized and supported the work of Sylvanus Thayer, who made the U.S. Military Academy at West Point a vital force in creating a corps of professionally trained officers.

The Regular Army was, nevertheless, kept quite small for the tasks it was assigned, which included policing the western and northern frontiers, a long war with the Seminole in Florida, and the establishment and manning of coastal fortifications. Standing at more than 10,000 in 1820, it was precipitately reduced by almost half in that year and maintained until 1835 at a strength of between 5,000 and 7,000 officers and men. There were temporary increases to between 10,000 and 12,000 between 1837 and 1842, because of troubles on the Canadian border, but on the eve of the Mexican War the army's strength stood at about 8,500 officers and men.

Mexican War (1846–48). The Regular Army underwent only limited expansion during the Mexican War, mainly through the filling up of understrength companies. The major portion of new troops were recruited as volunteers by the various states and were organized in accordance with their militia laws. Some ordinary militia were called up in the early stages of the war, but most militia units were soon dismissed and played little part in a war fought outside the borders of the country. The army expanded to a peak strength of around 50,000—regulars and volunteers—during the course of the war and demonstrated a remarkable proficiency, particularly in the artillery, which played a decisive role in overcoming the numerical superiority of the Mexicans in most battles. The graduates of West Point, mainly in junior officer positions, played no small part in the army's success during the Mexican War. The movement of Scott's army to Veracruz and subsequent support of its fighting march to Mexico City testified to a new maturity in the logistical services unknown in the War of 1812.

The immense new territories acquired in the Mexican War increased the army's responsibilities proportionately, and its peacetime strength rose somewhat, reaching 17,678 officers and men in 1858. In its role of protecting the emigrants to California and Oregon, the army encountered the mounted Indians of the Great Plains and the cavalry came into its own in a new type of Indian warfare. Some twenty-two distinct Indian wars were fought in the 1850–60 decade and in 1857 alone the War Department dispatched thirty-seven separate expeditions. Army detachments also played a major role in peace keeping in Kansas and Utah; and its topographical engineers extensively surveyed, explored, and mapped the new territories.

Civil War (1861–65). The U.S. Army expanded more than sixtyfold during the Civil War, reaching a peak strength of more than 1,000,000 officers and men (including ineffectives) in 1865. The Regular Army was increased only slightly—to an authorized strength of 42,000—and most of its regiments remained in the West in the old role of providing defense against the Indians. The Union army was mostly an army of state volunteer regiments, and some regiments, notably those composed of former slaves, were raised directly as United States Volunteers. As the volunteer spirit cooled, the federal government resorted to conscription to keep the ranks of volunteer regiments filled, though by far the major portion of Union soldiers enlisted voluntarily. A total of 2,500,000 men served at some time during the war—in 1,696 regiments of infantry, 272 of cavalry, and 78 of artillery. These regiments were grouped into higher formations of brigades, divisions, corps, and armies in much the same manner that then prevailed in Europe. Sixteen armies were organized during the war—most of them taking their names from the rivers along which they operated, for instance the armies of the Potomac, the James, and the Tennessee. The higher commands were generally held by West

Point graduates, though many of them were men who had resigned their regular commissions and reentered the army as officers in volunteer units—among them, Ulysses S. Grant and William T. Sherman. Down the line the volunteer army was initially officered by political generals and by regimental and company officers elected by their subordinates. The result was some delay in development of discipline and efficiency, but by the end of the war the Union army possessed these military virtues in full measure.

Post–Civil War Period (1866–98). With Gen. Robert E. Lee's surrender on Apr. 9, 1865, the great volunteer army was hastily demobilized; by mid-1866 only a regular force of 57,000 remained. In 1869 Congress cut the number of infantry regiments to twenty-five and authorized strength to 45,000; in 1876 it reduced the regimental tables of organization so as to limit the authorization to 27,442, a limit that was to remain virtually stationary down to the Spanish-American War. The army played a major role in the occupation of the South, and the last troops were not removed from duty there until 1877.

The army's major strength was again scattered at posts in the West, where between 1865 and 1891 the troops fought ten separate campaigns and 1,067 separate engagements with the Indians. Another major activity was the maintenance of order in strikes and other civil disorders at presidential order. The post-Civil War period was one of relative isolation from civil society, during which the army turned inward to develop a new professional spirit, typified by the most famous of its commanding generals of the period, Gen. William T. Sherman. It was a period that also saw the emergence of the National Guard of the states as the Organized Militia—the principal reserve in being in case of war—and the almost total disappearance of the ordinary militia as a military institution.

Spanish-American War (1898) and Subsequent Reforms. Despite the cultivation of a professional spirit among officers, the army that entered the Spanish-American War in 1898 was poorly prepared for an overseas venture. Its units were scattered across the country in company- and battalion-size organizations and had not the necessary training or experience in operations larger than those of a regiment. There was no agency charged with central planning or mobilization for war. Executive authority in matters of supply and administration was badly fragmented among the bureaus. There was constant dispute between the bureau chiefs, who would answer only to the secretary of war, and the commanding general, who supposedly exercised command over the whole army.

At the turn of the 20th century, the United States began to look beyond its own borders, and the army's old role of policing the frontiers gave way to new tasks overseas, beginning with the Spanish-American War in 1898. The army of the Spanish-American War was composed of the traditional elements—an expanded Regular Army (strength of 65,000 authorized) and state and federal volunteer units, the former almost entirely National Guard. At war's end the total force consisted of 274,717 men, of whom the major portion never left training camps in the United States. For the infantry in this war the three-battalion regiment finally became the standard organization. Of these regiments, both at home and in Cuba and the Philippines, sickness and disease took a far higher toll than enemy bullets. Medical care was inadequate, and supply and transportation functions badly executed, as the old administrative machinery proved inadequate to the occasion.

There followed a series of reforms, most of them initiated by Secretary of War Elihu Root between 1899 and 1903. The commanding general was replaced by a chief of staff heading up a general staff and responsible to the secretary of war for both management of the army and central planning. The Army War College was established and the whole school system modernized. The Dick Act of 1903 and succeeding legislation recognized the National Guard as the Organized Militia, provided for its entry into federal service in time of emergency, and began the process of bringing its training, organization, and equipment in line with those of the Regular Army. Although the Root reforms were imperfectly realized in the 1900–16 period, they started the process of modernization that was to carry the army through two world wars.

The army between 1900 and 1916 was a force that ranged between 65,000 and 108,000 officers and men. By the later date it was equipped with new and destructive weapons, such as the machine gun, and was beginning to experiment with motor transport and the airplane. Differently deployed than in the 19th century, it assumed new responsibilities outside the United States; for instance, suppressing the Philippine Insurrection (1899–1902), participating in the relief expedition to China during the Boxer Rebellion (1899), occupying Cuba (1899–1902), building the Panama Canal (1907–14), and conducting a punitive expedition to Mexico (1916).

The National Defense Act of 1916 enlarged the army and National Guard, added a new component to the army in the form of a Reserve Corps, and provided for training of officers in the Reserve Officers' Training Corps (ROTC) in the colleges.

World War I (1917–18) and Postwar Years. Despite these forward steps the army entered World War I unprepared; the raising, training, and supporting of a great national army during 1917–18 were a hectic experience. The World War I army was raised by the application of a genuine national selective service system, not by calling for volunteers; even the National Guard units were drafted into the federal service. All elements were welded into a national army without much distinction in regard to origin. The army was expanded, in the course of eighteen months, from 210,000 to 3,685,000 officers and men. The higher leadership, as in previous wars, came mainly from among West Point graduates; the great majority of junior officers were hastily trained in officer candidate schools. Nearly 2,000,000 men were shipped to France to form the American Expeditionary Forces under Gen. John J. Pershing, where it operated as an independent unit under its own commanders. Sixty-two square infantry divisions, consisting of four regiments each, were organized and forty-three were shipped to France. At home the massive effort in training troops and supporting the overseas army was directed by a reorganized War Department and general staff.

The national army of World War I was demobilized as rapidly as was the Union army following the Civil War, and by 1920 the army stood at 202,394 officers and men. The National Defense Act of 1920 attempted to establish a viable army structure based on the traditional principle of reliance on a citizen soldier reserve. It defined the army of the United States as an organization composed of three components—the Regular Army, the National Guard, and the Organized Reserve—each of which was to provide an appropriate share of troops in a general mobilization. The maximum authorized strength of the Regular Army was set at 17,717 officers and 280,000 enlisted men. For administrative purposes the country was divided into nine corps areas, supplanting the older territorial divisions. Each corps area was to have one Regular Army division, two National Guard divisions, and three divisions from the Organized Reserve—for a total of fifty-four on mobilization.

The structure created by the act of 1920 was never fleshed out. Congress appropriated only sufficient funds to maintain a Regular Army strength of 135,000–140,000 between 1922 and 1935, and this strength had only increased to 190,000 when war broke out in Europe in 1939. The regulars devoted much more time and effort than previously to training the reserve components; but the National Guard divisions remained badly understrength and the Organized Reserve had practically no enlisted strength to fill up paper divisions.

World War II (1940–45). After the Germans overran France in 1940 the entire National Guard was called to federal service, a one-year draft authorized, and most of the officers from the Organized Reserve called to active duty. At the time of Pearl Harbor the army numbered 1,643,500; but many of its units were still semitrained, and the whole army was woefully short of modern equipment.

The national army of World War II, raised and officered much as that of World War I had been, reached a peak strength of about 8,300,000 officers and men in 1945, of which number more than 5,000,000 were deployed overseas. In this war the U.S. Army, under leaders who had been trained in its schools in the interwar period, truly came of age. Not limited to a single overseas theater as in World War I, the army in World War II was deployed in major theaters in Western Europe; the Mediterranean; North Africa; the central, south, and southwest Pacific; and China, Burma, and India. In each theater army forces served as part of a unified command including all Allied ground, air, and naval forces present.

Within the United States, the army was reorganized into three major commands—Army Air Forces, Army Ground Forces, and Army Service Forces, each responsible for functions within its own sphere. In training and administering air forces totaling 2,300,000 men and 243 air groups, the Army Air Forces gained a semiautonomous status. Under Army Ground Forces, a balanced force of eighty-nine divisions (sixty-eight infantry, sixteen armored, and five airborne) was trained—all being shipped overseas and all but two seeing combat action. The infantry divisions were organized as triangular divisions of three regimental combat teams each, rather than as the square divisions of World War I. That the ground combat army was no larger testified to the heavy demands for air and service forces. Under Army Service Forces, nine service commands supplanted the corps areas in performing housekeeping functions in the United States; and the seven technical services carried out the detailed functions of research and development, procurement, storage, and distribution of supplies. The national army of World War II plainly exceeded in magnitude and complexity that of World War I.

Since 1945. Rapid demobilization again followed the end of the war, and by 1949 the active establishment had been reduced to 591,000 men in the ground forces, scattered on occupation duty and in general reserve in the United States. In 1947 the Air Force became a separate service, and all three services were brought together in the new Department of Defense. Within the framework of a unified defense establishment, the army's role became that of training for and conduct of land warfare, and it had all the concomitant tasks derivative from this general mission.

There were other ways in which the army changed in the postwar era. The nation assumed new responsibilities in world affairs and consequently had to maintain larger forces in being. In order to do so it had to rely on a peacetime draft. Except for a brief period in 1946–47 the postwar army was for twenty-eight years a mixed force of volunteers and draftees. It also became, during the Korean War, an integrated army in which blacks and whites served together in the same units with equal opportunities for advancement—a reversal of the policy, inaugurated during the Civil War, of admitting blacks into the army but placing them in segregated units.

The outbreak of the Korean War in June 1950 reversed the trend toward demobilization. By July 1951 the army had been increased to a total of 1,500,000 officers and men, making up sixteen divisions, seven of them in the Far East. Expansion was achieved by calling up National Guard and reserve units and individuals and by expanded draft calls, principally the latter.

Demobilization after the Korean War was far more gradual than after any earlier war, evidence of the necessity of keeping strong armed forces in being. But as the administration of President Dwight D. Eisenhower relied primarily on nuclear weapons, the army was reduced by 1959 to 862,000 men. Although fourteen divisions remained, some were in reality only training divisions, not suitable for combat deployment. The Berlin crisis in 1962–63 brought a call-up of reserves that increased army strength to sixteen divisions again, and sixteen were maintained after the reserves were demobilized, with a strength of approximately 975,000. Required supporting forces for the two divisions, however, remained in the reserve components, to be called up in case of war or emergency. Expansion began again with the decision to deploy ground forces in strength to Vietnam in mid-1965. By 1968 the army stood again at approximately the Korean peak of 1,500,000 officers and men (the equivalent of more than nineteen division forces); of these, 361,000 officers and men (the equivalent of more than eight division forces) were deployed in Vietnam at the height of the conflict there. The gradual withdrawal from Vietnam, starting in 1968, brought army strength down to 800,500 by July 1973, with further cuts in prospect. The expansion in the Vietnam War was almost entirely achieved by a combination of draft and enlistment, with a very limited call-up of reserve components.

Concomitant with the changes in its responsibilities and size after World War II, the army underwent a number of reorganizations. In 1946 the wartime structure was dismantled with the abolition of Army Service Forces and the restoration of the power of the general staff and of the technical and administrative services. Army Ground Forces was also stripped of most of its command functions and transformed into a training agency, Army Field Forces, in 1948, but most of its wartime functions were restored to the new Continental Army Command (CONARC) in 1956. In 1962 a new fundamental rearrangement took place with the creation of two new commands, Army Materiel Command and Combat Developments Command, on the level of CONARC. Many functions formerly performed by general staff sections were transferred to the commands, and the functions of the technical services, descendants of the bureaus that went back to Calhoun's time, were largely absorbed by the new Army Materiel Command. Combat Developments Command, as the name indicates, took over from CONARC the development of combat tactics and doctrine, while CONARC assumed a more complete control over schools, training, and operations in the continental United States. In 1973, in a reshuffling of functions, CONARC and Combat Developments Command were supplanted by two new commands, the Training and Doctrine Command and the Force Command.

Meanwhile, army forces overseas were distributed among army components of unified commands, the most important in Europe and the Pacific. The deployment pattern as it developed following the Korean War provided five divisions in Europe, two in Korea, and one in Hawaii—the balance of the divisions being in strategic reserve in the United States. The Vietnam War did not change the fundamental deployment pattern in Europe and Korea, although forces in these areas suffered shortages of personnel and equipment because of the higher priority of the Vietnam operation.

The army of the 1950's and 1960's employed increasingly sophisticated equipment and means of transportation and communication, necessitating the development of new tactical organizations and an increasingly complex logistical support system. In terms of division organization the triangular division of World War II survived the Korean War with some modifications but was replaced in 1956 by the pentomic division, consisting of five battle groups with a dual capability for atomic and conventional warfare. With the return to an emphasis on conventional war that came with the administration of John Kennedy, the pentomic division was replaced in 1962 by the reorganization objective army division (ROAD), an organization permitting increase or decrease in numbers of infantry battalions or other elements in the division, depending on its employment. In 1963 the army introduced the air assault division, whose primary characteristic was its air mobility for both men and equipment. In a sense it was an air cavalry division—with the helicopter playing the role that had traditionally belonged to the horse.

The completion of the withdrawal from Vietnam in March 1973 and the end of the draft on July 1, 1973, combined to mark the end of an era for the army. The withdrawal marked the end of seven years of fighting in Vietnam, and the end of the draft meant that the active army would once again become the volunteer force it had traditionally been in peacetime before World War II.

Peacetime Work. In addition to its primary task of preparing for and fighting wars, the army has throughout its history performed peacetime tasks that have contributed immensely to the development of the American nation. Among the most important of these have been exploration of the West; surveying of the transcontinental rail lines; improvement of rivers and harbors; building of the Panama Canal; and occupation work in the South during Reconstruction and in Cuba, Puerto Rico, the Philippines, Germany, Japan, and other areas in later periods. Army engineers have supervised the building of many important public facilities. Army doctors have made large contributions to the development of modern medicine, among them Walter Reed's proof that yellow fever is caused by a virus. Discoveries by army scientists and materials developed for army use have had great impact on civil society. The army has also been frequently called on by the president to maintain order in civil disturbances and to assist in the enforcement of federal laws. Its role in the relief of civil disasters, such as hurricanes, earthquakes, and floods, has been particularly important during the 20th century.

Army Aviation. As an element separate from the U.S. Air Force, army aviation had its beginnings in World War II, when light observation aircraft (Piper Cubs) were made organic to field artillery units. When a separate air force was created in 1947, this type of aircraft remained under army control. Meanwhile the army was experimenting with helicopters, and they proved invaluable during the Korean War for medical evacuation and other purposes. In 1952 an understanding was reached with the air force that the army should develop its own aviation for transport within the combat zone, subject to certain weight limits for fixed-wing aircraft. During the 1950's the army began development of many types of both fixed- and rotary-wing aircraft for observation, tactical movement of troops and supplies, aerial reconnaissance, command, liaison, and evacuation of casualties. By 1960 its inventory of aircraft was sizable; and it had developed an organization for training pilots, servicing planes, and utilizing the craft.

The air assault division, developed in 1963, was to depend almost entirely on the helicopter for its tactical mobility. And the proven utility of the helicopter in the Vietnam War gave further impetus to the employment of these craft in the regular ROAD divisions. A reassessment of the respective army and air force roles in 1966 placed the larger fixed-wing transports the army had developed under the air force, but the army retained primacy in the development of helicopters and smaller fixed-wing craft for its own use. By mid-1971 the army aircraft inventory included about 9,500 helicopters and about 2,500 other types of planes.

Army General Staff. Congress first created a general staff for the army in 1813, but it consisted simply of a group of heads of administrative bureaus. The modern general staff dates from 1903, when Congress, on the recommendation of Elihu Root, passed an act establishing the General Staff Corps and a chief of staff. A general staff of three divisions was subsequently established to assist the chief in managing current operations and to perform planning functions. This general staff was never able to fulfill completely the role Root envisioned for it; and the National Defense Act of 1916, reflecting congressional suspicions of a general staff, limited its numbers and functions. The United States entered World War I with an emasculated general staff, and a new and more powerful one had to be created in 1918 to give direction to the war effort. This general staff, under Gen. Peyton C. March as chief, had four directorates—Military Intelligence; War Plans; Operations; and Purchase, Storage, and Traffic. Each directorate possessed executive authority as well as planning functions.

Under the National Defense Act of 1920, March's directorates were replaced by a planning staff of five sections modeled on that used by Gen. Pershing in France—G-1 for personnel, G-2 for intelligence, G-3 for operations and training, G-4 for supply, and the War Plans Division. Though these general staff sections survived the reorganization of March 1942, all except War Plans Division were shorn of most of their powers with the creation of three major commands. The War Plans Division, renamed the Operations Division, became Gen. George C. Marshall's command post and something of a general staff in itself.

The reorganization of 1946 ended the preeminence of the Operations Division and restored the authority of other general staff sections; the general staff was organized as six coequal directorates with power to direct and supervise as well as to plan. In 1950 the Army Organization Act provided for an army staff to be composed of a chief of staff, a vice chief, not more than three deputy chiefs, not more than five assistant chiefs, and some thirteen heads of technical and administrative services—generally a reflection of the changes that had taken place since 1946. The secretary of the army was granted great flexibility in organizing the army staff and prescribing which part of it should be the general staff.

Under the provisions of this act, the army staff underwent major reorganizations in 1955–56 and in 1962–63. Smaller changes have been made since, the most notable being the creation of the position of assistant vice chief of staff in 1967. In 1973 under the chief, the vice chief, and his assistant, the following positions on the army staff were designated as general staff positions: deputy chiefs of staff for military operations, personnel, and logistics; the army comptroller; chiefs of research and development and of the Office of Reserve Components; and assistant chiefs of staff for force development and intelligence.

Insignia of Rank. Insignia of rank date from the Revolution, when Washington ordered that field grade officers wear colored cockades in their caps, general officers colored ribands across their coats, and noncommissioned officers stripes or epaulettes of colored cloth on arm or shoulder. In 1780 generals began to wear silver stars on their shoulders. The colonel's eagles date from 1832, and the various insignia for majors, captains, and lieutenants from 1836—though not precisely in their present form. Originally infantry colonels wore gold eagles, and other colonels wore silver ones. In 1851 the silver eagle was prescribed for all colonels, the silver leaf for lieutenant-colonels, and the gold leaf for majors. Insignia for captains and lieutenants were standardized in 1917, when second lieutenants, who had previously worn no insignia of rank, were authorized to wear the single gold bar. Meanwhile, the various chevrons of the noncommissioned officers were evolving into their present form. They were positioned at a spot on the sleeves just above the elbow in 1847, and then moved up to the shoulder.

Army Logistics. Logistics is the function of providing all the matériel and services a military force needs in peace or war. It includes procurement, supply, transportation, maintenance, construction, evacuation and hospitalization, and many other types of service. Logistics in the U.S. Army has become increasingly complex with the progress of the industrial and scientific revolutions. In modern war more soldiers are engaged in logistical pursuits than in combat.

During the American Revolution the Continental army had poor logistical support owing to lack of a native industry capable of producing weapons of war, the inability of Congress to mobilize the resources of the country, a primitive system of overland transportation, and poor functioning of the army's supply services. The situation was not vastly improved in the War of 1812, when logistical difficulties had much to do with poor American performance in the early stages. Development of a system equal to the needs of 19th-century warfare came largely after 1812 with the emergence of a strong native industry, vast improvements in transportation facilities, and development within the army of a better administrative apparatus. The army system was shaped around the War Department bureaus—notably quartermaster, ordnance, medical, subsistence, engineers, and signal—each of which had specified responsibilities for procurement, storage, and distribution of specific types of supplies and provision of specific services under the general supervision of the secretary of war.

The Civil War saw the emergence of such standard attributes of a military supply system as echeloned depots, classification of supplies, and methods of calculating requirements in terms of standard allowances for given bodies of men. A far-flung procurement organization emerged under the bureaus that, despite early scandals, performed well in drawing forth the material resources of the country. The railroads, on which the Union army relied primarily for military movements over distances, gave it an unprecedented mobility. Native productive capacity, and a depot and distribution system built around the railroads, made possible the support of armies in the field far larger than in earlier American wars.

Logistics in the two world wars of the 20th century was vastly more complex than in the Civil War. In both wars the United States had to support large forces overseas, and ocean shipping became the very center of army logistics. During World War I the army shipped more than 2 million men and 6 million short tons of supplies to France; during World War II it shipped more than 7 million men and nearly 127 million measurement tons of supplies to theaters spread around the globe. The total value of army procurement in World War II amounted to nearly $111 billion. There was a progressive increase in the quantity and variety of supplies and services needed to support a mechanized army. During the Civil War each Union soldier required 4 pounds of supplies per day, 3 pounds accounted for by rations, while each horse consumed about 26 pounds of forage; during World War II each soldier in the European theater required 66.8 pounds per day, only 7.2 pounds accounted for by rations, the largest item being 33.3 pounds of petroleum products to keep the army's motors turning.

There was a great proliferation of specialized units engaged in providing services. The various bureaus, during World War II known as technical and administrative services, continued to be responsible for detailed logistical functions in their respective spheres, though during World War I they were subordinated to Gen. George W. Goethals' Purchase, Storage, and Traffic Division and during World War II to Gen. Brehon B. Somervell's Army Service Forces. Overseas commands in both wars had their own logistics organizations, operating base and advance sections behind the armies to forward supplies and furnish service support. Specified reserve levels were maintained in depots all along the line from factory to troops, in order to maintain a continuous flow of supplies.

The logistical systems developed during World War II have since undergone modification to keep pace with technological change. Increased use of air transport has speeded movement; during the Vietnam War the vast majority of troops and many critical supplies were moved to the theater by air. Concentrated efforts have been devoted to eliminating the wasteful pipeline of World War II by providing for direct delivery from stateside sources to the user in the theater. In general the trend has been toward the functionalization of logistical organization, both in the combat and support areas. Thus in 1962 the Army Materiel Command assumed most of the functions of the commodity-oriented technical services in development, procurement, storage, and distribution. Throughout the army's logistical establishment in the 1960's, automatic data processing became the central feature of logistical systems. (*See also* Logistics.)

Army Posts. Posts established by the army played their most important role in American history in the extension of the frontier westward. These posts were usually established at the western fringe of settlement, or beyond at strategic places in Indian country. They were often the most important points along routes of travel and were trading centers as well as refuges for settlers. Many towns and cities that grew up around these forts still retain their names, Fort Wayne, Ind., for example.

The earliest army posts were inherited from the Revolution, the most notable being Fort Pitt, Pa., which served as a base for Gen. Anthony Wayne's expedition in 1793–94. After the War of 1812 the line of posts was pushed steadily westward, until by 1845 a chain of eleven forts extended from Lake Superior to the Gulf of Mexico. After the Mexican War posts were established at strategic points on the Great Plains along the routes to California and Oregon, and this network was vastly expanded during and after the Civil War. It was from these posts that the army carried on its long conflict with the Plains Indians. After the end of the Indian wars some of these posts—such as Fort Leavenworth and Fort Riley in Kansas and Fort Sill in Oklahoma—became permanent sites for army activities. The sites of newer army posts have been selected for such reasons as suitability as training centers or, in the case of logistical installations, proximity to transportation and industrial facilities and the availability of a supply of labor.

Army School System. Apart from the U.S. Military Academy, the first formal army school was for artillery instruction, established at Fort Monroe, Va., in 1824. The School of Application for Infantry and Cavalry, later to be known as the Command and General Staff College, was established at Fort Leavenworth, Kans., in 1881. Other branch and specialist schools followed. Between 1901 and 1914, as part of the Root reforms, a definite school system took shape, with the Army War College at the apex, including the Military Academy to train cadets for an officer career, the Command and General Staff College to prepare officers for staff and command positions in large units, and perhaps a dozen service schools for branch and specialist training.

World War I experience proved the value of the schools and the need for their expansion and refinement. During the 1920's a system of special service schools was developed—thirty-one in number—to provide training of both regular and reserve officers in the fundamentals of their branches and to train enlisted specialists. In 1924 the Army Industrial College was established, with the function of training regular officers in the techniques of industrial mobilization and wartime procurement. After World War II the Army War College and the Industrial College formed the nuclei for the National War College and the Industrial College of the Armed Forces, which served all three services. The army, however, retained the function of operating its own school system to meet its special needs and reestablished its own War College in 1950. That system continued to be organized along lines developed earlier, with the branch and specialist schools providing the fundamentals for officers and enlisted men and the War College and General Staff College providing higher-level training. The system, however, became vastly more complex and sophisticated as a result of changes in weapons, tactics, logistics and the role of the United States in world affairs. By 1970 it was offering training in a vast multiplicity of specialties hardly imaginable in the 1920's.

Army War College. The Army War College was established by Elihu Root in 1901 as the nucleus of a general staff, and it continued as a part of that body until 1914. As the capstone of the army educational system, its function has continuously been that of providing training of selected officers for higher command and general staff duties. In 1907 the college moved to a permanent location at Washington Barracks, D.C. (now Fort Lesley J. McNair). In 1917 it was closed for the duration of the war and reopened in 1920. Classes were suspended again in 1940 and only resumed in 1950 at Fort Leavenworth, Kans., the Fort McNair location having meanwhile been taken over by the National War College. In July 1951 the college was moved to Carlisle Barracks, Pa.

Army Hospitals. Hospitals of a primitive sort, often little better than pesthouses, were provided for soldiers during the Revolution, the War of 1812, and the Mexican War—usually in existing or improvised buildings. The Civil War saw a considerable advance with the adoption of the system of evacuation and hospitalization pioneered by Gen. Jonathan Letterman, surgeon general of the Army of the Potomac. Letterman's system involved field hospitals set up in tents where the sick and wounded could get immediate attention and pavilion hospitals set up in permanent locations from which the seriously wounded could be evacuated and given more careful treatment. After the Civil War, at various army posts, army surgeons established small hospitals. The Spanish-American War saw the introduction of permanent general hospitals for care of soldiers and medical research.

Though further refined, the army's hospital system in two world wars generally followed along the lines established earlier. Mobile field hospitals close behind the front lines received wounded men from collecting stations and forwarded them, if the wounds were serious enough, to evacuation hospitals farther to the rear. From evacuation hospitals patients who required still greater care were sent to base hospitals in the theater or, in the worst cases, back to general hospitals in the United States. The main improvement in this system in the Korean and Vietnam wars was the development of mobile surgical hospitals operating close behind the lines and the use of helicopters for evacuation of the wounded.

[P. M. Ashburn, *A History of the Medical Department of the United States Army;* James A. Huston, *The Sinews of War: Army Logistics, 1775–1953;* Maurice Matloff, ed., *American Military History;* Otto L. Nelson, Jr., *National Security and the General Staff;* Erna Risch, *Quartermaster Support of the Army: A History of the Corps, 1775–1939;* O. L. Spalding, *The United States Army in War and Peace;* Russell L. Weigley, *History of the United States Army.*]

ROBERT W. COAKLEY

ARMY ENLISTMENT. *See* **Enlistment.**

ARMY OF OCCUPATION (1918–23). As part of the Allied Army of Occupation, the American Third Army, commanded by Maj. Gen. Joseph T. Dickman, crossed into Germany in December 1918, taking station in the north sector of the Coblenz bridgehead. Units of the Third Army were stationed at various points within the American area and engaged in duties of occupation and training, including participation in civil administration of occupied territory, until July 2, 1919, when the Third Army was discontinued. It was succeeded by the "American Forces in Germany."

Maj. Gen. Edward F. McGlachlin, Jr., assumed command of this newly designated force until July 8,

1919, when its permanent commander, Maj. Gen. Henry T. Allen, reported. From January 1920, Allen worked in conjunction with the Rhineland High Commission. At noon on Jan. 27, 1923, American troops having left the Coblenz area, Allen relinquished command of the American area.

[Henry T. Allen, *The Rhineland Occupation*.]

ROBERT S. THOMAS

ARMY ON THE FRONTIER. This term applies to the activities of the U.S. Army stationed near the frontier settlements from the beginning of national existence until about 1890, the end of the settlers' frontier. The principal functions performed by this army were (1) guarding the frontier settlements from hostile Indians; (2) aiding the settlement of the West by developing and protecting the communication between the older settlements and the frontier, by exploring the West, constructing roads, and defending the overland trails, water routes, and later telegraph and railroad lines; and (3) policing the frontier until the civil governments could maintain order.

The western movement of settlers brought conflict with the Indians. Scores of Indian wars and campaigns were fought by the army. These wars were fought by the regular infantry and cavalry regiments occasionally aided by state militia and volunteers. The frontier soldiers were usually stationed in posts at strategic points defending the routes of communications, settlements, and Indian reservations. The strength of this army, about one half of the regular army in time of peace, ranged from 1,423 troops in 1790 in the Northwest Territory to over 26,000 in 1868, which was the height of the Indian wars on the Great Plains. The frontier posts had on the average a garrison of 200 troops. By 1867 over 100 posts were scattered throughout the West. As the Indian wars ended, after 1870, these posts were rapidly abandoned.

The army supplies were carried by boats, steamboats, ox and mule trains, pack mules and horses, and later by railroads, which stimulated the development of trade, farming, and ranching. The difficulty of supplying these remote army posts encouraged farming and urban enterprises around the posts, the beginning of permanent settlements.

The daily life of the frontier soldier was a hardy one. The soldiers built their shelter, escorted travelers, emigrants, and wagon trains on the trails, aided and protected surveying parties, constructed thousands of miles of trails and roads, supplied needy emigrants, patrolled trails and railroad lines, guarded river navigation, protected government and private property from hostile Indians and outlaws, assisted and fed friendly Indians, fought hostile Indians, and gave police assistance to the weak civil authorities on the frontier. Their shelters were usually log, stone, adobe, or sod huts constructed largely by their own labor. The hardships of the soldiers, the miserable quarters, inferior food, and the lonely life encouraged many desertions.

The army on the frontier disagreed with the Indian Bureau and the frontier civil authorities over the Indian policy. The frontiersmen in general demanded the destruction or removal of the Indians (*see* Indian Removals). The Indian Bureau attempted to protect the Indians, and the army to coerce them. When the Indians revolted the army made war upon the entire Indian tribe, punishing the innocent with the guilty, even to the extent of killing women and children in raids on villages or camps. The Indian Bureau and the army officials accused each other of being responsible for the Indian wars.

[C. Goodwin, *Trans-Mississippi West;* G. W. Manypenny, *Our Indian Wards;* N. A. Miles, *Serving the Republic;* F. L. Paxson, *History of the American Frontier,* and *The Last American Frontier;* R. E. Reigel, *America Moves West;* J. Winsor, *The Westward Movement.*]

RAYMOND L. WELTY

ARMY POSTS of the U.S. Army played an important part in the westward extension of the frontier. In the older eastern states they became centers for recruiting and drilling troops and guardians of the coastline at strategic points. These older forts followed European models of construction, and accommodations for the soldiers, officers, and their wives were usually comfortable. Not so those of the frontier, which were often in advance or on the fringe of the settled regions and usually speedily constructed by the soldiers themselves. President Thomas Jefferson introduced the factory or trading system in connection with the establishment of army posts as a means of dealing with the Indians. Settlements grew up around these posts, and after their abandonment, usually after a period of a few years, towns of the same name frequently remained. Important treaties with the Indians very often were made at the forts or at points near them under military protection. Many of these treaties were negotiated by the officers themselves.

A study of the extension of forts westward will show that they were usually slightly in advance of the frontier line of settlement and at some periods were constructed more rapidly than at others. The period after the War of 1812 was one in which forts were rapidly advanced throughout the old Northwest into territory formerly claimed by the British. As Spain and Mexico were pushed back in the Southwest, army posts followed, until by 1845 a line of eleven forts extended from Lake Superior to the Gulf of Mexico.

Indian raids during the Civil War on the Great Plains and the extension of mail routes and later railroads to the Pacific necessitated the building of forts at strategic points. Regular-army forts usually accommodating from two to six companies with artillery were supplemented by minor temporary or lightly held centers designated as camps or cantonments. The latter were usually little more than huts or shelters and often merely wooded, grassed, and watered areas suitable for a few days' stay.

The usual form for the larger posts, which indicates a fairly permanent station for troops, was in the form of a quadrangle constructed around a parade ground, with the officers' quarters, barracks, post traders, and hospital on one side and the stables and quartermaster's supplies on the other. The ends of the quadrangle might be occupied by the guardhouse, company kitchens, and workshops, and farther back by the laundresses' quarters. Not all new forts had such elaborate equipment.

Despite the lack of the amenities, life at some of these frontier posts was pleasant—in peacetime—for the younger set. Young West Pointers brought out their wives, who maintained as far as possible the social standards of their old homes, and "post hops," riding and hunting parties, and card games were enjoyed. Wild game was often plentiful, but this asset of the larder was supplemented when necessary by cattle drives from the east and south, thus introducing cattle to the Great Plains. Gardens and farms were laid out around the posts to provide vegetables, grains, and forage, and thus it was demonstrated that the prairies were not sterile because they had no trees. Flour mills were constructed at certain posts such as Snelling and Atkinson.

Most garrisons had post schools, libraries, newspapers, and magazines. Plays were given, and some of the most accurate and colorful literature of the new territory appears in the memoirs of army officers and their wives. After the abandonment of a post the buildings were usually sold and the land ceded or auctioned off. In a few cases the area was made into a national reserve.

[H. P. Beers, *Western Military Frontier;* U.S. War Department, Surgeon General Official Circular No. 8, *Report of the Hygiene of the United States Army With a Description of Military Posts.*]

CARL L. CANNON

ARMY SUPPLY. *See* **Army, United States.**

ARMY WAR COLLEGE. *See* **Army, United States.**

ARNOLD'S MARCH TO QUEBEC. In the summer of 1775 Col. Benedict Arnold went to Cambridge, Mass., and laid before Commander in Chief George Washington a plan for attacking Canada. Washington was sympathetic. The old classic route by way of Lake George, Lake Champlain, and the Richelieu River was assigned to Gen. Richard Montgomery. News of another passage by way of the Kennebec and Chaudière rivers had reached Washington. This route was assigned to a force under Arnold. On Sept. 19, Arnold's command left Newburyport, Mass., and went by sea to and up the Kennebec where 200 bateaux had been ordered to be ready. With these Arnold headed up the river. Made of green wood and ill-adapted to the upper rushing waters of the Kennebec, these bateaux were a tactical blunder that, however, did not daunt Arnold. Neither did he hesitate when Maj. Roger Enos turned back with one-fourth of the little army. On up the Dead River, full of ice, and through snowstorms, with insufficient food and clothing, Arnold led his force. Oct. 28 found them going across the carrying place which was actually the divide between the St. Lawrence and Atlantic watersheds. Arnold plunged ahead with an advance guard while the remainder were reduced to eating dogs and shoeleather. At Sertigan, Arnold arranged for supplies that refreshed his exhausted detachment so that they were able to go down the Chaudière and reach the St. Lawrence on Nov. 9, 1775. In the meantime Montgomery had reached Montreal, but Arnold went on across the St. Lawrence and was actually in front of Quebec before Montgomery arrived. Guy Carleton, the British commander at Montreal, evacuated that place and got into Quebec before Montgomery could join Arnold on Dec. 2. Carleton had 1,200 men while the combined American forces numbered scarcely 1,000. Nevertheless, in a blinding snowstorm, Montgomery and Arnold assaulted Quebec on the night of Dec. 31, 1775. The effort failed, Montgomery was killed and Arnold wounded. Arnold's march through the wilderness of Maine has been regarded as a noble example of perseverance and determination in the face of extreme hardship.

[J. H. Smith, *Arnold's March From Cambridge to Quebec*, and *Our Struggle for the Fourteenth Colony*.]

RANDOLPH G. ADAMS

ARNOLD'S RAID IN VIRGINIA. In December of 1780 Commander in Chief Sir Henry Clinton of the British armies in North America determined to send an expedition into Virginia. Its purpose was to conduct desultory raids into the tidewater region of that state and to block the mouth of the Chesapeake. The command was given to the traitor Benedict Arnold, because Clinton admired his intrepidity and believed he could induce some more Americans to desert. Leaving Sandy Hook on Dec. 20–21 and arriving at Hampton Roads Dec. 30, Arnold seized the small boats on the James River and pushed up that stream to Westover. Sending John Simcoe's rangers ahead, the force was moved on to Richmond, which Arnold occupied after a skirmish on Jan. 5, 1781. He destroyed the iron foundry at Westham and the American stores at Richmond. Arnold then reembarked on the James and fell down to Portsmouth, which he fortified and whence he sent various marauding and pillaging expeditions into the neighborhood until March, when he was joined and outranked by Maj. Gen. William Phillips. In April, Phillips and Arnold started another expedition up the James, reaching City Point on the 24th, whence they proceeded overland to Petersburg where 1,000 hogsheads of tobacco were destroyed, as were the small boats on the Appomattox. Arnold then returned to Osborn's on the James where he destroyed a small American fleet, marched to Manchester where 1,200 hogsheads of tobacco were destroyed, thence to Warwick where the flour magazines and mills were burned. In May the force fell down to Westover, thence to Brandon. Throughout these movements the British were harassed by the inferior forces of the Marquis de Lafayette and Anthony Wayne. Phillips died at Petersburg on May 13, 1781, and the chief command momentarily devolved on Arnold again. But at this time Lord Cornwallis came up with his superior forces and joined the detachment of Phillips and Arnold to his for the campaign of the summer of 1781.

[J. G. Simcoe, *Journal of the Operations of the Queen's Rangers*.]

RANDOLPH G. ADAMS

ARNOLD'S TREASON. Brig. Gen. Benedict Arnold of the Continental Army had fought gallantly for the American cause from Ticonderoga (1775) to Saratoga (1777). But by the spring of 1779 several motives led him to open up a treasonable correspondence with the British headquarters in New York. These were (1) irritation at repeated slights by Congress, (2) resentment at the authorities of Pennsylvania who had court-martialed him, (3) need for money, and (4) opposition to the French alliance of 1778. Throughout the rest of 1779 and 1780 he transmitted military intelligence about the American army to the British. On July 12, 1780, he "accepted the command at West Point as a post in which I can render the most essential services" (to the British). He demanded from the British £20,000 in case he could betray West Point and £10,000 in case he failed but himself went over to the British. Negotiations were carried on with Maj. John André, adjutant general of the British army. André visited Arnold at a point between the British and American lines Sept. 21, 1780. On Sept. 23, when returning from this meeting, André was captured by the Americans, and the incriminating documents found in his stocking were sent to Gen. George Washington. News of André's capture was also sent to Arnold, thus giving him time to escape down the Hudson River to the British before he could be arrested for treason. He became a brigadier general in the British army, went to England after the defeat of the British, and died there June 14, 1801.

[James Thomas Flexner, *The Traitor and the Spy;* Carl Van Doren, *Secret History of the American Revolution*.]

RANDOLPH G. ADAMS

AROOSTOOK WAR (1838–39), an undeclared and bloodless war occasioned by the failure of the United States and Great Britain to determine the boundary between New Brunswick and what is now Maine (*see* Northeast Boundary). In 1820 Maine became a state. Almost immediately, ignoring the British contention that all land north of Mars Hill, in Aroostook County, was British, the Maine legislature, jointly with Massachusetts, made grants to settlers along both branches of the Aroostook River. In 1827 the United States and Great Britain submitted the question to the king of the Netherlands. His compromise of 1831 was accepted by Great Britain, but rejected by the U.S. Senate in 1832. Finally, in January 1839, Rufus McIntire was appointed land agent, with authority to take a posse into the disputed area and oust Canadian lumberjacks working in the region. He was arrested by the Canadians, and within two months 10,000 Maine troops were either encamped along the Aroostook River or were on their way there. At the insistence of Maine congressmen, the federal government voted a force of 50,000 men and $10 million in the event of war. To prevent a clash Gen. Winfield Scott was dispatched to negotiate a truce with the lieutenant governor of New Brunswick. This he did, and Great Britain, convinced of the seriousness of the situation, agreed to a boundary commission, whose findings were incorporated in the Webster-Ashburton Treaty in 1842.

[H. S. Burrage, *Maine and the Northeastern Boundary Controversy.*]

ELIZABETH RING

ARPENT, an old French unit of land measure, both linear and superficial, now standardized in Louisiana at 192 feet, or a square of that dimension (equal to approximately five-sixths of an acre). French colonial land grants were described as fronting a given number of arpents on a river or bayou by forty arpents in depth and containing a certain number of superficial arpents.

WALTER PRICHARD

ARREST. The Fourth Amendment to the U.S. Constitution—applicable to state and city, as well as federal, law enforcement officers through the due process clause of the Fourteenth Amendment—guarantees "the right of the people to be secure in their persons . . . against unreasonable . . . seizures," and provides further that this right "shall not be violated . . . but upon probable cause." The Fourth Amendment does not use the term "arrest," but it is now established that an illegal arrest is an illegal "seizure" within the meaning of the amendment. Thus, although unfortunately they commonly occur, arrests based on mere suspicion or common rumor or otherwise lacking "probable cause" are unconstitutional at the local, as well as at the federal, level.

The Fourth Amendment provides that "no Warrants shall issue, but upon probable cause." Although the rule is otherwise with respect to searches, arrests for felonies may be made without warrants, even though it is practicable to obtain one. (Most states permit warrantless arrests for misdemeanors only if committed in the officer's presence.) But the Fourth Amendment also prohibits "unreasonable searches and seizures" generally; and because requirements in cases in which the police proceed without a warrant surely cannot be less stringent than when a warrant is obtained, "probable cause" or "reasonable grounds" is also required in such circumstances. Probable cause exists where the information within the officer's knowledge is sufficient to warrant a reasonable man to believe that a crime has, or is being, committed.

Although all arrests are seizures within the meaning of the Fourth Amendment, some seizures may not be arrests. In the 1968 "stop-and-frisk" cases (392 U.S. 1), the U.S. Supreme Court distinguished between "technical arrests" and less intrusive "seizures" (that is, brief detentions on the streets or "stops") and implied that the police may constitutionally "stop" or temporarily detain persons on the basis of facts and circumstances that would not support a full-blown arrest.

In the federal courts and in most state courts it is no defense to a prosecution that the defendant was illegally arrested or brought within the jurisdiction of the court by reason of a forcible abduction. "There is nothing in the Constitution that requires a court to permit a guilty person rightfully convicted to escape justice because he was brought to trial against his will" (342 U.S. 519, 522 [1952]). But whether an arrest is valid is nonetheless frequently a matter of practical importance. The police are authorized to conduct a limited search without warrant incident to a lawful arrest, and thus, the admissibility of evidence acquired in this way depends upon the validity of the arrest.

[William O. Douglas, "Vagrancy and Arrest on Suspicion," *Yale Law Journal,* vol. 70; Caleb Foote, "Safeguards in the Law of Arrest," *Northwestern University Law Review,* vol. 52; Wayne LaFave, *Arrest: The Decision to Take a Suspect Into Custody,* and " 'Street Encounters' and the Constitution," *Michigan Law Review,* vol. 67.]

YALE KAMISAR

ARREST, ARBITRARY, DURING THE CIVIL WAR. Freedom from arbitrary arrest, guaranteed in the writ of habeas corpus, has become synonymous in Anglo-Saxon tradition with civil liberty. The right to restrict this freedom nevertheless is recognized in England as a parliamentary function and in the United States as a constitutional exercise of power in time of "rebellion or invasion." Until 1861 this federal right had never been exercised, but the Civil War brought widespread restrictions of civil liberty. In order to cope with antiwar activities (*see* Copperheads), President Abraham Lincoln issued several proclamations by which the privilege of the writ of habeas corpus was suspended, first within limited areas and later (Sept. 24, 1862) throughout the entire nation.

The president's control of arbitrary arrest was frequently questioned, especially by Chief Justice

Roger B. Taney, who held (*ex parte Merryman*) that the legislative branch rather than the executive had this constitutional authority. Lincoln ably defended himself against dictatorship charges in various open letters, however (*see* Birchard Letter; Corning Letter). Executive control was maintained and extended, even after Congress required (Mar. 3, 1863) that political prisoners either be released or subjected to regular judicial procedure. The Department of State and later the War Department administered arrests. Passports were required, a secret service was organized, and Union officers and local police cooperated in apprehending suspects. Political prisoners were detained without hearing and usually released after brief imprisonment. Trial by military commissions, such as in the Vallandigham and Milligan cases, was exceptional. Although the authority for such commissions was not questioned by the Supreme Court during the war, their use outside the war zone for the trial of civilians was declared unconstitutional after the war.

The number of arrests for antiwar activities is not known exactly. One official list with 13,535 names is incomplete, while on the other hand Alexander Johnston's guess of 38,000 is exaggerated. No authoritative total has ever been reached. One famous series of arrests included the mayor and a judge of Baltimore and certain members of the Maryland legislature. Equally important, however, was the imprisonment of a number of northern editors and several public men including Congressman Henry May, former Gov. Charles S. Morehead of Kentucky, the mayor of Washington, and two diplomats (C. J. Faulkner and G. W. Jones), appointed during James Buchanan's administration, returning from abroad.

The Confederacy likewise made summary arrests to suppress disloyalty. Success was small, not only because political prisoners became popular martyrs, but because Confederate policy met the additional resistance of states'-rights opposition in numerous localities.

[F. L. Owsley, *State Rights in the Confederacy;* J. G. Randall, *Constitutional Problems Under Lincoln.*]

MARTIN P. CLAUSSEN

ARROWSMITH'S MAP. *A Map Exhibiting All the New Discoveries in the Interior Part of North America* was published in London, Jan. 1, 1795, by Aaron Arrowsmith, "Hydrographer to His Majesty." A large-scale map on a globular projection, it was printed on six sheets, measuring when joined 48½ by 57 inches. From notes furnished by members of the Hudson's Bay Company, numerous additions and corrections were made on the basic map. More than seventeen editions were published between 1795 and 1850, first by the author and later by his two sons, which attest the accuracy and importance of the map.

[Charles O. Paullin, *Atlas of the Historical Geography of the United States.*]

LLOYD A. BROWN

ARSENALS. An arsenal is an establishment for the manufacture, repair, receipt, storage, and issuance of ordnance. Historically, American arms manufacture favored governmental control rather than private production, as was the European practice, to insure the quality and uniformity of arms production. The Springfield, Mass., and Harpers Ferry, W.Va., armories were established in 1794 and 1796 respectively, to release the Republic from dependence upon foreign arms manufacture. With the organization of the army's Ordnance Department on May 14, 1812, arsenals came under its direction. By 1816 there were five federal arsenals: small arms were produced at Springfield and Harpers Ferry; artillery equipment and ammunition at Watervliet, N.Y.; small arms and gun carriages at Watertown, Mass.; and ammunition at Frankford, Pa. Arsenals at Rock Island, Ill., and Picatinny, N.J., were added at mid-century, whereas the Harpers Ferry arsenal was destroyed during the Civil War.

Up to and including World War II, American arsenal munition production was never enough to meet the wartime needs of the army; consequently, the expanded production needed in wartime was provided by the private sector. The arsenals were repositories of highly complex ordnance skills in peacetime and watchdogs of the expanding munitions industry in wartime. They provided weapons design and even plant design while monitoring production to ensure quality and interchangeability. Since the Korean War, arsenals no longer have the broad functions of the past; they contribute to only a small portion of the army's total ordnance requirements.

[C. M. Green, H. C. Thomson, and P. C. Roots, *The Ordnance Department: Planning Munitions for War;* J. A. Huston, *The Sinews of War: Army Logistics, 1775–1953.*]

DON E. MCLEOD

ART. *See* **Painting.**

d'ARTAGUETTE'S DEFEAT (1736). The governor of Louisiana, Jean Baptiste Le Moyne, Sieur de Bienville, decided in 1736 to exterminate the Chickasaw because of their long and successful opposition to the French (*see* Chickasaw-French War). He ordered Maj. Pierre d'Artaguette, in command of Fort de Chartres in the Illinois country, to lead a force from the north against the main Chickasaw villages in the northeastern part of the present state of Mississippi. Bienville, meanwhile, led a larger force up the Tombigbee River from the south, with the same objective. Obeying instructions, d'Artaguette collected 1,200 Indians and arrived at the villages on May 9, the date specified. There he waited in vain for Bienville, who was unavoidably detained, until the unrest of his Indians forced him into a fatal attack. In the course of the battle he was wounded, and he and a score of his countrymen, including the Sieur de Vincennes, François Marie Bissot, were captured by the Chickasaw. Bienville arrived toward the end of the month only to be defeated at the Battle of Ackia. After their victory the Chickasaw burned d'Artaguette and their other earlier captives at the stake.

[F. X. Martin, *History of Louisiana;* S. C. Williams, *Beginnings of West Tennessee.*]

GERALD M. CAPERS, JR.

ARTHUR D. LITTLE, INC. One of the first independent commercial research laboratories in the United States was founded by Arthur Dehon Little and Roger B. Griffin in Boston, Mass., in 1886. Its formation was a response to the slow pace of American industry in developing its own research facilities to utilize the rapid advances being made in science and technology. Initially most active in the handling of problems relating to paper manufacture, the company branched out into research on coal derivatives, lubrication, forest products, and textiles—conducting important developmental studies for a number of research-deficient industries. It was incorporated as Arthur D. Little, Inc., in 1909 and moved to the site of its present headquarters in Cambridge, Mass., in 1917. During World War I the company conducted special researches on airplane dopes and acetone production; from its work on gas mask materials it developed the "sucked-in" gas filter that was adopted as standard equipment by the U.S. Army. In 1918 a Canadian subsidiary, Arthur D. Little, Ltd., was formed to undertake a series of studies of the natural resources of the Dominion. The studies led to the formation of a new governmental agency in Canada, the Council for Scientific and Industrial Research.

On the death of Little, Aug. 1, 1935, the controlling interest in the company was willed to be held in trust for the benefit of the Massachusetts Institute of Technology. Since World War I the laboratory staff, grown to nearly eighty scientifically trained specialists, had contributed processes for pulp and papermaking; for production of alcohols and esters from oil refinery waste gases; and for production of nonflammable movie film, artificial silk, automobile finishes, stereotype mats, and phonograph records.

The success of Arthur D. Little, Inc., stimulated the development of industrial research facilities. While serving as a model for commercial research laboratories, the company assisted in the organization and staffing of the first centralized research department for the General Motors Corporation. Among the company's major contributions to the World War II effort was the invention of the compression still, which added greatly to the operational effectiveness of submarines. The company also has assisted in the expansion and diversification of the industry of Puerto Rico and in other regional studies. It conducts research in all areas of physical and engineering science, product and process development, life sciences and business, including operations research and technical evaluation. The staff of over 1,000 includes more than 500 scientists and engineers. The major activity continues to be research and development for private business and industry.

[Avery A. Ashdown, "Arthur Dehon Little," *Science,* New Series V, vol. 82; Earl P. Stevenson, *Scatter Acorns That Oaks May Grow: Arthur D. Little, Inc., 1886–1953.*]

JAMES A. MULHOLLAND

ARTICLES FOR GOVERNMENT OF THE NAVY. *See* **Uniform Code of Military Justice.**

ARTICLES OF CONFEDERATION. The Continental Congress decided even before independence that it was necessary to set up a confederacy based upon a written instrument. Several plans appeared in the press, and the subject was embraced in R. H. Lee's motion of June 7, 1776, on independence. On June 11 Congress voted to appoint a committee. This body set to work at once and on July 12 reported through John Dickinson a set of articles of confederation, of which eighty copies were printed for the use of members. Congress was so engrossed in war problems, however, that debates on the scheme dragged through more than a year. The principal disputes raged over the questions whether taxes should be apportioned according to the gross number of inhabitants counting slaves or excluding them—the South of course wishing them excluded; whether large and small states should have equality in voting; whether Congress should be given the right to regulate Indian affairs; and whether Congress should be permitted to fix the western boundaries of those states which claimed to the Mississippi. On Nov. 15, 1777, Congress finally approved a draft and sent it to the states, on the understanding that all must ratify it before it went into effect. This draft, declared a circular letter of Congress, "is proposed as the best which could be adapted to the circumstances of all; and as that alone which affords any tolerable prospect of a general ratification."

The Articles did not become the law of the land until Mar. 1, 1781. Nine states ratified as early as July 1778, but several of the smaller ones held back because of the question of western lands. Maryland in particular had urged that these lands be regarded as a common possession of all the states and felt aggrieved when the Articles contained a clause declaring that no state should be deprived of territory for the benefit of the United States. Maryland first declared that it would not ratify until its powerful neighbor, Virginia, ceased to advance extravagant western claims. But when New York had yielded and Virginia seemed certain to do so, Maryland on Mar. 1, 1781, signed the Articles through its delegates and made them effective.

Although the Articles have been harshly criticized and the very shrewdest critics at the time saw their inadequacy, they were generally regarded in 1781 as offering a sound national constitution. They provided for a "perpetual union" or "firm league of friendship" between the states. Each remained sovereign and independent and retained every right not expressly ceded by the Articles to the general government. A single agency of government was established—a Congress; the states were to appoint from two to seven delegates annually to it, and each state was to have one vote. Rhode Island thus obtained a parity with New York or Virginia. The costs of government and defense were to be defrayed from a common treasury, to which the states were to contribute in proportion to the value of their surveyed land and improvements. The states were likewise to supply quotas of troops, in proportion to the white inhabitants of each, upon congressional requisitions. To Congress was entrusted the management of foreign affairs, of war, and of the postal service; it was empowered to borrow money, emit bills of credit, and determine the value of coin; it was to appoint naval officers and superior military officers, and control Indian affairs. But none of these powers was to be exercised save by vote of a majority of all states, and the more important could not be exercised save by the vote of nine. On paper, almost every important national authority was turned over to Congress save three: the authority to raise money directly, the authority to enlist troops directly, and the authority to regulate commerce. But the paper powers proved to be very different from actual power.

It soon became evident that Congress was doomed to fail in its attempts to make the Articles workable. These attempts consisted chiefly in requests to the states for money that was never paid, pleas for troops which filled no army ranks, and petitions for special powers which the states never granted. At various points the powers of the states were supposedly limited. They were forbidden to enter into treaties, confederations, or alliances, to meddle with foreign affairs, or to wage war without congressional consent, unless invaded. Most important of all, they were to give to free inhabitants of other states all the privileges and immunities of their own citizens. A citizen of South Carolina, for example, who removed to Boston, at once became a citizen of Massachusetts. Interstate extradition of criminals was also provided. The states could impose duties, but not any which conflicted with the treaty stipulations of Congress. They were required to "abide by the determinations of Congress" on all subjects which the Articles left to that body. The states did respect each other's rights to a considerable extent (when two or more of them fell out, any one could submit the dispute to Congress). But they failed lamentably to respect the needs and requests of the national government. They refused to do what they should have done, especially in supplying money and men; they frequently did what they should have refrained from doing. A circular prepared by Congress not long after Maryland's ratification in 1781 declared: "The inattention of the States has almost endangered our very existence as a people."

Demands for amendment and invigoration of the Articles were made even before they became effective. New Jersey served notice on Congress Feb. 3, 1780, for example, that it was absolutely necessary to give the nation power to regulate commerce and to fix duties on imports. A committee which reported May 3, 1781, pointed to the chief defect of the Articles—the fact that they gave Congress no power to enforce its measures, and suggested a new article authorizing the employment of armed forces to compel recalcitrant states "to fulfill their Federal engagements." This would have led straight to civil war, and the plan failed. The years 1782–86 witnessed earnest efforts by Congress to obtain state consent to a federal impost, which would have furnished a stable revenue; earnest efforts also were made to obtain from the states a sufficient control over shipping to enable it to wage commercial warfare with nations discriminating against the United States. But some states, notably New York and Rhode Island, long proved stubborn; others were tardy; and when they did act, their laws were found to conflict. Again, while the states were bound to respect the treaties made by Congress, several of them indulged in gross violations of the Definitive Treaty of Peace. The close of the year 1786 found the Articles of Confederation in widespread discredit and many national leaders eager to find a wholly new basis for union. Yet the Articles, soon to give way to the Constitution, should not be regarded with contempt. They had served as a stepping stone to a new order; as John Marshall said later, they had preserved the idea of union until national wisdom could adopt a more efficient system. Had they not been agreed upon in time, the states might have fallen asunder after Yorktown.

[Merrill Jensen, *The New Nation;* Forrest E. McDonald, *E Pluribus Unum;* Edmund Morgan, *Birth of the Republic*.]

ALLAN NEVINS

ARTICLES OF WAR. *See* **Uniform Code of Military Justice.**

ARTICLE X of the League of Nations Covenant was of wholly American origin and was regarded by President Woodrow Wilson as an extension of the Monroe Doctrine to the whole world. In Wilson's mind the undertaking "to preserve as against external aggression the territorial integrity and existing political independence of all Members of the League" was not a pledge to go to war in advance of congressional consideration and decision. He interpreted the obligations of the article as moral, not legal.

Opponents of the covenant in the Senate made Article X their principal target. They argued that it was not the proper business of the United States to guarantee either new boundaries or old empires or to intervene in cases of revolution against oppression. They contended that moral obligations would be found as binding as legal ones. Consequently the Senate adopted a ponderous reservation repudiating any obligation under the article except as the Congress should provide in any particular case. This was unacceptable to Wilson not for its legal effect but for its embodiment of an attitude destructive to the principle of international responsibility. He contemplated territorial change accomplished through the peaceful operation of Article XIX rather than the traditional resort to violence.

[D. F. Fleming, *The United States and the League of Nations, 1918–1920*.]

HAROLD S. QUIGLEY

ARTILLERY in the U.S. Army dates from the revolutionary war, when units from Massachusetts and Rhode Island joined in the siege of Boston. The first artillery regiment of the Continental Army was raised in January 1776; by 1777 four Continental regiments were operating and constituted the regular artillery for the rest of the war. In the wars against the western Indians (1790–94) an artillery battalion was raised but was used mainly as infantry. Artillerymen manned the country's first coast defenses in 1794, leading to a traditional classification of U.S. Army artillery into field, siege and garrison, and coast artillery.

In 1808 a ten-company light or horse artillery regiment was authorized. Only one company was ever fully equipped, and because of the expense of maintaining the horses, it was dismounted the next year. A few units served as light artillery during the War of 1812, but most either doubled as infantry or manned coast defenses. In 1821 four artillery regiments of nine companies each were authorized, one of which was to be equipped with light guns and horses; and in 1847 the number of companies in each artillery regiment was increased to twelve. Although most artillery regiments fought in the Mexican War (1846–48) as infantry, a few functioned as light artillery and performed well. After the war the batteries of artillery were scattered among posts all over the United States, and in an economy move in 1856 the number of light batteries was reduced to four. When the Civil War began, a fifth artillery regiment of twelve batteries was organized. Thus, at the war's end the regular army had five artillery regiments, with a total of sixty batteries, mostly field artillery. In 1898 two additional regiments were organized and in 1899 two heavy batteries were added to each regiment, bringing the total number of batteries to ninety-eight.

In 1901 a major reorganization of artillery occurred. The seven regiments were broken into separate numbered batteries and companies of coast artillery within the Corps of Artillery. Coast and field artillery became full separate branches in 1907. The field artillery batteries were organized into three regiments of light, two mountain, and one horse artillery. Coast artillery remained in separate numbered companies within the Coast Artillery Corps. The number of field artillery regiments increased greatly during World War I, and coast artillery grew through the addition of antiaircraft units.

A need for more flexible, mobile units with greater firepower in World War II led to the breakup of regiments in both artillery branches. Elements were reorganized as separate battalions, batteries, and groups of field, coast, and antiaircraft artillery. They remained separate until the advent of the Combat Arms Regimental System in 1957, when the three components were reorganized as regiments, a system that perpetuates the histories of older units. In 1968 the Air Defense Artillery was established as a separate branch, and the artillery branch was dissolved when Field Artillery again became a separate branch in 1969. In 1972 there were fifty-eight field and twenty-two air-defense artillery regiments in the regular army.

American artillery has seen few major innovations introduced in the United States; mostly the ordnance of other nations has been copied and improved or adapted for use. The Colombaid guns of 1812 were among the first to be built for all elevations of fire while using the British explosive shell. Between 1840 and 1860 built-up guns of iron and steel together were experimented with, and cast guns were improved in range and weight of shot by John A. Dahlgren and T. J. Rodman. During the Civil War the Robert P. Parrott rifled muzzle-loading gun outranged its smoothbore contemporaries. From 1865 to the Spanish-American War a great deal of attention was paid to fortress guns, with innovations in mounts and fire control. From World War I to the present the American artillery has concentrated on improving the guns and their ammunition but has made few major innovations. One innovation, introduced just before World War II, was the proximity fuse. The latter carries a miniature radio set that sends a continuous impulse. As the shell approaches the target the impulse's echo duration becomes shorter, and at a predetermined interval the firing mechanism is activated. Most useful at first in antiaircraft guns, this fuse was adapted to regular artillery with devastating effect.

American inventiveness concentrated on fire control and laying techniques. By the Spanish-American War the artillery had perfected the indirect laying method and developed overhead fire procedures, leading to the technique of using map data to fire on unseen targets, a method used widely in World War I. American fire-control and gun-laying methods were so perfected by World War II that the United States fielded the most accurate, responsive, and widely feared artillery of the combatants. During this war and ever since, great reliance was made on the forward observer and the artillery-spotter aircraft to help direct the fire. One especially effective technique is the Time-On-Target (TOT), whereby any number and caliber of guns within range of a target can fire so that all their shells arrive at the same time.

[William E. Birkhimer, *Historical Sketch of the Organization, Administration, Materiel, and Tactics of the Artillery;* Fairfax Downey, *The Sound of the Guns.*]

WARNER STARK

"AS GOES MAINE, SO GOES THE NATION," a saying based upon the supposed accuracy of Maine's September election as a political barometer for the country, was originated by the Whigs after the presidential election of 1840.

[Claude E. Robinson, "Maine—Political Barometer," *Political Science Quarterly* (1932).]

ROBERT E. MOODY

ASHBURTON TREATY. *See* **Webster-Ashburton Treaty.**

ASHBY'S GAP, a pass in the Blue Ridge Mountains of Virginia leading from the Shenandoah Valley into eastern Virginia, often used by Confederate and Union armies in the several valley campaigns. In June 1863, J. E. B. Stuart's cavalry held this gap to prevent Gen. Joseph Hooker from interfering with Robert E. Lee's army in the march that led to Gettysburg.

[R. U. Johnson and C. C. Buel, eds., *Battles and Leaders of the Civil War,* vol. III.]

W. N. C. CARLTON

ASH HOLLOW, BATTLE OF. *See* **Harney Expedition.**

ASHLEY EXPEDITIONS, three expeditions sent out by William Henry Ashley aimed at launching the Rocky Mountain Fur Company in competition with the Hudson's Bay Company and the older established American companies. The more important results were the exploration of vast areas of the Rocky Mountain Northwest, the firmer hold of American interests on the disputed Northwest country, and the development of some of the more noted mountain men, including Jedediah Smith, Étienne Provost, Jim Bridger, Milton Sublette, Hugh Glass, and Thomas Fitzpatrick.

Organized in St. Louis in 1822 the first expedition, commanded by Andrew Henry, Ashley's lieutenant, came to grief near Great Falls, Mont., where Henry was attacked by the Blackfoot and driven out of the country. Ashley headed another expedition in the following spring, only to be attacked by the Arikara, on the Missouri River, and forced to retreat with heavy loss. Reinforced, the third expedition, in the charge of Jedediah Smith, pushed on to the Yellowstone, penetrated to the Green River Valley, the Utah trapping grounds, and learned from the Crow Indians the important location of South Pass, the effective discovery of which dates from that time. The party returned with a rich cache of furs, and Ashley set forth on a return winter trip. He crossed the Continental Divide by Bridger's Gap and reached the Green River near the crossing of the Oregon Trail. Bridger in the previous autumn had discovered Great Salt Lake.

Ashley replaced the fixed trading post with the annual rendezvous for collecting furs. The first mountain trappers' rendezvous was held in June 1825 and Ashley returned in the fall with a fortune in furs.

[H. M. Chittenden, *History of American Fur Trade;* H. C. Dale, *Ashley-Smith Expeditions;* W. J. Ghent, *Early Far West.*]

CARL L. CANNON

ASIA, TRADE WITH, burgeoned after the Revolution, which released American merchants from the restrictions of the British East India Company. Within a decade of the signing of the peace, ships from the Atlantic seaboard cities were bringing back tea, silks, and cottons from China and India and spices and coffee from the Dutch possessions in the East Indies. The great national trading companies' regulations in India and Indonesia and the lack of an export that China wanted were the principal difficulties American merchants encountered. All were eventually overcome. Americans were the only neutral mercantile people with the necessary skills to prosecute the commerce with Asia; in addition Yankee businessmen proved marvelously ingenious both in circumventing restrictions and in discovering exotic items wanted by the Chinese. The wars of the French Revolution soon delivered a great part of Europe's extracontinental trade into American hands.

The trade in some of these strange commodities would be deplored by later generations more interested in ecology and the well-being of Oriental populations than in commerce. It was American traders who almost exterminated the Northern Pacific sea otter and the Antarctic fur seal and seriously depleted the sandalwood of the Pacific islands. Trade in Turkish opium from Smyrna to Canton (the only port in China open to foreign trade) was an American monopoly because of the regulation forbidding British commerce in that drug of the "honorable company" (the British East India Company). Additionally, the Americans were able to compete very effectively with the British trade to China in Indian opium. It was this British and American commerce in narcotics that balanced payments, East and West, for at least the first half of the 19th century, thus bringing China into the world trading and financial community. It also provided the friction that produced the conflicts and subsequent treaties which "opened" the Celestial Empire, eventually bringing China into the world political arena.

Several developments changed trade patterns with the Orient later in the 19th century: America developed a mechanized textile industry that could undersell both Indian and Chinese cottons anywhere; the various East India companies lost their charters; Western merchants took the tea plant to India, Ceylon, and elsewhere; and Commodore Matthew C. Perry "opened" Japan in 1854. Thereafter, volume and value of commerce with Asia became relatively less important. China was a significant market for the American coarse cottons industry, and the Japan of the Meiji Restoration displaced China as America's major Asian trading partner. Revolutions and civil and world wars that badly disrupted American trade with China had a relatively minor or temporary effect on the commerce with Japan. Indeed, Japan's extraordinary economic development in the present century has rendered American trade with Japan more important than that with the rest of Asia combined.

It may be that the side effects of America's trade with Asia have been more important than the economic value of the commerce itself. China-trade fortunes and talent were of great significance in the American industrial revolution, for example. The establishment of American trading firms in Asia, as well as their members' close identification with other Westerners living there—even before the era of the treaty ports—created a distinctive attitude that carried over into American foreign policy from the moment of its inauguration in 1844 at least until World War II. Quite predictably this mental set helped provoke responses from Asians that American policy planners neither welcomed nor fully understood. Finally, the trade involved the United States very early with some remote but ultimately important areas of the world, such as Hawaii, Alaska, and South America—in fact, the entire Pacific Basin and the Indian Ocean. Thus, the Asian trade was a major influence in propelling the United States into areas and attitudes that were to be of unanticipated and fateful importance for the future. (*See also* China Trade.)

[Tyler Dennett, *Americans in Eastern Asia;* J. M. Downs, "American Merchants and the China Opium Trade, 1800–1840," *Business History Review* (1968), and "Fair Game: Exploitive Role-Myths and the American Opium Trade," *Pacific Historical Review* (1972); John K. Fairbank, *Trade and Diplomacy on the Pacific Coast, 1842–1854;* K. C. Liu, *Americans and Chinese*.]

JACQUES M. DOWNS

ASIENTO, a license granted in 1713 to the English South Sea Company by the Spanish government, as a result of the Treaty of Utrecht, whereby the company was given the exclusive right to sell a total of 144,000 African slaves in the Spanish colonies during thirty years or at the rate of 4,800 a year. For this privilege the company paid the Spanish crown $200,000.

A. CURTIS WILGUS

ASSASSINATIONS, POLITICAL. Violence has always been one response to conflict in periods of intense social and political controversy. The establishment of national independence, the relation of settlers to Indians, the slavery and secession questions, the trade union and ethnic movements, were all examples of intensified group conflict, engendering a persistent series of deadly attacks on people holding public office. Such attacks cannot be described as having a dominant rational political purpose; yet all have been related to politics and have had a political effect. By the mid-1970's there were eighty-one recorded assassinations or attempted assassinations of officeholders in the United States—and this number excludes attacks on politically prominent nonofficeholders, although many such attacks have had strong political motives and effects, as in the case of civil rights leader Martin Luther King, Jr.

On Jan. 30, 1835, an unsuccessful attempt was made to kill Andrew Jackson by Richard Lawrence, whose gun misfired. He was deemed a madman. The assassination of Abraham Lincoln on Apr. 14, 1865, was the first of great political consequence in the United States. In 1880 bitter quarrels among Republican leaders over patronage had their effect on Charles J. Guiteau, who importuned James A. Garfield from the day of his inauguration (Mar. 4, 1881) for a consular position. On July 2 he armed himself and shot the president as he was passing through the Union Railroad Station in Washington, D.C.; the president died on Sept. 19. On Sept. 6, 1901, William McKinley stood shaking hands at the Pan-American Exposition in Buffalo, N.Y., when he was mortally wounded by Leon F. Czolgosz, a young anarchist who had been influenced by Emma Goldman and others of her persuasion.

Former President Theodore Roosevelt was wounded in the chest on Oct. 14, 1912, as he made a political campaign speech in Milwaukee, Wis. His assailant, John N. Schrank, claimed, as he was hauled away, that he had acted at the behest of a vision of McKinley that commanded him to avenge the earlier assassination. Roosevelt stanched the blood with his fist and continued his speech. Franklin D. Roosevelt was the target of an assassination attempt on Feb. 15, 1933, in Florida by Joseph Zangara, who said he hated rulers and capitalists. Mayor Anton J. Cermak of Chicago, who was seated beside the president in his motorcar, was killed. On Nov. 1, 1950, Puerto Ricans Oscar Collazo and Griselio Torresola attempted to shoot their way into Blair House, the temporary residence of Harry Truman. The president was unharmed but a guard and Torresola were killed. Collazo was sentenced to death, but Truman commuted the sentence to life imprisonment. On Nov. 22, 1963, John F. Kennedy was shot and killed in Dallas, Tex. A commission established by his successor, chaired by Chief Justice Earl Warren, concluded that Lee Harvey Oswald was the lone assassin and that his motivation was obscure.

Kennedy's brother, Robert F. Kennedy, was shot on June 5, 1968, by Sirhan Sirhan with a small-caliber pistol immediately following a victory statement after the California presidential primary. His assassin claimed he was punishing the candidate for his pro-Israel statements (all the candidates had made similar statements). Kennedy died the following day.

These nine attacks span 133 years. Party affiliation, public policy, term of office, and political strength provide few clues to what triggered the attacks. Lincoln was the president of a divided nation; Garfield was the compromise candidate of a faction-torn party; and McKinley was the popular president of traditional American society, into whose midst came the political activists of turbulent Europe. The only common denominator among the attempts is that they correspond with a high level of civil strife. Every assassination attempt in American history occurred at or near a peak of either local or general civil strife.

With the exception of attacks on Republicans in the South during Reconstruction, only a small portion of the eighty-one incidents can be shown clearly to have been rationally calculated to advance political aims. The attack on Truman in 1950 by the two Puerto Rican nationalists was the only one made on a president under the aegis of an organized political group. Similarly the attacks on other officeholders were related to politics without being conspiratorial or political in the sense that the assailants were seeking power. Local politicians and candidates have been beaten or murdered on the orders of their rivals or rackets bosses, in reprisal for political infidelity or as part of a local political coup; but most such incidents are difficult to identify.

Of all the attacks against officeholders in U.S. history, perhaps only one qualifies as a rational political act—the attack on William Goebel, governor of Kentucky, in 1900. Goebel's Populist Democratic party narrowly won a three-way fight against Conservative Democrats and incumbent Republicans. Three men associated with the Republicans were convicted of the conspiracy that led to his assassination. Other politically identifiable attacks include the caning of Massachusetts Sen. Charles Sumner in 1856 by South Carolina Rep. Preston Smith Brooks, an act of outrage over an antislavery speech; the 1859 death of California Sen. David C. Broderick, shot by David S. Terry in a duel over slavery issues; the 1935 assassination of Louisiana Sen. Huey P. Long by Carl A. Weiss, apparently motivated by the fact that his father-in-law's judgeship had been taken away; and the wounding of five members on the floor of the House of Representatives by a group of Puerto Rican nationalists in 1954. The remainder of the eighty-one cases defy classification as "political" in terms of the motivation and personal characteristics of the assassins or would-be assassins, but they achieve a public dimension because of the choice of target and the political aftermath. In these cases the choice of target must be considered symbolic and the lone individual's motivation disturbed and ambiguous.

Political assassinations became a dire reality—and an ever-present public concern—during the 1960's, associated with the domestic troubles of the civil rights movement and the war in Vietnam. The deadly series of assassinations began with the 1963 murders of President Kennedy and civil rights leader Medgar W. Evers, followed by those of George Lincoln Rockwell, Martin Luther King, Jr., and Robert Kennedy, and ended with the 1972 unsuccessful attempt to kill presidential candidate George Wallace of Alabama. It seemed as though television and jet travel had summoned into being a worldwide stage for violence and terrorism. Political hijackings, kidnappings, and acts of violence by organized groups against diplomats, athletes, and celebrities evoked widespread attention and unease.

After the death of Robert Kennedy, President Lyndon B. Johnson appointed a commission (headed by Milton Eisenhower) to study social and political violence and recommend means of prevention. For the first time social scientists studied violence in Western nations as more than a meaningless aberration. In general it was found that the level of assassination and violence corresponded to the level of political turmoil and violence in general: it was concluded that the greater the level of civil strife, the more likely it is that high officeholders will be attacked. The violence of the 1960's, the commission found, was largely the result of disaffection that "weakens the consensus upon which the strength of government is based." And the commission found no "specific remedy for assassination and political violence in a democracy apart from the perceived legitimacy of the government and its leaders."

A study of past assassinations and attempted assassinations permits a number of conclusions. First, the more powerful and prestigious the office, the greater the likelihood of assassination. Second, the occupant of, or aspirant to, an elected public office is much more likely to be the victim of an assassination than the occupant of an appointed position, even if the latter is a powerful one (such as secretary of state or Supreme Court justice). One of every four U.S. presidents has been a target of assassination, as compared with approximately one of every 160 governors, one of every 142 senators, and one of every 1,000 congressmen. A vice-president has never been a target.

[William J. Crotty, ed., *Assassinations and the Political Order;* National Commission on the Causes and Prevention of Violence, *Assassination and Political Violence;* H. L. Nieburg, *Political Violence.*]

H. L. NIEBURG

ASSAY OFFICES. Assaying is done at all the federal mints, but special plants were established at New York in 1853; at Boise, Idaho, 1869; Helena, Mont., 1874; Deadwood, S.Dak., and Seattle, Wash., 1896; and Salt Lake City, Utah, 1908, for the receipt, testing, melting, and refining of gold and silver bullion and foreign coins and for recasting into bars, ingots, or discs. The early mints established at New Orleans, La., Charlotte, N.C., and Denver, Colo., were later turned into assay offices.

Other than the federal mints, there are now only two assay offices—New York and San Francisco. The New York Office also receives gold and silver bars as settlement for international balances.

[Jesse P. Watson, *The Bureau of the Mint.*]

Alvin F. Harlow

ASSEMBLY, FIRST AMERICAN. The colony established at Jamestown, Va., in 1607—under the charters of 1606, 1609, and 1612 of the Virginia Company of London—was governed by members of the company who assembled for Quarter Courts four times each year. In November 1618, the court ratified the Great Charter of Privileges, Orders, and Laws, giving the colony a generous measure of self-government. Sir George Yeardley was named the new governor of the colony, and he chose his wife's cousin, John Pory, to accompany him as secretary of Virginia, both to serve three-year terms. Upon arrival Pory was also made a member of the council, a small governing body appointed by the company. Yeardley's instructions called for the convening of an assembly as one step in the company's plan to give colonists the same "liberties, franchises, and immunities" as those enjoyed by residents of Britain. Thus the first legislature in any American colony gathered in July 1619 in the choir of the new church at Jamestown. It was attended by the governor, the four members of the council, and twenty-two burgesses—two from each of the eleven settlements making up the colony; Pory, who had served in Parliament from 1605 until 1611, was appointed speaker. The assembly, as Parliament did, exercised the privilege of determining the eligibility of its own members and actually denied seats to two burgesses. The work of the assembly fell into three categories: first, the members took into consideration the provisions of the new charter, endorsing some, but petitioning for clarification of portions of others; second, they passed laws growing out of the instructions issued to Gov. Yeardley and his predecessors; and third, they passed a series of local laws to govern the colony better.

[Richard L. Morton, *Colonial Virginia.*]

William S. Powell

ASSEMBLY, RIGHT OF, is protected by the federal and state constitutions. The First Amendment of the U.S. Constitution (1791) provides that Congress shall make no law abridging "the right of the people peaceably to assemble," and the Massachusetts constitution of 1780, to cite an early state document, declares that "the people have a right in an orderly and peaceable manner, to assemble to consult upon the common good." Although the right of peaceable assembly was once described by the Supreme Court as a by-product of the right of petition, Chief Justice Charles Evans Hughes declared in 1937 that it is "cognate to those of free speech and free press and is equally fundamental" (*De Jonge* v. *Oregon,* 299 U.S. 353, 364 [1937]). Indeed, it is regarded as so fundamental a right that its violation by a state is subject to review by the U.S. Supreme Court under the liberty guaranty of the due process clause of the Fourteenth Amendment (*Bates* v. *City of Little Rock,* 361 U.S. 516 [1960]).

Almost all constitutional clauses on the subject of assembly speak of "peaceful" or "orderly" assembly. Thus, like all other rights, the right of assembly is not unlimited. It is limited by the requirements of public order and public peace. In American law an unlawful assembly is usually defined as a gathering of three or more people, which has the common intent to attain a purpose, whether lawful or unlawful, that will interfere with the rights of others by committing acts in such fashion as to give firm and courageous people in the vicinity reasonable ground to apprehend a breach of the peace. To sustain a charge of unlawful assembly it must be proved that the defendants "assembled together" and intended to commit an unlawful act—such as intimidation, threats, boycott, or assault—or a lawful act in a violent, boisterous, or tumultuous manner. At the same time, it is clearly established in the law that a meeting cannot be prohibited merely because unpopular changes may be advocated. Thus the U.S. Supreme Court ruled in the famous case of *New York ex rel. Bryant* v. *Zimmerman,* 278 U.S. 63 (1928), that a terrorist organization such as the Ku Klux Klan may be required to submit a roster of its membership and a list of its officers to state authority, but that school teachers as a class (*Shelton* v. *Tucker,* 364 U.S. 479 [1960]), or an organization committed to lawful purposes, such as the National Association for the Advancement of Colored People (*Gibson* v. *Florida Legislative Investigation Committee,* 372 U.S. 539 [1963]), may not constitutionally be required to submit to any public authority a list of their associational ties or membership records. In *Henry* v. *City of Rock Hill,* 376 U.S. 776 (1964), the Court ruled squarely that the Constitution does not permit a local government to make the peaceful expression of unpopular views in a public place a criminal act. Furthermore, in contrast to British courts, American courts do not usually accept the view that the police may forbid a public meeting merely because they have reasonable grounds to believe that public disorder may result if the meeting is held. Even so, police discretion under either system of law is very great, and is not subject to effective judicial review. Finally, the right to hold meetings in streets, parks, or other public places is well recognized, but it ends where traffic obstruction or unlawful assembly, riot, or other breach of the peace occurs. While an ordinance forbidding all processions on the streets is clearly unreasonable, the city may require a prior permit, providing that the administrative official is not given an undefined or uncontrolled discretion. A leading decision on this point of law is *Niemotko* v. *Maryland,* 340 U.S. 268 (1951), which expressed strong disapproval of conferring upon local officials a "limitless discretion" in granting or denying permits for the holding of meetings in public places.

[David Fellman, *The Constitutional Right of Association,* chaps. 1–2.]

David Fellman

ASSEMBLY LINE, a system of manufacturing in which the work moves on a conveyor while each worker performs a specialized operation as the product goes by. The work operations may also be performed automatically. This technique was foreshadowed as early as the 15th century, when Venetian galleys were towed through the Arsenal while equipment and stores were installed from warehouses on either side. Christopher Polhem (1661–1751), a Swedish engineer, had the concept of rationalized production methods but lacked the technology to put his ideas into effect. At the beginning of the 19th century the English mechanical engineer Henry Maudslay designed a mechanized system for making pulley blocks and sheaves that enabled 10 men operating forty-four machines to do the work of 110 skilled craftsmen.

However, the assembly-line technique as such is largely an American development. In 1785 Oliver Evans built a gristmill near Wilmington, Del., in which a system of conveyors and chutes powered by waterwheels provided a continuous flow through the plant. This process became general in American flour milling. Subsequently, conveyor systems were used extensively to carry carcasses of animals through meat-packing plants, and in foundry operations to carry materials between the molding room and the foundry. One American contribution to the development of assembly-line production, the machine manufacture of standardized and interchangeable parts, was actually of European origin but came to fruition in the United States through the work of men like Eli Whitney and Samuel Colt. As early as the 1850's it was known in Europe as the "American system of manufacture." Another contribution, the concept of scientific management, was initiated in the 1890's in the time-and-motion studies of Frederick W. Taylor.

These various elements of the assembly line converged in the American automobile industry, and specifically in the Ford Motor Company, between 1908 and 1913. The company was faced with the problem of increasing the output of Model T cars while keeping the unit cost as low as possible. It is not certain who first suggested the moving assembly line, but the strongest evidence points to Clarence Avery, who had been Edsel Ford's high school manual training teacher. Early in 1913, the Ford Motor Company installed an assembly line for magnetos, with the result that assembly time was cut from eighteen minutes to five. Then a chassis assembly line was tried, with the chassis at first towed by rope and windlass while tests were made of such factors as optimum speeds and height. By Jan. 1, 1914, the production process was complete. It made possible complete chassis assembly in one and a half hours instead of the twelve and a half hours needed for stationary assembly, and engine assembly in six hours instead of twelve.

This initial example of complete assembly-line production was a major technological breakthrough that was followed not only by other automotive firms, but also by manufacturers of other commodities for which large output at low unit cost was wanted. Nevertheless it was a primitive technique by later standards. It required almost complete uniformity in the product, whereas by the 1950's data control processes permitted wide variations on the same assembly line.

In motor-vehicle manufacturing there are usually two main assembly lines, chassis and body, each fed by subassemblies for parts and components and eventually joining near the end of the process. The main and subassembly lines must be accurately synchronized. This technique is the core of modern mass production. It is also a capital intensive technique, requiring a heavy investment in equipment and tools, so that to be economically feasible it has to have a market capable of absorbing large quantities of the product. Estimates of the output needed to justify assembly-line production vary widely, but in the automobile industry the minimum for successful operation is not less than 200,000 units a year for a single assembly line working one 8-hour shift a day. The assembly line has therefore had an unpredicted impact: it increases production and reduces costs, but the investment it represents is also an incentive to create demand.

[Roger Burlingame, *Backgrounds of Power;* Siegfried Giedion, *Mechanization Takes Command;* Allan Nevins, with Frank E. Hill, *Ford: The Times, the Man, the Company.*]

JOHN B. RAE

ASSESSMENT OF CANDIDATES. *See* **Political Assessments.**

ASSINIBOINE (or **Assiniboin**). A vigorous and populous tribe of the northern Plains, the Assiniboine appeared in the 18th century on both sides of the Canadian border in Saskatchewan and Montana. Numbering about 10,000 in 1780, although hardly a fraction of that population by the mid-20th century, the Assiniboine played an important part in trade between whites and Indians, channeling firearms to other tribes. A Siouan-speaking people, they are held by tradition to be an offshoot of the Yanktonai Dakota, the split evidently having occurred in prehistoric times. The Assiniboine made their way into Manitoba, gradually moving westward to maintain contact with the Hudson's Bay Company posts. They adopted the horse, the tipi, and related Plains traditions, waging war over a long period against their former Dakota relatives.

[Robert H. Lowie, *The Assiniboine;* D. Rodnick, *The Fort Belknap Assiniboine of Montana.*]

ROBERT F. SPENCER

ASSINIBOINE, FORT, a post of the American Fur Company, west of Fort Union (near the present Montana–North Dakota border), which was the head of steamboat navigation on the Missouri River, 1834–35, and a depot for inland trade with the Assiniboine, Piegan, and Blackfoot.

[H. M. Chittenden, *The American Fur Trade of the Far West.*]

PAUL C. PHILLIPS

ASSISTANCE CLAUSE. Election laws, providing for the choice of an "honest and capable man" from each major party to "assist any voter in the preparation of his ballot when from any cause he is unable to do so" (Delaware, 1891) or for the voter's choice of "any qualified voter in the election district" for the same purpose (Pennsylvania, 1891), soon facilitated the delivery of bribed votes. Party members, serving as assistants, influenced the marking of ballots and rewarded the "fixed" voters with the token (pin, tag, acorn) for which the promised bribe would be paid. The 20th century saw increasing state legislation to abolish the assistants and check fraud in connection with bona fide assistance to disabled voters.

[J. A. Salter, *Boss Rule;* J. A. Woodburn, *Political Parties and Party Problems in the United States.*]

BAYRD STILL

ASSISTANT. The Massachusetts Bay Company Charter (1629) provided for eighteen assistants to be elected yearly by the freemen (stockholders). Seven, with the governor (or deputy governor), constituted a quorum (Court of Assistants) to manage the company's ordinary affairs. When the company became a commonwealth in Massachusetts, an assistant became a magistrate. Until deputies were admitted (1634), the Court of Assistants was the colony's sole legislature. As the colony's constitution matured, the assistants held four functions—legislative, executive, judicial, and "consultative" (that is, the governor's "standing council" with extensive powers "in the vacancy of the General Court"). The Connecticut Charter (1662) provided twelve assistants with similar powers.

[H. L. Osgood, *The American Colonies in the Seventeenth Century.*]

RAYMOND P. STEARNS

ASSOCIATED LOYALISTS OF NEW ENGLAND, or Loyal Associated Refugees, consisted of various associations formed by Col. Edward Winslow, Jr., in Rhode Island during its occupation by the British (December 1776–October 1779), to chastise the Americans for losses and indignities. They made several raids in Long Island Sound, capturing vessels, cattle, and prisoners.

[W. H. Siebert, "Loyalist Troops of New England," *The New England Quarterly,* vol. 4.]

WILBUR H. SIEBERT

ASSOCIATED PRESS. The formation of the Associated Press in May 1848 was the first successful attempt at cooperative news gathering on the eastern seaboard. The occasion was a meeting at the New York *Sun* office that resulted from persistent efforts of David Hale, co-owner of the New York *Journal of Commerce*. Four other participating newspapers were the *Herald, Tribune, Express,* and *Courier and Enquirer*—their representatives including such notable journalistic figures as James Gordon Bennett, Horace Greeley, and Henry J. Raymond. Although the papers were strong competitors, they agreed to divide the expense of telegraphic transmission of news from Washington, D.C., and from Europe on its arrival by ship at Boston.

At first this combination was vigorously opposed by telegraph companies, which had their own rudimentary news-sending arrangements. But by the outbreak of the Civil War the AP, as it came to be known, was reaching out over the country through member newspapers that both collected and disseminated, largely on a regional basis, news that was objectively written and concisely edited. During the Civil War the AP was exempted, because of its unbiased reporting, from the Department of State's brief order prohibiting telegraphic dispatches from Washington relating to either military or civil operations of the government. Monopolistic practices led to the formation in 1882 of a short-lived rival, to the shift in management from New York to Chicago under Melville E. Stone, and to a welter of controversies and investigations. After the Illinois Supreme Court outlawed the AP's exclusion of competitors from membership, the headquarters returned to New York in 1900, where the company was incorporated as a nonprofit cooperative.

While agreements with foreign press services brought in overseas news, the AP established correspondents around the globe who scored many beats in both war and peace. The monopoly continued in the United States until the formation of the United Press (1907) and the International News Service (1909). Landmark test cases took a variety of AP issues to the Supreme Court. In 1918 the Court upheld the AP's suit to prevent the International News Service from copying AP dispatches for distribution to INS members (248 U.S. 215). In 1937 the AP lost a leading New Deal labor case and was required to reemploy Morris Watson, discharged after he organized a unit of the American Newspaper Guild (301 U.S. 103). The practice of preventing distribution of news to rival nonmembers was finally outlawed as a violation of the Sherman Antitrust Act in 1945 (326 U.S. 1). In 1967 the AP won dismissal of the $2 million libel action brought by Gen. Edwin A. Walker against its report of his connection with rioting at the University of Mississippi (388 U.S. 130).

In addition to its news-reporting activities, the AP also provides wirephoto service (introduced in 1935) and financial news reports. In 1936 the sports department of the AP originated an annual and authoritative nationwide poll of sports editors and broadcasters for the selection of the ten best collegiate football teams, with the first team receiving the AP trophy and recognition as the national champion.

By 1974 the AP served 1,265 U.S. daily newspapers and 3,400 television and radio stations in the United States and a total of some 10,000 newspapers and broadcast stations in 104 countries. Its vast news net employed more than 150 reporters in Washington, D.C., alone. The annual budget exceeded $70 million. Many of the writers, editors, and managers of the AP have become notable in the world of journalism, for example, Kent Cooper, during whose general managership (1925–48) the AP contributed significantly to a new era in world communications. Twenty-seven staff members have won Pulitzer Prizes for news reporting and photography excellence. The first was won in 1922 by Kirke L. Simpson, for a series of stories on the burial of the Unknown Soldier. Joe Rosenthal's photograph of marines raising the flag on Iwo Jima won the prize in 1945, and Relman Morin's story of school integration rioting in Little Rock, Ark., won it in 1958.

[Edwin Emery, Philip H. Ault, and Warren K. Agee, *Introduction to Mass Communications;* Oliver Gramling, *AP: The Story of News;* Victor Rosewater, *History of Cooperative News-Gathering in the United States;* Peter M. Sandman, David M. Rubin, and David B. Sachsman, *Media.*]

IRVING DILLIARD

ASSOCIATIONS, one of the most effective pieces of revolutionary machinery used in the American Revolution. Before the Stamp Act the colonies were already familiar through merchant societies and political clubs with the idea of organization by agreement and pledge of support for some particular purpose. It was therefore an easy step for them, after the passage of that act, to use the device in nonimportation and nonconsumption agreements as a means of economic compulsion on Great Britain, enforced by another form of association, the Sons of Liberty. Local organizations were early linked up through committees of correspondence into an intercolonial association of the "true Sons of Liberty," whose chief aim appears to have been to keep a watchful eye on suspected enemies of the colonial cause. By 1773 nonimportation agreements and the Sons of Liberty had practically faded out of the picture, but came forcibly to the fore again when Parliament that year passed the act permitting the East India Company to export its tea to America without paying the usual English duties. Upon the passing of the Boston Port Bill following the Tea Party, the First Continental Congress, in 1774, adopted the famous "association," the members pledging themselves and their constituents not to import, export, or consume British goods until their grievances were redressed. The pledgers in this case provided the commercial boycott as sanction against both states and individuals who refused to join or broke their agreements. After the outbreak of hostilities, associations, both loyalist and patriot, were spontaneously formed, pledging the signers to serve their cause with their lives. During the course of the war, both England and its colonies found the association idea an effective device for recruiting troops.

[Carl Becker, *The Eve of the Revolution.*]

VIOLA F. BARNES

ASSOCIATORS, a military organization formed by Benjamin Franklin, Nov. 21, 1747, to defend the port of Philadelphia. Revolting against the pacific policy of the Quakers, they formed military companies and erected two batteries on the Delaware River. The Associators disbanded after the peace of Aix-la-Chapelle in 1748.

JULIAN P. BOYD

ASSUMPTION AND FUNDING OF REVOLUTIONARY WAR DEBTS. At the time of the organization of the American national government under the U.S. Constitution it was found that the national debt consisted of the following: foreign debt, $11,710,378; to domestic creditors, $42,414,085, including $2,000,000 of unliquidated debt. Alexander Hamilton as secretary of the treasury proposed to pay this at par in order that the credit of the national government might be established, although the domestic debt had been selling as low as 25 percent. This was finally agreed to after much popular opposition, since it meant that speculators who had bought up the securities would make large profits. In addition Hamilton also desired that the national government should assume the payment of the debts incurred by the individual states in carrying on the revolutionary war. This assumption of the state debts would increase the national debt by $18,271,786. From this proposal arose the celebrated "assumption" issue.

Some of the states had paid part of their revolutionary war debt while others had paid but little; also, some states were in far better financial condition than others, since they had suffered but little from the direct effects of the war. The state of New York was in a peculiarly advantageous position if an assumption measure was proposed. It was among the largest of the debtors, but aside from this obligation was in an unusually strong financial situation, due to the sale of public lands and the careful investment of state funds. The southern states whose population was smaller than that of the northern states were especially hostile to this assumption, which would place increased taxation for its payment upon the entire country, themselves included. Hamilton rightly claimed that assumption of the state debts would cause the creditors holding these securities to look to the national government for their payment, and thus increase their support of the new government at the expense of the states. He favored this as a strong believer in nationalism.

At the same time quite a controversy arose concerning the location of the new national capital. The southern states were especially anxious that it be placed on the banks of the Potomac River while other locations such as sites on the Susquehanna River in Pennsylvania and the Delaware River in New Jersey were advocated by the people of the middle and northern states. The issue of assumption was at first defeated in Congress, but finally, with the assistance of Thomas Jefferson, Hamilton procured an agreement by which southern votes in Congress were secured for the assumption of state debts in return for northern votes to locate the national capital on the banks of the Potomac River at the present city of Washington, D.C. It has been held that this agreement was accomplished by the action of Jefferson, then secretary of state, who invited Hamilton to dine with him at his home. Also, a few other friends were present at this social meeting for an informal conference. Jefferson, himself, reportedly stated that reasonable men could form a compromise by mutual satisfaction, which compromise was to save the Union. Since it would take time to build the national capital, it was further agreed that the government, then located at New York, should be transferred to Philadelphia for ten to fifteen years and after that to the present site of the national capital city at Washington.

Supposedly as a result of this informal agreement both the measures with regard to the assumption of state debts and the location of the national capital were carried through Congress in the spring of 1790.

[J. S. Bassett, *A Short History of the United States;* Gilbert Chinard, *Thomas Jefferson;* S. McKee, ed., *Hamilton's Papers on Public Credit, Commerce, Finance.*]

WILLIAM STARR MYERS

ASTOR FUR COMPANY. *See* **American Fur Company; Astoria; Pacific Fur Company.**

ASTORIA. John Jacob Astor planned an organized fur trade on a continental scale some time before American occupation of the upper Missouri country. To his American Fur Company, chartered in 1808, he added the Pacific Fur Company, organized in 1810, and proceeded to extend his organization from St. Louis to the mouth of the Columbia River in Oregon. Two expeditions were sent to Oregon: one by sea, and one along the route of the Lewis and Clark Expedition. The seagoing party, under Capt. Jonathan Thorn, embarked Sept. 6, 1810, in the *Tonquin* and after a stormy voyage reached the Columbia on Mar. 23, 1811. Within three weeks Astoria was established under the direction of Duncan McDougal, acting resident agent. In June Capt. Thorn and a trading party were massacred by Indians in Nootka Sound, and the lone white survivor blew up the ship *Tonquin,* killing himself and many Indians.

On July 15, 1811, a party of Canadians, sent by the rival North West Company to forestall the Americans, arrived at Astoria. In January 1812, a second party came from the North West Company post on the Spokane River. Then came the Astor Overlanders, thirty-four in number. They had left St. Louis Mar. 12, 1811, under the leadership of Wilson Price Hunt and had traveled up the Missouri and westward through the country of the Crow, over the Continental Divide to the Snake River, thence to the Columbia and the Pacific, where they arrived Feb. 15, 1812. In May, the Astor ship, *Beaver,* arrived. Activities were extended inland to the mouth of the Okanagan, to the Spokane, and to the Snake River. Robert Stuart and a small party of eastbound Astor Overlanders set out with dispatches for Astor in New York, June 29, 1812, ascended the Snake River to its head, became the first white men to cross the South Pass, wintered on the Platte, and arrived in St. Louis Apr. 30, 1813. They did not return, for news of the War of 1812 sounded the doom of the Astor enterprise. On Oct. 23, 1813, while Hunt was absent, McDougal and his associates, whose sympathies were with the British, sold all the Astor interests on the Columbia to the North West Company. Hunt returned to find Astoria in rival hands, the post renamed Fort George, and the British flag flying. Astoria was restored to the United States in 1818 in accordance with the Treaty of Ghent.

[H. M. Chittenden, *The American Fur Trade of the Far West.*]

CARL P. RUSSELL

ASTOR PLACE RIOT, in New York City, May 10, 1849, an outgrowth of a long-standing jealousy between the American actor Edwin Forrest and the English tragedian William Charles Macready, and essentially an expression of anti-British feeling mingled with class hatred. When police failed to disperse a pro-Forrest mob outside the Astor Place Opera House where Macready was playing *Macbeth,* the militia was called out; twenty-two people were killed and thirty-six wounded.

[M. J. Moses, *The Fabulous Forrest.*]

STANLEY R. PILLSBURY

ASTRONAUTICS. Derived from ''aeronautics'' (the science or art of flight in aircraft) the word ''astronautics'' gained currency in the late 1950's as it became obvious that men would soon be learning to navigate and fly spacecraft. Just as the legendary Greeks who sailed on the *Argo* in search of the Golden Fleece were called Argonauts and pioneering balloonists were named aeronauts, the first Americans to train for spaceflight were called astronauts. In 1959 the new National Aeronautics and Space Administration (NASA) selected seven military test pilots to train to be orbital circumnavigators, or astronauts, as part of the U.S. manned ballistic satellite program, Project Mercury. When the Soviet Union began the era of man in space on Apr. 12, 1961, with the flight of Yuri Gagarin, the popularization of the Russian term ''cosmonaut'' furnished a convenient tab for keeping score during a space-race decade of competition between cosmonauts and astronauts.

Although science fictioneers of the 19th century sometimes spoke of astronautics as the future mode of controlled human transport among the stars, the technical usage of the term was probably first introduced by the French aeronautical pioneer Robert Esnault-Pelterie. In 1929 he published a book entitled *L'astronautique,* expanding on several earlier papers dealing with the possibilities for interplanetary voyages. Applying the laws of celestial mechanics to manned spaceship ideas, such visionary pioneers as the Russian K. E. Tsiolkovsky, the American Robert H. Goddard, and the German Hermann Oberth, proved the feasibility of such ventures. Other transportation engineers and aeronautical scientists in the 1920's and 1930's—assuming a coming age of rocketry, superaviation, and superartillery—spoke of astronautics primarily in terms of the guidance, control, and navigation necessities for spaceships. Interplanetary travel then still seemed distant enough for all celestial bodies to be considered "stars"; thus, to navigate even to the moon, Venus, or Mars would be to perform a feat of astronautics. Although the term has been used generically to refer loosely to all man-made objects (mostly robots so far) that have probed the aerospace environment, it is now usually reserved in a specific sense to apply to the flight of humanly piloted vehicles that traverse outward beyond earth's stratosphere (above 50 miles or 100 kilometers).

Astronautics Programs. Rocket technology moved steadily toward intercontinental ballistic missilery during the 1950's. Combined with advances in high-performance military aviation; a bipolarized international rivalry; an arms race between the United States and the Soviet Union; the electronic computer revolution; and the development of telemetry, telecommunications, and various environmental, thermal, reaction, safety, mission, and configuration control systems, rocketry set the stage for man's escape from the gravitational envelope of the earth.

The years after 1961 witnessed a steady progression of programs and missions in astronautics. The most spectacular was inaugurated by President John F. Kennedy on May 25, 1961, when he asked Congress to authorize and appropriate moneys to NASA for a manned lunar landing and return within the decade. Project Mercury had just been preempted by the Soviets' Project Vostok, and the United States had had only fifteen minutes of experience in space with the suborbital Mercury-Redstone flight of Comdr. Alan B. Shepard, Jr. The presidential call was enthusiastically endorsed, and Project Apollo became a much larger and more complex program, designed to land on the moon rather than merely circumnavigate it.

The Mercury project achieved its design goals in February 1962 with the three-orbit mission of Col. John H. Glenn. Meanwhile, NASA needed an interim spaceflight program to fill the gaps in time and knowledge concerning rendezvous, docking, long-duration space flight, and technical improvements of many different sorts. Thus, Project Gemini was created for two-man operations; it also quickly developed into a major, first-class spacecraft program. So successful were its twelve missions, mostly in 1965 and 1966, that the United States finally gained a lead over the Soviet Union in the most spectacular events of the space race.

At the beginning of 1967 the Apollo program, with spacecraft to accommodate three-man crews for two weeks and with Saturn launch vehicles that promised to be able to inject over 100,000-pound payloads into translunar trajectories, seemed ready to launch a new, more truly astronautical, era. But a tragic fire during testing operations at the Cape Kennedy launch site snuffed out the lives of three astronauts; shortly thereafter, a cosmonaut was killed because his parachute landing system failed. Thus, a moratorium ensued for a year or so in astronautical achievements.

When Apollo operations resumed in 1968, the Saturn V launch vehicle and the command and service modules with all their appurtenances were in readiness. Because the lunar landing module was not, the second manned flight of the Saturn-Apollo systems was assigned to make the first lunar circumnavigation. In December 1968, Apollo 8—carrying Frank Borman, James A. Lovell, Jr., and William A. Anders—first broke the hold of earth's gravisphere. They circled the moon at less than 100 nautical miles altitude on Christmas Eve. Two more test missions were almost equally impressive. Consequently, on July 16, 1969, Apollo 11 was launched for the design goal of the decade. Four days later Neil A. Armstrong, followed by Edwin E. Aldrin, Jr., set foot upon the moon—in view of live television on earth—and thus took "one small step for [a] man, one giant leap for mankind."

Although this crowning achievement of the Apollo program was reinforced by six subsequent missions to the moon, one of which (Apollo 13) failed to land there, the accomplishments of lunar exploration have now been complemented by the achievements of three Skylab long-duration missions in earth orbit. These synoptic explorations of life in a space station and of earth's resources augur well for the future of astronautics. Using modified Apollo spacecraft, a demonstration of international cooperation and rescue capabilities, the Apollo-Soyuz Test Project, was scheduled for 1975. This project signaled the beginning of interplanetary spaceflight sponsored by international organizations seeking to send men to follow the many automatic spacecraft that have already probed the neighborhoods of Venus, Mars, and Jupiter.

[Eugene M. Emme, *Aeronautics and Astronautics, 1915–60;* Barton C. Hacker and James M. Grimwood, *On the Shoulders of Titans: A History of Project Gemini;* National Aeronautics and Space Administration, *Astronautics and Aeronautics;* Loyd S. Swenson, Jr., James M. Grimwood, and Charles C. Alexander, *This New Ocean: A History of Project Mercury;* Loyd S. Swenson, Jr., James M. Grimwood, and Courtney G. Brooks, *Apollo's Chariots: A History of the First Lunar Landing*.]

LOYD S. SWENSON, JR.

ASTRONOMY. Until about 1830, astronomy was little cultivated in the United States except by isolated individuals in the late 18th century, such as David Rittenhouse and Nathaniel Bowditch, and was largely limited to surveying and navigation. The years 1830–50 saw the founding of the first major American observatories—particularly the U.S. Naval Observatory in Washington, D.C. (1842), and Harvard Observatory in Cambridge, Mass. (1839). The first Harvard director, William C. Bond, erected a 15-inch refracting telescope, largest in the world except for its twin at Pulkovo, Russia. Other important observatories established before 1850 included those at New Haven, Conn., belonging to Yale College, and at Cincinnati, Ohio. The principal achievements of American astronomy in this early era were the use of the electric telegraph in determining geographical longitudes and Bond's invention of the chronograph for the precise timing of observations. The pioneer experiments in celestial photography at Harvard Observatory, where Bond took the first photograph of a star (Vega) in 1850, were of great future significance.

During the first half of the 19th century, Germany led the world in practical and mathematical astronomy. American science was greatly stimulated through the importation of German methods, especially by Ferdinand Hassler, Swiss-born founder of the U.S. Coast Survey (1807); Benjamin Apthorp Gould, who studied in Germany and founded the *Astronomical Journal* (1849); and Franz Brünnow, who became the first director of the observatory at Ann Arbor, Mich. (1854).

The rest of the 19th century saw the rapid growth and diversification of American activity in astronomy. Alvan Clark, a self-taught Massachusetts optician, and his sons quickly became the world's leading telescope makers, building a 26-inch refractor for the U.S. Naval Observatory, a 36-inch refractor for Lick Observatory in California (1888), and a 40-inch refractor for Yerkes Observatory in Wisconsin (1897). Simon Newcomb, director of the Nautical Almanac Office in Washington, D.C., prepared excellent tables of planetary motions, with the able cooperation of George W. Hill. Beginning in 1882, Edward C. Pickering of Harvard Observatory greatly advanced celestial photography. Under his leadership, hundreds of thousands of star-field photographs were taken, which aided in the wholesale discovery and study of variable stars. Edward E. Barnard began photographing the Milky Way with short-focus, large-aperture lenses in 1889 at Lick Observatory. His work revealed unsuspected structural features of the Milky Way, especially the dark nebulae, later identified as interstellar dust clouds.

Until almost 1900, most American astronomers were occupied with visual observations—measuring positions of stars, comets, and asteroids—or with calculation of orbits of solar-system objects. But then interest shifted increasingly toward astrophysics and stellar astronomy. Photographic observation methods quickly superseded visual ones in many applications, making study of stellar spectra a leading activity. At Lick Observatory, W. W. Campbell in the late 1890's devised improved spectrographs for the 36-inch refractor, with which he made wholesale determinations of the radial velocities of stars. Working with the Yerkes' 40-inch refractor, Frank Schlesinger perfected powerful new photographic techniques for measuring star distances between 1903 and 1905. Harvard Observatory's long-continued programs of spectral classification culminated in the nine-volume *Henry Draper Catalogue* of 225,300 stars (1918–24).

In this new astronomy, studies of the sun became prominent. Mount Wilson Solar Observatory in California was established in 1904, and there George Ellery Hale detected magnetic fields in sunspots (1908). Expeditions to distant parts of the world for observing total solar eclipses became usual. With the 60-inch reflector erected in 1908 at Mount Wilson, Harlow Shapley studied the distances of globular star clusters, using the Cepheid variable stars in these clusters as distance indicators. The asymmetric distribution of these clusters in space led Shapley in 1918 to his revolutionary conclusions that our Milky Way galaxy was much larger than suspected and that the sun was far from its center. The 100-inch Mount Wilson reflector began operating in 1919. With its aid, Edwin P. Hubble in 1923 detected Cepheid variables in the great Andromeda nebula, and soon established that this nebula is a galaxy very similar in size and contents to our own. Hubble's continuing researches led to his formulation (1929) of the relationship between the distances and red shifts of galaxies.

The interval between the world wars also saw a rapidly expanding understanding of stellar structure. Borrowing gas and radiation laws and atomic theory from physicists, astronomers learned how to evaluate temperatures and other physical conditions in the sun, stars, and nebulae. Among the leaders in this interpretative effort were H. N. Russell of Princeton, and Cecilia H. Payne and D. H. Menzel of Harvard. Especially prominent in observing stellar spectra were W. S. Adams of Mount Wilson Observatory and Otto Struve of the Yerkes and McDonald observatories.

A profound reorientation and explosive growth of American astronomy began in the late 1940's, triggered by wartime technological advances. Powerful new astronomical equipment included the 200-inch Hale reflector on Palomar Mountain in California, which went into operation in January 1949. Also newly installed at that time on Palomar was a 48-inch Schmidt telescope—an extremely fast, wide-field instrument for photographic sky surveys. Other improvements in the late 1940's included photoelectric devices that made accurate photometry of faint stars much easier and more efficient than before. The improvements, quickly adopted at many observatories, made visual and photographic photometry obsolete for most purposes. Later, very sensitive infrared photocells led to the detection of many extremely cool stars that are faint or unobservable in visible light. During the 1950's and 1960's, image-intensifier tubes were developed at Westinghouse Laboratories that have come into wide use as telescope accessories for recording spectra too faint for conventional photography.

Electronic computers revolutionized theoretical astronomy by making possible calculations previously too vast or intricate to carry out. Especially notable were the calculations of stellar models and their evolutionary changes, such as those made by Martin Schwarzschild of Princeton, and the refined studies of the moon's motion by W. J. Eckert. Celestial mechanics underwent a major revival, stimulated by enlarged computing facilities and by new problems introduced by artificial satellites and interplanetary probes.

Radio astronomy was largely an outgrowth of wartime developments in radio engineering, although as early as 1931 K. G. Jansky had detected radio noise of extraterrestrial origin. In 1942–43, intense radio emission from the sun was detected by G. C. Southworth. In 1951, H. I. Ewen and E. M. Purcell observed microwave line radiation (wavelength, 21 centimeters) emitted by hydrogen in interstellar gas clouds, and many observatories and government laboratories built large radio telescopes to study it. The 21-centimeter line soon proved a valuable tool for charting the spiral-arm pattern of our own galaxy.

The field of radio astronomy was broadened by discovery of violent bursts of radio noise from the planet Jupiter (1955). Strong radio sources outside our galaxy were first detected in 1949. Certain of these sources are quasars, believed to be among the remotest known objects and radiating energy so profusely that their physical explanation was a major unsolved mystery of the early 1970's. Radio astronomers gave much attention from 1968 on to the pulsars—cosmic radio sources emitting pulses at constant periods near one second. Such objects are generally interpreted as tiny, enormously dense, rapidly rotating collapsed stars. Another field (in which the National Radio Astronomy Observatory near Green Bank, W.Va., and the Kitt Peak National Observatory near Tucson, Ariz., took a leading role) has been the discovery of molecules of many species in interstellar gas clouds. Large radar telescopes at Arecibo, P.R., Lincoln Laboratory (Massachusetts), and the Jet Propulsion Laboratory (Pasadena, Calif.) have been used very successfully for radar studies of the moon and planets, especially Mars, Venus, and Mercury.

Astronomical observations from above the earth's atmosphere began just after World War II, when captured V-2 rockets were sent aloft from New Mexico with instruments to record the ultraviolet solar spectrum. Continued effort by scientists at the Naval Research Laboratory brought rocket astronomy to a high degree of perfection. Instrumented artificial satellites launched by the National Aeronautics and Space Administration (NASA) from the mid-1960's proved particularly effective for observing the sun at ultraviolet, X-ray, and gamma-ray wavelengths. Orbiting astronomical observatory (OAO) satellites made extensive ultraviolet observations of stars, and the Uhuru satellite surveyed the heavens for X-ray sources. The moon was mapped in minute detail by Orbiter spacecraft, and its surface was inspected by Surveyor and Apollo landings, while the planet Mars was viewed at close hand by Mariner craft.

By the early 1970's the nature of American astronomy had been completely transformed. Most practitioners were not trained astronomers but mathematicians, theoretical physicists, and engineers. The enormous expansion of the field, made possible only by government funding, resulted in a fragmentation into numerous specialized areas, creating serious communications problems.

[E. S. Holden, *Memorials of W. C. Bond and G. P. Bond;* B. Z. Jones and L. G. Boyd, *The Harvard College Observatory;* O. Struve and V. Zebergs, *Astronomy of the 20th Century.*]

JOSEPH ASHBROOK

ATCHISON, city in northeastern Kansas, located on the Missouri River, was established by Missourians in 1854 as a center for their efforts to make the territory a slave state. Its first newspaper, the *Squatter Sovereign,* was characterized as a "murder seeking, Abolitionist-hanging, murder-condoning, bloodthirsty Proslavery paper." In 1857 Samuel C. Pomeroy, an antislavery leader whose public career was to end in disgrace, joined with the proslavery promoters of Atchison in working for the development of the city, and excitement over slavery subsided. Three railroads subsequently were made to terminate at Atchison, including the Atchison, Topeka and Santa Fe. These activities made the city one of four major river centers struggling to dominate the railroad traffic to the West. It was the building of the first bridge across the Missouri, completed in 1869, that enabled Kansas City to outdistance its rivals. Edgar W. (Ed) Howe, editor of the *Atchison Globe* in later years, and author of the mordant *Story of a Country Town* (1884), was Atchison's most widely known citizen.

[Charles N. Glaab, *Kansas City and the Railroads: Community Policy and the Growth of a Regional Metropolis;* Richard C. Overton, *Burlington Route: A History of the Burlington Lines.*]

PAUL W. GATES

ATCHISON, TOPEKA AND SANTA FE RAILROAD. *See* **Railroads, Sketches.**

ATHERTON COMPANY. Maj. Humphrey Atherton, Gov. John Winthrop, the younger, and an incongruous intercolonial group of speculators formed a company that, by purchase from the Indians (1659) and foreclosure of a questionable Indian mortgage (1662), claimed title to nearly all the Narragansett country. Jurisdiction over the area was disputed between Connecticut and Rhode Island, whose charter claims conflicted; and the company, by supporting Connecticut and selling land to settlers, precipitated armed incidents and rendered vain all attempts at decision until the English Board of Trade (1727) gave Rhode Island jurisdiction and left the company's heirs no tenable claims to the land.

[Edward Field, *State of Rhode Island and Providence Plantations.*]

RAYMOND P. STEARNS

ATKINSON, FORT, one of the early posts located by the U.S. government along the Santa Fe Trail in Kansas. It was built of sod in Ford County on the Arkansas River by Maj. Hoffman in 1850. For this reason it was called Fort Sod and later Fort Sodom. It was besieged on one occasion by Comanche and Kiowa but was relieved. Abandoned in 1853, it was later temporarily reoccupied but was permanently abandoned in October 1854. Other forts of this name were located in Florida, Iowa (near Council Bluffs), Nebraska, and Wisconsin.

[F. W. Blackmar, *Kansas;* F. B. Heitman, *Historical Register of U.S. Army.*]

CARL L. CANNON

ATLANTA CAMPAIGN (1864). The Union advance southward to Atlanta began, May 5, 1864, simultaneously with Gen. U. S. Grant's advance to Richmond (*see* Wilderness, Battles of the). Gen. William T. Sherman's Union army numbered 110,000 men; Gen. Joseph Johnston's Confederate troops half that number. Sherman's superiority enabled him, with little risk, to maneuver Johnston from one position to another. If Johnston was to save his army and prevent Sherman from taking Atlanta, he could not afford to stand and fight unless conditions were favorable. He considered doing this at Cassville, halfway to Atlanta, but his subordinate commanders believed the risk too great. Ten days later a fierce battle took place at New Hope Church.

As the Confederates retreated nearer to Atlanta, fighting became more frequent. At Kenesaw Mountain, Sherman made a frontal attack against prepared positions, but was everywhere repulsed. The flanking operations were resumed. By July 6 Sherman had moved so near Atlanta that Johnston transferred his army south of the Chattahoochee River, into prepared positions along Peachtree Creek. On July 17 Johnston was relieved by a subordinate, John B. Hood, because he had "failed to arrest the advance of the enemy" (*see* Davis-Johnston Controversy). On July 20 Hood violently attacked, but was repulsed with heavy losses. The attack was resumed, but was again repulsed. Sherman's renewal of his flanking movements to cut Hood's line of supply and force him out of Atlanta brought on the Battle of Ezra Church. During August, Sherman edged closer to Hood's supply line. By the 31st he was across it. Hood evacuated Atlanta, Sept. 1, and moved his army south.

Capture and Burning of Atlanta. On Sept. 1 Sherman telegraphed President Abraham Lincoln:

"Atlanta is ours and fairly won." With the Confederates out of the city, all the people remaining in Atlanta were deported. After a brief rest, Hood started northward (*see* Hood's Tennessee Campaign). Sherman followed, but soon returned to Atlanta. On Nov. 16, the famous March to the Sea was begun.

Before setting out, Sherman ordered the complete destruction of the town. "Behind us," he wrote, "lay Atlanta smouldering and in ruins, the black smoke rising high in air and hanging like a pall over the ruined city." No city during the Civil War was so nearly completely annihilated.

[R. U. Johnson and C. C. Buel, eds., *Battles and Leaders of the Civil War;* William T. Sherman, *Memoirs*, vol. II.]

THOMAS ROBSON HAY

ATLANTIC, BATTLE OF THE, the 1939–45 struggle between Allied shipping and German submarines and Luftwaffe. Before the United States entered World War II, U.S. naval patrols gradually assumed the protection of anti-Axis merchantmen plying the broad neutrality zone. This move became necessary because President Franklin D. Roosevelt's pledge of "all aid short of war" to the Allies was antagonizing the Axis powers and causing incidents. On Sept. 4, 1941, some 200 miles southwest of Iceland, the American destroyer *Greer* replied with depth charges to a torpedo from the German U-652; neither vessel was damaged. The same was not true the following month: again south of Iceland, the American destroyer *Kearny* survived torpedo damage but, on Oct. 31, the *Reuben James* did not; it was the first American destroyer lost. By then, the U.S. Navy was convoying ships to a line 400 miles west of Ireland. Before the American declaration of war, the Axis—at the cost of fifty-nine German and nine Italian submarines and five surface raiders—had sunk 2,162 ships totaling 7,751,000 tons.

A month after Pearl Harbor an offensive by a few U-boats in American waters had incredible success since ships were still operating on a peacetime basis, unescorted and fully lighted. Belatedly, the United States organized the Tenth Fleet to bring all antisubmarine activities under a single command. An interlocking convoy system gradually developed from Gulf and Caribbean ports to Halifax in Nova Scotia or to Sydney on Cape Breton Island, where ships joined transatlantic convoys. German Adm. Karl Dönitz soon withdrew his U-boats to mid-ocean.

U-boats had great success against north Russian convoys. Most destructive was the concerted air and U-boat attack on Convoy PQ-17, which lost two-thirds of its thirty-three ships in July 1942. The Allies soon abandoned the north Russian run as too dangerous in summer. But burgeoning U.S. naval strength, as well as scientific advances, operations analysis, and improved radar, began to thwart U-boats. The development of support groups to aid endangered convoys was decisive. Convoy ONS-5, attacked by three wolf packs, lost twelve ships in May 1943; after support groups joined, no more ships were lost and six U-boats were sunk. Shaken, Dönitz largely abandoned attacks on convoys. U.S. hunter-killer groups using "jeep" aircraft carriers had increasing success also. Despite German improvements in structure and weapons, U-boats could never regain the initiative. Forays into the Mediterranean and the Indian Ocean sank few ships. By the last months of the war, the U-boats were nearly impotent.

Overall, U-boats destroyed 2,775 ships, at a cost to themselves of 781 out of the 1,175 completed U-boats. They could not stop the 300,000 successful transoceanic voyages.

[Samuel E. Morison, *The Battle of the Atlantic*, and *The Battle of the Atlantic Won;* S. E. Roskill, *The War at Sea.*]

HENRY H. ADAMS

ATLANTIC AND PACIFIC RAILROAD. This land grant railroad was chartered on July 27, 1866, to run along the thirty-first parallel, from Springfield, Mo., through Indian Territory, northern Texas, and Albuquerque, and across the Colorado River at Needles. The road was to receive twenty sections of land per mile in the states traversed (except Texas) and forty sections in the territories. Railroad building had reached Vinita, Indian Territory, when the panic of 1873 brought an end to operations. In 1876 the company was reorganized as a part of the St. Louis and San Francisco, but still cash for construction was not forthcoming. Four years later the Atchison, Topeka and Santa Fe bought a half interest in the old Atlantic and Pacific. Before through trains were run from California to St. Louis in 1883 it was necessary to reach a settlement with the Southern Pacific, which had built a line across California to Needles.

[Robert E. Riegel, *The Story of the Western Railroads.*]

DAN E. CLARK

ATLANTIC CABLE. *See* **Cables, Atlantic and Pacific.**

ATLANTIC CHARTER. The Atlantic Charter was signed Aug. 14, 1941, by President Franklin D. Roosevelt and Prime Minister Winston Churchill at a meeting in Argentia Bay off Newfoundland. The United States, still technically a neutral in World War II, already had taken a number of steps that brought it close to war. The charter, although less explicit, may be compared roughly to President Woodrow Wilson's Fourteen Points in that both declarations expressed idealistic objectives for a postwar world. The charter included the following points: the renunciation of territorial or other aggrandizement; opposition to territorial changes not approved by the people concerned; the right of people to choose their own form of government; equal access to trade and raw materials of the world; promotion of economic advancement, improved labor standards, and social security; freedom from fear and want; freedom of the seas; and disarmament of aggressor nations pending the establishment of a permanent system of peace.

Although only a press release as first issued, the charter was nonetheless well understood to be a pronouncement of considerable significance; and it soon acquired further authority when on Jan. 1, 1942, twenty-six countries (including the United States and Great Britain) signed the United Nations Declaration, which included among its provisions formal endorsement of the charter.

CHARLES S. CAMPBELL

ATLANTIC COAST LINE RAILROAD. *See* **Railroads, Sketches: Seaboard Coast Line.**

ATLANTIC COMMUNITY, a term referring to a supposed feeling of community arising from a common culture, embracing at most the whole Western Hemisphere and much of Europe, but as more commonly interpreted only North America and Western Europe. The area envisaged is sometimes viewed as having, beyond the community feeling, specific common interests sufficiently important to justify a common political or economic policy—perhaps even political union. To some extent the North Atlantic Treaty Organization reflects this sentiment.

CHARLES S. CAMPBELL

ATLANTIC FISHERIES DISPUTE. *See* **Fisheries Dispute, Arbitration of.**

ATOMIC BOMB, a military weapon deriving its energy from the fission or splitting of the nuclei of certain isotopes of the heavy elements uranium or plutonium. A nuclear device using plutonium was tested by the United States at Alamogordo, N.Mex., on July 16, 1945; and a bomb of this type was dropped on Nagasaki, Japan, in military operations on Aug. 9, 1945. A bomb using uranium-235 was dropped on Hiroshima, Japan, on Aug. 6, 1945.

The theoretical possibility of developing an atomic bomb or fission weapon became apparent to scientists throughout the world in 1939 soon after the discovery of nuclear fission in Germany. Although both Germany and England investigated the possibility of a weapon early in World War II, only the United States had sufficient resources and scientific manpower to undertake the project during the war. In the United States, feasibility studies began in laboratories in 1942 under the direction of Vannevar Bush and James B. Conant of the Office of Scientific Research and Development. Before the end of the year, three isotope-separation processes for the production of uranium-235 were under investigation, and Enrico Fermi had succeeded in achieving the world's first sustained nuclear chain reaction in Chicago on Dec. 2. The nuclear reactor provided a means of producing plutonium and promised ultimately to be a new source of power.

The Manhattan District of the U.S. Army Corps of Engineers, under the command of Brig. Gen. Leslie R. Groves, was responsible for coordinating the design and construction of the full-scale plants at Oak Ridge, Tenn., and Hanford, Wash., for the production of uranium-235 and plutonium, as well as for the design, fabrication, and testing of the weapon itself at a special laboratory at Los Alamos, N.Mex. During the two years preceding the test of the first weapon device at Alamogordo in July 1945, J. Robert Oppenheimer and a group of other scientists struggled with the design of two types of atomic bombs. Although the availability of sufficient uranium-235 for the gun-type weapon and the feasibility of the implosion-type for the plutonium weapon were not established before July 1945, both types of bombs were successfully produced for use during the war.

The atomic bombs dropped on Hiroshima and Nagasaki each released energy equivalent to about 20,000 tons of high explosive. More than 105,000 people died and 94,000 were wounded in these two attacks. Thus the bomb introduced a new method of warfare that posed unprecedented threats to the security of national states and civilian populations. In the postwar period, after unsuccessful attempts to establish international control of atomic energy under the United Nations, the United States and other nations embarked on the further development and production of nuclear weapons. The U.S. Atomic Energy Commission began a series of expansions of production facilities for uranium and plutonium and for the mass production of fission weapons. Other nations soon succeeded in producing atomic bombs—the Soviet Union in 1949; the United Kingdom in 1952; France in 1960; China in 1964; and India in 1974. Research and testing in the United States resulted in the design of a wide variety of fission weapons suitable for mass production and ranging from very small tactical devices to large strategic weapons. Fission weapons were also developed to serve as "triggers" for much more powerful thermonuclear or hydrogen bombs.

[Leslie R. Groves, *Now It Can Be Told;* Stephen Groueff, *Manhattan Project;* Richard G. Hewlett and Oscar E. Anderson, Jr., *The New World, 1939–1946;* Richard G. Hewlett and Francis Duncan, *Atomic Shield, 1947–1952.*]

RICHARD G. HEWLETT

ATOMIC ENERGY COMMISSION, UNITED STATES. The atomic bomb attacks on Japan in August 1945 thrust upon an unprepared U.S. Congress the task of devising legislation for the control and development of atomic energy. After almost nine months of public and congressional debate, President Harry Truman signed the Atomic Energy Act into law on Aug. 1, 1946. The new law created the Atomic Energy Commission, consisting of five commissioners to be appointed by the president to staggered terms of five years. The staff was to be directed by a general manager, who would serve as the chief executive officer of the agency. The law granted the commission absolute control over the development and use of atomic energy. All production facilities and nuclear reactors were to be government-owned; all technical information and research results were placed under commission control; and all such information was excluded from the patent system. The act also created the Joint Committee on Atomic Energy in the Congress, a Military Liaison Committee to operate between the commission and the Department of Defense, and a General Advisory Committee of outstanding scientists.

The new commission officially took control of the nation's atomic energy program on Jan. 1, 1947. Under the chairmanship of David E. Lilienthal, a public utility lawyer and chairman of the Tennessee Valley Authority, the commission set about refurbishing the production and research facilities built during the war. For this purpose the commission created a highly decentralized organization and continued the army's system of using private industrial and research contractors working in government facilities. Despite Lilienthal's interest in civilian uses of atomic energy, the emergence of the cold war required the commission initially to devote most of its resources to weapon development and production. This effort accelerated after the first Soviet nuclear detonation in August 1949, with high-priority research on the hydrogen bomb. In addition to building a stockpile of both tactical and strategic weapons, the commission under Chairman Gordon E. Dean expanded and strengthened research and development activities, including the construction of several experimental power reactors.

Early in the administration of Dwight D. Eisenhower, leadership of the commission passed to Lewis L. Strauss, an investment banker who had previously served on the commission under Lilienthal. Strauss spearheaded the administration's interest in promoting both industrial participation and international cooperation in atomic energy development. The new Atomic Energy Act of 1954 permitted private industry to own reactors and production facilities (but not fissionable material) and removed restrictions against the dissemination of technical information to other nations. The new act also broadened the commission's authority in licensing and regulating private atomic energy activities and removed the patent exclusion.

Although weapon development, testing, and production accelerated during the Eisenhower years, the commission under Strauss cast its public image in terms of the president's "Atoms-for-Peace" plan, announced late in 1953. The commission encouraged partnership with industry in building small-scale nuclear power plants that would demonstrate the technical, if not the economic, feasibility of nuclear power for civilian purposes. The commission also took the lead in establishing the International Atomic Energy Agency under the United Nations, negotiating a series of bilateral agreements to give research reactors and technology to friendly nations, and promoting under the auspices of the United Nations two international conferences that helped to demonstrate the peaceful potential of atomic energy. In many respects technical achievement could not match the expectations created in the Strauss era. John A. McCone, a West Coast industrialist who served as chairman during the last two years of the Eisenhower administration, faced new obstacles in both military and civilian development of atomic energy. Improvements in weapons became more difficult after the moratorium on atmospheric nuclear testing in 1958, and the demonstration power plants failed to achieve economically competitive civilian nuclear power.

In 1961 President John F. Kennedy appointed as chairman Glenn T. Seaborg, one of the pioneer scientists of the atomic energy program. Under Seaborg the commission launched a reappraisal of civilian nuclear power that helped to restore public confidence in its prospects and to concentrate resources in the most promising reactor systems. As the electric-power industry turned sharply toward nuclear plants, the commission enlarged its regulatory staff and in 1961 separated it from the operating staff, which continued to serve under the general manager. A 1964 amendment to the 1954 Atomic Energy Act also made possible private ownership of special nuclear materials, as well as facilities. Moving away from the military stance of its predecessors, the commission under Seaborg supported the Kennedy administration in negotiating the limited test ban treaty of 1963; advocated the development of nuclear explosives for peaceful purposes; expanded commission support of research and development, especially in the basic sciences, medicine, and space applications; and closed down most of the commission's facilities for the production of special nuclear materials.

The decade of stability the commission enjoyed during the Seaborg years ended in the summer of 1971 with the appointment of James R. Schlesinger, a former Rand Corporation economist, as chairman. Taking office during the height of the environmentalists' attack on the growing nuclear power industry, Schlesinger launched a broad reorganization of the commission. By the time he left the agency at the end of President Richard M. Nixon's first term, the commission had expanded its regulatory staff, streamlined the licensing and regulatory procedure, carried into the hardware stage the decision of the Seaborg commission to develop the fast-breeder power reactor, and opened new avenues for utilizing nuclear materials as an economic resource.

[Richard G. Hewlett and Oscar E. Anderson, Jr., *The New World, 1939–1946;* Richard G. Hewlett and Francis Duncan, *Atomic Shield, 1947–1952;* James R. Newman and Byron S. Miller, *The Control of Atomic Energy.*]

RICHARD G. HEWLETT

ATOMIC POWER REACTORS. The possibility of using the energy in the atomic nucleus as a power source was widely recognized soon after the discovery of nuclear fission late in 1938, but only the United States was able to devote any significant effort to atomic energy development during World War II. On Dec. 2, 1942, Enrico Fermi and others achieved the first self-sustained chain reaction at Stagg Field at the University of Chicago. This experiment made possible the construction of three large plutonium-producing reactors; each generated about 250,000 kilowatts of energy, but they were not utilized for electric power production.

Despite the initial popular belief that the use of nuclear power was imminent, technical progress was slow after the war. The U.S. Atomic Energy Commission (AEC), facing extreme shortages of uranium ore, supported only three small reactor projects before 1950. One of these, the Experimental Breeder Reactor No. 1, succeeded in generating a few kilowatts of electric power late in 1951, a record of more symbolic than practical achievement.

Growing industrial interest in nuclear power by 1952, basic revision in atomic energy legislation in 1954, and increasing ore supplies made a more ambitious program possible in the 1950's. The AEC adopted a five-year plan designed to test the feasibility of five different reactor systems. One of these, the Pressurized Water Reactor (PWR), designed and built by a joint AEC-Navy team under Rear Adm. H. G. Rickover, at Shippingport, Pa., produced 60,000 kilowatts of electricity for commercial use before the end of 1957. The AEC's Argonne National Laboratory, at Lemont, Ill., under Walter H. Zinn, successfully developed the Experimental Boiling Water Reactor (EBWR). The PWR and EBWR committed the United States almost exclusively to water-cooled reactors for the next two decades. By the end of 1957 the AEC had seven experimental reactors in operation, and American industry had started nine independent or cooperative projects expected to produce 800,000 kilowatts of electricity by the mid-1960's.

In contrast to the American emphasis on water-cooled reactors, both the United Kingdom and France chose to rely on gas-cooled systems. By 1957 the United Kingdom was building or planning twelve reactors with a total capacity of more than one million kilowatts; the French, five reactors totaling more than 350,000 kilowatts. The Soviet Union was planning a 200,000-kilowatt PWR and two smaller boiling water reactors.

Technical difficulties prevented any of these national plans from being realized by the early 1960's. In the United States the AEC countered the resulting pessimism by predicting the imminence of economically competitive nuclear power and concentrating resources on the most promising reactor designs—water-cooled reactors for the immediate future and sodium-cooled breeder reactors for later decades in the century. This confidence was fulfilled by early 1964, when an American power company first announced its decision, on the basis of economics alone, to construct a nuclear power plant. Despite a temporary dampening effect of challenges from environmentalists and licensing delays, the trend toward nuclear power accelerated again in the early 1970's. By the fall of 1972 the total nuclear gross generating capacity of all nations outside the Communist bloc had reached 32 million kilowatts. Of this total, the United States provided 13 million electrical kilowatts generated in twenty-eight operating plants. More than a hundred additional plants with a total capacity of over 116 million kilowatts had been ordered or were under construction in the United States.

[Atomic Energy Commission Naval Reactors Branch, *The Shippingport Pressurized Water Reactor;* Richard G. Hewlett and Oscar E. Anderson, Jr., *The New World, 1939–1946;* Richard G. Hewlett and Francis Duncan, *Atomic Shield, 1947–1952,* volumes in the official history of the U.S. Atomic Energy Commission; A. W. Kramer, *Boiling Water Reactors;* Philip Mullenbach, *Civilian Nuclear Power.*]

RICHARD G. HEWLETT

ATOMIC WEIGHT DETERMINATIONS became important as soon as the value of the English chemist John Dalton's atomic theory was recognized. As early as 1803 Dalton's notebooks carried estimates of relative weights of common atoms and molecules. Based on poor analyses and questionable assumptions, Dalton's atomic weights had no permanent influence. It was the Swedish chemist Jöns Jakob Berzelius who placed atomic weights on a sound footing between 1814 and 1826. He recognized the importance of accurate analysis for combining weights of reference elements and his values had a high level of precision. He was not as successful in his assumptions regarding atomic ratios in compounds; some of his values approached half or double the correct values. These problems remained unresolved until 1860 when Stanislao Cannizzaro, an Italian chemist, reintroduced Count Amedeo Avogadro's hypothesis (that equal volumes of gases at identical temperatures and pressures contain the same number of molecules) into chemistry. Application of the hypothesis made it possible to deduce the correct order of magnitude for atomic weights, leading to the introduction of the periodic table and the introduction of practical concepts of molecular structure.

Even before 1860, the Berzelius values were reexamined when his value for carbon was shown to be in error by the Frenchman J. B. Dumas in 1840. The Belgian chemist J. S. Stas helped Dumas correct the value for carbon, then spent the next twenty years in painstaking analyses toward improvement of the values for other elements. Stas's values were so highly regarded that little further corrective work was done between 1860 and 1885, although discoverers of new elements felt an obligation to measure their atomic weights.

From 1870 American chemists found in atomic weight determinations their first avenue to international reputation in chemical research. John W. Mallet of Virginia measured the atomic weights of lithium, aluminum, and gold with great accuracy; and J. P. Cooke of Harvard made a masterful study of antimony. In the 1880's E. W. Morley carried out his important determinations of the ratio of atomic weights of oxygen and hydrogen at Western Reserve University. Cooke and his student T. W. Richards also worked on the problem at Harvard, Richards going on during the rest of his life to become the world's leading investigator of atomic weights. He applied the principles of the new science of physical chemistry toward elimination of errors that had plagued his predecessors, arriving at values of extreme precision. Richards' laboratory at Harvard became a training ground of a new generation of atomic weight chemists, of whom G. P. Baxter (Harvard) and Otto Hönigschmidt (Munich) would do particularly distinguished work.

A new level of precision in atomic weight determinations became possible following J. J. Thomson's development of mass spectroscopy at Cambridge University shortly before 1914. His assistant, W. Aston, continued the work after World War I, developing the technique to a level of high precision. Further improvement in instrumentation took place in the laboratories of Arthur J. Dempster at the University of Chicago, Kenneth T. Bainbridge at Harvard, and Alfred O. Nier at the University of Minnesota in the period between 1925 and 1950. With the improved instrumentation it became possible to not only measure with great precision the mass of the several isotopes of an element, but the quantitative distribution of the several isotopes. By this means, the atomic weight of the naturally occurring elements might be determined with great accuracy.

[Aaron J. Ihde, *Development of Modern Chemistry,* and

"T. W. Richards and The Atomic Weight Problem," *Science*, vol. 164 (1969).]

AARON J. IHDE

ATROCITIES IN WAR. The history of warfare is replete with examples of atrocities, and American experience offers no exception. Americans have been the perpetrators as well as the victims of atrocities. Sometimes referred to as war crimes, atrocities generally have involved torture, maiming, or killing of civilians and noncombatants; destruction of nonmilitary targets; maltreatment and killing of wounded and prisoners of war; and use of weapons to cause superfluous damage or injury.

Many atrocities committed by Americans have occurred during guerrilla counterinsurgent wars, such as the American Indian wars, the Philippine Insurrection, and the war in Vietnam. Colonial Indian wars, such as the Pequot War (1637) and King Philip's War (1675–76), decimated or annihilated entire Indian societies in New England. Callous military tactics characterized the pacification of the Seminole in Florida and the forced removal of the Five Civilized Tribes from the southern states. Massacres such as those suffered by the Cheyenne at Sand Creek (1864) and at Summit Spring (1868), by the Piegan Blackfoot in Montana (1870), and by the Sioux at Wounded Knee (1889) are flagrant examples of atrocities by the U.S. Army on the frontier. Neither women nor children were spared; and many victims were sexually mutilated, disemboweled, and inflicted with other indignities, while the survivors were treated with indifference, their crops and herds destroyed. Revenge and retaliation for atrocities of equal brutality committed by the Indians often motivated such massacres.

Revelations that American soldiers in the Philippines were murdering civilians, destroying their villages, indiscriminately killing prisoners, using dumdum bullets and torture such as the "water cure" to defeat the Philippine insurgents led to the courts-martial of Brig. Gen. Jacob Smith and other officers in 1902. Smith was charged with "conduct prejudicial to good order and military discipline," because of his orders to kill prisoners and destroy civilian property in the course of his pacification efforts. Smith was found guilty, admonished by President Theodore Roosevelt, and forced into early retirement. Apologists for the military claimed that the unconventional tactics of the insurgents and the difficulty in distinguishing them from the native peasants justified the extraordinary measures. American military operations in South Vietnam were characterized by conditions similar to those in the Philippines, and allegations were made of similar atrocities perpetrated by American soldiers. The majority of the allegations concerning Vietnam atrocities were proven false, and other actions such as the use of napalm and crop destruction have been defended on the basis of military necessity. The most publicized, proven atrocity of the Vietnam War was the killing of unarmed civilians, mostly women and children, at the village of My Lai in 1968. Several American officers were punished for participation in this massacre or for failure to investigate its occurrence.

The number of proven atrocities in American military history is small in relation to the large number of men who have participated in the nation's wars. This is particularly true for conventional wars. Undisciplined volunteers were responsible for massacres on several occasions during the Mexican War, the most infamous occurring at Guadalupe on Mar. 25, 1847. The number of American war crimes during the two world wars was small, involving primarily individual acts of murder, sex crimes, and abuse of enemy prisoners of war. The number of such crimes was greater during the occupation after World War II than during combat.

American prisoners of war have suffered cruel and inhuman treatment during several wars. Deplorable conditions characterized the British prison ships of the American Revolution; the Confederate and Union prisons such as Andersonville, Rock Island, Elmira, and Camp Chase during the Civil War; the Japanese prison camps that housed the survivors of Bataan and Corregidor; and the Chinese Communist camps along the Yalu River during the Korean conflict.

Several international protocols and conventions have attempted to curb unnecessary violence and atrocities in war by prohibiting use of certain types of weapons and codifying rules of warfare pertaining to the protection of civilians, the treatment of wounded and prisoners of war, and the protection of cultural landmarks. The Nuremberg trials of German war criminals and the Japanese war crimes trials after World War II established that senior commanders are responsible for atrocities and war crimes perpetrated by subordinates.

[Dee Brown, *Bury My Heart at Wounded Knee;* Richard Hammer, *One Morning in the War;* Seymour M. Hersh, *My Lai 4;* Wilbur R. Jacobs, *Dispossessing the American Indian;* Francis J. Prucha, *The Sword of the Republic;* David Rees, *Korea: The Limited War;* Telford Taylor, *Nuremberg and Vietnam: An American Tragedy;* Russell F. Weigley, *History of the United States Army;* Leon Wolffe, *Little*

Brown Brother: How the United States Purchased and Pacified the Philippine Islands.]

VINCENT H. DEMMA

ATTAINDER, now obsolete in all democratic governments, a summary legal procedure whereby all the ordinary civil rights of the defendant are waived, the state proceeding against him by "bill," or legislative act. An attainted person suffered the loss of offices, property, and usually life; his children losing the inheritance of the estate and their noble rank, if any. The U.S. Constitution specifically prohibits the enactment of bills of attainder.

[T. P. Taswell-Langmead, *English Constitutional History*.]

BEN R. BALDWIN

ATTICA. The most violent prison riot in American history occurred at the Attica State Correctional Facility, located forty miles east of Buffalo, New York. On Sept. 9, 1971, approximately 1,000 of the prison's 2,254 inmates (85 percent of whom were black) seized control of the southeast portion of the prison compound. More than thirty guards and civilian employees were taken as hostages. The convicts issued a list of demands for higher wages; religious and political freedom; dietary, medical, and recreational improvements; and total amnesty and freedom from reprisals upon the surrendering of the hostages. Negotiations began between the inmates and Russell G. Oswald, New York State commissioner of corrections.

At the convicts' request civilian observers, representing the government, several newspapers, the radical Young Lords and Black Muslims, and other social and professional groups, were admitted to the prison. This ad hoc observers committee served as a liaison between Oswald and the convicts during four days of tense negotiations. Oswald offered a list of twenty-eight reforms that he was willing to grant. He acceded to nearly all the inmates' major demands except the ouster of Attica Superintendent Vincent R. Mancusi and total amnesty. The inmates insisted upon full immunity from all criminal charges. Gov. Nelson Rockefeller also rejected the amnesty plea and despite requests by the observers committee refused to travel to Attica to participate in negotiations.

At 7:46 A.M. on Sept. 13, 1971, Oswald read an ultimatum to the prisoners that reviewed his concessions and demanded the release of all hostages. In response, the prisoners displayed several hostages with knives held to their throats. At 9:46 A.M., 1,500 heavily armed state troopers, sheriff's deputies, and prison guards began an assault upon cellblock D. Twenty-nine inmates and ten hostages died from wounds suffered during the assault. Three convicts and one guard had died prior to the attack.

A preliminary report stated that nine hostages died from slashed throats and were emasculated or otherwise mutilated. Autopsies revealed that although some hostages were beaten and cut, all died from gunshot wounds in the assault and none was mutilated. The inmates had no firearms and apparently the hostages, dressed like convicts, were mistakenly killed by their would-be rescuers. On Sept. 16, Rockefeller appointed a five-man supervisory panel to prevent reprisals against inmates and protect their constitutional rights during the restoration of order. Charges of brutality after the uprising made by the committee were denied by prison officials.

After conducting extensive public hearings, a subcommittee of the U.S. Congress filed a report in June 1973, which criticized the tactics that the police and prison officials had used, and deplored the beatings and inadequate medical treatment of wounded inmates following the attack. A nine-member citizens fact-finding committee, headed by Robert B. McKay, dean of the New York University Law School, also conducted interviews and hearings. Their final report, Sept. 12, 1972, criticized Rockefeller for failing to visit Attica, cited the chaotic quality of the assault, and stated that the riot was a spontaneous uprising stemming from legitimate inmate grievances. Rockefeller, Oswald, and the chairman of a state congressional investigatory commission argued that the revolt was planned in advance by highly organized revolutionaries.

The criminal investigation of the Attica uprising, originally conducted by Deputy Attorney General Robert Fischer, led to forty-two indictments by a Wyoming County grand jury against sixty-two inmates involved in the rebellion. In April 1975, one inmate was convicted of murdering a guard. Shortly thereafter Anthony G. Simonetti, Fischer's successor, was accused of covering up evidence of brutality and incompetence by state police officials during the riot. The matter was investigated as the trials continued.

Poor conditions, racial tension, and the inmates' increased radical political awareness were some elements that precipitated the riot. The Attica uprising compelled the nation to reexamine its prisons and prison policy. Commissions, study groups, a massive quantity of verbiage, and some reform legislation resulted. Controversy continued to rage over the extent and effectiveness of these reforms.

[Tom Wicker, *A Time to Die*.]

WILLIAM DUNKEL

ATTORNEY GENERAL. *See* **Justice, Department of.**

AUBRY'S RIDE. Francis Xavier Aubry, after a successful trading venture in Santa Fe in 1848, determined to bring out a second caravan in the same year and allowed himself eight days to ride back to Missouri. Doubts being expressed by his friends, he wagered a considerable sum on his ability to do so. Ridden hard, his horse gave out on the Arkansas River. He pushed on fifteen or twenty miles to Mann's Fort, secured a remount, pressed onward, was pursued by Indians near Pawnee Fork, but reached Independence within less than the time specified.

[G. D. Brewerton, *Overland With Kit Carson*.]

CARL L. CANNON

AUBURN PRISON SYSTEM. The details of the separate or silent system were originally worked out in the prison being erected by New York at Auburn in the years following 1819. An act of that year and another of 1821 called for individual cells to displace the discredited congregate system. Rows of cells, 3½ by 7 by 7 feet in size, were erected in tiers, back to back, forming a cell block which was inclosed by the outer walls of the building. The plan differed strikingly from the Pennsylvania solitary pattern, but could trace a distant descent from the plans of the *maison de force* at Ghent. The cells provided separate sleeping quarters, from which the convicts marched in lockstep to the shops of contractors located in the prison yard. Strict rules of silence were enforced at all times. Religious services were conducted in chapels. The system was designed to isolate the convicts from each other and to encourage them to penitence without sacrificing the value of their labor. The fact that convict labor was thus available to the enterprising pioneers of the factory system in America helped to make Auburn the preferred pattern for state prisons during the next half-century.

[Blake McKelvey, *American Prisons*.]

BLAKE MCKELVEY

AUCTIONS. Based on the principle of competition on the part of buyers for the opportunity of purchasing an item or a lot of goods, the auction had its beginnings in antiquity. According to Herodotus, such institutions existed as early as 500 B.C. in Babylon, where once a year females of marriageable age were sold at auction on condition that they be wed; the scheme, incidentally, included a reverse-price, or subsidy, arrangement to stimulate the "purchase" of the plainer women. Later on, Roman soldiers in the field reportedly sold their loot at auction, *sub hasta* or "under the spear," to business agents who accompanied military expeditions for the purpose of acquiring war booty. The earliest reference to the term "auction" in the *Oxford English Dictionary* is dated 1595. There is ample evidence that both chattels and real property were sold by auction in 17th-century England; for example, Samuel Pepys reported witnessing an auction sale of ships in London in 1662. The firm of Sotheby's, world-famous auctioneers, was established in 1744, and Christie's, of similar renown, was inaugurated in 1766.

In early 18th-century trade with America, British manufacturers and exporters customarily assigned their goods to agents in some American port, who then sold the goods at auction. As auctioning became prevalent, orthodox functionaries were circumvented to some extent, with the result that they raised loud cries of protest and began to demand protective legislation. The problem was intensified because prices were much lower in Britain than in America, enabling foreign merchants to undermine American production and marketing operations by the exportation of low-cost British goods to America. The "dumping" of foreign goods on the American market, which was merely expedited by the auction method of sale, created serious public resentment and culminated in a strong campaign against auction sales generally.

Auctions played an important part in the infamous slave traffic of antebellum days. Because of its efficiency in relation to the task at hand (for example, concentration of traders at such sales with a resulting saving in time and effort), the auction method was employed almost exclusively in the purchase and sale of human chattels. The American slave trade was first restricted in 1808 when a federal statute was enacted proscribing the importation of slaves into the United States, and was finally outlawed by terms of the Thirteenth Amendment to the Constitution in 1865, which in effect prohibited ownership and thus sale of slaves by any means.

On the American frontier auctions were particularly useful. Thus, this method of transferring title was utilized in interneighborhood exchange transactions as well as in the sale of the fruits of agricultural effort in primary market centers. The scheme was of special usefulness in court-ordered sales resulting from bankruptcies, tax delinquencies, and the settling of estates. The auction was extensively used also as a selling instrument in the southern California land boom of the 1880's, in conjunction with seller-inspired rumors for bid-stimulation purposes.

The auction system used in America over the years has been mainly the English or ascending-price scheme, in which the auctioneer starts at some relatively low price and solicits successively higher bids and, finally, assuming there is no reservation price or that that price has been exceeded, knocks the goods down to the highest bidder. This is in contrast to the Dutch auction or upside-down system—used in the sale of vegetables, fruit, and flowers in the Netherlands—in which goods are offered on a declining price scale until, at some level, a buyer is found. It also differs from the simultaneous-bidding system—utilized in Japan, particularly in the marketing of fresh fish at the primary level—in which assembled bidders, at the signal of the auctioneer, use discrete finger signs in their bidding, the auctioneer instantly "reading" the top or winning bid from the sea of hands.

It should be pointed out that where highly developed market knowledge of the item being sold is confined to one or at most a few specialists (as may be true in the case of antiques and fine art pieces), it is possible for bidders to organize their efforts collusively for price-depressing purposes by confining competition to relatively low price levels. Buyer "rings" may make possible the acquisition of items of high market value at a fraction of the price they would yield in the absence of such restraint. Some countries (for example, England) have laws that purport to control buyer ring activities, but these are not very effective. Buyer collusion to depress prices can only be controlled by the employment of experts in the auction company's evaluation process and by the use of a reserve price below which the seller will not go in the sale of the item.

[Ralph Cassady, Jr., *Auctions and Auctioneering*.]

RALPH CASSADY, JR.

AUDUBON SOCIETY, NATIONAL, a citizens' organization that has been a major force in shaping America's wildlife protection and conservation movement. The society's roots go back to the latter part of the 19th century, when there were virtually no effective game laws: waterfowl were being shot by the wagonload to sell to restaurants; plumed birds were being slaughtered for feathers to decorate ladies' hats; and buffalo were being hunted almost to extinction. In an early attempt to protect wildlife, an Audubon society, named in honor of the artist and naturalist John James Audubon (1785–1851), was established in 1885 by George Bird Grinnell, editor of *Forest and Stream*. The organization was short-lived, but it led to the formation of a number of state Audubon societies; the membership included hunters who saw that without controls game would be wiped out and determined women who were appalled by the cruelty and waste in the destruction of wildlife. During the next several years progress was made at the state level, but it also became clear that there was need for a coordinated national effort for federal regulation. In 1905 twenty-five state Audubon societies joined to form the National Audubon Society.

During its first two or three decades the new national organization was concerned primarily with campaigning for bird protection laws and with direct protection of wildlife. But from its earliest days the society has also had broader wildlife and conservation interests. As early as the 1920's the society was actively campaigning for an international treaty to curb the menace of oil spills. By providing educational materials for schools and youth groups and offering workshops for the training of teachers, the society in the 1930's began teaching a doctrine that was not to become of general concern for almost another forty years: ecology. In 1974, through its 300,000 members and 320 local chapters, the National Audubon Society was working for wiser local and national policies to meet a wide range of environmental problems, from air and water pollution to strip-mining, land-use planning, and the effects of nuclear power generation.

[Carl W. Buchheister and Frank Graham, Jr., "From the Swamps and Back," *Audubon* (1973).]

ROBERT C. BOARDMAN

AUGHWICK, an Indian village on the Juniata River near the site of Fort Shirley, Pa., which in the 1750's served as a trading post and a home for Indian refugees from the Fort Duquesne vicinity.

SOLON J. BUCK

AUGUSTA, city in Georgia located at the head of navigation on the Savannah River, founded in 1735 by Gen. James Edward Oglethorpe. Until 1773 it remained the northwestern outpost of Georgia, dominating Indian trade and relations. Largely Loyalist, it fell twice into British hands (1779, 1780–81). For a short period, ending in 1795, it was the state capital. There a convention ratified the U.S. Constitution. Upland cotton and steam transportation made the city, temporarily, the greatest inland cotton market in the world. A government arsenal and a large powder mill made it a major source of supply for Confederate armies during the Civil War. In the 20th century Augusta remained an important cotton trading center and developed into a major textile manufacturing city. Since World War II the population has steadily decreased, the 1970 census indicating 59,864 persons living in the city.

[E. M. Coulter, *A Short History of Georgia.*]

CHESTER McA. DESTLER

AUGUSTA, a British vessel that, in 1777, led the attack against Commodore John Hazelwood's fleet defending Fort Mercer on the Delaware River. The Americans resisted, forcing a British retreat. Defense construction may have caused channel changes, and the *Augusta* grounded. The Revolutionists attacked, and, on Oct. 23, the *Augusta* exploded, losing over sixty men.

[Gardner W. Allen, *Naval History of the American Revolution.*]

JULIAN P. BOYD

AUGUSTA, CONGRESS OF, took place Nov. 5–10, 1763, in response to orders from the British government to the governors of Virginia, North Carolina, South Carolina, and Georgia that they collect representatives of the Southern Indians (Creek, Cherokee, Choctaw, Chickasaw, and Catawba), inform them that the French and Indian war had ended, and bring about a general settlement on trade and boundary difficulties. The governors from these colonies (lieutenant governor from Virginia) and John Stuart, superintendent of Indian affairs in the Southern District, met 700 Indians at Augusta, signed a treaty of friendship, and secured therein important land cessions in Georgia from the Creek.

[C. C. Jones, Jr., *History of Georgia,* vol. II; W. B. Stevens, *History of Georgia,* vol. II.]

E. MERTON COULTER

AUGUSTA, FORT, named for George III's mother. Constructed by Pennsylvania in 1756, near the site of present Sunbury, to defend the frontier after Gen. Edward Braddock's defeat and to forestall the French who supposedly intended to fortify the forks of the Susquehanna River, it protected frontiersmen from Indians and Tories until abandoned after 1780.

WILLIAM A. RUSS, JR.

AUGUSTA, TREATY OF (1773), made by Gov. James Wright of Georgia, and John Stuart, superintendent of Indian affairs in the Southern District, with chiefs of the Creek and Cherokee nations, at the suggestion of the Indians, who were hopelessly in debt to various groups of white traders. By this agreement George was ceded two tracts of land, one between the Altamaha and Ogeechee rivers and the other lying between the upper stretches of the Ogeechee and Savannah rivers, comprising in all more than 2.1 million acres, and from the sale of these lands the traders were to be paid. A great influx of settlers was attracted here just before the Revolution.

[C. C. Jones, Jr., *History of Georgia,* vol. II; W. B. Stevens, *History of Georgia,* vol. II.]

E. MERTON COULTER

AUGUSTA COUNTY, in Virginia, named in honor of Princess Augusta, wife of the Prince of Wales, was created on Nov. 1, 1738, from that portion of Orange County lying beyond the Blue Ridge. The newly created county was to remain part of the parent county until the number of inhabitants warranted the establishment of a separate government, which was not until Oct. 30, 1745. Territorially it included parts of the present states of Kentucky, Ohio, Indiana, Illinois, and western Pennsylvania, and nearly all of West Virginia. Here the Virginians came into conflict with Pennsylvania's claims, for both colonies had settlers in those parts of Pennsylvania west of the Alleghenies. Becoming alarmed at the influx of Virginia settlers, Pennsylvania had created, on Feb. 26, 1773, Westmoreland County, which included all of the present counties of Westmoreland, Fayette, Greene, Washington, and parts of Allegheny, Beaver, Indiana, and Armstrong. In 1774–75 Virginia created the district of West Augusta, which claimed the land of the newly created Westmoreland County. In 1776 Virginia attempted to strengthen title to these lands by dividing West Augusta into three new counties: Ohio, Yohogania, and Monongalia. These conflicting jurisdictional claims produced the Pennsylvania - Virginia boundary dispute, which was not settled until 1780. The immense territory of Augusta County was thus cut down, first by the creation of Botetourt County in 1769, Fincastle in 1772, the three counties in West Augusta, and later encroachments, until it reached its present-day status.

[Edgar W. Hassler, *Old Westmoreland: A History of Western Pennsylvania During the Revolution;* Joseph A. Waddell, *Annals of Augusta County, Virginia, From 1726 to 1871.*]

R. J. FERGUSON

AURARIA, the first settlement in Colorado, established in October 1858, and one of the towns started at the juncture of Cherry Creek and the South Platte, following gold discoveries earlier that summer (*see* Pikes Peak Gold Rush). In April 1860 it was consolidated with Denver, its rival, on the opposite bank of Cherry Creek.

[J. C. Smiley, *History of Denver.*]

MALCOLM G. WYER

AURORA, a Philadelphia newspaper founded in 1790 by Benjamin Franklin Bache as the *General Advertiser*. When Philip Freneau's *National Gazette* suspended publication, the *Aurora* took its place as the Jeffersonian Republican mouthpiece. It was notorious for its violent personal abuse and its attacks on the administrations of George Washington and John Adams, and charged that Washington had violated the Constitution. Forged letters of Washington were included. Shortly after his arrest and parole in 1798 on charges of libeling President Adams, Bache died. The *Aurora* was continued by William Duane, an assistant editor who married Bache's widow, but lost much of its effectiveness after 1800, when the capital was moved from Philadelphia to Washington.

[B. Faÿ, *The Two Franklins.*]

JULIAN P. BOYD

AUSTIN COLONY. On Jan. 17, 1821, the Spanish authorities in Mexico granted to Moses Austin permission to settle 300 families in Texas. After the death of the grantee, and after Mexico's successful revolt against Spain, the Mexican provisional government confirmed this concession to Stephen F. Austin, the "Father of Texas." Subsequently the younger Austin obtained contracts to settle 900 additional families, most of whom he had introduced by 1833. Austin's colonies formed the nucleus of the Anglo-American occupation of Texas.

[E. C. Barker, *The Life of Stephen F. Austin.*]

E. C. BARKER

AUTOMATION. The word "automation" was coined in 1946 by D. S. Harder, then vice-president of manufacturing for the Ford Motor Company. The word first appeared in print the following year in an article in *American Machinist* that described the Ford Motor Company's operations. In 1948–49 the company built what was called the first automated factory, which began operations in 1950, manufacturing automobile engines. Employing over 4,500 workers, this factory marked a significant increase in automaticity, notably in the making of cylinder blocks.

The term "automation" has many different definitions and is in some cases used interchangeably with "mechanization," "technological change," and "cybernation." The three key elements of automation are (1) automatic production machines; (2) machines to transfer materials between, and feed materials into, production machines; and (3) a control system that regulates the whole operation, including itself (feedback).

Production by automatic machines goes back in some industries to the early 19th century, and it was present in most by the 1870's. Devices for moving materials (endless screws and chains of buckets, for example) were in use in the "automatic" flour mill of Oliver Evans in 1785; transfer machines were in use at the Waltham Watch Company by 1888. Computers are the most powerful and flexible control devices, although feedback mechanisms that monitor the environment and adjust the mechanism accordingly are as old as thermostats and governors.

The development of the computer as a control mechanism greatly stimulated the concern over automation. Developed largely in the United States, the computer was used to some extent for scientific calculations before World War II, saw greatly expanded use during the war, and flowered as an instrument for data processing in the postwar period. Computers were first used as a control mechanism in 1957–58, when several electric power generating plants and oil refineries installed them to monitor performance and log data. By 1966 some 15,000–20,000 computers were in use.

After the coining of the word "automation" in 1946 and of "cybernetics" by Norbert Wiener in 1948, a growing public alarm arose over the social implications of the process. Arguing that it was something new in technology and was certain to lead to mass unemployment, some intellectuals and labor unions began to warn the public about its consequences. John Diebold's book *Automation—The Advent of the Automatic Factory* (1952) and the 1955 bargaining effort of the United Auto Workers were landmarks. Spokesmen for industry tended to deny that automation was really new and to minimize the idea that it would cause unemployment. The federal government tended to accept the latter view.

The public debate over automation died down by the end of the 1960's, in part because many unions successfully included protective clauses in their work contracts and also because massive, direct disemployment did not develop as expected. It has been estimated that if automation were introduced everywhere it was appropriate, it would adversely affect only 8 percent of the work force. The specific concern over automation, however, contributed to the government's general concern over structural unemployment in the early 1960's.

The most advanced automated factory constructed by the mid-1970's was the North Carolina Works of the Western Electric Company, built about 1960. There deposited-carbon resistors were manufactured at the rate of 20 per minute—the production, inspection, assembly, testing, and movement all automatically performed and controlled by computers with feedback loops. Such automaticity is not yet appropriate for most manufacturing, however, and automation's greatest impact to date is on office work.

[J. Bright, "The Development of Automation," in M. Kranzberg and C. Pursell, *Technology in Western Civilization*, vol. 2; B. Seligman, *Most Notorious Victory;* G. Terborgh, *The Automation Hysteria.*]

CARROLL PURSELL

AUTOMOBILE. Widespread interest in the possibilities of individualized, long-distance highway transportation grew after introduction of the geared, low-wheeled "safety bicycle" in 1885 and after quantity production reduced the price of a bicycle to about $30. Bicycle organizations in the United States and abroad began to agitate for improved roads and gained a broad base of support in the 1890's. The crest of the bicycle movement in the United States coincided with the climax of several decades of agrarian discontent that had singled out as a prime target the abuse of monopoly power by the railroads. Perceiving highway transportation as an alternative, farmers began to complain about the scandalous lack of good "farm to market" roads; improved roads became a popular political issue.

This revival of interest in highway transportation provided a fertile climate for commercial exploitation of the great advances made in automotive technology during the 1860–90 period. More compact and efficient power units had been developed, and the idea of substituting a motor for the horse occurred independently to many inventors in several nations. American accomplishment was most notable in steam-powered and electric-powered cars, which were rapidly to become backwaters of automotive technology. German and French inventors were well ahead of their American counterparts by the 1890's in development of the gasoline-powered automobile. By 1885, in Germany, Gottlieb Daimler and his assistant William Maybach had perfected a four-cycle internal-combustion engine, introduced by Nicholas Otto in 1876, and between 1885 and 1889 Daimler and Maybach built four experimental motor vehicles to demonstrate their 1.5 horsepower, 600-rpm engine, which weighed 110 pounds. Karl Benz, another German manufacturer of stationary gas engines, built his first car in 1886 and by 1891 had developed the automobile to the stage of commercial feasibility. Émile Constant Levassor, who had acquired the French manufacturing rights for the Daimler motor, created the basic mechanical arrangement of the modern motorcar in 1891 by placing the engine in front of the chassis instead of under the seats or in the back, an arrangement that made possible the accommodation of larger, more powerful engines. By 1895 automobiles were already a common sight on the streets of Paris.

Levassor demonstrated that the eventual displacement of the horse by the internal-combustion engine was more than an idle dream by driving one of his cars over the 727-mile course of the 1895 Paris-Bordeaux-Paris race at the then incredible speed of 15 mph, with the longest stop for servicing being only 22 minutes. The event stimulated a flurry of automotive activity in the United States. E. P. Ingersoll launched the first American specialized automobile journal, *Horseless Age;* the first European automobiles were imported for sale; the U.S. Patent Office was deluged with over 500 patents relating to motor vehicles; and the Chicago *Times-Herald* sponsored the first American automobile race, run over snow-covered roads in freezing temperatures on Thanksgiving Day, 1895.

Credit for the first successful American gasoline automobile is generally given to the winners of the *Times-Herald* race—Charles E. Duryea and J. Frank

Duryea of Springfield, Mass., bicycle mechanics who built their first car in 1893 after reading a description of the Benz car in *Scientific American* in 1889. It is now known that several American inventors built experimental gasoline automobiles prior to the Duryeas. However, these people made no lasting contribution to the implementation of the automotive idea in America. The Duryeas, in contrast, capitalized on the national publicity gained in winning the *Times-Herald* contest by initiating the manufacture of motor vehicles for a commercial market in the United States in 1896, when they made the first sale of an American gasoline-powered car and produced twelve more of the same design. Allowing for changes of name and early failures, thirty American automobile manufacturers produced an estimated 2,500 motor vehicles in 1899, the first year for which separate figures for the automobile industry were compiled in the *United States Census of Manufactures*. The most important of these early automobile manufacturers in volume of product was the Pope Manufacturing Company of Hartford, Conn., also the nation's leading bicycle manufacturer.

The market for motorcars expanded rapidly as numerous races, tours, and tests demonstrated that the automobile was superior to the horse. Three transcontinental crossings by automobile in 1903 inaugurated informal long-distance touring by the average driver. The most important organized reliability runs were the Glidden Tours, sponsored annually between 1905 and 1913 by the American Automobile Association. However, the central role played by motor vehicles in saving lives and property during the 1906 San Francisco earthquake capped the need for further reliability runs. Following the disaster, municipalities began to motorize emergency services, and the emphasis in formal tours shifted to gasoline economy runs. Speed tests and track and road races gave manufacturers publicity for their products and contributed much to the development of automotive technology. The clocking of a Stanley Steamer at near 128 mph at Daytona Beach, Fla., in 1906 was a spectacular demonstration of progress made since the turn of the century. Among the early competitions stressing speed, none excited the popular imagination more than the Vanderbilt Cup road races (1904–16).

Contrary to popular myth, there was great enthusiasm for the motorcar in the United States from its introduction. Municipal and state legislation intended to regulate motor vehicles developed slowly, reflected the thinking of the automobile clubs, and was typically far less restrictive than the uniform laws adopted by European nations. Years before Henry Ford conceived of his universal car for the masses, writers in popular periodicals confidently predicted the banishment of horses from cities and the ending of rural isolation and drudgery through the imminent arrival of the low-cost, reliable car. No one ever doubted that the automobile was cleaner and safer than the unsanitary, whimsical old gray mare. The automobile so excited the enthusiasm of the American people because no mechanical innovation in U.S. history has been so congruent with deeply ingrained traits of the American character. The automobile promised to revitalize the Jeffersonian agrarian myth in a new fusion of rural and urban advantages and to preserve and enhance the individualism and personal mobility threatened by the rise of an urban-industrial socioeconomic order. An absence of tariff barriers between the states and the higher per capita income and better income distribution relative to European countries were other factors encouraging Americanization of the automobile.

Some 458,500 motor vehicles were registered in the United States by 1910, making America the world's foremost automobile culture. Responding to an unprecedented seller's market for an expensive item, between 1900 and 1910 automobile manufacturing leaped from one hundred and fiftieth to twenty-first in value of product among American industries and became more important to the national economy than the wagon and carriage industry on all measurable economic criteria.

Automobile Manufacturing. Because the automobile was a combination of components already standardized and being produced for other uses—for example, stationary and marine gasoline engines, carriage bodies and wheels—the early automobile manufacturer was merely an assembler of major components and a supplier of finished cars. The small amount of capital and the slight technical and managerial expertise needed to enter automobile manufacturing were most commonly diverted from other closely related business activities—especially from the bicycle, carriage, and wagon trades, and from machine shops. Requirements for fixed and working capital were met mainly by shifting the burden to parts makers, distributors, and dealers. High demand for cars enabled the manufacturers to require advance cash deposits of 20 percent on all orders, with full payment upon delivery; and the process of assembling took much less time than the thirty- to ninety-day credit period the parts makers allowed. These propitious conditions for entry attracted some 515 separate companies into automobile manufacturing by 1908, the year in which Henry Ford introduced the Model T and William C. Durant founded General Motors.

The Association of Licensed Automobile Manufacturers (ALAM) attempted to restrict entry into, and severely limit competition within, the automobile industry. This trade association of thirty leading producers of gasoline-powered cars was formed in 1903 to enforce an 1895 patent on the gasoline automobile originally applied for in 1879 by George B. Selden. Litigation was begun against the Ford Motor Company and several other unlicensed "independents," who continued to make and sell cars without paying royalties to the association. A 1911 written decision sustained the validity of the Selden patent, while declaring that Ford and the others had not infringed upon it, because the patent did not cover cars using four-cycle engines. To avoid another divisive and costly patent controversy in the industry, the newly formed National Automobile Chamber of Commerce (which became the Automobile Manufacturers Association in 1932 and the Motor Vehicle Manufacturers Association in 1972) instituted a cross-licensing agreement among its members in 1914. This patent-sharing arrangement was probably the most effective antimonopoly measure to emerge from the Progressive Era, because it prevented use of the patent system to develop monopoly power in this vital industry.

The ALAM companies tended to emphasize higher-priced models that brought high unit profits, while Henry Ford and many other independents were more committed to the volume production of low-priced cars. Ransom E. Olds initiated volume production of a low-priced car, but the surrey-influenced design of his $650, one-cylinder, curved-dash Olds (1901–06) was soon outmoded. The $600, four-cylinder Ford Model N (1906–07) deserves credit as the first low-priced car with sufficient horsepower to be reliable. The rugged Ford Model T (1908–27) was even better adapted to the wretched rural roads of the day, and its immediate popularity skyrocketed Ford's share of the market for new cars to about 50 percent by the outbreak of World War I.

Mass production techniques perfected at the Ford Highland Park, Mich., plant in 1913–14—especially the moving-belt assembly line—progressively reduced the price of the Model T to a low of $290 for the touring car by 1927, making mass personal automobility a reality. Soon applied to the manufacture of many other items, Ford production methods resulted in a shift from an economy of scarcity to an economy of affluence; created a new class of semiskilled industrial workers; and opened new opportunities for remunerative industrial employment to the immigrant, the black migrant to the northern city, the physically handicapped, and eventually women. The five-dollar, eight-hour day instituted at Ford in 1914—which roughly doubled wages for a shorter workday—recognized dramatically that mass production necessitated mass consumption and mass leisure.

To compete with the Model T's progressively lower prices, the makers of moderately priced cars innovated modern consumer installment credit with the creation of the Guaranty Securities Company in 1915 and the General Motors Acceptance Corporation in 1919. Over 110 automobile finance corporations were in existence by 1921. Time sales accounted for about three-fourths of all automobile sales by 1926; and the finance corporations, wishing to diversify their risks, played an active role in encouraging installment purchases of many other types of merchandise. By the late 1920's this kind of buying was eroding the values of hard work, thrift, and careful saving sanctified in the Protestant ethic and so central to the socioeconomic milieu of perennial scarcity predicted by the classical economists.

Effect of the Automobile. American life was transformed during the 1920's by the mass-produced car, combined with the development of long-distance trucking and the small farm tractor (exemplified by the Fordson) in response to the demands of World War I. Regional, sectional, and rural-urban differences diminished. With the dispersal of the population into outlying areas, the locations of industrial plants and retail stores became decentralized. Larger trading areas killed off the village general store, lessened deposits in small local banks, forced the mail-order houses to open retail stores, and meant large-scale reorganization of both retail and wholesale trade. The quality of rural life was greatly upgraded as city amenities, especially far better medical care, were extended by the Model T; as the school bus replaced the one-room school with the consolidated school; and as the tractor removed much of the drudgery from farm labor. Ironically, the displacement of horses by the Fordson and the Model T raised the farmer's fixed costs while leading to chronic overproduction of staple crops, making the small family farm an increasingly inefficient economic unit.

The advent of the automobile had a tremendous effect on the cities too. A suburban real estate and construction boom initiated in the 1920's, although interrupted by the 1930's depression, continued into the 1970's. So did its related problems: a proliferation of inefficient local governmental units, mounting expenditures for municipal governments incurred in extending essential services, and a declining tax base and loss of vitality for the central city. Public health benefited from the disappearance of horses from cities; but street play for city children became increasingly hazardous, and automobile accidents became a major cause of deaths and permanent disabilities. Modern city planning arose to meet growing traffic congestion and parking problems; and accommodation to the motorcar through longer blocks, wider streets, and narrower sidewalks combined with a widening of the individual's range of associations to threaten the urban neighborhood as a viable form of community. Parental authority was undercut by the automobile date, which moved courtship from the living room into the rumble seat and replaced home entertainment with attendance at the movies or sports events. Recreational opportunities were greatly expanded as the automobile vacation to the seashore or the mountains became institutionalized and as the Sunday golf game or drive became alternatives to church attendance, the family dinner, and a neighborhood stroll. The pace of everyday life was accelerated, while the cost of automobile ownership came to constitute a heavy drain on the average family's budget.

By the mid-1920's automobile manufacturing ranked first in value of product and third in value of exports among American industries. The automobile industry was the lifeblood of the petroleum industry; one of the chief customers of the steel industry; and the biggest consumer of many other industrial products, including plate glass, rubber, and lacquers. The technologies of these ancillary industries were revolutionized by the new demands of motorcar manufacturing. The motorcar was responsible also for the rise of many new small businesses, such as service stations and tourist accommodations. Construction of streets and highways was the second largest item of governmental expenditure during the 1920's. Thomas C. Cochran, social and economic historian, noted this central role of automobility and concluded: "No one has or perhaps can reliably estimate the vast size of capital invested in reshaping society to fit the automobile. Such a figure would have to include expenditures for consolidated schools, suburban and country homes, and changes in business location as well as the more direct investments mentioned above. This total capital investment was probably the major factor in the boom of the 1920's, and hence in the glorification of American business."

In 1929, the last year of the automobile-induced boom, the 26.7 million motor vehicles registered in the United States—one for every 4.5 persons—traveled an estimated 198 billion miles, and that year alone government spent over $2.2 billion on roads and collected $849 million in special motor vehicle taxes. After the turn of the century, the automobile clubs became the main force in the good-roads movement, with motorists consistently favoring higher use taxes as one means of securing better roads. The Lincoln Highway Association, formed in 1913 to create a coast-to-coast hard-surfaced road, was disbanded after the Federal Aid Road Act of 1916 appropriated $75 million for improving rural post roads over a five-year period. Phenomenal growth in motor vehicle registrations and demonstration of the value of long-distance trucking in World War I led to the Federal Highway Act of 1921, which provided federal aid to the states, through fifty-fifty matching grants, for building a federal highway system. In 1929 gasoline taxes, collected by then in all states, amounted to $431 million in revenue and were the main source of revenue for highway expenditures.

Improvements in Technology. Improved roads and advances in automotive technology ended the Model T era. As the 1920's wore on, consumers came to demand much more from a car than the low-cost basic transportation that the utilitarian Model T afforded. The self-starter, which obviated the onerous and dangerous method of using a hand crank to start the car, gained rapid acceptance after its introduction in the 1911 Cadillac. The basic open-car design of the Model T became obsolete as closed cars increased from 10.3 percent of production in 1919 to 82.8 percent in 1927, making the automobile a year-round, all-weather vehicle. Ethyl gasoline, the octane rating of fuels, and better crankshaft balancing to reduce vibrations were the most important breakthroughs that led to the introduction of the high-compression engine in the mid-1920's. By then four-wheel brakes, low-pressure "balloon" tires, and wishbone-type front-wheel suspension also had appeared—resulting in a smoother, safer ride. Syncromesh transmission and safety plate glass in all windows were features of the 1928 Cadillac. Mass-produced cars of all colors became possible after Duco lacquer made its debut in the "True Blue" of the 1924 Oakland (the Model T had come only in black after 1913 because only black enamel would dry fast enough). The trend too was toward annually restyled, larger, more powerful, and faster six-cylinder cars; by the mid-1920's a Chevrolet with these advantages cost only a few hundred dollars more than a Model T.

Thus, Henry Ford's market strategy of a single, static model at an ever-decreasing price became outmoded in the 1920's. Under the leadership of Alfred P. Sloan, Jr., General Motors parlayed into leadership in the automobile industry the counterstrategy of blanketing the market with cars in several price ranges, constant upgrading of product through systematic research and testing, and the annual model change and/or planned obsolescence of product. And while Henry Ford continued to run his giant company as an extension of his personality, without even an organizational chart, General Motors pioneered development of the decentralized, multidivisional structure of the modern industrial corporation and became the prototype, widely copied after World War II, of the rational, depersonalized business organization run by a technostructure.

Competition between automobile manufacturers sharpened with the onset of market saturation. Replacement demand first exceeded demand from initial owners and multiple-car owners combined in 1927, and the 1929 total production of over 5.3 million motor vehicles was not again equaled until 1949. Despite that, almost half of American families still did not have a car in 1927; the inadequate income distribution of Coolidge prosperity meant a growing backlog of used cars on dealers' lots; and only about a third of the automobile dealers were making money. A trend toward oligopoly in the automobile industry, observable since 1912, accelerated as economies of scale and the vertical integration of operations became more essential for survival. The number of active automobile manufacturers dropped from 108 to 44 between 1920 and 1929; and Ford, General Motors, and Chrysler came to be responsible for about 80 percent of the industry's total output. The 1930's depression shook out most of the remaining independents; despite mergers among the independents that survived into the post–World War II period, in the mid-1970's only American Motors (formed from Nash-Kelvinator and Hudson in 1954) continued to challenge Detroit's Big Three. Closure of entry into automobile manufacturing was underlined by the failure of new firms, such as Kaiser-Frazer, to succeed in the post–World War II industry.

The major innovations in modern automotive technology not yet incorporated by the late 1920's were the all-steel body, the infinitely variable automatic transmission, and drop-frame construction, which dropped the passenger compartment from its high perch upon the axles to its now familiar position down between the front and rear wheels, lowering the height and center of gravity of the car. Increasingly since the 1930's, emphasis has been on styling—the factor contributing most to the high cost of the contemporary car through its implications for stamping processes. Streamlined styling was pioneered in the Chrysler "Airflow" models of the 1930's and in the 1947 Studebaker. The automatic transmission was introduced in the 1939 Oldsmobile and by the 1970's became standard equipment along with power brakes, power steering, radios, and air conditioning. Development of the high-compression, overhead-cam, V-8 engine led to a horsepower race in the 1950's that culminated in the "muscle cars" of the late 1960's. But the industry trend toward larger, more powerful, and more expensive cars was reversed by mounting consumer demand throughout the 1960's for the economical Volkswagen, a number of Japanese-built compacts, and domestic models such as the Nash Rambler and the Ford Mustang. By the early 1970's Big Three production had shifted toward emphasis on smaller, sportier, more economical models.

State of the Industry. The post–World War II American automobile industry could be considered a technologically stagnant industry, despite its progressive refinement of product and automation of assembly lines. Neither motorcars nor the methods of manufacturing them changed fundamentally over the next generation. The most promising improvements during the 1970's in the internal-combustion engine—the Wankel, the stratified charge, and the split-cycle rotary engines—were being pioneered abroad; and Saab and Volvo were making the first significant attempts to depart from traditional patterns of assembly-line production. Common Market and Japanese producers also led in meeting consumer demand for economy and compact cars at lower unit profits. American automobile manufacturers in the main responded to increasingly stiffer foreign competition by trying to cut labor costs through heightened factory regimentation intended to increase the workers' productivity on domestic assembly lines and through accelerated expansion of overseas subsidiaries. Notable increases in absenteeism, alcoholism, drug use, and neuroses among automobile workers further threatened the quality of Detroit's product. And with the growth of the multinational corporation in automobile manufacturing, it became more and more difficult to determine what indeed constitutes an American-made car. Detroit's share of the world market for cars slipped from about three-fourths in the mid-1950's to little more than a third by the mid-1970's.

Federal legislation affecting the automobile industry proliferated from the New Deal era on. The National Labor Relations Act of 1935 encouraged the unionization of automobile workers; and with the capitulation of General Motors and Chrysler in 1937 and Ford in 1941, the United Automobile Workers became an institutionalized power in the automobile industry. The federal government stepped in to correct long-standing complaints about the retail selling of automobiles with passage of the so-called Automobile Dealer's Day in Court Act (Public Law 1026) in 1956. Automotive design came to be regulated by the federal government with passage of the Motor Vehicle Air Pollution Act of 1965 and the National Traffic and Motor Vehicle Safety Act of 1966. Prices for new cars, as well as the wages of automobile workers, were made subject to governmental approval with the establishment in 1971 of wage and price controls as a measure to curb inflation. Progressive governmental regulation of the post–World War II automobile industry, however, was accompanied by the massive, indirect subsidization of the Interstate Highway Act of 1956, which committed the federal government to pay, from a Highway Trust Fund, 90 percent of the construction costs for 41,000 miles of mostly toll-free express highways.

Up to the 1960's American enthusiasm for the automobile remained remarkably constant through peace and war, depression and prosperity. Although during the Great Depression motor vehicle registrations declined slightly and factory sales dwindled to a low of 1.3 million units in 1932, the number of miles of travel by motor vehicle continued to increase, and automobility was one of the few aspects of American life that escaped disillusioned questioning. Full recovery from the depression was coupled with conversion of the automobile industry to meet the needs of the war effort. Manufacture of motor vehicles for the civilian market ceased early in 1942, with tires and gasoline severely rationed for the duration of the war. The automobile industry converted its resources to the manufacture of some seventy-five essential military items, contributing immeasurably to the Allied victory. After the war, the pent-up demand for cars and general affluence insured banner sales for Detroit, lasting into the late 1950's, when widespread dissatisfaction with the outcome of the automobile revolution began to become apparent.

Increasingly in the 1960's the automobile came to be recognized as a major social problem. Critics focused on its contributions to environmental pollution, urban sprawl, the rising cost of living, and accidental deaths and injuries. Much of the earlier romance of motoring was lost to a generation of Americans, who, reared in an automobile culture, accepted the motorcar as a mundane part of the establishment. While the automobile industry provided directly one out of every six jobs in the United States, its hegemony in the economy and society had been severely undercut over the preceding decades by proliferation of the size, power, and importance of government, which provided one out of every five jobs by 1970. With increased international involvement on the part of the United States, the rise of a nuclear warfare state, and the exploration of outer space, new industries more closely associated with the military-industrial complex—especially aerospace—became, along with the federal government, more important forces for change than the mature automobile industry.

These considerations notwithstanding, the American automobile culture continued to flourish in the 1960's. Drive-in facilities were extended from motion picture theaters and restaurants to banks, grocery stores, and even churches; automobile races attracted enthusiastic crowds; the cults of the hot rod and the sports car gained devotees; interest in restoring antique automobiles grew by leaps and bounds; and a new mass market for recreational vehicles resulted in an avalanche of campers and trail bikes descending on the national parks. The best indication of the automobile culture's continuing vitality was that in 1972 motor vehicle factory sales exceeded 11.2 million; registrations surpassed 117 million; and 83 percent of American families owned cars. In 1972 production lagged behind demand for new cars, and record-breaking factory sales for the third straight year were anticipated. To the average man the automobile remained an important symbol of individualism, personal freedom, and mobility in an increasingly collectivized and bureaucratized American society.

This phenomenal post–World War II proliferation of the U.S. automobile culture was abruptly halted in 1973–74 by an alleged fuel shortage, associated with a worldwide energy crisis. Critics charged that the fuel shortage was a ploy by the major oil companies to justify raising gasoline prices to boost profit margins; to squeeze out the independent dealers; and to gain public support for an expansion of offshore drilling and completion of the trans-Alaska pipeline. Nevertheless, domestic oil reserves in mid-1973 were reported to be only 52 billion barrels, about a ten-year supply. Projections were that crude petroleum imports would increase from 27 percent in 1972 to over

50 percent by 1980 and that all known world reserves of petroleum would be exhausted within fifty to seventy years. An embargo by the Arab oil-producing nations resulted by Jan. 1, 1974, in a ban on Sunday gasoline sales, a national 55-mph speed limit, five- to ten-gallon maximum limitations on gasoline purchases, and significantly higher prices at the pump. Despite short-range easing of the fuel shortage with the lifting of the Arab embargo, dwindling oil reserves promised, at the very least, increasingly higher gasoline prices that would impose inevitable limits on the further expansion of mass personal automobility anywhere in the world.

The end of a two-decade trend toward cars that guzzled more and more gasoline was underlined as sales of small cars increased to 39 percent (60 percent in Los Angeles) of the American market for the first quarter of 1973. By December, for the first time in history, sales of compacts and subcompacts surpassed sales of standard-sized cars, and projections were that smaller cars would soon account for two-thirds of the U.S. market. Consumers were responding to the inroads on purchasing power of runaway inflation and mounting taxes as well as to the fuel shortage. The American auto industry was ill-prepared for this marked shift in consumer preference, and for the first quarter of 1974 Detroit's sales slipped drastically. Large cars piled up on storage lots and in dealers' showrooms, and massive layoffs of automobile workers accompanied the shifting of assembly lines to the production of smaller models. Only American Motors, which had emphasized the small car since the mid-1950's, increased its sales. Among the Big Three, Ford held a comfortable lead in the conversion to the small car, with five compact and subcompact models.

Independently of the fuel shortage, by 1974 the worldwide automobile revolution had reached its zenith of probable development, and most observers anticipated more balanced transportation systems in the foreseeable future. The American market for motorcars was saturated with one car for every 2.25 persons (more cars than people in the Los Angeles area); the auto markets in Japan and in the developed countries of Europe were saturated in ratio of cars to available land and paved roads; and the low per capita incomes and poor income distribution in underdeveloped countries prohibited the creation of new auto cultures. The year 1973 marked the beginning of diversion of the Highway Trust Fund into nonhighway transportation, and California's freeway-building program, the most ambitious in the nation, was near collapse. Both General Motors and Ford inaugurated mass-transit divisions and were moving toward becoming total transportation corporations, whose main business by the end of the century was anticipated to become the designing of modular transportation systems for metropolitan areas. While the motor vehicle was still expected to play a major role in these transportation systems of the future, and it seemed that Detroit could continue prosperous and powerful through diversification and adaptation to small urban cars, by the mid-1970's the end undoubtedly had come to the "age of the automobile"—over two generations of American historical development dominated by the automobile and the automobile industry.

Automobile Racing. Contests emphasizing speed were of minimal importance in popularizing the automobile in the United States because the specialized cars used seemed remotely related to the average man's transportation needs. As early as 1905 the automobile trade journals expressed doubt that participation in races even had much advertising value for automobile manufacturers. The main value of track and road racing, therefore, was in providing grueling tests for advances in automotive technology; and this value became increasingly questionable with the institutionalization of systematic testing over specially designed courses. Nevertheless, automobile manufacturers have continued to support racing—with varying degrees of eagerness and openness. Few spectator sports can match the thrills and excitement of automobile racing, which early became a popular form of mass entertainment.

Organized automobile racing and time trials were supervised by the American Automobile Association until taken over by the newly formed U.S. Automobile Club in 1955. The last important American road race was run in 1916 at Santa Monica, Calif., for the Vanderbilt Cup; road racing remained popular in Europe, with Europeans generally excelling over Americans at the sport. The most famous American closed-circuit track event remains the Indianapolis 500-mile race, run since 1911 at increasingly higher speeds annually—except during wartime—over a brick-surfaced track. Dirt-track racing always has been popular throughout the country; the cars raced have ranged from specially designed midgets to modified stock cars. Drag racing—the attempt to achieve maximum acceleration over a short distance—became popular after World War II, and an annual drag-racing competition was inaugurated on the Bonneville Salt Flats (Utah). Bonneville also became the site of continuing attempts to set new land speed records in jet-propelled vehicles that bear more similarity to spaceships than to automobiles.

Sports Cars. Americans have contributed little toward perfecting the sports car—a small, high-performance car designed for highway use rather than organized racing. Sparked initially by GI's returning from England after World War II, an American sports car cult developed. The most important of a number of sports car organizations formed is the Sports Car Club of America, which has sponsored many sports-car competitions. European-made sports cars—especially the Porsche—continued in the mid-1970's to be most popular among devotees. In the 1950's Detroit introduced the Ford Thunderbird and the Chevrolet Corvette to compete with European sports cars, but the Thunderbird quickly evolved into a full-size, conventional car. In response to the growing youth market for smaller, sportier-looking cars, Detroit brought out a number of other models—such as the Ford Mustang—that look like, but lack the superior performance capabilities of, the true sports car.

[James J. Flink, *America Adopts the Automobile, 1895–1910;* John B. Rae, *The American Automobile,* and *The Road and the Car in American Life;* Emma Rothschild, *Paradise Lost: The Decline of the Auto-Industrial Age;* Lawrence J. White, *The Automobile Industry Since 1945.*]

JAMES J. FLINK

AUTO RACING. *See* **Automobile.**

AUTOSSEE, BATTLE OF (Nov. 29, 1813). During the Creek War, Gen. John Floyd, commanding 940 Georgia militia and several hundred friendly Creek Indians, crossed the Chattahoochee River into Mississippi Territory and attacked the Creek at Autossee, a Creek village near Tuckabatchee. Floyd's force drove the Creek from their villages, burned their houses, and killed 200 of them.

ROBERT S. THOMAS

AVERY SALT MINE, located at Avery Island, near New Iberia, La. Although a brine spring was discovered in 1791, it was not until May 1862 that the existence of a rock salt mass was revealed. The Confederate government worked the mine until the Union forces seized it and destroyed the equipment in April 1863. The mine has been worked continuously since 1883.

ELLA LONN

AVERYSBORO, BATTLE OF (March 16, 1865). W. J. Hardee's corps of Gen. J. E. Johnston's Confederate army, retreating through North Carolina, entrenched at the village of Averysboro and gave a portion of Gen. W. T. Sherman's Union army, under H. W. Slocum and H. J. Kilpatrick, a determined resistance for several hours; but inferior numbers compelled his retreat during the night.

[R. U. Johnson and C. C. Buel, eds., *Battles and Leaders of the Civil War.*]

ALVIN F. HARLOW

AVERY'S TRACE. In 1787 the North Carolina legislature provided for a lottery the proceeds of which were used to cut a way across the Cumberland Mountains in the Tennessee country in order to connect Washington District with the Cumberland settlements. Peter Avery blazed and cut a trace through the sites of the present towns of Harriman, Monterey, and Cookeville where the descent of the western escarpment of the Cumberland plateau began. The Cherokee claimed the region traversed by the trace and demanded toll for its use. Guards of militia became necessary where the party of travelers was not large or not well armed.

[W. E. McElwee, "The Old Road," *The American Historical Magazine,* vol. 8.]

SAMUEL C. WILLIAMS

AVIATION, the art and science of human flight, effectively began with successful balloon ascensions in France late in the 18th century. Balloon experiments were made in the United States during the 19th century, the most spectacular being the use of observation balloons by T. S. C. Lowe in behalf of the Union army during the Virginia campaigns of 1862–63. Of more significance were glider experiments conducted in the late 19th century by J. J. Montgomery, Octave Chanute, and the Wright brothers. These, along with similar experiments in Europe, provided the basic body of aerodynamic data necessary for the development of powered flight. Lighter-than-air powered flight was definitely a European achievement, accomplished during the first decade of the 20th century by the Brazilian Alberto Santos-Dumont in France and Count Ferdinand von Zeppelin in Germany.

Heavier-than-air flight was equally definitely an American achievement. Samuel P. Langley, astronomer and physicist, experimented with such flight from 1887 to 1903 and might have become the inventor of the airplane. In 1903 his engineer, Charles Manly, designed a remarkable power plant, a five-cylinder radial engine weighing 123 pounds and developing 52 horsepower. Langley tried twice, in October and December 1903, to launch his "aerodrome" from a catapult device on top of a houseboat in the Potomac River, but on both occasions the launch gear failed to function properly and the resultant derision caused Langley to abandon his efforts.

Powered heavier-than-air flight was first achieved by Orville and Wilbur Wright at Kitty Hawk, N.C., on Dec. 17, 1903. The brothers, bicycle mechanics from Dayton, Ohio, had a long period of trial and error behind this achievement. They had to build their own wind tunnel to work out correct tables of lift surfaces, and they were the first to formulate mathematical theories for propellers. The most important single factor in the success of the Wrights was their technique for warping the wings in coordination with the movements of the rudder and elevators, thereby solving the problem of maintaining lateral stability.

The Wright accomplishment was astonishingly ignored, even unknown, in the United States, even though subsequent flights were made in plain view just outside Dayton. Not until 1908, after spectacularly successful exhibition flights in Europe, were the brothers able to convince the War Department that they had indeed achieved powered flight and secure an order ($25,000) for America's first military airplane. Meanwhile, others had come into the picture. In 1907 Alexander Graham Bell had established the Aerial Experiment Association, located in Nova Scotia. Bell's own idea of a tetrahedral kite was impractical, and the association's principal contribution was to introduce Glenn Curtiss to aviation. Curtiss had been a builder of motorcycle engines and had made engines for Capt. Thomas Baldwin, a builder and demonstrator of small dirigibles. When his work for Baldwin brought him to Bell's attention, he became a member of the Aerial Experiment Association.

Curtiss' most important pioneering work was the design of seaplanes. He conceived the idea of putting a "step" in the float, thus breaking the surface tension of the water and enabling a floatplane to take off without excessive power. In 1908 he rebuilt Langley's aerodrome as a floatplane and flew it from Lake Keuka, N.Y., thereby enabling Langley's partisans to claim that he had actually preceded the Wrights. This action led the Wright brothers to put the Kitty Hawk plane in the Science Museum in London instead of in the Smithsonian (it was finally brought to the United States in 1947), and it undoubtedly was an added stimulus for them to sue Curtiss for patent infringement.

The Wrights claimed that their patents included any control system that changed the configuration of the wing, while Curtiss argued that the aileron, which he and most of the European pioneers used, constituted a different principle from wing-warping. The issue was never settled. When the United States entered World War I, the government required the contestants to pool their patents rather than impede production, and the lawsuit was abandoned.

There were other outstanding American feats in this pioneering era. Curtiss established a world speed record in 1910 (55 mph); and Lincoln Beachey, an altitude record of 11,642 feet in 1911. Lincoln P. Rodgers flew from New York to Long Beach, Calif., in 1911, taking 49 days in all, of which 82 hours and 14 minutes were in the air. The rest of the time was spent repairing the plane; it crashed nineteen times. In 1912 Glenn L. Martin, who had built his first experimental plane in Santa Ana, Calif., four years before, performed the not inconsiderable feat of flying to Catalina Island and back. The U.S. Navy was the first to launch a plane from a warship, from a platform on the U.S.S. *Birmingham* on Nov. 10, 1910, piloted by Eugene Ely. Two months later Ely made the first shipboard landing, on the *Pennsylvania*. In 1915 the navy achieved the first catapult launching from a moving vessel.

Nevertheless, when World War I broke out, American aviation had fallen far behind European aviation. There was no aircraft industry worth the name in the United States, and the only constructive step the government took was to found the National Advisory Committee for Aeronautics (NACA) in 1915. The United States went to war in 1917 with an air force consisting of a handful of obsolete planes. A massive building program had to depend on European models, and it began to produce about the time the war ended. The sole effective American contribution was the Liberty engine, a conventional twelve-cylinder, in-line engine whose merit was that it could be manufactured in quantity.

The deficiencies of American aviation brought action that resulted in improvement. Airmail service was begun by the U.S. Post Office in May 1918, using army planes to fly between Washington, D.C., and New York. The first transcontinental flight to be completed within twenty-four hours came in February 1921, by an army DH-4B flying between San Diego, Calif., and Jacksonville, Fla. More important, in May 1919 a navy flying boat (NC-4) completed a flight across the Atlantic, with stops at Bermuda and the Azores. Three others started the flight but failed to finish. In 1921 the military potential of air power was dramatically displayed by bombing tests off the Virginia capes, with captured German warships and the unfinished U.S.S. *Washington* as targets. Three years later four army Douglas biplanes set off around the world and two completed the journey, in an elapsed time of 172 days, 15.5 of them in the air.

There were difficulties. The Virginia capes tests exacerbated rivalries within the services, and these were intensified by the court-martial of Brig. Gen. William G. (Billy) Mitchell for insubordination in 1926. The Morrow Board, established by President Calvin Coolidge in 1926, resolved some of these problems and formulated a rational aviation policy, while the Kelly Air Mail Act of 1925 stimulated commercial aviation. Above all, the New York–Paris flight of Charles A. Lindbergh on May 20–21, 1927, provoked a tremendous outburst of popular enthusiasm for aviation.

This was also the period of American experimentation with lighter-than-air flight, undertaken by the navy because of the apparent usefulness of German zeppelins for reconnaissance during the war. The U.S.S. *Shenandoah* was modeled on a captured zeppelin; and the *Akron* and *Macon,* built by Goodyear, used German designs and technicians. All three were wrecked in storms: *Shenandoah* in 1925, *Akron* in 1933, and *Macon* in 1935. When the German *Hindenburg* was destroyed by fire while mooring at Lakehurst, N.J., in 1937, public opinion turned against airships, although the Hindenburg disaster would have been avoided if the ship had been able to use helium gas, the entire supply of which was held by the United States. The abandonment of airships was further expedited by phenomenal developments in airplanes. In the 1930's flying boats (seaplanes with hulls adapted for floating) reached the stage where they could perform most of the naval missions of the airship; they also made possible transoceanic commercial flight.

The most striking American achievement of the 1930's was the development of transport aircraft synthesizing in their design all-metal monocoque construction; retractable landing gear; controllable pitch propellers; wing flaps and wing slots; and, for the most part, radial, air-cooled engines with the cowling introduced by the NACA in 1928, which permitted effective cooling with reduced drag. Many of these features were European in origin, and most had been tried separately earlier. The principal American technical contribution, besides the engine cowling, was the controllable pitch propeller designed by Frank Caldwell at McCook Field (now Wright-Patterson Air Force Base) and later perfected at the Hamilton Standard Propeller Company. The result was to make the United States the world's leading manufacturer of transport aircraft. The end of the decade saw another landmark in American aviation when in 1939 Igor Ivan Sikorsky successfully flew an experimental helicopter.

In World War II, aviation emerged as an indispensable adjunct to military success. It early became obvious that adequate air support was essential to the success of surface operations. Among the features introduced or accelerated by the requirements of the war were naval battles in which all the fighting was done in the air, so that the aircraft carrier replaced the battleship as the basis of seapower; high-altitude flight in which oxygen masks and pressure suits were required (cabin pressurization was introduced late in the 1930's, but the needs of war production delayed its use); and airborne radar. Ground Control Approach (GCA) and Instrument Landing Systems (ILS) were also introduced, and extensive use was made of transport aircraft, especially landplanes, on intercontinental flights.

The United States had a major share in all of these. However, pioneering work on the major innovation of the war years, the jet engine, was done in Great Britain and Germany. The NACA had studied jet propulsion as early as 1923, but this and later studies quite accurately indicated that the jet at that stage would have a very short range. The first American-built jet plane was test flown on Oct. 2, 1942, at Muroc Dry Lake, Calif., using an American version of the British Whittle engine. Development was then pushed vigorously, but only the Germans used jet planes in combat in the war.

The demonstrated importance of aviation led to the appointment of the Finletter Commission in 1947 to formulate a long-range aviation policy. Its report, *Survival in the Air Age,* recommended annual military procurement of 30 to 40 million pounds of airframe weight as the minimum needed to maintain a healthy aviation industry in the United States, but the report became involved in political and interservice controversy and was never implemented. There was, however, vigorous development of the prospects that had emerged during the war of flight at high altitudes, where air turbulence was less likely; drag was reduced; and high speeds, including supersonic speeds, could be attained.

The sound barrier (speed of sound, about 761 mph at sea level) was broken on Oct. 14, 1947, by U.S. Air Force Maj. Charles Yeager, flying the Bell X-1; and the Mach number, a term designating relationship to the speed of sound, entered the American vocabulary. This flight was strictly an experimental operation. There were still acute problems to be solved because of the rapid increase of drag and boundary-layer turbulence as the speed of sound was approached. It took another decade of intensive research and development for jet aircraft to replace propeller-driven planes in most military and commercial operations. The jet engine itself was refined to outdo the piston engine in fuel consumption and reliability. High-speed, high-altitude flight required changes in airfoil design and brought the swept-back delta wing into general use. Wing loadings increased by a factor of 4 or 5 over what they had been in the 1930's. For short-winged planes (chiefly jet fighters) the "area rule" formulated by Richard T. Whitcomb at the NACA in 1952 produced a fuselage design that reduced drag sufficiently to make supersonic speed practical. The next step in airframe design was the "swing-wing" adopted for the F-111 in the 1960's. The F-111, however, had operational problems that led to its abandonment, and the only other attempt to use the swing-wing was in the projected Boeing supersonic transport, cancelled in 1971.

The development of the guided missile after World War II and the rapid growth of space exploration after the flight of Russia's Sputnik in 1957 brought a new dimension to aviation, symbolized when the NACA was absorbed into the new National Aeronautics and Space Administration (NASA) in 1958. The most spectacular innovations occurred in the area of missiles and space, but these properly belong under other categories. Aviation, in the conventional sense of the term, continued to make progress also. By 1960 experimental aircraft with rocket-propelled engines were launched from "mother" planes and attained altitudes of 136,000 feet. Operational airplanes also continued to establish performance records. Early in 1961 three U.S. Air Force B-52 bombers made a nonstop flight around the world, refueling in the air en route; and ten years later (Apr. 26, 1971) an air force SR-71 reconnaissance jet established a new record—combining duration, total distance covered, and altitude—for a flight of 10.5 hours, a distance of 15,000 miles at speeds in excess of Mach 3 (more than 2,000 mph), and altitudes over 80,000 feet.

[*American Heritage History of Flight;* Ronald Miller and David Sawers, *The Technical Development of Modern Aviation;* National Aeronautics and Space Administration, *Aeronautics and Astronautics, 1915–1960.*]

JOHN B. RAE

AVIATION AGENCY, FEDERAL. *See* **Federal Agencies.**

AVIATION INDUSTRY, the industry concerned with the manufacture of aircraft, aircraft engines, propellers, and other components—excluding electrical and electronic equipment and weapons for military aircraft. The American aviation industry began in 1909, when the Wright brothers formed a company to build airplanes and conduct flying schools. They were followed by Glenn Curtiss (also 1909), W. Starling Burgess (1910), Glenn L. Martin (1912), William E. Boeing (1915), and Allan and Martin Loughead (1915). Growth was slow because of minimal support from the government ($500,000 from 1909 to 1914), and the aviation industry in the United States and elsewhere has existed largely on sales to governments.

World War I found the United States with totally inadequate resources for aircraft design and construction. Total output in 1914 was forty-nine planes. A massive building program was initiated by the government, but it came under much criticism because planes were not produced in any quantity before the war ended. There were charges of mismanagement and corruption, with some foundation; but the real difficulty was failure to realize the complexity of the problem. An easy assumption made by Americans in World War I and repeated in World War II was that existing industrial resources—especially the automobile industry—could be converted on short notice to aircraft construction.

The war terminated a patent controversy between the Wrights and Martin on one side and Curtiss and Burgess on the other. Among them they controlled most of the basic airplane patents and each was claiming infringement by the other. Governmental pressure brought about the creation of the Aircraft Manufacturers' Association in 1917, with the administering of a cross-licensing agreement as its principal initial function. In the process, Wright and Martin merged as the Wright-Martin Company and Curtiss and Burgess as the Curtiss Aeroplane and Motor Company.

The wartime program produced, up to Nov. 1, 1919, some 14,000 planes, 42,000 engines, and 41,000 balloons and airships at a cost of over $365 million. About 300 plants and 20,000 workers were involved. When the armistice came, war contracts were abruptly terminated and the aviation industry virtually collapsed within a year. Most of the wartime entrants disappeared. The principal holdovers were the Wright Aeronautical Company, reorganized from Wright-Martin and now exclusively an engine manufacturer; Curtiss Aeroplane and Motor, briefly included in the Willys automotive empire; Boeing; and a reconstituted Glenn L. Martin Company. Two important new arrivals appeared in the early 1920's: Douglas, established in Los Angeles by Donald W. Douglas in 1920; and Consolidated, put together by Reuben Fleet from the remains of two wartime airplane companies, Dayton-Wright and Gallaudet, and located in Buffalo, N.Y.

The middle 1920's witnessed a steady, but still small-scale, growth of the industry, stimulated by the Kelly Air Mail Act of 1925, which put the carriage of airmail into private hands and therefore encouraged the development of more economical and efficient transport planes, and by the report of the Morrow Board in 1926, which provided a systematic five-year program of military and naval procurement. A number of new American airframe firms appeared, including Lockheed, a revival of the earlier Loughead company (the brothers changed the spelling of their name); Fairchild, originally a company engaged in aerial photography; and the companies founded by Igor Sikorsky, a brilliant Russian aeronautical engineer, and Anthony Fokker, the Dutchman who established a reputation as a designer of fighter planes for Germany in World War I. An outstanding entrant was William B. Stout's company, one of the first in the world to build all-metal aircraft. It was taken over by the Ford Motor Company in 1924 and produced the well-known Ford trimotor transport, the "tin goose." In addition, Wichita, Kans., emerged during the 1920's as the country's principal center for the manufacture of planes for general aviation—that is, planes that were neither military aircraft nor commercial transports.

The greatest advance of this period came in the design and production of radial air-cooled engines. Because Adm. William A. Moffett, head of the U.S. Navy Bureau of Aeronautics, believed that this type of engine was ideally suited to the navy's needs, he encouraged its development by Wright Aeronautical (later Curtiss-Wright) and a new firm, Pratt and Whitney. The pioneering American work on the radial air-cooled engine was done by Charles L. Lawrance, whose company was acquired by Wright Aeronautical in 1923. By the end of the decade the United States had attained a clear leadership, both qualitative and quantitative, in radial air-cooled engines.

There was also an American effort to enter the lighter-than-air field, again because of naval interest. The dirigible *Shenandoah* was completed in 1923 by the Naval Aircraft Factory in Philadelphia. In 1924 the Goodyear Zeppelin Corporation was formed, with both German designs and German technicians. This company built the *Akron* (1931) and the *Macon* (1933), both designed as carriers for four small airplanes. All three of these airships were wrecked in storms, with the result that further development of large dirigibles was abandoned.

The enthusiasm generated by Charles A. Lindbergh's New York to Paris flight in 1927 and the boom atmosphere of the late 1920's stimulated optimistic hopes about the growth of aviation and led to several efforts at large-scale combinations of aircraft manufacturers and air-transport companies. The most important were United Aircraft and Transport, started in 1928 by William E. Boeing, North American Aviation, and the Aviation Corporation (later AVCO). Such combinations did not fulfill the expectations of their promoters. The stock-market crash temporarily shut off the flow of capital into aviation, and in 1934 a political controversy over the award of airmail contracts resulted in legislation requiring the separation of manufacturing and transport companies. In general, the aircraft manufacturers weathered the depression of 1929–32 with reasonable success. The main exception was Lockheed, which went into receivership and was bought in 1932 by a syndicate under the leadership of Robert and Courtlandt Gross.

This period of financial stress was the prelude to an era of phenomenal achievement. A number of aeronautical technologies were synthesized into the design that became virtually universal for military and commercial transport planes—the all-metal, monocoque, low-wing monoplane, with retractable landing gear, controllable pitch propeller, wing flaps, and wing slots. There were both military and economic incentives to improve design, and the first planes to incorporate these features in the early 1930's were the Martin B-10 and the Boeing B-9 bombers and the Boeing 247 transport; the B-9 and the 247 had, in fact, the same basic design. What gave the American industry a commanding lead in developing and producing such planes was the rivalry between airlines and between manufacturers. The desire for a competitor to the 247 led to the development of the Douglas DC series, with the result that by 1939 the DC-3, introduced in 1935, dominated the world's airways. Commercial aviation also benefited from the introduction of long-range flying boats—the Sikorsky, Boeing, and Martin clippers—which made possible regular transoceanic service. As the decade ended, Boeing, Douglas, and Lockheed were all working on four-engined landplanes with pressurized cabins for high-altitude flight, but these did not go into regular commercial operation until after World War II. Simultaneously the American aviation industry became the leading producer of large bombers, beginning with the Boeing B-17 Flying Fortress in 1935.

There were also locational changes in the industry. In the mid-1930's the Pacific coast acquired the bulk of the country's airframe production when newcomers like North American (reconstituted from the holding company) and Northrop were added to the firms already in southern California and Consolidated moved from Buffalo to San Diego. Engine production was heavily concentrated in the Northeast. The industry was still small-scale. Its total output as late as 1939 was less than 6,000 planes for the year, and it ranked forty-first among American industries. On the world scene it led only in the production of transport aircraft; in military production the American industry was a minor factor. In the late 1930's five British aircraft firms and several German and Japanese firms exceeded any American company in volume of production and numbers employed.

World War II brought drastic changes. British and French orders began to stimulate expansion as early as 1938, and by 1940 American military demand was mushrooming; by 1943 the aviation industry was the country's largest producer and employer. This expansion was achieved partly by greater use of subcontracting and licensing but mainly by extensive construction of new facilities, government financed and located away from the supposedly vulnerable coastal areas. Most of these new plants were operated by airframe and aircraft engine companies, but some were run by automobile manufacturers. As in World War I, it became evident that automobile factories could not be converted to aircraft production, so that the automobile industry's contribution consisted of operating these wartime facilities plus making parts and components. Some of these plants, notably in Dallas and Fort Worth, Tex., remained permanent parts of the industry after the war.

Total output between 1939 and 1945 was approximately 300,000 aircraft, representing about 2 billion pounds of airframe weight. Peak employment in the aviation industry was 1,345,600 in 1943. The pressure to produce meant that there was much refinement and development of conventional aircraft types but little radical innovation. The American aviation industry, for instance, had very little to do with the development of jet propulsion. There was some experimental work; but the first American-built jets were based on British models, and none of them progressed far enough to be used in combat.

When the war ended, the aviation industry faced major readjustments. Military demand dropped sharply, but that was expected. The novel, and at the time imponderable, factors were the future of jet propulsion and the prospective replacement of manned military aircraft by ballistic missiles. In addition, the helicopter had begun to demonstrate a variety of potential uses during the war. A substantial growth in helicopter manufacture took place, partly through existing companies (Bell, Sikorsky Division of United Aircraft) but also through several new and specialized firms.

Jet airplanes developed much faster than had been anticipated, largely because of intensive research and development by the military. At the time of the Korean conflict (1950–52) fighter planes were jet-propelled but bombers still relied on piston engines. Within a very few years jet engines attained the range and fuel consumption suitable for bombers and transports. The plans for the Boeing B-47 were actually laid out before the end of World War II, and the B-47 was soon followed by the B-52. The prototype 707 flew in 1954, based on the design of the KC-135 air force tanker; it went into regular airline service in 1958. Douglas followed a year later with the DC-8, after some years of brilliant success with the piston-engined DC-6 and DC-7. The only other serious competitors in the field of large jet planes were Convair (formed from a wartime merger of Consolidated and Vulte) and Lockheed, and neither attained the success of Boeing and Douglas.

The most striking readjustment of the industry after World War II was that the airframe manufacturers became the prime producers of missiles and, after 1957, of space vehicles. One major company, Martin, withdrew entirely from aircraft manufacture, but this was an exceptional case. The missile was not a substitute for civil aircraft, either commercial or general, and combat in Vietnam demonstrated that the manned military airplane was far from obsolete. Nevertheless, by 1960 the aviation industry had become the aerospace industry.

These changes affected the structure of the industry. It continued to be acutely dependent on the government, to which it made 80 percent of its sales. Because of the new technologies, research and development became the largest single item of cost and the unique situation was created in which this industry had more managerial and technical personnel than production workers. Organizational changes occurred also. Convair went through a corporate upheaval and was absorbed by General Dynamics in 1953. Martin and North American, seeking reduced dependence on government contracts, merged with nonaviation firms to become Martin-Marietta and North American Rockwell (later Rockwell International) in 1961 and 1967, respectively, and some of the lesser concerns also merged with companies in other industries.

At the beginning of the 1970's the American aerospace industry still led the world in the design and manufacture of transport aircraft. From the first jets of the 1950's had come a diversity of models for long and short hauls, heavy and light loads. However, support for a supersonic transport (SST) was cut back in 1970 and withdrawn completely in 1971, although it was clear that Soviet and Anglo-French plans for such a plane would continue. Declining military demand and curtailment of the space program were causing distress, reflecting again the industry's acute dependence on governmental orders.

[W. G. Cunningham, *The Aircraft Industry: A Study in Industrial Location;* Lloyd Morris and Kendall Smith, *Ceiling Unlimited: The Story of American Aviation from Kitty Hawk to Supersonics;* J. B. Rae, *Climb to Greatness: The American Aircraft Industry, 1920–1960.*]

JOHN B. RAE

AWAKENING, SECOND, the name usually given the great religious revival that swept over the United States in the late 18th and early 19th centuries, following an era of extreme religious apathy. In the East it centered in the colleges where religion had been in sad plight, with apostasy rampant among the students. President Timothy Dwight of Yale University met the issue squarely and in chapel sermons and classroom discussions he won the respect of the students and prepared the way for a renewed religious interest. A revival began in 1802 that resulted in the conversion of a third of the student body. The Awakening spread to other colleges and soon a stream of young college graduates was entering every form of Christian work, particularly the Christian ministry and education and home and foreign mission enterprises.

In the West the Awakening was attended with great emotional excitement, under the preaching of such evangelists as James McGready, Barton W. Stone, and William McKendree. No churches were large enough to hold the vast crowds which assembled to hear the evangelists and as a result the camp meeting evolved. While at first largely a Presbyterian movement, the revival soon became interdenominational and spread rapidly throughout the West. Although greatly increasing church membership and raising the standard of western morals, there were some unfortunate results, such as excessive emotionalism and church schisms.

[Catharine C. Cleveland, *The Great Revival in the West, 1797–1805.*]

WILLIAM W. SWEET

AYLLÓN, EXPEDITIONS OF DE. In 1521 Lucas Vásquez de Ayllón sent from the West Indies an exploring expedition which visited the present Carolina coast, returning therefrom with a number of captured natives. In 1526 de Ayllón sailed in three caravels with 600 prospective settlers, African slaves, scores of horses, and orders to seek the ever-elusive Northwest Passage. The name of his settlement, San Miguel de Gualdape, is recorded, but its site has yet to be determined, some scholars having placed it south of Cape Hatteras, while others have placed it within the Chesapeake, either on the James River or the Potomac. Since the most extended account refers to severe cold, acceptance thereof would point to the more northerly site. The Spaniards suffered all the ills subsequently endured by the English at Jamestown in the form of malarial fevers, dissensions, and Indian assaults. The settlement was abandoned after one year and the survivors returned to the West Indies.

[Elroy M. Avery, *A History of the United States,* vol. I.]

MATTHEW PAGE ANDREWS

AYUBALE, BATTLE OF (Dec. 14, 1703), a frontier engagement between a force of 50 whites and 1,000 Indians under former Gov. James Moore of South Carolina and the defenders of the Spanish mission at Ayubale, near Tallahassee. Moore, who as governor (1700–03) had failed in an attempt to take the fort at St. Augustine, was given command of the expedition into Apalache to redeem his failure. He took Ayubale, devastated a wide area, badly crippled the Spanish in Florida, and carried away 1,300 Apalache Indian captives (or 600, according to the Spanish estimate), settling as Carolina dependents, on the east side of the lower course of the Savannah River, those not sold as slaves.

[J. T. Lanning, *Spanish Missions in Georgia;* D. D. Wallace, *History of South Carolina.*]

D. D. WALLACE

AYUNTAMIENTO (or ***Cabildo***), a Spanish and Spanish-American municipal council, with administrative, legislative, and judicial functions. Citizens sometimes joined it in open meeting, or *cabildo abierto*. Many cities in the United States, including St. Augustine, Fla., San Antonio, Tex., and Los Angeles, Calif., were governed by *ayuntamientos*.

[C. E. Chapman, *Colonial Hispanic America: A History*.]

CHARLES EDWARD CHAPMAN
ROBERT HALE SHIELDS

AZILIA, MARGRAVATE OF, the fantastic scheme of Sir Robert Montgomery to establish "a New Colony to the South of Carolina." Despite activities in Britain, he and others failed to settle the area between the Savannah and the Altamaha rivers, the Golden Islands region, within the three years conditioning his grant of 1717 from the Carolina proprietors.

[V. W. Crane, *The Southern Frontier, 1670–1732*.]

H. B. FANT

BACHELOR HOUSES. To protect the colony from being burdened with the indigent and to maintain moral standards, Connecticut as early as 1636 forbade heads of families from entertaining single young men without permission. Nor could an unmarried young man keep house alone without consent under penalty of a fine. The Connecticut Code of 1650 (*see* Ludlow's Code) and the New Haven laws of 1656 extended this prohibition to single persons of either sex. Similarly strict laws against strangers are found in the Massachusetts codes of 1641, 1648, and 1660.

[E. W. Capen, *The Historical Development of the Poor Law of Connecticut*.]

RICHARD B. MORRIS

BACKLASH. The word "backlash" entered the lexicon of American politics in the mid-1950's. Initially it referred to the hostile reaction of conservative southerners in the Democratic party to the liberal stance adopted by the national Democratic party on domestic issues, particularly race relations. Passage of the Civil Rights Act of 1957 increased the alienation of southern Democrats from the national political party that had dominated politics in the South for a century. In the 1960's, during the administrations of presidents John F. Kennedy and Lyndon B. Johnson, the term achieved prominence, and its application was no longer limited to the South. The national Democratic party adopted a series of reform programs aimed at upgrading the social, economic, and political status of Afro-Americans. Passage of the Economic Opportunity Act of 1964, the Civil Rights Act of 1964, the Voting Rights Act of 1965, and the Open Housing Act of 1968 evoked opposition among traditional supporters of the Democratic party. The hostile response to these initiatives in civil rights and domestic legislation among blocs of rank-and-file voters considered Democrats since at least the New Deal era was referred to as backlash.

During the 1960's the term was increasingly used to identify voters who supported the candidacy of Alabama Gov. George C. Wallace for the presidency. In 1964 Wallace entered several northern Democratic primaries and captured a significant minority of the vote, ranging from one-third to two-fifths of rank-and-file Democrats. In his bid for the presidency in 1968 under the third-party banner of the American Independent party, Wallace's following was similarly said to be from the backlash of white citizens. Nevertheless, at this time the term "backlash" was used to characterize not only regular Democrats' reactions against reform legislation and support for Wallace but also, more generally, resistance to reform among white citizens who felt that Afro-Americans were demanding too much, too fast, with too much conflict and violence.

Whereas peaceful, nonviolent protest by Afro-Americans during the early 1960's gave way to massive civil disorders from 1964 through 1968 in northern cities, backlash against these events was said to consist in a change in attitudes among white citizens who recoiled against the demands by Afro-Americans for equality of treatment in the areas of housing, education, law enforcement, and employment. Those who used the term "backlash" to describe these events did not establish beyond question, however, exactly which white attitudes had changed or how much.

[W. Brink and L. Harris, *Black and White: A Study of U.S. Racial Attitudes Today;* R. Hamilton, *Class and Politics in the United States*.]

DAVID J. OLSON

BACKWOODS AND BACKCOUNTRY. The term "backwoodsman" was not applied to those who, in the first century of colonization, settled in the wilder portions of New England. It became common when pioneers began advancing the frontier farther south—moving into and beyond the mountains of Pennsylvania, Virginia, and the Carolinas, regions which came to be known to the coast states as the backcountry. For generations after the great westward movement began, about 1769–70, this backcountry, comprising the present Middle West, West Virginia, Kentucky, Tennessee, and other inland areas farther south, was predominantly forest. Until 1800 roads fit for wheeled vehicles were rare and short, and most traveling was done by water or mere horse trail. There were still only a few small cleared areas in southwestern Virginia, now Kentucky, when, in 1776, the settlers chose two agents to ask protection of Virginia. As a result "Kentucky County" was created, and in 1777 two burgesses were sent to the Virginia legislature. During the Revolution backwoodsmen under George Rogers Clark (*see* Clark's Northwest Campaign) took Kaskaskia (July) and Vincennes (December) in Illinois from the British in 1778. In Tennessee they first organized the Watauga Association and then the State of Franklin. An undisciplined but, as usual, efficient army of backwoodsmen annihilated Maj. Patrick Ferguson's force at the Battle of King's Mountain, in western North Carolina. Later, under their idol, Andrew Jackson, they fought the Creek War and won the Battle of New Orleans. Their prowess in war bred in them a group consciousness and pride. When Jackson was inaugurated in 1829 the backwoodsmen flocked to Washington and made the occasion, including the White House reception, so turbulent and uproarious that old Federalists and Whigs thought the era of mob rule had come. During that period the word "backwoodsman" acquired an opprobrium which it never afterward lost.

[E. Douglas Branch, *Westward;* Seymour Dunbar, *History of Travel in America;* Theodore Roosevelt, *The Winning of the West.*]

ALVIN F. HARLOW

BACON'S REBELLION, a revolt in Virginia in 1676 led by Nathaniel Bacon, Jr., a young planter, against the aged royal governor, Sir William Berkeley. The revolt has, since the time of the American Revolution, usually been interpreted as an attempt at political reform directed against the allegedly oppressive rule of the governor. Recent scholarship has questioned this thesis and emphasized the controversy over Indian policy, over which Berkeley and Bacon disagreed, as a fundamental cause of, rather than a pretext for, the rebellion.

When Indian depredations occurred on the northern and western frontiers in the fall of 1675 and spring of 1676, Bacon demanded the right to lead volunteers against all Indians, even those living peacefully within the colony, in retaliation. Berkeley, fearing unjust dispossession and slaughter of the friendly Indians, refused. Bacon ignored the governor's restriction and led volunteers to the southern frontier in May 1676, where he slaughtered and plundered the friendly Occaneechee Indians. When the governor attempted to call him to account, Bacon marched to Jamestown and, at gunpoint, forced the assembly of June 1676 to grant him formal authority to fight the Indian war, which he then prosecuted against another friendly tribe, the Pamunkey. When Berkeley attempted to raise forces to reestablish his own authority, Bacon turned on the governor with his volunteers. Civil war ensued. Berkeley was driven to the eastern shore of Virginia. Jamestown, the capital, was burned. For a few months Bacon's word was law on the mainland. But suddenly, in October 1676, he died. Berkeley, having recruited forces on the eastern shore, returned to the mainland, defeated the remaining rebels, and, by February 1677, reestablished his authority. Soon thereafter 1,000 troops, sent by Charles II to suppress the rebellion, arrived, accompanied by commissioners to investigate its causes. Berkeley's strict policy toward the defeated rebels was severely censured by the commissioners who attempted to remove him from the governorship. Berkeley returned to England in May 1677 to justify himself but died on July 9, before seeing the king.

[Wilcomb E. Washburn, *Governor and the Rebel: A History of Bacon's Rebellion in Virginia.*]

WILCOMB E. WASHBURN

BACTERIOLOGY AND VIROLOGY. Some colonial intellectuals undoubtedly knew about the "little animals" of Anthony van Leeuwenhoek and other 17th- and early 18th-century microscopic discoveries through their reading in the *Philosophical Transactions* of the Royal Society and other contemporary publications. However, it is doubtful that any investigator on the western side of the Atlantic actually undertook direct studies of minute organisms until well into the 19th century. Cotton Mather—in his unpublished "Angel of Bethesda"—is the only American writer known to have given credence during the 18th century to the hypothesis propounded by Athanasius Kircher and Benjamin Marten that epidemic diseases are caused by and spread through the agency of microscopic organisms. Early in the 19th century John Crawford, a Baltimore physician, drew the ridicule of most of his professional colleagues for advocating a similar "germ" theory of disease. After Crawford, in the absence of real proofs for such a theory, few other American medical scientists up until the 1870's were willing to argue against the majority, who swore by one or another of a variety of miasmatic theories of disease.

During the 1830's and 1840's new potentialities for biomedical research arose with the appearance of greatly improved microscopes equipped with the recently developed achromatic lenses. A handful of American medical investigators—prominent among them, Joseph Leidy of Philadelphia and John L. Riddell of New Orleans—who acquired good achromatic microscopes during this period, made a beginning in the scientific study of fungi and other minute organisms. At midcentury, in fact, some scientists were using their instruments to try to establish a connection between the organisms they observed and epidemic diseases, such as cholera, malaria, and yellow fever. Their failure to establish any connections, together with the undeniable success of sanitary work based upon assumptions that disease arose in dirt and miasmas, brought further experiment along this line almost to a halt during the 1860's and much of the 1870's. Only in the early 1880's was substantial interest in bacteriology rekindled in the United States, after a spate of advances in Europe—Joseph Lister's introduction of antiseptic surgery, Robert Koch's discovery of the tubercle bacillus and identification of the comma bacillus of cholera, and Louis Pasteur's successful inoculation against rabies and other animal diseases.

In 1885 barely half a dozen American scientists were pursuing bacteriological research. However, this number mushroomed during the next two or three decades as the United States hastened to take advantage of and catch up to the European scientific work; for it was realized that bacteriology had fundamental and important implications for agriculture, botany, and other sciences—and particularly for medicine. A number of Americans went to Europe at that time, especially to Germany, to learn about the demanding new laboratory methods and bacteriological techniques, and those scientists passed along the new knowledge upon their return. Still others absorbed the new techniques from the rapidly proliferating literature. By the mid-1880's bacteriological instruction was being given at such universities as Illinois, Harvard, Johns Hopkins, Michigan, and Pennsylvania, and the Massachusetts Institute of Technology (MIT). Application of these techniques to infectious disease control began a few years later when public health laboratories were established, among the first being those of the Massachusetts State Board of Health and the city health departments of Providence, R.I., and New York. Early bacteriological activities at those laboratories included the testing of water supplies, the diagnosis of diphtheria, and the preparation of vaccines and sera.

Some of the most important bacteriological contributions by Americans before World War I were made in federal government laboratories. In the Department of Agriculture, Daniel Salmon, chief of the Bureau of Animal Industry, investigated the causal organism of swine cholera and in the 1890's organized a meat inspection service that used microscopes to detect trichinosis in pork for export. In 1893 two of his scientists, Theobald Smith and F. L. Kilborne, brought much greater scientific distinction to the department by their unraveling of the tick transmission of Texas cattle fever, one of the earliest demonstrations anywhere of the role of the insect vector (an intermediate host that carries disease). Smith subsequently also carried out important studies in the bacteriology of human diseases, particularly tuberculosis, in posts in Boston, Mass., and Princeton, N. J. In addition to Smith's work significant bacteriological contributions were made by several other early Department of Agriculture scientists, including the soil bacteriologist Charles Thom and the plant pathologist Erwin F. Smith. In yet another area of inquiry, the zoologist Charles Wardell Stiles identified a new variety of American hookworm and subsequently not only determined its wide distribution in the South but also played a leading role in efforts at eradicating and controlling it.

In the army George Sternberg was a productive pioneer in the early 1880's, through his translation of Antoine Magnin's general bacteriology text as well as through his extensive original research, which included the isolation of the pneumococcus. Even more important was his success in 1893 in organizing the Army Medical School, an institution that gave army physicians specialized training in preventive medicine and such new medical sciences as bacteriology, a particularly significant initiative in view of the growing global involvement of the United States in tropical areas and the consequent need for combating tropical diseases. Sternberg's venture was amply justified within a few years by the notable findings in Cuba of the Yellow Fever Commission under Walter Reed, with its electrifying demonstration of the transmission of that disease by the mosquito.

By the 20th century bacteriology had become the epitome of the new science—rigorous and demanding in its methods, surprisingly fruitful and effective in its results. Devotees of bacteriology quickly began banding together to organize their own societies and create their own journals. The second generation of bacteriologists, many of whom had studied under William T. Sedgwick at MIT, spread out across the country to staff new university departments. Others joined developing research facilities, such as Chicago's McCormick Institute for Infectious Diseases, under Ludvig Hektoen. In the U.S. Marine Hospital Service, a one-man bacteriological research effort by J. J. Kinyoun expanded after 1900 with the formation of the Hygienic Laboratory, under Milton Rosenau. Among other activities the laboratory became responsible for the standardization and control of vaccines and other biologicals. After World War II its microbiological and other research developed enormously with the growth of the laboratory into the National Institutes of Health.

For much of the early 20th century, the nation's principal biomedical research center was the Rockefeller Institute for Medical Research, founded in 1906. Under Simon Flexner, scientists of the institute undertook a wide range of bacteriological studies along with other medical investigations. In the course of this work they collectively came to represent the prototype of the 20th-century American laboratory researcher, an image passed on to the public by Sinclair Lewis in *Arrowsmith* and by popularizers, such as Paul de Kruif.

After the remarkable early years, in which scientists identified one disease after another with particular bacteria, the period after World War I saw relatively fewer new bacteria isolated and fewer headlines about such research. But many of the difficult tasks of bacteriology still remained and were vigorously pursued: sorting out the varieties of bacteria and learning their behavior; developing accurate means of diagnosis; determining immune mechanisms in animals and human beings and preparing sera or vaccines; and probing the subbacterial world of the viruses. Steadily improved laboratory techniques and equipment greatly advanced all these studies—and none more than virology. Here, after years of uncertainty and confusion, the most dramatic impetus came with the introduction of the electron microscope, developed mainly in Europe during the 1930's but put into commercial production by the laboratories of the Radio Corporation of America just before World War II. With this instrument the American study of such long-frustrating virus diseases as poliomyelitis and influenza greatly accelerated after the war, a study that was climaxed by the development of the successful Salk and Sabin vaccines as a result of massive nationwide and international research efforts. Virology has also been enlisted for several years in a substantial effort against the common cold, while increased research is being directed toward the possibility that at least some forms of cancer may be caused by viruses.

Society's demand for research upon and control of bacteria and viruses has shown no abatement over the years. Meanwhile, the tasks of science in meeting this demand have become steadily more complicated and difficult. Not the least of the current challenges are such phenomena as the evolutionary changes of some diseases and their causative organisms; the increasing resistance of others to vaccines and drugs; and the still undetermined effects on such organisms of the gross alterations being made on man's environment.

[William Bulloch, *The History of Bacteriology;* Paul F. Clark, *Pioneer Microbiologists of America;* William D. Foster, *A History of Medical Bacteriology and Immunology.*]

JAMES H. CASSEDY

BAD AXE, BATTLE OF (Aug. 3, 1832). The Sauk and Fox Indians, dissatisfied with lands to which the federal government had moved them, recrossed the Mississippi River in April 1832 and, under Black Hawk's leadership, attacked white settlers. They were defeated by an American force of 1,300 men, commanded by Gen. Henry Atkinson, at the mouth of the Bad Axe River, midway between Prairie du Chien and La Crosse, Wis.

ROBERT S. THOMAS

BAD LANDS, a severely eroded area in South Dakota, created by precipitation of volcanic ash, sand, and Fuller's earth, perhaps borne by wind, from eruptions in the far Northwest that buried several hundred square miles more than 300 feet in depth. Water erosion carved this material into many fantastic forms. The precipitation engulfed vast herds of antediluvian monsters where they had been feeding in the swamps, the remains of which were later exposed by erosion. The federal government established the region as the Badlands National Monument in 1939 and built a system of highways into the more scenic regions of the park. The Bad Lands were discovered by fur traders early in the 19th century, and for more than 150 years scientific societies, museums, and educational institutions have engaged in unearthing the paleontological treasures, so long entombed. Included in these relics are fossil mammoths, elephants, Brontotheriums, Protoceras, camels, horses, and many of the Carnivora whose descendants are still extant. In these fastnesses the Sioux took refuge when pursued by the U.S. Army in the Messiah War of 1890. The term "badlands" is now used to describe any area with a similarly eroded topography, as in North Dakota.

[C. R. Swartzlow and R. F. Upton, *Badlands National Monument,* United States National Park Service Natural History Handbook.]

DOANE ROBINSON

BAGHDAD PACT, originated on Feb. 24, 1955, as an agreement between Iraq and Turkey to "cooperate for their security and defense." Britain adhered to it in April, Pakistan in September, and Iran in October 1955. Pact members established a council of ministers; a secretariat with headquarters in Baghdad; and committees for economic cooperation, military planning, and countersubversion.

Although the United States had encouraged the concept of a "northern tier" alignment to block any Soviet attempt to penetrate the strategic Middle East, it never officially joined the Baghdad Pact, not wishing to further sharpen Soviet and Egyptian opposition to it or to increase Israeli apprehensions. Nevertheless, the United States became formally associated with committees of the pact, designated observers to attend council meetings, and provided considerable assistance, especially financial.

Pact members, with American aid, fostered better military planning and coordination, expanded regional transportation and communication facilities, and increased technical and economic cooperation among themselves. There were, however, adverse reactions to the pact. By building up Iraqi power and splitting the Arab world, it aroused the hostility of Egypt and Arab nationalists. Moreover, it was so unpopular in Iraq that it helped bring about the overthrow of the pro-Western monarchy of King Faisal II in 1958—the new government withdrew from the pact in March 1959. The pact also failed to contain the USSR, which hurdled the northern tier as early as September 1955 by arranging a large-scale arms deal with Egypt. Following Iraq's withdrawal, the other pact members, with American support, re-formed as CENTO (Central Treaty Organization), with headquarters in Ankara, Turkey.

[John C. Campbell, *Defense of the Middle East;* Waldemar Gallman, *Iraq Under General Nuri;* George Lenczowski, *The Middle East in World Affairs;* Kenneth Love, *Suez: The Twice-Fought War.*]

FRED J. KHOURI

BAGOT-RUSH AGREEMENT. *See* **Great Lakes Disarmament Agreement.**

BAHAMA ISLANDS, former British colony, consisting of a chain of 760 islands, located fifty miles off the southeast coast of Florida. (The island nation has been independent since July 1973.) Although granted to the Carolina proprietors in 1670, the Bahamas were passed by during the most active age of colonization and had only a meager development before 1718. Pirates found their innumerable harbors most convenient. After 1718, with separation from the Carolinas, colonists increased and pirates diminished; nevertheless illegal trading still featured in the economic life. In the preliminaries of the American Revolution, the islanders supported the American opponents of British policy and later aided them with military supplies. During the Civil War, the islands served as a base for blockade runners. The American prohibition experiment of the 1920's greatly stimulated interest in the Bahamas, the islands serving as a port for the rumrunners. The islanders have sought by various attractions to maintain the contacts thus inaugurated. During World War II the U.S. government leased areas for military bases, and in 1950 signed an agreement with Great Britain permitting the United States to establish a proving ground and missile-tracking station. American investments in the islands and the ever-increasing number of tourists have continued to bring even closer relations.

[C. Atchley, *The West Indies.*]

CHARLES F. MULLETT

BAILEY* V. *DREXEL FURNITURE COMPANY, 259 U.S. 20 (1922), a case in which the U.S. Supreme Court invalidated a 1919 act of Congress that had levied a tax of 10 percent on the products of business concerns employing children under the age of sixteen. The Court held that the measure was not a valid exercise of the taxing power, since it was an attempt to bring under congressional control matters whose regulation belongs solely to the states.

P. ORMAN RAY

BAKER, BOBBY, CASE. Robert G. ("Bobby") Baker, secretary to the U.S. Senate majority at the time of his resignation under fire in 1963, was one of the most powerful congressional staff members of his time. His personal business ventures, which a Senate committee later found to involve abuse of his trusted political position, became a national scandal that briefly threw the spotlight on the sometimes unchecked power of little-known, but influential, Capitol Hill aides.

A poor boy from Pickens, S.C., Baker rose from Senate page to top Senate assistant with the special help of Majority Leader Lyndon B. Johnson and Sen. Robert S. Kerr of Oklahoma. Despite the fact that one of his mentors had become president, Baker was indicted in January 1966 on nine charges, including grand larceny and attempted tax evasion. His conviction and prison sentence of from one to three years were based partly on evidence that he had pocketed approximately $100,000 he had solicited from business interests as campaign payments and tried to conceal the transactions in his income tax declarations. After four years of appeals and litigation over admittedly illegal government eavesdropping, Baker entered Lewisburg Penitentiary in January 1971. Paroled in June 1972, he returned to an apparently flourishing motel enterprise, but not to politics.

[Congressional Quarterly, *Congress and the Nation, 1945–1964.*]

JOHN P. MACKENZIE

BAKER'S CABIN MASSACRE (Apr. 30, 1774), the murder of six or seven unarmed Mingo Indians by a party of whites at Baker's Cabin, on the Virginia side of the Ohio River, near present-day Steubenville, Ohio. As a result Chief Logan went on the warpath, charging that his sister and other near relatives had been killed.

[R. G. Thwaites and Louise P. Kellogg, *A Documentary History of Dunmore's War.*]

EUGENE H. ROSEBOOM

***BAKER* V. *CARR*,** 369 U.S. 186 (1962), decided by a six to two decision by the Supreme Court, established the rule that the federal courts could review claims of discrimination against voters arising out of legislative malapportionment. Nonjusticiability of malapportionment had been commented on in an extended opinion by Justice Felix Frankfurter in *Colegrove* v. *Green* (1946): Frankfurter voiced the view that congressional apportionment is a matter "of peculiarly political nature and therefore not meet for judicial determination. . . . Courts ought not to enter this political thicket. The remedy for unfairness in districting is to secure State legislatures that will apportion properly, or to involve the ample powers of Congress." In fact, as Justice William Brennan, Jr., pointed out in *Baker*, on the matter of justiciability Frankfurter spoke for only three of the seven justices of the Court who participated in the decision in *Colegrove*.

The complaint in *Baker* was that although the Tennessee constitution had required since 1870 that a census be taken every ten years and that the legislature be apportioned according to the number of qualified voters in each county, all attempts to reapportion from 1901 to 1961 had failed; that as a result of changes as the state's population had grown, the relative standings of the counties in terms of qualified voters had altered significantly—the record showing that in 1961, 37 percent of the voters of Tennessee elected twenty of the thirty-three senators, while 40 percent of the voters elected sixty-three of the ninety-nine members of the house.

The impact of *Baker* was to open the doors to judicial consideration of issues related to apportionment, but the Supreme Court was careful to limit its holding by insisting, first, that the Court possesses jurisdiction of the subject matter and, second, that a justiciable cause of action be stated upon which appellants would be entitled to appropriate relief. The case was remanded to the lower court. Although the Supreme Court did not rule on constitutional standards for apportionment until two years later, the *Baker* decision stimulated immediate judicial, legislative, or referendum actions on the issue of legislative apportionment in at least forty-three states. After his retirement Chief Justice Earl Warren wrote that he viewed *Baker* v. *Carr* as the most important case during his years on the Supreme Court. In opening the way for *Reynolds* v. *Sims* (1964) to establish the "equal population" principle, *Baker* was, according to Warren, the "parent case of the one man, one vote doctrine."

[R. B. McKay, *Reapportionment.*]

CALVIN B. T. LEE

BAKESHOP CASE. *See* ***Lochner*** v. ***New York.***

BALANCE OF TRADE. Following the mercantilistic tradition, an excess of merchandise exports over imports is usually called a favorable balance of trade, and the reverse an unfavorable balance—the original assumption being that the difference was paid in specie, the acquisition of which made a nation economically strong. This theory is fallacious but persistent. It confuses money with wealth and is incompatible with any demand-and-supply theory of the value of money. It leaves out of consideration all "invisible" items, such as capital loans, shipping charges, tourist expenditures, immigrant remittances, and interest payments. Inclusion of these is necessary to calculate the more significant balance of international payments. In the long run the value of the wealth (including bullion) and services flowing out of a country tends to equal that of those flowing in, except for excesses of bad debts or other losses in one direction or the other.

The American colonies had an unfavorable balance of trade because they were a new country and the settlers were constantly buying on credit or depending on England for capital for new undertakings. Mercantilistic England encouraged American extractive industries and discouraged manufacturing. In 1770 the colonies south of Pennsylvania had a nearly even trade balance with England; Pennsylvania and those north imported eight times as much from England as they exported to that country, making up the difference largely by a favorable trade balance with the West Indies and by their carrying business.

After the Revolution the new nation still wanted English manufactures but found it difficult to pay for them because England's markets were closed to many American products and trade with the British West Indies was illegal. The new trade to China, treaties with Prussia and Sweden, and finally Jay's Treaty improved matters a little, but the development of cotton growing and the outbreak in 1793 of what soon became the Napoleonic wars helped much more. Both France and England bought heavily of American products and made increasing use of American shipping services. Between 1790 and 1807 the American merchant marine engaged in foreign trade tripled. After 1806 England took successful steps to stop American commercial growth, and from English intervention in American trade the War of 1812 developed. Following the war foreign manufactured goods flooded American markets and hurt infant industries. Protection sentiment increased, producing progressively higher tariffs in 1816, 1824, and 1828. Thereafter rates fell (except in 1842). Higher tariffs at home and abroad, a postwar depression, and greater interest in developing the West all cut down the rate of growth of U.S. foreign commerce and its importance relative to domestic commerce. Foreign trade picked up after 1830. Europeans, particularly the English, invested approximately $150 million, much of it in American internal improvements—railroads, turnpikes, some banks, and especially canals. But European investment ended abruptly with the panic of 1837 and defalcation by several states. Between 1838 and 1849 the U.S. trade balance was slightly favorable. During the 1850's both imports and exports (notably cotton) expanded rapidly until the Civil War. Foreign trade declined during the war because of the northern blockade and the activity of southern cruisers.

During the prosperity following the war American foreign trade grew from $405 million in 1865 to $1.2 billion in 1873. The Homestead Act, wars in Europe, immigration, railroad building, and increasing use of agricultural machinery caused a rise in food exports. A five-year depression began in 1873. In 1874 the U.S. trade balance again became favorable, largely because interest payments on foreign capital in the United States exceeded new foreign investments. The annual balance after that was favorable for nearly a century, until 1971—except for 1876, 1888, 1889, and an unusual situation in 1942–45 because of lend-lease. A great expansion of foreign trade began after 1897. Thenceforth capital loans abroad grew nearly as fast as foreign loans to the United States. Tourist expenditures and immigrant remittances became important.

During World War I the United States supplied the Allies with enormous quantities of food and war matériel. Between July 1, 1914, and Dec. 31, 1919, the U.S. trade balance was favorable by $18.6 billion—$4 billion being paid in specie, $2.6 billion in returned securities, and the balance in capital loans, three-quarters governmental (*see* Debts, Foreign). In 1916 the United States ceased being a debtor nation and became a creditor.

The 1920's were a prosperous era. Since U.S. high tariffs made imports difficult, the only way to continue to sell abroad was to make heavy loans. The United States loaned $12 billion during the decade, while foreigners invested $7 billion in the United States. Of course a loss occurred from scaling down the war debts. Notable borrowers were Latin-American nations, whose prospects were sometimes too optimistically regarded, and Germany, which was thereby helped to pay reparations to the Allies (*see* Dawes Plan; Young Plan), which in turn were able to pay on their war debts to the United States. Then came the crash of 1929. Numerous Latin-American nations, largely dependent on the marketing of one or two commodities, defaulted. U.S. loans to Germany declined, and after the Hoover moratorium in 1931 Germany ceased paying reparations and the Allies stopped paying their debts. Losses on foreign investments, however, were no greater proportionately than on domestic ones.

U.S. foreign trade improved starting in 1934. Numerous reciprocal trade treaties lowered U.S. tariff walls, which had reached a peak in 1930, and encouraged a freer flow of trade. Among various advantages to be expected from this change in policy, one was that it would facilitate the payment of debts to U.S. investors abroad—for after some lapse of time a creditor nation should usually receive back annually more in interest and returned principal than it lays out in new loans. The United States did not, however, achieve an unfavorable trade balance. First lend-lease and later foreign aid programs (about $5 billion annually) interfered.

World War II stimulated exports enormously although much of the increase was in lend-lease shipments of war matériel to the Allies. The United States did not expect payment, but those who simultaneously provided imports did, so that in effect the nation had an unfavorable balance of trade between 1942 and 1945. During the next five years the United States exported vast quantities of goods to help rebuild a war-ravaged world. One-quarter of these exports went to Europe. Merchandise exports were almost double merchandise imports, exceeding them between 1946 and 1950 by $6 billion annually. Despite the Korean War (1951–53) the favorable balance hovered around $5 billion until the mid-1960's, although it was then less than one-quarter of merchandise exports. The balance of payments, including all the invisible items, turned against the United States in 1958, and gold began to flow out of the nation on a regular basis. In 1966 even the favorable merchandise balance began to shrink, until in 1971 it turned unfavorable by $2 billion, and it worsened sharply in 1972. (It became slightly favorable again in 1973.) Rising prices of American goods, increasingly efficient competition from abroad (notably Japan and Germany), the costly Vietnam War, and the tendency toward protection vis-à-vis the United States by the European Common Market explain the shift in some measure.

One thing seems clear in an age that has seen service industries surpassing product industries: It is more than ever futile to analyze merchandise exports (which average 4 percent of the gross national product) and imports without reference to other items in the balance of international payments.

[Board of Governors of the Federal Reserve System, *Federal Reserve Bulletin* (annual analysis of balance of payments); W. C. Gordon, *International Trade;* Emory Johnson, *Domestic and Foreign Commerce of the United States;* D. Kemmerer and C. C. Jones, *American Economic History;* U.S. Department of Commerce, *Historical Statistics of the United States: Colonial Times to 1957;* J. P. Young, *The International Economy.*]

DONALD L. KEMMERER

BALCONES ESCARPMENT, a geologic fault extending across Texas from Del Rio to Red River west of Denison. Visible on the surface eastward from Del Rio and northeastward from San Antonio to Austin, the fault continues below the surface to the east of Waco and Fort Worth. It very nearly divides Texas into two geographical regions: the region east of the fault is humid and contains nearly all of the most populous cities; the soil in the region to the west is hard and dry.

L. W. NEWTON

BALFOUR AND VIVIANI-JOFFRE MISSIONS. In April 1917, after the United States entered World War I, a mission headed by Arthur James Balfour, British foreign secretary, and another by René Viviani, French minister of justice, and Marshal Joseph Joffre, former commander of the French armies, visited the United States. The British discussed questions of the purchase of war materials, military equipment, merchant tonnage, and cooperation of the British and American navies; they proposed the sending of American troops to France to be trained and incorporated in the British and French armies. Joffre, on the other hand, urged the creation of an American army, even though this might take longer, and this plan was adopted. Balfour discussed terms of peace with E. M. House, U.S. special representative, and then with President Woodrow Wilson, but it is not clear whether he disclosed specifically the terms of the "secret treaties" between the Allies.

[Blanche E. C. Dugdale, *Arthur James Balfour;* W. G. Lyddon, *British War Missions to the United States, 1914–1918;* C. Seymour, *The Intimate Papers of Colonel House.*]

BERNADOTTE E. SCHMITT

BALIZE, a pilot village and fortification established in 1722 on the principal mouth (then usually called Southeast Pass) of the Mississippi River, about a half mile from the Gulf of Mexico and nearly a mile below the bar at the then entrance to the river proper, roughly 110 miles from New Orleans. Built by the French as first line of defense for Louisiana, it afforded slight protection because the mud would not hold strong works, there was frequent demolition by storms and floods, and other passes were negotiable by light craft. The Spanish maintained it, but the United States abandoned it for defenses some thirty miles upstream (forts Jackson and St. Philip).

[P. de Charlevoix, *Histoire et description générale de la nouvelle France,* vol. VI.]

MACK SWEARINGEN

BALLADS. When George Lyman Kittredge wrote, in the introduction of a volume of selections from Francis James Child's monumental work, *The English and Scottish Popular Ballads* (1904), that "A ballad is a song that tells a story or a story told in song" only one collection of American folk songs had been published (*Allen's Slave Songs of the United States,* 1867). Since that time hundreds of titles have been added to the literature of American balladry. Not all of the items in these books, of course, fit the definition of a ballad but they indicate the great richness of America's heritage of traditional balladry and an astonishing fertility in the production of indigenous folk songs. Versions of the so-called Child ballads have been found all over the United States, along with large numbers of the 18th- and 19th-century come-all-ye's. Often these ballads have been adapted to the locale that has preserved them and always new ballads have grown out of the traditional matrix. Among people, whether untutored or educated, whose lives are isolated, the desire for entertainment usually breeds songs that tell stories. American frontiers have been lonely.

In subject matter the ancient ballads and the indigenous product are generally widely different. The former sing of highborn ladies, the men of fortune and renown, while their American prototypes, composed by hard-handed miners, mountaineers, cowboys, sailors, and lumberjacks, follow the pattern of the come-all-ye's and are peopled with working-class characters. Undoubtedly the most popular of indigenous types are the occupational ballads, the bad-man ballad, the murder ballad, and the vulgar or bawdy ballad. In the occupational ballad singers celebrate the hardships or the glories of some type of work or else they recount a feat of daring, the tragic death of a worker, or some comic incident of camp life. "Foreman James Monroe," "James Bird," "The Buffalo Skinners," "Red Iron Ore," "Joe Bowers," "Casey Jones," and "The Erie Canal" are familiar examples.

As the English loved Robin Hood because he took from the rich to give to the poor, so the American folksinger has commemorated Jesse James, Sam Bass, and Pancho Villa. Indeed, the sympathies of the folksinger have always been with the rebel against society. Thus the 19th-century American ballad persistently attributes crime to the influence of a bad environment ("liquor and bad company") and then is likely to quote the criminal's confession where he apologizes for his deed. White ballads ordinarily run in this vein, although in the case of such horrible murders as that of Pearl Bryant or in the feud songs of the southern mountains, the singers express their indignation at the deeds.

The vulgar ballad has universal popularity from the forecastle to the college campus. Transmitted by word of mouth and finding no occupational or class barriers, these ballads usually have fine tunes and are often couched in fresh and vigorous language.

Afro-American ballads stand in a class by themselves, for while the main body of Afro-American songs is not strictly narrative in form, the race has produced America's most original and interesting narrative songs in English—"John Henry," "Frankie," "Casey Jones," "Po' Laz'us." Perhaps these Afro-American songs do not equal in grace and finish the older English lays, but in them are found the same fresh imagery, the same direct and incisive narrative technique, along with new interest in the internal emotional problems of the characters. Certain work ballads, such as "Po' Laz'us" and "John Henry," orally composed and transmitted in big construction camps, have an epic vigor. Moreover, while the pioneer or occupational isolation that produced the best white ballads has been broken, the Afro-American community has kept its folk solidarity and has responded fruitfully to the influence of radio, television, and recordings by producing new songs of high quality.

[G. M. Laws, *Native American Balladry;* John A. Lomax and Alan Lomax, *American Ballads and Folk Songs;* Louise Pound, *American Ballads and Folk Songs.*]

JOHN A. LOMAX

BALLINGER-PINCHOT CONTROVERSY (1909–11), a bitter contention over the conservation of natural resources. Early in William H. Taft's administration an order of former President Theodore Roosevelt withdrawing from sale certain public lands containing waterpower sites in Montana and Wyoming was cancelled. Gifford Pinchot, chief of the Forest Service, protested and publicly charged Secretary of the Interior Richard A. Ballinger with favoritism toward corporations seeking waterpower sites. Pinchot defended L. R. Glavis, Land Office investigator, dismissed for accusing Ballinger of being a tool of private interests by favoring certain claims to valuable Alaskan mineral lands. Pinchot likewise was dismissed. A joint congressional investigating committee exonerated Ballinger. But, failing to regain public confidence, Ballinger resigned in March 1911. The incident widened the split in the Republican party between the conservative (Taft) and progressive (Roosevelt) factions.

[F. A. Ogg, *National Progress*.]

GLENN H. BENTON

BALLOONS. In early June 1784—just a year after the first success of the Montgolfier brothers at Annonay, France—Peter Carnes raised a 35-foot, hot-air balloon at Bladensburg, Md. Later that month Carnes's tethered balloon carried thirteen-year-old Edward Warren aloft at Baltimore. The first American to make a free ascent, however, was John Jeffries, who bought a brief ride in the hydrogen balloon of Jean-Pierre Blanchard, a Frenchman, at London the last day of November 1784; five weeks later Jeffries and Blanchard crossed the English Channel—Dover to Calais—in the same vehicle. Blanchard made the first free ascent in the United States at Philadelphia in January 1793.

Not until October 1830 did an American make a balloon ascent in the United States; that was Charles Ferson Durant, at Castle Garden (Battery Park) at the tip of Manhattan Island. John Wise, the most prominent American aeronaut of his day, made his 230th ascent from St. Louis in July 1859 and landed twenty hours later in Henderson, N.Y., a distance of 809 miles. The first aerial photographs in the United States were taken over Boston by William Black from the balloon of Thaddeus S. C. Lowe in October 1860. In July 1861 Lowe ascended from the Mall in Washington, D.C., and sent to the White House the first telegraph message from the air. President Abraham Lincoln was so impressed that he advocated the use of balloons in the Civil War; and Lowe organized an aeronautic corps that performed valuable reconnaissance in 1862 at Fair Oaks (May), Gaines's Mill (June), Fredericksburg (December), and at Chancellorsville (May 1863) before the military balloon service was abandoned. Captive balloons were used extensively for reconnaissance and fire control throughout World War I. In World War II Japan launched some 9,000 unmanned bomb-carrying balloons to ride the jet stream toward the United States; about 10 percent reached American soil.

The U.S. Weather Bureau uses hundreds of small balloons daily to study atmospheric conditions. In May 1961 the U.S. Navy's Strato Lab V polyethylene balloon, with a capacity of 10 million cubic feet, carried two men to a record altitude of 113,740 feet. Balloons are used in a wide variety of such scientific research as celestial measurements by infrared telescope and cosmic ray studies. In 1972 an Australian-American research team launched a balloon with a capacity of 46 million cubic feet to monitor outer space X rays. It remained aloft for twenty-six hours, with a half-ton payload, and reached an altitude of 148,000 feet. Fully expanded, such a balloon could contain forty-six Washington Monuments. Manned balloon flights have continued. On Feb. 18, 1974, T. L. Gatch took off from Harrisburg, Pa., to cross the Atlantic. He was lost without trace after last being reported west of the Canary Islands on Feb. 22.

[Roger Pineau, *Ballooning 1782–1972* (Smithsonian Institution exhibit catalog, 1972).]

ROGER PINEAU

BALLOT, a method of voting by way of a form that lists the voter's options. The ballot was preceded by other methods of voting. In colonial times, voice voting and even such unorthodox procedures as letting corn or beans designate votes were used. With the formation of the Union, the paper ballot emerged as the dominant voting method, and many states allowed the voter to make up his own ballot in the privacy of his home. Almost immediately the political parties, motivated by a desire to influence the vote, started to print ballots as substitutes for the handwritten ones, a practice that was constitutionally upheld by a Massachusetts supreme court decision in 1829. These "party strip" ballots listed only the candidates of a single party on them and were peddled to the voters by "party hawkers" on or before election day. Voting such ballots was almost always done in public—contrary to the notion of a secret vote cherished today. Under this system, the parties were able to influence the vote by pressuring voters to take their ballot, virtually ensuring a straight-ticket vote, and forcing them to vote in public so that their actions could be clearly observed by party workers.

The system of party ballots led to widespread intimidation and corruption, which were not corrected until the ballot reform period of the 1890's. Between 1888 and 1896, civic groups and "good government" people convinced over 90 percent of the states to adopt a new ballot patterned after one introduced in Australia in the 1850's to eliminate vote corruption in that country. The Australian ballot was the exact opposite of the earlier party ballots. It was official (being prepared and distributed by the government rather than by the political parties), consolidated (placing the candidates of both major parties on the same ballot instead of on separate ballots), and secret (eliminating the "public vote"). Still in use in all states, it successfully eliminated much of the partisan intimidation and vote fraud that had existed; it also facilitated split-ticket voting.

The arrangement of candidates' names on the Australian ballot varied among the states. Massachusetts arranged the candidates' names by political office; Indiana, by party affiliation. These examples influenced other states and became known as the "Massachusetts office bloc" and "Indiana party column" formats of the Australian ballot. With the gradual advent of the voting machine in the 1900's, the basic principles of the Australian ballot remained intact, and the voting machine became in essence a mechanical Australian ballot.

[E. C. Evans, *A History of the Australian Ballot System in the United States;* J. G. Rusk, "The Effect of the Australian Ballot Reform on Split-Ticket Voting: 1876–1908," *American Political Science Review*, vol. 64 (1970).]

JERROLD G. RUSK

BALL'S BLUFF, BATTLE OF (Oct. 21, 1861). Inconsequential as a military affair, this engagement had important results. Union Col. E. D. Baker, senator from Oregon and a personal friend of President Abraham Lincoln, was killed; the Union troops, through mismanagement, were defeated. Discontented Radicals and a critical public blamed Gen. G. B. McClellan. Congress inaugurated the Committee on the Conduct of the War to investigate Ball's Bluff and other Union failures. McClellan, on orders from the secretary of war, arrested Gen. C. P. Stone, charged with responsibility both for the defeat and for Baker's death. No formal charges were ever made. After six months' imprisonment Stone was released by a special provision in the Confiscation Act of July 17, 1862. The Union Army of the Potomac questioned their leader's ability "A fatal hesitation took possession" of McClellan. A movement against Richmond, Va., was deferred pending further preparation.

[R. U. Johnson and C. C. Buel, eds., *Battles and Leaders of the Civil War.*]

THOMAS ROBSON HAY

BALTIMORE, city and seaport at the upper end of the Chesapeake Bay on the Patapsco River and Maryland's largest city. It was almost 100 years after the landing of the colonists in 1634 at Saint Mary's, the first settlement in Maryland, that Baltimore was founded, in 1729. The new settlement was named in honor of the second proprietor of Maryland, Charles Calvert, Baron Baltimore.

Whereas the founding of Saint Mary's, and of Annapolis in 1649, had stemmed ultimately from political and religious factors, the founding of Baltimore stemmed from the need for a port in the area. Baltimore was not, however, dissociated from the Roman Catholic tradition of the colony and in 1808 became the seat of the first Roman Catholic archdiocese in the United States.

During the Revolution and the War of 1812 privateers built and manned in Baltimore played a conspicuous part. It was at Baltimore that the tide was turned in the latter war, during the night of Sept. 12–13, 1814, when the port was successfully defended against the British after the sack of Washington. During the British bombardment of Fort McHenry during this battle Francis Scott Key was inspired to write "The Star-Spangled Banner."

Economic Development. Needing an outlet for the tobacco grown in the area, the founders of Baltimore sought and obtained a port charter in 1729. Toward the middle of the 18th century, with the discovery of markets for flour in Ireland and Scotland, many of the ubiquitous tobacco fields of the area were converted to wheat tillage. A substantial shipbuilding industry grew with the development of the Baltimore clipper, which carried the vigorous trade of the port to Europe and the Caribbean. At the outbreak of the Revolution, Baltimore was a busy seafaring and commercial town of 6,700 inhabitants, the third-ranking port in the colonies. After the Revolution, commerce boomed and the population grew. Trade in the Caribbean led to the importation of iron, laying a foundation for heavy industry. In 1790 the population had grown to 13,501, and in 1797 Baltimore became a city.

Baltimore's shipbuilding industry grew apace during the first half of the 18th century. Commerce also flourished, and by 1830, Baltimore had a population of 80,620. Looking to the west for increasing wheat supplies for its flour trade and threatened by the opening of the Erie Canal in 1825, Baltimore began construction in 1827 of the Baltimore and Ohio Railroad, the first steam-operated railway in the United States. During the late 19th century and in the 20th century one of the major factors in Baltimore's success as a port was its relative proximity to the Middle West, as compared with other East Coast ports; the resulting freight differential has kept it a leader in the export of bulk cargoes.

The tide of Baltimore's growth was stemmed during the second half of the 19th century by political strife and the Civil War, climaxed in 1904 by a fire that destroyed about 140 acres in the downtown area. With expanding trade after World War I the port revived. The restoration of active trading with the Caribbean changed the thrust of Baltimore's economy from commerce to heavy industry, as new iron mines and oil wells were opened in the Caribbean area. Shipbuilding continued, but as a heavy industry in merchant vessels. The city's industry was dominated, however, by primary metal manufacturing; the Bethlehem Steel Company, the largest tidewater steel mill in the United States, had an annual ingot capacity of 8.2 million tons.

In 1970 the port was handling more than 40 million short tons of cargo annually, and the annual value of foreign trade was more than $1 billion. Baltimore's rank among the nation's ports had fallen to sixth, but the city maintained its sixth rank in population with nearly one million inhabitants.

Culture. Whereas the social life of Baltimore has been dominated by the tobacco aristocracy, its culture has been the product of its merchant class. The city continues to be known for its rows of red-brick houses with white marble steps, most of which are replacements for the similar Georgian houses of early merchants, destroyed by the fire of 1904. In the early 19th century wealthy merchants were engaging the foremost Greek revival architects of the country—particularly Maximilien Godefroy and Benjamin Latrobe—to design their public buildings and residences, notably the First Unitarian Church (1818). In the second half of the century, commercial fortunes were turned toward philanthropy. In 1867 Johns Hopkins founded Johns Hopkins Hospital and the Johns Hopkins University, the first in the country to be geared to the German emphasis on sustaining graduate education and research. In 1868 George Peabody founded the Peabody Institute, including a conservatory of music still ranked among the major schools of music in the country. In 1884 Enoch Pratt founded a free library.

As the fire of 1904 changed the physical appearance of Baltimore, so the burst of mercantile and industrial activity following World War I changed its cultural complex. The decline in refinement is decried and satirized in the writings of H. L. Mencken. The process continued during the depression of the 1930's and into World War II, as slums spread throughout the city. After World War II, Baltimore pioneered in attacking urban blight and slum conditions through a minimum standard housing code and a housing court, the first in the country. The racial integration of the public school system was effected in 1954, as the city's Afro-American population came more and more to dominate the urban center, constituting 46 percent of the city's population in 1970.

[Francis F. Beirne, *The Amiable Baltimoreans;* C. C. Hall, *Baltimore: Its History and Its People;* Hamilton Owens, *Baltimore on the Chesapeake;* J. Thomas Scharf, *The Chronicles of Baltimore.*]

BALTIMORE, BATTLE OF (Sept. 12, 1814). After the burning of Washington, D.C., a British land force of 8,000, commanded by Gen. Robert Ross, attempted to capture Baltimore. Ross, killed in battle, was successfully opposed by a force of Maryland and Pennsylvania militia and volunteers.

ROBERT S. THOMAS

***BALTIMORE* AFFAIR,** an attack by a Chilean mob in Valparaíso on Oct. 16, 1891, upon a party of 117 sailors on shore leave from the U.S.S. *Baltimore;* two Americans were killed and several others seriously wounded. This hostility emerged from the mistaken feeling that during Chile's civil war the United States had sympathized unduly with the Chilean government, the *Balmacedistas* whom the Congressionalists overthrew. The new government did not punish the assailants and offered neither apology nor explanation until President William H. Harrison laid the matter before Congress and, on Jan. 21, 1892, threatened an end to diplomatic relations. Chile sent a note of apology on Jan. 26 and later paid $75,000 to the injured men and to the relatives of the two dead sailors. This is the nearest the United States has ever come to actual conflict with a South American nation.

[H. C. Evans, *Chile and Its Relations With the United States.*]

OSGOOD HARDY

BALTIMORE AND OHIO RAILROAD. *See* **Railroads, Sketches: Chesapeake and Ohio.**

BALTIMORE BELL TEAMS, named for the small bells suspended in metal arches over the hames to speed the horses and sound warning on narrow, crooked roads. These teams hauled country produce to Baltimore and returned with goods for homes and local merchants. Such teams made regular trips from points as far southwest as Knoxville, Tenn., and operated until 1850 or later, when they were superseded by canals and railroads.

JOHN W. WAYLAND

BALTIMORE CLIPPER, a term applied to the fast topsail schooners developed in and around the Chesapeake Bay in the revolutionary period and later to the square-rigged vessels having the same general lines which were built in the Chesapeake region. In postrevolutionary days they came into general notice largely because their speed enabled them to be used effectively both in privateering and in the slave trade. *Ann McKim* (1833) was the ultimate expression of the type and is regarded by some as the link between the Baltimore clipper and the clipper ship. Its length (143 feet) was great by prevailing standards compared to its beam (31 feet). It had the characteristic Baltimore clipper drag in that it drew 11 feet forward and 17 aft. *Ann McKim*'s stem was sharp, but its greatest beam was so far forward that it was bluffer bowed than the later clipper ship. Its freeboard was low and carrying capacity small, and hence it was primarily a speed model. The three masts were tall and light with a sharp rake, but it was ship-rigged with courses, topsails, topgallant sails, and royals on each mast.

[Howard Irving Chappelle, *The Baltimore Clipper, Its Origin and Development;* Jacques and Helen LaGrange, *Clipper Ships of America and Great Britain.*]

HAMILTON OWENS

BALTIMORE COUNCILS, PROVINCIAL AND PLENARY. Ecclesiastical legislation in the Roman Catholic church of the United States began with a synod of the priests under Bishop John Carroll of Baltimore in 1791. The regulations adopted served to administer church affairs until 1829, when the first Provincial Council of Baltimore was held. There were seven of these councils (1829, 1833, 1837, 1840, 1843, 1846, and 1849). By the year 1852 the church had been divided into several provinces, and while provincial councils were held in these provinces under their archbishops, three plenary councils were held in Baltimore in 1852, 1866, and 1884. The legislation of these three national assemblies was concerned with explanations of Catholic faith, with regulations for the administration of the sacraments, with feasts and fast days, with clerical life and discipline, with ecclesiastical property tenure, and with Catholic education and social welfare agencies.

[Peter Guilday, *A History of the Councils of Baltimore: 1791–1884.*]

PETER GUILDAY

BALTIMORE FIRE (Feb. 7–8, 1904), the third greatest conflagration in American history. It destroyed most of the central business district over an area of 150 acres. Damages were estimated at about $150 million. Better streets and more fire protection were indirect results.

W. C. MALLALIEU

***BALTIMORE* INCIDENT.** While convoying merchant vessels to Havana during naval hostilities with France, Capt. Isaac Phillips in the U.S. sloop *Baltimore* encountered a British squadron on Nov. 16, 1798. Facing superior force, and with strict injunctions to avoid conflict with British vessels, Phillips, under protest, submitted to the mustering of his crew and the removal of all seamen without papers showing American citizenship. Fifty-five were taken off, but only five were finally retained. Phillips was afterward summarily dismissed from the navy, and stringent orders were issued requiring American national vessels to resist forcibly any similar insult to the flag.

[G. W. Allen, *Our Naval War With France.*]

ALLAN WESTCOTT

BALTIMORE RIOT, an attack on Pennsylvania and Massachusetts militia en route to Washington, Apr. 19, 1861, by Baltimoreans who considered them invaders. The railroad was not continuous through Baltimore, horses drawing the cars from one terminal to the other. After a few troops had gone through, the connecting tracks were blocked with anchors and other obstacles, which forced later contingents to march. The crowd pursued them with stones, bricks, and a few pistol shots. The militia, who had broken into a run, fired backward over their shoulders and forward at the people lining the street ahead of them. The mayor endeavored to quiet the crowd, and finally, near the Washington terminal, the police succeeded in holding the people back until the troops entrained. Four militiamen and twelve civilians were killed and an unknown number wounded.

[George W. Brown, *Baltimore and the Nineteenth of April, 1861.*]

GEORGE FREDERICK ASHWORTH

BANK, FEDERAL RESERVE. *See* **Federal Reserve System.**

BANK DEPOSITS. On the basis of their origin, bank deposits fall into two categories. A saver may deposit money in a bank for safekeeping and for the purpose of earning interest—a primary deposit. Or a bank may enter the amount of a loan on a borrower's checking account—a secondary, or created, deposit. Early banks had two basic ways of lending their credit, namely by issuing bank notes, which are the bank's demand promissory notes, or by creating deposits. It was long assumed that in the pre–Civil War period banks did most of their lending in the form of bank notes, but recent research indicates that bank deposits against which checks might be written were probably more important than has been presumed. If there were early figures for check clearings or even if early banks had drawn a sharper distinction between time (savings) deposits and demand deposits, the matter would be clearer. Yet economist Condy Raguet included deposits in his definition of money supply (1839), and former Secretary of the Treasury Albert Gallatin (1801–14) had similar views. Statements of both the first Bank of the United States and the second generally showed more deposits than bank notes, and the same situation prevailed among Boston's banks between 1803 and 1837. But in rural areas bank notes were used more than deposits. The Farmer's Bank of Maryland was the first to pay interest on deposits (1804), a practice that became general by the 1830's and remained so even after the distinction between time and demand deposits became sharper shortly before the Civil War. (The federal government did not keep separate aggregate statistics on them until 1892.)

After the National Banking System was set up in 1863, the use of checks drawn on demand deposits rapidly outdistanced the use of bank notes. Checks became the chief means of payment although most people—including practically all Populists and even some economists—persisted in believing that only coin, greenbacks, and National Bank notes were "money." Between 1866 and 1913 the deposits of national banks, the most important group of commercial banking institutions, grew from $565 million to $6,052 million; but their bank notes totaled only $727 million in 1913. David Kinley's National Monetary Commission report of 1910 said the nation did about 88 percent of its business by check.

Between mid-1914 and mid-1920 (the Federal Reserve System opened on Nov. 16, 1914) demand deposits adjusted seasonally of all banks doubled from $10.1 billion to $19.6 billion. Wartime needs of the government and sharply reduced reserve requirements against deposits in the Federal Reserve Act were both responsible for the growth of these so-called invisible greenbacks of World War I. Demand deposits adjusted seasonally rose from $18 billion in mid-1922 to $22.5 billion in mid-1929, then fell to a low of $14.4 billion in mid-1933—moves that reflected, and also helped cause, the boom and then the depression of those years. The Banking Act of 1933 forbade banks to pay interest on demand deposits, and the Banking Act of 1935 gave the Federal Reserve System the authority to as much as double reserve requirements against deposits. This authority was used when the 1934 devaluation of the dollar stimulated an unhealthy growth of deposits. During World War II demand deposits adjusted seasonally rose from $33.6 billion in mid-1940 to $88.8 billion in mid-1946, again playing the role of invisible greenbacks. They increased unduly again during the Korean War (1951–53) and grew from $132.3 billion to $169.6 billion from December 1964 to December 1970, the height of the war in Vietnam. One would expect a rise in population and in real income to increase deposits, but wars cause a disproportionate increase. What the printing press was to 18th- and 19th-century war financing, banks' giving the government deposits in exchange for Treasury IOU's is to 20th-century wars—known as monetizing the debt. Excessive government spending in peacetime can also cause a disproportionate increase in deposits.

From 1914 on, National Bank reserve requirements for time deposits were less than those for demand deposits, the theory being that these funds would be used for long-term loans and that depositors would have to wait thirty days to withdraw them. In practice, however, time deposits were convertible into demand deposits almost at will and thus were as much "money" as were demand deposits. If one adds the time deposit growth of the 1922–29 boom, or of any of the later war periods, to the demand deposit and currency growth, the extent of the monetary inflation is shown to be greater than it appears by the more usual method of computation. Another little-noticed form of deposit, the savings and loan share or deposit—also reflecting buying power and acting as fuel for inflation—continued to grow very fast. These deposits totaled $235 billion in mid-1974, three-fifths the total of commercial bank time deposits. It must be taken into consideration, however, that neither of these types of savings deposits turns over, or changes hands, as often as demand deposits do (another dimension of the measure of deposits as "money"), which somewhat lessens their importance.

For well over a century bank deposits have been a major form of saving and the nation's most important form of money. (*See also* Bank Failures; Banking; Banks, Savings; Federal Reserve System; Savings and Loan Associations.)

[J. V. Fenstermaker, *The Development of American Commercial Banking, 1782–1837;* M. Friedman and M. Schwartz, *A Monetary History of the United States, 1867–1960;* David Kinley, *The Use of Credit Instruments in Payments in the United States.*]

DONALD L. KEMMERER

BANK FAILURES. American financial history down to 1934 was characterized by an appalling number of bank failures, because the majority of banks were local enterprises, not regional or national institutions with numerous branches. Lax state government regulations and inadequate examinations permitted many banks to pursue unsound practices. With most financial eggs in local economic baskets, it took only a serious crop failure or a business recession to precipitate dozens or even hundreds of bank failures. On the whole, state-chartered banks had a particularly poor record.

At the outset of the 19th century inability of a bank to redeem its notes in specie might cause it embarrassment, and later on states imposed penalties in those circumstances, but such an inability did not automatically signify failure. The first bank to fail was the Farmers' Exchange Bank of Glocester, R.I., in 1809. The statistics of bank failures between 1789 and 1863 are inadequate, but the losses were unquestionably large. John Jay Knox estimated that the losses to noteholders were 5 percent per annum, and bank notes were the chief money used by the general public. Not until after 1853 did banks' deposit liabilities exceed their note liabilities. During the three decades between 1830 and 1860 weekly newssheets called Bank Note Reporters gave the latest discount quoted on the notes of weak and closed banks. Worthless bank notes were a risk that all businesses had to allow for. Although some states—such as New York in 1829 and 1838, Louisiana in 1842, and Indiana in 1834—established sound banking systems, banking as a whole was characterized by many failures.

The establishment of the National Banking System in 1863 introduced needed regulations for national (nationally chartered) banks. These were more numerous than state banks, down to 1894, and were larger on the average. But even their record left much to be desired. There were 515 national bank suspensions during the fifty years 1864–1913, and only two years passed without at least one suspension. State banks suffered 2,491 failures during the same period. The nation had 1,532 banks in 1863 and 26,664 in 1913. The worst year was the panic year of 1893, with almost 500 bank failures. The establishment of the Federal Reserve System in 1913 did little to improve the record of national banks, all of which had to join it. They suffered 825 failures between 1914 and 1929 and an additional 1,947 failures by the end of 1933. During the same twenty years there were 12,714 state bank failures. By 1933 there were 14,771 banks in the United States, half as many as in 1920, and most of that half had disappeared by the failure route. During the 1920's Canada, employing a branch banking system, had only one failure. Half a dozen states had experimented with deposit insurance plans without success. Apparently the situation needed the attention of the federal government.

The bank holocaust of the early 1930's—9,106 bank failures in four years, 1,947 of them national banks—culminating in a nationwide bank moratorium in March 1933, at last produced the needed drastic reforms. In 1933 Congress forbade Federal Reserve member banks to pay interest on demand deposits and founded the Federal Deposit Insurance Corporation (FDIC). The FDIC raised its initial capital by selling two kinds of stock. Class A stock (paying dividends) came from assessing every insured bank 0.5 percent of its total deposits—half paid in full, half subject to call. All member banks of the Federal Reserve System had to be insured. Federal Reserve Banks had to buy Class B stock (paying no dividends) with 0.5 percent of their surplus—half payable immediately, half subject to call. In addition, any bank desiring to be insured had to pay 0.083 percent of its average deposits annually. The FDIC first insured each depositor in a bank up to $2,500; in mid-1934 Congress put the figure at $5,000; on Sept. 21, 1950, the maximum became $10,000; on Oct. 16, 1966, the limit went to $15,000; on Dec. 23, 1969, to $20,000; and on Nov. 27, 1974, to $40,000. At the end of 1971 the FDIC was insuring 98.6 percent of all commercial banks and fully protecting 99 percent of all depositors. But it was protecting only about 64 percent of all deposits, savings deposits being protected at a high percentage but business deposits at only about 55 percent. Considerable bank examining is called for, and the FDIC examines more than 50 percent of the banks in the nation, which account for about 20 percent of banking assets. It does not usually examine member banks of the Federal Reserve System, which tend to be the larger banks. There is a degree of rivalry between the large and small banks, the FDIC being looked upon as the friend of the smaller banks.

Whereas in the 1920's banks were failing at an average rate of about 600 a year, during the first nine years of the FDIC (1934–42) there were altogether 487 bank closings because of financial difficulties, mostly of insured banks, and 387 of these received disbursements from the FDIC. During the years from 1943 to 1972, the average number of closings dropped to five per year. From 1934 to 1971 the corporation made disbursements in 496 cases involving 1.8 million accounts, representing $1.215 billion in total deposits, of which 97.5 percent has been paid. The FDIC in 1973 had $5.4 billion in assets. Through this protection people today are spared that traumatic experience of past generations, a "run on the bank" and the loss of a large part of their savings. For example, in 1974 the $5 billion Franklin National Bank of New York, twentieth in size in the nation, failed. It was the largest failure in American banking history. The FDIC, Federal Reserve, and comptroller of the currency arranged the sale of most of the bank's holdings, and no depositor lost a cent.

[Davis R. Dewey, *State Banking Before the Civil War;* William H. Dillistin, *Bank Note Reporters and Counterfeit Detectors, 1826–1866;* Oliver M. W. Sprague, *History of Crises Under the National Banking System;* C. B. Upham and E. Lamke, *Closed and Distressed Banks.*]

DONALD L. KEMMERER

BANK FOR INTERNATIONAL SETTLEMENTS. The Bank for International Settlements (BIS) evolved from the Hague Agreement of Jan. 20, 1930, which in turn was predicated on the report in March 1929 of the committee of reparation experts headed by Owen D. Young (*see* Young Plan). The BIS was incorporated in and received its charter from Switzerland on Feb. 25, 1930. Located in Basel, it began business May 17, 1930, with an authorized capital of 500 million Swiss gold francs (about $100 million then), one-quarter paid in by 1961. The central banks of Belgium, Britain, France, Germany, and Italy and two banking groups, one Japanese and one American, guaranteed the original subscription. The Japanese group sold out in 1951. The United States has never taken a "seat" in the BIS although Americans have served as president and in other managerial posts. Eight European central banks have recently dominated the BIS, and all the central banks of Western Europe are members. It is a European central banks' bank: only they may elect its board.

The chief activity of the BIS is executing any banking operations the central banks request. Under its statutes it may also "act as trustee or agent in regard to international financial settlements entrusted to it under agreements with the parties concerned." Thus in its early days it handled the Young Plan reparation payments, and later those of the European Payments Union and of the European Coal and Steel Community. Since 1964 it has worked for the Group of Ten (representatives of the major banking nations) and more recently helped with the European Monetary Agreement. But unlike a central bank, the BIS may not issue notes, accept bills of exchange, make advances to governments, or acquire a predominant interest in any business enterprise. Between 1964 and March 1973 the BIS more than quadrupled its balance sheet total to 25 billion gold Swiss francs.

Although its property and holdings are immune from expropriation in time of peace or war, the BIS had to tread carefully during World War II. Toward the end of the war, in 1944, the Bretton Woods Conference recommended its liquidation. The bank survived, however, because it does not duplicate the operations of the International Monetary Fund or the World Bank, but complements them.

[R. Auboin, "The Bank for International Settlements, 1930–55," Princeton University Essays in International Finance; Bank for International Settlements, *Forty-Third Annual Report,* and *Eight European Central Banks;* H. H. Schloss, *The Bank for International Settlements.*]

DONALD L. KEMMERER

BANKHEAD COTTON ACT, approved Apr. 21, 1934, designed to supplement the cotton production control provisions of the Agricultural Adjustment Act of 1933. While not actually placing limits upon the growing of cotton by individual farmers, the act established a national quota and levied a tax of 50 percent of the central market price (but not less than five cents per pound) upon cotton ginned in excess of the individual quota. This tax was the essence of the act. Following the decision of the Supreme Court invalidating the Agricultural Adjustment Act, Congress repealed the Bankhead Act (Feb. 10, 1936).

R. P. BROOKS

BANKING. The fundamental functions of a commercial bank during the past two centuries have been making loans, receiving deposits, and lending credit either in the form of bank notes or of "created" deposits. The banks in which people keep their checking accounts are commercial banks.

There were no commercial banks in colonial times, although there were loan offices or land banks, which made loans on real estate security with limited issues of legal tender notes. Robert Morris founded the first commercial bank in the United States, the Bank of North America, chartered Dec. 31, 1781. It greatly assisted the financing of the closing stages of the Revolution. The second bank was the Bank of Massachusetts, chartered Feb. 7, 1784; the third was the Bank of New York, which began without a charter June 9, 1784; and the fourth was the Bank of Maryland in 1790. By 1800 there were twenty-eight state-chartered banks and by 1811 there were eighty-eight.

Alexander Hamilton's financial program included a central bank to serve as a financial agent of the Treasury, provide a depository for public money, and be a regulator of the currency. Accordingly the first Bank of the United States—de facto the fifth—was founded Feb. 25, 1791, with a twenty-year charter. It was the nation's largest commercial bank. Its $10 million capital (huge for that day) and favored relationship with the government aroused much anxiety, especially among Jeffersonians. The bank's sound but unpopular policy of promptly returning bank notes for redemption in specie and refusing those of non-specie-paying banks, together with a political feud, were largely responsible for the narrow defeat of a bill to recharter it in 1811. Stephen Girard bought the bank and building. Between 1811 and 1816 both people and government were dependent on state banks, whose number increased to 246 and whose note circulation quadrupled. Nearly all but the New England banks suspended specie payments in September 1814 because of the War of 1812 and their own unregulated credit expansion.

The country soon recognized the need for a new central bank, and Congress established the second Bank of the United States on Apr. 10, 1816, also with a twenty-year charter. Its $35 million capitalization and favored relationship with the Treasury likewise aroused anxiety. Instead of repairing the overexpanded credit situation that it inherited, it aggravated it by generous lending policies. That precipitated the panic of 1819, in which it barely saved itself and incurred widespread ill will. Thereafter, under Nicholas Biddle, it was well run. As had its predecessor it required other banks to redeem their notes in specie, but most of the banks had come to accept that policy, for they appreciated the services and the stability provided by the second bank. The bank's downfall grew out of President Andrew Jackson's prejudice against banks and monopolies; the memory of the bank's role in the 1819 panic; and most of all, Biddle's decision to let rechartering be a main issue in the 1832 presidential election. Many persons otherwise friendly to the bank, faced with a choice of Jackson or the bank, chose Jackson. He vetoed the recharter. After Sept. 26, 1833, the government placed all its deposits with the "pet banks" (politically selected state banks) until it set up the Independent Treasury System in the 1840's. Between 1830 and 1837 the number of banks, bank note circulation, and bank loans all about tripled. Without the second bank to regulate them, the banks overextended themselves in lending to speculators in land. The panic of 1837 resulted—bringing with it a suspension of specie payments, many failures, and a depression that lasted until 1844.

For thirty years (1833–63) the country was without an adequate regulator of bank currency. In some states the laws were very strict or banking was forbidden, while in others the rules were lax. Banks made many long-term loans, especially on real estate, and they resorted to many subterfuges to avoid redeeming their notes in specie. Conditions were especially bad in parts of the Midwest and South, where there was some "wildcat" banking—the practice of lending notes at town branches but redeeming in specie only at a main office hidden away in a remote spot where only wildcats abounded. This practice probably began in Michigan. Almost everywhere bank tellers and merchants had to consult weekly publications known as Bank Note Reporters for the current discount on bank notes and turn to the latest Bank Note Detectors to distinguish the hundreds of counterfeits and notes of failed banks. This situation constituted an added business risk and necessitated somewhat higher mark-ups on merchandise. In this bleak era of banking, however, there were some bright spots. These were the Suffolk Banking System of Massachusetts (1819–63), which kept New England notes at par; the moderately successful Safety Fund (1829–66) and Free Banking (1838–66) systems of New York, the latter copied, but achieving less success, in fourteen other states; the Indiana (1834–65), Ohio (1845–66), and Iowa (1858–65) systems; and the Louisiana Banking System (1842–62), which was the first to require a minimum percent of specie reserve behind liabilities and insisted also that loans be short term. Inefficient and corrupt as some of the banking was before the Civil War, the nation's expanding economy found it an improvement over the system of land banks, personal loans, and long-time borrowing from merchants on which the 18th-century economy had depended.

Secretary of the Treasury Salmon P. Chase began agitating for an improved banking system in 1861, one important motive for which was his desire to widen the market for government bonds. The National Banking Act creating the National Banking System was passed Feb. 25, 1863, and completely revised June 3, 1864. Its head officer was the comptroller of currency. It was based on several recent reforms, especially the Free Banking System's principle of bond-backed notes. But the reserve requirements for bank notes were high, and the law forbade real estate loans and branch banking, had stiff organization requirements, and imposed burdensome taxes. State banks at first saw little reason to join, but in 1865 Congress levied a prohibitive 10 percent tax on their bank notes, effective July 1, 1866, which drove most of these banks into the new system. There were 1,644 national banks by Oct. 1, 1866, and they were required to use the word "National" in their name. The use of checks had been increasing in popularity in the more settled regions long before the Civil War, and by 1853 the total of bank deposits exceeded that of bank notes. After 1865 the desire of all banks, both state and national, to avoid the various new restrictions on bank notes doubtless speeded up the shift to this more convenient form of bank credit. By the 1890's it was estimated that about 85 percent of all business transactions were settled by check payments. Since state banks were less restricted, their number increased again until it passed that of national banks in 1894. Most large banks were national, however. Improvements in state banking laws began about 1887.

The National Banking System constituted a substantial improvement over the pre–Civil War hodgepodge of banking systems. But it had three major faults and several minor ones. The first major fault was the perverse elasticity of the bond-secured bank notes, of which the supply did not vary in accordance with the needs of business. The second fault was the decentralization of bank deposit reserves, which operated in the following way. There were three classes of national banks. The lesser ones kept part of their reserves in their own vaults and deposited the rest at interest with the larger national banks, especially with the New York City banks; these in turn loaned a considerable part of the funds on the call money market to finance stock speculation. In times of uncertainty the lesser banks demanded their outside reserves; call money rates soared; security prices tobogganed; and some good as well as many weak banks were ruined by runs. The third major fault was that there was no central bank to take measures to forestall such crises or to lend to deserving banks in times of distress. Among the minor faults were a slow and cumbersome check collection system and inadequate use of commercial paper.

Four times—1873, 1884, 1893, and 1907—panics highlighted the faults of the National Banking System. Improvised use of clearinghouse certificates in interbank settlements somewhat relieved money shortages in the first three cases; "voluntary" bank assessments collected and loaned by a committee headed by J. P. Morgan gave relief in 1907. In 1908 Congress passed the Aldrich-Vreeland Act to investigate foreign central banking systems and suggest reforms and to permit emergency bank note issues. The nation used these emergency issues on only one occasion, when a panic occurred at the outbreak of World War I in August 1914. The Owen-Glass Act of 1913 superimposed a central banking system on the existing national banking system. It required all national banks to "join" the new system, which meant to buy stock in it immediately equal to 3 percent of their capital and surplus, thus providing the funds with which to set up the Federal Reserve System, which was accomplished in 1914. State banks might also join by meeting specified requirements, but by the end of 1916 only thirty-four had done so. A majority of the nation's banks have always remained outside the Federal Reserve System, although the larger banks have usually been members. The Federal Reserve System largely corrected the faults to which the National Banking System had been prey. Admittedly the Federal Reserve had its faults and did not live up to expectations, especially during 1919–20, 1927–29, after World War II, and 1965–75. Nevertheless the nation's commercial banks had a policy-directing head and a refuge in distress to a greater degree than they had ever had before. Thus ended the need for the Independent Treasury System, which finally wound up its affairs in 1921.

Between the opening of the Federal Reserve System on Nov. 16, 1914, and May 1974, the commercial banking system grew and changed, as might be expected in a nation whose population more than doubled and whose real national income septupled during that period. The number of banks declined from 27,864 in mid-1914 to 14,741 in 1974; the number of national banks, from 7,518 to 4,659. (Bank failures between 1920 and 1933 were the principal cause of these declines, mergers being a minor reason.) Demand deposits meanwhile grew from $10 billion to $237 billion; and time deposits, from $8.6 billion to $393 billion. Loans grew from $15.2 billion to $510 billion, a thirty-four-fold increase; investments, on the other hand, rose from $5.5 billion to $188 billion—30 percent in Treasury securities—a thirty-four-fold increase. Wholesale prices quadrupled in that same period. Every decade during the interval saw some further significant developments in commercial banking.

Only a few national banks gave up their charters for state ones to avoid having to join the Federal Reserve System, but during World War I many state banks became members of the system—there were 1,374 in it by 1920. All banks helped sell Liberty bonds and bought short-term Treasuries between bond drives, which was one reason for a more than doubling of the money supply (currency and demand deposits) and also of the price level from 1914 to 1920. A major contributing factor for these doublings was the sharp reduction in reserves required under the new Federal Reserve System as compared with the pre-1914 National Banking System.

By 1921 there were 31,076 banks, the all-time peak; many were small family-owned state banks. Every year local crop failures, other disasters, or simply bad management wiped out several hundred of them. By 1929 the number of banks had declined to 25,568. Admittedly mergers eliminated a few names, and the growth of branch, group, or chain banking provided stability in some areas, the Bank of America in California being an outstanding example. But the 1920's are most remembered for stock market speculation. Several large banks, such as New York's National City and Chase National, had a part in this speculation—chiefly through their investment affiliates, which were essentially investment banks. The role of investment adviser gave banks great prestige until the panic of 1929, when widespread disillusionment from losses and scandals brought them discredit.

The 1930's witnessed many reforms growing out of the more than 9,000 bank failures between 1930 and 1933 and capped by the nationwide bank moratorium of March 6–9, 1933. To reform the commercial and central banking systems as well as to restore confidence in them, Congress passed two major banking laws, one on June 16, 1933, and the other on Aug. 23, 1935. These laws gave the Federal Reserve System firmer control over the banking system, especially over the member banks. They also set up the Federal Deposit Insurance Corporation to insure bank deposits, and soon all but a few hundred small banks belonged to it. That move greatly reduced the number of bank failures. Other changes included banning investment affiliates, prohibiting banks to pay interest on demand deposits, loosening restrictions against national banks' having branches and making real estate loans, and giving the Federal Reserve Board the authority to raise (to as much as double) member bank legal reserve requirements against deposits. As a result of the depression the supply of commercial loans dwindled and interest rates fell sharply. Consequently, banks invested more in federal government obligations, built up excess reserves, and imposed service charges on checking accounts. The 1933–34 devaluation of the dollar, which stimulated large imports of gold, was another cause of those excess reserves.

During World War II the banks once again helped sell war bonds. They also converted their excess reserves into government obligations and increased their own holdings of these from $16 billion in 1940 to $84 billion in 1945. Demand deposits more than doubled. Owing to bank holdings of government obligations—virtually convertible into cash—and to Federal Reserve commitments to the Treasury, the Federal Reserve had lost its power to curb bank-credit expansion. Price levels nearly doubled during the 1940's.

By the Federal Reserve–Treasury "accord" of March 1951, the Federal Reserve System regained its freedom to curb credit expansion, and thereafter interest rates crept upward. That development improved bank profits and also led banks to reduce somewhat their holdings of federal government obligations. Term loans (five to ten years) to industry and real estate loans increased. Banks also encountered stiff competition from rapidly growing rivals, such as savings and loan associations and personal finance companies. On July 28, 1959, Congress eliminated the difference between reserve city banks and central reserve city banks for member banks. The new law kept the same reserve requirements against demand deposits (10–22 percent), but it permitted banks to count cash in their vaults as part of their legal reserves.

Interest rates rose spectacularly all during the 1960's, prime commercial paper reaching 9 percent in 1970, then dropped sharply in 1971, only to rise once more, hitting 12 percent in mid-1974. Whereas consumer prices had gone up 23 percent during the

1950's, mostly early in the decade, they rose 31 percent during the 1960's, especially toward the end of the decade as budget deficits mounted, and climbed another 24 percent by mid-1974. Money supply figures played a major role in determining Federal Reserve credit policy from 1960 on.

Money once consisted largely of hard coin. With the coming of commercial banks it came also to include bank notes and demand deposits. But the difference between these and various forms of "near money," such as time deposits, savings and loan association deposits, and federal government E and H bonds—all quickly convertible to cash—is slight. Credit cards, increasingly prevalent during the 1950's and particularly during the 1960's, carry the confusion a step further. How does one add up the buying power of money, near money, and credit cards? As new forms of credit become more like money, it becomes increasingly difficult for the Federal Reserve to regulate the supply of credit and prevent booms.

In more than 190 years commercial banks have come to serve the economy in several important ways. They provide a safe place in which to keep savings; they are an institution from which short-term borrowers, and to some extent long-term borrowers too, can borrow funds (with the result that savings do not lie idle and unproductive); and they supply the nation with most of its money. (*See also* Banks, Export-Import; Banks, Savings; Federal Reserve System; Investment Banks; Savings and Loan Associations.)

[*Annual Reports of the Comptroller of the Currency;* Board of Governors of the Federal Reserve System, *The Federal Reserve System, Annual Reports,* and *Federal Reserve Bulletin;* L. V. Chandler, *The Economics of Money and Banking;* J. V. Fenstermaker, *The Development of Commercial Banking, 1782–1837;* Milton Friedman and M. Schwartz, *A Monetary History of the United States, 1867–1960;* B. Hammond, *Banks and Politics in America;* J. T. Holdsworth, *The First Bank of the United States;* E. W. Kemmerer and D. L. Kemmerer, *ABC of the Federal Reserve System;* Paul A. Samuelson and H. E. Krooss, *Documentary History of Banking and Currency in the United States;* W. B. Smith, *Economic Aspects of the Second Bank of the United States;* Paul Trescott, *Financing American Enterprise;* R. Westerfield, *Money, Credit and Banking;* J. A. Wilborn, *Biddle's Bank: The Crucial Years* (esp. p. 133).]

DONALD L. KEMMERER

BANKING, BRANCH AND GROUP. The first Bank of the United States had eight branches; the second bank had twenty-nine. Thereafter, what meager developments there were in branch banking before the 20th century took place under state authority, very little occurring between 1860 and 1890. The National Banking Act of 1863 forbade national banks to have branches.

The Federal Reserve Act of 1913 permitted foreign branches to a limited degree; in 1918 state banks having branches and wanting to join the Federal Reserve System were authorized to keep them; and the McFadden-Pepper Act of 1927 allowed national banks to set up a limited number of branches in the parent bank's city provided the state permitted branch banking.

During the 1920's hundreds of small state banks failed because of dependence on a single local crop or industry. Canadian and English experience indicated that branch banking offered a partial solution. Accordingly, the Banking Act of 1933 permitted national banks to establish branches, under certain restrictions, in states allowing branch banking. Thus a few score state banks were attracted into the national system.

In 1936 eighteen states permitted statewide branch banking, and seventeen permitted it within limited areas. At the time there were 3,581 branches in existence. In 1969 there were still eighteen states permitting branch banking, although the number of states permitting it within limits had increased to twenty; but there were many more branches. At the end of 1973 the 14,172 commercial banks had 26,251 branches and "additional offices." California had the most highly developed branch system. The Federal Reserve banks had twenty-four branches.

Where branch banking is prohibited or discouraged, resort has been made to chain banking or group banking, the original distinction between these being that chains are owned by one or more individuals, whereas groups are owned by holding companies. The federal government paid little attention to chain banking until about 1963, when the House Committee on Banking and Currency broadened the definition of chain banking, investigated its extent among the nation's 200 largest banks, found considerable indication of a community of interest among them, and submitted a report. Group banks held only 6 percent of bank deposits in the 1930's and 1940's but grew noticeably in the 1950's from the addition of new bank affiliates by existing systems. Such uncontrolled concentration of financial resources caused public concern, and Congress held hearings, finally passing the Bank Holding Company Act of 1956, which made the Federal Reserve's board of governors the supervisory agency in this field. At the board's suggestion, Congress amended the act in 1966. In December 1970 there were 121 registered bank holding companies, holding $78 billion in deposits, or 16.2 percent of all commercial bank deposits. But holding companies controlling only one bank were exempt from the 1956 law; between 1955 and April 1970 their number grew from 117 to 1,116 and their deposits from $11.6 billion to $138.8 billion, representing 32.6 percent of commercial deposits. Many of these holding companies carried on a variety of nonbanking activities. Alarmed by this rapid growth, Congress, by a Dec. 31, 1970, law ended the exemption of one-bank holding companies—all are under Federal Reserve control.

[Association of Registered Bank Holding Companies, *The Bank Holding Company;* G. T. Cartinhour, *Branch, Group and Chain Banking;* D. R. Dewey, *State Banking Before the Civil War;* Gerald C. Fischer, *Bank Holding Companies;* W. R. Lamb, *Group Banking;* R. B. Westerfield, *Historical Survey of Branch Banking in the United States.*]

DONALD L. KEMMERER

BANKING, STATE. State investment in banks was common before the panic of 1837. The idea behind it frequently was that bank profits would lead to abolition of taxes. This idea had its roots in the early 18th century, when most of the colonies at one time or another had loan offices or land banks, which were as close as the colonists came to having banks. The interest payments from the loans made by these institutions brought in enough revenue to pay the expenses (chiefly administrative salaries) of the provincial governments. For example, between about 1724 and 1754 such income paid most of the cost of New Jersey's government.

In the 19th century sometimes the state was sole owner of a bank, as in South Carolina, but more commonly it was part owner, as in Indiana. In some cases the ventures were profitable; in others they were disastrous. In Illinois, where the state owned $3.6 million of stock, there was failure and in 1843 divorce of bank and state. In Mississippi, Arkansas, and Florida, where the investment was nearly $12 million, the result was repudiation of a debt that has never been paid. In Louisiana, where the bonds issued to aid banks amounted to $19 million, there was collapse and reform under the Specie Reserve System of 1842 (*see* Louisiana Banking System).

Among the successful state-owned banks, the State Bank of Missouri was the most important. It continued in operation through the panics of 1837 and 1857; and in 1862, when it entered the national system as a private bank, the state sold its stock for a premium. The State Bank of Indiana passed through the panics and emerged in 1857, when its charter expired, with a net profit to the state of more than $2 million, still the basis of the school fund. The Bank of the State of South Carolina also withstood the panics and continued through the Civil War as one of the strongest institutions in the country.

State banking was one of three alternatives from which states chose following a growing public distrust of banks after the panic of 1819, the political struggle with Andrew Jackson over renewing the charter of the second Bank of the United States, and especially the panic of 1837. Some states forbade banking altogether: seven of thirty-one states were doing so in 1852. Others—the majority, including New York, Michigan, and Louisiana—elected to regulate banking more closely. Still others—Indiana, Missouri, and Ohio—made banking a state monopoly, or at least set up a state-owned bank. Some indecisive ones tried one solution, then another; Iowa, for instance, went from prohibition to state banking.

With the passage of the July 1865 amendment to the National Banking Act, imposing a 10 percent tax on state bank notes after July 1, 1866, so as to force all state banks to join the National Banking System, state-owned banks disappeared. State-chartered banks found a way around the law by encouraging borrowers to use check currency.

[J. R. Cable, *The Bank of the State of Missouri;* B. Hammond, *Banks and Politics in America;* L. C. Helderman, *National and State Banks: A Study of Their Origin;* H. McCulloch, *Men and Measures of Half a Century.*]

DONALD L. KEMMERER

BANKING ACTS OF 1933 AND 1935. The Banking Act of 1933, approved June 16, 1933, contained three groups of provisions as follows: (1) provisions designed to increase the power of the Federal Reserve Board to control credit, especially with respect to loans to brokers and customers secured by stocks and bonds; (2) provisions dealing with the commercial banks, of which by far the most important was the one providing for the insurance of bank deposits under the supervision of the Federal Deposit Insurance Corporation; and (3) provisions designed to separate commercial and investment banking functions by prohibiting commercial banks from operating investment affiliates and by prohibiting investment banking houses from carrying on a deposit banking business.

The Banking Act of 1935, approved Aug. 23, 1935, contained three titles. Title I amended the deposit insurance provisions of the Banking Act of 1933. Title II provided for a rather drastic reorganization of the Federal Reserve Board and changed the name of that body to the Board of Governors of the Federal Reserve System. Certain changes were also made in the management of the Federal Reserve banks. Powers over discount and open market operations of the Reserve banks were increased and centralized in the Board of Governors, and the discount base was very materially broadened. Title III contained a series of technical amendments to the banking laws governing the operations of the commercial banks.

[F. A. Bradford, *Money and Banking*.]

FREDERICK A. BRADFORD

BANKING CRISIS OF 1933, the outcome of the large number of bank failures during the years 1931–32 combined with the wave of hoarding which swept the country and markedly weakened the banking structure. The attempts of the Reconstruction Finance Corporation to avoid final disaster were in large measure nullified by the publication of the names of borrowing banks, a procedure not calculated to restore confidence to frightened depositors.

Banking difficulties in Michigan finally caused Gov. William A. Comstock to declare a bank moratorium in that state on Feb. 14, 1933. Alarm quickly spread to neighboring states. Moratoria were declared in four other states by the end of February, and in seventeen additional states during the first three days of March. Finally, on Mar. 4, banks in the remaining states closed their doors and the country was left devoid of banking facilities.

The situation was serious and prompt action was imperative. Congress, called in special session by President Franklin D. Roosevelt, passed the Emergency Banking Act of 1933 on Mar. 9, thus providing machinery for reopening the banks. Under this act, only sound banks were to be reopened while those of questionable soundness were to be placed in the hands of conservators, to be opened later if conditions permitted.

The bank moratorium, which had been proclaimed by the president on Mar. 6, was extended a few days to permit the provisions of the act to be put into effect. Sound banks were reopened on Mar. 13, 14, and 15. By the latter date, banks controlling about 90 percent of the banking resources of the country were again in operation and the banking crisis of 1933 was at an end.

[J. I. Bogen and M. Nadler, *The Banking Crisis;* F. A. Bradford, *Money and Banking;* L. Sullivan, *Prelude to Panic*.]

FREDERICK A. BRADFORD

BANK NOTES. *See* **Money.**

***BANK OF AUGUSTA* V. *EARLE*,** 13 Peters 519 (1839), involved the right of a Georgia bank to recover on a bill of exchange purchased in Alabama. The Supreme Court, speaking through Chief Justice Roger B. Taney, held that though a state might exclude the creature of another state, yet in the silence of any positive rule it would be presumed that "foreign" corporations were by comity permitted to make contracts. Taney's opinion became the leading authority on the law of foreign corporations.

[Charles Warren, *The Supreme Court in United States History*.]

CHARLES FAIRMAN

***BANK OF COMMERCE* V. *NEW YORK CITY*,** 2 Black 620 (1863). The Supreme Court held that the state could not tax capital invested in federal securities—thereby strengthening the financial position of the government in the midst of the Civil War.

[T. R. Powell, "Indirect Encroachment on Federal Authority by the Taxing Power of the States," *Harvard Law Review*, vols. 31, 32.]

CHARLES FAIRMAN

BANK OF NORTH AMERICA, America's first government-incorporated bank, chartered by the Continental Congress in 1781, commenced operations in Philadelphia on Jan. 7, 1782. Organized by Robert Morris, the bank supplied vital financial aid to the government during the closing months of the American Revolution. Original depositors and stockholders included Thomas Jefferson, Alexander Hamilton, Benjamin Franklin, John Paul Jones, James Monroe, John Jay, and Stephen Decatur.

[A. W. Whittlesey, *Highlights in the 125-Year History of The Pennsylvania Company*.]

A. W. WHITTLESEY

BANK OF THE STATE OF SOUTH CAROLINA. *See* **South Carolina, State Bank of.**

BANK OF THE UNITED STATES. First Bank of the United States (1791–1811). As the result of a proposal by Secretary of the Treasury Alexander Hamilton for the establishment of a national bank, an act incorporating subscribers to the Bank of the United States was approved by President George Washington and became law on Feb. 25, 1791. Under the provisions of the law the bank, which was to be located in Philadelphia, was to have a capital of $10 million, composed of 25,000 shares of $400 par value. One-fifth of the capital was subscribed by the government, the rest by private investors. Private subscriptions were limited to 1,000 shares, and no shareholder was to have more than thirty votes. Foreign shareholders were not permitted to vote by proxy.

The management of the bank was vested in a board of twenty-five directors, elected by the shareholders. The board of directors was authorized to elect a president who was to receive compensation, the directors serving without pay. Only American citizens might be directors of the bank.

The bank was empowered to carry on a commercial banking business, was not permitted to deal in commodities or real estate, and was limited to 6 percent in the interest it might charge on loans. The bank was authorized to issue circulating notes totaling up to $10 million, the amount of its capital.

The Bank of the United States opened its doors for business on Dec. 12, 1791. It was efficiently managed and furnished the country, through its main office and eight branches, with sound banking service throughout its chartered life of twenty years. The bank served satisfactorily as fiscal agent for the government and exerted a salutary controlling influence on the note issues of the state banks by refusing to accept state bank notes that were not redeemable in specie. In spite of the manifest advantages of a national bank, the charter of the first bank was not renewed in 1811, doubt as to its constitutionality being the controlling factor. The bank therefore wound up its affairs, eventually paying shareholders $434 on each share held.

Second Bank of the United States (1811–36). After a brief and unsatisfactory period of state banking, the second Bank of the United States was incorporated under a law of Apr. 10, 1816. The charter provisions were similar to those of the first bank except that the capital and note issue limits were increased to $35 million. The president of the United States was also authorized to appoint five of the twenty-five directors.

The second Bank of the United States was badly managed under its first president, William Jones, who retired in 1819. Langdon Cheves, who succeeded Jones, spent his administration in getting the bank back to a sound position. In 1823 Nicholas Biddle assumed the presidency, and from then until 1833 the bank was well and capably managed, extending sound banking service to the country through its main office and twenty-five branches.

A dispute between Biddle and President Andrew Jackson led to the withdrawal of government deposits in 1833 (*see* Removal of Deposits) and a severe contraction of the bank's business. Efforts to obtain a renewal of the second bank's charter proved futile, and the institution ceased to function as a national bank upon the expiration of its charter in 1836.

[R. C. H. Catterall, *The Second Bank of the United States;* J. T. Holdsworth and D. R. Dewey, *The First and Second Banks of the United States.*]

FREDERICK A. BRADFORD

***BANK OF THE UNITED STATES* V. *HALSTEAD*,** 10 Wheaton 51 (1825), concerned the applicability of state legislation regulating the procedural processes to federal courts within the respective states. The Supreme Court upheld the power of federal courts to alter forms of proceedings to meet changing conditions on general (implied) grounds relating to the judicial power and from specific legislative grants.

PHILLIPS BRADLEY

***BANK OF THE UNITED STATES* V. *PLANTER'S BANK OF GEORGIA*,** 9 Wheaton 904 (1824). Chief Justice John Marshall here enunciated the rule that a suit against a corporation chartered and partly owned by a state was not a suit against the state itself. "It is, we think, a sound principle that when a government becomes a partner in any trading company, it divests itself, so far as concerns the transactions of that company, of its sovereign character, and takes that of a private citizen." The rule was later applied to banks wholly owned by a state (*see Briscoe* v. *Bank of the Commonwealth of Kentucky*).

[A. J. Beveridge, *John Marshall.*]

PHILLIPS BRADLEY

BANKRUPTCY LAWS existed in England in the 18th century but were limited to creditor-initiated proceedings against traders, bankers, brokers, factors, and underwriters. The subject of bankruptcy laws was not considered by the federal convention of 1787 until late in its proceedings. Charles Pinckney was the author of the first draft of the bankruptcy clause of the Constitution; it was adopted with practically no debate, with only one dissenting vote.

Congress did not immediately exercise the power "to establish . . . uniform laws on the subject of bankruptcies throughout the United States" (Article I, Section 8). The first American bankruptcy legislation on the federal level was enacted in 1800 as a result of the unsettled economic conditions arising out of widespread speculation in the shares of a multitude of newly incorporated companies dealing in land and in government scrip. The first legislation closely resembled the English statutes of the time. It applied only to traders, merchants, and brokers and provided only for involuntary bankruptcies, that is, creditor-initiated proceedings. It was essentially a liquidation provision—the assets of the bankrupt being seized and sold to satisfy the claims of creditors. A bankrupt was permitted to retain a certain percentage of his assets and could be discharged from any unsatisfied indebtedness by the consent of two-thirds of his creditors. The act of 1800 was a temporary measure, expressly limited to five years. The return to prosperity, coupled with growing public dissatisfaction with the workings of the act, resulted in its repeal in 1803.

The second national bankruptcy act was passed in 1841. It too was the product of hard times—the great panic of 1837 and the resulting depression. The second act was not limited to involuntary bankruptcies; debtor-initiated proceedings, that is, voluntary bankruptcies, were also permitted. Additionally, this second bankruptcy act eliminated creditor control of discharge: any debtor who surrendered his property and complied with the orders of the court could obtain a discharge. The act of 1841, like the act of 1800, was largely a product of financial stringency and was repealed after only eighteen months of operation, as economic conditions improved. Financial stress brought on by the Civil War resulted in the enactment of the third federal bankruptcy statute in 1867. The act of 1867 followed in many respects the patterns of its predecessors. It did, however, extend both voluntary and involuntary bankruptcy to moneyed and commercial corporations. The act of 1867 was repealed in 1878; the repeal was at least in part attributable to widespread abuses on the part of the courts in administering it.

Thus, during the first one hundred years of the nation's history, federal bankruptcy laws were in force for a total of only fifteen years. During the intervals between the repeal of one federal bankruptcy act and the passage of the next, state laws governed the debtor-creditor relationship. Such laws were not satisfactory. They were limited in scope because of the constitutional grant of power to Congress; they were not uniform; and they often discriminated against out-of-state creditors.

The panic of 1893 rekindled interest in national bankruptcy legislation, and in 1898 Congress enacted a bankruptcy bill drafted primarily by Colonel Torrey, a St. Louis attorney hired by various commercial interests. The act of 1898 has continued in force to the present day, the last serious attempts to repeal it having been in 1910. The act has been amended more than ninety times since its passage, most extensively in 1938 by the Chandler Act. As a result of amendments designed to combat the depression of 1929, the Bankruptcy Act contains not only liquidation provisions similar in nature to the earlier bankruptcy enactments but also a number of specialized rehabilitation provisions such as section 77, providing for the reorganization of railroads, and chapter X, regulating the reorganization of large publicly held corporations under the supervision of the Securities and Exchange Commission.

[Stefan Riesenfeld, *Creditors' Remedies and Debtor's Protection;* Charles Warren, *Bankruptcy in United States History.*]

DAVID G. EPSTEIN

BANKS, EXPORT-IMPORT. The various export-import banks of Washington have had as their goal the promotion of U.S. trade—and more notably exports than imports—that might otherwise be lost because it seemed too risky, or required too long-term a loan, to appeal to private business. The 1945 Export-Import Bank Act provides that the bank is not to compete with private capital—and at times its activities have, in effect, taken the form of subsidizing some U.S. exports, allegedly to offset the help foreign governments are giving their exporters or to overcome the barriers these governments have erected against U.S. imports.

The first Export-Import Bank of Washington was created by executive order and chartered Feb. 12, 1934, to facilitate trade with the Soviet Union. By a law of Jan. 31, 1935, it continued as a federal agency. The second Export-Import Bank was organized in March 1934 to finance the purchase and minting of silver for Cuba. In June 1936 it was merged with the first Export-Import Bank. On July 31, 1945, the bank became an independent federal agency. The Reconstruction Finance Corporation provided most of its early funds; the federal government later subscribed to $1 billion of its common stock. Trade with the USSR did not materialize, and the bank has chiefly aided trade and internal development in Latin America, although China in the 1940's and a number of European countries and even Canada have felt its benefits. It has extended short-term credits for the export of agricultural products, such as cotton and tobacco, when financing was not available from private institutions. More important, it has granted one-to-five-year credits to firms seeking to export heavy industrial machinery, farm machinery, and railroad equipment. Finally, it has extended credit to firms unable to withdraw their funds from countries with exchange restrictions. The bank has cooperated with the Department of State in encouraging projects that will promote the internal economic stability of friendly nations.

The federal Treasury owns all the Export-Import Bank's capital stock, $1 billion. The bank may borrow up to $6 billion from the Treasury on a revolving basis although debt-ceiling restraints often limit its borrowings. It must get its authorizations annually from Congress. Other sources of funds are private capital markets and its own earnings. Losses by the bank have been minor. Theoretically it can support—through loans, guarantees, and insurance—trade to the extent of $16.125 billion. In practice, in fiscal 1973 it supported $10.5 billion of exports. From its inception through fiscal 1973 it supported $63 billion in export sales, half of them between 1970 and 1973. In 1973 alone it processed over 8,800 transactions.

[Export-Import Bank of the United States, *Annual Report: Fiscal Year 1973;* Howard S. Piquet, *The Export-Import Bank of the United States.*]

DONALD L. KEMMERER

BANKS, INVESTMENT. *See* **Investment Banks.**

BANKS, LAND. *See* **Agriculture.**

BANKS, NATIONAL. *See* **Banking.**

BANKS, POSTAL SAVINGS. *See* **Postal Service, United States.**

BANKS, PRIVATE, historically, are the original form of banking. Private banks are strictly defined as individuals or partnerships engaged in any of the functions of banking—deposit, exchange, loan, discount, or sale of securities. Like any private business their obligations were originally protected by the personal liability of the individual or partnership. They were the product of the era of laissez-faire and developed in America on the model of the great English banking houses.

With the growth of social control of business—and banking was one of the earliest areas of economic life to yield to this—the number of private banks declined. Some states prohibit their operations entirely, and in all there has been an increasing tendency to subject them to the same control as corporations and curtail the field of their operations. The function of note issue, little used by most private banks, was no longer practiced after the passage of the National Banking Act in 1863.

Private banks continued to exist because of a real need for their services, the lack of regulation, and a tradition of personal integrity. Perhaps the most famous house of private bankers in America has been that of J. P. Morgan.

Some of the banks that developed before the Civil War with charters for speculative businesses such as railroads, insurance companies, and canal companies may be regarded as private banks. An example of these was the Manhattan Company, organized ostensibly for the purpose of supplying New York City with water. Stephen Girard's bank was another. It occupied the building of the first Bank of the United States in Philadelphia after 1811. Another example was George Smith's Bank of Milwaukee, which, organized to carry on insurance, converted itself into a bank.

[L. C. Helderman, *National and State Banks.*]

LEONARD C. HELDERMAN

BANKS, SAVINGS. The first savings bank in the United States was the Provident Institution for Savings in Boston, which was chartered Dec. 13, 1816. The Philadelphia Savings Fund Society was chartered earlier, Dec. 2, 1816, but did not begin business until Feb. 25, 1819. Between 1816 and 1820 ten mutual savings banks were chartered, all in the Northeast. By 1914 there were 634 mutual savings banks with nearly 8 million depositors and $4 billion in savings. By the end of 1973 there were 484 of these banks in eighteen states, still chiefly in the Northeast, with $106 billion in deposits. Two-thirds of these funds were invested in loans on real estate. Since 1935 mutual savings banks have been eligible for membership in the Federal Reserve System, but few have joined.

After the Civil War stock savings banks were organized in a number of states. Their number reached 1,529 by mid-1915 and then declined to 341 in 1935, with $700 million in deposits. The Postal Savings System, founded in 1910 largely to serve immigrants, accepted savings at the post office but actually deposited them in nearby savings banks. This system experienced a temporarily rapid growth during the early 1930's when so many banks were failing. Its peak year was 1947, with some 4.2 million depositors and more than $3 billion in deposits. By mid-1965 the system had only one million depositors, with balances totaling $344 million. It was then outdated since the Federal Deposit Insurance Corporation gave depositors adequate protection and other institutions paid higher interest rates than the Postal Savings System. Congress terminated the system in March 1966.

Both state-chartered and national savings banks offer customers savings account service and are definitely the most important form of savings institution. Time deposits of these banks totaled $373 billion in May 1974. In addition, savings and loan associations have given both savings banks and commercial banks severe competition. Since 1929 their "deposits"—which are actually shares in the association but are treated as savings deposits—have grown from $6.2 billion to $235 billion, in May 1974.

[Board of Governors of the Federal Reserve System, *All Bank Statistics,* and *Federal Reserve Bulletin;* Federal Deposit Insurance Corporation, *Annual Report;* F. J. Sherman, *The Modern Story of Mutual Savings Banks.*]

DONALD L. KEMMERER

BANKS, WILDCAT. *See* **Banking.**

BANNOCK. A Great Basin tribe speaking a language belonging to the Shoshonean branch of the Uto-Aztecan linguistic family, the Bannock ranged from southeastern Idaho both west and east, into the Snake River region in Idaho and into Wyoming. Like other residents of the Great Basin—including the northern Paiute, to whom they appear most closely related—the Bannock were adapted to the arid environment of the area and to the subsistence provided by it. Divided into small bands, the tribe moved widely, gathering wild seeds and insects and sometimes massing for communal rabbit and antelope hunts. When first contacted, some of the Bannock had assimilated Plains traits by virtue of the presence of horses. But unlike their neighbors to the east, such as the Wind River Shoshone and the eastern Ute, they did not adopt the Plains war pattern. Their small population was reduced early by smallpox and reservation confinement. A revolt in 1878, the so-called Bannock War, was a reaction by them against reservation life; it was, however, quickly suppressed.

[Julian H. Steward, *Basin-Plateau Aboriginal Socio-Political Groups.*]

ROBERT F. SPENCER

BANNOCK WAR (1878), the last major uprising among the American Indians in the Pacific Northwest except for the revolt of a small group of Shoshone known as the Sheepeaters, in Idaho in 1879. Threat of starvation impelled the Bannock to leave the Fort Hall Reservation in Idaho, in 1878, to find sustenance through gathering and hunting. They were angered to find the hogs of settlers rooting up the camass bulbs upon which they relied heavily for food, and under the leadership of Buffalo Horn, they began to attack settlers. The Bannock were joined by a few other northern Paiute under a leader named Egan. Pursued by troops under Gen. O. O. Howard, the Indians suffered heavy losses in two engagements. They then began to scatter in small groups and gradually drifted back to the reservation. Hostilities had ceased by October 1878.

[Ross Arnold, *Indian Wars of Idaho;* George F. Brimlow, *The Bannock Indian War of 1878;* Brigham D. Madsen, *The Bannock of Idaho.*]

KENNETH M. STEWART

BAPTIST CHURCHES. The Baptist movement originated in 17th-century English Puritanism. One strand of its tradition can be traced to the Separate Puritan Congregation of John Smith and Thomas Helwys that was established in Holland in 1608. Another strand is derived from the Particular Baptists, a group that separated from Henry Jacob's Southwark congregation in England in 1638. This group was strongly related to the Calvinist tradition in doctrine and to the Non-Separating Congregationalists in its understanding of the church.

In the United States, Roger Williams helped to establish the first Baptist congregation in Providence, R.I., in 1639. The center of the colonial Baptist movement was in the Middle Colonies, where the Philadelphia Baptist Association, established in 1707, united churches that stretched from Virginia to Massachusetts. The expansion of the churches as a result of the Great Awakening led to the formation of the

Ketochten Association in Virginia (1765) and the Warren Association in Rhode Island (1767). The associational system that was developed during this period stressed cooperation between the congregations, particularly in the area of evangelism.

In 1814, the Baptists established a General Convention to support the missionary work of Adoniram Judson in Burma. Other national Baptist societies were established in the early 19th century to handle such matters as publications and home missions. These conventions were not, strictly speaking, denominational structures but only charitable organizations to which congregations voluntarily subscribed.

The Baptist churches split in 1845, largely over the issue of slavery. From its beginning, the Southern Baptist Convention adopted a more denominational pattern than had been customary and empowered the central body to act semiautonomously in the areas delegated to it. This centralizing tendency has continued in the Southern Convention until 1975, when the actual polity of the church should be described as semipresbyterian. The Baptists in the North moved more slowly toward a centralized denominational organization and relied on the voluntary society model until 1907, when the Northern Baptist Convention was formed. The Northern Convention became the American Baptist Convention in 1950 and, after strengthening the denominational structure, became the American Baptist Churches in the U.S.A. in 1973.

The Afro-American Baptist congregations and denominations grew after the Civil War because of racial discrimination in the older Baptist organizations. In 1880, the National Baptist Convention of America was formed. This influential group split in 1907, with the larger faction adopting the name of the National Baptist Convention, U.S.A., Inc. (*see* Afro-American Church).

Although the tensions caused by modern trends in theology arose earlier among Baptists in the urban North, they have plagued all Baptist groups in the 20th century. The Northern Baptists have split twice over theological issues, once in 1932 and again in 1947, and the Southern Baptists have sacrificed several seminary professors to maintain unity. In the opinion of many Baptist theologians, these intradenominational quarrels have seriously weakened the various Baptist churches' capacity to bear witness to their distinctive beliefs.

Although Baptists have adopted confessions of faith, these confessions have been regarded as noncompulsory summaries of principles. There are, however, distinctive Baptist affirmations: belief in religious liberty, in the independence of the local congregation, and in the doctrine of soul liberty. Most Baptists, but not all, hold a theology derived from the Evangelical Calvinism of the 18th century.

There are twenty-six Baptist denominations in the United States as well as many independent congregations that have no associational connection. Approximately 95 percent of all Baptists belong to eight major organizations: Southern Baptist Convention, 12,000,000 members; National Baptist Convention, U.S.A., Inc., 6,400,000 members; National Baptist Convention of America, 2,600,000 members; American Baptist Convention, 1,400,000 members; National Primitive Baptist Convention, 1,000,000 members; American Baptist Association, 870,000 members; Conservative Baptist Association of America, 300,000 members; and General Association of Regular Baptist Churches, 204,000 members.

[W. W. Barnes, *The Southern Baptist Convention, 1843–1953;* E. L. Eighmy, *Churches in Cultural Captivity: A History of the Social Attitudes of Southern Baptists;* H. H. Hobbs, *What Baptists Believe;* W. S. Hudson, ed., *Baptist Concepts of the Church;* D. D. Pelt and R. L. Smith, *The Story of the National Baptists.*]

GLENN T. MILLER

BAR ASSOCIATION, AMERICAN. *See* **American Bar Association.**

BARATARIA, the name of a bay, a village, and a bayou on the Gulf Coast of Louisiana, sixty miles south of New Orleans and forty miles west of the mouth of the Mississippi. The Barataria region is inseparably connected in history and legend with the smuggling operations of Jean and Pierre Laffite, who maintained headquarters there from 1810 to 1815. Though regarded as pirates by the United States, the Laffites claimed to operate as privateers under letters of marque and reprisal issued by the Republic of Cartagena (now part of Colombia), on the northern coast of South America, which had declared its independence from Spain in 1810. (*See also* Galveston Pirates.)

[Lyle Saxon, *Lafitte the Pirate.*]

WALTER PRICHARD

BARBADOS, island nation in the West Indies, member of the Commonwealth of Nations, was first settled in 1627 by the British. As a British colony,

Barbados traded extensively—and not always legitimately—with New England, New York, and Virginia throughout the colonial period, mainly exchanging sugar, cotton, molasses, and ginger for foodstuffs. Moreover, many settlers went from Barbados to the Carolinas.

Despite the abolition of slavery on the island in 1834, Barbados' sugar industry continued to prosper. By 1970 sugar and sugar products made up 50 percent of the island's domestic exports, but since 1968 tourists, mainly from the United States and the United Kingdom, have brought more foreign currency into the country.

[C. Atchley, *The West Indies*.]

CHARLES F. MULLETT

BARBARY WARS. Tripolitan War (1801–05). After the Revolution the United States, following the example of European nations, made annual payments to the Barbary states (Morocco, Algiers, Tripoli, and Tunis) for unmolested passage along North Africa's Barbary Coast. Constant difficulties, however, ensued, such as the episode of the *George Washington*, and in 1801 Tripoli declared war and seized several Americans and their vessels. The war, entirely naval except for the Derna expedition, was feebly prosecuted by the commanders first dispatched, but in 1803 Commodore Edward Preble was sent out with the *Constitution, Philadelphia,* and several brigs and schooners. His arrival galvanized the entire force into vigorous action. Making a naval demonstration before Tangiers, which brought the Emperor of Morocco to make amends for treaty violations, Preble set up a strict blockade of Tripoli itself. Here on Oct. 31, 1803, the *Philadelphia* ran on a reef just outside the harbor and was captured by the Tripolitans, who a few days later floated it and anchored it under the guns of the citadel. But on Feb. 16, 1804, Lt. Stephen Decatur and eighty other officers and men recaptured and burned it in a daring night attack.

During August and September 1804, Preble, in addition to blockading, harassed the Tripolitan shipping and fortifications with frequent attacks in which the small gunboats fearlessly entered the harbor to enable the crews to board and capture piratical craft while the larger ships kept up a protective fire on batteries. Such activity reached a climax on Sept. 4, when the *Intrepid* with its cargo of gunpowder and explosive shells was maneuvered into the harbor at night. Apparently the explosion occurred prematurely, for all the participants were killed and little damage was done to the Tripolitan shipping.

When, soon after, Preble was relieved by Commodore Samuel Barron, and Barron was relieved in turn the next spring by Commodore John Rodgers, the Bey of Tripoli was ready to conclude peace. He was partly induced to this by the success of the Derna expedition, which had captured Derna and was threatening to march on Tripoli itself. The treaty, somewhat hastily concluded, June 4, 1805, abolished all annual payments, but provided for $60,000 ransom money for the officers and crew of the *Philadelphia*.

War with Algiers (1815). Although payments were continued to the other Barbary states, the absence of American naval vessels in the years preceding the War of 1812 encouraged Algiers to seize American merchantmen such as the *Mary Ann,* for which $18,000 was paid Algiers, and to threaten others such as the *Allegheny,* where an increased payment was demanded and secured. Immediately after the determination of the war, Decatur, now a commodore, and William Bainbridge were ordered to the Mediterranean with an overwhelming force (*see* Decatur's Cruise to Algiers). By June 1815, within forty days after his departure from New York, Decatur, the first to arrive, had achieved his immediate mission. Capturing the Algerian flagship *Mashuda* in a running fight off Gat and appearing off Algiers, he demanded and secured a treaty humiliating to the once proud piratical state—no future payments, restoration of all American property, the emancipation of all Christian slaves escaping to American men-of-war, civilized treatment of prisoners of war, and $10,000 for a merchantman recently seized. As Tunis and Tripoli were forced to equally hard terms and an American squadron remained in the Mediterranean, the safety of American commerce was assured.

[G. W. Allen, *Our Navy and the Barbary Corsairs;* Ray W. Irwin, *The Diplomatic Relations of the United States With the Barbary Powers, 1776–1816*.]

WALTER B. NORRIS

BARBECUE, an outdoor entertainment distinguished by the serving of meat cooked, often as whole carcasses, on racks over open pits of coals. Apparently originating in Virginia about 1700, probably in connection with local fairs where foot-races, dancing, fiddling contests, and other sport and pastimes were engaged in, the barbecue was especially popular on the southwestern frontier. During the first period of nationalism the universal celebration of the Fourth of July did much to shape the barbecue as an institution. Beef and other meats were donated, and bread, condiments, and often beer or lemonade were served free to all comers. There were oratory, music, dancing, and various sports, including tournaments, roping contests, and other equestrian games. Candidates for public office were invited to expound their platforms, and they and their partisans were quick to take advantage of the barbecue as a campaigning device.

[American Heritage, *American Heritage Cookbook and Illustrated History of American Drinking and Eating.*]

MODY C. BOATRIGHT

BARBED WIRE. "Free grass" and the open range were doomed by advancing values and population. Without absolute control of his land and stock, no ranchman could afford extensive improvement. If he provided ample water, the stock belonging to other men would tramp out his range in getting to it; if he bought high-grade bulls, his neighbors would get the use of them, while at the same time scrub bulls of other brands ran with his cows. Colorado alone of the range states enforced laws against scrub breeders.

Cattle, some rovers always excepted, would, after being located normally, remain on a given range; but droughts and blizzards made them drift, a hundred—sometimes two hundred—miles. Moreover, open range meant open road for thieves. "Slick" wire would not hold range stock; plank fences were too expensive; hedges of *bois d'arc,* wild roses, and other growth proved impracticable. Only small bunches of cattle could thrive under herd, and herding was costly; the lineriders of the big outfits were helpless when northers and blizzards struck.

Following various patents on barbed wire (twisted wire with coiled barbs), in 1873 Joseph F. Glidden, a prairie farmer of Illinois, gave it commercial practicability and the next year sold the first piece. Factories developed. Fencing proceeded outward from privately owned land near settlements. John W. Gates in the late 1870's put up a "bob" wire fence on Alamo Plaza in San Antonio to demonstrate its being "bull proof and horse high." Before the plains were fenced into pastures, cowmen cooperated to build drift fences across long distances. By 1890 most of the range land under private ownership had been fenced, but it was decades later before some of the federal and state lands of western states were fenced.

With fencing came wire-cutting "wars" in Texas and elsewhere, brought on by men accustomed to using land without owning it and resentful of being shut out. Many big outfits fenced in vast tracts to which they had no right. But barbed wire came to stay. It revolutionized the whole range industry, cutting off trail driving and free grazing, making the improvement of breeds and the watering of the range by wells and tanks inevitable. It also aided in the development of stock-farming.

[W. P. Webb, *The Great Plains.*]

J. FRANK DOBIE

BARBED WIRE PATENT CASE, 143 U.S. 275 (1892), settled a long dispute as to patent rights for the invention of barbed wire between the assignees of Joseph Glidden and Jacob Haish. The latter claimed that exclusive rights could not be set up because there were various types of barbed wire in local use at the time the Glidden patent was granted. The court decided, however, in favor of this patent on the ground that Glidden had "taken the final step in the invention which has turned a failure into a [commercial] success. In the law of patents it is the last step that wins."

PHILLIPS BRADLEY

BARGEMEN, a term that was used interchangeably with keelboatmen, bargers, and keelers, and applied to men engaged in operating river boats that traveled upstream as distinct from flatboats. French and American bargemen employed on the Missouri and upper Mississippi rivers were also hunters and trappers. Most full-time bargemen worked on the lower Mississippi and the Ohio River and its tributaries. After 1820 they gradually disappeared as the steamboat, turnpike, and railroad took over transportation.

The bargemen were traditionally the roughest element in the West, prodigious drinkers, fighters, gamblers, pranksters, and workers, and the respectable elements along the rivers are said to have lived in terror of them. Their chief pleasuring resorts were New Orleans, Natchez, St. Louis, Shawneetown, and Louisville. They wore red shirts as a sort of occupational badge. A number of bargemen were famous in their day and Mike Fink, the most notorious and acknowledged kingpin, became the hero of a cycle of legends.

[Leland D. Baldwin, *The Keelboat Age on Western Waters;* Walter Blair and Franklin J. Meine, eds., *Half Horse, Half Alligator.*]

LELAND D. BALDWIN

BARNBURNERS, nickname of a faction of the Democratic party in New York State in the 1840's. They were first called Radicals and were the progressive element in the party. The name "Barnburner" was given them as early as 1843, and accepted by them at the state Democratic convention of 1847. It was based on the story of the Dutch farmer who was willing to burn his barn to get rid of the rats. Barnburners opposed further expenditures for canals, wanted a limitation on the state debt, and a direct state tax. They advocated a constitutional convention, and when it was called in 1846, they controlled it. In national affairs, they favored the Wilmot Proviso and opposed the extension of slavery. They seceded from the state convention of 1847 and from the 1848 Democratic national convention. They nominated Martin Van Buren for president and then united with the Free Soilers. This movement defeated Lewis Cass, the Democratic candidate. After this election they gradually returned to the Democratic party, but when the Republican party was formed most of the younger Barnburners joined, bringing elements of leadership and voting strength.

[H. D. A. Donovan, *The Barnburners*.]

AUGUSTUS H. SHEARER

BARN RAISING, a custom representative of the combination of cooperative labor and social festivity common in frontier days. The custom still survives in some sections.

Before the day set for the barn raising, carpenters cut the lumber. On the day of the great event, all the neighboring farmers, with their families, would assemble. In the morning all the men cooperated in erecting, with the simplest of tools, the framework of the barn. Prizes were sometimes offered for the exhibition of the greatest feat of strength. Dinner prepared by the combined efforts of the women present was then served. Later the occasion took on a more strictly social aspect. The program included games, athletic events, and a dance. Wrestling, jumping competition, and prizefighting were common.

Barn raisings have had most significance in sections of the Middle and West Central states where large structures were erected.

H. H. SHENK

BARNSTORMING. In 1815, at the instance of N. L. Usher of Lexington, Ky., a theatrical troup, which included Noah M. Ludlow, was led by Samuel Drake from Albany into the West. They often slept in barns and played in theaters that were little better than barns. William Turner, James Caldwell, Sol Smith, Mary Duff, and Eliza Riddle were among the barnstormers who brought contemporary farce and melodrama as well as Shakespeare and Sheridan to Cincinnati, St. Louis, Nashville, New Orleans, and many smaller frontier centers in the days before railroads. By analogy, itinerant fliers and stunt pilots about 1912–22 were also called barnstormers.

[William Carson, *The Theatre on the Frontier;* William Dunlap, *A History of the American Theatre*.]

HARVEY L. CARTER

BARNUM'S MUSEUM. In December 1841, P. T. Barnum bought Scudder's American Museum at Broadway and Ann Street, New York. It was enlarged as Barnum's American Museum, opening weekdays at sunrise with a single fee of twenty-five cents. The museum had on exhibit not only thousands of curios and relics but also living curiosities and "transient novelties" (such as the midget Charles Stratton, billed as "Gen. Tom Thumb"). There was also a lecture room seating 3,000, in which plays were given. Fire destroyed building and contents, July 13, 1865. Barnum's less-famous New American Museum, opened Nov. 13, 1865, on Broadway between Spring and Prince streets, was also burned (1868).

[G. S. Bryan, ed., *Struggles and Triumphs*, Barnum's autobiography.]

G. S. BRYAN

BARRIER FORTS, ATTACK ON (1856), the first use of armed force against China by the United States. On Nov. 15, during intermittent warfare between the Chinese and the British, Commander A. H. Foote, in the sloop *Portsmouth* below Canton, was fired upon by the four Barrier Forts. Foote retaliated on Nov. 20 by attacking the forts with a force of 287 sailors and marines, spiking the guns and blowing up the walls. The American loss was seven killed and twenty-two wounded. Although Secretary of State William L. Marcy criticized the action as hasty, Foote's aggressiveness secured greater safety for Americans trading in China.

[J. M. Hoppin, *Life of Andrew Hull Foote*.]

WALTER B. NORRIS

***BARRON* V. *BALTIMORE*,** 7 Peters 243 (1833). John Barron, owner of a wharf in Baltimore, Md., contended that the city, by grading and paving streets, had diverted streams from their natural courses toward his facility, causing increased sedimentation that rendered his water too shallow for business. The city, Barron argued, had deprived him of property without due process of law, violating the Fifth Amendment. The question was whether or not the specific amendment, and more generally the Bill of Rights, applied to state and local authority as well as to the central government. Chief Justice John Marshall dismissed the case in a unanimous opinion of the Supreme Court, commenting that the issue was "of great importance, but not much difficulty." The Constitution was established by the people "for their own government, and not for the government of the individual states," he affirmed. Reviewing the origins of the first ten amendments in the state ratifying conventions and the language of Article I, Sections 9 and 10, of the Constitution, Marshall concluded that the Bill of Rights restrained the federal government alone and was not binding on the states. Subsequent Supreme Court rulings have modified this decision.

[C. Herman Pritchett, *The American Constitution.*]

JOHN J. TURNER, JR.

BARTER, strictly, the exchange of goods for goods without using money, for example, the furs obtained from the Indians for beads, liquor, and firearms. As the people on the frontier usually lacked money they bartered horses, farms, tobacco, wool, and rice. Less strictly but more important, barter is involved in transactions carried on in terms of money which utilize goods for part of the payment. The farmer's wife trades butter and eggs for groceries. The accounts are kept in money, but actually it is an exchange of goods for goods. Many real-estate deals are of this nature. The old radio or auto is part payment for the new one. Many security transactions involve giving old securities for new ones. Clearinghouses of banks and stock exchanges involve a similar procedure. They offset the debits and the credits and pay only balances.

[B. M. Anderson, Jr., *The Value of Money.*]

JAMES D. MAGEE

BARTLETT'S EXPLORATIONS. As U.S. commissioner on the Mexican boundary question, John Russell Bartlett made explorations in 1850–53 into Texas, New Mexico, California, and adjacent Mexican states. Scientists accompanied the party, and the results were published with interesting illustrations in 1854.

[John Russell Bartlett, *Personal Narrative of Explorations and Incidents Connected With the United States and Mexican Boundary Commission.*]

CARL L. CANNON

BASCOM, FORT, established on the Canadian River in New Mexico in 1868 by Gen. George W. Getty acting under Gen. Philip H. Sheridan's orders. Its purpose was to protect the frontier against raids of the Cheyenne, Kiowa, Comanche, and Arapaho. It was abandoned in 1870.

[C. C. Rister, *Southwestern Frontier, 1856–1881.*]

CARL L. CANNON

BASEBALL was born in obscurity, and its early history is a mishmash of mythology, unsubstantiated facts, and rampant sentimentality. Actually almost nothing is known of its origins. While some authorities have attempted to trace its ancestry back to various bat-and-ball games played by children even before George Washington became president, others insist with unconscious irony that the national pastime was derived from the English games of cricket and rounders. All experts agree, however, that a game in which a bat, ball, and bases were used was being played throughout the United States during the early years of the 19th century. In New England it was called town ball, which Oliver Wendell Holmes reported that he played as an undergraduate at Harvard College in the 1820's. In other parts of the country, it was apparently a team game that had evolved from one old cat. In both instances the playing field was a square rather than a diamond, and the batter stood midway between what are now home plate and first base.

One of baseball's most enduring myths is that the game was "invented" by Abner Doubleday in Cooperstown, N.Y., in 1839, and the National Baseball Hall of Fame and Museum was built in Cooperstown in 1939 to commemorate this legend. But baseball scholars—and there are many of them—have conclusively demonstrated that Doubleday had nothing to do with the game's beginnings or development and that in all likelihood the first games bearing some resemblance to modern baseball were played in New York City rather than in Cooperstown. In any event, in 1845, a group of New York sportsmen—several years later A. G. Spaulding, one of the most famous of the early professional ballplayers, called them "gentlemen to the manner born" and "men of high taste"—organized the Knickerbocker Baseball Club and drew up a set of rules, among which were several provisions that would be readily recognized by present-day fans. For the next few years baseball was played almost exclusively in and around New York City by the Knickerbockers and other teams composed of gentlemen sportsmen. If democracy in sports is equated with mass participation, baseball in its formative years was undeniably an aristocratic game. In this respect its history is similar to that of every other popular American sport except basketball.

During the decade preceding the Civil War several baseball clubs were organized in the larger cities of the Northeast. Many of these clubs, moreover, were composed of players from all walks of life, for interclub competition put a premium on skills that had nothing to do with an individual's social background. By 1860 more than fifty clubs belonged to the National Association of Baseball Players; several played regular schedules and charged admission; and one, the Excelsiors of Brooklyn, in 1860 toured from Buffalo to Baltimore taking on—and beating—all comers. The Civil War broke up the clubs and their schedules, but long before Appomattox baseball had become the most popular game among the troops (at least those in the northern armies) behind the lines. The demobilized soldiers took the game back with them to their home towns. A short time after the war baseball was being played in most towns in the North and many in the South, and a year after the end of the war more than 200 clubs were members of the National Association. In 1865, however, the fielders still did not wear gloves, the catcher still caught the ball on the first bounce, and the pitcher still used an underhand delivery. It would be at least another twenty-five years before the game was standardized into the form in which it is played today.

Baseball, like most other American sports, soon became a business enterprise. Although amateur clubs had occasionally paid some of their stars, the first all-professional team was the Cincinnati Red Stockings, which in 1869 toured the nation without losing a game. In the next few years other professional teams were formed, but from the outset the success of professional baseball was jeopardized by repeated instances of bribery, the widespread gambling that attended almost every game, and the lack of any overall organization. The clubowners, however, were businessmen, and like other entrepreneurs of the period they quickly recognized the advantages of monopoly over unregulated competition and of organization over chaos. Accordingly, in 1876, teams from eight cities established the National League of Professional Baseball Clubs. This organization, which is still in existence, gradually eliminated competition, introduced regularly scheduled games, and formulated and codified most of the rules under which baseball is played today.

During the half-century after the formation of the National League, professional baseball became a complex, ingeniously organized industry that was dominated by the major league clubowners. The pattern was set as early as 1882, when the American Association was organized under rules set down by the National League. In subsequent years minor leagues were established with National League approval in every section of the country. The structure was completed with the formation of the American League in 1901 and the establishment of the World Series in 1903. The result was an economic pyramid that has fittingly come to be called organized baseball. At the top of the pyramid were the major league team owners; at the bottom, the lowest minor league teams. All were held together by rules governing the exchange and contracts of players, who on at least one occasion banded together and complained that they were "bought, sold and exchanged like sheep." In that no team or league could be formed without the sanction of the organization, this was a monopoly. And like all monopolies it fought off interlopers, defeating the National Brotherhood of Baseball Players in the Brotherhood War in 1889–90 and a group of financiers who in 1914–15 attempted to operate the Federal League as a third major league.

Since World War I no two individuals have had a more profound effect on both the game and business of baseball than George Herman ("Babe") Ruth and Kenesaw Mountain Landis. Babe Ruth, an alumnus of a Baltimore orphanage, grew up to hit more home runs (60) in a season (1927) than any other player (a record not surpassed until 1961) and to receive a higher salary than the president of the United States. Ruth was almost singlehandedly responsible for changing baseball from a defensive game characterized by the bunt, squeeze, steal, and hit-and-run, into an offensive contest in which strategy was subordinated to sheer power as represented by the home run. Landis, a U.S. district judge, was named commissioner of baseball by the clubowners in 1921 as a result of the "Black Sox" scandal in which eight members of the Chicago White Sox accepted bribes to throw the 1919 World Series. Landis, who was to serve as "czar" of baseball until his death in 1944, barred from organized baseball the Chicago players who had accepted bribes and restored public confidence in the game by the strict discipline he imposed on the players and management. During his long reign the clubowners introduced many innovations, such as night baseball, ladies' days, radio broadcasts of the games, and farm systems.

Aside from practice games in spring training, the two major leagues have confined their rivalry to the World Series and All-Star games. At the end of the regular season in 1903 Pittsburgh, the pennant winner in the National League, challenged Boston to a series in which Boston won, five games to three. In the following year the New York Giants, leaders in the National League, refused to meet the American League winner, but in 1905 both leagues agreed to a set of rules that both regularized and institutionalized the World Series. Despite wars, depressions, and acts of nature, the World Series has been played every autumn since 1905 with the championship going to the winner of four games, except in the years 1919–21 when the title went to the team that won five games. The All-Star Game, which is played in midseason between teams of the outstanding representatives of both leagues, was the brainchild of a Chicago sportswriter who inaugurated it as a promotional stunt to take place during the 1933 Century of Progress Exposition in Chicago. At least one All-Star Game has been played in various major league cities since then, except for 1945, with the players being generally selected by their fellow players or the fans. The managers of the preceding year's pennant winners serve as the managers of the respective All-Star teams and are given some voice in the choice of players. Although some iconoclasts have suggested interleague games be held on a regular basis during the season, this proposal has never appealed to a majority of the clubowners in the two leagues.

In recent years professional baseball has not been altogether immune to the forces that have reshaped so many other aspects of American life. Almost a decade before the 1954 Supreme Court decision requiring racial integration in the schools, Jackie Robinson broke the color line in organized baseball, playing for the Montreal Royals in the International League in 1946 and the Brooklyn Dodgers in the National League in following years. By 1960 black players had become commonplace in organized baseball. Baseball was also markedly affected by new patterns of recreation and leisure. Television, while making new fans, did not necessarily create new customers, and it all but wrecked the minor leagues. The omnipresent automobile made a stadium's parking lot as important as its concession for the sale of hot dogs (which, incidentally, were "invented" at a big-league baseball park), while it succeeded in luring away many fans who formerly would have been in the bleachers.

Despite changes in popular tastes and customs, professional baseball has remained not only a business but also a monopoly. After the formation of a new league was announced in 1959, organized baseball responded by absorbing some of its potential competitors and expanding each league from eight to ten teams. Meanwhile the owners continued their pursuit of profits by establishing new teams and by shifting franchises to areas where it was hoped there were more paying customers, a larger television audience, and local officials willing to build new baseball parks. By 1973 each league consisted of twelve teams spread from the Atlantic to the Pacific and from Montreal to Texas and Georgia. At the same time the owners had to contend with a players' union, which in April 1972 conducted a thirteen-day strike that forced the postponement of the regular opening of the season. The players, moreover, continued to agitate for an alteration in the "reserve clause," which bound a player to his club until he retired or was traded, and in 1972 the Supreme Court in the Curt Flood case suggested that either the owners or Congress should modify the clause.

Baseball is a participant as well as a spectator sport, and for generations the game has been played by Americans from all social classes on teams representing colleges, schools, towns, factories, and clubs. All American boys may not play—or even like—baseball, but it is virtually impossible for any American boy to grow up without knowing a great deal about the game. He learns it at the playground or in physical education classes at school; he is urged—more often than not by his parents—to play on a local Little League team; and he is bombarded with news of professional baseball by his friends, by newspapers, and by radio and television announcers. In the 1970's, American girls began to take a greater interest in the game and, despite some opposition, joined a number of Little League teams. In 1974 President Gerald Ford signed a law making it illegal to bar girls from Little League teams. It is true that fishing and bowling are more popular participant sports than baseball and that horse racing is a more popular spectator sport, but it is also true that baseball, if not the national pastime, is a national cult. The only other nations in which baseball enjoys a comparable status are Japan and some Latin-American countries.

Baseball has always had certain features that set it off from other American sports. No other game combines team play and individual virtuosity with such felicity, and few other games provide both players and spectators with such sharp contrasts between the predictable and the unexpected. Baseball, moreover, is preeminently a game of statistics, for virtually every bit of action in a baseball game, season, and career can be reduced to figures, all of which eventually end up in the record books. These statistics are endlessly fascinating to many fans and also serve to give baseball a kind of continuity that is unique in the history of American team sports. Baseball, with its emphasis on statistics, may even have made a contribution to American education, for it is likely that many boys first learned about percentages, not in grade school, but from their own efforts to figure out batting averages or the standing of a favorite major league team.

[Allison Danzig, *The History of Baseball;* Murray Olderman, *Nelson's 20th Century Encyclopedia of Baseball;* Lawrence S. Ritter, *The Glory of Their Times;* Harold Seymour, *Baseball: The Early Years,* and *Baseball: The Golden Age.*]

HAROLD C. SYRETT

BASKETBALL. The only major sport of wholly American origin, basketball was invented at the outset of winter 1891 by James Naismith, a physical education instructor at the Springfield, Mass., Young Men's Christian Association (YMCA) Training School. Gym classes having been forced indoors by cool weather, students balked at the dull exercises and gymnastics they were required to perform. Naismith, sympathetic with the students' fondness for outdoor warm-weather sports but cognizant that rugged games played indoors can damage both gymnasiums and people, devised a game that forbade running with the ball and tackling, discouraged high-velocity throwing, and allowed each participant to share in ball handling and scoring.

Naismith's first game was a success, even though only one basket was scored. Within months, basketball was incorporated into the programs of other YMCA's, which began to form leagues in 1893. Women quickly took up the game in Springfield and elsewhere. Smith College and Vassar College pioneered in college women's basketball, and Geneva College in Pennsylvania, Mount Union College in Ohio, and the University of Iowa first introduced the sport to male students in 1892. On Feb. 9, 1895, the first intercollegiate game on record took place between the Minnesota State School of Agriculture and Hamline University. Intercollegiate leagues began forming in New England and other eastern states in 1901, and other regions of the country followed shortly thereafter. Professional, amateur, and industrial teams took form as well, and the sport proved well suited to the intramural and competitive programs of public and private schools.

From its American origin, the game has become second only to soccer in worldwide popularity. The Fédération Internationale de Basketball Amateur (FIBA) was established in 1932 and has grown to include 132 national basketball federations. Basketball was introduced into the Olympic Games in 1936; the United States monopolized gold medals in men's basketball until Russia's disputed last-second championship victory over the United States in 1972.

Basketball's infancy was characterized by wide variations in rules and equipment as well as by more violent physical contact than Naismith had envisioned. In 1901 the Amateur Athletic Union (AAU) joined with the Springfield YMCA to form a basketball rules committee to control amateur and industrial teams. In 1908 college rules were drawn up by the National Collegiate Athletic Association (NCAA). The AAU, the YMCA, and the NCAA formed a Joint Basketball Rules Committee in 1915, initiating the process of standardizing the rules for all their members. The National Basketball Committee of the United States and Canada now meets annually to effect rules changes for collegiate, high school, AAU, and YMCA basketball. Special rules for women's basketball were first formulated by Clara Baer of Newcomb College in New Orleans, La., in 1895 and officially adopted in Springfield in 1899. Since 1970 rules changes have made women's basketball almost identical with men's, reflecting the increasing proficiency of women players.

While basketball has been esteemed for its purely recreational values—as attested by ubiquitous baskets in vacant lots and driveways and by thousands of intramural basketball programs for both boys and girls—the game has proved immensely popular as a competitive sport. The YMCA and the AAU sponsored leagues and tournaments from the earliest days of the game, and the AAU has held annual national tournaments since 1897 for men and since 1926 for women. Regional and statewide high school tournaments became commonplace early in the 20th century, and various promoters held national high school tournaments until the National Federation of State High School Athletic Associations banned them in 1934. No qualms, however, attended the development of nationwide collegiate tournaments in the 1930's. In fact, college basketball reached big-time status in that decade, when air travel began to facilitate intersectional games of wide public interest. In 1934 Ned Irish's successful promotion of a contest between Notre Dame and New York University in Madison Square Garden in New York City proved the financial possibilities of promoting college basketball on a large scale. Large public arenas were soon erected or opened to basketball, and colleges, especially after World War II, built larger facilities. The National Association of Intercollegiate Athletics established a tournament in 1937 that draws leading teams from small colleges. New York City sportswriters inaugurated the National Invitational Tournament in 1938, and in the following year the NCAA held the first of its national tournaments, the winner of which is usually recognized as the national champion. To provide tournament opportunity to smaller or less highly competitive schools, the NCAA since 1957 has sponsored a college-division tournament in addition to the university-division tournament.

Accompanying these developments were changes in the game itself that increased its spectator appeal. Intersectional play facilitated greater uniformity of rules and officiating and attracted national interest to some teams and players. Elimination in 1937 of the center jump after each basket greatly speeded up play, as did the introduction of the fast break, pioneered in the 1930's by Frank Keaney's Rhode Island State College "point-a-minute" teams. With increased public attention given to gifted college players, they soon began to be groomed for subsequent careers in professional basketball.

Professional teams appeared before 1900, as amateur teams found that revenue from ticket sales was greater than fees for renting gymnasiums. A professional National Basketball League was formed in 1898 but lasted only until 1903, manifesting the ephemeral nature of early professional leagues and many early professional teams. Players frequently played for several teams at once, the exclusive contract not becoming common until utilized by the Original Celtics, the most successful team of the 1920's. Other famous teams of those early years were the Troy Trojans, the Buffalo Germans, the New York Wanderers, and—in the 1930's—the New York Renaissance, an all-black team of outstanding ability. These and other teams enjoyed great success on barnstorming tours, a tradition still carried on with great success by the Harlem Globetrotters, organized in 1927. A new National Basketball League was formed in 1938 in the upper Midwest, and in 1946 several arena owners who had successfully sponsored college basketball games established the Basketball Association of America. These two rival leagues merged in 1949 to form the National Basketball Association. This league and the American Basketball Association, initiated in 1967, now dominate professional basketball, regularly replenishing their ranks by the organized drafting of outstanding college players.

[Zander Hollander, ed., *The Modern Encyclopedia of Basketball;* James Naismith, *Basketball: Its Origin and Development.*]

RICHARD R. BENERT

BASTOGNE, a town in the Belgian Ardennes, scene of an epic defense by American troops during the Battle of the Bulge in World War II. Controlling a vital road network, Bastogne was an obvious goal when German armies on Dec. 16, 1944, launched a surprise counteroffensive. The Allied commander, Gen. Dwight D. Eisenhower, rushed a combat command of the 10th Armored Division to Bastogne, followed by the 101st Airborne Division. A desperate delaying action by the 28th Infantry Division and part of the 9th Armored Division east of Bastogne enabled the 10th Armored's tanks to reach Bastogne ahead of the Germans and screen assembly of the airborne troops. Contingents of the Fifth Panzer Army encircled Bastogne the night of Dec. 20, but because the main German objective was to cross the Meuse River to the west, all-out attack was delayed. When the Germans on Dec. 22 demanded surrender, the American commander, Brig. Gen. Anthony C. McAuliffe, responded with derision: "Nuts!" That same day the U.S. Third Army began to drive to Bastogne's relief, and clearing weather on Dec. 23 enabled American planes to drop supplies. Although the Germans attacked strongly on Christmas Day, the defenses held, and on Dec. 26 tanks of the 4th Armored Division broke the siege. Heavy fighting nevertheless remained as the Germans for another week tried desperately to take the town. Reinforced by more troops of the Third Army, the defenses held, so that on Jan. 3, 1945, the Third Army was able to begin an offensive aimed at eliminating the "bulge" the Germans had created in American lines. The Belgians after the war erected a monument (*Le Madrillon*) at Bastogne in tribute to the American stand there and elsewhere in the Battle of the Bulge.

[H. M. Cole, *The Ardennes: Battle of the Bulge,* in *U.S. Army in World War II;* S. L. A. Marshall, *Bastogne: The First Eight Days.*]

CHARLES B. MACDONALD

BATAAN-CORREGIDOR CAMPAIGN. A few hours after the surprise attack on Pearl Harbor, Dec.

7, 1941, precipitating U.S. entry into World War II, Japanese air units from Taiwan attacked Clark Field to destroy the backbone of American air power in the Philippines. Major landings by Lt. Gen. Masaharu Homma's Fourteenth Army north and south on Manila on Dec. 22 and 24 caught defending forces under Gen. Douglas MacArthur in a trap. MacArthur was forced to retire into a defense zone on the Bataan peninsula. His retreat was skillful, and on Jan. 7, 1942, he reported, "I am on my main battle line, awaiting general attack." Homma obliged on Jan. 9. MacArthur's largely Filipino reservist army, backed up by a division of American and Filipino Scout regulars, retreated to a secondary line and then held, inflicting heavy losses, especially with artillery.

By February Homma's attack had been defeated, but MacArthur's men were gravely short of food, quinine to combat malaria, and supplies of all sorts. A tight Japanese blockade had isolated the Philippines. In early March, at President Franklin D. Roosevelt's order, MacArthur broke through the blockade by PT boat to escape to Australia. Homma attacked again on Apr. 3 and quickly cut through the starving defenders. On Apr. 9, 1942, Bataan surrendered; 79,500 men laid down their arms; and many hundreds perished afterward from weakness and brutal treatment by guards on the infamous death march to prison camps in central Luzon.

Corregidor, a fortress island in Manila Bay, held out for three weeks more under MacArthur's former subordinate, Gen. Jonathan M. Wainwright. Japanese artillery and aircraft bombarded the island, destroying most above-ground structures and forcing thousands to take shelter in tunnels, including the famous Malinta Tunnel, which contained the headquarters, hospital, and nurses' quarters. On the night of May 5–6 Japanese Fourth Division troops gained a foothold, inducing Wainwright to surrender the 16,000 defenders the next day. After the war Homma was tried as a war criminal in Manila and executed.

[J. H. Belote and W. M. Belote, *Corregidor: The Saga of a Fortress;* Stanley Falk, *Bataan: The March of Death;* Louis Morton, *The Fall of the Philippines.*]

JAMES H. BELOTE
WILLIAM M. BELOTE

BATEAU, a keelless, flatbottomed, sharp-ended craft, built of plank and propelled by oars, setting poles, or square sails and steered by oar or rudder. Large bateaux employed eighteen or twenty rowers and carried forty tons or more. Missouri bateaux were often called Mackinaw boats. Bateaux were superseded on the Ohio and Mississippi rivers before 1800 by keelboats.

[Leland D. Baldwin, *The Keelboat Age on Western Waters.*]

LELAND D. BALDWIN

BATHTUBS AND BATHING. The first mention of the use of bathtubs in the United States dates back to the early 1820's. The most advanced installation took place in Philadelphia between 1832 and 1837 when the Stephen Girard estate built a row of model houses. This was made possible by the water supply provided by the Schuylkill Water Works. The water rate for a bathtub in 1836 was $36.00 per year. In that year, despite an effort to ban them on sanitary grounds (their use was prohibited between Nov. 1 and Mar. 15 as a health measure), Philadelphia had 1,530 bathtubs. In 1845 Boston made their use unlawful except on the advice of a physician. Hartford, Providence, and Wilmington made heavy water charges for their use. By 1860 most first-class New York hotels had bathtubs.

The "rain bath" was introduced during the middle of the 19th century. In 1850 Harper and Gillespie of Philadelphia installed the first bathtub in the White House, for President Millard Fillmore. It was not replaced until President Grover Cleveland's administration in the early 1890's.

[William Chauncy Langdon, *Everyday Things in American Life;* Lawrence Wright, *Clean and Decent.*]

CAROL ARONOVICI

BATON ROUGE, capital city of Louisiana, located on the Mississippi River. Founded by the French about 1720 as an important military and trading post, it became English by the Treaty of Paris in 1763, Spanish in 1783, French again in 1800, and was claimed by Spain (along with West Florida) at the time of the Louisiana Purchase (1803). After the successful West Florida Revolution in 1810 (*see* Baton Rouge, Seizure of), it was annexed to the United States. In 1822 the city became the site of the U.S. military post and arsenal for the southwestern district, and remained such until 1877, except during a part of the Civil War. The city was made the state capital in 1849.

During the 20th century Baton Rouge became an industrial center. Standard Oil Company built a huge refinery in 1909, attracted by its river port that can accommodate ocean-going vessels and the nearby oilfields. Other industries built plants in the area, and the city was an important synthetic rubber center during World War II. The population increased 300 percent in 1940–50, reaching about 166,000 in 1970.

[Alcée Fortier, *History of Louisiana,* vol. I.]

WALTER PRICHARD

BATON ROUGE, BATTLE OF (Aug. 5, 1862). To regain control of the lower Mississippi, the Confederates planned to recapture Baton Rouge, La., then occupied by Union forces. Confederate Gen. John C. Breckinridge's land forces were to be supported by the ironclad ram, *Arkansas*. He attacked the town from the east and forced the Union troops to the levee where their gunboats protected them. Unsupported by the *Arkansas,* which had broken down, Breckinridge withdrew.

[Alcée Fortier, *A History of Louisiana.*]

W. B. HATCHER

BATON ROUGE, SEIZURE OF. Baton Rouge, on the Mississippi River, was in a portion of Spanish West Florida (between the Mississippi and the Perdido) to which the United States mistakenly asserted title as a part of the Louisiana Purchase, but of which it had not attempted to take possession. In September 1810, American settlers in West Florida seized Baton Rouge, organized a convention, declared their independence of Spain, and invited the United States to annex their territory. President James Madison disregarded their pretensions to independence, but promptly gave orders for the occupation of West Florida as territory belonging to the United States, and Baton Rouge was occupied by American troops early in December.

[I. J. Cox, *The West Florida Controversy.*]

JULIUS W. PRATT

BATTELLE MEMORIAL INSTITUTE was set up in Columbus, Ohio, by the will of steel industry heir Gordon Battelle, who wanted to encourage creative research and invention, primarily in the field of metallurgy. The institute was incorporated in 1925 and began operations in 1929 with an endowment of about $3.5 million from the estates of Battelle and his mother. Unlike that at the earlier Mellon Institute, research at Battelle was carried out exclusively by the staff, on behalf of private industry. Battelle rather than Mellon, then, provided the model for the modern nonprofit contract research institute. Research ideas generally grew out of ideas that needed to be made commercially feasible. Battelle's endowment permitted a certain number of institute-sponsored projects, but most research was undertaken for specific firms and, especially later, governments. When helping to develop xerography gave the institute a share in the profits of that process, its resources increased greatly. After World War II branches were set up in Geneva, Frankfurt, and, later, Richland, Wash., and the institute thrived on the new prestige of research. Work in all of the sciences was developed, and by the late 1960's Battelle's annual contract total was well over $100 million.

[George A. W. Boehm and Alex Groner, *The Battelle Story: Science in the Service of Mankind.*]

JOHN C. BURNHAM

BATTERY, the 21-acre area lying at the extreme southern tip of Manhattan Island at the confluence of the Hudson and East rivers. It was originally fortified by the Dutch, and in 1693 the British governor, Benjamin Fletcher, ordered the installation of a supplementary battery of cannon on the rocky island some 300 yards offshore. Construction of the large fort that dominates the park was begun in 1808 and after the War of 1812 it was named Fort Clinton in honor of DeWitt Clinton, mayor of New York City. The island was connected to the mainland by a drawbridge.

By 1822, when the property was ceded to New York City, landfill had completely connected the two areas. The following year the fort was converted into an auditorium—Castle Garden. The Marquis de Lafayette was received at Castle Garden on his return to America in 1824 and in 1850 Jenny Lind made her American debut there. The surrounding park had become one of New York's most popular recreation areas.

From 1855 to 1890 the building served as the immigration station for New York. When the facility was moved to Ellis Island the New York Aquarium was installed. During the construction of the Brooklyn-Battery Tunnel, which passes under the park, the aquarium was moved to Coney Island.

The fort was renamed Castle Clinton National Monument in 1946 and restored to its 19th-century appearance. The Battery is the embarkation point for Liberty Island, site of the Statue of Liberty, and the park contains memorials to the poet Emma Lazarus, the explorer Giovanni da Verrazano, and Americans killed in Europe during World War II.

[Rodman Guilder, *The Battery;* Nathan Silver, *Lost New York.*]

BATTERY, ELECTRIC. The electrochemical battery, first described by the Italian scientist Alessandro Volta in 1800, proved to be one of the seminal discoveries in the history of electrical science. It not only provided scientists—among them, Humphry Davy and Michael Faraday—with an important new investigative tool but also became a key element in the creation of the first major electrical industry, the telegraph industry. Important contributions to the improvement and application of the battery during the first half of the nineteenth century were made by Robert Hare and Joseph Henry. During the 1820's Hare, a Philadelphia chemist, developed batteries of improved efficiency and high current capacity, at the time variously described as calorimotors, galvanic deflagrators, and quantity batteries. Henry used the quantity battery during the 1830's in laboratory experiments with relays, powerful electromagnets, and remote signal circuits. During the 1840's, Samuel Morse, Leonard Gale, and Alfred Vail developed the Henry apparatus into a successful commercial telegraph system. Attempts were made, particularly by Thomas Davenport and Charles G. Page, to develop battery-powered electric propulsion units for boats or land vehicles, but by 1850 there was a general consensus that battery-driven motors could not compete economically with the steam engine.

A new phase of battery development began in the second half of the 19th century following the introduction of the rechargeable lead-plate storage battery and the direct-current dynamo, which could economically recharge the new type of cell. Large quantities of storage batteries, also known as secondary batteries or accumulators, were employed in electric power and lighting systems because of their ability to store energy at times of light load and release it during peak load conditions. Significant American contributions to the improvement of storage batteries were made by Charles Brush in the 1880's and by Thomas Edison around 1900. The Edison battery used iron and nickel with an alkaline electrolyte, achieving more than twice the storage capacity of the older lead-plate type. The battery was brought into the daily lives of millions of Americans for the first time when the storage battery began to be used to power automobile starter motors and headlights and when battery-powered radio receivers appeared just after World War I. The annual value of storage batteries manufactured in the United States reached almost $100 million by 1925.

Since World War II there has been a pronounced trend toward more diverse application of electric batteries—in household appliances and toys, for example, as well as in the ubiquitous transistor radio receiver. In the 1970's concern about the air pollution caused by automobiles using internal-combustion engines has led to renewed interest in battery-powered automobiles as a possible replacement. The advent of more exotic batteries, such as solid-state solar cells and fuel cells, has already resulted in the design of compact and lightweight power systems for communications satellites and space capsules. These developments have not yet had much impact at the consumer level, but the fuel cell has been widely discussed as a promising power source for electric cars.

[Percy Dunsheath, *A History of Electrical Engineering.*]

James E. Brittain

BATTLE FLEET CRUISE AROUND THE WORLD, undertaken in 1907–09 by order of President Theodore Roosevelt as a demonstration of national strength. The fleet, consisting of sixteen American battleships, sailed from Hampton Roads, Va., bound for San Francisco, on Dec. 16, 1907, under the command of Rear Admiral Robley D. Evans, by way of Rio de Janeiro and the Strait of Magellan. On May 6, 1908, the fleet reached San Francisco where, on May 9, Evans was relieved by Rear Admiral Charles M. Thomas. Five days later Thomas turned over his command to Rear Admiral Charles S. Sperry, who sailed from San Francisco for Hawaii on July 7. The squadron visited New Zealand, Australia, the Philippines, China, and Japan, finally returning by way of the Suez Canal and the Mediterranean. It reached Hampton Roads on Feb. 22, 1909, after an absence of 434 days, of which 190 were spent in actual cruising. A month had been spent in Magdalena Bay in target practice and another month in Manila Bay in battle practice. The battle fleet visited every continent on the globe, sailed over every navigable ocean, and crossed the equator four times. The officers of the fleet were entertained and feted by the rulers of nearly all countries visited, and naval greetings were exchanged with the warships of fourteen different nations.

[R. D. Evans, *An Admiral's Log;* Franklin Matthews, *Back to Hampton Roads,* and *With the Battle Fleet.*]

Louis H. Bolander

"BATTLE HYMN OF THE REPUBLIC," one of the most popular and inspiring of American patriotic hymns, written in 1861 by Julia Ward Howe. In the autumn of 1861 Mrs. Howe and her husband were in Washington, D.C., interested in hospital work under the Sanitary Commission. They had been outside the city on a mission in connection with their work and were returning in a carriage through an exceedingly dark night. They met a regiment of troops which was marching up the road and singing the familiar song known as "John Brown's Body," the music of which was written by William Steffe about 1852. Mrs. Howe remarked as the soldiers were passing that these were poor words to be set to such a glorious tune. Mrs. Howe continued to turn the matter over in her mind and awakened from her sleep late that night. She arose and wrote down the entire hymn, beginning with the words "Mine eyes have seen the glory of the coming of the Lord."

The poem was printed in the *Atlantic Monthly* for February 1862. It at once became popular and spread over the entire country. Not only is it in all collections of patriotic American songs but is included in the hymnals of a number of churches as well.

[J. E. Richards and M. H. Elliott, *Julia Ward Howe*, vol. I.]

WILLIAM STARR MYERS

BATTLE MONUMENTS COMMISSION, AMERICAN. *See* **Federal Agencies.**

BATTLESHIPS. *See* **Warships.**

BATTLESHIPS, DUMMY. On Feb. 24, 1863, a scow with turret of tar-smeared barrel staves, wooden guns, clay furnace, pork barrel funnel, and ludicrous mottoes painted across its false paddle box was floated down the Mississippi River by federal seamen, and caused the Confederates below Vicksburg to destroy the newly captured ironclad *Indianola*. A similar dummy released on a flood tide, Feb. 20, 1865, drew fire from Confederate batteries along Cape Fear River for several hours. The success of these facetious experiments was largely due to the sensation created by the monitor type of battleship.

[Richard S. West, Jr., *The Second Admiral, A Life of David Dixon Porter*.]

RICHARD S. WEST, JR.

BATTS-FALLAM EXPEDITION, first recorded crossing of the Appalachian Mountains, the expedition was sent out from Fort Henry (site of Petersburg, Va.) in 1671 by Col. Abraham Wood for the "finding out the waters on the other side of the mountains in order to discovery of the South sea." The leader was Capt. Thomas Batts, and the expedition was journalized by Robert Fallam. The party of five, including an Appomattoc Indian chief, set out Sept. 1, crossed the Blue Ridge and the Allegheny range, and pushed down the valley of the New River to where that stream reaches the line of West Virginia, Sept. 17.

[C. W. Alvord and Lee Bidgood, *The First Explorations of the Trans-Allegheny Region*.]

SAMUEL C. WILLIAMS

BAYARD-CHAMBERLAIN TREATY, drafted by a joint commission at Washington, D.C., Feb. 15, 1888, to clarify the respective powers and rights of Great Britain and the United States in the waters of Newfoundland and the adjacent provinces. The Treaty of Washington, extending valuable privileges to American fishermen in Canadian waters, had been abrogated as of July 1, 1885, and more stringent and somewhat obscure provisions of the Convention of 1818 were in effect. Rigorous enforcement by the Canadian authorities, seizure and forfeiture of U.S. vessels, retaliatory legislation, and jingoistic fulminations by press and politicians had created a situation that threatened peaceful relations. The new treaty provided for a joint commission to define American rights in Canadian waters, recognized exclusive Canadian jurisdiction in bays whose outlets were less than six miles in width, remedied several minor American grievances, and promised further concessions should the United States remove tariff duties on Canadian fish. The Senate rejected the treaty on Aug. 21, 1888, but more than twenty years later, when the protracted fisheries dispute was arbitrated at The Hague, the substance of several of its more significant provisions appear in the award that the tribunal rendered against American claims.

[Joseph I. Doran, *Our Fishery Rights in the North Atlantic;* Allan Nevins, *Grover Cleveland*.]

W. A. ROBINSON

***BAYARD* V. *SINGLETON*,** North Carolina Superior Court (1787). This case is important because it is the first reported decision under a written constitution overruling a law as unconstitutional. The defendant moved for dismissal of the case according to an act of the legislature which required the courts to dismiss, upon affidavit, suits against persons holding forfeited Tory (enemy alien) estates. The court overruled the motion and declared that the constitution of the state gives every man a right to a decision concerning property by jury trial. If the legislature could thus alter or repeal the constitution it would thereby destroy its own existence, and might even take away, summarily, one's life.

[H. T. Lefler, *North Carolina History Told by Contemporaries.*]

ROBERT W. WINSTON

Grand Ohio Company, or Walpole Company, in which the Indiana land grant was merged, but Wharton excluded John Baynton and George Morgan, thus incurring their bitter enmity. The outbreak of the Revolution caused this project to collapse. (*See also* Vandalia Company.)

[A. T. Volwiler, *George Croghan and the Westward Movement, 1741–1782.*]

JULIAN P. BOYD

BAYNTON, WHARTON AND MORGAN, a firm of Philadelphia merchants that virtually monopolized the rich western trade at the close of the French and Indian War and that by its contacts in Philadelphia, Lancaster, Pittsburgh, Kaskaskia, and London exploited the West in one of the most significant commercial enterprises of the day. Before the legal opening of Indian trade, the firm sent the first cargo of goods westward (1765) under protection of passes by George Croghan, deputy superintendent for Indian affairs. This premature attempt to capture Indian trade infuriated the Pennsylvanian frontiersmen known as Black Boys, who attacked the pack train and destroyed the shipment. Soon, however, the firm had 600 pack horses and wagons on the road between Philadelphia and Pittsburgh and some 300 boatmen on the Ohio River.

Its unscrupulous business methods, Gen. Thomas Gage's curtailment of Indian trading posts and his restrictions on the Indian department, together with the collapse of trade due to illicit French suppliers and the growing competition of another Philadelphia firm, David Franks and Company, combined to cause a sharp decline in its fortunes during 1767. The company entered into voluntary receivership and withdrew completely from the Illinois trading venture in 1772.

To recoup its losses and those of the "Suffering Traders" of 1763, Baynton, Wharton and Morgan, with the firm of Simon, Trent, Levy and Franks, organized the Indiana Company to secure land grants for losses incurred through Indian attacks. Samuel Wharton and William Trent represented their respective firms. Sir William Johnson's ingenious handling of the Indians at Fort Stanwix in 1768 resulted in the Six Nations ceding to this company 2.5 million acres of land, now a part of West Virginia. Immediate objections arose, royal confirmation was withheld, and Wharton and Trent were sent to London to negotiate for the Indiana Company. Here the claims of other groups brought about the formation in 1769 of the

BAY OF PIGS INVASION (Apr. 17, 1961), the abortive attempt by Cuban exiles—organized, financed, and led by the U.S. Central Intelligence Agency (CIA)—to overthrow the revolutionary regime of Premier Fidel Castro in Havana. The landing by the 1,453 men of Brigade 2506 on the swampy southwestern coast of Cuba turned within seventy-two hours into a complete disaster as the Castro forces captured 1,179 of the invaders and killed the remaining 274. For the United States and for President John F. Kennedy, who had authorized the operation in his third month in the White House, the Bay of Pigs became a bitter political defeat as well as a monumental failure in a large-scale intelligence enterprise. The invasion is also believed to have inspired the Soviet Union to install missiles with nuclear warheads in Cuba the following year, leading to what constituted the most dangerous postwar crisis between Washington and Moscow.

The plans for the Bay of Pigs were conceived by the CIA during 1960, toward the end of the Eisenhower administration, on the theory—proved by events to have been totally erroneous—that a landing by the exiles' brigade would touch off a nationwide uprising against Castro. This was the essential intelligence miscalculation that most of the key participants subsequently acknowledged.

To prepare for the invasion, the CIA trained the force in secret camps in Guatemala for nearly six months. But long before the landing, it was widely known in the Cuban community in Florida (and, presumably, the information was also available to Castro agents) that such a landing was in the offing. This was the second major intelligence failure: the inability to preserve secrecy. Finally, the invasion failed because Kennedy, as he had forewarned his aides, refused to provide U.S. air support for the brigade. Castro's aircraft easily disposed of the exiles' tiny air force and proceeded to sink the invasion ships and cut down the men holding the Bay of Pigs beachhead.

The final act came in December 1962, twenty

months later, when Castro released the 1,179 Bay of Pigs prisoners in exchange for $53 million worth of medical supplies and other goods.

[Haynes Johnson, *The Bay of Pigs;* Tad Szulc and Karl E. Meyer, *The Cuban Invasion.*]

TAD SZULC

BAYONNE DECREE. *See* **Napoleon's Decrees.**

BAYOU, a term used throughout the South, but especially in the Mississippi River delta region of Louisiana and Mississippi. Numerous bays, creeks, sloughs, and small elongated lakes in the delta—and even the irrigation canals for the rice fields of Texas, Arkansas, and Louisiana—are commonly referred to as bayous; but the word is more specifically used to distinguish the sluggish or stagnant offshoots of rivers that meander through the marshes or alluvial lowlands. Rivers in the level delta area tend to wind back and forth, and in times of flood the heavy flow of water cuts into the bank at each curve until eventually it breaks through and creates a new channel for the river. A crescent of stagnant brown water is thus left isolated as a bayou beside the new bed of the stream. Most etymologists think the term probably came from the Choctaw Indian word *bayuk* ("small sluggish stream"); others insist that it is derived from the French word *boyau* ("gut or channel").

Many of the larger bayous are historically important: Bayou Pierre near Jackson, Miss., was familiar to thousands traveling the Natchez Trace as a major obstacle to be crossed at Grindstone Ford; and Bayou Barataria was frequently used by the famed pirate Jean Laffite. During the Civil War the Confederates used the bayous flowing into the Gulf of Mexico to run weapons, ammunition, medical supplies, and other contraband goods through the Union blockade.

The natural beauty of the bayous, with their banks lined with moss-draped live oaks, was appreciated by many antebellum planters, who built colonnaded mansions close by. In fact, because boats were virtually the only means of transportation, almost all civilization in early Louisiana seemed to be associated in one way or another with the bayous. In modern times the recreational potential of the bayous has been recognized in Louisiana, where they have been incorporated into some of the state parks.

ROBERT W. TWYMAN

BAYOU TECHE EXPEDITION, a Union raid directed by Gen. Nathaniel Banks in April and May 1863, from Brashear City (Berwick Bay) to Alexandria, La., on Red River, to disperse the Confederate state government at Opelousas and thus to prevent Confederate reinforcements being sent from that quarter to Vicksburg, then besieged by Gen. Ulysses S. Grant.

[A. Fortier, *History of Louisiana,* vol. IV.]

WALTER PRICHARD

BAY PATH, a trail from the Connecticut River to Massachusetts Bay at or near Boston. Conversely, the same trail from the bay to the Connecticut River would be the Connecticut Path. Some writers reserve the name Bay Path for such a trail in Massachusetts and that of Connecticut Path for one in Connecticut. There seems no question that from 1648 there was a route known as the New Path westward through Weston, Sudbury, Marlborough, Worcester, Brookfield, and Brimfield to Springfield. Similarly, there is no question that after 1683 another path ran southwestward from the vicinity of Boston to Woodstock, Conn., and thence westward to Hartford. Obviously the New Path was not used by the earliest settlers in the Connecticut Valley, but some claim that the second or southern route was the Old Path used by the Thomas Hooker party in 1636 and by the other early colonists. There is, however, considerable evidence that the Old Path followed a middle route coinciding in part with the eastern section of the southern path and with the portion of the New Path west of Brimfield. Competent recent authorities have tended to accept this middle route as the original Old Path used in the 1630's. But the evidence is incomplete and not incontrovertible. Nor is the existence of the second route earlier than 1683 adequately supported by contemporary evidence. It is even possible that the original Old Path did not follow exactly any one of the three routes. All three routes assume a path between Springfield and Hartford which would have been on the east bank of the Connecticut River at least as far south as East Windsor.

[Levi B. Chase, *The Bay Path and Along the Way.*]

GEORGE MATTHEW DUTCHER

BAY PSALM BOOK, a hymnal used in Massachusetts Bay Colony, and the earliest book known to have been printed within the present boundaries of the United States. Begun in 1639 and finished in 1640, it was printed in Cambridge, Mass., as *The Whole Booke of Psalmes* by Stephen Daye, the first printer of the English colonies. Eleven copies are known to exist, of which only four are perfect.

[C. Evans, *American Bibliography;* Zoltán Haraszti, *The Enigma of the Bay Psalm Book.*]

CARL L. CANNON

BEALL'S RAID ON LAKE ERIE. On Sept. 19, 1864, John Beall, a Confederate soldier recently made an acting master in the navy, seized the steamer *Philo Parsons* on Lake Erie in an attempt to capture the Union revenue cutter *Michigan* and free Confederate prisoners on Johnson's Island, at the entrance to Sandusky Bay, Ohio. The plot failed when Beall's men revolted. He was captured three months later near Buffalo, N.Y., and tried on charges of being a spy, found guilty, and executed.

[Isaac Markens, *President Lincoln and the Case of John Yates Beall;* F. J. Shepard, "The Johnson's Island Plot," *Publications of the Buffalo Historical Society* (1906).]

BEAR FLAG REVOLT (1846) climaxed a decade of suspicion and jealousy between the Anglo-Californians of the Sacramento Valley and the Mexican authorities. Unlike the American residents of Monterey and Los Angeles, many of whom were closely connected with prominent California families through business relations, friendship, or marriage, the American residents of northern central California formed a community by themselves. Restive under Mexican rule and overanxious to assert their "racial superiority," they had a deep-seated fear of their fate if the California authorities should get them completely under control.

Some color was indeed given to this fear by the treatment accorded the fur traders Jedediah S. Smith and James O. Pattie in the previous decade and especially by the deportation in 1840 of Isaac Graham and some forty of his friends. Accordingly it is not surprising that, when the settlers learned of the Hawk's Peak episode and John C. Frémont's withdrawal from California in March 1846, they should have believed the rumors that the government planned to seize and expel all foreigners in the province.

Uneasiness gave place to alarm when the news came (later proved false) that 250 Californians were advancing on Sacramento. The Americans immediately repaired to Frémont's quarters at the Marysville Buttes, where, in the middle of May, he had encamped on his return from Oregon. This much criticized defiance of the local authorities by Frémont was declared by him to be "the first step in the conquest of California." The next step was the seizure, early in June, by Ezekial Merritt and a dozen other Americans of a large band of government horses which Gen. José Castro, military commandant at Monterey, had obtained from Gen. M. G. Vallejo at Sonoma and which were being driven to San José by way of Sutter's Fort. This was an act of war and it was decided that the third step must be the capture of Sonoma, the chief stronghold of the Californians north of the Bay Region. The actual capture of the quiet little pueblo at early dawn, June 14, 1846, was a rather ludicrous affair. After a scene of no little confusion and considerable imbibing of Vallejo's wine, simple articles of capitulation were arranged and signed.

Then followed the erection of the Republic of California under the leadership of William B. Ide. To signalize it, William Todd designed a flag from a piece of unbleached cloth five feet long and three feet wide. Facing a red star was a grizzly bear, which gave both the flag and the republic its familiar name. A proclamation setting forth the justification and purposes of the revolution was prepared; but before the new government could get under way, Commodore John D. Sloat reached Monterey, claiming California for the United States. On July 9, 1846, the American flag replaced the bear flag.

[R. G. Cleland, *A History of California: The American Period;* W. B. Ide, *Who Conquered California?*]

OSGOOD HARDY

BEAR HUNTERS AND BEAR STORIES. When Meriwether Lewis and William Clark in 1806 returned from their historic expedition into the Far West, they published to the world, along with other wonders, accounts of the grizzly bear and its ferocity. A naturalist named it *Ursus horribilis*—and in hunters' stories the grizzly has ever since been horrible. The grizzly is especially ferocious when cornered, and often imagines itself cornered when it is not. Stories like that of Hugh Glass and his hand-to-hand fight with a grizzly became an enduring part of American lore. The fights between bulls and grizzlies arranged by early Californians were an American counterpart to English bearbaiting but more heroic.

The discovery of the grizzly increased the fame of the more widespread black bear, known indeed to have killed a few men, though the "bear hug" is a fable. Bear hunters became folk heroes as distinct as keelboatmen or Indian fighters. In 1827 Davy Crockett of Tennessee was sent to Congress almost purely on his reputation as a "bar hunter"; he killed 105 bears in one season. Empowered by mother wit, he so narrated his exploits with bears that his autobiography remains an American classic. Mighty hunters like Wade Hampton of South Carolina followed Crockett. The tall tale has had no richer subject than the bear.

Although by 1925 the grizzly came dangerously close to extinction, it lives on in national parks, in the paintings of western artists like Frederic Remington and Charles M. Russell, in many books, and in folk tales.

[Joaquin Miller, *True Bear Stories;* John G. Neilhardt, *The Song of Hugh Glass;* Theodore Roosevelt, *The Wilderness Hunter;* William H. Wright, *The Grizzly Bear.*]

J. Frank Dobie

BEAR PAW MOUNTAINS, BATTLE AT (Oct. 1–5, 1877). At the end of their long campaign, which began in Idaho, June 1877, the Nez Perce under Chief Joseph were surrounded by Gen. Nelson A. Miles's command in the Bear Paw Mountains of northern Montana. After a brave resistance, Joseph surrendered, ending the Nez Perce War.

Paul I. Wellman

BEAR RIVER, site in California of gold deposits discovered in July 1848, some six months after the strike at John Sutter's mill. Some of the most picturesque mining camps in California collected on the river and its tributaries, including Red Dog, Dutch Flat, and You Bet.

[O. C. Coy, *Gold Days.*]

Carl L. Cannon

BEAR RIVER, BATTLE OF (Jan. 29, 1863). Utah Indians, among the more peaceful of American Indians, had occasionally preyed upon Mormon settlers and emigrants on the Overland mail route. The hostilities were a result of encroachment by whites on Indian tribal lands. To subdue and control the Indians Col. Patrick E. Connor, commander of federalized California volunteers sent to Camp Douglas (Salt Lake City) in 1862, led his troops to Bear River. There, with scarcely 200 effectives, he fought four hours against 300 well-armed Indians, smashing their villages, capturing their animals and stores, and killing over 200 of them. His own loss was fifteen killed and forty-eight wounded.

Robert S. Thomas

BEAUBIEN LAND CLAIM, an effort to homestead a portion of the Fort Dearborn military reservation at Chicago. The claimant, Jean Baptiste Beaubien, had long lived on the tract as a trader, and in 1835 he entered some seventy-five acres of it at the land office. The commandant ignored this title, and a prolonged legal contest ended in its rejection by the U.S. Supreme Court in 1839. Immense wealth hinged upon the issue, and the contest aroused intense local public interest.

[Henry H. Hurlbut, *Chicago Antiquities.*]

M. M. Quaife

BEAUFORT, city in South Carolina, founded by the British in 1711 on Port Royal Island. First visited in 1521 by the Spanish, early attempts (all unsuccessful) at settlement were made by the French (1562), English (1670), and Scots (1684). Beaufort was the second permanent settlement in South Carolina.

The city remains a port of entry. Preservation of colonial buildings and other historic landmarks have made Beaufort a tourist center. The population in 1970 was just under 10,000.

[H. A. M. Smith, "Beaufort, the Original Plan and Early Settlers," *South Carolina Historical Magazine,* vol. 9 (1908).]

BEAUHARNOIS, FORT, a French post and Jesuit mission, erected in 1727 on Lake Pepin in Minnesota to keep the Sioux from attacking France's new line of communication between Lake Superior and the West, and to prevent the Sioux from allying with the Fox Indians. It was abandoned about 1728.

Grace Lee Nute

BEAVER DAM CREEK, BATTLE OF. *See* **Mechanicsville, Battle of.**

BEAVER DAMS, BATTLE OF (June 24, 1813). Col. C. G. Boerstler with a detachment of about 600 men left Fort George, near Niagara, N.Y., the evening of June 23, under orders to march by way of Queenston, Ont., to the De Cou house above Beaver Dams to disperse James Fitzgibbon's British irregulars and Indians. Fitzgibbon was warned of Boerstler's advance and ambushed the Americans on the

24th a little east of Beaver Dams. After two hours of fighting, the Americans were forced to surrender.

[Louis L. Babcock, *The War of 1812 on the Niagara Frontier*.]

ROBERT W. BINGHAM

BEAVER HATS. America produced quantities of beaver fur, but men's beaver hats were all imported until about the middle of the 17th century. Virginia in 1662 sought to stimulate manufacture by offering a subsidy of ten pounds of tobacco for every good hat made from native fur or wool. Once begun, hat manufacture in America grew rapidly. By 1731 the hatmakers of London were complaining to Parliament that New England and New York were producing 10,000 hats annually and exporting them not only to British possessions, but to Spain, Portugal, and the West Indies. In 1732 Parliament forbade American makers to export hats, even among the American colonies. Seven years' apprenticeship was also required, and no Afro-Americans were permitted to work at the trade. New England calmly ignored or evaded the law, which remained in force until the revolutionary war. Silk hat manufacture began in earnest about 1835 and the beaver hat diminished in popularity.

[J. Leander Bishop, *History of American Manufactures, 1608–1860;* H. H. Manchester, *Sixty Centuries of Hatmaking*.]

ALVIN F. HARLOW

BEAVER MONEY. Lack of currency in the Pacific Northwest led to the private coinage of gold dust into coins called beaver money because a beaver was pictured on each coin. They were also stamped with their weight, the initials of the partners of the issuing company, and the date 1849. These illegal but useful coins quickly disappeared from circulation because they contained 8 percent more gold than the U.S. coins.

[Charles H. Carey, *A General History of Oregon Prior to 1861*.]

ROBERT MOULTON GATKE

BEAVER TRADE. *See* **Fur Trade.**

BECKNELL'S EXPEDITIONS. William Becknell, sometimes referred to as the "father of the Santa Fe Trail," left Franklin, Mo., for Santa Fe, N.Mex., June 10, 1821, on a trading expedition. He is believed by most authorities to be the first American merchant to reach the New Mexican capital after the establishment of Mexican independence. After a profitable trade he returned to Missouri in January 1822. His success was responsible for the rapid development of commercial relations with Santa Fe. Later in the year he made a second trip in which he departed from the regular trail along the Arkansas River by crossing the Cimarron River, thus tracing out the Santa Fe Trail. This trip was also notable because wagons were used on the plains for the first time.

[William Becknell, *Journal of Santa Fe Expedition, 1821;* W. J. Ghent, *Early Far West*.]

CARL L. CANNON

BEDFORD, FORT. Fort Raystown, Pa., built about 1750 by Col. John Armstrong as a frontier defense, was in July 1757 much enlarged and strengthened by Col. Henry Bouquet for the use of Gen. John Forbes's expedition during the French and Indian War. Here Bouquet was joined in September by Forbes and the Virginia troops under Col. George Washington for the advance along the Forbes Road, which began four miles westward. Rechristened Fort Bedford (1759), it was the principal depot for supplies and troops between Carlisle and Fort Pitt. The fort withstood a six weeks' siege during Pontiac's conspiracy, but in 1769 was bloodlessly yielded to James Smith's Black Boys. Dilapidated, it was abandoned before the Revolution. A marker has been placed at the site of the fort.

E. DOUGLAS BRANCH

BEDFORD-STUYVESANT, a section of the borough of Brooklyn in New York City, is the core area of the largest contiguous Afro-American ghetto in the United States. Most of the 655,000 blacks residing in Brooklyn in 1970 lived in Bedford-Stuyvesant and the adjoining areas of Fort Greene, Crown Heights, Brownsville, and East New York. Although lacking precise, legal boundaries, Bedford-Stuyvesant has traditionally been bounded by Washington Avenue, Myrtle Avenue, Broadway, and Atlantic Avenue.

During the late 19th century, when the area became densely populated, Bedford and Stuyvesant were considered neighboring but distinct sections centered upon local avenues of the same names. Both were overwhelmingly white and middle class. After World War I, blacks began moving into the neighborhood in considerable numbers. Although it was still predominantly white and middle class in 1930, Bedford-Stuyvesant was attracting more and more black settlers. During succeeding decades this trend was accelerated by the availability of better and cheaper housing than in Harlem, which already was heavily populated; the linkage of the area to Manhattan by subway; the unsuitability of the section's large single-family houses for families without servants and their conversion to multiple-dwelling units; the aging of the area's original inhabitants and the departure of their children; and the internal dynamism of ghetto expansion. By 1950 more than half the section's population was black and 61 percent of Brooklyn's blacks were concentrated there. Subsequently the black population expanded into adjacent sections.

The political success of black Americans in Bedford-Stuyvesant began with the election of Bertram Baker to the state assembly in 1948, but progress was slow. Shirley Chisholm's election to the U.S. House of Representatives in 1968 represented a major advance, although Brooklyn blacks remained underrepresented.

[Harold X. Connolly, *A Ghetto Grows in Brooklyn.*]

HAROLD X. CONNOLLY

BEDINI RIOTS, public demonstrations against the papal nuncio, Monsignor Gaetano Bedini, on Dec. 31, 1853, and Jan. 14, 1854, on the occasion of his visit to Cincinnati, Ohio. Nativistic, Know-Nothing, and anti-Catholic prejudice had been aroused by press and speeches, prior to his arrival. On the night of Dec. 31 a disorderly mob marched to the cathedral rectory, but was dispersed after rioting had broken out and one citizen and one policeman had been injured fatally. There was no violence during the demonstration on Jan. 14, but an effigy of Monsignor Bedini was burned and threats were made against the Catholic clergy and churches.

[M. E. Thomas, *Nativism in the Old Northwest.*]

ALFRED G. STRITCH

BEECHER ISLAND, BATTLE OF (1868). Col. George A. Forsyth, leading fifty experienced scouts in search of Indians who had pillaged western Kansas, encamped, Sept. 16, 1868, on the Arikaree River, fifteen miles south of Wray, Colo. Attacked next morning by about 1,000 Cheyennes and Sioux, led by Roman Nose, the scouts moved onto Beecher Island. The Indians made several unsuccessful charges, then settled to a siege. Despite wounds and death, the scouts held on. Emissaries eluded the Indians at night, and on the ninth day troops arrived. Five scouts were dead and eighteen wounded.

[George A. Forsyth, *The Story of the Soldier.*]

LEROY R. HAFEN

BEECHER'S BIBLES, the term applied to the Sharps rifles during the Kansas struggle between the free-state and the proslavery elements. In March 1856, at New Haven, Conn., Henry Ward Beecher addressed a meeting at which a subscription was taken to equip a company of free-state emigrants to Kansas. Beecher said that for slaveholders in Kansas a Sharps rifle was a greater moral argument than a Bible and that the emigrants should, therefore, be equipped with rifles. The first rifle was subscribed by Benjamin Silliman of the Yale College faculty, the second by the pastor of the church in which the meeting was held, and Beecher pledged the last twenty-five for his church, the Plymouth Church of Brooklyn.

[J. F. Rhodes, *History of the United States.*]

JAMES ELLIOTT WALMSLEY

BEEF TRUST CASES. In 1902 three large meat packers—Swift, Armour, and Morris—formed the National Packing Company in an effort to secure control of packing houses in Kansas City, East St. Louis, and Omaha. The government promptly attacked these and three other concerns, charging monopolistic practices that had resulted in a large degree of control over the slaughtering and packing of meat. In 1905 the Supreme Court in *Swift and Company* v. *United States* (196 U.S. 375) upheld the government charges for the most part, but failed to order dissolution of the National Packing Company, and monopolistic practices continued. Thereupon the government sought an injunction, but the individuals involved successfully pleaded immunity from criminal prosecution because they had previously been compelled to testify against themselves. In 1910 further attacks on the packers were again unsuccessful, but in 1920, after an extensive Federal Trade Commission investigation, the packers agreed to dispose of their varied stockyard interests, their retail meat markets, and the wholesaling of lines not directly related to meat packing.

[Harry W. Laidler, *Concentration of Control in American Industry.*]

R. E. WESTMEYER

BEEKEEPING. The honeybee, *Apis mellifera,* is not native to North America. The common black bees of

Europe were imported to Virginia in 1621; subsequently, the Italian, Egyptian, Cyprian, Tunisian, Carniolan, and Caucasian strains of bees were imported. The spread of honeybees throughout the United States was slow; they were not found in Florida until 1763 or in California until 1856. Procedures for shipping live swarms of bees in packages without combs, and the shipment of bees by the postal and railway systems near the end of the 19th century and the beginning of the 20th century, led to a more rapid distribution of honeybees.

Rev. Lorenzo L. Langstroth, of Andover, Mass., is known as the father of American beekeeping. His utilization of the ⅜-inch space between combs (bee space) made possible the development of the modern movable-frame hive (1852), which, with minor modifications, is still being used. Langstroth was also noted for his book *Langstroth on the Hive and the Honey-Bee: A Bee Keeper's Manual.* His contemporary Moses Quinby wrote *Mysteries of Beekeeping Explained.* The publication of these two books in 1853 marked the real beginning of beekeeping in the United States. Both Langstroth and Quinby made major contributions to practical beekeeping that led ultimately to a new industry. For example, the development of the movable-frame hive, the wax foundation, the bee smoker, the honey extractor, package bee shipments, and techniques of queen production in the latter part of the 19th century revolutionized beekeeping. In the same period, two trade journals that are still published made their first appearance: *The American Bee Journal* (1861) and *Gleanings in Bee Culture* (1873). The American Bee Association, formed in 1860, was the first national organization of beekeepers. In 1974 there were two organizations: the American Beekeeping Federation and the American Honey Producers Association.

Much of the progress of the industry in the 20th century can be attributed to earlier research in apiculture conducted by state and federal scientists: for example, controlled bee breeding was made possible by the development of instrumental insemination of queens by Lloyd R. Watson. This technique, subsequently improved by others, enabled bee breeders to develop and maintain stocks for specific purposes: bees that gather more nectar, bees that are adapted to various environmental conditions, and bees that are more efficient in pollination of specific crops. Research in the United States has led also to the discovery of the pathogenic agent of American foulbrood disease, the use of chemotherapeutic agents for the control of bee diseases, and improved bee management and technology, which produce larger honey yields, more efficient methods of harvesting and processing honey, and more efficient use of bees for pollination.

In 1899 the beekeeping industry produced 30,983 tons of honey and 882 tons of beeswax. In 1970, 4.6 million colonies produced 117,395 tons of honey and 2,324 tons of beeswax, which were valued at $40.8 million and $2.8 million, respectively. Even more important, these bees are beneficial, and in some cases essential, to the pollination of agricultural crops valued at $6 billion.

[F. C. Pellett, *History of American Beekeeping.*]

H. SHIMANUKI

BEEKMAN PATENT, a tract sixteen miles square in Dutchess County, N.Y., embracing the present towns of Beekman, Union Vale, a portion of La Grange, and nearly all of Pawling and Dover, granted to Col. Henry Beekman on Apr. 22, 1697, by the British governor, Benjamin Fletcher. The death of Fletcher's successor, Richard Coote, Earl of Bellomont, cut short an attempt to vacate the patent as an extravagant grant. A new patent for the same land was issued by the next governor, Viscount Edward Hyde Cornbury, in 1703.

[Frank Hasbrouck, *History of Dutchess County.*]

A. C. FLICK

BEER. *See* **Brewing.**

BEES, a social gathering combining work and pleasure, and often competition. In the New England and middle colonies and on the early and midwestern frontiers various communal activities formed an important exception to the ordinarily individualistic habits of American farm families. The motivation was both economic and social. Log rollings and barn raisings necessitated collective effort; corn husking and threshing were most efficiently done by common endeavor. Machinery and specialized labor ended all these practices except for the threshing ring, which continues where farms are not large and farming is diversified. Corn husking, cradling, threshing among men, sewing, quilting, apple paring among women, roused the competitive spirit, made sport of work, and gave public recognition to the champion worker. Courting opportunities were afforded the young people. The finder of a red ear at a husking bee was awarded an extra pull at the jug. Sociability, neighborliness, and conversation were promoted. The educational counterparts of these activities were spelling bees and ciphering matches. Maple sugaring-offs in the North and cane sorghum boilings in the South made party occasions of work. The roundup in the cattle country was an adaptation of the same general principle. Competitive aspects survive in rodeos and various contests at agricultural fairs.

[P. W. Bidwell and J. I. Falconer, *History of Agriculture in the Northern United States, 1620–1860.*]

HARVEY L. CARTER

BEET SUGAR. Sugar beets, which probably grew wild in Asia, were cultivated at an early time in Egypt and southern Europe. A German chemist, Andreas Marggraf, demonstrated in 1747 that sugar from beets was identical with cane sugar. Early in the 19th century, when France was cut off from overseas sugar supplies, Napoleon Bonaparte established the sugar beet industry. Although the industry declined with Napoleon's downfall, it gradually revived, spreading first to Germany and then to much of the rest of Europe.

Four small factories were constructed in the United States between 1838 and 1856, but all failed. The first successful one was established by E. H. Dyer at Alvarado, Calif. (22 miles east of San Francisco), in 1870 and operated through 1967. The next successful plants were established in Watsonville, Calif. (1888); Grand Island, Nebr. (1890); and Lehi, Utah (1891). During the 1870's Maine and Delaware offered a bonus for beet sugar manufactured within their limits, and factories destined to operate only a few years were built at Portland and Wilmington, respectively. The Portland factory inaugurated the practice of contracting with farmers for a specific acreage of sugar beets that would be raised from seed furnished by the company. This plan of operation, adapted from French practices, has persisted to the present. Despite the activity in Maine and Delaware, production in the United States has tended to concentrate in irrigated areas in the West.

By 1910 more beet than cane sugar was produced in the continental United States; in 1920 the output exceeded one million tons; and in 1972 it was about 3.5 million tons, which was more than one-fourth of the sugar consumed in the United States. In the 1970's some sixty plants were producing beet sugar in eighteen states, more than one-third of the total factory capacity being located in California and Colorado.

One reason that the beet sugar industry was established so slowly in the United States is the large amount of hand labor required in growing beets. During the 1930's, studies began on the mechanization of growing and harvesting beets. Machines for planting, cultivating, and harvesting beets—all requiring specialized technological changes—were developed by the beginning of World War II. Their adoption was hastened by shortages of hand labor during the war and by postwar prosperity. In 1948, 40.8 man-hours of fieldwork were required to produce enough beets for a ton of sugar; in 1971, only 15.5.

The United States has protected its sugar industry by tariffs and other means since 1803. Since 1934 the secretary of agriculture has determined American sugar consumption requirements and assigned quotas to U.S. and foreign production areas.

[Leonard J. Arrington, *Beet Sugar in the West.*]

WAYNE D. RASMUSSEN

BELGIAN RELIEF, the means by which some 7.3 million Belgian civilians, inside the German army lines during World War I, received necessary food imports through the Allied blockade. Created as a temporary committee in October 1914 by a group of Americans, with the approval of their government, the Commission for Relief in Belgium (CRB) became the neutral channel through which more than 5.1 million tons of provisions and supplies passed into Belgium and were distributed by local Belgian committees. From 1915 some 1.8 million French civilians in the occupied areas of northern France were included in the relief.

The functions of the CRB were to secure basic foodstuffs by purchase or gift, to transport these commodities into Belgium, and to guarantee their equitable distribution under the supervision of American or other neutral volunteer workers. Delicate semidiplomatic relationships with belligerent and neutral powers, and public opinion widely mobilized, kept the door to Belgium open. Relief requirements were met by gifts amounting to $52 million in cash and kind collected by volunteer committees in the United States, the British Empire, and elsewhere; by British and French government subsidies totaling $314 million; and by U.S. government loans of $380 million made to Belgium and France in 1917–19. Altogether the CRB disbursed nearly $895 million with an administrative expense of less than one-half of one percent. The price level of breadstuffs in Belgium remained about 15 percent below commercial prices in surrounding countries.

Herbert Hoover directed and controlled the complicated operations and gained the acclaim that led to his rise in government. Hoover resigned as chairman of the CRB when the United States entered the war in 1917.

[G. I. Gay, *Statistical Review of Relief Operations;* G. I. Gay and H. H. Fisher, *Public Relations of the Commission for Relief in Belgium.*]

PERRIN C. GALPIN

BELKNAP, FORT, built in 1850 on the Salt Fork of the Brazos River in central Texas to afford frontier protection and to guard the Lower Indian Reserve set aside by Texas. The tribes on the reserve were the Caddo, Anadarkho, Waco, Tahwaccaro, and Tonkawa. The fort was named for Gen. William Goldsmith Belknap.

[J. Pike, *Scout and Ranger,* Carl L. Cannon, ed.]

CARL L. CANNON

BELKNAP SCANDAL, one of the series of scandals that marked President Ulysses S. Grant's second administration. Cora Le Roy Belknap, first wife of Secretary of War William W. Belknap, secured a lucrative post tradership at Fort Sill for John S. Evans. Mrs. Belknap reportedly received $6,000 per year for this service. After her death it was alleged that the money was paid to Secretary Belknap. On Mar. 2, 1876, the House of Representatives voted unanimously to impeach the secretary; Belknap resigned the same day. The impeachment trial held in April and May resulted in acquittal; twenty-two of the twenty-five members voting for acquittal declared that the Senate had no jurisdiction over a resigned officer.

[W. B. Hesseltine, *Ulysses S. Grant, Politician.*]

W. B. HESSELTINE

BELLEAU WOOD, BATTLE OF. The German Seventh Army, under Gen. Max von Boehn, driving southward from the Chemin des Dames toward Paris, on May 31, 1918, approached the Marne at Château-Thierry. Just west of there the American Second Division, under the command of Maj. Gen. Omar Bundy, hastened in support of the French Twenty-first Corps, the left corps of the French Sixth Army. Forcing back minor French units, by June 3 the Germans uncovered the American front line, which stood fast and stopped them. On June 6 the Americans assumed the offensive. Against bitter resistance the Fourth Marine Brigade, commanded by Brig. Gen. James Harbord, recaptured Bouresches and the southern edge of Belleau Wood, while on its right the Third Infantry Brigade advanced nearly to Vaux.

Continuing their local offensive, the Americans took most of Belleau Wood on June 8–11, and despite desperate counterattacks completed its capture on June 21. At noon, July 1, following an intense artillery preparation, the Third Infantry Brigade stormed Vaux and La Roche Wood. The division front, everywhere established on favorable ground, was turned over to the American Twenty-sixth Division, July 9, the Second Division retiring to a support position.

American losses were severe—nearly 8,000 killed, wounded, or missing. Approximately 1,600 German prisoners were taken. In 1923 the site was made a permanent memorial to the Americans who died during the battle and, by order of the French government, the site was renamed Bois de la Brigade Marine.

[Joseph M. Hanson, *History of the American Combat Divisions;* Charles R. Howland, *A Military History of the World War.*]

JOSEPH MILLS HANSON

BELLEFONTAINE, the first permanent settlement of English-speaking people in the Old Northwest. The spring which gave it its name, "la belle fontaine," was located a short distance south of the present town of Waterloo, Ill. The first settlers, mainly veterans who had served with George Rogers Clark, established themselves with their families at Bellefontaine in the fall of 1779. At an election held there in 1782 fifteen Americans voted. The federal census of 1800 enumerated 286 inhabitants, making Bellefontaine the third largest settlement in the Illinois Territory. As Illinois became more populous, Bellefontaine, never a compact village, gradually lost its identity.

[C. W. Alvord, *Kaskaskia Records, 1778-1790,* and *The Illinois Country, 1673–1818.*]

PAUL M. ANGLE

BELLEFONTAINE, FORT, built on the south side of the Missouri River, four miles from its junction with the Mississippi, under orders of Gen. James Wilkinson, in the fall of 1805, by Lt. Col. Jacob Kingsbury and two companies of the First Infantry. It was constructed on low land near Coldwater Creek and named for a spring there. After the flood of 1810 the fort was moved to the top of a nearby hill where it served as military headquarters for the Middle West until the erection of Jefferson Barracks in 1826.

[Kate L. Gregg, "Building of the First American Fort West of the Mississippi," *Missouri Historical Review* (1936).]

KATE L. GREGG

BELLE ISLE, an island in the James River at Richmond, Va., used as a prison for enlisted men captured by the Confederacy. In use continuously after the Battle of Bull Run in 1861, the prison held approximately 10,000 men under harsh conditions by the end of 1863. At that time, because the prisoners constituted a drain on the food supply and were the objectives of several cavalry raids (*see* Dahlgren's Raid), the captives were sent to a new prison at Andersonville, Ga.

[W. B. Hesseltine, *Civil War Prisons.*]

W. B. HESSELTINE

BELLEVUE WAR. William W. Brown, owner of a hotel at Bellevue, Jackson County, Iowa, was believed to be the leader of a gang of outlaws in that vicinity. When Sheriff William A. Warren attempted to arrest Brown and several other men on April 1, 1840, a fight resulted. Four of the posse and three of the alleged bandits (including Brown) were killed, and thirteen of Brown's band were captured. The following day the citizens voted on the penalty, dropping white beans in a box for hanging, red beans for whipping. The red beans predominated and the men were flogged and sent down the Mississippi River.

[John C. Parish, "White Beans for Hanging," *The Palimpsest,* vol. I; Harvey Reid, *Thomas Cox.*]

RUTH A. GALLAHER

BELL TELEPHONE LABORATORIES. As the world's largest and probably best-known institution for organized industrial research, the Bell Telephone Laboratories (Bell Labs) has provided much of the stimulus for an ongoing revolution in telecommunications based on solid-state electronics and information theory. The prime responsibility of Bell Labs is the engineering of the Bell telephone system's communications network as an integrated system. In discharging this responsibility, Bell Labs has developed a wide range of new technologies beneficial to telephone companies and other industries, and the federal government in the military area.

Bell Labs was formally organized as a nonprofit corporation in 1925 although the Bell telephone system had supported substantial, organized scientific and engineering research since the 1880's. A succession of fundamental contributions emanated from Bell Labs prior to World War II. Karl G. Jansky's pioneering observations of extraterrestrial radio waves reported in 1932 were later recognized as the foundation for the new science of radio astronomy. The work of Harold S. Black on feedback amplifier theory and of George C. Southworth on waveguides during the 1930's opened important new areas to development. Clinton J. Davisson's electron diffraction experiments at Bell Labs in the 1920's won him the Nobel Prize in physics in 1937 (shared with G. P. Thomson of Cambridge University). Fundamental work on noise in electronic circuits by H. Nyquist and J. B. Johnson established the limitations on the ability to detect threshold electrical signals and led to the creation of the information theory by Claude E. Shannon in the 1940's. The experience gained in coordinating the efforts of groups of scientists and engineers in the creation of complex electronic communications systems enabled Bell Labs to play a key role in the development of a large variety of radar systems during World War II.

The resumption of solid-state research at Bell Labs after the war culminated in the successful development of the transistor, announced in 1948. This discovery initiated a new era of solid-state electronics, with wide-ranging applications to computers, satellite communications, and consumer goods. The importance of the research that led to the transistor was recognized by the award of a Nobel Prize to William Shockley, John Bardeen, and Walter Brattain in 1956.

Other notable inventions and developments from Bell Labs are the coaxial cable, the introduction of the use of Boolean algebra for switching, and the invention of the AND and OR gates in the late 1930's, the latter making possible the subsequent development of the digital computer. Research at Bell Labs since World War II has been related to such areas as the development of solar batteries, optical masters, acoustics, magnetic materials, polymer science, and suboceanic and satellite communications.

The headquarters of Bell Labs are at Murray Hill, N.J., with additional research and development facilities at twenty other locations in various parts of the United States.

[American Telephone and Telegraph Company, *Events in Telephone History;* George Shiers, *Bibliography of the History of Electronics.*]

JAMES E. BRITTAIN

BELMONT, BATTLE OF (Nov. 7, 1861), Ulysses S. Grant's first Civil War battle and first defeat. Gen. John C. Frémont ordered the attack on Belmont, Mo., to prevent Gen. Leonidas Polk at Columbus, Ky., from aiding the Confederates in Missouri. Steaming from Cairo, Ill., on the Ohio River, Grant landed five miles above Belmont and drove Gen. G. J. Pillow's men to the river and set fire to their camp. Polk, crossing with reinforcements and aided by the Columbus batteries, drove Grant to his transports and retreat.

[U. S. Grant, *Personal Memoirs;* R. U. Johnson and C. C. Buel, eds., *Battles and Leaders of the Civil War*.]

W. C. Mallalieu

"BELOVED MAN"/"BELOVED WOMAN." The translation of the terms "beloved man" and "beloved woman" from various American Indian languages of the Southeast admits of some question. Since the term for "beloved" may also be translated "honored" or "esteemed," the designation reflects an honorable status ascribed to persons either because of achievement or because of birth. Suggested is the concept of status ranking, existent in aboriginal times among such tribes as the Creek, Muskogee, Choctaw, Chickasaw, and Natchez.

The term has both political and social connotations: Among the Creek there was a loose confederacy, one paralleled in the north by the League of the Iroquois, itself originally a Southeastern group of tribes. Creek towns and groups of towns, depending on local arrangement, might have a paramount chief, the *miko,* a man from a maternal clan that possessed the rights to the office. The *miko* represented his town or united group of towns in federation deliberations and acted as judge, supervisor of granaries, and ceremonial leader. He possessed an internal council made up of a vice-chief, a speaker, and a group of veterans, men conversant with tradition and noted for military success. These were the "beloved men." Because office passed through the maternal clan, the clan itself selected the persons who were to fill the positions held by the clan as hereditary rights. Women in the generation of the mother of the officeholder, "beloved women," could exert political pressures both on the selection of chiefs and on their administration.

The general matrilineal pattern as well as the interplay of the political and the clan characterize the native Southeast. Patterns of officeholding and clanship, including the interaction between men and the women of the clan, were well defined. A somewhat aberrant variation appears among the Natchez of the lower Mississippi, who, through an interlocking system of hereditary ranks—again with a maternal emphasis—created a caste-like structure having a paramount chief, the Sun; lesser ranks of nobles, "honored men"; and commoners. In view of the early disruption of the Southeastern native cultures, it is not possible to designate with exactness the precise role of the "beloved man" and the "beloved woman" in all instances.

[John R. Swanton, *Indians of the Southeastern United States*, and *Social Organization and Social Usages of the Indians of the Creek Confederacy*.]

Robert F. Spencer

BELTRÁN-ESPEJO EXPEDITION. When the military escort of the Augustin Rodríguez expedition (1581) returned from New Mexico, the Franciscans on the frontier at Santa Barbara (southern Chihuahua) were alarmed for the safety of Rodríguez and another missionary, Francisco López, who had remained at Puaráy. With fifteen volunteer soldiers Bernardino Beltrán started north (November 1582) to rescue his colleagues. Upon reaching the Pueblo country, he learned that they had been killed; but the soldiers refused to return before exploring the country.

There is no account from Beltrán regarding what happened; knowledge rests on later statements of soldiers, especially Diego Perez de Luxán and Antonio de Espejo. Espejo, desiring to emulate Hernando Cortes by developing a "new" Mexico, largely financed the expedition and tried to dominate it. His report added much detailed information of the Pueblo country and people; his exaggerations regarding population, resources, and mining prospects were somewhat discounted by Luxán.

The expedition failed in its immediate objective, but its favorable reports of the country strengthened the resolve of secular and religious authorities to colonize New Mexico and evangelize its inhabitants. (*See also* Rodríguez-Chamuscado Expedition.)

[H. E. Bolton, ed., *Spanish Exploration in the Southwest;* Diego Perez de Luxán, *Expedition Into New Mexico Made by Antonio de Espejo, 1582–1583,* G. P. Hammond, ed.]

Lansing B. Bloom

BEMIS HEIGHTS, BATTLES OF. *See* **Freeman's Farm, Battles of.**

BENEFIT OF CLERGY, originally a plea exempting the clergy from criminal process of the English royal courts; but ultimately a commutation of the death sentence in certain felonies for all prisoners who could read, which last requirement was dropped by the 18th century. In colonial times it was in general use in the South and occasionally in New England, notably in the Boston Massacre case. Statutes abolishing this privilege appear after the Revolution, but until the eve of the Civil War it was still allowed in the southern states, where its use meant sparing a master's valuable property in his slave.

[A. L. Cross, "Benefit of Clergy in the American Criminal Law," *Proceedings*, Massachusetts Historical Society, vol. 61.]

RICHARD B. MORRIS

BENNING, FORT. Camp Benning (redesignated as Fort Benning in 1922) was established near Columbus, Ga., during World War I. By consolidation of the Small Arms Firing School (Camp Perry, Ohio), the Infantry School (Fort Sill, Okla.), and the Machine Gun School (Augusta, Ga.), a model infantry school was established at Benning in 1920. It is now the nation's largest infantry center.

[Charles J. Sullivan, *Army Posts and Towns*.]

ROBERT S. THOMAS

BENNINGTON, BATTLE OF (Aug. 16, 1777). Toward the middle of August 1777, British Gen. John Burgoyne planned a raid on the American stores at Bennington, Vt. His purpose was fourfold: to encourage the Loyalists; frighten New England; replenish his stock of provisions; and mount a regiment of heavily equipped German dragoons. Accordingly, these dragoons, lumbering along on foot in their enormous jackboots and stiff leather breeches, were made the nucleus of the raiding force, which, under the command of German Col. Frederick Baum, amounted, with Tories, Canadians, Indians, and a handful of English, to about 800 men. On nearing Bennington, Baum learned that American Gen. John Stark had assembled about 2,600 troops at Bennington to oppose him, and he sent to Burgoyne for reinforcements. Col. Heinrich von Breyman, with 500 men, was sent to his assistance. In the meantime Stark, hearing of Baum's advance, marched to meet him. On Aug. 15 it rained, and both armies remained in their lines. The following afternoon Stark attacked. Baum's command was too widely dispersed. His auxiliaries were scattered, and his regulars, hastily entrenched on a hill overlooking the Walloomsac River, were surrounded and most of them captured. In the meantime Breyman, ignorant of the battle, approached. Stark, now reinforced by Col. Seth Warner with 350 men, re-formed and attacked. The Germans retreated and were pursued until dark. The Americans took about 700 prisoners. The successful outcome of the engagement did much to improve the morale of the American forces.

[H. B. Dawson, *Battles of the United States;* Hoffman Nickerson, *The Turning Point of the Revolution*.]

A. C. FLICK

BENTON, FORT. After 1830 the American Fur Company established several trading posts near the navigation-head of the Missouri River. One of these, Fort Lewis (established 1844), a large, bastioned, log structure, was moved in 1846 to the site of the present town of Fort Benton, Mont., where it retained its original name until 1850, when it was renamed for Thomas Hart Benton, who allegedly saved the company from prosecution for selling whiskey to the Indians. The post was subsequently rebuilt with adobe bricks. During the Montana gold rush, beginning in 1862, Fort Benton became a main port of entry to the mines. A town with the same name sprang up around it and the fur company sold out to a mercantile firm in 1865.

[H. M. Chittenden, *The American Fur Trade;* A. J. Craven, ed., "Affairs at Fort Benton from Lt. Bradley's Journal," *Contributions to the Historical Society of Montana*, vol. III.]

JAY MONAGHAN

BENTONVILLE, BATTLE OF (Mar. 19–21, 1865). Gen. J. E. Johnston, in command of the small Confederate force in North Carolina, hoping to prevent a junction of the Union generals W. T. Sherman and U. S. Grant, here attacked on Mar. 19 the left wing of Sherman's army, which was moving rapidly northward (*see* Carolinas, Sherman's March Through). Though outnumbered, Johnston succeeded in fighting a drawn battle, but lost at least 2,000 men. Desultory fighting occurred during the next two days, but by the night of Mar. 21 most of Sherman's army was concentrated at the spot, and Johnston retired.

[R. U. Johnson and C. C. Buel, eds., *Battles and Leaders of the Civil War*.]

ALVIN F. HARLOW

BENT'S FORT, first known as Fort William, completed by William Bent, his three brothers, and Ceran St. Vrain about 1832, on the north bank of the Arkansas River, some seven miles east of present La Junta, Colo. The founders are said to have previously built a temporary stockade farther up the river. Located on the mountain branch of the Santa Fe Trail, Bent's Fort participated in both the mountain fur trade and the overland commerce to Santa Fe, becoming the outstanding trading post of the Southwest. It was rectangular in form, about 180 by 135 feet. The walls, of gray adobe, were two to four feet thick and fifteen high, with bastions at two diagonal corners. Within, low earth-roofed rooms faced an interior court. An adjoining adobe corral housed stock and equipment.

Cheyenne and Arapaho brought buffalo robes and skins for barter at the fort and from it white traders carried wares to Indian villages. An annual wagon train freighted furs to Missouri and returned with Indian goods. The fort outfitted trappers and traders, sheltered travelers, and was a depot for military expeditions before and during the Mexican War. William Bent married a Cheyenne, Owl Woman, reared his family at the fort, and became Colorado's first citizen. According to unverified tradition, the government wanted the fort, but offered an inadequate price. Bent thereupon partially destroyed it and deserted it in 1849. Moving forty miles downriver, he erected Bent's New Fort, 1853. He leased this structure, built of stone, to the government in 1859 and retired. Next year additional barracks were built and the post was named Fort Wise, after the governor of Virginia. In 1861 the name was changed to Fort Lyon, honoring Gen. Nathaniel Lyon. Floods endangering the buildings in 1866, Fort Lyon was moved about twenty miles up the river to its present location. The site of the 1832–49 fort was made a national historic site in 1960.

[David Lavender, *Bent's Fort.*]

LeRoy R. Hafen

***BEREA COLLEGE* V. *KENTUCKY*,** 211 U.S. 45 (1908), involved the right of Berea College to teach black and white students at the same time in the same classroom. Kentucky law had declared such interracial educational activity to be illegal and the supreme court of the state upheld the statute. The U.S. Supreme Court dodged the major issue of interracial education and decided the case on the narrow grounds involving the right of the state to change or amend the charter of a corporation. It held that the law did not prohibit the teaching of blacks and whites at the same place at different times or at different places at the same time, but provided the states with the means to outlaw interracial education. Such an amendment of the charter of Berea College was held to violate no provision of the Constitution. The decision reinforced and expanded the *Plessy* v. *Ferguson* ("separate, but equal") doctrine (1896).

Henry N. Drewry

BERGEN PRIZES. Capt. Pierre Landais of the *Alliance*, an American vessel of John Paul Jones's squadron in European waters, captured three British merchantmen (*Betsy, Union, Charming Polly*) in 1779. When bad weather forced Landais into Bergen, Norway, England requested and obtained restoration of the vessels from the Danish-Norwegian government. Jones, in person, demanded indemnification at Copenhagen. The Danish foreign minister, Count Andreas Peter von Bernstorff, negotiated with the United States for years. It was proved finally that an Anglo-Danish treaty of 1600 obligated Denmark to England. Hence under international law it could not be forced to indemnify the United States. Congress reimbursed Landais in 1806 and the heirs of Jones in 1848.

[S. P. Fogdall, *Danish-American Diplomacy, 1776–1920.*]

S. P. Fogdall

BERING SEA FISHERIES. *See* **Seal Fisheries.**

BERLIN, TREATY OF, the separate peace treaty between the United States and Germany, signed Aug. 25, 1921, and proclaimed Nov. 14 of the same year, entered into after the Senate rejected the Treaty of Versailles. This treaty is unique, first because of its brevity and second because it is an index-treaty, in that its provisions merely refer to provisions of the Treaty of Versailles that are either accepted or rejected by the United States. Provisions thus taken over were those with respect to colonies, disarmament, reparations, and responsibility for the war. The most important features rejected were the League of Nations, the International Labor Organization, and the boundaries provisions. Approximately two-thirds of the Treaty of Versailles, including its harshest provisions, was thus accepted by the United States through the Treaty of Berlin.

Clarence A. Berdahl

BERLIN AIRLIFT, history's largest exclusively aerial supply operation. For eleven months (1948–49)

American and British planes sustained more than 2 million West Berliners and occupation troops after the Soviet Union blocked surface routes into Berlin in an effort to force withdrawal of the occupation forces of the West. Under World War II agreements the Soviet Union occupied eastern Berlin; the United States, Britain, and France occupied zones in western Berlin, with surface access presumably assured through the Soviet zone of Germany and air access assured along three twenty-mile-wide corridors. This four-power administration soon degenerated under such acts of Soviet intransigence as the flooding of the city with Soviet-printed currency. Starting in January 1948, the Soviets periodically closed access routes. After boycotting four-power occupation agencies, they halted all surface traffic into West Berlin on June 23 and denied coal and electricity from the Soviet zone.

Convinced the Soviets would stop short of war, the American commander, Gen. Lucius D. Clay, obtained U.S. government approval for an airlift requiring a minimum of 140,000 tons per month, an undertaking on a scale never before attempted. U.S. C-47 aircraft began flying into West Berlin's Tempelhof airfield on June 25, and British planes into Gatow airport on June 30. As larger U.S. Air Force C-54's, U.S. Navy R-5D's, and British Avro Yorks became available, tonnage reached a record 12,940 tons in one day on Apr. 16, 1949. One landing and takeoff occurred, on the average, every three minutes. The Soviets harassed some flights, but, as Clay predicted, stopped short of war. Hurt by reciprocal denial of imports from West Germany, they raised the blockade May 12, 1949, although the airlift continued into September.

The operation cost thirty-one American, thirty-nine British, and nine German lives. A total of 276,926 flights carried 2,323,067 tons. The U.S. cost alone was $234 million. Despite the success of the airlift, Soviet harassment of Berlin continued at intervals over the years, although not again to the extent evidenced by the blockade.

[Frank Donovan, *Bridge in the Sky;* Jean Edward Smith, *The Defense of Berlin.*]

CHARLES B. MACDONALD

BERLIN BLOCKADE. The Soviet blockade of Berlin, beginning on June 23, 1948, and the responding American-British airlift to keep West Berlin alive, was the most dramatic of the early cold war confrontations. Shortly after the defeat of Germany, the Soviet Union and the United States began to compete for the support of their former enemy. The United States and its allies, in control of most of Germany's population and industry, held the advantage. Initially seeking West Germany's economic recovery to promote the Marshall Plan's broader purpose—the economic reconstruction and growth of Western Europe—the United States in early 1948 imposed stringent German currency reforms and moved toward the creation of a West German constitution and government. These actions precipitated the Soviet blockade of the western half of Berlin, in an attempt to prevent the revival of West German power. Despite the stakes at issue, both powers were unwilling to risk war. Troops were not sent to reopen the Berlin corridor by challenging the Red Army, and the Soviets did not challenge the airlift. After 321 days of successful American and British sustenance of West Berlin's population with necessary supplies, the Soviets terminated the blockade. (*See also* Berlin Airlift.)

[W. Phillips Davison, *The Berlin Blockade;* Oran R. Young, *The Politics of Force.*]

JOHN W. SPANIER

BERLIN DECREE. *See* **Napoleon's Decrees.**

BERLIN WALL. In 1961 Premier Nikita Khrushchev of the Soviet Union renewed his three-year-old threat to transform West Berlin into a "free city" before that year ended: if the West would not agree, the Soviets would sign a peace treaty with East Germany, abrogate the right of its World War II allies to be in Berlin, and make their further stay dependent upon East German consent. East Germany could then intensify pressure until the Western position became untenable. The Soviets hoped that this strategy would resolve the problem of a satellite whose population was escaping to West Berlin in ever larger numbers. The United States, for its part, felt that Western presence and access to the western half of Berlin were nonnegotiable. President John F. Kennedy believed that elimination of the West from Berlin would erode the faith of European allies in American power and commitments, thereby neutralizing Western Europe. Soviet and American interests thus appeared irreconcilable.

When on Aug. 13, 1961, the Communists built a wall dividing Berlin, they apparently ended the refugee issue. But American inaction left a profound impression of a lack of resolve at a time when many Europeans believed that the distribution of power was turning in favor of the Soviet Union. These beliefs, probably shared by Khrushchev, were corrected by the outcome of the Cuban missile crisis, which also ended the Berlin confrontation.

[John Mander, *Berlin: Hostage for the West;* Hans Speier, *Divided Berlin;* Oran R. Young, *The Politics of Force.*]

JOHN W. SPANIER

***BERMUDA* ADMIRALTY CASE.** In December 1865 the U.S. Supreme Court handed down a judgment in a case involving the British-owned steamship *Bermuda,* the case turning on the issue of continuous voyage.

During the Civil War, British flag vessels had made frequent sailings from British ports, such as Liverpool, loaded with war supplies destined for the Confederacy. Some ships, instead of running the blockade, had delivered their cargoes to British islands near the Atlantic coast—Nassau in the Bahama Islands and Hamilton in the Bermudas suddenly becoming busy ports. There the cargo had been then transferred to light, fast ships for delivery to the South.

In the winter of 1862 the *Bermuda* sailed from Liverpool. It arrived safely at St. George's in the Bermuda Islands, and on Apr. 23, 1862, continued its voyage, allegedly bound for Nassau. Its cargo included artillery, ammunition, small arms, Confederate uniform insignia, and Confederate postage stamps. On Apr. 27, while some 400 miles from Charleston, S.C., it was captured off Great Abaco Island by the Union warship *Mercedita.* Sent to Philadelphia, the *Bermuda* became the subject of legal action brought against it as a prize.

The federal district court held that the evidence proved the ship intended to complete its voyage and deliver its cargo either at Nassau or to a Confederate port—by itself or by transshipment. In a judgment delivered by Chief Justice Salmon P. Chase, the Supreme Court affirmed the action of the lower court: the vessel and cargo, even if neutral, were condemned for the reason that ultimate destination was to ports under blockade (the doctrine of continuous voyage), which justified seizure and condemnation. Further, it was affirmed that such destination equally justified seizure of contraband en route to ports not under blockade. Because the *Bermuda* cargo had been consigned to enemies and because most of it was contraband, the Supreme Court held that it must share the fate of the ship.

[Thomas A. Bailey, *A Diplomatic History of the American People;* Carlton Savage, *Policy of the United States Toward Maritime Commerce in War,* vol. I, and *Wallace's Reports of Supreme Court Decisions,* vol. III.]

PAUL B. RYAN

BERMUDA CONFERENCE (1957). After the deep Anglo-American rift caused by the Suez War in 1956, President Dwight D. Eisenhower and Harold Macmillan, the new British prime minister, met in Bermuda in March 1957 to bring the two allies closer together once again. European unity and the continued testing of nuclear weapons were stressed, and the two leaders announced an agreement whereby the United States would supply Britain with intermediate-range missiles.

JOHN W. SPANIER

BERMUDA ISLANDS, a cluster of more than 300 islands located 570 miles east of Cape Hatteras, N.C. America has had close contacts with these islands from the first settlement by colonists shipwrecked on their way to Virginia in 1609 (*see* Somers' Voyage) to the present. From 1612 to 1615 the islands were included under the Virginia Company charter, but thereafter they had a separate history, first as a company colony and then as a crown colony (1684). The settlers concentrated on tobacco (*see* Tobacco Contract), and the colony developed rapidly. Throughout the colonial period there was considerable trade with the mainland where, in addition, many Bermudans sought opportunities denied them in the islands. During the American Revolution the inhabitants opposed British colonial policy and sent delegates to the Continental Congress to secure relief from the trade embargo against loyal colonies. They achieved their end by furnishing gunpowder and other supplies to the rebels.

During Prohibition (1919–33) rum smuggling from Bermuda to the United States was a highly profitable venture. In 1941 sites for U.S. naval and air bases were leased. Bermuda is now a popular tourist area, with a permanent population of about 52,000.

[Hudson Strode, *The Story of Bermuda.*]

CHARLES F. MULLETT

BERNARD, FORT, a small trading post between Horse Creek and Fort Laramie in Wyoming on the Oregon Trail. It was noted by many overland emigrants before and after the California gold rush of 1849, but there is no definite information about the owner or how long it continued. A trappers' trail from

Bent's Fort to the south in Colorado joined the Oregon Trail at this post. Taos and Santa Fe traders freighted flour here to trade to emigrants bound for the coast.

[A. B. Hulbert, *Forty-Niners.*]

CARL L. CANNON

BETHABARA, the first town planted (1753) by German Moravians from Pennsylvania in Wachovia, N.C. Its early settlers were noted for advanced agricultural practices, especially their "medicine garden," which produced over fifty kinds of herbs. Bethabara grew slowly and is now only a small village, known locally as Oldtown.

[J. H. Clewell, *History of Wachovia.*]

HUGH T. LEFLER

BETHEL COMMUNITY (1844–77), a minor communist experiment established in Shelby County, Mo., by William Keil and followers (chiefly German) from Ohio and Pittsburgh, Pa. Keil preached moral living, subscribing to no religious faith, and dominated an unincorporated, self-sustaining, orderly, prosperous community that expanded to four towns. Property and labor were shared, though private earnings were allowed. A sister colony was fostered in Aurora, Ore., in 1855. Both dissolved, dividing their property upon Keil's death in 1877.

[Robert J. Hendricks, *Bethel and Aurora.*]

FLOYD C. SHOEMAKER

BETHESDA HOUSE OF MERCY, an orphanage and school, founded by the Reverend George Whitefield, near Savannah, Ga., in 1739. Whitefield died in 1770, and the project faltered before 1800. Savannah's venerable Union Society, sponsor of present Bethesda, revived the use of the site for orphanage purposes in 1855.

[Luke Tyerman, *The Life of the Rev. George Whitefield.*]

H. B. FANT

BEVERAGES, NON-ALCOHOLIC. *See* **Soft Drink Industry.**

BIBLE. The fact that the appearance of the two most widely used of the early English translations of the Bible was contemporaneous with the beginning of English colonization of America is of great historical importance. The Genevan Bible, the work of exiled Protestant scholars who had fled to Geneva to escape Catholic Queen Mary's persecutions, was in fact the Puritan's Bible. Its convenient size and relative cheapness, together with its verse divisions and Calvinistic notes, made it immensely popular. From 1560, the year of its first publication, to 1640 it passed through 160 editions and was undoubtedly the Bible most used by the first two generations of American Puritans.

Even after the appearance of the King James, or Authorized, Version (1611), the Genevan Bible continued to hold its own, although doubtless the Authorized Version found greater favor outside New England. The availability of these two great versions from the beginning of colonization helps to explain the influence exerted by the Bible in American colonial life. During the entire colonial period the Bible was easily first among moral and cultural influences upon the ordinary English-speaking citizen. The Bible in German, printed in 1740–43 by Christopher Sower, Sr., a printer of the Dunker denomination from Germantown, Pa., was the first Bible to appear in a European language in America. It exercised a corresponding influence upon the growing number of German colonists.

Among the questions to be decided when the western movement of the population began after the Revolution was whether the nation was to be Christian or pagan in its outlook. And no single factor had a larger part in determining what direction the nation would take than the widespread distribution of the Bible throughout the West by such agencies as the American Bible Society (1816), the American Tract Society (1825), and the American Sunday School Union (1824). These agencies, together with the evangelical churches and the direct influence they exerted, made the Bible a necessity in almost every American home. As a result of the great revivals that swept over the nation throughout most of the 19th century, Bible reading and study in the home as well as in the Sabbath schools and denominational colleges were stressed as the best means of cultivating the Christian life. Family worship became a practice in tens of thousands of American homes, where a chapter of the Bible was read, a hymn sung, and a prayer offered as part of the daily family routine.

The Bible has had an important role in advancing every reform movement in American history—as witness the antislavery, temperance, and peace movements. Unfortunately it has also been used to support glaring evils and to oppose progress, and it has given birth to numerous erratic movements.

Bible reading and study have greatly declined, and the influence of the Bible has decreased correspondingly. Certainly Bible reading in the home has lessened, doubtless largely because the Bible is no longer considered the infallible guide in every department of life, as it once was. Yet the Bible is still in great demand and exercises a wide influence, as indicated by the fact that the United Bible Societies, a world fellowship of fifty-six Bible societies, distributed 5,903,807 Bibles and 13,960,707 Testaments in 1973, and the increase of Bible-related publications has not slackened (well over 4,000 titles were listed in 1971).

[P. Marion Simms, *The Bible in America.*]

William W. Sweet

BIBLE COMMONWEALTH, a term that has been applied by modern historians to the Puritan colonies of Massachusetts and New Haven, Conn., where the right to vote was limited to church members and an effort was made to bring all activities into harmony with the Bible. This effort is best illustrated by *An Abstract of the Lawes of New England* . . . (London, 1641), a code prepared by John Cotton which became the basis for the government of the New Haven colony. With the exception of the chapters dealing with inheritance and crime, the provisions of this code were not biblical but were based upon the early practices of Massachusetts. Insofar as possible, however, all provisions were supported by marginal scriptural citations.

[I. M. Calder, *The New Haven Colony.*]

Isabel M. Calder

BIBLES, PRINTING OF. The first book printed within the limits of the present United States of which any copy survives was the hymnal known as the *Bay Psalm Book,* which contained portions of the Bible. The first complete Bible produced was John Eliot's translation into the Algonkin language printed at Cambridge in 1663 (second edition, 1685). In 1688 William Bradford projected the printing of a Bible in Philadelphia, but nothing came of it or of John Fleeming's proposal in Boston in 1770. Partly because the printing of the King James Version was an Oxford monopoly, three editions of Martin Luther's Bible in German appeared in America (Germantown, Christopher Sower, 1743, 1763, 1776) before any were printed in English. Robert Aitken published the first American Bible in English in Philadelphia, 1781–82. Isaiah Thomas is responsible for the legend of an English Bible printed surreptitiously in Boston about 1752, but no such book was attested by contemporaries, nor is any copy known to exist. Thomas printed the first Greek New Testament, Worcester, 1800. The first printing of the Douay Version (Roman Catholic) was in Philadelphia in 1790.

[E. B. O'Callaghan, *List of Editions of the Holy Scriptures . . . Printed in America Previous to 1860.*]

Randolph G. Adams

BICAMERAL LEGISLATURES in the United States have as their antecedents the British Parliament and colonial legislatures. They have been used by the national government and by almost all of the states since the adoption of the Constitution. After Vermont adopted the two-house legislature in 1836, the bicameral pattern prevailed in all states until Nebraska established a unicameral legislature in 1934. No other state has emulated this action. At the municipal level, nearly all cities use the single-chamber city council.

The bicameral legislature was developed as a device for resolving political conflict through compromise. For instance, the members of one house might be elected, and the members of the other house appointed. One house might be based on geographical subdivisions, while the other might simply represent population. Or differing political interests might be emphasized in each house: one might speak mainly for property owners and the economically powerful and the other might represent all the people. (However, a heterogeneous group of voters now selects the members of both houses in a bicameral legislature.) The length of term and the size of the district represented may differ for the two houses.

In a bicameral legislature, proponents claim, unwise and precipitous legislation is prevented: bills are reviewed more carefully; and checks and balances are promoted. These assertions remain essentially unproven. Moreover, the Nebraska experience has yielded mixed results and so has done little to resolve any controversy. Bicameral legislatures at the national and state levels are retained for several reasons. The constitutions creating them are difficult to amend, and few are willing to make the attempt. There is little public pressure for change. The superiority of the unicameral legislature has not been demonstrated conclusively. Those political interests who benefit from the existing organization of legislatures fear the uncertainties of change. Finally, the present pattern serves the purposes of many incumbent public officials.

[A. C. Breckenridge, *One House For Two;* William J. Keefe and Morris S. Ogul, *The American Legislative Process.*]

MORRIS S. OGUL

BICYCLING. Invented mainly in France and England, bicycles had their first vogue in America in the late 1860's. The sudden popularity soon collapsed but was revived a decade later when Albert A. Pope began importing them from England and later manufacturing them. Chiefly through his efforts, which included continuous propaganda for better roads, bicycling became, during the 1880's and 1890's, one of the most popular American sports. Change in design and model made bicycling more practical. Their use was thus widened to include business as well as pleasure. For a while bicycling was pushed into the background by motorcycles and automobiles and by the development of golf, tennis, and other outdoor sports.

A short revival of interest in bicycling occurred in the 1930's (200,000 bicycles were sold in 1932), but the biggest resurgence of interest occurred in the 1960's and early 1970's. Numerous bicycle clubs were started and many U.S. cities and parks set aside areas as bicycle paths. In major American cities more and more bicycles were used for recreation and transportation to avoid automobile traffic congestion. In 1973, 15.3 million bicycles were sold in the United States, 5.2 million of which were imports. It is estimated that in the early 1970's approximately 50 million people in the United States participated in cycling sports.

H. U. FAULKNER

BIDDLE MISSION. Charles A. Biddle, sent by President Andrew Jackson to Nicaragua, Guatemala, and Panama to determine expediency of Isthmus of Panama canal negotiations, secured from New Granada (Colombia) a concession (June 22, 1836) for himself and associates to construct a trans-isthmian road or railway, and for steam navigation of the Chagres River. Jackson, infuriated because of Biddle's use of a governmental mission to secure a private concession, disclaimed official connection with the affair. Biddle's death (Dec. 21, 1836) saved him a presidential reprimand.

[E. T. Parks, *Colombia and the United States, 1765–1934.*]

E. T. PARKS

BIDLACK TREATY. On Dec. 12, 1846, Benjamin A. Bidlack, American chargé d'affaires in Bogotá, signed a treaty with New Granada (Colombia). The terms of the treaty removed tariff discrimination against American commerce and provided for the guarantee of the neutrality of the Isthmus of Panama "with a view that the free transit . . . [across it] may not be interrupted." New Granada's rights of sovereignty over the isthmus were also guaranteed.

On thirteen occasions (1856–1903) American troops were landed to protect the transit route. In 1903 President Theodore Roosevelt argued that this treaty "vested in the United States a substantial property right" in the isthmus. When Panama seceded (Nov. 3, 1903) it was held by the American government that the covenant ran with this land (*see* Hay-Bunau-Varilla Treaty).

[H. C. Hill, *Roosevelt and the Caribbean;* E. T. Parks, *Colombia and the United States, 1765–1934.*]

E. T. PARKS

BIG BLACK RIVER, BATTLE AT (May 16–17, 1863). After his defeat at Champion's Hill in Mississippi, Confederate Gen. John C. Pemberton retreated to the Big Black River. It was hoped that the river's bridge could be held long enough to permit the army to cross before Gen. Ulysses S. Grant could attack in force. Everything was in confusion; there seemed to be no leadership. On the morning of May 17 Grant's advance troops appeared. Pemberton was driven in retreat into Vicksburg.

[F. V. Greene, *The Mississippi.*]

THOMAS ROBSON HAY

BIG BONE LICK, a salt spring in Boone County, Ky., one and one-half miles east of the Ohio River. The earliest known white man to visit this place was Capt. Charles Lemoyne, Baron de Longueuil, who came in 1729. Christopher Gist visited it in 1751; and in 1773 James Douglas, a Virginia surveyor, described the animal fossils that he found on the surface. Here were found the bones of mastodon, Arctic elephant, and other animals of the glacial epochs. In 1803 and 1806 Dr. William Goforth made a collection of fossils which he entrusted to the English traveler Thomas Ashe. Ashe in turn sold these to the Royal College of Surgeons in London, and to private Irish and Scotch collectors. Thomas Jefferson made a collection of some of the bones, and natural history museums at Lexington, Cincinnati, Philadelphia, and Boston collected the remaining skeletons. The large prehistoric animals were attracted to the Big Bone Lick by the seepage of brine from an underlying basal coal measure. Pioneers found that 500 gallons of this water made one bushel of salt.

[W. R. Jillson, *Big Bone Lick*.]

T. D. CLARK

BIG BOTTOM MASSACRE (Jan. 2, 1791). Shawnee Indians surprised a new settlement on the Muskingum River in Ohio; stormed the blockhouse; and killed eleven men, one woman, and two children. Three settlers were captured while four others escaped into the woods. The Ohio Company of Associates acted immediately afterward to provide greater protection for settlers.

ROBERT S. THOMAS

BIG BROTHER MOVEMENT. In 1903, a small group of men in Cincinnati, Ohio, following an appeal by Irvin F. Westheimer, a young stockbroker, agreed to take an interest individually in fatherless boys in that city. The movement was formalized in New York City a year later by Ernest K. Coulter, clerk of the children's court. At present there are 210 member agencies of a national organization, Big Brothers of America, formed in 1947, with headquarters in Philadelphia, Pa., and officially chartered by an act of Congress in 1958. As of January 1974 about 100,000 Big Brother–Little Brother assignments were active throughout the United States. A similar but separate confederation of Big Brothers' agencies exists in Canada, with approximately fifty agencies serving 20,000 boys.

RAYMOND J. HOFFMAN

BIG HOLE, BATTLE OF (Aug. 9, 1877). During the Nez Perce War, Col. John Gibbon, with a number of volunteers and mounted infantrymen, attacked Chief Joseph's camp on the Big Hole River in Montana at daybreak. The surviving Nez Perce drove the soldiers back and disabled or killed sixty-nine soldiers before withdrawing. Eighty Indians had died, over two-thirds of them women and children. In 1963 the site was designated Big Hole National Battlefield.

WILLIAM S. LEWIS

BIG HORN MOUNTAINS, a range of the Rocky Mountains lying mainly in north central Wyoming, but extending into southern Montana. Discovered in 1743 by Pierre Gaultier de Varennes, Sieur de La Vérendrye, soon they were frequented by American fur traders. In 1811 Big Horn Mountains were crossed by Wilson Price Hunt and the overland Astoria expedition. The mountains were the site of the Fetterman massacre (1866) and the Battle of the Little Bighorn (1876).

DAN E. CLARK

BIG KNIVES, or Long Knives, was a term used by the western Indians to designate the English colonists. After 1750 it was restricted to the colonists of Virginia, in contradistinction to those of New York and Pennsylvania. George Rogers Clark spoke of himself and his men as Big Knives in speeches to the Indians in 1778 after the capture of Illinois. From the latter part of the Revolution through the War of 1812, the term was used to designate Americans. The origin is thought to be in the use of steel knives and swords by the colonists, perhaps contrasted with the stone knives of the early Indians.

LOUISE PHELPS KELLOGG

BIGLOW PAPERS, originally, nine satirical poems in Yankee dialect directed against the Mexican War, which, in the opinion of their author, James Russell Lowell, had as its object the acquisition of slave territory. From 1846 to 1848 the jingling rhymes like "What Mr. Robinson Thinks" spread from newspaper to newspaper. In 1848 Lowell gathered the nine poems into a collection, elaborating on them until the original intent of the lyrics was all but lost. To the spokesman Hosea Biglow was added the pundit editor Rev. Homer Wilbur, who was endless in his comment. Written in haste, with youthful extravagance and zeal, the satires sparkle with fun and at times bite like acid.

Beginning in 1862, Lowell ran in the *Atlantic Monthly* a second series of the papers, this time satirizing the South. Some of the lyrics, like "Jonathan to John," display flashes of the old-time fire, but the poet, less youthful now, had to force himself into the satiric mood. The jingles of Hosea Biglow with their misspellings could not voice the national tragedy. As a result the final collection, 1867, with its chaos of embellishment, its beautiful nature poetry, and its long essay on Yankee dialect, is, unlike the first series, hardly to be rated as primarily satiric.

FRED LEWIS PATTEE

BIG MOCCASIN GAP, in extreme southwestern Virginia, admitted Daniel Boone and other pioneers through the Clinch Mountains into Kentucky. Not far from it were the blockhouses, built by Capt. John Anderson in 1777, where parties formed for the journey over the Wilderness Road. The line established by the Treaty of Lochaber, 1768, and surveyed by John Donelson in 1770 crossed the road near this gap.

[A. B. Hulbert, *Boone's Wilderness Road;* W. A. Posey, *The Wilderness Road.*]

JONATHAN T. DORRIS

BILLETING, quartering of military troops, a European practice rarely resorted to in America. Regiments usually camped out or occupied forts and barracks erected at colonial expense. Increased troop arrivals during the French and Indian War made billeting an issue, beginning in New York and Philadelphia, in 1756. To shelter soldiers, the Mutiny Act of 1765 required colonial governments, when barracks were not available, to billet troops in inns, barns, and uninhabited houses, and to furnish certain provisions. As "a common resort of arbitrary princes," billeting aroused resistance in Charleston (1764), New York (1766), and Boston (1768), largely arising from unwillingness to accede to any money legislation by Parliament and to any military enforcement of unpopular measures. This resistance fed on traditional British aversion to standing armies. Billeting, though paid for, led directly to the Boston Massacre. The Quartering Act of 1774, designed to permit billeting within Boston, had little to do with the final issue, which was already joined. Billeting was objected to in the Declaration of Independence and was prohibited in the Bill of Rights, in the Third Amendment.

[C. M. Clode, *Military Forces of the Crown;* G. O. Trevelyan, *The American Revolution;* C. H. Van Tyne, *Causes of the War of Independence.*]

ELBRIDGE COLBY

BILL OF RIGHTS. The term "bill of rights" does not appear in the U.S. Constitution. It is, however, commonly used to designate the first ten amendments; and often it is used with latitude to include as well some later amendments affecting rights or liberties, such as the Nineteenth Amendment, granting the right of suffrage to women.

At the constitutional convention in 1787 George Mason proposed that the Constitution be "prefaced with a bill of rights." He argued that with the aid of state bills of rights already in existence, "a bill [of rights] might be prepared in a few hours." (Indeed, Mason was an old hand at the drafting of such documents, for he was the author of the Virginia Declaration of Rights, adopted in 1776 and the model for all later state bills of rights.) Elbridge Gerry moved the appointment of a committee to prepare a bill of rights, but the motion lost by a five-to-five vote. Accordingly, the Constitution as submitted for ratification contained no bill of rights. It did, however, include some important guarantees of personal rights and liberties: the privilege of the writ of habeas corpus was not to be suspended except in cases of rebellion or invasion (Article I, Section 9); no bill of attainder or ex post facto law was to be passed (Article I, Section 9); all crimes were to be tried by jury (Article III, Section 2); and no religious test could be required as a qualification to any office (Article VI).

When the Constitution came before the ratifying conventions, its opponents joined with advocates of a bill of rights in arguing that the Constitution was defective. They were answered by Federalists, in particular James Wilson and Alexander Hamilton, who argued that such personal guarantees were both unnecessary and dangerous because their inclusion in the Constitution might imply that the federal government had powers that in fact had not been conferred on it. "Why, for instance, should it be said," Hamilton asked rhetorically in *Federalist* 84, "that the liberty of the press shall not be restrained, when no power is given by which restrictions may be imposed?" James Madison tended to think along the same line, but in time he was won over to the side that favored a bill of rights. In a letter to Thomas Jefferson (Oct. 17, 1788), he wrote that notwithstanding the objections that he could see, he conceded that a bill of rights might nonetheless be useful in the following ways:

> 1. The political truths declared in that solemn manner acquire by degrees the character of fundamental maxims of free Government, and as they become incorporated with the national sentiment, counteract the impulses of interest and passion. 2. Although it be generally true . . . that the danger of oppression lies in the interested majorities of the people rather than in usurped acts of Government, yet there may be occasions on which the evil may spring from the latter source; and on such, a bill of rights will be a good ground for an appeal to the sense of the community.

The consequence of the debate over political philosophy and constitutional theory and interpretation was that some states sent along with their ratifications amendments that they wanted to see adopted by the new government (more than a hundred such amendments were proposed by the ratifying conventions).

On May 4, 1789, two months after the First Congress convened, Madison gave notice to the House of Representatives, where he sat as a member, that he intended to bring up the subject of amendments to the Constitution. On June 8 he proposed that the House resolve itself into a committee of the whole on the state of the Union to consider eight resolutions on amendments to the Constitution. Several members argued that there were more pressing matters; however, the House agreed that the matter would be referred to a committee of the whole. On July 21, Madison moved that the House become a committee of the whole to take up his amendments. The motion lost, and the amendments were then referred to a select committee of ten members, which included Madison. On Aug. 13 the House resolved itself into a committee of the whole to consider the select committee's report.

Madison spoke for incorporating the amendments into the body of the Constitution itself at appropriate places, so that then "they will stand upon as good a foundation as the original work." Furthermore, he said, the text of the Constitution would then be simpler than if the amendments were to consist of separate and distinct parts. The matter was debated, and at that point Madison's proposal won.

The select committee recommended fourteen amendments. The House, as a committee of the whole, considered and debated them for five days, and, with some changes, approved them all. On Aug. 19 the House took up the amendments as reported by the committee of the whole. Its first action was to decide that the amendments be appended as a supplement to the Constitution and not be distributed throughout the original document. But for this action, it would not be possible to speak of any one part of the Constitution as the Bill of Rights. On Aug. 20 and 21 the House considered the amendments and affirmed, except for some changes, the previous action it had taken as a committee of the whole; on Aug. 22 it referred the amendments to a committee of three "to arrange the said amendments." The committee submitted its report on Aug. 24, and the House voted a resolution proposing seventeen amendments to the states for ratification. The House then forwarded the amendments to the Senate.

The record of the Senate proceedings is extremely meager. It shows that debate was taken up the following week, but it is doubtful that the Senate devoted more than two normal session days to the subject. It approved some articles and rejected others, and on Sept. 9 it reconsidered some of the actions it had previously taken. On Sept. 21 the Senate asked for a conference with the House to straighten out differences. As a result, the House reduced its original seventeen amendments to twelve, and these the Senate approved on Sept. 25. Thus, the Bill of Rights had been before Congress from June 8 to Sept. 25, 1789; but it is doubtful that more than a total of seven or eight session days had been devoted to consideration of the amendments.

On Nov. 20, 1789, New Jersey became the first state to ratify the amendments; Virginia, on Dec. 15, 1791, was the eleventh state to do so, completing the ratification process. On the latter date the Bill of Rights became effective. (Although Dec. 15 is not a legal or public holiday, by an act of Congress it is observed as Bill of Rights Day.) Two amendments failed of ratification, those related to the apportionment of representatives and the compensation of members of Congress—matters that were hardly germane to a bill of rights.

While Congress was trying to reach agreement on the amendments, in Paris on Aug. 26, 1789, the Constituent Assembly for the new French republic issued the Declaration of the Rights of Man and of the Citizen; and when the new French constitution came into force in 1791, the declaration was prefixed to it. In its generalities the declaration was modeled after the American Declaration of Independence. In their practical provisions, both the French declaration and the American Bill of Rights were modeled after the bills of rights of the American states—notably, the Virginia Declaration of Rights; the Massachusetts Bill of Rights (1780), drafted largely by John Adams; and the Virginia Statute for Establishing Religious Freedom (1786), drafted by Thomas Jefferson.

But both the Americans and the French had learned from the English models also: the Magna Charta (1215), the Petition of Right (1628), and the Bill of Rights (1689). Jefferson, Madison, and Mason had been influenced, directly or indirectly, by the writings of John Locke and John Milton, the pamphlets of Thomas Paine, the long tradition of natural law, the idea of a higher law implicit in the Hebrew Scriptures, Stoic philosophy, medieval political thought, and English revolutionary and constitutional theory.

In some four hundred words, the original Bill of Rights provides—in its more important articles—for freedom of religion, speech, press, and assembly and the right of petition (First Amendment); a guarantee against unreasonable searches and seizures (Fourth Amendment); a prohibition of double jeopardy, coerced testimony against oneself in any criminal case, and a prohibition against depriving any person of his life, liberty, or property without due process of law and against the taking of private property for public use without just compensation (Fifth Amendment); the right to a speedy and public trial, the right to be confronted by accusing witnesses, and the right to assistance of counsel (Sixth Amendment); the right to trial by jury (Seventh Amendment); a prohibition against excessive bail or fines and against cruel and unusual punishments (Eighth Amendment). The Ninth Amendment is a statement of the general principle that the provision of certain rights in the Constitution shall not imply the denial of other rights "retained by the people"; and so, too, the Tenth Amendment states that the powers not delegated to the federal government or prohibited to the states are reserved to the states or to the people. (*See also* Amendments to the Constitution.)

The Supreme Court in 1833 in an opinion by Chief Justice John Marshall declared that the first ten amendments were adopted to guard against abuses by the federal government and not against encroachments by the states. This position, although repeatedly contested, was insistently reaffirmed by the Court. After adoption of the Fourteenth Amendment, it was contended that the procedural safeguards prescribed in the Bill of Rights are "fundamental principles of liberty and justice" and are therefore essential ingredients of due process of law applicable against the states; but the Court, except for Justice John M. Harlan (born 1833), rejected this argument. With respect to substantive provisions, Justice Harlan, in 1907, argued that the First Amendment freedoms of speech and press are "essential parts of every man's liberty" and are therefore protected by the Fourteenth Amendment's guarantee that no state may deprive a person of his "liberty" without due process of law. But this was in a dissenting opinion. Justice Louis D. Brandeis expressed the same view in 1920 but also in a dissenting opinion. The first constitutional breakthrough came in *Meyer* v. *Nebraska* (1923), in which the Court declared unconstitutional a state statute that prohibited any school, public or private, from teaching any subject in a language other than English. The Court's opinion by Justice James McReynolds broadly defined the "liberty" protected by the due process clause of the Fourteenth Amendment. And, two years later, in *Gitlow* v. *New York,* the Court said that it would "assume" that freedom of speech and press "are among the fundamental personal rights and 'liberties' protected by the due process clause of the Fourteenth Amendment from impairment by the states."

In subsequent cases decided in the 1930's the Court "assimilated" into the Fourteenth Amendment the First Amendment freedoms of religion and assembly; and in 1947, in *Everson* v. *Board of Education,* it held that the First Amendment ban on "establishment of religion" was applicable to the states by the Fourteenth Amendment. The Court has not, however, "incorporated" into the Fourteenth Amendment all the guarantees of the first eight amendments. The Court has proceeded slowly and on a case-by-case basis, and while there has been a definite line of progress, it has by no means been a straight line. It was not until 1963 that the Court, overruling a case it had decided in 1942, held that the Sixth Amendment right to counsel was applicable to the states under the due process clause of the Fourteenth Amendment. The chief proponent of the proposition that the framers of the Fourteenth Amendment intended that the entire Bill of Rights be applicable to the states was Justice Hugo Black, but his position was strongly challenged by Justice Felix Frankfurter and Justice John M. Harlan (born 1899). The intermediate position, which generally prevailed, was formulated by Justice Benjamin Cardozo in *Palko* v. *Connecticut* (1937). This position was that there is no total incorporation, but that only those guarantees in the Bill of Rights that are found to be "implicit in the concept of ordered liberty" become effective against the states. These must be rights found to be "of the very essence of ordered liberty"—such rights that "neither liberty nor justice would exist if they were sacrificed"—they must be principles of justice "so rooted in the traditions and conscience of our people as to be ranked as fundamental."

The constitutional guarantees are obviously not an exhaustive enumeration of basic human rights. From time to time other rights clamor for recognition. Accordingly, the Court has said that specific guarantees of the Bill of Rights "have penumbras, formed by emanations from those guarantees that help give them [i.e., the guarantees] life and substance" (Justice William O. Douglas in *Griswold* v. *Connecticut,* 1965). Among such rights recognized by the Court are the right to travel, the right of parents to send their children to a private school, the right to procreate, the right to privacy, and the right of association. This class of "peripheral" rights is, of course, not closed. One rationale for them is that without these rights, specifically enumerated rights would be less secure.

The Supreme Court under Chief Justice Earl Warren (1953–69) was especially vigilant and creative in the process of defining and implementing the Bill of Rights. It made the due process clause and the equal protection clause of the Fourteenth Amendment, especially when intertwined with the First Amendment, familiar terms to millions of citizens. Working closely with Chief Justice Warren were justices Black, Douglas, William J. Brennan, Arthur J. Goldberg, Abe Fortas, and Thurgood Marshall. Among their predecessors who made significant contributions to a recognition of the primacy of the Bill of Rights in American society and government were the first Justice Harlan; justices Oliver Wendell Holmes, Brandeis, Cardozo, Frank Murphy, Wiley B. Rutledge; and chief justices Harlan F. Stone and Charles E. Hughes.

[Z. Chafee, Jr., *Three Human Rights in the Constitution,* and *How Human Rights Got Into the Constitution;* N. Dorsen, ed., *The Rights of Americans;* M. R. Konvitz, *Bill of Rights Reader: Leading Constitutional Cases, Fundamental Liberties of a Free People,* and *Expanding Liberties;* L. W. Levy, *Legacy of Suppression: Freedom of Speech and Press in Early American History;* L. H. Pollock, ed., *The Constitution and the Supreme Court,* vol. II; R. A. Rutland, *The Birth of the Bill of Rights, 1776–1791.*]

MILTON R. KONVITZ

BILLS OF CREDIT, a term applied to noninterest-bearing government obligations that circulate as money, although commonly applied in the United States to issues by the colonies and, later, by the Continental Congress and states during the revolutionary war. Since the establishment of the national government, such issues have been known as treasury notes or United States notes.

Bills of credit in the colonies began with an issue of £7,000, shortly increased to £40,000, in Massachusetts in 1690. This was followed by similar action by New Hampshire, Rhode Island, Connecticut, New York, and New Jersey before 1711, South Carolina in 1712, Pennsylvania in 1723, Maryland in 1734, Delaware in 1739, Virginia in 1755, and Georgia in 1760. In most cases the bills were issued to excess and depreciated sharply in value. Parliament finally prohibited such paper currency in New England in 1751 and in the other colonies in 1764.

As soon as the colonies broke away from England, they again began to emit bills of credit in large amounts. The Continental Congress, unable to obtain necessary funds from other sources, authorized $241,552,780 of bills from 1775 to 1779 inclusive, while the various states put out $209,524,776 of bills during the same period.

[D. R. Dewey, *Financial History of the United States.*]

FREDERICK A. BRADFORD

BILLS OF RIGHTS, STATE. The bill of rights adopted by Virginia in 1776 preceded those of the other states, and was the model upon which the national Bill of Rights, the first ten amendments of the U.S. Constitution, was drawn up. The Virginia declaration, in large part the work of George Mason, was adopted on June 12 by the colonial House of Burgesses, which met as a convention. The document was in large part a restatement of English principles drawn from such sources as Magna Carta, the Petition of Right, and the English Bill of Rights. It still stands in practically the original form as the beginning of the present constitution of Virginia.

While other and later state constitutions have copied the Virginia provisions somewhat, they also have added other provisions according to local or contemporary needs. The second great bill of rights was the Declaration of Rights of the Commonwealth of Massachusetts, adopted in 1780. It was stated in thirty provisions while that of Virginia was stated in sixteen. The Massachusetts bill of rights goes into greater detail than that of Virginia, stressing such things as the right of the people to bear arms, a condemnation of ex post facto laws, bills of attainder, and the quartering of soldiers in time of peace. The Puritan religious influence is shown in the statement that "it is the right as well as the duty of all men in society, publicly, and at stated seasons, to worship the Supreme Being, the great Creator and Preserver of the universe." The final article is a more lengthy and specific statement of the principle of separation of powers. This bill of rights also stands as a part of the original constitution of Massachusetts and still remains in force today.

The bills of rights in other or later-formed states show the results of contemporary events and influence and are often much more lengthy. Thus, slavery is prohibited in the bills of rights of Maryland, Nevada, and in almost all the southern states. This is a direct result of the Civil War and the Reconstruction period. The constitution of New Mexico contains the odd and legally questionable statement that "the people of the State have the sole and exclusive right to govern themselves as a free, sovereign and independent State."

While many of the bills of rights of the various

states set forth matters that are never questioned and establish prohibitions of powers already beyond the competence of the state governments, there is no doubt that their effect in general is healthy and constructive. They specifically state and emphasize the fundamental principles upon which American government and society are founded.

[E. S. Corwin, *The Constitution and What It Means Today;* Allan Nevins, *The American States During and After the Revolution, 1775–1789.*]

WILLIAM STARR MYERS

BILOXI, city in southeastern Mississippi located on the Gulf of Mexico, the first settlement in and capital of the Louisiana Territory. It was settled by Pierre Lemoyne, Sieur d'Iberville, in 1699, with 200 French colonists, as Fort Maurepas on the Biloxi Bay (near the present Ocean Springs, Miss.). The capital was relocated to the present site in 1719. New Orleans replaced Biloxi as the territory's capital in 1722. Biloxi was incorporated as a village in 1872 and as a city in 1896. Seafood is the city's chief industry. Its 1970 population numbered 48,486.

BIMETALLISM. In 1791 the world's leading countries were on a bimetallic monetary standard under which both silver and gold served as a basis of coinage. Following Alexander Hamilton's recommendations, based upon previous reports by Thomas Jefferson and Robert Morris, the U.S. Congress also established a bimetallic standard. The Coinage Act of Apr. 2, 1792, provided for a gold eagle ($10 gold piece) of 247.50 grains, 100 percent fine; a silver dollar of 371.25 grains; and subsidiary silver coins (half-dollar, quarter-dollar, disme, and half-disme) of proportional weight.

The American silver dollar circulated at face value in Latin America even though it weighed less than the Latin-American dollar. Consequently, most of what was minted was exported and did not circulate to any significant extent. In 1806 President Jefferson by executive order put a stop to this practice by suspending the coinage of silver dollars.

Gold coins were also under pressure because the mint ratio of silver to gold (15 to 1) undervalued gold. An owner of gold could sell it to the mint at the congressionally set price of $19.40 an ounce; but in the free market, where prices were set chiefly by supply and demand, he could get approximately $20 an ounce. In accordance with Gresham's law the undervalued metal in a bimetallic system will cease to circulate once the disparity between the mint and the market ratios becomes large enough to yield a profit after all selling costs are paid. Until the Napoleonic wars the disparity between silver and gold was not large enough to cover selling costs and still yield a profit. But in 1821 England adopted the gold standard. This move raised the demand for gold, pushing its price beyond the point at which Gresham's law began to work, and gold all but disappeared from circulation.

After the Napoleonic wars many proposals were made to devalue gold, but the scarcity of the metal did not seem to permit it. Then gold was discovered in the Appalachians in the 1830's, and Congress reduced the gold content of the eagle to 232.0 grains by act of June 28, 1834. On Jan. 18, 1837, the weight was increased to 232.2 grains, making the mint ratio of silver to gold 15.988 to 1. Gold was thus overvalued at the mint, but it was not until 1844 that Gresham's law caused all silver coins to disappear from circulation. In order to bring subsidiary silver back, Congress by an act of Feb. 21, 1853, reduced the half-dollar from 206.25 grains, 9/10 fine, to 192 grains, 9/10 fine. Other coins were reduced proportionately.

Civil War inflation drove all specie out of circulation; the country was on an irredeemable paper standard from 1861 to 1879. But it was assumed that specie payments would be resumed (and the Resumption Act of 1875 so provided). Meanwhile, in light of the fact that the silver dollar had not circulated for thirty years, the coinage laws were rewritten; the act of Feb. 12, 1873, dropped the silver dollar and made the gold dollar the monetary standard.

A series of events in the early 1870's had reduced the demand for silver. In 1871–73 Germany went on the gold standard and demonetized silver; the Latin Union countries thereupon closed their mints to silver; Scandinavia adopted the gold standard; and Russia, in 1876, suspended silver coinage. More common use of bills of exchange in the India trade also reduced the demand. At the same time the silver supply increased some 20 percent because of new discoveries in the old mines of Nevada.

The price of silver fell sharply, and silverites and quantity theorists who were interested in raising the price level denounced the 1873 coinage act as "the crime of 1873." They insisted that the act had been a Machiavellian plot by the creditor classes to prevent price recovery. The act's authors, on the other hand, insisted that silver had been dropped because silver dollars had not circulated for a generation. For many years most scholars agreed with them; but more recent scholars, less frightened by threats of inflation than their predecessors, have resurrected the charge that the act of 1873 was passed in anticipation of a decided decline in the price of silver; if silver had not been demonetized, bimetallism at 16 to 1 would have driven gold out of circulation.

From 1873 on, silverites tried to restore free silver, but they had only partial success. The Bland-Allison Act of Feb. 28, 1878, instructed the U.S. Treasury to purchase at market prices at least $2.5 million of silver a month to be coined into dollars at the old rate of 412.5 ounces, 9/10 fine. The Bland-Allison Act was replaced by the Sherman Silver Purchase Act of June 17, 1890, which required the purchase of 4.5 million ounces per month. The Sherman Act in turn was repealed on Nov. 1, 1893, in the continuous struggle between the "easy-money free silverites" and the "sound-money forces."

The discovery of substantial gold reserves in Alaska and South Africa, together with more efficient methods of refining gold, put a temporary end to the money debate. As much greater quantities of gold fattened the money supply, prices rose, dampening the arguments of the silverites. At the same time, checkbook money was slowly but surely making hard money relatively less important, especially psychologically. A monetary problem did occur during World War I, but it did not create any emotional outbreak. As in every major war and as in every depression except that of 1873–78, the country suspended domestic specie redemption.

World War I also did something for silver. The Pittman Act of Apr. 23, 1918, authorized the Treasury to melt 350 million silver dollars, to sell the silver at $1 or more an ounce, and to buy 371.25 grains of pure silver for each dollar's worth sold.

The depression of the 1930's restored interest in bimetallism, the gold standard, and the money supply. On Apr. 5, 1933, President Franklin D. Roosevelt by proclamation suspended the gold standard. The Thomas Amendment to the Agricultural Adjustment Act (May 12, 1933) authorized the president to devalue the gold dollar up to 50 percent, to accept up to $200 million in silver at 50 cents an ounce in payment of war debts, and to restore bimetallism. By the Gold Reserve Act of Jan. 30, 1934, the weight of the gold dollar was reduced from 23.22 to 13.71 grains, making gold worth $35 an ounce instead of $20.67.

Again, something was done for silver. By various acts between 1933 and 1935 the government was instructed to buy all newly mined domestic silver at $1.2929 an ounce (the old 16 to 1 ratio) less a seigniorage, which varied from 50 percent to 77.57 percent.

During the 1960's the United States abandoned all but a small vestige of a metallic standard. The acts of Mar. 3, 1965, and Mar. 18, 1968, eliminated the gold reserve against Federal Reserve deposits and Federal Reserve notes. An act of July 23, 1965, put an end to the minting of standard silver coins; and an act of Aug. 15, 1971, temporarily suspended the international right to convert dollars into gold. Subsequently, on Apr. 3, 1972, the dollar was devalued 8.57 percent, making the price of gold $38 an ounce. Less than a year later (Feb. 12, 1973) the dollar was devalued an additional 10 percent and the price of gold was raised to $42.22 an ounce. Meanwhile, two markets were established for gold, the arbitrary market of $42.22 an ounce and a free market in which gold at one time reached almost $200 an ounce.

[H. E. Krooss, *Documentary History of Banking and Currency;* J. L. Laughlin, *History of Bimetallism in the United States;* David A. Martin, "1853: The End of Bimetallism in the United States," *Journal of Economic History,* vol. 33 (1973); W. K. Nugent, *Money and American Society, 1865–1880.*]

HERMAN E. KROOSS

BINGHAM PURCHASE. In 1786, when Massachusetts, which then included Maine, disposed of large tracts of unsettled timberlands in Maine by lottery, William Bingham, a wealthy Philadelphia banker, drew several townships and purchased others, with a total area of one million acres. Gen. Henry Knox had signed a contract to buy another tract of one million acres, but his duties as secretary of war prevented his developing it, and Bingham took that over also.

[William Bingham, *Description of Certain Tracts . . . in the District of Maine.*]

ALVIN F. HARLOW

BIOCHEMISTRY. The origins of biochemical studies in America clearly derive from antecedent studies in Europe, arising from the work of Justus von Liebig at Giessen and Munich, Max Joseph von Pettenkofer and Carl von Voit at Munich, Ernst Felix Hoppe-Seyler at Tübingen and Strasbourg, and Wilhelm Kühne at Heidelberg. The American origins are shrouded in obscurity because of parallel developments out of agricultural and medical chemistry during the 19th century, there having been no clear merging of the two areas until the 1930's. The American students of Liebig and even those of Pettenkofer and Voit mostly moved into laboratories concerned with agricultural problems involving plant growth and animal feeding; those of Hoppe-Seyler and Kühne tended to place stress on problems associated with human physiology—particularly blood, urine, and other body fluids.

Proteins received a great deal of attention from both groups—the agricultural chemists being concerned mainly with the protein content of feeds and their utilization by farm animals; the physiological chemists searching for underlying composition, but without significant success, because the complexity of proteins was not appreciated. In the late 19th century Thomas B. Osborne at the Connecticut Agricultural Experiment Station carried out some masterful work on the isolation and purification of plant proteins and ultimately sought to unravel their amino acid composition, utilizing techniques developed in Germany by Emil Fischer and Emil Abderhalden. The last years of the 19th century also saw the beginnings of extensive studies on the energy requirements of animals and the energy values of various foods and feeds. W. O. Atwater, F. G. Benedict, and H. P. Armsby were leaders in such research at the turn of the century, utilizing respiration calorimeters large enough to study human beings and large farm animals.

In the early decades of the 20th century the agricultural chemists were largely responsible for the unfolding of nutritional knowledge of vitamins and minerals, even though the earliest recognition of the antiberiberi factor was made in Java by Christiaan Eijkman, a Dutch bacteriologist. In 1912, Sir Frederick Gowland Hopkins and Casimir Funk called clear attention to the dietary need of trace organic nutrients and Funk introduced the term "vitamine," which later came to be written "vitamin." The studies of Osborne and Lafayette B. Mendel at the Connecticut Agricultural Experiment Station and of Elmer V. McCollum at the Wisconsin station led to the recognition, in 1913, of the growth-promoting activity of a trace substance—later known as vitamin A—in butterfat. McCollum also clarified the role of a water-soluble material that he identified as vitamin B and that was curative for beriberi. Early in the 1920's, McCollum at Johns Hopkins University and Harry Steenbock at the University of Wisconsin further clarified the role of fat-soluble substances in the prevention of rickets, the name vitamin D being given to this factor. Steenbock showed that ultraviolet light converted foods sterols into vitamin D during irradiation. The Steenbock patents led to the commercial fortification of milk, yeast, and other foods with vitamin D through the irradiation process. During the 1920's and 1930's other American and European investigators clarified the nature of the B-complex, particularly important work being done by Robert R. Williams working independently, Joseph Goldberger of the U.S. Public Health Service, Conrad A. Elvehjem of Wisconsin, and Roger Williams of Oregon State College. The work of these men and their students inaugurated a whole new understanding of nutrition and led, through practical application of this knowledge to food selection and fortification, to the virtual elimination of such diseases as scurvy, rickets, beriberi, and pellagra.

Composition and properties of body fluids received much attention from physiological chemists associated with medical schools and research centers, such as the Rockefeller Institute for Medical Research (now Rockefeller University). Lawrence J. Henderson of Harvard University pioneered in the application of physical chemistry to physiological systems, particularly the maintenance of equilibrium in body fluids, such as the blood. D. D. Van Slyke of the Rockefeller Institute extended these principles to gas-transport equilibria in the blood, and A. Baird Hastings worked extensively on acid-base equilibria of the blood under varying conditions, first at Rockefeller Institute and after 1926 at the University of Chicago. The mechanism of blood clotting came under the careful scrutiny of W. H. Howell at Johns Hopkins University. Otto Folin of Harvard was noteworthy for his introduction of analytical methods for the determination of components of body fluids, particularly blood and urine. Such tests quickly became important in diagnosis and treatment of disease.

American biochemists pioneered in the study of intermediary metabolism with the use of isotopic tracers. At Columbia University in the 1930's Rudolf Schoenheimer and David Rittenberg utilized heavy hydrogen and nitrogen-15 to show the active breakdown of fats and proteins in animal tissues. When radioisotopes—particularly carbon-14, discovered by Reuben Kamin—became widely available after World War II, they were used extensively. Melvin Calvin at the University of California developed the techniques necessary for the study of photosynthesis, and these techniques were fruitfully used for the study of fermentation and the metabolism of proteins, fats, and carbohydrates. Vincent du Vigneaud carried out particularly significant work between 1935 and 1960 in the reactions of sulfur-containing compounds and of active methyl groups.

American biochemists have also contributed extensively to the understanding of enzymes, protein synthesis, and the transmission of genetic information. In 1926 James B. Sumner crystallized jack-bean urease, thus demonstrating the protein nature of enzymes. John H. Northrup crystallized pepsin a few years later, and by 1974 nearly a hundred enzymes had been prepared in crystalline form, many of them in America. In the 1960's William Stein and Stanford Moore of Rockefeller University and C. B. Anfinsen of the National Institutes of Health succeeded in establishing the amino acid sequence and structure of ribonuclease. Phoebus Levene had spent many years at the Rockefeller Institute studying the chemical composition of nucleic acids without recognizing their function. The nature of genetic mechanisms came under extensive study after O. T. Avery at the institute recognized the role of nucleic acids in hereditary processes in 1944. James Watson joined Francis Crick of Cambridge University in 1951 to establish the double helix structure of DNA. American molecular biologists—notably Max Delbrück, A. D. Hershey, S. E. Luria, R. W. Holley, H. G. Khorana, and M. W. Nirenberg—played an important role in clarifying the function of nucleic acids in protein synthesis between 1950 and 1970.

[R. Chittenden, *The Development of Physiological Chemistry in the United States;* E. V. McCollum, *A History of Nutrition;* Gunther Stent, *The Coming of the Golden Age.*]

AARON J. IHDE

BIRCH, JOHN, SOCIETY. *See* **John Birch Society.**

BIRCHARD LETTER, a public letter, June 29, 1863, to M. Birchard and eighteen other Ohio Democrats in which President Abraham Lincoln defended the administration's treatment of antiwar agitators. Lincoln offered to rescind the sentence of banishment (May 5, 1863) to the Confederacy of C. L. Vallandigham, an Ohio politician who had violated General Order No. 38, forbidding any expression of sympathy for the Confederacy, if a majority of those to whom the letter was addressed would subscribe to certain pledges in connection with the prosecution of the Civil War.

[J. G. Nicolay and John Hay, *Complete Works of Abraham Lincoln.*]

PAUL M. ANGLE

BIRCH BARK. The bark of the paper birch (*Betula papyrifera*) was used by Indians of the Great Lakes country and adjacent Canada for covering canoes, wigwams, food containers, and cooking vessels. A kettle of this bark will boil food safely, if it does not touch the flames. Small sheets of birch bark were used for picture writing with a stylus by the Chippewa (Ojibwa) and a few other Indians. Its use for canoes and shelters extended into Alaska, thence to Siberia.

[W. J. Hoffman, *The Beginnings of Writing;* J. H. Saloman, *Indian Crafts and Lore.*]

CLARK WISSLER

BIRDS. During the 16th, 17th, and 18th centuries some travelers, missionaries, and colonists included in their writings minor comments on birds seen. But there were two notable naturalists: Mark Catesby (1679–1749), who wrote and illustrated the *Natural History of Carolina, Florida, and the Bahama Islands* in two folio volumes (1731–43), and William Bartram (1739–1823), who was known for his *Travels Through North & South Carolina, Georgia, East & West Florida* (1791) and for being the mentor of Alexander Wilson (1766–1813).

The 19th century saw both the beginning and a great development of American ornithology. Wilson is known as the father of American ornithology for his *The American Ornithology* in nine folio volumes (1808–14), in which 280 species are given scientific names and descriptions and in which colored illustrations are provided for most. Overlapping Wilson in time was J. J. Audubon, whose *The Birds of America* (1827–38), in four double elephant folios of 435 hand-colored plates, has been called "the greatest monument erected by art to nature." The text to the plates, *Ornithological Biography* (1831–39), in five octavo volumes, lists names of 506 species.

The period from the time of Audubon until the 1880's was one in which the number of faunal studies and descriptions of new species from across the continent rapidly increased. The genius of Spencer F. Baird and of Elliott Coues brought order to the nomenclature and classification of the developing science. Baird and his co-workers surveyed the field in *A History of North American Birds: Land Birds* (1874) and *The Water Birds of North America* (1884). Coues's classical *Key to North American Birds* (1872) went through six much-revised editions, the last appearing in 1927 and still useful.

In the 1880's an important part of ornithology was collecting specimens for the purpose of documenting records, providing descriptions, and preservation for further study. Many large collections were built by wealthy individuals. In the middle and latter part of the century these collections began to be consolidated in the large natural history museums that were being established, notably in Washington, D.C.; Philadelphia; New York City; Cambridge, Mass.; and Chicago. With these museums came the first professional ornithologists to curate, add to, and study the collections.

In the late 19th century, scientific ornithology, to many, was the finding, naming, describing, and classifying of birds. Knowledge of the living bird was considered natural history or popular ornithology. But even while "scientific" ornithology was giving a fairly complete account of American avifauna (the last new bird species to be described in North America was in 1889), inquiring students were beginning to explore distributional, behavioral, and ecological aspects of the living bird in wider concepts of biological theory, the new natural history.

A symptom of this change and a powerful impetus to its progress was the founding in 1883 of the American Ornithologists' Union for "the advancement of its members in ornithological science," with forty-seven active and eighty-seven associate members. Arrangements were made for annual meetings; the publication of a quarterly bird journal, *The Auk;* the preparation of a code of nomenclature; and a checklist of North American birds (several times revised and listing 760 species in its 1957 edition). The union had a membership of 3,300 in 1974.

In 1883 life history studies were mostly accumulations of general information on individual species. By the 1930's outlines at least of the life histories of most American birds were known, and from extensive studies of various individual species more general ideas began to emerge: they concerned stimulus for the annual cycle, especially migration; the role of territory; the psychological aspects of behavior, contributing to the development of ethology; and ecological aspects of bird life.

During the early part of the 20th century some American ornithologists began to be interested also in foreign birds, both their systematics and their other biological aspects. Some students traveled in lesser known parts of the world studying birds and made important contributions to the understanding of regional avifauna, such as those of Africa and South America; and important worldwide collections were built up in the large natural history museums.

From the 1930's on, the study of birds continued to receive more impetus and to go in new directions. The subspecies concept (leading to the development of trinominal names for recognizable geographical varieties of a species, introduced about 1900) became the raw material for the study of adaptation and of evolution at work. Students of bird orientation and navigation, in migration and homing, began considering the possible roles of lines of terrestrial navigations, Coriolis force, and celestial clues, such as star patterns and sun-arc and time factors, while radar provided quantitative data for analysis of migrations. Protein analysis, electrophoresis, and other refined techniques are being used in searching out phylogenetic relationships between birds. Electrical devices for sound recording promise advances in basic knowledge of communication systems and behavioral motivations. Ornithologists look forward also to mathematical models of birds and their habitats and distributional patterns.

With these advances ornithology has become a subject for specialization by university professors and graduate students (in more than fifty American colleges and universities). Some universities are building up their own museums because, even with sophisticated equipment and an emphasis on concepts and living birds, museum specimens (such as dried bird skins, skeletons, and carcasses preserved in liquid) are necessary for study, reference, and documentation.

Present-day highly trained American specialists in ornithology, abetted by a body of gifted amateurs, are contributing to basic biology. With access to foreign journals, fieldwork abroad, and attendance at international meetings, their horizons are now worldwide. (*See also* Audubon Society, National; Bird Sanctuaries.)

[E. G. Allen, "The History of American Ornithology Before Audubon," *Transactions of the American Philosophical Society,* vol. 41; American Ornithologists' Union, *Fifty Years' Progress of American Ornithology: 1883–1933;* C. G. Sibley, *Ornithology: In a Century of Progress . . . 1853–1953;* A. Wolfson, ed., *Recent Studies in Avian Biology.*]

A. L. Rand

BIRD SANCTUARIES are natural areas set aside for birds, where they can nest, feed, or roost free from harm or disturbance by human beings. In these areas they are protected from being shot by hunters; protected from indirect effects of human action, such as disturbance that may frighten a nesting bird from its eggs at a critical time; or—the reason for an increasing number of sanctuaries in recent years—protected from loss of vital habitat, as when a marsh that is important as a feeding area for migrating waterfowl is acquired as a sanctuary in order to prevent the area from being filled in, drained, or otherwise changed. Normally a place is picked as a sanctuary because it has natural advantages for the purpose, but there may also be man-made improvement, such as special planting to attract a particular species or water impoundment to offer an improved habitat for waterfowl.

When sanctuaries were first being established around the turn of the 20th century, it was thought that a sanctuary should guard the protected birds against natural enemies, such as weasels and snakes, and even against hawks and owls. Most wildlife biologists now believe that predators are a vital part of the natural scheme of things and that, within reasonable limits, all wildlife within a sanctuary should be protected. In fact, such areas are now more often called wildlife sanctuaries, and some of them are sanctuaries for hawks, wolves, and other predators that need protection.

Historically there is good reason to associate birds with sanctuaries. The natural tendency for many species of birds to congregate in large numbers in a certain habitat makes them particularly vulnerable prey for hunters and also makes it possible for a fence and a warden to protect a species by protecting comparatively small, key areas. When the first bird sanctuaries were established, huge numbers of egrets and other plumed birds were being killed along the Florida coast, their plumes ripped out to sell in the feather trade to decorate ladies' hats, and the carcasses left to rot. Still larger numbers of waterfowl and shorebirds were being butchered as they fed in the marshes near large eastern cities, to be carted off and sold to restaurants. The first bird sanctuaries came into being when the American Ornithologists' Union and the National Audubon Society began providing funds to hire wardens to patrol some of these areas in order to enforce wildlife laws. At that time bird protection was a dangerous business; at least one early Audubon warden was murdered by poachers. The federal government also made an early start in providing sanctuaries. In 1903 President Theodore Roosevelt began setting aside some government-owned lands, by executive order, as federal bird reservations. A major development in the growth of the federal refuge system was the imposition in 1934 of a fee (the so-called duck stamp) for hunting waterfowl. Duck stamp monies are earmarked for acquisition of wildlife refuge lands. Today the National Wildlife Refuge System, under the U.S. Interior Department's Bureau of Sports, Fisheries, and Wildlife, maintains (as of January 1974) 341 units, covering some 30.5 million acres.

Through much of its history the federal refuge system has been concerned principally with game species, thus directly aiding the hunters whose money supports the refuge program. (Since 1960 the federal government, and many state governments, have been taking an increasing interest in nongame species.) The Audubon Society, which, with a string of more than forty sanctuaries from Maine to California, maintains the nation's largest private refuge system, has for the most part left game-bird sanctuaries to the government and concentrated on nongame species. Its refuges range in size from a rocky islet off the coast of Maine that is used by nesting seabirds to a 26,000-acre tract of Louisiana bayou and coastal marsh. It has also acquired an important nesting area in northern Colorado for the golden eagle, the rare prairie falcon, and other birds of prey, and a stretch of the Platte River in Nebraska, a vital stopover point for migrating sandhill cranes, vast numbers of waterfowl, and the extremely rare whooping crane.

[Carl W. Buchheister and Frank Graham, Jr., *Audubon;* Charles H. Callison, *America's Natural Resources.*]

ROBERT C. BOARDMAN

BIRD'S INVASION OF KENTUCKY, one phase of an extensive series of operations planned by the British for the year 1780, whereby the entire West, from Canada to Florida, was to be swept clear of both Spaniards and colonists (*see* British Plan of Campaign in the West). From Detroit, Col. Henry Bird led an Indian army, accompanied by a few white men, against the settlers of Kentucky. The settlements of Martin's Station and Ruddle's Station were easily overwhelmed, but lack of provisions compelled a retreat. Over 300 prisoners were carried back to Detroit.

[M. M. Quaife, "When Detroit Invaded Kentucky," *Burton Historical Collection Leaflet,* vol. 4.]

M. M. QUAIFE

BIRD'S POINT, early fortification in Missouri, neighbor to both Charleston, Mo., and Cairo, Ill., opposite the mouth of the Ohio River where it joins the Mississippi. Of strategic importance in guarding both rivers, it was first fortified by the Spanish in 1795. Col. U. S. Grant was in command of this district for a time, and a few skirmishes took place here during the Civil War.

[U. S. Grant, *Personal Memoirs;* Louis Houck, *History of Missouri.*]

STELLA M. DRUMM

BIRTH CONTROL MOVEMENT. While most colonial and early national Americans were governed by the biblical injunction to increase and multiply, individual instances of birth control occurred, largely through such means as sexual abstention and abortion. Family limitation was established practice in certain religious communities—for example, through selective breeding by the Perfectionists at Oneida Colony, N.Y. Birth control became a concern of other Americans beginning in the 1830's and 1840's in the context of feminist and health reform agitation. Birth control publicists of this era, notably Robert Dale Owen of New York and Charles Knowlton of Massachusetts, faced widespread social disapproval and even harassment. Nevertheless, there was some experimentation with contraceptive devices plus a steady, if slow and partly underground, growth in demand for birth control information.

Beginning in 1873 the adoption of federal and state Comstock laws—named for their most zealous advocate, Anthony Comstock—caused birth control pamphlets to be classed as obscene and barred from the mails and made it difficult even for physicians to write on the scientific aspects of contraception. Most members of the medical profession accepted the prevailing morality in declining to provide advice on the subject, and not until 1912 did a president of the American Medical Association, the pediatrician Abraham Jacobi, venture to endorse birth control in public.

Significant relaxation of the restrictive legislation against birth control did not come until a decade or so after 1912, when Margaret Sanger challenged the measures in the courts—first through publication of contraceptive information and then, in 1916, by opening a birth control clinic in Brooklyn, N.Y. With the rapid establishment of other clinics the National Birth Control League was formed in 1917, forerunner of the Planned Parenthood Federation of America. During the next several decades this body was the focal point of many legal battles and of the opposition to birth control of various civic and religious bodies, especially the Roman Catholic church. After World War II, however, there was a steady acceleration in public acceptance of family limitation—partly a new Malthusian response to economic realities and partly a manifestation of trends toward greater sexual freedom and women's rights. This acceptance has in turn led to such developments as expanded sponsorship of educational and clinical programs by the Planned Parenthood Federation and other private organizations; greater support for medical research in related fields, such as reproductive biology; extensive programs to produce cheap and effective contraceptive devices and drugs; and finally, beginning in the 1960's, unprecedented federal involvement in a variety of foreign and domestic birth control activities.

[Norman E. Himes, *Medical History of Contraception;* David M. Kennedy, *Birth Control in America: The Career of Margaret Sanger;* David J. Rothman and Sheila M. Rothman, eds., *Birth Control and Morality in Nineteenth-Century America: Two Discussions.*]

JAMES H. CASSEDY

BISHOP HILL COLONY, a theocratic communist colony, founded in Henry County, Ill., in 1846 by Erik Jansson, who brought there some 1,500 emigrants from Sweden where they had been persecuted because of their conversion to perfectionism. The colony was incorporated in 1853 and was dissolved in 1860. In 1879 many members of the former colony lost their farms to liquidate its debts and the costs of years of litigation.

[M. A. Mikkelsen, *The Bishop Hill Colony;* G. M. Stephenson, *The Religious Aspects of Swedish Immigration.*]

G. M. STEPHENSON

BISMARCK SEA, BATTLE OF (Mar. 2–4, 1943). To reinforce the Japanese garrison at Lae, New Guinea, eight Japanese transports carrying 7,000 troops, escorted by eight destroyers, left Rabaul, New Britain, about midnight on Feb. 28, 1943. Hidden initially by bad weather, the convoy was spotted by Allied patrol planes on Mar. 1 and 2 in the Bismarck Sea. Heavy bombers struck the ships on Mar. 2, but the biggest attack came the following day as the convoy entered Huon Gulf. Brushing aside feeble Japanese air cover, at about 10 A.M. more than 300 American and Australian bombers and fighters unleashed a devastating attack. Some of the medium bombers used a new "skip-bombing" technique, coming in at very low levels, in the manner of torpedo planes, and dropping delay-fuse bombs that bounced from the water to explode against the sides of Japanese ships. These attacks on Mar. 3 and 4 and a quick strike by American motor torpedo boats sank all eight transports as well as four destroyers, at a cost of only four Allied planes. More than half the Japanese troops were killed, the rest being rescued by Japanese destroyers and submarines. The Japanese never again sent convoys to Lae; subsequent attempts at reinforcement were made only by individual high-speed ships or small coastal craft.

[Wesley Frank Craven and James Lea Cate, eds., *The Army Air Forces in World War II*, vol. IV, *The Pacific: Guadalcanal to Saipan, August 1942 to July 1944;* Samuel Eliot Morison, *History of United States Naval Operations in World War II*, vol. VI, *Breaking the Bismarcks Barrier, 22 July 1942–1 May 1944*.]

STANLEY L. FALK

BISON. *See* **Buffalo.**

BIT, an archaic term for a currency value of one-eighth of a dollar, used chiefly in the South and Southwest, when depreciation of colonial paper money, problems of exchange, coinage, and lack of specie caused the circulation of the Spanish real, a silver coin of that value.

[Neil Carothers, *Fractional Money*.]

JOHN FRANCIS, JR.

BIZERTE, a city on the north coast of Tunisia, important during World War II for its port and airfields. In November 1942, German and Italian forces occupied the area in order to contest the Allied forces that had invaded French Northwest Africa. During the following Tunisian campaign, the Axis used the port and airfields advantageously.

On Apr. 22, 1943, when Gen. Sir Harold Alexander's Anglo-American troops attacked Gen. Jürgen von Arnim's Italo-German forces in the northeastern corner of Tunisia, Bizerte was the objective of the American forces engaged. After hard fighting, particularly on Hill 609, Gen. Omar N. Bradley's U.S. Second Corps entered Bizerte on May 7, the same day that British units seized Tunis. This Axis defeat (200,000 prisoners were taken) opened the way for future Allied operations across the Mediterranean into Europe. Bizerte subsequently served as an Allied loading point for the invasions of Sicily and southern Italy and as a supply depot during these and other Mediterranean campaigns.

[George F. Howe, *Northwest Africa: Seizing the Initiative in the West*, U.S. Army in World War II.]

MARTIN BLUMENSON

BLACK BALL LINE, the first and most celebrated of the lines of transatlantic sailing packets from New York. Its popular nickname came from the black disk carried on the fore-topsail and the house flag. On Oct. 27, 1817, came the announcement of regular monthly sailings. Service started at Liverpool on Jan. 4, 1818, and at New York the next day. In 1822 it was increased to semimonthly sailings with eight ships. The line was started by five New York textile and cotton merchants, all but one of whom were Quakers. Jeremiah Thompson is credited with the original idea. After 1834 it was operated by Capt. Charles H. Marshall. The line continued for exactly sixty years, terminating in 1878. During that time forty-three different ships were used.

[R. G. Albion, *Square-Riggers on Schedule*.]

ROBERT G. ALBION

BLACK BELT, a crescent-shaped area extending along the Alabama River in Alabama and up the Tombigbee River in northeastern Mississippi. About three-fourths of its 5,000 square miles lies in Alabama, including seventeen counties that make up nearly one-fourth the entire area of the state. This region derives its name from the black soil that is prevalent here in contrast to the red clays to the north and south. The Black Belt is a prairie that lies much lower than the surrounding country because of the decomposition of the soft limestone rock under the soil. This rock decomposition has given it a remarkably fertile soil, making it one of the best agricultural regions of the entire South.

The portion of the Black Belt in Alabama was first opened for settlement by the Creek cession of 1816. However, the pioneers were suspicious of the unusual black soil, and it was not until the Jacksonian migration of the 1830's that the region began to be settled. The Mississippi portion was opened at this time, too, as the Choctaw and Chickasaw moved west of the Mississippi. Because of the high fertility of the soil and the accessibility to market at Mobile it was inevitable that the Black Belt should become a plantation region producing great crops of cotton by slave labor. From 1830 to 1860 the Black Belt of Alabama was the most prosperous portion of the state, held the most slaves, produced the most cotton, and was the bulwark of the Whig party. All the rivers of Alabama, except the Tennessee, water the region, and three of the five state capitals—Cahaba, Tuscaloosa, and Montgomery—were located there.

With the coming of the Civil War, the Black Belt

turned from cotton production to the raising of foodstuffs and furnished throughout the war a great part of the food supplies for the Confederate armies. As it had almost no railroad connections with the West or North it remained practically untouched by the northern armies. After the war it again became the leading cotton-producing region of the South until 1880. Unable to meet the competition of Texas cotton, it turned more and more to diversified farming and the raising of food crops, although it remained the principal cotton region east of the Mississippi River.

[T. P. Abernethy, *The Formative Period in Alabama;* U. B. Phillips, *American Negro Slavery.*]

R. S. COTTERILL

BLACK BOYS, Pennsylvania frontiersmen who, in 1763, 1765, and 1769, came together under the leadership of James Smith to defend the frontier against the Indians. In 1765, fearful of traders who might supply guns to the Indians, the Black Boys burned a packhorse train belonging to Baynton, Wharton and Morgan, a company engaged in the Indian trade (*see* Sideling Hill). The frontiersmen disguised themselves during their attacks by blackening their faces.

[Neil Swanson, *The First Rebel;* A. T. Volwiler, *George Croghan and the Westward Movement.*]

JULIAN P. BOYD

BLACKBURN'S FORD, BATTLE AT (July 18, 1861). On his advance to Bull Run, Union Brig. Gen. Irvin McDowell ordered Gen. Daniel Tyler's division to reconnoiter toward Manassas Junction. Tyler found Confederate Gen. James Longstreet's brigade in position behind Bull Run at Blackburn's Ford, attacked, and was decisively repulsed. The morale of McDowell's army suffered from this initial reverse.

[R. U. Johnson and C. C. Buel, eds., *Battles and Leaders of the Civil War,* vol. I.]

JOSEPH MILLS HANSON

BLACK CAPITALISM implies black economic development, with the objective of encouraging economic independence among Afro-Americans, through the ownership and operation of business enterprises and increased employment opportunities, especially at the managerial level in private business.

Early federal programs aimed at making capital and business facilities available to Afro-Americans were focused on the development of black enterprises catering chiefly to black populations. The self-defeating character of this approach was recognized and a new goal of making blacks integral participants in the overall enterprise system gradually emerged during the late 1960's. Primary barriers to achieving this goal have been prejudice, a lack of capital and entrepreneurs, and a paucity of business experience among Afro-Americans. Despite evident progress by 1970, blacks, constituting 11.1 percent of the total population, owned less than 2 percent of all firms and took in less than one percent of total annual American business receipts; employed blacks constituted only 9.6 percent of the total employed and an infinitesimal proportion of business managers.

The black economic development that began in the first half of the 19th century, in the form of small grocery stores and such services as food catering, gardening, and barbering, prospered until Reconstruction created a climate hostile to its continuation, and 20th-century immigration spawned competition for many traditionally black enterprises. The National Business League, founded by Booker T. Washington in 1900, helped Afro-Americans, and still helps, along with at least 140 other organizations that concentrate on assisting black businesses.

Since receiving increasing attention after the 1965 War on Poverty program encouraged black leaders and white businessmen, with federal assistance, to provide more economic opportunities for blacks, the fostering of black capitalism has become increasingly controversial. Some think it is a ruse to keep blacks from participating fully in the economic system, while others think it is the principal means by which blacks may eventually control their economic destinies. The disagreements stem mainly from the great expectations associated with black capitalism programs and the very poor results achieved.

[Frederick E. Case, *Black Capitalism: Problems in Development–A Case Study of Los Angeles;* Theodore L. Cross, *Black Capitalism;* President's Advisory Council on Minority Business Enterprise, *Minority Enterprise and Expanded Ownership: Blueprint for the 70s.*]

FREDERICK E. CASE

BLACK CAVALRY IN THE WEST (1866–91). Established by an act of Congress in 1866, the Ninth and Tenth Cavalry regiments spent over twenty-five years on the frontier. During that time these black troopers fought Indians, bandits, horse thieves, and Mexican revolutionaries. The Ninth Cavalry was ordered into Texas in 1867, while the Tenth assumed field duties in Kansas. The Ninth spent eight years along the Rio Grande housed in rundown posts and serving under the most trying of conditions; they, together with the black infantry, contributed to the eventual pacification of the Texas frontier. The Tenth Cavalry was assigned to Texas in 1875, and the Ninth received orders sending them to New Mexico. In 1881 the Ninth was assigned to duty in Kansas and in Indian Territory. It was their task to keep the "Boomers," settlers who tried to occupy an area in Indian Territory, out of the Indian country. After four years the Ninth was transferred to Nebraska, Wyoming, and Utah. They participated in the Pine Ridge campaign, the last major Indian uprising. The Tenth Cavalry, after relieving the Ninth in Texas, remained along the Rio Grande and took an active role, with the black infantry, in running the Apache warrior Victorio back into Mexico. Ten years later, in 1885, the regiment was sent to Arizona to participate in the campaign against Geronimo. Its final effort was the capture of the Apache chief Mangas Coloradas.

Both regiments served in the West with distinction and gallantry. Their service covered the expanses of Kansas, Texas, Indian Territory, Nebraska, New Mexico, Arizona, Colorado, and the frigid plains of the Dakotas. A dozen Medals of Honor decorated the uniforms of black cavalrymen, plus many commendations for valor conferred upon individual soldiers. These troopers were called "buffalo soldiers" by the Indians, supposedly because they saw a similarity between the hair of the black troopers and that of their sacred animal of the plains. It was a title of respect.

[Arlen L. Fowler, *The Black Infantry in the West, 1869–1891;* W. H. Leckie, *The Buffalo Soldiers*.]

ARLEN L. FOWLER

BLACK CODES. The term "black codes" refers to legislation enacted in the former Confederate states in 1865 and 1866 for the purpose of limiting the freedom of recently freed blacks. It is sometimes considered to include southern antebellum legislation that restricted the action and movements of slaves, although such laws are more frequently referred to as slave codes. Persons using the term "black codes" to include all such laws see them as originating in the 17th century, continuing until the Civil War, and being reenacted in slightly modified form immediately after the war.

The laws passed in 1865–66 by the several states differed from one another, but their general concern was the same: they were intended to replace the social controls of slavery, which had been swept away by the Emancipation Proclamation and the Thirteenth Amendment, and to assure the South that free blacks would remain in a position subordinate to whites. Typical of the legislation were provisions for declaring blacks to be vagrants if they were unemployed and without permanent residence. As vagrants they were subject to being arrested, fined, and bound out for a term of labor if unable to pay the fine. Penalties existed for refusing to complete a term of labor as well as for breaking an agreement to work when it was entered into voluntarily; persons encouraging blacks to refuse to abide by these restrictive laws were themselves subject to penalties. In like manner, orphans could be apprenticed to work for a number of years. In many of these cases the whites to whom blacks were assigned turned out to be their former owners. Blacks could not testify in court cases involving whites and were often prohibited from bearing firearms. Intermarriage between the races was forbidden. Of the states with the most restrictive legislation, Mississippi limited the types of property blacks could own, and South Carolina excluded blacks from certain businesses and from the skilled trades.

Being strikingly similar to the antebellum slave codes, the black codes were, at the very least, not intended to protect the rights to which Afro-Americans were entitled as free men—and it is no overstatement to say that they aimed to reinstate the substance of the slave system without the legal form.

Enactment of black codes in the southern states was a factor in the conflict within the federal government, between the executive and legislative branches, for control of the process of Reconstruction. More than any other single factor it demonstrated what Afro-Americans could expect from state governments controlled by those who had actively supported the Confederate cause. Northern reaction to the codes helped to produce Radical Reconstruction and the Fourteenth and Fifteenth amendments, which temporarily removed such legislation from the books. Following Reconstruction, many of the provisions of the black codes were reenacted in the Jim Crow laws that continued in effect until the Civil Rights Act of 1964.

[John Hope Franklin, *From Slavery to Freedom;* Theodore B. Wilson, *The Black Codes of the South;* C. Vann Woodward, *The Origins of the New South*.]

HENRY N. DREWRY

BLACKFOOT. One of the most numerous and powerful of the tribes of the northwestern Plains, the Siksika ("black feet") were so named because their moccasins were black from the ash of prairie fires or were simply dyed black. While population figures are surmised with difficulty, especially because of the involvement of the Siksika with other and related Algonkin-speaking tribes, the Blackfoot nation at its peak, between 1700 and about 1870, may have had as many as 15,000 members. Spread from the North Saskatchewan River to the southern tributaries of the Missouri in Montana, the Blackfoot nation comprised several subtribes, which may all have had a common source in the area of Algonkin speech to the east. The Blackfoot proper; the Piegan and the Blood tribes, who were their close relatives; the Algonkin Atsina, who were an Arapaho offshoot; and the Athapascan Sarsi formed a military federation that was significant in the balance of power in the northwestern Plains in the 18th century.

The Blackfoot complex is one of classic Plains culture: bison hunting; the war and coup-counting patterns; movements of individual bands; and the great seasonal convocations for intensive hunting. The Blackfoot are also of interest in that they were in process of modifying their kinship organization at the time of their first contact with Europeans in the mid-16th century. Originally patrifocal, they began to model their institutions after those of the neighboring Crow and were developing matrilineal institutions. They had the best-developed system of military associations (divisions of warriors) based on age-grading.

[J. C. Ewers, *The Blackfeet,* and *The Horse in Blackfoot Indian Culture.*]

ROBERT F. SPENCER

BLACK FRIDAY (Sept. 24, 1869), the climactic day of an effort by Jay Gould, James Fisk, Jr., Abel Rathbone Corbin, and one or two associates to corner the ready gold supply of the United States. The nation then being on a paper-money basis, gold was dealt in as a speculative commodity on the New York exchange. Gould and Fisk first enlisted Corbin, who had married President Ulysses S. Grant's sister; they then drew the new head of the New York subtreasury, Daniel Butterfield, into the scheme and unsuccessfully tried to involve Grant's private secretary, Horace Porter. On June 15, 1869, they entertained Grant on Fisk's Bristol Line steamboat, attempted to learn the Treasury's gold policy, and argued that it was important to keep gold high in order to facilitate sales of American grain in Europe. Grant was noncommittal. A gold corner did not seem difficult if government nonintervention could be assured, for New York banks in the summer of 1869 held only about $14 million in gold, not more than a million was in local circulation, and time would be required to bring more from Europe. On Sept. 2 Gould began buying gold on a large scale; on the 15th Fisk began buying heavily and soon forced the price from 135 to 140. The movement excited much suspicion and fear, and the *New York Tribune* declared it the "clear and imperative duty" of the Treasury to sell gold and break up the conspiracy. Secretary of the Treasury George S. Boutwell visited New York but decided not to act; meanwhile Grant had gone to Washington, Pa., and was out of touch until he returned to Washington, D.C., on Sept. 22. On the 23rd, with gold at 144, the New York panic grew serious.

The climax of Black Friday found Fisk driving gold higher and higher, business profoundly disturbed throughout the nation, and the New York gold room a pandemonium as scores were ruined. As the price rose to 160 Boutwell in Washington urged the sale of three million dollars of the gold reserve, Grant suggested five, and the Secretary telegraphed an order to sell four. Gould, perhaps forewarned by Butterfield, had already begun selling, and gold sank rapidly to 135; Fisk immediately found means to repudiate his contracts. The episode caused heavy indirect losses to business and placed an ugly smirch on the Grant administration. Gould and Fisk made an $11 million profit.

[G. S. Boutwell, *Reminiscences of Sixty Years in Public Affairs;* F. C. Hicks, ed., *High Finance in the Sixties;* James Schouler, *History of the United States,* VII.]

ALLAN NEVINS

BLACK HAWK WAR (1832), a conflict between the United States and a faction of Sauk (or Sac) and Fox Indians, waged mainly in Illinois and Wisconsin. The leader of the Sauk and Fox was an aging chief named Black Hawk, who was the rival of another Sauk chief, Keokuk. Keokuk had been receptive to ceding land to the whites and with his faction of the Sauk and Fox had moved across the Mississippi River to Iowa in 1823. Black Hawk, who had fought on the side of the British in the War of 1812, declined to evacuate his village at Rock Island, Ill.

At issue was a treaty made at St. Louis in 1804, under the terms of which the Sauk and Fox supposedly agreed to cede all their lands on the eastern side of the Mississippi River in return for being allowed to remain undisturbed until the country should be opened to settlement. Black Hawk vehemently denied the validity of the treaty, maintaining that the party of Sauk and Fox who had signed the treaty had had no authority to do so and had been deceived while intoxicated. The issue became acute in 1831, when white settlers preempted the site of Black Hawk's village. Black Hawk was aroused and threatened resistance. Hostilities with the Indians were narrowly averted that year when an army of regulars and Illinois militiamen was assembled, but Black Hawk yielded to this threat of force and withdrew across the Mississippi.

Early in 1832, despite the opposition of Keokuk, Black Hawk, with 400 warriors and their families, crossed back into Illinois and moved toward Rock Island. Again the militia was called out, the settlers were alerted, and Gen. Henry Atkinson ordered Black Hawk to return to Iowa. Emissaries from Black Hawk were shot in cold blood. Black Hawk refused to comply with Atkinson's directive, and war erupted. Black Hawk retired up the Rock River, attacking and burning frontier settlements, with the soldiers in pursuit. The troops, poorly disciplined and inexperienced in Indian warfare, were at first unable to retaliate effectively. They were later strengthened, and Black Hawk, hard pressed, realized the futility of resistance and made offers of peace, which were ignored. On July 28 Black Hawk was overtaken by a force of volunteers under Gen. James D. Henry and was crushingly defeated; sixty-eight warriors were killed and many more wounded.

The remnant of Black Hawk's forces was pursued across southern Wisconsin to the mouth of the Bad Axe River, where on Aug. 3 they were massacred as they attempted to cross the Mississippi into Iowa. Black Hawk himself escaped but was later captured by the Winnebago, who turned him over to American troops for the reward. After imprisonment, he was taken to Washington, D.C., where, incongruously, he was honored. He was then allowed to return to the remnant of his tribe in Iowa, where he died in 1838.

Under the terms of the Black Hawk Purchase, signed on Sept. 21, 1832, the Sauk and Fox agreed to cede 6 million acres of land in eastern Iowa, a tract of 400 square miles being reserved along the western bank of the Mississippi for Keokuk and his followers, as a reward for having refrained from participation in the Black Hawk War.

[Cecil Eby, *"That Disgraceful Affair," The Black Hawk War;* William T. Hagan, *The Sac and Fox Indians;* Donald Jackson, ed., *Autobiography of Black Hawk.*]

KENNETH M. STEWART

BLACK HILLS, a group of mountains in western South Dakota and northeastern Wyoming, located mainly in the Black Hills National Forest. The hills are formed by an upthrust of the archean rock through the overlying strata to a maximum height of 7,242 feet above sea level. Harney Peak is the granite (archean) core of the upthrust. From the surrounding prairie through the foothills to Harney Peak, an upcrop of each stratum rises in regular order—the shales, redbeds (gypsum), sandstone, schists, limestones, and granite—as they are folded back, affording an unusual opportunity to study the geological formations underlying the region. The Black Hills were embraced within the Great Sioux Reservation as defined by the Laramie Treaty of 1868. Gold was found in the hills by miners accompanying Gen. George A. Custer's expedition of 1874, which set out from Fort Abraham Lincoln (Bismarck) to find a practicable highway to Fort Laramie. The discovery created much excitement, but the federal government sought to protect the rights of the Indians until these rights could be eliminated by treaty. When early efforts to accomplish this release failed because the Indians refused to accede to government terms, the government raised the embargo and gold hunters rushed into the diggings in vast numbers. This invasion led to the Black Hills War, the high point of which was the destruction of Custer's army on the Little Bighorn in June 1876. After this affair the government forced a treaty of relinquishment and civil government was established.

The miners first assembled at Custer, S.Dak., where 15,000 passed the winter of 1875–76. Gold having been found in Deadwood Gulch, there was a stampede from Custer to the new diggings early in 1876, and Deadwood quickly became the most exciting and picturesque gold camp on the continent. The diggings at that time were entirely in placer gravel, but before autumn the Homestake gold mine had been established at Lead and passed into the hands of San Francisco capitalists. The Homestake mine was developed and for over a hundred years has yielded fabulous sums. Its engineers believe its stores of ore cannot be depleted for many years to come. There are extensive gold deposits in and about Keystone, and that region is very heavily mineralized. Mica, spodumene, amblygonite, feldspar, arsenic, gold, silver, and galena are produced in commercial values. More than 100 valuable minerals are present.

Custer State Park is very extensive and scenically attractive. President Calvin Coolidge, with his staff, made it his summer home in 1927. The region is also the site of Wind Cave National Park, Mount Rushmore National Memorial, and Jewel Cave (S.Dak.) and Devils Tower national monuments.

[Donald Jackson, *Custer's Gold;* Watson Parker, *Gold in the Black Hills,* and *Black Hills Ghost Towns.*]

DOANE ROBINSON

BLACK HILLS WAR (1876). The Black Hills of western South Dakota and adjacent northeastern Wyoming traditionally had been hunting grounds, as well as sacred territory, for the western bands of the Sioux (or Dakota). Under the terms of the Laramie Treaty of 1868, the Black Hills were recognized as part of the Great Sioux Reservation. Although whites were to be excluded from the reservation, persistent rumors of mineral wealth attracted goldseekers there. In 1874, yielding to the demands of the prospectors, the government dispatched troops into the Black Hills under Gen. George Armstrong Custer, ostensibly to establish sites for army posts, although the troops were accompanied by prospectors. When Custer announced that the Black Hills were a goldseeker's paradise, the gold rush was on.

When the Sioux threatened war over the intrusions, the government offered to purchase the land, but the Indians refused to sell. In November 1875 all Indians who had been roaming off the reservation hunting buffalo were ordered to report to their agents, but few of them complied. In March 1876 Gen. George Crook headed north from the Platte River to round up the absentee bands.

In the middle of March the soldiers fought an inconclusive battle with the Northern Cheyenne, who were reinforced by Oglala Sioux under their war leader, Crazy Horse. In June the military mounted a three-pronged invasion of the Indian country, with Crook again leading the attack. Crook was stopped on Rosebud Creek in south-central Montana by Crazy Horse and the Oglala, after which he withdrew. Crazy Horse joined a large encampment of Northern Cheyenne on the Little Bighorn River, in Montana, where Custer and his troops were to lose their lives on June 25, 1876.

After their victory at the Little Bighorn the Indians did not pursue their advantage but dispersed, celebrating and hunting. After that, they were unable to cope with renewed offensives by the military. There were a few skirmishes, but by the spring of 1877 most of the warriors had straggled in to the agencies to be disarmed, except for some who went to Canada with chiefs Sitting Bull and Gall.

Under the terms of a treaty in 1877 the Sioux were obliged to cede the Black Hills for only a fraction of their value, and the area was opened to the goldminers.

[George Hyde, *Spotted Tail's Folk;* Robert Utley, *The Last Days of the Sioux Nation.*]

KENNETH M. STEWART

BLACK HORSE CAVALRY, the name applied to a bipartisan group of corruptionists in the New York legislature who during the last quarter of the 19th century preyed particularly on corporations. They usually blackmailed by introducing bills damaging to the business of corporations that would be killed if sufficient money were forthcoming.

[Theodore Roosevelt, *An Autobiography.*]

HAROLD ZINK

BLACK INFANTRY IN THE WEST (1866–91). A new chapter in American military history opened in the summer of 1866. Congress for the first time authorized six regiments of black troops (each regiment to consist of ten sixty-six-man companies) to be included in the regular army. Two of the regiments were designated cavalry and four, infantry. The infantry units were activated as the Thirty-eighth, Thirty-ninth, Fortieth, and Forty-first Infantry regiments. The Thirty-ninth and Fortieth Infantry were assigned to the South and the Thirty-eighth and Forty-first were sent to the West. In 1869 congressional reorganization of the army consolidated the Thirty-eighth and Forty-first Infantry regiments into the Twenty-fourth regiment, and the Thirty-ninth and Fortieth regiments into the Twenty-fifth.

In 1870 the black regiments moved out on the Texas frontier and began a tour of duty along the Rio Grande that was to last a decade. In this ten-year period the black infantrymen participated in many of the army forays into Mexico and contributed to the eventual defeat of the Apache warrior Victorio and the general pacification of the Texas frontier.

The two regiments separated in 1880, with the Twenty-fourth Infantry moving to Indian Territory and the Twenty-fifth Infantry to Dakota Territory. The Twenty-fourth Infantry was to remain in Indian Territory for eight years before being assigned to Arizona and New Mexico territories, where they would finish out the period of Indian wars. While in Arizona a noncommissioned officer of the Twenty-fourth Infantry won the Medal of Honor for his heroic part in defense of an army paymaster during a robbery attempt. The Twenty-fifth Infantry meanwhile was ordered in 1880 to Dakota Territory, where some units were assigned the task of guarding Sitting Bull and his people at Fort Randall. They remained in Dakota Territory until the summer of 1888, when they were moved to Montana Territory. The Pine Ridge campaign (1890–91) on the Northern Plains found units of the Twenty-fifth Infantry on hand, but not participating in the actual fighting.

[Arlen L. Fowler, *The Black Infantry in the West, 1869–1891;* W. H. Leckie, *The Buffalo Soldiers.*]

ARLEN L. FOWLER

BLACK JACK, BATTLE OF (June 2, 1856), the first engagement of the Kansas Border War. In retaliation for John Brown's massacre at Pottawatomie Creek, a Missouri band under Capt. Pate seized two of Brown's sons. Brown attacked Pate at Black Jack, near Baldwin, Kans. After minor casualties on each side Pate surrendered with twenty-one men. Both bands were dispersed by Col. Edwin V. Sumner of the regular army.

[W. E. Connelley, *Standard History of Kansas and Kansans.*]

WILLIAM M. BALCH

BLACK LAWS. Ohio enacted laws in 1804 and 1807, compelling registration of all Afro-Americans in the state, forbidding any free black to remain without giving $500 bond against his becoming a public charge, and denying validity to an Afro-American's testimony in trials where whites were involved. These laws were an issue in the state campaign of 1846, and in the legislative session of 1848–49, with the Free Soil party leading the attack upon them, they were repealed.

[Charles B. Galbreath, *History of Ohio.*]

ALVIN F. HARLOW

BLACK LEGION, a secret terrorist society active in Michigan in 1936 that murdered a number of blacks and whites whom the society's members felt had violated their peculiar moral standards. The legion first attracted public notice by its murder, May 12, 1936, of Charles A. Poole of Detroit. The resultant criminal prosecutions and sweeping expression of public condemnation soon drove the order into obscurity and to dissolution.

M. M. QUAIFE

BLACKLEGS, a term, now used in a general sense, which once had a special significance, being associated peculiarly with the history of "Natchez-Under-the-Hill," the tenderloin district of Natchez. It referred to professional gamblers possessing large capital, associated in perfectly organized gangs which robbed, murdered, and plundered with impunity in the early period of the old Southwest.

[Robert Coates, *The Outlaw Years.*]

JAMES W. SILVER

BLACKLISTING, a practice of employers to exclude from the job market individuals who are, or are believed to be, union men, labor agitators, or active in strike activities. Originating in the labor troubles of the 1830's, blacklisting, along with the use of agents provocateurs and injunctions, was one of the most widely used of antiunion weapons. Lists of suspects were usually available from an employer upon request, and on some occasions lists were circulated through employers associations. The use of the blacklist continued through the labor agitation following the Civil War, especially as violent conflicts between labor and business escalated in the late 19th century. The need for secrecy undoubtedly played a part in the formation in 1869 of the Knights of Labor, which did not fully cast off its status as a secret organization until 1881. Despite attempts to curb blacklisting, the ease with which employers could communicate with one another without surveillance made the use of the blacklist a fact of life for American labor until the advent of the New Deal. The passage of the National Labor Relations Act, or Wagner Act, in 1935 brought a measure of effective control. The establishment of the right to collective bargaining by the Wagner Act and the subsequent maturation of relations between business and labor significantly diminished the use of the blacklist in labor relations.

A new dimension in blacklisting emerged following World War II with the development of the cold war. Investigations into Communist activities in America resulted in the expulsion of Communists from trade unions and of Communist-dominated unions from national labor organizations. The most glaring example of blacklisting resulted from congressional investigations of government employees and persons employed in the arts, particularly in the motion picture industry. The most celebrated such case of the postwar period was that of the so-called Hollywood Ten, who went to jail rather than answer questions concerning their political affiliations. With the rise of McCarthyism in the early 1950's, the

House Un-American Activities Committee, under Chairman John S. Wood, made an exhaustive investigation into Communist influence in the entertainment world. Unlike the Hollywood Ten, the unfriendly witnesses in this probe used the Fifth Amendment, rather than the First Amendment, to defy the committee. Saved by this strategy from going to jail for contempt of Congress, they were consequently included in a show-business blacklist and barred from employment in motion pictures, television, and radio for the next decade. Although blacklisted writers managed to continue working under assumed names, most cinema actors either left the country or found other employment. Some were able to find employment in the theater because legitimate theater organizations, such as the Actor's Equity Association and the League of New York Theatres, were able to enforce a mutually agreed-upon antiblacklisting resolution.

[John R. Commons, *History of Labour in the United States;* Robert Vaughn, *Only Victims.*]

JOSEPH A. DOWLING

BLACK MUSLIMS. The Black Muslim (Nation of Islam) movement was founded in Detroit in 1930 by Wali Farad. According to Black Muslim doctrine, Farad was an incarnation of God who came to America to rescue Afro-Americans from their bondage to the "blue-eyed devils" of the white race. In 1934, Farad was succeeded by Elijah Muhammad; under Muhammad's leadership, the Black Muslims established mosques in most of America's major cities and achieved a membership of more than 100,000 by the early 1960's. One of the movement's most prominent leaders was Malcolm X, until his break with the sect in 1963 (*see* Organization of Afro-American Unity).

The Black Muslims denounce Christianity as a means of white oppression and preach black racial superiority. This doctrine and the Muslim belief that blacks should retaliate against attacks made on them caused many whites during the early 1960's to perceive the Black Muslims as a dangerous movement. However, the Muslims have avoided confrontations with white authorities and have obeyed America's laws while minimizing contact with whites. The Nation of Islam is a prosperous, slowly growing organization whose members embrace a strict asceticism.

[E. U. Essien-Udom, *Black Nationalism;* C. Eric Lincoln, *The Black Muslims in America;* Malcolm X, *Autobiography of Malcolm X.*]

RICHARD P. YOUNG

BLACK NATIONALISM, the belief that the African origins and the American experiences of blacks have created in the United States a nation within a nation and that the interest of Afro-Americans can best be served by recognition of this ethnic unity. Black-nationalist views cover a range of beliefs, including positive acceptance of blackness, some degree of separation from the white majority, and creation of a national homeland. In the 19th century it found expression in the creation of black churches and fraternal organizations, in the emigration schemes sponsored by blacks, and in the opposition to the efforts of the American Colonization Society to return American blacks to Africa. In the 20th century cultural nationalism, pan-Africanism, community control, and a variety of separatist movements have characterized expression of black nationalism. Among the leaders from the 18th century to the 20th have been Paul Cuffe, Martin R. Delany, James T. Holly, Edward W. Blyden, W. E. B. Du Bois, Noble Drew Ali, Malcolm X, and Imamu Baraka.

Through most of its history, black nationalism appears as a response to the treatment of Afro-Americans by whites. In the 1970's it became more aggressive and assertive, attempting to deal with a range of issues, of which resistance to racism was but one feature.

[Theodore Draper, *The Rediscovery of Black Nationalism;* E. U. Essien-Udom, *Black Nationalism: The Search for Identity in America.*]

HENRY N. DREWRY

BLACK PANTHERS. The Black Panther party was organized in Oakland, Calif., in 1966 by two young Afro-American militants, Huey P. Newton and Bobby G. Seale, who in 1974 still dominated the party. Ideologically, the party represents a synthesis of black nationalism and Marxism: the Panthers believe in black liberation and sponsor programs to develop cohesiveness in the black community, but they also favor building coalitions with radical elements from other races.

In 1967, the Panthers organized the residents of Oakland's ghetto for purposes of self-defense against the city's police. On May 2, the party gained national publicity when thirty armed Panthers demonstrated on the steps of the California capitol to protest the passage of a bill that infringed on the Panthers' right to bear arms. The Panthers immediately became a symbol of black militancy to the entire nation; after this incident, party branches were established throughout the United States.

The Black Panthers achieved their greatest impact in 1968 when the party's minister of information, Eldridge Cleaver, published *Soul On Ice,* a best-selling defense of the black liberation movement. In addition, the Black Panthers merged with the Student Nonviolent Coordinating Committee (SNCC), whose principal leaders were named to prominent party positions. This merger quickly collapsed over the question of forming alliances with nonblacks, and Cleaver later left the party because of tactical disputes. In addition, the Panthers' notoriety and militancy triggered police harassment. Newton and Seale were arrested on numerous occasions and subjected to lengthy trials and imprisonment before their release. In the early 1970's, it appeared that the party was near extinction, but in a dramatic change of tactics, the Black Panthers turned to electoral politics, centering their attention on Oakland, where Seale unsuccessfully ran for mayor in 1973.

[Philip S. Foner, ed., *The Black Panthers Speak;* Gene Marine, *The Black Panthers;* Bobby Seale, *Seize the Time: The Story of the Black Panther Party and Huey P. Newton.*]

RICHARD P. YOUNG

BLACK PATCH WAR, the result of attempts of Kentucky and Tennessee tobacco growers to overcome monopolistic control of markets and prices. By 1906 producers were sufficiently organized to threaten control of the trust. In the Black Patch or fire-cured tobacco area, which embraced counties in southwestern Kentucky and adjoining districts in Tennessee, aggressive methods imposed by association members, and retaliation by nonmembers, resulted in much violence. During 1907 and 1908 night riding by the "silent brigade" was prevalent. Speculation in warehouse receipts, increased production in unrestricted areas, adverse court decisions, and general friction, hostility, and suspicion doomed the movement to deterioration.

[John G. Miller, *The Black Patch War.*]

FRED COLE

BLACK POWER means the control by black people of the political, social, economic, and cultural institutions that affect their daily lives. The phrase came to prominence in the summer of 1966, when Stokely Carmichael and Willie Ricks of the Student Nonviolent Coordinating Committee (SNCC) proclaimed it upon the completion of the march through Mississippi begun by James Meredith. The term had been used earlier in a number of ways: *Black Power* (1954), Richard Wright's book on Ghana; in the conference held in Chicago during the summer of 1965 to establish an organization of black power; and in Adam Clayton Powell's speeches at Howard University and before Congress in the spring of 1966, when he urged that Afro-Americans seek black power. The term now embraces a wide variety of ideologies and specific strategies for the advancement of Afro-Americans. Initially, as a result of the SNCC experience in registering black voters in the Deep South during the early 1960's, it meant that blacks should have political control of those areas in the South in which they constitute a majority of the population. This meaning was soon extended to the advocacy of black control of urban ghettos and of all the institutions that affect the lives and destinies of Afro-Americans. Black-power strategies cover the spectrum from black capitalism and electoral politics to armed struggle. Black-power goals range from pluralism (equal group status within American society) to separatism (an autonomous black city, county, state, or nation), to socialist revolution (replacing white American capitalism with black socialism). Most blacks tend to view black power as just another stratagem for uniting themselves as a group to enable them to achieve equality as individuals within American society.

[Joel D. Alberbach and Jack L. Walker, "The Meaning of Black Power: A Comparison of Black and White Interpretations of a Political Slogan," *American Political Science Review,* vol. 64 (1970); Robert L. Scott and Wayne Brockriede, *The Rhetoric of Black Power.*]

JOHN H. BRACEY, JR.

BLACK ROCK, BOMBARDMENT OF (Oct. 13, 1812). In reprisal for the capture of two British sloops by a small American naval force, Black Rock (at the northern end of the village of Buffalo, N.Y.) was subjected to a heavy bombardment. The short range of the guns on the American shore prevented an effective answer, and considerable damage to the village was caused. During the bombardment news came of the American defeat at Queenston Heights and a week's armistice was arranged to permit the burial of the dead.

[L. L. Babcock, *The War of 1812 on the Niagara Frontier;* R. W. Bingham, *The Cradle of the Queen City.*]

JULIAN PARK

BLACKSMITHING. In colonial times the blacksmith was an important factor of the community. The first colony at Jamestown, Va., in 1607, brought over a blacksmith. The Plymouth colony in 1626 ruled that "no smiths shall use their science or Trade . . . for any streangers . . . til . . . the necessity of the Colony be served." About 1635 Lynn, Mass., assigned twenty acres to the blacksmith. In 1642 Plymouth ordered smiths to "repaire armes speedyly," and to take corn for their pay. In 1650 New Netherland sought "a blacksmith conversant with the treatment of horses and cattle." In 1694 a blacksmith's apprentice at Elizabeth, Va., after seven years' service, was to receive a full set of tools and clothing. In 1810 Pennsylvania reported 2,562 blacksmith shops, doing $1,572,627 worth of work. In 1850 the United States had 100,000 blacksmiths and whitesmiths, in addition to gunsmiths and machinists.

The basic equipment of the blacksmith shop was forge and bellows, anvil and slack tup, hammer and tongs, swage and cutter, chisel and punch, and file and drill. The blacksmith not only made shoes for horses and oxen and applied them, but also made such hardware as latches, hinges, andirons, farm tools, nails, hammers, axes, chisels, and carving tools. In horse-drawn society he was the mainstay of transportation: he welded and fitted wagon tires and hub rings and made and fitted all metal parts of wagons, carriages, and sleighs. The village smith was frequently called on to furnish ice skates, toy wagons, and doll carriages. Moreover, he was the single source of decorative ironwork for fine houses—wrought-iron gates and fences and the spikes for the tops of brick walls. Most skilled of all blacksmiths were those who shaped iron to the precise and intricate needs of ships, which often stayed at sea for years before returning to port for repair and refitting. Warships and whaling vessels generally carried their own blacksmiths to repair fittings and guns at sea and to make grappling hooks and harpoons.

In the latter part of the 20th century blacksmiths had all but disappeared from the American scene. A few—known as tool dressers rather than blacksmiths—dressed picks and mattocks, air drills, stone chisels, and various knives used in industry. Others—known as farriers—were to be found in rural areas caring for racing and riding horses, though these were more in demand for their veterinary practices than for their knowledge of ironworking.

[Alex W. Bealer, *The Art of Blacksmithing.*]

HERBERT MANCHESTER

BLACKSTOCK'S HILL, BATTLE OF. *See* **Enoree, Battle of.**

BLACK SWAMP, a term once applied to much of northwestern Ohio but more accurately to an area lying chiefly in the drainage basin of the Maumee River, including all or parts of a dozen present-day counties. Most of this region was once under the waters of Lake Erie. It is so level and swampy that drainage difficulties, the prevalence of malarial diseases, and its general inaccessibility for a long time retarded settlement. After 1850, when drainage and transportation problems began to be solved, the region underwent a rapid development and today constitutes one of the richest farming sections of the state.

[Henry Howe, *Historical Collections of Ohio,* vol. II.]

EUGENE H. ROSEBOOM

***BLACK WARRIOR* AFFAIR.** The *Black Warrior,* an American steamer, touched at Havana, Cuba, Feb. 28, 1854, on its eighteenth voyage to New York. In technical conformity with law, but contrary to informal agreements, a cargo manifest was demanded by Spanish authorities. Failing this, the ship was seized, but was restored to its owners on payment of a $6,000 fine, subsequently remitted. The controversy called forth able papers by William L. Marcy, secretary of state, but the tactics of Pierre Soulé, American minister to Spain, temporarily threatened war. Linked somewhat with the Ostend Manifesto, the issue hung fire until August 1855, when Spain paid an indemnity of $53,000.

[A. A. Ettinger, *The Mission to Spain of Pierre Soulé;* Henry L. Janes, "The Black Warrior Affair," *American Historical Review,* vol. 12 (1907).]

LOUIS MARTIN SEARS

BLACKWATER, BATTLE OF (Dec. 18, 1861). While campaigning against Confederate Gen. Sterling Price in Missouri, part of Gen. John Pope's command, under Col. J. C. Davis, surrounded an enemy force at the Blackwater River at the mouth of Clear Creek (vicinity of Warrensburg), and compelled its surrender. This was part of Pope's campaign to strip Price of supplies and munitions.

ROBERT S. THOMAS

BLADENSBURG, BATTLE OF (Aug. 24, 1814). Maj. Gen. Robert Ross, with 4,500 British troops, landed on the Patuxent River in Maryland, Aug. 19–20, thus compelling Commodore Joshua Barney to destroy his gunboat flotilla in that river. The British force then turned toward Washington. About 6,000 District of Columbia and Maryland militia, a few regulars, and Barney's seamen constituted the defensive force under Maj. Gen. William Winder. Ross reached Bladensburg Aug. 24. Across the river, on rising ground, Winder hastily and unskillfully posted his army, already worn down by three days' futile maneuvering, sleepless nights, and scanty food. The British, advancing steadily under artillery fire, drove back the American light troops after crossing the bridge, and approached the second line. Showers of Congreve rockets so terrified the raw militia that two regiments disintegrated immediately. A Baltimore regiment offered some resistance but broke when ordered to fall back. Barney's naval contingent, firing eighteen-pounders, checked Ross for a time, retreating only when its flanks were uncovered by fleeing infantry supports, its ammunition expended, and Barney wounded. A general retirement, ordered by Winder, was effected in fair order, the British being too exhausted to pursue vigorously. Halting briefly at Capitol Hill, the Americans marched on to Georgetown. Ross entered Washington and burned the Capitol, presidential mansion, and public buildings. President James Madison, Secretary of War John Armstrong, Secretary of State James Monroe, and Attorney General Richard Rush were on the field during part of the battle. American losses were insignificant, those of the British rather severe. A congressional investigation whitewashed all concerned, but the uselessness of undisciplined militia against British regulars was again demonstrated. Winder was exculpated by a court of inquiry, and Armstrong, made the scapegoat by the public, was compelled to resign. Failure of the administration to adopt defensive measures in time may be considered the true explanation of the disaster.

[J. S. Williams, *History of the Invasion and Capture of Washington.*]

CHARLES WINSLOW ELLIOTT

BLADENSBURG DUELING FIELD, five miles from Washington, D.C., but in the jurisdiction of Maryland, where statutes against dueling were more lax than in the District of Columbia. Thirty to fifty duels were fought there by statesmen, military and naval officers, and civilians from 1802 until 1851. The most famous were the mortal wounding of Commodore Stephen Decatur by Commodore James Barron (1820) and the killing of Sen. A. T. Mason of Virginia by his brother-in-law, J. M. McCarthy (1819).

[D. C. Seitz, *Some Famous Duels.*]

RICHARD J. PURCELL

BLAND-ALLISON ACT, the first of several U.S. government subsidies to silver producers in depression periods. The five-year depression following the panic of 1873 caused cheap-money advocates (led by Representative R. P. Bland of Missouri) to join with silver-producing interests in urging return to bimetallism. The silver dollar had been omitted from the list of coins by a mint reform act, which lent itself to the political sobriquet of the "Crime of '73," and silver had depreciated with other commodities. The silver advocates demanded restoration of free coinage of silver at a ratio of 16 to 1, approximately $1.29 an ounce.

Free coinage, as the symbol of justice for the poor, was seized upon by greenbackers and others determined to prevent resumption of specie payments and to make government obligations payable in silver. When Bland's bill for free coinage, passed by the House (Nov. 5, 1877), jeopardized Secretary of the Treasury John Sherman's plans for resuming specie payments, Sherman substituted limited purchases for free coinage, through a Senate amendment sponsored by Sen. W. B. Allison of Iowa. The producers accepted the arrangement as likely to restore silver to $1.29.

The law, passed Feb. 28, 1878, over President Rutherford B. Hayes's veto, required government purchase, at market prices, of $2 million to $4 million worth of silver bullion monthly, and coinage into legal tender 16-to-1 dollars, exchangeable for $10 silver certificates receivable for public dues and reissuable. The president was directed to arrange an international bimetallic conference to meet within six months. These provisions signified victory for producers over inflationists, defeat of international bimetallists by national bimetallists, a drain on the Treasury through the customs in times of uncertainty, and failure for the conference.

[H. B. Russell, *International Monetary Conferences.*]

JEANNETTE P. NICHOLS

BLAST FURNACES, EARLY. From the earliest days of colonization, Englishmen pointed out that the smelting of iron in the New World for England's manufacturers would be advantageous to the mother country in view of the diminishing English forests that furnished fuel for the production of iron. The first attempt to build blast furnaces in the colonies was made in Virginia by the London Company. The project was not successful. The Puritans in Massachusetts established the first successful ironworks as early as 1644. The colonial iron industry, however, made slow progress in the 17th century.

Not until the 18th century did the smelting of iron in America become important. The colonial iron industry then went through a process of remarkable development. By the outbreak of the American Revolution there were more blast furnaces in the American colonies than in England and Wales, and American furnaces produced more pig iron and castings than English furnaces.

Colonial blast furnaces were patterned after those of the mother country. Built of stone, they were usually about 25 feet square at the bottom and from 25 to 30 feet high. Although square, they were larger at the bottom than at the top, thus resembling truncated pyramids. The blast, forced through a single tuyere into the furnace, was produced by large bellows driven by water power. Before 1800, blowing cylinders were substituted for bellows at a number of furnaces. American furnaces continued to use charcoal fuel and cold blast until just before 1840 when some ironmasters began using anthracite coal. Later, coke displaced anthracite and charcoal as a furnace fuel. (*See also* Iron and Steel Manufacture.)

[Arthur C. Bining, *British Regulation of the Colonial Iron Industry,* and *Pennsylvania Iron Manufacture in the Eighteenth Century;* V. S. Clark, *History of Manufactures in the United States, 1607–1860.*]

ARTHUR C. BINING

BLEASE MOVEMENT. In the early 1900's, Coleman L. Blease, South Carolina politician, attempted to appeal to the political consciousness of the underprivileged white class. By studiously imitating former Gov. Benjamin Tillman's vehement attacks on Afro-Americans, aristocrats, and clerical politicans, Blease became something of the popular idol Tillman had formerly been. Elected governor in 1910, his administration was bizarre, but not criminal. He pardoned extravagantly and answered the snubs of the opposition with abusive language. Although the combined opposition of Tillman and the upper classes could not prevent the reelection of Blease in 1912, his influence thereafter declined and his repeated attempts to win high office usually ended in failure. Blease lacked a constructive program and the prudence of a successful organizer. But his agitations had permanently quickened the political consciousness of the cotton-mill operatives and other poor whites.

[D. D. Wallace, *The History of South Carolina.*]

FRANCIS B. SIMKINS

BLEEDING KANSAS. *See* **Border War.**

BLENNERHASSETT ISLAND in the Ohio River below the mouth of the Little Kanawha River (an Indian rendezvous) and two miles south of Parkersburg, W.Va., was first known as Backus Island for Elijah Backus, who purchased it in 1792. It is famous as the site of Blennerhassett House, where Aaron Burr and Harman Blennerhassett, who purchased the north end of the island in 1798, are alleged to have plotted treason against the United States. (*See also* Burr Conspiracy.)

[William H. Safford, *The Life of Harman Blennerhassett.*]

CHARLES H. AMBLER

BLESSING OF THE BAY, second seaworthy vessel built in the colonies, preceded only by the *Virginia,* a thirty-ton pinnace that had been built by the Popham Colony at the mouth of the Kennebec River, Maine, in 1607. The *Blessing of the Bay,* a thirty-ton bark, mostly of locust, was built at a cost of £145 for Gov. John Winthrop at Mistick (now Medford), Mass., by Robert Molton and other shipwrights sent to New England in 1629 by the Company of the Massachusetts Bay, and was launched July 4, 1631. It went to sea Aug. 31, 1631, and carried on a coastwise trade as far south as the Dutch town of New Amsterdam.

[John Robinson and G. F. Dow, *Sailing Ships of New England.*]

R. W. G. VAIL

BLIND. *See* **Handicapped, Education of the.**

BLIZZARDS are defined in the United States as snowstorms accompanied by winds of 32 mph or more, low temperatures, and visibility reduced to less than 500 feet. If temperatures fall to 10°F. or lower and winds are over 45 mph, the term "severe blizzard" is applied. In popular terminology, any snowstorm of long duration or accompanied by appreciable wind is called a blizzard in both England and America. Much of the snow that obscures vision in a real blizzard consists of fine, dry snow picked up from the ground by wind. Reports of drifts 25 to 30 feet deep under blizzard conditions are not unusual; and the effect of such storms is to tie up transportation (railroads in the 1880–1900 period and highways in the 20th century) and to isolate whole communities for days. In the 19th century such isolation resulted in great suffering and scores of deaths; more recently airlifts to relieve human and animal starvation, as well as better highways and communications, have reduced the number of deaths. Only occasionally are hunters or motorists caught in a sudden cold wave and blizzard, as on Mar. 15, 1941, when at least seventy persons died in a fast-moving blizzard that hit North Dakota, Minnesota, Wisconsin, and Michigan after an unusually warm spell on a weekend. Deaths on the highways or elsewhere during blizzards are usually caused by heart attacks brought on by struggling through or shoveling snowdrifts, rather than by more direct effects of the blizzard itself.

Snow accumulations of from 5 to 30 feet often occur in snowstorms of long duration, especially in the mountains of the Pacific Northwest region or in the New England–New York State region. Even though accumulations of snow are not produced by blizzards, they cause great economic loss when residents of towns or farms are isolated, communications and transportation break down, and normal activities are paralyzed. In fact, even a few inches of snow may tie up an entire metropolitan area, resulting in losses running into millions of dollars; and when a real blizzard strikes a large city, losses—including time lost in production or business—can run into tens of millions of dollars for one storm.

The most widespread blizzard conditions in history occurred in connection with an intense cold wave that moved from the Canadian Prairies on Feb. 9–11, 1899, to the Gulf coast, southern Texas, Florida, and the entire Atlantic coast on Feb. 14. Ample warnings made possible by certain facts—that barometric pressure on Feb. 11 was the highest ever recorded (31.42 inches) in the Canadian provinces and that record pressure with temperatures ranging from −40°F. to −61°F. occurred throughout the northern plains—prevented much loss of life, livestock, and property in the South and East. However, winds of from 50 to 70 mph and temperatures dropping to −15°F. in downtown Washington, D.C., and zero in the Gulf states and Texas, frozen rivers, ruined crops and orchards, record snows, and other disastrous occurrences made this event a major catastrophe. The most famous blizzard, the Blizzard of '88, occurred on Mar. 11, 1888. New England and New York were paralyzed by four-foot snowdrifts after 60-mph winds had buffeted the entire area. Earlier that year, Jan. 12, the Great Plains were hit. At Bismarck, N.Dak.; Huron, S.Dak.; and Topeka, Kans., winds of from 54 to 66 mph, deep snow, and temperatures falling sixty degrees in eighteen hours resulted in a loss of 200 lives—many of them schoolchildren on their way home. Other memorable blizzards were the storm of 1873, when 70 died in the northern plains; that of January 1886 in Kansas, when 100 died; the Knickerbocker snowstorm in Washington, D.C., Jan. 27–29, 1922, when 100 died from the collapse of the Knickerbocker Theater; and the Feb. 12–14, 1923, blizzard, when 27 froze to death in the Dakotas.

Records show that historic blizzards have occurred somewhere in the United States almost every year since chronicles began. During some decades blizzards have occurred in specific areas almost every year, whereas during other periods none has occurred. In the northern plains eighteen notably disastrous blizzards that tied up railroads and caused suffering and loss of livestock occurred between 1871 and 1905; on the other hand, during the period 1905–23, only three blizzards (in 1917, 1920, and 1923) were notable. The Dakotas and Minnesota were hit by five similar blizzards in the 1960's. Toward the south and east notable blizzards occur less often—in Kansas only eleven times in 100 years, 1912 and 1958 having the worst, while in Oklahoma and Texas only five notable blizzards have occurred since 1878, although northers occur every year. The Great Lakes region has had relatively few blizzards (nine since 1894, the worst in 1970 in Chicago). New England suffers in about one year out of five; and the Deep South has had only seven notable blizzards since 1800.

[David M. Ludlum, *Early American Winters,* vols. I, II.]

MALCOLM RIGBY

BLOCKADE, the closing by sea of the coasts and ports of an enemy in such a manner as to cut off entirely his maritime communications. Blockades and disputes about blockades have played a prominent part in American diplomatic and naval history. As a nation with a small navy and a large merchant marine, the United States originally sought to limit, as far as possible, the scope and uses of blockades. The Continental Congress, in its 1784 plan for foreign treaties, specified that only blockades maintained by actual patrolling squadrons in close proximity to the enemy's coast and ports could be accepted as legitimate.

During the Napoleonic wars both Britain and France, in their efforts to cripple each other, went far beyond the definition of blockade of the Continental Congress. In May 1806 Britain declared the whole of the European coast, from the Elbe River to the port of Brest, to be under blockade, although the British had far too few ships really to close off and patrol such a vast area. Napoleon responded with the so-called Berlin and Milan decrees, which closed all the ports of Europe under his control to British shipping and to ships that had called at a British port or submitted to search by British cruisers. The United States vigorously protested these British and French edicts on the ground that they went far beyond the traditional practice of blockade. The British system of "mock blockades" was later to be cited by President James Madison, in his war message to Congress in June 1812, as one of the principal American grievances against England.

The American view of blockade was eventually embodied in the Declaration of Paris, adopted by the great powers in 1856. The declaration stipulated that a blockade, in order to be binding, must be "maintained by a force sufficient really to prevent access to the coast of the enemy." (Ironically, the United States did not sign the Declaration of Paris because it objected to another provision in the agreement outlawing privateers.)

At the onset of the Civil War, President Abraham Lincoln proclaimed a blockade of the entire coast of the Confederacy. This blockade, which was a major factor in the Union victory, was scrupulously observed by the British, who viewed it as establishing a valuable precedent for actions they might wish to take in a future war. The United States, finding itself in the unaccustomed position of dominant naval power, resorted to devices even more far-reaching than those it had condemned in the Napoleonic era. One such device was the doctrine of continuous voyage, which held that ships destined for a neutral country could be seized if it could be proven that their cargo was destined ultimately for a blockaded port (*see Bermuda* Admiralty Case; Enemy Destination).

By the time of World War I the development of submarines, mines, and long-range artillery had made the traditional "close" blockade, prescribed by the Declaration of Paris, militarily impossible. Britain resorted during the war to a "distant" blockade, utilizing mine fields and patrols of cruisers on the high-seas approaches to Germany. The United States protested this departure from accepted practice, but it was the German "submarine blockade" of the British Isles that most outraged American opinion. In February 1915 the Germans announced that the waters around the British Isles constituted a war zone in which all enemy ships were liable to destruction without warning by submarines and in which neutral ships would sail at their own risk. This "blockade"—construed to be a flagrant violation of traditional practice—shocked and angered Americans and led to complications that were eventually to bring the United States into the war on the side of the Allies. In World War II the United States and Britain employed a long-range air and naval blockade against Germany, while the Germans again engaged in unrestricted submarine warfare against the Allies.

During the Cuban missile crisis of 1962 the United States imposed a "quarantine" of Cuba in order to halt the delivery of offensive weapons to the island and force the removal of Soviet missiles that had been installed there. In the opinion of some experts, this action in effect constituted a "pacific blockade"—that is, a blockade imposed by one nation upon another nation with whom it is ostensibly at peace and applied only to certain ships and cargoes entering or leaving the blockaded ports.

[Thomas A. Bailey, *A Diplomatic History of the American People;* C. John Colombos, *The International Law of the Sea.*]

RONALD SPECTOR

BLOCKADE RUNNERS, CONFEDERATE. On Apr. 16, 1861, President Abraham Lincoln proclaimed a naval blockade of the Confederacy's 3,500 miles of coastline. The effectiveness of the blockade increased after early Union victories along the coast. The risk of capture averaged one in ten in 1861 and increased to one in three by 1864. The trade with other countries by running the blockade proved highly lucrative. The value to the Confederacy is told in the record of 1.25 million bales of cotton run out and in 600,000 small arms and other munitions, endless supplies of provisions, clothing, hospital stores, manufactures, and luxuries run in. The goods entering the Confederacy were valued at $200 million. Had it not been for the blockade runners, the Confederate armies more than once would have been on the verge of starvation; and except for the increasing stringency of the blockade, the runners would probably have enabled the South to win its independence by keeping a federal squadron of 600 vessels occupied. Furthermore, runners afforded the one means of outside communication. On the debit side must be ranged the facts that the traffic drained away the gold supply, thus contributing to depreciation of Confederate currency; that it drew attention to the ports, probably precipitating attacks upon their defenses; that the yellow fever scourge in Wilmington, Del., was traceable to a blockade runner; and that the traffic, stimulating a hunger for speculation and the riotous living of the blockade-running gentry, demoralized many citizens.

[F. C. Bradlee, *Blockade Running During the Civil War;* F. L. Owsley, *King Cotton Diplomacy;* J. R. Soley, *The Blockade and the Cruisers*.]

ELLA LONN

"BLOCKS OF FIVE." This phrase acquired notoriety during the Benjamin Harrison–Grover Cleveland election of 1888 when W. W. Dudley, Republican campaign treasurer, issued a circular on Oct. 24, to Indiana followers, suggesting that they "divide the floaters into blocks of five," each in charge of a trusted leader with the necessary bribes who would insure the proper delivery of the vote.

[Ellis P. Oberholtzer, *A History of the United States Since the Civil War,* vol. V.]

HARVEY WISH

BLOCS, a name given to organized voting groups in American legislative bodies, and more loosely, to associations of pressure groups attempting to lobby in American legislatures. In either case, the purpose of organization is to create a group of legislators who will vote together consistently on certain specified issues. Strictly defined, blocs are persistent and highly organized, being based on closely shared interests and commanding a high degree of loyalty from their members. The farm bloc, formed in the Senate in 1921, is perhaps the best example of one. Consisting of about twenty-five western and southern senators, it had its own established committee structure and developed a substantial program of bills of interest to farmers. Together with a parallel group of House members, it secured the passage of a number of bills in the 1920's. A progressive bloc of Senate and House members also operated briefly in the early 1920's. A liberal bloc in the House in the 1930's lent support to New Deal legislation. A protectionist bloc, a wet bloc, a dry bloc, and a veterans' bloc were all active in Congress around 1940. In 1959, a group of more than one hundred House Democrats organized the Democratic Study Group, a liberal body having some of the features of earlier blocs.

After World War II the veterans' bloc and the protectionist bloc, which had existed both inside and outside Congress prior to the war, lost much of their influence. A labor bloc and a civil rights bloc rose to prominence in their place; but neither had an organization in Congress, and their structure outside Congress was little more than ad hoc. Neither group could expect the kind of voting consistency from its congressional supporters that the older lobbies had received: no longer dominated by a single constituency interest, most legislators had lost the political motivation to vote as bloc members.

[Congressional Quarterly, *Congress and the Nation,* vol. I; Julius Turner, *Party and Constituency*.]

ROBERT EYESTONE

"BLOOD IS THICKER THAN WATER." Commodore Josiah Tattnall, in command of the American squadron in the East Indies waters, made this adage a part of American history when explaining why he had given aid to the British squadron in an attack on Taku forts at the mouth of the Pai River June 25, 1859, thereby infringing strict American neutrality.

[Tyler Dennett, *Americans in Eastern Asia*.]

KEITH CLARK

BLOODY ANGLE (May 12, 1864), the climax in the first phase of Gen. U. S. Grant's Wilderness campaign in Virginia. Union troop movements at Spotsylvania indicated Grant planned a heavy attack. Gen. Robert E. Lee was uncertain where the blow would fall. Early in the morning Grant moved in force against the salient, or "bloody angle," in Lee's line. Because of surprise, lack of artillery, and the force of the onslaught the salient was overrun. To restore the broken line and save his army, Lee proposed to lead the counterattack. Officers and men remonstrated, crying, "General Lee to the rear." Lee's example fired his troops with intense ardor. The opposing lines met; the Union advance was halted and forced back. Lee put in every available man. All day and far into the night the battle raged. Neither side could advance. Early next morning Lee retired to prepared positions and the fighting ceased.

[R. U. Johnson and C. C. Buel, eds., *Battles and Leaders of the Civil War*.]

THOMAS ROBSON HAY

BLOODY ISLAND, a sand bar in the Mississippi River, opposite St. Louis, Mo., which became densely wooded and a rendezvous for duelists. Appearing first above water in 1798 its continuous growth menaced St. Louis harbor. Beginning in July 1837 Capt. Robert E. Lee, of the Army Corps of Engineers, devised and established a system of dikes and dams that washed out the western channel and ultimately joined the island to the Illinois shore.

[Stella M. Drumm, "Robert E. Lee and the Improvement of the Mississippi River," *Missouri Historical Society Collections*, vol. 6.]

STELLA M. DRUMM

BLOODY MARSH, BATTLE OF (July 7, 1742), the principal and decisive engagement in the war of Jenkins' Ear. In the summer of 1742 a Spanish force collected in Havana and St. Augustine, consisting of about fifty sails and a number of men, estimated in contemporary accounts to be from 2,800 to 4,000, invaded Georgia. They made a landing preparatory to attacking Frederica, the strongest English settlement in Georgia. James Oglethorpe immediately marched out a hurriedly organized force and attacked. He routed the Spaniards, and in the retreat he posted in ambush on the edge of a marsh three platoons and a company of Highlanders. When a group of about 400 Spaniards unsuspectingly marched into the glade, Oglethorpe's forces attacked them and killed about 200 and forced the remainder to retreat to the south end of the island. A few days later the whole remaining force returned to Florida.

[H. E. Bolton and M. Ross, *The Debatable Land;* C. C. Jones, *A History of Georgia;* W. B. Stevens, *A History of Georgia.*]

E. MERTON COULTER

BLOODY MONDAY, the name given the election riots, Aug. 6. 1855, in Louisville, Ky. These riots grew out of the bitter rivalry between the Democrat and Know-Nothing parties. Rumors were started that foreigners and Catholics had interfered with the process of voting. A street fight occurred, twenty-two persons were killed, scores were injured, and much property was destroyed by fire.

[W. H. Perrin, J. H. Battle, G. C. Kniffen, *Kentucky, History of the State.*]

T. D. CLARK

BLOODY POND, BATTLE OF (Sept. 8, 1755). The British expedition to capture Crown Point, N.Y., under the command of Sir William Johnson, had reached the southern extremity of Lake George when word was received of the approach of a body of 1,400 French, Canadians, and Indians commanded by Baron Ludwig Dieskau. The following morning Johnson sent out 1,000 men; the troops fell into an ambush and the survivors retreated to the English camp. An attack on the camp followed but was beaten off. Several hundred Canadians and Indians left the field and returned to plunder the scene of the morning fight. They were resting by a pool when they were attacked by a scouting party. After a short but bloody fight, the Canadians and Indians fled. The bodies of the dead were thrown into the pool, which henceforth was called Bloody Pond.

A. C. FLICK

BLOODY RUN, BATTLE OF (July 31, 1763). Pontiac's siege of Fort Detroit began May 9, 1763. During the night of July 30–31, Capt. James Dalzel and a detachment of 280 relief troops marched eastward along the Grand Marias River to surprise Pontiac. Instead the column was itself furiously assailed at Parent's Creek (ever since called Bloody Run) and driven back to the fort. Dalzel was slain and sixty of his men were killed or wounded. (*See also* Pontiac's War.)

M. M. QUAIFE

BLOODY SHIRT, part of the expression, "waving the bloody shirt," this term is used to describe the attempts made in political campaigns (especially in 1872 and 1876) by Radical Republicans to defeat the Democrats by impassioned oratory designed to keep alive the hatreds and prejudices of the Civil War period.

[W. A. Dunning, *Reconstruction, Political and Economic.*]

HALLIE FARMER

BLOOMER DRESS, a loose-fitting costume of knee-length dress and Turkish pantaloons buttoned at the ankle, introduced in Seneca Falls, N.Y., by Elizabeth Smith Miller in February 1851 and popularized by Amelia Bloomer, editor of the feminist journal *Lily*. For its physical comfort and as a symbol of the suffrage movement, the dress survived six years of ridicule but was extinguished by the revival of the hoopskirt.

[E. D. Branch, "The Lily and the Bloomer," *The Colophon* (1932).]

E. DOUGLAS BRANCH

BLOUNT CONSPIRACY takes its name from William Blount, U.S. senator from Tennessee in 1796–97. The conspiracy was connected with the Yazoo land frauds of 1796 and its main purpose seems to have been to raise the value of western lands by driving the Spaniards out of Louisiana and Florida. This was to be accomplished by a land force of western frontiersmen and Indians with the aid of a British fleet. The British minister in the United States, Robert Liston, gave the conspirators some encouragement and sent one of them to London. The conspiracy was exposed when an incriminating letter written by Blount to one of his agents fell into the hands of the administration and was transmitted by President John Adams to the Senate (July 3, 1797). Blount was promptly expelled from that body. Impeachment proceedings against him were considered but dropped because of his expulsion. The exposure of the conspiracy had repercussions in the domestic politics and foreign relations of the United States, and there is some reason to believe that Aaron Burr's later conspiracy was connected with this one.

[Frederick J. Turner, "Documents on the Blount Conspiracy," *American Historical Review,* vol. 10; Arthur P. Whitaker, *The Mississippi Question, 1795–1803.*]

ARTHUR P. WHITAKER

BLUE AND GRAY, familiar names for the armies of the North and South during the Civil War, derived from the fact that the Union Army wore blue uniforms while the Confederates wore gray. As sectional hatred died, these terms superseded the harsher names of the 19th century.

FRED B. JOYNER

BLUEBACKS, Confederate paper currency, first issued under an act approved one month after the establishment of the Confederate government. From an initial issue of $1,000,000, the treasury notes grew to $800,000,000 by Apr. 1, 1864, when deflationary measures were taken that reduced the outstanding currency to $480,036,095 on Oct. 1, 1864.

WILLIAM M. ROBINSON, JR.

BLUE-COLLAR WORKERS, those members of the nonagricultural labor force who perform manual labor, whether skilled, semiskilled, or unskilled, and, typically, work for hourly wages. The percentage of manual workers in the total work force has changed only slightly since 1900 (from about one-third to nearly one-half), although the proportion of female blue-collar workers has significantly declined.

WILLIAM H. ISSEL

BLUE EAGLE EMBLEM, a blue-colored representation of the American thunderbird, with outspread wings, proclaimed on July 20, 1933, as the symbol of industrial recovery by Hugh S. Johnson, the head of the National Recovery Administration. All who accepted the president's Reemployment Agreement or a special Code of Fair Competition were permitted to display a poster on which was reproduced the blue eagle together with the announcement "Member N.R.A. We Do Our Part." On Sept. 5, 1935, following the invalidation of the compulsory code system, the emblem was abolished and its future use as a symbol was prohibited.

[Hugh S. Johnson, *The Blue Eagle From Egg to Earth.*]

ERIK MCKINLEY ERIKSSON

BLUEGRASS COUNTRY, some 8,000 square miles of east central Kentucky, encircled by the Ohio River on the north and the Knobs on the east, south, and west. The terrain, with some exceptions, has a gracefully undulating surface over a limestone foundation. The land is specially adapted to the growth of bluegrass, for which the region has been named. The inner portion with Lexington at the center is a beautiful district of shaded, winding roads, fine farms, and prosperous villages and towns.

The first settlers of Kentucky came to this region in one of the greatest migrations of American history. Over the Wilderness Road, by way of Cumberland Gap, trekked most of these multitudes. Here the pioneers Daniel Boone and Simon Kenton became national heroes. At Harrodsburg the first permanent settlement in Kentucky was made; the first Anglo-Saxon government west of the Alleghenies was organized at Boonesborough; the first college (now Transylvania University) in the West, which was attended by Jefferson Davis, was established at Lexington; Abraham Lincoln came to Lexington to court Mary Todd. These and many other places and incidents in the Bluegrass country constitute a historic environment probably unequaled in the Ohio Valley.

[Thomas D. Clark, *Kentucky: Land of Contrast;* Darrell Haug Davis, *Geography of the Blue Grass Region of Kentucky.*]

JONATHAN T. DORRIS

BLUE LAWS, originally, colonial laws regulating conduct, particularly on the Sabbath. Rev. Samuel A.

Peters wrote an account of the so-called blue laws of Connecticut in *A General History of Connecticut, by a Gentleman of the Province,* published on blue paper in London in 1781. The term was taken up by various later editors of the laws to refer specifically to the legislation of the New Haven colony. Such instances as punishments of a rebellious child by being forced to work for his father as a prisoner with a lock on his leg and of a young unmarried couple being fined twenty shillings for kissing were considered typical blue laws. Despite some distortions, it is true that rigid Sabbath, sex, and sumptuary regulations prevailed generally in Puritan New England. But blue laws were not original among the Puritans nor unique with them in this country. To some degree blue laws could be found in every one of the American colonies. Compulsory church attendance and laws forbidding sports, travel, and work on the Sabbath were found in the South as well, perhaps the most sweeping Sunday law being the Georgia act of 1762. Blue laws became in the main dead letters after the Revolution, but from time to time there have been attempts to revive them all along the line. National prohibition, anticigarette legislation, and the activities of the Lord's Day Alliance and other groups attest to the survival of the blue law spirit to some degree. Blue laws still exist, but only as regulations determining the types of businesses that can operate on Sunday.

[G. Myers, *Ye Olden Blue Laws.*]

RICHARD B. MORRIS

BLUE LICKS, BATTLE OF (Aug. 19, 1782), an engagement between 182 Kentucky pioneers and 240 Indians and Canadians, in the British service, raiding into Kentucky from the Ohio country and the vicinity of Detroit. It occurred near the lower Blue Lick Springs on the middle fork of Licking River. A precipitate attack was launched by Kentuckians, from several pioneer stations, against the foe lying in ambush. After a fierce conflict of a few minutes, the right wing of the Kentuckians gave way and the entire body retreated in confusion, with losses of about seventy killed and captured. The losses of the Indians and Canadians were never ascertained. Notwithstanding the adverse outcome of the battle, no invasion by Indians in force ever afterward occurred within the borders of Kentucky. The site is now Blue Licks Battlefield State Park.

[Bennett H. Young, *History of the Battle of the Blue Licks;* Samuel M. Wilson, *Battle of the Blue Licks.*]

SAMUEL M. WILSON

BLUE LIGHTS. In December 1813, American frigates under Cmdr. Stephen Decatur prepared to run out of the harbor of New London, Conn., where they had been blockaded by the British since May. Decatur saw blue lights burning near the mouth of the river in sight of the British blockaders. Convinced that these were signals to betray his plans he abandoned the project. Suspicion was directed against the members of Congress who pressed for peace, and the odious epithet of "Bluelight Federalists" long was applied to extreme Federalists.

[James Schouler, *History of the United States of America.*]

CHARLES MARION THOMAS

BLUE LODGES, secret proslavery societies formed in western Missouri during 1854 to thwart northern antislavery designs to make Kansas a free territory under the Kansas-Nebraska Act. They not only promoted the migration of proslavery settlers to Kansas but occasionally crossed the border to participate in the election of proslavery members to the territorial government.

[L. W. Spring, *Kansas, the Prelude to the War for the Union.*]

ASA E. MARTIN

BLUE RIDGE TUNNEL, constructed in 1850–58 by the Blue Ridge Railroad, the state of Virginia, and the Virginia Central Railroad, at a cost of $488,000, through Blue Ridge Mountain under Rockfish Gap, between Afton and Waynesboro, Va. It was for some time the longest tunnel in America. In 1870 it was acquired by the Chesapeake and Ohio Railroad.

[William Couper, *Claudius Crozet, 1789–1864.*]

JOHN W. WAYLAND

BLUE SKY LAWS, legislative enactments designed to prevent the fraudulent flotation or sale of corporate stocks and bonds. Kansas enacted the first blue sky law in May 1911, and this statute was followed by similar ones in forty-five other states. There are three types of these laws: (1) fraud statutes, the principle of which is to follow and punish the security swindler under the criminal law; (2) dealers-license statutes, which endeavor to prevent fraud by restricting security traffic to carefully selected professional dealers, as well as by revoking licenses for violation of the statutes; and (3) specific approval statutes, regulating and controlling only the securities sought to be sold within the state, through specific permits of sale. Blue sky laws have been supplemented by the Securities Act of 1933 and the Securities Exchange Act of 1934, which regulate and control interstate dealings in securities and the operation of the organized security exchanges respectively.

FRANK PARKER

BLUESTEM PASTURES, prior to 1929 called Flint Hills, a region in east central Kansas about 50 miles east-to-west (Wilson to Marion counties) and about 130 miles north-to-south (Pottawatomie County to the south line), extending into Oklahoma to include that part of Osage County that lies between the Verdigris and the Arkansas rivers, where the region is called the Osage pastures. Originally all eastern Kansas was covered mostly with bluestem grasses, but because of the hilly character of the country and the presence of extensive outcroppings of limestone rock, settlement left this part of the area largely in grass. During the late 1880's the pastures were fenced and served not only the local herds but the transient herds from the Southwest, which by this time were moved by rail instead of by the long drive. The bluestem is unusually rich in feed value for grass-fattening livestock during the spring and early summer, and eventually the region became the most important pasture country in the central prairie-plains area. Supplemented by the corn and alfalfa lands of the valleys, the region became also an important breeding center and the home of the great herds of W. J. Todd, Dan Casement, and R. H. Hazlett.

[Paul Wallace Gates, *50,000 Acres: Conflicts Over Kansas Land Policy, 1854–90.*]

JAMES C. MALIN

BLUFFTON MOVEMENT, in South Carolina, an attempt in 1844 to invoke "separate state action" against the tariff of 1842, after John C. Calhoun's failure to secure the presidential nomination and the northern Democrats' abandonment of the South on the tariff had apparently destroyed hope for relief within the Democratic party. Though many of the Blufftonites undoubtedly contemplated disunion, the object of their leader, Robert Barnwell Rhett, seems rather to have been a "reform" of the Union giving further safeguards to southern interests. The movement collapsed within a short time, largely through its repudiation by Calhoun.

[Laura A. White, *Robert Barnwell Rhett: Father of Secession.*]

JAMES W. PATTON

BLUNDER, FORT. *See* **Rouse's Point Boundary Controversy.**

BOARD OF TRADE AND PLANTATIONS, the main British colonial office from its creation, May 15, 1696, until the eve of the American Revolution. It replaced the older committee of the Privy Council, called Lords of Trade and Plantations. It was a paid board of five members, the chief officers of state being also ex officio members. It had charge of poor relief in England, regular commercial relations with other nations, the enforcement of the trade and navigation acts, the general supervision of colonial administration, and the examination of colonial laws to see they were not harmful to British interests nor contrary to the English common law. It heard and investigated complaints of merchants and recommended imperial legislation in its field. It supervised the negotiation of important commercial treaties and kept in touch with the regular consular service. Its voluminous records today are the chief source for American colonial history in its imperial aspects. (*See* Colonial Policy, British.)

The board was a part of the regular political party system and its members changed with the usual party shifts. Under a dominant character like the Duke of Newcastle it had little power—most of the business being transferred directly to Newcastle's office. In 1748 George Dunk, Earl of Halifax, was appointed president of the board. He began at once to make his position important. Investigations were made and reports compiled of what had been going on in America for the previous thirty years. Plans were developed for strengthening the position of the royal governors. Instructions were revised, judges were made dependent upon the crown for their salaries and their terms of office, and the struggle began between the agents of the crown and the leaders of the colonial legislatures. By his energy, Halifax made himself practically a secretary of state for the colonies, secured control of the colonial patronage, and was admitted to the cabinet in 1756. His influence was powerful in colonial affairs many years after his retirement from the board in 1761. Wills Hill, Earl of Hillsborough, who became a full secretary of state for the colonies, was directly responsible for many of the unfortunate policies between 1764 and 1772 that ultimately led to the Revolution. His most offensive colonial activities were connected with his attempt to force Massachusetts to rescind its famous Circular Letter and his use of troops in Boston, culminating in the Boston Massacre.

The permanent secretaries of the board were among the best-informed men on colonial affairs in England. Another important officer was a solicitor and clerk of reports whose duties were to prepare all formal reports, to assemble information for use of the board, and to represent it before other departments of the government. The most famous of these was John Pownall, who served from 1745 to 1758 and personally prepared the reports associated with the work of Halifax. Another important officer was an attorney to whom all colonial laws were sent for examination and report as soon as they arrived from America. These reports on colonial laws subjected every American statute to a constitutional test.

[O. M. Dickerson, *American Colonial Government: A Study of the British Board of Trade in Its Relation to the American Colonies*.]

O. M. DICKERSON

BOARDS OF TRADE. *See* **Chambers of Commerce.**

BODY OF LIBERTIES. *See* **Massachusetts Body of Liberties.**

BOG IRON MINING. Bog ore is a brown hematite deposited in pond and bog bottoms and was found by the early American settlers in the coastal lowlands from Massachusetts to Delaware. Since it was near water transportation and easily dug or raked from pond bottoms or picked up on marsh meadows, it was the first important source of native iron supply, although superior but less accessible and tractable rock ores were also known to exist in America. These hematites were employed in the earliest New England works at Lynn and Braintree, Mass., where they were smelted with charcoal in small furnaces that cast, directly from the ore, kettles and other hollowware, as well as pig for refining into bars for nails and implements. American bog ore castings, such as kettles, were preferred in colonial households as tougher and lighter than imported ironware. Bog ores had been largely displaced by rock ores by the time of the Revolution and virtually ceased to be used toward the middle of the following century. The latest furnaces employing them extensively were built in Ohio on the south shore of Lake Erie about 1825. The newly opened Erie Canal was used to ship pig to Albany for casting stove plates.

[James M. Swank, *History of the Manufacture of Iron*.]

VICTOR S. CLARK

BOISE, FORT, a fur trading post of the Hudson's Bay Company in Idaho. First built in 1834 on the Boise River about seven miles above its mouth, it was relocated in 1838 near the confluence of the Boise and Snake rivers. It was a small, adobe-walled fort, famous as a stopping point on the Oregon Trail. Partially destroyed by flood waters in 1853, it was finally abandoned after the Indian war of 1855.

[C. J. Brosnan, *History of the State of Idaho*.]

CORNELIUS JAMES BROSNAN

BOLLMAN CASE. In *ex parte* Bollman and Swartwout (1807) the Supreme Court upheld its power to issue a writ of habeas corpus to review a commitment by an inferior federal court, and upon hearing ordered the release of two petitioners held on charges of treason as participants in the Burr conspiracy. Justus Erich Bollman and Samuel Swartwout, by separate routes, had carried copies of a letter in cipher from Aaron Burr to Gen. James Wilkinson at New Orleans. Wilkinson arrested them and sent them to Washington, where they were committed for trial by the circuit court for the District of Columbia. While the case was pending in the circuit court President Thomas Jefferson attempted, unsuccessfully, to induce Congress to suspend the privilege of the writ of habeas corpus. In holding that the evidence had been insufficient to support a charge of treason, Chief Justice John Marshall said for the Supreme Court that "there must be an actual assembling of men for the treasonable purpose, to constitute a levying of war." But, he added, if that be proved, then a conspirator, however remote from the scene of action, would be guilty. This dictum proved embarrassing when, a few months later, Marshall presided at the trial of Burr.

[A. J. Beveridge, *The Life of John Marshall;* Charles Warren, *The Supreme Court in United States History*.]

CHARLES FAIRMAN

BOLL WEEVIL, a beetle which eats the buds and young bolls of cotton, may have existed in Mexico and Central America for centuries. About 1892–93 it crossed into Texas, somewhere near Brownsville, and in 1894 was found in cotton fields 125 to 175 miles northward. Thereafter it advanced north and east at the rate of about 100 miles per year, until by 1923 it had reached the Atlantic coast. In 1930 it was said that 90 percent of the cotton-growing area was infested, though the fight against it had decreased its ravages in the worst spots. The peak year of the pest was 1921. (The cotton growers' woes were increased in 1916 by the appearance of the pink bollworm, another probable immigrant from Mexico.) It is estimated that the boll weevil destroys three to five million bales of cotton annually.

[U.S. Entomology Bureau, *An Annotated Bibliography of the Mexican Cotton Boll Weevil,* circular 140.]

ALVIN F. HARLOW

BOLTERS, party members who do not support the regular nominee of their party or its platform. The "bolt" may occur at the convention, as in 1912 when Theodore Roosevelt and his followers withdrew from the Republican party (*see* Progressive Party), or it may occur after the convention or primary has been held.

[C. W. McKenzie, *Party Government in the United States.*]

C. H. HAMLIN

BOMBING. Although aerial bombing during World War I never advanced much beyond the experimental stage, experience during that war provided the basis for continuing controversy over the nature, place, and role of military and naval aviation. Central figures in the controversy were the Italian Giulio Douhet for his 1921 book *Command of the Air;* Sir Hugh Trenchard for innovations as commander of the RAF, 1919–29; and the American Brig. Gen. William ("Billy") Mitchell, whose unbridled advocacy of air power led eventually to his court-martial. The 1930's witnessed a continuing series of technological advances in aircraft design, featuring increases in speed, range, ceiling, and load-carrying capacity. By 1939 both the U.S. Army Air Corps (USAAC) and the U.S. Navy had conceptualized (but as yet had no experience with) the means by which they would employ aircraft in bombing roles.

Principal emphasis in the USAAC was on long-range strategic bombing, best defined as bombing of the sources (industry, transportation, fuel, power) as opposed to the manifestations (armies and navies) of an enemy's strength. Also recognized was the need for tactical bombing, or close-in support of ground forces on the battlefield. The navy's interest lay primarily in dive-bombing in support of landing operations, striking targets protected by terrain from the low trajectory of naval artillery.

The performance of the German Luftwaffe early in World War II (Poland, Rotterdam, the Battle of Britain) caught the world's attention, as did the spectacular Japanese aerial attack at Pearl Harbor. The USAAC became the U.S. Army Air Forces (USAAF) in February 1942 and rapidly built up to unprecedented size, for the U.S. and British Combined Chiefs of Staff recognized that several years would pass before Adolf Hitler's Fortress Europe could be struck by any other means than through the air. Beginning in August 1942, the USAAF joined the RAF Bomber Command in the attack on Germany and occupied Europe that continued almost until VE Day. Controversy has continued to surround these campaigns—concerning both their military effectiveness and moral appropriateness. A presidential commission concluded after the war, however, that "Allied air power was decisive in the war in Western Europe."

In the Pacific theater, USAAF and navy bombing prior to late 1944 was devoted primarily to supporting landing operations and destroying Japanese shipping. Continual bombing of Japan proper began in November 1944 from bases in the Marianas, greatly intensifying after March of 1945 and culminating in the dropping of two atomic bombs on Aug. 6 and 8, 1945. Japan's surrender prior to the planned invasion proved the effectiveness of these attacks, occurring, as they did, concurrently with a tight naval blockade.

With the National Security Act of 1947, the USAAF became a separate service, the U.S. Air Force (USAF), testifying to the then widely held assumption that wars of the future would be won by those nations capable of conducting atomic (later nuclear) warfare most efficiently on short notice. This assumption lay behind the subsequent buildup of the USAF's Strategic Air Command (SAC) into the most powerful air striking force in the world, armed with both bombers and intercontinental ballistic missiles (ICBM's). It also accounted for the tendency to look on the Korean War experience as an aberration, not to be taken seriously as a portent of things to come. The bombing in Indochina from 1965 to 1972, involving both the USAF and the U.S. Navy, was conducted under a series of tactical and strategic restrictions that frustrated the airmen assigned to the task but that they nonetheless honored, often to their considerable peril. The effectiveness of bombing in support of ground forces was acknowledged from the start; that of independent air operations in North Vietnam and Laos was controversial from the start and appears destined to remain so.

[Wesley F. Craven and James L. Cate, eds., *The Army Air Forces in World War II;* E. M. Emme, ed., *The Impact of Air Power;* R. F. Futrell, *The USAF in Korea;* R. Littauer and N. Uphoff, eds., *The Air War in Indochina;*

C. Webster and N. Frankland, *The Strategic Air Offensive Against Germany, 1939–45.*]

DAVID MACISAAC

BONANZA KINGS. John W. Mackay, James G. Fair, James C. Flood, and William S. O'Brien organized the Consolidated Virginia Silver Mine near Virginia City, Nev., from a number of smaller claims on the Comstock lode, in 1871. Later they added the nearby California mine. For three years after large ore bodies were uncovered in 1874 the two mines produced $3 million per month. In 1876, for exhibition purposes, $6 million was taken in one month from both mines. Production began to fall off in 1879 but in twenty-two years of operation the two mines yielded $150 million in silver and gold and paid over $78 million in dividends. The term "bonanza" was applied to the large ore body that lay in a vertical rift of the hanging wall of the Comstock lode.

[T. A. Rickard, *History of American Mining.*]

CARL L. CANNON

BONANZA WHEAT FARMING in the Red River Valley of the North during the period 1875–90 was an important factor in the settlement and development of the spring wheat region. The Cass-Cheney farm, first and most widely known of the bonanzas, was established in 1875 when George W. Cass, president of the Northern Pacific Railroad, and E. P. Cheney, a director of the road, exchanged almost worthless Northern Pacific bonds for land held by the railroad in the Red River Valley. Cass took ten sections, Cheney eight, and an experienced wheat farmer contracted to handle operations. Yields for the next decade were uniformly high. Capital was attracted to the region, and many Northern Pacific bondholders followed the example set by Cass and Cheney. By 1890 over 300 farms in the valley exceeded 1,000 acres; a half dozen or more exceeded 15,000 acres. Some of the farms were individually owned; others were corporations. Few bonanzas were established after 1890, and most of the older farms were broken up within the next quarter century.

[H. E. Briggs, "Early Bonanza Farming in the Red River Valley of the North," *Agricultural History,* vol. 6 (1932).]

ROBERT H. BAHMER

BONDS, GOVERNMENT. *See* **Debt, Public.**

BONHOMME RICHARD -SERAPIS *ENCOUNTER* (Sept. 23, 1779), one of the most notable victories in American naval history. John Paul Jones's flagship, the *Bonhomme Richard,* originally an Indian merchantman renamed in honor of Benjamin Franklin, was proceeding with Jones's tiny fleet up the east coast of England in quest of English cargoes. Although worn-out and unseaworthy, it carried forty-two guns. About noon, Jones sighted two enemy ships of war, the *Serapis* and the *Countess of Scarborough,* convoying ships loaded with naval stores. He maneuvered his ship close to the *Serapis* and both opened broadside fire. Jones had placed some of his guns below, and two of the larger ones on the lower deck burst, killing and wounding several men. This catastrophe necessitated using only the lighter guns and musketry. The slaughter on both sides was terrible, and the American ship was leaking badly. After an hour's fighting, Jones answered the British challenge to surrender: "I have not yet begun to fight." The two vessels became locked together and the battle raged for more than two hours longer. Jones was hampered by treachery of a captain in his own fleet, but by using British prisoners to man the pumps he stayed afloat and wore down the enemy to the point of exhaustion and surrender.

[E. S. Maclay, *History of the United States Navy.*]

ARTHUR R. BLESSING

BONITO IN CHACO CANYON. A large prehistoric pueblo ruin known as Bonito stands in Chaco Canyon, N.Mex., northeast of Gallup. The shallow canyon contains thirteen main ruins, part of them contemporary and all belonging to the prehistoric period known as Pueblo III, or the Grand period in Pueblo culture. Bonito, as determined by the tree-ring dating method, was occupied during the interval A.D. 919–1130. It was originally four stories high and contained about 500 rooms, the architecture resembling that of modern Indian villages near Santa Fe. The ruin was partially excavated in 1896–99 by the Hyde Expedition and in 1921–23 by the National Geographic Society. Chaco Canyon was proclaimed a national monument in 1907.

[*National Geographic Magazine,* vols. 39 (1921), 41 (1922), 44 (1923).]

CLARK WISSLER

BONNEVILLE DAM. *See* **Hydroelectric Power.**

BONNEVILLE EXPEDITION. Capt. B. L. E. Bonneville, U.S. Army, headed a party of trappers and traders in the Far West that started from Fort Osage in Missouri, May 1, 1832. The well-known Platte-South Pass route was followed to Green River. Here, a few miles above the mouth of Horse Creek in a region favored by the mountain men as a place of annual rendezvous, Fort Bonneville was built. Abandoned shortly after completion, it was frequently called "Fort Nonsense." Bonneville moved to the headwaters of the Salmon River, then continued to move during most of the time that he was in the mountains. So thoroughly did he cover the Rocky Mountains and the Columbia drainage basin, and so good was his mapmaking that he may be credited with having been the first to gain true geographic knowledge of the Far West. A branch expedition organized by Bonneville left Green River, July 1833, under Joseph Reddeford Walker, crossed Salt Lake Desert, descended Humboldt River, crossed the Sierras north of Yosemite Valley, and spent the winter at Monterey. In the spring, it returned through the Sierras via Walker's Pass, across the Great Basin, and up Bear River, joining Bonneville June 1, 1834.

Washington Irving made a compelling story of Bonneville's manuscript, which ranks at the top of the literary contributions of the fur traders.

[Washington Irving, *The Adventures of Captain Bonneville.*]

CARL P. RUSSELL

"BONNIE BLUE FLAG," the title of a popular Confederate ballad that was sung throughout the South during the period of secession. Authorities disagree as to the author, as to where it was first sung, and as to the meaning of bonnie blue flag. It was, however, sung often by Harry McCarthy; it was sung in New Orleans and in Richmond theaters in 1861. The blue flag of South Carolina was the blue field of the United States flag bearing first a single star for South Carolina, which later, according to the song, "grew to be eleven," and was used before the adoption of an official flag.

CARL L. CANNON

BONUS ARMY, a spontaneous gathering of unemployed World War I veterans who, late in May 1932, began marching and hitchhiking to Washington, D.C., in small groups from all over the United States until about 15,000 were assembled there. The needy veterans, seeking some economic relief from Congress, eventually united in petitioning for immediate payment of the adjusted compensation, or "bonus," certificates approved by Congress in 1924 but not payable until 1945.

The problems of food, shelter, and sanitation for the impoverished veterans embarrassed Washington, and there was latent danger of disorder. But the leader, Walter W. Waters, maintained almost military discipline and expelled Communist agitators, while patriotism permeated the ranks. Although Washington's chief of police tried to provide quarters, most of the men built wretched hovels in which they lived.

In mid-June, Congress, by a narrow margin, defeated the bonus bill, but the disappointed "Bonus Expeditionary Force" stayed on, haunting the Capitol grounds. Late in July, the veterans were ordered to evacuate. Most of the veterans departed, but about 2,000 failed to do so. An attempt by police to remove the remaining veterans resulted in the death of two policemen and two veterans. On July 28, on instructions from the president, U.S. troops drove them from their quarters in public buildings and from their camps, using tanks, infantry, and cavalry. (*See also* Bonuses, Military.)

[E. Francis Brown, "The Bonus Army Marches to Defeat," *Current History* (1932); Walter W. Waters, *B.E.F., The Whole Story of the Bonus Army.*]

JOSEPH MILLS HANSON

BONUS BILL, CALHOUN'S. On Dec. 16, 1816, John C. Calhoun recommended that the House of Representatives appoint a committee to inquire into the expediency of creating a fund for internal improvements from the profits derived from the second national bank. With the appointment of the committee, Calhoun, as chairman, introduced a bill on Dec. 23, 1816, to set apart as a permanent fund for internal improvements the $1.5 million bonus exacted from the bank as a price of the charter and the profits from the $7 million of the bank stock owned by the United States. Although the bill was passed, President James Madison vetoed it, Mar. 3, 1817, on the ground that it was unconstitutional, but suggested an amendment to the Constitution that would remove all doubts upon the subject.

GEORGE D. HARMON

BONUSES, MILITARY, gratuities or benefits, usually paid in a lump sum, to veterans of military service. They should be distinguished from pensions, which are a continuing compensation paid to disabled veterans or their dependents. Until World War II bonuses paid to veterans in the United States took the form of both cash payments and land grants. The practice began in 1776 when the Continental Congress voted to reward men of the Continental army with grants of land that ranged in size from 100 acres for noncommissioned officers and privates to 1,100 acres for a major-general. Public lands in Ohio (U.S. Military District) were reserved for location of the bounties, and warrants totaling more than 2 million acres were eventually issued. In 1778, acting on a suggestion by George Washington, the Congress voted to give, at the end of the war, an additional five years' pay to commissioned officers and a sum of about $80 to all others as a bonus.

During the first half of the 19th century, bonuses took the exclusive form of land grants. An act of 1811 extended to veteran noncommissioned officers and privates, with five years of service, a grant of 160 acres of the public domain. In 1846 Congress awarded 160 acres of land to noncommissioned officers and privates who had served in the war with Mexico. In 1850 an act granted 80 acres to any veteran of the War of 1812 excluded under the act of 1811, to commissioned officers of the Mexican War, and to any person who had served in an Indian war since 1790. Finally, in 1855, Congress raised the minimum land grant for all previous laws to 160 acres and lowered all previous eligibility requirements to fourteen days' service or participation in one battle. Although warrants for more than 65 million acres were issued under these various laws, very little of the land was actually taken up by veterans, since the warrants could be sold to other persons or exchanged for interest-bearing or treasury scrip. A large market for the warrants developed and most of the bonus lands fell into the hands of speculators.

Civil War veterans of the Union Army received bonuses adjusted to the length of service, a maximum of $100 being paid to those who had served three years. In 1875 President Ulysses S. Grant vetoed a congressional measure that would have equalized the bonus payments of all Union soldiers. The veterans of the Spanish-American War were not given a bonus, and the issue was not raised again until after World War I.

Although servicemen received a mustering-out bonus of $60 at the end of World War I, the American Legion led a movement for an additional bonus. At its fall convention in 1919 the legion took the position that ex-servicemen were entitled to "adjusted compensation"—that is, the difference between the money they actually received while in the service and the larger amount they could have earned had they remained at home. A bill to grant such a bonus was vetoed by President Warren G. Harding in 1922 but subsequently passed over President Calvin Coolidge's veto in 1924. Veterans were to receive $1.00 for each day of domestic service and $1.25 for each day served overseas, actual payment being in the form of paid-up twenty-year endowment insurance policies, deferred until 1945. More than 3.5 million interest-bearing adjusted compensation certificates were issued, with a total value of $3.5 billion. With the coming of the depression and massive unemployment, the American Legion demanded immediate cash payment of the certificates. In 1931 Congress passed over President Herbert Hoover's veto a compromise bill under which veterans could borrow 50 percent of the cash value of their certificates at 4.5 percent interest. That measure did not quiet the veterans, however; and subsequent demands for full and immediate payment were highlighted by the Bonus Army incident in the summer of 1932. Somewhere between 12,000 and 15,000 veterans assembled in Washington to demand cash payment of their certificates. Fearing violence, Congress appropriated $100,000 to provide transportation home for the veterans, and most departed. The few thousand petitioners who remained were forcibly driven out of the city by federal troops on July 28. The issue was finally resolved in January 1936, when Congress passed over President Franklin D. Roosevelt's veto a bill authorizing immediate payment of the certificates.

While the United States was still involved in World War II, Congress passed the Servicemen's Readjustment Act of 1944, popularly called the GI Bill of Rights. The act provided a comprehensive program of veterans' benefits, including unemployment compensation, education and job training, and guaranteed housing and business loans. Through the date of its termination in July 1949, the unemployment compensation program paid almost $4 billion in "readjustment allowances" to nearly 9 million veterans. The education and job training program, which terminated in July 1956, provided educational benefits at the secondary and college level and on-the-job training to almost 10 million veterans at a cost exceeding $13 billion. The insured-loan program came to an end for most veterans in July 1962, and by that date more than 5 million applicants had obtained loans totaling more than $50 billion.

In July 1952 Congress passed the Veteran's Readjustment Act, which extended the benefits of the earlier measure to veterans of the Korean conflict. Eligible under the act were service personnel honorably discharged on or before Jan. 31, 1955. Thus, veterans of service discharged during the decade after Feb. 1, 1955, were not eligible for benefits. Eleven years later, however, Congress passed still another GI Bill, the Veteran's Readjustment Benefits Act of 1966. In addition to extending benefits of the previous measures to veterans of the military conflict in Vietnam, it also applied retroactively to those who had served for more than 180 days after Jan. 31, 1955. Thus, the act of 1966 seemed to commit the nation for the first time to the idea that peacetime veterans are entitled to receive the same benefits as wartime veterans. In December 1974 Congress passed, over President Gerald Ford's veto, the Vietnam Era Veteran's Readjustment Act. The main provisions of the act extended the period of educational benefits from thirty-six to forty-five months and increased the monthly payments to veterans enrolled in college by 23 percent.

[Paul W. Gates, *History of Public Land Law Development;* Elmer E. Lewis, *Laws Relating to Veterans, 1914–1941;* Davis R. B. Ross, *Preparing for Ulysses;* Gilman G. Udell, *Supplement to Compilation of Veterans Laws, 82nd–91st Congresses.*]

SEDDIE COGSWELL

BOOBY TRAPS. Traps executed in warfare have existed since antiquity, but the modern booby trap appeared in World War I. The booby trap is a device that explodes when a hidden or apparently harmless object is disturbed; the explosion occurs before the victim can recognize and react to the danger.

The Germans and Japanese used booby traps extensively during World War II, usually as defensive weapons. The Korean War saw wide use of booby traps by the Chinese and North Koreans. Booby traps were a major weapon in the Vietnam War, their employment by the Vietcong and North Vietnamese being so common that they served as offensive as well as defensive weapons. Supply caches were extensively booby-trapped, as were known routes of communications and approaches to hidden base camps. The Vietcong used nonexplosive traps also, particularly sharpened stakes hidden in vegetation at likely helicopter landing zones. U.S. troops seldom used booby traps in World War II and the Korean War, but frequently in Vietnam, where the "mechanical ambush," a pellet-firing mine activated by a hidden trip wire, was employed.

JOHN ALBRIGHT

BOODLE, a term for money used for graft or bribery, first applied by sensational newspapers (1884–86) to members of the New York Board of Aldermen who were charged with accepting bribes in connection with the granting of a franchise for a street railroad on Broadway. Thereafter, the term came into common use to signify bribery in general and particularly in municipal governments.

[M. Ostrogorski, *Democracy and the Organization of Political Parties.*]

P. ORMAN RAY

BOOK AUCTIONS. The first book auction in America for which a definite record exists is the sale held by Ambrose Vincent in Boston, May 28, 1713. No copy of the catalog, possibly a broadside, is known. The earliest surviving catalog recorded in George L. McKay's *American Book Auction Catalogues, 1713–1934* (1937) is that of the library of the Rev. Ebenezer Pemberton, sold in Boston July 2, 1717. The McKay compilation includes a detailed account of auction houses and important libraries by Clarence S. Brigham. The auction, a comparatively new method of disposing of books, spread rapidly. Sales also took place in New York, Philadelphia, Virginia, and Charleston, S.C., in the second quarter of the century, but few catalogs, if issued, have survived. The manuscript catalog of the library of John Montgomerie, governor of New York, sold in May 1732, is in the New York Public Library.

Among the earliest and most active auctioneers was Robert Bell of Philadelphia, who held numerous sales from 1768 to 1784. After the death of William Byrd of Westover, Va., forty wagonloads from his library, one of the largest in the country, were sent to Bell to sell by auction. In 1784 the Pennsylvania assembly passed an act requiring auctioneers to be appointed and licensed. Bell attacked the action, without success, in the pamphlet *Bell's Address to Every Freeman . . . concerning a Tyranical Embargo now laid upon the Free-Sale of Books by Auction.* Noted auctioneers in Philadelphia included Moses Thomas (entered business in 1823), Samuel T. Freeman (1826), and Stan V. Henkels (1883); in Boston, Joseph Leonard (1842) and C. F. Libbie and Company (1878). By the late 19th century, activity centered in New York, where auctioneers included Royal Gurley (1831), James Ewing Cooley (1833), Lemuel Bangs (1837), George A. Leavitt (1857), Bangs Merwin and Company (1858), and John Anderson (1903, later Anderson Galleries). Thomas E. Kirby formed the American Art Association (1887), acquired by Cortland F. Bishop (1923), who also acquired the Anderson Galleries (1927), merging the two as the American Art

Association–Anderson Galleries (1929); the latter was dissolved shortly after the formation of Parke-Bernet Galleries (1938), which was bought out by Sotheby of London (1965), now known as Sotheby Parke Bernet, Inc. (1973). Swann Auction Galleries (1942) is still active.

Noted sales include the later library of Thomas Jefferson (1829); the library of George Washington (1876); and the library of George Brinley of Hartford (1878–93), which was the largest collection of books relating to America ever formed. Other collections strong in American history include those of Henry C. Murphy (sold in 1884) and of Brayton Ives (1891), whose library also included important early English literature. The Thomas Winthrop Streeter collection of North American history, particularly on the West, grossed more than $3 million (1966–69). Libraries of American literature include those of Charles B. Foote (1894), Frank Maier (1909), Jacob C. Chamberlain (1909), and Stephen H. Wakeman (1924), who had brought together an extensive collection strong in 19th-century New England writers. The Robert Hoe library, rich in many fields, was the most valuable library ever sold by auction (1911–13) in America. Sales of rare editions in English literature include the collections of Winston H. Hagen (1919), Herschel V. Jones (1919–23), Beverly Chew (1924–25), John L. Clawson (1926), all especially devoted to Elizabethan literature; George Barr McCutcheon (1925–26), Jerome D. Kern (1929), John Spoor (1939), A. Edward Newton (1941), Frank J. Hogan (1945–46), and Edward Hubert Litchfield (1951); John Quinn (1923–24), mainly late 19th- and early 20th-century books and manuscripts, particularly Irish literature; Anson Conger Goodyear (1927), American and English literary autographs; Oliver R. Barrett (1950–52), Abraham Lincoln and other autograph material; the Marquis of Lothian (1932), early books and manuscripts; Cortland Field Bishop (1938–48); and Lucius Wilmerding (1950–51), early bindings and rare English and French literature.

[Wesley Towner, *The Elegant Auctioneers.*]

MICHAEL PAPANTONIO

BOOK COLLECTING. *See* **Collecting: Books and Manuscripts.**

BOOK PUBLISHING. The history of book publishing in the United States began in mid-September 1638 with the arrival in Boston of the English ship *John,* bearing the press that the Rev. Josse Glover, who died on the voyage over, had meant to set up in Boston. Glover's widow settled in Cambridge, where the press was set up and operated by two sons of the locksmith Stephen Day, who had traveled to Boston with the Glovers. Eighteen-year-old Matthew Day, consequently, became the nation's first printer.

In the hands of the Days and later of the family of Samuel Green, the Cambridge press printed more than 200 books before its demise in 1692. Perhaps the most important was the *Whole Booke of Psalmes,* a metrical translation from the Hebrew better known as the *Bay Psalm Book,* which initiated Cambridge press production in 1640 and was the first book printed in America.

Book publishing was slow to rise. It was a cottage industry through the 17th and 18th centuries, often the occupation of a whole family. For some time materials had to be imported, and a native literature was late in developing. Books were only a part of the colonial printer's output. The print shop also turned out magazines and newspapers, selling its output in the front part of the store, along with notions of every variety, and confining the machinery to the back. Print shops became the center of political and intellectual activity, as well as meeting places for dissenters in the years preceding the Revolution. Not until the early 19th century did newspaper and magazine publishing begin to develop separately. Bookselling and book publishing were inseparable, for the most part, during the first half of that century, and some of the old-line houses continued to maintain retail bookselling establishments well into the 20th century.

By the end of the 17th century, book publishing had made only a modest beginning. It was still in the hands of printers who were also publishers, but sometimes practiced their trade on behalf of others. Copyright was virtually unknown, and censorship was rigid. What was to come could be seen in the variety of work emerging from the presses. Most of the categories of modern publishing were in existence; but unfortunately the technology of printing had scarcely advanced since the 15th century, so the products of the press were not distinguished for craftsmanship or beauty.

In the 18th century, there were tentative starts in virtually every field of publishing and a probing toward the development of markets. Boston was still the center of the book trade, but the balance was shifting toward Philadelphia and soon would shift to New York. This was a natural economic development, since the latter two cities were growing larger, attracting more business, and so creating an increased market for sales, at the same time bringing together large numbers of intellectuals and craftsmen. The press also moved constantly westward from the eastern seaboard, carrying the colonial pattern of printing with it and establishing at least some kind of publishing in every part of the country. The long struggle for copyright was beginning, almanacs were best-sellers, and religious and other kinds of specialized publishing were bringing a new diversity to the trade. Children's books and textbooks were helping to broaden literacy, thus creating a new and constantly expanding adult market.

Modern publishing began in the early 19th century, and Mathew Carey of Philadelphia, an Irish radical who became a solid member of the American establishment, is widely regarded as the first modern publisher. The house he founded, after many transformations, still exists under the name of Lea and Febiger. Books were sold in the years before the Civil War in a variety of ways: through trade fairs, trade sales, and book auctions; in bookshops; and by subscription. A major development was the beginning of paperback publishing in 1842, when two newspaper "supplements," *Brother Jonathan* and *The New World,* were launched and quickly became such a threat to established publishers that they began to issue paperbacks in series.

A technological revolution started about 1825 with the invention, first, of the flatbed press and then of the revolving cylinder press. It was all that the burgeoning industry needed to reach what was beginning, with the sharp rise in population and in literacy, to be a mass market. Thousands of volumes could be turned out in a short space of time, where once they had been produced slowly by the hundreds. Cheap fiction, including the dime novel, came out of this revolution in printing, which soon embraced hardcover books as well.

Most of the great houses known today were founded in the half-century before the Civil War. In New York, chronologically, there were John Wiley and Sons, Harper, Appleton, A. S. Barnes, Putnam, Dodd, Mead, Baker and Scribner, D. Van Nostrand, and E. P. Dutton. In Philadelphia, besides Mathew Carey's successors, the major publishers were J. B. Lippincott Company and the Blakiston Company. In Boston, Ticknor and Fields was the dominant house of the period; the major Boston houses that survived the century were Houghton Mifflin and Little, Brown. Cincinnati was beginning to rise as a publishing center, subscription publishing was thriving in Hartford, and after the war Chicago grew strong enough to take over from Cincinnati.

By the end of the Civil War, the structure of the general publishing house had been established and the specialty houses were developing rapidly. Authors still had few rights and only domestic copyright protection. Publishing was considered an "occupation for gentlemen," and indeed the heads of publishing houses were different from the entrepreneurs of the industrial expansion. Distribution of books had already been identified as the growing industry's major bottleneck; it remains so today. Most important, perhaps, publishers had emerged by 1865 as the chief purveyors of ideas in the cultural life of the nation.

Between the Civil War and World War I book publishing came to full flower, rooted more deeply in the national culture than any other means of communication and influencing it more than any other medium until the advent of television. After the Civil War, a new generation emerged to build on what the founders had established. Among the new leaders were Henry Holt, George E. Brett (who established the American branch of Macmillan), Thomas Y. Crowell, P. F. Collier, I. K. Funk, David McKay, Frank N. Doubleday, S. S. McClure, George Doran, Albert and Charles Boni, Alfred A. Knopf, and Ben W. Huebsch. It was a period that also saw the rise of the university press, with that of Cornell University appearing first, in 1869.

The mass market continued to expand at an astonishing rate, with the help of public libraries and public education. An overwhelming quantity of fiction was published between 1890 and 1910, and for a time in the 1890's such authors as Rudyard Kipling and George du Maurier had a tremendous popular following in America. Book publishers also played an important role in World War I as a transmission belt for British propaganda and as mobilizers of public sentiment.

The 1920's saw a literary renaissance and the rise of another generation of publishers, including Bennett Cerf and Donald Klopfer (Random House), Leon Shimkin and M. Lincoln Schuster (Simon and Schuster), and Alfred Harcourt and Donald Brace (Harcourt, Brace). During World War II millions of books were supplied to soldiers and an already burgeoning mass market was extended, leading to the steadily growing importance of the paperback industry and to the phenomenon of the 1970's in which it was possible for an author to earn a million dollars from a book before publication, from paperback, motion picture, and other subsidiary rights.

In the 1960's and early 1970's, Wall Street realized publishing was a "growth" industry, and conglomerates and industries not necessarily related to books acquired publishing houses. This era of mergers and acquisitions seemed to be virtually over by 1974, with much less damage to the basic integrity of the business than had been feared. As the nation neared its two hundredth anniversary, book publishing remained the primary free forum for ideas in the United States.

[Hellmut Lehmann-Haupt et al., *The Book in America;* Charles Madison, *Book Publishing in America;* John Tebbel, *A History of Book Publishing in the United States.*]

JOHN TEBBEL

BOOKS, CHILDREN'S. Reading matter designed for colonial children consisted largely of works intended to instruct or improve, little books like *Spiritual Milk for Boston Babes* (1646) by John Cotton and the *New England Primer* (published some time before 1690 by Benjamin Harris and appearing in countless editions). Most of the early books were English imports or American printers' reissues, some with slight changes made to Americanize them. Among the most significant were British books reprinted by Hugh Gaines and, later, Isaiah Thomas, both of whom issued John Newbery's *The History of Little Goody Two Shoes* (1775 and 1787). Thomas also brought out Newbery's *Mother Goose's Melodies* (1786). Tiny toybook versions of English, French, and other fairy tales and fables were published by a string of printers on the East Coast, along with chapbook issues of religious texts and instructive works of natural science.

In the 1830's, Washington Irving and Christopher Pearse Cranch introduced American stories of the fantastic at the same time that Samuel Griswold Goodrich and Jacob Abbott began to flood the market with their endless series of didactic geographical and travel stories (the *Peter Parley* and *Rollo* books, respectively). Both men were vehemently against fairy tales. Abbott's pleasant Franconia stories were his best writing. For many decades of the 19th century, the American Sunday School Union and other tract societies poured out a stream of little books advocating religion and condemning vice. By the 1850's Nathaniel Hawthorne was introducing Greek mythology in his *Wonder-Book for Boys and Girls* (1852) and *Tanglewood Tales* (1853). The 1860's and 1870's saw a fresh kind of storywriting, with Mary Mapes Dodge creating *Hans Brinker* (1865); Louisa May Alcott, *Little Women* (1868) and its sequels; Thomas Bailey Aldrich, *The Story of a Bad Boy* (1870); and Mark Twain, *Tom Sawyer* (1876) and other stories. John Bennett's *Master Skylark* (1897) brought credit to the end of the century. Alongside these—from the 1880's on—came the flashy dime novels; the formula-style Horatio Alger, Jr., series; and many other popular series for girls as well as boys. While the boys had farm stories and western and sea adventures, the girls were offered pious heroines (such as Elsie Dinsmore) but also Susan Coolidge's "Katy" books (1872–86), Lucretia Hale's *The Peterkin Papers* (1880) and its sequel (1886), and Margaret Sidney's *Five Little Peppers* (1881) and its sequels. Howard Pyle, artist-reteller of the great legends and creator of new fairy tales inspired by folklore, made a major contribution at the turn of the century, as did Frank Stockton with his literary fantasies and Joel Chandler Harris with his dialect stories from *Uncle Remus: His Songs and Sayings* (1880) and its sequels based on black folklore. There was little true or lasting poetry for children. Exceptions were Sarah Josepha Hale's "Mary Had a Little Lamb" in her *Poems for Our Children* (1830) and Clement C. Moore's "A Visit from St. Nicholas" (1823). F. O. C. Darley and Howard Pyle each turned the song "Yankee Doodle" into a picture book (1865 and 1881).

The 20th century saw a continuation of English imports and an increase in translations from foreign-language books for children, as well as increased American production. Early in the century L. Frank Baum achieved success with his Oz books, and other series writers also flourished. By 1922, critics began to look to recognition of quality in children's literature through the awarding of the annual John Newbery medal for writing and, by 1938, the Randolph Caldecott medal for picture-book illustration—each award established by Frederic G. Melcher and administered by the American Library Association. The first National Book Award for children's books was awarded in 1969, recognizing children's books as part of the mainstream of literature, and lists of notable children's books also came into being.

VIRGINIA HAVILAND

BOOMER MOVEMENT, a term applied to attempts of settlers to occupy an area in Indian Territory during the period from 1879 to 1885. The Five Civilized Tribes of Indians formerly owned all of the present state of Oklahoma except the Panhandle (*see* Cimarron, Proposed Territory of). In 1866 as a punishment for having participated in the Civil War on the side of the South, they were compelled to cede to the United States as a home for other Indians the western half of their domain. During the next ten years several tribes of Indians were given reservations on these lands, but a fertile region of some 2 million acres near the center of Indian Territory was not assigned to any tribe and came to be known as the "unassigned lands" or Old Oklahoma.

Early in 1879 E. C. Boudinot, a railway attorney of Cherokee descent, published a newspaper article stating that this was public land, and so open to homestead entry. Widely reprinted, this article created great excitement. Later in the same year a colony of homeseekers under the leadership of C. C. Carpenter sought to enter the Indian Territory and occupy this area but was prevented by troops under Gen. John Pope.

In 1880 David L. Payne became the leader of these so-called "boomers." Payne organized the movement, charging a small fee for membership in his "Oklahoma colony." During the next four years he and his followers made eight attempts to settle the region but in every case were ejected by soldiers. Upon his death at Wellington, Kans., in 1884 his lieutenant, W. L. Couch, led an expedition to the forbidden area but was promptly removed by the military. The struggle was then transferred to the national capital, and on April 22, 1889, the unassigned lands were opened to settlement under the provisions of an act of Congress.

[E. E. Dale and J. L. Rader, *Readings in Oklahoma History*.]

EDWARD EVERETT DALE

BOOMTOWNS, settlements that sprang up or rapidly increased in size as the result of some mineral or industrial development. Rochester, N.Y., was one of the earliest notable examples, its growth after 1825 as the result of the building of the Erie Canal and the development of the Genesee waterpower being phenomenal for the period. There were a few boomtowns in the Middle West, but the finest specimens began to be seen only with the discoveries of gold and silver in the Far West. San Francisco itself in 1849–51 was a remarkable example. Simultaneously, in the gold regions, before there were any sawmills, villages of tents, with an occasional log hut, sprang up and their occupants quickly formed city governments. By the time lumber began to be sawed county governments were being organized, and the crudest of small frame shacks became courthouses. Virginia City and other Nevada towns were mushroom growths from silver ore; meanwhile, in the 1860's, gold strikes contributed to the establishment of many others in Idaho, Montana, and Colorado, mostly ephemeral, though Helena, Mont., and Denver, Colo., proved to be permanent. Gold brought Deadwood, S.Dak., into being in 1876. Two cities built on silver evolved swiftly in 1878: Tombstone, Ariz., a new foundation; and Leadville, Colo., long a somnolent hamlet, but whose population leaped from 300 to 35,000 in two years. Oil City, Pa., in 1859 was the first of a long series of petroleum boomtowns, later continued in Ohio, Indiana, Oklahoma, and Texas. The opening of a portion of the Indian Territory to colonization in 1889 created Guthrie and Oklahoma City almost overnight. Immediately afterward, new gold discoveries in Colorado did the same for Cripple Creek and Creede. Hopewell, Va., was a typical creation of World War I munition plants, and other precocious towns arose in Florida during the land-speculation excitement of the 1920's. Similarly, beginning in 1956, Cape Canaveral, Fla., developed into a prosperous town, with over 35,000 inhabitants employed in the U.S. space program. However, cutbacks in federal appropriations for space flights and space research in the 1970's brought severe economic stress to the area. Construction of the Alaskan pipeline began in 1974, and boomtowns sprang up along the pipeline's route as work progressed.

[John M. Clampitt, *Echoes From the Rocky Mountains;* Alvin F. Harlow, *Old Waybills*.]

ALVIN F. HARLOW

BOONDOGGLING. On April 3, 1935, Robert C. Marshall, a witness before the Aldermanic Committee to Investigate the Relief Administration in New York City, testified that he taught various crafts, including "boondoggling," to workers on relief, and described "boondoggles" as gadgets or useful articles made out of scrap material. The term boondoggling was thereafter rather loosely used by critics of the New Deal throughout the country to ridicule so-called useless make-work and unproductive educational, recreational, and research projects for relief workers.

STANLEY R. PILLSBURY

BOONE-CALLAWAY KIDNAPPING. The settlement of Boonesborough on the Kentucky River had been left in peace by the Indians until Sunday, July 14, 1776, when three girls were captured as they were floating in a canoe on the river. They were Jemima, daughter of Daniel Boone, and Elizabeth and Frances, daughters of Col. Richard Callaway. The settlement was thrown into a turmoil and a rescue party was organized by Boone. Meanwhile the girls were hurried north by their captors toward the Shawnee towns across the Ohio River. The girls attempted to mark their trail until threatened by the Indians.

The third morning, as the Indians were building a fire for breakfast, the rescuers came up. "That's Daddy's gun," cried Jemima, as one Indian was toppled into the fire. The others ran off leaving their plunder, which the whites took. The girls were escorted home in triumph. Jemima soon married one of the rescuing party, Flanders Callaway. Elizabeth Callaway married Samuel Henderson, and Frances, John Holder. The episode served to put the settlers in the Kentucky wilderness on guard and prevented straying beyond the fort.

[John Bakeless, *Daniel Boone;* George W. Ranck, *Boonesborough;* R. G. Thwaites, *Daniel Boone*.]

LOUISE PHELPS KELLOGG

BOONESBOROUGH, former village on the south side of the Kentucky River, in the present county of Madison, founded Apr. 2, 1775, by Daniel Boone. Dispatched from the Watauga treaty ground by members of the Transylvania Company to mark out a roadway to lands purchased from the Cherokee, Boone and his companions blazed a trail across Cumberland Gap and through the wilderness to the mouth of Otter Creek on the Kentucky River. There they erected a stout stockaded fort that served as a rallying point of defense for the harassed settlers throughout the Revolution. At Boonesborough, May 23–27, 1775, the Transylvania proprietors called a convention to consider the needs of the colony. The novel proceedings and enactments had no legal sanction, but probably had a useful effect on morale.

On July 14, 1776, three young girls, one a daughter of Boone, were captured near the fort by Indians, but within three days were rescued unharmed (*see* Boone-Callaway Kidnapping). On Apr. 15, 1777, Boonesborough was subjected to an Indian attack, and on July 4 of the same year the assault was renewed on a larger scale. The fiercest siege and assault of all occurred Sept. 7–20, 1778. The Shawnee chiefs, Black Fish and Moluntha, together with a French-Canadian, Lt. Antoine Dagneaux de Quindre, were in command of a large body of Indians supported by a few British militiamen from Detroit, and this combined force attacked the little fortress, but failed to bring about its downfall and finally withdrew.

[John Bakeless, *Daniel Boone;* George W. Ranck, *Boonesborough*.]

SAMUEL M. WILSON

BOONE'S STATION, the stockaded home of Daniel Boone from 1780 to 1786, settled by Daniel's brother, Israel, in 1776, on Boone's Creek in Fayette County, Ky., near the present village of Athens. Here John Filson interviewed Daniel Boone in 1784 for his *Adventures of Colonel Daniel Boone*.

[George W. Ranck, *Boonesborough*.]

JONATHAN T. DORRIS

BOONTON IRON WORKS, an important ironmaking center, founded about 1770 by Samuel Ogden, who, with others in his family, purchased a six-acre tract along the Rockaway River, near Boonton, Morris County, N.J. Here rolling and slitting mills were erected that engaged in the manufacture of nail rods and bar iron. With the building of the Morris Canal in 1830 the New Jersey Iron Company was organized. This company built a new plant costing $283,000 and imported skilled mechanics from England. Under Fuller and Lord (1852–76) the enterprise tended to become an integrated industry with ore and timber reserves, canal boats, furnaces, mills, and auxiliary plants. After 1881 the business slowly declined. The plant closed in 1911.

[C. S. Boyer, *Early Forges and Furnaces in New Jersey*.]

C. A. TITUS

BOONVILLE, BATTLE OF (June 17, 1861). In the first engagement of the Civil War in Missouri, troops of the Missouri state guard (prosouthern) under Col. John S. Marmaduke were defeated by Gen. Nathaniel Lyon at Boonville, a strategic point on the Missouri River. The engagement began about five miles below Boonville. Union forces occupied the town and gained control of the river, and Confederate strength in Missouri was weakened.

[Walter Williams and Floyd C. Shoemaker, *Missouri, Mother of the West*, vol. II.]

FLOYD C. SHOEMAKER

BOOT AND SHOE MANUFACTURING. Bootmakers and shoemakers arrived early in the history of each of the colonies to provide the settlers with much-needed products. After acquiring leather from nearby tanneries, cobblers, frequently working at home, used hand tools and centuries-old techniques to cut out the various parts, to sew together the pieces to make the upper, and to attach the upper to the sole, as they shaped each shoe over a wooden last or form. Despite the widespread existence of these craftsmen, a nascent industry had begun to develop in eastern Massachusetts by the end of the colonial era. Lynn had become a leading center after John Adam Dagyr and other immigrants had introduced the most recent European hand processes, permitting colonists to make products that competed successfully with foreign imports.

In order to supply the demands of a growing population after the revolutionary war, merchant capitalists slowly reorganized the trade. They purchased leather from both American and foreign markets, cut the materials, hired craftsmen to make the shoes in their homes or small shops, and sold the finished products. This domestic, or putting-out, system of manufacture meant the cobbler worked for the merchant. Two kinds of specialization emerged: shoemakers in a region would specialize in a particular type of shoe, or craftsmen would specialize in only one step in the manufacturing process. Improving transportation networks and growing financial resources permitted shoe manufacturers in Massachusetts and the Middle Atlantic states to exploit southern and western markets.

Factories and mechanization came to this large industry after 1850, as entrepreneurs gradually recognized the usefulness of consolidating the various processes at one location, where better supervision of the increasingly specialized steps could occur. Within these central shops, or factories, machines were perfected that imitated specific hand processes. Of the more than 5,000 American patents issued before 1900 for improvements in shoemaking, three developments proved most significant: the adaptation of the Howe sewing machine to stitching uppers; the invention by Lyman R. Blake, a black mechanic, of a device for sewing the upper to the sole (the machine bears the name of Col. Gordon McKay, who improved and marketed it during the Civil War); and the perfection by Charles Goodyear, Jr., by 1875 of Auguste Deystouy's welt-stitching machine for joining the upper and sole. The advantages of machines, especially those that were power driven, encouraged the further subdivision of processes, with the result that more than 170 steps existed by the end of the century. Mechanization had increased labor productivity, or reduced the time required to make a shoe, by more than 80 percent and yielded a product of superior construction and styling.

As increased productivity and parallel consumer demand for a greater diversity of styles led to the creation of large, integrated factories, employees turned toward trade unionism, and in 1895 formed the International Boot and Shoe Workers Union. In 1899 the principal producers of shoemaking machinery formed the United Shoe Machinery Company, which still controlled this industry in the mid-1970's. In 1905 the shoe manufacturers formed the National Boot and Shoe Manufacturers Association.

Although New England and the Atlantic seaboard dominated shoemaking, other centers of manufacture in western New York, the Midwest, and the upper South emerged before World War I, using materials from throughout the world. Consolidation reduced the number of firms to 1,449 in 1919, but these companies had 211,000 employees and an output of 331 million pairs of shoes. Americans exported almost $75 million worth of leather footwear a year.

After World War I the shoemaking industry experienced difficulties. Although Americans refined techniques, foreign machinery manufacturers competed successfully. Imported shoes and a trend toward canvas and rubber shoes eroded the domestic market. Synthetic leather materials forced firms to adopt costly new technology. A more affluent society encouraged companies to design new styles, which then presented inventory problems. As competition and the size of the required capital investment rose, many inefficient firms either closed or consolidated.

In 1967 American shoe manufacturing establishments numbering 951 produced $2.75 billion worth, or 380 million pairs, of shoes and provided work for almost 200,000 people. The majority of these firms employed between 100 and 500 workers. No longer one of the largest American industries by then, boot and shoe manufacturing still contributed substantially to the economy and provided a needed consumer product.

[Ralph B. Bryan, *Hide and Leather and Shoes' Encyclopedia of the Shoe and Leather Industry;* Blanche Evans Hazard, *The Organization of the Boot and Shoe Industry in Massachusetts Before 1875;* Edgar M. Hoover, Jr., *Location Theory and the Shoe and Leather Industries;* Carl Kaysen, *United States United Shoe Machinery Corporation.*]

LUCIUS F. ELLSWORTH

***BOOTH* V. *UNITED STATES*,** 291 U.S. 339 (1934). In 1919 Congress passed an act permitting certain federal judges to retire with full pay, at the age of seventy. On June 16, 1933, new legislation reduced their pay 15 percent. Retired Judge Wilbur F. Booth thereupon sued the government. The Supreme Court unanimously ruled in his favor, holding that a retired judge did not "relinquish his office," and so, under Article III, Section 1, of the Constitution, his pay could not be reduced.

ERIK MCKINLEY ERIKSSON

BOOTLEGGING, a term derived from the early Indian traders' custom of carrying a bottle of liquor in the boot, especially applied to illicit deliveries of alcoholic beverages. The bootlegger is a peddler whose name differentiates his activities from those of the merchant who unlawfully purveys from a shop known variously as a blind tiger, blind pig, or speakeasy. The manufacture of illicit hard liquor is termed "moonshining," and the product, variously known, is often referred to as mountain dew.

Since the activity is illicit, no reliable estimates can be given as to its scope. In those times and places in which alcoholic beverages can be obtained lawfully at reasonable prices bootlegging has little reason for being; but heavy taxation or legal efforts to prevent the sale of liquor create a demand for an illicit supply. Between the effective date of the Eighteenth Amendment prohibiting manufacture of or traffic in liquor (Jan. 16, 1920) and its repeal (Dec. 3, 1933) the consumption of bootleg liquor in the United States was probably about 100 million gallons a year.

The profits derived from bootlegging depend somewhat upon the source of the beverage and somewhat upon the methods of retailing. During Prohibition liquor was smuggled across the borders, brought in by boat, alcohol lawfully possessed for manufacturing purposes was sold for beverages, and a relatively small amount was distilled without license. In the larger cities powerful bootlegging organizations arose that arranged for a steady supply of hard liquor and beer, often themselves controlling illicit distilleries and breweries and smuggling operations, and set up a complete system of retailing, both through luxurious speakeasies that furnished a variety of entertainment as well as food and illicit drink and through the private calls of bootleggers upon regular customers. These organizations tried to create monopolies and were ready to murder competitors or their spies. The St. Valentine's Day massacre of 1929 in a populous section of Chicago's North Side was the slaughter of seven unarmed rivals by one of these bootlegging gangs.

To meet the rising tide of crime several steps were taken. The original National Prohibition Enforcement Act of 1919, the Volstead Act, was amended by the more much severe Jones Act of 1929. This law raised the maximum penalty for bootlegging to a fine of $10,000 plus five years in prison, but it carried a rider stipulating that it was the intent of Congress to apply this drastic punishment to major offenders only. A year later, a federal grand jury sitting at Chicago uncovered what was termed the largest liquor ring since the advent of Prohibition. The indictment of thirty-one corporations and 158 individuals cited violations in New York, Chicago, Detroit, Cleveland, Philadelphia, St. Louis, Minneapolis, St. Paul, Los Angeles, and North Bergen, N.J. This group was charged with the diversion of more than 7 million gallons of alcohol in the seven years preceding indictment and was alleged to have done a total business in excess of $50 million. The state of Michigan went so far as to declare bootlegging a felony and to provide that on a third conviction for felony the convict might be sentenced to life imprisonment.

Before the end of 1930 more than 200 persons had been killed in the process of enforcement of the Volstead Act, and moderates were beginning to question whether the enforcement of Prohibition was feasible. The public revealed this attitude in a *Literary Digest* poll, May 24, 1930, by returning 30.5 percent of their votes in favor of continuance and strict enforcement of the Prohibition amendment, 29.1 percent in favor of modification to permit light wines and beer, and 40.4 percent in favor of repeal of the Eighteenth Amendment.

A limited number of bootleggers has always operated and probably will continue, but since the quality of their merchandise and public support are both uncertain, their sales volume doubtless will remain relatively small. The federal Bureau of Alcohol, Tobacco, and Firearms reported seizing 15,000 stills in 1958. Only 1,300 were seized in 1974, but the bureau estimates that it confiscates one-third to one-half of all operating stills.

[Herbert Asbury, *Great Illusion;* J. H. S. Bossard and Thorstein Sellin, eds., "Prohibition: A National Experiment," *Annals of American Association for the Promotion of Social Science,* vol. 158 (1932).]

ROBERT G. RAYMER

BORAX (sodium tetraborate) became important in the European Middle Ages as a flux for soldering—that is, for cleaning the surfaces of metal pieces to be joined by being melted together. A measure of the small scale of early technology is that, despite this restricted application, borax became an important commodity in international trade. Native European sources were unknown, and the nature of this mysterious material was long a puzzle to chemists. So was its place of origin. First known to be imported from the Far East, borax was ultimately found to come from Tibet—almost the only source known until the discovery (1776) and exploitation (1820) of Italian springs of boric acid (hydrogen tetraborate), which could be converted by the addition of soda (sodium carbonate) into borax. From the 1830's to the 1860's Italy was the principal source of borax. Traces of borax were also reported from other localities, including South America. In the 1860's desert areas now in Chile began to supply borax.

The key figure in the discovery of borax in North America was John A. Veatch, who found it in California in 1856, first in springs at the north end of the Sacramento Valley (Tehama County) and then in larger quantities in a cutoff bay of Clear Lake (Lake County). Veatch himself stated that the discovery was accidental, sparked by the presence in the region of an Englishman who had formerly worked for a London borax company. The California Borax Company was organized to exploit this source, and the company struggled for a decade to extract and purify a material encrusted on the bottom of an isolated wilderness lake. Veatch's explorations had taken him in the meantime to southern California, where in 1857 he found borax in the waters of mud volcanoes in the Colorado desert. Within the next decade borax was found in surface encrustations in Nevada and southern California, and exploitation of these more convenient sources was begun. In 1871 the *Mining and Scientific Press* of San Francisco reported borax to be "all the rage," with production in progress at Columbus, Fish, and Teal marshes in Esmeralda County, Nev. In 1880 production began in Death Valley, Calif., where for a decade the famous twenty-mule-team wagons carried it out of this below-sea-level depression to the railroad junction at Mojave, 160 miles away.

These surface deposits of borax were largely sodium calcium tetraborate (ulexite), known from their appearance as cotton balls, and their conversion to true borax—chemically simple but difficult in practice—was mastered only in the mid-1880's. After this time American producers not only satisfied the American market and began exportation, but they drove the price down to a level that caused most of them to fail. The principal survivor, Francis M. ("Borax") Smith, engaged Stephen Mather (later the first director of the National Park Service) to promote borax, an effort that manifested itself in 1896 in a pamphlet advertising 200 "recipes" for borax. Thus began a successful advertising campaign that greatly expanded the demand for a material that had become inexpensive—especially in washing powders, glass, and ceramic glazes.

By 1896 Smith controlled nearly all American sources of borax, but that same year, through difficulties with his other investments, he was forced to merge with the English borax company Redwood and Sons to form a company now known as U.S. Borax. The exploitation of shallow deposits terminated after the beginning of mining operations in 1927 at a site determined by drilling in the Mojave Desert, now marked by the company town, Boron. In the 1970's production there and at Searles Lake, Calif., exceeded one million tons per year, and satisfied the borax requirements of the United States, Western Europe, Japan, and many other parts of the world.

[Henry G. Hanks, *Report on the Borax Deposits of California and Nevada;* Robert Shankland, *Steve Mather of the National Parks;* John R. Spears, *Illustrated Sketches of Death Valley and Other Borax Deserts of the Pacific Coast.*]

ROBERT P. MULTHAUF

BORDER FORTS, EVACUATION OF (1796). By the French and Indian War Great Britain conquered the western country, and by the Proclamation of 1763 constituted it a permanent Indian preserve. This policy was reversed by the Quebec Act (1774), which annexed the entire Northwest to Quebec Province. Thereby the older colonies, which had fought to obtain the West, found themselves excluded from all share in it. During the Revolution they again renewed the struggle for the West, and at its close obtained it, with the Mississippi River and the line through the middle of the Great Lakes–St. Lawrence system as the western and northern boundaries of the new nation (*see* Definitive Treaty of Peace, 1783).

Elsewhere in the treaty Great Britain agreed to evacuate all places held by its armies within the United States "with all convenient speed." These included Carleton Island (Fort Haldimand), Oswego (Fort Ontario), Niagara, Detroit, and Michilimackinac, guarding the fur trade route between Montreal and the far Northwest and serving as natural centers of control of the interior Indian tribes, allies of Great Britain in the late war. Gov. Frederick Haldimand and the Montreal traders were appalled by the boundary provisions of the treaty, the governor fearing the surrender of the posts would precipitate a general Indian uprising, the merchants foreseeing their own financial ruin. The early American overtures for the transfer were evaded, therefore, while their later appeals at London were met by the excuse that the Americans had not complied with the treaty in the matter of collection of debts owed to British merchants (*see* British Debts) and in the treatment accorded the Loyalists.

For a decade Great Britain pursued a policy of opportunism, meanwhile retaining the posts and exercising *de facto* control over the Northwest. In 1793, however, it entered the continental revolutionary wars, while in America President George Washington was prosecuting the conquest of the Northwestern Indian Confederacy (*see* Wayne Campaign). Faced with a war in Europe, the British Ministry did not want another in America. By the Jay Treaty (ratified in 1795) the evacuation of the western posts by June 1, 1796, was promised. The Americans proved less ready to receive than the British were to deliver them. Detroit was taken over July 11; Oswego on July 15; Niagara on Aug. 10; and Michilimackinac, Sept. 1. With the transfer American rule over the country adjacent to the Great Lakes was first established, but west of Lake Michigan and on Lake Superior British authority continued dominant until after the War of 1812.

[Alfred L. Burt, *The Old Province of Quebec;* Louise P. Kellogg, *The British Regime in Wisconsin and the Northwest;* A. C. McLaughlin, "The Western Posts and the British Debts," American Historical Association *Annual Report* (1894).]

M. M. QUAIFE

BORDER RUFFIANS, citizens of western Missouri who endeavored to establish slavery in Kansas Territory. The term originated in 1855 with Gen. B. F. Stringfellow's assault upon A. H. Reeder, governor of the territory, and was first used by the *New York Tribune*. Missourians readily adopted the name, and border ruffian stores, hotels, and riverboats capitalized upon it. Antislavery presses and orators soon expanded the term to include all proslavery southerners in Kansas. Some of the ruffians were of the carousing type, but indiscriminate usage included such respectable leaders as Sen. David R. Atchison. Border ruffians voted illegally in Kansas elections, raided Lawrence and other towns, stole horses, and in general molested the free-state families (*see* Kansas Struggle). Much of their overzealous work was inspired by similar depredations committed by antislavery Kansans upon Missourians, and once such practices had begun, a spirit of lawlessness prompted both groups to use extreme measures. (*See also* Border War.)

[W. E. Connelley, *A Standard History of Kansas and Kansans.*]

WENDELL H. STEPHENSON

BORDER SLAVE STATE CONVENTION, also called the Peace Convention or Peace Conference, met in Washington, D.C., Feb. 4–27, 1861, at the invitation of the Virginia legislature, in an attempt to satisfy the states of the far South on the slavery issue. Twenty-two states were represented, with the border states most active. The seven states that had already seceded did not send delegates, nor did Arkansas, Wisconsin, Minnesota, California, and Oregon. Former President John Tyler of Virginia, chosen president of the convention, stated its purpose: "to bring back the cotton states and thereby restore the Constitution and the Union of the States." The Crittenden Compromise plan, which formed the basis of discussion, was so modified by further compromise in the course of the deliberations that the final recommendations of the convention satisfied no one. The recommendations, submitted to Congress on Feb. 27, constituted the last attempt at conciliation on the slavery question in the territories.

[J. G. Randall, *The Civil War and Reconstruction.*]

C. MILDRED THOMPSON

BORDER STATE REPRESENTATION. *See* **Secessionist Movement.**

BORDER STATES, a designation applied to the tier of slave states bordering on the North, consisting of Delaware, Maryland, Virginia, Kentucky, and Missouri. They were largely southern in sentiment, though many of their economic ties were with the North. They owe their chief significance to their reaction toward secession and the Civil War. None seceded except Virginia, from which West Virginia separated. Kentucky set up and maintained for a few months in 1861 the unique policy of neutrality, and all except Delaware sent considerable numbers of soldiers to the Confederacy. Kentucky and Delaware were the only border states to cling to slavery until the Thirteenth Amendment abolished it.

[E. C. Smith, *The Borderland in the Civil War*.]

E. MERTON COULTER

BORDER WAR (1854–59). The opening of the Kansas Territory to slavery in 1854 promoted emigration from the Northeast of antislavery groups (*see* Emigrant Aid Movement), the arrival of squatters and speculators, and the presence of an adventurous element recruited from both North and South. While claim jumping provoked dissension, the slavery issue was predominant. Recurring personal altercations led proslavery and free-state groups to organize regulating associations and guerrilla bands. It is impossible to determine which side committed greater excesses in lynching, horse stealing, pillaging, and pitched battles. The first eighteen months of settlement witnessed sporadic shootings, killings, and robberies, including the Wakarusa War, December 1855, which brought over 1,000 border ruffians into the territory. "Bleeding Kansas" soon became a grim reality. The sack of Lawrence, May 21, 1856, by a posse of border ruffians and John Brown's massacre of five proslavery men at Pottawatomie three days later started a four months' reign of terror. Free-state men won victories at Black Jack, Franklin, Fort Saunders, Fort Titus, Slough Creek, and Hickory Point; their opponents pillaged and later burned Osawatomie (Aug. 30, 1856), but official intervention prevented them from further destroying Lawrence. A semblance of order restored by Gov. John W. Geary in the fall was of brief duration. The Marais des Cygnes massacre of nine free-state men, May 19, 1858, was the last wholesale slaughter. In the same year disturbances in Linn and Bourbon counties reached critical proportions. Major conflict terminated in 1859, albeit sporadic disorders continued until the Civil War inaugurated a new chapter in Kansas-Missouri relations. Anticipating a congressional appropriation that did not materialize, territorial commissioners approved claims for losses resulting from border trouble totaling over $400,000, which, though exaggerated, give some notion of the extent of property damage.

[F. W. Blackmar, *The Life of Charles Robinson;* D. W. Wilder, *Annals of Kansas*.]

WENDELL H. STEPHENSON

BORGNE, BATTLE OF LAKE (Dec. 14, 1814), the naval engagement preceding the Battle of New Orleans. The British, with a force of light barges commanded by Capt. Lockyer, captured the five American gunboats commanded by Lt. Thomas Catesby Jones guarding the Malheureux Island passage. This cleared the eastern approach to the city and avoided the fortifications along the river. The defeated Americans inflicted such heavy losses upon their captors as to contribute to the many delays in their attack on New Orleans, which made it possible for the lately arrived Gen. Andrew Jackson to organize the defense of the city.

[A. T. Mahan, *The War of 1812 in Its Relations to Sea Power;* Theodore Roosevelt, *The Naval War of 1812*.]

U. T. BRADLEY

BOROUGH. Numerous colonial towns were patterned after the English borough, which was a trading community or town that had obtained some degree of corporate organization and certain rights of self-government. The colonial boroughs received their charters from the governors and were governed by a mayor and recorder, appointed by the governor, and aldermen elected by the freemen. Sitting as a common council, these officials passed bylaws regulating trade, industry, and labor, binding out orphans, supervising poor relief, fixing the assize of bread, and admitting the freemen, who in early days possessed a monopoly of retail trade, although in later times such regulations were generally relaxed. Sitting as a mayor's or sessions court, these same officials handled both civil and criminal business. After the Revolution borough charters were granted by the state legislatures. The suffrage was widened, and the mayor came to be elected by popular vote and gained increasing authority in borough management.

[R. B. Morris, *Select Cases of the Mayor's Court of New York City;* A. E. Peterson and G. W. Edwards, *New York as an Eighteenth Century Municipality*.]

RICHARD B. MORRIS

BOSQUE REDONDO, a reservation of forty square miles on the Pecos River in east-central New Mexico, near Fort Sumner, to which 8,000 Navaho and 400 Mescalero Apache were removed in 1863. The government planned to teach the Navaho a new way of life, to transform them into peaceful, sedentary farmers. Although the plan was unsuccessful in that respect, it did end the raiding activities of the Navaho. During their four-year confinement the Navaho were able to raise only a fraction of the crops necessary for their sustenance, and many of them died. The reservation was abolished when the Navaho were allowed to return to their homeland in 1868.

[Lynn R. Bailey, *Long Walk;* Lawrence C. Kelly, *Navajo Roundup;* James D. Shinkle, *Fort Sumner and the Bosque Redondo Indian Reservation.*]

KENNETH M. STEWART

BOSSES AND BOSSISM, POLITICAL. Anyone who controls voters in an authoritative, organized, and arbitrary manner in an American political entity, especially a city, county, or state, is traditionally known as a political boss. Bossism is a phenomenon of the latter half of the 19th century and the first half of the 20th century and has been linked with the immigration, urbanization, and machine politics of that era. Its decline after World War II has been attributed by some to changes in immigration policy and in big-city demography; to growth in federal government power, which produced programs to meet big-city needs and thereby undercut local organizations; and to a decline in the structure, function, and appeal of political parties.

The traditional definition of a boss has been modified to some extent. Although a boss is an outstanding practitioner of machine politics, not all machine political leaders are bosses. To be a boss in the classic sense means to dominate a polity—a city, county, or state. Machine politics concentrates on patronage, service, and favors in exchange for electoral loyalty. It minimizes issues, ideology, and impersonal rationality while maximizing personal contact and organized access to government. Many practice machine politics, but bosses do it so successfully that they control a local or state government, determining personnel, services, and policies, acting as intermediaries with the larger political world.

Famous city bosses—including William Marcy Tweed, Richard Croker, Charles Francis Murphy, Ed Flynn (all of New York), James McManes (Philadelphia), Frank Hague (Jersey City), James Michael Curley (Boston), Edward H. Crump (Memphis), Abraham Ruef (San Francisco), Thomas J. Pendergast (Kansas City, Mo.), and George B. Cox (Cincinnati)—showed some common patterns. They developed machines (or inherited machines) commanding voter loyalty, using organization, jobs, favors, ethnic and cultural recognition, party identification, and other factors to give security, especially to urban working classes and aspiring white-collar classes. At the same time, government policy favors were given to upper- and middle-class community leaders in exchange for elitist support. Much the same pattern was followed by state bosses like Matthew Stanley Quay and his successor Boies Penrose (Pennsylvania), Thomas Collier Platt (New York), Thomas Taggart (Indiana), Huey P. Long (Louisiana), and Harry Flood Byrd (Virginia), with some variations in the composition of the popular base. City bosses could sometimes parlay their power into domination of state politics. Bosses have not come exclusively from either of the two major political parties, but more big-city and southern state bosses have been identified with the Democratic party. By the 1970's the remaining outstanding big-city boss was Chicago's Mayor Richard J. Daley, who had dominated its Democratic machine for two decades, but who had become something of an anachronism.

Bossism probably reached its peak in America early in the 20th century. At this juncture progressivism attacked, among other things, boss rule and big-machine politics. It advocated economy, efficiency, business-type values, nonpartisan local elections, middle-class and Protestant ethics, and managerial government. Its solution to the evils of politics was to "take politics out of government," and vice versa. Progressive reformism in the 20th century combined with other factors previously mentioned to make bossism less viable and produce its decline.

As the power of bosses decreased, they began to be assessed more empathetically. Social scientists and novelists alike explained that bosses filled a functional need for many in city life, stabilized the political system, and provided influence channels and economic benefits, such as tax favors, franchises, and other public subsidies to businesses, as well as protection in some instances to racketeers and leaders of organized crime.

The "new" politics of the 1960's took another view, saying essentially that bosses were always on the side of the elite, shortchanging the masses they pretended to help. But this view also gave little credit to progressivism as a viable alternative. It argued for new political movements rather than either progressivism or a return to bossism.

[H. F. Gosnell, *Machine Politics: Chicago Model;* W. D. Miller, *Mr. Crump of Memphis;* Mike Royko, *Boss;* J. T. Salter, *Boss Rule;* J. H. Wilkinson, *Harry Byrd;* T. Harry Williams, *Huey Long;* Harold Zink, *City Bosses in the United States.*]

J. LEIPER FREEMAN

BOSTON, capital of Massachusetts, located on Massachusetts Bay. Capt. John Smith explored and mapped the vicinity of Boston in 1614. In 1621 a party from Plymouth visited the site of Boston, the peninsula called Shawmut by the Indians, and other landmarks. Individual settlers in the next few years located there and across the Charles River. Following the Great Migration of 1630, John Winthrop's group first settled at Charlestown but soon moved over to the Shawmut peninsula. On Sept. 7 of that year it was ordained by the Court of Assistants, sitting at Charlestown, that the new town be named Boston. In 1632 Boston was made the capital of Massachusetts Bay Colony, and that year the first meetinghouse was erected. The first post office was opened in 1639; in 1652 a mint began operations; and in 1686 the first bank in Boston, which was also the first in the colonies, was established. A printing press was set up in 1674 (although there had been one in Cambridge, across the Charles River, since 1638), and in 1704 the *Boston News-Letter* appeared. By that time Boston was becoming the largest and most important town in America. Its population in the middle of the 18th century was about 15,000. It was one of the earliest and chief centers of rebellion against the government of England (*see* Boston Massacre; Boston Tea Party), and the first armed conflicts of the revolutionary war (*see* Bunker Hill; Lexington and Concord) took place in its environs. Gen. George Washington forced the British to evacuate it in March 1776, and thereafter its peace was undisturbed during the war.

In government Boston was merely a town administered by selectmen until 1822, when it received a city charter. During the 19th century it became the cultural center of the continent and took pride in its nicknames, the "Hub" and the "Athens of America." The names of Louis Agassiz, Richard Henry Dana, Ralph Waldo Emerson, Nathaniel Hawthorne, Oliver Wendell Holmes, Henry W. Longfellow, James R. Lowell, Francis Parkman, Henry Thoreau, and John Greenleaf Whittier; the city's institutions of learning, numerous literary, historical, scientific, and musical societies, clubs, and coteries; its Beacon Hill crowded with the homes of old, aristocratic families; and its numerous colonial landmarks—all gave Boston a unique distinction and atmosphere. It was the nation's leading port until well into the 19th century, when it lost its supremacy to New York because of its lack of water communication to the west—although it still retained considerable foreign commerce. The city suffered numerous disastrous fires in the 17th and 18th centuries, but the worst in its history was that of 1872, when sixty acres in the business district were swept with fire, resulting in a $75 million loss, including 800 buildings. By the filling in of tidal marshes and inlets, Boston's original area of 783 acres was by 1930 expanded to 1,800 acres. Gradual absorption of suburbs brought the city's area by that date to 47.8 square miles.

Both before and after World War II Boston continued to expand, and by 1970 the metropolitan area included seventy-eight cities and towns; the population of the city proper was 641,071 and that of the metropolitan area, 2,753,700. Since World War II, Boston's industry has become decentralized, spreading throughout the metropolitan area, while commerce has remained centered in the city; machinery, electrical goods, and shoes are high in the area's list of manufactures, and Boston is the world's leading wholesale wool market. Still a major fishing port, with an annual catch valued at more than $10 million, Boston ranked sixteenth in the nation as a commercial port in 1970.

Of the fifty-two colleges and universities in the vicinity—notably Harvard University and the Massachusetts Institute of Technology in Cambridge—Boston itself is the home of twenty, including Boston and Northeastern universities. Boston is also a medical center, including the notable Massachusetts General Hospital. Boston's cultural tradition continues, for example, in the American Academy of Arts and Sciences (1780) and the Boston Atheneum (1807). The Boston Museum of Fine Arts, founded by public subscription in 1871, houses one of the finest collections in the world, and the Boston Symphony Orchestra continues as one of the most renowned in the United States.

[Justin Winsor, *The Memorial History of Boston;* Van Wyck Brooks, *The Flowering of New England.*]

ALVIN F. HARLOW

BOSTON, SIEGE OF. On the day after the Battle of Lexington (April 19, 1775) the Massachusetts Committee of Safety called out the militia. On April 22 the Massachusetts Provincial Congress resolved that an army of 30,000 men should be raised, Massachusetts to furnish about half, the other New England colonies the rest. Progress was slow: the old militia regiments could not be held together, and new ones had to be raised. On June 17 the Battle of Bunker Hill was fought, which, while technically a British success, had the moral effect of an American victory.

On July 3, George Washington, chosen as commander in chief by the Continental Congress, assumed command. He found the British holding Bunker Hill and Boston Neck; the Americans faced them, their left in Somerville, their right in Roxbury, and their center in Cambridge. It was evident that the makeshift force could not be relied upon; so in the face of the enemy a beginning was made upon organizing a continental army in place of the colonial contingents (*see* Washington's Eight Months Army).

During the winter no serious operations were undertaken. The Americans needed all their energies for organization; moreover, they were practically without artillery and ammunition. On the British side, the commanders could see no advantage in starting a campaign that they could not press to a finish.

In January 1776, the guns captured at Ticonderoga (May 10, 1775) reached Cambridge. On March 4, Washington seized Dorchester Heights, from which his guns commanded the city and harbor. The British forces were now in an untenable position, and on the 17th they embarked for Halifax. The Americans immediately occupied Boston.

[Richard Frothingham, *The Siege of Boston.*]

OLIVER LYMAN SPAULDING

BOSTON & MAINE. *See* **Railroads, Sketches.**

***BOSTON-BERCEAU* ACTION** (Oct. 12, 1800). Off Guadeloupe during naval hostilities with France, the U.S. frigate *Boston* (thirty-six guns), commanded by Capt. George Little, captured the French corvette *Berceau* (twenty-four guns) after a twelve-hour chase and a stubborn engagement extending intermittently from 4:30 until after 10 P.M. Though almost completely dismantled, the *Berceau* was towed into Boston as a prize.

[G. W. Allen, *Our Naval War With France.*]

ALLAN WESTCOTT

BOSTON COMMITTEE OF CORRESPONDENCE, a revolutionary body of propaganda and administration that became an important factor in promoting American unity and made possible the first Continental Congress through the spread of committees elsewhere. The parent body was appointed by a Boston town meeting, Nov. 2, 1772, upon motion of Samuel Adams. It consisted of twenty-one men headed by James Otis. The committee formulated public opinion and communicated Boston's position on colonists' rights to other Massachusetts cities, requesting that similar committees be set up. Within a few months eighty committees had been organized in Massachusetts. The Boston committee also played a role in the early conduct of hostilities and facilitated the transition of Massachusetts from royal government to independent statehood.

[William V. Wells, *The Life and Public Services of Samuel Adams.*]

LLOYD C. M. HARE

BOSTON COMMON, a forty-five-acre tract in Boston, bought by the city in 1634 as a pasture and parade ground. It is located between Beacon and Tremont streets, just below the Massachusetts State House, and is the city's chief pride. Where the British troops were entrenched in 1775, Boston citizens now walk under the trees while their children ride in the swan boats on the Frog Pond. Famous preachers and orators have spoken at the Boston Common. In the Central Burying Ground lie many Bostonians as well as the British soldiers killed at the Battle of Bunker Hill, and monuments to famous citizens, including the Augustus Saint-Gaudens memorial to Col. Robert Gould Shaw, border the paths. In fair weather Bostonians come to the common to hear band concerts, to enjoy such entertainments as puppet shows, and to borrow books from a mobile lending library; in all weather soap-box orators declaim on the issues of the day.

[S. G. Drake, *Old Landmarks and Historic Personages of Boston;* M. A. DeWolfe Howe, *Boston Common.*]

R. W. G. VAIL

BOSTON MANUFACTURING COMPANY, organized in 1813 by Boston merchants previously engaged in the India trade, including Francis Cabot Lowell. It built at Waltham, Mass., the first complete textile factory in America, combining power spinning and weaving, on looms invented by one of the proprietors. This proved a pilot plant for the larger factories later built at Lowell, Mass., which became the first American mill city.

VICTOR S. CLARK

BOSTON MASSACRE. British regulars arriving (Oct. 1, 1768) to maintain order in Boston produced soldier-civilian tensions that came to a head on the evening of Mar. 5, 1770. Seven grenadiers of the Twenty-ninth Regiment, led by Capt. Thomas Preston, marched to the relief of an eighth, on duty at the customshouse in King (now State) Street and beset by a taunting crowd of civilians. Preston, unable to disperse the crowd, loudly ordered his men, "Don't fire," while the mob was shouting "Fire and be damned!" The soldiers fired, killing three men instantly; two died later.

In October 1770 Preston, defended by John Adams and Robert Auchmuty, assisted by Josiah Quincy, Jr., was tried for murder and acquitted by a Boston jury. It has never been satisfactorily explained why the radicals Adams and Quincy undertook to represent Preston and, later, the soldiers; moreover, some surviving documents suggest that the jury in Preston's case was "packed." The soldiers—defended by Adams, Quincy, and Sampson Salter Blowers—won acquittals a month later, the jurors coming from towns outside Boston. Four civilians, accused of firing from the customshouse windows, were tried in December 1770; even though they lacked defense counsel, the evidence against them was so thin that the jurors peremptorily acquitted all.

[Hiller B. Zobel, *The Boston Massacre.*]

HILLER B. ZOBEL

"BOSTON MEN," a term derived from the hailing place of the first Yankee ships trading along the northwest coast of America, used to distinguish Americans from other white men or "Kling Chautsh" men (Englishmen and Canadians). The expression was incorporated and used in the Chinook jargon.

[G. Gibbs, *Dictionary of the Chinook Jargon.*]

WILLIAM S. LEWIS

"BOSTONNAIS" (or "Bastonais"), a term once applied by French-Canadians to Americans. It dates back to the invasion of Canada under Gen. Richard Montgomery in 1775, and possibly to that of Sir William Phips in 1690. Meaning "people of Boston," it was given to all English colonists on the Atlantic seaboard and finally to all Americans.

LAWRENCE J. BURPEE

BOSTON NEWS-LETTER, the first newspaper published without interruption during the colonial period. Number one included the week Apr. 17 to 24, 1704. The original publisher was John Campbell, postmaster, and the first printer was Bartholomew Green. In 1723 Green became the owner and changed its name to *The Weekly News-Letter*. When Green died in 1732 his son-in-law, John Draper, took over as publisher. Draper died in 1762, leaving the paper to his son, Richard, who changed the title to *The Boston Weekly News-Letter and New England Chronicle.* Richard Draper published his pro-British sentiments in the paper until his death in 1774. His widow continued publication until Feb. 22, 1776, when British troops and Loyalists, including Mrs. Draper, evacuated Boston.

No complete file is known, but the New-York Historical Society, the Massachusetts Historical Society, and the American Antiquarian Society at Worcester, Mass., have comparatively good files.

[James Melvin Lee, *History of American Journalism.*]

CARL L. CANNON

BOSTON POLICE STRIKE. About three-quarters of the Boston police force went on strike, Sept. 9, 1919, when the police commissioner refused to recognize their right to affiliate with the American Federation of Labor. Mayor Andrew J. Peters and a citizens' committee headed by James J. Storrow made compromise proposals relating to pay and working conditions in order to prevent the strike, but the police commissioner rejected them. The strike thus precipitated left Boston almost unprotected, and riots, disorders, and robberies occurred.

At the time of the strike, Boston's police commissioner was appointed, not by the mayor of the city, but by the governor of the state. Before the strike occurred Calvin Coolidge, then governor, was urged by the mayor and the Storrow committee to intervene but refused to act. When the rioting occurred Peters called out the Boston companies of the militia, restored order, and broke the strike. With the city already under control, Coolidge ordered the police commissioner again to take charge of the police and called out the entire Massachusetts militia, declaring: "There is no right to strike against the public safety by anybody, anywhere, any time." This action gave Coolidge a reputation as a courageous defender of law and order, which led to his nomination for vice-president (1920) and his eventual succession to the presidency.

[William Allen White, *A Puritan in Babylon: The Story of Calvin Coolidge,* and *The Autobiography of Calvin Coolidge.*]

CLARENCE A. BERDAHL

BOSTON PORT ACT, the first of the Coercion Acts, passed by Parliament on Mar. 31, 1774. To punish Boston for the Boston Tea Party, the act ordered the port of Boston closed on June 1, 1774, until the townspeople paid for the tea destroyed on Dec. 16, 1773, and proved to the crown's satisfaction they were peaceable subjects. Because Boston alone was punished, Lord North believed the colonies would not "take fire." It was a costly mistake: the cry was raised in America that the Port Act was merely a prelude to a "massacre of American liberty"; the colonies rallied to Boston's aid; and the Continental Congress was called to concert opposition to the mother country.

[J. T. Adams, *Revolutionary New England;* C. H. Van Tyne, *The Causes of the War of Independence.*]

JOHN C. MILLER

BOSTON RESOLUTIONS OF 1767, an expression of the longing of many Massachusetts patriots to restore puritanic simplicity in New England and strengthen patriotism by barring the importation of British luxuries. In 1767, when New England's declining prosperity made economy essential and the Townshend Acts threatened fresh British oppression, Samuel Adams secured the passage in the Boston town meeting of resolutions pledging the citizens to abstain from the use of many British manufactures, chiefly articles of luxury. Outside of New England, however, the movement had little success, and it was soon merged with the nonimportation agreement.

[C. H. Van Tyne, *The Causes of the War of Independence.*]

JOHN C. MILLER

BOSTON RESOLUTIONS OF 1810, a forecast of New England separatism in the approaching War of 1812. In these resolutions, passed Feb. 9, the Massachusetts legislature condemned the severity of President James Madison toward Francis James Jackson, the notorious British minister, exculpated Jackson, and endeavored to compel renewed diplomatic intercourse with Great Britain.

[Henry Adams, *History of the United States, 1801–1817,* vol. V.]

LOUIS MARTIN SEARS

BOSTON TEA PARTY. On the night of Dec. 16, 1773, 342 chests of tea belonging to the East India Company were thrown into Boston harbor by American patriots. This audacious destruction of British property was caused by the Boston Whigs' fear that if the tea were landed, its cheap price would prove an "invincible temptation" to the people. This, it was believed, would give the East India Company a monopoly of the American tea trade and establish the right of Parliament to raise a colonial revenue by means of port duties. Therefore, when it was learned at the town meeting of Dec. 16 that Gov. Thomas Hutchinson was determined to refuse the patriots' demand that the tea ships be permitted to return to England without paying the duty required by law, Samuel Adams exclaimed that the meeting could do nothing more to save the country. His words were the signal for a war whoop from the "Indians"—Sons of Liberty disguised with blankets and dusky complexions—waiting outside the meetinghouse. With the cry of "Boston harbor a tea-pot this night," the patriots streamed down to the waterfront, where, surrounded by an immense crowd of spectators, they made short work of the tea.

The Boston Tea Party was called "the boldest stroke which had yet been struck in America." It marked the beginning of violence in the dispute, hitherto waged chiefly with constitutional arguments, between mother country and colonies, and it put the most radical patriots in command throughout America. The efforts of the British government to single out Massachusetts for punishment served only to unite the colonies and hasten them into war with England.

[John C. Miller, *Sam Adams, Pioneer in Propaganda;* C. H. Van Tyne, *The Causes of the War of Independence.*]

JOHN C. MILLER

BOSTON TEN TOWNSHIPS, a tract of 230,400 acres north of the Susquehanna River in New York, including parts of Broome, Tioga, and Cortland counties, claimed by both New York and Massachusetts until, by the Treaty of Hartford in 1786, a compromise was effected whereby New York was granted sovereignty and Massachusetts right of preemption of the soil. Subsequently, in 1787, right of purchase from the Indians was granted by Massachusetts to Samuel Brown and ten associates. (*See* Phelps-Gorham Purchase.)

[R. L. Higgins, *Expansion in New York.*]

A. C. FLICK

BOTANICAL GARDENS are specialized parks that serve as focal points to display the diversity among plants and provide regionally significant demonstrations of the most beautiful and cultivable flowering plants and ferns from the world catalog of more than 300,000 extant species. Botanical gardens are universally concerned with applying botanical and horticultural information to the improvement of human life, especially in urban and suburban settings.

Most botanical gardens have education programs and carry out public service activities. The larger gardens also have programs for basic research, principally in systematic botany, but also in such ancillary disciplines as ecology, biochemistry, pathology, and plant breeding.

Historically, botanical gardens in America are derived from European models, the earliest of which were established in Pisa and Padua, Italy, in the mid-1500's as collections of medicinally useful plants for study by medical students—reflecting the origin of botanical science as a cornerstone of early medicine. Subsequently, botanical gardens became testing grounds and display areas for the plant treasures taken back from the early exploration of the Americas and Africa. In England, botanical gardens became centers of excellence in landscape architecture, with great collections of diverse plants exhibited not only for their intrinsic value but also as components of a larger design. Most American botanical gardens tend to be based on the English model.

Among the earliest botanical gardens in the United States were John Bartram's Garden, established near Philadelphia in 1728 and now a public park; André Michaux's Garden, established at Charleston, S.C., in 1787, now part of that city; and the Elgin Botanical Garden, established in New York in 1801 where Rockefeller Center now stands. The oldest existing American garden is the Missouri Botanical Garden, founded in St. Louis in 1859. There are approximately 150 botanical gardens in the United States, of which one-third are located in the Northeast and a lesser concentration in the Southwest. Administratively, most botanical gardens are operated by municipalities, universities, or private organizations. A large proportion have evolved as outgrowths of private estates.

Botanical gardens range in size from one acre to several hundred or even thousands of acres. Among the largest are the New York Botanical Garden (including the associated Cary Arboretum), 2,050 acres, and the Missouri Botanical Garden (including the associated arboretum and natural reserve), 1,725 acres—both strongly oriented to research and professional training, and both maintaining large herbaria, libraries, and laboratories. Longwood Gardens, at Kennett Square, Pa., with 1,200 acres, and Callaway Gardens, at Pine Mountain, Ga., with 2,500 acres, are both major display gardens.

In addition to these vast gardens there are a number of very active and significant gardens, including the Brooklyn Botanic Garden, Matthaei (University of Michigan) Botanical Garden, Chicago Botanical Garden, Fairchild Tropical Garden (Coral Gables, Fla.), Rancho Santa Ana Botanic Garden (Claremont, Calif.), Los Angeles State and County Arboretum, and University of California Botanic Garden (at Berkeley).

HOWARD S. IRWIN

BOTANY. The plants taken to Europe in the 16th century by René de Laudonnière's expedition to the Florida-Georgia region and by Thomas Harriot from the Roanoke area were reported in John Gerard's *Herball* (1597). These and the discoveries of John Tradescant the younger from the vicinity of Yorktown, Va., were included in John Parkinson's *Theatrum* (1640). The oldest Virginia specimens preserved today were taken by John Banister. His specimens and drawings were published separately by Robert Morison, John Ray, and Leonard Plukenet and, with Virginia specimens and descriptions sent by John Clayton to Johann Gronovius, Carl Linnaeus' associate in Leiden, were enumerated in *Flora virginica* (1739–43). This was the earliest book expressly devoted to a flora common to the Atlantic coastal plain. The descriptions and drawings of Carolina plants in Mark Catesby's *Natural History* and important collections made by Pehr Kalm, especially from Pennsylvania and New Jersey, with a few specimens from Cadwalader Colden along the Hudson River and John Bartram along Delaware Bay, were the essence of Linnaeus' knowledge of the plants of the eastern United States, as incorporated in his pivotal *Species plantarum* (1753).

Bartram—a self-educated Quaker farmer, friend of Benjamin Franklin, and founding member of the American Philosophical Society—established the first botanic garden in 1728. He searched from Lake Ontario to the St. Johns River, Fla., and forwarded seeds and specimens to Linnaeus, Gronovius, Johann Dillenius, Catesby, Peter Collinson, and John Fothergill. In company with his son, William, he discovered plants endemic to the southeastern states, including the famed *Franklinia;* William Bartram's *Travels* (1791), an important source book for the naturalist today, promptly became a literary classic. Benjamin Smith Barton—physician, professor of materia medica and natural history—illustrated his *Elements of Botany* (1803), the first botany text published in the United States, largely with William Bartram's drawings. Barton planned a more comprehensive continental flora than André Michaux's and to that end employed the German Frederick Pursh and, later, the Englishman Thomas Nuttall to botanize for him. Barton intended to include novelties of the Meriwether Lewis and William Clark expedition; but Pursh, apprehending inexorable delays, published his own *Flora Americae septentrionalis* (1814), the year before Barton's death. Nuttall lived to botanize from Georgia to the mouth of the Columbia River and from San Diego to Michilimackinac. His *Genera* (1818), although presented in the already outmoded Linnaean classification, is a fundamental reference.

The engineer Stephen H. Long's expedition to the Rocky Mountains was the first government-sponsored expedition to document importantly knowledge of the zonation of floras and faunas. In his report on the expedition, John Torrey adopted the natural system of classification of Bernard de Jussieu for the first time in America in a major publication. Edwin James, who also took part in the expedition, botanized (July 1820) on the summit of Pikes Peak—the first 14,000-foot peak to be climbed for scientific purposes. Botanical exploration increased rapidly during succeeding decades, bearing fruit in Torrey and Asa Gray's *Flora of North America* (1838–43). Harvard's Gray, an advocate of Darwinism in America, became the leading botanist of the 19th century and the only one to be enshrined in the Hall of Fame. One of Gray's many associates, the St. Louis physician George Engelmann, encouraged Henry Shaw to establish the Missouri Botanical Garden in 1859. Albert Kellogg, who went to California with the gold rush, became resident botanist there, and advocated that Pacific Coast discoveries be published locally.

The "new systematics"—vividly set forth in Edgar Anderson's *Plants, Life and Man* (1952)—has shifted the emphasis from individual specimens to plant populations. Chemotaxonomy is a growing topic, and computer technology promises to be useful in botany.

Dimension was added to the study of botany when the first American microscope with an efficient achromatic lens appeared. Charles Edward Bessey opened the first student laboratory in 1871: he had one microscope. Graduate work abroad (principally in Germany), immigrant botanists, Darwinian concepts, and the question of mechanism versus vitalism stimulated laboratory science and departmentalized botany. Edward Charles Jeffrey, for example, became the first professor of vegetable histology (later plant morphology) at Harvard in 1902; and his *Anatomy of Woody Plants* (1917) and C. J. Chamberlain's *Gymnosperms, Structure and Evolution* (1934) evidenced increasing interest in evolution and phylogeny. Plant physiology had been introduced by Joseph Priestley when he came to America as an exile in 1794, but little progress in this field was made before the beginning of the 20th century. D. T. MacDougal, who had worked with desert plants, wrote the first American text on plant physiology (1901). The physicist L. J. Briggs and the plant ecologist H. L. Shantz worked out the wilting coefficients of plants. Between 1930 and 1940 knowledge of photosynthesis and hormone actions progressed, as did understanding of photoperiodism, crystallization of urease, and membrane responses. Nitrogen fixation; the role of auxin, giberellins, and abscisic acid; and herbicides assumed prominence. Tissue culture, initiated by W. J. Robbins in 1930, inspired research in factors necessary for growth and differentiation. Light-requirement studies, coupled with advances in refrigeration, led to the development of growth chambers with controlled conditions. With the advent of the electron microscope, morphogenesis and ultrastructure were favored by plant physiologists. Molecular biology, which originally concentrated on bacteria, now studies development in higher plants.

The pharmacological use of plants themselves declined with the isolation and synthesis of active ingredients. However, few drugs of any value have been synthesized. Most of the world's plants have not yet been analyzed for potential utility, and renewed attention is now being given to native uses of plants as drug sources.

Plant pathology was first taught in a botany course at the University of Illinois in 1873 and as a separate course at Harvard in 1875—at first with only slight attention given to the effects of the environment on plant diseases. The ability of bacteria to induce plant disease was demonstrated in the years 1879–85. Understanding of viruses progressed when studies showed that no symptoms were produced in some hosts (1918) or under certain environmental conditions (1922), and virus strains were demonstrated in 1925. Wendell M. Stanley, Nobel laureate in 1946, purified a virus strain in 1935. Nematology became differentiated from plant pathology, and a separate professional society was consequently organized in 1961. Algal studies, at first taxonomic in emphasis, were diversified as Gilbert Smith probed the origins of gametes and as physiological investigations led to algae as potential food in space travel.

The first American experiment in genetics, reported by Cotton Mather in 1716, concerned Indian corn, a subject still prominent in genetic laboratories. A development important to genetics occurred in the

19th century, with the opening of the West and the inauguration of land grant colleges (1862), which stressed agricultural botany. Following the rediscovery of Mendelian inheritance in 1900, genetics attracted renewed botanical and zoological experimentation. Two crop plants, tomatoes and tobacco, stimulated a new field of study, cytogenetics.

Paleobotany—originally purely descriptive because of an expanding coal industry and the discovery of fossil beds in the West—came to embrace the study of paleoclimates, fossil pollens, migration of floras, and more critical reinterpretation. Man's influence on his environment, expounded as early as 1864 by George Perkins Marsh in *Man and Nature,* assumed importance with the Dustbowl; ecologists Paul B. Sears and Frederick Clements focused on soil conservation as a national policy. Whereas botanists formerly worked as individuals, the present trend, especially in experimental biology, is toward teamwork.

[Joseph Ewan, ed., *A Short History of Botany in the United States;* William C. Steere, ed., *Fifty Years of Botany.*]

JOSEPH EWAN

BOUCHARD EXPEDITION, an effort on the part of the Buenos Aires revolutionary authorities in 1818 to bring into the anti-Spanish liberal cause the inhabitants of California. Hippolyte de Bouchard, with the *Argentina* and *Santa Rosa,* came to California by way of the Hawaiian Islands, and, Nov. 20, 1818, captured Monterey. Other landings at Santa Barbara and Capistrano showed that the Californians were not anxious for liberation from Spain. Accordingly, Bouchard sailed for Chile, and California remained in the Spanish empire until Apr. 11, 1822, when a special junta declared it dependent upon Agustín de Iturbide's Mexican empire.

[C. E. Chapman, *A History of California: The Spanish Period.*]

OSGOOD HARDY

BOUGAINVILLE (Nov. 1, 1943). The amphibious landing on Bougainville, the largest of the Solomon Islands, was made by Lt. Gen. A. A. Vandegrift's U.S. First Marine Amphibious Corps, at Cape Torokina on the western coast. The terrain behind the beaches was the worst possible, consisting of swamp and jungle. The objective was to gain locations for airfields within easy striking distance of Rabaul, on New Britain Island. In spite of a scarcity of amphibious shipping, a make-do shore party, and worthless naval gunfire support, this was, at the time, the best-planned and executed amphibious operation of the war: 33,861 men had been put ashore by Nov. 13. The Japanese had about 270 men at Cape Torokina and approximately 58,000 military personnel throughout the rest of the island. Even though the Japanese moved many troops into the Allied perimeter, by Nov. 30 the objective was achieved and the perimeter was defended by a well-anchored defense. From Nov. 1 to Dec. 15 the marines suffered 423 killed and 1,418 wounded; the Japanese, approximately 2,500 killed.

[G. C. Dyer, *The Amphibians Come to Conquer.*]

W. M. DARDEN

BOULDER DAM. *See* **Hydroelectric Power.**

BOUNDARY DISPUTES BETWEEN STATES. At the time of the adoption of the U.S. Constitution (1788), apparently only Pennsylvania and Maryland of the original thirteen states had no pending question as to the correctness of their boundaries. Since the adoption, more than half the states of the United States have been involved in some kind of disagreement with one or more neighboring states concerning boundaries. These disputes have for the most part been minor in nature, and their settlement has been brought about by mutual agreement with or without the consent of Congress, by congressional action alone, or by the Supreme Court. In great part the disputes over boundaries have developed because of the interpretation of colonial grants or charters, of treaties, or of general international law. A few controversies have arisen about boundaries established by Congress either before or at the time of the admission of new states.

Of the disputes having their origin in colonial arrangements, probably the first to be settled was that between North Carolina and South Carolina. This was ended by a survey in 1815 that extended the 1772 line to the corner of Georgia. The Massachusetts–Rhode Island dispute originated in the Plymouth colony grant of 1630 and the Rhode Island charter of 1663. In spite of a Supreme Court case in 1846 that Rhode Island lost, the dispute was not settled until the two states agreed on a boundary line by a compact. This was assented to by Congress in 1858. The agreement was revised in 1899 by mutual consent and a line was established that could be more readily marked. The boundary dispute between Connecticut and New York, which began before 1650, was settled by the two states in 1880, Congress approving their action in

1881. The Massachusetts–New Hampshire boundary controversy, which originated in the Massachusetts charter of 1629, was settled in 1895 by an agreement on the generally recognized boundary of the time. Cases decided by the Supreme Court concerning boundaries of colonial origin include *Rhode Island* v. *Massachusetts,* 4 Howard 591 (1846); *Georgia* v. *South Carolina,* 257 U.S. 516 and 259 U.S. 572 (1922); *Vermont* v. *New Hampshire,* 289 U.S. 593 (1933); and *New Jersey* v. *Delaware,* 291 U.S. 361 (1934).

The disputes that have been settled by congressional action alone have related chiefly to boundaries originally established between territories by act of Congress. Notable among these are changes in the boundaries of Michigan with respect to the states of Indiana and Ohio. The Michigan-Indiana boundary was moved north by the act admitting Indiana to statehood, in order to give that state an outlet on Lake Michigan; while the serious dispute with Ohio from 1818 to 1837 resulted in a move of the Michigan-Ohio boundary north, to put the Toledo area in Ohio. It was the act admitting Michigan to the Union in 1837 that made this change in the Ohio boundary; as recompense for its loss of the disputed territory, Michigan was given what is now the upper peninsula of that state. A protracted Illinois-Wisconsin dispute was settled with the admission of Wisconsin into the Union in 1848.

A relatively large number of boundary disputes between states have been settled by decisions of the Supreme Court. Where specific treaties have been involved, these have been interpreted and followed by the Court. This was true in the dispute between Missouri and Kentucky; the court ruled that since the treaty signed by France, Spain, and England in 1763 set the Mississippi River as the boundary, it "has remained . . . as they settled it" (*Missouri* v. *Kentucky,* 78 U.S. 395, 401 [1871]). The Definitive Treaty of Peace of 1783 with Great Britain set the western boundary of the United States, and its terms were followed in setting all or part of the boundaries of the states along the Mississippi River. This same treaty also determined the northern boundary of Florida and set the Chattahoochee River as part of the Alabama-Georgia boundary. The 1819 treaty with Spain defined the Oklahoma-Texas boundary (except the Panhandle portion) and the southern boundaries of Oregon and Idaho. The Rio Grande portion of the New Mexico–Texas boundary was a heritage from the Treaty of Guadalupe Hidalgo of 1848.

In the determination of boundary questions between states of the Union not involving specific treaties, the Supreme Court applies the principles of general international law. Water boundaries in rivers and bays have given rise to many more disputes than land boundaries. In this regard the Court has held that the doctrine of the thalweg (that is, that the main channel of navigation is the middle of a river rather than a line equidistant between the two banks) is applicable between states unless the boundary has been fixed in some other way, such as by agreement, practical location, or prescription. This principle was used by the Court in its determination of the boundary between New Jersey and Delaware on the Delaware River in 1934 (291 U.S. 361). Along the unstable Missouri River, boundary cases have been decided by application of the rules of international law concerning change by avulsion or accretion—for example, in *Nebraska* v. *Iowa,* 143 U.S. 359 and 145 U.S. 798 (1892). The rule of international law regarding cession of territory on a river boundary was followed in determining the Ohio River boundary. This was held to be the north, or far, bank at low water, based upon the cession by Virginia to the United States of territory to the northwest of the Ohio River. In the construction of this grant it was held that Virginia (the territory involved now comprises Kentucky and West Virginia) must have intended to retain the river (*Handly's Lessee* v. *Anthony,* 5 Wheaton 374 [1820]; *Indiana* v. *Kentucky,* 136 U.S. 479 [1890]).

Other river-boundary cases decided by the Supreme Court include *Iowa* v. *Illinois,* 147 U.S. 1 (1893); *Missouri* v. *Nebraska,* 196 U.S. 23 (1904) and 197 U.S. 577 (1905); and *Washington* v. *Oregon,* 211 U.S. 127 (1908).

Boundaries in waters other than rivers have been subject to dispute, and in several instances an economic factor has been involved. Oyster beds were at least partly the cause of disputes decided by the Supreme Court in *Louisiana* v. *Mississippi,* 202 U.S. 1 (1906), which concerned the boundary from the mouth of the Pearl River to the high sea. The same issue was involved in *Smith* v. *Maryland,* 18 Howard 71 (1855). Fishing rights were among the questions involved in Supreme Court decisions in 1926 and 1935 on the Michigan-Wisconsin boundary in Green Bay and Lake Michigan (*Michigan* v. *Wisconsin,* 272 U.S. 398 [1926] and *Wisconsin* v. *Michigan,* 297 U.S. 547 [1936]). Oil wells in the bed of the Red River made the precise location of the Oklahoma-Texas boundary very important, and the Court decided this matter in *Oklahoma* v. *Texas,* 269 U.S. 314 (1926).

While disputes over boundaries between states have been somewhat heated in a few instances—as in the Georgia–North Carolina dispute over Walton County in 1803, the Ohio-Michigan dispute of 1818–37, and the Iowa-Missouri controversy in 1839—in general, as distinct from regional disputes, boundary questions have not had a disrupting effect.

Questions of state boundaries continue to arise, though, as the more recent case of the Rio Grande attests. The Rio Grande as far west as the southern boundary of New Mexico was set as the boundary between the United States and Mexico by the Treaty of Guadalupe Hidalgo in 1848, following the war with Mexico. In 1853, by the Gadsden Purchase, the United States acquired the territory from the Rio Grande west to the Colorado River. This involved the territory now included in the southwest part of the state of New Mexico and the southern part of the state of Arizona. The boundary between Upper and Lower California was set as the boundary by the Treaty of Guadalupe Hidalgo. The Rio Grande changed course in the vicinity of El Paso, and the resultant dispute as to the true boundary was settled in 1963 (formalized in 1967) by what is known as the Chamizal Treaty.

[Edward M. Douglas, *Boundaries, Areas, Geographic Centers and Altitudes of the United States and the Several States;* Dixon Ryan Fox, *Yankees and Yorkers;* Charles O. Paullin, *Atlas of the Historical Geography of the United States;* James Brown Scott, *Judicial Settlement of Controversies Between States of the American Union;* Marvin Lucian Skaggs, *North Carolina Boundary Disputes Involving Her Southern Line.*]

PAUL C. BARTHOLOMEW

BOUNTIES, COMMERCIAL, have played an important role in American economic development. In the colonial period Great Britain paid bounties on the export from the American colonies of hemp, flax, tar, potash, indigo, and a number of other commodities in an effort to stimulate their production and to diminish Britain's previous dependence for these items on foreign nations. North Carolina and South Carolina profited the most from these bounties, and the production of naval stores and indigo became, with rice cultivation, their chief occupation. The loss of these bounties after the Revolution brought disaster to those engaged in the production of naval stores and indigo. The colonial governments also offered bounties to encourage the manufacture of such goods as linen, woolens, iron, glass, brick, and salt, and after 1775 they redoubled their efforts to build up domestic manufactures by combining cash bounties, financial subsidies, and tariff protection.

Following the Revolution, states continued to give bounties for the growing of wheat, flax, and even corn; for the production of hemp, glass, and sailcoth; and at least six states offered bounties for the production of silk. The federal government offered bounties for various commercial purposes and achieved the same result indirectly by requiring the navy to buy only rope made from American hemp and by sending scientists abroad to find better strains of sugarcane and other plants that might be adapted to American conditions. On the eve of the Civil War the southern states, which felt that up to 1860 bounties, tariff protection, and subsidies to internal improvements had chiefly benefited other sections, incorporated a provision in the Confederate constitution that forbade them. In 1890 the United States offered a bounty of two cents a pound on sugar produced within the country and states have likewise given bounties to the beet sugar industry. Such bounties coupled with high tariff protection and huge subsidies in the Far West for irrigation projects have been responsible for the growth of the sugar beet industry.

In the 20th century bounties continued to be used by the states to rid them of wolves and other carnivorous animals, but tariffs and quotas have been relied upon by the United States to stimulate and protect industry.

[G. L. Beer, *British Colonial Policy, 1754–1763;* O. Handlin and M. F. Handlin, *Commonwealth: A Study of the Role of Government in the American Economy;* F. W. Taussig, *Some Aspects of the Tariff Question.*]

PAUL WALLACE GATES

BOUNTIES, FISHING. *See* **Fishing Bounties.**

BOUNTIES, LAND. *See* **Land Bounties.**

BOUNTIES, MILITARY. When war forces were raised by volunteering instead of by conscription or militia obligations, bounties stimulated recruiting. For Indian and French campaigns, colonies offered cash inducements, sometimes solely to induce enlistments, sometimes for bringing clothing or weapons into service. The practice was adopted during the Revolution by both Congress and the states. In January 1776, $6.66 was offered to fill the Canada expedition; in June $10 for three-year enlistments or reenlistments; in September $20 and 100 acres for enrollments for the duration of the war. To fill militia quotas, states offered their own bounties, so that states and Congress bid against one another and sums mounted until Congress was offering $200 and New Jersey $1,000. Bounty jumping and reenlisting were prevalent.

With the peace, bounties shrunk to $6 in 1791 for Indian campaigns, but climbed after the Whiskey Rebellion to $16 and 160 acres. During the War of 1812 offers increased to $124 and 320 acres. They were abolished in 1833 but were resumed in 1847 to raise and reenlist men for the Mexican War. Civil War bounties (*see below*) repeated revolutionary history, with the exception of land grants. Bounties disappeared after Appomattox, and recruiting bounties were expressly forbidden by the Selective Service Act of 1917.

ELBRIDGE COLBY

Civil War Bounties. The system of granting land as a bounty for army enlistment used during the Revolution was not followed in the Civil War, except for the favored position of servicemen under the Homestead Act. From the start of war in 1861 states and localities stimulated recruiting by grants of money. Since July 1861, Congress had allowed a $100 bounty for three-year men. The passage of the Militia Draft Act in July 1862 provided $25 for nine-month and $50 for twelve-month volunteers.

Officials everywhere pressed for larger bounties, and on Mar. 3, 1863, Congress passed the Enrollment Act, which legalized the earlier practice of giving $100 to conscripts and substitutes. Also, since those able to do so could avoid the draft on payment of $300, for several months an equivalent sum was given to all three-year, and $400 to all five-year, volunteers. But, since these bounties were divided over the term of service and were included in the monthly pay, they merely served as an addition to the legal wages.

A worse system prevailed for state bounties. It was considered a disgrace for any congressional district to have to submit to a draft, so funds were raised to the utmost limit to fill the quotas by offering bounties before the federal draft began. In consequence, the richer districts by offering $1,000 or more could entice volunteers from poorer localities and fill their quota with ease, whereas the low-bounty regions were badly depleted of manpower by the exodus and then had to give an additional quota by draft. Furthermore, there arose the loathsome profession of bounty brokers, who not only recruited men and then robbed them of much of their bonus but also resorted to bribery to secure the muster of broken-down derelicts who had to be discharged later. The bounty-jumper problem was greatly aggravated by these practices.

In four years' time the federal government paid over $300 million in bounties, and in 1864–65 alone the states and localities paid about the same amount. The total mercenary fees for the Civil War, including local bounties in the first two years and substitute fees, amounted to about $750 million dollars.

FRED A. SHANNON

[T. Cross, *Military Laws of the United States;* Fred A. Shannon, *Organization and Administration of the Union Army;* E. Upton, *Military Policy of the United States.*]

BOUNTY JUMPER, a product of the system of military bounties in the Civil War. Aided and abetted by bounty brokers, men would enlist, collect bounties, desert, and then reenlist elsewhere, repeating the process until finally caught. One deserter was sentenced to four years' imprisonment after confessing to jumping bounties thirty-two times. The large initial bounty payments was one of the major causes of the more than 268,000 desertions from the ranks of the Union Army.

[F. A. Shannon, *Organization and Administration of the Union Army.*]

FRED A. SHANNON

BOUQUET'S EXPEDITION (1763–65). At the outbreak of Pontiac's War, Col. Henry Bouquet was sent with 500 regulars to relieve Fort Pitt. Leaving Carlisle, Pa., he marched westward, and after defeating the Indians at the Battle of Bushy Run he relieved the beleaguered fort. Bouquet's force was too small to march against the Delaware and Shawnee in the Ohio country, but in 1765 the Pennsylvania assembly voted an adequate force for the expedition. Desertions from the militia, however, forced Bouquet to call for Virginia volunteers to meet him at Fort Pitt. After many delays he collected some 1,500 men and in October 1765 marched unopposed to the Muskingum River, near the mouth of the Tuscarawas. There he was met by chiefs bringing in eighteen white prisoners and suing for peace. Bouquet demanded the return of all the captives; and, taking the principal chiefs as hostages, he moved south to the forks of the Muskingum in the heart of the Indian country. Here he waited until some 200 prisoners had been surrendered to him.

He then made peace with the Indians, directed them to go to Sir William Johnson to make treaties, and took hostages for the performance of this obligation and for the delivery of about 100 prisoners still in the hands of the Shawnee. He returned to Fort Pitt, and the Indians subsequently delivered there the remaining captives. Bouquet's expedition overawed the Indians and ended the reign of terror on the border. (*See also* Bradstreet's Lake Erie Expedition.)

[Francis Parkman, *The Conspiracy of Pontiac*.]

SOLON J. BUCK

BOURBON COUNTY, established by Georgia in 1785, on the Mississippi River, lying north of the 31st parallel and extending to the mouth of the Yazoo River, above Natchez. Being largely a land speculation, it was to be governed by fourteen men mentioned in the act; and when a land office should be opened, the price per acre should not be more than twenty-five cents. As Spain had not yet evacuated this territory and as the United States disputed Georgia's claim to these western lands, the act was repealed three years later.

[E. C. Burnett, "Papers Relating to Bourbon County, Georgia, 1785–1786," *American Historical Review*, vol. 15; A. P. Whitaker, *Spanish-American Frontier*.]

E. MERTON COULTER

BOURBONS, or **Redeemers,** the name applied to the white southern politicians who gained control of their state governments at the end of the Reconstruction era in the 1870's. They called themselves Redeemers because they believed they had redeemed their states from Republican and black control. Their political detractors called them Bourbons with the implication that, like the ruling monarchs of France, they were so wedded to the ideas and practices of the past that they forgot nothing and learned nothing. Neither term accurately describes the men and their programs. Most were conservative Democrats—joined by some former southern Whigs—who favored economy in government, financial retrenchment, reduced taxes, and severely limited state services. Above all, they were commercial-minded men who openly aligned themselves with the Republican, industrial North in order to exploit the natural resources of the South for personal gain. They willingly sacrificed long-held tenets of agrarianism and states' rights in order to advocate southern industrial development. The Populist revolt in the 1890's was an unsuccessful attempt by agrarians to overthrow Bourbon rule.

[C. Vann Woodward, *Origins of the New South, 1877–1913*.]

MONROE BILLINGTON

BOURGEOIS, a title used in the fur trade, especially in the Northwest, to refer to the leader of a unit. The bourgeois was governor of the pack train, master of the canoe brigade, and despot of the trading post. His word was law and his orders were implicitly obeyed. He was responsible for the well-being of the men and the success of the trade venture. When the great companies were organized the bourgeois were the wintering partners.

[L. E. Masson, ed., *Les Bourgeois de la Compagnie du Nord-Ouest*, a collection of diaries kept by bourgeois published in Quebec (1889); Grace Lee Nute, *The Voyageur*.]

LOUISE PHELPS KELLOGG

BOURGMONT'S EXPLORATIONS. Étienne Veniard de Bourgmont, first French scientific explorer of the Missouri River, commanded Fort Detroit in 1706. By 1712 he was exploring the lower Missouri Valley. His "Route to follow to mount the Missouri River" (ca. 1714) and "Exact Description of Louisiana" (ca. 1717) show he reached the Platte River. Search for a route to the fabulous silver mines of New Mexico and activities of the Spanish made imperative a French post in Missouri. Authorized by Louis XV, in 1723 Bourgmont led an expedition up the Mississippi River from New Orleans and with the help of friendly Missouri Indians built Fort Orleans on the north bank of the Missouri River in Carroll County, Mo. In 1724 he conducted an overland trip to the village of the Kansas Indians near present Doniphan, Kans., effecting peace with them and, further to the southwest, with the Padouca.

[G. J. Garraghan, *Chapters in Frontier History*.]

DOROTHY PENN

BOUWERIES. When the Dutch West India Company took over Manhattan Island in 1626 (*see* New Netherland), it divided a large tract of land in what is now New York City's lower east side into six bouweries or farms, erected buildings on them, and leased them to tenants. One large farm, known as the Company's Bouwerie, just west of these, was retained and operated to aid in providing for the company's officers and servants. Other tracts of forest land were granted to individuals, who cleared them and created their own bouweries.

[J. H. Innes, *New Amsterdam and Its People*.]

ALVIN F. HARLOW

BOWDITCH'S *AMERICAN PRACTICAL NAVIGATOR*. In 1799 Nathaniel Bowditch published in the United States an expanded, corrected, revised edition of J. H. Moore's standard work, *The Practical Navigator*. By the third edition (1802), the work was so changed that it bore Bowditch's name and the new title *The New American Practical Navigator*. It quickly became the standard work used by American seamen and has played the important part of guiding the navigator in every American adventure on the sea.

More than sixty editions have appeared since its introduction, bringing up-to-date methods to the mariner. In 1866 the copyright and plates were bought by the U.S. Navy Hydrographic Office. *The New American Practical Navigator* is not only a notable book; it is an American nautical institution.

GERSHOM BRADFORD

BOWERY, a district in lower Manhattan in New York City which has developed around a street of the same name. The street was first known in the 17th century as Bouwerie Lane or Bouwerie Road, because it led from New Amsterdam out to the bouwerie or farm of Gov. Peter Stuyvesant. Later it was the beginning of the road to Boston, and the first mail between New York and Boston started over it in 1673. By 1800 the slums growing up around it determined its future character. Some famous theaters were located on it; but it eventually attained worldwide notoriety because of the swindling, political chicanery, prostitution, crime, and gang warfare carried on in its vicinity. The district is still frequented by the homeless and derelicts.

[Alvin F. Harlow, *Old Bowery Days*.]

ALVIN F. HARLOW

BOWIE KNIFE. Devised either by Rezin P. Bowie or his brother James, who died in the siege of the Alamo, the knife both in origin and use has been the subject of a cycle of heroic folk tales. It achieved fame in the Sandbar duel in 1827. Although supplanted largely by the six-shooter, it was for four decades a part of the regular equipment of frontiersmen and backwoodsmen from Florida to California. The mountain men used a modified form of it. The Texas Rangers rode with it. The pirates of the Mississippi River disemboweled their victims with it. Its steel of superb temper, the blade well guarded, handle and blade so balanced that it could be thrown as well as wielded, it was both economical and practical for skinning, cutting up meat, eating, fighting duels, stabbing enemies, hammering, and performing other services.

J. FRANK DOBIE

BOWLES'S FILIBUSTERING EXPEDITIONS. In the early 1780's William Augustus Bowles, after an adventurous life among the Creek Indians, traveled to the Bahamas where he became acquainted with Lord Dunmore, governor of the islands, and with the trading house of Miller, Bonnamy and Company. Bowles became the agent of this commercial house, reinforced with the benevolent and probable financial interest of Lord Dunmore, and in this capacity he sought the trade of the Creek, which at this time was rather securely held by another English firm, Panton, Leslie and Company, who had secured their concessions from Spain and from Alexander McGillivray, the half-breed Creek chief.

In pursuance of his aims, Bowles appeared on the west coast of Florida in 1788 with a cargo of goods, which he liberally distributed among the Indians, without arousing the suspicion of McGillivray, but suspected of evil designs by the Spaniards. It was probably the purpose of Bowles to attack the Spaniards through Indian allies, but the desertion of some of his men caused him to leave. In 1791, the year after McGillivray had made the Treaty of New York with the United States, Bowles returned to Florida with the idea of supplanting McGillivray in Creek leadership, being aided by the unpopularity of that agreement. Cunningly he plundered the storehouse of Panton, Leslie at Saint Marks, but fell prey to Spanish duplicity when he agreed to go to New Orleans to treat with the authorities there. For the next few years he was held prisoner in Havana, Madrid, Cádiz, and the Philippines. Escaping he returned to Nassau, in 1799, and soon put out for Florida on his third and last filibustering expedition. The next year he attacked the Spanish fort at Saint Marks, successfully seized it, and held it for a few months. Being forced out he escaped into the hinterland, where for the next few years he was a menace to the Spaniards. At the suggestion of the United States, the Spaniards offered a reward of $4,500 for his capture and in May 1803 he was seized on American soil through a ruse by American authorities, Spain, and Great Britain. He died two years later in Morro Castle, Havana. Bowles's whole career in Florida had been directed assiduously against the Spanish power and in the interest of Great Britain generally, but more specifically to promote the commercial ambitions of Miller, Bonnamy and Company.

[J. W. Caughey, *McGillivray of the Creeks;* A. Stephens, ed., *The Life of General W. A. Bowles;* A. P. Whitaker, *The Mississippi Question, 1795–1803;* G. White, *Historical Collections of Georgia*.]

E. MERTON COULTER

BOWLING GREEN, a park in New York City, originally a small open space in front of the fort at the foot of Broadway, sometimes called the Parade. It was leased for a bowling green in 1733. A lead statue of George III was erected there in 1770 and destroyed by the populace at the outbreak of the Revolution in 1775.

[I. N. Phelps Stokes, *The Iconography of Manhattan Island.*]

ALVIN F. HARLOW

BOWYER, FORT, ATTACK ON (Sept. 15, 1814). From this fort, commanding the entrance to Mobile Bay, Maj. William Lawrence, with 130 troops, inflicted a mortifying defeat upon a British combined land and sea force of six vessels and 1,300 men, under Capt. Henry Percy, killing 162 and wounding 70 British while suffering only 8 American casualties.

[Oliver L. Spaulding, *The United States Army in War and Peace.*]

ROBERT S. THOMAS

BOXER REBELLION, an antiforeign uprising in China by members of a secret society known as Boxers, beginning in June 1900. A total of 231 foreigners and many Chinese Christians were murdered. On June 17 the Boxers began a siege of the legations in Peking. The United States joined Great Britain, Russia, Germany, France, and Japan in a military expedition for the relief of the legations, sending 5,000 troops for this purpose. The international relief expedition marched from Taku to Tientsin and thence to Peking, raising the siege on Aug. 14. The United States did not join in the punitive expedition under German Commander in Chief Count von Waldersee. In July Secretary of State John Hay issued a circular note to "preserve Chinese territorial and administrative entity," and during the Peking Congress (Feb. 5–Sept. 7, 1901) the United States opposed the demand for a punitive indemnity, which might lead to the dismemberment of China. The Boxer protocol finally fixed the indemnity at $333 million, provided for the punishment of guilty Chinese officials, and permitted the major nations to maintain legation guards at Peking and between the capital and the sea. The U.S. share of the indemnity, originally set at $24.5 million but reduced to $12 million, was paid by 1924.

[Tyler Dennett, *Americans in Eastern Asia;* H. B. Morse, *The International Relations of the Chinese Empire.*]

KENNETH COLEGROVE

BOXING. *See* **Prizefighting.**

BOYCOTTING. A boycott is a collective refusal to purchase commodities or services from a manufacturer or merchant whose employment or trade practices are regarded as unfair. Occasionally the economic boycott has been used by consumers against aggressor nations. Its chief use is by organized workers to secure better conditions of employment. Means for effecting a boycott include the distribution of cards, handbills, and lists of grievances and picketing.

In the United States the courts have made a distinction between primary and secondary boycotts. The former involves refusal of patronage by employees directly concerned in an industrial dispute; the latter involves attempts to persuade or coerce third parties to boycott an employer.

Considerable uncertainty and confusion characterize the law of boycotts in the United States, but a few general principles are fairly well established. In most jurisdictions it is not unlawful for an association of aggrieved workers to withhold patronage. Moreover, it does not appear to be unlawful in the several states for such workers to ask or persuade others to assist in their cause. It is illegal, however, to use physical violence, coercion, or intimidation. The behavior of pickets must be peaceful, and customers must be accorded complete freedom in entering and leaving the boycotted establishment.

The pivotal point in the law of boycotts is the use of pressure against third parties. Because most manufacturers do not distribute their goods directly but through wholesalers and retailers, organized labor can make a boycott effective only by bringing pressure upon such dealers. This is in essence a secondary boycott, which is regarded as unlawful in most jurisdictions. In Arizona, California, and Oklahoma all peacefully conducted boycotts have been held legal, and some of the lower courts of New York have sustained them. In Missouri and Montana the printing and distributing of circulars for purposes of boycott may not be directly enjoined by the courts.

The boycott was held unlawful in the United States as early as 1886. In 1908 the Supreme Court in the Danbury hatters case decided that the secondary boycott constitutes a conspiracy in restraint of trade under the provisions of the Sherman Antitrust Act (1890). The Court held that treble damages might be recovered for losses sustained by the manufacturer through the interstate boycott. In the Buck Stove and Range

Company case (1911), the same tribunal decided that all means employed to make effective an unlawful boycott are illegal, even though in themselves such means are innocent. Disregard of an injunction in this case by certain officials of the American Federation of Labor resulted in citation for contempt and jail sentence for one year. Although the sentence was subsequently set aside, the decision greatly discouraged the use of the boycott in labor disputes.

An attempt to escape from the restrictions of the Sherman act was made through section 20 of the Clayton Antitrust Act (1914), which prohibits the use of the injunction to restrain employees from picketing, boycotting, and advising others to withhold patronage from an employer when such activities are carried on by peaceful and lawful means. In the Duplex Printing Press Company case (1921), however, the Supreme Court ruled that all methods employed to make effective interstate boycotts involving third parties are unlawful.

Boycotts have also been used by unorganized groups appealed to through the press, mail, radio or television, or, in local instances, person to person. Informed by national news of a strike in California by the United Farm Workers, for example, some people across the nation stopped buying lettuce and other vegetables from that state. In the late 1960's, in protest against the policy of apartheid, U.S. college students carried on a campaign to force their institutions to rid their endowment funds of the securities of South African companies. On the local level consumer boycotts against anti-black discrimination on buses and in restaurants were successfully carried out in southern cities during the same decade.

Probably less successful, but still of some consequence, have been consumer boycotts in the 1970's against high meat prices. With national television networks, viewed daily by a large part of the total population, concerted boycotting action may be easier to achieve than ever before, and by means that make legal suppression difficult if not impossible.

[Francis B. Sayre, *Cases on Labor Law*.]

GORDON S. WATKINS

BOYDTON PLANK ROAD, ENGAGEMENT AT (Oct. 27–28, 1864). While moving Union troops on the Boydton Plank Road where it crossed Hatcher's Run, near Petersburg, Va., a gap opened between Gen. Winfield S. Hancock's Second Corps and Gen. G. K. Warren's Fifth Corps. Confederates pushed into this opening and attacked Hancock's right and rear, provoking a bloody battle.

[R. U. Johnson and C. C. Buel, eds., *Battles and Leaders of the Civil War*.]

ROBERT S. THOMAS

BOY SCOUTS OF AMERICA, incorporated Feb. 8, 1910, and granted a federal charter by Congress June 15, 1916. This organization is based on the principles established in England by scouting's founder, Lord Baden-Powell, in 1907, and modified to meet the needs of American youth. The purpose of the Boy Scouts of America is to provide for boys and young adults an effective educational program designed to build desirable qualities of character; to train them in the responsibilities of participatory citizenship; and to develop in them physical and mental fitness.

There are three programs: Cub Scouting, for boys who have completed the second grade or are eight years of age or older but not yet eleven; Scouting, for boys who have completed the fifth grade or are eleven years of age or older but not yet eighteen; and Exploring, for young men and women who have completed the eighth grade or are fifteen years of age or older but not yet twenty-one. A volunteer movement at all levels, the scouting program in the United States depends on more than a million and a half scoutmasters, den leaders, and Explorer advisers, who volunteer their time and talents. Scouts are organized in patrols, under a boy leader, and in troops, under a scoutmaster. Entering scouting as a Scout, a boy may advance through Second Class, First Class, Star Scout, Life Scout, and finally to Eagle Scout. The official Scout uniform is protected by act of Congress.

Between 1910 and 1973, 55,100,376 persons were associated with the movement in the United States. The world scouting membership (December 1972) was 12,520,925 in 106 countries.

PETER H. JOHNSON

BOZEMAN TRAIL, traced by John M. Bozeman, 1863–65, as the shortest and easiest route for emigrants to the gold fields of Virginia City, Mont. The trail continued the route from the South Platte at Julesburg (Fort Sedgwick), Colo., past Fort Laramie, where it crossed the Oregon Trail, to the Powder River crossing at Fort Connor, Wyo. Thence it passed eastward of the Big Horn Mountains to the Yellowstone River and westward to Virginia City.

A caravan first used the trail in the summer following the Powder River campaign in October 1865. Notwithstanding the Treaty of Laramie in 1851 the Sioux resented the invasion, and when forts Reno, Phil Kearny, and C. F. Smith were established (1865–66) for emigrant protection they went on the warpath. Red Cloud's War followed. By 1868 all posts along the trail had been abandoned. Following suppression of the Sioux in 1877 (*see* Sioux Wars) the Bozeman Trail became an important route for cattle moving north from Texas into Wyoming and Montana.

[E. A. Brininstool and G. R. Hebard, *The Bozeman Trail.*]

PAUL I. WELLMAN

BRADDOCK'S EXPEDITION. On Apr. 14, 1755, Gen. Edward Braddock, appointed commander of all the British forces in America, was dispatched with two regiments for a campaign in the French and Indian War. The first objective was Fort Duquesne. The regulars and the colonial forces rendezvoused at Fort Cumberland, to start for Fort Duquesne by the route later called Braddock's Road. Wagons and horses were secured from Pennsylvania with Benjamin Franklin's aid; Indian allies came from Aughwick, but most of them deserted when Braddock ordered their families home.

The army, 2,200 strong, started west June 7, but had advanced only to Little Meadows (near Grantsville, Md.) by June 16. Then, on the advice of Lt. Col. George Washington, his aide-de-camp, Braddock pushed on rapidly with some 1,200 men and a minimum of artillery, leaving a command under Col. William Dunbar to bring up the heavier goods. On July 9 the expedition crossed and recrossed the Monongahela near Turtle Creek. Up to this point every precaution had been taken against surprise, but apparently the officers now grew overconfident. A hill commanding the route was left unoccupied, and the troops marched in an order too close for safety.

From Fort Duquesne Capt. Daniel Beaujeu led some 250 French and 600 Indians to oppose Braddock. He had not laid his ambush when the two parties unexpectedly met. The British opened fire, putting most of the French to flight and killing Beaujeu. His subordinate rallied the Indians to seize the hill that Braddock had neglected and to surround the British line. The van of the English, falling back, became entangled with the main body so that order was lost and maneuvering was impossible. For three hours the British stood under a galling fire; then Braddock ordered a retreat. The general was mortally wounded; many of the officers were killed; the retreat became a rout. Washington, sent to Dunbar by Braddock, reported the defeat and dispatched wagons for the wounded.

Dunbar, now in command, ordered quantities of stores destroyed, and retreated rapidly to Fort Cumberland. Refusing the request of Virginia and Pennsylvania that he build a fort at Raystown (Bedford, Pa.) and defend the frontier, he marched to Philadelphia in August and left the border to suffer Indian raids. Though Braddock's expedition failed, it demonstrated that an army could be marched over the Alleghenies, it taught the troops something of Indian fighting, and its very mistakes contributed to the success of the Forbes Expedition.

[Stanley Pargellis, "Braddock's Defeat," *American Historical Review* (1936); Francis Parkman, *Montcalm and Wolfe.*]

SOLON J. BUCK

BRADDOCK'S ROAD ran from the Potomac River at Wills Creek (Cumberland, Md.) to the Monongahela at Turtle Creek. The section from Wills Creek to the upper Youghiogheny River was opened by the Ohio Company, probably in 1752. In 1754 George Washington, then a lieutenant colonel, improved the road to Great Meadows and extended it to Christopher Gist's plantation (six miles northeast of the present Uniontown, Pa.). In 1755, Gen. Edward Braddock's expedition used the road and extended it almost to Fort Duquesne. After Braddock's defeat the road facilitated Indian raids; still later it became a highway for western emigration and part of it was incorporated in the National Road. (*See also* Cumberland Road.)

[A. B. Hulbert, *Historic Highways of America;* J. K. Lacock, "Braddock Road," *Pennsylvania Magazine of History and Biography* (1914).]

SOLON J. BUCK

BRADSTREET'S FORT FRONTENAC EXPEDITION. After the disaster at Ticonderoga in July 1758, Lt. Col. John Bradstreet led a successful raid that went far to restore British morale during the French and Indian War.

Taking command in early August of 2,600 men secretly mobilized in the Mohawk Valley, Bradstreet moved swiftly forward along the waterways. He reached Oswego on Aug. 24 and, crossing Lake Ontario, effected a surprise which enabled him to capture Fort Frontenac at Cataraqui (present Kingston) on the 27th. Both the post and the French shipping were put to the torch. This bold campaign broke the French hold of the water routes by which the western posts were supplied, contributing to the evacuation of Fort Duquesne later in the same year and to the surrender of Fort Niagara in 1759.

[George W. Schuyler, *Colonial New York,* vol. II.]

ARTHUR POUND

BRADSTREET'S LAKE ERIE EXPEDITION (1764). Col. John Bradstreet emerged from two wars with high credit, first as Sir William Pepperell's capable assistant at the capture of Louisburg in 1748, and later as the conqueror of Fort Frontenac in 1758. Unfortunately, his record suffered from his next assignment: command of the expedition of 1764 to the Great Lakes area to place Indian relations on a peace footing following the uprising under Pontiac.

On the shores of Lake Erie, Bradstreet revealed ignorance of Indian affairs by concluding improper treaties with unimportant delegations of Delaware and Shawnee. In this he went beyond his instructions; worse yet, he did not recover possession of all prisoners held by the former foes. To Col. Henry Bouquet, advancing from the Forks of the Ohio, fell the duty of pushing far into Ohio to restore white prestige.

Bradstreet proceeded to Detroit, where he was only partially successful. While returning, he failed to carry out instructions to move on mutinous Scioto villages, a dangerous situation in that quarter being saved by Bouquet's steadiness. Delaying too long on the Sandusky shore, Bradstreet's forces, near to mutiny, encountered severe hardships. His reputation as a popular hero did not survive.

[A. Pound, *Native Stock.*]

ARTHUR POUND

BRADY PHOTOGRAPHS, a collection of over 7,000 photographs (two negatives, in most cases) taken by Mathew B. Brady and his associates during the Civil War at an expenditure of over $100,000. They included portraits of officers and soldiers and scenes at the front and in the rear, along the battle lines from Washington to New Orleans.

The project bankrupted Brady, and the War Department acquired the plates and some negatives at public auction in 1874 for $2,840. Some copies of the photos are known to have passed into private hands. The largest collections are now in the National Archives and the Library of Congress.

[James D. Horan, *Mathew Brady: Historian With a Camera;* F. T. Miller, *The Photographic History of the Civil War.*]

THOMAS ROBSON HAY

BRAIN TRUST. Prior to his nomination as the Democratic candidate for the presidency in 1932, Franklin D. Roosevelt had brought together three close advisers, Raymond Moley, Rexford G. Tugwell, and Adolph A. Berle, Jr., all professors at Columbia University. These three continued to aid Roosevelt during his campaign for election and, after his inauguration on Mar. 4, 1933, they became prominent in the councils of the chief executive. They were given salaried offices in Washington—Moley in the Department of State, Tugwell in the Department of Agriculture, and Berle in the Reconstruction Finance Corporation. They and all economists, lawyers, and scholars who subsequently joined the administration were indiscriminately dubbed the brain trust, whether or not they were close to the president. The impression was created that they were responsible for everything that was done, so the expression "brain trust" became a symbol for all New Deal experimentation.

[Ernest K. Lindley, *The Roosevelt Revolution.*]

ERIK MCKINLEY ERIKSSON

BRANDS, PRIVATE AND NATIONAL. From the beginning of American commerce, much merchandise offered for sale has been identified by marks of origin, ownership, or sponsorship. On casks and boxes they were literally "brands," but the term was loosely used to cover other kinds of craftsmen's or merchants' marks. The trademarks of merchants or other distributors have been set apart as a class called private brands to distinguish them from the trademarks of manufacturers. The manufacturer's trademarked merchandise may be distributed and advertised nationally; the private-branded merchandise usually has only sectional distribution.

The rivalry between the two classes originated in the latter part of the 19th century, but did not become clearly evident until the 20th century. The earliest manufacturers of trademarked products who used national advertising to stimulate consumer demand met little opposition from wholesalers and dealers. Their articles were usually of a new type or manifestly superior to unidentified bulk goods. But gradually, nationally advertised brands entered commodity fields where the dealer's influence had been dominant. Here he already had his own private brand, or an unadvertised brand that allowed a larger margin of profit. The manufacturer's brands, procurable through other channels, weakened his hold on his customers.

For this reason and others, the large department stores, mail-order houses, and chains promoted the sale of private brands they controlled and established new ones. Some of these private brands were made by manufacturers who marketed their own nationally advertised brands. Often the only important difference was that one was sponsored by a manufacturer and bore a craftsman's mark, the other by a distributor and bore a merchant's mark. (*See also* Trademarks.)

G. B. HOTCHKISS

BRANDY STATION, BATTLE OF (June 9, 1863). Ordered by Union Gen. Joseph Hooker to ascertain whether Robert E. Lee's army was moving northward, Gen. Alfred Pleasonton's federal cavalry, 7,981 strong, with 3,000 infantry, crossed the Rappahannock River in Virginia. At Beverly Ford, John Buford's Union cavalry division drove part of J. E. B. Stuart's 10,292 cavalry toward Fleetwood Hill and Brandy Station. Two other divisions, crossing below, attacked Stuart's rear at Fleetwood. Stuart hurried troops to action, precipitating the greatest cavalry conflict of the Civil War. The Confederates retained the field, but Pleasonton learned that Lee was marching toward Maryland.

[John W. Thomason, Jr., *Jeb Stuart.*]

JOSEPH MILLS HANSON

BRANDYWINE CREEK, BATTLE OF (Sept. 11, 1777), fought in Chester County, Pa., ten miles northwest of Wilmington, Del. The British and Hessian troops commanded by the generals Sir William Howe, Lord Cornwallis, and Baron Wilhelm von Knyphausen composed a force of 18,000. The American army under Gen. George Washington numbered 11,000, of whom a large number were militia. Following a feint attack by the Hessians on the Americans at Chad's Ford, the British crossed the east side of the creek at Jeffrie's Ford, continued southward, and suddenly attacked Gen. John Sullivan's troops near Birmingham Meetinghouse. The Americans, although outnumbered, fought gallantly, but were compelled to retire. Washington had received faulty news concerning the approach of the British. At night he withdrew his army toward Philadelphia without demoralization, despite 1,000 casualties.

[C. W. Heathcote, *History of Chester County.*]

CHARLES W. HEATHCOTE

BRANNAN PLAN, a farm price-support plan using direct payments to the farmer, under certain conditions, as a substitute for price supports, first proposed by Charles Brannan, secretary of agriculture, in April 1949. The proposal aroused considerable opposition, its opponents characterizing it as unsound and fantastically expensive. Its supporters called it a rational approach to income protection for agriculture and a more effective and less costly way to subsidize the farmer when subsidy is needed. The plan has been urged in Congress a number of times, usually in amended form, but it has never been approved.

[R. M. Christensen, *The Brannan Plan;* Allen Matusow, *Farm Policies in the Truman Years.*]

THOMAS ROBSON HAY

BRATTLEBORO. *See* **Dummer, Fort.**

BRAZIL, CONFEDERATE EXPATRIATES TO. Perhaps nearly half of the eight or ten thousand southerners who immigrated to foreign lands after the Civil War went to Brazil. The expatriates formed associations and sent advance agents to the southern empire to make arrangements and to select lands for homes. Coming from every southern state and some northern states, they represented every social class and profession. Many had been leaders in the Old South. At first the chief embarkation point was New Orleans; later it became New York. Rio de Janeiro received nearly all the immigrants, though the colonists settling on the Amazon River went via Pará.

The greater number settled in colonies located in the wilderness of the provinces of Paraná, São Paulo, Rio de Janeiro, Espírito Santo, and Pará. Most of them tried agriculture and stock raising. They were comparatively successful at Villa Americana, in the hinterland of São Paulo, which at its peak was a thriving community of several hundred families. The colonial experiments as a rule were not successful and broke up after a few months' or at most a few years' endurance, the colonists going to São Paulo, or, more often, returning to the United States. The failures were due to lack of access to markets; unsatisfactory labor supply (the Brazilian slaves could not be kept in isolated interior communities); climatic conditions, tropical insects, and disease; lack of capital; and homesickness for friends and relatives. Yet many traces still remain of these southern expatriates in Brazil.

[Lawrence F. Hill, "The Confederate Exodus to Latin America," *Southwestern Historical Quarterly* (1935, 1936).]

LAWRENCE F. HILL

BRAZITO, BATTLE AT (Dec. 25, 1846). En route to Chihuahua, N.Mex., Gen. Alexander W. Doniphan, with 500 Missouri volunteers, reached the east bank of the Rio Grande by midafternoon, Dec. 25. He received Juan Ponce de León's messenger, under a black flag, demanding surrender. In the ensuing thirty-minute fight, the Americans' superior fire and tactics triumphed. Ponce fled in disorder, losing a hundred killed and wounded to the American loss of seven slightly wounded.

[Justin Smith, *The War With Mexico.*]

ROBERT S. THOMAS

BREDA, PEACE OF, signed July 21, 1667, by England and France after the naval war between England and Holland in which France joined the latter, provided for the restoration of Acadia to France and confirmed the English possession of New Netherland. King Charles II's order (1668) for Acadia's return was delayed by the claims of Thomas Temple to part of the region, based on a grant from Oliver Cromwell (1656). Restoration took place in 1670, France returning to England at the same time part of the island of St. Christopher.

[F. G. Davenport, ed., *European Treaties Bearing on the History of the United States,* vol. II.]

ROBERT E. MOODY

BREED'S HILL. *See* **Bunker Hill.**

BRETHREN. The Brethren, popularly known as Dunkers or Dunkards, are descendants of a pietist sect founded by Alexander Mack that began to migrate to America in 1719. Like many pietist groups, the Brethren grew during the Great Awakening, and from that time they have tended to assume an evangelical posture. Early Brethren congregations attached great importance to the Lord's Supper, which they preceded by foot-washing and a love feast and concluded with the kiss of peace. Although in the past the Brethren have emphasized plain dress, they have tended toward a more moderate position on the issue in recent years. The largest Brethren denomination is the Church of the Brethren with 181,000 members. This group grew rapidly in the 1960's. Other Brethren denominations are the National Fellowship of Brethren Churches, 33,000; the Brethren Church (Ashland, Ohio), 16,000 members; and the Old German Baptist Brethren, 4,200 members.

[Martin Grove Brumbaugh, *A History of the German Baptist Brethren in Europe and America;* Donald F. Durnbaugh, *The Brethren in Colonial America;* Donald F. Durnbaugh and L. W. Shultz, *A Brethren Bibliography.*]

GLENN T. MILLER

BRETTON WOODS CONFERENCE, also known as the United Nations Monetary and Financial Conference, held in New Hampshire, July 1–22, 1944, and attended by forty-four nations. The conference was held to make plans for postwar international economic cooperation similar to the groundwork for political cooperation laid by the Atlantic Charter and the declaration at the Moscow Conference of Foreign Ministers. Agreement was reached for an International Monetary Fund of $8.8 billion, as assigned at the conference (American quota $2.75 billion), to promote exchange stability and expansion of international trade, and for an International Bank for Reconstruction and Development (the World Bank, as it came to be called) with authorized capital of $10 billion (American subscription $3.175 billion). Four of the nations attending did not sign—Haiti, Liberia, New Zealand, and the Soviet Union.

CHARLES S. CAMPBELL

BREWING. Like winemaking, brewing has existed for millennia as an art; only in the past century has it become an applied science. Beer came from England to America with the earliest settlers. At that time brewing could be called a household industry, carried on by farmers and tavern keepers. But commercial breweries selling to local areas that could be reached by horse and wagon were soon started. William Penn, for example, established such a business in Pennsbury in 1683, not only to make a profit but also to encourage the drinking of beer rather than hard liquor, in the interest of temperance.

The ancient process of brewing began by heating and soaking barley to force germination. The end product, called malt, was mixed with water and boiled to form what brewers called the wort. Hops were added to the boiling liquid to give it a pleasant bitter taste and an aroma. After straining, the wort was fermented for a few days by adding yeast. Until the 20th century, brewers governed the proportions of the ingredients and the exact timing of the process by age-old recipes or simply rule-of-thumb. The reputation of a commercial brewery depended greatly on the skill of its brewmaster.

Early American beer was of the English type, fermented with yeast that floated on top of the wort. Near the middle of the 19th century the rapidly increasing flow of German immigrants to America brought their type of beer. The kind of yeast they used stayed at the bottom of the wort, and after its removal the fermented wort was aged, or "laggered," at low temperatures for some weeks. The milder and more aromatic German lager soon captured most of the beer market, and the English type of fermentation was confined to ale.

From about 1875 on, technological and scientific changes took place in brewing that made the amateur or small-scale operator unable to compete with the up-to-date, large brewery. The railroad made it possible for breweries with limited local markets, such as those in Milwaukee, Wis., to seek nationwide distribution—which, in turn, required beer able to withstand temperature changes, bumping, and the lapse of time. From the 1880's on, pasteurization checked bacterial growth; chemical additives were eliminated (enforced by law in 1907); bottling became mechanized; and carbonation was controlled and artificial. In order to make their way into the territories of local brewers, the national shippers developed means of influencing local sellers, ranging from discounts and credits to purchases of saloon properties.

The brewing industry that revived after the years of Prohibition, between 1919 and 1933, had most of the same large producers but operated in a quite different environment from the old one. As Prohibition had accustomed people to drinking hard liquor, it took a dozen years to build the market for beer back to its size before World War I, and in 1970 consumption was still slightly less per capita than in 1914. Meanwhile, the motor truck, cans, and more exact chemistry aided the competitive position of the larger breweries. There were only 150 brewers in 1970 as compared to 1,400 in 1914, and fewer than a dozen sold their product throughout the nation. Since all these companies could make reliable beer with many desirable qualities and were forbidden by federal law from controlling outlets, competition was chiefly in marketing and rapid adjustment to changes in public taste.

[Thomas C. Cochran, *The Pabst Brewing Company*.]

THOMAS C. COCHRAN

BRIAND-KELLOGG PACT. *See* **Kellogg-Briand Pact.**

BRIAR CREEK, BATTLE OF (Mar. 3, 1779). Col. Mark Prevost, British commander, trapped and routed a force of about 1,200 southern militia and regular Continentals under Col. John Ashe at Briar Creek, in Severn County, Ga. The American loss was 150 killed and wounded, 189 captured. The British lost but 16 killed and wounded.

[Charles Stedman, *History of the American War*.]

ROBERT S. THOMAS

BRICKER AMENDMENT, the popular designation for a series of proposals (1952–57), in varied form, to amend the U.S. Constitution, primarily to ensure that treaties and executive agreements inconsistent with the Constitution could not become effective in domestic law. These were sponsored as Senate joint resolutions, in the 82d through the 85th Congresses, by Sen. John W. Bricker of Ohio, but failed to obtain sufficient support for enactment.

The formal basis for these proposals was an interpretation, long asserted but not widely approved, of Article VI, Section 2, of the Constitution—the supremacy clause—which designates the Constitution, federal statutes "made in pursuance thereof," and treaties "made, or which shall be made, under the authority of the United States" as the supreme law of the land. It was argued that under the law as it stands those statutes consistent with the Constitution ("made in pursuance thereof") are so qualified, while no such requirement is made for treaties, leaving what Bricker called a gap in the Constitution; it was further argued that the framers of the clause intended that treaties made under the Articles of Confederation, as well as those concluded after adoption of the Constitution, should bind the states and so used broad language to include the former, which were not chronologically pursuant to the Constitution. Bricker cited Justice Oliver Wendell Holmes's remark in *Missouri* v. *Holland,* 252 U.S. 416, 433 (1920): "It is open to question whether the authority of the United States means more than the formal acts prescribed to make the convention," but ignored Holmes's view that there were other constitutional limitations on the treaty power. The Supreme Court has not yet held any treaty unconstitutional, but has consistently declared that there are criteria for doing so, as in *Reid* v. *Covert,* 354 U.S. 1 (1957). Bricker feared that United Nations treaties on human rights would impair domestic jurisdiction and therefore wished to increase state powers to limit the effectiveness of treaties—but many supporters of the amendment did not share this motivation.

An amendment declaring treaties and executive agreements inconsistent with the Constitution to be without legal effect would have attracted wide support, including that of President Dwight D. Eisenhower. But Bricker insisted upon adding to this a limitation upon the scope of the treaty power, which would have conditioned the internal effectiveness of any treaty regulating subjects within the reserved powers of the states upon implementation by state legislation. He sought also to subject executive agreements to closer congressional scrutiny and approval—an objective still attractive to the Congress—but failed to develop procedures appropriate to the several varieties of such agreements.

[Louis Henkin, *Foreign Affairs and the Constitution;* Charles H. McLaughlin, "The Scope of the Treaty Power in the United States," *Minnesota Law Review,* vol. 42 (1958), vol. 43 (1959); Walter Weise, *Der Kampf um das Bricker Amendment.*]

CHARLES H. MCLAUGHLIN

BRICKS. *See* **Building Materials.**

BRIDGER, FORT, a frontier trading post and later a fort of the U.S. Army, located on Black's Fork, Uinta County, Wyo. It was named after James ("Jim") Bridger, trapper and scout, who with his partner, Louis Vasquez, built it in 1843 and operated it for a number of years. Although trading in pelts was carried on, Bridger's post is best known as a way station and supply point for emigrants bound for Oregon, Utah, and California (*see* Oregon Trail). Its establishment marks the beginning of caravan travel to the Pacific Coast. The post was taken over by Mormon colonists from Utah about 1855; was burned by the Mormons on the approach of U.S. troops in the Mormon War of 1857; was rebuilt as a military post by the U.S. Army in 1858; and was finally abandoned in 1890. For many years it was famous as a mail, express, and telegraph station. It is now the site of a state park.

[J. C. Alter, *Jim Bridger.*]

RUPERT N. RICHARDSON

BRIDGES. Timber and Masonry Bridges. The construction of permanent bridges over broad waterways was a costly enterprise that the American colonies could seldom undertake. The earliest bridges were split logs or hewn timbers laid between timber cribs or rubble stone abutments. These were superseded by pile-and-beam structures consisting of long stringers spanning between abutments and intermediate transverse rows of piles, each bound together by a horizontal cap piece and diagonal braces. Examples notable for size were the Great Bridge over the Charles River at Cambridge, Mass. (1662), and the York River bridge at York, Maine (1761). A variation on the traditional form was the span built by Enoch Hale over the Connecticut River at Bellows Falls, Vt., in 1785, in which the chief supporting elements were massive timbers arranged in the form of crude polygonal arches.

Masonry bridges were extremely rare in the colonies because of the high cost of quarrying and dressing stone as well as laying up the blocks. The first was a three-arched structure built in 1693 to carry Frankford Avenue over a stream in Philadelphia, but the record shows few others for more than a century.

The great age of timber bridge construction was inaugurated by Timothy Palmer, who built the first timber truss span for the channel crossing of the bridge over the Merrimack River at Newburyport, Mass. (1792). His greatest work was the Permanent Bridge over the Schuylkill River at Philadelphia (1798–1806). A similar structure over the same stream was the Colossus of Lewis Wernwag (1809–13), which included wrought-iron bracing elements in place of the timber forms in Palmer's trusses. Wernwag's bridges ushered in a prolific period of invention in timber trusses. Theodore Burr patented a combination arch and truss in 1817, having built the first bridge of this type in 1803–04. Ithiel Town in 1820 patented the lattice truss, the first truss to be free of arch action and hence to exert only a vertical force at the abutments. Simpler and more widely useful forms came with the patents of Stephen Long (1830), William Howe (1841), and Caleb and Thomas Pratt (1844).

Masonry arch bridges continued to be rare until the advent of the railroad. The first two designed for rail traffic were built by the Baltimore and Ohio Railroad: the Carrollton Viaduct at Baltimore (1829) and the Philips Viaduct at Relay, Md. (1835), both of which are still standing. The railroads continued to construct masonry bridges throughout the 19th century, but the masonry arch was rapidly superseded by concrete around 1890.

Iron and Steel Truss Bridges. The first iron truss bridge in the United States was built by Earl Trumbull in 1840 to carry a roadway over the Erie Canal at Frankfort, N.Y. The Howe truss was adopted for the first iron railroad bridge, erected at Manayunk, Pa., in 1845 by Richard Osborne. This was also the first bridge to contain both cast and wrought iron, but the metals were incorrectly distributed to take full advantage of their special physical properties. The decade following erection of the Manayunk span was the heroic age of the iron truss: the Pratt invention was quickly adapted to iron construction, and it was followed by still other patents, chiefly those of Squire Whipple (1847), Wendel Bollman (1852), and Albert Fink (1854). The Whipple truss was the most widely used for big railroad bridges up to 1890, while the redundant Bollman and Fink trusses were confined largely to the railroads with which the two men were associated.

The rapid progress in bridge design emboldened the engineers to create the massive iron and steel bridges required by broad waterways and heavy rail loads. The Ohio River proved to be the challenge and the testing ground: the first of the long-span forms was built at Steubenville, Ohio, by the Pittsburgh and Steubenville Railroad (1863–65), with a channel span of 320 feet. Length steadily increased as the railroads constructed iron and then steel bridges over the Ohio at Cincinnati, Louisville, and Cairo. The substitution of steel for iron in truss bridges came with the construction of the Chicago and Alton's Missouri River bridge at Glasgow, Mo. (1878–79).

The development of the cantilever truss to the point at which it could carry rail loads occurred largely during the same decade. The first use was in the Kentucky River bridge of the Cincinnati Southern Railway (1876–77), the work of Charles Shaler Smith. It was followed by ever-lengthening spans at Niagara Falls (1883), Poughkeepsie, N.Y. (1886–88), and Memphis, Tenn. (1888–92), by which date steel had largely come to replace iron.

Iron and Steel Arch Bridges. The iron arch bridge was slow to develop in the United States—the first having been built by Richard Delafield at Brownsville, Pa., 1836–39, sixty years after it had appeared in England. The possibilities of the form came suddenly to prominence with the construction of Eads Bridge spanning the Mississippi River at Saint Louis, Mo. (1868–74). The triumph of James B. Eads, this bridge was the first in the United States to be built of steel and had the longest arch spans at the time. The hinged arch was introduced by Joseph M. Wilson of Philadelphia in 1869 and was within twenty years adopted for the 509-foot spans of William R. Hutton's Washington Bridge in New York (1887–89).

Suspension Bridges. From a strictly chronological standpoint the suspension bridge antedates iron truss and arch forms, but these were derived from long-established timber and masonry prototypes. The suspension bridge with a rigid level deck carried by iron chains was invented by James Finley, who built the first one at Uniontown, Pa., in 1801 and received a patent on his invention in 1808. Except for an unsuccessful attempt by Josiah White and Erskine Hazard to use wire for the cables of a bridge at Philadelphia in 1816, the wire-cable form was the achievement of Charles Ellet and John A. Roebling. Ellet's greatest bridge, at Wheeling, W.Va. (1846–49), failed in a storm and had to be rebuilt by Roebling, who had already established his reputation with suspension aqueducts built for the Pennsylvania State and the Delaware and Hudson canals. Roebling's triumphs came in stunning succession: Niagara Falls (1851–55), Cincinnati (1856–67), and Brooklyn, N.Y. (1869–83), were the most prominent—the last embracing the longest single span in the world at the time.

Steel and Concrete Bridges. With the long tradition of timber, iron, and early steel forms behind them, the engineers in 1900 were prepared to produce spectacular works. The simple steel truss reached its greatest length, 723 feet, in the railroad bridge over the Ohio River at Metropolis, Ill. (1914–17); and the continuous form, its greatest weight and length, 1,550 feet, in another Ohio River span, the rail bridge at Sciotoville, Ohio (1914–17). Cantilever trusses made it possible to stretch the main span of the New Orleans Public Belt Highway Bridge to 1,575 feet in 1958. The heaviest steel arch is still the Hell Gate Bridge at New York City (1914–16), designed by Gustav Lindenthal for a four-track rail line, and the longest is the Bayonne, N.J., highway bridge (1928–31) of Othmar Ammann.

New York's East River spans, following the Brooklyn Bridge, brought the steel tower to suspension bridge construction and thus formed the precedents for the modern classics of the type: George Washington at New York (1927–31), its 3,500-foot double-deck main span once the longest and still the heaviest; Golden Gate at San Francisco (1933–37), for twenty-seven years the longest clear span at 4,200 feet; Verrazano-Narrows at New York (1959–64), its 4,260-foot main span now the longest in the world. Othmar Ammann was chief engineer of the New York bridges, and Joseph B. Strauss, of the San Francisco.

The first reinforced concrete bridge, based in part on earlier plain concrete forms, was built in Golden Gate Park, San Francisco, in 1889 by Ernest Ransome. The concrete arch grew steadily in size and refinement of form. The Tunkhannock Creek Viaduct of the D. L. and W. Railroad (1911–15) is still the largest concrete bridge in overall dimensions. The 460-foot arch ribs in the Westinghouse Bridge at Pittsburgh, Pa. (1930–31), were for more than thirty years the longest, but the length has been exceeded by two highway bridges in the state of Washington.

The introduction of rigid frames and box girders in the early 20th century led to a great increase in length and improvement in appearance of the conventional girder bridge that originally appeared in iron in 1841.

[Carl W. Condit, *American Building: Materials and Techniques;* David B. Steinman and Sara Ruth Watson, *Bridges and Their Builders.*]

CARL W. CONDIT

BRIDGEWATER, BATTLE OF. *See* **Lundy's Lane, Battle at.**

BRISCOE* V. *BANK OF THE COMMONWEALTH OF KENTUCKY, 11 Peters 257 (1837). The Bank of Kentucky was entirely owned by the state and its officers and directors were appointed by the state legislature. The question was whether notes issued by such a bank constituted a subterfuge by which the state in effect was emitting bills of credit in the sense forbidden by the Constitution. The Supreme Court found the notes to be backed by the resources of the bank and not the credit of the state and the bank to be a separate entity capable of suing and being sued; therefore, such notes were not bills of credit in the prohibited sense. This case completely repudiated the decision in *Craig* v. *Missouri.*

[A. J. Beveridge, *John Marshall.*]

HARVEY PINNEY

BRISTOE CAMPAIGN (Oct. 9–22, 1863). Gen. Robert E. Lee crossed the Rapidan River in Virginia, Oct. 9, turning the right flank of Union commander George G. Meade, and advanced toward Washington. Using parallel roads Meade marched rapidly to cover the capital. He reached Centreville first, his rear guard, under Gen. G. K. Warren, severely repulsing Gen. A. P. Hill's corps at Bristoe Station, Oct. 14. A battle under favorable conditions proving impossible, Lee returned to the Rappahannock River.

[Douglas S. Freeman, *R. E. Lee,* vol. III.]

JOSEPH MILLS HANSON

BRISTOL TRADE. During the early 16th century Bristol found its location in southwestern England a great advantage in capturing trade with America; by the 17th century it had become the foremost English port. Throughout the 16th century Bristol merchants showed a steady willingness to support overseas expansion in the realms of trade, fisheries, and exploration. Richard Hakluyt the geographer, Sir Ferdinando Gorges, a Newfoundland fishery syndicate, and other important elements in American development had Bristol contacts. Moreover, prevailing winds and ocean currents enabled the city's traders to share in the profitable Caribbean commerce. In the later 17th century Bristol became the port of departure for many colonists bound for America. Although the city lost its commercial priority in the 18th century, it still shared heavily in western enterprises, especially through the slave trade and the fisheries. On the eve of the American Revolution it was the second city in Britain, and its merchants greatly influenced British colonial policy.

[*Cambridge History of the British Empire,* vol. I; C. P. Lucas, *The Beginnings of English Overseas Enterprise.*]

CHARLES F. MULLETT

BRITISH CAMPAIGN OF 1777. As the year 1776 ended, the British ministry came to think of the problem in America as one of reconquest, rather than of policing. A reasoned procedure was evolved in consultation with Gen. Sir John Burgoyne, lately returned to London from Canada. The plan decided on provided for an expedition to proceed from Montreal southward along the familiar Champlain-Hudson route. A large army moving up the Hudson from New York would meet Burgoyne at Albany, after which a subsidiary force might proceed eastward down the Connecticut River. As Burgoyne moved from Montreal, an auxiliary force would go up the St. Lawrence River to Oswego and, with Indian aid, would strike into the Mohawk Valley. It was also proposed that a force of southern Indians, blacks, and British regulars be used "to awe the Southern provinces." A "numerous fleet" would "sweep the whole coast." It was believed that the plan, properly concerted and carried out, "might possibly do the business [of ending the colonial revolt] in one campaign."

To carry out this plan, the British force in the colonies would be reinforced from England. American auxiliaries of every description—Tories, Canadians, and Indians—would be recruited, and foreign regular troops would be hired for service in America (*see* Hessians). An unusual complement of guns was to be taken, as it was expected some of the numerous forts along the proposed route of invasion would need to be besieged and reduced by gunfire.

Because the active theater of war was comprised in a long, narrow band along the North Atlantic seaboard, bisected from north to south by the Champlain-Hudson route, it was clear that if this route could be occupied and held, the revolt would soon come to an end. In fact, such occupation was "the indispensable first step in reconquering the colonies."

The reasoning was correct, but the plan failed because of the shortcomings of the commanding general, because of the physical barriers of river, forest, and terrain, which impeded transport and troop movements, and because of the difficulty of securing adequate supplies of food and munitions. Final important causes were the uncertain allegiance of Canada and of the American Tories, and the overrating of Indian cooperation. The American opposition, at opportune moments, capitalized on these handicaps and was finally able to win a decisive victory. (*See* Bennington, Battle of; Burgoyne's Invasion; Highlands of the Hudson; Oriskany, Battle of.)

[Hoffman Nickerson, *The Turning Point of the Revolution.*]

THOMAS ROBSON HAY

BRITISH DEBTS, the debts owed by the American colonial merchants and planters to British merchants before the Revolution and which, obviously remaining unpaid during the war, continued a subject of dispute between the United States and England until 1802. The debts were a natural consequence of the economic system prevalent in the colonies. The merchants of the northern colonies and the planters of the southern colonies bought practically all of their manufactured articles from English merchants. The merchants of the northern colonies depended on their trade and the southern planters upon their prospective crops to pay the balances due in England. The result, from 1763 to 1775, was a rather constant indebtedness of some £3,000,000—most of which was owed by the southern planters. Stoppage of payment on these debts was frequently resorted to by the colonies in their fight against the colonial legislation of Parliament in the period, 1763–75. And the possibility of wiping out the indebtedness by war was one of the contributing causes of the Revolution.

During the Revolution all of the states enacted laws affecting these debts. In the states north of Maryland most of the debts were owed to Loyalists, while in the southern states most of the debts belonged to the British merchants. Some of the laws confiscated Loyalist estates, including debts (England later claimed that debts due to Loyalists should be included with those due to British merchants); some laws sequestered the debts due to British merchants; others confiscated such debts; while still others banished or restricted the activities of the agents of the British merchants; other laws, such as paper money legislation, just as effectively abolished or barred the collection of the debts. In Maryland £144,536 of debts due to British merchants were paid into the state treasury; in Virginia about £287,000; and in North Carolina over £50,000.

These debts were an important problem in the negotiation of the Definitive Treaty of Peace in 1782–83. At one time the British ministers were ready to make peace without any guarantee for the Loyalists and merchants. However, John Adams, more interested in the fisheries than in the debts of the planters and having "no notion of cheating anybody," was responsible for the provision (article IV) that the debts due before the war were to be paid in sterling. Article V required that Congress should recommend to the several states the restoration of the confiscated estates of the Loyalists. Article IV met with determined opposition in the southern states and article V in all of the states. Practically all of the states either delayed or refused compliance. British merchants and their agents were denied admission to some states; courts were frequently closed to the debt cases; installment laws were passed; wartime interest was disallowed; and in some cases the debts were declared to have been terminated by the war and the wartime legislation of the states. On the other hand, Afro-American slaves were carried off by the British troops; American posts along the Canadian border were occupied by the British (*see* Border Forts, Evacuation of); and Indians were incited to attack the frontier.

With the adoption of the Constitution, opposed by many of the debtors, a new chapter in the debts controversy opened. The federal courts facilitated the collection of many of the debts; and the new administration was able to negotiate more effectively with England relative to the infractions of the treaty of peace. After Gouverneur Morris' mission to London an English minister, George Hammond, was sent to the United States. However, the negotiations between Hammond and Thomas Jefferson failed to settle the debt question. Nothing more was done until the strained relations of 1792–93 led to the mission of John Jay and the famous Jay's Treaty. By article VI of this treaty the United States accepted liability for such of the debts as could not at that date be recovered due to legal impediments imposed by the states. A five-man commission, to adjudicate the claims, sat at Philadelphia from May 29, 1797, to July 31, 1799. Claims to the amount of £5,638,629 8s. 1d. were received. The commissioners were unable to agree on such important matters as the jurisdiction of the commission, the nature of legal impediments, the question of the solvency of debtors, and wartime interest. The entire matter, therefore, fell again into the regular diplomatic channels. A final settlement was negotiated by Rufus King and the ministry of Henry Addington on Jan. 8, 1802. By the terms of this settlement the United States was to pay, in lieu of its liability under article VI of Jay's Treaty, the lump sum of £600,000. An English commission sat until 1811 adjusting the claims. It found only about 20–25 percent of the claims good, but even so was able to pay, with the £600,000, only about 45 percent of the approved claims.

[J. B. Moore, *International Adjudications,* vol. III.]

BEN R. BALDWIN

BRITISH PLAN OF CAMPAIGN IN THE WEST. British authorities, during the spring of 1780, were prepared to carry out a comprehensive plan for the recapture of the Illinois country and to attack St. Louis, New Orleans, and other Spanish posts on the Mississippi River. Spain, allied with France, was then the enemy of Great Britain. Four simultaneous movements were begun. Col. Henry Bird with a force from Detroit was directed to "amuse" George Rogers Clark at the Falls of the Ohio. Gen. John Campbell, from Pensacola, after taking New Orleans was to proceed up the Mississippi to Natchez, where he was to be joined by a force which was to have captured St. Louis. Capt. Charles de Langlade was to advance down the Illinois River while another party was ordered to watch Vincennes.

No part of the plan proved successful. Bird, after taking two small posts in Kentucky, retreated. Campbell, frightened at the display of strength by Gov. Bernardo de Galvez at New Orleans, remained at Pensacola. A force of British and Indians from Michilimackinac, after their first repulse at St. Louis, withdrew. Langlade retreated precipitately upon learning of the approach of Illinois cavalry.

[James A. James, *The Life of George Rogers Clark.*]

JAMES A. JAMES

BRITISH TRAVELERS IN AMERICA, EARLY. Precisely because the British and American peoples have so much in common, early British travelers were quick to note points of difference. Few failed to mention with disapproval the great use of ice and iced drinks, the sallow unhealthy look, the lack of recreation, the addiction to boarding houses, and the omnipresent rocking chair habit. American men bore additional charges of constant tobacco chewing, indiscriminate, though admittedly accurate, spitting, and sprawling with feet on chairs and tables. As for abstract social traits, Americans were credited with hospitality, good nature, and high sexual morality, but condemned for low political and business ethics, inquisitiveness, bragging, and hypersensitivity to British criticism.

Henry Wansey (visiting in 1794) and especially John Melish (1806–11) made valuable observations concerning economic life in the East and the South. Morris Birkbeck (1817–18) viewed the western frontier realistically, but with confidence in its future development. The actor John Bernard (1797–1819) excelled in genial anecdotal description. The irrepressible journalist, William Cobbett (1792–1800, 1817–18), was no more critical of America than of his own native country. Henry B. Fearon (1817–18), a trustworthy and penetrating observer, who covered 5,000 miles, concluded that the United States was the poor man's land of opportunity. On the other hand, Isaac Weld (1795–97) and Thomas Ashe (1806) were neither favorable nor always reliable; Charles William Janson (1807) was often mendacious; W. Faux (1815) was a deliberately abusive faultfinder.

After 1825 professional commentators began to replace the earlier incidental observers. British condescension toward Jacksonian democracy became evident. Frances Trollope (1827–31) was ill-tempered in tone, and her generalizations concerning particulars which she disliked led her many European readers to unfair conclusions and infuriated Americans. Captain Basil Hall (1827–28) wrote with an aristocratic political bias, and even a capable observer like Frederick Marryat (1837–39) could not approve American "mob government." Harriet Martineau (1834–36) commended Americans' shortcomings with excellent judgment. In common with nearly all British travelers she wrote scathingly of slavery. Charles Dickens (1842, 1867–68), America's most famous visitor, made justifiable criticisms, but Americans overlooked the fact that he had not spared his own country and resented it that he should criticize America at all. With the coming of such impartial observers as James Silk Buckingham (1837–40), the geologist Sir Charles Lyell (1841, 1845–46, 1852, 1853), and Alexander Mackay (1846–47), the pendulum of opinion swung back in America's favor. America must have had its attractions to change Isabella Bird (1855) from antagonism to admiration and to induce J. Richard Beste (1852) to travel for pleasure by canal, river, rail, and wagon with a wife and eleven children.

The works of these travelers as a result of their visits to America are: Thomas Ashe, *Travels in America in 1806;* J. Richard Beste, *The Wabash; or Adventures of an English Gentleman's Family in the Interior of America;* Isabella Bird, *The Englishwoman in America;* Morris Birkbeck, *Notes on a Journey in America;* James Silk Buckingham, *America: Historical, Statistic, and Descriptive,* and *The Slave States of America;* William Cobbett, *A Year's Residence in the United States of America;* Charles Dickens, *American Notes for General Circulation;* W. Faux, *Memorable Days in America: Being a Journal of a Tour to the United States;* Henry Bradshaw Fearon, *Sketches of America. A Narrative of a Journey of Five Thousand Miles Through the Eastern and Western States of America;* Basil Hall, *Travels in North America, in the Years 1827 and 1828,* and *Forty Etchings, From Sketches Made With the Camera Lucida, in North America, in 1827 and 1828;* Charles William Janson, *The Stranger in America;* Charles Lyell, *Travels in North America;* Alexander Mackay, *The Western World; or, Travels in the United States in 1846–47;* Captain Frederick Marryat, *A Diary in America, With Remarks on its Institutions,* parts one and two; Harriet Martineau, *Retrospect of Western Travel,* and *Society in America;* John Melish, *Travels in the United States, in the Years 1806, 1807, and 1809–11;* Frances M. Trollope, *Domestic Manners of the Americans;* Henry Wansey, *The Journal of an Excursion to the United States, in the Summer of 1794;* Isaac Weld, *Travels Through the States of North America, and the Provinces of Upper and Lower Canada, During the Years 1795, 1796, and 1797.* (*See also* French Travelers in America.)

[Jane L. Mesick, *The English Traveler in America, 1785–1835;* Allan Nevins, *American Social History as Recorded by British Travelers;* H. T. Tuckerman, *America and Her Commentators.*]

HARVEY L. CARTER

BROAD SEAL WAR. Following the closely contested election of 1838, two groups sought admission to Congress from New Jersey (New Jersey then electing its congressmen on a general ticket). Both held commissions bearing the great (broad) seal of the state; only the Whig commissions, however, were legally executed and signed by the governor. Charging their opponents with fraud and facing loss of control of the House, the Democratic majority refused to seat all but one Whig. When it was proved that the county clerks in Cumberland and Middlesex counties had suppressed the returns in certain townships that would have given the Democrats a majority, the House, on Feb. 28, 1840, voted to seat the five Democratic claimants.

[I. S. Kull, ed., *New Jersey, A History.*]

C. A. TITUS

BROADSIDES, a name given to sheets of paper printed on one side only. In 17th-century America broadsides were used for poetical effusions, news items, and political propaganda. In the Revolution they were used for political purposes, often reprinted in the printer's newspaper. Later they were used in political, antislavery, and temperance campaigns; also for song sheets, especially during the Civil War. Parodies often resulted. Broadsides were also used for memorials, obituaries, accounts of trials, executions, sometimes in crude poetry. Newspaper carriers used them for New Year's offerings. They have also been used for official proclamations and posters. Broadsides are ephemeral, become scarce, and increase in value. Good collections are in a few libraries.

[Carl Berger, *Broadsides and Bayonets: The Propaganda War of the American Revolution.*]

AUGUSTUS H. SHEARER

BROADWAY, a street in New York City running the length of Manhattan. Most of the lower course of Broadway is said to follow the routes of old Indian trails. In New Amsterdam its first quarter mile was called the Heerewegh or Heere Straat. The name was anglicized to Broadway about 1668. Two public wells were dug in the middle of it in 1677 and abolished in 1806. The first paving, a ten-foot strip of cobblestones on each side of an earthen center, was done in 1707. The first sidewalks, four blocks on both sides, were laid in 1790. George Washington for a time during his presidency lived at 39 Broadway. In 1852 a franchise was granted for a cable-car line on Broadway, then the city's chief residential street. The line, which was fought in the courts for more than thirty years, was finally built in 1885, but long before that time the street had ceased to be residential and had become the main business thoroughfare of the city. As it progressed northward, it followed in general the line of the Bloomingdale Road to 207th Street. Beyond the Harlem River it becomes a part of the road to Albany. The first subway line under it was begun in 1900. In the latter 19th century theaters congregated along it, first below and then above Longacre (now Times) Square, until its name became a symbol for the American theater. The first arc electric street lights in New York were placed on Broadway in 1880 and the brilliant lighting in the early 20th century brought it the nickname of the Great White Way.

[Stephen Jenkins, *The Longest Street in the World.*]

ALVIN F. HARLOW

BRODHEAD'S ALLEGHENY CAMPAIGN. Col. Daniel Brodhead set out from Fort Pitt, Aug. 11, 1779, with 600 regulars, volunteers, and a few Delaware warriors against the Seneca on the upper Allegheny. A party of Indians coming downstream was defeated, but warned the villages, and the inhabitants fled. After destroying their houses and corn, Brodhead returned to Pittsburgh. Provisional treaties were made with the Wyandot and a branch of the Shawnee that for a short time saved the frontier from invasion. (*See also* Sullivan-Clinton Campaign.)

[Louise P. Kellogg, *Frontier Advance on the Upper Ohio,* and *Frontier Retreat on the Upper Ohio.*]

JAMES A. JAMES

BRONCO, a Spanish word, early used in America to characterize hostile Indians as opposed to *Indios mansos*—gentle Indians. In time the Spaniards applied the adjective to wild horses, a usage peculiar to America. Frontiersmen borrowed the adjective and converted it into a noun, sometimes spelled *bronk* or *broncho.* The mustang is not synonymous with the bronco until caught and more or less broken. Loosely, a bronco is a range horse, a cow horse—more specifically and accurately, a range horse that pitches or bucks. Through Wild West shows, rodeos, cowboy reunions, frontier days celebrations, and the Calgary Stampede, the bronco is familiar to the American public; it is found in the remuda of every sizable ranch. The range horse is basically of Spanish (Andalusian and Arabian) stock, but in the Americas it developed a buck virtually unknown in Europe or Asia. There horses are traditionally "gentled"; but by Indians, cowboys, vaqueros, and gauchos they are "broken," usually a rough process hardly conducive to gentleness.

[William H. Carter, *The Horses of the World;* William R. Leigh, *The Western Pony.*]

J. FRANK DOBIE

BRONSON* V. *RODES, 7 Wallace 229 (1868), an action on a New York executor's bond of 1851 to repay a loan "in gold or silver coin." In 1865 the obligor tendered payment in U.S. notes, which Congress had declared "lawful money and a legal tender in payment of debts." The tender was refused and the obligor sued to cancel a mortgage securing the bond. Decrees in his favor by two state courts were reversed by the U.S. Supreme Court, which held that "express contracts to pay coined dollars are not debts which may be satisfied by the tender of U.S. Notes."

C. SUMNER LOBINGIER

BROOK FARM INSTITUTE OF AGRICULTURE AND EDUCATION, a cooperative community that grew out of the realistic social criticism of the day, touched by German Transcendentalism. George Ripley was the indefatigable and brave center of the group, which moved to a farm of 200 acres in West Roxbury, Mass., in April 1841. The members undertook to build a community in which manual and intellectual labor might be united and men and women live in a simple but cultivated society. They worked hard, erected new buildings, and did their best with the poor soil.

Ripley came to believe more organization was necessary, and an adaptation of the Fourier phalanx was adopted in 1845, with the primary departments of agricultural, domestic, and mechanic arts. Since communal living and centralized efficiency were basic to their new doctrine, they built a large phalanstery. Fire destroyed it in 1846 while the members were celebrating its completion. Money was depleted, they could not pay the promised 5 percent on investments, and the experiment had to end, but not in great debt.

Though not a financial success, Brook Farm was a great social success. Gaiety, entertainment, music, spirited talk, a successful progressive educational program with outside pupils, and a generous economic democracy were there. Although the great Transcendentalists had too little faith in external reform to join the group, Nathaniel Hawthorne, Charles A. Dana, and John S. Dwight were members and the famous of Boston and Concord came often to talk or lecture. Their interest has kept the farm in memory.

[J. R. Codman, *Brook Farm;* Lindsay Swift, *Brook Farm.*]

ALLAN MACDONALD

BROOKINGS INSTITUTION, a pioneer in the organized, independent study of problems of government relating to organization and administration, development and evaluation of policies, and the training of public service personnel. The antecedent Institute for Governmental Research was established in 1916 by a group of businessmen and educators concerned with improving the efficiency of government. Robert S. Brookings, a public-spirited St. Louis businessman, arranged financial support for the fledgling institute and also established an Institute for Economic Research and a Graduate School of Government and Economics. In 1928 he combined these to form the Brookings Institution.

Brookings Institution studies are intended to be—and are generally viewed as being—factually and analytically authoritative contributions to the public's consideration of policy issues. Some have had an immediate and direct impact upon federal actions, such as the Budget and Accounting Act of 1921, the organization of the Marshall Plan, and legislation dealing with presidential transitions. The federal government has now accepted problems of organization and personnel training as matters of its own continuing concern. Though not neglecting these areas of its earlier interest, Brookings, in consequence, has concentrated its efforts upon the analysis of public issues and evaluations of program accomplishments.

[Charles B. Saunders, Jr., *The Brookings Institution: A Fifty Year History*.]

CLARENCE H. DANHOF

BROOKLYN, a borough of New York City, located at the southwestern extremity of Long Island. The earliest recorded land grants within present-day Brooklyn date from the mid-1630's, although previous settlement by Dutch farmers seems a distinct possibility. After ferry service was established between New Amsterdam and Long Island about 1640, a town called Breuckelen, after a village in Holland, was established about a mile from the ferry slip and organized in 1646. Breuckelen (also known as Brookland, Brooklyn, and other variants) was only one of the six small towns (Bushwick, Flatbush, Flatlands, Gravesend, and New Utrecht) constituting Kings County in 1680. Population growth was modest until the 19th century, when it was spurred by the introduction of more reliable steam ferries to and from New York City in 1814 and by Irish and German immigration. In 1816 Brooklyn village, with a population of about 4,000, was chartered. Brooklyn achieved city status in 1834 and became the dominant community in Kings County, annexing Williamsburg and Bushwick in 1855 and the other outlying areas in later years, until in 1896 it had become coterminous with Kings County. Brooklyn city then ranked fourth in the country in both population and manufactures and served as a major port facility. Despite its size and independence, Brooklyn never attained full freedom from neighboring New York City. Ferry service had long tied the two together; Brooklyn Heights in the 1820's was advertised as New York's first suburb. Whereas the opening of the Brooklyn Bridge in 1883 encouraged continued growth in Brooklyn, it also connected it more securely to Manhattan, thus facilitating Brooklyn's merger with New York City in 1898.

The completion of the Williamsburg Bridge in 1903 and the Manhattan Bridge in 1909, plus the expansion of the rapid transit system throughout Brooklyn and into Manhattan, stimulated additional demographic growth. By 1925 Brooklyn had become, and still remains, the most populous borough in New York City, totaling 2,602,012 in 1970. One-fourth of this population was black and concentrated in Bedford-Stuyvesant and its environs, constituting the largest predominantly black ghetto in the United States.

[Henry R. Stiles, *A History of the City of Brooklyn;* Harold C. Syrett, *The City of Brooklyn, 1865–1898;* Ralph Foster Weld, *Brooklyn Village, 1816–1834*.]

HAROLD X. CONNOLLY

BROOKLYN BRIDGE, the first bridge built across the East River between New York City and Brooklyn, and at the time the longest of all suspension bridges. There had been talk of bridging the river as early as 1840. The corporation to build the structure was organized in 1867, the city of Brooklyn subscribing for $3 million of the stock and New York for $1.5 million. John A. Roebling was chosen chief engineer, but he died in 1869, and his son Washington completed the task. The bridge was thirteen years in building, and cost $15.5 million. It was opened on May 24, 1883.

[David McCullough, *The Great Bridge*.]

ALVIN F. HARLOW

BROOKLYN HEIGHTS, BATTLE OF. *See* **Long Island, Battle of.**

BROOKS-BAXTER WAR, a dispute between Elisha Baxter and his political opponent, Rev. Joseph Brooks, in the 1872 election for Arkansas' governor. Brooks contested his resulting loss, but the legislature supported Baxter. Baxter was inaugurated on Jan. 6,

1873. In the spring of 1874 Brooks secured a favorable state supreme court decision, but President Ulysses S. Grant ruled that the decision rested with the state legislature, which supported Baxter's claims, May 11, 1874.

[John M. Harrell, *The Brooks and Baxter War*.]

CHARLES J. FINGER

BROOKS-SUMNER AFFAIR. Sen. Charles Sumner, in the course of his famous speech, "The Crime Against Kansas," on May 19, 1856, ridiculed Sen. Andrew P. Butler of South Carolina for his devotion to "the harlot, Slavery." Two days after these remarks, Butler's nephew, Preston S. Brooks, a member of Congress from South Carolina, sought out the Massachusetts senator at his desk and, rebuking him for his insult, struck him over the head repeatedly with a cane. When the attack ended Sumner sank to the floor with injuries that incapacitated him for some years. This demonstration, and the investigation ordered by the House, heightened the tension of the sectional controversy. Brooks, who was saved from expulsion by the two-thirds rule, was praised in the South and rewarded with reelection.

ARTHUR C. COLE

BROTHERHOOD OF LOCOMOTIVE ENGINEERS. *See* **Railroad Brotherhoods.**

BROWN, FORT, at Brownsville, Texas, was established in 1846 by Gen. Zachary Taylor and named for Maj. Jacob Brown, who was killed later in that year in its defense against a Mexican attack. It was captured and held for a short time in 1859 by the Mexican brigand Juan Cortina and in the last year of the Civil War was taken from the Confederates by Union troops. From 1865 to 1944 its 288 acres were occupied by a U.S. garrison. It was declared surplus in 1946.

L. W. NEWTON

BROWNISTS, a term applied to groups in England (ca. 1580–1660) that openly separated from the established church. The term was derived from Robert Browne, author of *Reformation Without Tarrying for Anie,* 1583. Browne advocated an essentially Congregational polity, a church made up only of the visible elect who were to choose and install their own officers. Later Separatists, including the Pilgrims at Plymouth, probably owed much to Browne, as also did the settlers of Massachusetts Bay, although the latter always insisted that they had never separated from the Church of England.

[Perry Miller, *Orthodoxy in Massachusetts.*]

PERRY MILLER

BROWNSTOWN AND DETROIT TREATIES. At Detroit, Nov. 17, 1807, Gov. William Hull negotiated the cession of the Indian title to the southeast quarter of Michigan plus the portion of Ohio lying north of the Maumee. Between this tract and the settled portion of the United States lay an extensive area still in Indian possession (Ottawa, Wyandot, Chippewa, and Potawatomi). Accordingly, at Brownstown, Nov. 25, 1808, Hull negotiated a second treaty whereby title to a roadway 120 feet wide, running from Maumee Rapids to Lower Sandusky (modern Fremont) and thence southward to the Greenville Treaty line, was secured. The object of the Brownstown Treaty was to make possible travel by land to Detroit, without trespassing upon the Indian domain.

M. M. QUAIFE

BROWNSVILLE AFFAIR. Around midnight on Aug. 13, 1906, in Brownsville, Tex., an armed group of men fired indiscriminately for about ten minutes into homes and stores adjacent to Fort Brown, which was garrisoned by the black soldiers of companies B, C, and D of the First Battalion, Twenty-fifth Infantry. One townsman was killed and a policeman was wounded. Witnesses alleged that those doing the shooting were the soldiers. The next morning a handful of cartridges of a type used by the U.S. Army was found outside the fort; yet when the company commanders inspected the men's rifles that same morning, none appeared to have been fired, and an inventory revealed none of the fort's cartridges missing. A series of military inquiries and civilian grand jury investigations failed to establish the identity of those who did the shooting. On Oct. 4 an ultimatum from President Theodore Roosevelt was read to the assembled soldiers, then stationed at Fort Reno, Okla., stating that all would be discharged "without honor" unless they produced the guilty men. All maintained their innocence. Because of their "conspiracy of silence," all 167 enlisted men who had been garrisoned at Brownsville were cashiered from the army. Although Sen. Joseph B. Foraker of Ohio initiated an investigation by the Senate Committee on Military Affairs, the only result was to raise further doubts regarding the propriety of the president's action. A military court of inquiry convened by the War Department in January 1909 determined without an announced explanation that fourteen of the soldiers were eligible to reenlist. Although none of the men was ever permitted to confront or cross-examine his accusers and none was proved guilty of the crime, their discharges stood until sixty-six years later when, on Sept. 22, 1972, Secretary of the Army Robert F. Froehlke directed that the discharges be changed from "without honor" to "honorable."

[John D. Weaver, *The Brownsville Raid.*]

GEORGE L. MACGARRIGLE

BROWN UNIVERSITY was founded in 1764 in Warren, R.I., as Rhode Island College, the seventh oldest institution of higher learning in the United States. Established by Baptist clergy, the college set forth a liberal outlook in its charter, emphasizing nonsectarian principles in admissions policy and curricula. The first president, James Manning, was elected and the first students admitted in 1765; the first college commencement was held in 1769. Early efforts to relocate the school permanently resulted in its being moved to Providence in 1770. During the American Revolution, the college was closed and its University Hall was used as a barracks and hospital for American and French troops.

In 1804, the college was renamed Brown University in honor of Nicholas Brown, a generous benefactor. Francis Wayland, elected Brown's fourth president in 1827, introduced electives and a new curriculum that emphasized applied science and engineering. After the Civil War intercollegiate sports were introduced; the first master of arts degree was awarded in 1888, followed in 1889 by the awarding of the first degree of doctor of philosophy. Under the administration of Elisha Benjamin Andrews, elected Brown's eighth president in 1889, nine new departments in instruction were created, and undergraduate enrollment and faculty size increased greatly. In 1891, Pembroke College, a coordinate undergraduate school for women, was established. With William Herbert Perry Faunce as president from 1899 to 1929, the university enlarged its curriculum, inaugurated study for honors, and formally established the Graduate School.

Henry Merritt Wriston, university president from 1937 to 1955, raised Brown's status from that of a regional school to a rank of eminence among the outstanding universities of the country. Wriston brought in many outstanding faculty members, instituted important changes in the curriculum, and made the college more residential in character. An innovative six-year program leading to the degree of master of medical science was instituted in 1963. With the merger of Brown University and Pembroke College in 1971, all courses in the university became coeducational.

[Donald Fleming, *Science and Technology in Providence, 1760–1914: An Essay on the History of Brown University in the Metropolitan Community.*]

MARY GREENBERG

BROWN* V. *BOARD OF EDUCATION OF TOPEKA, two cases reaching the U.S. Supreme Court in 1954 and 1955 that were concerned with the legality of separation by race in public education. In the first case the Court held that segregation in public schools at all levels was illegal. In the second case it held that the pace of desegregation in schools was the responsibility of school authorities, would depend on the problems and conditions facing the individual community, and should be carried out "with all deliberate speed." After the 1955 decision, the case was returned to federal district courts for implementation. While *Brown* v. *Board of Education,* 347 U.S. 483 (1954), reversed *Plessy* v. *Ferguson* (1896), with its "separate but equal" ruling on railroad accommodations, the 1954 ruling came as a culmination of the legal debate on segregation in education before the courts since 1938. The earlier debate included the cases of *Gaines* v. *Canada* (1938), *Sipuel* v. *University of Oklahoma* (1948), *Sweatt* v. *Painter* (1950), *McLaurin* v. *Oklahoma State Regents* (1950), and *Byrd* v. *McCready* (1950). The *Brown* decision reflected no major shift of positions by the Court. The furor caused by the decision is more of a reflection on the opposition to the finding than on the novelty of the legal position.

Oliver Brown sued the Topeka, Kans., Board of Education when his daughter was denied admission to the school near her home because of her race. En route to the Supreme Court the case was combined with cases from three other states and one from the District of Columbia (*Davis* v. *County School Board of Prince Edward County, Harry Briggs, Jr.* v. *R. W. Elliot, Gebhart* v. *Bolton,* and *Bolling* v. *Sharpe*). In its 1954 decision the Court held that to separate Afro-American school children by race induces a sense of inferiority that retards educational and mental development, that "separate education facilities are inherently unequal," and that the plaintiffs were "by reason of the segregation complained of, deprived of the equal protection of the laws guaranteed by the Fourteenth Amendment." The decision limited its disapproval of the *Plessy* doctrine of "separate but equal" to education. Nevertheless it was construed to mean that racial segregation was not permissible in other public facilities; later Court action supported this view.

[Morroe Berger, *Equality by Statute;* Loren Miller, *The Petitioner.*]

HENRY N. DREWRY

BROWN* V. *MARYLAND, 12 Wheaton 419 (1827), a case relating to the right of a state to control the sale of imported merchandise. It afforded Justice John Marshall an opportunity to supplement his first opinion on the meaning of the commerce clause of the Constitution as originally stated in *Gibbons* v. *Ogden*.

Affirmed by the court of appeals, the case came to the Supreme Court on a writ of error. Marshall's opinion reversed the affirmation on the ground that the Constitution prohibits a state from levying imposts or duties on imports or exports, except what may be "absolutely necessary for executing its inspection laws." The principles stated have been upheld by nearly all courts that have dealt with the subject of commerce. (*See also* Original Package Doctrine.)

[A. J. Beveridge, *John Marshall,* vol. 4.]

THOMAS ROBSON HAY

BRUSSELS MONETARY CONFERENCE (Nov. 22–Dec. 17, 1892), authorized by the Sherman Silver Purchase Act, failed because Great Britain rejected American proposals for increasing silver coinage; the Americans rejected the British plan for small European silver purchases. This, with other circumstances, caused the repeal of the Sherman silver act.

W. C. MALLALIEU

BRYAN-CHAMORRO TREATY, a treaty between the United States and Nicaragua, signed by Secretary of State William Jennings Bryan and Nicaragua's Washington minister, Emiliano Chamorro, on Aug. 5, 1914. It granted to the United States in perpetuity the exclusive right to build an interoceanic canal in Nicaragua, subject to a subsequent agreement regarding details of construction and operation; and also a ninety-nine-year lease of Great and Little Corn islands and a right to establish a naval base in the Gulf of Fonseca. Nicaragua received $3 million.

Costa Rica and El Salvador protested against the treaty. Costa Rica claimed that an arbitral award by President Grover Cleveland in 1888 had bound Nicaragua not to make grants for canal purposes without consulting Costa Rica because of its interest in the San Juan River. El Salvador asserted that the waters of the Gulf of Fonseca belonged jointly to El Salvador, Nicaragua, and Honduras. Both appealed to the Central American Court, which decided that Nicaragua had violated its neighbors' rights and should take steps to restore the legal status existing before the treaty. It did not declare the treaty itself invalid, because it had no jurisdiction over the United States. Nicaragua refused to accept the decision and the treaty remained in force. The proposed naval base was never established and the Corn Islands remained under Nicaraguan jurisdiction, except for a small area used by the United States for a lighthouse.

[Thomas A. Bailey, "Interest in a Nicaraguan Canal, 1903–1931," *Hispanic American Historical Review,* vol. 16 (1936); I. J. Cox, *Nicaragua and the United States, 1909–1927.*]

DANA G. MUNRO

BRYAN'S STATION was established in 1779 in Kentucky (near Lexington) by four Bryan brothers from North Carolina. The occupants of this parallelogram of some forty cabins withstood several Indian attacks, the most important of which occurred in August 1782, when they were besieged by about 300 Indians and Canadians under Capt. William Caldwell and Simon Girty. The Battle of Blue Licks occurred about sixty miles northeast three days later.

[Reuben T. Durrett, *Bryan's Station.*]

JONATHAN T. DORRIS

BUCCANEERS, or Freebooters, terms commonly applied to the adventurers who infested the West Indies in the 16th, 17th, and 18th centuries. Among themselves they were known as Brethren of the Coast. It seems probable that a group of Normans early settled on an island, perhaps Tortuga, and organized themselves into a small band, living off wild animals and preying upon the neighboring Spanish colonies. They formed a picturesque lot, traveling in pairs, living in the open, dyeing their clothes in blood, and going about heavily armed. The Spaniards soon began to attack these groups and to destroy the wild cattle and swine that were their principal source of food. Driven to self-defense and finally to open warfare with Spain, they took to the sea and began a career of piracy, plunder, murder, and rapine, attacking Spanish commerce and colonial towns. This life appealed to many individuals of various nationalities, and the number of buccaneers increased rapidly. But about 1670 a partial stop was put to this piracy in the Caribbean and some of the buccaneers went to the Pacific to continue their profession. Finally by the Treaty of Ryswick in 1697 buccaneering was practically suppressed. Among the picturesque leaders of the buccaneers were Pierre La Grand, François l'Olonnais, Sir Henry Morgan, Jacques Cassard, Edward Teach (Blackbeard), Bartholomew Roberts, and François Thurot.

[Maurice Besson, *The Scourge of the Indies;* Alfred Sternbeck, *Filibusters and Buccaneers.*]

A. CURTIS WILGUS

BUCKBOARDS. Originally designed for personal transportation in mountain regions, these distinctively American four-wheeled vehicles, with one seat resting upon elastic boards fastened directly to the axles, were widely used in newly settled sections.

HARVEY L. CARTER

BUCKLAND RACES (Oct. 19, 1863). Confederate Gen. J. E. B. Stuart, with Gen. Wade Hampton's cavalry division, covering Robert E. Lee's retirement from Bristoe to the Rappahannock near Buckland Mills, Va., turned on H. J. Kilpatrick's pursuing Union cavalry, while Fitzhugh Lee's division charged the Union flank. Kilpatrick was routed, fleeing five miles to Haymarket and Gainesville. The Confederates derisively called the affair "Buckland Races."

[J. W. Thomason, Jr., *Jeb Stuart.*]

JOSEPH MILLS HANSON

BUCKSHOT WAR. As a result of the state election of 1838, members of the Democratic party and members of the Whig and Anti-Masonic opposition both claimed control of the Pennsylvania House of Representatives. Two speakers were elected. A mob, largely from Philadelphia, assembled in Harrisburg, threatened violence, and forced Thaddeus Stevens, leader of the opposition, Charles B. Penrose, and Thomas H. Burrowes to escape from the senate chamber through a window. Gov. Joseph Ritner called for U.S. troops which President Andrew Jackson refused, whereupon the governor called out the Philadelphia militia, requisitioning among other equipment thirteen rounds of buckshot cartridges, whence the name "Buckshot War." The opposition was defeated when three Whigs voted with the Democrats, thus enabling them to organize the house and restore order.

[H. R. Mueller, *The Whig Party in Pennsylvania.*]

H. H. SHENK

BUCK STOVE AND RANGE CASE. In 1906 the metal polishers in the Buck Stove and Range Company, St. Louis, struck for a nine-hour day. The American Federation of Labor put the company on their "unfair list," whereupon the company obtained a sweeping injunction forbidding this boycott. For refusal to obey, Samuel Gompers, John Mitchell, and Frank Morrison were sentenced to prison for contempt, but did not serve. The case was outlawed in 1914 by the Supreme Court under the statute of limitations (*see* Clayton Act).

[H. W. Laidler, *Boycotts and the Labor Struggle.*]

H. U. FAULKNER

BUCKTAILS (1818–26), a faction of the New York Democratic-Republican party opposed to the canal policy of Gov. DeWitt Clinton. The name was originally applied to Tammany Society members and was taken from the Tammany insignia, a deer's tail worn in the hat.

[J. D. Hammond, *Political History of the State of New York.*]

MILTON W. HAMILTON

BUDGET, DIRECTOR OF THE. *See* **Office of Management and Budget.**

BUENAVENTURA RIVER, a mythical river, erroneously depicted on early Spanish and American maps. The maps showed a river flowing from the Rocky Mountains into Great Salt Lake and emptying into the Pacific Ocean. Some overland emigrant parties even expected to reach California in boats. As late as 1844 John C. Frémont was searching for this fabulous river.

[Allan Nevins, *Frémont, the West's Greatest Adventurer.*]

JEANNE ELIZABETH WIER

BUENA VISTA, BATTLE OF (Feb. 22–23, 1847). During the Mexican War Gen. Zachary Taylor had advanced his army of 4,700 men from Monterrey to a mountain pass south of Saltillo. Near the hacienda of Buena Vista he encountered a Mexican force under Gen. Antonio López de Santa Anna three times the size of his own. Though the Americans lost ground the first day, they won a brilliant victory on the second, and the Mexicans withdrew. Taylor gained a reputation which aided him in his bid for the presidency, but the further conquest of Mexico was entrusted to Gen. Winfield Scott.

[N. W. Stephenson, *Texas and the Mexican War*.]

L. W. NEWTON

BUFFALO, or more properly the American bison, at the time of the discovery of the New World ranged over about one-third of the continent from sixty-three degrees north latitude in Canada to about twenty-five degrees north latitude in Mexico, and from the Blue Mountains of Oregon to the western portions of New York, Pennsylvania, Virginia, and the Carolinas. The chief habitat was the plains between the Missouri River and the Rocky Mountains. Fossil remains date to the mid-Pleistocene period.

Easily hunted and of large size—the males reaching 2,000 pounds—the buffalo were everywhere a favorite source of food for the Indians and frontier settlers. As civilization advanced westward the animals were exterminated and by 1850 few if any remained east of the Mississippi. The dry plains, however, still contained numbers so vast as to be almost impossible of computation. Gen. Philip H. Sheridan, in 1866, estimated 100 million buffalo in the region between Camp Supply in Indian Territory and Fort Dodge, Kans., and this was only part of the western buffalo.

Plains Indians based their civilization and religion to a large extent on the buffalo, as those farther east based theirs on the maize. Methods of killing included stalking, stampeding herds over cliffs, and driving them into culs-de-sac. When horses were introduced in the plains, the methods of pursuit and the surround were added. Every part of the buffalo was useful to the Indians, who depended on the bison for food, shelter, weapons, and clothing. Natural increase kept pace with the slaughter until the advent of the white man.

The building of the Union Pacific and Kansas Pacific railroads, the early trains of which were sometimes stopped by herds crossing the tracks, led to the disappearance of the animals in the central plains, and by 1875 there were two distinct groups, the northern and southern. The railroads furnished transportation outlets and in the 1870's hide and meat hunters began a systematic and wholesale destruction, shipping robes and meat to the East. By 1878 the southern herd was practically extinct, although the four last survivors were not killed until 1899. Similarly the northern herd was exterminated by 1844, except for a few individuals. Buffalo bones, gathered by settlers, later were important in commerce.

William T. Hornaday, of the National Museum, first called the nation's attention to the virtual disappearance of the buffalo in 1886. He made a census in 1889 which showed a total of only 1,091 American bison existing throughout the world. This was the low ebb. Many individuals became interested, and in 1905 the American Bison Society was organized. Through its efforts public consciousness was aroused and there are now managed herds on government reservations, with nearly 1,400 buffalo, small groups of buffalo in state parks, and many private breeders, eliminating the danger of complete extinction.

[Wayne Gard, *The Great Buffalo Hunt;* Francis Haines, *The Buffalo;* Tom McHugh, *The Time of the Buffalo;* Frank G. Rose, *The North American Buffalo.*]

PAUL I. WELLMAN

BUFFALO, the second largest city in New York State, located at the eastern tip of Lake Erie, twenty miles southeast of Niagara Falls. It was named for Buffalo Creek, which in the French occupation was known as Rivière aux Chevaux. There are many theories to account for the translation of *chevaux* to buffalo; none has been fully substantiated. When in 1799 Dutch land speculators (the Holland Land Company) bought most of the Phelps-Gorham purchase, consisting of a million acres west of the Genesee River, they commissioned Joseph Ellicott to survey and offer for sale lots in a village on Buffalo Creek, to be called New Amsterdam. The Dutch name never was generally used, and when the village became the county seat in 1807 it officially took the new name. The town was completely burned by the British and Indians in December 1813, but was rapidly rebuilt. It became the terminus of the Erie Canal in 1825 and was a city by 1832.

Buffalo's location aided its development during the 20th century into a major industrial city and port. The city has been a port on the St. Lawrence Seaway since 1957, and is one of the most active ports on the Great Lakes. It is connected to Canada by a railroad bridge and the Peace Bridge (opened 1927). Its many industries, including steel, electric products, and grain storage, have access to the enormous amount of hydroelectric power supplied by Niagara Falls and have helped Buffalo grow to a city of over 460,000 inhabitants.

[R. W. Bingham, *The Cradle of the Queen City;* F. H. Severance, *An Old Frontier of France.*]

JULIAN PARK

BUFFALO CHIPS, the dried excrement of the American bison, widely used for fuel by American Indians and the first white men on the Great Plains.

EVERETT DICK

BUFFALO TRAILS. The first thoroughfares of North America, save for the time-obliterated paths of mastodon, musk-ox, and Mound Builders, were the traces made by buffalo and deer in seasonal migration and in quest of—or between—feeding grounds and salt licks. Many of these routes, hammered by countless hoofs instinctively following watersheds and the crests of ridges in avoidance of summer muck and winter snowdrifts, were followed by the Indians as courses to hunting grounds and as warriors' paths; they were invaluable to explorers and adopted by pioneers. Buffalo traces were characteristically north and south; but their major east-west trails—through Cumberland Gap, along the New York watershed, from the Potomac River through the Allegheny divide to the Ohio headwaters, through the Blue Ridge Mountains to upper Kentucky—anticipated the courses of trunk railways. Sen. Thomas Benton saluted these sagacious pathmakers by stating that the buffalo blazed the way for the railroads to the Pacific.

[A. B. Hulbert, *Historic Highways of America,* vol. I.]

E. DOUGLAS BRANCH

BUFFER STATE. *See* **Indian Barrier State.**

BUFFINGTON ISLAND SKIRMISH (July 19, 1863), in Meigs County, Ohio, contributed to the capture of the Confederate raider, Gen. John Morgan, who was seeking to escape across the Ohio River at a ford opposite Buffington Island (*see* Morgan's Raids). Delayed overnight, he was almost surrounded by Union cavalry next day and the battle ended in a rout. Morgan and 1,200 men escaped, but the raid finally ended in his capture at Salineville on July 26.

[Whitelaw Reid, *Ohio in the War,* vol. I.]

EUGENE H. ROSEBOOM

BUFORD EXPEDITION. As part of the effort to make Kansas a slave state (*see* Border War; Kansas Struggle), Col. Jefferson Buford of Eufaula, Ala., in April 1856 organized and equipped for settlement, mostly at his own expense, 400 men mainly from Alabama, Georgia, and South Carolina. In Kansas, Buford's men participated in many of the conflicts between the free and slave state factions.

[W. L. Fleming, "The Buford Expedition to Kansas," *American Historical Review,* vol. 6.]

HENRY T. SHANKS

BUILDING AND LOAN ASSOCIATIONS. For a century after the founding of the first building and loan association in Frankford, Pa., in 1831, these were local private cooperative credit agencies lending on home mortgages, generally with monthly amortization payments. In 1875 New York provided the first state supervision of such agencies; in 1877 Pennsylvania associations formed a league; and in 1892 came nationwide organization. The strength of the local associations was in low cost of operation, which depended on members' knowledge of neighborhood real estate values. Their weaknesses were dependence of the individual association solely on its own resources and inability to combat widespread economic fluctuations. Sporadic failures during the depression of the 1890's became epidemic in the catastrophic depression of the 1930's. At that time the federal government provided subsidies to the building and loan associations that carried corresponding regulation. The Reconstruction Finance Corporation (1932) made loans to building associations; in the same year the Federal Home Loan Bank System provided a central credit facility to supplement resources of the member institutions. The Home Owners Loan Act of 1933 promoted the chartering of associations under the Federal Home Loan Bank Board, creating an organization somewhat like the Federal Reserve System. In 1934 the Federal Savings and Loan Insurance Corporation, guaranteeing mortgages, was a benefit of the National Housing Act. In addition to these direct aids, the emphasis placed by the government on home building was a powerful help. This was true because savings in the associations is countercyclical, greater in dull times when, in the absence of special government programs, home construction lapses and the associations lack opportunities to invest their funds.

Federal Housing Administration and Veterans Administration loans by building associations have increased, though in 1971 conventional loans still constituted almost 86 percent of the funds extended (FHA and VA loans involve red tape delays, and associations sometimes have found the fixed rate of interest unacceptable). The assets of savings and loan associations stood at the end of 1972 at $243.6 billion, more than double the figure of eight years earlier. These organizations are the third largest financial intermediary in the nation; only commercial banks and life insurance companies have greater assets. Laws and regulations have broadened the services of the associations, permitting the transfer of savings to third parties and the financing of mobile homes.

[G. M. Gerloff, ed., *Federal Home Loan Bank System;* Savings and Loan League, *Savings and Loan Fact Book.*]

BROADUS MITCHELL

BUILDING MATERIALS. The Indian peoples of North America had developed mature building techniques suitable to Neolithic cultures long before Europeans established their first settlements on the continent. The materials of Indian construction were always those that were locally available and could be easily worked by primitive hand-and-tool techniques. In the eastern area of America, forests covered most of the land, and building accordingly consisted of gabled, domed, or vaulted frames built up of branches or light trunks and covered with bark, thatch, or wattle and daub. On the prairies the cunningly made collapsible tent of nomadic tribes was constructed of a conical framework of saplings covered with skins. Permanent structures in the northern areas were circular in outline, framed in substantial timbers, and covered with a thick layer of mud and grass for insulation against the cold and for protection against snow and wind. In the Sierras, where snow was the chief problem, steeply pitched frames of trunks and branches were covered with heavy slabs of wood rudely shaped from trunks split by wind. Variations on these structures, built with larger openings and covered with thatch, appeared in the warmer coastal areas.

In the deserts of the Southwest, where wood was scarce and heat insulation a necessity, the large communal structures known as pueblos were constructed in tiered series of rectangular apartments with thick walls of adobe (sun-dried brick) and with roofs composed of branches laid on transverse log beams and covered in turn with a heavy blanket of clay. In the canyons of upper New Mexico and lower Colorado, suitable clays for brick were scarce, but there were extensive outcroppings of sandstone that could be easily broken off into building stones. The Indians who penetrated the canyons constructed their pueblos of thin sandstone tablets laid up with astonishing skill either on the alluvial floor or on shelves and notches eroded in the canyon walls.

The Europeans who established the American colonies in the 17th century brought their knowledge of materials and techniques from their native lands, but during the first few years of settlement they were often compelled to adopt the simpler Indian techniques. The English, Dutch, German, and French who settled the seaboard and Gulf coast areas brought variations on framing in sawn timbers, which were usually covered with clapboard siding for walls and shingles for roofs—the latter gradually giving way to slate and tile in the more elegant houses, especially those built by the Dutch. Construction in thick wooden planks set vertically came to be common in parts of the Connecticut Valley, while construction of solid walls built up of horizontally laid logs was introduced by Swedish settlers in the Delaware Valley. The only stone in these early structures was confined to foundations and chimneys. Joints were originally the mortise-and-tenon form secured by wooden pegs, but hand-wrought nails began to be used early in the 17th century and machine-made varieties in the late 18th century.

In the more costly forms of buildings, brick laid up in lime mortar slowly replaced timber construction in the English-speaking areas, but expensive stone masonry was confined largely to the Dutch settlements of the New York area. Adobe brick was nearly universal as a structural material in the Spanish Southwest, while kiln-baked stucco-covered brick was confined mainly to the mission churches of the 18th century, the domed and vaulted construction of which could be accomplished only in the stronger, more manageable material.

All the traditional materials of European building came into use during the colonial period, and they were continued throughout the predominantly agrarian phase in the history of the Republic. Heavy power-sawed timbers were used as posts, sills, girders, rafters, joists, and braces in buildings and truss bridges; deep laminated timbers of bolted planks were developed early in the 19th century for the arch ribs of bridges; the thinner sections, like the two-by-four that was soon to become universal, became the basis of the light balloon frame invented in 1833.

Carefully dressed masonry work of both stone and brick began to appear in large and elegant forms as the nation expanded. The common and long-familiar structural forms of walls, buttresses, vaults, and domes were used in public buildings, while massive arches of Roman form were adapted to the requirements of railway viaducts from 1830 on.

Iron. The most far-reaching revolution in the building arts came with the introduction of iron as a primary building material. Although it was first used as early as 1770 in England, it did not appear in the United States until about 1810, and then only in the form of wrought-iron braces and ties for timber arch-and-truss bridges. Cast-iron columns were first used in Philadelphia in 1822, and the cast-iron building front combined with interior cast-iron columns reached a well-developed form in New York by 1848. The first cast-iron arch bridge was erected in 1836–39, exactly sixty years after the English prototype. The first iron truss, again composed entirely of the cast metal, was introduced in 1840. Cast iron, however, is relatively weak in tension and therefore had to be replaced by wrought iron for beams and other horizontal elements as buildings and bridges grew larger and the loads upon them increased. The wrought-iron roof truss was introduced in 1837 and the combination cast- and wrought-iron bridge truss in 1845, both in the Philadelphia area. Wrought-iron floor beams of a depth adequate to the new commercial structures appeared almost simultaneously in three New York buildings in 1854. The first, though unsuccessful, application of metal wire to the suspension bridge was made in Philadelphia in 1816, but the continuous history of this valuable invention did not begin until 1842, when a second wire-cable suspension bridge was completed over the Schuylkill River.

Concrete and Steel. The rise of the new industrial nation following the Civil War was marked by two fundamental innovations in building construction: the introduction of steel and concrete as primary materials. The first appeared initially in two bridges erected almost simultaneously: James B. Ead's bridge at St. Louis (1868–74) is a steel-arch structure, and the deck of John A. Roebling's Brooklyn Bridge (1869–83) is suspended from steel cables. The history of steel in buildings is more complex. The first elevator buildings of New York and Chicago were constructed in combinations of masonry bearing walls and internal iron columns. The iron frame was expanded and elaborated during the 1870's and early 1880's to the point at which all internal loads were carried on cast-iron columns and wrought-iron floor beams. The decisive steps in skeletal or skyscraper construction came in Chicago: the first steel girders were introduced in the Home Insurance Building (1884–85), and the first all-steel frame came with the second Rand McNally Building (1889–90). Certain of these pivotal innovations in framed construction were anticipated in the Produce Exchange of New York (1881–84).

Hydraulic concrete, originally a Roman invention, was revived in the late 18th century. Composed of lime (as a cementing agent), water, sand, and gravel or broken stone aggregate, it is virtually unlimited in use because its plastic state before setting allows it to be cast in any structural shape. The hydraulic property comes from the presence of clayey materials in the lime, and before the technique of artificially producing the proper mixture was developed, builders had to depend on a supply of natural cement rock from which the hydraulic lime could be made. The regular use of concrete in the United States began in 1818, when deposits of cement rock were discovered in New York during construction of the Erie Canal. The first poured concrete house was constructed in 1835, and the first of precast block in 1837, both in the immediate area of New York City. The American manufacture of artificial cement was established in 1871; the use of mass concrete in walls, footings, jetties, dams, and arch bridges spread rapidly during the remainder of the century.

Plain concrete has little tensile strength and must be reinforced with iron or steel rods in order to sustain tensile and shearing stresses. Although the first experiments in this novel technique were carried out in England, France, and Germany, the first reinforced concrete structure was a house built in Port Chester, N.Y., 1871–76. The leading American pioneer in large-scale commercial and industrial building was Ernest Ransome, who built the first reinforced concrete bridge in 1889 and developed mature forms of reinforced concrete framing during the 1890's.

Few entirely new structural materials were introduced after 1900, but ferrous metals emerged in various chemical and mechanical alterations. The 20th century saw the revival of chromium steel for the skyscrapers of the 1920's and the adaptation of self-weathering steel to structural uses in 1962. The major innovation in methods of joining members came with the application of electric arc welding to steel framing in 1920. Aluminum made its initial appearance as a structural material in 1933, when it was used for the floor framing of a bridge at Pittsburgh, Pa. Its role expanded to the primary structural elements of a bridge at Massena, N.Y., in 1946. The use of stressed-skin construction, with aluminum as a sheathing material, came with an experimental house of 1946, although similar construction in thin steel plate had been introduced in 1928.

The materials of reinforced concrete remained unchanged but were used in novel ways with the coming of shells (1934) and prestressed members (1938). Wood returned to large buildings in the form of heavy glued-laminated ribs and beams, appearing for the first time in the United States in 1937. Tubular forms of steel and aluminum came with the first geodesic dome of 1947. Plastics as a sheathing material were introduced in two conservatory buildings in St. Louis in 1962, but their use as a structural material came only in the 1970's.

Nonstructural Materials in Buildings. Nonstructural materials include a great multitude of substances, which may be conveniently divided into those used for the building envelope and its internal enclosures and those suitable for mechanical and electrical utilities. In the first category are the traditional materials of plaster, stucco, paint, varnish, finishing oils, and glass—followed in the late 19th century and the 20th century by glass block and by synthetic wallboards of plaster, cement, glued wood fibers, and plywood. Insulating and sheathing materials include asbestos, tile, lightweight concrete, cork, various fibers, plastic foams, and plastic sheets. In the second category are plain and galvanized sheet metal; pipe of brass, copper, iron, steel, and clay; wire; electrical insulation of rubber; plastics; glass; fibers; and a variety of ceramic materials. Prefabricated buildings and railroad cars by the mid-20th century came to be composed of synthetic materials manufactured out of every kind of traditional building material.

[Carl W. Condit, *American Building: Materials and Techniques;* James M. Fitch, *American Building: The Historical Forces That Shaped It.*]

CARL W. CONDIT

BUILDINGS. *See* **Architecture.**

BULGE, BATTLE OF THE, a German counteroffensive in World War II, so named from a 40-mile-wide and 60-mile-deep bulge created in American lines. It was the greatest pitched battle ever fought by U.S. troops, involving 600,000 Americans, more than three times the number that fought on both sides at Gettysburg.

As German armies retreated from France in late summer 1944, Adolf Hitler believed that once winter weather had limited the effectiveness of Allied aircraft, he might regain the initiative by a counteroffensive in the semimountainous Ardennes region of Belgium and Luxembourg, scene of German triumphs in 1914 and 1940 and a sector that the Americans held thinly in order to concentrate troops elsewhere for attacks. Over objections of his field commanders, who deemed resources inadequate for such a plan, Hitler aimed at the Belgian port of Antwerp, intending thereby to cut off to the north the British 21st Army Group and the U.S. First and Ninth armies; these forces eliminated, he hoped to gain a negotiated peace on the western front.

While holding the Allies through the autumn to minor penetrations beyond the German frontier, the German commander, Field Marshal Gerd von Rundstedt, secretly massed more than 200,000 men and 1,200 tanks in the wooded Eifel region opposite the Ardennes. Through snow and fog on Dec. 16, three German armies struck along a 60-mile front against seven American divisions of the First Army's 5th and 8th Corps. Surprise was total, but only at one point did the Germans achieve the swift breakthroughs essential to success of their plan: a tank-infantry task force of the 1st SS Panzer Division penetrated north of Saint Vith and continued westward virtually unchecked.

In the north the U.S. 78th Infantry Division held at Monschau, and the 2nd and 99th divisions, in an epic stand, staved off tanks of the Sixth Panzer Army at Elsenborn Ridge. Although two regiments of the 106th Division were surrounded and eventually captured near Saint Vith, the reserve 7th Armored Division helped deny that town's road net to the Fifth Panzer Army for six days. In the center the 28th Infantry Division fought a grudging delaying action across northern Luxembourg, slowing a German drive on the Belgian road center of Bastogne. In the south, near Echternach, the 4th Division and part of the 9th Armored Division gave some ground to the German Seventh Army but successfully blocked the southern shoulder of the penetration. Even when surrounded, American troops fought with grim determination, and stragglers often delayed German columns with hastily formed roadblocks. The German drive was thus seriously slowed, contained at both shoulders, and constricted by lack of roads.

On the second day the supreme Allied commander, Gen. Dwight D. Eisenhower, and the Twelfth Army Group commander, Lt. Gen. Omar N. Bradley, rushed reinforcements. Two-thirds of the 10th Armored Division headed for the southern shoulder, the rest for Bastogne along with the 101st Airborne Division. The 82nd Airborne Division hurried to blunt the task force of the 1st SS Panzer Division. Other units began to build a line westward from the Elsenborn

Ridge lest the Germans turn north toward supply depots around Liège.

In spite of the American defense German gains by the fourth day, Dec. 19, had split the Twelfth Army Group, severing lateral communications between the Third Army to the south and the First and Ninth armies. This prompted Eisenhower to put the northern armies under the Twenty-first Army Group commander, Field Marshal Bernard L. Montgomery, which later led to recrimination when American commanders held that Montgomery claimed undue credit for the German defeat.

The Germans surrounded Bastogne on Dec. 20. The American Third Army on the 22nd began to drive to Bastogne's relief, and German panzer divisions striving for the Meuse River were slowed by gasoline shortages. On Dec. 23 the weather cleared, enabling Allied planes to attack German columns and drop supplies at Bastogne. When the 2nd Armored Division on Christmas Day wiped out a panzer division at Celles, four miles from the Meuse, that was the high-water mark of the counteroffensive.

Admitting that the Meuse and Antwerp were beyond reach, Hitler nevertheless hoped to anchor his south flank on Bastogne and drive north to encircle American troops near Aachen. Thus, severe fighting continued at Bastogne, even after the 4th Armored Division lifted the siege on Dec. 26. The First and Third armies, nevertheless, began to counterattack Jan. 3, 1945, driving to a juncture north of Bastogne at Houffalize on Jan. 16 and precipitating slow German withdrawal. The last of the "bulge" was eliminated on Jan. 28.

The Americans incurred 81,000 casualties—19,000 killed, and 15,000 captured; British casualties totaled 1,400. German losses totaled approximately 100,000. Each side lost 800 tanks. The counteroffensive delayed a final Allied offensive against Germany for six weeks, but in expending his last reserves, Hitler had crippled the defense of Germany on both eastern and western fronts.

[H. M. Cole, *The Ardennes: Battle of the Bulge*.]

CHARLES B. MACDONALD

BULLBOATS. When Hudson's Bay Company traders first visited the Mandan Indians in 1790 they found that the tribe possessed tublike boats with frameworks of willow poles, covered with raw buffalo hides. Later, frontiersmen who ascended the Missouri River noted this light, convenient shallow-draft boat. From 1810 to 1830, American fur traders on the tributaries of the Missouri regularly built boats eighteen to thirty feet long, using the methods of construction employed by the Indians in making their circular boats. These elongated bullboats were capable of transporting two tons of fur down the shallow waters of the Platte.

[Phil E. Chappell, *A History of the Missouri River*.]

CARL P. RUSSELL

BULLDOZE. In 1875, during the Reconstruction period, a federal marshal was investigating an attempt to assassinate a registrar of voters in East Feliciana Parish, La. The natives refused him all information, and as the marshal stood pondering he was approached by a half-witted German who shouted, "Bull dooza mit der hooza!" The expletive had no meaning whatsoever, but to the frightened marshal it sounded like a threat from the Ku Klux Klan and he fled, which result was so satisfactory that the term "bulldoze" came into general use throughout the South, with the generic meaning to intimidate in a bullying manner.

[T. Jones Cross, "The True Etymology of Bulldoze," *Proceedings of the Historical Society of East and West Baton Rouge* (1918).]

MILLEDGE L. BONHAM, JR.

BULL GARRISON HOUSE, located on Tower Hill, South Kingstown, R.I. On Dec. 15, 1675, during King Philip's War, it was attacked and burned by the Narragansett Indians, fifteen of its defenders losing their lives.

HOWARD M. CHAPIN

BULLION. *See* **Bimetallism.**

BULL MOOSE PARTY, a popular nickname given to the Progressive party of 1912–16, which nominated Theodore Roosevelt for the presidency at a national convention in Chicago, Ill., in August 1912. The Progressives seceded from the Republican party following the renomination of President William H. Taft. The name itself was a tribute to Roosevelt, who often used the term "bull moose" to describe the strength and vigor of a person.

Thus he wrote, following his nomination for the vice-presidency on the Republican ticket in 1900, in a letter to Sen. Mark A. Hanna, "I am as strong as a bull moose and you can use me to the limit." Also, when shot by a would-be assassin in Milwaukee, Wis., on the evening of Oct. 14, 1912, he insisted on immediately filling an engagement to speak, saying to the audience, "It takes more than that to kill a bull moose."

The party was in large part reunited with and reabsorbed into the Republican party during the campaign of 1916, after the nomination of Charles Evans Hughes, who was acceptable to Roosevelt and the leading Progressives.

[J. B. Bishop, *Theodore Roosevelt and His Time.*]

WILLIAM STARR MYERS

BULL RUN, FIRST BATTLE OF (July 21, 1861), the first major engagement of the Civil War, known in the Confederacy as the Battle of Manassas, has been described as "the best planned and worst fought battle." The principal Union army, under Gen. Irvin McDowell, was mobilized about Washington. Union Gen. Robert Patterson, with a smaller army, was sent to "retain" Confederate Gen. Joseph E. Johnston in the Shenandoah Valley. Gen. Pierre G. T. Beauregard, with his southern army, occupied the line of Bull Run Creek, which lies across the main highways from Washington southward. His advance force under Gen. M. L. Bonham was based at Fairfax Courthouse to watch McDowell's army. McDowell had available about 30,000 men and forty-nine guns; Beauregard, about 22,000 men and twenty-nine guns; Johnston, about 9,000 to Patterson's 12,000. None of these armies was thoroughly organized or disciplined.

Public opinion compelled President Abraham Lincoln to order McDowell to move forward. The Union advance guard drove in Bonham's pickets on July 17. In accordance with previous orders, Bonham withdrew to Centreville, waited until dark, then retired behind Bull Run where the road from Washington to Richmond crossed at Mitchell's Ford and where Beauregard expected the main attack. The Confederates were disposed as follows: Gen. Richard S. Ewell held the right at Union Mills Ford below the Orange and Alexandria Railroad; Gen. D. R. Jones protected McLean's Ford two miles upstream; Gen. James Longstreet held Blackburn's Ford a mile above; Bonham was a mile and a half farther on; Col. P. St. George Cocke guarded Ball's Ford and Lewis' Ford, one and one-half miles and two and one-half miles above Mitchell's Ford; a mile farther Col. N. G. Evans held the Stone Bridge where the Warrenton Turnpike crossed Bull Run. Thus the Confederate line extended about eight miles behind a shallow, meandering creek. Ewell was supported by Gen. T. H. Holmes' brigade, while Col. Jubal Early was behind Jones and Longstreet. Gen. Daniel Tyler, commanding McDowell's advance force, on his own initiative, made a reconnaissance in force on July 18, but was sharply repulsed by Longstreet and Bonham aided by Early (*see* Blackburn's Ford, Battle at).

Eluding Patterson, Johnston and part of his army reached Bull Run on Saturday, July 20. Though the ranking officer, Johnston did not assume personal direction of the Confederate operations until the middle of the ensuing battle, meanwhile stationing his troops on the slope behind Beauregard's line. McDowell and Beauregard planned to turn each other's flank. Ewell, on the Confederate right, was to cross Bull Run at daylight of July 21, the other brigades to follow. Beauregard's order did not reach Ewell. Longstreet, after crossing, waited in vain for word of his attack. By 7 A.M., when Jones received his orders, Union brigade commanders William T. Sherman and Robert C. Schenck were attacking the Confederate left at the Stone Bridge, Col. Ambrose E. Burnside, at the same time, attempting to flank this end of the Confederate line. Evans, at the Stone Bridge, promptly deployed his scant half brigade to meet these movements. Johnston sent Gen. T. J. Jackson and Col. John Imboden to support Evans and soon Gen. G. E. Bee and Col. Wade Hampton followed. Fierce fighting raged from Bull Run to the Henry house plateau to which the Confederates were driven. Here Bee lost his life and Jackson won the nickname "Stonewall." The arrival of another portion of Johnston's army turned the tide in favor of the Confederates. The federal troops were driven across Bull Run in disorder, pursued along the Warrenton Turnpike. No fighting of any consequence had taken place on the Confederate right.

When the break took place on the right, Johnston ordered Bonham and Longstreet to move in pursuit. The Union withdrawal turned into a rout as the troops streamed back in the direction of Washington. The Confederate pursuit started from Mitchell's Ford in the direction of Centreville at which point it was halted, the Confederates later returning to Bull Run. Bitter controversy afterward ensued between Jefferson Davis, Johnston, and Beauregard as to the responsibility for not pursuing the defeated federal troops into Washington. Military critics think this was not feasible. The staff work and courier service on both sides were miserable and a heavy rainstorm added to the confusion and uncertainty. From some 13,000 men actually engaged, the Union lost about

500 killed, 1,000 wounded, and 1,200 missing; the Confederates, with about 11,000 engaged, lost about 400 killed, 1,600 wounded, and 13 missing. The Confederates also captured twenty-five guns and much other material. But it was a Pyrrhic victory. The South was made overconfident while the North was spurred to earnest effort.

[R. U. Johnson and C. C. Buel, eds., *Battles and Leaders of the Civil War,* vol. I; R. M. Johnston, *Bull Run: Its Strategy and Tactics.*]

MILLEDGE L. BONHAM, JR.

BULL RUN, SECOND BATTLE OF, also known as the Battle of Manassas, was initiated by the decision of Gen. Robert E. Lee, Aug. 24, 1862, at Jefferson-ton, Va., to send the 23,000 troops of Gen. T. J. ("Stonewall") Jackson to break the communications of Maj. Gen. John Pope's Army of Virginia, which was unassailably placed on the upper stretches of the Rappahannock River, Va. Jackson started before day-light, Aug. 25, passed Thoroughfare Gap and, on the evening of the 26th, reached Bristoe Station. The next day Jackson plundered Pope's base at Manassas Junction and proceeded to Groveton Heights, five miles northwest of Manassas. There, on the 28th, he attacked Gen. Rufus King's division. On Aug. 29 Pope in turn attacked Jackson, who with difficulty beat off repeated assaults. Lee, meantime, had brought up the remainder of his army, 32,000 men, and had formed them on Jackson's right. By nightfall of the 29th Lee's line formed an obtuse angle from north to south (Gen. James Longstreet) and thence southwest to northeast (Jackson). Pope, reinforced by a large part of the Army of the Potomac, renewed the attack on Jackson on the 30th, but failed to confront Longstreet with sufficient force. Lee accordingly ordered a general attack which swept Pope from his positions. Heavy rain on Aug. 31 delayed pursuit and made possible the retreat by Pope within the Washington defenses. Pope blamed his defeat on Gen. Fitz-John Porter, who Pope felt had failed to carry out orders. Porter was cashiered and was not vindicated until 1886, but Pope himself was not again trusted with field command. Pope's losses, Aug. 16 to Sept. 2, were 1,747 killed, 8,452 wounded, and 4,263 missing or captured; those of Lee were 1,553 killed, 7,812 wounded, and 109 missing.

[D. S. Freeman, *R. E. Lee,* vol. 2; J. C. Ropes, *The Army Under Pope.*]

DOUGLAS SOUTHALL FREEMAN

BULLWHACKER. *See* **Mule Skinner.**

BUMMERS, a nickname applied to foragers of Gen. W. T. Sherman's army during its march to the sea in 1864 and north through the Carolinas.

JOSEPH MILLS HANSON

BUNCOMBE. *See* **Bunkum.**

BUNDLING, a mode of courtship in colonial days where the parties instead of sitting up together went to bed together, with their clothes on. This custom, inherited from Europe, apparently originated as a matter of convenience and necessity where space and heat were lacking. It was confined largely to the poorer classes. Its prevalence seems to have ended in the late 18th century with the general improvement of living conditions.

[Henry Reed Stiles, *Bundling: Its Origin, Progress and Decline in America.*]

HUGH T. LEFLER

BUNKER HILL (June 17, 1775). To force the British from Boston, on the night of June 16 the American militia besieging the town sent 1,200 men to seize Bunker Hill, on the peninsula of Charlestown. Instead, the detachment built a small redoubt on Breed's Hill, nearer Boston but easily flanked. Working silently, they were not discovered until daybreak, when British warships, anchored below, opened an ineffective fire. Col. William Prescott, commanding in the redoubt, strengthened his left flank, toward the Mystic River, by a breastwork, a rail fence stuffed with hay, and a slight defense of stones on the beach. The defenders of these were joined by perhaps 2,000 men, and were commanded by Maj. Gen. Israel Putnam, while in the redoubt Brig. Gen. Joseph Warren served as a volunteer. Meanwhile, under the command of Maj. Gen. Sir William Howe, 2,000 British infantry, with a few field guns, landed below the redoubt.

Dividing his men into two wings, early in the afternoon Howe attacked both the redoubt and the rail fence, expecting first to turn the fence by a column along the beach, which would make it easily possible to storm in front. The attack was bloodily repulsed by the provincials, chiefly New Hampshire men under John Stark, and the remainder of the British withdrew after being but briefly in touch with the Americans. At the second attack the British advanced on both wings with great courage; but the provincials, as before holding their fire until the regulars were close, cut them to pieces and forced their withdrawal. Still trusting to the desperate frontal attack, in the final attempt Howe merely feinted against the fence, and for the first time attacked the redoubt with the bayonet. For the first time, also, his fieldpieces got within effective range and drove the defenders from the breastwork. What would have happened had the Americans had enough powder cannot be known; but Prescott's men were out of ammunition and, after a first severe fire, on his order, quit the redoubt. In this assault fell Maj. John Pitcairn, British commander at Lexington, and Joseph Warren. The defenders of the fence covered the American retreat. After an engagement lasting less than two hours, the British were masters of the peninsula, but with heavy casualties of 1,054, while the Americans lost, in killed, wounded, and prisoners, but 441. At first regarded by the Americans as a defeat, Bunker Hill, because of the way in which militia resisted regulars, came to be regarded as a moral victory, leading to a dangerous overconfidence in unpreparedness.

[Allen French, *First Year of the American Revolution;* Richard Frothingham, *History of the Siege of Boston;* Don Higginbotham, *The War of American Independence.*]

ALLEN FRENCH

BUNKER HILL MONUMENT, commemorating the Bunker Hill battle during the Revolution, its cornerstone laid by the Marquis de Lafayette in 1825, was dedicated in 1843, Daniel Webster being chief orator at both events.

ALVIN F. HARLOW

BUNKUM, or Buncombe, a term that, by 1828, had come into general use in political Washington to mean speechmaking designed for show or public applause and, later, insincere public talk or action. It is reputed to have originated a few years earlier in connection with a speech that Felix Walker made in Congress to please Buncombe County, N.C., in his congressional district.

[J. H. Wheeler, *Historical Sketches of North Carolina, From 1584 to 1851,* vol. II.]

E. MERTON COULTER

BURCHARD INCIDENT. Rev. Samuel D. Burchard, representing several hundred clergymen supporting the Republican presidential candidate, James G. Blaine, addressed the candidate in a speech at New York's Fifth Avenue Hotel on Oct. 30, 1884. In his speech Burchard described the Democrats as the party of "rum, Romanism, and rebellion." Blaine's failure to offset the diatribe cost him Irish support and the election.

[David S. Muzzey, *James G. Blaine.*]

JEANNETTE P. NICHOLS

BUREAUCRACY. In its most general sense the term "bureaucracy" may refer to all administrative organizations, public or private. Most narrowly, the term refers to the administration of government through bureaus, or specialized administrative units. The Federal Bureau of Investigation and the Internal Revenue Service are well-known examples of bureaus that are subdivisions of larger departments—Justice and Treasury, respectively. As commonly used, bureaucracy refers primarily, though not exclusively, to government bodies and tends to carry negative connotations, with regard to such alleged defects as excessive size, impersonality, and unresponsiveness to requests for service.

Concern about the sheer size of government bureaucracy seems well grounded in fact. When Congress created the federal bureaucracy in 1789 by establishing the departments of State, Treasury, and War, a relative handful of persons was thereby employed; by 1800 the federal civil service employed only about 3,000 persons. By 1830 the figure exceeded 10,000 (about 0.1 percent of the total population); by 1930 the civil service had grown to more than 600,000 employees (roughly 0.5 percent of the population); in 1970 the federal civil service numbered nearly 3 million (almost 1.5 percent of the population). If military personnel are included, figures more than double. State and local bureaucracies have also grown apace: by 1970 they employed approximately 9 million persons, slightly more than half of whom were school personnel.

Such growth has been a product both of an increase in population and, most importantly, of an expansion in the scope of services that citizens expect government to provide. To some extent the growth is a result of technology: an increasingly complicated and sophisticated society has required correspondingly increased investment in its governance. But much of the growth of bureaucracy reflects changes in social values. Government is now expected to provide kinds of services (such as medical insurance or auto safety regulation) not previously thought necessary or appropriate. Significantly, the greatest expansion of the federal bureaucracy occurred coincident with the expanded social and economic programs of President Franklin D. Roosevelt's New Deal.

As bureaucracy has grown it has changed, and so have attitudes toward it. The greatest initial fear concerning it was that bureaucratic routines might become overly rigid and personnel might become mere "timeservers." The concept of rotation in office—whereby officials are replaced before they have served extended periods in their positions—was introduced to guarantee fresh talent. However, notably under President Andrew Jackson, this idea degenerated into the spoils system, administrative appointments being awarded on the basis of political services rendered, almost without regard for qualification or competence.

Reacting to the excesses of the spoils system, reformers sought the implementation of a merit system for recruitment and promotion, and the protection of tenure for officeholders. Such reform was substantially secured by way of the Pendleton Act of 1882, and the system thus established has been extended subsequently to cover most of the federal bureaucracy. Similar reforms have been implemented at state and local levels. With these reforms, a new perspective on bureaucracy was developed. The bureaucracy came to be seen as essentially apolitical, rather than as an active political agent. The distinction between politics (making policy) and administration (implementing policy) was stressed.

Experience with a professional civil service has shown that the role of bureaucracy in policymaking was not merely an artifact of the spoils system, but an integral aspect of American politics. Given the size and technical complexity of the problems of modern government, legislative bodies must draft laws in general form, leaving the bureaucrats to develop specific guidelines for their implementation and to give them substance through case-by-case application. Moreover, with complexity has come reliance upon the expertise of the administrator, not only in the application of law but also in its formulation as well: bureaucrats have become major sources of proposals for new legislation at all levels of government.

While the policymaking role of bureaucracy has come to be accepted, it has also engendered criticism. Critics worry about legislatures' surrendering power to nonelected officials, about the influence that interest groups are able to develop at the administrative level, and about the inefficiency of cumbersome administrative organizations in responding to problems or directives. In a time when many are concerned that the presidency has become too powerful vis-à-vis the legislative branch of the U.S. government, there is an equally serious concern that the bureaucracy has become so vast that the president himself has little control over much of what is done in the executive branch of government.

In response to some of these concerns reforms have been undertaken to improve the administrative process through systematic techniques of planning and budgeting. Emphasis has been placed upon quantitative analysis of programs in terms of cost-benefit criteria and upon comprehensive program review and planning efforts. While results of these reforms have been mixed, fears have been expressed that this general approach will tend to move policy control even further from elected legislative bodies. In any event such developments and controversies highlight the centrality of bureaucracy to many aspects of contemporary American government and politics.

[Anthony Downs, *Inside Bureaucracy;* John M. Pfiffner and Robert Presthus, *Public Administration.*]

CHARLES WALCOTT

BURGESSES, HOUSE OF. *See* **Colonial Assemblies.**

BURGHERS, citizens of an incorporated city who, under the Dutch (1657), enjoyed great or small burgher rights, and under the English were entitled by birth or admission by the magistrates to the designation of freemen. In New York and Albany only freemen, who had paid the required fees, could do business or ply a trade.

[A. C. Flick, ed., *History of the State of New York.*]

A. C. FLICK

BURGOYNE'S INVASION. In the late spring of 1777, Gen. John Burgoyne prepared to invade New York from Canada by the Lake Champlain–Hudson River route (*see* British Campaign of 1777). Lt. Col. Barry St. Leger was given command of a small expedition, which was to ascend the St. Lawrence River, cross Lake Ontario, and advance on Albany by the Mohawk Valley. Both commanders were instructed that their principal objective was junction with Sir William Howe. An order was prepared, but through a mischance never sent from England, commanding Howe to proceed up the Hudson River. In spite of this fateful blunder, Howe knew the British plans, for he had received a copy of Burgoyne's instructions.

Burgoyne's army was made up of 3,700 British regulars, 3,000 German troops, 250 Canadians and Tories, and 400 Indians. With his well-equipped force he proceeded up Lake Champlain in late June and on July 1 was within four miles of Ticonderoga, which, with Mt. Independence east of the lake, was garrisoned by about 2,300 Continentals under Gen. Arthur St. Clair. In spite of militia reinforcements St. Clair wisely abandoned the fortress the night of July 5–6. Engagements with pursuing British at Hubbardton, Skenesboro (now Whitehall), and Fort Anne did not prevent St. Clair from saving his army to form the nucleus of later resistance. The taking of Ticonderoga increased the confidence of the British and was at first a severe shock to the patriots; later, it proved a stimulus to resistance.

Burgoyne's progress now became very deliberate. He was retarded by his extensive baggage and by the fact that the transportation of his artillery up Lake George required all available boats, while his army proceeded overland. To oppose him there were 2,000 Americans under Gen. Philip Schuyler at Fort Edward; but Schuyler was reinforced July 12 by about 1,700 men from St. Clair's command and 600 Continentals from Peekskill. Retreating before Burgoyne's slow advance, Schuyler felled trees across the roads and encouraged the country people to burn their standing crops and drive off their cattle. His steadiness was of the utmost value to the American cause.

Meanwhile Howe, evidently believing the rebellion nearly crushed and that Burgoyne did not require his active cooperation, left Sir Henry Clinton at New York to make a sortie up the Hudson with such troops as could be spared from the garrison and went to Philadelphia.

Fortune now began to turn against Burgoyne. A raiding force dispatched to secure patriot stores at Bennington, Vt., was overwhelmed, Aug. 16, by Gen. John Stark's New Hampshire militia and Seth Warner's small force. St. Leger, besieging Fort Stanwix, managed, at Oriskany, to repulse a relieving body of militia under Gen. Nicholas Herkimer, but his Indian allies fled in panic at news of the approach of a patriot force under Benedict Arnold, and he abandoned his campaign.

Gen. Horatio Gates, now in command of the American army near the mouth of the Mohawk, had about 6,000 effective troops. Reinforced by Gen. Daniel Morgan's Virginia riflemen, he moved northward and entrenched at Bemis Heights, about eight miles south of the hamlet of Saratoga, now Schuylerville. Burgoyne, whose Indian scouts had fled, was close upon the American army before he realized its presence. The first Battle of Freeman's Farm was fought Sept. 19. Both armies remained in position, and Burgoyne waited, hoping for news of Clinton's expected advance up the Hudson, but Clinton got no farther than the Highlands of the Hudson. Meanwhile Gates's numbers were increasing, bodies of New England militia were gathering in Burgoyne's rear, and the British supplies were running dangerously low. It was necessary to fight or to retreat. By Oct. 7 Burgoyne's effective troops numbered about 5,000, while the Americans in front of him were nearly 8,000. A reconnaissance in force to examine the American left was repulsed, the British were driven back into their lines, and a determined attack led by Gen. Arnold threatened their whole position (*see* Freeman's Farm, Second Battle of). Burgoyne now had no alternative and fell back toward Saratoga. His movement was so deliberate that the Americans were able to surround him, and on Oct. 17, finding himself opposed by over 17,000 regulars and militia, with less than 3,500 infantry ready for duty, he surrendered his army to Gates. (*See also* Convention Army; Franco-American Alliance of 1778.)

[George A. Billias, ed., *George Washington's Opponents*.]

RALPH FOSTER WELD

BURKE ACT of 1906 amended the Dawes General Allotment Act of 1887 by changing the time that Indians would be enfranchised as citizens and subject to the civil and criminal jurisdictions of the states in which they resided. Under the Dawes Act the Indian became a citizen immediately upon receipt of a "trust patent," under the term of which he did not receive title to his land for twenty-five years. It was considered that many Indians at that time were unprepared for citizenship, and that many of them had been exploited in connection with their voting rights. The Burke Act provided that the Indian would become a citizen only at the end of the twenty-five-year trust period, when he became the unrestricted owner of his land. The secretary of the interior was given the right to abbreviate the probationary period in individual cases in which the Indians concerned had shown themselves competent to manage their own affairs. Accordingly, competency commissions were established in various parts of the country to pass on the qualifications of Indian applicants for citizenship.

[G. E. E. Lundquist, *The Red Man in the United States*.]

KENNETH M. STEWART

BURLINGAME TREATY, articles added to the Treaty of Tientsin (1858) between the United States and China, signed July 28, 1868. These articles acknowledged Chinese territorial jurisdiction in China, left trade privileges in China to the discretion of the Chinese government, and established free immigration between the countries (*see* Chinese Exclusion Acts). It placed China on the most-favored-nation plane with regard to treatment of consuls and immunity and privileges in travel, residence, and education of Chinese subjects in the United States. It guaranteed nonintervention by the United States in Chinese domestic administration. It was signed in Washington by William H. Seward, secretary of state, Anson Burlingame, acting as envoy extraordinary and minister plenipotentiary of the emperor of China, a Chinese envoy, and a Manchu envoy.

[Frederick Wells Williams, *Anson Burlingame and the First Chinese Mission to Foreign Powers*.]

ROGER BURLINGAME

BURLINGTON COMPANY, a group of eight investors of Burlington, N.J., which absorbed various mortgages of George Croghan between 1768 and 1770. The mortgages, issued to Gov. William Franklin and assigned by him to the company, included one for £3,000 on 40,000 acres of Croghan's Otsego, N.Y., purchase. Franklin, besides personal loans to Croghan, had purchased a 50 percent stock interest in the company for £1,500 (1772). The remaining original shareholders sold their stock and rights, including Franklin's mortgages, to Andrew Craig and William Cooper, who, without notifying Franklin, instituted sheriff's sale proceedings under a judgment of 1773 and, by questionable methods, purchased the Otsego tract for £2,700 (January 1786). Efforts of Franklin and Croghan's heirs to contest title proved fruitless.

[A. T. Volwiler, *George Croghan and the Westward Movement, 1741–1782*.]

C. A. TITUS

BURLINGTON ROUTE. *See* **Railroads, Sketches: Burlington Northern.**

BURLINGTON STRIKE. On Feb. 27, 1888, locomotive enginemen of the Burlington Railway, members of the Brotherhood of Locomotive Engineers, struck for higher wages and abandonment of the system of classification. The strike was supported by the Knights of Labor. As it dragged on, violence flared, trains were wrecked, men were shot, and property was burned or otherwise destroyed. The brotherhood finally gave in, but the railway damage was enormous. By Feb. 1, 1889, train operations were normal.

[John R. Commons, *History of Labor in the United States*, vol. II.]

THOMAS ROBSON HAY

BURMA ROAD AND LEDO ROAD. Construction of a 400-mile military highway from Ledo, India, to join with an existing 717-mile road to Burma from Kunming, China, was one of the largest engineering projects of World War II.

In 1937 the Chinese had started a crash project to get a passable military road between Kunming and Lashio, Burma, a railhead on a railway to Rangoon. This road to Burma used existing caravan traces dating back to the 13th century. It was handmade, snaking across the formidable terrain of Yunnan Province and cutting across the grain of the lower Himalayas and the gorges of the Mekong and Salween rivers. By 1940 the Burma Road was a backcountry highway, being graded, graveled, and bridged to carry ten tons. There were difficulties, however. Bullied by Japan, the British closed their 117-mile Burma sector in 1940 for a short time. Japanese air power endangered growing traffic; the Chinese in 1941 countered with protective American Air Volunteers, famed as "Flying Tigers." Finally, Japan's conquest of Burma in 1942 blockaded China's land route to Rangoon.

When Lashio fell, a Chinese division fled to India. In June 1942 Gen. Joseph W. Stilwell, American theater commander in China, Burma, and India, conceived a project to use this Chinese army in India to retake north Burma and build a 400-mile military highway to link up with the Burma Road at Wanting. Chinese and British allies showed no enthusiasm for a second Burma campaign, urging instead an all-American air transport route to aid China. Monsoon weather, Burma's jungles, and a determined enemy were arguments used against Stilwell.

Stilwell's strategy persisted. The Ledo Road project started in October 1942, but it made little progress during 1943. Stilwell's Chinese began gaining victories in the Hukwang Valley in early 1944, and the road moved toward China. The capture of Myitkyina, Burma, on Aug. 3, 1944, forecast the joining of the Ledo Road to the Burma Road and Kunming. Opened Jan. 27, 1945, the combined highways were officially named the Stilwell Road.

The Ledo portion of the road was engineered by 17,000 Americans, under Gen. Lewis A. Pick; the fatalities totaled 1,133 men, 625 of whom died in combat. "Pick's Pike" cost $150 million. Sixty-four truck companies—pitifully short of the 375 planned to operate convoys—delivered 150,000 tons of heavy artillery, 25,000 trucks, and miles of gasoline pipeline to parallel the road to Kunming.

Controversy over the Ledo Road's worth plagued the effort from its beginning and it was a contributing factor in Stilwell's recall. Nevertheless, the new Ledo Road revived China's interest in modernizing its Burma Road. Hard to evaluate, these military highways had a great impact on China's morale and ability to finish the war. Sufficient lend-lease supplies arrived on them to flesh out thirty Chinese divisions in 1945, and these divisions were able to stop an eleven-division Japanese drive in East China.

[Leslie Anders, *The Ledo Road;* Tan Pei-Ying, *The Building of the Burma Road.*]

CHARLES F. ROMANUS

BURNING SPRING, located in present Kanawha County, W.Va., near Malden, referred to by pioneers as "one of the wonders of the world." It is not known when this "boiling pot," which could be ignited and extinguished at will, was first seen by white persons, but in 1755 Mary Ingles, a captive, assisted Indians in making salt there. The 250-acre tract on which the spring was located was patented by generals George Washington and Andrew Lewis, but Washington never saw it. It was his intention to give the spring site to the "public forever," but instead it went to his nephew, Lawrence Augustine Washington who, in turn, sold it to the owners of a salt plant.

[John P. Hale, *Trans-Allegheny Pioneers;* West Virginia Geological Survey (1914), *Kanawha County.*]

CHARLES H. AMBLER

BURNS FUGITIVE SLAVE CASE (1854), one of three famous fugitive slave cases arising in Boston, Mass., after the enactment of the Fugitive Slave Law of 1850. Part of the Vigilance Committee (1850–61) planned to rescue Anthony Burns, an escaped slave, from an upper room of the courthouse. They battered in a door of the building at night, May 26, entered, and one of them shot and killed the U.S. marshal. Despite the committee's efforts, U.S. Commissioner Edward G. Loring remanded Burns to his owner in Alexandria, Va. On June 2 throngs witnessed the slave's departure. Several rich citizens paid $1,300 for his freedom in 1855 and Burns returned to Massachusetts. Following the Burns case, enforcement of the Fugitive Slave Law declined.

[W. H. Siebert, *The Underground Railroad in Massachusetts;* C. E. Stevens, *Anthony Burns.*]

WILBUR H. SIEBERT

BURNT CORN, BATTLE OF (July 27,1813), an encounter between Creek Indians and Alabama frontiersmen on Burnt Corn Creek. On their return from Pensacola, where aid had been received from the British, a party of Creek Indians was attacked by three companies of frontiersmen under command of Col. James Caller. The Indians defeated the Alabamians, killing two and wounding fifteen.

JOHN B. CLARK

BURR CONSPIRACY, one of the most involved and mysterious episodes in early American history, and the climax of the dramatic struggle for power between President Thomas Jefferson and Aaron Burr, vice-president during Jefferson's first term. Essentially it was a compound of personal and political rivalry, discredited ambition, and land hunger.

Burr's exact intentions probably cannot ever be known. Following his duel with Alexander Hamilton in 1804, Burr became a creature of circumstances, hoping and scheming to regain something of his one-time popularity and power. To accomplish this he chose what he considered the most likely road to wealth and power—land conquest or seizure in Spanish territory west of the Mississippi.

Burr's first act was an attempt to attach England to his cause. Failing in this, he enlisted those who might be of help, yet never disclosed his exact intentions. Harman Blennerhassett, a trusting, visionary Irishman, who lived on an island in the Ohio River, was only one, though the most bizarre and reputedly the heaviest of the contributors to their venture. Burr went to the West, down the Mississippi River to New Orleans, and back overland, seeking friendly help and necessary funds. Returning to the East he sought successively to draw France and then Spain into his web of intrigue, but to no avail.

Before leaving Philadelphia in the summer of 1806, Burr wrote to his friend and co-conspirator Gen. James Wilkinson, who commanded the American army on the Mississippi, that the expedition would start for New Orleans before the end of the year. But Wilkinson, thoughtful for his own safety and uncertain as to Burr, declined to be involved further. Instead, when Burr's advance flotilla reached the lower Mississippi, Wilkinson ordered its members arrested. As Burr came down he, too, was seized and then paroled. He attempted to escape to Spanish territory, but was again captured and taken East for trial. Burr was acquitted of treason and high misdemeanor, but the "conspiracy" had already collapsed.

[Thomas P. Abernethy, *The Burr Conspiracy;* Herbert S. Parmet and M. B. Hecht, *Aaron Burr.*]

THOMAS ROBSON HAY

BURR-HAMILTON DUEL. The most famous duel in American history resulted in the mortal wounding of Alexander Hamilton at the hands of Aaron Burr, July 11, 1804. Burr issued his challenge ostensibly because Hamilton refused to disavow a "despicable opinion" of Burr, which he was reported to have expressed during Burr's unsuccessful New York governorship campaign in 1804. Actually, Burr vengefully blamed Hamilton for his defeat for the presidency of the United States in 1801. Hamilton had deflected Federalist votes to Jefferson, the Republican, rather than see his party elevate a man he deeply distrusted. Thus dashed—and snubbed as vice-president—Burr hoped to console himself as governor of New York. Hamilton feared that once in that office Burr would seek to head as dictator a secession, then brewing, of the New England and middle states from the Union.

Hamilton, morally opposed to dueling, doubted that his technical demurrer to Burr's charge would be accepted. Explaining his motives for meeting Burr, he admitted that he had been "extremely severe" in criticizing Burr's political and private character and said he believed that "the ability to be in future useful . . . in . . . public affairs" required him to conform to the prevailing code of honor. He rejected the plea of Rufus King, one of the few friends who knew of the threatened encounter, that he refuse to go to the field. He resolved, however, to throw away his first and perhaps even his second fire.

The duel took place beneath the Palisades at Weehawken, N.J. As Hamilton fell, he discharged his pistol wildly and, his second believed, involuntarily. After suffering excruciating pain from the ball lodged in his spine, Hamilton died the next day. Amid shocked mourning for Hamilton, Burr fled from the murder findings of coroners' juries. These charges were later quashed, but Burr's remaining years were doomed to discredit.

[Harold C. Syrett and Jean G. Cooke, *Interview at Weehawken: The Burr-Hamilton Duel as Told in Original Documents.*]

BROADUS MITCHELL

BURR TRIAL. The constitutional aspects of this trial have to do largely with the interpretation of the constitutional provision concerning treason. Aaron Burr was indicted for treason in 1807 and brought to trial in the U.S. Circuit Court at Richmond, Va., before Chief Justice John Marshall sitting as a circuit judge. The political passions of the times and the friction between President Thomas Jefferson and Marshall carried over into the trial and render appraisal difficult. An early incident of the trial was the Marshall opinion that a federal court might issue a subpoena *duces tecum* to the president of the United States. In guiding the jury as to the law of treason the chief justice gave an interpretation so restricting the meaning of the words "levying war" that in the case at hand only the assemblage at Blennerhassett Island could come within it. Burr, however much he may have counseled, advised, or planned that assemblage, was not present. Under the Marshall interpretation his absentee connection was not sufficient to render him guilty of treason. Marshall held that the broader definition asked by counsel for the prosecution would include the English doctrine of constructive treason, which the phrasing of the constitutional provision was intended to exclude. This statement of the law resulted in a verdict of acquittal. The chief justice was sharply criticized for inconsistency and bias, in that in a dictum in an earlier case in the Supreme Court involving two of Burr's messengers (*see* Bollman Case) he had stated the law in a way which seemingly should have linked Burr with the treasonable assemblage.

[*Reports of the Trials of Colonel Aaron Burr for Treason and for a Misdemeanor;* Thomas P. Abernethy, *The Burr Conspiracy;* Herbert S. Parmet and M. B. Hecht, *Aaron Burr.*]

CARL BRENT SWISHER

BUSHWHACKERS. This term, originally used in the early 18th century to describe a backwoodsman, was applied during the Civil War by federal soldiers to Confederate guerrilla fighters, with a distinct implication of private plunder. Used in Missouri as synonymous with border ruffians, it was more commonly applied in the mountain sections of Virginia and Kentucky.

JAMES ELLIOTT WALMSLEY

BUSHY RUN, BATTLE OF (Aug. 5–6, 1763). Col. Henry Bouquet's expedition to relieve Fort Pitt was attacked by Delaware, Mingo, Shawnee, and Huron Indians near Bushy Run, twenty-five miles east of Pittsburgh, Pa. After a day of indecisive fighting, the men rested. In the morning Bouquet, feigning retreat, drew the Indians forward to receive a flanking fire. The Indians, completely routed, fled, but the British had suffered a loss of over 100 men.

SOLON J. BUCK

BUSINESS, BIG. The term "big business," when used in the context of American economic development, refers to the concentration of industrial and financial power that began in the post–Civil War period. During that period the United States was undergoing a rapid change from an agrarian, rural, handicraft economy to an industrial, urban, factory economy. This transformation—and its attendant concentration of economic power—was encouraged by a political climate that produced the passage of generous tariff, banking, railroad, and immigration legislation, as well as a social environment that promoted initiative, competition, and exploitation of natural resources.

The first of the big businesses were the railroads, which proliferated in numbers and distances covered during the 1870's and 1880's. Spurred by the large financial incentive of federal subsidies, the number of railroads grew far out of proportion to the amount of available traffic. Railroad entrepreneurs engaged in disastrous competition quickly saw the profitability of cooperation and consolidation. All that remained to be done during the period was the selection of a suitable legal and organizational device that would ensure efficient cooperation.

The extension of transcontinental railroads and the consolidation of competing lines resulted in the creation of a national transportation network and a national market. Local producers, faced by vigorous competition from afar and by a larger market, sought control over competitors and increased market share through combination and consolidation. Successful consolidation in one economic function (horizontal integration) often prompted consolidation of component functions (vertical integration) by the same firm. Such consolidation and integration not only eliminated competition and provided security for the entrepreneurs involved, but also made possible greater production and marketing efficiency.

Popular protest mounted as society became aware of real or imaginary abuses resulting from an economy that was becoming dominated by a single firm or several large firms in almost every area of activity. Protesters first turned to producers' and consumers' cooperatives, but these attempts at self-help were unsuccessful. Soon protesters sought government action. Their efforts resulted in the passage of the Interstate Commerce Act (1887), which was intended to regulate railroad activities, and the Sherman Antitrust Act (1890), which was intended to regulate industrial size and competition. These acts, and subsequent legislation, proved ineffective. Consequently, new demands were periodically made for economic reform. During the Progressive and New Deal eras, regulatory legislation was passed that constituted a further attempt to deal with concentrated industrial and financial power.

Much of the difficulty of enacting effective regulatory legislation has been the result of the persuasiveness of business lobbies in combating the efforts of their critics, and there has been the additional problem of composing a definition of "bigness" that will eliminate the real, or perceived, evils of size and concentration of economic power while retaining the benefits derived therefrom. Since the mid-20th century the problem of size and concentration of economic power has manifested itself in the creation of conglomerate enterprises.

[Edward Chase Kirkland, *Industry Comes of Age;* Glenn Porter, *The Rise of Big Business, 1860–1910.*]

ROSARIO JOSEPH TOSIELLO

BUSINESS, PUBLIC CONTROL OF. By statute and administrative action, public control of business has become more inclusive and less fettered since World War I than it was before. Two developments are notable: private enterprises, besides being variously restrained, are publicly assisted to function, and even to survive; and comprehensive laws and public agencies modify the economy and thereby affect the operation of areas of business. The growth in scope of public control amounts to an alteration not only in degree but also in kind. The existing discipline of and solicitude for business, both direct and incidental, has many causes—including historical events, progress in science and technology, and transformations in enterprise itself. Broadly, prior to World War I governmental intervention was justified because the public was dependent upon business, whereas since then business has been increasingly dependent upon government. The distinction between the freedom of private proprietors—in industry, commerce, agriculture, finance, and services—and the demands of society has become blurred.

The American colonies inherited from England a penchant for competition in the production of goods and services. During the 17th century mercantilist government reliance on monopolies—and indeed promotion of them—was waning, soon to be replaced by the advocacy of free individual initiative as the guarantee of an abundancy of products at reasonable prices. Certain types of proprietors—innkeepers, ferrymen, millers—since their enterprises were affected with a public interest, were forbidden to refuse their services to applicants. The holders of a monopoly, such as a bridge or toll road, were also regulated in their charges. With the development of public utilities (companies furnishing water, light, heat, and telephone and telegraph communication), in which competition was wasteful, the grant of franchises presupposed the supervision of rates.

Railroads, though not classified as public utilities, early came under state supervision. After the lines were extended to be interstate, and competition between them led to discriminatory abuses, the Interstate Commerce Act of 1887 forbade unreasonable rates, favoritism to certain shippers, and unfairness to local communities served by a single line (for example, a higher charge for a shorter haul than for a longer haul over the same tracks). Though the federal law was inspired by the pressures of large, well-organized groups of small shippers, the Interstate Commerce Commission for twenty years was frustrated in administering the act. The railroads were ingenious in evading orders, and the courts to which they appealed against the commission were excessively legalistic and permissive. The Hepburn Act of 1906 gave the commission authority to set maximum rates, effective in thirty days unless the carrier in that time obtained a court order to the contrary. But the railroads were able to continue to discriminate in short hauls until the Mann-Elkins Act of 1910 removed the qualifying language that had been the refuge of those who challenged the law. The Shipping Act of 1916 provided limited supervision of common carriers by water, at that time the railroads' chief competitors.

The experiments with public restraints on transportation were matched by state and then federal statutes attempting to preserve competition in commerce. "Trust" became the generic term for a business combination—though holding companies, "gentlemen's agreements," and outright mergers were resorted to also. The Sherman Antitrust Act of 1890 was short and simple, but by the same token its undefined terms were subject to elusive interpretation. It made illegal "every contract, combination in the form of trust or otherwise, or conspiracy in restraint of trade . . . among the . . . States, or with foreign nations." The courts stood in the way of enforcement. At first they acted unexpectedly against labor unions, while holding that the monopoly in sugar refining was immune because each of its plants was exclusively in the jurisdiction of the state in which it was located. Later the concept of commerce was broadened to embrace manufacturing for interstate shipment.

The powerful movement toward business consolidation rendered invalid the desire for competition that had long prevailed among small businesses. Nevertheless, the Clayton Act of 1914 amended the Sherman law by punishing particular monopolistic practices that were listed. The exercise was substantially futile; for not all misdemeanors were included, and substitutes for those prohibited were created with alacrity. In anticipation of such nimble behavior, the Federal Trade Commission was set up in the same year to detect and report monopolistic infractions, and by its cease-and-desist orders to relieve the clogged court dockets. Its history has been mixed, though the tendency has been to save at the spigot while losing at the bung.

These approaches to public control of business—and there were many others not here mentioned—suddenly took a positive turn in the economic mobilization during American engagement in World War I. It was evident that free-market forces alone could not be relied upon to direct materials, capital, and labor into defense uses. The War Industries Board, Food Administration, Fuel Administration, and Emergency Fleet Corporation were the chief agencies of government control at this time; as the railroads under private management proved unable to meet traffic needs, the government leased the lines and reduced waste in their operation. The period of wartime controls was short, basically two years, and haste and inexperience made for more dependence on persuasion than was possible later.

Economic demobilization was prompt after World War I, on popular demand, and the nation entered the prosperous 1920's. Presidents in that decade were content to give business its head. After the stock market collapsed in the autumn of 1929 and a catastrophic business year followed, it was indisputable that the total economy was sinking into alarming depression. President Herbert Hoover abandoned his faith in "rugged individualism" so far as to champion agricultural controls; federal appropriations for relief of the unemployed; and the Reconstruction Finance Corporation, to make loans to railroads, banks, and other major business enterprises. His gestures toward public succor were in themselves little and late, but they formed precedents for the enormously expanded program of the New Deal that followed.

President Franklin D. Roosevelt's inauguration occurred in a dreary scene of banks closing, industrial production shrunk to less than half the previous performance, staple farm crops at giveaway prices, and a third of the nation's workers jobless. Swiftly, in the emergency, the federal government came to the rescue in every sector of the economy. All but a few banks were reopened, ample credit was dispensed to financial enterprises, public relief payments were expanded, and homes were protected against foreclosure. The Agricultural Adjustment Act constituted a breadline for farmers, and the National Industrial Recovery Act gave manufactures and commerce the coveted liberty of collusion in return for minimum wages, maximum hours, and the right of workers to organize and bargain collectively. The antitrust acts were suspended; the "big stick" of Theodore Roosevelt, which he boasted he would wield against overbold business, became the crutch supplied by Franklin Roosevelt to limping enterprise.

With entrance of the United States into World War II, government controls of the economy were redoubled: government-set materials priorities; consumer rationing; price, wage, and profit limits were established to cope with scarcities, instead of overabundance. The business letdowns following the war were minor. The next episodes of wage and price fixing—in 1971–73—were intended to reduce the inflation resulting from the long Vietnam War; they met with little or no success, though at last unemployment was somewhat lessened.

The responsibilities of the federal government, which profoundly influences the economy, had greatly increased in variety and extent beginning with the depression of the 1930's. The Tennessee Valley Authority, social security, and defense spending (including the undertaking of atomic energy production and control and the space program) were supplemented by fiscal policies of the Treasury and monetary maneuvers of the Federal Reserve System. All these were continuing conditioners of private enterprise.

Significant developments in the policing of business after World War II involved federal action. Fair employment practices were mandated on behalf of workers belonging to minority groups. Consumer protection markedly increased in scope and intensity, notably by means of the Food and Drug Administration, a reanimated Federal Trade Commission, and the Environmental Protection Agency. The Environmental Protection Agency, established in 1970, combined existing scattered antipollution programs and adopted new aims, including control of automotive effluents and radiation. The Federal Power Commission was concerned with energy sources such as nuclear reactors, natural gas, offshore drilling for oil, and higher voltage transmission lines for electricity. In the traditional field of preservation of competition, prosecution of vertical and horizontal business combinations—and mergers—was more successful than attacks on recently emerged conglomerate consolidations. The Department of Transportation was established in 1967 to embrace numerous existing agencies, focusing on coordinating and constructing facilities for economy and convenience. Distress of the railroads promoted a public corporation, Amtrak, to revive passenger service on railroads. The Department of Health, Education, and Welfare was formed in 1953; its 300 programs to improve living conditions modified and supplemented private enterprise. Efforts of the states toward business regulation have been encouraged by federal initiative and are subject to federal guidelines but remain relatively spasmodic and weakly staffed.

Overall, the policies of the federal government in international finance, monetary management, trade, and overseas aid have profoundly affected domestic business prosperity and prices. Such events as the energy crisis of 1973—precipitated by restriction on oil shipments on the part of disgruntled Arab states but having deeper cumulative causes—indicate that the prospect is for enlarged and more varied intervention of the government in the American economy.

[Marshall E. Dimock, *Business and Government;* Harold Koontz and Richard W. Gable, *Public Control of Economic Enterprise*.]

BROADUS MITCHELL

BUSINESS CYCLES. According to a definition formulated in 1946 by the economists Wesley C. Mitchell and Arthur F. Burns (*Measuring Business Cycles*), business cycles are

> a type of fluctuation found in the aggregate economic activity of nations that organize their work mainly in busi-

Table 1
Business Cycle Expansions and Contractions in the United States: 1854 to 1970

Business cycle reference dates		Duration in months			
				Cycle	
		Contraction (trough from previous peak)	Expansion (trough to peak)	Trough from previous trough	Peak from previous peak
Trough	**Peak**				
December 1854	June 1857	(X)	30	(X)	(X)
December 1858	October 1860	18	22	48	40
June 1861	April 1865	8	*46*	30	*54*
December 1867	June 1869	*32*	18	*78*	50
December 1870	October 1873	18	34	36	52
March 1879	March 1882	65	36	99	101
May 1885	March 1887	38	22	74	60
April 1888	July 1890	13	27	35	40
May 1891	January 1893	10	20	37	30
June 1894	December 1895	17	18	37	35
June 1897	June 1899	18	24	36	42
December 1900	September 1902	18	21	42	39
August 1904	May 1907	23	33	44	56
June 1908	January 1910	13	19	46	32
January 1912	January 1913	24	12	43	36
December 1914	August 1918	23	*44*	35	*67*
March 1919	January 1920	*7*	10	*51*	17
July 1921	May 1923	18	22	28	40
July 1924	October 1926	14	27	36	41
November 1927	August 1929	13	21	40	34
March 1933	May 1937	43	50	64	93
June 1938	February 1945	13	*80*	63	*93*
October 1945	November 1948	*8*	37	*88*	45
October 1949	July 1953	11	*45*	48	*56*
August 1954	July 1957	*13*	35	*58*	48
April 1958	May 1960	9	25	44	34
February 1961	November 1969	9	*105*	34	*114*
November 1970		*12*	(X)	*117*	(X)
Average, all cycles:					
27 cycles, 1854–1970		19	33	52	[1] 52
11 cycles, 1919–1970		15	42	56	[2] 60
5 cycles, 1945–1970		11	49	60	[3] 59
Average, peacetime cycles:					
22 cycles, 1854–1961		20	26	45	[4] 46
8 cycles, 1919–1961		16	28	45	[5] 48
3 cycles, 1945–1961		10	32	42	[6] 42

NOTE: Italicized figures are the wartime expansions (Civil War, World Wars I and II, Korean War, and Vietnam War), the postwar contractions, and the full cycles that include the wartime expansions.

[1] 26 cycles, 1857–1969.
[2] 10 cycles, 1920–1969.
[3] 5 cycles, 1945–1969.
[4] 21 cycles, 1857–1960.
[5] 7 cycles, 1920–1960.
[6] 3 cycles, 1945–1960.

Source: National Bureau of Economic Research, Inc.

Table 2
Selected Measures of Duration, Depth, and Diffusion of Business Cycle Contractions (1920–70)

	Business Cycle Contraction, from Peak (top line) to Trough (next line)										
	Jan. 1920 July 1921	May 1923 July 1924	Oct. 1926 Nov. 1927	Aug. 1929 March 1933	May 1937 June 1938	Feb. 1945 Oct. 1945	Nov. 1948 Oct. 1949	July 1953 Aug. 1954	July 1957 April 1958	May 1960 Feb. 1961	Nov. 1969 Nov. 1970
DURATION											
Business cycle chronology	18 mos.	14 mos.	13 mos.	43 mos.	13 mos.	8 mos.	11 mos.	13 mos.	9 mos.	9 mos.	12 mos.
GNP, current $	n.a.	6	12	42	9	6	12	12	6	6	[c]
GNP, constant $	n.a.	3	3	36	6	n.a.	6	12	6	12	15
Industrial production	14	14	8	36	12	27	15	8	14	13	14
Nonfarm employment	n.a.	n.a.	n.a.	43	11	22	13	16	14	10	8
DEPTH [a]											
GNP, current $	n.a.	−4.9%	−3.0%	−49.6%	−16.2%	−11.9%	−3.4%	−1.9%	−2.6%	−0.3%	[c]
GNP, constant $	n.a.	−4.1	−2.0	−32.6	−13.2	n.a.	−1.9	−3.4	−3.9	−1.6	−1.5%
Industrial production	−32.4%	−17.9	−7.0	−53.4	−32.4	−38.3	−9.9	−10.0	−14.3	−7.2	−8.1
Nonfarm employment	n.a.	n.a.	n.a.	−31.6	−10.8	−10.1	−5.2	−3.4	−4.3	−2.2	−1.6
Unemployment rate											
Maximum level	11.9 [d]	5.5 [d]	4.4 [d]	25.2	20.0	4.3	7.9	6.1	7.5	7.1	6.1
Increase	+10.3 [d]	+2.6 [d]	+2.4 [d]	+22.0	+9.0	+3.4	+4.5	+3.6	+3.8	+2.3	+2.7
DIFFUSION											
Nonfarm industries, maximum percentage with declining employment [b]	97% (Sept. '20)	95% (Apr. '24)	71% (Nov. '27)	100% (June '33)	97% (Dec. '37)	n.a.	90% (Feb. '49)	87% (Mar. '54)	88% (Sept. '57)	82% (Aug. '60)	83% (June '70)

[a] Percentage change from the peak month or quarter in the series to its trough month or quarter, over the intervals shown above. For the unemployment rate, the maximum figure is the highest for any month during the contraction and the increases are from the lowest month to the highest, in percentage points.

[b] Since 1948, based on changes in employment over six-month spans in 30 nonagricultural industries, centered on the 4th month of the span. Prior to 1948 based on cyclical changes in employment in 41 industries.

[c] No decline.

[d] The maximum figures are annual average (monthly data not available) for 1921, 1924, 1928, 1933; increases, in percentage points, are for 1919–21, 1923–24, 1926–28, and 1929–33.

Source: U.S. Department of Commerce, U.S. Department of Labor, Board of Governors of the Federal Reserve System, National Bureau of Economic Research. For a fuller version of this table see Solomon Fabricant, "The 'Recession' of 1969–70," in Victor Zarnowitz, ed., *The Business Cycle Today*, NBER (1972), pp. 100–110.

ness enterprises; a cycle consists of expansions occurring at about the same time in many economic activities, followed by similarly general recessions, contractions, and revivals which merge into expansion phase of the next cycle; this sequence of changes is recurrent but not periodic; in duration business cycles may last from more than one year to ten or twelve years; they are not divisible into shorter cycles of similar character with amplitudes approximating their own.

This definition resulted from extensive observation of economic data for a number of countries over periods ranging back to the late 18th century and up to the 1930's. Studies of more recent data have, for the most part, confirmed the continued existence of business cycles conforming to the definition. However, certain developments have led to long-term changes in the character of the cycle. These include secular shifts in the character of economic activity, such as the shift toward greater employment in service industries, including government; the creation of new institutions, such as bank deposit insurance and unemployment insurance; and the attention given by government to the use of fiscal and monetary policy to modify the business cycle, particularly to offset any tendency toward recession. In general, cyclical fluctuations since the 1950's, both in the United States and abroad, have been milder than in the past, and the contraction phase has often been characterized by a reduced rate of growth in aggregate economic activity rather than an absolute decline. Thus the term "growth cycle" has come to be applied to these milder fluctuations. The shift has generally been accompanied by a higher rate of inflation during the expansion phase of the cycle, often extending into the contraction phase.

Chronologies of business cycles have been constructed for a number of countries. The one in common use for the United States was developed by the National Bureau of Economic Research, Inc. (*see* Table 1). On an annual basis, it extends from 1834 to 1970 and covers thirty-two expansions and thirty-two contractions. The monthly and quarterly chronology begins in 1854 and covers twenty-seven cycles.

Table 2 gives a record of the chief characteristics of the eleven business cycle contractions (recessions) in the United States from 1920 to 1970. Most of the contractions have lasted about a year or less. Only two were substantially longer: the eighteen-month contraction during 1920–21 and the forty-three-month contraction during 1929–33. These intervals (the top line of Table 2) represent the consensus among a number of different measures of economic activity, some of which are also shown in the table.

Business contractions vary not only as to length but also as to depth. In the Great Depression after 1929, gross national product (GNP) fell by nearly one-half, and even after allowance for the accompanying fall in the price level, the drop was nearly one-third. None of the contractions since then has approached such magnitude. The declines in real GNP have ranged from 1.5 to 4 percent. Similarly, the unemployment rate, which by 1933 had climbed to about 25 percent, has not gone higher than from 6 to 8 percent in subsequent recessions.

Severe business contractions have wide repercussions throughout the economy—affecting not only production and employment but also prices, profits, interest rates, wages, consumer buying, and many other aspects of economic life. Mild contractions are more scattered in their effects. This phenomenon of diffusion is illustrated in the bottom line of Table 2, in terms of the percentage of industries (out of thirty that cover the entire nonfarm sector) in which employment declined. Even in the milder contractions—like those of 1926–27, 1960–61, and 1969–70—the percentage of industries registering declines ranged from 71 to 83. In the severe contractions of 1920–21, 1929–33, and 1937–38, the percentage ranged from 97 to 100, virtually encompassing all industries.

[Martin Bronfenbrenner, ed., *Is the Business Cycle Obsolete?;* Arthur F. Burns, *The Business Cycle in a Changing World;* Milton Friedman and Anna Schwartz, *A Monetary History of the United States, 1867–1960;* Wesley C. Mitchell, *Business Cycles and Their Causes;* Joseph A. Schumpeter, *Business Cycles: A Theoretical, Historical and Statistical Analysis of the Capitalist Process;* Victor Zarnowitz, ed., *The Business Cycle Today.*]

GEOFFREY H. MOORE

BUSINESS FORECASTING, the function of a large and flourishing group of specialists with its own professional organization, the National Association of Business Economists. Business forecasting takes place on three levels: at the national level; at the industry or market level; and at the individual firm level. Large corporations have their own economics departments for such forecasting—sometimes as part of operations research or market research—which are staffed by economists and statisticians who have advanced degrees. Since the largest corporations are in the national market, their staff economists must forecast domestic economic trends as a whole, trends for the specific industry in which the company operates, and trends concerning the market share of the corporation itself. In addition to such in-corporation activity, there are many private consulting firms or branches of financial firms—such as banks and securities dealers—who provide forecasting services to firms, both in a supplemental way and on an overall basis for firms that do not have their own forecasting staffs.

Nearly all business forecasting in America is strongly quantitative. Numerical forecasts of the main national accounts, national economic indicators, industry time series, and firm accounting statements are regularly prepared. At a minimum, businesses need annual forecasts. It is popular to combine forecasts for one, two, or three years ahead and to include quarterly forecasts spanning the same time horizon. Some firms need monthly or weekly forecasts, whereas others must peer into the future for two or three decades. In the latter category are life insurance corporations, forest product manufacturers, mining companies, public utilities, and, generally, firms engaged in long-term projects or activities.

The growth of multinational corporations, many of which are based in America, has made it imperative for such companies to forecast the outlook for the whole world economy in addition to that for the domestic economy. Overseas activity levels, world trade, U.S. trade, and U.S. balance of payments are the main items that command much of the attention of present-day business forecasters.

By and large, there are two approaches to business forecasting. In the judgmental approach, economists with perceptive vision of the contemporary environment and prevailing trends fit the statistical magnitudes of the economy into future patterns that appear to be plausible. These are checked for internal consistency and compared with special studies on developments in individual markets. The judgmental approach is quantitative but informal. The other approach is through formal model building. Mathematical models with statistically estimated coefficients are fitted together into logical, dynamic systems. With given historical data, information about economic policy, and expert opinion on particular areas of the economy as inputs, the model is used to predict outputs over a forecast time horizon. These models are now on-line in large computers and are used repeatedly in forecast calculations as input information changes. There is a growing reliance on these formal computerized models, modified with expert opinion. Business forecasting by government is now done in this way.

Over the years, especially since the end of World War II, the data base for business forecasting has grown stronger, more detailed, and more reliable. The improvement of data, together with the development of intricate models and heavy reliance on the computer for fast results, has greatly changed the practice of business forecasting. Now remarkably more informative and more accurate, it is widely used throughout business and government.

L. R. KLEIN

BUSINESS MACHINES. Blaise Pascal, the French philosopher and mathematician, invented the adding machine in 1642, when he was nineteen. The machine, of a type that can now be bought in any drug store for about a dollar, consisted of a series of toothed wheels with visible numbers inscribed on them for counting. Although it worked, it was not popular. Neither was the machine for multiplying and dividing invented (1672–73) by another famous philosopher, the German G. W. Leibniz. The crucial feature of Leibniz' machine was a wide drum wheel on which were cut teeth of varying lengths. By the sliding of this wheel on its axis along a series of gear wheels, the machine could be made to multiply. Numerous other calculating machines were subsequently invented, most of them variations of the Pascal or Leibniz machines, but the only one of any consequence was the arithmometer of the Alsatian Thomas of Colmar, a machine similar to that of Leibniz, introduced in 1820; it enjoyed a modest commercial success—1,500 were made over sixty-seven years—and inspired imitators after the expiration of Thomas' patent. Among the numerous unsuccessful machines was the first calculating machine, so designated in a U.S. patent granted to George W. Edelman of Philadelphia (Dec. 22, 1846).

The large-scale application of business machines did not begin with the calculating machine, but with the typewriter and the cash register; these were American inventions, in the sense that the first commercially successful examples were introduced in the United States. A typewriting machine was patented in England in 1714 by Henry Mill and was followed by many others. The first one patented in the United States was the typographer of W. A. Burt of Detroit (1829); it has been called the first that "is known to have been capable of practical work." But the machine that finally succeeded—which gave the name "typewriter" to the whole class of such machines—was developed between 1866 and 1873 by C. L.

Sholes, Carlos Glidden, and Samuel Soulé of Milwaukee, Wis. The machine worked, but its success stemmed in part from the association of James Densmore, an astute businessman, and a manufacturing agreement (1873) with the prosperous firearms manufacturing company, E. Remington and Sons.

The cash register appeared at about the same time (1879). Conceived by a Dayton, Ohio, businessman, James Ritty—reportedly inspired by a ship's engine-room telegraph he observed on an Atlantic voyage—it was simply a cashbox to which was attached a conspicuous register (and bell) on which the amount of a sale was "rung up." Ritty's attempt to sell it failed, until he was joined by Joseph Patterson, now legendary as the prototype of the supersalesman. The machine was primarily designed to discourage pilferage by clerks and met a cold reception until Patterson equipped his salesmen with miniature models that could be concealed until the salesman was in the "boss's office." Thus was launched the National Cash Register Company.

The success of the typewriter and cash register owed more to promotion than to demand, in consequence of a campaign in which the most brilliant idea was perhaps the "invention" of the female typist. By the 1890's schools flourished throughout the country for teaching ladies to type, giving many a longed-for excuse to remove themselves from the environment of the home. Resistance to the business machine was overcome, and a flood of successful inventions appeared. The parade was led by the irrepressible Thomas A. Edison, whose mimeograph (1875) began the history of the reproducing machine; whose stock ticker (1868) was the parent of the teletyping machine; and whose phonograph (1877) was soon adapted to use as a dictating machine.

The calculating machine was carried along on this wave, but its history remained complicated. A new principle for a multiplying machine, based on a gear wheel with retractable teeth (instead of the sliding gear wheel with teeth of varying length that characterized the Leibniz/Thomas machines), was introduced in 1886 by Willgodt Odhner, a Swede living in Saint Petersburg, Russia. It was manufactured there at a rate of about ten times that averaged by the Thomas arithmometer during its half-century of existence and was soon produced in comparable quantities in Sweden and Germany. The German version, Brunsviga, became the prototype of increasingly more complicated and versatile mathematical machines. Meanwhile, an American from Cincinnati, Ohio, F. S. Baldwin, had apparently anticipated Odhner by a year with a machine based on the same principle. But Baldwin, a professional inventor, had sold only ten machines by 1886 when he retired to further experimentation for twenty-five years. A calculating machine industry had developed by the time he associated himself in 1911 with Jay R. Monroe to form the Monroe Calculating Machine Company. This industry had grown up around the simple adding machine—and particularly the comptometer introduced by Dorr E. Felt in 1885 and the W. S. Burroughs calculator of 1892. Although there were essential differences between them, both these machines were based on the motion of toothed sectors (that is, pie-shaped segments of a circle) under the control of keys so placed along their length as to vary the distance traveled when the keys were depressed. These calculators sacrificed efficient multiplication for more rapid addition (and subtraction), which was more important to the accountant. They popularized the term "adding machine," and within a very short time outdistanced all competitors, in terms of quantity production. The United States came to rival Germany as the center of the calculating machine industry; indeed it was reported that the Burroughs machine was even preferred by the German post office.

The demands of commercial arithmetic account for most subsequent modifications of calculating machines, and the development was rapid. Burroughs recognized at the outset the desirability of a printed record, and his machine was consequently adapted to this purpose. The business machine promoters were also tampering with that sacred book—the ledger—and, in 1894, the loose-leaf ledger was adapted to mechanical accounting. By 1910 the accountant had available a bookkeeping machine that performed all four arithmetic operations in a loose-leaf ledger without removing the sheets from the binder or the binder from the machine. The printing feature of these machines was a challenge to the typewriter manufacturers, and the following year saw J. T. Underwood offering a typewriter modified into a billing machine with an adding register.

The supremacy of the American calculating machine industry was largely the result of its adherence to the needs of business; its leading rival, the German industry, was developing more sophisticated, but less salable, machines, capable of scientific calculations. A number of inventors of the middle 19th century had developed complicated (and expensive) machines for scientific calculations, but their work had come to nothing. The most famous of these was the Englishman Charles Babbage; but the group also included an

American, George Grant, who exhibited a scientific calculator at the Philadelphia Exposition of 1876. Grant is reported to have remarked, years later, that he "spent an immense amount of time on a difference engine or tabulating calculating machine and stopped because it was purely scientific and science is a beggar."

The first important calculating machine for science was after all American. This was the punched-card tabulating machine introduced by Herman Hollerith of Washington, D.C., for use in compiling the 1890 census. Hollerith's machine, which simultaneously sorted and counted cards on which data had been placed in a coded pattern of holes, utilized a principle that Babbage had used and that goes back to the French Jacquard tapestry loom of 1801. But Hollerith continued to improve it, leaving the government to form his own factory, which in 1911 joined with others to form the C-T-R Company, now known as International Business Machines. The company was directed from 1914 by Thomas J. Watson, who had been a protégé of Patterson at National Cash Register; and the machines were subsequently developed with the requirements of business accounting in mind. Attempts by the U.S. Census Bureau to avoid exclusive dependence on Hollerith subsequently led to the development of a rival system by James Powers, which was marketed commercially (from 1927) by the Remington Rand Company, successor to the pioneer typewriter manufacturer. Both systems were shown by L. J. Comrie, in the late 1920's, to be as adaptable to the needs of scientific calculation as to business accounting, and then merged into the evolving computer.

Of other business machines, the most remarkable development has taken place in the reproducing machine. Edison's mimeograph was joined about 1906 by a machine using a photographic process, and photostatic copies became predominant until about 1950. Since then, the most common process has been xerography, an electrostatic system invented in 1937 by Chester F. Carlson. (*See also* Computers; Phonograph; Typewriter.)

[L. J. Comrie, *The Hollerith and Powers Tabulating Machines;* H. Hollerith, "Mechanical Methods Used in Compiling Data of the 11th U.S. Census," *Proceedings of the American Association for the Advancement of Science* (1892); E. M. Horsburgh, *Modern Instruments and Methods of Calculation;* Perley Morse, *Business Machines;* L. W. Truesdale, *The Development of Punched Card Tabulation at the Bureau of the Census;* J. A. V. Turk, *Origin of Modern Calculating Machines.*]

ROBERT P. MULTHAUF

BUSING, the transporting of children by bus to school to achieve desegregation or racial balance. Before 1960 the yellow school bus had been a symbol of progress representing the nation's transition from the one-room schoolhouse to the comprehensive consolidated school, although the effect of much of this early busing was to preserve racial segregation. In 1930, 7.4 percent of America's 26 million public schoolchildren rode school buses; by 1970 this had climbed to 43.4 percent, or 18.2 million of 42 million children. The Supreme Court had ordered school desegregation in 1954, and the court's unanimous 1971 decision in *Swann* v. *Charlotte-Mecklenburg Board of Education* reaffirmed that busing was a legitimate tool. In 1970 lower federal courts began ordering busing to eliminate racial segregation in such nonsouthern cities as Denver and Detroit, and northern congressmen began joining their southern colleagues in seeking antibusing legislation, even though the U.S. Office of Education estimated that only 2 to 3 percent of all busing was for desegregation purposes. A 1971 Gallup poll found a 77 percent national opposition to busing, with blacks split almost evenly. In March 1972 President Richard M. Nixon proposed a package of antibusing measures, including a moratorium act and hints of the ultimate need for a constitutional amendment. In June Congress passed a Higher Education Act with compromise antibusing provisions, chiefly the Broomfield amendment (Rep. William S. Broomfield of Michigan), that delayed implementation of court busing orders until appeals had been exhausted. In May 1973 the Supreme Court upheld an appeals court ruling that barred Richmond, Va., from merging its predominantly black city schools with predominantly white suburban schools by busing across school district lines. In a landmark decision in July 1974 the Court ruled by a vote of five to four that the federal district and appeals courts in a Detroit case (*Bradley* v. *Milliken*) had unconstitutionally approved the merger of suburban and city schools for purposes of desegregation. Busing remained a legitimate instrument for furthering integration, but not across school district lines.

["Education for a Nation," *Congressional Quarterly* (1972).]

HUGH DAVIS GRAHAM

BUSY BEES OF DESERET, the Mormon settlers (1848) in the territory that became Utah. Deseret is the "land of the honeybee" of the Book of Mormon.

WHEELER PRESTON

BUTE, FORT, or Manchac Post, named for the British prime minister, John Stuart, third Earl of Bute, was established in 1763 at the junction of Iberville River (or Bayou Manchac) with the Mississippi River, and remained an important British military and trading post in West Florida until captured by Spanish forces under Bernardo de Galvez of Louisiana on Sept. 7, 1779.

[Alcée Fortier, *History of Louisiana*, vol. II.]

WALTER PRICHARD

BUTLER'S ORDER NO. 28. Gen. Benjamin F. Butler became military commander of New Orleans, May 1, 1862, following the fall of the city to Union troops. The marked hostility of the inhabitants of the city to the federal government was exhibited in insults to which Union officers and soldiers were subjected by the women. Accordingly on May 15, Butler issued an order to the effect that any female insulting or showing contempt for any officer or soldier of the United States should "be treated as a woman of the town plying her avocation." The order evoked a storm of protest at home and abroad and was a cause of Butler's removal from command of New Orleans, Dec. 16, 1862.

[James Ford Rhodes, *History of the United States*, vol. IV.]

JAMES E. WINSTON

BUTLER'S RANGERS, a regiment of Loyalists, recruited in 1777 by Col. John Butler with the consent of Sir Guy Carleton to serve with the Indians against the colonists. Eight companies were recruited. Their uniforms consisted of a green coat and waistcoat faced with red, buff breeches, white leggings, and a hat of the Foot Regiment pattern. From their headquarters at Fort Niagara, the Rangers embarked on forays that spread terror throughout New York and Pennsylvania. They perpetrated the Wyoming Valley invasion in July 1778, and took part in Sir John Johnson's raid on the Mohawk settlements in 1780. The regiment was disbanded in June 1784.

[E. Cruikshank, *The Story of Butler's Rangers*.]

ROBERT W. BINGHAM

BUTTE DES MORTS COUNCIL. Lewis Cass, governor of Michigan Territory, and Thomas L. McKenney, Indian commissioner, held a council with the Chippewa, Menomini, and Winnebago at Little Butte des Morts, north of Lake Winnebago, near where the Fox River flows out. A treaty was signed there Aug. 11, 1827, adjusting boundaries and the relations of these tribes with the Indians migrating to Wisconsin from New York.

LOUISE PHELPS KELLOGG

BUTTERFIELD CLAIMS. In 1854 two ships, loaded with war materials, cleared at New York for St. Thomas in the Danish West Indies. Suspicion arose that they were destined for Venezuelan rebels. Because of lack of evidence they were cleared in a libel suit. When they arrived at St. Thomas, trouble arose again because of their suspicious character. The owners presented a large claim for damages because the vessels were detained by the Danish government. Thirty-four years of negotiations ended in a Danish-American arbitration treaty (1888), as a result of which the claim was disallowed on the ground that the Danish government had observed strictly the neutrality laws involved. The name is derived from the firm that handled the negotiations.

[S. J. M. P. Fogdall, *Danish-American Diplomacy, 1776–1920*.]

S. P. FOGDALL

BUTTERFIELD OVERLAND DISPATCH. Because of much travel to Colorado after the discovery of gold there, D. A. Butterfield, backed by New York capital, organized a joint-stock express and passenger carrying service between the Missouri River and Denver. In July 1865, the route via the Smoky Hill River in central Kansas was surveyed, and soon thereafter coaches were in operation. Ben Holladay, acting for a competing organization, bought the Butterfield Overland Dispatch in March 1866 when eastern express companies threatened to take it over and establish a service between the Missouri River and Sacramento, Calif.

[LeRoy Hafen, *The Overland Mail*.]

C. C. RISTER

BUTTERFIELD OVERLAND MAIL. *See* **Southern Overland Mail.**

BYRD'S POLAR FLIGHTS. North Pole. On Apr. 5, 1926, Commander Richard E. Byrd sailed on the S.S. *Chantier* for Kings Bay, Spitsbergen, in Norway, which he intended using as the base for a flight to the

North Pole. The vessel arrived in the bay on Apr. 29. The only pier in the harbor was occupied by a Norwegian gunboat; therefore, it was necessary to ferry the big trimotor Fokker airplane, *Josephine Ford,* ashore through the drifting ice, which choked the bay, on a raft constructed from four ship's boats. This operation was successfully accomplished, and preparations for the flight commenced. After being held up by defects in the plane's skis for some days, Byrd and his pilot, Floyd Bennett, eventually took off for the North Pole shortly after midnight on May 9. The flight proceeded uneventfully until the airplane was one hour's flight short of the pole, at which time a leak was discovered in an oil tank. In spite of this they continued onward. At 9:02 A.M., Greenwich civil time, the pole was reached. After circling around it, the course was set for Spitsbergen. The return flight was uneventful, and the motors continued to function in spite of the oil leak.

South Pole. Early in the Antarctic spring of 1929 Byrd made a flight from his base at Little America to the foot of the Queen Maud Mountains and laid down a gasoline base. On Nov. 29, 1929, at 3:29 P.M., the polar flight party took off in the Ford airplane, *Floyd Bennett,* for the pole. At 9:15 they started up the Liv Glacier Pass for the Polar Plateau. The plane was so heavily loaded that it could not gain enough altitude to clear the head of the glacier. It was necessary to dump several hundred pounds of emergency food to lighten the plane enough to clear the "hump." Once over the plateau the plane made good time. At 1:14, Greenwich civil time, the pole was reached. A few minutes later the course was changed to head back to the mountains. This part of the flight developed into a race against clouds moving in from the east. After a short flight to the east the plane was landed at the fuel base. At six o'clock the return journey to Little America began. Shortly after ten the party landed at the camp.

[Richard E. Byrd, *Little America.*]

R. E. BYRD

CABANNE'S TRADING POST, established ten miles above Omaha on the west side of the Missouri River between 1822 and 1826 for the American Fur Company by John Pierre Cabanne. Between 1833 and 1840 the post was moved to Bellevue, Nebr., and placed under the management of Peter A. Sarpy.

[Hiram Chittenden, *The American Fur Trade of the Far West.*]

EVERETT DICK

CABEZA DE VACA, TRAVELS OF. In 1527, at the age of about thirty-seven, Álvar Núñez Cabeza de Vaca went to America as treasurer of the expedition led by Pánfilo de Narváez, which landed near the present city of Tampa, Fla., in April 1528. After a brief and disastrous exploration of the country the colonists built five horsehide boats and sailed for Cuba. A hurricane sank all but the one commanded by Cabeza de Vaca, and it soon was wrecked on the Texas coast. From the fall of 1528 to the spring of 1536 Cabeza de Vaca and his companions endured untold hardships, including imprisonment by Indians, in a 6,000-mile journey through the American Southwest and northern Mexico. After arriving safely in New Spain, Cabeza de Vaca returned to Old Spain to ask Charles V for the governorship of "La Florida." Instead he was given the governorship of Paraguay. His account of his travels was printed in 1555 at Valladolid, Spain, under the title *Relación y Comentarios.*

[Morris Bishop, *The Odyssey of Cabeza de Vaca.*]

A. CURTIS WILGUS

CABILDO, the Spanish governmental organization for the province of Louisiana. It was established by Alexander O'Reilly, an Irish officer in the Spanish army, in 1769, superseding the French superior council, and was abolished when France regained possession of the province in 1800. In addition to the governor, who presided, the cabildo consisted of two ordinary alcaldes (judges in New Orleans), the provincial alcalde (judge outside New Orleans), alferez real (royal standard bearer), alguacil mayor (high sheriff), depositary-general (treasurer and storekeeper), receiver of fines (collector), attorney-general-syndic (public prosecutor), mayordomo-de-propios (municipal treasurer of New Orleans), and the escribano (clerk). The cabildo met in the Government House (Casa Capitular or Principal), known today as the Cabildo.

[J. S. Kendall, *History of New Orleans,* vol. I.]

WALTER PRICHARD

CABINET. This body, which has existed since the presidency of George Washington, rests on the authority of custom rather than the Constitution or statute. It is generally composed of the heads of the major federal administrative departments: State; Treasury; Defense; Justice; Interior; Agriculture; Commerce; Labor; Health, Education and Welfare; Housing and Urban Development; Transportation. In terms of money spent, number of persons employed, and scope of legal authority, these are the most significant units of the administration. The heads of these departments are presidential appointees, subject to confirmation by the Senate and serving at the pleasure of the president.

Although all presidents have, periodically, held formal cabinet meetings, the role of the cabinet in presidential decision making has generally been limited. The importance of the cabinet varies depending on the particular president (Dwight D. Eisenhower and Lyndon B. Johnson relied on the cabinet more than Franklin D. Roosevelt or John F. Kennedy did), but as a collective body it does not play a central role in any administration. Frequently cabinet meetings are largely symbolic; they are held because of the expectation that such meetings should take place. The cabinet collectively may lack significance; but individual members can have great influence in an administration because of their expertise, political skill, or special relationship to the president (for example, John Mitchell as attorney general under Richard M. Nixon; Secretary of Defense Robert McNamara under Kennedy and Johnson; and Attorney General Robert Kennedy under Kennedy). Frequently and increasingly, cabinet members are overshadowed by the expanding White House staff (personal assistants to the president). Also of considerable importance in any administration are informal advisers to and confidants of the president.

The cabinet in the United States, unlike that in most parliamentary systems, does not function as a collegial executive; the president clearly is the chief executive. Cabinet members in the course of their work find that their survival and success generally do not depend on their colleagues or on any sense of collegiality; rather, they must often fend for themselves. Particularly crucial are their own relationships to the president, the clientele of their agency, and Congress. Also, in contrast to parliamentary systems, U.S. cabinet members may not serve in the legislative body at the same time. If a person is a member of Congress when appointed to the cabinet, that person must resign the congressional seat.

[Richard F. Fenno, Jr., *The President's Cabinet;* Louis Koenig, *The Chief Executive*.]

DALE VINYARD

CABIN RIGHTS, sometimes called "tomahawk rights," "corn rights"—even "sugar-camp rights" or, later, "settlement rights." Construction of a cabin, clearing of a small tract, or the making of other improvements on unoccupied and unclaimed land on the frontier was commonly held to be sufficient for granting title. At a later time when revenue needs led to the sale of public land, such improvements might entitle the squatter to a preferential or preemption right to buy the land from the government, state or federal, at the lowest established price. If a settler was unfortunate enough to squat upon unimproved land showing no evidence of private ownership and made his improvements only to be subject to ejectment when the absentee owner appeared, under Virginia law he was entitled to the value of his improvements or the right to buy the title at its value before he made his improvements, if he had a color of title (tax payment). In either case the value of the "occupancy" right or the land without improvements was to be determined by a local jury.

[Amelia C. Ford, *Colonial Precedents of Our National Land System As It Existed in 1800;* Paul W. Gates, *Landlords and Tenants on the Prairie Frontier*.]

PAUL W. GATES

CABLES, ATLANTIC AND PACIFIC. Telegraphy had barely been successfully established on land in the mid-1840's when thoughts turned to bridging the Atlantic Ocean. The recently discovered plastic material gutta-percha was available for insulating the copper wire; furthermore, by the early 1850's steamships large enough to make the operation feasible were being built. Starting in 1850 short lines were laid across the English Channel and in the Mediterranean. Enough of these were successful for some of their supporters to be optimistic about the chances for more ambitious ventures.

American contributions to the first Atlantic cables centered around Cyrus Field, who had made a fortune in New York in the wholesale paper business and who became a tireless promoter of the cable enterprise. Field and a few friends financed a line up to and across Newfoundland, but the money and expertise for the ocean route were to be found in England, where Field spent much of his time in succeeding years. Money was raised primarily from the merchants of London, Liverpool, and Manchester; the British and American governments supplied guaranteed subsidies for a working cable as well as ships for the laying operations. The British steamship *Agamemnon* and the American steamship *Niagara,* each with half the needed cable, made an unsuccessful attempt to lay a transatlantic cable in 1857. In 1858 they met at mid-ocean to try again. The line broke three times—each time requiring a new start—before, on Aug. 5, a single-wire connection was made between Valencia, Ireland, and Trinity Bay, Newfoundland. The event was greeted with great excitement, especially in America. Unfortunately, attempts to use high-voltage pulses aggravated flaws in the cable; its condition deteriorated rapidly; and it failed entirely by Oct. 20.

Failure made it difficult to raise more money. But other cable successes helped to restore faith; and the Civil War emphasized the need for rapid transoceanic communications. In 1865 the entire length of a transatlantic cable was loaded on board the *Great Eastern*. It broke two-thirds of the way across. But on Aug. 27, 1866, a renewed attempt was successful; the 1865 cable was then picked up and completed.

An additional cable was laid across the Atlantic as early as 1869, and in 1884 John W. Mackay, who had made a fortune in mining, and James Gordon Bennett of the *New York Herald* laid the first two American-sponsored cables. Many others followed. Over the years specialized techniques were developed to cope with the greatly attenuated, blurred signal that came through these 2,000-mile spans. Two basic modes of operation emerged, one developed by the Eastern Company (British) with its long chains of cables to the Far East, the other by Western Union (American) with its dominance—in the 20th century—of the high-density North Atlantic routes. In 1956 procedures were finally perfected for submerging repeaters, or amplifiers, with the cable; this greatly increased the information capabilities, making telephone transmission possible. Repeatered cables continued to be improved, and the older types disappeared completely.

Strong interest in a Pacific cable was expressed in the United States and Canada from 1870 on, but the commercial and political demands were not great enough, and not until 1902 was the first (British) Pacific cable laid; it ran from Vancouver to Australia and New Zealand. In 1903 the first link of an American Pacific cable (promoted by Mackay) was completed between San Francisco and Hawaii; it was extended to Guam and the Philippines in the years that followed. (About twenty years later it was discovered that 75 percent of Mackay's Pacific cable was owned by British and Danish cable companies.)

British interests dominated the world's cables in the 19th century. After 1900 they lost some ground to other national interests, notably American. The American operations, especially those of the American Telephone and Telegraph Company, have played an especially large role in the development of repeatered cables. The importance of submarine cables has been immeasurable politically, militarily, and commercially and, as many of those who celebrated the short-lived cable of 1858 realized, their effect has often been psychological, reducing U.S. separation from the rest of the world from a matter of weeks to a matter of seconds.

[Bern Dibner, *The Atlantic Cable;* Bernard Finn, *Submarine Telegraphy: The Grand Victorian Technology;* Leslie B. Tribolet, *The International Aspects of Electrical Communications in the Pacific Area.*]

BERNARD S. FINN

CABOT VOYAGES. Early in 1496 a petition was placed before Henry VII of England in the name of John Cabot, an Italian navigator, and his three sons, Sebastian, Lewis, and Sanctius, for the privilege of making explorations in the New World. Letters patent dated Mar. 5, 1496, were granted to the Cabots, and in the spring of 1497 they sailed west from Bristol. Coasting southward they discovered, it is believed, Cape Breton Island and Nova Scotia. The following year letters patent were granted to John Cabot alone, authorizing him to make further explorations along the eastern coast of North America. The discoveries made on this voyage were supposedly recorded on a map and globe made by the explorer. Both are now lost. Because there is no firsthand data concerning the Cabot voyages, Sebastian Cabot has often been confused with his father, John. Important contributions to geographical knowledge were made by the Cabots, although the descriptions of the regions they explored apply to no portion of the United States.

[G. E. Nunn, *The La Cosa Map and the Cabot Voyages;* J. A. Williamson, *Voyages of the Cabots and the English Discovery of North America Under Henry VII and Henry VIII.*]

LLOYD A. BROWN

CABRILLO EXPEDITION. In the hope of finding a direct route from Spain to the East Indies through Spanish waters, Juan Rodríguez Cabrillo and Bartolomé Ferrelo sailed on June 27, 1542, from Navidad, Mexico, and on Sept. 28 reached a port that they named San Miguel. They were in fact at San Diego Bay and thus were the discoverers of California. After getting as far north as Drake's Bay, they were forced back to the Santa Barbara Islands where Rodríguez died. Ferrelo carried on and is believed to have reached the vicinity of the Rogue River in Oregon.

[H. E. Bolton, *Spanish Explorations in the Southwest, 1542–1706.*]

OSGOOD HARDY

CABUSTO, BATTLE OF (November 1540). Cabusto, a Chickasaw town situated on the Black Warrior River near old Erie (Ala.), was the scene of one of Hernando de Soto's conflicts with the Indians. A series of engagements was fought around the old town, in which it is claimed that about 8,000 Indians participated. With Cabusto as a base, de Soto broke through the palisaded defenses of the Indians north of the river and advanced up the Tombigbee Valley. (*See also* De Soto Expedition.)

[A. B. Meek, *Romantic Passages in Southwestern History.*]

A. B. Moore

CACIQUE, a term adapted by the Spanish from the northern South American–Caribbean Carib language, in which it referred to a village, to a tribal chieftain or headman, or to both. The Spanish, having incorporated the word, then came to apply it to chiefs elsewhere in their American domains. Although the word is encountered now and again in South America, it has come to have special meaning among the Pueblo Indians of the Rio Grande area. Among the Keresan-speaking Pueblos, for example, the cacique, often a secret figure, represents peace and spiritual leadership, embodying in his presence and person the sense of tribal well-being.

[E. C. Parsons, *Pueblo Indian Religion.*]

Robert F. Spencer

CAHABA OLD TOWNS, a cluster of villages along the Cahaba River, some six miles northeast of Marion, Perry County, Ala. From Fort Claiborne in Monroe, Col. Gilbert Russell in the spring of 1814 was sent northward to Cahaba Old Towns in a futile effort to provide defense against the Creek Indians.

John B. Clark

CAHOKIA, the first permanent white settlement of consequence in Illinois, founded March 1699 by priests of the Seminary of Quebec who established the Mission of the Holy Family. Their chapel, which became the nucleus of the village, was located near the left bank of the Mississippi River, a short distance south of the present city of East Saint Louis. Cahokia took its name from the adjacent Indian village, which in 1699 contained about 2,000 Tamaroa and Cahokia.

The mission at Cahokia quickly attracted French settlers, principally from Canada, occasionally from Louisiana. Their number, however, was never large. A census in 1723 enumerated only twelve white residents, while at Kaskaskia and Fort de Chartres, the other principal settlements, 196 and 126 were counted. In 1767, after many French had moved to Saint Louis because of the cession of the Illinois country to Great Britain, Cahokia contained 300 whites and 80 blacks—about half the population of Kaskaskia. By 1800 its population had increased to 719, while that of Kaskaskia had dropped to 467.

Throughout the 18th century Cahokia exemplified several of the features of a typical French village. There was a common pasture land and a large common field divided into strips for cultivation. The church was the center of village life and the priest the most influential resident. Most of the inhabitants were *coureurs de bois,* voyageurs, and traders who mingled freely with the Indians. English and American travelers usually criticized their squalor and lack of enterprise, but they noted also a carefree gaiety impervious to the hardships and uncertainties of their way of life.

Although Cahokia became the seat of Saint Clair County, the first county organized in Illinois, its growth was not commensurate with that of the territory. In 1927 the village was incorporated, and in 1970 had a population of more than 20,000.

[C. W. Alvord, *Cahokia Records, 1778–1790;* Gilbert J. Garraghan, "New Light on Old Cahokia," *Illinois Catholic Historical Review* (1928).]

Paul M. Angle

CAHOKIA MOUNDS. The prehistoric settlement of Cahokia in the alluvial plain of the Mississippi River valley, about 4 miles northeast of present-day East Saint Louis, is the largest archaeological site north of central Mexico. A focus of development of the Mississippian culture in the Midwest between A.D. 700 and about 1450, Cahokia probably attained the status of a true city with a population estimated at 30,000 by A.D. 1000–1100. A mapping project undertaken by Melvin Fowler has demonstrated that the site was carefully planned with many of the mounds constructed with horizontal compass orientations in mind. At least 100 large platform and burial mounds and many smaller ones are within the 6-square-mile tract of the settlement or within its immediate area. Monks Mound, the largest platform mound at Cahokia and the third largest temple mound in the New World, is 300 by 200 meters at its base and 30 meters high. At one time several buildings of wattle and daub were apparently on the summit of this huge terraced earth construction, which covers 15 acres. The inhabitants of this prehistoric city lived both within and outside a wooden palisade surrounding Monks Mound and other platform and burial mounds situated around the sides of a large central plaza. Clear evidence of social stratification has been discovered by archaeologists at the south end of the plaza in a low mound that marks the point of convergence of important horizontal angles within the planned city. A male buried on a platform of 20,000 cut shell beads was found below a posthole nearly a meter in diameter that once held a huge post signifying the point of convergence. A number of retainer burials were also uncovered in the mound, including a pit with forty-one young "sacrificed" females. Another retainer burial containing four males and two females had among the grave goods a copper-wrapped staff, nineteen gaming pieces, about two bushels of uncut mica, and two caches of stone projectile points containing a total of over 700 points. Rings of posts 240 to 480 feet in diameter that once stood outside the main palisade have been interpreted as calendrical wood henges. Large numbers of often high-quality artifacts occur throughout the site, including polished, painted, and engraved ceramics tempered with crushed shell. Clearly the center of a chiefdom or early state-level society, Cahokia had immense influence throughout the Midwest. Although the presence of a planned city with flat-topped platform mounds, plazas, fortifications, and a large stratified society suggests the diffusion of ideas from Mexico or even more direct contacts, no Mexican artifacts have ever been discovered at the site. The cultural climax at Cahokia waned by A.D. 1300, and by the time the first European explorers paddled down the Mississippi only the remnants of the huge earthen mounds stood as testaments to the city's former greatness.

[*Explorations Into Cahokia Archaeology*, Illinois Archaeological Survey, bulletin 7.]

GUY GIBBON

CAHUENGA, TREATY OF, signed on Jan. 13, 1847, ending California's part in the Mexican War. After preliminary negotiations, at the old Cahuenga ranch house, Capt. John C. Frémont and Andres Pico, leader of Mexican forces in California, signed a document, the liberal terms of which were in complete accord with President James Polk's conciliatory policy.

[R. G. Cleland, *A History of California: The American Period*.]

OSGOOD HARDY

CAIRO, city in southern Illinois, the "Eden" of Charles Dickens' *Martin Chuzzlewit*, founded in 1837 by the Cairo City and Canal Company, after an earlier effort (1818) had failed. For fifteen years the town grew slowly, but the sale of lots, which commenced in 1853, and the completion of the Illinois Central Railroad attracted settlers, and by 1860 the population exceeded 2,000. During the Civil War, Cairo was of great strategic importance, and for several months both Gen. U. S. Grant and Andrew H. Foote had headquarters there (*see* Belmont, Battle of). Because of its low elevation and location at the juncture of the Ohio and Mississippi rivers, its existence depends upon extensive levees, but even these have failed to prevent several severe inundations.

[John M. Lansden, *A History of the City of Cairo, Illinois*.]

PAUL M. ANGLE

CAIRO CONFERENCES. On their way to the Teheran Conference, President Franklin D. Roosevelt and Prime Minister Winston Churchill met with Generalissimo Chiang Kai-shek at Cairo (Nov. 22–26, 1943) to discuss the war against Japan and other Far Eastern matters. (Stalin was not present because Russia was not then fighting Japan.) The three conferees issued a declaration of intent: to take from Japan all the Pacific islands occupied by it since 1914; to restore to China all territory "stolen" by Japan, such as Manchuria, Formosa, and the Pescadores Islands; and to give Korea its independence "in due course."

Returning from Teheran, Roosevelt and Churchill met with President İsmet İnönü of Turkey at the second Cairo Conference (Dec. 4–6, 1943). No significant agreements were reached, and İnönü declined to commit his country to entering the war.

CHARLES S. CAMPBELL

CAJON PASS, between the San Gabriel and San Bernardino mountains, the best route from the Mojave Desert to southern California. It was probably first known to white men when in March 1776 it was traversed by Father Francisco Garcés. The first American to discover the pass was Jedediah Smith (November 1826). Shortly afterward it became a part of the route between California and Santa Fe.

OSGOOD HARDY

CALAMITY HOWLER, a phrase contemptuously used by political opponents of the discontented Populists and agrarians during the late 1880's and 1890's. The term signifies a noisy pessimist, particularly one who disagrees with the measures and policies of the ruling political party and who foretells the economic ruin of a geographical section or the nation. It first appeared in print, it is thought, in the *Congressional Record,* Mar. 2, 1892, page 1,654. Representative Jeremiah Simpson of Kansas, in speaking to a bill appropriating funds for charitable institutions in Washington, D.C., said, "If the destitution is so great here in the capital of the country, what must it be in the other portions of our Union? It seems to me time that we had some calamity howlers here in Washington as well as in Kansas."

HARRY R. WARFEL

CALDER* V. *BULL, 3 Dallas 386 (1798), the *locus classicus* wherein the Supreme Court defined an ex post facto law: one which makes criminal an act not punishable when committed; or retrospectively increases the punishment; or alters the rules of evidence in order to convict the offender. Thus it was not unconstitutional for the Connecticut legislature to grant a retrial in a civil case.

CHARLES FAIRMAN

CALHOUN'S *DISQUISITION ON GOVERNMENT,* John C. Calhoun's reasoned views on government as seen from the point of view of the permanent minority (the South). Begun in 1843, finished to Calhoun's own satisfaction in five years' time, it elaborates the doctrine of his *South Carolina Exposition and Protest.* Its keynote is the idea of a concurrent majority. Simple majority government always results in despotism over the minority unless some way is devised to secure the assent of all classes, sections, and interests.

The argument is close-knit and convincing if one accepts the belief of Calhoun that the states retain absolute sovereignty over the Constitution and can do with it as they wish. This doctrine could be made effective by nullification. But Calhoun believed that the clear recognition of rights on the part of the states on the one hand and of the national majority on the other would prevent matters ever coming to a crisis. South Carolina and other southern states, in the three decades preceding the Civil War, had provided legislatures in which the vested interests of land and slaves dominated in the upper houses, while the popular will of the numerical majority prevailed in the lower houses. This was done in conscious acceptance of the doctrine of the *Disquisition.*

[Richard K. Cralle, ed., *Works of John C. Calhoun,* vol. I.]

JAMES ELLIOTT WALMSLEY

CALHOUN'S *EXPOSITION.* After the passage of the Tariff of Abominations the South Carolina legislature resolved that it was "expedient to protest against the unconstitutionality and oppressive operation of the system of protective duties" and appointed a committee to report thereon. In 1828, at the request of William C. Preston of the committee, John C. Calhoun prepared his *South Carolina Exposition and Protest* in which he declared the tariff of 1828 "unconstitutional, unequal and oppressive; and calculated to corrupt public virtue and destroy the liberty of the country." Drawing on the 1798 Virginia and Kentucky Resolutions, Calhoun proposed nullification as the constitutional remedy: South Carolina should call a convention which would interpose the state's veto, to be binding upon its citizens and the general government unless three-fourths of the states should amend the Constitution. Amended and published, although not adopted, by the legislature, Calhoun's *Exposition* was applied four years later in the nullification of the tariff acts of 1828 and 1832.

[Frederic Bancroft, *Calhoun and the South Carolina Nullification Movement;* John C. Calhoun, *Works,* vol. VI; D. F. Houston, *A Critical Study of Nullification in South Carolina.*]

FLETCHER M. GREEN

CALICO RAILROAD, the derisive name applied to the Lyons, Iowa, Central Railroad that was to have been built across Iowa from Lyons to Council Bluffs. The company was organized in 1853. Iowa residents purchased stock, and Iowa counties voted bonds to help build the road. Early in 1854 work on the track between Lyons and Iowa City was begun and progressed rapidly. The funds, however, were inadequate and some were misappropriated. As a result, work was stopped in June and some 2,000 engineers, contractors, and laborers were left without their pay and without work. The Iowa counties were compelled to redeem their bonds. The railroad company had a store at Lyons, and the goods, including a supply of calico, were distributed in partial payment to the workers.

[Ruth Irish Preston, "The Lyons and Iowa Central Railroad," *Annals of Iowa,* third series, vol. IX.]

RUTH A. GALLAHER

CALIFORNIA. Aboriginal California. The ancestors of the original Californians probably migrated from Asia during the last Ice Age, between 15,000 and 30,000 years ago, across the bridge of ice that then connected Asia and North America. For thousands of years until the arrival of the Spaniards the society of the California Indians remained at the level of the Stone Age, lacking agriculture and based on hunting and gathering. This condition, which misled the Spaniards and later the Anglo-Americans into supposing that the California Indians were an "inferior race," was in fact the result of the geographical and cultural isolation created by the Pacific on the west and the mountains and deserts to the east and south.

Spanish Exploration and Colonization. The extreme isolation that so long sheltered the California Indians made California nearly the last part of the Western Hemisphere to become a European colony. Although the Spanish founded their first settlement on the Pacific coast as early as 1519, at Panama, they permitted 250 years to elapse before founding their first settlement in Alta (upper) California, at San Diego in 1769. The small ships of that period required several months to sail northward against the prevailing winds from the northwest and the powerful California current flowing southward along the coast. The long voyages were especially cruel because the cause of scurvy—the absence of fresh fruits and vegetables—was not discovered until the 1770's.

The name "California," originally the name of a mythical land of Amazons in a Spanish novel written by Garcí Ordóñez de Montalvo about 1500, was first applied to Baja (lower) California, probably in the 1530's. Alta California was discovered in 1542 when Juan Rodríguez Cabrillo explored parts of its coast. In 1602–03 Sebastían Vizcaíno made the first usable maps of the coastline, and named and charted the Bay of Monterey. When at last a "sacred expedition" founded the little settlements at San Diego in 1769 and at Monterey in 1770, the plan was that of José de Gálvez, an intensely ambitious visitor general who wished to make it appear that New Spain was flourishing and expanding under his leadership. Captain Gaspar de Portolá was the military leader of the expedition, and Father Junípero Serra founded the first group of what would ultimately be twenty-one Franciscan missions extending along El Camino Real from San Diego to Sonoma.

The Mexican Province, 1821–46. Lacking the population and resources for the effective colonization of its remote northwestern frontiers, New Spain tried to make Spanish colonists out of the native Indians through the mission system. But this attempt failed, and when the missions were finally "secularized" under Mexican rule, the mission lands and cattle simply passed into the hands of a few hundred ranchers who secured huge land grants from the Mexican governors. Cowhides, known as "California bank notes" and worth about two dollars each, became the province's main commercial product. Richard Henry Dana's account of the hide trade, in *Two Years Before the Mast* (1840), pointed out how easily the United States could acquire California and how weak and unprosperous it had remained under Mexico. At the end of the Mexican period in 1846, the population other than full-blooded native Indians was only about 7,000.

Early American Period, 1846–79. When Mexico ceded California to the United States at Guadalupe Hidalgo on Feb. 2, 1848, the signers of the treaty were unaware that gold had been discovered nine days earlier, on Jan. 24, at John A. Sutter's sawmill on the south fork of the American River. Before the end of 1849 the gold rush had increased California's population above 60,000, the number required for statehood, and a convention at Monterey had drawn up a constitution forbidding slavery. State government was in *de facto* operation for nearly a year before Congress, deadlocked in dispute over the territorial expansion of slavery, finally admitted California to the Union as a part of the Compromise of 1850. The gold rush tremendously accelerated the growth of California; it greatly stimulated the economies of the United States and of the world through a much-needed increase in the money supply; and it was one of the most romantic adventure stories in modern history, as Bret Harte's fiction attests. But it brought only tragic disappointment to most of those who flocked to the diggings. At the peak in the early 1850's a miner might average twenty dollars a day, but his expenses averaged eighteen dollars. Consequently the state was full of bitterly disillusioned men who remained in it only because they had no money for transportation back to their homes. For early California society the gold rush set a tone of greed, crime, violence, and disorder. Lynchings in the mining camps were followed by more formal but equally extralegal "committees of vigilance" in San Francisco and other towns. Mistreatment of Indians, Mexicans, and Chinese in the mining areas introduced a long tradition of racial oppression in Anglo-American California.

Mining remained the dominant industry of the region until the 1870's, for the discovery of the great silver deposits of the Comstock Lode in 1859 made up for the gradual decline of gold production. Manufacturing developed slowly, and the early growth of farming was stunted by the long period (averaging seventeen years) required to perfect in the American courts the land titles based on Mexican land grants. A great drought in the early 1860's nearly wiped out the cattle industry; but wheat growing began to flourish later in the same decade, especially in the great Central Valley, and at the same time wine production increased rapidly in the coastal valleys of northern California. The citrus industry developed phenomenally in southern California in the 1870's and after.

The Central Pacific, the western part of the first transcontinental railroad, was completed in 1869 with the aid of huge federal loans and land grants, and with the use of Chinese labor. Theodore Judah, the young engineer who conceived the project, died in 1863, and this left full control to four small businessmen of Sacramento—Leland Stanford, Collis P. Huntington, Mark Hopkins, and Charles Crocker—who became the Big Four of California and made enormous fortunes by achieving a virtually complete monopoly of both rail and steamship transportation. This monopoly enabled the Southern Pacific, as the railroad was later called, to dominate not only the economy but also the government and politics of California. Its manipulations of freight rates, land prices, and politicians are brilliantly described in Frank Norris' novel *The Octopus* (1901). The opening of the railroad failed to bring the expected surge of prosperity to California, and the 1870's were a time of depression and widespread unemployment. The so-called Workingmen's party of California, organized in 1877 and led by the demagogic Denis Kearney, a self-educated Irish immigrant, demanded radical change in general and Chinese exclusion in particular. Its followers were not union labor men, but rather the unemployed and the unorganized. In 1878 the party elected most of the San Francisco delegates to the state constitutional convention that produced California's second constitution, ratified in 1879. This became the longest written constitution in the world, except for those of India and Louisiana. Because of the widespread fear of corruption by legislators, the constitution included innumerable details that should have been left to legislation, and thus it ultimately required hundreds of amendments.

Political Corruption and Reform. The new constitution attempted some important political and economic reforms, but conservative forces were able to discredit and nullify these provisions, partly by attributing them to the radical influence of the Workingmen. The new railroad commission, for example, was entirely ineffective, and the Southern Pacific's political machine continued to have far more control over state and local politics than the state government had in its attempts to regulate the railroad. The Southern Pacific and various urban public utility corporations were allied with corrupt politicians. In 1906 a graft prosecution in San Francisco began the process of overthrowing this system by exposing the corruption of the city's Union Labor party regime, masterminded by the brilliant but cynical lawyer Abraham Ruef. Simultaneously a "good government" movement gained control in Los Angeles, and in 1907 the leaders of these two movements joined with other California progressives, notably the journalist Chester Rowell of Fresno, to form the Lincoln-Roosevelt Republican League. In 1910 this organization won control of the statewide Republican party, and succeeded in nominating and electing Hiram W. Johnson as governor along with a strong progressive majority in the legislature.

In a remarkable series of reforms in 1911, the progressives established effective regulation of the railroad and other public utilities, a workmen's compensation plan, and the state's first budget system. They also enacted the initiative, the referendum, and the recall. The direct primary, adopted in 1909, had already taken the nomination of state party candidates away from state party conventions and given it directly to the voters. These measures were based on the belief of the progressives, and of the Populists before them, that government should be taken out of the hands of party bosses and given directly to the people. This doctrine was carried to an extreme in 1913 with the adoption of the cross-filing system (in effect until 1959), which permitted a candidate to file for the nomination of more than one party. Such measures greatly weakened the power and responsibility of political parties in California. Republicans were able to take credit for the adoption of the progressive reforms; and through cross-filing many Republican incumbents in the legislature were able to obtain the Democratic nominations as well as their own, and thus win reelection in the primaries. For several decades this made California almost a one-party Republican state, and thus further weakened its party system.

Movies, Oil, and Water. The "cow counties" of southern California remained thinly populated through the 1890's, but early in the 20th century the region's warm winters and moderate summers began to attract a great surge of population growth. The climate led the infant motion picture industry to "discover" California in 1907, and the movies in turn advertised southern California throughout the country. Movie cameras were not yet advanced enough to make films indoors, and the large number of sunny days in the winter made year-round filming possible. Moreover, almost any outdoor scene that film might require, from a historic battlefield to a desert, could be duplicated somewhere among the infinitely varied landscapes of the area. Within a few years the great majority of all motion pictures were being made in Hollywood, where the first studio was established in 1911.

Another industry that played a vital part in California's growth was oil, and this "black gold" became far more valuable than its yellow counterpart had ever been. The first discoveries were made in Ventura County in the 1860's. In 1892 Edward L. Doheny found rich deposits of oil in Los Angeles. Great new fields were opened in the early 20th century in the San Joaquin Valley; in the 1920's in the Los Angeles basin, Huntington Beach, Santa Fe Springs near Whittier, and Signal Hill in Long Beach; and in 1937 in Wilmington. The availability of oil and gasoline was a factor in making the use of the automobile more widespread in southern California than anywhere else in the world. By 1970 California had accounted for more than one-sixth of the nation's total oil output.

The oil refining industry demanded enormous quantities of water; growing cities needed even more for domestic consumption; and California's burgeoning agriculture depended on irrigation because of the long dry summers. Some of the state's most controversial problems grew out of these needs for water. San Francisco tapped Hetch Hetchy, a beautiful valley in Yosemite National Park, but the damming and flooding of Hetch Hetchy were delayed for many years by bitter resistance from nature lovers led by John Muir, the founder of the Sierra Club. Long aqueducts brought water to Los Angeles—first from the Owens Valley in 1913, and then from the Colorado River, where Hoover Dam was finished in 1936. Irrigation water from the great Central Valley Project, begun in the 1930's and built by the Federal Bureau of Reclamation, could be sold only for units of land no larger than 160 acres. This limitation on federally subsidized water dated from the Newlands Reclamation Act of 1902. The refusal of Congress to modify the limitation led the state government to undertake a vast project of its own to provide water for larger farms and for other uses. In 1960 the voters approved the largest bond issue in the history of an American state, for the Feather River Project to bring water from the northern Sierra to the arid western San Joaquin Valley and to southern California.

The Great Depression. California was particularly vulnerable to the ravages of the depression of the 1930's. Its agriculture had specialized in luxury foods, such as oranges, which were the first to be dropped from tightened family budgets. During the 1920's hundreds of thousands of elderly people from the Middle West had moved to southern California to retire, and had now lost their savings in bank failures. By 1934 nearly one-fifth of the people of California were on relief; more than one-fourth of those who were employable could find no jobs; and it was particularly hard for old people to find employment. Dr. Francis E. Townsend, an elderly physician of Long Beach, became a major power in politics with his plan for "revolving pensions" that would be given to everyone over sixty, and would have to be spent within sixty days.

The Republican administration of President Herbert Hoover was generally blamed for the depression; and the fact that Hoover was overwhelmingly defeated in 1932, not only in his own state of California but even in his home county of Santa Clara, suggested that California would certainly elect a New Deal Democratic governor in 1934. But radicalism ruined the hopes of the liberal Democrats when Upton Sinclair, who had previously run twice for governor as a Socialist, defeated the moderate New Dealer George Creel for the Democratic nomination in 1934. Creel complained that the resulting choice between the radical Sinclair and the right-wing Republican incumbent Gov. Frank F. Merriam was "a choice between epilepsy and catalepsy." But Sinclair's EPIC plan (End Poverty in California) was so socialistic that it frightened many conservative Democrats into voting for Merriam, who won easily. In 1938 Culbert L. Olson finally became the first and only Democratic governor of California in the first half of the 20th century, but he lacked majority support in the legislature and his attempts at a New Deal for California were badly frustrated.

World War II and After. The huge wartime expenditures of the federal government in California—largely for the building of ships and aircraft—not only brought the state out of the depression but launched it into a period of unprecedented growth. Unfortunately the war also produced a tragic mistake, when the federal government ordered the removal of all persons of Japanese ancestry, regardless of citizenship, to "relocation" camps in the interior.

California's governor from 1943 to 1953 was Earl Warren, a Republican who began his career as a conservative, but who became steadily more liberal throughout his life. A great admirer of Hiram Johnson, and particularly of Johnson's ideas of "nonpartisanship," Warren was able to win the votes of so many Democrats that in 1946 he became the only governor of California to win both the Democratic and Republican nominations, and in 1950 the first governor of California ever elected to a third term. In 1953 President Dwight D. Eisenhower appointed him chief justice of the Supreme Court, and by 1969, when he retired, the Warren Court had come to stand for a remarkable series of decisions, particularly in the areas of civil rights of racial minorities and of persons accused of crimes. Notable Warren opinions include the school desegregation ruling (1954) and the "one man, one vote" cases concerning state legislative apportionment (1962).

In 1958 a Republican blunder made possible the election of a Democratic governor, Edmund G. Brown. Conservative U.S. Sen. William F. Knowland attempted a frontal assault against organized labor by running for governor of California on a platform of a state "right to work" law that would have outlawed the union shop. California labor unions rallied to defeat Knowland. Brown's administration, from 1959 to 1967, followed what his first inaugural address described as "the path of responsible liberalism." He rejoiced in the state's phenomenal population growth and declared a public holiday to celebrate the day in 1963 when it was estimated that California passed New York to become the most populous state. California's annual production and income in 1965 were surpassed only by the United States, the Soviet Union, West Germany, Britain, and France. But in the later 1960's the state's economic and population growth slowed down. Deep cutbacks in federal spending in the aircraft, aerospace, and electronics industries brought sudden unemployment to thousands of scientists, engineers, and technicians in California, and from 1969 to 1971 California shared in a nationwide economic recession, complicated by continuing inflation.

The climate of southern California, which had long attracted so many new residents, suffered a disastrous setback with the coming of smog. First noticed in Los Angeles in 1943, air pollution gradually made several urban areas unpleasant, and even hazardous to health. Water pollution, urban and suburban sprawl, and overcrowding also contributed to a new concern for the environment and to fear of a deterioration in the quality of life.

Other major problems developed in the field of race relations. The Japanese-Americans rebounded from their wartime oppression to achieve a high degree of social advancement, but Afro-Americans, Mexican-Americans (Chicanos), and Indians (native Americans) remained in relative poverty. The demand for labor during World War II had brought hundreds of thousands of Afro-Americans to California, largely from the rural South. They were concentrated in all-black neighborhoods in a few cities, and the liberal efforts of Governor Brown and the Democratic legislature to break down the residential segregation practices of the real estate industry produced a severe white backlash. In 1964 the white majority of the state's voters overwhelmingly approved an initiative constitutional amendment repealing all of the state's fair-housing laws. This action was itself later nullified by the U.S. Supreme Court as a denial of equal protection, but in the meantime Afro-American resentment against it contributed to the terrible riot in the black ghetto of Watts in southern Los Angeles in August 1965.

The Mexican-Americans became by far the largest ethnic minority in California. In 1970 they numbered 3 million out of the state's population of 20 million, or about 15 percent. There were more persons of Mexican ancestry in Los Angeles than in any other city except the capital of Mexico itself. Most of them were concentrated in the eastern part of Los Angeles, or in other urban barrios. Others engaged in migrant agricultural labor and lived in rural slums in even deeper poverty. Hope for improvement of their condition arose in the 1960's when César Chavez led the first successful agricultural labor union in California.

A period of mass disruptions on college and university campuses began with the "free speech movement" at Berkeley in 1964 and increased with the growth of American involvement in the war in Vietnam. Public resentment against student rebels combined with public resistance against increased taxes to produce a strong conservative reaction in state politics. Ronald Reagan was swept into office as governor in 1966 as the leader of this revival of conservatism—on a pledge to "cut, squeeze, and trim" the costs of government, including the costs of public higher education. Reagan's earlier career in the movies and television had given him a charismatic personal appeal, and the very fact that he had never before held political office strengthened his stance as a "citizen politician." To describe his political philosophy and program Reagan adopted the slogan "the Creative Society," stressing his belief that private enterprise with the greatest possible freedom from government control was the most important creative force in America.

When Richard M. Nixon—former congressman, senator, and presidential candidate—was defeated for the governorship of California by Brown in 1962, many newspapers opined that the voters had "retired him from politics." Yet in 1968 Nixon became the first native son of California to be elected president of the United States. (He was triumphantly reelected in 1972, but a few months later his presidency was tragically discredited by the Watergate scandals involving the tactics that had been used to secure his reelection, and he resigned in August 1974.) California had thus produced a conservative Republican governor and a conservative Republican president. This was a significant political change, even though the conservatives failed to control either the state legislature or Congress. Liberal governors like Warren and Brown had not only welcomed the state's headlong growth, but had believed in using government and government money to aid that growth. The shift in executive leadership coincided with a shift to a new set of general values. For Californians, the greatest numbers had always been the greatest good. Now they were coming to feel that growth should be measured in qualitative rather than quantitative terms. When Edmund G. Brown, Jr., became governor in 1975, many of his ideas and policies reflected this change in outlook.

[H. H. Bancroft, *California;* Walton Bean, *California, An Interpretive History;* J. W. Caughey, *California;* C. E. Chapman, *A History of California: The Spanish Period;* R. G. Cleland, *A History of California: The American Period.*]

WALTON BEAN

CALIFORNIA ALIEN LAND LAW. To check the increasing competition of Japanese immigrant farmers, the California legislature passed the Alien Land Law of 1913. The act was amended and extended by popular initiative in 1920 and by the legislature in 1923 and 1927. These laws expressly permitted aliens who were eligible for American citizenship to acquire, enjoy, and transfer real property in the state to the same extent as citizens of the United States. On the other hand, individual aliens who were not eligible for citizenship and corporations in which a majority of members were such aliens, or in which a majority of the capital stock was owned by them, were permitted to hold real property only as stipulated in existing treaties between the United States and their respective countries. The law was repealed in 1955 after it was ruled that the law violated the Fourteenth Amendment.

P. ORMAN RAY

CALIFORNIA BANK NOTES. In the 1820's California became well known to the New England states through the hide and tallow trade. Californians depended on Boston ships for all goods of foreign manufacture and generally paid for them with hides, commonly known as California bank notes, and averaging $1.50 to $2.00 in value.

OSGOOD HARDY

CALIFORNIA BATTALION. On July 5, 1846, at Sonoma, Capt. John C. Frémont absorbed into his command most of the American settlers and adventurers who had begun the Bear Flag Revolt on June 14. The total of 234 men was, at Monterey on July 23, enlisted by Commodore Robert F. Stockton as the Navy Battalion of Mounted Riflemen. Augmented to some 400 volunteers, the California Battalion served through the remainder of the American campaign against the Spanish Californians, participating under Frémont in Stockton's first capture of Los Angeles, Aug. 13, and later receiving the final surrender of Gen. Andres Pico's Californians to Frémont at the Cahuenga ranch on Jan. 13, 1847. It was mustered out of service, unpaid, April 1–19, 1847. The question of merging the battalion with the regular U.S. forces under Gen. Stephen W. Kearny was an important part of the Kearny-Frémont controversy, which led to Frémont's later arrest and court-martial.

[H. H. Bancroft, *History of California*, vol. V; Allan Nevins, *Frémont, the West's Greatest Adventurer.*]

RUFUS KAY WYLLYS

CALIFORNIA TRAIL, a term applied to various through trails to California, the earliest ones being up the peninsula (1769) and northwest from Sonora (1774). From Santa Fe the Old Spanish Trail, made known (1776) by the Juan de Escalante expedition, followed the Chama River, crossed Colorado into Utah, and later was extended southwest to Los Angeles. Early traders and trappers also went west through

Zuni, then southwest by Salt River and west by the Gila, or (later) from Zuni west to the Mohave country. Still other trails followed the Rio Grande south, then struck west to the headwaters of the Gila. In the 1840's gold-seekers converged in the Salt Lake Valley via the Platte River, Pueblo–Fort Bridger, and Frémont trails, then continued west into northern California.

[R. P. Bieber, "The Southwestern Trails to California in 1849," *Mississippi Valley Historical Review*, vol. 12 (1925).]

LANSING B. BLOOM

CALIFORNIA* V. *CENTRAL PACIFIC RAILROAD COMPANY (1888). The Supreme Court held that, under the commerce and other clauses, Congress has power to construct interstate means of transportation directly or by charter through corporations, and that California could not tax the franchise thus granted by the United States.

[Charles Warren, *The Supreme Court in U.S. History*.]

JAMES D. MAGEE

CALOMEL, or mercurous chloride, was used throughout the 19th century in the United States as a popular medication, especially for malarial fevers. Although known in colonial days, calomel first came to be widely used as a result of its administration by Benjamin Rush in the Philadelphia yellow fever epidemic of 1793. Rush attempted to remove the "poison" by bleeding and strong purgatives (calomel, rhubarb, and jalap), a practice borrowed from John Mitchell of Virginia (1741). One of Rush's pupils, John Esten Cooke, extending the theory to practically all diseases, gave wide currency to the practice through his lectures and writings at Transylvania University (1827–37). He advised repeated and strong doses, even a dram in extreme cases. At the Louisville Medical Institute (1837–44) Cooke found complaints against his teaching, which finally caused his resignation. A milder dosage known as Cooke's pills (one to two grams of calomel with aloes, rhubarb, and soap) was popular for many years. While W. A. Hammond was surgeon general (1862–64), calomel and tartar emetic were banned from the supply list, but were later restored. Calomel is still used, but rarely, as a cathartic, diuretic, and antiseptic.

[Richard H. Shryock, *Medicine and Society in America, 1660–1860*, and *The Development of Modern Medicine*.]

W. C. MALLALIEU

CALUMET. *See* **Pipe, Indian.**

CALUMET AND HECLA MINE, a copper mine in the Keweenaw Peninsula of Lake Superior in northwest Michigan. For some years previous to its discovery by Edwin J. Hulbert in 1859 copper exploration and mining had been taking place in the region. Hulbert uncovered the conglomerate lode in 1864. The geological deductions that led to this result were based upon the discovery of masses of breccia scattered upon the ground, which suggested to Hulbert a search for the mother lode. The Calumet and the Hecla mines opened as separate undertakings under Hulbert's management, but in 1866 Alexander Agassiz was sent out from Boston to superintend the initial stages of development. The problem of separating the conglomerate copper from its rock matrix was solved with great difficulty. The country was then very remote and wild, having only water transportation in the summer and none in the winter. In spite of difficulties the two original mines paid dividends in 1869 and 1870, and in 1871 were consolidated into the Calumet and Hecla Mining Company. Other mining companies were opened in the vicinity, at first under distinct corporations, but by 1923 most of them had consolidated with the Calumet and Hecla Company.

Several shafts reached a depth of over a mile on the vertical and considerably over that on the vein or incline. Early milling methods did not recover all the copper from the rock, and the old tailings have been reworked with modern methods with remarkable results. (*See also* Copper Industry.)

[T. A. Richard, *A History of American Mining*.]

LEW A. CHASE

CALVINISM, in its broadest sense, is the entire body of conceptions arising from the teachings of John Calvin. Its fundamental principle is the conception of God as absolutely sovereign. The statement of Calvinism most influential in America was the Westminster Confession (1647). Its doctrinal portion was accepted by the New England Congregationalists and embodied in their Cambridge Platform (1648). American Presbyterians coming from Scotland and North Ireland were sternly Calvinistic. The Synod of Philadelphia, the oldest general Presbyterian body in America, passed the Adopting Act in 1729, which required all ministers and licentiates to subscribe to the Westminster Confession. Other Calvinistic bodies in America are the two reformed churches, the Dutch and the German, and all other Presbyterian bodies.

[W. W. Sweet, *Story of Religions in America.*]

WILLIAM W. SWEET

CALVO DOCTRINE, enunciated in 1885 by Carlos Calvo, Argentinian diplomat and jurist, held that foreigners should be denied the right to appeal to their own governments for enforcement of contracts. Latin American governments often will include a Calvo clause in a contract with a foreigner in which the foreigner gives up the right of appeal to his own government for such enforcement. The Calvo doctrine is to be distinguished from the Drago doctrine, given validity by the Hague Convention of 1907, prohibiting the use of force in the collection of public debts.

[A. S. Hershey, "The Calvo and Drago Doctrines," *American Journal of International Law* (1907, 1926).]

CAMBODIA, BOMBING OF. As part of the American involvement in the war in Vietnam, bombing operations in Cambodia began on Mar. 18, 1969. The operations were initially conducted by B-52's and were begun to reduce a threat to U.S. ground forces that were being withdrawn as part of President Richard M. Nixon's program to end U.S. ground involvement. At the time of the decision to begin these B-52 strikes, American casualties were running at a rate of about 250 a week. The North Vietnamese had established huge stockpiles of arms and munitions in Cambodian sanctuaries, from which they continually launched attacks across the border into South Vietnam against American troops. These enemy forces would then quickly return to their sanctuaries to rearm and prepare for further action. The air strikes, in conjunction with other factors—such as the reduction of the overall vulnerability of American forces as they relinquished the major combat roles to South Vietnamese forces—cut the number of American ground casualties in half.

Limited tactical air operations in Cambodia began on Apr. 24, 1970, preparatory to ground operations during the American-Vietnamese incursion. The purpose of these strictly controlled operations, made with the acquiescence of the government of Cambodia, was to destroy long-standing North Vietnamese base areas and supply depots near the Cambodian border and cause the North Vietnamese to disperse their forces further. After the withdrawal of U.S. ground troops from Cambodia on June 30, 1970, tactical air and B-52 strikes continued at the request of the Cambodian government. These missions were approved by Federal Armée National Khmer (FANK) representatives prior to execution. Air strikes continued, again at the request of the Cambodian government, until Aug. 15, 1973, when they were terminated as a result of congressional action. These operations lasted four and a half years, but they represented only about one percent of the total U.S. air activity in the Vietnam War.

PHILIP D. CAINE

CAMBRIDGE, a city in northeastern Massachusetts, settled in 1630. Originally intended as the seat of government of the Massachusetts Bay Colony, the town was early abandoned by Gov. John Winthrop and others in favor of Boston, leaving Deputy Gov. Thomas Dudley and Simon Bradstreet to found New Towne, as Cambridge was first called. For a time Rev. Thomas Hooker's company settled there (1632–36) before removing to Connecticut. Their places were taken by the company of Rev. Thomas Shepard, who became the first permanent minister of the town. The name was changed to Cambridge in 1638, two years after the founding of Harvard College. In 1639 Stephen Day set up the first printing press in North America at Cambridge. Since then the city has been a major cultural and literary center.

Cambridge is also the site of the Massachusetts Institute of Technology and the Smithsonian Astrophysical Observatory. These institutions, along with Harvard University, have made scientific and industrial research a major activity of the city. The 1970 population of the city was just over 100,000.

[S. A. Drake, *History of Middlesex County;* L. R. Paige, *History of Cambridge.*]

R. W. G. VAIL

CAMBRIDGE AGREEMENT, a decision made and signed by Puritan members of the Massachusetts Bay Company on Aug. 26, 1629, that if the charter and company could be legally transferred to New England, they would migrate there with their families. By accepting the agreement and overcoming the legal obstacle concerning removal, the company, originally organized for purposes of trade, shifted its emphasis of interest from commerce to religion. Although the joint stock remained under the direction of English businessmen for some time, henceforth the control of the plantation was in the hands of Puritans, who, dissatisfied with the prospect of religious and political reform at home, looked to the Massachusetts project as an opportunity to establish a Calvinistic utopia. The sequel to the Cambridge Agreement was the Great Migration of March 1630, when more than 1,000 Puritans transferred families and effects to New England for the purpose of building a colony based on their ideas of close union of church and state.

[C. M. Andrews, *The Colonial Period of American History,* vol. I.]

VIOLA F. BARNES

CAMBRIDGE PLATFORM, a resolution drawn up by a synod of ministers from Massachusetts and Connecticut (August 1648), which met pursuant to a request of the Massachusetts General Court. The New England authorities desired a formal statement of polity and a confession of faith because of the current Presbyterian ascendancy in England and the activities of local Presbyterians such as Dr. Robert Child. The platform, written by Richard Mather, endorsed the Westminster Confession and for ecclesiastical organization upheld the existing Congregational practice. The Cambridge Platform remained the standard formulation in Massachusetts through the 18th century and in Connecticut until the Saybrook Platform of 1708.

[Perry Miller, *Orthodoxy in Massachusetts;* Williston Walker, *The Creeds and Platforms of Congregationalism.*]

PERRY MILLER

CAMDEN, BATTLE OF (Aug. 16, 1780). Following Gen. Benjamin Lincoln's disaster at Charleston, Gen. Horatio Gates was given command of the American army in the South, consisting of 1,400 regulars under Baron (Johann) de Kalb and 2,052 militia. Marching southward from Hillsboro, N.C., Gates occupied Rugelys Mill, a strong position about thirteen miles northeast of Camden that had been occupied by the British under Lord Rawden. Gates unwisely sent 400 regulars to help Thomas Sumter cut the British lines of communication far to the southeast (*see* Hanging Rock, Action at). Failing to attack promptly, he allowed Lord Cornwallis time to arrive with reinforcements. The two generals decided to surprise each other. Cornwallis, with 2,000 veterans, marched northward and met Gates marching southward early in the morning of Aug. 16. The Americans were exhausted from long marches, many helpless with dysentery, and more than half were militia who had never been under fire. The two forces met near Camden, S.C. At the first attack the militia fled. The regulars, standing their ground, were surrounded and almost annihilated. De Kalb was mortally wounded and captured. The Americans lost 2,000 killed, wounded, and captured, seven cannon, 2,000 muskets, and their transport. The British loss was 324. Gates fled to Hillsboro and vainly attempted to rally his demoralized army and call out more militia, but his day was over. On Dec. 2 he was replaced by Nathanael Greene. Many Americans fled to the swamps and mountains and carried on guerrilla warfare.

[John W. Fortescue, *History of the British Army,* vol. III; Edward McCrady, *The History of South Carolina in the Revolution.*]

NELSON VANCE RUSSELL

CAMDEN-YORKE OPINION. A written opinion, professional and not judicial in character, was given in 1769 by Lord Camden, who was at the time lord chancellor of Great Britain, and Charles Yorke, who was later to be raised to the same eminent position. It related to the rights of private persons who had taken conveyances of lands from native tribes of India and supported such titles, grants from the king not being necessary. It was held that the king only had sovereignty over the inhabitants as English subjects. The opinion was seized on by certain western land companies in America as applicable to any purchases they might make from the aborigines as proprietors of the soil. Many public men and lawyers in America concurred in the soundness of the opinion, Patrick Henry among them. When the matter came to judicial test in the United States after the Revolution, the contrary view prevailed: titles to lands acquired from the American Indian tribes were void when the state had not given consent; the real title was held to be in the state as sovereign.

[C. W. Alvord, *Mississippi Valley in British Politics.*]

SAMUEL C. WILLIAMS

CAMELS IN THE WEST. As a result of the Mexican War, the United States added 529,189 square miles to its area. This territory contained no railroads, and the difficulties of transportation were so great that an effort was made to establish fast express routes across this new country by using camels. Congress in 1855 appropriated $30,000 to purchase camels in Egypt and Asia. Seventy-six camels were brought to Texas (1856). Twenty-eight of them were taken to California (1857) to be used on mail and express routes through the desert country, but after a few trips their use was discontinued. They were sold at auction in 1864, most of them being taken to Nevada and used to carry freight to and from the mines. Those remaining in Texas were sold to circuses and zoological gardens. The only other importation of camels was in 1860–62. Forty-five animals were brought from Siberia to San Francisco by Otto Esche, a German merchant, who planned to use them on eastbound express routes. He never started this service but sold most of the camels to a mining company in British Columbia. Years later wild camels were occasionally seen in the Northwest, in Nevada, and especially in Arizona. All American camels are now extinct.

[Lewis B. Lesley, "Uncle Sam's Camels," *California Historical Society Quarterly* (1930).]

A. A. GRAY

CAMINO DEL DIABLO, or the Devil's Highway, an old and difficult trail connecting a series of desert water holes northwestward from the Rio de Sonoita to the Gila River near its confluence with the Colorado River. Apparently it was first traced by white men when the Jesuit missionary Eusebio Francisco Kino traversed it in February 1699. The trail crossed the present boundary of Mexico and the United States some forty miles northwest of the border town of Sonoita, and thence crossed the Tule Desert westward to the southeastern end of the Gila Range, following the latter's eastern slope to the Gila River. As a shortcut from the settled portion of Sonora through the lands of the Papago to the Colorado and thence into California, it was frequently used by travelers, including Juan Bautista de Anza's exploring party of 1774 to California.

[H. E. Bolton, *Rim of Christendom,* and *Outpost of Empire;* K. Bryan, *Guide to Desert Watering Places.*]

RUFUS KAY WYLLYS

CAMPAIGN RESOURCES. Both human and material resources are necessary to acquire, retain, and nurture political power. These resources can be purchased or volunteered and—to be used effectively—must be organized, patterned, and channeled in varying combinations. Political power is built on three constituencies: (1) the electoral, in which efforts are made to move (or sometimes for strategic reasons not to move) people to register and vote; (2) the financial, which represents mainly wealth, goods, and services and in which money is converted to other resources by enabling the purchase of goods and services that are not or cannot be volunteered; and (3) the organizational, in which individuals and groups coalesce in various ways, through political parties or independently, to help or hinder political objectives. Each of these constituencies interacts with the others in the processes of campaigning to win nomination and election and in bargaining for political power and influence.

Human resources include personal energies, intelligence, and skills. Staff and volunteer energies must be structured into the manpower demands of modern campaigning. "Intelligence" is used in two senses here: to mean the seeking of information for campaigns and the application of thought processes to the organization of human and material resources in winning combinations. Professional and technical skills are necessary in the organizational, publicity, and financial management of modern campaigns. These skills rate high in increasing campaign costs, because many of the skills needed—for instance, in producing and disseminating publicity; organizing registration, fund-raising, or get-out-the-vote drives; providing organizational and financial management—cannot be volunteered but must be purchased. For these purposes professional campaign managers, media consultants, and advertising specialists must be employed. Furthermore, each brings attendant costs in human and material needs. Human resources, of course, also include the personal qualities of the candidate; and his organization's ability to shape a favorable image, as well as to develop issues and exploit events, are crucial factors in a successful campaign.

Material resources include the money, goods, and services necessary for modern campaigning. Expenditures fall roughly into four general categories: (1) overhead, including the maintenance of campaign headquarters and staff; (2) field activity, including meetings, rallies, travel, and other expenses incurred in bringing the candidate into direct contact with the voters; (3) publicity, which means all forms of advertising, literature, and means of communication, including radio and television; and (4) election-day activities, including expenditures for election-day work, poll watchers, cars, and drivers. The effectiveness of any campaign technique or category of expenditure over another has not yet been measured, but many campaign activities clearly are essential. There is no uniformity in patterns of spending. In campaigns for major offices, broadcasting and related costs in producing presentations are sometimes the largest item in a campaign and are the highest single functional campaign cost in the nation. At the local level, on the other hand, the largest functional expenses relate to registration and election-day activities.

Goods and services paid for by a corporation or by a labor or other special-interest organization are prohibited under federal law and in some states. When "in-kind" contributions of goods and services are permitted, the law may require that they be disclosed and a value put upon them in the same manner as money contributions (*see* Publicity Laws).

If money is unique because it can be converted into other resources, other resources can in turn be converted into political money. The politician can use the privileges of public office to award contracts, fill jobs, and make decisions that attract dollars. Skillful use of ideology, issues, and the perquisites and promises of office attract financial support to political actors—both in legitimate forms as contributions or dues and in illegitimate ways, as scandals demonstrate from time to time.

Political money, however, is only symbolic of true political goals. The real competition is for power, prestige, and other satisfactions. Instrumental in this struggle, money's importance lies in the ways in which it is used by people to gain influence, is converted into other resources, or is used in combination with other resources to achieve political ends. Because of its universality, money is a tracer element in the political process, marking the tracks both of the individual or group seeking influence and of the candidate and party seeking election to office. Revelation of their financial transactions and associated behavior deepens understanding of the flows of influence and power.

American candidates and parties spent record amounts—about $425 million—on political activity at all levels in 1972. This record spending was more than triple the $140 million spent twenty years earlier. The 1972 spending was in four major areas: $135 million to elect a president, including prenomination campaigns and minor party candidates; $98 million to nominate candidates and elect a Congress, including labor, business, professional, and miscellaneous committee expenditures not disbursed to and spent by candidates; $95 million to nominate candidates and elect governors, other statewide officials, and state legislators and to campaign for and against state ballot issues and constitutional amendments; and $95 million to nominate candidates and elect the hundreds of thousands of county and local public officials.

Considerable disagreement exists as to whether funds for campaigning should come exclusively or partially from private or public sources or in combination. The Revenue Act of 1971, amended by the Federal Election Campaign Act of 1974, provides that individuals be allowed a credit against their federal income tax in an amount equal to one-half of all contributions to qualified candidates or committees, not to exceed $25 in the case of a single return or $50 in the case of a joint return; alternatively, an individual may claim a deduction from his federal taxable income in an amount not to exceed $100 on a single return or $200 on a joint return. The purpose is to encourage more small contributions by providing limited tax incentives for political contributions, thus causing federal-government sharing of some of the costs of politics. The amended act also provides for a tax checkoff whereby taxpayers can direct that $1 of the tax paid on a single return or $2 on a joint return be diverted to a fund for distribution to nominated candidates for president who want the funds, who meet requirements of sufficient support, and who agree not to raise funds privately; provides for expenditure ceilings and limited matching subsidies for candidates for presidential nomination, once a threshold level of private contributions is raised; and further provides optional but limited government funding for the political parties to hold the national nominating conventions. The long-range implication of these provisions is that the federal government will assume direct responsibility for certain candidates for the presidency in the general election period. By 1974 eleven states had some form of tax incentive for political contributions tied to state income taxes. Moreover, four states have some form of dollar tax checkoff applicable to state income taxes, and two states provide a tax surcharge permitting taxpayers to add $1 to the tax bill; the monies generally go to designated political parties or neutral funds for party distribution according to formula. Three states have forms of government funding for gubernatorial elections, New Jersey (effective in 1977) and Maryland and Minnesota (effective in 1978).

[Alexander Heard, *The Costs of Democracy*.]

HERBERT E. ALEXANDER

CAMPAIGNS, POLITICAL, are organized efforts to win elections in order to gain public office or to gain power, influence, or prestige. Campaigns are drives for votes made by political parties and candidates and their auxiliary organizations, culminating in elections that are won by a majority or plurality, as determined by constitutional or legal provisions. Campaigns are held for nomination or for election: nomination campaigns include primary and runoff primary elections, conventions, and caucuses; the final phase is the campaign for general or special election. Not all campaigns are directed at winning an election. If victory seems impossible, the campaign may attempt to affect the outcome (for example, in a presidential election it may try to splinter a potential majority in the electoral college); it may attempt to educate the electorate over a long period of time, as minor and single-issue parties do; it may attempt to focus attention on and crystallize an issue or series of issues, as factional contests do in primaries; or it may attempt to project an individual for future consideration for public office or for purposes of ego satisfaction.

In addition, campaigns are waged for or against initiatives, referenda, ballot measures, bond issues, and constitutional amendments in states and localities. Except in some states or in special circumstances, such campaigns are not hotly contested, since the element of personal rivalry is absent. Petition campaigns are undertaken to obtain enough voter signatures for the candidate or party to qualify on the ballot; petition drives may also be conducted when recall elections are permitted.

Political campaigns in the United States range from the White House to the courthouse, from the quadrennial presidential contests to countless state, county, and local races for executive, legislative, judicial, special district, and special unit offices. In all, some 521,000 public offices are filled by elections, not counting campaigns for nomination to run for many of those offices or for party offices (*see* Campaign Resources).

Campaigns are designed to reach a growing electorate, swelled both by natural increases and by the extension of the right of suffrage, provided successively to poor white males prior to 1850, to Afro-Americans after the Civil War, to other minorities under the 1965 and 1970 Voting Rights acts, to women under the Nineteenth Amendment to the Constitution, and to young people under the Twenty-sixth Amendment. In 1972 there were almost 140 million persons eligible to register and vote, and about 55 percent of them voted in the presidential election. The proportion of those actually registered who cast ballots was a somewhat higher 76 percent.

The rapid expansion of the electorate helped to trigger the development of political parties as coalescing and unifying bodies in elections. The two major parties, the Democratic and the Republican, grew into the largest, most extensive nongovernmental organizations in the nation—serving crucial functions in recruiting candidates and workers, registering voters, getting voters to the polls, and presenting an information flow about election alternatives. The parties collect funds, conduct campaigns through their own or auxiliary bodies, and activate widespread participation. Although large, the parties are decentralized and thus are subject to two strong countertendencies that have emerged: reform movements seeking to democratize politics have sometimes removed the nominating function from the party organization by legally substituting primaries for party conventions; and the increased socioeconomic levels of the electorate have led to greater independence in voting; this tendency has been reinforced by new technologies, such as television, that stress the individual candidate over his party label.

One vital campaign function is to inform—to convey information, knowledge, and opinions to potential voters. Ideally this function is intended to stimulate rational voting decisions. In actuality, campaigns are appeals to reason mixed with emotion. Differences about the roles of governments and about public policies make factional divisions inevitable. Competing philosophies require publicity, and in the American experience, supporters of differing views and candidates have been quick to take to the printed word, and not only at election times. The system of newspaper support of, or support by, one political faction or the other—often supplemented by government printing subsidies—developed early. The printed word was used not only in newspaper columns and in letters to the editors but also in party pamphlets, campaign biographies, and throwaways. Pictures, buttons, banners, and novelty items appeared. Rallies were held. The first use of radio in political campaigns occurred in 1924. The years 1948–52 marked the beginning of television presentations. Modern developments also include public opinion polling; jet and helicopter travel; and use of computers for registration and voting analyses and for fund, mail, and telephone drives.

New methods of campaigning tend to supplement existing ones, and little displacement of the old by the new has occurred. Of course, forms of campaigning do change: for example, when newspapers became more independent and divorced from direct party or factional control and government subsidies ended, parties and candidates turned to direct purchased advertising as well as to indirect attempts to influence editorial and news columns. Events and press releases are now timed to meet press deadlines. Television has reordered campaigns, with itineraries, speeches, and national nominating conventions planned according to the dictates of prime time.

Political campaigns can be divided into four subcampaigns: for funds, for the support of party leaders and party organizations, for the support of interest-group leaders and organizations, and for the support of the electorate at large. Considerable dialogue has been held regarding the form, length, and content of political campaigns. Critics object to certain practices in the conducting and funding of campaigns (*see* Publicity Laws). Considerations of ethics and fair play are ever present.

[Stanley Kelley, Jr., *Political Campaigning: Problems in Creating an Informed Electorate*.]

HERBERT E. ALEXANDER

CAMPAIGNS, PRESIDENTIAL, have taken place in the United States every fourth year, beginning in 1788. They include both the process of candidate nomination and the subsequent campaign for election. Since the 1830's, nomination has centered on national party conventions called to choose individuals to run for president and vice-president and to adopt the party's platform. Delegate selection for these conventions was for a long time wholly extralegal and determined by local party traditions. Early in the 20th century some states set up presidential primaries to choose delegates and record voter preferences among the aspiring candidates. In the late 1960's a further reform movement began to broaden the ability of party members to participate in delegate selection and to reduce the influence of party organizations.

An incumbent president who desires renomination usually obtains it without a convention contest. If he does not want it or has already served two terms, the convention makes the final choice, sometimes only after a lengthy and bitter struggle. Since the late 1950's, rapid modes of transportation and ease of communication have often enabled one candidate to build up a strong lead prior to the convention and to win on the first ballot. Thus, the preconvention campaign has become the decisive part of the nominating process. Broadening public participation has reduced the role of state party leaders and hence has also reduced past practices of convention bargaining among politicians who control blocs of delegates.

Candidates for president were often chosen from among successful governors, especially the governors of key states like Ohio and New York, which have large blocs of electoral votes. Men who had made their reputations as military leaders were also frequent choices. After World War II the trend was away from governors in favor of U.S. senators because of greatly increased American concern with foreign relations and the greater national "visibility" senators can acquire.

Once chosen, the presidential candidate selects a new national party chairman and sets up his own campaign organization. In the 19th century the nominee himself did little stumping and conducted instead a "front porch" campaign, but the 20th century saw a tendency for increased candidate involvement, often reaching a frantic pace after the middle of the century. From the 1920's on, radio figured prominently in getting the candidates' messages disseminated; since the 1952 campaign, television has been the key medium. Generally the media increased in importance as grass-roots party organization declined in vigor and usefulness. Public relations experts and opinion pollsters also came to occupy crucial roles in campaign management.

Little has changed overall in the extent to which presidential campaigns emphasize general appeals and slogans rather than focus on clear-cut issues. With communications improvements, these appeals are more often carefully designed for national audiences instead of being tailored to each local group encountered on a campaign tour. Nevertheless, the New Deal era and the elections of 1964 and 1972 did see issues posed more sharply than is usual.

[Nelson Polsby and Aaron Wildavsky, *Presidential Elections;* Gerald Pomper, *Nominating the President: The Politics of Convention Choice*.]

ELMER E. CORNWELL, JR.

Campaigns of 1788 and 1792. These first two campaigns had no formal nominations, only one presidential candidate, and little opposition to the second choice. The Constitution ratified, the Continental Congress delayed three months before fixing the first Wednesday in January 1789 for choosing electors, the first Wednesday in February for their voting, and the first Wednesday in March for starting the new government. Pennsylvania, Maryland, and Virginia elected electors; the Massachusetts legislature chose from elected electors; New Hampshire's election failed and its legislature appointed electors, as did those of the remaining states. Thirteen states could cast ninety-one votes; but two states had not ratified, and one (New York) failed to elect or appoint electors; four electors failed to vote. George Washington received sixty-nine votes, one of the two votes of every elector. John Adams received thirty-four of the second votes, and the other thirty-five were scattered among ten different candidates (John Jay, Robert Harrison,

John Rutledge, John Hancock, George Clinton, Samuel Huntington, John Milton, James Armstrong, Edward Telfair, and Benjamin Lincoln).

In 1792 fifteen states could cast 132 electoral votes. Alexander Hamilton's financial measures and the consolidation of national power (*see* Federalist Party) roused an opposition (Jeffersonian Antifederalists), which centered its efforts on the defeat of Adams by the Antifederalist George Clinton, since to defeat Washington was seen to be futile. The attempt failed. Washington's vote was again unanimous, and Adams defeated Clinton by seventy-seven votes to fifty.

[Edward A. Stanwood, *A History of the Presidency*.]

JOHN C. FITZPATRICK

Campaign of 1796. For the first time, the national election was contested by political parties. The French Revolution, the Genêt affair, and the Jay Treaty resulted in bitter partisanship. Without the modern machinery of nomination, the Federalists informally agreed upon John Adams as Washington's successor; with him they chose Thomas Pinckney. With more enthusiasm the Democratic-Republicans (*see* Republican Party, Jeffersonian) chose their leaders, Thomas Jefferson and Aaron Burr. Electors were chosen in sixteen states—in six by popular vote, in ten by the legislature. Of the total electoral votes Adams secured seventy-one, Jefferson sixty-eight, Pinckney fifty-nine, Burr thirty, and the remaining forty-eight were divided among nine others.

[Edward A. Stanwood, *A History of the Presidency*.]

FRANK MONAGHAN

Campaigns of 1800 and 1804. The election of 1800 marks a turning point in American political history. Its preliminaries were expressed in the Virginia and Kentucky Resolutions proffered by Thomas Jefferson and James Madison as a party platform. Its party machinery, still more essential to success, was directed by Aaron Burr with supplemental support in Pennsylvania and South Carolina.

Burr had already established the nucleus of a political machine that was later to develop into Tammany Hall. With this organization he swept New York City with an outstanding legislative ticket, gained control of the state assembly, and secured the electoral votes of New York for the Democratic-Republicans (*see* Republican Party, Jeffersonian). He had already secured a pledge from the Democratic-Republican members of Congress to support him equally with Jefferson. Hence the tie vote (seventy-three each) that gave him a dubious chance for the presidency. The Federalist candidates were John Adams, sixty-five votes, and Charles Cotesworth Pinckney, sixty-four votes.

Publicly disclaiming any intent to secure the presidency, Burr was, nevertheless, put forward by the Federalists in order to defeat Jefferson and bring about another election (*see* Jefferson-Burr Election Dispute). A slight majority in the House of Representatives enabled them to rally six states to Burr and divide the vote of two others, thus neutralizing the vote of the eight states that supported Jefferson. The contest was prolonged through thirty-five fruitless ballotings; on the thirty-sixth, by prearrangement, a sufficient number of Federalists cast blank ballots to give Jefferson ten states and the presidency.

This narrow escape from frustrating the popular will led the incoming administration to pass the Twelfth Amendment to the Constitution, separating the balloting for president and vice-president, in time for the 1804 election. Jefferson covertly helped eliminate Burr in New York, and the party caucus brought George Clinton forward as candidate for the vice-presidency. Burr, already divining his political ostracism, attempted to recover ground as an independent candidate for governor of New York. Representative Federalists of New England sought his support in their plans for disunion, but he refused to commit himself to such a program. The Federalists selected Pinckney as their presidential candidate, and chose Rufus King for the vice-presidency. Jefferson, preeminently successful in the more important measures of his administration, was triumphantly reelected in 1804 as president with Clinton as vice-president.

[Edward A. Stanwood, *A History of the Presidency*.]

ISAAC J. COX

Campaigns of 1808 and 1812. Candidates for the Democratic-Republican nomination in 1808 were James Madison, the choice of Thomas Jefferson; James Monroe, somewhat tainted by affiliation with John Randolph and the Quids, who were anathema to the outgoing administration; and George Clinton, a New Yorker not favored by the Virginia dynasty. Jefferson's own refusal to consider a third term confirmed the two-term tradition for a president. At the party caucus Madison received eighty-three votes; his rivals, three each.

The Federalist opposition was led by Charles Pinckney and Rufus King, but the chief obstacle to the Madison slate came from his own party, notably in Virginia and Pennsylvania, where William Duane, a powerful journalist, was unreconcilable. The malcontents finally voted the party ticket, and in the electoral college Madison obtained 122 out of 176 votes. Clinton ran far behind on the presidential ticket, but became vice-president by a wide margin. Defeated for the presidency, the Federalists nevertheless made serious inroads upon the Republican majority in the House of Representatives.

In 1812 Madison secured his renomination by a tacit rather than a formal yielding to the demands of Henry Clay and the war hawks. Clinton having died in office, the vice-presidential nomination, tendered first to John Langdon of New Hampshire, went to Elbridge Gerry of Massachusetts. Opposition to the party slate was led by DeWitt Clinton of New York, who finally accepted nomination from the prowar Republicans, with the endorsement of the Federalists. Jared Ingersoll of Pennsylvania was nominated as his running mate. The electoral college gave Madison 128 votes, as against 89 for Clinton. Vermont and Pennsylvania stood by Madison, but New York was led by Martin Van Buren into the Clinton column. Gerry and the ticket could not carry the candidate's own state of Massachusetts, notwithstanding his recent election as governor. Thus, at the beginning of the War of 1812, the Republican party was seriously divided.

[K. C. Babcock, *The Rise of American Nationality;* Edward Channing, *The Jeffersonian System.*]

LOUIS MARTIN SEARS

Campaigns of 1816 and 1820. There was no campaign by parties in 1816 worth the name, none at all in 1820. President James Madison's choice was James Monroe, old Jeffersonian protégé, secretary of state and war. Some Democratic-Republicans favored Gov. Daniel D. Tompkins of New York. Younger Republicans, interested in nationalist measures following the War of 1812, including a bank, protective tariffs, and internal improvements to speed the development of the West, preferred William H. Crawford, secretary of the treasury and citizen of Georgia. They gave him fifty-four votes in the congressional caucus to sixty-five for Monroe. In the electoral college Monroe overwhelmed Rufus King, signer of the Constitution and statesman of note, but a Federalist whose party now was thoroughly discredited by the Hartford Convention. Monroe was given 183 votes to 34 for King.

Newer sectional conflicts and rivalry among the younger leaders embittered the Era of Good Feelings, but President Monroe was secure. He was reelected in 1820, with only one dissenting electoral vote (cast by William Plummer of New Hampshire for John Quincy Adams). Federalists saw a greater menace to their propertied interests rising with the democracy of the West; it was to dethrone "King Caucus" (the congressional caucus nominating system) and the Virginia dynasty in the free-for-all campaign of 1824.

[Edward A. Stanwood, *A History of the Presidency.*]

ARTHUR B. DARLING

Campaign of 1824. With the second inauguration of James Monroe in 1820, preparations began for the next campaign, which was to mark the beginning of the transition from federalism to democracy with resulting voter realignment under new party emblems. The five candidates were prominent in national affairs and represented sections or factions rather than parties. In general, the politicians supported William H. Crawford; John Quincy Adams represented business; John C. Calhoun, the South and the rising slavocracy; Henry Clay, the expanding West; and Andrew Jackson, the people everywhere. The first three were cabinet members, Clay was speaker of the House, and Jackson was the country's most popular military figure.

Crawford was virtually eliminated by a paralytic stroke; Jackson was brought in late by his friends; Clay's support was never impressive; and Calhoun withdrew and became candidate for vice-president on both the Adams and Jackson tickets. No candidate received a majority electoral vote. Jackson secured the greatest number, 99; Adams, 84; Crawford, 41; and Clay, 37. Selection was made by the House of Representatives and Adams was chosen. Jackson's supporters charged that a "corrupt bargain" had been made when it was learned that Clay threw his support to Adams in exchange for the position of secretary of state.

[Bennett Champ Clark, *John Quincy Adams;* Marquis James, *Andrew Jackson: Portrait of a President.*]

THOMAS ROBSON HAY

Campaigns of 1828 and 1832. In 1828 President John Quincy Adams stood for reelection on the National Republican ticket and Andrew Jackson of Tennessee made his second campaign for the presidency, his supporters now being called Democrats. Designated the people's candidate by the action of friends in the legislature of his own state, Jackson won and held the necessary support of influential leaders in New York, Pennsylvania, and South Carolina. The campaign was waged throughout the administration of Adams. It was not marked by any clear-cut declaration of political principle or program, and Jackson came to think of it as a personal vindication. Of the twenty-four states, Delaware and South Carolina still expressed their choice by vote of the legislature. In twenty-two states the elections were held in the period from late October to early December. There was a great increase in the popular vote cast, and both candidates shared in the increase: 647,286 being cast for Jackson and 508,064 for Adams. The electoral vote stood 178 for Jackson to 83 for Adams. John C. Calhoun of South Carolina was again elected vice-president. In many parts of the nation there was evidence of a more effective organization of the vote than in any previous contest, yet over and above all considerations in this election was the appeal that the frontier hero made to an increasing body of democratically minded voters. Jackson himself was the cause of an alignment of public opinion in the years that followed (*see* Jacksonian Democracy). Jackson men controlled the Congress, and platforms and programs were supported by leaders and sections and groups, but not by clearly defined political parties.

Naturally Jackson stood for reelection in 1832, although he had spoken in favor of a single term, and the campaign to renominate him began at once. After December of 1831, when Henry Clay returned to the Senate, he, rather than Adams, received the support of most of those who were opposed to Jackson. This did not include Calhoun, who in 1830 had broken with Jackson. Clay was formally presented by a national convention that met in December of 1831. He was endorsed by a national convention of young men, which prepared a platform in a meeting held in May of 1832. In that month a national convention of Jackson supporters nominated Martin Van Buren of New York for the vice-presidency. In this election the recently gathered Anti-Masonic party supported William Wirt of Maryland. The campaign not only witnessed the general use of the national party convention, but platforms were presented and cartoons freely used, and there was concentration of popular attention upon the pageantry of parades. Aside from the personal contest between Jackson and Clay the issue between the two centered on Jackson's attack on the Bank of the United States and particularly his veto of the bill for the recharter of the bank, a bill that had the backing of the supporters of Clay in both houses of Congress. Twenty-four states participated in this election, and all except South Carolina provided a popular vote. The electorate endorsed the administration of Jackson, for the distribution of the vote in twenty-three states gave Jackson 687,502, Clay 530,189, and Wirt 101,051. In the electoral college the vote stood Jackson 219, Clay 49, Wirt 7, with 11 votes representing the vote of South Carolina cast for John Floyd of Virginia.

[Claude G. Bowers, *Party Battles of the Jackson Period;* S. R. Gammon, *The Presidential Campaign of 1832.*]

EDGAR EUGENE ROBINSON

Campaign of 1836. Made up chiefly of Anti-Masons, National Republicans, and anti-Jackson Democrats, the Whig party, formed in 1834, naturally lacked unity. Because of this, the Whig leaders decided to put forward several sectional candidates in the 1836 presidential campaign. Accordingly, Judge Hugh L. White was entered in the race through nomination by legislative caucuses in Tennessee and Alabama, held in January 1835. At about the same time, Judge John McLean was nominated by a legislative caucus in Ohio, but he withdrew from the race in the following August. Sen. Daniel Webster was nominated by a Massachusetts legislative caucus, also in January 1835. Still another candidate of the Whigs was Gen. William H. Harrison, who was formally nominated by both Anti-Masonic and Whig state conventions in Pennsylvania in December 1835.

Meanwhile, at the Democratic National Convention held in Baltimore on May 21–22, 1835, Martin Van Buren, who was President Andrew Jackson's personal choice, had been unanimously nominated for the presidency. No platform was adopted by the convention, but a committee was authorized to draw up an address. Published in the party organ, the Washington *Globe,* on Aug. 26, 1835, this address presented Van Buren as one who would, if elected, continue "that wise course of national policy pursued by Gen. Jackson." For all practical purposes, this address may be regarded as the first platform ever issued by the Democratic party.

When the election returns were finally in, Van Buren had won the presidency with 170 electoral votes and a popular vote of 765,483 to 739,795 for his opponents. White received 26 electoral votes, Webster 14, and Harrison 73, while South Carolina bestowed its 11 votes on W. P. Mangum. No candidate for the vice-presidency received a majority of the electoral vote, so on Feb. 8, 1837, the Senate chose the Democratic candidate, Richard M. Johnson, over his leading rival, Francis Granger.

[Edward A. Stanwood, *A History of the Presidency.*]

ERIK MCKINLEY ERIKSSON

Campaign of 1840. Distinctive in American history as the first national victory of the Whig party, the campaign of 1840 was unique for its popular and emotional appeal, organized on an unprecedented scale. To the Whigs belongs the credit of introducing into a presidential battle every political device calculated to sway the "common man."

The Whig convention, assembled at Harrisburg, Pa., Dec. 2, 1839, nominated Gen. William Henry Harrison of Indiana for president and John Tyler of Virginia for vice-president. No attempt was made to frame a platform; indeed, the only bond uniting the various groups under the Whig banner was a determination to defeat the Democrats. The Democratic convention held at Baltimore, May 5, 1840, was united on Martin Van Buren for president, but the choice of a vice-president was left to the state electors. A platform on strict construction lines was adopted.

The Whigs conducted their campaign at a rollicking pitch. Harrison was adroitly celebrated as the "Hard Cider and Log Cabin" candidate, a phrase which the Democrats had used in contempt. Popular meetings, "log cabin raisin's," oratory, invective against Van Buren the aristocrat, songs and slogans ("Tippecanoe and Tyler Too") swamped the country. In the election Harrison polled an electoral vote of 234, a popular vote of 1,274,624; Van Buren received 60 electoral votes and 1,127,781 popular votes. A minor feature in the campaign was the appearance of an abolition (the Liberty) party, whose candidate, James G. Birney, received 7,069 votes. Although the causes for Van Buren's defeat should be traced back to opposition to Jackson, the Panic of 1837, the unpopular Seminole War, and the campaign methods employed by the Whigs contributed largely to Harrison's success.

[D. B. Goebel, *William Henry Harrison;* Edward A. Stanwood, *A History of the Presidency.*]

DOROTHY BURNE GOEBEL

Campaign of 1844. No outstanding Democratic candidate could muster the necessary two-thirds vote in the 1844 convention, so James K. Polk of Tennessee, the first "dark horse," was nominated, with George M. Dallas of Pennsylvania as running mate, on a platform demanding "the re-annexation of Texas and the re-occupation of Oregon" and in favor of tariff reform. The Whigs nominated Henry Clay of Kentucky and Theodore Frelinghuysen of New Jersey, on a platform favoring protective tariff and a national bank but quibbling on the Texas annexation issue, which alienated some of the Whigs. The Liberty party unanimously selected James G. Birney as its presidential candidate. Polk carried New York by a small popular majority and was elected, with 170 electoral votes to 105 for Clay. The popular vote was Polk, 1,338,464; Clay, 1,300,097; Birney, 62,300.

[Edward A. Stanwood, *A History of the Presidency.*]

WALTER PRICHARD

Campaign of 1848. The Whig nominee, Zachary Taylor, who sidestepped the burning issue of slavery extension, coasted to victory on his military reputation with Millard Fillmore as his vice-president. His Democratic opponent, Gen. Lewis Cass of Michigan, straddled the slavery extension question by advocating state sovereignty. The new Free Soil party, specifically opposed to extension and headed by Martin Van Buren, split the Democratic vote in New York and thus contributed materially to Taylor's triumph. (Gerrit Smith, the National Liberty party candidate and staunch abolitionist, advised those who would not vote for an abolitionist to vote for Van Buren, rather than Cass.) Taylor carried half the states, eight in the South and seven in the North. The popular vote was Taylor, 1,360,967; Cass, 1,222,342; Van Buren, 291,263; Smith 2,733. The electoral vote was Taylor, 163; Cass, 127.

[Edward A. Stanwood, *A History of the Presidency.*]

HOLMAN HAMILTON

Campaign of 1852. The Whig party in 1852 was apathetic and demoralized by the slavery issue. Democratic victory seemed almost certain, but the question of greatest interest was who would be the Democratic candidate. After many ballots, the leading Democrats, Lewis Cass, James Buchanan, and Stephen Douglas, were eliminated and a dark horse, Franklin Pierce of New Hampshire, was nominated with William R. King of Alabama. The Whigs nominated the military hero Gen. Winfield Scott; the Free-Soilers nominated the antislavery leader John P. Hale of New Hampshire. Both major parties endorsed the Compromise of 1850, so there were no issues and little contest. Pierce carried all states save Massachusetts, Vermont, Kentucky, and Tennessee. The popular vote was Pierce, 1,601,117; Scott, 1,385,453; Hale, 155,825. The electoral vote was Pierce, 254; Scott, 42.

[Roy F. Nichols, *Franklin Pierce.*]

ROY F. NICHOLS

Campaign of 1856. The Republican party in its first presidential campaign nominated John C.

Frémont of California. Its platform opposed slavery expansion and condemned slavery and Mormonism as twin relics of barbarism. The American, or Know-Nothing, party nominated Millard Fillmore, who had succeeded to the presidency following the death of Zachary Taylor. The Democrats nominated James Buchanan. John C. Breckinridge was selected as his running mate. Their conservative platform stressed states' rights, opposed sectionalism, and favored a somewhat ambiguous plank, giving popular sovereignty to the territories. The electoral vote was Buchanan, 174; Frémont, 114; Fillmore, 8. The popular vote was Buchanan, 1,832,955; Frémont, 1,339,932; Fillmore, 871,731. The Republicans rejoiced in their showing, having won the votes of eleven free states, while the Democrats congratulated themselves upon having saved the Union.

PHILIP G. AUCHAMPAUGH

Campaign of 1860. The Democratic National Convention met amid great excitement and bitterness over the slavery issue, at Charleston, S.C., April 23, 1860. The delegates from the eight states of the far South (Southern Democrats) demanded the inclusion of a plank in the platform providing that Congress should guarantee slave property in the territories. This was refused, and after several days of useless wrangling and failure to unite the convention upon a candidate, adjournment was taken to Baltimore on June 18 following. At this meeting the convention nominated Stephen A. Douglas of Illinois for president, and later the national committee nominated Herschel V. Johnson of Georgia for vice-president. The platform pledged the party to stand by the Dred Scott decision or any future Supreme Court decision that dealt with the rights of property in the various states and territories. Southern Democrat delegates met separately at Baltimore on June 28, and nominated John C. Breckinridge of Kentucky for president and Joseph Lane of Oregon for vice-president. The platform reaffirmed the extreme southern view with regard to slavery. Meanwhile, the remains of the old-line Whig and American (Know-Nothing) parties had met in a convention at Baltimore on May 9 and adopted the name of the Constitutional Union party, also the platform of "the Constitution of the country, the Union of the States and the enforcement of the laws." They nominated John Bell of Tennessee for president and Edward Everett of Massachusetts for vice-president and attempted to ignore the slavery and other sectional issues, with a plea for the preservation of the Union.

The Republican National Convention had met in Chicago on May 16. By means of the platform issues of nonextension of slavery and of a homestead law and by advocacy of a protective tariff, the agricultural elements of the northern and western parts of the country and the industrial elements of Pennsylvania, New England, and other northern and eastern sections of the country were united. At first it seemed that the convention would nominate either William H. Seward of New York or Salmon P. Chase of Ohio, but a deadlock between their respective supporters being threatened the convention nominated Abraham Lincoln of Illinois on the third ballot. Hannibal Hamlin of Maine was nominated for vice-president on the second ballot.

The split in the Democratic party made possible the election of Lincoln. He received 180 electoral votes as against 72 for Breckinridge who carried the extreme southern states, and 39 for Bell who carried the border states. Douglas received but 12 (9 from Missouri and 3 of the 7 from New Jersey). The popular vote totaled 1,865,593 for Lincoln, 1,382,713 for Douglas, 848,356 for Breckinridge, and 592,906 for Bell. The combined opponents thus received 958,382 votes over Lincoln, who was a minority president during his first administration.

[W. S. Myers, *The Republican Party, A History;* Edward A. Stanwood, *A History of the Presidency.*]

WILLIAM STARR MYERS

Campaign of 1864. A national convention was called in the name of "the executive committee created by the national convention held in Chicago on the sixteenth day of May 1860." The use of the name Republican was carefully avoided. The convention met in Baltimore on June 7, 1864, and named itself the National Union Convention. The Republican leaders desired to appeal to Union sentiment and do away as far as possible with partisan influence. The platform, which was unanimously adopted, was a statement of "unconditional Union" principles and pledged the convention to put down rebellion by force of arms. Abraham Lincoln was nominated for a second term by the vote of every delegate except those from Missouri, who had been instructed to vote for Gen. Ulysses S. Grant. The nomination then was made unanimous. Andrew Johnson of Tennessee, a leading Southern Democrat who had been staunch in his loyalty to the Union, was nominated for vice-president.

The Democratic party met in convention on Aug. 29, at Chicago. Its platform declared the war a failure and advocated the immediate cessation of hostilities and the restoration of the Union by peaceable means. The convention nominated Gen. George B. McClellan for president and George H. Pendleton for vice-president. McClellan accepted the nomination but at the same time virtually repudiated the platform, for he was thoroughly loyal to the cause of the Union.

At first it appeared that the Democrats might defeat Lincoln, but the victories of the Union army in the field proved that the war was not a failure and rallied the people to the support of Lincoln and Johnson and the Union cause. The election took place on Nov. 8. For the first time in U.S. history certain states, those of the South, deliberately declined to choose electors for the choice of president. Lincoln carried every state that took part in the election but New Jersey, Delaware, and Kentucky. He received 212 electoral votes. McClellan received 21. Lincoln was given a popular majority of only 403,151 in a total of 4,010,725. This election was one of the most vital in the history of the country since upon its result might depend the perpetuation of the national Union.

[W. S. Myers, *General George B. McClellan;* Edward A. Stanwood, *A History of the Presidency.*]

WILLIAM STARR MYERS

Campaigns of 1868 and 1872. The issues in 1868 were southern Reconstruction and the "Ohio Idea" (payment of the national debt in greenbacks). Horatio Seymour of New York and Frank Blair of Missouri, the Democratic nominees, ran on a platform calling for a restoration of the rights of the southern states and payment of the war bonds in greenbacks. Alarmed by Democratic victories in 1867, the Republicans nominated the war hero, Ulysses S. Grant, and Schuyler Colfax of Indiana. Their platform acclaimed the success of Reconstruction and denounced as repudiation the payment of the bonds in greenbacks.

Personal attacks on the candidates and Republican "waving the bloody shirt" featured the campaign. An effort to replace the Democratic nominees in October failed but foreshadowed defeat. Grant received 214 electoral votes to Seymour's 80, and nearly 53 percent of the popular vote, receiving 3,013,421 votes to 2,706,829 for Seymour. Seymour carried eight states. The result was a personal victory for Grant rather than for Republican policies.

Dissatisfaction with the Reconstruction policy and a desire for reform led to a Liberal Republican organization, supported by tariff and civil-service reformers, independent editors, and disgruntled politicians. The new party nominated Horace Greeley, with B. Gratz Brown of Missouri, to oppose Grant's reelection in 1872. (Grant's running mate in this campaign was Henry Wilson of Massachusetts.) Its platform demanded civil-service reform, universal amnesty, and specie payment. The tariff issue was straddled to please Greeley, a protectionist. The Democrats accepted the Liberal Republican platform and nominees. The Greeley campaign lacked enthusiasm, and he was mercilessly lampooned. Grant received 286 electoral votes to Greeley's 66 and over 55 percent of the popular vote, receiving 3,596,745 votes to 2,843,446 for Greeley. Greeley died shortly after the election and before the electoral college met. His electoral votes were scattered among four other candidates.

[C. H. Coleman, *The Election of 1868;* E. D. Ross, *The Liberal Republican Movement.*]

CHARLES H. COLEMAN

Campaign of 1876. This campaign is especially notable because it resulted in the famous disputed presidential election. The leading aspirant for the Republican nomination was James G. Blaine of Maine. His name was presented to the national convention at Cincinnati by Robert G. Ingersoll in a striking speech in which he dubbed Blaine "the Plumed Knight." Among the other candidates were Benjamin H. Bristow of Kentucky, Roscoe Conkling of New York, Oliver P. Morton of Indiana, and Rutherford B. Hayes of Ohio. For six ballots Blaine led the field, but his involvement in a scandal brought to light a few weeks before the Republican convention caused a stampede to Hayes on the seventh ballot, resulting in his nomination. William A. Wheeler of New York was named as his running mate. The platform endorsed the Resumption Act and eulogized the Republican party for its work during the Civil War and Reconstruction.

Thomas F. Bayard of Delaware, Allen G. Thurman of Ohio, Winfield Scott Hancock of Pennsylvania, and Thomas A. Hendricks of Indiana sought the Democratic nomination, but the logical contender was Gov. Samuel J. Tilden of New York, who was named on the first ballot. Hendricks was then nominated for the vice-presidency. The scandals of the Grant administration were denounced in unsparing terms and "reform" was declared to be the paramount issue. Repeal of the clause of the act of 1875 providing for the resumption of specie payments was advocated, but Tilden personally was known to be a sound-money man rather than a Greenbacker. The platform also declared in favor of civil-service reform.

In the campaign the Democratic speakers dwelt heavily upon the scandals under Republican rule and contended that only through a change of men and parties could there be any real reform. Republican orators resorted to "bloody shirt" tactics (that is, revived the Civil War issues), questioned Tilden's loyalty during that conflict, and praised Hayes's military record—four honorable wounds and a brevet major generalcy. In the North the campaign was a quiet one, but in some of the southern states attempts to intimidate Afro-American voters produced violent disorders and considerable bloodshed.

Early returns on election night indicated the election of Tilden, but presently it appeared that the result would be in doubt. When the electoral college met and voted, Tilden received 184 unquestioned votes, Hayes 165. The 4 votes of Florida, the 8 votes of Louisiana, the 7 votes of South Carolina, and 1 vote of Oregon were claimed by both parties. After a protracted, bitter dispute, Congress created an electoral commission of five senators, five representatives, and five judges of the Supreme Court to help decide the result. Of the senators, three were to be Republicans and two Democrats; of the representatives, three were to be Democrats and two Republicans; four of the judges, two Republicans and two Democrats, were designated by their districts, and they were to choose the fifth judge. It was expected that the fifth judge would be David Davis, but his election to the Senate by the Democrats in the Illinois legislature gave him an excuse to decline the thankless task. The choice then fell upon Joseph P. Bradley, who had been appointed to the bench as a Republican, but some of whose decisions made him acceptable, temporarily, to the Democrats.

In case the two houses of Congress voting separately refused to accept any return, the dispute was to be referred to the commission, whose decision was to be final unless it was rejected by both houses. The two houses, voting separately on strict party lines, did disagree. Decision, therefore, rested with the commission, which, in all cases, by a vote of eight to seven (Bradley voting with the majority), refused to go against the election results as certified by the state authorities (in the case of Oregon by the secretary of state) and declared in favor of the Republican contenders. In each case the Senate accepted this decision, the House rejected it. All the disputed votes were therefore counted for Hayes and Wheeler and they were declared elected.

[J. H. Dougherty, *The Electoral System of the United States;* P. L. Haworth, *The Hayes-Tilden Election.*]

PAUL L. HAWORTH

Campaign of 1880. Taking place during a business revival and with no definite issue before the country, the 1880 campaign was routine politics. The Republicans overcame a serious split between groups headed by James G. Blaine and Roscoe Conkling by nominating James A. Garfield, a member of neither faction, over former President Ulysses S. Grant, supported by the Conkling wing for a third term. The Conkling faction was appeased by the nomination of Chester A. Arthur for the vice-presidency. Against Garfield the Democrats nominated Winfield Scott Hancock, a nonpolitical Civil War general; but their party had no positive program, was discredited by its factious opposition to the Hayes administration, and was defeated by a close vote. The Republicans carried the "doubtful states" and regained control over Congress. The popular vote was Garfield, 4,453,295; Hancock, 4,414,082. The electoral vote was Garfield, 214; Hancock, 155.

[E. E. Oberholtzer, *United States Since the Civil War,* vol. IV; T. C. Smith, *Life of James A. Garfield.*]

THEODORE CLARK SMITH

Campaign of 1884. Fought primarily between James G. Blaine, Republican, and Grover Cleveland, Democrat, the campaign of 1884 was one of the most vituperative in American history. There were several reasons why it became relentlessly personal in character. From the moment of Blaine's nomination at Chicago on June 6 he came under heavy fire from the reform element of all parties. He was believed to be allied with the spoils element in Republican politics; he had an unhappy record for baiting the South; he favored certain big business interests; and his railroad transactions had raised a suspicion that he had used his position as speaker of the House for personal profit. To divert attention from these attacks certain Republicans published evidence that Cleveland, nominated on July 10 at Chicago, was the father of an illegitimate son born in Buffalo some ten years earlier. There were virtually no serious issues between the two parties; both had good reason not to meddle seriously with the currency question or tariff, and international affairs attracted little attention. One leading feature of the campaign was the secession of a large body of Republicans who could not stomach

Blaine and who became Cleveland Democrats, or Mugwumps. Another feature was the open enmity of Tammany Hall, under political boss John Kelly, for Cleveland, and the success of it and other malcontents in carrying many Irish voters over to Blaine or to the new Antimonopoly party headed by Benjamin F. Butler. After exchanges that one observer compared to the billingsgate of quarreling tenement dwellers, the two parties approached election day running neck and neck. Democratic victory was finally decided by the vote of New York state, in which the Rev. Samuel D. Burchard's "rum, Romanism and rebellion" speech at a reception for Blaine, the "Belshazzar's feast" of Republican millionaires and politicians at Delmonico's just before election, and Roscoe Conkling's knifing of Blaine all played a part. Cleveland and his running mate, Thomas A. Hendricks, obtained a popular vote of 4,879,507 against Blaine's 4,850,293, and an electoral vote of 219 against Blaine's 182. Butler's popular vote was just over 175,000, and that of John P. St. John, Prohibition candidate, was just over 150,000.

[Allan Nevins, *Grover Cleveland—A Study in Courage*.]

ALLAN NEVINS

Campaign of 1888. The tariff was the chief issue of this campaign, which resulted in the election of Republican candidate Benjamin Harrison over Grover Cleveland by a majority of the electoral college but not of the popular vote. The Republicans had approached the election with scant hope of victory, for Cleveland had proved an admirable president, when his annual message of 1887, devoted entirely to arguments for tariff reform, gave them new heart. The issue was one on which they could rally nearly all manufacturers, most general business, and perhaps a majority of workingmen. Benjamin Harrison, who represented extreme high-tariff demands, was nominated by the Republicans at Chicago on June 25, after James G. Blaine had withdrawn for reasons of health, and John Sherman and Walter Q. Gresham, whose tariff views were moderate, had failed to gain strength. Levi P. Morton was named for vice-president. Harrison, supported by Blaine, by manufacturing interests who were induced by the Republican chairman, Matthew S. Quay, to subscribe large campaign funds, and by Civil War veterans hungry for pension legislation, waged an aggressive campaign. His speechmaking abilities made a deep impression on the country. Cleveland, who was renominated by the Democrats at St. Louis early in June, felt that his presidential office made it improper for him to do active campaigning; his running mate, former Sen. Allen G. Thurman of Ohio, was too old and infirm to be anything but a liability to the party; and campaign funds were slender. Worst of all for the Democrats, their national chairman, Sen. Calvin S. Brice of Ohio, held high-tariff convictions, was allied with big business, and refused to put his heart into the battle. Two weeks before election day the Republicans published an indiscreet letter by Lord Sackville-West, the British minister, hinting to a supposed British subject that Cleveland would probably be more friendly to England than Harrison; and though Cleveland at once had Sackville-West recalled, the incident cost him many Irish-American votes. Cleveland received 5,537,857 popular votes, Harrison 5,447,129; but Cleveland had only 168 electors against Harrison's 233. Clinton B. Fisk of New Jersey, Prohibition candidate, polled 249,506 votes; Alson J. Streeter of Illinois, Union Labor nominee, 146,935.

[Edward A. Stanwood, *A History of the Presidency*.]

ALLAN NEVINS

Campaign of 1892. Grover Cleveland was reelected over Benjamin Harrison in 1892 by a majority the size of which surprised observers of both parties. Cleveland had been named on the first ballot at the Democratic convention in Chicago, although David B. Hill of New York had made a demagogic attempt to displace him. Adlai E. Stevenson was selected for the vice-presidency. Harrison, who had estranged the professional politicians of his party, who had quarreled with its most popular figure, James G. Blaine, and who had impressed the country as cold and unlikable, was reluctantly accepted by the Republicans at Minneapolis on June 10. It was impossible to repudiate his administration. However, the McKinley Tariff of 1890 had excited widespread discontent, the Sherman Silver Purchase Act of the same year had angered the conservative East, and heavy federal expenditures had caused general uneasiness. Cleveland's firm stand on behalf of the gold standard and low tariffs and his known strength of character commended him to large numbers of independent voters. One factor adverse to the Republicans was the great strength manifested by the Populists, who polled 1,040,000 votes for James B. Weaver of Iowa and James G. Field of Virginia, most of this coming from old Republican strongholds in the Middle West. Another factor was the labor war at Homestead, Pa., which showed that the highly protected steel industry did not properly pass on its tariff benefits to the worker. Cleveland, with a popular vote of 5,555,426, had 277 electors; Harrison, with a popular vote of 5,182,690, had 145; while Weaver won 22 electoral votes.

[Allan Nevins, *Grover Cleveland—A Study in Courage*.]

ALLAN NEVINS

Campaign of 1896. Following this campaign and election, a twenty-two-year period ended in which neither major party had been able to control the national government for more than the life of a single Congress; it ushered in a period of Republican domination which lasted until 1911.

Favored by Marcus A. Hanna's cannily managed campaign, William McKinley of Ohio was named on the first ballot by the Republican convention meeting at St. Louis. Garret A. Hobart was selected as the vice-presidential candidate. The traditional party platform was adopted with the exception of a declaration for the gold standard until bimetallism could be secured by international agreement. A bloc of western delegates bolted and organized the Silver Republican party.

There was no dominant candidate for the Democratic nomination. The important contest was over the platform. As presented to the delegates, it was an antiadministration document favoring free silver at the sixteen-to-one ratio, criticizing the use of injunctions in labor disputes, and denouncing the overthrow of the federal income tax. In its support William Jennings Bryan delivered his "Cross of Gold" oration and endeared himself to the silver delegates by his effective answers to the criticisms of the administration orators.

The enthusiasm growing out of that speech gave impetus to Bryan's candidacy for the presidential nomination. Back of this was also the long campaign he had waged by personal conferences, speeches, and correspondence with the inflationist delegates from the South and West. Another factor was the bolting Republicans and the Populists, who saw themselves being forced to support the Democratic nominee and demanded someone not too closely identified with the regular Democratic party platform. Bryan appealed to the delegates as the Democrat who could unite the silver and agrarian factions.

The Populists, Silver Republicans, and National Silver party members joined the Democrats in support of Bryan. The administration Democrats placed a National Democratic ticket in the field to hold conservative Democratic votes away from him, nominating John M. Palmer of Illinois as their presidential candidate.

The campaign was highly spectacular. The Democrats exploited Bryan's oratory by sending him on speaking tours back and forth across the country during which enormous crowds came out to hear him. In sharp contrast, the Republican management kept McKinley at his home in Canton, Ohio, where carefully selected delegations made formal calls and listened to "front porch" speeches by the candidate. More important were the flood of advertising, the funds for building local organizations, and the large group of speakers on the hustings, which were maintained by Hanna's organization. The metropolitan press, like the other business groups—except the silver miners—was essentially a unit in opposing Bryan. The results showed a sharp city-versus-rural division, with Bryan carrying the Solid South and most of the trans-Missouri states. The remainder, including California, Oregon, North Dakota, Kentucky, and Maryland, went to McKinley. With him were elected a Republican House and a Senate in which various minor party members held a nominal balance of power. The popular vote was unusually large, each candidate receiving larger totals than any previous candidate of his party, McKinley's vote being 7,102,246 and Bryan's 6,492,559. The electoral vote was 271 and 176, respectively.

[E. E. Robinson, *The Evolution of American Political Parties*.]

ELMER ELLIS

Campaign of 1900. The presidential candidates and most of the issues of the 1896 campaign were carried over to the 1900 campaign. With the trend of prices upward, the pressure for inflation had declined, and the expansion of American control over new territories had created the issue of imperialism.

At the Republican convention in Philadelphia a combination of circumstances forced Marcus A. Hanna and President William McKinley to accept Theodore Roosevelt as the vice-presidential candidate. The party's position on the new territories was defined as American retention with "the largest measure of self-government consistent with their welfare and our duties."

When the Democrats met at Kansas City they once again selected William Jennings Bryan as their presidential candidate, but they were unwilling to accept the conservatives' proposal to forget the last platform and make anti-imperialism the only issue. The 1896 platform was reindorsed, an antitrust plank added, and imperialism designated the "paramount issue."

The campaign lacked the fire of 1896. The Republicans emphasized the "full dinner pail" and the danger threatening it from the Democratic platform; the Democrats stressed the growth of monopolies under the McKinley administration and the danger of imperialistic government. The result was a more emphatic Republican victory than in 1896, one generally interpreted as an endorsement of both McKinley's domestic and foreign policies. The popular vote was McKinley, 7,218,491; Bryan, 6,356,734. McKinley obtained 292 electoral votes to 155 for Bryan. This election made Roosevelt's elevation to the presidency automatic upon McKinley's death in September 1901.

[E. E. Robinson, *The Evolution of American Political Parties;* Edward A. Stanwood, *A History of the Presidency.*]

ELMER ELLIS

Campaign of 1904. Theodore Roosevelt, who succeeded to the presidency on the death of William McKinley in 1901, ardently hoped to be nominated and elected "in his own right." The death of Marcus A. Hanna of Ohio, whom the big business interests of the country would have preferred, made possible the president's nomination by acclamation when the Republican convention met in Chicago, June 21. Charles W. Fairbanks of Indiana was chosen for the vice-presidency.

The Democrats, meeting at St. Louis, July 6, pointedly turned their backs upon "Bryanism" by omitting from their platform all reference to the money question (*see* Free Silver) and by nominating for president Alton B. Parker, a conservative New York judge, who at once pledged himself to maintain the gold standard, and for vice-president, Henry Gassaway Davis, a wealthy West Virginia octogenarian. Business leaders, more afraid of the Democratic party than of Roosevelt, contributed so heavily to the Republican campaign chest that Parker rashly charged "blackmail." Corporations, he said, were being forced to contribute in return for the suppression of evidence that the government had against them. Roosevelt, indignantly denying the charge, won by a landslide that reclaimed Missouri from the Solid South and gave him 336 electoral votes to Parker's 140 and a popular plurality of 2,544,238. Prohibitionist, Populist, Socialist, and Socialist-Labor candidates received only negligible support.

[Edward A. Stanwood, *A History of the Presidency.*]

JOHN D. HICKS

Campaign of 1908. Theodore Roosevelt, though at the height of his popularity, refused to run for a second elective term in 1908, but swung his support in the Republican convention to William Howard Taft, who was nominated. James S. Sherman of New York was selected for the vice-presidency.

The Democratic convention was as completely dominated by William Jennings Bryan, who became its nominee. Party differences were not significant. After an apathetic campaign Bryan carried only the Solid South, Kansas, Colorado, and Nevada, though he received about 44 percent of the popular vote, securing 6,412,294 to Taft's 7,675,320. Taft's electoral vote was 321; Bryan's 162. The Republicans won the presidency and both houses of Congress.

[Samuel Eliot Morison and Henry Steele Commager, *The Growth of the American Republic.*]

CHESTER LLOYD JONES

Campaign of 1912. This campaign marked the culmination of the progressive movement in national politics and resulted in the return of the Democrats after sixteen years of Republican presidents.

The struggle for the Republican nomination became a sanguinary battle between the progressive and conservative wings, aided in each case by personal followings and some division of support from large interests. In the beginning it was the progressive Sen. Robert M. LaFollette of Wisconsin against the incumbent, William Howard Taft. But former President Theodore Roosevelt, who had been largely responsible for Taft's nomination in 1908, entered the race to rally behind him Republicans who believed Taft had been too friendly with the conservative Old Guard. The influence in Taft's hands was sufficient to return delegates pledged to him in most cases where they were named by conventions, but either Roosevelt or La Follette was successful in states where presidential primaries were held save one. The conservative-controlled national committee placed Taft delegates on the temporary roll in all contests, and the small majority resulting gave Taft the nomination. Roosevelt was later nominated by the newly organized Progressive (Bull Moose) party, consisting largely of Republican bolters.

The contest for the Democratic nomination was also hard fought with both of the leading candidates accepted as progressives. Beauchamp ("Champ") Clark of Wisconsin led from the beginning and had an actual majority in the convention for a time, but when William Jennings Bryan transferred his support to the second progressive, Woodrow Wilson, a shift began that resulted in the latter's nomination. The choice for vice-president was Thomas R. Marshall. All three party platforms were unusually favorable to progressive policies. Wilson, backed by a united party, won easily, and Roosevelt was second. There was an unusual amount of shifting of party loyalties, although most Democrats voted for Wilson and most Republicans for Roosevelt or Taft. Wilson's popular vote was 6,296,547, Roosevelt's was 4,118,571, and Taft's was 3,486,720. The electoral vote was, respectively, 435, 88, and 8. The Democrats won majorities in both branches of Congress. In spite of the three-way contest, a fourth candidate, Eugene V. Debs, Socialist, secured approximately 900,000 votes.

[E. E. Robinson, *The Evolution of American Political Parties;* Edward A. Stanwood, *A History of the Presidency.*]

ELMER ELLIS

Campaign of 1916. This campaign reunited the Republican party and determined that American foreign policy should be left in Woodrow Wilson's hands. The Republicans reunited when, after the nomination of Charles Evans Hughes, Theodore Roosevelt, already nominated by the rapidly declining Progressive party, announced support of the ticket.

There was no opposition to the renomination of President Wilson and Vice-President Thomas R. Marshall. The Democrats defended the policies of the administration, especially the Underwood Tariff and the measures for the regulation of business. They also praised the foreign policy as one which had kept the United States out of war and preserved national honor. The Republicans attacked the policies of the administration, promised a stronger foreign policy, and were supported by the more extreme partisans of both alliances in the European war.

The results were in doubt for several days because of the close vote in several states. Wilson won the presidency, carrying Ohio, New Hampshire, the South, and most of the border and trans-Missouri states, including California, with an electoral vote of 277, against 254 for Hughes. The popular vote was Wilson, 9,127,695; Hughes, 8,533,507. Congress remained Democratic only because independent members of the House were friendly.

[E. E. Robinson, *The Evolution of American Political Parties.*]

ELMER ELLIS

Campaign of 1920. The debate on the League of Nations determined the alignment of political forces in the spring of 1920. The Republicans were confident: the wounds of the intraparty strife of 1912 had been healed; the mistaken strategy of 1916 admitted; and the conservative mood of the country was easily interpreted. They met in convention in Chicago, could not agree upon any one of the leading preconvention candidates, Frank O. Lowden, Hiram Johnson, or Leonard Wood, and nominated Warren G. Harding, senator from Ohio, on the tenth ballot. Calvin Coolidge, governor of Massachusetts, was nominated for the vice-presidency.

The Democrats met in San Francisco. None of the discussed candidates, William G. McAdoo, Alfred E. Smith, John W. Davis, A. Mitchell Palmer, or James M. Cox, commanded a great following. Cox, governor of Ohio, was nominated on the forty-fourth ballot, with Franklin D. Roosevelt, thirty-eight-year-old assistant secretary of the navy, as vice-presidential nominee. The Socialist party, meeting in May, nominated Eugene Debs for the fifth time. A Farmer-Labor ticket appeared also.

None of the platforms was unexpected or significant on domestic issues. The Republicans attacked the president and opposed American entrance into the League of Nations. The Democratic national committee supported Wilson's appeal for a "solemn referendum" on the covenant of the League; Cox waged a persistent and vigorous campaign. Harding, remaining at his home for the most part, contented himself with vague generalizations. Neither candidate had been nationally known at the outset of the contest, and no clear-cut issue developed and no real contest transpired. The total vote cast was 26,733,905. The Nineteenth Amendment had been proclaimed in August, and in every state women were entitled to vote. Harding won more than 60 percent of the total vote cast. Cox won the electoral vote in only eleven states, receiving 127 electoral votes to Harding's 404. The Socialist vote was 919,799, but the strength of all the third parties totaled only about 5.5 percent.

[E. E. Robinson, *The Presidential Vote, 1896–1932.*]

EDGAR EUGENE ROBINSON

Campaign of 1924. As in 1920, the candidates in 1924 were new in a presidential canvass. The Republican convention meeting in Cleveland, with a few scattering votes in dissent, nominated Calvin Coolidge, who as vice-president had succeeded to the presidency in August 1923 when President Warren Harding died. The vice-presidential nomination, refused by several, was accepted by Charles G. Dawes of Illinois. The platform was marked by extreme conservatism.

The Democrats met in New York and were in almost continuous session for two and a half weeks.

Not only was there serious division upon the matter of American adherence to the League of Nations and upon the proposed denunciation of the Ku Klux Klan, but also upon the choice of the nominee. Each of the two leading candidates, Alfred E. Smith and William G. McAdoo, was sufficiently powerful to prevent the nomination of the other, and finally on the one hundred and third ballot the nomination went to John W. Davis of West Virginia. Gov. Charles W. Bryan of Nebraska was nominated for vice-president. The platform called for a popular referendum on the League of Nations.

The Conference for Progressive Political Action brought about a series of meetings and eventually a widespread support of Sen. Robert M. La Follette in his independent candidacy, with Burton K. Wheeler as his running mate. La Follette's platform, in which appeared most of the progressive proposals of the previous twenty years, was endorsed by the Socialist party and the officers of the American Federation of Labor. So real did the threat of the third party candidacy appear to be that much of the attack of the Republicans was on La Follette, who waged an aggressive campaign.

The total vote cast exceeded that of 1920 by 2.36 million, but because of the vote cast for La Follette (nearly 5 million), that cast for Republican and for Democratic tickets was less than four years earlier, Coolidge securing 15,718,211 votes, and Davis 8,385,283. La Follette carried Wisconsin (13 electoral votes). Coolidge topped the poll in thirty-five states, receiving 382 electoral votes, leaving the electoral vote for Davis in only twelve states, or 136 votes.

[E. E. Robinson, *The Presidential Vote, 1896–1932.*]

EDGAR EUGENE ROBINSON

Campaign of 1928. On Aug. 2, 1927, President Calvin Coolidge announced that he did not choose to run for president in 1928. The majority of the leaders of the Republican party were undecided with regard to the candidate they should support. A popular movement having its strength in the rank and file of the voters forced the nomination of Secretary of Commerce Herbert Hoover on the first ballot at the Republican National Convention, which met at Kansas City, Mo., in June. The platform contained strong support of the usual Republican policies such as a protective tariff and sound business administration. It advocated the observance and rigorous enforcement of the Eighteenth Amendment. Charles Curtis of Kansas was nominated for vice-president.

The Democrats met at Houston, Texas, and on June 28 nominated New York Gov. Alfred E. Smith, the first Catholic to be nominated for the presidency. They then nominated Arkansas Sen. Joseph T. Robinson for vice-president. The platform did not differ strikingly from that of the Republicans. The contest became one between rival personalities. Smith, an avowed "wet," took a stand in favor of a change in the Prohibition amendment, and advocated that the question of Prohibition and its enforcement be left to the determination of the individual states.

At the election on Nov. 6, Hoover was overwhelmingly successful. He carried forty states, including five from the Old South, with a total of 444 electoral votes. Smith carried eight states with an electoral vote of 87. The popular plurality of Hoover over Smith was 6,375,824 in a total vote of 36,879,414.

[W. S. Myers, *The Republican Party.*]

WILLIAM STARR MYERS

Campaigns of 1932 and 1936. The presidential campaign of 1932 began in earnest with the holding of the Republican National Convention at Chicago on June 14–16. President Herbert Hoover and Vice-President Charles Curtis were renominated on the first ballot. The platform praised the Hoover record, including his program for combating the depression. After a long debate a "wet-dry" plank on Prohibition was adopted which favored giving the people an opportunity to pass on a repeal amendment.

The Democratic National Convention was also held at Chicago, June 27–July 2, 1932. On the fourth ballot, Gov. Franklin Delano Roosevelt of New York was nominated for the presidency, defeating Alfred E. Smith and ten other candidates. John Nance Garner of Texas was selected as the vice-presidential candidate. The platform pledged economy, a sound currency, unemployment relief, old-age and unemployment insurance under state laws, the "restoration of agriculture," and repeal of the Eighteenth Amendment together with immediate legalization of beer.

After a campaign featured by Roosevelt's promise of "a new deal," the elections were held on Nov. 5. The popular vote for each party was as follows: Democratic, 22,809,638; Republican, 15,758,901; Socialist, 881,951; Socialist-Labor, 33,276; Communist, 102,785; Prohibition, 81,869; Liberty, 53,425; and Farmer-Labor, 7,309. The electoral vote was 472 for the Democrats and 59 for the Republicans.

In 1936 the Republican National Convention was held at Cleveland beginning on June 9. Gov. Alfred M. Landon of Kansas and Frank Knox, a Chicago publisher, were nominated for the presidency and vice-presidency, respectively. The platform strongly denounced the New Deal administration, from both constitutional and economic viewpoints. It pledged the Republicans "to maintain the American system of constitutional and local self-government" and "to preserve the American system of free enterprise."

The Democratic National Convention assembled at Philadelphia on June 25 for what proved to be a ratification meeting for the New Deal. President Roosevelt and Vice-President Garner were renominated without opposition. The platform vigorously defended the New Deal and pledged its continuance.

When the election was held on Nov. 3, the Democrats again won an overwhelming victory, carrying every state except Maine and Vermont. The popular vote for each party was as follows: Democratic, 27,752,869; Republican, 16,674,665; Union, 882,479; Socialist, 187,720; Communist, 80,159; Prohibition, 37,847; and Socialist-Labor, 12,777. The Democrats received 523 electoral votes while the Republicans received only 8.

ERIK MCKINLEY ERIKSSON

Campaign of 1940. Although either Robert A. Taft, Arthur H. Vandenberg, or Thomas E. Dewey was expected to be the Republican candidate, the nomination was won by Wendell L. Willkie at Philadelphia, June 28, on the sixth ballot. As president of a large utilities corporation Willkie had fought the New Deal, but in foreign affairs he was an internationalist, and with Europe at war, this fact commended him to the liberal element of the party, which carried his nomination against the Old Guard. The nomination of a liberal by the Republicans, together with the international crisis, in turn made the nomination of Franklin D. Roosevelt by the Democrats (Chicago, July 16) a practical certainty, even though his running for a third term was unprecedented. Foreign affairs dominated the campaign. Both candidates promised aid to the Allies; both promised at the same time to keep the United States out of foreign wars. Roosevelt and Henry A. Wallace, secretary of agriculture, received 27,307,819 popular and 449 electoral votes against 22,321,018 popular and 82 electoral votes for Willkie and Charles L. McNary of Oregon.

CHRISTOPHER LASCH

Campaign of 1944. Thomas E. Dewey, governor of New York, was nominated by the Republican convention in Chicago on June 26 with little opposition. John W. Bricker of Ohio was chosen as his running mate. President Franklin D. Roosevelt, running for a fourth term, encountered even less opposition at the Democratic convention in Chicago. The real struggle revolved around the choice of a vice-presidential candidate. With Roosevelt's support Vice-President Henry Wallace could probably have been nominated for another term, but the opposition to Wallace from within the party convinced the president that a compromise candidate had to be found. James F. Byrnes of South Carolina was acceptable to the White House and to the party conservatives, but not to labor, in particular not to Sidney Hillman of the Congress of Industrial Organizations. Accordingly Sen. Harry S. Truman of Missouri was nominated on the second ballot, July 20. In the November election Roosevelt received 25,606,585 popular and 432 electoral votes to Dewey's 22,014,745 popular and 99 electoral votes. The Democrats preserved their control of both houses of Congress.

CHRISTOPHER LASCH

Campaign of 1948. The Republicans, having gained control of Congress in 1946, confidently expected to turn the apparently unpopular Truman administration out of power in the autumn elections, and for the first time in the party's history renominated a defeated candidate, Thomas E. Dewey, at the convention meeting in Philadelphia on June 21. The Democrats, on the other hand, suffered from severe internal conflicts. Truman's nomination at Philadelphia on July 15 caused no enthusiasm. Radicals left the party and, meeting in the same city on July 22, nominated Henry A. Wallace and Sen. Glen Taylor of Idaho as the candidates of the Progressive party. Southerners, offended by the civil rights planks of the Democratic platform, also seceded and at Birmingham, Ala., July 17, formed the States' Rights Democratic party, with Gov. J. Strom Thurmond of South Carolina and Gov. Fielding L. Wright of Mississippi as their candidates. Under these circumstances Truman's candidacy appeared to be hopeless. The president, however, proved to be a whistle-stop campaigner of unexpected ability. Moreover, he enjoyed the support not only of organized labor and of Afro-American voters but as it turned out, to the great surprise of prophets and pollsters, of midwestern farmers as well. The election was close—Truman retired for the evening on election night thinking he had lost. He and Alben W. Barkley of Kentucky polled 24,105,812 popular and 304 electoral votes against 21,970,065 popular and 189 electoral votes for Dewey and Gov. Earl Warren of California. Thurmond polled 1,169,063 popular votes and the 38 electoral votes of South Carolina, Alabama, Mississippi, and Louisiana. Wallace won 1,157,172 popular votes. The Democrats regained control of Congress by small majorities.

[Samuel J. Lubell, *The Future of American Politics*.]

CHRISTOPHER LASCH

Campaign of 1952. After a long and bitter struggle, the internationalist wing of the Republican party succeeded on July 11 in bringing about the nomination of Gen. Dwight D. Eisenhower against the opposition of Sen. Robert A. Taft and his supporters. The Democrats, following the Republicans to Chicago ten days later, turned to Gov. Adlai E. Stevenson of Illinois, who consented to become a candidate only at the last moment. In the following campaign Stevenson suffered from revelations of corruption in the Truman administration, from the widespread dissatisfaction with the seemingly inconclusive results of the war in Korea, and from the vague feeling that it was "time for a change." Eisenhower's personal appeal, moreover, was immense. He and Sen. Richard M. Nixon of California polled 33,936,234 votes to 27,314,987 for Stevenson and Sen. John J. Sparkman of Alabama. The Republicans carried the electoral college, 442 to 89. They carried the House of Representatives by a narrow margin and tied the Democrats in the Senate.

[Samuel J. Lubell, *Revolt of the Moderates*.]

CHRISTOPHER LASCH

Campaign of 1956. Adlai E. Stevenson was renominated on the first ballot by the Democrats at Chicago, with Sen. Estes Kefauver of Tennessee as his running mate. President Dwight D. Eisenhower and Vice-President Richard M. Nixon were renominated by the Republicans at San Francisco with equal ease. The campaign, however, was far from being a rehash of 1952. Stevenson, having been advised that his serious discussions of issues in 1952 had been over the voters' heads, agreed to pitch his campaign at a somewhat lower level. The results disappointed his more ardent supporters without winning him any votes. The Suez crisis, occurring on the eve of the election, further strengthened the administration's position by creating a national emergency. In the election the president polled 35,590,472 popular and 457 electoral votes to Stevenson's 26,022,752 popular and 73 electoral votes. As in 1952, Eisenhower broke into the Solid South, carrying not only Florida, Virginia, and Tennessee, which he had carried in 1952, but Texas, Oklahoma, and Louisiana as well. In spite of his personal triumph, however, the Democrats carried both houses of Congress.

CHRISTOPHER LASCH

Campaign of 1960. The Democrats nominated Sen. John F. Kennedy of Massachusetts at Los Angeles in July, with Sen. Lyndon B. Johnson of Texas as his running mate. The Republicans, meeting at Chicago two weeks later, nominated Vice-President Richard M. Nixon and Henry Cabot Lodge of Massachusetts. The most striking feature of the campaign was a series of televised debates, in which the candidates submitted to questioning by panels of reporters. By sharing a national audience with his lesser-known opponent, Nixon in this manner may have injured his own cause. Indeed, the debates, in view of the closeness of the result, may have been the decisive factor in Kennedy's victory. The final vote was not known until weeks after the election. Kennedy received 34,227,096, Nixon 34,108,546, and minor candidates 502,773. Despite the fact that Kennedy won by only 118,550 votes and had only 49.7 percent of the total vote as compared with 49.6 percent for Mr. Nixon, the President-elect won 303 electoral votes to Nixon's 219. At forty-three, Kennedy was the youngest man ever elected to the presidency (although not the youngest to occupy the office). He was also the first Roman Catholic ever to become president.

[Theodore White, *The Making of the President 1960*.]

CHRISTOPHER LASCH

Campaign of 1964. Upon assuming office following the assassination of President John F. Kennedy in November 1963, Vice-President Lyndon B. Johnson acted quickly to restore public calm and to achieve many of President Kennedy's legislative goals. Lyndon Johnson was subsequently nominated by acclamation by the Democrats, meeting in Atlantic City, N.J. The only uncertainty there was the choice of a vice-presidential nominee. After the earlier veto by Johnson of Attorney General Robert F. Kennedy, brother of the slain president, the choice of Johnson and the party fell to Minnesotan Hubert H. Humphrey, assistant majority leader of the Senate.

Conflict over the presidential nomination centered in the Republican party. New York's Gov. Nelson Rockefeller represented the moderate and liberal factions that had dominated the party since 1940. A new, conservative group was led by Arizona's Sen. Barry M. Goldwater, who offered "a choice, not an echo." Presidential primaries indicated the limited appeal of both candidates, but no viable alternative emerged. Goldwater accumulated large numbers of delegates in the nonprimary states, particularly in the South and West, and sealed his first-ballot victory with a narrow win in the California primary. Rep. William E. Miller of New York was selected as his running mate.

The main issues of the 1964 campaign were presented by Goldwater, who challenged the previous party consensus on a limited welfare state and the emerging Democratic policy of accommodation with the Communist world. The Democrats defended their record as bringing peace and prosperity, while pledging new social legislation to achieve a "Great Society." The armed conflict in Vietnam also drew some attention. In response to an alleged attack on American warships in the Gulf of Tonkin, the president ordered retaliatory bombing of North Vietnam, at the same time pledging "no wider war."

In the balloting, Lyndon Johnson was overwhelmingly elected, gaining 43,129,484 popular votes (61.1 percent) and a majority in forty-four states and the District of Columbia—which was voting for president for the first time—for a total of 486 electoral votes. Goldwater won 27,178,188 votes (38.5 percent) and six states—all but Arizona in the Deep South—for a total of 52 electoral votes. There was a pronounced shift in voting patterns, with the South becoming the strongest Republican area, and the Northeast the firmest Democratic base.

[Philip E. Converse, Aage R. Clausen, and Warren E. Miller, "Electoral Myth and Reality: The 1964 Election," *American Political Science Review*, vol. 59 (1965); John Kessel, *The Goldwater Coalition;* Theodore H. White, *The Making of the President 1964*.]

GERALD M. POMPER

Campaign of 1968. The presidential election took place in an atmosphere of increasing American civil disorder, evidenced in protests over the Vietnam War, riots in black urban neighborhoods, and assassinations of political leaders. On Mar. 31, President Lyndon B. Johnson startled the nation by renouncing his candidacy for reelection. His withdrawal stimulated an intense contest for the Democratic nomination between Minnesota's Sen. Eugene McCarthy, New York's Sen. Robert F. Kennedy, and Vice-President Hubert H. Humphrey. Kennedy appeared to have the greatest popular support, his campaign culminating in a narrow victory over McCarthy in the California primary. On the night of this victory, Kennedy was assassinated. Humphrey abstained from the primaries but gathered support from party leaders and from the Johnson administration. At an emotional and contentious convention in Chicago, Humphrey was easily nominated on the first ballot. Maine's Sen. Edmund S. Muskie was selected as the vice-presidential candidate.

Former Vice-President Richard M. Nixon was the leading candidate for the Republican nomination. He withstood challenges from moderate Gov. Nelson Rockefeller of New York and conservative Gov. Ronald Reagan of California. Gaining a clear majority of delegates on the first ballot at the party's convention in Miami Beach, he then named Gov. Spiro T. Agnew of Maryland as his running mate. A new party, the American Independent party, was organized by Gov. George C. Wallace of Alabama and was able to win a ballot position in every state. Curtis LeMay, former air force general, was selected as the new party's vice-presidential candidate.

The campaign centered on the record of the Johnson administration. Nixon denounced the conduct of the war and promised both an "honorable peace" and ultimate withdrawal of American troops. He also pledged a vigorous effort to reduce urban crime and to restrict school desegregation. Wallace denounced both parties, calling for strong action against North Vietnam, criminals, and civil rights protesters. Humphrey largely defended the Democratic record, while also proposing an end to American bombing of North Vietnam.

The balloting brought Nixon a narrow victory. With 31,785,480 votes, he won 43.4 percent of the national total, thirty-two states, and 301 electoral votes. Humphrey won 31,275,166 votes, 42.7 percent of the total, thirteen states and the District of Columbia, and 191 electoral votes. Wallace gained the largest popular vote for a third-party candidate since 1924—9,906,473 votes and 13.5 percent of the popular total. The five southern states he captured, with 46 electoral votes, were too few to accomplish his strategic aim, a deadlock of the electoral college.

[Lewis Chester, Godfrey Hodgson, and Bruce Page, *An American Melodrama;* Philip E. Converse et al., "Continuity and Changes in American Politics: Parties and Issues in the 1968 Election," *American Political Science Review*, vol. 63 (1969); Richard Scammon and Ben Wattenberg, *The Real Majority*.]

GERALD M. POMPER

Campaign of 1972. The Nixon administration provided the campaign setting in 1972 by a series of American policy reversals, including the withdrawal of most American ground forces from Vietnam, the imposition of wage and price controls, and presidential missions to Communist China and the Soviet

Union. President Richard M. Nixon's control of the Republican party was undisputed, resulting in a placid party convention in Miami, where he and Vice-President Spiro T. Agnew were renominated.

In the Democratic party, major party reform resulted in more open processes of delegate selection and increased representation at the convention of women, racial minorities, and persons under the age of thirty. At the same time, a spirited contest was conducted for the presidential nomination. The early favorite, Maine's Sen. Edmund S. Muskie, was eliminated after severe primary defeats. Alabama's Gov. George C. Wallace raised a serious challenge but was eliminated from active campaigning by an attempted assassination. The contest then became a two-man race between South Dakota's Sen. George S. McGovern and former Vice-President Hubert H. Humphrey, the 1968 candidate. A series of upset primary victories and effective organization in local party caucuses culminated in a direct victory for McGovern in the California primary and a first-ballot nomination in Miami, the convention city. The vice-presidential Democratic position was awarded to Missouri's Sen. Thomas Eagleton. After the convention adjourned, it was revealed that Eagleton had been hospitalized three times for mental depression. He was persuaded to resign, and the Democratic National Committee then, at McGovern's suggestion, named Sergeant Shriver as his running mate. With Wallace disabled, the American Independent party named Rep. John G. Schmitz of California as its presidential candidate.

The Democrats attempted to focus the campaign on the alleged defects of the administration, including the continuation of the war in Vietnam, electronic eavesdropping by the Republicans on the Democratic national headquarters at Washington's Watergate complex, and governmental favors for Republican party contributors. The full extent of these improprieties was not revealed, however, until the following year. Aside from defending the Nixon record, the Republicans attacked the Democratic candidate as advocating radical positions on such issues as amnesty for war resisters, marijuana usage, and abortion and as inconsistent on other questions. Much attention centered on 25 million newly eligible voters, including the eighteen-year-olds enfranchised by constitutional amendment.

The final result was an overwhelming personal victory for Nixon, who won the highest total and proportion of the popular vote in electoral history. Nixon won 47,169,905 popular votes (60.7 percent) and 521 electoral votes from forty-nine states. McGovern won 29,170,383 popular votes (37.5 percent), but only 17 electoral votes (from Massachusetts and the District of Columbia). Despite this landslide, the Republicans failed to gain control of the House and lost two seats in the Senate.

[Walter Dean Burnham, *Critical Elections and the Mainsprings of American Politics;* Theodore H. White, *The Making of the President 1972.*]

GERALD M. POMPER

CAMPAIGN SONGS, partisan ditties used in American political canvasses and especially in presidential contests. In the 19th century the words of these songs were commonly set to established melodies, such as "Yankee Doodle," "Marching Through Georgia," "Rosin the Bow," "Auld Lang Syne," "John Brown's Body," "Dixie," and "O Tannenbaum" ("Maryland, My Maryland"); or to tunes widely popular at the time, such as "Few Days," "Champagne Charlie," "Wearing of the Green," or "Down in a Coal Mine," which served for "Up in the White House." Perhaps the best known of them was "Tippecanoe and Tyler Too," in which words by Alexander C. Ross were adapted to the folk tune "Little Pigs." First heard at Zanesville, Ohio, this song spread rapidly over the country, furnishing a party slogan. The *North American Review* stated that what the *Marseillaise* was to Frenchmen, "Tippecanoe and Tyler Too" was to the Whigs of 1840. In 1872 an attempt was made to revive the air for "Greeley Is the Real True Blue." The words, sometimes with music, of 19th-century campaign songs were distributed in paper-covered songbooks or songsters. Among these were the *Log Cabin Song Book* (1840) and *Hutchinson's Republican Songster for the Campaign of 1860,* compiled by J. W. Hutchinson. Glee clubs were often organized to introduce campaign songs and to lead audiences and marchers in singing them. The songs were real factors in holding the interest of crowds, emphasizing issues, developing enthusiasm, and satirizing opponents.

In the 20th century, with changes in the methods of campaigning, particularly the use of, first, radio and then television, the campaign song declined as a popular form of expression. In his 1932 presidential campaign Franklin D. Roosevelt adopted the nonpolitical melody "Happy Days Are Here Again." By the 1960's campaign songs no longer presented issues, but instead presented an emotional feeling attached to a campaign. John F. Kennedy's campaign song was adapted from the popular tune "High Hopes," and in Lyndon Johnson's 1964 campaign the theme song from the Broadway hit show *Hello, Dolly* was adapted to "Hello, Lyndon."

[S. L. Cook, *Torchlight Parade;* Irwin Silber, *Songs America Voted By*.]

G. S. BRYAN

CAMPBELLITES. *See* **Disciples of Christ.**

CAMP BUTLER, a training camp for Illinois volunteers, established in August 1861, and used until June 1866. It was located six miles east of Springfield. Here nearly a third of the Illinois regiments were mustered into the federal service and later discharged. After the capture of Fort Donelson, Tennessee, in February 1862 by Union troops, Camp Butler was also used as a prison camp, housing at one time as many as 3,600 captured Confederates.

[Helen E. Sheppley, "Camp Butler in the Civil War Days," *Journal of the Illinois State Historical Society* (1933).]

PAUL M. ANGLE

CAMP CHASE, located just west of Columbus, Ohio, served the dual purpose of training camp and military prison during the Civil War. As the war continued, its importance as a prison camp increased and Confederate prisoners continued to be received in large numbers until the cessation of hostilities. The prison population was greatest in 1863 when some 8,000 Confederate soldiers were confined there. In 1864 a Confederate plan to release the prisoners at Johnson's Island in Lake Erie, seize Sandusky, and release the prisoners at Camp Chase miscarried.

[William H. Knauss, *The Story of Camp Chase*.]

FRANCIS R. AUMANN

CAMP DOUGLAS, established in September 1861 for the concentration and training of Illinois volunteers. It covered sixty acres near the then southern limit of Chicago. After the fall of Fort Donelson, Tennessee, in February 1862, Camp Douglas served also as a prison camp, 30,000 Confederates being confined there at one time or another. It was dismantled in November 1865.

[A. T. Andreas, *History of Chicago*.]

PAUL M. ANGLE

CAMP GRANT MASSACRE. On Apr. 30, 1871, the Arivaipa band of Apache, hoping to settle down and lead peaceful lives, was encamped near Camp Grant, Ariz. In an early morning attack the sleeping Apache were slaughtered by a party of citizens of Tucson, assisted by Papago Indians. Most of the Arivaipa men were away at the time, hunting with their chief, Eskiminzin, and so, of 108 Indians slain only 8 were men. Twenty-nine children were taken prisoner, to be sold as slaves in Mexico. The perpetrators of the massacre were arrested, but they were acquitted at once by a Tucson jury. However, newspaper reports of the carnage shocked readers all over the nation and influenced the formulation of a new federal Indian policy, which came to be known as President Ulysses S. Grant's peace policy. The objective was to assemble all the Apache on reservations "and to promote peace and civilization among them."

[Odie B. Faulk, *The Geronimo Campaign;* Ralph H. Ogle, *Federal Control of Western Apaches, 1848–1886;* Dan L. Thrapp, *The Conquest of Apachería*.]

KENNETH M. STEWART

CAMP JACKSON AFFAIR. Capt. Nathaniel Lyon, an antisecessionist in command of the U.S. arsenal in Saint Louis, Mo., received information in late April and early May 1861 that Missouri authorities, including the secessionist governor Claiborne F. Jackson, were planning to capture the arsenal in order to arm troops under prosouthern leaders. Lyon collected and armed a number of politico-military organizations as Home Guards and removed the remaining guns to Illinois. Jackson therefore took advantage of a Missouri law and ordered Brig. Gen. D. M. Frost, a secessionist, to establish an encampment for the purpose of drilling and disciplining militiamen. Frost, with about 600 militiamen, set up Camp Jackson in the western part of Saint Louis. On May 8, the camp received a quantity of arms from Jefferson Davis. Lyon learned of the arrival of the arms, and a week later, with about 8,000 men, seized without resistance the militiamen at Camp Jackson. While being marched to the prison, a large crowd, sympathetic to the prisoners, had gathered. The crowd was fired upon by Lyon's troops and about twenty-eight men, women, and children were killed and a number wounded. Many of the militiamen were opponents of secession, and all were subsequently released on parole, subject to exchange as prisoners of war.

[R. U. Johnson and C. C. Buel, eds., *Battles and Leaders of the Civil War,* vol. I.]

STELLA M. DRUMM

CAMP MEETINGS. Outdoor religious meetings were a feature of the evangelical revival in both England and America in the 18th century. Baptists held meetings similar to the later camp meetings during the American Revolution. A meeting conducted jointly by Presbyterian and Methodist ministers at Gasper River, in Logan County, Ky., in July 1800, is generally accepted as the first regular camp meeting. Held in a wood, near a supply of water, the encampments usually lasted four days or longer. There were several services each day, and sometimes four or five ministers spoke at the same time from different parts of the campground. The animated evening services of the frontier assemblies, accentuated by pine knots flickering in the dense darkness, were usually tense with excitement and frequently marked by emotional actions such as jerking, falling, barking, rolling, and dancing.

Camp meetings were not confined to the frontier, but extended throughout the United States during the early 19th century. Steamboats carried many hundreds of people at excursion rates from eastern cities to nearby camp meetings. In many cases cottages replaced tents and permanent auditoriums were erected. During the late 19th century, popular educational movements, such as Chautauqua (New York), and summer resort communities, such as Ocean Grove, N.J., developed from camp-meeting beginnings. Many summer assemblies still function as outgrowths of the camp meeting.

[Catherine C. Cleveland, *The Great Revival in the West, 1797–1805;* Charles A. Johnson, *The Frontier Camp Meeting*.]

W. B. POSEY

CAMPOBELLO FIASCO, an attempt by the John O'Mahony Fenians to seize the island of Campobello, New Brunswick, for Ireland in April 1866. The British, aware of the plan, sent a vessel to Eastport, Maine, and increased their garrisons. Three U.S. vessels and a number of troops successfully intercepted shipments of Fenian arms and prevented violations of American neutrality laws. Disheartened, the Fenians returned home to plan anew.

[J. Stephens, *Fenian Brotherhood*.]

EZRA H. PIEPER

CAMPS AND CANTONMENTS OF WORLD WAR I. To build the camps and cantonments required for housing and training of U.S. National Guard and National Army divisions during World War I, the Construction Division of the army was created in May 1917. This unit, later known as the Cantonment Division, was first commanded by Brig. Gen. Isaac W. Littell—later by Brig. Gen. R. C. Marshall, Jr., under whose administration it became a part of the office of the chief of staff.

The secretary of war (Newton D. Baker) ordered the building of sixteen cantonments with wooden barracks for the new National Army and, in addition, sixteen National Guard camps where troops would be quartered in tents with wood floors, with wooden buildings for kitchens and mess halls. Projected dates for calling conscripted men to the colors forced construction work to be crowded practically within a ninety-day period.

Each National Army cantonment contained, in addition to the barracks, quarters, and administration buildings, a hospital, warehouses, railroad tracks, permanent highways, water supply, electricity, sewerage, refrigeration, welfare buildings, sewage-disposal plant, remount depot, target range, and, in many cases, a power station. Each cantonment could accommodate a "Pershing" division, approximately 28,000 men. The National Guard camps, in addition to the tent facilities, included the principal installations of the National Army cantonments, but on a limited scale. With the exception of two donated parcels, land for cantonments was purchased; sites for National Guard camps were all loaned gratis or rented.

By Sept. 1, 1917, the thirty-two construction projects were housing troops, and a month later all tent camps were substantially complete. On Nov. 15 the same was true of the cantonments. Physical work of building was done by civilian labor (reaching a peak of 200,000 men), employed by contractors working on a cost-plus emergency contract. The average cost of construction per cantonment was $11.6 million, exclusive of land; for the National Guard tent camps, the average was $2.4 million.

National Army cantonments built were Custer at Battle Creek, Mich.; Devens, Ayer, Mass.; Dodge, Des Moines, Iowa; Dix, Wrightstown, N.J.; Funston, Fort Riley, Kans.; Gordon, Atlanta, Ga.; Grant, Rockford, Ill.; Jackson, Columbia, S.C.; Lee, Petersburg, Va.; Lewis, American Lake, Wash.; Meade, Admiral, Md.; Pike, Little Rock, Ark.; Sherman, Chillicothe, Ohio; Taylor, Louisville, Ky.; Travis, San Antonio, Tex.; and Upton, Yaphank, Long Island, N.Y.

National Guard camps built were Beauregard at Alexandria, La.; Bowie, Fort Worth, Tex.; Cody, Deming, N.Mex.; Doniphan, Fort Sill, Okla.; Frémont, Palo Alto, Calif.; Green, Charlotte, N.C.; Hancock, Augusta, Ga.; Kearney, Linda Vista, Calif.; Logan, Houston, Tex.; MacArthur, Waco,

Tex.; McClellan, Anniston, Ala.; Sevier, Greenville, S.C.; Shelby, Hattiesburg, Miss.; Sheridan, Montgomery, Ala.; Wadsworth, Spartanburg, S.C.; Wheeler, Macon, Ga.

In addition to the above, three embarkation camps were built: Merritt, Tenafly, N.J.; and Stewart and Hill, Newport News, Va. Two quartermaster camps were constructed: Ordway, Washington, D.C.; and J. E. Johnston, Jacksonville, Fla. Total capacity in men for the National Army cantonments was 654,786; for the National Guard camps, 438,042.

After cessation of hostilities, the government salvaged a vast quantity of material and disposed of all remaining installations either at auction or by sales preceded by advertising for sealed bids.

ROBERT S. THOMAS

CAMP WILDCAT, a natural fortification in the Rockcastle Hills of Laurel County, Ky., where Union troops, under Col. T. T. Garrard, decisively repulsed Gen. Felix Zollicoffer on Oct. 21, 1861.

JONATHAN T. DORRIS

CANADA, CONFEDERATE ACTIVITIES IN, directed against northern prison camps were reported as early as November, 1863, but were unorganized until the arrival in Canada of Confederate commissioners Jacob Thompson, J. P. Holcombe, and C. C. Clay in May 1864.

A peace movement in July and a ''Northwest conspiracy'' in August having failed, an effort was made to seize federal ships on Lake Erie in John Beall's raid in September, and an attack was made on Saint Albans, Vt., in October 1864. About this time plans to release Confederate prisoners in northern prison camps uniformly failed.

Plots to burn northern cities, including New York and Cincinnati, followed. In New York eleven hotels and Barnum's Museum were fired on Nov. 25, 1864, but the blazes were quickly extinguished. A train-wrecking effort near Buffalo in December, to release captured Confederate generals, failed and one plotter was executed.

Confederates in Canada supplied cash for buying gold, shipping it to England, and selling it in order to depress federal currency values. Two million dollars were thus shipped with no permanent result. About $300,000 was spent by Confederates in Canada in promoting these various futile schemes.

[John W. Headley, *Confederate Operations in Canada and New York.*]

CHARLES H. COLEMAN

CANADA AND THE AMERICAN REVOLUTION. Attempts at Alliance. For strategic reasons, it seemed essential to win Canada to the cause of the American Revolution. Accordingly, on Oct. 24, 1774, the Continental Congress dispatched a letter appealing to the Canadians, dwelling upon the supposed grievances of Canadians against the British government and inviting them to send delegates to the next Congress; it added that if they refused to be friends they would be treated as foes. Massachusetts made similar overtures on its own account, appointing a committee to correspond with the Canadians, and early in 1775 sent John Brown to Canada to advance the cause. In the absence of any actual rising in the province, Congress later in the year decided to seize Canada by force (see below); and in 1776 it supplemented its military effort by sending to Montreal a mission composed of Benjamin Franklin, Samuel Chase, and Charles Carroll, and equipped with a printing press to assist in spreading revolutionary propaganda. The mission made little impression upon Canadian opinion and retired from Canada at the end of May, after the siege of Quebec had been raised by troops from England. The failure to win the French-Canadians to the American cause was due in great part to traditional animosities, largely based on religion, which were reinforced by resentment aroused by the exactions of the American army; while even the English-speaking merchants, bound by close commercial ties to London, were unfavorable to actual secession from the British Empire. Various proposals for enterprises toward Canada made later in the war were thwarted by the mutual jealousy between the French and the Americans; neither party wished its ally to gain control of the colony.

American Invasion of Canada. In attempting the conquest of Canada, the Continental Congress wished not only to effect a diversion favorable to the colonial operations around Boston, but, still more, to deprive Britain of a base for attack upon the revolutionary colonies. The idea was encouraged by the capture of Ticonderoga and Crown Point, which secured the route northward. Hopes of success were increased by the knowledge that there were few regular troops in Canada, and the plausible expectation of a rising of the French-Canadians. After some hesitation, Congress authorized Gen. Philip Schuyler (June 27, 1775) to undertake the invasion. Active direction of the expedition, however, fell to Brig. Gen. Richard Montgomery.

A hasty enterprise against Montreal resulted only in the capture of Ethan Allen by the British (Sept. 25,

1775). The real gateway of Canada, St. Johns on the Richelieu River, held by a large proportion of Canada's regular garrison, fell after a siege lasting from Sept. 17 to Nov. 2, during which the invaders were strengthened by ammunition and provisions obtained by the capture of Fort Chambly. Montreal was occupied Nov. 13, 1775.

Sir Guy Carleton, governor of the province, fled to Quebec, which was already threatened by the force which Benedict Arnold had brought up by the tremendously difficult Kennebec route (*see* Arnold's March to Quebec); but even after Arnold's junction (Dec. 2) with Montgomery's depleted army, the colonial troops available for the siege of Quebec numbered only about 1,000. The one assault which was attempted (Dec. 31) failed completely, Montgomery being killed; and in spite of considerable reinforcements, toward spring the siege ended abruptly with the opening of navigation, when the first of 10,000 regulars arrived from England (May 5, 1776). On May 16 a British force from the west captured 400 Americans at Cedars, above Montreal; on June 7 part of the American main force strengthened by a brigade under Gen. John Sullivan, who assumed command, met disaster at Three Rivers. On June 15 Montreal was evacuated. Sullivan's force and the small body under Arnold from Montreal were reunited at St. Johns. On June 18 the last Americans left that fortress. Carleton's pursuit was delayed while he built a fleet, which destroyed Arnold's (*see* Valcour Island, Battle of), but it was too late in the season for further operations, and invasion of the colonies was postponed until 1777 (*see* Burgoyne's Invasion).

The failure of the American invasion was due to inadequate military measures, to British sea power, and to the generally neutral attitude of the French-Canadians. It has been argued that the campaign was advantageous to the revolutionary cause in the end by forcing the British to divert the reinforcements of 1776 to the St. Lawrence, thus causing a dispersion of the royal forces that led to the decisive success at Saratoga the following year.

C. P. STACEY

Gates's Proposed Expedition. The opposition to George Washington as commander in chief did not subside with the exposure of the Conway Cabal. In the hope of achieving control, early in 1778 Gen. Horatio Gates and his friends fixed on an invasion of Canada. The interest and support of the Marquis de Lafayette were enlisted; he was to be the leader of this fantastic "iruption into Canada" in the dead of winter. In February 1778 he went to Albany, but nothing had been done. Lafayette was enraged and humiliated. By April he was back with Washington. Gates and his friends had blundered again. Six months later they attempted, unsuccessfully, to revive the plan.

THOMAS ROBSON HAY

[A. L. Burt, *The Old Province of Quebec;* Don Higginbotham, *The War of American Independence;* Justin H. Smith, *Our Struggle for the Fourteenth Colony;* G. M. Wrong, *Canada and the American Revolution.*]

CANADA AND THE WAR OF 1812. Since the destruction of British power in Canada was a primary object of those responsible for bringing on the War of 1812 (*see* War Hawks), it was inevitable that the United States in the course of that war should attempt the conquest of the colony. In 1812 an attempted invasion on the Detroit frontier resulted in disaster and an enterprise on the Niagara, the Battle of Queenston Heights, met the same fate. The next year brought more success: Oliver Hazard Perry's victory in the Battle of Lake Erie permitted a successful invasion of western Upper Canada (Battle of the Thames) and the Detroit frontier region remained in American hands until the end of the war. Farther east, the Americans successfully raided York, but initial successes on the Niagara were followed by a check at Stoney Creek, and no permanent foothold was gained; and the campaign against Montreal was a total failure (Chrysler's Field and Chateaugay). In 1814 the United States again attempted to invade Canada on the Niagara, but though the American troops now gave a better account of themselves, particularly at Chippewa, Lundy's Lane, and Fort Erie, no conquest of territory resulted.

Among the causes of the American failures, the military unpreparedness of the United States and the large degree of skill with which the defense was conducted by the British regular troops in Canada are important. The determined resistance of the Canadian population was contrary to American expectations and was also a powerful factor. Finally, the American strategic plans were in general decidedly unsound, in that they wasted the country's military resources in ill-conceived enterprises against Canada's western settlements instead of concentrating them in an effective offensive movement against the essential British line of communication in the St. Lawrence Valley.

[Sir C. P. Lucas, *The Canadian War of 1812;* A. T. Mahan, *Sea Power in Its Relations to the War of 1812;* Julius W. Pratt, *Expansionists of 1812.*]

C. P. STACEY

CANADIAN-AMERICAN RECIPROCITY. Faced with the ending of British imperial preference in the 19th century, the Canadian business community turned for trade to the North American continent. Under threats of a movement for annexation to the United States originating in 1849 with Montreal merchants, the British government supported reciprocal trade with the Americans as an alternative, using maritime fishing rights as an enticement to interest Washington. In 1854, the Elgin-Marcy Reciprocity Treaty was negotiated. The treaty, which was to remain in force for ten years from 1855 and was abrogable on one year's notice, gave Americans access to Atlantic fisheries north of the thirty-sixth parallel and listed most Canadian raw materials and agricultural produce as goods reciprocally admitted duty-free. Historians have disagreed over the effects of the treaty but now generally accept that the economic prosperity that followed in British North America was largely the result of other factors. The United States abrogated the treaty in 1866, ostensibly because of problems arising from the Civil War but principally because it was not considered economically advantageous to American interests. For British North America, confederation of the British provinces into the Dominion of Canada (1867) offered a new economic possibility.

From Confederation to 1911, reciprocity was an aim of all Canadian governments, although political rhetoric made it a party issue: the Conservative party, which stood publicly for nationalism and protectionism ("the National Policy"), succeeded in associating the Liberals with free trade, commercial union, and continentalism. The government of Sir Wilfrid Laurier fell in 1911 in an election fought in large part over a draft treaty supported by several prominent American politicians—among them President William Howard Taft—as a prelude to annexation. After 1911, reciprocity ceased to be a significant strategy for North American trade and thereafter was not a major issue.

[L. Ethan Ellis, *Reciprocity, 1911;* D. C. Masters, *The Reciprocity Treaty of 1854;* L. B. Shippee, *Canadian-American Relations, 1849–1874.*]

J. M. BUMSTED

CANADIAN-AMERICAN RELATIONS. The Canadian-American relationship is an unusual one in a number of ways. The two nations share one of the longest common borders in the world—nearly 5,000 miles, if Alaska is included. This frontier is technically undefended, giving rise to much discussion of how the two nations pioneered mutual disarmament, even though the lack of defense is more mythical than real. Canada and the United States are each other's best customers, with more goods moving across the Great Lakes than over any other localized water system in the world. However, the cultural impact of the more populous nation upon the smaller has caused Canada to fear a "creeping continentalism," or "cultural annexation," by the United States—a fear that led to strains in the Canadian-American relationship in the 1960's and 1970's. Indicative of the cultural problem is Canadian resentment of use of the term "American" as solely applicable to the United States, since Canadians are Americans too in the geographical sense.

To understand the Canadian-American relationship, one must be aware of three problems. The first is that until the 20th century, Americans tended to assume that one day Canada would become part of the United States—especially since it continued to be (and technically still is) a monarchy that democratic Americans who espoused the notion of Manifest Destiny felt should be added to "the area of freedom." The second is that Canadians found themselves caught between the United States, which they feared would absorb them, and Great Britain, whose colony they were; and thus Canadian statesmen often used the cry of "Americanization" to strengthen ties with Britain. The third is that the Canadian population has been roughly one-third French-speaking for a century and a half, and this bilingual and bicultural condition has complicated the North American relationship.

In a sense, one cannot separate Canadian-American relations from Canadian history. This is especially so for two reasons. Of the two score or more distinct steps by which a colonial dependency of Britain became a self-governing colony and then a fully independent nation, most were taken in Canada first or arose from a Canadian precedent or over a Canadian initiative. Thus, Canada represents the best and most complete example of progressive decolonization in imperial history; and the Canadian-American relationship must be understood as one involving sharp contrasts between a nation, the United States, that gained its independence by revolution, and a nation, Canada, that sought its independence by evolution. Further, despite similarities of geography, patterns of settlement, technology, and standards of living, Canadians came to differ in numerous and fundamental ways from Americans. The most important areas of difference (apart from those arising from Canada's bilingual nature) were (1) that Canada did not experience a westward movement that paralleled the Turnerian frontier of the American West; (2) that Canada's economy was, especially in the 18th and 19th centuries, dependent upon a succession of staples—principally fish, furs, timber, and wheat—which prevented the development of an abundant and diversified economy like that of the United States; and (3) that Canadians could not at any time become isolationists, as Americans did, since they felt under threat from an immediate neighbor, which the United States did not. Most Americans are ignorant of these basic differences in the histories of the two nations—perhaps the single greatest cause of friction in Canadian-American relations, for, as Canadians argue, they know much American history while Americans know little of Canadian history.

The history of the relationship itself has been marked by periods of sharp hostility tempered by an awareness of a shared continental environment and by the slow emergence of a Canadian foreign policy independent of either Great Britain or the United States—a policy, moreover, that has given Canada middle-power status in the post–World War II world. The original hostility arose from the four intercolonial wars (sometimes referred to as the Great War for Empire) in which the North American colonies of Britain and France were involved from 1689 until 1763. The English Protestant settlers of the thirteen seaboard colonies were at war with the French Catholic inhabitants of New France until, in the French and Indian War, Britain triumphed and Canada passed to the British by the Peace of Paris (1763). Thereafter, Canadians were caught up on the fringes of the American Revolution: Benjamin Franklin traveled to Montreal in an unsuccessful attempt to gain revolutionary support there, and rebel privateers raided the Nova Scotian coast. The Treaty of Paris, in 1783, created the new United States and left what thereafter was called the British North American Provinces in British hands. The flight of nearly 40,000 Loyalists from the United States to the new provinces of Upper Canada (later Canada West and now Ontario) and New Brunswick and to the eastern townships of Lower Canada (later Canada East and now Quebec) assured the presence of resolutely anti-American settlers on the Canadian frontier.

Relations between the United States and Britain, and thus with Canada too, remained tense for over three decades. Loyalists in Canada resented the loss of their American property and, later, the renunciation by some American states of their debts for Loyalist property confiscated during the American Revolution. The British regained certain western forts on American soil, contrary to the treaty of 1783, to assure control over the Indians; and American frontiersmen believed that the British encouraged Indian attacks upon them. Although Jay's Treaty of 1796 secured these forts for the United States, western Americans continued to covet Canada. A combination of such war hawks, a controversy over British impressment of American seamen, and the problem of neutral rights on the seas led to an American declaration of war against Britain in 1812. A series of unsuccessful invasions of Canada nurtured anti-Americanism there, while the burning of York (now Toronto), the capital of Upper Canada, became an event for the Canadian imagination not unlike the stand at the Alamo and the sinking of the *Maine* to Americans. The Treaty of Ghent, signed in 1815, restored the *status quo ante* but ended British trade with American Indians, removing a major source of friction. The Rush-Bagot Agreement of 1817 placed limitations on armed naval vessels on the Great Lakes and became the basis for the myth—since the agreement did not apply to land fortifications—that the Canadian-American border henceforth was undefended.

A second period of strain along the border began in 1837 and extended until 1871. Rebellions in both Canadas in the former year were put down by the British government, but not before American filibustering groups—and particularly the Hunters Lodges—provoked a number of border incidents, especially over the *Caroline;* further, the leaders of the rebellion sought refuge in the United States. Two years later a dispute over the Maine boundary led to a war scare. Although the border was settled by the Webster-Ashburton Treaty of 1842, the Oregon frontier remained in dispute until 1846. In the 1850's, Canada flourished, helped in part by trade with the United States encouraged by the Elgin-Marcy Reciprocity Treaty of 1854 (after an abortive annexation manifesto was released by a body of Montreal merchants, forcing the British to support such trade). During the Civil War, relations deteriorated: Canadians were felt to be antinorthern, and they bore the brunt of Union resentment over Queen Victoria's Proclamation of Neutrality. The *Trent* affair of 1861 brought genuine danger of war between the North and Britain and led to the reinforcement of the Canadian garrisons. Canadians anticipated a southern victory and an invasion by the northern army in search of compensatory land; therefore, detailed defensive plans were developed, the emphasis on siege warfare and "General Winter." The *Alabama* affair; Confederate use of Canadian ports and towns for raids on Lake Erie, Johnson's Island, and Saint Albans; and the imposition of passport requirements along the border by American customs officials gave reality to Canadian fears. Ultimately Canada enacted its own neutrality legislation. Moreover, concern over the American threat was one of the impulses behind the movement, in 1864, to bring the Canadian provinces together into a confederation, as achieved by the British North America Act in 1867. In the meantime (and again in 1871), there were raids by Fenians from the United States. These raids and congressional abrogation of the reciprocity treaty in 1866 underscored the tenuous position of the individual colonies. Thus, the formation of the Dominion of Canada on July 1, 1867, owed much to the tensions inherent in the Canadian-American relationship.

These tensions were much eased by the Treaty of Washington in 1871. From this date on, the frontier between the two countries became progressively "unguarded," in that no new fortifications were built. The treaty provided for the arbitration of the *Alabama* claims and a boundary dispute over the San Juan Islands. Although this agreement strengthened the principle of arbitration and although Canada was represented for the first time on a diplomatic matter (by its prime minister, Sir John A. Macdonald), the treaty was unpopular in Canada, giving rise to the oft-repeated charge that Britain was willing to "sell Canada on the block of Anglo-American harmony" and that Canada was an American hostage to Britain's good behavior in the Western Hemisphere. Significantly, Canadians then began to press for independent diplomatic representation.

Problems between Canada and the United States after 1871 were, in fact, more economic and cultural than strictly diplomatic. Disputes over the Atlantic fisheries, dating from before the Revolution, and over questions relating to fur seals in the Bering Sea were resolved by arbitration. As the United States refused to renew reciprocity of trade, Canada turned in 1878 to the national policy of tariff protection. A flurry of rumors of war accompanied the Venezuela boundary crisis in 1895; and the Alaska boundary question, unimportant until the discovery of gold in the Klondike, exacerbated old fears, especially as dealt with in 1903 by a pugnacious Theodore Roosevelt. Perhaps the last gasp of fear of direct annexation was heard in 1911, when the Canadian electorate indirectly but decisively turned back President William Howard Taft's attempt to gain a new reciprocity treaty that many thought might lead to a commercial, and ultimately political, union. American neutrality in 1914, at the outbreak of World War I, was resented in English-speaking Canada, and relations remained at a low ebb until the United States entered the war in 1917.

A period of improved Canadian-American relations followed. An international joint commission had been created in 1909 to adjudicate on boundary waters, and a massive influx of American settlers onto the Canadian prairies between 1909 and 1914 had been welcomed by the Canadian government. With the coming of World War I, the economies of the two nations began to interlock more closely. In 1927 Canada achieved full diplomatic independence by exchanging its own minister with Washington; by 1931, when all dominions were declared to be fully autonomous and equal in stature, Canada clearly had shown the United States how it could take the lead in providing the hallmarks of autonomy for other former colonies as well. During the U.S. experiment with prohibition—which Canada did not share—minor incidents arose, the most important of which was the American sinking of the Canadian vessel *I'm Alone* in 1929; but harmonious arbitration of this specific case in 1935, following America's repeal of Prohibition in 1933, eliminated the causes of the friction. Canadians were disturbed that the United States failed to join the League of Nations, but they welcomed American initiatives toward peacekeeping in the 1920's and 1930's. With the outbreak of World War II in Europe and the rapid fall of France in 1940, Canadians were willing to accept the protection implied by President Franklin D. Roosevelt in his Ogdensburg Declaration of Aug. 18, and Roosevelt and Prime Minister William Lyon Mackenzie King established the Permanent Joint Board on Defense, which continues to exist.

Military cooperation continued during and after America's entry into World War II. The Alaska Highway was jointly constructed; Canadian forces helped against the Japanese in the Aleutian Islands; and both Canada and the United States became charter members of the North Atlantic Treaty Organization in 1949. A collaborative series of three early-warning radar systems was constructed across Canada during the height of the cold war, and in 1957 a North American Air Defense Command (NORAD) was created. Increasingly Canada came to play the role of peacekeeper in the world—at Suez, in the Congo, in Southeast Asia, and in 1973 in Vietnam. Although Canada entered into trade relations with Cuba and Communist China at a time when the United States strenuously opposed such relations, diplomatic relations remained relatively harmonious. Nor did relations deteriorate when Canadians protested against American nuclear testing in the far Pacific Northwest, or when Canada gave refuge to over 40,000 young Americans who sought, during the Vietnam War, to avoid military service.

This harmony was offset by continued and increased economic and cultural tension. In the 1930's the two countries erected preferential tariff barriers against each other, and despite an easing of competition in 1935, Canadians have continued to be apprehensive of the growing American influence in Canadian industry and labor. Disputes over the role of American subsidiary firms in Canada; over American business practices, oil import programs, and farm policy; and over the influence of American periodicals and television in Canada led to a resurgence of "Canada First" nationalism under Prime Minister John Diefenbaker in the late 1950's and early 1960's. Still, Queen Elizabeth II and President Dwight D. Eisenhower in 1959 together opened the Saint Lawrence Seaway, long opposed by the United States; the flow of Canadian immigrants to the United States continued; and relations, while no longer "easy and automatic," as Prime Minister Lester B. Pearson once described them, remained open to rational resolution. The growth of a French-Canadian separatist movement; diverging policies over the Caribbean and, until 1972, the People's Republic of China; and American ownership of key Canadian industries (especially the automobile, rubber, and electrical equipment sectors) promised a future not without dispute.

[J. B. Brebner, *The North Atlantic Triangle;* Gerald M. Craig, *The United States and Canada;* John Sloan Dickey, ed., *The United States and Canada.*]

ROBIN W. WINKS

CANADIAN-AMERICAN WATERWAYS. A large number of bodies of water on the North American continent extend across national boundaries and have posed considerable difficulty for the nations involved. For much of the period since 1535, when Jacques Cartier first navigated the Saint Lawrence River to what is now Montreal, attention has been focused particularly on the transportation potential of the Saint Lawrence system and its links to the Great Lakes. Natural obstacles in the path of a North American dream of a fully navigable passageway from the lakes to the sea via the Saint Lawrence have gradually been eliminated—at first by competition between the United States and Canada and subsequently by cooperation between the two countries. The Welland Canal, connecting Lake Ontario and Lake Erie, for example, was originally built by Upper Canadian interests in response to the American opening of the Erie Canal. American initiative during the Civil War constructed canals at Sault Sainte Marie, opening Lake Superior. Thus, despite frequent pronouncements of the need for international cooperation in improving water transport, most of the 19th-century activity by both nations was motivated primarily by economic competition, with overtones of military demands for a waterway completely within national boundaries.

Not until the 1890's was serious consideration given to joint construction of a Saint Lawrence waterway, and then, for better than half a century, various proposals were opposed by one nation or the other. Finally, in 1954, the U.S. Congress agreed to a Canadian initiative of 1951 for construction of a seaway capable of handling the largest oceangoing vessels. The decisive factors in bringing about the agreement were the need to transport iron ore and a Canadian threat to develop the electric power potential of the waterway with or without American assistance. The Saint Lawrence Seaway was officially opened in 1959 and handles largely bulk cargo, especially iron ore and wheat.

Since the 1960's transportation and navigation have played a decreasing role in Canadian-American waterway considerations. Most of the new factors—such as pollution, water supply, flood control, and hydroelectric power—were covered in the Boundary Waters Treaty of 1909, which created an international joint commission to deal with them. Many of the issues surfaced in the negotiations leading to the Columbia River Treaty of 1961 and its subsequent modification in 1964. While the United States and Canada have been able to agree in principle on the need to clean up the Great Lakes, disagreement over responsibility and financial commitment has hampered action. A mounting wave of Canadian nationalism beginning in the late 1960's produced substantial opposition to any plans for joint cooperation in exploiting water resources, on the grounds that such activity would inevitably result in a sellout of Canadian natural resources to the United States.

[John V. Krutilla, *The Columbia River Treaty: The Economics of an International River Basin Development;* William R. Willoughby, *The St. Lawrence Waterway: A Study in Politics and Diplomacy.*]

J. M. BUMSTED

CANADIAN AND U.S. BOUNDARY DISPUTES. *See* **Northeast Boundary; Northwest Boundary Controversy.**

CANADIAN ANNEXATION MOVEMENT. In 1849 Canadian urban and commercial interests, primarily in Montreal, sponsored a movement to annex Canada to the United States. This was an attempt to offset the serious decline in trade, prices, and property values in Canada that had resulted from the capture of western trade by the Erie Canal route, by granting of bonding privileges by the United States, by repeal of the Corn Laws and imperial preference, and by failure of the United States to satisfy the Canadian demand for reciprocity in natural products in 1848 and 1849. An annexation manifesto, issued on Oct. 10, 1849, received over 1,000 signatures, including some of the most prominent political and financial leaders of Montreal. Widespread opposition, counter manifestoes, and return of prosperity ended the movement within six months.

[C. D. Allin and G. M. Jones, *Annexation, Preferential Trade and Reciprocity.*]

ALBERT B. COREY

CANADIAN INDIANS. With the exception of the Eskimo culture area, the various Canadian Indians manifest a cultural continuity with those directly to the south, and the Eskimo culture area impinges on that of Alaska. Similarly, there is a direct cultural continuum from the interior of Alaska through the Yukon and Northwest territories to the southern tier of Canadian provinces.

The Indians of Canada through the eastern side of the continent are all, again with the exception of the Eskimo, to be linked with the Algonkin speech family. The extinct Boethuk of Newfoundland were probably Algonkin speakers, while the Montagnais-Naskapi of interior northern Quebec give way to the various Woodland Algonkins of the Great Lakes, inclusive of the Saint Lawrence Valley. Algonkin speech spread into the central woodlands of Ontario and Manitoba among the Ojibwa (or Chippewa) and included the Cree, a tribe that ranged from James Bay to the Saskatchewan River, and such Plains-Prairie peoples as the Blackfoot in Saskatchewan and Alberta. Some of these groups followed the general subarctic pattern of life, dependent primarily on hunting and gathering and lacking agriculture, but the strong cultural imprint of the North American Plains carries over to the cultures of some, such as the Blackfoot.

The area of northwestern Canada and Alaska was inhabited by the various vaguely defined tribes and tribelets of boreal forest and tundra adaptation. Some of the Algonkin Cree fell into this pattern; others became adapted to Plains bison-hunting life. Beginning with the Chipewyan and moving northwest, Athapascan speech is encountered, a language family that moves without interruption to the Yukon Valley of Alaska, among, for example, the Beaver, the Slave, the Kaska, and the tundra-dwelling groups designated Dogrib and Yellowknives. In Alberta and eastern British Columbia there is an extension northward of the gathering, salmon-fishing Plateau peoples. On the Canadian side are encountered the Salishan-speaking tribes Lillooet, Shuswap, and Kutenai, apparently remotely Algonkin.

The Canadian areas stand out distinctly. The British Columbia coasts offer the dramatic cultures of the Northwest Coast: for example, the Tlingit, Haida, and Tsimshian in the North; the Kwakiutl, Nootka, and Bella Coola in the central regions; and the various Salishan groups clustering about Puget Sound and the lower Fraser Valley. The groups in this area are notable for their art; their use of wood, seen especially in their splendid houses; and their system of ritual economic exchanges, the potlatches. The Eskimo cultures of Canada, spreading from the Mackenzie delta to the Labrador coasts and including the northern islands and the shores of Hudson Bay, have their own distinctive configuration, one slightly different from those of Alaska or Greenland: small bands, the snow house or snow-covered tent, and a dependence on sealing and caribou-hunting.

In the Canadian interior, because of the presence of French fur traders for more than two centuries, there has been much interracial mixing. The descendants of such unions, the so-called métis, play an important role in the northwest. Like that of the United States, Canadian Indian policy has vacillated. The effects of treaty and reservation life are still to be felt.

[Diamond Jenness, *The Indians of Canada.*]

ROBERT F. SPENCER

CANADIAN RIVER, a part of the Arkansas River system in the southwest United States. Early French traders and explorers followed its course west into the Spanish territory. The name possibly was given to the river by early French hunters and traders who came from Canada. The upper part was called Rio Colorado by the Spanish. By the Treaty of Doak's Stand in 1820, Canadian River was made the northern boundary of the Choctaw nation. Early emigrants to California followed the south bank of the Canadian on to Santa Fe.

[J. B. Thoburn and M. H. Wright, *Oklahoma, A History of the State and Its People;* Grant Foreman, *Pioneer Days in the Early Southwest.*]

ANNA LEWIS

CANAL BOATS. *See* **Canals.**

CANAL LANDS. *See* **Canals.**

CANAL RING, a group of corrupt contractors and politicians who conspired shortly after the Civil War to defraud the state of New York by overcharging for repairs and improvement of the state's canal system. It defied an investigation in 1868 and for years was powerful enough to prevent interference and to defeat unfriendly candidates for office.

[D. S. Alexander, *Political History of the State of New York.*]

ALVIN F. HARLOW

CANALS. Since 1607, American river systems have provided an essential element in internal transportation. However, full-scale navigation ceased at the fall line. The earliest canals—such as the Patowmack Company's works at Great Falls, Md. (constructed 1786–1808), and the Western Inland Lock Navigation Company's canal at Little Falls, N.Y. (1795)—bypassed the fall line. Other early canals skirted mill dams and other river channel obstructions. The Middlesex Canal (1793–1804), connecting Boston with the Merrimac River, and the Santee and Cooper Canal (1790's), connecting these two rivers above Charleston, S.C., fully launched America into canal construction.

Lack of skilled engineers, compounded by the crude surveying equipment available, hampered canal construction efforts. Samuel Thompson erred over 30 feet in elevation (in 18 miles) in his Middlesex Canal survey. William Watson, his replacement, brought knowledge of English canals and more accurate surveying abilities to the project. The Erie Canal (1817–25) became the great school for American canal engineers and civil engineering in general. Benjamin Wright, its first chief engineer, derived his principal experience primarily from surveying the Erie route and working for the Western Inland Lock Navigation Company. Under his tutelage evolved the famed Erie school, including David Bates, James Geddes, John Jervis, Nathan Roberts, and Canvas White. Erie school engineers spread throughout the United States, working in all aspects of civil engineering, frequently moving from one job to another and field-training others in engineering disciplines. After leaving the Erie Canal, Roberts worked on the Pennsylvania Main Line Canal (1826–34) and the Chesapeake and Ohio (C & O) Canal (1828–50); built the bridge across the Potomac River at Harpers Ferry; and helped plan river navigation improvements at Muscle Shoals, Tenn. Some became engineers from necessity. Josiah White, a merchant, promoted the Lehigh Canal (1827–29), did his own engineering, and held several patents for canal lock construction.

Two main groups financed canals: states and private companies. When a canal would open up a large new territory and the canal's chances for financial success were limited, the state tended to provide the necessary capital. When a canal focused on a single natural resource (for example, coal) or was linked to a clearly established trade route, it usually was privately financed. Except for the Erie Canal, most state systems were financial disasters in spite of substantial land subsidies; for example, Indiana received 1,457,366 acres; Ohio, 1,100,361 acres; and Michigan, 1,250,000 acres. Indiana approached bankruptcy in the 1830's because of poor fiscal management and its commitment to canal construction. On the other hand, private companies—such as the Lehigh Coal and Navigation Company, the Delaware and Hudson (D & H) Company, and the Delaware and Raritan Company—prospered.

Private companies usually escaped the problems of poor construction based on contract favoritism, fiscal mismanagement, and pressures to locate in certain areas for political rather than sound engineering or business reasons. Not every private company was immune. On the C & O Canal, the lock tender's houses near the terminus are stone, further along brick, then frame, and finally log, demonstrating the declining condition of the company as construction progressed.

Financing took many forms. State systems received direct cash outlays or federal land subsidies. Both states and private companies issued stock. In several instances—for example, the Morris Canal (1825–31), the C & O Canal, and the Whitewater Canal (1836–43)—company script was issued. Lotteries helped finance construction of a canal in the District of Columbia and of the Amoskeag Falls Canal (1812–30), the Cumberland and Oxford Canal (1827–29), and the

Union Canal (1821–27). The profits received from tolls on the Erie Canal helped to build the New York system of lateral canals. However, tolls rarely met expectations, and construction-recovery cost based upon projected revenue from tolls usually proved disastrous. Finally, some companies received outright grants from towns and villages in order to entice the canal into their area.

The principal engineering elements of a canal are the source of water supply, the canal bed, and locks to raise boats from one level to another. The main water supply for canals is a dam that feeds water either directly into the canal or into a feeder leading into the canal. Frequently, slack-water navigation is part of a canal system. The Lower Division of the Lehigh Canal, for instance, consisted of eight sections of canal and nine slack-water pools. The C & O Canal and the Schuylkill Canal (1816–25) also used slack-water navigation.

Canal beds were not uniform. A bed could have a shape varying from 45 to 60 feet at the top, with sloping side walls leading to a bottom between 30 and 45 feet wide. At first, canal depth was 4.5 to 5 feet, but most canals were deepened to 6 feet as boat drafts became larger.

Next to canalboats, locks varied most in size from one canal to another. Distance inside the chamber from gate to gate varied from 70 to 220 feet; width, from 9 to 24 feet. Lift ranged from 2 to 30 feet. Some locks were constructed of cut stone; others were composite locks consisting of loosely laid-up stone with board planking to hold the rubble in place. The completely wooden lock, number 1, on the Delaware and Raritan Canal (1831–34) at Bordentown, N.J., was a rarity. Balanced-beam miter gates ("V" gates with large wooden arms to help move them) were found both upstream and downstream. On the Delaware Canal (1827–30), Lehigh Canal, and portions of the C & O Canal, a drop or "fall" gate was used on the upstream end. Locks were named after the function they performed (for example, lift lock, guard lock, outlet lock, and tide lock). Almost all locks were lifting locks. Many canals had a weigh lock to determine the quantity of goods in a boat for toll purposes.

Other engineering elements were stop gates (to control water in long, open levels in case of a breach or during repairs), waste weirs, overflows (to maintain proper water level), culverts, and aqueducts. Many of these remains are engineering landmarks, such as the Monocacy Creek aqueduct and Paw Paw tunnel on the C & O Canal, the Roebling cable aqueduct across the Delaware River at Lackawaxen from the D & H Canal (1825–29), the Lockport flight (canal locks resembling a set of stairs) and Schoharie Creek aqueduct on the Erie Canal, the high lift locks of the Upper Division of the Lehigh Canal, and the floating towpath across Musconetcong Lake on the Morris Canal. Canal engineering also found unique answers to specific problems. Rather than large lock flights to overcome a rapid rise in elevation, as found on the Black River Canal (1838–55) in New York, the Morris Canal turned to a system of inclined planes that generated power for the plane cars with hydraulic Scotch turbines. The Allegheny Portage Railroad (Hollidaysburg to Johnstown, Pa.), part of the Pennsylvania Main Line Canal, utilized inclined planes powered by steam.

The most individual units on canals were the canalboats. Basically there were two types—packet (passenger) boats and freight boats. Packet boats, the fastest boats on a canal and usually pulled by horses, lasted only until railroads developed. Travelers' accounts from the middle of the 18th century (among them, Charles Dickens) picture both the joys and discomforts of the packet boat. Freight boats fall into two types—company boats and private boats. Company boats frequently were of one general style of construction for each canal, carried between 75 and 125 tons, and were identified by special colors and markings. Private boats were all shapes and sizes, with each owner trying to add his own touch of originality. In almost all cases, freight boats were pulled by mules. As canals declined, alternatives to mule power were sought, such as trolley cars, electric traction or mine cars, tractors, and self-propelled boats. All proved to be failures. In New York a group of boats called "line boats" carried both freight and passengers.

Finally, canal operation required personnel—lock tenders, maintenance men, ratters, level walkers, carpenters, and section bosses. A boat crew consisted of a minimum of a captain and driver, with a helper and second driver added when boating could be conducted 24 hours a day. Canal construction also drew heavily upon immigrant groups, especially the Irish and Germans.

Canals continue to play a key role in America. Both the Erie Barge Canal and the Chesapeake and Delaware Ship Canal are vital transportation links. Canal landmarks are becoming the basis for parks and other recreational development and, in several cases, are being restored to their 19th-century operating order. Canal museums are found in Syracuse, N.Y.; Canal Fulton, Ohio; and Easton, Pa. Canal societies have been formed in Maryland, Massachusetts, New York, Ohio, and Pennsylvania.

[Carter Goodrich, ed., *Canals and American Economic Development;* Ralph D. Gray, *The National Waterway;* Alvin C. Harlow, *Old Towpaths;* Harry N. Scheiber, *Ohio Canal Era;* Ronald E. Shaw, *Erie Water West.*]

HARRY L. RINKER

CANAL ZONE. *See* **Panama Canal and Canal Zone.**

CANARY ISLANDS, a Spanish island group off the northwest coast of Africa, which served as a way station for Spain's New World voyages, besides supplying wine for Spanish America and skilled workers for West Indian sugar plantations. The New England colonies early began a profitable intercourse with the Canaries, together with Portugal's Madeiras and Azores, involving mainly the exchange of lumber and fish for wine. Although illegal according to English interpretation of the Navigation Act of 1663, trade with the Canaries continued until the early 19th century, causing much friction between New England and royal authorities.

[G. L. Beer, *The Old Colonial System, 1660–1754;* W. B. Weeden, *Economic and Social History of New England, 1620–1789.*]

CHARLES EDWARD CHAPMAN
ROBERT HALE SHIELDS

CANDLES lighted most American homes, public buildings, and streets until gas (1820's) and kerosene lamps (1850's) replaced them. Housewives made many kinds of candles—bear grease, deer suet, bayberry, beeswax (expensive, for state occasions largely), tallow dip (commonest), from well-rendered mutton fat, and spermaceti. Every autumn the housekeepers filled their leather or tin candle boxes to last through the winter. First, women prepared wicks from rough hemp, milkweed, or cotton spun in large quantity. Then followed the long hard task of dipping or molding several hundred candles by hand. The homemaker was the only manufacturer until the 1700's when an itinerant candlemaker could be hired. Later, professional chandlers prospered in the cities. Although factories were numerous after 1750, the home-dipping was continued as late as 1880. There was a large market for sperm candles in the West Indies, where in 1768 over 500,000 pounds of sperm and tallow candles were purchased from the colonies. The total production from both factories and homes reached an estimated $8 million in 1810. The New England factories, which produced the most, imported supplies of fat from Russia. There were large plants, also, in New Orleans, St. Louis, and Hudson, N.Y. South Carolina and Georgia produced quantities of seeds and capsules from tallow trees used extensively for candlemaking in the South. Allied industries grew rapidly for making metal and pottery candle holders.

[Alice Morse Earle, *Home Life in Colonial Days;* Arthur H. Hayward, *Colonial Lighting;* Marion Nicholl Rawson, *Candle Days.*]

LENA G. FITZHUGH

CANE RIDGE REVIVAL, the culmination of a great spiritual awakening in Kentucky, which began at the close of the 18th century (*see* Great Revival). This special manifestation of religious fervor occurred in August 1801, at a camp meeting near the Cane Ridge Meeting House in Bourbon County. The number attending has been estimated at 20,000. The revivalists underwent fervid physical and vocal exercises that indicated an extraordinary religious experience. The Disciples of Christ developed from the intellectual quickening of the movement.

[Alonzo Willard Fortune, *The Disciples in Kentucky;* James R. Rogers, *The Cane Ridge Meeting House.*]

JONATHAN T. DORRIS

CANNING INDUSTRY. In 1795 the French government offered a prize for a better way of preserving food than by smoking or salting and thus encouraged the beginning of canning. The prize was awarded in 1809 to Nicolas Appert, a Parisian confectioner, who had developed a workable method of preserving food in bottles. Despite numerous claims to the contrary, he is now generally considered the father of the canning process.

The history of the canning process can be considered in terms of three milestones: the practical work of Appert, who developed the process; the scientific discoveries of Louis Pasteur, who, in the latter half of the 19th century, explained the basic scientific theory of the process; and the technological developments of William Lyman Underwood and Samuel Cate Prescott, who applied science to the process.

Appert's method consisted of the following steps: (1) enclosing in bottles the food to be preserved; (2) corking the bottles carefully; (3) submerging the bottles in boiling water for varying lengths of time, depending on the food; and (4) removing the bottles and cooling them. In 1810 Appert wrote a treatise describing his process. A year later this was published in English, with a second edition appearing a year after that. An American edition was printed in 1812 from the second English edition.

Pioneers of American canning were Thomas Kensett, Sr., and his father-in-law, Ezra Daggett, working in New York beginning in 1819, and William Underwood, of Boston, who started in 1821. All three used the Appert method with bottles, although the "tin" can—its name derived from the English canister—had been introduced in the United States by Peter Durand in 1818. The tin-coated steel container did not come into widespread use until 1839. Sometime in 1895, William Lyman Underwood, grandson of the first Underwood, and Samuel Cate Prescott, a young instructor at Massachusetts Institute of Technology, began a collaboration that was to have a great effect on the development of canning. Their research confirmed that bacteria caused food spoilage, as shown earlier by other scientists, notably Louis Pasteur in the 1860's, and that heating to temperatures above the boiling point was needed for sterilization of the product. These men showed, and were the first to recognize, the importance of heat penetration in canning. They were also the first to recommend incubation tests.

Of the many process and machine developments since—including higher heat for shorter periods of time—perhaps that of the hydrostatic sterilizer stands out. In addition to providing consistent sterilization, this unit results in tremendous savings in steam and water costs and has the ability to adjust readily to different sizes of cans and bottles. In the sterilizer, cans are preheated in a water column, then sterilized in a superheated steam chamber, and finally carried through a second water leg for cooling. When the cans are discharged, they are cool enough to label. One such installation cost about $750,000, but it cut the labor force for the operation from approximately twenty-five to one. While not all such changes produce such dramatic results, the canning industry has been forced by rising labor costs to substitute machines wherever feasible. The trend toward machine harvesting is leading to the development of new and tougher varieties that do not need to be hand-picked.

A related trend is toward longer operation, which makes possible the maintenance of a different labor force than is possible on seasonal operation. A related development is that of huge aseptic tanks for storing partially processed tomatoes, so that the finish processing can be done through the year in accordance with market demands rather than only in season.

The trend toward big business is manifesting itself in the canning industry in two ways. The companies are getting larger as small ones either are bought out, combine, or go out of business. Particularly in quality control, the small canner can no longer compete. Also, more and more growers are forming bargaining associations to negotiate with the canners on crop prices. Such associations appeared first in California, but they now exist nationwide. The 1973 annual volume of products canned was over a billion cans.

[A. W. Bitting, *Appertizing, or the Art of Canning: Its History and Development;* S. A. Goldblith, *The Science and Technology of Thermal Processing.*]

RICHARD L. MCKEE

CANNONISM, a term common during Joseph G. Cannon's service as speaker of the House of Representatives (1903–11) when the great powers of that office were used in the interest of the ultraconservative elements and to defeat progressive legislation.

[D. S. Alexander, *History and Procedure of the House of Representatives.*]

W. A. ROBINSON

CANOE. American Indians constructed several kinds of canoes, including the birchbark canoe of the Eastern Woodland tribes and the dugout canoe, or pirogue, used by the Southeastern Indians and many Western Indians. The Algonkin-speaking Indians of the Northeast had learned the secret of making birchbark canoes long before the whites reached North America, and the pioneers found the canoe so useful in traveling on inland waterways that they quickly adopted it. The great advantage of birchbark canoes is their lightness, which makes it possible to portage them easily. The canoes are responsive enough to be guided through rapids with precision. If repairs are needed, the necessary materials can be found growing almost anywhere along the route. Until railroads became common, the canoe was the chief vehicle for reaching much of the northern part of the continent, and it was extremely useful to explorers and fur trappers.

The pirogue, the traditional dugout canoe of the Indians of the Southeast, was usually shaped from the trunk of a cypress tree, hollowed out by burning and scraping. In some, both ends were squared, and in others, only one. The pirogue drew only an inch or so of water, and it was well-suited to being poled through the vegetation-clogged bayous. Indians in other parts of the East also made dugouts, and around the Caribbean area the dugouts were equipped with sails.

On the northern Pacific Coast of North America, excellent dugout canoes, elaborately carved and painted, were made from the giant cedar and other light woods, some of the canoes being as much as a hundred feet long. The Eskimo kayak is a specialized variant of the canoe, with a frame of whale ribs or driftwood, over which sealskins are stretched to make a watertight covering. Another Eskimo craft, the umiak, is a less sophisticated type, since the hide covering is used only along the bottom and sides. The Chumash and Gabrielino Indians of the southern California coast and the offshore Channel (Santa Barbara) Islands made plank canoes, the planks being lashed together and caulked with asphalt.

[Harold E. Driver, *Indians of North America.*]

KENNETH M. STEWART

CANTIGNY, AMERICAN ATTACK AT. The American First Division, under command of Gen. Robert L. Bullard, on Apr. 25, 1918, joined the French First Army. It occupied the sector facing Cantigny, held by the German XVIII Army. To test the Americans' offensive ability in their first active sector, the French command ordered the new division to capture Cantigny. After careful preparations the Twenty-eighth Infantry attacked at 6:45 A.M., May 28. The assailants, assisted by French tanks, took all objectives, with 250 prisoners, in forty-five minutes. Thereafter the Americans repulsed several violent German counterattacks, losing 1,067 killed and wounded, but maintaining their position.

[J. M. Hanson, "History of the American Combat Divisions," *The Stars and Stripes;* C. R. Howland, *A Military History of the World War.*]

JOSEPH MILLS HANSON

CANTON FUR TRADE developed from the search for some staple, other than specie, which American merchants could exchange for the teas and silks of China. Furs met with a ready sale; the cargo of the first American vessel, the *Empress of China,* to Canton, Feb. 22, 1784, included furs. But only such rare furs as otter, seal, beaver, and fox were acceptable. Boston merchants decided to seek sea otter skins on the Northwest coast. The *Columbia* (Sept. 30, 1787–Aug. 9, 1790) returned from Canton with a cargo of teas exchanged for sea otter skins by the natives. Others hastened to follow. By 1796 American vessels were engaged in contraband fur trade with the Californians and by 1804 were borrowing Aleutian sea otter hunters, on shares, from the Russian governor at Novarkhangelsk. In 1783, in the southern Pacific, the mass slaughter of the fur seal had begun. When, after the War of 1812, the fur trade with Canton was renewed, the growing scarcity of the sea otter, increased competition, and a consequent decline in profits reduced the American vessels engaged from thirteen in 1821 to two in 1830. Trading in furs with Canton became merely one aspect of a more general Pacific trade and by 1837 the old Northwest fur trade no longer existed.

[F. R. Dulles, *The Old China Trade;* Samuel Eliot Morison, *Maritime History of Massachusetts, 1783–1860.*]

KENNETH WIGGINS PORTER

CANTONMENTS. *See* **Camps and Cantonments of World War I.**

CANVASS, a word used to describe two political processes. First, it means to ascertain by direct personal approach how citizens intend to vote in a coming election. In the late 19th and early 20th centuries such canvasses were often made ninety, sixty, and fifteen days before an election. The practice is somewhat less common now because of the polls made locally by newspapers and nationally by magazines of wide circulation and polls taken by the more sophisticated methods of the professional polling services.

Second, in a somewhat looser sense, to canvass means to make a campaign for the support of a given candidate, either by the candidate or his supporters, or for a party ticket.

ROBERT C. BROOKS

CAPE ANN, eastern peninsula of Massachusetts, known in 1605 to Samuel de Champlain as Le Cap aux Isles. In 1606 he entered the cape's harbor. Capt. John Smith in 1614 called it Cape Tragabigzanda, after a Turkish lady, but it was renamed Cape Ann for the wife of James I. In 1623 the Dorchester Company of merchants in England established a fishing station at the cape, to which came disaffected settlers from Plymouth and Nantucket. Among these Roger Conant was a leader. In 1624 he quieted friction over fishing rights asserted for Plymouth by Myles Standish. For ships of that time the fishing grounds were too distant and, since the soil was poor, the enterprise failed in 1626. For twenty years the settlement languished, until Rev. Richard Blynman arrived in 1642. The city of Gloucester, on Cape Ann, began to grow as a deep-sea fishing port, absorbing Portuguese and Italian crews, and has never lost its eminence.

A moorland section of the cape, called Dogtown, was abandoned after the 18th century, and its odd settlers became figures of rather sordid romance. Other sections, Annisquam and Pigeon Cove, were given over to artists. Their works, together with Rudyard Kipling's *Captains Courageous* and J. B. Connolly's *Out of Gloucester,* have kept Cape Ann in the public eye. Off the shore of west Gloucester is the reef of Norman's Woe, scene of Henry Wadsworth Longfellow's "Wreck of the Hesperus."

[Charles B. Hawes, *Gloucester by Land and Sea.*]

CHARLES KNOWLES BOLTON

CAPE BRETON EXPEDITION. *See* **Louisburg Expedition.**

CAPE COD, peninsula in southeastern Massachusetts, a landmark for early explorers, and possibly the Promontory of Vinland of the Norse voyagers (985–1025). Giovanni da Verrazano in 1524 approached it from the south, and Esteban Gomes the next year called it Cape St. James. Bartholomew Gosnold in 1602 gave it the name that survives. Samuel de Champlain charted its sand-silted harbors in 1606 and Henry Hudson landed there in 1609. Capt. John Smith noted it on his map of 1614, and at last the Pilgrims entered the "Cape Harbor" on Nov. 11, 1620. Aside from Barnstable and Sandwich (1638) and Yarmouth (1639), the cape's towns developed slowly. Provincetown was a group of huts until the 18th century. A channel from Massachusetts Bay to Buzzards Bay is shown on Cyprian Southack's map of 1717, but the Cape Cod Canal had a troubled development from 1870 to 1914. The federal government purchased it in 1928.

Whaling and cod fishing arose in the 18th century but lost out to New Bedford and Gloucester. Oysters and clams still bring wealth to Wellfleet. Salt by evaporation of sea water became an industry before 1800. Cranberry growing started about 1816 at North Dennis. At Falmouth and elsewhere shipbuilding flourished before and after the Revolution. Sandwich was famous from 1825 to 1888 for its glassworks. Whaling started migration of Portuguese from Lisbon, from the Azores, and the Cape Verde Islands. The cape has a long chronicle of shipwrecks, to which the ancient gravestones bear testimony. Ribs of the *Sparrow-Hawk* (1626) are at Pilgrim Hall. The U.S. submarine "S4" sank off Wood End, Dec. 17, 1927; its crew of forty slowly died of suffocation, while sending out messages by Morse code.

During the summer months the fishing ports are exceptionally busy and the villages and towns become heavily populated resorts. In 1961 Cape Cod was designated a national seashore.

[William Berchen and Monica Dickens, *Cape Cod;* John Hay and Peter Farb, *The Atlantic Shore;* Charlton Ogburn, Jr., *The Winter Beach.*]

CHARLES KNOWLES BOLTON

CAPE FEAR, ACTION AT. *See* **Fisher, Fort, Capture of.**

CAPE FEAR RIVER SETTLEMENTS. Discovered by Giovanni da Verrazano sailing for Francis I of France in 1524, the Cape Fear region of what is now North Carolina was the site of a short-lived Spanish colony of 500 men, women, and black slaves in 1526. Both Spanish and English explorers visited the area in succeeding years, but the first English attempt at settlement was made in 1662 by a group of New England men under the guidance of William Hilton. For unknown reasons the colony was abandoned, but Hilton returned the next year with a colony from Barbados to establish the county of Clarendon. With its own governor and assembly, Clarendon flourished until 1667, when the death of the governor, lack of support from abroad, and Indian warfare caused the settlers to abandon the colony. Little further interest was shown in the region until after the removal of the Indian and pirate menace during the second decade of the 18th century. In 1713 Landgrave Thomas Smith of Carolina received a grant for Smith Island at the mouth of the Cape Fear River, and soon afterward settlers from South Carolina and from Albemarle, N.C., began to move into the region. In 1725 the town of Brunswick was laid out on the west bank of the river, about 14 miles from the sea. Eight years later Wilmington was founded and became the colony's chief port. From 1732 until 1775 thousands of Scottish Highlanders, including Flora MacDonald, settled on the upper Cape Fear River. Naval stores, lumber, and rice became the most important products of the region.

[Lawrence Lee, *The Lower Cape Fear in Colonial Days;* Duane Meyer, *The Highland Scots of North Carolina.*]

WILLIAM S. POWELL

CAPE GIRARDEAU. As early as 1765, a bend in the Mississippi River about sixty miles south of the French village of Sainte Geneviève in Missouri had been referred to as Cape Girardot or Girardeau. The settlement there dates from 1793 when the Spanish government, which had secured Louisiana in 1762, granted Louis Lorimier, a French-Canadian, the right of establishing a trading post. His grant gave him extensive trading privileges and a large tract of land surrounding his post. Lorimier was made commandant of the district and prospered from the returns on his land sales and trade with the Indians.

[Louis Houck, *History of Missouri.*]

W. J. HAMILTON

CAPE HORN, southernmost point of the Americas, lies practically due south of Eastport, Maine, easternmost city of the United States. Traditionally the most dreaded of ocean headlands both because of the almost ceaseless storms for which it is noted and the fact that it lies within the southern ice line, Cape Horn was first sighted by the Dutch navigators Jakob Le Maire and William Schouten when on a voyage toward the East Indies in 1616. They were the first to enter the Pacific Ocean by way of Cape Horn, previous navigators having used the Straits of Magellan. Schouten named the point Cape Hoorn after the town of Hoorn in Holland where he was born. The difficulty of making the westbound passage of Cape Horn in sailing ships played a part in retarding the growth of California, but the discovery of gold on Sutter's ranch near Sacramento in the latter part of 1848 stimulated both the passage of the cape and the growth of the American merchant marine. Because of the necessity always to contend with the rigors of Cape Horn when making a coast-to-coast voyage, American shipbuilders were compelled to produce fast, weatherly, and immensely strong vessels. The stimulus given by the rapid growth of the trade to California went far to put American square-rigged ships in the forefront of the world. Famous Cape Horn ships of this period include the *Flying Cloud, Andrew Jackson* (which shared the record of eighty-nine days, New York to San Francisco), *Sea Witch, Great Republic, John Gilpin, Flying Fish,* and *James Baines* (which logged the fastest speed ever recorded under sail, twenty-one knots). The rigors of the Horn passage, the growth of intercontinental trade, the greater development of the U.S. Navy, and the difficulty of adequately protecting the Pacific and the Atlantic coasts turned the attention of the United States to the building of the Panama Canal. From that time the importance of the route around Cape Horn, used long previously only by freight ships, most of them steamers, rapidly declined. The last American sailing ship to beat round Cape Horn was probably the schooner *Wanderbird,* in 1936.

[Alan Villiers, *The War With Cape Horn.*]

ALAN VILLIERS

CAPITAL, NATIONAL, LOCATION OF. It has been put forth that the selection of a site for the national capital during the early days of the Republic played an important part in Secretary of the Treasury Alexander Hamilton's successful establishment of the national credit. Immediately after the Continental Congress hastily adjourned (1783) from Philadelphia to New York, because of Pennsylvania's failure to protect it from the insults of mutinous soldiery (*see* Pennsylvania Troops, Mutinies of), agitation was begun in Congress for establishing a permanent seat of government. Nearly every one of the eastern and Middle Atlantic states offered a location or urged a claim. The struggle continued for five years and carried over into the Congress under the Constitution. Supposedly, in 1790 Hamilton, cleverly using the desire of the southern states to obtain the capital, traded, through Secretary of State Thomas Jefferson, Pennsylvania support for the Potomac River location, in return for Virginia support for his plan of the assumption of the states' revolutionary war debts. The location act was approved July 16, 1790, and Virginia fulfilled its bargain by voting for the act (approved Aug. 4) making provision for the public debt. Twentieth-century research has cast a number of doubts as to whether this bargain ever took place.

[Claude G. Bowers, *Jefferson and Hamilton.*]

JOHN C. FITZPATRICK

CAPITALISM, an economic system in which the ownership and control of land, natural resources, and capital; the production and marketing of goods; the employment of labor; and the organization and operation of the system as a whole are entrusted to private enterprise working under competitive conditions. The right to own property, the freedom to make contracts, and the freedom of entrepreneurs to make their own decisions, set prices, and make a profit are basic assumptions of the system, with acquisition of such consumers' goods as food and clothing as the goal. The accumulation, control, and use of capital (primarily by private enterprise) is the way that goal is most quickly reached.

Capital, which economists define as "produced goods intended for further production," includes such items as tools, machines, coal, oil, industrial supplies, and unfinished or unsold goods. Although cash and bank deposits are sometimes called "liquid capital" because they may be directed to any use the possessor wishes, they really are only titles to capital. Capital is man-made and can be created only through someone's saving. Interest is the rental price for its use. Generous use of capital, moreover, is the basis of mass production. The nations with the most capital per person have the highest standard of living.

Capital is produced in all types of economies—whether they be truly communistic; state socialistic, as the Soviet Union is; welfare; or fascistic—but methods of producing capital differ. In a capitalistic economy, capital creation is largely voluntary on the part of citizens and private firms because they are free to set prices and make a profit, subject always to the limitations of competition. In state socialism most capital is created by government decisions imposing forced savings (fewer consumer goods) on the people.

The percentage of the average individual's income drained off by government taxes and then presumably returned to him in the form of goods and services provided by the government can be a measure of the country's economic system. If taxes equal 1 or 2 percent, the system is anarchistic; 3 to 33 percent, capitalistic; 34 to 67 percent, socialistic; and over 67 percent, communistic. Some authorities use other percentages.

The first two English colonies in America were handicapped at the outset by lack of capital and lack of the profit motive. The Pilgrims did not bring a horse, cow, or plow. Their meager supplies soon gave out, and there was a period of starvation. Little incentive existed in either Virginia or Plymouth for the individual to work hard to build up a surplus, since the settlers were expected to put all their produce into a common fund from which all would be supported and out of which the companies financing the expeditions would receive repayment and profit—essentially a communistic system so far as the settlers were concerned. John Smith later remarked, "When our people were fed out of the common store and laboured jointly together . . . the most honest among them would hardly take so much true paines in a weeke as now for themselves they will doe in a day. . . ." When the settlers were permitted greater freedom of enterprise and allowed to accumulate private property, the colonies prospered and grew. Over a century and a half later, the Constitution in many ways reemphasized this way of life.

The Industrial Revolution in the capitalistic United States, just as in England earlier, was a spontaneous development, arriving when technology was sufficiently advanced and the rate of saving was about double the rate of capital depreciation. In a socialistic state, in contrast, development is not spontaneous, and the government decides when it will build a factory or a railroad.

In a truly capitalistic economy neither giant private monopolies nor government regulatory bodies should interfere with the operation of the free market system. Even under laissez-faire no such free market system has ever actually existed. But abuses by trusts in the late 19th century and after provided good reason for increasing government regulation of big business. Later on wars and major depressions provided others. After the mid-1960's, chronic inflation supplied excuses for still more regulation, including a growing amount of price fixing by government. Thus, by the early 1970's the federal government was regulating virtually every business in some way. Many big ones (steel, auto, oil, public transportation) either had to get government permission to raise prices or were very limited in how much they could freely raise them. And whereas tax collectors of federal, state, and local governments in 1902 took only 10 percent of the national income, by 1969 they drew off 42 percent. If the United States could any longer be said to have a capitalistic economy, it is only in comparison with the state socialistic economies of Eastern European nations or with the somewhat less socialistic economies of Sweden, Britain, and a few others. The kind of capitalism under which the United States had made its material advances in the 19th century no longer exists.

[R. Blodgett, *Comparative Economic Systems;* R. Blodgett and D. L. Kemmerer, *Comparative Economic Development;* T. C. Cochran and T. B. Brewer, *Views of American Economic Growth;* M. I. Goldman, *Comparative Economic Systems;* D. L. Kemmerer and C. C. Jones, *American Economic History;* C. Nettels, *The Roots of American Civilization;* W. W. Rostow, *The Stages of Economic Growth;* C. Snyder, *Capitalism the Creator*.]

DONALD L. KEMMERER

CAPITAL PUNISHMENT refers to the imposition of the death penalty as an optional or mandatory punishment for the commission of certain types of crimes, thereby known as capital crimes. No definitive agreement has existed among the capital punishment jurisdictions of the United States as to what constitutes a capital offense. Furthermore, most jurisdictions adopted an optional procedure that granted judges or juries the authority to decide whether the death penalty or some other form of punishment would be imposed. Therefore, the death penalty has not been applied in a strictly uniform manner. There is sufficient similarity of application, however, to separate the types of capital crime into four categories. These are (1) crimes against the government, such as treason, espionage, and capital perjury; (2) crimes against property when life is threatened, such as arson, burglary, and train wrecking; (3) crimes against the person, which include murder, rape, and felony murders associated with kidnapping, assault, and robbery; and (4) miscellaneous crimes, a collection of assorted offenses created by panic legislation.

The principal arguments for capital punishment center upon a fundamental belief in retribution, retaliation, and deterrence. Proponents of the death penalty firmly believe it to be a just punishment that corresponds to the type of injury inflicted; a process to rid society of deviants; and, primarily, a device to inhibit people from committing capital crimes.

The advocates of abolition of the death penalty promote rehabilitation over death. They consider capital punishment both uncivilized and ineffective as a deterrent. Their position is supported by studies showing that, over time, the homicide rates in states with the death penalty and states without it are approximately the same; that changes in homicide rates are a result of societal and cultural differences; that emotional and prejudicial considerations on the part of judges and juries generally determine when the death penalty is used, turning it into a weapon of discrimination, primarily against the poor and against Afro-Americans; and, finally, that capital offenders rarely consider execution when they commit their crimes.

Capital punishment was adopted from the English system. The colonies, however, resisted the harsher characteristics of the English penal code and retreated from it during and after the American Revolution. Prompted by the growth of societies that advocated abolition of capital punishment, a major shift away from such punishment developed in the middle of the 19th century: Pennsylvania abolished public executions in 1834, and Michigan officially abolished the death penalty in 1847. These accomplishments were muted by the Civil War, when some states that had followed Michigan's example reinstated the death penalty. The opponents of capital punishment renewed their attack at the turn of the century. Their efforts, again impeded by war—the two world wars—were persistent; and a clear trend away from capital punishment became evident by the late 1960's.

In the 1960's and 1970's, opponents of the death penalty increasingly challenged the major principles of capital punishment in the courts. Their litigation resulted in a growing reluctance on the part of the states to execute capital offenders. Executions dropped from a high of 152 in 1947 to 7 in 1965, and none after 1967. In 1971, thirty-nine of the fifty-four U.S. jurisdictions (the fifty states, the District of Columbia, Puerto Rico, the Virgin Islands, and the federal criminal jurisdiction) provided for the death penalty as part of their system of criminal justice; fifteen jurisdictions had either abolished or restricted its use. In 1972, the Supreme Court ruled in *Furman* v. *Georgia* (408 U.S. 238) that the optional death penalty, as it applied in this and companion cases, was unconstitutional because it violated the Eighth (cruel and unusual punishment) and Fourteenth amendments of the Constitution.

The Court refrained from deciding whether the death penalty itself was cruel and unusual punishment; rather, it concentrated on the way in which judges and juries arbitrarily and infrequently imposed the death sentence. In essence, capital punishment as an optional sentence, which it was in the vast majority of cases, was abolished in the United States.

The *Furman* ruling may be viewed as a major achievement in the long struggle of the opponents of the death penalty. One immediate effect of the ruling was the commutation of the death sentence to life imprisonment for all 600 prisoners awaiting execution. This was followed by a series of appellate court rulings that state laws imposing the optional death penalty for certain kinds of capital offenses were unconstitutional.

The decision stimulated an intense national discussion on the merits of capital punishment. National surveys indicated that public opinion favored the use of the death penalty in certain types of cases. Legislation reinstating the death sentence for specific crimes was introduced in Congress and some state legislatures. The states acted quickly and began to pass new capital punishment laws featuring optional and mandatory death penalties for specific crimes. New York's optional death sentence was one of the first to be tested in the courts. The Supreme Court, in refusing to review the appellate court ruling that declared that new law unconstitutional, reaffirmed its decision in *Furman*.

[Hugo A. Bedau, ed., *The Death Penalty in America;* Gerald Gunther, "The Supreme Court 1971 Term," *Harvard Law Review*, vol. 86 (1972); Thorsten Sellen, ed., *Capital Punishment*.]

DONALD M. BOROCK

CAPITATION TAXES. The federal government is forbidden by Article I, Section 9, of the Constitution from levying a capitation or other direct tax, "unless in Proportion to the Census of Enumeration" laid down in Section 2. Section 9, however, in accord with colonial practices of placing taxes on the importation of convicts and slaves, permits a tax or duty to be imposed on persons entering the United States, "not exceeding ten dollars for each person." The poll-tax restriction did not apply to the states. Following colonial precedents, the state employed this tax, generally placed on all males above twenty-one, sometimes above sixteen, regardless of income or property. In southern states the poll tax was often made a prerequisite to the exercise of the suffrage, thus disqualifying the Afro-American or controlling his vote. The ratification of the Twenty-fourth Amendment in 1964 outlawed the use of the poll tax in federal elections. In 1966 the Supreme Court ruled that the poll tax as a prerequisite for voting in a state election was unconstitutional under the Fourteenth Amendment.

RICHARD B. MORRIS

CAPITOL AT WASHINGTON. In a disappointing public competition in 1791 of amateur and professional architectural plans for the capitol building, Stephen Hallet's, though not satisfactory, was judged the best. William Thornton, by permission, submitted a more artistic design, and Hallet was employed to make working drawings of it and to superintend the construction. Accused of substituting his own plan for Thornton's, Hallet was dismissed in 1794 and James Hoban, an Irish architect, succeeded him. The cornerstone was laid with Masonic ceremonies by President George Washington, Sept. 18, 1793; but the center portion had not been erected when the British burned the public buildings in 1814. Rebuilding commenced in 1815, under Benjamin H. Latrobe, and the center portion of Acquia freestone with a low dome, designed by Charles Bulfinch, was finished in 1827. The present north and south wings of Massachusetts marble (the fluted pillars are from Maryland) were begun in 1851, from designs of Thomas Ustick Walter, and finished in 1857–59. The present dome of cast iron, an adaptation of Michelangelo's St. Peter's basilica (Rome) and Sir Christopher Wren's St. Paul's (London), was begun in 1856 and finished in 1865. It is surmounted by Crawford's heroic bronze of Freedom, 19½ feet high. The dome is, roughly, 300 feet in height. In 1959–60 the east front was extended over 30 feet, despite protests by preservation and architectural groups.

[W. B. Bryan, *History of the National Capitol.*]

JOHN C. FITZPATRICK

CAPPER-VOLSTEAD ACT (Feb. 18, 1922), also known as the Cooperative Marketing Act. As a consequence of the depression of agricultural prices subsequent to World War I, farm organizations intensified their drive for government aid and managed to get a farm bloc established in Congress. Sen. Arthur Capper was a member of this bloc, and the Capper-Volstead Act was a part of the farm legislative program. The act authorized various kinds of agricultural producers to form voluntary cooperative associations for purposes of producing, handling, and marketing farm products—that is, it exempted such associations from the application of the antitrust laws. The secretary of agriculture was given power, on his own motion, to prevent such associations from achieving and maintaining monopolies. He could hold hearings, determine facts, and issue orders ultimately subject to review by federal district courts. The act is an example of legislative aid to agricultural cooperatives and of the delegation of adjudicative power to an administrative agency.

HARVEY PINNEY

CAPRON TRAIL, one of the important east-west trails of Florida, probably first run about 1850, the date of the establishment of Fort Capron (Saint Lucie County). It passed from Fort Capron through Fort Vinton, Fort Drum, Fort Kissimmee, Fort Clinch, Fort Meade, to Fort Brooke (Tampa). Fort Capron and the Capron Trail commemorated the valor of Capt. Erastus A. Capron, who was killed Aug. 20, 1847, at the Battle of Churubusco in Mexico.

[Frederick W. Dau, *Florida Old and New.*]

KATHRYN T. ABBEY

CAPUCHINS, members of a branch of the Franciscan Friars Minor, founded by Matteo da Bascio of Urbino, Italy, in 1525. A major arm of the 16th-century Counter-Reformation, the Capuchins dedicated themselves to missionary work in the 17th century, putting themselves under the Congregation for the Propagation of the Faith (1622). They were the first missionaries in Maine (1630) and established a central mission at Port Royal, Nova Scotia (1633), from which they served the eastern part of Canada and the northern United States. They were placed in charge of missionary work in Louisiana in 1722 and had the area of their mission expanded to include the east bank of the Mississippi River four years later. This latter area was ceded to the Jesuits in 1750. The French monks were replaced in 1766 by Spanish Capuchins, who served the region until 1807. The modern history of the order begins in 1857 when two brothers, Gregory Haas and John Fry, established a friary at Mount Calvary, Wis. In the mid-1970's there were over 1,200 members of the order in the United States.

[Otto Jeron, "The Capuchins in America," *Historical Records and Studies,* vol. 5; T. MacVicar, "Franciscans, Capuchins," *New Catholic Encyclopedia,* vol. V; C. E. O'Neill, *Church and State in French Colonial Louisiana.*]

GLENN T. MILLER

CARACAS MIXED COMMISSIONS were established subsequent to the 1902 crisis in the Venezuelan debt controversy. After negotiations at Washington, D.C., in which the United States played a decisive part, protocols were signed in February and March 1903, between Venezuela and ten creditor powers (Great Britain, Germany, Italy, France, Belgium, the Netherlands, Norway-Sweden, Mexico, Spain, and the United States), providing for settlement of claims by commissions consisting of one member appointed by each party and a neutral umpire. Venezuela allotted 30 percent of customs revenues at La Guayra and Puerto Cabello for payments awarded. The commissions sat at Caracas (June–December 1903) and awarded sums ranging from over 10,000,000 bolivars (francs) to Belgium to 174,000 bolivars to Norway-Sweden. The United States received about 2,250,000 bolivars. All claims were drastically cut down except for those of Belgium and Mexico. Great Britain, Germany, and Italy (the blockading powers) were given priority in payment by an arbitration tribunal at The Hague.

CHARLES C. GRIFFIN

CARAVANS, OUTFITTING OF. A visitor to the West in 1860 estimated that 20,000 wagons were in use transporting settlers and supplies, requiring around 100,000 oxen and 40,000 mules to pull them. Western towns such as St. Louis, Fort Smith, Little Rock, San Antonio, Denver, and Salt Lake City did a thriving business in consequence. At one of these (or others equally active), people bound for the Far West had a last opportunity to purchase necessities. Food (such as meal, flour, sugar, coffee, and bacon), clothing, blankets, guns and ammunition, and farm implements (such as an ax, hoe, shovel, and an occasional plow) were a few of the purchases. In addition, wagons were generally burdened with household goods (a bedstead, a framed picture of grandfather or grandmother, a favorite chair, and perhaps one or more heirlooms) and other sundry things considered as necessities. Many of those traveling the Oregon Trail to the Columbia or the Platte route to California discarded much of this impedimenta before they arrived at their destination. In consequence many intermediate towns and communities profited. Settlers at Salt Lake City and in the Great Basin did a thriving exchange trade with the forty-niners, buying worn-out horses and cattle or exchanging potatoes and flour for the excess burdens of the travelers. Likewise Denver was to profit as a supply center during Colorado's gold-rush days, 1858–65.

The great rush for western lands following the enactment of the federal homestead law of 1862 greatly increased caravan traffic, and in every town of considerable size along the frontier there was one or more well-known supply firms. One general supply store at Fort Griffin, Texas, during a one-day period (1877), sold goods to the value of better than $4,000, of which $2,500 represented guns and ammunition. Other supplies were plows, farm tools, staple groceries, wagons, kerosene, dry goods, seed, and feed for livestock. Such large quantities of supplies were required that numerous freighting firms were organized and long trains of wagons were on every well-traveled road.

[Alexander Majors, *Seventy Years on the Frontier;* F. L. Paxson, *History of the American Frontier.*]

C. C. RISTER

CARAVAN TRAFFIC ON THE GREAT PLAINS existed from approximately 1825 to 1875 and reached its maximum development during the first few years after the Civil War. During this period both immigrant and trade caravans were employed, particularly after the beginning of the Oregon movement (1842), the Mormon migration (1847), and the discovery of gold in California (1848).

The first important caravan traffic across the Great Plains was via the Santa Fe Trail. William Becknell drove the first wagon from western Missouri to Santa Fe in 1822. This was eight years before Jedediah Smith, David E. Jackson, and William Sublette took a party of eighty-one men and ten large wagons (drawn by five mules each) from Saint Louis to the trappers' rendezvous on the Wind River in Wyoming;

and it was ten years before Capt. B. L. E. de Bonneville conducted still another wagon train across South Pass. Caravans of twenty-five wagons or more were used largely to transport trade goods over the Santa Fe Trail valued at $35,000 in 1824, $90,000 in 1826, and $150,000 in 1828. The distance traveled from Franklin, Mo., to Santa Fe was 870 miles. After the first few years, Lexington, some 60 miles farther west, was the point of departure; and still later, Independence, 100 miles farther west, was the starting point.

Caravan movements over the Oregon Trail were equally significant, although perhaps not so important commercially. Elm Grove, located 12 miles southwest of Independence, was a favorite starting point, and later West Port. At Elm Grove, beginning in 1842, settlers came in covered wagons each spring, elected their captains, guides, and other officers, and began the long trek westward via the Oregon Trail. The caravan of 1842, organized by Dr. Elijah White, traveled as far as Fort Hall, Idaho, before the wagons were abandoned. From here the people traveled on foot, horseback, or by raft down the Snake and Columbia rivers. The following year upward of 1,000 immigrants moved over the same route in many wagons, some of which reached the banks of the Columbia River.

During the 1850's, caravans, large and small, were thronging all roads across the Great Plains. Randolph B. Marcy conducted a caravan of 100 wagons from Fort Smith to New Mexico via the Canadian River in 1849, on the first leg of its journey to California; and Indian agent William Bent estimated 60,000 immigrants to have crossed the plains along the Arkansas route in 1859. Heavy freight caravans plied the routes between San Antonio and Chihuahua, between Santa Fe and Chihuahua, and from points in Nebraska, Kansas, and Colorado to the Far West by 1860. A well-known road from Council Bluffs to the Great Salt Lake via Fort Bridger was traveled by thousands of Mormon pilgrims from 1847 to 1860.

The Army Appropriation Bill of 1853 made available $150,000 to be spent by the secretary of war, Jefferson Davis, to survey routes for western railways, and soon after, four surveys were made. This promised a new era that was formally initiated by the first Union Pacific Act of 1862. Seven years later the first transcontinental line was completed. But caravan trade and travel remained for a decade, until railroads could offer adequate facilities.

[W. J. Ghent, *The Early Far West, A Narrative Outline, 1540–1850;* Josiah Gregg, *Commerce of the Prairies;* Col. Henry Inman and Col. William F. Cody, *The Great Salt Lake Trail;* Alexander Majors, *Seventy Years on the Frontier;* F. L. Paxson, *History of the American Frontier.*]

C. C. RISTER

CARDIFF GIANT. In 1868 George Hall had a human figure weighing 2,966 pounds carved from Iowa gypsum in Chicago. He transported the "giant" to Cardiff, N.Y., and secretly buried it on the Newell farm. In 1869 it was discovered by men digging a well. It was exhibited as a petrified prehistoric giant, creating much excitement and deceiving many people until the hoax was exposed by Othniel C. Marsh of Yale University.

DEXTER S. KIMBALL

CAREY DESERT LAND ACT. Because the Desert Land Act of 1877 had failed in its objective of encouraging the irrigation of desert lands of the western states—although it had enabled speculators and cattlemen to acquire ownership of 8 million acres of public lands—Congress tried a second experiment to make the dry lands productive. Doubting federal power to reclaim dry lands, Congress in the Carey Desert Land Act of 1894 sought to encourage the states to take the leadership in reclamation by granting them up to a million acres, which in turn were to be available to cooperating developers. Unfortunately, the units of land individuals could acquire from the states were too small to attract capital for the building of diversionary dams and ditches. Another problem was that larger possible projects, being interstate in character, were beyond individual state promotion. Congress next turned to the Department of the Interior, under the Newlands Reclamation Act of 1902, to use most of the proceeds from public-land sales and mineral leases for the building of irrigation projects.

[Paul W. Gates, *History of Public Land Law Development;* E. Louise Peffer, *The Closing of the Public Domain: Disposal and Reservation Policies.*]

PAUL W. GATES

CARIBBEAN POLICY. The interest of the United States in the Caribbean dates from the earliest days of the Republic. Initially and through the 1830's, American attention was focused mainly on Cuba, all efforts being directed at assuring that it would remain in Spain's weak hands and not fall to England or France. During the 1840's, U.S. policy toward Cuba became more assertive, propelled by the South's desire to add another slave state to the Union. It was then that a series of attempts to purchase the island began and that prominent southerners assisted the efforts by some Cubans to annex their country to the United States. Also during this period Central America became an object of American interest as the location for a projected interoceanic canal; treaties were signed with Colombia, Nicaragua, and Honduras to assure U.S rights to build the canal. This move ran counter to British designs in the area, but a clash was averted with the signing in 1850 of the Clayton-Bulwer Treaty, whereby the two countries agreed to share jurisdiction over any canal that might be built in Central America. Restrained in both Cuba and Central America, the United States next turned its attention to the Dominican Republic. In 1854 and 1866 negotiations were begun to permit use of that country's largest bay as a U.S. naval station, and in 1869 the negotiations were broadened to include annexation of the entire country. The move, however, was unsuccessful. Failure also followed an effort to purchase the Danish West Indies in 1866, and for the next two decades U.S. concern with the Caribbean was sharply reduced.

By the 1890's the question of an isthmian canal again became primary. With Britain beset by challenges to its European position, the United States was able to pursue a more aggressive Caribbean policy aimed at securing control of the approaches to the projected canal. The new U.S. policy involved the use of American military forces as well as diplomatic maneuvering and culminated in 1898 in the Spanish-American War. The war left the Caribbean under U.S. hegemony, with Puerto Rico as an American colony and Cuba under temporary occupation (the latter would assume quasi-protectorate status in 1902 under the Platt Amendment). The question of jurisdiction over the canal was settled by the Hay-Pauncefote Treaty in 1900, wherein Britain renounced its claims. Construction was still delayed by Colombia's reluctance to grant the necessary strip of land across the Isthmus of Panama, but in 1903 a U.S.-instigated rebellion severed Panama from Colombia. The land was then turned over to the United States, and construction began.

With U.S. supremacy attained and the canal under way, the next step was to remove any pretext for European intervention. For this purpose the United States assumed the role of gendarme in the area, a policy expressed officially in 1905 in the Roosevelt Corollary to the Monroe Doctrine. Customs receiverships under U.S. supervision were instituted to deal with countries defaulting in their international debts, and military intervention was used to deal with revolutionary disorders. The interventions were particularly frequent under President Woodrow Wilson; they included thorough and long-lasting takeovers of the governments in Haiti and the Dominican Republic.

After World War I, the Caribbean policy of the United States gradually became less overbearing. In Central America there was a shift toward intraregional arbitration and joint action, evident in the Washington treaties of 1923. In Cuba the Crowder Commission, a special board managing Cuba's public finances, completed its functions in 1924; and in the same year the intervention in the Dominican Republic was brought to a close. The trend continued during the administration of Herbert Hoover with the abrogation of the Roosevelt Corollary, and culminated in President Franklin D. Roosevelt's Good Neighbor Policy, whereby the United States officially abandoned military intervention in Latin America. Consequently the Platt Amendment was abrogated in 1933, as was a treaty with Panama also authorizing U.S. intervention. The following year the last troops were withdrawn from Haiti.

For the next two decades noninterventionism was the trend in U.S. Caribbean policy. By the early 1950's, however, the policy once again assumed a more aggressive character, influenced by the cold war and the fear of Communist infiltration. Such considerations led to the overthrow of President Jacobo Arbenz Guzmán's leftist regime in Guatemala, with U.S. support, in 1954. The aggressiveness became more pronounced in the 1960's after Cuba's gravitation toward the Soviet bloc. Accordingly, aid was given in 1961 to the abortive Bay of Pigs invasion of Cuba by anti-Castro exiles; in January 1962, on U.S. initiative, Cuba was excluded from the Organization of American States; and later in the year the island was blockaded during the missile crisis. The next assertion of U.S. power occurred in 1965 in the Dominican Republic, where 42,000 U.S. Marines were landed during a period of intense revolutionary unrest. It seemed that these political disturbances offered a good chance for a repeat of Cuba's recent history and that therefore the United States would, as in the past, resort to military action to prevent them. However, an inter-American force soon replaced the marines, and that force withdrew after elections were held the next year. In the next decade the United States made no major moves in the Caribbean, although the lack of any serious political upheavals in the area does not warrant the assumption of a major change in policy.

[Samuel Flagg Bemis, *The Latin American Policy of the United States;* Edwin Lieuwen, *U.S. Policy in Latin America.*]

FRANCISCO S. PÉREZ-ABREU

CARILLION, FORT. *See* **Ticonderoga, Fort.**

CARLISLE, a borough of southern Pennsylvania, founded 1751, which became the center of the Scotch-Irish settlement in the Cumberland Valley. At the crossroads of important Indian trails and the site of Fort Louther, it was a refuge and trading center for pioneers and the site of a treaty signing between the Ohio Indians and Benjamin Franklin (1753). Carlisle also served as a station on the Underground Railroad.

[C. P. Wing, *History of Cumberland County, Pa.*]

MULFORD STOUGH

CARLISLE COMMISSION. *See* **Peace Commission of 1778.**

CARLISLE INDIAN INDUSTRIAL SCHOOL, the first off-reservation school for American Indians in the United States, was established in 1879 in Pennsylvania by Capt. R. H. Pratt, under whose twenty-five year direction it grew from 136 to 1,000 students. Instruction included practical training in farming, horticulture, dressmaking, cooking, laundering, housekeeping, and twenty trades. A distinctive feature was the outing system. Pupils were urged to spend a year working on farms or in homes or industries of the neighborhood. The school's football team, including the great athlete Jim Thorpe, became famous by defeating strong, established college teams during the 1907, 1911, and 1912 seasons. The school was closed in 1918.

[Elaine Goodale Eastman, *Pratt, the Red Man's Moses.*]

MULFORD STOUGH

CARLOTTA, CONFEDERATE COLONY OF. In 1865 many ex-Confederates left their native land for Mexico. Emperor Maximilian encouraged this exodus by appointing Commodore M. F. Maury imperial commissioner of immigration. Military and civil colonies were to be established along the railway between Veracruz and Mexico City. The best-known colony was Carlotta, 500,000 acres in the Cordova Valley, named in honor of the empress. Among reasons for the colony's failure were a hostile American press, lack of funds, improper colonization methods, forcible land seizure and occupation, disturbed political conditions in Mexico, local hostility, and the opposition of the U.S. government.

[George D. Harmon, "Confederate Migration to Mexico," *Hispanic American Historical Review* (1937).]

C. C. RISTER

CARLSBAD CAVERNS, the largest underground chambers ever discovered, located in southeastern New Mexico, were found by Jim White, a Texas cowboy, in 1901. The caverns became a national monument in 1923 and a national park (46,753 acres) in 1930. Largest of the explored part of the caverns is the Big Room, more than three-quarters of a mile long, 625 feet wide, and 350 feet high.

S. S. MCKAY

CARMELITES, one of the oldest of Catholic orders, believed to have been founded by Saint Berthold about 1195 in Palestine. Traditionally, their rule has stressed extreme asceticism, absolute poverty, abstinence from meat, and solitude. In the late Middle Ages, the order was reorganized along the lines of the mendicant orders, and in 1452 the Order of Carmelite Sisters was formed. In the 16th century it was divided by the reforms of Saint John of the Cross and Saint Theresa of Ávila. Those that accepted the reforms are called "discalced" (unshod or barefoot); those that rejected them, "calced." The friars, influenced by the missionary revival of the 17th century, were temporarily assigned the care of the eastern part of Louisiana in 1622. Only one brother is definitely known to have gone to the area, which was transferred to the Capuchins in 1726. The first discalced sisters entered the United States in 1790 and established a nunnery in Port Tobacco, Md. The sisters, who have been more influential in the United States than the friars, have been noted for their mission of contemplation and prayer.

[A. Fortier, *History of Louisiana;* C. E. O'Neill, *Church and State in French Colonial Louisiana;* J. Smet, "Carmelites," *New Catholic Encyclopedia,* vol. V.]

GLENN T. MILLER

CARMELO RIVER enters the Pacific Ocean from the southeast about five miles southwest of Monterey,

Calif. It was discovered in 1602 by Sebastián Vizcaíno, who exaggerated it to the proportions of a mighty river. It was long sought by subsequent explorers.

OSGOOD HARDY

CARNEGIE CORPORATION OF NEW YORK, a private grant-making foundation, was created by Andrew Carnegie in 1911 to promote the advancement and diffusion of knowledge and understanding between the people of the United States and the British dominions and colonies. Of its $135 million endowment, $10 million was to be used in the British dominions and colonies. Capital assets in 1974, at market value, were about $270 million.

Carnegie himself was the president of the governing board of trustees until his death in 1919, and the corporation, his largest single charity, was chiefly under his personal direction. After his death the trustees elected a full-time president as the corporation's chief executive officer. One of Carnegie's lifelong interests was the establishment of free public libraries to make available to everyone a means of self-education. He, personally, and the corporation in its early years provided more than $56 million in funds for 2,509 library buildings throughout the English-speaking world. The library building program ended in 1917.

Although its purposes are broadly stated, the corporation customarily selects a few areas in which to concentrate its grants over a period of years. In the early 1970's grants were made primarily to institutions and organizations for the improvement of education at the preschool, elementary, secondary, and higher-education levels. The corporation is also interested in certain aspects of governmental affairs. Cutting across these program areas is a continuing interest in increasing education opportunities for minorities. The Commonwealth Program devotes 7 percent of the corporation's income to education projects of universities in developing countries. A full listing of the corporation's activities is in its annual report, and a few projects are described in more detail in a quarterly publication.

AVERY RUSSELL

CARNEGIE FOUNDATION FOR THE ADVANCEMENT OF TEACHING, a private operating foundation, was established in 1905 by Andrew Carnegie with an initial $10 million endowment (increased in 1908 to $15 million). It was incorporated in 1906 by an act of Congress "to provide retiring pensions, without regard to race, sex, creed, or color, for the teachers of universities, colleges and technical schools in the United States, the Dominion of Canada, and Newfoundland [and] to do and perform all things necessary to encourage, uphold, and dignify the profession of the teacher and the cause of higher education." As of June 30, 1973, pension payments of $82,877,862 had been given to 6,214 individuals. Once the foundation's primary purpose, in 1974 the pension program was being phased out.

Over the years several notable studies have been undertaken by the foundation in medical, legal, engineering, and dental education; college athletics; and teacher-training. The Pennsylvania Study (1926–38) revealed the course-credit system's weakness as a measure of academic progress. A program of tests for entrance to graduate and professional schools (1937–48) was merged with other testing organizations to create the Educational Testing Service. The Carnegie Commission on Higher Education, a six-year project begun in 1967, studied and made recommendations about higher education for the 1970's and beyond. The Council on Policy Studies in Higher Education, slated to be the foundation's principal organ, was formed in 1974 to report on various educational problems.

Many foundation programs have received financial support from the Carnegie Corporation of New York, and the two foundations share offices and some senior officers. The foundation has a board of trustees (twenty-five members) and an endowment in 1975 with a market value of $23 million. It publishes an annual report and periodic bulletins on its studies.

RICHARD H. SULLIVAN

CARNEGIE HERO FUND COMMISSION, created in 1904 for the purpose of making annual awards from a trust income of $5 million, given by Andrew Carnegie, to recognize acts of heroism in the United States and Canada. The commission awards medals and often financial rewards out of this trust fund. The financial rewards may be in the form of a single cash award, pensions for dependents of those killed while performing a heroic act, pensions for those disabled while performing a heroic act, or, in the case of young heroes, funds for higher education.

FRED A. EMERY

CARNEGIE INSTITUTION OF WASHINGTON. In 1901 Andrew Carnegie offered the federal government $10 million in bonds of the U.S. Steel Corporation as an endowment to finance the advancement of knowledge. His gift was declined, and he gave the money in 1902 to establish the private Carnegie Institution, which was renamed the Carnegie Institution of Washington when, in 1904, it received a congressional charter of incorporation. The wealthiest organization of its kind in the country, the institution was intended to encourage original research by providing opportunities to exceptional men. The trustees decided to accomplish this purpose by spending a small part of the income on grants to individuals and the bulk of it on large, well-organized projects. Carnegie, pleased by this conception, added $2 million to the endowment in 1907 and another $10 million in 1911. Under presidents Daniel Coit Gilman (1902–04) and Robert S. Woodward (1904–20), the institution created ten major departments in various fields of the physical and biological sciences as well as in history, economics, and sociology. Under presidents John C. Merriam (1920–38), Vannevar Bush (1939–56), Caryl P. Haskins (1956–71), and Philip Abelson (1972–), the emphasis on large projects remained the standard policy of the institution. Bush eliminated the last vestige of the program of grants to individuals. Over the years the ten departments evolved into six in different parts of the country, each distinguished in its field: the Mount Wilson Observatory; the Geophysical Laboratory; the Department of Terrestrial Magnetism; the Division of Plant Biology; the Department of Embryology; and the Department of Genetics. The facilities of the institution were mobilized for defense research in both world wars. After World War II, the institution's administration chose to avoid major financing by federal grants and, receiving a new capital gift of $10 million from the Carnegie Corporation of New York, the institution continued to operate almost wholly on income from endowment.

DANIEL J. KEVLES

CARNIFEX FERRY, BATTLES AT. An Ohio regiment posted at this river-crossing (Gauley River) in West Virginia was routed on Aug. 26, 1861, by a Confederate brigade under Gen. John B. Floyd, who thereupon entrenched and remained there until attacked on Sept. 10 by Gen. William S. Rosecrans' small army. After a sharp action, Floyd, slightly wounded, retreated with his command during the night.

[R. U. Johnson and C. C. Buel, eds., *Battles and Leaders of the Civil War*, vol. 1.]

ALVIN F. HARLOW

CAROLANA, a colony projected by Daniel Coxe, a British physician and land speculator, who by 1698 had acquired title to the Sir Robert Heath grant of 1629, under which he claimed the region in the rear of the Carolina settlements and including the lower Mississippi Valley. The expedition that was sent out to plant the colony landed at Charleston, S.C., but one ship sailed up the Mississippi River for 100 miles, turning back when Jean Baptiste Le Moyne, Sieur de Bienville, informed the captain, on Sept. 15, 1699, that the French already occupied the region. Coxe reasserted his claim to the territory, but his colony never materialized.

[Samuel Ashe, *History of North Carolina;* Edward McCrady, *The History of South Carolina Under the Proprietary Government.*]

WALTER PRICHARD

CAROLINA, FUNDAMENTAL CONSTITUTIONS OF, the most pretentious of the attempts to establish a feudal aristocracy in English America, were drawn up in 1669 by John Locke under the direction of his employer and patron, the Earl of Shaftesbury. Between that date and 1698 at least five revisions were issued by the Lords Proprietors. Outstanding features were the provisions for a provincial nobility of proprietors, landgraves, and caciques having permanent ownership of two-fifths of the land; for a grand council made up of proprietors and their councillors which should have the executive and judicial authority, and—through its control of the initiative—should likewise control legislation; for an established Anglican Church and religious toleration; and for serfdom and slavery.

Shelving the top-heavy system for a time at the beginning of settlement, the proprietors set up revised grand councils in North Carolina and in South Carolina, but in the former the Fundamental Constitutions had little weight. In South Carolina they greatly strengthened the tendency toward a dominant landed aristocracy, and to them may be traced the ballot and certain land-ownership requirements for voting and officeholding. The attempts of the proprietors to force the complete system upon the assembly came to a climax and failure about 1700.

[Samuel Ashe, *History of North Carolina;* Edward McCrady, *The History of South Carolina Under the Proprietary Government.*]

R. L. MERIWETHER

CAROLINA PROPRIETORS. The first Carolina patent was granted by Charles I to Sir Robert Heath in 1629. By its terms the province extended from ocean to ocean between the thirty-first and thirty-sixth parallels. This patent was declared forfeited by Charles II on the ground of nonuse, and in 1663 he issued a charter with the same bounds to eight joint proprietors: Edward Hyde, Earl of Clarendon; George Monck, Duke of Albemarle; William, Lord Craven; John, Lord Berkeley; Anthony Ashley Cooper, Lord Ashley (later Earl of Shaftesbury); Sir George Carteret; Sir John Colleton; and Sir William Berkeley. In 1665 the boundaries were extended to include the territory from 29° to 36°30′ north latitude. "Declarations and Proposals," the first organic law, issued by the proprietors in 1663, promised land to settlers who should emigrate within five years, representation of freeholders in a provincial assembly, and liberty of conscience. The Fundamental Constitutions of Carolina, formulated by John Locke in 1669, never went into effect in the colony.

The enterprise resulting in loss, proprietary neglect became chronic. Great discontent was caused by the indifference of the proprietors during the war with the Tuscarora (1711–12) and the Yamasee War (1715–16) and by their lack of support when the province was threatened from the West Indies by the French and the Spanish (1706, 1719) and when it was attacked by pirates (1718). Proprietary orders destructive of provincial interests brought about a revolutionary movement in South Carolina (1719), which the crown thereupon took over as a royal colony, leaving North Carolina to the proprietors until purchase of the proprietorship of both provinces for the crown (1729). Lord Carteret retained his interest in the form of a strip of land lying south of Virginia and estimated at an eighth of the original grant (*see* Granville Grant).

[Samuel A. Ashe, *History of North Carolina;* Edward McCrady, *The History of South Carolina Under the Proprietary Government;* D. D. Wallace, *History of South Carolina.*]

D. D. WALLACE

CAROLINA ROAD. *See* **Virginia Path.**

CAROLINAS, SHERMAN'S MARCH THROUGH THE. In February 1865, Union Gen. William T. Sherman's army left Savannah on its way northward "to make South Carolina feel the severities of war" and to unite with Gen. Ulysses S. Grant in Virginia. By Feb. 17 the army was at Columbia, S.C., which was burned. None in Sherman's army ever admitted responsibility for this act. On March 10 the army was at Fayetteville, N.C. As Sherman advanced, opposition became stronger. At Bentonville on Mar. 19 the advance was delayed several days, but by the 25th Sherman was at Goldsboro. On April 13 he had reached Raleigh.

The news of Robert E. Lee's surrender caused Gen. J. E. Johnston to negotiate for the surrender of the Confederate Army. A conditional agreement was signed, April 18, but was repudiated because of too liberal terms. On the 26th Johnston surrendered on the same terms Lee had received.

Sherman marched nearly 500 miles in about eight weeks, impeded as much by the multitude of slaves and their families who mingled with the marching troops as by the opposition, although weak and unorganized, of Confederate troops.

[R. U. Johnson and C. C. Buel, eds., *Battles and Leaders of the Civil War.*]

THOMAS ROBSON HAY

***CAROLINE* AFFAIR.** In November 1837, William Lyon Mackenzie launched a rebellion in Upper Canada. Defeated by government forces, Mackenzie and his followers fled to Navy Island in the Niagara River. Sympathizers on the American side of the river supplied them with food, arms, and recruits, using the American-owned steamer *Caroline*. On the night of Dec. 29, a body of Canadian troops crossed to the American side and seized the *Caroline,* killing Amos Durfee, an American, in the struggle. The steamer was towed into midstream, set afire, and turned adrift. President Martin Van Buren, through the State Department, protested vigorously to the British minister at Washington and lodged a protest at London, all of which was ignored. For a time feeling ran high on both sides of the border, and steps were taken to forestall invasion from Canada and to prevent Americans from violating the frontier. The case dragged on for some years and meanwhile became complicated by the arrest, in New York, of Alexander McLeod, a Canadian sheriff, for the murder of Durfee. As an adjunct of the Webster-Ashburton Treaty the affair was settled in 1842 by an expression of regret on the part of England that there had not been an immediate explanation and apology for the occurrence.

[Alexander DeConde, *A History of American Foreign Policy.*]

MILLEDGE L. BONHAM, JR.

CAROLINE ISLANDS. In the American drive across the Central Pacific in World War II, commanded by Adm. Chester W. Nimitz, commander in chief of the U.S. Pacific Fleet and Pacific Ocean areas, Truk atoll, near the center of the Caroline Islands, was originally targeted for an amphibious assault. After an air strike against Truk by Rear Adm. Marc A. Mitscher's Fast Carrier Force on Apr. 17–18, 1944, Nimitz decided to bypass the eastern and central Carolines. Truk was thereafter "neutralized" by a second fast carrier raid on Apr. 29 and by routine land-based heavy bomber attacks.

To protect the right flank of Gen. Douglas MacArthur's return to the Philippines, key positions in the Palaus in the western Carolines were selected for amphibious landings. Rear Adm. Theodore S. Wilkinson commanded the expeditionary force under overall command of Third Fleet commander Adm. William F. Halsey. Pelelieu Island, strongly fortified and defended by about 13,000 Japanese, was assaulted on Sept. 15 by the First Marine Division, later supported by the Eighty-first Infantry Division. Organized resistance ended on Nov. 27 at the cost of almost 10,500 American casualties. Meanwhile, elements of the Eighty-first Infantry Division had captured the neighboring island of Angaur and had occupied undefended Ulithi atoll, 360 miles to the northeast. Ulithi was promptly converted into a major U.S. naval base.

[Jeter A. Isely and Philip A. Crowl, *The U.S. Marines and Amphibious War;* F. O. Hough, *The Assault on Pelelieu;* Samuel E. Morison, *History of United States Naval Operations in World War II,* vols. VIII and XII; Robert R. Smith, *The Approach to the Philippines.*]

PHILIP A. CROWL

CARONDELET, a Mississippi River steamboat with a sloping iron casemate and thirteen guns, built at Saint Louis by James B. Eads. It fought at Fort Henry and Fort Donelson. In April 1862, under Commander Henry Walke, it forced the evacuation of Island Number Ten by running past the batteries at night to safeguard Union troops crossing below.

[R. U. Johnson and C. C. Buel, eds., *Battles and Leaders of the Civil War.*]

WALTER B. NORRIS

CARONDELET CANAL, named for the Spanish governor who sponsored it in 1794 as a navigation and drainage project. The canal extended a mile and a half from New Orleans to Bayou Saint John, thus opening water communication between the city and Lake Pontchartrain and eliminating the necessity of the long Mississippi River voyage.

[J. S. Kendall, *History of New Orleans.*]

WALTER PRICHARD

CARONDELET INTRIGUE. Baron Francisco Luis Hector de Carondelet was one of the governors of Spanish Louisiana who intrigued with western communities of the United States, notably Kentucky, for the purpose of detaching them from the Union. His purpose was to thwart the policy of the United States to secure unchallenged access to the Mississippi River, thus endangering Spanish Louisiana and New Spain. The movement came to an end with the ratification (1795) of Pinckney's Treaty.

[Samuel Flagg Bemis, *Pinckney's Treaty;* Arthur Preston Whitaker, *The Spanish American Frontier, 1783–1795.*]

SAMUEL FLAGG BEMIS

CARPENTERS' HALL, Philadelphia, on Chestnut Street between Third and Fourth streets, was built by the Carpenters' Guild in 1770 as a meeting place for its members. It was here the first Continental Congress convened, on Sept. 5, 1774.

[J. T. Schraft, *History of Philadelphia.*]

CHARLES W. HEATHCOTE

CARPETBAGGERS were northerners who went to the South just after the end of the Civil War and, sooner or later, became active in politics as Republicans. The term was a derogatory epithet utilized by their political opponents to stigmatize them as settlers who were so transitory and propertyless that their entire goods could be carried in carpetbags, a then common kind of valise covered with carpeting material. Some individuals may have fitted this stereotype, but no single term—certainly not one devised by their partisan foes—can accurately describe the diverse group of northerners who participated in southern politics as Republicans during Reconstruction. Few of the carpetbaggers were wealthy or prominent when they came to the South, but few, on the other hand, were penniless vagabonds. Primarily they were aspiring young men who, like earlier frontiersmen, moved from their homes to improve their personal lives and status. Many had gained wartime experience in the South while serving as soldiers in the Union army or as agents of the Treasury Department and the Freedmen's Bureau. Others had been sent as missionaries from the North to minister to the educational and religious needs of former slaves.

Whatever drew them to the South, most of the so-called carpetbaggers arrived before the Reconstruction Act of 1867 offered them political opportunities by enfranchising black southerners and disqualifying many former Confederate officeholders. In the constitutional conventions elected in 1867–68, they took an active part in shaping the new state constitutions. When the new governments were established, hundreds of northerners served as Republican state and local officials. At least forty-five sat in the U.S. House of Representatives and seventeen in the Senate; ten were state governors. As is true with any group of political leaders, their conduct and influence varied from state to state and from county to county. Some were corrupt; others were honest. Some were capable; others were inept. Their attitudes toward black southern Republicans varied from close, dedicated alliance to open, hostile opposition. Whenever their Democratic opponents gained control of a state in the 1870's—whether by election or by violence—the role of the carpetbaggers declined rapidly. Many returned to the North or continued their migration toward the West; others remained in the South for the rest of their lives. They disappeared almost completely as a distinguishable class in southern politics after the federal government in 1877 abandoned the enforcement of various Reconstruction measures.

[Richard N. Current, *Three Carpetbag Governors;* Jonathan Daniels, *Prince of Carpetbaggers: M. S. Littlefield;* Otto Olson, *Carpetbagger's Crusade: The Life of Albion Winegar Tourgée*.]

JOSEPH LOGSDON

CARPET MANUFACTURE. Carpets first appeared in American homes about 1700. For over a century the meager domestic supply was a product of households, itinerant handicraftsmen, or small shops operated by marketers who contracted with workers to supply them with carpets made in the workers' homes. Aided by favorable tariff rates, the transition to the factory system began in 1791 when William P. Sprague set up a plant in Philadelphia. Linking the Jacquard apparatus (which enabled the weaving of intricate patterns) to the hand looms in 1828 gave a further impetus to this movement; and by 1835 the industry was dominated by sizable mills located chiefly in the eastern coastal states. At this early date practically all varieties of modern floor coverings were already being produced. Inventions by Erastus B. Bigelow and Halcyon Skinner between 1840 and 1875 made power weaving possible, and by the latter date production was organized along modern lines in large plants, employing in some instances over 1,000 workers. Lower production costs, expanding national income, and a general acceptance of carpets as a status symbol combined to make their use increasingly commonplace after 1870. This trend was reflected in the output of the industry, which on a per capita basis increased from approximately one-half square yard in 1870 to a full square yard by 1900.

A marked shift in the industry's growth rate did occur after the turn of the century. One reason for this shift, which by 1950 had reduced output back to its 1870 level of about one-half square yard per capita, was that as the use of carpets became increasingly widespread after 1900, they began to lose their prestige value. The major factor accounting for the industry's failure to maintain a higher rate of production relative to the population growth during the first half of the 20th century was the growing competition from an expanding variety of available goods and services such as radios, refrigerators, washing machines, automobiles, and vacation travel.

From the low point reached at mid-century, the industry's growth trend once again shifted, and by the early 1970's, output had risen to over 850 million square yards, or approximately four square yards per capita. Two developments that enabled the industry to reduce the prices of its products to consumers were largely responsible for sales growth. One was a greater substitution of synthetic fibers and cotton for the more expensive carpet wool. The second was the shift from the production of woven carpets and rugs to tufted floor coverings that were less durable than the woven varieties, but much less costly to manufacture.

[A. H. Cole and H. F. Williamson, *The American Carpet and Rug Industry*.]

HAROLD F. WILLIAMSON

CARRIAGE MAKING. Horse-drawn vehicles were made in the colonies from the earliest days of settlement. Prior to the Revolution, pleasure vehicles were rare and confined to towns. Most country travel was on horseback because of poor roads.

Extensive road building and a rapid increase of horse-drawn vehicles began with the birth of the Republic, testifying to the territorial expansion of the country, the greater mobility of its population, and the democratization of travel. Famous builders of wagons and stagecoaches established themselves at strategic points like Troy, N.Y., and Concord, N.H. (*see* Concord Coach).

After carriages for the well-to-do, such as the fifty-nine owned in New York in 1770, ceased to measure the demand for personal wheeled transportation, private conveyances developed along popular lines typical of American manufactures. The first example of this was the one-horse shay, or chaise, a light vehicle with two high wheels adapted to the rough roads and numerous fords of the still undeveloped country. For fifty years these were so popular that proprietors of carriage shops were usually known as chaise-makers.

By the middle of the 18th century the chaise was superseded by the four-wheel buggy, the most typical American vehicle prior to the cheap motor car. It was simpler, lighter, stronger, and cheaper than other corresponding conveyances.

Carriage making, long since a factory industry, reached the height of its development in 1904. Since then it has declined rapidly. The number of horse-drawn vehicles of all kinds made in America in 1939 was less than 50,000, compared with 1,700,000 thirty years earlier. The number of wage earners engaged in making such vehicles in 1939 had fallen to less than 5 percent of the number at the opening of the century. By the 1950's the industry produced only racing sulkies and a few made-to-order buggies.

[Victor S. Clark, *History of Manufactures in the United States;* Ralph Moody, *Stagecoach West;* Ezra M. Stratton, *The World on Wheels.*]

VICTOR S. CLARK

CARRIAGE TAX, CONSTITUTIONALITY OF. In the case of *Hylton* v. *United States* (1796), the question of whether a tax on carriages imposed by an act of Congress (June 5, 1794) was a direct tax, and therefore subject to the rule of apportionment, was decided in the negative. Three justices, Samuel Chase, William Paterson, and James Iredell, sitting without their colleagues, decided unanimously that the tax was an excise or duty and not a direct tax. The case is chiefly interesting as the first in which the constitutionality of an act of Congress was directly reviewed by the Court.

[Charles Warren, *History of the Supreme Court of the United States.*]

PHILLIPS BRADLEY

CARRION CROW BAYOU, BATTLE OF, fought on Oct. 14–15, 1863, when the Confederates attempted to turn back a federal raid up the Bayou Teche from Berwick Bay to Opelousas and Washington, La. Other skirmishes occurred there later in the year (Nov. 3, 11, and 18), during the return of the federal raiders to New Iberia.

[C. A. Evans, ed., *Confederate Military History,* vol. X.]

WALTER PRICHARD

CARRIZAL, SKIRMISH OF (June 21, 1916). Two troops of the Tenth Cavalry, on a reconnaissance mission, attempted to force passage through the town of Carrizal in Chihuahua, Mexico (*see* Mexico, Punitive Expedition Into). Four hundred Carranzistas, representatives of the Mexican government, resisted. In the skirmish that followed the American troops were defeated and forced to withdraw, leaving two officers and forty-three enlisted men killed, wounded, or taken prisoner. This incident resulted in an exchange of sharp notes between the two governments and the massing of troops for quick action. Further conflict was avoided by the appointment of a joint commission and the eventual withdrawal of American troops from Mexico.

[Frank Tompkins, *Chasing Villa.*]

C. A. WILLOUGHBY

CARTAGENA EXPEDITION, organized in 1741 in England and composed of thirty ships of the line, some ninety other vessels, 15,000 sailors, and 12,000 land troops, was designed to capture the great Spanish stronghold of the Caribbean region (*see* King George's War). At Jamaica the expedition was reinforced by 3,600 troops from the colonies, consisting of five companies from Massachusetts, two from Rhode Island, two from Connecticut, five from New York, three from New Jersey, eight from Pennsylvania, three from Maryland, four from Virginia, and four from North Carolina. The attacks on Cartagena, from Mar. 9 to Apr. 11, failed, and about two-thirds of the land force was lost from illness and in battle.

[H. L. Osgood, *The American Colonies in the 18th Century.*]

PERCY SCOTT FLIPPIN

CARTER'S VALLEY SETTLEMENT. John Carter, later leader in the Watauga settlement, located a trading house on the west side of the Holston River in Tennessee country below Long Island of Holston and a few miles south of the Virginia line in 1770, and that section of the Holston Valley has ever since borne the name of Carter's Valley. Carter sold supplies to emigrants who came to Long Island to begin the water journey to the Natchez district, and also to the Cherokee out on hunts. The Indian chiefs objected to this trading post, and in 1772 it was robbed by the Indians and abandoned by Carter, who removed to the Watauga. In the early part of 1776 another settlement of the valley was attempted only to be broken up in the summer of that year. Settlements by the hardier of the pioneers were renewed in 1777, and they thereafter held the fertile region in fair security.

[S. C. Williams, *Dawn of Tennessee Valley and Tennessee History.*]

SAMUEL C. WILLIAMS

CARTER* V. *CARTER COAL COMPANY, 298 U.S. 238 (1936). In this case the Guffey Coal Act, regulating wages, hours, conditions of work, and prices in the coal industry, was declared unconstitutional on grounds that the production of coal is not within the interstate commerce power and that the act also made an unconstitutional delegation of legislative power. The price-fixing provisions were not passed upon. Seven states presented briefs on behalf of the act, arguing that the problems of the coal industry could not be solved by independent state action.

HARVEY PINNEY

CARTHAGE, BATTLE OF (July 5, 1861). Defeated at Boonville by Union Gen. Nathaniel Lyon, the Missouri secessionists under Gov. Claiborne Fox Jackson and Gen. Sterling Price retreated into southwest Missouri, hoping for reinforcements from Arkansas. Anticipating this, Lyon sent Col. Franz Sigel to Springfield. Sigel advanced to check the retreating enemy until Lyon arrived. Near Carthage on July 5, although greatly outnumbered, he attacked Jackson. Defeated, Sigel retreated to Springfield. Impeded by high waters, Lyon arrived a week later. Encouraged by victory and reinforcements, the secessionists prepared to advance on Springfield.

[E. M. Violette, *A History of Missouri.*]

GLENN H. BENTON

CARTOGRAPHY. Commercial Mapping. Commercial or nongovernmental mapping and mapmaking in the United States began immediately after the Revolution with proposals by William Tatham, Thomas Hutchins, Simeon De Witt, and other topographers and geographers who had served in the army to compile and publish maps of the states and regions of the United States. Since then a wide variety of maps, atlases, and three-dimensional cartographic models have been published. The three most widely published and used types are the geographical national and world atlases, county atlases, and individual maps.

Geographical atlases and maps were first published in the United States in the early 1790's—for example, Matthew Carey's *American Atlas,* published in Philadelphia in 1795. By the 1820's the best work was being done by H. C. Carey and L. Lea, Samuel E. Morse and S. Breese, Henry S. Tanner, and John Melish. Melish's *Map of Pennsylvania* (1822) and Herman Böyë's *Map of the State of Virginia* (1826) are excellent examples of large-scale state maps. Prior to the introduction of lithography in about 1830, maps were printed from copper engravings. Use of lithography expedited publication of maps in variant forms and made them appreciably less expensive. With this and related technical improvements there was a rapid increase in commercial map publication. The principal centers of publication during most of the 19th century were Philadelphia, Boston, New York, and Chicago. This technical development in cartography coincided with the rapid expansion of the United States into the West and into various parts of the world, which excited a considerable interest in maps, either as individual state and county sheets, or in atlases.

By mid-century, map publication was accelerated by the introduction of the rotary steam press, zinc plates, the transfer process, glazed paper, chromolithography, and the application of photography to printing. Two major map publishers, August Hoen of Baltimore and Julius Bien of New York, set the high standards of cartographic excellence during the second half of the 19th century. They were responsible for many of the outstanding examples of cartographic presentation, especially those included in government publications. The Hoen Company was still producing maps in the mid-1970's. Others who contributed significantly to the development of techniques of survey, compilation, and map reproduction were Robert Pearsall Smith and Henry Francis Walling. Beginning with the second half of the 19th century a uniquely American commercial map publication was the county atlas and, to some extent, the city and town map. Significantly, this was the period during which the fire insurance and underwriters map was developed, which was perfected in great detail and, until the 1960's, kept up-to-date for most cities and towns of the United States by the Sanborn Map Company.

Commercial map publication during the 20th century expanded to include a wide variety of subjects, such as recreational, travel, road, automobile, airline, sports, and astronautical exploration maps catering to a rapidly growing interest in graphic information.

During and after World War II there was a rapid acceleration in commercial map production. To a considerable extent this was a response to the requirements of a nation at war in all parts of the world. Government mapping and mapmaking agencies contracted out to commercial map publishing firms large orders for many kinds of maps and atlases. Aerial and satellite photography, especially since World War II, has become a fundamental source of information in map compilation. The best modern maps are objects of artistic excellence as well as accurate selective graphic representations of a portion of the earth's surface.

Federal Mapping and Mapmaking. In a resolution of the Continental Congress on July 25, 1777, Gen. George Washington was empowered to appoint Robert Erskine geographer and surveyor on Washington's headquarters staff. Under Erskine and his successors, Simeon De Witt and Thomas Hutchins, more than 130 manuscript maps were prepared. From these beginnings a considerable mapping program by the federal government has evolved that since the early days of World War II literally covers the world and, since 1964, the moon.

In 1785 the Congress established in the Department of the Treasury the General Land Office, which became responsible for the survey of the public domain. The activity of this office has, in varying forms, continued to this day. Increase in maritime commerce and the need for maps of the coast brought about, in 1807, the creation of an office for the survey of the coasts, which, with several modifications and a lapse between 1819 and 1832, has continued through to the present as the U.S. Coast and Geodetic Survey. The rapid movement of population to the West and the large acquisition of lands by the Louisiana Purchase increased the need for exploration, survey, and mapping, much of which was accomplished by topographical engineer officers of the War Department.

Between 1819 and the eve of the Civil War, the mapping activities of the federal government increased greatly. A topographical bureau established in the War Department in 1819 was responsible for a nationwide program of mapping for internal improvements and, through detailed topographic surveying, for maps and geographical reports. A cartographic office was set up in the U.S. Navy Depot of Charts and Instruments in 1842 that was instrumental in the mapping of the Arctic and Antarctic regions and the Pacific Ocean and in supplying the navy with charts. In the 1850's the Office of Explorations and Surveys was created in the Office of the Secretary of War, with a primary responsibility for explorations, surveys, and maps of the West—especially for proposed and projected railroad routes to the Pacific coast.

During the Civil War the best European surveying, mapmaking, and map-reproduction techniques were blended with those of U.S. cartographic establishments—especially in the Union and Confederate armies. By the end of the war, which had disclosed the inadequacy of map coverage for military as well as civilian enterprise, U.S. mapmaking was equal to any in Europe. A few of the mapping agencies that were created between the Civil War and World War I to serve major continuous national needs include the Bureau of the Census, which, beginning in 1875, published thematic demographic maps and atlases compiled principally from returns of the census; the Geological Survey, created in 1879 to prepare large-scale topographic and other maps, almost exclusively of the United States and its territories; the Hydrographic Office of the navy, established in 1866 to chart foreign waters; the Corps of Engineers, expanded greatly to undertake a major program of mapping and surveying for internal improvements; and the Weather Bureau, organized in 1870 in the Signal Office of the War Department to prepare daily, synoptic, and other kinds of weather maps.

World War I created a large and immediate need for maps by the military, especially in Europe. Mapmaking and map-reproduction units were organized and established in France. Some of the maps were made from aerial photographs and represented the beginning of modern quantitative mapping with a respectable degree of accuracy. New techniques of compilation and drafting and improved methods of rapid reproduction developed during the war accelerated and widened the opportunities for mapping during the 1920's and 1930's.

During the Great Depression many specialized agencies were created to map a wide variety of cultural and physical features, the understanding of which was essential to economic recovery. Thematic and special-purpose maps—many of which were included with government reports—came into their own. Significant among the specialized agencies were the Bureau of Agricultural Economics, the Tennessee

Valley Authority, the Climatic and Physiographic Division, the National Resources Committee and Planning Board, and the Federal Housing Administration. Geographers played a leading role in the development of techniques for presentation, especially in thematic and resource maps, and in field mapping.

A rapid proliferation of mapping agencies in the federal government occurred during World War II. The principal types of maps of this period were topographic maps, aeronautical and nautical charts, and thematic maps. Several hundred geographers in Washington, D.C., alone were given responsibilities for mapmaking and geographical interpretation, particularly in the compilation of thematic maps. The wide use of aerial photography during the depression was expanded to universal application, especially for the making of large-scale topographic maps. The Aeronautical Chart and Information Service, the Hydrographic Office, and the Army Map Service, with their numerous field units, were the primary agencies of production.

The period after World War II witnessed the spread of large-scale mapping into the Arctic and Antarctic regions. The development of color-sensitive photographic instruments, of highly sophisticated cameras in space vehicles, of automated cartography combining electronics with computer technology, of sensing by satellites in prescribed earth orbits, and of a host of other kinds of instrumentation has made possible a wide variety of almost instantaneous mapping or terrain imagery of any part of the earth as directed. As mapping has become an exact science, maps have become a fundamental source of information and a basic record in most agencies of the federal government.

[*Imago Mundi: A Periodical Review of Early Cartography* (1932–); Lloyd Brown, *The Story of Maps;* Martin P. Claussen and Herman R. Friis, *American and Foreign Maps Published by the U.S. Congress, 1789–1861: Historical Catalog and Index;* Philip L. Phillips and Clara E. Le Gear, *A List of Geographical Atlases in the Library of Congress;* U.S. National Archives, *Guide to Cartographic Records in the National Archives;* John A. Wolter, "Some Materials for the Writing of American Cartography," *Bulletin of the Geography and Map Division,* no. 88 (1972).]

HERMAN R. FRIIS

CARTOONS, POLITICAL. Early cartoons were woodcuts or engravings. Benjamin Franklin printed his "Join or Die" snake cartoon in the *Pennsylvania Gazette,* May 9, 1754, and it was widely copied in the colonial period. Paul Revere and other artists depicted the Stamp Act and the Boston Massacre in separately issued engravings. The ratification of the Constitution was celebrated by Benjamin Russell with the rising columns of the "Federal Edifice" cartoon in the *Massachusetts Centinel* (1788); but woodcut cartoons were used sparingly in newspapers. From the Jackson period through the Civil War many poster cartoons, wood engravings, and lithographs were produced. These often contained portraits of political figures, with lettering issuing from their mouths. Civil War cartoons appeared in periodicals such as *Harper's Weekly* and *Vanity Fair.* The modern cartoon, a pen drawing with effective caricatures, was the creation of Thomas Nast of *Harper's Weekly* in the period following the Civil War. He popularized such symbols as the Republican elephant and the Tammany tiger. The first newspaper editorial cartoons were those of Walt McDougall used by the *New York World* in 1884 and they were followed by those of Homer Davenport and Frederick Opper, creators of the dollar-marked suit and bloated "trust" figures in the *Journal.* Since World War II major newspapers have carried daily "editorial" cartoons that interpret or comment on political news or events. Outstanding cartoonists included Herbert Block ("Herblock") of the *Washington Post* and Daniel Fitzpatrick of the *St. Louis Post-Dispatch.*

[William Murrell, *A History of American Graphic Humor, 1747–1938;* Allan Nevins and Frank Weitenkampf, *A Century of Political Cartoons: Caricature in the United States from 1800 to 1900.*]

MILTON W. HAMILTON

CARVER CLAIM grew out of the assertion that at Saint Paul on May 1, 1767, the Sioux nation granted to Jonathan Carver, traveler and author, an extensive tract embracing approximately the northwestern one-fourth of modern Wisconsin. The federal government rejected the claim early in the 19th century, after fifty years of exploitation by many land speculators.

[M. M. Quaife, "Jonathan Carver and the Carver Grant," *Mississippi Valley Historical Review,* vol. 7.]

M. M. QUAIFE

CARVER'S *TRAVELS*. The first person to visit and publicly describe the region of the upper Great Lakes and the upper Mississippi River was Capt. Jonathan Carver of Massachusetts. His tour, performed in 1766–68, was described in his *Travels,* first published in London in 1778. The book proved immensely popular, and many editions, in several different languages, were issued. During the 20th century the reliability of the narrative has been keenly debated by scholars; examination of Carver's manuscript journal establishes that it differs in important respects from the published version. Research points to the conclusion that while Carver actually made the tour he describes, he suppressed the fact that he performed it as a hired agent of Maj. Robert Rogers, who was intent on finding the Northwest Passage to the Pacific Ocean, rather than on his own responsibility.

[Louise P. Kellogg, *The British Regime in Wisconsin and the Northwest.*]

M. M. QUAIFE

CARY'S REBELLION, an uprising in colonial North Carolina occasioned by the disfranchisement of the Quakers, a numerous sect in that province. In 1707 Thomas Cary, deputy governor, was deposed at the solicitation of the Quakers, but for two years he refused to abandon his office. In 1710 the proprietors sent Edward Hyde as governor, and Cary revolted, although he had promised to support Hyde. With Virginia aid, Cary was defeated, captured, and sent to England on a treason charge, but was never tried.

[R. D. W. Connor, *North Carolina.*]

HUGH T. LEFLER

CASABLANCA CONFERENCE (Jan. 14–24, 1943), a meeting between President Franklin D. Roosevelt and Prime Minister Winston Churchill to resolve military problems, primarily the strategy that was to follow victory in North Africa, and to unite the disparate factions representing Free French Forces. The American proposal to assault the European continent was overruled in favor of the British plan for an invasion of Sicily and Italy. The public announcement by Roosevelt (Jan. 24) that "the elimination of German, Japanese, and Italian war power means the unconditional surrender by Germany, Italy, and Japan" became the subject of much controversy.

[Herbert Feis, *Churchill, Roosevelt, Stalin: The War They Waged and the Peace They Sought;* U.S. Department of State, *Foreign Relations of the United States: The Conference at Washington, 1941–1942, and Casablanca, 1943.*]

RAYMOND G. O'CONNOR

CASCADES OF THE COLUMBIA, falls and rapids in the Columbia River at the present site of the Bonneville Dam. They were a cause of great difficulty to the early explorers and fur traders and were especially dreaded by the settlers, who often preferred the toil and hardships of crossing mountain passes to the dangers to life and property encountered in descending these cascades.

DAN E. CLARK

CASCO TREATY OF 1678 brought to a close the hostilities between the Indians of the Abnaki and Pennacook confederacies in New England and the English settlers of Massachusetts Bay and sought to reestablish the friendly relations between the Indians and English that had characterized the northern settlements previous to the outbreak of King Philip's War in 1675. By the terms of this treaty all captives were to be surrendered without ransom. The treaty also stipulated that the English should give the Indians one peck of corn annually for each family settled on Indian lands, with the exception of Maj. Phillips of Saco, a great proprietor, who was required to give a bushel.

[Francis Parkman, *A Half-Century of Conflict,* vol. I.]

ELIZABETH RING

CASCO TREATY OF 1703, an unsuccessful attempt by Gov. Joseph Dudley of Massachusetts Bay to prevent further Indian hostilities from breaking out along the northern frontier. War was already going on in Europe between England and France (*see* Queen Anne's War), and the Indians of the Abnaki and Pennacook confederacies in New England from whom trouble was expected were under the influence of French Jesuits. Accordingly, Dudley arranged a meeting with the several chiefs and their tribes to confer with him and his councillors to reconcile whatever differences had arisen since the last treaty (1678). They met in Casco, Maine, June 20, 1703. The Indians made professions of peace, disavowing any conspiracy with the French to exterminate the English. They then presented the governor with a belt of wampum and ended the ceremony with an exchange of volleys. The Indians undoubtedly intended to make the white leaders their victims on the spot, but the white and Indian leaders were so placed that one group could not be destroyed without the other. Within two months the eastern Indians were again on the warpath and the people of New England prepared for another period of surprise attacks from Indian enemies.

[Charles E. Clark, *The Eastern Frontier. The Settlement of Northern New England, 1610–1763;* H. M. Sylvester, *Indian Wars of New England,* vol. III.]

ELIZABETH RING

CASIMIR, FORT. *See* **New Castle.**

CASKET GIRLS were women imported into Louisiana by the Compagnie des Indes as wives for settlers. Their name derives from the small chests (*cassettes*) in which they carried their clothes. They were conspicuous by reason of their virtue. Normally women were supplied to the colonists by raking the streets of Paris for undesirables or by emptying the houses of correction. The casket girls, however, were recruited from church charitable institutions and, although poor, were practically guaranteed to be virtuous. For this reason it later became a matter of pride in Louisiana to show descent from them rather than from the more numerous prostitutes. The first consignment reached Biloxi in 1719 and New Orleans in 1727–28. They inspired Victor Herbert's operetta *Naughty Marietta*.

[Charles Gayarré, *History of Louisiana;* Dunbar Rowland, *Mississippi, the Heart of the South.*]

MACK SWEARINGEN

CASTINE, a town on the east side of Penobscot Bay, Maine, incorporated 1796, occupies a peninsula called Pentegoet by the French and Majorbagwaduce by the English. Strategically located in respect to the Penobscot Indians and their trade and within the area in dispute between the English and the French, the place was a center of international rivalry from the earliest days. The trading post established in 1630 by Edward Ashley and the Plymouth colonists in the right of the Beauchamp and Leverett patent passed into the control of the French in 1635 by the Treaty of Saint-Germain. English again by conquest in 1654, it was returned to the French in 1670 by the Treaty of Breda, the trade being dominated by the Baron de Saint Castine until his return to France in 1701. From the beginning of the Indian wars in 1688 until 1759, the Indians, instigated by the French, prevented settlement by the English. Soon after 1763 the first English settlers took possession.

[George A. Wheeler, *History of Castine, Penobscot and Brooksville.*]

ROBERT E. MOODY

CASTLE THUNDER, a tobacco warehouse in Richmond, Va., used (1861–65) by the Confederates to confine political prisoners and occasional spies and criminals charged with treason. Similar in general purposes to the Old Capitol prison in Washington, it had an unsavory reputation, and its officers were accused of unnecessary brutality toward their charges. After the fall of Richmond the prison was used by the federal authorities to house Confederates charged with crimes under international law.

W. B. HESSELTINE

CASTORLAND COMPANY, organized in Paris in 1792 as the Compagnie de New Yorck to colonize French aristocrats and others dissatisfied with conditions following the French Revolution. Land in Lewis County, N.Y., part of the Macomb Purchase, was bought from William Constable. Settlers arrived in 1796; within four years the colony had failed. The transplanted French people, unfit for the vigorous open life and hard work of the frontier, preferred more civilized communities.

[A. M. Sakolski, *The Great American Land Bubble.*]

THOMAS ROBSON HAY

CATALINA, SANTA, an island located about twenty-five miles southeast of Los Angeles harbor, discovered Oct. 7, 1542, by Juan Rodríguez Cabrillo. In 1602 Sebastián Vizcaíno named the island for St. Catherine of Alexandria. The chief bay, Avalon, during the Spanish and Mexican period was one of the most frequented ports of refuge for smugglers, hunters of sea otters and seals, and hide and tallow traders. The island became a resort area after purchase in 1919 by William Wrigley.

[C. F. Holder, *The Channel Islands of California;* J. N. Stewart, *Catalina's Yesterdays.*]

OSGOOD HARDY

CATHOLICISM. In colonial times most of the Roman Catholics in America lived in Maryland, which had been founded by the Catholic Calvert family as a land of sanctuary for all Christians. These Maryland Catholics were deprived of their religious freedom and many civil rights—temporarily by the Puritans in the 1650's and permanently by the Anglicans after the Revolution of 1688. From then on, they were excluded from voting and holding public office, forbidden to have churches or schools, and subjected to many other legal disabilities and even, for a while, to double taxation. Nevertheless, a few families became wealthy landowners. In the 18th century some Catholics, including many from Germany, settled in Pennsylvania, where they enjoyed *de facto* toleration. Hardly any were to be found in the other colonies, where their religion was proscribed in law and in practice. A majority of the colonial Catholics supported the American Revolution. Charles Carroll of Carrollton signed the Declaration of Independence; Daniel Carroll of Maryland and Thomas FitzSimons of Pennsylvania sat in the Constitutional Convention; and John Barry and Stephen Moylan were the most prominent of those who served in the armed forces during the Revolution. Yet only gradually did the Catholics acquire full civil rights in the several states.

The spiritual care of colonial Catholics was provided mainly by Jesuits, who were subject to their provincial in England up to the suppression of the Society of Jesus in 1773; the clergy and laity also came under the jurisdiction of the vicar-apostolic of the London district until the Revolution severed all ecclesiastical ties with England. In 1784 the sacred Congregatio de Propaganda Fide in Rome appointed as superior of the mission in the United States a native of Maryland and former Jesuit, John Carroll, cousin of Charles Carroll. Five years later he was elected first bishop of Baltimore by his fellow priests. There were then about 35,000 Roman Catholics living chiefly in the Middle Atlantic states and in the French villages of the western country. Carroll became an archbishop in 1808 when his see was raised to metropolitan rank and four suffragan dioceses were created (Boston, New York, Philadelphia, and Bardstown, Ky.).

The infant church owed its growth largely to European assistance. During and after the French Revolution many priests came from that country, and bishops of French birth were numerous in the first half of the 19th century. Financial aid was furnished by the Society for the Propagation of the Faith (founded at Lyons in 1822); the Leopoldine Foundation (Vienna, 1828); and the Ludwig-Missionsverein (Munich, 1838). The principal obstacle to the church's development before 1830 was the occasional insubordination of refractory (mostly Irish) priests and lay trustees, who resisted episcopal authority over their parishes and provoked temporary schisms and scandals.

Catholic educational and charitable institutions date from 1727, when the first French Ursulines arrived in New Orleans to conduct a school for girls, an orphanage, and a hospital. In the East, Georgetown Academy was opened for students of every religion in 1791; and in the same year the first seminary, Saint Mary's, was founded by French Sulpicians in Baltimore. Elizabeth Bayley Seton, after founding the first native religious community for women, the Sisters of Charity of Saint Joseph, established a school for girls at Emmitsburg, Md., in 1809; members of this sisterhood also began the first Catholic orphanage and hospital in the East—both at Philadelphia—in 1814 and 1828, respectively. By 1840 there were at least 200 Catholic schools, half of which were located west of the Alleghenies. The first Catholic weekly newspaper was the *United States Catholic Miscellany,* founded at Charleston, S.C., by Bishop John England in 1822.

This same farsighted prelate promoted regular meetings of the American hierarchy in order to ensure uniformity of discipline and cooperation in solving common problems. The bishops assembled seven times from 1829 to 1849 in the Provincial Councils of Baltimore. After the erection of more metropolitan sees, three plenary councils were held at Baltimore in 1852, 1866, and 1884; each published a pastoral letter in addition to decrees on many subjects. From 1890 to World War I the archbishops met annually in different cities.

Between 1830 and 1860 the Roman Catholic population of the United States increased from 318,000 to 3,103,000; of the latter total nearly 2,000,000 were immigrants. This sudden influx of numerous foreign Catholics gave rise to the American nativist movement, which vilified "Romish" beliefs and practices and impugned the loyalty and patriotism of Catholics by means of sensational newspapers, books, and lectures exposing alleged plots against American democracy and fantastic cases of moral corruption. Anti-Catholic sentiment exploded violently in the wanton burning of the Ursuline convent at Charlestown, Mass., in 1834, and in the bloody riots in Philadelphia in 1844. Organized nativism attacked the church through the American Protestant Association (founded in 1842) and, in the political field, through the Know-Nothing party in the 1850's. After the beginning of the Civil War, anti-Catholic bias tended to subside; thereafter it was active only locally, except when it was stirred up nationally by the American Protective Association in the 1890's and the Ku Klux Klan in the 1920's.

On the questions of slavery and emancipation Catholics were divided along sectional lines, but the bishops collectively maintained unity within the church by refraining from official statements that might be interpreted as interference in political affairs. Although they inculcated Pope Gregory XVI's condemnation of the slave trade, Catholic moralists did not regard slavery as evil per se; nor did the faithful, who mostly adhered to the Democratic party, support abolitionism. During the Civil War, Catholics fought on both sides, the most renowned among them being William Rosecrans for the Union and Pierre Beauregard for the Confederacy. At the request of President Abraham Lincoln's government John Hughes, archbishop of New York, went to Paris to advocate French neutrality; Archbishop Hughes also favored conscription and helped to quell the draft riots in his own city. On the battlefields and in the military hospitals Catholic sisters rendered generous service as nurses.

In 1863 the country had about 100,000 Catholic Afro-Americans, slave and free; the majority of them lived in Louisiana. In spite of the exhortations of the Plenary Council of 1866, the church made little progress among the black race for several reasons: a scarcity of personnel and means, a preoccupation with Catholic immigrants, indifference, the opposition of various Protestant denominations, and the unattractiveness to blacks of white Catholicism. After World War II Catholic bishops in many places anticipated public opinion and court decisions by ending racial segregation in churches and schools. In the 1960's black clerical, religious, and lay leaders formed several organizations, such as the National Office for Black Catholics, to satisfy the particular needs of Afro-Americans. Although the priests now called Josephites (introduced from England in 1871), the Sisters of the Blessed Sacrament (founded by Katharine Drexel in 1891), and other Catholic religious communities are devoted to this apostolate, the number of black Catholics in 1973 was estimated at only 900,000 (less than 4 percent of the total black population).

As for relations with the Holy See, the Catholic church in the United States remained under the direct supervision of the sacred Congregatio de Propaganda Fide until 1908. It was not noticeably affected by the presence of an American minister at the papal court from 1848 to 1868. In 1869–70 the American church was represented at the First Vatican Council by forty-eight bishops and one abbot, many of whom did not want the definition of the dogma of papal infallibility but accepted it in the end. The first American cardinal was John McCloskey, archbishop of New York, who was elevated to the Sacred College in 1875. Since 1893 the pope has had an apostolic delegate residing in Washington, D.C., as an observer and representative to the American church. Also, several American prelates have been nuncios and delegates in other countries and have held various offices in the Roman Curia. Between 1962 and 1965, 246 American bishops and abbots, as well as several theologians and other scholars, attended one or more of the four sessions of the Second Vatican Council and contributed especially to the writing and passing of its Declaration on Religious Freedom.

The greatest impetus to Catholic educational efforts in the United States was given by the Third Plenary Council of Baltimore (1884). Not only were parents commanded to procure a religious education for their children by sending them, if possible, to Catholic schools; but also priests were ordered to erect an elementary school in each parish—a goal that was never attained and since the 1960's has been abandoned. On the highest educational level, the Catholic University of America in Washington, D.C., was opened in 1889 as the first Catholic center for graduate study in both the sacred and the profane sciences. To coordinate all these undertakings the National Catholic Educational Association was established in 1904. Bishop Hughes tried in vain to lighten the financial burden of Catholics by requesting a share of the public school funds in New York in the 1840's, and Archbishop John Ireland of Saint Paul also failed in his attempt to achieve the same end by incorporating the parochial schools into the public school system of Minnesota in the 1890's. Since World War II certain forms of state aid to children attending Catholic schools, such as free bus transportation and the loan of textbooks, have been upheld by the Supreme Court; but the attempts of some states to supplement the salaries of teachers of secular subjects or to purchase services for the teaching of secular subjects in nonpublic schools have been declared unconstitutional. Mainly because of the rising costs (in part caused by the loss of teaching sisters, brothers, and priests who had to be replaced by lay teachers at higher salaries) the number of Catholic parochial and private elementary schools declined from 10,931 with 4,566,809 pupils in 1965 to 8,647 with 2,717,898 pupils in 1974; the number of high schools declined from 2,465 with 1,095,519 enrolled in 1965 to 1,702 with 911,730 enrolled in 1974; and the number of colleges and universities declined from 304 with 384,526 students in 1965 to 258—although with more students (407,081)—in 1974. Religious instruction was being given to 5,253,738 Catholic children attending public elementary and high schools in 1974, mainly through the Confraternity of Christian Doctrine.

It was particularly through its school system that the Roman Catholic church preserved the faith of the children of immigrants and at the same time eased their entrance into American society. Between 1881 and 1890 about 1,250,000 Catholics immigrated to the United States, and only slightly fewer came in the next decade, bringing the total Catholic population to 12,041,000 at the turn of the century. Within the following ten years 2,316,000 more arrived. A certain national antagonism was evidenced by the suggestion of Peter Paul Cahensly, the German founder of the Saint Raphael Societies for the protection of Catholic European emigrants, that the newer nationalities also be represented in the hierarchy; the majority of the bishops, who were of Irish birth or descent, resisted this proposal as contrary to the rapid Americanization of the newcomers. The only large and lasting schism in the history of American Catholicism began in 1907 with the organization of the Polish National Catholic Church. Otherwise it seems probable that relatively few of the immigrants have been lost to the church beyond the normal leakage due to other causes. Most of the losses have occurred in the cities, where a majority of the Catholic immigrants settled. To foster the growth of the church in isolated districts, especially in the Southwest, the Catholic Church Extension Society was founded in 1905; and to strengthen the faith in farming areas, the National Catholic Rural Life Conference was founded in 1923.

In the 19th century, American Catholics had few resources to devote to the preaching of the gospel in non-Christian lands, but the First American Catholic Missionary Congress, held in 1908, aroused interest in this work. Three years later the first native American religious community intended exclusively for the foreign missions, the Maryknoll Fathers, was established at Maryknoll, N.Y. The Catholic Students' Mission Crusade was inaugurated in 1918. The number of foreign missionaries reached a peak of 9,655 in 1968 and by 1972 fell to 7,649 (4,307 men and 3,342 women), of whom 376 were lay persons. Meanwhile, American Catholics were contributing about two-thirds of the general fund of the international Society for the Propagation of the Faith.

Most American Catholics have always belonged to the working class, and their leaders have long been concerned with the social order. In 1887 Cardinal James Gibbons, archbishop of Baltimore, and others defended the Knights of Labor against more conservative prelates, who would have had the union condemned as a forbidden secret society by the church. Certain recommendations of the bishops' statement of 1919 were so progressive that they were called socialistic by opponents. The most influential thinker and writer in this field before World War II was the Rev. John A. Ryan. In 1937 the Association of Catholic Trade Unionists was founded, and in the same decade the first labor schools were opened in several cities. Catholics have also sought to forestall juvenile delinquency by various programs, the most successful being that of the Catholic Youth Organization founded in Chicago in 1930.

In 1917 the National Catholic War Council was formed to coordinate the activities of the dioceses and societies with the national emergency. After the armistice this council was transformed into the permanent National Catholic Welfare Conference, which acted in an advisory capacity under an administrative board of ten bishops and functioned through several departments—for education, lay organizations, press, social action, legislation (proposed in Congress), and youth. In 1966 the conference was reorganized and expanded into the National Conference of Catholic Bishops (a strictly ecclesiastical body for pastoral purposes) and its operational secretariat and service agency, the United States Catholic Conference (a civil corporation with broader social concerns).

Vigorous as American Roman Catholicism has been, it has produced few officially recognized exemplars of extraordinary personal sanctity. Its only canonized saints are Mother Frances Xavier Cabrini (died 1917), a naturalized citizen who founded the Missionary Sisters of the Sacred Heart for the care of the immigrants, and Elizabeth Bayley Seton (died 1821). Also remarkable for heroic virtue were Blessed Philippine Duchesne (died 1852), a French religious of the Sacred Heart who labored for thirty-four years in Missouri; and Blessed John Nepomucene Neumann, a Bohemian who ministered as a priest in the United States and then as bishop of Philadelphia (died 1860).

Since World War II Catholic laymen have come to play a more active role in the church. Such men as Orestes A. Brownson and James McMaster wielded much influence as editors of Catholic magazines and newspapers even before the middle of the 19th century; and local societies began to federate as early as 1855 in the German Catholic Central Verein. In the 20th century, lay organizations for the most part have been brought together successively in the American Federation of Catholic Societies (founded 1901) and in the National Council of Catholic Men and the National Council of Catholic Women, which were established in 1920 and united in 1971 in the National Council of Catholic Laity. After World War II the laity in cooperation with the clergy fostered the Cana Movement and the Christian Family Movement for the application of Catholic principles to the married state and parenthood and the retreat movement for a deepening of the spiritual life amid secular occupations. In the late 1960's some laymen through organizations and publications became outspoken in criticism of ecclesiastical authorities, while others united to preserve traditional beliefs and values. Outside the church, the characteristic defensiveness of Catholics, which was reinforced by the defeat of the Democratic party's Catholic candidate for the presidency in 1928, Alfred E. Smith, amid widespread anti-Catholic bigotry, was overcome to a large extent by the election of another Catholic candidate, John F. Kennedy, in 1960. Some Catholics took a prominent part in the civil rights movement and in the antiwar movement of the 1960's and 1970's.

The Second Vatican Council (1962–65) wrought striking changes in the American Catholic church. In some respects church discipline (for example, regarding mixed marriages, fasting, and abstinence from meat) was relaxed. The liturgy, revised in form and translated into English to permit more congregational participation, was introduced everywhere but was not universally welcomed, while some radical individuals and groups began to hold unauthorized services. Friendly relations, common prayer, joint social action, and theological discussions with other Christian denominations and with Jews were promoted, especially by the Bishops' Committee for Ecumenical and Interreligious Affairs on the national level and by diocesan commissions. The permanent diaconate, to which men over thirty-five, whether married or single, may be ordained after special training, was established. The pentecostal or charismatic movement spread, particularly on college campuses, as did the cursillo movement among adults. (The cursillo is a three-day course of spiritual renewal or awakening that attempts to convey by experience a new sense of the dynamic and personalistic aspects of the Christian faith and a new insight into the nature of the Christian community.) While continuing to support their charitable institutions locally and the Catholic Relief Services (founded 1943) for overseas aid, Catholics joined in the struggle against poverty on the national level by launching the Campaign for Human Development in 1969.

In some areas, unrest and decline overshadowed the renewal intended by the Vatican Council. Although the program of studies for candidates for the priesthood was reformed, vocations decreased, so that of the 596 seminaries and novitiates with 48,992 students existing in 1965, only 402 with 19,348 students remained in 1974. Similarly, most of the religious orders of men and women rewrote their constitutions but lost numerous members and failed to enlist many new ones; the sisters dropped off most sharply from 181,421 in 1966 to 139,963 in 1974. Priests organized themselves on the diocesan level in official senates or unofficial associations, many of which formed the National Federation of Priests' Councils in 1968. Meanwhile, because of abandonment of the ministry, death, and paucity of ordinations their number fell from 59,892 in 1967 to 56,712 in 1974. More effort was made to utilize the mass media, especially through the establishment of diocesan offices for communications; but the number and circulation of Catholic newspapers and magazines declined, and many Catholic publishing houses went out of business. Finances were strained by diminished church attendance, by the expense of maintaining old parishes in the inner city while building new ones in the suburbs, and by the need to provide spiritual care for the large numbers of Spanish-speaking faithful in some places. Uncertainty about Catholic doctrine was increased; for instance, by the public protest of many teachers of theology and religion against Pope Paul VI's encyclical on artificial contraception in 1968. The number of conversions in 1974 was the second lowest since 1939, and the number of baptisms, reflecting the national birthrate, began a downward trend in 1962. For these reasons, as well as reduced immigration and multiplying defections from the faith, the rate of growth was declining. The total in 1974, nevertheless, was the highest ever recorded—48,465,438 (22.95 percent of the population of the United States)—more Roman Catholics than in any other country except Brazil and Italy. The country was divided into 32 archdioceses and 133 dioceses, having 17,784 parishes with, and 649 without, resident pastors.

[Harold A. Buetow, *Of Singular Benefit: The Story of Catholic Education in the United States;* John Tracy Ellis, *American Catholicism,* and *A Guide to American Catholic History;* John Tracy Ellis, ed., *Documents of American Catholic History;* Thomas T. McAvoy, *A History of the Catholic Church in the United States;* Hugh J. Nolan, ed., *Pastoral Letters of the American Hierarchy, 1792–1970;* Edward R. Vollmar, *The Catholic Church in America: An Historical Bibliography.*]

ROBERT TRISCO

CATLIN'S INDIAN PAINTINGS. From 1829 to 1838 George Catlin, a young, self-taught artist, roamed the trans-Mississippi wilderness, sketching and painting some 600 Indian portraits, scenes of native life, and landscapes. His expedition up the Missouri by the steamboat *Yellowstone* and downstream by canoe in the summer of 1832 with a long stay at Fort Clark produced a splendid Mandan ethnological series of portraits and ceremonies. In 1834 he accompanied the First Dragoons into Texas and the Comanche country and spent the following two seasons on the upper Mississippi and Minnesota rivers among the Sioux and other northern tribes. Catlin exhibited his collection in Europe for years after 1838 and added the 603 items of the so-called Catlin Cartoon Collection. The original collection, held as security by Joseph Harrison, Jr., for a loan extended to Catlin, was presented to the Smithsonian Institution in 1879 by Mrs. Harrison.

[George Catlin, *Letters and Notes of the Manners, Customs, and Condition of the North American Indians;* Washington Matthews, "The Catlin Collection of Indian Paintings," *Annual Report of the Board of Regents of the Smithsonian Institution* (1892).]

WILLOUGHBY M. BABCOCK

CATSKILL MOUNTAINS, a group of mountains of the Appalachian system in New York that took their name from the many wildcats roaming their hemlock-wooded slopes during the early days of New Netherland. The Dutch thought the mountains haunted. Rip Van Winkle's long sleep, after his tipsy encounter with the crew of the *Half Moon,* as told by Washington Irving, is supposed to have occurred in Schneider's Hollow in the Catskills. The mountains are now a major resort area.

[H. A. Haring, *Our Catskill Mountains.*]

A. C. FLICK

CATTLE were brought to America before 1600 by the Spanish settlers of Florida. A shipment in 1611 started cattle raising in Virginia, and the Pilgrims began with a few of the Devonshire breed in 1624. Black and white Dutch cattle were brought to New Amsterdam in 1625 and Flemish cattle to Virginia in 1621. Large yellow cattle were imported from Denmark into New Hampshire by John Mason in 1633. Although losses of cattle during the ocean voyages were heavy, they increased rapidly in all the colonies and soon were being shipped to the West Indies. Cattle grazed upon common or public lands, giving rise to brands and roundups early in American history. Since controlled breeding was impossible in these circumstances, the types of cattle became intermingled and no distinction was made between dairy and beef animals. Some dairying was done even though milk yields were small and butter and cheese were generally of poor quality. As settlers moved west, they took their cattle with them.

Interest in improved livestock, based upon English efforts, came at the close of the American Revolution when Bakewell, or improved Longhorn cattle, were imported, followed by Shorthorns, sometimes called Durhams, and Devons. Herefords were first imported by Henry Clay in 1817. Substantial numbers of Aberdeen Angus did not reach the United States from Scotland until after the Civil War. By the 1880's some of the Shorthorns were being developed as dairy stock. Meanwhile, in the 1860's, other dairy breeds had been established—the Holstein-Friesian breed, based upon stock from Holland, and the Brown Swiss. Even earlier, Ayrshires, Jerseys, and Guernseys had become known as dairy cattle.

Even as distinctive breeds of beef and dairy cattle were becoming established, a new cattle industry was rising in the Great Plains. During the Civil War longhorned cattle, descendants of Spanish stock, grew up unchecked on the Texas plains. After other attempts to market these cattle failed, John G. McCoy made arrangements to ship them from the railhead at Abilene, Kans., and in 1867 the long drives from Texas to the railheads began. By 1880 more than 4 million cattle had been driven north. Many of the cattle were held for breeding on the northern plains, giving rise to the range cattle industry, which was based on grazing on public lands and limited care by cowboys. Many of these herds were owned by eastern and foreign capitalists. Overgrazing, disastrous weather, and settlement by homesteaders brought the range cattle industry to an end after 1887.

The ranch cattle industry—based upon owned and leased land, winter pasture and feed, and controlled breeding—led to more effective beef production. The Hereford and Angus continued to dominate the beef breeds; but after World War II the Charolais, originating in France, and the Santa Gertrudis, Brangus, and Beefmaster, originating in the United States and carrying some Brahman blood, began to gain prominence. Because of high feed costs in the 1970's, some ranchers were producing grass-fed beef instead of feed-fed beef.

While dairy breeds have not changed, productivity per cow has increased greatly; dairy technology has improved; and the areas of supply have been extended. Homogenization, control of butterfat percentage, and drying have changed traditional milk production and consumption. The industry has also become subject to high standards of sanitation.

The problems of both beef and dairy interests have been dealt with by a combination of public and private agencies. State and federal departments of agriculture have enforced inspections, quarantines, and various eradication measures to combat disease. The federal government has provided a system for maintaining prices of milk. Experiment stations have conducted studies in breeding, nutrition, and comparative production. Producers themselves have organized cow-testing circuits and artificial-breeding cooperatives for dairy cattle. Associations of the leading breeders have been formed to regulate registry and to promote the interests of the group; the first herdbooks to be issued were those of Shorthorns (1846) and of Jerseys (1868).

In 1960, 24,606,000 dairy cattle produced 123,220 million pounds of milk; in 1974, 15,227,000 produced 114,857 million pounds. There were 72 million beef cattle and calves in the United States in 1960, and 112 million in 1974. Over 34 million cattle and calves were slaughtered for food in 1960 and over 37 million in 1973.

[H. M. Briggs, *Modern Breeds of Livestock;* Edward E. Dale, *The Range Cattle Industry;* James W. Thompson, *A History of Livestock Raising in the United States, 1607–1860.*]

WAYNE D. RASMUSSEN

CATTLE ASSOCIATIONS, organizations of cattlemen after 1865 on the western ranges. In scope these were local, district, sectional, and national and, like miners' associations and squatter claim clubs, functioned on the frontiers. The Colorado Cattle Growers' Association was formed as early as 1867. The Southwestern Cattle Growers' Association of Kansas and the Montana Stock Growers' Association began in 1884. The Wyoming Stock Growers' Association, organized in 1873, had a membership of 400 in 1886 from nineteen states. Its cattle, real estate, plants, and horses were valued in 1885 at $100,000,000. In 1884 the National Cattle and Horse Growers' Association was organized at St. Louis.

A president, secretary, treasurer, and executive committee were the usual officials to administer an association's affairs and to make reports at the annual or semiannual meetings. In the Wyoming Stock Growers' Association, brand inspectors supervised the sale and transportation of one million cattle in 1885. Roundup districts were laid out, rules for strays or mavericks adopted, and thousands of brands recorded. Associations cooperated with local and state officials and were alert to urge favorable legislation by Congress.

[Ora B. Peake, *The Colorado Range Cattle Industry;* Louis Pelzer, *The Cattlemen's Frontier.*]

LOUIS PELZER

CATTLE BRANDS, although traceable back to ancient Egypt, are peculiarly associated with ranching. The institution of ranching as taken over from Mexico by Texas and California included brands. They are burned on range horses also. Attempted substitutions for firebranding have proved impracticable. After all, suffering from the process is brief and thought not to be intense. The brand is a mark of ownership and every legitimate brand is recorded by either state or county, thus preventing duplication within a given territory. Identification of range stock is necessary among honest people as well as against thieves, in fenced pastures as well as on open range.

In form, brands are made up of (1) letters, (2) figures, and (3) geometric designs, symbols, or representations of objects. Combinations are endless. Because brands reduce the value of hides and also induce screw worms, they are now generally smaller and simpler than they were when cattle were less valuable. They may or may not signify something peculiar to the originator, but usually they do have a significance. A seaman turned rancher gave the anchor brand; a cowman who won a big game of poker on a hand of four sixes adopted 6666 as his brand; a rancher honored his wife Ella with "E Bar." Brands are the heraldry of the range. Reading and calling them is an art known only to range men. A straight line burned on the side of a cow may be a "Dash," a "Bar," a "Rail." The letter H set upright cannot be misread; lying on its side, however, it is "Lazy H"; in an oblique position, "Tumbling H"; joined to a segment of circle under it, "Rocking H"; separated from the segment, "H Half-Circle."

[J. Frank Dobie, *On the Open Range.*]

J. FRANK DOBIE

CATTLE DRIVES. Contrary to popular conception, long-distance cattle driving was traditional not only in Texas but elsewhere in America long before the Chisholm Trail was dreamed of. The Spaniards, the establishers of the ranching industry in the New World, drove herds northward from Mexico as far back as 1540. In the 18th century and on into the 19th the Spanish settlements in Texas derived most of their meager revenue from horses and cattle driven into

Louisiana, though such trade was usually contraband (*see* Natchitoches). Meantime in the United States, herds were sometimes driven long distances. In 1790 the boy Davy Crockett helped drive "a large stock of cattle" 400 miles from Tennessee into Virginia; twenty years later he took a drove of horses from the Tennessee River into southern North Carolina. In 1815 Timothy Flint "encountered a drove of more than 1,000 cattle and swine" being driven from the interior of Ohio to Philadelphia. The stock in the states was gentle, often managed on foot. The history of trail driving involves horses as well as cattle.

Notwithstanding antecedent examples, Texans established trail driving as a regular occupation. Before they revolted from Mexico in 1836, they had a "Beef Trail" to New Orleans. In the 1840's they extended their markets northward into Missouri—Sedalia, Baxter Springs, Springfield, and Saint Louis becoming the principal markets. During the 1850's emigration and freighting from the Missouri River westward demanded great numbers of oxen, the firm of Russell, Majors and Waddell in 1858 utilizing 40,000 oxen. Texas longhorn steers by the thousands were broken for work oxen. Herds of longhorns were driven to Chicago, and one herd at least to New York.

Under Spanish-Mexican ownership, California as well as Texas developed ranching, and during the 1830's and 1840's a limited number of cattle were trailed from there to Oregon. But the discovery of gold in California arrested for a while all development there of the cattle industry and created a high demand for outside beef. During the 1850's, although cattle were occasionally driven to California from Missouri, Arkansas, and perhaps other states, the big drives were from Texas. Steers worth $15 in Texas were selling in San Francisco for as high as $150. One Texas rancher in 1854 hired for $1,500 a famous Indian fighter to captain his herd of 1,000 steers to California; thirty-five armed men accompanied it. These drives were fraught with great danger from both Indians and desert thirst.

During the Civil War, Texas drove cattle throughout the states for the Confederate forces. At the close of the war Texas had probably 5 million cattle—and no market. Late in 1865 a few cowmen tried to find a market. In 1866 there were many drives northward without a definite destination and without much financial success; also to the old but limited New Orleans market, following mostly well-established trails to the wharves of Shreveport and Jefferson (Texas). In 1867 Joseph G. McCoy opened a regular market at Abilene, Kans. The great cattle trails, moving successively westward, were established and trail driving boomed. In 1867 the Goodnight-Loving Trail opened up New Mexico and Colorado to Texas cattle. By the tens of thousands they were soon driven into Arizona. In Texas itself cattle raising was expanding like wildfire. Caldwell, Dodge City, Ogallala, Cheyenne, and other towns became famous because of trail-driver patronage.

During the 1870's the buffaloes were virtually exterminated and the Indians of the Plains and Rockies were at the same time subjugated, penned up, and put on beef rations. An empire was left vacant. It was first occupied by Texas longhorns, driven by Texas cowboys. The course of empire in America has been west, but over much of Oklahoma, Kansas, Nebraska, the Dakotas, Wyoming, Montana, and parts of Nevada and Idaho the precursors of this movement were trail men from the South. The Long Trail extended into Canada. In the 1890's herds were still driven from the Panhandle of Texas to Montana, but trail driving virtually ended in 1895. Barbed wire, railroads, and nesters ended it. During three swift decades it had moved over ten million cattle and one million range horses, stamped the entire West with its character, given economic and personality prestige to Texas, made the longhorn the most historic brute in bovine history, glorified the cowboy over the globe, and endowed America with its most romantic tradition relating to any occupation—a peer to England's tradition of the sea.

[Andy Adams, *The Log of a Cowboy;* J. H. Cook, *Fifty Years on the Old Frontier;* E. E. Dale, *The Range Cattle Industry;* J. Evetts Haley, *Charles Goodnight;* J. M. Hunter, *The Trail Drivers of Texas;* E. S. Osgood, *The Day of the Cattleman;* W. M. Raine and Will C. Barnes, *Cattle;* Walter P. Webb, *The Great Plains.*]

J. Frank Dobie

CATTLE RUSTLERS, or cattle thieves, have been a problem wherever cattle have been run on the range on an extensive scale. Rustlers drove off cattle in herds when Texas was a republic; they now carry them off in trucks in many states. Their methods have varied from open and forceful taking of cattle in pitched battles to that of sneaking away with "dogie" or motherless calves. The former method, never prevalent, passed with the open range; the latter method is still a favorite.

Cattle are branded to distinguish their ownership, but rustlers sometimes changed the old brand by tracing over it with a hot iron to alter the design into their own brand—a practice known as "burning brands."

The taking of large and unbranded calves from the cows and then placing them in the rustler's brand was and is a favorite method. But the principal loss by 20th-century rustlers is through their use of automobiles and trucks. They kill cattle on the range and haul away the beef, and they load calves in their trucks at night and are hundreds of miles from the scene by morning.

Laws for the recording of brands for the protection of livestock owners have long been rigid. But when the laws proved insufficient, cowmen came together in posses, in vigilance committees, and finally in local and state associations to protect their herds (*see* Cattle Associations). The greatest deterrent in the 1880's was the fencing of the land with wire. That retarded the mobility of the rustler, but the automobile and the opening of roads greatly accelerated it, and there are still rustlers on the range.

J. EVETTS HALEY

CATTLE TICK FEVER, the worst plague of the western range during the trail-driving days (1865–95). It caused widespread outbreaks of what was variously known as Spanish, Texas, and tick fever and pleuro-pneumonia, although for years the cause was unknown. Many states established quarantines against the Texas longhorns. The tick has now been virtually eradicated by dipping.

J. EVETTS HALEY

CAUCUS, a term applied to a face-to-face meeting of party members in any community or legislative body for the purpose of discussing and promoting the affairs of their particular political party. There are, however, various applications of the term.

First, "caucus" means a meeting of the respective party members in a local community, for the purpose of nominating candidates for office or for electing delegates to county or state party conventions. Such a caucus is generally open to all voters in the community who identify with, or meet specified requirements as members of, the particular party involved. Such a nominating caucus was used in the colonies at least as early as 1725 and particularly in Boston, where several clubs, attended largely by ship mechanics or caulkers, endorsed candidates for office before the regular election and came to be known as caucus clubs. The gentry also organized their "parlor caucuses" for the same purpose, and this method of nomination soon became the regular practice among the emerging political parties. It was entirely unregulated by law until 1866, but abuses became so flagrant that, despite some legal regulation after that date, control by bosses came under more and more criticism. By the early 1900's the caucus had given way, first, to party nominating conventions and, finally, to the direct primary. A few states still permit the use of caucuses for nomination of candidates for local offices or selection of delegates to larger conventions.

A second application of the term "caucus" is to the party caucus in Congress, which is a meeting of the respective party members in either house to organize, determine their position on legislation, and decide other matters. The Federalists certainly held party caucuses as early as 1796; the Republicans followed suit; and the caucus was firmly established at least by 1825. In general this caucus has three purposes or functions: (1) to nominate party candidates for speaker, president pro tem, and other House or Senate offices; (2) to elect or provide for the selection of the party officers and committees, such as the floor leader, whip, Committee on Committees, Steering Committee, Policy Committee; and (3) to decide what action to take with respect to policy or legislation, either in broad terms or in detail.

Caucus decisions may be binding—that is, requiring a member to vote with his party—or merely advisory. In the case of election of party officers, a mere majority may bind; on issues of party policy, a two-thirds majority is generally required. Whether formally binding or not, caucus decisions are generally followed by the respective party members; bolting is likely to bring punishment in the form of poorer committee assignments, loss of patronage, and the like. Party leaders have varied in their use of the caucus as a means of securing cohesive party action. The caucus was notably effective as used by the Democrats during the administration of Woodrow Wilson (1913–18) and by the Republicans in the 1920's. During the next three decades a tendency developed to consider these party meetings mere conferences rather than binding caucuses; and for many years since the New Deal period the Democrats, in particular, seldom held caucuses or conferences on legislation, possibly out of concern that party disunity would be revealed. This neglect of caucus did not seem to undermine the authority of strong congressional leaders like Sam Rayburn, Lyndon Johnson, and Everett Dirksen, but other party leaders were losing too much ground to committee chairmen operating from more independent bases of power. During the late 1960's and early 1970's all the congressional caucuses or conferences underwent a revival, with much of the impetus for reform and reinvigoration coming from junior members.

A very special application of the party caucus in Congress was the congressional caucus (1796–1824), which was the earliest method of nominating presidential candidates. No provision was made in the Constitution for presidential nomination, clearly on the assumption that the presidential electors should exercise their own individual choice; and no nominations were made for the first two presidential elections, since George Washington was the choice of all. But Washington's retirement having been announced and political parties having been organized for the particular purpose of controlling the national administration, the Federalist members of Congress met in secret conference in 1796 and agreed to support John Adams and Thomas Pinckney for president and vice-president; shortly afterward the Republican members met and agreed on Thomas Jefferson and Aaron Burr. In 1800 the respective party members met again for the same purpose, and after that date the congressional caucus met openly as a presidential nominating caucus. This system became increasingly unpopular. Many thought it contrary to the spirit of the Constitution, if not actually unconstitutional, for members of Congress thus virtually to select the president. The friends of Andrew Jackson were particularly bitter against the congressional caucus, since he was never its choice, and it was denounced by mass meetings throughout the country. In 1824 only about one-fourth of the members of Congress attended, nominating William H. Crawford, who stood third in the electoral vote. The congressional caucus never met again, being succeeded in the next decade by the national convention system.

[Clarence A. Berdahl, "Some Notes on Party Membership in Congress," *American Political Science Review*, vol. 43 (1949); Robert L. Peabody, "Party Leadership Change in the United States House of Representatives," *American Political Science Review*, vol. 61 (1967); Floyd M. Riddick, *The United States Congress: Organization and Procedure*.]

CLARENCE A. BERDAHL
ROBERT L. PEABODY

CAVALRY, HORSE, a branch of the U.S. Army, used with varying effectiveness from the American Revolution through the Indian wars in the West. In 1775 and 1776 the Continental army fought with a few mounted militia commands as its only cavalry. In December 1776 the Congress authorized 3,000 light horse and the army organized four regiments of cavalry. Because these regiments were never even at half strength, George Washington recommended that they be converted to legions in 1780. The four legions and various partisan mounted units were used mainly for raiding; they were seldom employed in pitched battles. At the end of the war, all cavalry commands were discharged. During the next fifty years when regular cavalry units did exist, they were organized for short periods of time and comprised only a minute part of the army. Most states, however, possessed organized mounted militias, and these commands were employed by the army under the terms of the Militia Act of 1792.

Indian trouble along the western frontier revived the need for federal horse soldiers. In 1832 Congress passed "An Act to Authorize the President to Raise Mounted Volunteers for the Defense of the Frontier." Organized along the lines of emergency state militia, the six Mounted Volunteer Ranger companies showed the value of using mounted government troops in the West but also proved that a more efficient, less expensive force was needed. With little or no training or discipline, the volunteers had cost the government almost $154,000 more than a regiment of dragoons; the army needed a more permanent organization. On Mar. 2, 1833, Congress replaced the Mounted Rangers with the Regiment of United States Dragoons, a ten-company force mounted for speed but trained to fight both mounted and dismounted. In May 1836 the Second Regiment of Dragoons was formed to fight in the Seminole War.

Ten years later, after the commencement of the Mexican War, Congress augmented the two dragoon regiments with the Regiment of Mounted Riflemen; a third dragoon regiment; and several voluntary commands. The only new organization to escape the standard army reductions at the conclusion of hostilities was the Mounted Riflemen. In 1855 the government enlarged the mounted wing by two additional regiments—the First Cavalry and the Second Cavalry. According to the general orders, these new regiments were to be a distinct, separate arm of the army. Mounted forces from 1855 until 1861 were divided into dragoons, mounted riflemen, and cavalrymen.

During the Civil War the U.S. Cavalry evolved into an efficient organization. In August 1861 the army redesignated the regular horse regiments as cavalry, renumbering them one through six according to each organization's seniority. The First Dragoons thereupon became the First Cavalry. Not until the Confederate cavalry corps demonstrated the efficiency of mass tactics and reconnaissances, however, did the Union cavalry begin to imitate the southern horse soldiers. By the end of the war, the cavalry corps had demonstrated devastating effectiveness. After the Civil War, the six regiments were not able to perform all duties assigned. Consequently, in July 1866 Congress authorized four additional regiments—the Seventh, Eighth, Ninth, and Tenth. The new regiments increased the number of cavalry troops from 448 to 630 and the total manpower from 39,273 to 54,302. The Ninth and Tenth Cavalry represented a departure from past traditions. These regiments were manned by black enlisted men and noncommissioned officers commanded by white officers (*see* Black Cavalry in the West). During the western Indian wars, the cavalry performed adequately under adverse conditions. Much of the time there were too few troops for so vast a region and such determined foes; a cost-conscious Congress rarely provided adequate support.

After the conclusion of the Indian wars in the early 1890's, the horse cavalry declined in importance. Some troops served as infantry during the Spanish-American War, and the cavalry was revived briefly during Gen. John Pershing's punitive expedition into Mexico. But during World War I only four regiments were sent to France, after which the mechanization of armies made the horse cavalry obsolete.

[James M. Merrill, *Spurs to Glory: The Story of the United States Cavalry;* Francis Paul Prucha, *The Sword of the Republic: The United States Army on the Frontier, 1783–1846;* Robert M. Utley, *Frontiersmen in Blue: The United States Army and the Indian, 1848–1865,* and *Frontier Regulars: The United States Army and the Indian, 1866–1891.*]

EMMETT M. ESSIN III

CAVALRY, MECHANIZED. *See* **Armored Vehicles.**

CAVE-IN-ROCK, a cave in Hardin County, Ill., on the Ohio River, about thirty miles below the mouth of the Wabash. In pioneer times it was used as an inn patronized by flatboatmen. It often served as a rendezvous for outlaws who robbed flatboats going down the river. Among its early occupants were Sam Mason and his gang of river pirates and highwaymen and the bloodthirsty Harpe brothers.

[Otto A. Rothert, *The Outlaws of Cave-in-Rock.*]

OTTO A. ROTHERT

CAYUSE WAR (1847–50). In 1836 a Presbyterian mission was established among the Cayuse Indians by the medical missionary Marcus Whitman at Waiilatpu, near the present city of Walla Walla in southeastern Washington. By 1842 the Indians had become hostile and apprehensive at the increasing numbers of white immigrants in the area. During the winter of 1846–47 a large part of the Cayuse tribe died in a measles epidemic. Apparently blaming the missionaries for the catastrophe, the Cayuse attacked and destroyed the mission, killing Whitman, his wife, and twelve others. A military expedition comprising both regular troops and volunteers pursued the Cayuse, who fled to the mountains. There were no decisive engagements, and the struggle dragged on until the spring of 1850, when in order to make peace five Cayuse men gave themselves up, thus ending the war. The five were later tried and hanged.

[Clifford M. Drury, *Marcus M. Whitman, M.D., Pioneer and Martyr;* Ray M. Glassley, *Indian Wars of the Pacific Northwest;* Alvin M. Josephy, *The Nez Perce Indians and the Opening of the Northwest;* Frances Fuller Victor, *The Early Indian Wars of Oregon.*]

KENNETH M. STEWART

CEDAR CREEK, BATTLE OF (Oct. 19, 1864). Following the Battle of Fisher's Hill, Va., the Union and Confederate armies marched up and down the Shenandoah Valley (*see* Shenandoah Campaign), the former destroying property and crops as it went. Union Gen. Philip H. Sheridan finally halted his army across Cedar Creek, east of Fisher's Hill. Shortly afterward he went to Washington. The Confederate army unexpectedly attacked and after defeating the Union troops halted unnecessarily. The delay was fatal. Returning from Washington, Sheridan rode (*see* Sheridan's Ride) from Winchester, twenty miles away, rallied his men, and led them back into battle. The Confederates were defeated, suffering heavy losses. A Confederate victory was turned into a rout. Thereafter, both armies were transferred to Richmond.

[John B. Gordon, *Reminiscences of the Civil War;* R. U. Johnson and C. C. Buel, eds., *Battles and Leaders of the Civil War.*]

THOMAS ROBSON HAY

CEDAR MOUNTAIN, BATTLE OF (Aug. 9, 1862), the first encounter in the Second Bull Run campaign. Union Gen. John Pope's advance under Nathaniel Banks at Cedar Run, near Culpeper, Va., was opposed by Gen. T. J. Jackson's Confederate troops, under Richard S. Ewell and William H. Winder. Though outnumbered, Banks advanced, but, after bitter fighting, his troops were repulsed everywhere. Following a brief pursuit Jackson withdrew to join Gen. Robert E. Lee's army. The Confederates, numbering over 20,000, lost about 1,300; the Union troops, numbering about 8,000, lost nearly 2,400.

[R. U. Johnson and C. C. Buel, eds., *Battles and Leaders of the Civil War*.]

THOMAS ROBSON HAY

CÉLORON'S LEAD PLATES, markers used by the French in the French-English rivalry over the Ohio Valley. By 1749 the English were pressing across the Alleghenies into the rich valley beyond the mountains. Unable to make reply in kind, the governor of New France sent an army, led by Pierre Joseph Céloron, to enforce its authority on the Ohio. Céloron descended the river as far as the Great Miami, where he turned northward toward Detroit. En route, in frequent councils, he urged the Indians to cease all intercourse with the English and warned the English to leave the country. At strategic points along the Ohio, lead plates were planted, bearing an inscription reciting the French monarch's title to the country. One of them was found prior to 1821 at Marietta, Ohio, and is now owned by the American Antiquarian Society. Another plate was found at Point Pleasant, W.Va., and since 1849 has belonged to the Virginia Historical Society at Richmond. Both the English and the Indians ignored the admonitions of Céloron; the ownership of the Ohio Valley remained to be determined by the French and Indian War.

[M. M. Quaife, "Pierre Joseph Céloron," *Burton Historical Collection* Leaflet, VII.]

M. M. QUAIFE

CEMENT. In newly discovered lands adventurers seek gold; colonists seek limestone to make cement. American colonists made their first dwellings of logs, with log fireplaces and chimneys plastered inside, caulked outside, with mud or clay. To replace these the first bricks were imported. Brick masonry requires mortar; mortar requires cement, which was first made of lime burned from oyster shells. In 1662 limestone was found at Providence, R.I., and manufacture of "stone" lime began. Some limes made better cement than others, but not until 1791 did John Smeaton, English engineer, establish the fact that argillaceous (silica and alumina) impurity gave lime improved cementing value. Burning such limestones made hydraulic lime—a cement that hardens under water. Some of the colonial limes unwittingly may have been hydraulic, but it was after the beginning of the country's first major public works, the Erie Canal, 1817, that American engineers learned to make and use a true hydraulic cement (one that had to be pulverized after burning to slake, or react with water). The first masonry on the Erie Canal was contracted to be done with common quick lime; when it failed to slake a local experimenter pulverized some and discovered a "natural" cement, that is, one made from natural rock. Canvass White, subsequently chief engineer of the Erie Canal, pursued investigations, perfected manufacture and use, obtained a patent, and is credited with being the father of the American cement industry. During the canal and later railway building era, demand rapidly increased and suitable cement rocks were discovered in many localities: 1818, Fayetteville, N.Y.; 1828, Rosendale, N.Y.; 1829, Louisville, Ky.; 1836, Cumberland, Md.; 1838, Utica, Ill.; 1850, Siegfried's Bridge (Coplay), Pa.; 1875, Milwaukee, Wis.; 1883, Mankato, Minn. Cement made at Rosendale, N.Y., was the most famous; that at Coplay, Pa., the most significant, because it became the first American Portland cement. The name Portland cement was given by an English bricklayer, Joseph Aspdin, in 1824, to a cement made by burning and pulverizing briquets of an artificial mixture of limestone (chalk) and clay, because the hardened cement resembled a well-known building stone from the Isle of Portland. Manufacture of Portland cement developed abroad at the same time the manufacture of natural cements was spreading in America. Soon after the Civil War, Portland cements, because of their more dependable qualities, began to be imported. Manufacture was started at Coplay, Pa., about 1870, by David O. Saylor, by selecting from his natural cement rock that was approximately of the same composition as the Portland cement artificial mixture. The Lehigh Valley around Coplay contained many similar deposits, and until 1907 this locality produced annually half (at first much more) of all the cement made in the United States. By 1900 the practice of grinding together ordinary limestone and clay, burning or calcining the mixture in rotary kilns, and pulverizing the burned clinker had become so well known that the Portland cement industry spread rapidly to all parts of the country, and by 1971 there were 174 plants across the country. Production increased from 350,000 barrels in 1890 to 410 million barrels in 1971. At first cement was used only for mortar in brick and stone masonry. Gradually mixtures of cement, sand, stone, or gravel (aggregates) with water (known as concrete), poured into temporary forms where it hardened into a kind of conglomerate rock, came to be substituted for brick and stone, particularly for massive work like bridge abutments, piers, dams, and foundations.

[Robert W. Leslie, *History of the Portland Cement Industry in the United States*.]

NATHAN C. ROCKWOOD

CEMETERIES, NATIONAL. Before the Civil War, military dead were usually interred in cemetery plots at the post on which the man's unit was stationed. The Mexican War established the precedent of burying American dead on foreign soil, when Americans were buried in Mexico City. The Civil War, with its national army concepts, large concentrations of troops, and horrendous casualties, demonstrated the need for more and better military burial procedures. By War Department General Order 75 (1861), formal provisions for recording burials were established for the first time; and General Order 33 (1862) directed commanders to "lay off plots . . . near every battlefield" for burying the dead. Also in 1862, Congress authorized the acquisition of land for national cemeteries; by year's end fourteen had been opened. Basically, two types were developed: those near battlefields and those near major troop concentration areas, such as at Arlington, Va. (established in 1864).

After the Spanish-American War, Congress authorized the return of remains for burial in the United States at government expense if the next of kin desired it rather than burial overseas. Of Americans killed in World War I, approximately 40 percent were buried abroad. Only 12.5 percent of the number returned were interred in national cemeteries. Beginning in 1930, twenty-four cemeteries were transferred from the War Department to the Veterans Administration and, after 1933, thirteen more were given over to the Department of the Interior. After World War II, approximately three-fifths of the 281,000 Americans killed were returned to the United States, 37,000 of them to be interred in national cemeteries. By 1951, all permanent overseas cemeteries had been placed under the control of the American Battle Monuments Commission.

In 1974 the United States had 115 national cemeteries, battle monuments, and memorials. Eligibility requirements for interment have varied over the years, but now generally include members and former members of the armed forces; their spouses and minor children; and, in some instances, officers of the Coast and Geodetic Survey and the Public Health Service.

[B. C. Mossman and M. W. Stark, *The Last Salute: Civil and Military Funerals, 1921–1969.*]

JOHN E. JESSUP, JR.

CENSORSHIP. The Press. Censorship of the printed word has been the focus of legal, political, and social conflict throughout American history. In the colonial and early national periods, censorship was usually politically motivated. In the famous (and unsuccessful) prosecution of John Peter Zenger, printer of the *New York Weekly Journal,* in 1735, the charge was "seditious libel," the legal phrase for the crime of criticizing the government. And despite the First Amendment to the U.S. Constitution ("Congress shall make no law . . . abridging freedom of speech, or of the press"), both Federalists and Republicans prosecuted opposition newspaper editors for seditious libel in the early national period. In 1836, by contrast, Congress rejected, partly on grounds of freedom of the press, President Andrew Jackson's efforts to bar "incendiary" abolitionist publications from the mails. The major 20th-century outbreak of political censorship came under the war-inspired espionage and sedition laws of 1917–18. In a case arising from this legislation (*Schenck* v. *United States,* 1919), Supreme Court Justice Oliver Wendell Holmes, Jr., enunciated the "clear and present danger" test subsequently used by civil liberties lawyers to restrict sharply the government's powers of political censorship.

Since the mid-19th century, press censorship has more typically arisen from moral rather than political considerations. In the turbulent post–Civil War era, the supposed moral threat of "obscene" books and magazines aroused great alarm; and in 1873 the New York Society for the Suppression of Vice and the New England Watch and Ward Society were founded to combat these evils. In that year, spurred by Anthony Comstock of the New York antivice group, Congress outlawed the mailing of "obscene," "lewd," or "lascivious" publications. In succeeding years, many states enacted legislation against the sale of such works. Under these laws, federal postal and customs officials, local magistrates, and private antivice champions like Comstock suppressed a wide range of written work, including hard-core pornography; erotic classics (Boccaccio, Ovid, Rabelais); literature dealing with marriage reform, birth control, or abortion; and occasional works by established contemporary authors. These censorship activities, reflecting the genteel moral code of the day, generally won at least tacit support from major publishers, philanthropists, social workers, and the social elites of various American cities.

From the outset, however, the censors had their critics—for example, Theodore Schroeder, author of *"Obscene" Literature and Constitutional Law* (1911)—and with the new literary realism and the decline of the genteel code in the 1920's, the obscenity laws came under increasing challenge. A succession of novels attacked by Comstock's successor John S. Sumner were cleared in the New York courts, while in Boston the Watch and Ward Society met defeat in its efforts to suppress H. L. Mencken's *American Mercury* magazine (1926) and in other cases.

The issue of federal censorship emerged sharply in 1929–30, during debate over the Smoot-Hawley tariff, when Sen. Bronson M. Cutting of New Mexico attacked the censorship powers of the U.S. customs service—powers dating from 1842. Owing to Cutting's efforts, the new tariff law provided that works should be judged as a whole rather than on isolated passages, that recognized classics should be treated in a special category, and that court proceedings should replace purely administrative censorship. It was under this liberalized procedure that federal district judge John M. Woolsey, in a landmark decision of 1933, permitted the importation of James Joyce's hitherto-banned *Ulysses*.

Postal censorship efforts continued against such works as Erskine Caldwell's *God's Little Acre* (1933) and Lillian Smith's *Strange Fruit* (1944). The postal authorities were supported in these activities by Roman Catholic groups such as the National Organization for Decent Literature, which had largely supplanted the Protestant-dominated vice societies in spearheading the antiobscenity cause. In spite of this support, many of the post office rulings were reversed in the courts, most notably in the *Esquire* magazine case of 1943.

The U.S. Supreme Court first addressed itself to the obscenity issue in the *Roth* v. *United States* decision of 1957, which set forth a legal definition of obscenity considerably more permissive than those long accepted in this area of constitutional law. "The test of obscenity," declared the Court, "is whether to the average person, applying contemporary community standards, the dominant theme of the material appeals to prurient interest." Under this new standard, the Supreme Court cleared D. H. Lawrence's *Lady Chatterley's Lover* in 1960, and lower courts generally adopted a more lenient stance.

Although the broad trend since the 1920's was toward a decline in censorship, periodic upswings occurred, particularly in times of rapidly changing social and sexual mores. The decade of the 1960's was such a time. In 1966 the Supreme Court upheld the conviction and prison sentence of Ralph Ginzburg, publisher of *Eros* magazine, noting particularly his advertisements, appealing "to the prurient interests." In the Postal Act of 1967, Congress provided for criminal proceedings against mailers of "erotically arousing" or "sexually provocative" advertisements who continue to mail to any citizens who have formally indicated to the postal authorities their desire not to receive such unsolicited material. In 1973, under Chief Justice Warren Burger, the Supreme Court continued its tougher line on the obscenity issue, holding five to four that "contemporary community standards" may be local rather than national and that in the absence of clear evidence pro or con, lawmakers and the courts have the right to assume a causal connection between pornography and antisocial behavior. Commenting editorially on this decision, the *New York Times* declared that it would "make every local community and every state the arbiter of acceptability, thereby adjusting all sex-related literary, artistic, and entertainment productions to the lowest common denominator of toleration."

Motion Pictures, Radio, and Television. The commercial debut of Thomas Edison's "Kinetoscope" in 1894 launched not only a revolution in popular entertainment but also a fresh chapter in the long history of censorship. As the popularity of motion pictures spread, so did efforts to regulate the new medium, and within a few decades numerous cities and states had established licensing boards empowered to ban or cut any film deemed obscene, immoral, or otherwise objectionable. In 1915 the Supreme Court upheld such prior-restraint censorship, holding that the exhibition of motion pictures was "a business pure and simple" and not subject to First Amendment protection. In 1952, overturning a New York ban on *The Miracle* (an Italian film denounced as sacrilegious by the Roman Catholic hierarchy), the Supreme Court reversed its 1915 position and declared motion pictures "a significant medium for the communication of ideas" and thus fully shielded by the First Amendment. Several subsequent decisions by the high court imposed increasingly stringent procedural restraints on the dwindling number of state and municipal licensing boards. In June 1973, a more conservatively inclined Supreme Court majority reopened the censorship door a bit, ruling that a movie (or book or periodical) that offended local community standards might legitimately be banned in that area, even if freely circulated elsewhere.

Customs authorities, local police, and various private organizations have also played a role in movie censorship. In 1968, for example, the Bureau of Customs seized a Swedish film, *I Am Curious (Yellow)*, only to have its action reversed in federal court. By contrast, when the New York City police in 1972 closed a theater exhibiting an explicit sex film called *Deep Throat,* the suppression was upheld in a subsequent criminal court trial. Of the private organizations, the most influential is the National Catholic Office for Motion Pictures (formerly the Legion of Decency) founded in 1934 by the American Catholic bishops. The film ratings of this body are highly influential, and producers sometimes consult with it during the filming and editing process, seeking to avoid a damaging rating.

Over the years the movie industry responded to censorship threats with various self-regulatory schemes. The first of these, the National Board of Review, organized with industry support in 1909 to preview and evaluate films, soon lost credibility. In 1922, reacting to the establishment of a movie licensing board in New York State and the rise of censorship pressures elsewhere, the industry trade association, the Motion Picture Producers and Distributors of America, appointed former Postmaster General Will H. Hays as its president, with a mandate to oversee the moral tone of the movies. After considerable delay the "Hays Office" in 1930 promulgated a highly detailed, but initially ineffective, production code. Four years later, under continued censorship and boycott threats (especially from the Legion of Decency), the Production Code Administration, a powerful and semiautonomous enforcement agency, was established under Joseph I. Breen. As the movie industry became less monolithic and public attitudes more permissive, the code gradually lost effectiveness as a means of self-regulation. In 1968, to forestall legislative moves toward a mandatory film classification system and to provide a guide to theater owners and patrons, the industry began assigning each movie a rating indicating something of its character and appropriateness for youth. By the late 1970's, although the broad drift was clearly toward greater tolerance as to what might be viewed—at least by adults—within the darkened confines of a movie theater, censorship was still a far from negligible factor.

The emergence of radio in the 1920's and television in the 1950's posed quite a different set of issues, since both utilize a limited range of electronic frequencies and are thus necessarily subject to public licensing and regulation. In 1927 Congress established the Federal Radio Commission (FRC); seven years later, in the Communications Act of 1934, the FRC was transformed into the Federal Communications Commission (FCC), with licensing and regulatory power over both radio and television broadcasting. While given a broad mandate to serve "the public interest, convenience, or necessity," the new agency was subjected to this explicit proviso: "Nothing in this Act shall be understood or construed to give the Federal Communications Commission the power of censorship." Aside from insisting that broadcasters present both sides of controversial issues, the FCC during its first thirty-five years generally construed its regulatory power quite narrowly. Under the chairmanship of Dean Burch, a former head of the Republican National Committee who took office in 1969, it moved in a more activist direction. In 1971 the commission narrowly rejected Burch's proposal to reprimand the Columbia Broadcasting System (CBS) television network for an allegedly biased documentary on military spending, and in 1973 the FCC launched an investigation of obscenity in the electronic media—especially in the popular "call-in" radio shows. In 1969 Vice President Spiro T. Agnew attacked the network news agencies as "a tiny and closed fraternity of privileged men," and in 1972 the head of the White House Telecommunications Policy Office proposed that the FCC licensing process involve more scrutiny of program content. The forced resignation of President Richard M. Nixon in 1974 terminated what had seemed to many to be a concerted move toward increased government influence in shaping the content of radio and television broadcasting.

On other fronts, the Federal Trade Commission exercises a regulatory function in the area of radio and television advertising, and all states but Texas and Colorado have prohibited broadcasts of court proceedings. More typically, commercial broadcasting, as a private profitmaking enterprise, has been shaped not by censorship or government control but by a complex set of pressures rooted in considerations of the marketplace and in the industry's own assessment of the public taste. Codified in the Television Code of the National Association of Broadcasters (an organization founded in 1922), this unwillingness to flaunt conventional standards of propriety has influenced countless programming decisions, most notoriously in the 1969 CBS cancellation of "The Smothers Brothers," a highly popular, but iconoclastic and sometimes risqué, comedy show.

[Erik Barnouw, *A Tower in Babel: A History of Broadcasting in the United States;* Fred W. Friendly, *Due to Circumstances Beyond Our Control;* William A. Hachten, *The Supreme Court on Freedom of the Press;* H. L. Nelson, ed., *Freedom of the Press From Hamilton to the Warren Court;* J. C. N. Paul and M. L. Swartz, *Federal Censorship;* Richard S. Randall, *Censorship of the Movies;* Charles Rembar, *The End of Obscenity.*]

PAUL S. BOYER

CENSORSHIP, MILITARY. Although occasional instances of military censorship—for example, Gen. Andrew Jackson's jailing in 1815 of a New Orleans newspaper editor who published military information—took place before the Civil War, it was not until the Civil War that systematic military censorship began. Aimed at suppressing prosouthern sentiments in the press and keeping vital military information from the enemy, censorship in the Civil War, vigorously enforced by Secretary of War Edwin Stanton, included army control of telegraph lines; post office confiscation of disloyal newspapers; imprisonment of newspaper editors; and confiscation and sale of their presses. During the Spanish-American War the slight attempts at controlling the press by exclusion from cable terminals in Florida were easily foiled by the use of dispatch boats carrying uncensored messages from Cuba.

Censorship in World War I, like that in World War II, reflected limited prewar planning. In World War I the strongest military and civil censorship to date in America was to be seen in the Espionage Act of June 1915, certain executive orders issued by President Woodrow Wilson, and voluntary suppression of military information by the press—watched over by the (George) Creel Committee, but not consistently honored. Field military censorship included some examination of outgoing mail sent by troops in France and control of correspondents' dispatches sent from the front, although occasionally uncensored material did get into print. A censorship board in the United States controlled telephone, telegraph, and overseas cables.

By late evening of Dec. 7, 1941, the day the United States entered World War II, censorship of outgoing cables was executed by the navy in New York City, and within days, a combination of voluntary and official censorship of military information was operating. On Dec. 18, 1941, the Office of Censorship was established by law with Byron Price, formerly of the Associated Press, as its head. Radio, land lines, and overseas cables became subject to censorship, and censorship codes for press and radio were created and enforced. Overseas censorship imposed on mail and press communications during this war was the strongest in American history; all mail and dispatches were examined and censored. To protect the secrecy of D-Day, even diplomatic correspondence was censored in London.

Mail was not screened in the Korean War, although press dispatches from the combat zone were censored. During the war in Vietnam there was no mail or press censorship, and information was protected from press disclosure only by security regulations preventing its release to the press.

[Departments of the Army, Navy, and Air Force, *Field Press Censorship;* Robert E. Summers et al., *Wartime Censorship of Press and Radio, 1942.*]

JOHN ALBRIGHT

CENSUS, U.S. BUREAU OF THE, administers Section 2 of Article I of the U.S. Constitution, which provides for a decennial census to apportion the House of Representatives. With the progressive delegation over the years of many other data-gathering functions, the bureau has become the nation's leading producer of basic statistical sources.

The first census of 1790 could have been limited to statewide aggregates of population, differentiating only between slaves and free persons and omitting Indians, who did not pay taxes. Nevertheless, the census takers were required to list heads of families; the number of persons in each household; and, for an estimate of military or industrial manpower, the number of free white males at least sixteen years old. Thus, from the first enumeration the legislative and executive branches considered plans for using the constitutional mandate to obtain data that were deemed in the national interest. By 1850 Congress required details about every inhabitant except untaxed Indians.

Congress, under the economic stress of the Napoleonic Wars, provided as a part of the census of 1810 for the publication of detailed data about domestic manufactures—the first major expansion beyond population statistics. On the basis of recommendations by Rep. Adam Seybert of Pennsylvania, Secretary of State John Quincy Adams developed a questionnaire for manufacturing establishments as part of the census of 1820. In 1830 this questionnaire was omitted because Adams had expressed dissatisfaction with the quality of the 1820 returns. Ten years later social statistics (occupations, dependent persons, literacy, and schools) and data about economic institutions (manufacturing, mining, agriculture, and commerce) were included in the census. The superintendent of the 1870 census, Gen. Francis Amasa Walker—a leading economist, statistician, and administrator—directed the production of the *Statistical Atlas* (1874), which includes statistical charts, graphic illustrations of census data, and maps of rainfall, temperature, geology, and economic activities.

The tenth census was a comprehensive centennial survey planned originally for 1875 by Walker with the collaboration of Rep. James A. Garfield. It became, instead, the 1880 census, which included, for the first time, the untaxed Indians. The personal data comprised names, ages, places of birth of the individuals and their parents, marital status, health, attendance at school, literacy, and occupation. Related social statistics included detailed data about dependent and delinquent classes, the growth of cities, morbidity and mortality, police departments, benevolent and educational organizations, and religious bodies. Highly qualified special agents prepared reports on vital statistics, agriculture, major industries (manufacturing, mining, insurance, lumbering, transportation, and publishing), the use of power and machinery in industry, wages and prices, the factory system, and strikes and lockouts. The twenty-two volumes of special studies that resulted were supplements to the statistical *Compendium of the Tenth Census (June 1, 1880)*. They included historical essays and analyses of the quantitative data by such prominent public figures as the geologists John Wesley Powell, Clarence King, and Raphael Pumpelly; manufacturer-economist Edward Atkinson; and zoologist Spencer F. Baird. The Census Office spent eight years compiling the statistical and analytical reports for 1880. The 1890 census was of comparable magnitude, but the reports were completed sooner with the aid of Herman Hollerith's punched cards and electrical tabulating machine.

The Census Office abandoned the comprehensive inventory method in 1900, providing instead for the collection of nonpopulation data during the intercensal decennial period. Service and distributive trades were added to the censuses in 1929 and transportation companies in 1963. Housing questionnaires were included with the population inquiries for the census of 1940. Since the late 1930's the Bureau of the Census has developed sampling techniques to estimate and publish current demographic and economic data. In 1941 the bureau was made responsible for the statistics on foreign trade that have been recorded since 1789. The bureau conducts, in addition, special surveys for other federal agencies.

During the 19th century Congress delegated responsibility for the census reports successively to the president, State Department, and Department of the Interior. From 1850 to 1900 a superintendent of the census was appointed under the secretary of the interior to direct each census. Until 1880 U.S. marshals supervised operations and appointed assistants to obtain the census information. The act for the 1880 census gave the superintendent authority to direct the census and to recruit and organize a field staff of supervisors and enumerators. An act of Mar. 6, 1902, provided for a permanent census office within the Interior Department. This office, headed by a director, was transferred the following year to the newly established Department of Commerce and Labor, where it later became known as the Bureau of the Census. (In 1913 the bureau was included in the separate Department of Commerce.) The activities of the bureau continued to expand; several associate directors of the bureau are active in planning and directing research in statistical methodology and standards, demographic and housing censuses, economic censuses and surveys, and data-processing plans and operations.

Census records have become primary sources for demographic and social research and genealogy. Because the published returns before 1850 were inaccurate and incomplete, it is preferable to use the original returns for this period. The separate returns for the 1810 census of manufactures, submitted to the Treasury Department and analyzed by political economist Tench Coxe, have been lost; but the original notes by several assistant marshals appear on many population schedules. Except for a fragment, returns for the 1890 census were lost in a fire. Later population schedules were converted to microfilm and the originals destroyed. Access to these microfilm copies for the 20th century has been limited to employees of the bureau to protect private information. To meet the increasing demands for data at the lowest level of aggregation, the bureau began publishing details about "small" geographic areas—usually counties and metropolitan areas but also census tracts and even blocks within a city. These data were made available in printed, machine-readable form or in the form of special tabulations paid for by the user. The extensive manuscript and the published cartographic output of the bureau are also available to researchers.

[National Archives, *Preliminary Inventory of the Records of the Bureau of the Census;* U.S. Bureau of the Census,

Historical Statistics of the United States, Colonial Times to 1957 (and continuation to 1962); U.S. Bureau of the Census and Library of Congress, *Catalog of United States Census Publications, 1790–1945.*]

MEYER H. FISHBEIN

CENT. The U.S. cent came from the adoption of the dollar as the unit and its division decimally. Colonial accounts were kept in pounds, shillings, and pence, but the circulation was mostly Spanish dollars. A privately issued coin dated 1783 (called the Washington cent) had the word "cent" on it. Vermont and Connecticut in 1785 coined cents, but Massachusetts, in 1786, was the first state to have the word on its coin. The Fugio, or Franklin, cent in 1787 was the first cent issued under the authority of the United States. Cents were minted regularly by the federal government starting with 1793.

[Neil Carothers, *Fractional Money.*]

JAMES D. MAGEE

CENTENNIAL EXPOSITION, celebrating the one hundredth anniversary of the Declaration of Independence, held in Philadelphia in 1876, was the first great international exposition held in America. It was ten years in the planning and building; it covered more than 450 acres in Fairmount Park; its total cost was more than $11 million. Thirty-seven foreign nations constructed pavilions, many in their native architectural styles. The 167 buildings of the exposition housed more than 30,000 exhibitors from 50 nations. The gates were opened on May 10, and during the 159 days that followed there were 8,004,274 cash admissions. There were seven principal divisions in the exposition: mining and metallurgy, manufactured products, science and education, fine arts, machinery, agriculture, and horticulture. The Woman's Building, an innovation in expositions, demonstrated the relative emancipation of women in America.

There was no midway or similar amusement, for nothing could have competed with the intense public interest in the working models of many new machines and processes. The architecture was confused, but impressive. The influence of various foreign exhibits evoked a new interest in interior decoration in America. In this exposition the world, for the first time, saw industrial America on display. Americans realized that the machine age had arrived and that their country was, in many ways, at last coming of age. The centennial exposition was honest, homely, and revealing; it provided an immense stimulus to the growing aesthetic, social, and industrial consciousness of America.

[Dee Brown, *The Year of the Century: 1876.*]

FRANK MONAGHAN

CENTINEL OF THE NORTH-WESTERN TERRITORY, published in Cincinnati by William Maxwell, the first newspaper in the Northwest Territory. It appeared Nov. 9, 1793, and weekly thereafter until June 1796, when it was merged with *Freeman's Journal.* Subscription was "250 cents" per annum, and 7 cents a single copy. The motto of the *Centinel,* "Open to all Parties—but influenced by none," expressed the publisher's aims: to afford an isolated community a medium to make known its varied wants and to record local happenings, as well as those of the outside world. A complete file is in the library of the Cincinnati Historical Society.

BEVERLEY W. BOND, JR.

CENTRAL AMERICAN COURT OF JUSTICE, a tribunal established in 1907 by the five Central American republics (Costa Rica, El Salvador, Guatemala, Honduras, and Nicaragua) in accordance with a treaty signed at the Central American Peace Conference held in Washington in 1907 under the sponsorship of the United States and Mexico. It consisted of five judges, one selected by each signatory state. It was given jurisdiction over all controversies arising among the signatories regarding which a diplomatic understanding could not be reached. The court was also authorized to hear cases of an international character brought by a citizen of one of the five republics against one of the other governments. The court was installed at Cartago, Costa Rica, on May 25, 1908. In 1916 and 1917 suits were brought in the court by Costa Rica and Salvador to prevent Nicaragua from carrying out the terms of the Bryan-Chamorro Treaty of 1914 between the United States and Nicaragua regarding a canal route. The court decided both cases against Nicaragua. Nicaragua refused to accept the decision and the United States failed to support the court, thus putting the tribunal in a futile position. When the period of ten years for which the court was established expired in 1918 nothing was done to renew it, and the court was dissolved.

[M. O. Hudson, *The Permanent Court of International Justice.*]

BENJAMIN H. WILLIAMS

CENTRAL INTELLIGENCE AGENCY. The surprise Japanese attack on Pearl Harbor in December 1941 revealed there were grave shortcomings in U.S. intelligence operations. Steps were taken to improve this situation in World War II, especially through the establishment of the Office of Strategic Services (OSS). After the war, President Harry S. Truman determined that he was receiving contradictory and uncoordinated intelligence information from many separate government sources. Therefore, by an executive directive of Jan. 22, 1946, he established the Central Intelligence Group (CIG), whose job was to coordinate, correlate, evaluate, and disseminate intelligence information relating to the national security. It was also to perform such other functions related to foreign intelligence activities as it might be assigned. In 1947 the National Security Act was passed by Congress, establishing the Central Intelligence Agency (CIA) under the direction of the National Security Council. Its functions, similar to those of the CIG, were described in broad terms in the act but detailed by the National Security Council within the terms of the act. They include the clandestine collection of foreign intelligence information.

The act also established the position of director of central intelligence. The director is the president's principal adviser on foreign intelligence and heads the U.S. Intelligence Board, which is composed of the heads of the principal intelligence agencies of the government. He also heads the CIA. The director is responsible for the production of national intelligence estimates and other intelligence papers required for the formulation of national security policy. The CIA does not make policy; it provides evaluated factual data on the basis of which the senior policymakers of the government may make informed decisions. The director of central intelligence, as head of the intelligence community (that is, all the foreign intelligence components of the government), is also charged with the responsibility of preparing an annual consolidated program budget to insure coordinated use of national intelligence resources.

The National Security Act specifically places on the director of central intelligence the responsibility of protecting intelligence sources and methods from unauthorized disclosure. It is the protection of sources and methods that requires secrecy, lest such a source or method be lost forever through inadvertent disclosure. The act further provides that the CIA shall have no police powers or internal security functions. The latter are the province of the Federal Bureau of Investigation; the CIA operates only in the field of foreign intelligence.

Since the 1950's, beginning with the development of the high-altitude U-2 reconnaissance aircraft, highly advanced scientific and technical methods for the collection of intelligence have been developed and utilized. These systems have enabled the United States to negotiate and monitor adherence to agreements such as the Nuclear Test Ban Treaty and the Strategic Arms Limitation Treaty.

The activities of the CIA are monitored by special subcommittees of the Armed Services and Appropriations committees of the Senate and the House of Representatives. Press stories on the role of the CIA in covert political actions overseas have increased public debate on U.S. involvement in such activities. In recognition of widening congressional interest in the CIA, there have been adjustments in both houses in the composition of the structure of the committees appointed to oversee the CIA.

[A. W. Dulles, *The Craft of Intelligence;* L. B. Kirkpatrick, *The U.S. Intelligence Community.*]

CENTRALIZATION. In national affairs, centralization usually refers to the growing concentration of authority in the federal government over fields formerly occupied in part, or not at all, by the state governments. Centralizing tendencies have been most conspicuous since the adoption of the Fourteenth Amendment, which gave a veto upon state legislative acts to the federal courts and thus placed in the hands of the courts the protection of fundamental property rights. But centralization has been stimulated mainly through congressional legislation regulating and protecting interstate commerce, particularly through investigative and regulatory agencies centering in Washington (*see* Interstate Commerce Commission; Federal Agencies). Centralization has been accelerated through federal grants-in-aid—federal appropriations of money for a great variety of state enterprises or needs. For example, Congress may not require a state to construct and maintain a system of highways of specified length, width, and materials or to maintain a state highway department. Yet, through its power to appropriate money and to prescribe conditions with which a state must comply if it wishes to share in the federal funds, the national government, through the Bureau of Public Roads in the Department of Agriculture, is able to do indirectly what it cannot do directly.

Centralization is viewed with alarm by some, who fear that it will result in the reduction of the states to mere administrative areas of the national government, like the French *départements*. By others, centralization is viewed as inevitable once national unity has been attained and social and economic interests have developed to a point where they overlap state boundaries.

In state affairs, centralization refers to the expanding activities of state governments, whereby they have assumed supervision, direct control, or actual performance of activities previously carried on inadequately, if at all, by counties, cities, or other local governments. Such centralization has appeared notably in connection with the support of schools, highway construction and maintenance, charities, correctional institutions, and public health.

[A. F. Macdonald, *Federal Aid*, and *American State Government and Administration;* F. A. Ogg and P. O. Ray, *Introduction to American Government*.]

P. ORMAN RAY

CENTRAL OF GEORGIA RAILROAD. *See* **Railroads, Sketches.**

CENTRAL OVERLAND CALIFORNIA AND PIKES PEAK EXPRESS was chartered by the Kansas legislature in February 1860. It absorbed the stage lines running from St. Joseph, Mo., to Denver and to Salt Lake City. Through its president, William H. Russell, it launched the famous Pony Express. In May 1860 it obtained a contract for mail service from Utah to California. Maintenance of frequent stage service and heavy losses from the Pony Express brought embarrassment to the C. O. C. and P. P. Express. Employees dubbed it "Clean Out of Cash and Poor Pay." On Mar. 21, 1862, Ben Holladay purchased the holdings at public sale for $100,000.

[L. R. Hafen, *The Overland Mail*.]

LEROY R. HAFEN

CENTRAL PACIFIC–UNION PACIFIC RACE, a construction contest between the two companies bidding for government subsidies, land grants, and public favor. The original Pacific Railway Act (1862) authorized the Central Pacific to build eastward from the California line and the Union Pacific to build westward to the western Nevada boundary. This legislation was unpopular with the railroad companies, and they planned to build beyond the designated boundaries. Their attitude led to amendments to the Pacific Railway Act (1865–66), which authorized the roads to continue construction until they met. The amendments precipitated a historic race, 1867–69, because the company building the most track would receive the larger subsidy.

The competing companies projected their lines 300 miles in advance of actual construction, which was technically within the law. But when surveys crossed and recrossed, the railroad officials got into legal battles and the crews into personal ones. When the two roads were about 100 miles apart, Congress passed a law compelling the companies to join their tracks at Promontory Point, Utah, some 50 miles from the end of each completed line. The final, and most spectacular, lap of the race was made toward this point in the winter and spring of 1869, the tracks being joined on May 10. Neither company won the race because there was no definite goal on Promontory Point that had to be reached. The race was a dead heat if anything because both tracks reached the immediate vicinity at about the same time.

[Gen. G. M. Dodge, *The Dodge Records*.]

J. R. PERKINS

CENTRAL ROUTE, the overland route used most extensively during the twenty years following 1848, by immigrants bound for California. There were many deviations. From Independence or other points on the Missouri River the immigrants followed the Platte, went through South Pass in Wyoming, went around to the north of Great Salt Lake, followed the Humboldt River to the sinks, and proceeded to California by different passes through the Sierras. Beginning with 1851, mail service was maintained over this route.

[Cardinal Goodwin, *The Trans-Mississippi West;* L. R. Hafen, *The Overland Mail*.]

RUPERT N. RICHARDSON

CENTURY OF DISHONOR, a book by Helen Maria Hunt Jackson, published in 1881, which publicized the cause of the American Indian to an unprecedented degree. It was, in effect, an indictment of the government of the United States for its repeated failure to keep treaties made with, and promises made to, native American Indians. It was influential in promoting reforms in Indian affairs.

KENNETH M. STEWART

CENTURY OF PROGRESS INTERNATIONAL EXPOSITION, held in Chicago, 1933–34, one of the greatest financial successes in the history of world fairs. It was planned during a period of prosperity and successfully held in the midst of a great depression. It was designed to celebrate the one hundredth anniversary of the founding of Chicago and to demonstrate a century's progress in many fields. The original plans were scaled down several times to meet the exigencies of shrinking budgets. During the 170 days beginning May 27, 1933, there were 22,565,859 paid admissions; during the 163 days beginning May 26, 1934, there were 16,486,377. Official foreign participation was extremely limited. The schematic pattern of the fair was vague and confusing, but the modernistic architecture of the exposition has exerted much influence and the color effects have made themselves clearly evident in commercial design.

FRANK MONAGHAN

CEREAL GRAINS collectively form man's most important food source. In the United States, cereals ranking in importance according to acreage harvested (1970) are maize (corn), wheat, oats, sorghum, barley, rice, rye, and sugarcane. Most cereal grains belong to the grass family *Gramineae*. Millets and buckwheat belong to different botanical families and are unimportant economically in the United States.

Indians raised maize extensively long before the arrival of Christopher Columbus. European settlers quickly adopted it because the plants grew almost anywhere, required little attention after planting, and yielded good returns. Pioneers for generations afterward found that maize best suited their homesteading, transportation, and marketing circumstances. The "corn belt" developed in the 19th century from Ohio to Nebraska after a mechanical revolution harnessed the horsepower necessary for extensive cultivation. The automatic checkrow planter (1875) and the mechanical corn picker (1880) increased farmers' efficiency. In 1916 Donald F. Jones developed a system for producing modern hybrid seed, and by 1925 improved varieties were commercially available. Farmers in 1970 produced almost twice as much maize as in 1900 on nearly one-third less land.

Columbus introduced wheat, barley, and sugarcane to the New World in 1493. New York and Pennsylvania produced wheat extensively in the 17th century. After repeal of the English Corn Laws (1847), American wheat exports increased in the world market. Improved plows, reapers, and threshers were then available to expand production. Washington, California, and North Dakota became important wheat-producing states by 1890. As with maize, improved varieties that were drought- and disease-resistant and gave higher yields led to increased wheat production on less land during the 20th century. The 1970 Nobel Peace Prize winner, Norman Borlaug, received the award for his work in the breeding of wheat and maize, both major ingredients in the world's food supply.

Since barley, oats, and rye withstand cold weather better than other cereals, these crops appealed to farmers in Montana, the Dakotas, and Minnesota, where they were raised most extensively. Besides food, barley and rye were used to make alcoholic drinks. Oats were also valuable because of oat flour's antioxidant quality in various food preparations.

African slaves brought sorghum to America, but it remained unimportant until droughts and insect plagues ruined Great Plains farming in the 1880's. Farmers turned to sorghum because it was a xerophyte (drought-resistant plant) and immune to grasshopper attack. Texas has become the biggest producer of sorghum.

Rice culture began when South Carolina settlers imported rice from Madagascar in 1695. By 1808, Georgia farmers were raising a variety of African rice on dry land. In 1970 Arkansas, Texas, Louisiana, and California grew the most rice.

Sugarcane came to Louisiana from San Domingo in 1742, but commercial production did not develop until 1795. When Louisiana seceded in 1861, the northern states looked to the Hawaiian Islands for its sugar. Louisiana regained U.S. leadership in sugarcane production later in the century. The states producing most of America's sugarcane in 1970 were Louisiana, Florida, and Hawaii.

[S. G. Harrison, *The Oxford Book of Food Plants;* John T. Schlebecker, *The Use of the Land: Essays on the History of American Agriculture,* and *Whereby We Thrive: A History of American Farming, 1607–1972.*]

G. TERRY SHARRER

CEREALS, MANUFACTURE OF. In slightly over a century a combination of market forces, consumer demands, and innovative individuals transformed American breakfast habits and produced a multibillion dollar consumer industry. Ferdinand Schumacher, a German immigrant, began the cereals revolution in 1854 with a hand oats grinder in the back room of a small store in Akron, Ohio. His German Mills American Oatmeal Company, the nation's first commercial oatmeal manufacturer, marketed the product as a substitute for breakfast pork. Improved production technology (steel cutters, porcelain rollers, improved hullers), combined with an influx of German and Irish immigrants, quickly boosted sales and profits. In 1877, Schumacher adopted the Quaker symbol, the first registered trademark for a breakfast cereal. The acceptance of "horse food" for human consumption invited competition; Henry Parsons Crowell went into the business in 1882, and John Robert Stuart followed suit three years later. Crowell, operating at Ravenna, Ohio, consolidated all operations—grading, cleaning, hulling, cutting, rolling, packaging, and shipping—under one roof. Stuart's Chicago Imperial Mill and his mill in Cedar Rapids, Iowa, also offered formidable competition.

To combat Schumacher's dominant position, Stuart and Crowell joined forces in the Oatmeal Millers Association in 1885 and initiated a price war. A fire the next year at his Jumbo Mill in Akron forced Schumacher to submit to a union with Stuart and Crowell in the Consolidated Oatmeal Company. In 1888 the three combined the nation's seven largest mills into a holding company, the American Cereal Company. By the turn of the 20th century, technology, entrepreneurship, and the "Man in Quaker Garb" had given Quaker Oats a national market and produced yearly sales of $10 million.

As the manufacture of oatmeal assumed big business proportions, a new industry—ready-to-eat precooked cereals—came into existence. Shredded wheat, probably the first ready-to-eat cereal, appeared in Denver in 1893. Henry Perky, the developer, soon pushed his product into a receptive national market and built the Shredded Wheat Company, which the National Biscuit Company purchased in 1928. Another cereal manufacturer, William Danforth, began about the same time, entering the Robinson Commission Company in 1893. With financial help from his father Danforth acquired control of the firm and began manufacturing dairy and chicken feed and Purina whole wheat cereal. He capitalized on the 1890's health food craze and succeeded in having his cereal named the official breakfast food of the popular Dr. Ralston health clubs. Sales boomed, and cereal became a major part of the business. The Ralston-Purina Company early in the 20th century decided to concentrate on the feed business and indeed became the nation's largest feed producer, so that although the checkerboard-square products familiar to urban America did come out of the early endeavor, it accounts for less than 10 percent of the company's volume.

Despite Danforth's and Perky's successes, the primary thrust toward the new breakfast-food concept came from John H. Kellogg and William K. Kellogg and from Charles W. Post. The Michigan cereal industry rose from a combination of sincere religious belief and commercial interest in health foods. A medically trained Seventh-Day Adventist, Dr. John H. Kellogg experimented with cereals because of the dietary strictures of his faith. As early as 1875, subsisting on a vegetable diet while in New York studying medicine, he remarked: "My cooking conveniences were very limited. It was very difficult to prepare cereals. It often occurred to me that it should be possible to purchase cereals at groceries already cooked and ready to eat." Kellogg's inventive, broad-ranging mind moved toward this goal after he assumed control of the Adventist Battle Creek Sanitarium. Granola, his first cereal product, closely resembled toasted bread crumbs. In 1891 Kellogg applied for a patent for a flaked-food process, and two years later he formed the Kellogg's Sanitas Food Company to handle the development and marketing of his food ideas. In 1895 he launched cornflakes, which immediately captured the public imagination and, in the 19th-century pattern of overcompetition, produced forty rival manufacturers in the Battle Creek area.

The most serious competition to Kellogg came from Charles W. Post, who exploited the health food concept and moved beyond the local market. Post, a former Kellogg patient, began with Postum, a cereal coffee substitute that eliminated most of the caffeine found in regular coffee. In 1898 Grape-nuts, the concentrated cereal with a nutty flavor, made its debut. Late in the 1890's Post joined the cornflake battle. He originally called his product Elijah's Manna, but religious protest and trademark laws forced a name change to Post Toasties. Good business sense, determination, and powerful advertising produced a multimillion dollar fortune for Post in a few years. Post's death in 1914 facilitated the merger of his company with the Jello firm and began the process of mergers that culminated in the powerful General Foods Corporation.

William K. Kellogg, after serving for many years as his brother's administrative assistant, unhappily watched the Post fortune grow at what he considered to be the expense of the Kellogg family. In 1906, hoping to salvage years of research, William Kellogg established the Kellogg Toasted Corn Flake Company without his brother, Dr. Kellogg. William Kellogg moved rapidly away from his brother and the health food concept, opting for heavy advertising and commercial taste appeal. His signature on every package became the company trademark and insurance of quality. During the 1920's the company expanded by embracing technological advances and new products. In 1925 William Kellogg introduced Rice Krispies, an exploded rice cereal. More durable packages with waxite liners insured freshness and better shipping. By 1930 Kellogg's produced 40 percent of American ready-to-eat cereals. By the time of William Kellogg's death, nine major plants distributed products worldwide.

Early in the 20th century, the Quaker Oats Company (formed in 1901 to replace the American Cereal Company) jumped into the world market. Thanks to the complementary talents of its three founders—Schumacher, the pioneer innovator; Stuart, the manager and financial organizer; and Crowell, the creative merchandiser, advertiser, and promoter—sales increased 150 percent in the century's first decade. Alexander Anderson's steam-pressure method of shooting rice from guns created puffed rice and wheat and further stimulated profit. Crowell's intensive advertising campaign in the 1920's and 1930's featured promotions with such celebrities as Babe Ruth, Max Baer, and Shirley Temple. Sponsorship of the popular "Rin-Tin-Tin" and "Sergeant Preston of the Yukon" radio shows aided the company's expansion during the depression. The World War II boom boosted annual sales to $90 million, and by 1956 sales topped $277 million. In 1964, the firm that had begun 110 years before with a hand grinder sold over 200 products, grossed over $500 million, and claimed that 8 million people ate Quaker Oats each day.

National advertising—which contributed much to the growth of Quaker Oats, Kellogg's Corn Flakes, and Post products early in the 20th century—facilitated the emergence in the 1920's of the fourth largest American cereal manufacturer, General Mills. In 1921, James Ford Bell, president of Wasburn, Crosby Company, a Minneapolis milling firm, began experimenting with rolled wheat flakes. After tempering, steaming, and cracking wheat and processing it with syrup, sugar, and salt, it was prepared in a pressure cooker for rolling and then dried in an electric oven. A few short years later, Wheaties had become the "Breakfast of Champions." In 1928 four milling companies in Minneapolis, California, Utah, Texas-Oklahoma, and Detroit consolidated as the General Mills Company. The new firm expanded packaged food sales by heavy advertising, including sponsorship of such radio programs as "Skippy," "Jack Armstrong, The All-American Boy," and baseball games. Endorsements by Jack Dempsey, Johnny Weissmuller, and others verified the "Breakfast of Champions" slogan. By 1941 Wheaties claimed 12 percent of the U.S. cereal market. Experiments with the puffing process produced Kix, a puffed corn cereal, and Cheerios, a puffed oats cereal. Further product innovation and diversification brought total General Mills sales to over $500 million annually (18 percent in packaged foods) by the early 1950's.

The cereal industry followed the pattern of many American manufacturing organizations. Responding to perceived needs and consumer demands, innovators launched new products. From these beginnings emerged combines with larger capital bases to handle the business of production, distribution, and marketing. Imaginative firms utilized the growing mass media both to acquaint consumers with their products and to create demand—a process that eliminated many small producers and eventually created an oligopolistic industry controlled by four major producers. The ready-to-eat cereal industry has now come full circle. Beginning with supposed health foods (Kellogg's original granola), the industry has moved in less than a century back to health foods and even to the reintroduction of granola.

[John Calhoun Baker, *Directors and Their Function: A Preliminary Study,* part 4; Richard Ellsworth Day, *Breakfast Table, Autocrate: The Life Story of Henry Parsons Crowell;* James Gray, *Business Without Boundary: The Story of General Mills;* Arthur F. Marquette, *Brands, Trademarks, and Good Will: The Story of the Quaker Oats Company;* Horace B. Powell, *The Original Has This Signature—W. K. Kellogg;* John Harrison Thornton, *The History of the Quaker Oats Company.*]

THOMAS B. BREWER

CERRO GORDO, BATTLE OF (April 18, 1847). Advancing into the interior of Mexico after taking Veracruz, Gen. Winfield Scott found a Mexican army under Gen. Santa Anna entrenched on the National Road, eighteen miles below Jalapa. David E. Twiggs's division stormed two fortified hills after a turning movement suggested and guided by Capt. R. E. Lee. James Shields's brigade gained the rear of the position, and the Mexicans fled. Santa Anna escaped, leaving 3,000 prisoners, guns, baggage, and $11,000 in specie. The American loss was 431.

[Justin H. Smith, *The War With Mexico.*]

CHARLES WINSLOW ELLIOTT

CHAD'S FORD. *See* **Brandywine Creek, Battle of.**

CHAIN GANGS, a form of convict labor occasionally used by southern sheriffs in antebellum days, much as they had been used by the wardens of debtor prisons in the North and in England during the latter part of the 18th century. But the wide and systematic employment of chain gangs took place during the first decades after the Civil War, when lessees took full control over most of the convicts in the southern states. In place of the old ball-and-chain, the lessees substituted shackles fastened to both ankles of each convict and joined by a chain that permitted only short steps; a long chain was then strung through one of the links of each short chain, thus binding scores of convicts together. Compelled to work, eat, and sleep together, the prisoners lived under the basest sort of conditions.

In the late 1880's protests against the convict leases (*see* Convict Labor Systems) led to their gradual abandonment in favor of penal plantations, which usually dispensed with the chains. But it was not long before an increasing demand for good roads prompted the county sheriffs to hold a larger portion of the convicts for labor on the local roads, reviving the chain-gang system for this purpose. By the late 1890's the major portion of the convicts of Georgia, Florida, North Carolina, South Carolina, and other southern states were coupled together in road gangs. Humanitarian protests gradually led to state inspection of the county road gangs in several states and to state operation of the system in Georgia. The introduction of road-making machinery antiquated the chain gang and enabled the reformers to carry their opposition to the system to partial success in most of the states, but chain gangs still persist in many counties throughout a large section of the South.

[Blake McKelvey, *American Prisons;* J. F. Steiner and R. M. Brown, *The North Carolina Chain Gangs.*]

BLAKE MCKELVEY

CHAIN STORES, a group of retail stores in the same general kind of business under the same ownership or management. The U.S. Bureau of the Census began a continuing study of U.S. distribution in 1929 and at that time defined chains as firms with four or more stores. Beginning with the 1948 *Census of Business,* the Bureau of the Census abandoned the use of the term "chain stores" because of the inherent arbitrariness of any numerical definition of the term and in its place substituted the term "multiunit establishment firms." Data are currently published for seven categories of multiunit establishment firms ranging in size from two or three stores to 101 or more stores. Industry use of the term "chain stores" generally refers to firms with eleven or more stores. The industry definition of chain stores also includes the centralization of purchasing and warehousing. Multiunit department-store firms frequently do not include such centralized operations and therefore are not considered chains.

There have been sporadic instances of chains of stores at different times and places, but the date commonly cited as the beginning of modern chain-store history in the United States is 1859, the year from which the Great Atlantic & Pacific Tea Company dates its origin. Sears, Roebuck and Company, the world's largest retailer, began as a mail-order business in 1886 but did not start to build its chain of stores until the 1920's. Although other well-known large chains were established before 1900, chains were still in an embryonic stage at the turn of the century. Government statistics show that only fifty-eight chains existed in the entire United States in 1900. This number more than quadrupled by 1910 and tripled again by 1920. Diffusion of the chain-store phenomenon accelerated during the first three decades of the 20th century. The period between the end of World War I and the depression of the 1930's was the era of most rapid growth. By 1929 chain stores accounted for 22 percent of total U.S. retail sales. Their growth was therefore considerably greater than the general expansion in retail trade from 1900 to 1929.

The success of the chains was the result of a variety of factors, but their ability to charge lower prices than independents was probably most important. Chain stores were able to reduce their unit costs by volume buying and by purchasing directly from manufacturers. Another chain economy resulting from large volume was the ability to use specialized personnel in general management, real estate, accounting, purchasing, advertising, and other departments. Chains also engaged in manufacturing goods and contracting with manufacturers for the production of items with their own brand names. Their size made it possible for them to press manufacturers for lower prices.

One response of independent retailers and wholesalers to strong competition from chain stores was the attempt to use political power to neutralize the price economies of the chains. Many states passed anti–chain-store taxes during the 1930's that tended to raise chain prices. These discriminatory taxes were adverse to consumer interest in lower prices and were generally prohibited by judicial decisions before World War II. The focus then shifted to retail price maintenance laws or so-called fair-trade laws, which permit the establishment of legal minimum retail prices. Fair-trade laws are state laws that were made possible by the passage of the 1937 Miller-Tydings Enabling Amendment to the Sherman Antitrust Act. Enforcement of these laws in the states that have them has been difficult because consumers oppose them and they are difficult to enforce in a dynamic market,

Another response of independents and wholesalers to chain competition was to attempt to adopt the same economies as the chains. An example in the food industry has been the formulation of affiliated groups of independent retailers and wholesalers, a move that gave the retailers many of the economies of the chains.

The *Census of Business* of 1967 showed that chains with two or more stores accounted for 40 percent of total U.S. retail sales. Even with the extensive growth of chains, single-store independents account for 60 percent of total U.S. retail sales. Chains are more important in certain areas, accounting for 83 percent of total variety-store sales and 61 percent of total grocery-store sales. In 1967 there were 204 firms operating 101 or more stores. These 204 large chains accounted for 19 percent of total U.S. retail sales. The largest chains, though, have grown since World War II at a lower rate than medium-size chains. Chain stores have been an important factor in distribution because their introduction of savings in the distribution process and the resulting competitive pressure on prices induced other retail firms to imitate their innovations.

[Godfrey M. Lebhar, *Chain Stores in America, 1859–1962;* Tom Mahoney and Leonard Sloane, *The Great Merchants;* Daniel I. Padberg, *Economics of Food Retailing.*]

GEORGE PRENDERGAST

CHAIRMAKING. Among the numerous woodworking industries in the American colonies furniture making soon reached a point where it supplied articles for export to the South and to the Caribbean. The most common product was chairs, which are often recorded in coastal and sugar island cargoes. Their manufacture, which was already specialized before the Revolution, was recognized as a distinct branch of furniture making in the census of 1810. Rockers, said to be an American invention, were popular in Spanish America. Vessels leaving Baltimore for points around Cape Horn in a single day in 1827 carried 12,000 chairs.

An expanding commercial market early invited quantity production and the use of mechanical aids in manufacture. Philadelphia chair shops had steam-driven machinery before 1825. About 1850 a Fitchburg, Mass., factory producing principally for export had a capacity of sixty-five dozen chairs a day, and employed special machines to shape interchangeable parts that were boxed separately for shipment and assembled at their destination. Until after 1890 Massachusetts made more chairs than any other state. Towns like Ashburnham, Gardner, and Westminster were centers for their production.

Chair design has accommodated itself to period fashions. Nevertheless popular types like the Windsor chair have remained in general use since introduced at Philadelphia about 1700, where they were known at first as Philadelphia chairs. Windsors were advertised during the 18th century by cabinetmakers who specialized in them. Chairs are not as large a fraction of furniture output today as they were when household equipment was less elaborate. Modern statistics record them by groups like household, office, public building, wood, wicker, and metal chairs. (*See also* Furniture.)

[Thomas H. Ormsbee, *The Story of American Furniture;* Victor S. Clark, *History of Manufactures in the United States; United States Census of Manufactures.*]

VICTOR S. CLARK

CHALMETTE NATIONAL HISTORICAL PARK, located about five miles below New Orleans, on the east bank of the Mississippi River, marks the site of the Battle of New Orleans (1815) where Gen. Andrew Jackson defeated the British. Originally a sugar plantation owned by Ignace de Lino de Chalmette, a wellborn French Creole, the thirty-acre site is now divided into two sections. The first section is the actual battlefield, which housed the plantation home Chalmette and his wife were forced to abandon. Their home was burned as a war measure. The second section is occupied by the now inactive Chalmette National Cemetery. The Chalmette Monument, started in 1855, was completed in 1908, and the monument and surrounding grounds were declared a national historical park on Aug. 10, 1939.

[Grace King, *Creole Families of New Orleans.*]

CHAMBERSBURG, BURNING OF (July 30, 1864). Union Gen. David Hunter, defeated by the Confederate commander, Gen. Jubal A. Early, in the course of his retreat up the Shenandoah Valley wantonly burned crops, homes, and villages. In retaliation, Early dispatched a cavalry force under Gen. John McCausland to Chambersburg, Pa., in adjacent Union territory, to demand a ransom of $100,000 in gold or $500,000 in greenbacks, failing the delivery of which, he was ordered to burn the town. McCausland went as directed. No ransom of the amount demanded could be paid. The town was burned.

[R. H. Early, ed., *Gen. Jubal A. Early: Autobiographical Sketch and Narrative*.]

THOMAS ROBSON HAY

CHAMBERS OF COMMERCE, voluntary associations of business and professional men approaching the problems of the community from the business angle. The Chamber of Commerce of New York is the oldest such organization in America, its original charter having come from King George III in 1768.

In general, American chambers of commerce follow the British, rather than the Continental, types and usually are broader in the scope of their activities than even the British prototype.

In most of the older American cities the chambers of commerce were developed from two types of previous organizations. The first of these was the Board of Trade, established originally for the purpose of regulating or supervising trading activities. In Boston, Baltimore, Minneapolis, Milwaukee, St. Louis, and Cincinnati, as well as in other cities, the present chamber of commerce has, as at least one of its component parts, a former trading body and some even continue this activity. In the chambers growing out of trading bodies the growth usually has been effected by merger with other types of organization, the basis of combination being a common concern with civic affairs.

The second type of older American chamber is the organization characterized by having been originally a group of taxpaying businessmen—a taxpayers' league or a Civic Association—united for defense, or to foster some civic interest.

The most common activities engaged in by American chambers of commerce include industrial and commercial development and expansion, and dealing with problems connected with agriculture, transportation, publicity, charity solicitation (community chests), regulation and promotion of trade, and commercial arbitration.

The Chamber of Commerce of the United States (established in 1912) is a federation of local chambers and other business organizations and individuals that applies similar principles to national affairs. One of its principal activities is the conducting of referenda on legislative matters and other public questions.

[W. G. Bruce, *Commercial Organizations*.]

PAUL T. CHERINGTON

CHAMBLY, FORT, a British fort, built in 1775 and located at the foot of the Richelieu River rapids in Canada on the site of Fort St. Louis (erected 1764). The fort was captured by the Americans on Oct. 20, 1775 (*see* Canada and the American Revolution), and held until the spring of 1776, when it was evacuated and burned as the Americans retreated southward to Ticonderoga.

[J. H. Smith, *Our Struggle for the Fourteenth Colony*.]

ROBERT S. THOMAS

CHAMPAGNE-MARNE OPERATION (July 15–18, 1918). This German offensive in France had several objectives. One was to correct their faulty supply in the Marne salient; another was to draw reserves to assure success in the offensive planned against the British in Flanders. The attack was made by three armies of the German Crown Prince Group. The plan was for the 7th Army (under the command of Gen. Max von Boehn) to cross the Marne east of Château-Thierry and advance up the valley to Epernay. The 1st Army (Gen. Bruno von Mudra) and 3rd Army (Gen. Karl von Einem) were to attack east of Reims in the direction of Epernay, swing south of the forest of Reims, and capture Épernay and Châlons. The attack was definitely halted east of Reims on the first day by the efficient defense plans of the 4th French Army (under the command of Henri J. E. Gouraud). West of Reims some fourteen divisions crossed the Marne, but, unaided by the attack east of Reims and without artillery support, this attack soon bogged down. Orders were given on the 17th for their withdrawal, preparatory to a general withdrawal, from the Marne salient. The 3rd, 42nd, and part of the 28th American Divisions participated. The approximate number of Americans engaged was 85,000. The 38th Infantry Regiment (3rd Division) here won the sobriquet "Rock of the Marne" (*see* Aisne-Marne Operation).

[Girard L. McEntee, *The Military History of the World War*.]

GIRARD L. MCENTEE

CHAMPAIGN COUNTY RESCUE CASES, arising from an attempt to enforce the Fugitive Slave Act, involved the conflict of state and federal authorities. In April 1857 Udney Hyde harbored, on his farm near Mechanicsburg, Champaign County, Ohio, a fugitive slave from Kentucky. The slaveowner sent three U.S. deputy marshals and five Kentuckians for the slave on May 21. Friends summoned by Hyde from

Mechanicsburg scared the posse away, but it returned six days later and carried off four citizens. At South Charleston the posse assaulted an Ohio sheriff for trying to serve a writ of habeas corpus, but next morning was overtaken by officers and a crowd and bound over to the Common Pleas Court of Clark County. Proslavery sympathizers appealed to Judge Humphrey H. Leavitt of the U.S. District Court at Cincinnati, who assumed jurisdiction and released the defendants as having rightfully performed their duties and not being amenable to the state's laws. The payment of $950 by Hyde's neighbors for the slave's manumission terminated federal suits against leading obstructors.

WILBUR H. SIEBERT

CHAMP D'ASILE. In 1817 a group of Napoleonic exiles under the leadership of the French army officer Frédéric Lallemand made a fortified camp in Texas on the Trinity River, about ninety miles from the coast, calling it Champ d'Asile. It was charged that they hoped to take Mexico and rescue Napoleon from St. Helena. Scarcely were the forts and dwellings completed when the Spanish, who claimed the territory, forced the colonists to withdraw to Galveston Island. There they remained for weeks, the victims of hunger, sickness, and tropical storms. At last, aided by the pirate Jean Laffite, they made their way to the French settlements in Louisiana.

[Anne Boreman Lyon, "The Bonapartists in Alabama," *The Gulf States Historical Magazine* (1903); Jesse R. Reeves, *The Napoleonic Exiles in America, 1815–1819.*]

FANNIE RATCHFORD

CHAMPION'S HILL, BATTLE OF (May 16, 1863). When Confederate Gen. John C. Pemberton at Edward's Station learned that Gen. U. S. Grant's army was about to move westward from the vicinity of Jackson, Miss., toward Vicksburg, he decided to attack. It was necessary to defeat Grant to prevent being shut up in Vicksburg. By the morning of May 16, 1863, the Confederates had moved eastward to Champion's Hill. While Grant concentrated his army, Pemberton, uncertain as to what to do, halted his troops to await the expected attack. Grant handled his troops with energy and decision. The Union attack was successful. After hours of battle, Pemberton's army was driven from the field toward Vicksburg.

[F. V. Greene, *The Mississippi.*]

THOMAS ROBSON HAY

CHAMPLAIN, LAKE. *See* **Lake Champlain.**

CHAMPLAIN'S INDIAN ALLIANCE. In 1608 Samuel de Champlain made an alliance with the Indians of the St. Lawrence and with the Huron from the interior; in 1609 their chiefs called upon him to assist them in a campaign against their enemies, the Iroquois. Champlain, with a small contingent of Frenchmen, accompanied the Indian war party up Richelieu River and through Lake Champlain. At its southern end in a battle, July 29, two chiefs were killed by bullets from Champlain's arquebus. The Iroquois, astonished at the firearms, broke and fled.

It has been asserted by many early historians of Canada that the Iroquois thenceforth became the enemies of the French colony and that by this act Champlain endangered his life work. This view attributes too much influence to a single battle, although Champlain in 1610 and 1615 again attacked the Iroquois with his Algonquian and Huron allies. The strategic position of the Iroquois and their ability to obtain firearms from the Dutch at Albany created a situation that made the Iroquois the natural enemies of New France. Champlain could not have foreseen that the Dutch would settle on the Hudson River and that his obligation to help his allies created the situation. Had he not kept his promise to them, he could not have maintained his position at Quebec.

[H. P. Biggar, ed., *Champlain's Works,* vol. II; L. P. Kellogg, *French Régime in Wisconsin and the Northwest.*]

LOUISE PHELPS KELLOGG

CHAMPLAIN'S VOYAGES. A sojourn of two years in Mexico and the West Indies (1599) prepared Samuel de Champlain for his first Canadian voyage (1603) when he served as an observer for the expedition of Aymar de Chaste, authorized by Henry IV of France to make a general survey and fix settlements. Champlain prepared a cartographic survey of the St. Lawrence region including the gulf, Gaspé and Isle Percé, and the Saguenay River, resulting in an account prolific in valuable information (*Des Sauvages*). In 1604 under Pierre du Guast, Sieur de Monts, he explored Nova Scotia. A year later he explored the New England coast, mapping 1,000 miles of coastline. He returned to France in 1607. With a commission as lieutenant governor, he set out in 1608 with a group of settlers who founded Quebec. Other voyages of 1610, 1611, 1613, and a number made in the 1620's, made him the acknowledged master of all that related to New France. His final voyage was in 1633, and in the two years before his death he greatly expanded the colony of Quebec.

[Marcel Trudel, "Samuel de Champlain," *Dictionary of Canadian Biography,* vol. I.]

ARTHUR C. PARKER

CHAMPOEG CONVENTION. On May 2, 1843, Oregon settlers met at Champoeg in the Willamette Valley to create a civil government which was to continue until either Great Britain or the United States established control over the Oregon country. The plan was contested by the British settlers, who looked upon it as pro-American. This provisional government was the only one in the Pacific Northwest until the Oregon territorial government was established by the United States on Mar. 3, 1849.

[Charles H. Carey, *A General History of Oregon Prior to 1861.*]

ROBERT MOULTON GATKE

CHANCELLORSVILLE, BATTLE OF (May 1–4, 1863). In April Gen. Joseph Hooker, with almost 130,000 men, lay across the Rappahannock River from Fredericksburg, Va. Entrenched behind Fredericksburg, Gen. Robert E. Lee awaited another attack such as that of Union Gen. A. E. Burnside in the previous December. In the absence of Gen. James Longstreet's divisions in southeastern Virginia, Lee had approximately 60,000 men.

Beginning April 27, Hooker in rapid movements got four army corps across the Rappahannock River on Lee's left flank, while maintaining his old lines and sending an army corps of 20,000 men under John Sedgwick across the river below Lee's right flank. On May 1, with the forces on Lee's left, Hooker advanced across the river beyond Chancellorsville, only to retire behind Chancellorsville on the approach of the enemy. Lee, threatened by Hooker's movements, ran the risk of having his communication with Richmond cut and being caught in an encircling trap. The greatest danger being on his left, Lee, leaving a force of about 10,000 men at Fredericksburg under Gen. Jubal A. Early, marched with the remainder of his troops toward Chancellorsville. The opposing armies, late in the day of May 1, took position for battle on lines nearly perpendicular to the Rappahannock. At night Lee and Gen. T. J. ("Stonewall") Jackson, conferring upon their dangerous situation, decided on a daring measure, that of dividing their forces and having Jackson with about 30,000 men march the next day around Hooker's right flank, while Lee with less than 20,000 men held the line in front of Hooker. Accordingly on May 2, while Lee deployed his men in skirmishes against Hooker, Jackson moved rapidly around Hooker's right flank.

In spite of adequate information of Jackson's movement, the army corps on Hooker's extreme right were unprepared when Jackson, late on May 2, fell upon them with irresistible fury. Gen. O. O. Howard's corps was routed, and another corps badly demoralized. In the confusion and darkness greater disaster might have happened had not Jackson been dangerously wounded by the fire of his own troops and carried from the battlefield. In the renewed conflict of May 3, a cannonball struck a pillar against which Hooker was leaning. Dazed by the effect and in doubt about the security of his army, Hooker withdrew his troops to the banks of the river, where they remained throughout May 4 in disorder and uncertainty.

Lee, meanwhile, turned back to deal with Sedgwick's corps, which had routed the Confederate force under Early and was rapidly approaching Chancellorsville. Under the fierce attack of Lee's veterans, Sedgwick likewise retired to the Rappahannock, which he crossed during the night of May 4. When, on May 5, Lee advanced again beyond Chancellorsville, Hooker withdrew the Union forces north of the river. In the entire campaign Hooker lost 17,287 men (1,606 killed, 9,762 wounded, 5,919 missing) and Lee 12,764 (1,665 killed, 9,081 wounded, 2,018 captured). But Lee suffered the irreparable loss of Jackson, who after days of intense suffering died of his wounds.

[John Bigelow, *The Campaign of Chancellorsville.*]

ALFRED P. JAMES

CHANTIER in the fur trade of the Far West signified the place near the larger posts where lumber was made up, boats and canoes built, and other craftsmanship necessary for the post performed. The word comes from the French *chantier* ("shipyard").

[H. M. Chittenden, *History of the American Fur Trade of the Far West.*]

CARL L. CANNON

CHANTILLY, BATTLE OF (Sept. 1, 1862), occurred during Union Gen. John Pope's withdrawal to Fairfax Courthouse in Virginia after his defeat at the second Battle of Bull Run. Confederate Gen. T. J. ("Stonewall") Jackson, seeking to command the road on which Pope was retreating, encountered federal troops protecting the line of retreat. A sharp engagement followed, accompanied by a terrific thunderstorm. Losses were heavy; the Union generals Isaac I. Stevens and Philip Kearny were killed. Jackson could not interrupt Pope's retreat, and the federals reached Fairfax Courthouse without further disaster.

[R. U. Johnson and C. C. Buel, eds., *Battles and Leaders of the Civil War,* vol. II.]

W. N. C. CARLTON

CHAPARRAL, from Spanish *chaparro,* as used by Mexicans, who gave the word to the Southwest, generally means any kind of thick or thorny brush, but never timber. In California, chaparral is specifically the manzanita oak; in parts of Texas, it is called the black chaparral. Chaparral peculiar to arid and semiarid regions of the Southwest includes granjeno, mesquite, allthorn, and huisache; the bushes are often interspersed with various kinds of cacti, agaves, and yuccas. Only dogs, horses, and men used to the chaparral can run in it, and the "brush popper," armored in leather and ducking, is a distinctly different type from the plains cowpuncher. The leaves of chaparral growth are as slender as the thorns are sharp, preventing evaporation. Some varieties afford good browsing; others are as bitter as gall. Before the era of overgrazing, a solid turf and frequent grass fires kept the brush down. Now it usurps millions of acres once prairie.

[J. Frank Dobie, *A Vaquero of the Brush Country.*]

J. FRANK DOBIE

CHAPBOOKS were cheap popular pamphlets, generally printed on a single sheet and folded to form twenty-four pages or less, often crudely illustrated with woodcuts, sold by chapmen. Published in the tens of thousands in America until about 1850, these books were most numerous from about 1800 to 1825. Famous authors and peddlers of American chapbooks were Rev. Mason Locke Weems of Virginia (author of the Washington cherry tree story), Josiah Priest of New York, and Chapman Whitcomb of Massachusetts. Prominent among the publishers were Andrew Steuart of Philadelphia, Isaiah Thomas of Worcester, Fowle and Draper and Nathaniel Coverly of Boston, and Samuel Wood and Sons and Mahlon Day of New York. The beginning of popular literature in the United States, with emphasis on the wonderful, the sad, and the humorous, chapbooks were for over 100 years the only literature available in the average home except the Bible, the almanac, and the newspaper. They contained fairy tales, lives of heroes and rascals, riddles, jests, poems, songs, hymns, speeches, accounts of shipwrecks, Indian captivities, highwaymen, deathbed scenes, executions, romances, astrology, palmistry, etiquette books, letter-writers, valentine-writers, and moral and (sometimes) immoral tales.

[W. W. Watt, *Shilling Shockers of the Gothic School;* H. B. Weiss, *American Chapbooks.*]

R. W. G. VAIL

CHAPLIN HILLS, BATTLE OF. *See* **Perryville, Battle of.**

CHAPULTEPEC, BATTLE OF (Sept. 13, 1847). The western approaches to Mexico City are commanded by Chapultepec, a rocky eminence, 200 feet high, crowned with stone buildings. During the Mexican War, after vigorous bombardment, Gen. Winfield Scott launched Gen. G. J. Pillow's division against the southern slopes. The garrison resisted desperately, but the Americans mounted the walls on scaling ladders and captured the castle on the summit. Gen. John A. Quitman's and Gen. William J. Worth's divisions then attacked the Belén and San Cosme gates, and the city surrendered the next morning. The American loss (for the day) was 138 killed, 673 wounded. Mexican casualties are unknown, but 760 were captured.

[Justin H. Smith, *The War With Mexico,* vol. II.]

CHARLES WINSLOW ELLIOTT

CHARITY ORGANIZATION MOVEMENT. In founding the London Charity Organization Society in 1869, English poor-law reformers introduced the charity organization movement. It spread to the United States, and by 1904 there were 104 societies in America, the first having been established in Germantown, Pa., in 1873. The movement had as its goals the more businesslike and scientific handling of poverty cases by private agencies and the tightening of public policies toward indigents and beggars. Ideally, charity organization would end politicking, fraud, and the dole on the public level, and overlapping and counterproductive philanthropy by private groups and individuals.

Philosophically, the charity organization movement was of a piece with self-help concepts popularized by Samuel Smiles in England and Horatio Alger,

Jr., in the United States: apart from the mentally enfeebled, orphans, and others deemed to require institutional care, unfortunates in society should be encouraged to elevate themselves through moral exertion and individual enterprise; moreover, the poor would always be a problem if governments and charitable societies callously or sentimentally failed to force them upward. In practice, these Victorian concepts of discipline were to guide poor relief through volunteer "friendly visitors" from the local Charity Organization Societies or Associated Charities, who would screen needy applicants and forward reports for action to private agencies.

In time the charity organization movement overshadowed the agencies it had been formed to assist, taking on direct burdens of aid. The Charity Organization Society of the City of New York (1882), successor to such forerunners as the New York Association for Improving the Condition of the Poor of the 1840's, was a case in point. By the late 19th century the New York Charity Organization Society had established the Penny Provident Fund to foster savings, the Provident Loan Society to provide low interest rates on loans, workrooms to educate unskilled women in marketable occupations, such as laundering, and a woodyard, where knowing citizens could direct beggars to labor for their daily bread.

Some critics felt the charity organization movement lacked heart. John Boyle O'Reilly, a Boston poet, wrote: "The organized charity scrimped and iced/ In the name of a cautious, statistical Christ." Others scored the growing tendency to pay the formerly voluntary friendly visitors and thus withhold funds from the poor themselves. But, meanwhile, the movement was moving toward greater professionalization in the welfare field. Its paid visitors pioneered in the case method by treating families and individuals as separate problems, not merely as members of an impoverished class. Social scientists, including John R. Commons, used societal records for research. Journals, including the Philadelphia society's *Monthly Register* (1880) and the New York society's *Charities* (1891, *Charities and the Commons* after 1905); nationwide cooperation through the National Association of Societies for Organizing Charities (1888); and greater emphasis on professional preparation, particularly exemplified in the New York School of Philanthropy (1898)—all marked steps toward more rational and systematic treatment of poverty problems.

In the 20th century, growing specialization occurred in many areas of social welfare, including public health, housing, and recreation. Local, state, and national responsibility for resolving problems caused by poverty and by associated social ills, spurred on by the social security commitments of the 1930's, reached a climax with creation of the cabinet-level departments of Health, Education, and Welfare (1953) and Housing and Urban Development (1965). The Family Welfare Association (1911) reflected a change in private relief work, as the charity organization movement's terminology (charity, paupers, indigents) gave way to new terms (social welfare, clients, recipients). Finally, formation of the American Association of Social Workers (1922) signified a new status for those concerned with efficiency and competency in meeting the challenges of social distress.

[Vaughn Davis Bornet, *Welfare in America;* Robert H. Bremner, *From the Depths;* Frank Dekker Watson, *The Charity Organization Movement in the United States.*]

CHARLES WETZEL

CHARITY SCHOOLS. During the colonial period, free education generally meant instruction for poor and underprivileged children. Numerous schools were established in the American colonies and were organized and supported by benevolent persons and societies, a practice that served to fasten on the idea of free education an odium that was difficult to remove. The pauper-school conception came directly from England and persisted far into the 19th century. Infant-school societies and Sunday-school societies engaged in such work. Schools were sometimes supported in part by rate bills: charges levied upon parents according to the number of their children in school. Declaration of poverty exempted parents from the payment of rate bills, and it also often put the element of charity in certain educational practices. In the history of education in the United States, philanthropy and charity have played important parts, on the theory that the level of life among the masses could thus be raised and their moral, religious, and economic conditions be improved. As a result many kinds of charity schools were established, and in some instances the children not only were instructed but were provided with food, clothes, and lodging. Generally the curriculum was of the most elementary character.

[Frank P. Graves, *A Student's History of Education;* Edgar W. Knight, *Education in the United States.*]

EDGAR W. KNIGHT

CHARIVARI. *See* **Shivaree.**

CHARLES RIVER BRIDGE CASE, 11 Peters 420 (1837). In 1785 the Massachusetts legislature incorporated the Proprietors of the Charles River Bridge for the purpose of erecting a toll bridge between Boston and Charlestown. In 1828, long before the expiration of the charter, the legislature incorporated the Warren Bridge Company to build another bridge a few rods from the first. The new bridge was to become free to the public within six years. Was the second charter unconstitutional as impairing the obligation of the first? (*See* Contract Clause.)

The case was carried from the highest court in Massachusetts to the Supreme Court of the United States, where it was first argued in 1831. Chief Justice John Marshall would have held the second grant invalid, but because of absences and disagreement it was impossible to reach a decision until 1837. By that time new appointments had worked a transformation in the Court, which now upheld the constitutionality of the second charter with only two dissenting votes. In an opinion that marked the leaning against monopolistic power characterizing Jacksonian political philosophy (*see* Jacksonian Democracy), Roger B. Taney, the new chief justice, developed the rule that corporate charters are to be construed strictly in favor of the public.

[C. B. Swisher, *Roger B. Taney;* Charles Warren, *The Supreme Court in United States History.*]

CHARLES FAIRMAN

CHARLESTON, the second largest city in South Carolina, located in the southeastern section of the state. In 1680 the English, who had settled ten years earlier at Albemarle Point on the Ashley River, moved down to the present site of Charleston on the peninsula that lies between the confluence of the Ashley and Cooper rivers. With a deep harbor, a dry path to the backcountry, and myriad coastal creeks and inlets, Charleston became the chief marshaling point for the exportation first of deerskins and then of rice and indigo. By 1704 Charleston was a walled city, a formidable English rival to Spanish Saint Augustine. After Gov. Sir Nathaniel Johnson had parried a French-Spanish invasion attempt in 1706, Fort Johnson was built on James Island at the mouth of the harbor. Until 1790 Charleston was the capital of South Carolina.

The Charleston Indian trade was the city's first source of wealth. English cloth, tools, trinkets, and firearms, which were cheaper than those the Spanish and the French could supply, were exchanged for deerskins and furs. Although the proprietors and the planters originally contended for the trade, Charleston merchants successfully organized the traders who made yearly visits to the Cherokee and the Creek. Charleston merchants flourished from the 1730's to 1808, exporting rice and indigo to Europe and lumber to the West Indies and importing manufactured goods from England, household necessities from New England, and slaves from Africa. Factors gathered the country produce in storehouses on their wharves while the merchants freighted the vessels for foreign destinations. The Exchange (1771), modeled after the customshouses of Bristol and Liverpool, was the site where the tea was stored in 1773, and the last royal governor was welcomed in 1775.

Charleston's merchants and planters sat in South Carolina's Commons House of Assembly, and until 1730 Charleston itself was governed by commissions established by the assembly; subsequently the commissions were elected by the people of the city each Easter Monday. Merchants served as the commissioners of the pilotage, of fortifications, of the streets, and of the markets and workhouse and as firemasters; artisans served as packers and woodmeasurers.

During the Revolution, Charleston was three times successfully defended against the British. On June 28, 1776, Sir Peter Parker's fleet was repulsed as it attempted to sail past the hastily erected fort of palmetto logs on Sullivan's Island defended by the men of Col. William Moultrie. In 1779 Gen. Augustine Prevost's land force was also unsuccessful in its attempt to take the city. The capture of Charleston took place on May 12, 1780, after Sir Henry Clinton had landed his army on the sea islands, crossed the Ashley River, and invested the city from the landward side. Adm. Marriot Arbuthnot blocked the entrances to the harbor, and the British held Charleston until Dec. 14, 1782.

In order to stabilize society after the Revolution, the city was incorporated on Aug. 13, 1783, and a city government with an intendant and thirteen wardens was established. The reassembling low-country elite was able to muffle the radical challenge within the city but had to consent to the demands of the growing backcountry planting interests to remove the capital from Charleston to Columbia. The convention that ratified the Constitution of the United States was held in Charleston, however, on May 23, 1788; Charleston and the low-country parishes voted overwhelmingly for South Carolina's entry into the Union.

With the wars of the French Revolution and Napoleon's reign, Charleston like other American ports had a new burst of commercial prosperity, and

Charleston's last great age of commerce, from 1791 to 1808, gave rise to the many fine private houses and beautiful gardens for which Charleston is now best known. The Charleston single and double houses, adapted to the climate by their piazzas and decorated in the fashionable Adam style, were built by many merchant princes, such as Josiah Smith, William Blacklock, and Nathaniel Russell. Charleston Gardens benefited from the nurseries of André Michaux established on Charleston Neck in 1786; from them came the camellias that soon grew in profusion at Middleton Place on the Ashley River, laid out about 1740 by Henry Middleton, and at Otranto on Goose Creek, the home of the noted botanist Alexander Garden. Following this tradition, the Magnolia Gardens were created by the Rev. John Grimke Drayton in the 1840's and the Cypress Gardens by the Kittredge family in the 20th century.

President Thomas Jefferson's embargo of 1808, British Orders in Council, French decrees, and the War of 1812 disrupted trade. The merchants tied to European firms departed, their places gradually taken by representatives of northern firms, who redirected Carolina trade to Europe through northern ports. As steam replaced sail, this tendency increased. The local merchant community declined in influence and in status, and the city came to be dominated by the rice planters from the Waccamaw and the Combahee rivers and the cotton planters from the sea islands. The influx of refugee French from Santo Domingo in the 1790's had brought not only another new important group but also the fear of a slave revolt—and this was enhanced by the scare raised by the former slave Denmark Vesey and his cohorts in 1822. In the middle of the 1820's the site of the old tobacco inspection warehouse was turned into a city guardhouse and then into a military college, The Citadel (1842). At the time of nullification (1832) the city was divided, but on Dec. 20, 1860, the convention that met in St. Andrew's Hall voted unanimously for secession from the Union.

The first shot in the Civil War was fired from Fort Johnson upon Fort Sumter, at the mouth of Charleston harbor, on Apr. 12, 1861. Fort Sumter, which was surrendered to the Confederates on Apr. 14, kept the Union navy out of Charleston harbor during the ensuing siege of Charleston. For almost four years blockade runners scudded past the severely pounded walls of Fort Sumter, while the Confederates experimented with torpedoes and submarines. The victories at Secessionville on James Island on June 16, 1862, and at Battery Wagner on Morris Island on July 18, 1863, kept the Union troops at bay, but the city fell on Feb. 17, 1865. The great fire of Dec. 11, 1861, however, had done more damage than the enemy's bombardment.

Blighted by Civil War losses and Reconstruction troubles, Charleston made a beginning in postwar recovery with the development of the fertilizer industry started in 1867. Since then importation of ores has led to the development of a profitable oil-refining industry. In substantial measure, however, Charleston's economy has been supported since 1901 by the presence of a U.S. Navy installation on the Cooper River, originally a navy yard and now, after expansions during World War I and World War II, a base. In 1970 Charleston ranked forty-sixth among harbors in the continental United States, having handled only slightly more than 6 million tons of cargo during the previous year.

The city's population remains substantially stable in numbers, as Afro-Americans move from outlying parishes into the heart of the city and middle-class whites move into the suburbs; in 1970 the population was 66,945, having increased by only approximately 1,000 during the previous decade.

[Mrs. St. Julien Ravenel, *Charleston, The Place and the People;* George C. Rogers, Jr., *Charleston in the Age of the Pinckneys.*]

GEORGE C. ROGERS, JR.

CHARLESTON, capital city of West Virginia, took its name from Charles Clendenin, whose son George acquired lands at the junction of the Elk and Kanawha rivers in the year 1787. Here was located Fort Lee, a refuge for wilderness settlers for a generation following the French and Indian War. Here Gen. Andrew Lewis halted his army in his march from Lewisburg to Point Pleasant in Dunmore's War. In 1791 Daniel Boone lived in a cabin in the suburbs of the present city and represented the county in the Virginia Assembly.

Charleston was a pivotal point in the early part of the Civil War and changed hands between Confederate and Union forces a half-dozen times.

[Phil M. Conley, *West Virginia Encyclopedia;* Roy Bird Cook, *The Annals of Fort Lee.*]

MORRIS P. SHAWKEY

CHARLESTON AND HAMBURG RAILROAD. *See* **South Carolina Railroad.**

CHARLESTON GARDENS. The Revolution and the Civil War took heavy toll of the 18th- and 19th-century gardens of Charleston, S.C., and neighboring parishes. Middleton Place has the only surviving colonial garden, laid out about 1740 by Henry Middleton. Its formal terraces rise from the west bank of the Ashley River; and the camellias and evergreens planted by André Michaux are its special pride. Magnolia Gardens, on the Ashley, were created during the 1840's by the Rev. John Grimke Drayton. Informal in style, their charm lies in the brilliance of massed azaleas, considered the finest in the world. Cypress Gardens, near Summerville, on the Cooper River, is the outstanding 20th-century garden achievement. The winding waterways of the old Dean rice plantation are utilized as its setting. Thousands of tourists visit the gardens every spring.

MARGARET B. MERIWETHER

CHARLESTON HARBOR, DEFENSE OF. On June 1, 1776, a British squadron, led by Sir Henry Clinton and Peter Parker, anchored off Sullivan's Island, at the entrance to Charleston Harbor, S.C. The city was held by 6,000 militia, while a much smaller force, led by Col. William Moultrie, was stationed on the island. On June 28 the British tried to batter down the island fort, only to find that their shots buried themselves in the green palmetto logs of the crude fortification. After the loss of one ship, the British retired and soon sailed for New York. Thus the Carolinas averted the threatened British invasion of the South.

[Edward McCrady, *South Carolina in the Revolution.*]

HUGH T. LEFLER

CHARLESTON INDIAN TRADE. As the only considerable English town on the southern coast, Charleston, S.C., was from the time of its settlement in the late 17th century in a position to reap a golden harvest from the trade to the Indians in English woolens, tools, weapons, and trinkets. These goods, cheaper and better than those of the Spanish and French, soon became indispensable to the Indians and made the trade not only the first road to wealth in the colony but likewise the chief means by which the Carolinians drove back the Spanish and, after 1700, competed with the French for control of the region from the Tennessee River to the Gulf of Mexico.

At first the proprietors and planters contended for the trade, but by 1700 it was the Charleston merchants who financed the traders and received the profits. After the French and Indian War the growth of Savannah, Ga., and the acquisition by the British of Pensacola caused the center of the southern Indian trade to shift westward.

[V. W. Crane, *The Southern Frontier.*]

R. L. MERIWETHER

CHARLESTON RIOT. On Mar. 28, 1864, a fight occurred in Charleston, Ill., between soldiers on leave and Copperheads, that resulted in nine killed and twelve wounded. Fifteen Copperheads were held for military trial but on President Abraham Lincoln's order were released to the civil authorities. Two were indicted, tried, and acquitted. Others involved escaped arrest.

CHARLES H. COLEMAN

CHARLESTOWN, former city of Massachusetts, now part of Boston, founded July 4, 1629, by Thomas Graves; Francis Bright; Ralph, Richard, and William Sprague; and about 100 others, who preceded the Great Migration. John Winthrop's company stopped here for some time in 1630, before deciding to settle across the Charles River at Boston. The Battle of Bunker Hill was fought at Charlestown (June 1775) at which time the town was set afire by the British.

[Richard Frothingham, *History of Charlestown;* J. F. Hunnewell, *A Century of Town Life: A History of Charlestown, 1775–1887.*]

R. W. G. VAIL

CHARLEVOIX'S JOURNEY. The journey of the French Jesuit Pierre François Xavier de Charlevoix to America and Canada (1720–22) was an attempt on the part of the French authorities to discover a route to the Western Sea, through the continent of North America. The regent of France, not wishing to have his purpose known, disguised the journey as a tour of inspection of the posts and missions of interior America. Charlevoix left France in July 1720, arrived at Quebec in September, too late to join the flotillas that ascended to the "upper country." In May 1721 he went around the Great Lakes, arriving in Mackinac in time to accompany the new commandant at La Baye to his post. There he conversed with Sioux Indians on their knowledge of the Western Sea. Finding it too late for an excursion to Lake Superior, Charlevoix decided to visit Louisiana. He entered Illinois by the St. Joseph–Kankakee route and at Kaskaskia spent the winter interviewing traders from the Missouri. From Kaskaskia he went down the river to New Orleans, where he spent fifteen days, and continued to Biloxi, where in February 1722 he fell ill. Not being able to remount the Mississippi as he had planned, Charlevoix returned to France, where he arrived in December 1722. His recommendations to the regent resulted in a post among the Sioux, established in 1727. He wrote of his experiences in America in *Histoire et description générale de la Nouvelle France,* published in 1744 and first translated into English in 1761.

[Louise Phelps Kellogg, *French Régime in Wisconsin and the Northwest.*]

LOUISE PHELPS KELLOGG

CHARLOTINA, the name proposed for a colony, the establishment of which was suggested in a pamphlet appearing in Edinburgh in 1763, entitled *The Expediency of Securing our American Colonies by Settling the Country Adjoining the River Mississippi, and the Country upon the Ohio, Considered.* Had such a colony been erected it would have included the region lying between the Maumee, Wabash, and Ohio rivers, the upper Mississippi, and the Great Lakes.

[C. W. Alvord and C. E. Carter, *The Critical Period, 1763–1765.*]

WAYNE E. STEVENS

CHARLOTTE, FORT, the name given to the French Fort Condé at Mobile when the English took over the town at the close of the French and Indian War in 1763. Fort Charlotte was captured by the Spaniards in March 1780 and was held by them until U.S. troops under Gen. James Wilkinson took possession in April 1813 (*see* Mobile Seized). After the purchase of Florida by the United States in 1819, Fort Charlotte was of no further importance and was gradually demolished.

[P. J. Hamilton, *Colonial Mobile.*]

R. S. COTTERILL

CHARLOTTE, TREATY OF CAMP (October 1774), ended Dunmore's War with the Shawnee. The site was on Pickaway plains, Pickaway County, Ohio; the Earl of Dunmore marked the name with red chalk on a peeled oak. Here Chief Cornstalk, defeated by Col. Andrew Lewis at Point Pleasant, made a treaty, agreeing that the tribe would give up all prisoners, would not hunt south of the Ohio River, and would obey trade regulations of the British government.

LOUISE PHELPS KELLOGG

CHARTER, ATLANTIC. *See* **Atlantic Charter.**

CHARTER COLONIES were promoted through private enterprise under charters from the crown. They were founded by trading companies, by squatters later incorporated, and by lords proprietors. Colonies founded by trading companies for the most part either disappeared or changed their status early. The Virginia Company lost its charter in 1624, the New England Council surrendered its patent in 1635, the Providence Island colony was conquered by Spain in 1641, and the Massachusetts Bay Company became a theocracy; thus the Bermuda Company was the only trading company in control of a colony through the greater part of the 17th century. Connecticut and Rhode Island, founded as squatter colonies by dissenters from Puritan Massachusetts, received charters of incorporation early in the Restoration period. The predominating type throughout the 17th century was the proprietary colony. Of this sort was James I's grant of all the Caribbean islands to the Earl of Carlisle, Maryland, and Maine, in the early part of the century, and after 1660 the Carolinas, New York, the Jerseys, the Bahamas, and Pennsylvania.

Similar institutions of government developed in all of the charter colonies. All ultimately had a governor, council, and house of representatives, the governor and council chosen by company or lord proprietor, and in the corporation colonies, indirectly by the people. The house of representatives, first the voluntary concession of the trading company, as in Virginia and Bermuda, later became a generally accepted institution in all chartered colonies except New York. Government in the corporation colonies was the freest from outside control. Perhaps because they were settled without the mediation of trading company or proprietor, the inhabitants of those colonies from the beginning cherished a conception of government based on sovereignty of the people.

When the Restoration government turned its attention to the building of a colonial policy, it found charters obstacles in the path. Several colonies were royalized, and, with the view of ultimate consolidation of all colonial possessions into a few large units, the Dominion of New England was established. Its failure brought temporary reaction in favor of charter colonies, but throughout the 18th century the process of royalization went on until by 1776 only two proprieties, Maryland and Pennsylvania, and two corporation colonies, Connecticut and Rhode Island, remained. Except in the corporation colonies the people seem to have preferred royal rule.

[C. M. Andrews, *Colonial Period of American History*.]

VIOLA F. BARNES

CHARTERED COMPANIES, British trading companies that played an important part in colonization in the New World, though they did not originate for that purpose. The joint-stock company was already in existence in many countries in the 16th century as an effective means of carrying on foreign trade, and when the New World attracted the interest of merchants, companies were formed for purposes of trade in that direction. Since production of certain desired articles required the transportation of laborers, colonization became a by-product of the trading company. The first English company to undertake successful colonization was the Virginia Company, first chartered in 1606 and, through two subcompanies, authorized to operate on the Atlantic coast between thirty-four and forty-five degrees north latitude. The original project was somewhat enlarged and developed more in detail by later charters in 1609 and 1612 to the London branch of the Virginia Company, and in 1620 to the Council for New England, the successor to the Plymouth branch. Down to the Puritan Revolution this method of sponsoring colonization predominated. The Newfoundland Company of 1610, the Bermuda Company of 1615, an enlargement of an earlier project under the auspices of the Virginia Company, the Massachusetts Bay Company of 1629, and the Providence Island Company of 1630 represent the most important attempts at trade and colonization. After the Puritan Revolution, the lord proprietor superseded the trading company as preferred sponsor of colonization, both king and colonists becoming increasingly distrustful of corporations. Massachusetts and Bermuda, the last of the companies in control of colonization, lost their charters in 1684, but the former had long since ceased to be commercial in character.

[C. M. Andrews, *The Colonial Period of American History*, vol. I; H. L. Osgood, *The American Colonies in the Seventeenth Century*.]

VIOLA F. BARNES

CHARTER OAK. *See* **Connecticut Charter of 1662.**

CHARTER OF LIBERTIES, drafted in 1683 by New York's first assembly, approved by James, Duke of York, as an instrument of government for his province. Recalling the rights of Englishmen and the principles of the great liberty documents, this charter described the framework of government, the functions of governor, council, and a legislative assembly representative of the qualified freeholders, and guaranteed the freedom of the assembly (which was to meet at least once in three years), trial by jury, due course of law in all proceedings, protection of the property of women, freedom from feudal exactions, exemption from quartering of soldiers, and especially religious toleration for all Christians.

[J. R. Brodhead, *History of the State of New York*.]

RICHARD J. PURCELL

CHARTER OF PRIVILEGES, granted by William Penn to Pennsylvania, Oct. 28, 1701, guaranteed freedom of worship to all who professed faith in "*One* almighty God." All who believed in Jesus Christ were eligible for office. A unicameral legislature was established and the council ceased to be a representative body.

[J. Paul Selsam, *The Pennsylvania Constitution of 1776;* W. R. Shepherd, *History of Proprietary Government in Pennsylvania*.]

J. PAUL SELSAM

CHARTERS, MUNICIPAL, the written instruments authorized or granted by the state by virtue of which cities or similar entities are given their corporate existence, powers, structure of government, and legislative and administrative procedures. The term usually also encompasses amendments to such charters, including those made by applicable general and special state laws. In the colonial period, municipal charters—perhaps not over twenty-five in total number—were confined to the royal and proprietary colonies, where they were granted by the governor. They dealt primarily with property rights, the control of certain public institutions, and local courts.

With the Revolution, the granting of municipal charters became a function of state legislatures, first by special act (still used in a few states where not constitutionally prohibited), and later by general enabling acts, usually availed of by petition and popular election, sometimes by local selection of one of several optional laws. Beginning with Missouri in 1875, a majority of the states now provide, usually constitutionally, for home-rule charters. These charters are prepared by local commissions in already existing municipal corporations, adopted by the electorate, and amended by means of council or voter initiative and approval by the voters. Typical home-rule provisions attempt to give the charter supremacy over the legislature in dealing with municipal affairs, but these have provided a difficult yardstick for the courts. Except as limited in home-rule states, the power of the legislature is paramount over a municipal charter, which is held not protected by the contract clause of the U.S. Constitution.

Traditionally, municipal charters have spelled out municipal powers in great detail, in part because of a judicial rule of strict construction of municipal powers widely known as Dillon's rule. In the 20th century charters have tended to be much shorter, relying on brief, comprehensive statements of authority and leaving more to be specified by ordinance. The concept of a municipal charter has not generally been extended to such political subdivisions as counties, townships, and school districts, although in about a dozen states the home-rule charter privilege has been granted to counties beginning in California in 1911.

[Charles R. Adrian and Charles Press, *Governing Urban America;* National Municipal League, *A Model City Charter;* William Winter, *The Urban Polity.*]

ORVILLE C. PETERSON

CHARTRES, FORT DE, seat of civil and military government in the Illinois country for more than half a century, near Kaskaskia in Randolph County, Ill., named in honor of the son of the regent of France. Building of the fort began in 1719 and was completed the following year. Built of wood, and exposed to the flood waters of the Mississippi River, the fort quickly fell into disrepair. In 1727 it was rebuilt, but by 1732 it was so dilapidated that Louis St. Ange, the commandant, built a new fort with the same name at some distance from the river. By 1747, when a general Indian uprising seemed imminent, this too had fallen into such bad condition that repair was considered impossible; the garrison was withdrawn to Kaskaskia.

In 1751 the French government decided to build a new fort at Kaskaskia, but the engineer in charge, Jean Baptiste Saucier, decided on a location near the old fort. Foundations were laid in 1753; three years later the structure was substantially finished. Costing 200,000 livres, the new Fort de Chartres was an irregular quadrangle with sides 490 feet long and stone walls 2 feet 2 inches thick. Ten years after its completion a competent English officer described it as "the most commodious and best built fort in North America." It was capable of housing 400 men, although its garrison rarely exceeded half that number.

Fort de Chartres, transferred to the British on Oct. 10, 1765, was the last French post in North America to be surrendered under the Treaty of Paris. Renamed Fort Cavendish, it was the seat of British rule in the Illinois country until 1772, when it was abandoned and destroyed.

[C. W. Alvord, *The Illinois Country, 1673–1818.*]

PAUL M. ANGLE

CHARTRES, FORT DE, TREATY, the name given to an agreement made by George Croghan, deputy superintendent of Indian affairs, with the western Indians in 1766, in which the Indians acknowledged the authority of the king of England and agreed to return prisoners and stolen horses and to permit the establishment of trading posts. The conference was held at Fort de Chartres, beginning on Aug. 25, 1766. Twenty-two tribes, including the Kaskaskia, Piankashaw, Kickapoo, Miami, Sauk, and Fox, were present; later three other tribes adhered to the pact. The peace established at this conference lasted for the duration of British rule in the Illinois country.

[A. T. Volwiler, *Croghan and the Westward Movement.*]

PAUL M. ANGLE

CHASE IMPEACHMENT was generally considered as part of a concerted Jeffersonian Republican effort to curb the power of the federal bench. Associate Justice Samuel Chase, an arbitrary personage with an abusive tongue and an unswerving confidence in the righteousness of the Federalist party, which had elevated him to the bench, was charged in articles of impeachment with unbecoming conduct and disregard of law. Chase was impeached by the House of Representatives on May 12, 1804. The outcome of the Senate trial hinged largely on the question whether his conduct, admittedly objectionable, constituted "high crimes or misdemeanors." His acquittal, Mar. 1, 1805, was probably a distinct gain for judicial independence.

[Charles Warren, *The Supreme Court in United States History.*]

W. A. ROBINSON

CHATEAUGAY, BATTLE OF (Oct. 25, 1813). During the autumn of 1813, Maj. Gen. Wade Hampton advanced along the Chateaugay River into Canada to Montreal with over 4,000 troops. On Oct. 22 he halted about fifteen miles from the St. Lawrence. Here, three days later, he attempted to dislodge 800 hostile troops barring his farther progress. In this engagement the British suffered only twenty-five casualties, the Americans double that number. Hampton abandoned his drive to Montreal and retired to U.S. territory.

[Henry Adams, *History of the United States*, vol. VII.]

JAMES RIPLEY JACOBS

CHÂTEAU-THIERRY BRIDGE, AMERICANS AT (May 31–June 1, 1918). German troops entered Château-Thierry on May 31, having broken the French front on the Aisne. French Gen. Ferdinand Foch, rushing troops to stop the Germans, sent the American Third Division, under the command of Joseph T. Dickman, to the region of Château-Thierry, where, aided by French Colonials, the Americans prevented the enemy from crossing the Marne on May 31 and June 1. The German attacks in the area then ceased.

JOSEPH MILLS HANSON

CHATTANOOGA CAMPAIGN (October–November 1863). Before the Battle of Chickamauga the Union troops under Gen. U. S. Grant, released by the capture of Vicksburg, had begun to move eastward. Confederate Gen. Braxton Bragg had failed to follow through after Chickamauga. All he could do was to "besiege" W. S. Rosecrans' Union army in Chattanooga, Tenn. Grant, placed in general command of all Union forces in the West, replaced Rosecrans with G. H. Thomas and instructed him to hold Chattanooga "at all hazards." Food was running short and supply lines were constantly interrupted. Grant's first act was to open a new and protected line of supply, via Brown's Ferry. Reinforcements arrived. Vigorous action turned the tables on Bragg, whose only act was to weaken himself unnecessarily by detaching Gen. James Longstreet on a fruitless expedition to capture Knoxville. Bragg then awaited Grant's next move. President Jefferson Davis visited the army and tried, unsuccessfully, to restore confidence.

On Nov. 24, 1863, Union Gen. Joseph Hooker captured Lookout Mountain on the left of Bragg's line. The next day Grant attacked all along the line. The Confederate center on Missionary Ridge gave way; the left had retreated; only the right held firm and covered the retreat southward into northern Georgia. A brilliant rear-guard stand at Ringgold Gap halted Grant's pursuit. The Union troops returned to Chattanooga; the Confederate Army went into winter quarters at Dalton, Ga.

[R. U. Johnson and C. C. Buel, *Battles and Leaders of the Civil War*, vol. III.]

THOMAS ROBSON HAY